INTRODUCTION TO
PHILOSOPHY

INTRODUCTION TO PHILOSOPHY

Classical and Contemporary Readings

THIRD EDITION

Edited by

John Perry
Michael Bratman

New York   Oxford
Oxford University Press
1999

Oxford University Press

Oxford   New York
Athens   Auckland   Bangkok   Bogotá   Buenos Aires   Calcutta
Cape Town   Chennai   Dar es Salaam   Delhi   Florence   Hong Kong   Istanbul
Karachi   Kuala Lumpur   Madrid   Melbourne   Mexico City   Mumbai
Nairobi   Paris   São Paulo   Singapore   Taipei   Tokyo   Toronto   Warsaw

and associated companies in
Berlin   Ibadan

Copyright © 1999 by Oxford University Press, Inc.

Published by Oxford University Press, Inc.
198 Madison Avenue, New York, New York 10016

Library of Congress Cataloging-in-Publication Data
Introduction to philosophy : classical and contemporary readings /
   edited by John Perry and Michael Bratman.—3rd ed.
         p.   cm.
   Includes bibliographical references and index.
   ISBN 0-19-511204-0 (paper)
   1. Philosophy—Introductions.   I. Perry, John, 1943–   .
II. Bratman, Michael.
BD21.I54   1998
100—dc21   97-47072
                                                  CIP

9 8 7 6 5 4 3

Printed in the United States of America
on acid-free paper

For our children

Jim, Sarah, and Joe Perry
Gregory and Scott Bratman

Contents

Part VI: Puzzles and Paradoxes   785

Introduction

A. Zeno's Paradoxes

B. Metaphysical and Epistemological Puzzles and Paradoxes

C. Puzzles of Rational Choice

D. Paradoxes of Logic, Set Theory, and Semantics

Preface to the Third Edition

—•—

We are pleased that our *Introduction to Philosophy* has continued to be used in teaching a new generation of students about the joys and the disciplines of philosophy. In preparing this third edition we have tried to benefit from thoughtful responses by many teachers of philosophy to a survey of use of the second edition. We also benefited from, and are grateful for, various efforts—most notably those of Edwin Curley—to alert us to errata in the earlier edition.

We have made a number of changes that we think are improvements. We have added an introductory essay, "On the Study of Philosophy." Each of the major parts of the collection has been subject to some change and/or reorganization. The most substantial changes have been to Part II, "God and Evil," and Part V, "Ethics and Society." Part IV, "Minds, Bodies, and Persons," now includes a separate subsection on consciousness, and John Perry's *Dialogue on Personal Identity and Immortality*." The "Puzzles and Paradoxes" section has been reorganized and supplemented, and the glossary is somewhat expanded. We are grateful to Scott Bratman for his editorial help.

J.P.
M.B.

Preface to the First Edition

In this anthology we have collected a variety of readings for use in a course or sequence of courses designed to introduce students to philosophy. We have based the selection on two courses we have taught numerous times at Stanford University: "God, Self, and World" and "Value and Obligation." The first is an introduction to metaphysics and epistemology, the second to ethics. These are one-quarter courses, usually taught in sequence, with a fair number of students taking both.

These courses are built around classic texts supplemented by shorter selections from the past and present. We have included in this anthology not only texts that we have found successful but also others that a survey of colleagues at Stanford and other institutions have identified as suitable. Thus, the total number of selections is larger than can be reasonably covered in even a two-quarter sequence, and instructors will want to pick those that fit their approach. We have included some footnotes from the original selections but have eliminated others. In some cases footnotes were eliminated because they could not be understood in the context of the selection; in other cases this was done simply to save space. The remaining footnotes have been renumbered.

Punctuation and other matters of style have been altered to conform with American conventions, with a couple of exceptions. In cases where quotation marks are clearly used for mentioning linguistic items—and the author's practice indicates an intent to note this specific use of such marks—punctuation that is not part of the mentioned item has not been moved inside the marks. In other cases single quotes have been left where they would normally be replaced by double quotes, as they appeared to be making a distinction of importance to the author.

Part VI, "Puzzles and Paradoxes," consists of short statements of some famous, interesting, and philosophically relevant mind-benders. We have found these useful in several ways in introducing students to philosophy: as paper assignments, as subjects for the odd short lecture after an exam or a vacation, as challenges for motivated students, or as materials to be worked into other sections of the book. We hope others find them as much fun to teach with as we have. We are grateful to Carl Ginet of Cornell University who shared with us his experience of using such puzzles to introduce students to philosophy.

College students of the present era tend to be preoccupied with preparation for a career—a preoccupation one can hardly criticize, given the expense of a college education and the concerns of parents as well as a civilization rich in opportunities for those who are technically prepared and full of pitfalls for those who are not. But, for most students, college will be the only opportunity to address the enduring problems of human existence; to examine carefully and thoughtfully the beliefs and values inherited from culture and parents; to gain an appreciation of the unsettled questions at the foundations of science and culture; and to develop habits of orderly, but imaginative, thinking. It is the job of the teacher of philosophy to encourage and assist students in taking advantage of this opportunity, and we feel there could be few callings as exciting and fulfilling. We hope this anthology will be of some value to our like-minded colleagues.

Stanford, Calif.   J. P.
May 1985   M.B.

On the Study of Philosophy

WELCOME TO PHILOSOPHY. FOR some of you, it will be the most practical subject you will study in college.

Why would we say that? Doesn't philosophy have a reputation for being *impractical*? Isn't it abstract and theoretical—the very opposite of practical?

Philosophy can be abstract and theoretical. But the study of philosophy can be practical in that it affects what you do with your life. This is because the abstractions and theories pertain to the basic concepts and values with which you confront experience.

Humans do things for reasons. We want certain things, and we believe that acting in certain ways will get us those things. So we act. Rocks don't act for reasons, but we do. It's part of what makes us human. Our desires and beliefs provide us with those reasons. Values and concepts are the building blocks of desires and beliefs. Thus our values and concepts play a big role in determining what we do and who we are.

Humans also reflect on and criticize the reasons we do things. Do we have good reasons for our reasons? Why do we want what we want? Why do we believe what we believe?

Having the capacity to reflect on one's reasons is another part of being human. It's a capacity that divides us from most of our fellow animals. We not only believe things, we can think about why we believe things. We not only want things, we can ask ourselves why we want them.

All humans have this capacity to reflect on their beliefs and desires, on their basic concepts and values. But not everyone likes to do so. It is the love of this activity that draws a person to philosophy. Do you worry about whether there is a God? What the difference between the future and the past is? Why we can't turn around in time as we can in space? Whether you are really a brain in a vat in someone's experiment? Whether other humans have minds, or

just you? How you would know if blue things looked to you just like green things look to everyone else? How you can be free, if every physical event has a physical cause? Have you ever wondered what made it wrong to lie and cheat? Whether democracy was really better than other political systems, or just the one you happened to grow up in? If this all sounds like you, taking a philosophy course may be one of the most enjoyable and most liberating experiences of your life.

Why should reflecting on one's beliefs and desires be liberating? Because in a very real sense your beliefs and desires, because they motivate what you do, define who you are. But where did those desires, values, and beliefs come from? Are they merely the accidental result of where you were born, who your parents and teachers and friends were? Philosophy can be liberating because it helps us reflect on the basic concepts with which we deal with experience and the desires that motivate us to do what we do, and to put our personal stamp on them. We can never fully escape limitations on our vision that result from the particular time and place we live. But through reading and thinking we can examine and challenge ideas that seem natural from our perspective with ideas that come from quite different points of view. Those of our values and concepts that survive this process will be more truly our own.

While college may seem like a hectic time, it is the best opportunity that most of us have to reflect intensively on who we are, to examine the source of our own way of looking at things, and seriously to consider alternatives. One of the saddest things that can happen to a person is to realize that she has committed a large part of her life to goals that upon reflection don't seem very important, on the basis of beliefs that upon reflection don't seem very plausible. Because your philosophy class gives you tools and opportunity to reflect on your basic values and concepts, and to develop habits of reflection, it may be the most practical course you take in college.

The philosophy class in which you are enrolled, and for which this book is a text, is part of a long tradition, stretching back to ancient times, of reflecting on the most basic values and beliefs that humans have. Philosophy means thinking as hard and as clearly as one can about some of the most interesting and enduring problems that human minds have ever encountered. Some of these problems have been discussed since ancient times. What makes acts right or wrong? You can read what the ancient philosopher Plato, the eighteenth-century philosopher David Hume, and the contemporary philosopher Tom Nagel have to say about it. What is it to be conscious? You can read what the seventeenth-century philosopher René Descartes, the pioneer of computer theory Alan Turing, and the contemporary philosopher John Searle think about that. Other problems are as timely as your morning paper. Is there anything wrong with a woman renting out her body? You can read what Debra Satz thinks about that. Is it immoral to get an abortion? You can read what Rosalind Hursthouse, reflecting on ideas of the ancient philosopher Aristotle, says about that.

To read philosophy well one must read slowly and aggressively. This may mean breaking some habits. There is a lot of emphasis today on reading fast. This is the age of information. To take advantage of the information available to us (even to cope with it) or to master that which is important for our job, for responsible citizenship, or for a full life—or at any rate for the final or the midterm—you have to learn to absorb large amounts of information in limited amounts of time. The college student, one hears, must learn to read at a minimum of 1000 words a minute. And 2000 or 3000 words is better; and those who really want to get ahead should read so fast that the only limiting factor in the speed with which they read is the speed with which they can turn pages.

These skills may be suitable for some types of reading, but not for philosophy. Good philosophers develop arguments and theories of some intricacy: arguments that are designed to convince the reader of the author's position on important issues. Reading such works is valuable insofar as one grapples with the ideas—fighting not only to understand the author but also, once one does, fighting with him or

her for control of one's mind. One should not be easily convinced of one position or another on issues so weighty as the existence of God, the indirectness of our knowledge of the external world, or the nature of justice.

Of course, all generalizations are a bit suspect. When one is reading for pleasure or to absorb straightforward information from a reliable source, speed-reading can be fine. But, if one derives pleasure from reading philosophy, it should be the pleasure of grappling with important and sublime ideas, not the exhilaration of racing through a thriller. And, when one learns from reading philosophy, it should be a result of being forced to think through new ideas and grasp new concepts, not simply the uploading of a data file from the text to the mind.

College students will have learned that mathematics and other technical material cannot be read in overdrive. But, philosophy can be deceptive. It cannot be claimed that good philosophy always makes good reading, but some philosophy does. A lot of philosophy, including a good portion of the famous historical works included in this anthology, make pleasant reading. They do not contain symbols, equations, charts, or other obvious signs of technicality and intricacy. One can just sit down and read Hume, or even Descartes, getting a feel for the author's position and style and the historical perspective of the work. When these texts are assigned in courses that survey the literature of various periods—with an eye toward getting a sense of the flow of ideas and concerns—as parts of larger assignments that cover hundreds of pages a week, one may have little choice but to read philosophy in this way, that is, just to get a feel for what is going on.

But appearances to the contrary, philosophy is inevitably technical. The philosopher constructs arguments, theories, positions, or criticisms in an attempt to persuade his or her most intelligent and perceptive opponents. The ideas and issues dealt with have a long history: to say something new, interesting, and persuasive, the philosopher must build his or her case with care. The result may be understood on various levels; to understand it at the deepest level, the reader must adopt the stance of the intelligent and perceptive opponent, thus coming to understand the case the philosopher is trying to make. This is what we mean by reading aggressively.

To read philosophy in this way, one should imagine onself in a dialogue with the philosopher—as if the philosopher were one's roommate (or an intelligent and articulate new roommate) trying to convince one of a startling new idea.

To see this approach at work, let's consider an example. Here is a passage from Descartes's "First Meditation."

Today, then having rid myself of worries and having arranged for some peace and quiet, I withdraw alone, free at last earnestly and wholeheartedly to overthrow all my beliefs.

To do this, I do not need to show each of my beliefs to be false; I may never be able to do that. But, since reason now convinces me that I ought to withhold my assent just as carefully from what is not obviously certain and indubitable as from what is obviously false, I can justify the rejection of all my beliefs if I can find some ground for doubt in each. And, to do this, I need not take on the endless task of running through my beliefs one by one: since a building collapses when its foundation is cut out from under it. I will go straight to the principles on which all my former beliefs rested.

Let's start with the second paragraph. The first place to pause is the word *this*. Whenever one encounters a demonstrative pronoun or other device by which the author refers back to something earlier, one should pause and make sure one knows to what it refers.

DESCARTES: To do this . . .
YOU: Wait a minute. To do what? Oh yes, I see, *to overthrow all your beliefs*.

But what is to overthrow one's beliefs? This sort of phrase ought immediately to occasion a demand for clarification.

Y: What do you mean, "Overthrow all your beliefs" anyway? Every one of them? You must be kidding? You are trying to make yourself believe everything you now believe is false? Can that really be what you mean?

Of course, Descartes isn't your roommate and, in fact, is long dead. So he can't respond to you. Still, you should mentally—or on the margin of your book—note this question.

Y: Well, of course you can't respond. But this sounds pretty odd. I will keep my eye open for clarification of just what it is you are trying to do.
D: As I was saying: To do this, I do not need to show each of my beliefs to be false; I may never be able to do that.
Y: Well, I didn't have to wait long. It's a relief that you aren't going to show all of your beliefs to be false. Still, it sounds as if this is something you want to do but simply don't think you could. The point of even wanting to seems a bit obscure. Go ahead.
D: But, since reason now convinces me . . .
Y: Reason. Reason. I wonder what exactly you mean by that. Hmm, this is the first use of the word. I mean, I know the meaning of the word *reason*, but it sounds as if you have something rather definite in mind. Actually, I use the word as a verb rather than a noun. Maybe I had better look it up in the dictionary. Here we are: "A statement offered in explanation." That doesn't seem to fit. *Motive*, *cause*, likewise. *Sanity*. That must be as in, "He has lost his reason." Or *intelligence*. One of these must be the closest. The latter seems better. So you are saying that your intelligence convinces you that you should be a great deal more cautious about what you believe—that's what this seems to amount to. Still, I have a hunch that more is packed into your use of the word *reason* than I can get out of the dictionary. The prof said you were a rationalist and that they put great emphasis on the power of reason. I'll keep it in mind that this is a key word and look for other clues as to exactly what you mean by it.
D: . . . That I ought to withhold my assent just as carefully from what is not obviously certain and indubitable as from what is obviously false; I can justify the rejection of all my beliefs if I can find some ground for doubt in each.
D: Wait a minute. You just said a mouthful. Let

me try to sort it out. Let's see. *Withhold my assent.* So you said you were going to overthrow your beliefs at the end of the last paragraph. Then, you said to do this you don't need to show that they are false. So *withholding assent* must be how you describe the in-between position—you have quit believing something, although you haven't shown it false, you don't believe the opposite either.

Wait a minute. Does that make sense? If I don't believe that 3 + 5 = 8, don't I automatically believe that it's not the case that 3 + 5 = 8? Hmm. I guess not. Suppose it was 358 + 267. Until I add it up, I neither believe it does equal 625 nor believe that it doesn't. So I guess that's where one is at when one is *withholding assent.*

Here is another mouthful: "Not obviously certain and indubitable." I'll look up the last word. *Unquestionable: Too evident to be doubted.* How is that different from certain? If your *Meditations* is one of the all-time classics, why are you being redundant in this show-offy way? Maybe I should give you the benefit of the doubt.

Let's see, the contrast is between *certain and indubitable*—no, wait, *obviously certain and indubitable*—and *obviously false.* Clearly one withholds one's assent from what is obviously false. So what you are saying is that you are going to do the same for *everything*, except that which is obviously certain and indubitable. And your reason, which seems to amount to your intelligence, is what leads you to do this. OK, proceed.

D: . . . I can justify the rejection of all my beliefs . . .

Y: You seem to go back and forth between a pretty sensible position—not believing what you aren't really sure of—and something that sounds a bit weird. Before you said you were going to try to overthrow *all* your beliefs; now you are trying to justify rejecting *all* your beliefs. I must admit, even though you have quite a reputation as a philosopher, this project strikes me as sort of extreme.

D: . . . If I can find some ground for doubt in each . . .

Y: Oh dear, another technical sounding phrase: *ground for doubt.* I better pull out my *Webster's* again. Well, you aren't using *ground* to mean dirt and you don't mean the bottom of a body of water, so you must mean *basis for belief or argument.* It sounds as if you are going to look for some basis for an argument *against* every single one of your beliefs. *That* sounds like quite a project. I wonder how come your *Meditations* is so short if you are really going to go through each one of your beliefs.

D: And, to do this, I need not take on the endless task of running through my beliefs one by one . . .

Y: Well, that's a relief.

D: . . . Since a building collapses when its foundation is cut out from under it, I will go straight to the principles on which all my former beliefs rested.

Y: Relying on a metaphor at a crucial point, eh? I thought the prof said that was a dubious practice. She said we should look at the assumptions underlying the appropriateness of the metaphor. So it looks like you think your beliefs form a *structure* with a *foundation.* The foundation is principles. All your beliefs rest on—i.e., I suppose, depend on in some way—certain principles. For this all to make sense, these principles must be beliefs. So what you are saying is that you are going to isolate certain beliefs, on which the rest depend. If you have a ground for doubt for a principle, you will quit believing it, not in the sense of taking it to be false or believing the opposite, but in the sense of withholding your assent. In so doing, you will automatically have a ground for doubt for all other beliefs that depend on the dubious principle.

D: Well, I guess that's an intelligible project. It still seems like it ought to take a lot longer than 50 pages. We shall see . . .

This is what it is like to read aggressively.

But being part of the philosophy tradition doesn't just mean reading about what others have thought. It means thinking yourself, long and hard, about the problems that interest you, and writing about them.

Now there may be a bit of a problem here. We said that in taking this philosophy class you are joining a tradition that goes back to Hume and Descartes and Aristotle and Plato. We have invited you to think about big issues and basic concepts. But when you get your writing assignments, your teacher will no doubt warn you against trying to be too deep and profound.

Imagine going to the ballet. You are impressed with the ballerina, and decide that you want to become one. The day of your first ballet lesson arrives. You have visions of a whole new world opening up to you; you imagine yourself gliding across the floor, spinning, jumping. But you find that your ballet lesson isn't like that at all. You spend a lot of time stretching and doing other exercises that you don't remember anyone doing when you saw *Swan Lake*.

Your first experience writing philosophy is going to be like that. You have read some of the works of the great philosophers. You are eager to share with the world some of your own deep philosophical thoughts, and to attack head on some big problems. But what you will be asked to do, in all likelihood, is to write a very short and very clear essay on a very restricted topic. And when your teacher grades the essay, she may miss all the profundity and focus on the fact that you didn't state with absolute clarity some mundane things she should have known anyway.

A good ballet requires numerous small precise movements on the part of the dancer, the ones she has practiced over and over for years. But these are not visible without close inspection; instead one sees a beautiful, creative, and seemingly effortless movement of the whole dancer. Somewhat similarly, as one reads a good philosophy article the original ideas, broad themes, and central conclusions will be apparent. But underneath there will be a solid structure of close argumentation, where the philosopher gives you reasons for adopting her view and for rejecting the views of others. So don't be discouraged because you are being asked to master this skill. Plato, Descartes, Hume, Lewis, and Anscombe all went through the same thing.

Here are some of the skills you need to master to do well in philosophy:

- Analyzing statements and arguments.

When you were working to understand Descartes in the passage we went through earlier, you were analyzing his statements. You were making sure you understood each word, and knew the possible ambiguities.

In a good philosophical essay the statements will add up to arguments, with premises and a conclusion. (For more about arguments, see the entry *deductive argument* in the glossary and the related entries.) You need to learn to spot the main conclusions the philosopher is arguing for, and the premises she uses to establish them.

- Imagining alternatives to familiar views and situations.

Nothing is more important to a philosopher than a good imagination. If you encounter a generalization, you should try to see if you can think of a counterexample. If you encounter a view that seems strange or absurd, you should try to see if you can imagine what experiences would lead someone to hold that view.

- Stating things explicitly, clearly, and succinctly.

Saint Paul said, "Faith, Hope and Charity, but the greatest of these is Charity." As a novice philosopher, your motto should be "Truth, Profundity, Clarity, but the greatest of these is Clarity." The reason is this. Our language is built around familiar ideas and situations. Philosophers often need to express thoughts that push the limits of language, because they want to consider unfamiliar ideas and odd situations. When doing this, it's relatively easy to sound profound, but very difficult to be clear. But if you are not clear, you cannot be sure that what you say is true, nor can you get the help of others to figure out whether it is.

Looking constantly for concrete examples that nail down what you are getting at is one of the best ways of keeping your thinking and writing clear. Another is to imagine a reader of your own work, who is reading it as slowly and aggressively as we encouraged you to read the philosophical works you encounter. Indeed, don't just imagine such a reader, become such a reader, rooting out unclarity and ambiguity in your own work.

• Thinking creatively.

A lot of philosophy is analysis and criticism: criticism of the concepts and values you inherit, criticism of the ideas you encounter in the work of others, and criticism of your own ideas. But one of the most important values of the philosophical tradition has been the new concepts and values that emerge from the stubborn reflection on old ones. At the beginning of virtually every social and scientific revolution, there stands a philosopher who not only questioned some idea or practice of her age, but was able to suggest something better.

If you can develop these skills as a philosophy student, then there is another way in which philosophy may be a very practical pursuit for you. Most professions highly value persons who can carry the analysis of a position or an argument to a deeper level, who can identify and untangle assumptions, and who can communicate effectively about complicated matters. Our world is a world replete with documents, deliberations, and decisions. The person who can bring rigor, clarity, and imagination to bear on dealing with these documents, deliberations, and decisions can make an enormous contribution in any number of areas of life.

In all these senses, then, philosophy can be a practical pursuit for the college student. Our fondest hope for this book is that it encourages those students with a bent toward reflection to plunge into philosophy and to reap the rewards its study can bring.

PART I

Philosophy and
the Meaning of Life

The Value of Philosophy

BERTRAND RUSSELL

Bertrand Russell (1872–1970) taught at Cambridge University, but he lost his position because of his pacifism during World War I. A leader, with G. E. Moore of the early twentieth-century revolt against idealism, Russell's work in logic and epistemology was one of the main influences on twentieth-century analytical philosophy. His works include *The Principles of Mathematics, Principia Mathematica* (with Alfred North Whitehead), *The Problems of Philosophy, Our Knowledge of the External World*, and numerous other books.

———•——

HAVING NOW COME TO THE END of our brief and very incomplete review of the problems of philosophy, it will be well to consider, in conclusion, what is the value of philosophy and why it ought to be studied. It is the more necessary to consider this question, in view of the fact that many men, under the influence of science or of practical affairs, are inclined to doubt whether philosophy is anything better than innocent but useless trifling, hair-splitting distinctions, and controversies on matters concerning which knowledge is impossible.

This view of philosophy appears to result, partly from a wrong conception of the ends of life, partly from a wrong conception of the kind of goods which philosophy strives to achieve. Physical science, through the medium of inventions, is useful to innumerable people who are wholly ignorant of it; thus the study of physical science is to be recommended, not only, or primarily, because of the effect on the student, but rather because of the effect on mankind in general. This utility does not belong to philosophy. If the study of philosophy has any value at all for others than students of philosophy, it must be only indirectly, through its effects upon the lives of those who study it. It is in these effects, therefore, if anywhere, that the value of philosophy must be primarily sought.

From *The Problems of Philosophy*. Copyright © 1969 by Oxford University Press. Reprinted by permission of the publisher.

But further, if we are not to fail in our endeavour to determine the value of philosophy, we must first free our minds from the prejudices of what are wrongly called "practical" men. The "practical" man, as this word is often used, is one who recognizes only material needs, who realizes that men must have food for the body, but is oblivious of the necessity of providing food for the mind. If all men were well off, if poverty and disease had been reduced to their lowest possible point, there would still remain much to be done to produce a valuable society; and even in the existing world the goods of the mind are at least as important as the goods of the body. It is exclusively among the goods of the mind that the value of philosophy is to be found; and only those who are not indifferent to these goods can be persuaded that the study of philosophy is not a waste of time.

Philosophy, like all other studies, aims primarily at knowledge. The knowledge it aims at is the kind of knowledge which gives unity and system to the body of the sciences, and the kind which results from a critical examination of the grounds of our convictions, prejudices, and beliefs. But it cannot be maintained that philosophy has had any very great measure of success in its attempts to provide definite answers to its questions. If you ask a mathematician, a mineralogist, a historian, or any other man of learning, what definite body of truths has been ascertained by his science, his answer will last as long as you are willing to listen. But if you put the same question to a philosopher, he will, if he is candid, have to confess that his study has not achieved positive results such as have been achieved by other sciences. It is true that this is partly accounted for by the fact that, as soon as definite knowledge concerning any subject becomes possible, this subject ceases to be called philosophy, and becomes a separate science. The whole study of the heavens, which now belongs to astronomy, was once included in philosophy; Newton's great work was called "the mathematical principles of natural philosophy." Similarly, the study of the human mind, which was a part of philosophy, has now been separated from philosophy and has become the science of psychology. Thus, to a great extent, the uncertainty of philosophy is more apparent than real: those questions which are already capable of definite answers are placed in the sciences, while those only to which, at present, no definite answer can be given, remain to form the residue which is called philosophy.

This is, however, only a part of the truth concerning the uncertainty of philosophy. There are many questions—and among them those that are of the profoundest interest to our spiritual life—which, so far as we can see, must remain insoluble to the human intellect unless its powers become of quite a different order from what they are now. Has the universe any unity of plan or purpose, or is it a fortuitous concourse of atoms? Is consciousness a permanent part of the universe, giving hope of indefinite growth in wisdom, or is it a transitory accident on a small planet on which life must ultimately become impossible? Are good and evil of importance to the universe or only to man? Such questions are asked by philosophy, and variously answered by various philosophers. But it would seem that, whether answers be otherwise discoverable or not, the answers suggested by philosophy are none of them demonstrably true. Yet, however slight may be the hope of discovering an answer, it is part of the business of philosophy to continue the consideration of such questions, to make us aware of their importance, to examine all the approaches to them, and to keep alive that speculative interest in the universe which is apt to be killed by confining ourselves to definitely ascertainable knowledge.

Many philosophers, it is true, have held that philosophy could establish the truth of certain answers to such fundamental questions. They have supposed that what is of most importance in religious beliefs could be proved by strict demonstration to be true. In order to judge of such attempts, it is necessary to take a survey of human knowledge, and to form an opinion as to its methods and its limitations. On such a subject it would be unwise to pronounce dogmatically; but if the investigations of our previous chapters have not led us astray, we shall be compelled to renounce the hope of finding philosophical proofs of religious beliefs. We cannot, therefore, include as part of the value of philosophy any definite set of answers to such questions. Hence, once more, the value of philosophy must not depend upon any supposed body of definitely ascertainable knowledge to be acquired by those who study it.

The value of philosophy is, in fact, to be sought largely in its very uncertainty. The man who has no tincture of philosophy goes through life imprisoned in the prejudices derived from common sense, from the habitual beliefs of his age or his nation, and from convictions which have grown up in his mind without the co-operation or consent of his deliberate reason. To such a man the world tends to become definite, finite, obvious; common objects rouse no questions, and unfamiliar possibilities are contemptuously rejected. As soon as we begin to philosophize, on the contrary, we find, as we saw in our opening chapters, that even the most everyday things lead to problems to which only very incomplete answers can be given. Philosophy, though unable to tell us with certainty what is the true answer to the doubts which it raises, is able to suggest many possibilities which enlarge our thoughts and free them from the tyranny of custom. Thus, while diminishing our feeling of certainty as to what things are, it greatly increases our knowledge as to what they may be; it removes the somewhat arrogant dogmatism of those who have never travelled into the region of liberating doubt, and it keeps alive our sense of wonder by showing familiar things in an unfamiliar aspect.

Apart from its utility in showing unsuspected possibilities, philosophy has a value—perhaps its chief value—through the greatness of the objects which it contemplates, and the freedom from narrow and personal aims resulting from this contemplation. The life of the instinctive man is shut up within the circle of his private interests: family and friends may be included, but the outer world is not regarded except as it may help or hinder what comes within the circle of instinctive wishes. In such a life there is something feverish and confined, in comparison with which the philosophic life is calm and free. The private world of instinctive interests is a small one, set in the midst of a great and powerful world which must, sooner or later, lay our private world in ruins. Unless we can so enlarge our interests as to include the whole outer world, we remain like a garrison in a beleaguered fortress, knowing that the enemy prevents escape and that ultimate surrender is inevitable. In such a life there is no peace, but a constant strife between the insistence of desire and the powerlessness of will. In one way or another, if our life is to be great and free, we must escape this prison and this strife.

One way of escape is by philosophic contemplation. Philosophic contemplation does not, in its widest survey, divide the universe into two hostile camps—friends and foes, helpful and hostile, good and bad—it views the whole impartially. Philosophic contemplation, when it is unalloyed, does not aim at proving that the rest of the universe is akin to man. All acquisition of knowledge is an enlargement of the Self, but this enlargement is best attained when it is not directly sought. It is obtained when the desire for knowledge is alone operative, by a study which does not wish in advance that its objects should have this or that character, but adapts the Self to the characters which it finds in its objects. This enlargement of Self is not obtained when, taking the Self as it is, we try to show that the world is so similar to this Self that knowledge of it is possible without any admission of what seems alien. The desire to prove this is a form of self-assertion and, like all self-assertion, it is an obstacle to the growth of Self which it desires, and of which the Self knows that it is capable. Self-assertion, in philosophic speculation as elsewhere, views the world as a means to its own ends; thus it makes the world of less account than Self, and the Self sets bounds to

the greatness of its goods. In contemplation, on the contrary, we start from the not-Self, and through its greatness the boundaries of Self are enlarged; through the infinity of the universe the mind which contemplates it achieves some share in infinity.

For this reason greatness of soul is not fostered by those philosophies which assimilate the universe to Man. Knowledge is a form of union of Self and not-Self; like all union, it is impaired by dominion, and therefore by any attempt to force the universe into conformity with what we find in ourselves. There is a widespread philosophical tendency towards the view which tells us that Man is the measure of all things, that truth is man-made, that space and time and the world of universals are properties of the mind, and that, if there be anything not created by the mind, it is unknowable and of no account for us. This view, if our previous discussions were correct, is untrue; but in addition to being untrue, it has the effect of robbing philosophic contemplation of all that gives it value, since it fetters contemplation to Self. What it calls knowledge is not a union with the not-Self, but a set of prejudices, habits, and desires, making an impenetrable veil between us and the world beyond. The man who finds pleasure in such a theory of knowledge is like the man who never leaves the domestic circle for fear his word might not be law.

The true philosophic contemplation, on the contrary, finds its satisfaction in every enlargement of the not-Self, in everything that magnifies the objects contemplated, and thereby the subject contemplating. Everything, in contemplation, that is personal or private, everything that depends upon habit, self-interest, or desire, distorts the object, and hence impairs the union which the intellect seeks. By thus making a barrier between subject and object, such personal and private things become a prison to the intellect. The free intellect will see as God might see, without a *here* and *now*, without hopes and fears, without the trammels of customary beliefs and traditional prejudices, calmly, dispassionately, in the sole and exclusive desire of knowledge—knowledge as impersonal, as purely contemplative, as it is possible for man to attain. Hence also the free intellect will value more the abstract and universal knowledge into which the accidents of private history do not enter, than the knowledge brought by the senses, and dependent, as such knowledge must be, upon an exclusive and personal point of view and a body whose sense-organs distort as much as they reveal.

The mind which has become accustomed to the freedom and impartiality of philosophic contemplation will preserve something of the same freedom and impartiality in the world of action and emotion. It will view its purposes and desires as parts of the whole, with the absence of insistence that results from seeing them as infinitesimal fragments in a world of which all the rest is unaffected by any one man's deeds. The impartiality which, in contemplation, is the unalloyed desire for truth, is the very same quality of mind which, in action, is justice, and in emotion is that universal love which can be given to all, and not only to those who are judged useful or admirable. Thus contemplation en-

larges not only the objects of our thoughts, but also the objects of our actions and our affections: it makes us citizens of the universe, not only of one walled city at war with all the rest. In this citizenship of the universe consists man's true freedom, and his liberation from the thraldom of narrow hopes and fears.

Thus, to sum up our discussion of the value of philosophy; Philosophy is to be studied, not for the sake of any definite answers to its questions, since no definite answers can, as a rule, be known to be true, but rather for the sake of the questions themselves; because these questions enlarge our conception of what is possible, enrich our intellectual imagination and diminish the dogmatic assurance which closes the mind against speculation; but above all because, through the greatness of the universe which philosophy contemplates, the mind also is rendered great, and becomes capable of that union with the universe which constitutes its highest good.

The Province of Philosophy

J. J. C. SMART

J. J. C. Smart (1920–   ) has written *Philosophy and Scientific Realism, Between Science and Philosophy*, and *Ethics, Persuasion and Truth*. He has been a professor of philosophy at the University of Adelaide and at Australian National University.

———•———

NO ONE ANSWER CAN BE GIVEN TO the question "What is philosophy?" since the words "philosophy" and "philosopher" have been used in many ways. Some people, for example, think of philosophy as offering the consolations of a religion, and of the philosopher as a

man who receives with equanimity the buffetings of life. This has very little to do with the way in which academic people, including myself, use the word "philosophy." I do not feel particularly unqualified to be an academic philosopher because I am not "philosophical" when I am bowled out first ball at cricket. As I propose to use the word "philosophy" it will stand primarily for an attempt to think clearly and comprehensively about: (a) the nature of the universe, and (b) the principles of conduct. In short, philosophy is primarily concerned with what there is in the world and with what we ought to do about it. Notice that I have said both "to think clearly" and "to think comprehensively." The former expression ties up with the prevailing conception of philosophy as linguistic or conceptual analysis, and the latter ties up with another common conception of philosophy as the rational reconstruction of language so as to provide a medium for the expression of total science.[1]

Thus, a man might analyze biology in a certain way. He might argue, as I shall do, that living organisms, including human beings, are simply very complicated physico-chemical mechanisms. This man might also analyse physics as the ordering and predicting of sense experiences. For the sake of argument let us concede that such a man might be thinking clearly, he would not be thinking *comprehensively*. As biologist he would be thinking of man as a mechanism, as very much a part of nature, a macroscopic object interacting with its environment. As physicist, however, he would be thinking of this great world of nature as just a matter of the actual and possible experiences of sentient beings, and so, in a sense, he would be putting nature inside man.[2] To think comprehensively he would have to discover a way of thought which enabled him to think both as a biologist and as a physicist. Presumably a comprehensive way of thought would be one which brought all intellectual disciplines into a harmonious relationship with one another. It may turn out that there are some realms of discourse, such as theology, which cannot be brought into a harmonious relationship with the various sciences. Any attempt to do so may result in violence to logic or to scientific facts, or may involve arbitrariness and implausibility. (Consider, for example, the implausibility of a theory which asserts that the mechanistic account of evolution by natural selection and mutation is broadly true but that there is a special discontinuity in the case of man, to whom was super-added an immortal soul.) If this is so, such anomalous branches of discourse will have to be rejected and will not form part of the reconstruction of our total conceptual scheme.

So much, for the moment, about the "nature of the universe" or "world view" part of philosophy. Let us now briefly consider the second part of phi-

losophy, which is concerned with the principles of conduct. . . . . as has been generally recognised in modern philosophy, it is not possible to deduce propositions about what ought to be done purely from propositions about what is the case. It follows that the principles of conduct are by no means unambiguously determined by our general philosophy. Nevertheless, in their laudable objection to those who would deduce ethics from the nature of the world (and in particular to some of those biologists who would base ethics on the theory of evolution and the like) philosophers have tended to obscure the fact that our general philosophical and scientific beliefs may strongly influence our ethical principles. For example, if one of our principles of conduct were that we should do what is commanded by a personal God and if our world view were one which left no place for such a God, then this principle of conduct would have to be given up, or at least we should have to find some other reason for adhering to it. In this [selection], which will be naturalistic in temper, I do not wish to concern myself with the general question of the legitimacy or illegitimacy of theology. The example of theology was brought up simply to show in a vivid way that metaphysics can be relevant to ethics. We must certainly not jump from the impossibility of deducing "ought" solely from "is" to the untenable position that our general philosophical and scientific views have no bearing on our ethical ones.

Philosophy and the Elimination of Nonsense

I have been suggesting a conception of philosophy as the attempt to acquire a synoptic view of the world. On this account of philosophy it shares the tentative character of the sciences. We must never think that we have acquired, even in outline, the final truth, for science inevitably provides surprises for us, and we may have to make important revisions of even our most general notions. We may hope, however, that our synoptic account will be nearer to the final truth than is that of common sense. Now in recent years it has been argued in some quarters that in philosophy we are not concerned, as scientists are, with the distinction between truth and falsity, but with that between sense and nonsense. As philosophers, according to this conception, it is not our business to say what the world is in fact like: we must leave this to scientists and historians. What we can do, and what we are by our training peculiarly fitted to do, is to help to ensure that we, together with scientists and historians, at least utter falsehoods: that we and they do not fall into nonsense which has not even achieved the distinction of an intelligible falsehood. Let me illustrate the notion of nonsense by means of an example based on *Alice in Wonderland*.[3] Suppose that a man came and said that he had seen a miaowing and blinking cat's head which was unattached to a body. I should be disposed in this case to disbelieve the man, and to say that what he told me was *false*. I should feel that I *understood* him: that I knew what it would be like for such an event as he reported to occur, but that I did not believe that any such event ever had or would occur. His report would contradict various secure beliefs that I possessed, particularly in the field of animal physiology. Now let us suppose that the man had reported not that he had seen a cat's head by itself but that he had seen simply a grin by itself. Not even a grinning mouth unattached to a head, but simply a grin all on its own. In this case I should not know what was meant at all. I should not be disposed to say that I understood what the man said, even though I disbelieved in the truth of his report. I should say, rather that what he said was nonsense, neither true nor false, and so I could not even disbelieve him.

Now it is indubitable that there are sentences which have appeared to be meaningful and which nevertheless have turned out to be nonsense. I shall mention one such sentence in a moment. And so even though the remarks of traditional philosophers (say, about the famous trio of topics, God, Freedom, and Immortality) may not be obvious nonsense, like the report of the catless grin, they may be nonsense all the same.

Here is a sentence, couched entirely in the respectable terminology of pure mathematics, which at first sight may appear to some readers (assuming that they have not encountered it before) to be perfectly meaningful, though perhaps rather dry and abstract. It was first concocted by Bertrand Russell.

(Russell's paradox.) The sentence is: "The class of all classes not members of themselves is a member of itself." There appear to be plenty of classes of objects which are not members of themselves. The class of criminals is not a criminal (the police do not have to seek the *class of criminals* after they have arrested all criminals), and the class of football teams in the league is not a further football team. Most classes therefore appear not to be members of themselves. But some classes do appear to be members of themselves: certainly the class of classes does. For is not the class of classes a class? It would therefore seem to be perfectly intelligible to pose the question of whether the class of all classes not members of themselves is or is not one of those classes which are members of themselves. Unfortunately, this question admits neither the answer "yes" nor the answer "no." For if the class of all classes not members of themselves is a member of itself, then it follows that it is one of those classes which are not members of themselves. And if it is not a member of itself, then it *is* a member of itself. Either way we get a contradiction. It follows that we can neither say that the sentence "the class of all classes not members of themselves is a member of itself" expresses a truth, nor can we say that it expresses a falsehood. We are forced to conclude that it is meaningless.[4]

The above paradox is particularly important and instructive, because it shows how unsuspected possibilities of nonsense can break out even in the rigorous and austere terminology of mathematics. For those readers who may not find abstractions about classes to their taste I shall mention a similar, though less important paradox, which may be even more succinctly stated. Consider the sentence "This sentence is false." The sentence is about itself. Is it true or false? It can be neither, because if it is true it is false and if it is false it is true. It is important to note that the above paradoxical sentences are not mere contradictions. You can assert the negation of a contradiction. That is, a contradiction is just plain false. "$2 + 2 = 5$" is a contradiction, and so "$2 + 2 \neq 5$" is a truth. Contradictions have their uses, for they occur in proofs by *reductio ad absurdum*. If you can deduce "$2 + 2 = 5$" you can normally deduce that the negation of one or other of the premises is true. I have said "normally" here, because it is important to use *reductio ad absurdum* methods only when you are reasonably sure of the meaningfulness of the sentence you are trying to prove. If the sentence you are trying to prove is meaningless it may be like one of the paradoxical sentences above and you may be able to deduce a contradiction both from it *and* from its negation. In which case the deduction of a contradiction from its negation does not ensure its truth. This consideration may be of interest to some readers, in that it may throw light on the fact that certain mathematicians, the so-called "intuitionists," Brouwer and his school, reject proof by *reductio ad absurdum* in circumstances in which classical mathematicians do not. It is, of course, the case that there are sentences which classical mathematicians regard as meaningful and which the intuitionists hold to be meaningless.

The sort of possibility of nonsense to which I have been drawing attention in the last few paragraphs is a subtle and insidious one. Nonsense of a sort has always been recognised: consider "I married a prime number" and "Virtue is triangular." It is an insight of the last fifty years (though foreshadowed by the philosophically subtle humour of Lewis Carroll) that there can be important and nonobvious possibilities of nonsense. This insight was generalised by Wittgenstein and by those much influenced by him into a complete philosophy of philosophy.

It is clear that some technique for recognising non-obvious nonsense is highly desirable, and I should agree that the development and application of such a technique is at least part of the task of philosophy. How does this connect up with my conception of philosophy as the development of a synoptic outlook? Can the elimination of nonsense change our world view? At first sight the answer to this is in the negative. If the nonsense really is nonsense it cannot form part of a world view, even a false one. So it looks as though elimination of nonsense removes dead wood but does not affect the living branches of our knowledge. This answer is, however, too hasty. It may well be that by using nonsensical premises, in addition to a set A of meaningful ones, we may be able to deduce a set B of meaningful sentences which are not deducible from A alone. I shall show how to deduce the false but meaningful sentence. "The moon is made of green cheese" from the nonsensical sentence "This sen-

tence is false." Let us represent the sentence "This sentence is false" by the symbol "S" for short.

From "This sentence is false" we can deduce "This sentence is not false." That is, from S we can deduce not-S. However, from S we can deduce "S or the moon is made of green cheese." But not-S (which we have already deduced) together with "S or the moon is made of green cheese" enables us to deduce "The moon is made of green cheese."

Thus given the nonsense "This sentence is false" we can deduce that the moon is made of green cheese. We have been able to do this because the nonsense in question issues in a contradiction, and from a contradiction we can, by the method of the last paragraph, deduce any sentence whatever. It is not obvious, however, that all nonsensical sentences issue in a contradiction. Some seem so far off the rails of meaningful discourse that it is not even possible to use them to demonstrate their own senselessness. Thus, it is not obvious that "I married a prime number" or "A bodiless grin appeared in the room" issue explicitly in contradiction. Nevertheless, my derivation of the proposition that the moon is made of green cheese should make it plausible that a philosopher should be able to deduce false conclusions from true premises if he makes his deduction through unrecognised nonsense. The deduction would, of course, be an incorrect one, but it would be incorrect in a very unobvious and subtle way. The detection of its incorrectness would depend on the detection of hidden nonsense. A good example of this sort of thing, in the history of philosophy, suggested to me by D. M. Armstrong, is perhaps Aristotle's deduction of the false, though meaningful, proposition that the heavenly bodies are of a different substance from that of the earth. His deduction is by way of the nonsense that the heavenly bodies obey laws of the same nature as the laws of logic, i.e., laws of a sort of logical hardness.

It may be thought that my example of a deduction that the moon is made of green cheese proves too much. For if it proves anything it proves that from "This sentence is false" (or from a simple non-paradoxical contradiction such as "$2 + 2 = 5$") we could deduce anything whatever. But philosophers, however metaphysical they may be, are not satisfied to assert any proposition whatever. There are some propositions which they wish to assert and there are other propositions which they wish to deny. A system of thought which harboured a contradiction would, on the contrary, degenerate into the happy assertion of anything whatever. To this objection we must reply that in practice a system will degenerate in this way only if the contradiction is detected. If the contradiction is not detected it cannot in practice provide a route for the deduction of any proposition whatever. It is like a way out of prison which is quite unknown to the prisoners:[5] as far as they are concerned it might as well not exist, and the bolts and bars do not lose any of their effectiveness.

I conclude therefore that it must not be supposed that the view that philosophy consists only in the elimination of nonsense implies the proposition that philosophy has no effect on our world view. It may cause us to shed some of our beliefs about the world because it may enable us to see that we have accepted these beliefs only on the strength of a fallacious deduction through a nonsensical part of language. This conclusion is far stronger than another one, which is conceded by most philosophers, that the elimination of nonsense leads to clarity of thought and so helps the progress of the sciences.

Philosophy as More Than the Elimination of Nonsense

That philosophy is at least the elimination of nonsense and the clarification of thought is something of which I have not the least doubt. However, I should also wish to argue that philosophy is more than this, and that it is the business of the philosopher to decide between various synoptic hypotheses on grounds of plausibility. Of course, scientists have to decide between hypotheses, and with a slight over-simplification we may say that they do so by means of observation and experiment. It may be, however, that no available method of experiment and observation will decide between two hypotheses. The philosopher may legitimately, I think, feel it within his province to speculate on the relative plausibilities of the two hypotheses if they are of such generality and importance as to affect our overall world view. For example, in the sequel I shall be concerned to argue for the plausibility of the view

that the human brain is no more than a physical mechanism, that no vitalistic or purely psychical entities or laws are needed to account for its operations. This type of philosophical thinking links up closely with the purely clarificatory sort of philosophy, since part of my strategy will be to try to expose confusions in a priori philosophical arguments for the opposite hypothesis. Of course, those who produce such a priori arguments will probably deny that what they are arguing for is a "hypothesis": they will hold that their view is true as a matter of logic, just as a mathematical proposition perhaps is. I shall, however, indicate why I think that such philosophers are too sanguine in regarding philosophy as pure logic.

A philosopher might have to decide between two hypotheses for which there not only is no available empirical test but for which there could be no possible empirical test. I shall illustrate this point by reference to the hypothesis that the universe began to exist ten minutes before I began writing this sentence, but with everything just as it was ten minutes ago.[6] (Fossils in the rocks, photographs in the pocket, memory traces in the brain, light rays in interstellar space, and so on.)[7] Of course this is not a hypothesis which any philosopher is likely to hold, though the English naturalist and biblical theologian Philip Gosse produced a very similar theory in order to reconcile geology and the book of Genesis.[8] Gosse held that the world was created only a few thousand years ago, exactly as stated in the book of Genesis, but that God had also created the various eroded canyons, fossils as if of prehistoric animals and plants, and so on. In short, he held that the world was created a few thousand years ago just as in fact it was (on the usual geological and evolutionary account) at that time. Clearly Gosse's theory was immune to empirical refutation, and he was extremely pained when both the scientific world and the theological world spurned his ingenious reconciliation. Nevertheless, though it is not a live philosophical theory, the hypothesis that the world began ten minutes ago, just as it was ten minutes ago, will serve to illustrate my methodological point. It is clear that no experiment or observation could upset the hypothesis that the world began ten minutes ago just as it was ten minutes ago. If I mention our memories of last week's football match the reply will be that these are not true memories: the football match never happened, but we came into existence ten minutes ago complete with pseudo-memories of the non-existent game. If I point to newspaper photographs of the football match the reply will be that the newspaper, complete with photographs, itself began to exist ten minutes ago. And so on.

Some philosophers would say that since there could be no experimental or observational way of deciding the question whether or not the world came into existence ten minutes ago just as it was ten minutes ago, the assertion or denial that the world began ten minutes ago is without sense. This seems to me to be unplausible. There seems to be nothing contradictory in the notion of a world suddenly springing into existence in this way. Moreover, suppose that I am suffering from an intense toothache. I should not take kindly to the view that in a year's time there would be no meaningful difference between the hypothesis that the world exists now, complete with my toothache, and the hypothesis that the world will spring into existence next year, just as it will be next year, with pseudo-traces, such as memories and empty gums, as if of my present toothache.

It is hard, therefore, without losing all sense of reality, to deny that the hypothesis that the world began ten minutes ago just as it was ten minutes ago is a meaningful one. (Though an unbelievable one.) Indeed, though there are no possible observations or experiments which could distinguish between this hypothesis and the more usual one, there are considerations, hard though they may be to formulate, of simplicity and plausibility, which should determine us to reject the "ten minutes ago" hypothesis. For this hypothesis presents us with a cosmology depending on a highly complex and arbitrary set of initial conditions. If the "ten minutes ago" hypothesis is accepted, then we have to take as a brute fact, for which no explanation could possibly be given, that ten minutes ago there were certain footprints on the beach at Glenelg, South Australia, that there were certain light waves in the depths of intergalactic space, that there were certain definite "photographs" in my breast pocket, that there were certain types of pseudo-prehistoric bones in the rock strata.[9] All these facts would have to be taken as just "flat" and in principle inexplicable. Now it is true

that on any hypothesis there is an element of arbitrariness in nature. Why have we five fingers rather than four or six? Nevertheless this arbitrariness can be understood as due to the element of sheer accident involved in the large-scale non-accident of evolution by natural selection. This arbitrariness, and other sorts of arbitrariness, such as the occurrence of hard rocks here and soft rocks there, of blue stars here and red stars there, is, on the normal hypothesis that the world has existed for a very long time, much what we should expect. It would be surprising rather if everything were neat and orderly. But this sort of arbitrariness is not like the extraordinary and universal arbitrariness of the initial conditions which we find in the "ten minutes ago" hypothesis.

The example of the hypothesis that the universe began to exist ten minutes ago seems to show that it is possible to choose, on grounds of plausibility, between two hypotheses between which there can be no empirical test. I shall myself consider one important case of this sort [in *Philosophy and Scientific Realism*] when I shall argue for the view that our conscious experiences are to be *identified* with brain processes. Another possible view would be that our conscious experiences are not identical with brain processes but that they are *correlated* with brain processes. Here once more we have, as we shall see, two hypotheses between which no empirical test could decide. I shall argue on plausible grounds for the former (materialistic) hypothesis against the latter (dualistic) hypothesis. Before I can do this I shall, of course, have to argue that certain a priori philosophical arguments against materialism are not as cogent as they seem at first sight to be. The plausible arguments I shall use are of various sorts, but one of these is worthy of specific mention. This is *Occam's razor*. It depends on the precept "Do not multiply entities beyond necessity." This is a familiar maxim not only of philosophical method but also of scientific method. For example, if biochemical reactions will explain a certain phenomenon of cell growth, then there is no need to postulate, in addition to the biochemical reactions which we know to occur anyway, a life force or some irreducibly biological law of nature. (Occam himself is popularly supposed to have applied his razor to the metaphysical problem of universals, though I gather that there is a good deal of doubt about the historical accuracy of this.) It might turn out that in cases where we need to talk of universals, such as justice and whiteness, we could manage equally well by talking of the *words* "just" and "white." If we can think of words as marks on paper and the like (the trouble, of course, is that words, unlike particular inscriptions, themselves turn out to be universals), then we can effect an economy. For we know that ink marks on paper and the like occur anyway, and if they will do all the explanatory tasks that are needed we need not bring in the airy fairy and altogether dubious entities justice and whiteness.

I suspect that considerations of plausibility, turning on the notions of simplicity and arbitrariness, of Occam's razor and the like, have an important and indeed indispensable place in philosophical argument. This is partly because philosophy is carried out in a natural language, not in some artificial language, with rigid formation and transformation rules explicitly laid down as in a formal logical or mathematical system. Hence, though it is often possible to *persuade* another philosopher that he has landed himself in inconsistency or in nonsense, and that he must therefore give up certain of his tenets, it is never possible to *prove* this to him. He can always patch up the inconsistencies and nonsenses in his language by means of supplementary rules and hypotheses. We shall have to present an alternative in chapter 6 [of *Philosophy and Scientific Realism*] to the so-called libertarian theory of free-will. At first sight this theory is easy to refute, for the libertarian seems to hold that acting freely is something intermediate between being determined and acting by pure chance. Logic would seem to leave no room for such an intermediate possibility. The libertarian will reply that if I define "pure chance" as "not being determined," then his "acting freely" is a sub-species of what I call "pure chance."[10] This sub-species is not properly pure chance, but consists in acting from reasons, not from causes. I then reply to the libertarian with the stock philosophical arguments showing that reasons are not a sort of para-cause and that acting from reasons is not incompatible with acting from causes. The obdurate libertarian is sure to prepare yet another line of defence and get round this objection in some way. (As I well know from inconclusive philosophical discussions on this topic.)

This characteristic inconclusiveness of philosophical argument is a fact familiar to all philosophers. If they were to take it seriously more of them would be favourably disposed to my conception of philosophy as in part depending on merely plausible considerations. If a philosopher keeps on patching up his theory we may try to persuade him that his way of talking is becoming more and more baroque and is ill-fitting to our scientific knowledge. The libertarian philosopher of free-will may, if he is ingenious enough, render himself immune to our logical arguments, but only at the cost of great artificiality in his theory, and at the price of bringing in a great discontinuity in the story of animal evolution. Just where in the line of evolution, the primates, or sub-men, or early men, does this "soul," or power of free choice in the libertarian sense, become superadded to man as he appears in the usual biological story? It would, moreover, have to be very special creation: it is impossible that the evolution of such a metaphysical entity could be explained in the usual mechanistic terms, natural selection acting on gene pools (a gene being a complex nucleic acid). Of course, if the philosopher is happy with the baroque quality of his theory and with its artificiality of fit with total science, then there is no more to be done. In many cases, however, plausible considerations of the sort I have suggested may have a persuasive force that purely abstract considerations of consistency and the like may not have. With ingenuity these last can be got round, but if the methods of getting round them have to be supplemented every century, or every decade, in order to take account of advances in sciences, then it will be a very romantically minded philosopher who will not begin to feel uneasy.

Synoptic Philosophy and Man's Place in Nature

If philosophy is concerned, in the manner suggested above, with the rational reconstruction of our conceptual scheme, then it quite obviously covers a very wide field.[11] There will therefore be some important issues which, for the purposes of this [selection], I shall be content to leave to one side. For example, I shall not be concerned with the much-vexed question of Platonism versus nominalism, that is, whether in addition to the concrete objects or events which exist in space and time we must postulate abstract objects as well. For example, do mathematicians assert the reality of *numbers* and *classes*? The two parts of the previous question can indeed be amalgamated if we accept Frege's and Russell's analysis of numbers as classes of classes of objects. In any case, in higher mathematics it is essential to introduce infinite classes, i.e., classes of numbers. That a class is an abstract object can most easily be seen if we consider the null class, which can be described e.g., as the class of twentieth-century terrestrial unicorns. The null class is a perfectly good class, and because it has no members there is no temptation to confuse it with the "heap" of its members. A class, unlike a heap, has a number. Consider the class of students who are in this room at a certain moment. It has, say, ten members. Contrast the spatially scattered "heap" of human protoplasm in this room. This has no number. It is made up of ten persons and 10^{15} living cells and goodness knows how many molecules or atoms.[12] Now science, since it includes mathematics, apparently has to mention classes. Does this mean that we must accept classes as real things postulated by science, on a par, perhaps, with electrons or the far side of the moon?[13] The reason why I shall not discuss this issue of Platonism versus nominalism, or of the reality of abstract entities, is that it has little relevance to the question of man's place in the universe. The connecting theme of this book will be the attack on anthropocentric or near-anthropocentric strains of thought in philosophy. I shall attack phenomenalist and subjectivist theories of mind and matter, space and time. The question of whether the universe contains Platonic entities is neutral to these issues.

Of course, the days when man was thought to be physically at the centre of the universe are long over, but as I shall try to show, a disguised anthropocentricity still prevails in many fields of philosophy. For example, traditional phenomenalism in a sense puts this great world of nature "inside sentience": indeed, as we shall see, phenomenalism has appealed to no less a man than F. P. Ramsey on account of its apparent power to tame the vast astronomical spaces that threatened to overawe him. Moreover, I shall be concerned to refute the more recent phenomenalism, not of tables and chairs but of electrons and

protons, which has attempted to deny the full-blooded reality of the sub-microscopic world, i.e. of objects of an order of magnitude very much smaller than those of macroscopic or roughly man-sized objects. In later chapters I shall attack anthropocentricity in prevailing theories of the secondary qualities and of consciousness, and I shall be concerned to put man in his place by defending the view that he is nothing more than a complicated physical mechanism. The ground for this part of the book is prepared by a chapter on the relations between physics and biology. The chapter on space and time might be thought to be outside the scope of the book, but the reader will, if he perseveres, discover that even in such notions as of past, present, and future there is a concealed anthropocentricity. In the final chapter there is a discussion of the relevance and lack of relevance of a materialistic metaphysics for ethics.

NOTES

1. In thinking of philosophy as rational reconstruction of language I have been very much influenced by Hilary Putnam and by W. V. Quine. See, for example, Quine's *Word and Object* (Technology Press of M.I.T., 1960).

2. On this point see chapter II [*Philosophy and Scientific Realism* (Routledge and Kegan Paul, London, 1963)]. It is interesting that theoretical physicists, when they venture into philosophy, commonly tend to be phenomenalists, and biologists tend to be materialists.

3. Lewis Carroll, *Alice in Wonderland* (Everyman edition, J. M. Dent, London, 1952), p. 56.

4. I here neglect the possibility of other ways of dealing with Russell's paradox, such as Zermelo's. The cautious reader should consult the essay "The Demarcation between Science and Metaphysics" (especially pp. 263–73) in K. R. Popper's *Conjectures and Refutations* (Routledge and Kegan Paul, London, 1963), which came into my hands while this book was in the press. Popper's argument suggests that we should draw a less sharp line between nonsense and falsehood than I have done. This would strengthen the main argument of this chapter, which is that philosophy is concerned with world view.

5. I think that this simile is originally due to Wittgenstein.

6. If someone raises the relativistic objection that "ten

minutes ago" has no unambiguous meaning we can say "ten minutes ago with reference to some specified inertial frame of reference."

7. See Bertrand Russell, *Analysis of Mind* (Allen and Unwin, London, 1921), pp. 159–60.
8. An interesting account of Philip Gosse's theory is given in Martin Gardner, *Fads and Fallacies in the Name of Science* (Dover Inc., New York, 1957), pp. 124–27.
9. I am also neglecting the arbitrariness of our choice of criterion of simultaneity at a distance, which is implied by the special theory of relativity.
10. This paragraph was already written and set up in print before I saw the two lucid notes by Richard Acworth and C. A. Campbell in *Mind*, Vol. 72, 1963, pp. 271–72 and 400–405. These reply to a former article of mine and point out that the libertarian could defend himself by partitioning the field which I call 'pure chance.'
11. W. V. Quine has recently argued against the tenability of the analytic-synthetic distinction. (See his *Word and Object, op. cit.*, also his *From a Logical Point of View* (Harvard University Press, 1953).) According to this laws of logic and of pure mathematics are not different in kind from very high-level laws of physics. It would also seem to follow

from his view that there would be an arbitrariness in the formation rules which we lay down for a system. Indeed, there are varying expedients in mathematical logic to eliminate the class of all classes paradox, and some sentences which would be meaningless in Whitehead and Russell's system are allowed in Quine's *Mathematical Logic* (Harvard University Press, 1958). There is perhaps a certain arbitrariness in whether we regard something as meaningless or as a high-level falsehood. (Thus, it could be taken not as meaningless that there are catless grins, but that it follows from certain very high-level assumptions that there are none.) If Quine's views on the nature of logic are accepted, then the first of the two conceptions of philosophy that I have sketched in this chapter collapses into the second. If so, this only strengthens my position in this book. Since Quine's views are controversial, I do not wish to commit myself on this issue, which is a highly technical one, and which would in any case lead us away from the main preoccupations of this book. See also footnote 4.
12. Cf. W. V. Quine, *From a Logical Point of View* (Harvard University Press, 1953), p. 114.
13. For a discussion of this issue see especially Quine, op. cit.

The Absurd

THOMAS NAGEL

Thomas Nagel (1937–   ) is professor of philosophy at New York University. His publications include *The Possibility of Altruism, Mortal Questions,* and *The View From Nowhere.*

———•———

MOST PEOPLE FEEL ON OCCASION that life is absurd, and some feel it vividly and continually. Yet the reasons usually offered in defense of this conviction are patently inadequate: they *could* not really explain

why life is absurd. Why then do they provide a natural expression for the sense that it is?

I

Consider some examples. It is often remarked that nothing we do now will matter in a million years. But if that is true, then by the same token, nothing that will be the case in a million years matters now. In particular, it does not matter now that in a million years nothing we do now will matter. Moreover, even if what we did now *were* going to matter in a million years, how could that keep our present concerns from being absurd? If their mattering now is not enough to accomplish that, how would it help if they mattered a million years from now?

Whether what we do now will matter in a million years could make the crucial difference only if its mattering in a million years depended on its mattering, period. But then to deny that whatever happens now will matter in a million years is to beg the question against its mattering, period; for in that sense one cannot know that it will not matter in a million years whether (for example) someone now is happy or miserable, without knowing that it does not matter, period.

What we say to convey the absurdity of our lives often has to do with space or time: we are tiny specks in the infinite vastness of the universe; our lives are mere instants even on a geological time scale, let alone a cosmic one; we will all be dead any minute. But of course none of these evident facts can be what *makes* life absurd, if it is absurd. For suppose we lived forever; would not a life that is absurd if it lasts seventy years be infinitely absurd if it lasted through eternity? And if our lives are absurd given our present size, why would they be any less absurd if we filled the universe (either because we were larger or because the universe was smaller)? Reflection on our minuteness and brevity appears to be intimately connected with the sense that life is meaningless; but it is not clear what the connection is.

Another inadequate argument is that because we are going to die, all chains of justification must leave off in mid-air: one studies and works to earn money to pay for clothing, housing, entertainment, food, to sustain oneself from year to year, perhaps to support a family and pursue a career—but to what final end? All of it is an elaborate journey leading nowhere. (One will also have some effect on other people's lives, but that simply reproduces the problem, for they will die too.)

There are several replies to this argument. First, life does not consist of a sequence of activities each of which has as its purpose some later member of the sequence. Chains of justification come repeatedly to an end within life, and whether the process as a whole can be justified has no bearing on the finality of these end-points. No further justification is needed to make it reasonable to take aspirin for a headache, attend an exhibition of the work of a painter one admires, or stop a child from putting his hand on a hot stove. No larger context or further purpose is needed to prevent these acts from being pointless.

Even if someone wished to supply a further justification for pursuing all the things in life that are commonly regarded as self-justifying, that justification would have to end somewhere too. If *nothing* can justify unless it is justified in terms of something outside itself, which is also justified, then an infinite regress results, and no chain of justification can be complete. Moreover, if a finite chain of reasons cannot justify anything, what could be accomplished by an infinite chain, each link of which must be justified by something outside itself?

Since justifications must come to an end somewhere, nothing is gained by denying that they end where they appear to, within life—or by trying to subsume the multiple, often trivial ordinary justifications of action under a single, controlling life scheme. We can be satisfied more easily than that. In fact, through its misrepresentation of the process of justification, the argument makes a vacuous demand. It insists that the reasons available within life are incomplete, but suggests thereby that all reasons that come to an end are incomplete. This makes it impossible to supply any reasons at all.

The standard arguments for absurdity appear therefore to fail as arguments. Yet I believe they attempt to express something that is difficult to state, but fundamentally correct.

II

In ordinary life a situation is absurd when it includes a conspicuous discrepancy between pretension or aspiration and reality: someone gives a complicated speech in support of a motion that has already been passed; a notorious criminal is made president of a major philanthropic foundation; you declare your love over the telephone to a recorded announcement; as you are being knighted, your pants fall down.

When a person finds himself in an absurd situation, he will usually attempt to change it, by modifying his aspirations, or by trying to bring reality into better accord with them, or by removing himself from the situation entirely. We are not always willing or able to extricate ourselves from a position whose absurdity has become clear to us. Nevertheless, it is usually possible to imagine some change that would remove the absurdity—whether or not we can or will implement it. The sense that life as a whole is absurd arises when we perceive, perhaps dimly, an inflated pretension or aspiration which is inseparable from the continuation of human life and which makes its absurdity inescapable, short of escape from life itself.

Many people's lives are absurd, temporarily or permanently, for conventional reasons having to do with their particular ambitions, circumstances, and personal relations. If there is a philosophical sense of absurdity, however, it must arise from the perception of something universal—some respect in which pretension and reality inevitably clash for us all. This condition is supplied, I shall argue, by the collison between the seriousness with which we take our lives and the perpetual possibility of regarding everything about which we are serious as arbitrary, or open to doubt.

We cannot live human lives without energy and attention, nor without making choices which show that we take some things more seriously than others. Yet we have always available a point of view outside the particular form of our lives, from which the seriousness appears gratuitous. These two inescapable viewpoints collide in us, and that is what makes life absurd. It is absurd because we ignore the doubts that we know cannot be settled, continuing to live with nearly undiminished seriousness in spite of them.

This analysis requires defense in two respects: first as regards the unavoidability of seriousness; second as regards the inescapability of doubt.

We take ourselves seriously whether we lead serious lives or not and whether we are concerned primarily with fame, pleasure, virtues, luxury, triumph, beauty, justice, knowledge, salvation, or

mere survival. If we take other people seriously and devote ourselves to them, that only multiplies the problem. Human life is full of effort, plans, calculation, success and failure: we *pursue* our lives, with varying degrees of sloth and energy.

It would be different if we could not step back and reflect on the process, but were merely led from impulse to impulse without self-consciousness. But human beings do not act solely on impulse. They are prudent, they reflect, they weigh consequences, they ask whether what they are doing is worthwhile. Not only are their lives full of particular choices that hang together in larger activities with temporal structure: they also decide in the broadest terms what to pursue and what to avoid, what the priorities among their various aims should be, and what kind of people they want to be or become. Some men are faced with such choices by the large decisions they make from time to time; some merely by reflection on the course their lives are taking as the product of countless small decisions. They decide whom to marry, what profession to follow, whether to join the Country Club, or the Resistance; or they may just wonder why they go on being salesmen or academics or taxi drivers, and then stop thinking about it after a certain period of inconclusive reflection.

Although they may be motivated from act to act by those immediate needs with which life presents them, they allow the process to continue by adhering to the general system of habits and the form of life in which such motives have their place—or perhaps only by clinging to life itself. They spend enormous quantities of energy, risk, and calculation on the details. Think of how an ordinary individual sweats over his appearance, his health, his sex life, his emotional honesty, his social utility, his self-knowledge, the quality of his ties with family, colleagues, and friends, how well he does his job, whether he understands the world and what is going on in it. Leading a human life is a full-time occupation, to which everyone devotes decades of intense concern.

This fact is so obvious that it is hard to find it extraordinary and important. Each of us lives his own life—lives with himself twenty-four hours a day. What else is he supposed to do—live someone else's life? Yet humans have the special capacity to step back and survey themselves, and the lives to which they are committed, with that detached amazement which comes from watching an ant struggle up a heap of sand. Without developing the illusion that they are able to escape from their highly specific and idiosyncratic position, they can view it *sub specie aeternitatis*—and the view is at once sobering and comical.

The crucial backward step is not taken by asking for still another justification in the chain, and failing to get it. The objections to that line of attack have already been stated; justifications come to an end. But this is precisely what provides universal doubt with its object. We step back to find that the whole system of justification and criticism, which controls our choices and supports our claims to rationality, rests on responses and habits that we never question, that we should not know how to defend without circularity, and to which we shall continue to adhere even after they are called into question.

The things we do or want without reasons, and without requiring reasons—the things that define what is a reason for us and what is not—are the starting points of our skepticism. We see ourselves from outside, and all the contingency and specificity of our aims and pursuits become clear. Yet when we take this view and recognize what we do as arbitrary, it does not disengage us from life, and there lies our absurdity: not in the fact that such an external view can be taken of us, but in the fact that we ourselves can take it, without ceasing to be the persons whose ultimate concerns are so coolly regarded.

III

One may try to escape the position by seeking broader ultimate concerns, from which it is impossible to step back—the idea being that absurdity results because what we take seriously is something small and insignificant and individual. Those seeking to supply their lives with meaning usually envision a role or function in something larger than themselves. They therefore seek fulfillment in service to society, the state, the revolution, the progress of history, the advance of science, or religion and the glory of God.

But a role in some larger enterprise cannot confer significance unless that enterprise is itself significant. And its significance must come back to what we can understand, or it will not even appear to give us what we are seeking. If we learned that we were being raised to provide food for other creatures fond of human flesh, who planned to turn us into cutlets before we got too stringy—even if we learned that the human race had been developed by animal breeders precisely for this purpose—that would still not give our lives meaning, for two reasons. First, we would still be in the dark as to the significance of the lives of those other beings; second, although we might acknowledge that this culinary role would make our lives meaningful to them, it is not clear how it would make them meaningful to us.

Admittedly, the usual form of service to a higher being is different from this. One is supposed to behold and partake of the glory of God, for example, in a way in which chickens do not share in the glory of coq au vin. The same is true of service to a state, a movement, or a revolution. People can come to feel, when they are part of something bigger, that it is part of them too. They worry less about what is peculiar to themselves, but identify enough with the larger enterprise to find their role in it fulfilling.

However, any such larger purpose can be put in doubt in the same way that the aims of an individual life can be, and for the same reasons. It is as legitimate to find ultimate justification there as to find it earlier, among the details of individual life. But this does not alter the fact that justifications come to an end when we are content to have them end—when we do not find it necessary to look any further. If we can step back from the purposes of individual life and doubt their point, we can step back also from the progress of human history, or of science, or the success of a society, or the kingdom, power, and glory of God, and put all these things into question in the same way. What seems to us to confer meaning, justification, significance, does so in virtue of the fact that we need no more reasons after a certain point.

What makes doubt inescapable with regard to the limited aims of individual life also makes it inescapable with regard to any larger purpose that encourages the sense that life is meaningful. Once the fundamental doubt has begun, it cannot be laid to rest.

Camus maintains in *The Myth of Sisyphus* that the absurd arises because the world fails to meet our demands for meaning. This suggests that the world might satisfy those demands if it were different. But now we can see that this is not the case. There does not appear to be any conceivable world (containing us) about which unsettlable doubts could not arise. Consequently the absurdity of our situation derives not from a collison between our expectations and the world, but from a collision within ourselves.

IV

It may be objected that the standpoint from which these doubts are supposed to be felt does not exist— that if we take the recommended backward step we will land on thin air, without any basis for judgment about the natural responses we are supposed to be surveying. If we retain our usual standards of what is important, then questions about the significance of what we are doing with our lives will be answerable in the usual way. But if we do not, then those questions can mean nothing to us, since there is no longer any content to the idea of what matters, and hence no content to the idea that nothing does.

But this objection misconceives the nature of the backward step. It is not supposed to give us an understanding of what is *really* important, so that we see by contrast that our lives are insignificant. We never, in the course of these reflections, abandon the ordinary standards that guide our lives. We merely observe them in operation, and recognize that if they are called into question we can justify them only by reference to themselves, uselessly. We adhere to them because of the way we are put together; what seems to us important or serious or valuable would not seem so if we were differently constituted.

In ordinary life, to be sure, we do not judge a situation absurd unless we have in mind some standards of seriousness, significance, or harmony with which the absurd can be contrasted. This contrast is not implied by the philosophical judgment of ab-

surdity, and that might be thought to make the concept unsuitable for the expression of such judgments. This is not so, however, for the philosophical judgment depends on another contrast which makes it a natural extension from more ordinary cases. It departs from them only in contrasting the pretensions of life with a larger context in which *no* standards can be discovered, rather than with a context from which alternative, overriding standards may be applied.

V

In this respect, as in others, philosophical perception of the absurd resembles epistemological skepticism. In both cases the final, philosophical doubt is not contrasted with any unchallenged certainties, though it is arrived at by extrapolation from examples of doubt within the system of evidence or justification, where a contrast with other certainties *is* implied. In both cases our limitedness joins with a capacity to transcend those limitations in thought (thus seeing them as limitations, and as inescapable).

Skepticism begins when we include ourselves in the world about which we claim knowledge. We notice that certain types of evidence convince us, that we are content to allow justifications of belief to come to an end at certain points, that we feel we know many things even without knowing or having grounds for believing the denial of others which, if true, would make what we claim to know false.

For example, I know that I am looking at a piece of paper, although I have no adequate grounds for claiming I know that I am not dreaming; and if I am dreaming then I am not looking at a piece of paper. Here an ordinary conception of how appearance may diverge from reality is employed to show that we take our world largely for granted; the certainty that we are not dreaming cannot be justified except circularly, in terms of those very appearances which are being put in doubt. It is somewhat farfetched to suggest I may be dreaming; but the possibility is only illustrative. It reveals that our claims to knowledge depend on our not feeling it necessary to exclude certain incompatible alternatives, and the dreaming possibility or the total-hallucination possibility are just representatives for limitless possibilities most of which we cannot even conceive.[1]

Once we have taken the backward step to an abstract view of our whole system of beliefs, evidence, and justification, and seen that it works only, despite its pretensions, by taking the world largely for granted, we are *not* in a position to contrast all these appearances with an alternative reality. We cannot shed our ordinary responses, and if we could it would leave us with no means of conceiving a reality of any kind.

It is the same in the practical domain. We do not step outside our lives to a new vantage point from which we see what is really, objectively significant. We continue to take life largely for granted while seeing that all our decisions and certainties are possible only because there is a great deal we do not bother to rule out.

Both epistemological skepticism and a sense of the absurd can be reached via initial doubts posed within systems of evidence and justification that we accept, and can be stated without violence to our ordinary concepts. We can ask not only why we should believe there is a floor under us, but also why we should believe the evidence of our senses at all—and at some point the framable questions will have outlasted the answers. Similarly, we can ask not only why we should take aspirin, but why we should take trouble over our own comfort at all. The fact that we shall take the aspirin without waiting for an answer to this last question does not show that it is an unreal question. We shall also continue to believe there is a floor under us without waiting for an answer to the other question. In both cases it is this unsupported natural confidence that generates skeptical doubts; so it cannot be used to settle them.

Philosophical skepticism does not cause us to abandon our ordinary beliefs, but it lends them a peculiar flavor. After acknowledging that their truth is incompatible with possibilities that we have no grounds for believing do not obtain—apart from grounds in those very beliefs which we have called into question—we return to our familiar convictions with a certain irony and resignation. Unable to abandon the natural responses on which they depend, we take them back, like a spouse who has run off with someone else and then decided to return; but we re-gard them differently (not that the new attitude is necessarily inferior to the old, in either case).

The same situation obtains after we have put in question the seriousness with which we take our lives and human life in general and have looked at ourselves without presuppositions. We then return to our lives, as we must, but our seriousness is laced with irony. Not that irony enables us to escape the absurd. It is useless to mutter: "Life is meaningless; life is meaningless . . ." as an accompaniment to everything we do. In continuing to live and work and strive, we take ourselves seriously in action no matter what we say.

What sustains us, in belief as in action, is not reason for justification, but something more basic than these—for we go on in the same way even after we are convinced that the reasons have given out.[2] If we tried to rely entirely on reason, and pressed it hard, our lives and beliefs would collapse—a form of madness that may actually occur if the inertial force of taking the world and life for granted is somehow lost. If we lose our grip on that, reason will not give it back to us.

VI

In viewing ourselves from a perspective broader than we can occupy in the flesh, we become spectators of our own lives. We cannot do very much as pure spectators of our own lives, so we continue to lead them, and devote ourselves to what we are able at the same time to view as no more than a curiosity, like the ritual of an alien religion.

This explains why the sense of absurdity finds its natural expression in those bad arguments with which the discussion began. References to our small size and short lifespan and to the fact that all of mankind will eventually vanish without a trace are metaphors for the backward step which permits us to regard ourselves from without and to find the particular form of our lives curious and slightly surprising. By feigning a nebula's-eye view, we illustrate the capacity to see ourselves without presuppositions, as arbitrary, idiosyncratic, highly specific occupants of the world, one of countless possible forms of life.

Before turning to the question whether the absurdity of our lives is something to be regretted and if possible escaped, let me consider what would have to be given up in order to avoid it.

Why is the life of a mouse not absurd? The orbit of the moon is not absurd either, but that involves no strivings or aims at all. A mouse, however, has to work to stay alive. Yet he is not absurd, because he lacks the capacities for self-consciousness and self-transcendence that would enable him to see that he is only a mouse. If that *did* happen, his life would become absurd, since self-awareness would not make him cease to be a mouse and would not enable him to rise above his mousely strivings. Bringing his new-found self-consciousness with him, he would have to return to his meager yet frantic life, full of doubts that he was unable to answer, but also full of purposes that he was unable to abandon.

Given that the transcendental step is natural to us humans, can we avoid absurdity by refusing to take that step and remaining entirely within our sublunar lives? Well, we cannot refuse consciously, for to do that we would have to be aware of the viewpoint we were refusing to adopt. The only way to avoid the relevant self-consciousness would be either never to attain it or to forget it—neither of which can be achieved by the will.

On the other hand, it is possible to expend effort on an attempt to destroy the other component of the absurd—abandoning one's earthly, individual, human life in order to identify as completely as possible with that universal viewpoint from which human life seems arbitrary and trivial. (This appears to be the ideal of certain Oriental religions.) If one succeeds, then one will not have to drag the superior awareness through a strenuous mundane life, and absurdity will be diminished.

However, insofar as this self-etiolation is the result of effort, will-power, aceticism, and so forth, it requires that one take oneself seriously as an individual—that one be willing to take considerable trouble to avoid being creaturely and absurd. Thus one may undermine the aim of unworldliness by pursuing it too vigorously. Still, if someone simply allowed his individual, animal nature to drift and respond to impulse, without making the pursuit of

its needs a central conscious aim, then he might, at considerable dissociative cost, achieve a life that was less absurd than most. It would not be a meaningful life either, of course; but it would not involve the engagement of a transcendent awareness in the assiduous pursuit of mundane goals. And that is the main condition of absurdity—the dragooning of an unconvinced transcendent consciousness into the service of an immanent, limited enterprise like a human life.

The final escape is suicide; but before adopting any hasty solutions, it would be wise to consider carefully whether the absurdity of our existence truly presents us with a *problem*, to which some solution must be found—a way of dealing with prima facie disaster. That is certainly the attitude with which Camus approaches the issue, and it gains support from the fact that we are all eager to escape from absurd situations on a smaller scale.

Camus—not on uniformly good grounds—rejects suicide and the other solutions he regards as escapist. What he recommends is defiance or scorn. We can salvage our dignity, he appears to believe, by shaking a fist at the world which is deaf to our pleas, and continuing to live in spite of it. This will not make our lives un-absurd, but it will lend them a certain nobility.[3]

This seems to me romantic and slightly self-pitying. Our absurdity warrants neither that much distress nor that much defiance. At the risk of falling into romanticism by a different route, I would argue that absurdity is one of the most human things about us: a manifestation of our most advanced and interesting characteristics. Like skepticism in epistemology, it is possible only because we possess a certain kind of insight—the capacity to transcend ourselves in thought.

If a sense of the absurd is a way of perceiving our true situation (even though the situation is not absurd until the perception arises), then what reason can we have to resent or escape it? Like the capacity for epistemological skepticism, it results from the ability to understand our human limitations. It need not be a matter for agony unless we make it so. Nor need it evoke a defiant contempt of fate that allows us to feel brave or proud. Such dramatics, even if carried on in private, betray a failure to appreciate the cosmic unimportance of the situation. If *sub specie aeternitatis* there is no reason to believe that anything matters, then that does not matter either, and we can approach our absurd lives with irony instead of heroism or despair.

NOTES

1. I am aware that skepticism about the external world is widely thought to have been refuted, but I have remained convinced of its irrefutability since being exposed at Berkeley to Thompson Clarke's largely unpublished ideas on the subject.
2. As Hume says in a famous passage of the *Treatise*: 'Most fortunately it happens, that since reason is incapable of dispelling these clouds, nature herself suffices to that purpose, and cures me of this philosophical melancholy and delirium, either by relaxing this bent of mind, or by some avocation, and lively impression of my senses, which obliterate all these chimeras. I dine, I play a game of backgammon, I converse, and am merry with my friends; and when after three or four hours' amusement, I would return to these speculations, they appear so cold, and strain'd, and ridiculous, that I cannot find in my heart to enter into them any farther' (bk. 1, pt. iv, sect. 7; Selby-Bigge edition, p. 269).
3. "Sisyphus, proletarian of the gods, powerless and rebellious, knows the whole extent of his wretched condition: it is what he thinks of during his descent. The lucidity that was to constitute his torture at the same time crowns his victory. There is no fate that cannot be surmounted by scorn" (*The Myth of Sisyphus*, trans. Justin O'Brien [New York: Vintage, 1959], p. 90; first published, Paris: Gallimard, 1942).

Apology: Defence of Socrates

PLATO

Plato (ca. 428–ca. 348 B.C.) is regarded by many as the greatest philosopher of all time; it has been said that all philosophy is merely a footnote to his work.

—•—

17a I DON'T KNOW HOW YOU, FELLOW Athenians, have been affected by my accusers, but for my part I felt myself almost transported by them, so persuasively did they speak. And yet 5 hardly a word they have said is true. Among their many falsehoods, one especially astonished me: their warning that you must be careful not to be taken in b by me, because I am a clever speaker. It seemed to me the height of impudence on their part not to be embarrassed at being refuted straight away by the facts, once it became apparent that I was not a clever 5 speaker at all—unless indeed they call a "clever"

speaker one who speaks the truth. If that is what they mean, then I would admit to being an orator, although not on a par with them.

As I said, then, my accusers have said little or nothing true; whereas from me you shall hear the whole truth, though not, I assure you, fellow Athenians, in language adorned with fine words and phrases or c dressed up, as theirs was: you shall hear my points made spontaneously in whatever words occur to me—persuaded as I am that my case is just. None of you should expect anything to be put differently, because it would not, of course, be at all fitting at my 5 age, gentlemen, to come before you with artificial speeches, such as might be composed by a young lad.

One thing, moreover, I would earnestly beg of you, fellow Athenians. If you hear me defending

From *Defence of Socrates*, *Euthyphro, and Crito*, translated by David Gallop. Copyright © 1997 by Oxford University Press. Reprinted by permission of the publisher and translator.

myself with the same arguments I normally use at
10 the bankers' tables in the market-place (where many
d of you have heard me) and elsewhere, please do not
be surprised or protest on that account. You see, here
is the reason: this is the first time I have ever appeared before a court of law, although I am over 70;
so I am literally a stranger to the diction of this place.
5 And if I really were a foreigner, you would naturally excuse me, were I to speak in the dialect and
18a style in which I had been brought up; so in the present case as well I ask you, in all fairness as I think,
to disregard my manner of speaking—it may not be
as good, or it may be better—but to consider and
attend simply to the question whether or not my
5 case is just; because that is the duty of a judge, as it
is an orator's duty to speak the truth.

To begin with, fellow Athenians, it is fair that I
should defend myself against the first set of charges
falsely brought against me by my first accusers, and
b then turn to the later charges and the more recent
ones. You see, I have been accused before you by
many people for a long time now, for many years
in fact, by people who spoke not a word of truth. It
is those people I fear more than Anytus and his
crowd, though they too are dangerous. But those
5 others are more so, gentlemen: they have taken hold
of most of you since childhood, and made persuasive accusations against me, yet without an ounce
more truth in them. They say that there is one
Socrates, a "wise man," who ponders what is above
c the earth and investigates everything beneath it, and
turns the weaker argument into the stronger.

Those accusers who have spread such rumour
about me, fellow Athenians, are the dangerous ones,
because their audience believes that people who inquire into those matters also fail to acknowledge the
5 gods. Moreover, those accusers are numerous, and
have been denouncing me for a long time now, and
they also spoke to you at an age at which you would
be most likely to believe them, when some of you
were children or young lads; and their accusations
simply went by default for lack of any defence. But
the most absurd thing of all is that one cannot even
d get to know their names or say who they were—except perhaps one who happens to be a comic play-
wright. The ones who have persuaded you by malicious slander, and also some who persuade others

because they have been persuaded themselves, are
all very hard to deal with: one cannot put any of 5
them on the stand here in court, or cross-examine
anybody, but one must literally engage in a sort of
shadow-boxing to defend oneself, and cross-examine without anyone to answer. You too, then, should
allow, as I just said, that I have two sets of accusers:
one set who have accused me recently, and the other c
of long standing to whom I was just referring. And
please grant that I need to defend myself against the
latter first, since you too heard them accusing me
earlier, and you heard far more from them than
from these recent critics here.

Very well, then. I must defend myself, fellow 5
Athenians, and in so short a time must try to dispel 19a
the slander which you have had so long to absorb.
That is the outcome I would wish for, should it be
of any benefit to you and to me, and I should like
to succeed in my defence—though I believe the task 5
to be a difficult one, and am well aware of its nature. But let that turn out as God wills: I have to
obey the law and present my defence.

Let us examine, from the beginning, the charge
that has given rise to the slander against me—which b
was just what Meletus relied upon when he drew
up this indictment. Very well then, what were my
slanderers actually saying when they slandered me?
Let me read out their deposition, as if they were my
legal accusers:

"Socrates is guilty of being a busybody, in that he
inquires into what is beneath the earth and in the 5
sky, turns the weaker argument into the stronger, c
and teaches others to do the same."

The charges would run something like that.
Indeed, you can see them for yourselves, enacted in
Aristophanes' comedy: in that play, a character
called "Socrates" swings around, claims to be walking on air, and talks a lot of other nonsense on sub- 5
jects of which I have no understanding, great or
small.

Not that I mean to belittle knowledge of that sort,
if anyone really is learned in such matters—no matter how many of Meletus' lawsuits I might have to
defend myself against—but the fact is, fellow
Athenians, those subjects are not my concern at all. d
I call most of you to witness yourselves, and I ask

you to make that quite clear to one another, if you have ever heard me in discussion (as many of you have). Tell one another, then, whether any of you 5 has ever heard me discussing such subjects, either briefly or at length; and as a result you will realize that the other things said about me by the public are equally baseless.

In any event, there is no truth in those charges. Moreover, if you have heard from anyone that I un- e dertake to educate people and charge fees, there is no truth in that either—though for that matter I do think it also a fine thing if anyone *is* able to educate people, as Gorgias of Leontini, Prodicus of Ceos, 5 and Hippias of Elis profess to. Each of them can visit any city, gentlemen, and persuade its young people, 20a who may associate free of charge with any of their own citizens they wish, to leave those associations, and to join with them instead, paying fees and be- ing grateful into the bargain.

On that topic, there is at present another expert here, a gentleman from Paros; I heard of his visit, because I happened to run into a man who has spent 5 more money on sophists than everyone else put to- gether—Callias, the son of Hipponicus. So I ques- tioned him, since he has two sons himself.

"Callias," I said, "if your two sons had been born as colts or calves, we could find and engage a tutor b who could make them both excel superbly in the re- quired qualities—and he'd be some sort of expert in horse-rearing or agriculture. But seeing that they are actually human, whom do you intend to engage as their tutor? Who has knowledge of the required 5 human and civic qualities? I ask, because I assume you've given thought to the matter, having sons yourself. Is there such a person," I asked, "or not?"

"Certainly," he replied.

"Who is he?" I said; "Where does he come from, and what does he charge for tuition?"

"His name is Evenus, Socrates," he replied; "He comes from Paros, and he charges 5 minas."

I thought Evenus was to be congratulated, if he c really did possess that skill and imparted it for such a modest charge. I, at any rate, would certainly be giving myself fine airs and graces if I possessed that knowledge. But the fact is, fellow Athenians, I do not.

Now perhaps one of you will interject: "Well 5 then, Socrates, what is the difficulty in your case?

What is the source of these slanders against you? If you are not engaged in something out of the ordi- nary, why ever has so much rumour and talk arisen about you? It would surely never have arisen, un- less you were up to something different from most d people. Tell us what it is, then, so that we don't jump to conclusions about you."

That speaker makes a fair point, I think; and so I will try to show you just what it is that has earned me my reputation and notoriety. Please hear me out. Some of you will perhaps think I am joking, but I 5 assure you that I shall be telling you the whole truth.

You see, fellow Athenians, I have gained this rep- utation on account of nothing but a certain sort of wisdom. And what sort of wisdom is that? It is a human kind of wisdom, perhaps, since it might just be true that I have wisdom of that sort. Maybe the c people I just mentioned possess wisdom of a super- human kind; otherwise I cannot explain it. For my part, I certainly do not possess that knowledge; and whoever says I do is lying and speaking with a view to slandering me—

Now please do not protest, fellow Athenians, even if I should sound to you rather boastful. I am not myself the source of the story I am about to tell 5 you, but I shall refer you to a trustworthy author- ity. As evidence of my wisdom, if such it actually be, and of its nature, I shall call to witness before you the god at Delphi.

You remember Chaerephon, of course. He was 21a a friend of mine from youth, and also a comrade in your party, who shared your recent exile and restoration. You recall too what sort of man Chaerephon was, how impetuous he was in any un- dertaking. Well, on one occasion he actually went to the Delphic oracle, and had the audacity to put the following question to it—as I said, please do not 5 make a disturbance, gentlemen—he went and asked if there was anyone wiser than myself; to which the Pythia responded that there was no one. His brother here will testify to the court about that story, since Chaerephon himself is deceased.

Now keep in mind why I have been telling you b this: it is because I am going to explain to you the origin of the slander against me. When I heard the story, I thought to myself: "What ever is the god saying? What can his riddle mean? Since I am all

5 too conscious of not being wise in any matter, great or small, what ever can he mean by pronouncing me to be the wisest? Surely he cannot be lying: for him that would be out of the question."

So for a long time I was perplexed about what he could possibly mean. But then, with great reluctance, I proceeded to investigate the matter somewhat as follows. I went to one of the people who c had a reputation for wisdom, thinking there, if anywhere, to disprove the oracle's utterance and declare to it: "Here is someone wiser than I am, and yet you said that I was the wisest."

So I interviewed this person—I need not mention his name, but he was someone in public life; and when I examined him, my experience went 5 something like this, fellow Athenians: in conversing with him, I formed the opinion that, although the man was thought to be wise by many other people, and especially by himself, yet in reality he was not. d So I then tried to show him that he thought himself wise without being so. I thereby earned his dislike, and that of many people present; but still, as I went away, I thought to myself: "I am wiser than that fellow, anyhow. Because neither of us, I dare say, 5 knows anything of great value; but he thinks he knows a thing when he doesn't; whereas I neither know it in fact, nor think that I do. At any rate, it appears that I am wiser than he in just this one small respect: if I do not know something, I do not think that I do."

Next, I went to someone else, among people thought to be even wiser than the previous man, and e I came to the same conclusion again; and so I was disliked by that man too, as well as by many others.

Well, after that I went on to visit one person after another. I realized, with dismay and alarm, that I was making enemies; but even so, I thought it my duty to attach the highest importance to the god's 5 business; and therefore, in seeking the oracle's 22a meaning, I had to go on to examine all those with any reputation for knowledge. And upon my word, fellow Athenians—because I am obliged to speak the truth before the court—I truly did experience something like this: as I pursued the god's inquiry, I found those held in the highest esteem were practically the most defective, whereas men who were

supposed to be their inferiors were much better off 5 in respect of understanding.

Let me, then, outline my wanderings for you, the various "labours" I kept undertaking, only to find that the oracle proved competely irrefutable. After I had done with the politicians, I turned to the poets—including tragedians, dithyrambic poets, and b the rest—thinking that in their company I would be shown up as more ignorant than they were. So I picked up the poems over which I thought they had taken the most trouble, and questioned them about 5 their meaning, so that I might also learn something from them in the process.

Now I'm embarrassed to tell you the truth, gentlemen, but it has to be said. Practically everyone else present could speak better than the poets themselves about their very own compositions. And so, once more, I soon realized this truth about them too: it was not from wisdom that they composed their c works, but from a certain natural aptitude and inspiration, like that of seers and soothsayers—because those people too utter many fine words, yet know nothing of the matters on which they pronounce. It was obvious to me that the poets were in much the same situation; yet at the same time I re- 5 alized that because of their compositions they thought themselves the wisest people in other matters as well, when they were not. So I left, believing that I was ahead of them in the same way as I was ahead of the politicians.

Then, finally, I went to the craftsmen, because I was conscious of knowing almost nothing myself, d but felt sure that amongst them, at least, I would find much valuable knowledge. And in that expectation I was not disappointed: they did have knowledge in fields where I had none, and in that respect they were wiser than I. And yet, fellow Athenians, 5 those able craftsmen seemed to me to suffer from the same failing as the poets: because of their excellence at their own trade, each claimed to be a great expert also on matters of the utmost importance; and this arrogance of theirs seemed to eclipse their wis- e dom. So I began to ask myself, on the oracle's behalf, whether I should prefer to be as I am, neither wise as they are wise, nor ignorant as they are ignorant, or to possess both their attributes; and in re- 5 ply, I told myself and the oracle that I was better off as I was.

The effect of this questioning, fellow Athenians, 23a was to earn me much hostility of a very vexing and trying sort, which has given rise to numerous slanders, including this reputation I have for being "wise"—because those present on each occasion 5 imagine me to be wise regarding the matters on which I examine others. But in fact, gentlemen, it would appear that it is only the god who is truly wise; and that he is saying to us, through this oracle, that human wisdom is worth little or nothing. b It seems that when he says "Socrates," he makes use of my name, merely taking me as an example—as if to say, "The wisest amongst you, human beings, is anyone like Socrates who has recognized that with respect to wisdom he is truly worthless."

That is why, even to this day, I still go about seek- 5 ing out and searching into anyone I believe to be wise, citizen or foreigner, in obedience to the god. Then, as soon as I find that someone is not wise, I assist the god by proving that he is not. Because of this occupation, I have had no time at all for any ac- c tivity to speak of, either in public affairs or in my family life; indeed, because of my service to the god, I live in extreme poverty.

In addition, the young people who follow me around of their own accord, the ones who have plenty of leisure because their parents are wealthiest, enjoy listening to people being cross-examined. Often, too, 5 they copy my example themselves, and so attempt to cross-examine others. And I imagine that they find a great abundance of people who suppose themselves to possess some knowledge, but really know little or d nothing. Consequently, the people they question are angry with me, though not with themselves, and say that there is a nasty pestilence abroad called "Socrates," who is corrupting the young.

Then, when asked just what he is doing or teaching, they have nothing to say, because they have no idea what he does; yet, rather than seem at a loss, 5 they resort to the stock charges against all who pursue intellectual inquiry, trotting out "things in the sky and beneath the earth," "failing to acknowledge the gods," and "turning the weaker argument into the stronger." They would, I imagine, be loath to

admit the truth, which is that their pretensions to knowledge have been exposed, and they are totally ignorant. So because these people have reputations e to protect, I suppose, and are also both passionate and numerous, and have been speaking about me in a vigorous and persuasive style, they have long been filling your ears with vicious slander. It is on the strength of all this that Meletus, along with Anytus and Lycon, has proceeded against me: Meletus is aggrieved for the poets, Anytus for the craftsmen and 5 politicians, and Lycon for the orators. And so, as I 24a began by saying, I should be surprised if I could rid your minds of this slander in so short a time, when so much of it has accumulated.

There is the truth for you, fellow Athenians. I have spoken it without concealing anything from you, ma- 5 jor or minor, and without glossing over anything. And yet I am virtually certain that it is my very candour that makes enemies for me—which goes to show that I am right: the slander against me is to that effect, and such is its explanation. And whether you b look for one now or later, that is what you will find.

So much for my defence before you against the charges brought by my first group of accusers. Next, I shall try to defend myself against Meletus, good 5 patriot that he claims to be, and against my more recent critics. So once again, as if they were a fresh set of accusers, let me in turn review their deposition. It runs something like this:

"Socrates is guilty of corrupting the young, and of failing to acknowledge the gods acknowledged by the city, but introducing new spiritual beings in- c stead."

Such is the charge: let us examine each item within it.

Meletus says, then, that I am guilty of corrupting the young. Well I reply, fellow Athenians, that 5 Meletus is guilty of trifling in a serious matter, in that he brings people to trial on frivolous grounds, and professes grave concern about matters for which he has never cared at all. I shall now try to prove to you too that that is so.

Step forward, Meletus, and answer me. It is your 10 chief concern, is it not, that our younger people shall d be as good as possible?

—It is.

Very well, will you please tell the judges who influences them for the better—because you must obviously know, seeing that you care? Having discov-
5 ered me, as you allege, to be the one who is corrupting them, you bring me before the judges here and accuse me. So speak up, and tell the court who has an improving influence.

You see, Meletus, you remain silent, and have no answer. Yet doesn't that strike you as shameful, and as proof in itself of exactly what I say—that you have never cared about these matters at all? Come then,
10 good fellow, tell us who influences them for the better.

—The laws.

e   Yes, but that is not what I'm asking, excellent fellow. I mean, which *person*, who already knows the laws to begin with?

—These gentlemen, the judges, Socrates.

What are you saying, Meletus? Can these people
5 educate the young, and do they have an improving influence?

—Most certainly.

All of them, or some but not others?

—All of them.

My goodness, what welcome news, and what a generous supply of benefactors you speak of! And
10 how about the audience here in court? Do they too
25a have an improving influence, or not?

—Yes, they do too.

And how about members of the Council?

—Yes, the Councillors too.

5   But in that case, how about people in the Assembly, its individual members, Meletus? They won't be corrupting their youngers, will they? Won't they all be good influences as well?

—Yes, they will too.

So every person in Athens, it would appear, has
10 an excellent influence on them except for me, whereas I alone am corrupting them. Is that what you're saying?

—That is emphatically what I'm saying.

Then I find myself, if we are to believe you, in a most awkward predicament. Now answer me this.
b Do you think the same is true of horses? Is it everybody who improves them, while a single person spoils them? Or isn't the opposite true: a single per-

son, or at least very few people, namely the horse-trainers, can improve them; while lay people spoil them, don't they, if they have to do with horses and make use of them? Isn't that true of horses as of all 5 other animals, Meletus? Of course it is, whether you and Anytus deny it or not. In fact, I dare say our young people are extremely lucky if only one person is cor- c rupting them, while everyone else is doing them good.

All right, Meletus. Enough has been said to prove that you never were concerned about the young. You betray your irresponsibility plainly, because you have not cared at all about the charges on which you bring me before this court.

Furthermore, Meletus, tell us, in God's name, 5 whether it is better to live among good fellow citizens or bad ones. Come sir, answer: I am not asking a hard question. Bad people have a harmful impact upon their closest companions at any given time, don't they, whereas good people have a good one?

—Yes.   10

Well, is there anyone who wants to be harmed d by his companions rather than benefited?—Be a good fellow and keep on answering, as the law requires you to. Is there anyone who wants to be harmed?

—Of course not.   5

Now tell me this. In bringing me here, do you claim that I am corrupting and depraving the young intentionally or unintentionally?

—Intentionally, so I maintain.

Really, Meletus? Are you so much smarter at your age than I at mine as to realize that the bad 10 have a harmful impact upon their closets companions at any given time, whereas the good have a ben- e eficial effect? Am I, by contrast, so far gone in my stupidity as not to realize that if I make one of my companions vicious, I risk incurring harm at his hands? And am I, therefore, as you allege, doing so much damage intentionally?

That I cannot accept from you, Meletus, and nei- 5 ther could anyone else, I imagine. Either I am not corrupting them—or if I am, I am doing so unin- 26a tentionally; so either way your charge is false. But if I am corrupting them unintentionally, the law does not require me to be brought to court for such mistakes, but rather to be taken aside for private instruction and admonition—since I shall obviously

stop doing unintentional damage, if I learn better.
5 But you avoided association with me and were unwilling to instruct me. Instead you bring me to
court, where the law requires you to bring people
who need punishment rather than enlightenment.

Very well, fellow Athenians. That part of my
b case is now proven: Meletus never cared about these
matters, either a lot or a little. Nevertheless, Meletus,
please tell us in what way you claim that I am corrupting our younger people. That is quite obvious,
isn't it, from the indictment you drew up? It is by
teaching them not to acknowledge the gods ac-
5 knowledged by the city, but to accept new spiritual
beings instead? You mean, don't you, that I am corrupting them by teaching them that?

—I most emphatically do.

Then, Meletus, in the name of those very gods we
are now discussing, please clarify the matter further
c for me, and for the jury here. You see, I cannot make
out what you mean. Is it that I am teaching people to
acknowledge that some gods exist—in which case it
follows that I do acknowledge their existence myself
as well, and am not a complete atheist, hence am not
guilty on that count—and yet that those gods are not
5 the ones acknowledged by the city, but different ones?
Is that your charge against me—namely, that they are
different? Or are you saying that I acknowledge no
gods at all myself, and teach the same to others?

—I am saying the latter; you acknowledge no
gods at all.

d   What ever makes you say that, Meletus, you
strange fellow? Do I not even acknowledge, then,
with the rest of mankind, that the sun and the moon
are gods?

—By God, he does not, members of the jury,
5 since he claims that the sun is made of rock, and the
moon of earth!

My dear Meletus, do you imagine that it is
Anaxagoras you are accusing? Do you have such
contempt for the jury, and imagine them so illiter-
ate as not to know that books by Anaxagoras of
10 Clazomenae are crammed with such assertions?
e What's more, are the young learning those things
from me when they can acquire them at the book-
stalls, now and then, for a drachma at most, and so
ridicule Socrates if he claims those ideas for his own,
especially when they are so bizarre? In God's name,

do you really think me as crazy as that? Do I acknowledge the existence of no god at all?

—By God no, none whatever.   5

I can't believe you, Meletus—nor, I think, can
you believe yourself. To my mind, fellow Athenians,
this fellow is an impudent scoundrel who has
framed this indictment out of sheer wanton impu- 27a
dence and insolence. He seems to have devised a sort
of riddle in order to try me out: "Will Socrates the
Wise tumble to my nice self-contradiction? Or shall
I fool him along with my other listeners?" You see, 5
he seems to me to be contradicting himself in the
indictment. It's as if he were saying: "Socrates is
guilty of not acknowledging gods, but of acknowledging gods"; and yet that is sheer tomfoolery.

I ask you to examine with me, gentlemen, just
how that appears to be his meaning. Answer for us, 10
Meletus; and the rest of you, please remember my b
initial request not to protest if I conduct the argument in my usual manner.

Is there anyone in the world, Meletus, who acknowledges that human phenomena exist, yet does
not acknowledge human beings?—Require him to
answer, gentlemen, and not to raise all kinds of con- 5
fused objections. Is there anyone who does not acknowledge horses, yet does acknowledge equestrian
phenomena? Or who does not acknowledge that
musicians exist, yet does acknowledge musical phenomena?

There is no one, excellent fellow: if you don't wish
to answer, I must answer for you, and for the jurors
here. But at least answer my next question yourself. c
Is there anyone who acknowledges that spiritual phenomena exist, yet does not acknowledge spirits?

—No.

How good of you to answer—albeit reluctantly
and under compulsion from the jury. Well now, you
say that I acknowledge spiritual beings and teach 5
others to do so. Whether they actually be new or old
is no matter: I do at any rate, by your account, acknowledge spiritual beings, which you have also
mentioned in your sworn deposition. But if I acknowledge spiritual beings, then surely it follows
quite inevitably that I must acknowledge spirits. Is 10
that not so?—Yes, it is so: I assume your agreement,
since you don't answer. But we regard spirits, don't d
we, as either gods or children of gods? Yes or no?

—Yes.

Then given that I do believe in spirits, as you say,
5 if spirits are gods of some sort, this is precisely what
I claim when I say that you are presenting us with
a riddle and making fun of us: you are saying that
I do not believe in gods, and yet again that I do believe in gods, seeing that I believe in spirits.

On the other hand, if spirits are children of gods,
some sort of bastard offspring from nymphs—or
from whomever they are traditionally said, in each
10 case, to be born—then who in the world could ever
e believe that there were children of gods, yet no
gods? That would be just as absurd as accepting the
existence of children of horses and asses—namely,
mules—yet rejecting the existence of horses or asses!

In short, Meletus, you can only have drafted this
either by way of trying us out, or because you were
5 at a loss how to charge me with a genuine offence.
How could you possibly persuade anyone with even
the slightest intelligence that someone who accepts
28a spiritual beings does not also accept divine ones, and
again that the same person also accepts neither spirits nor gods nor heroes? There is no conceivable way.

But enough, fellow Athenians. It needs no long
defence, I think, to show that I am not guilty of the
5 charges in Meletus' indictment; the foregoing will
suffice. You may be sure, though, that what I was
saying earlier is true: I have earned great hostility
among many people. And that is what will convict
me, if I am convicted: not Meletus or Anytus, but
b the slander and malice of the crowd. They have certainly convicted many other good men as well, and
I imagine they will do so again; there is no risk of
their stopping with me.

Now someone may perhaps say: "Well then, are you
not ashamed, Socrates, to have pursued a way of life
which has now put you at risk of death?"
5   But it may be fair for me to answer him as follows: "You are sadly mistaken, fellow, if you suppose that a man with even a grain of self-respect
should reckon up the risks of living or dying, rather
than simply consider, whenever he does something,
c whether his actions are just or unjust, the deeds of
a good man or a bad one. By your principles, presumably, all those demigods who died in the plain
of Troy were inferior creatures—yes, even the son

of Thetis, who showed so much scorn for danger,
when the alternative was to endure dishonour.
Thus, when he was eager to slay Hector, his mother, 5
goddess that she was, spoke to him—something like
this, I fancy:

My child, if thou dost avenge the murder of thy
    friend, Patroclus,
And dost slay Hector, then straightway [so runs the
    poem]
Shalt thou die thyself, since doom is prepared for
    thee
Next after Hector's.

But though he heard that, he made light of death 10
and danger, since he feared far more to live as a base d
man, and to fail to avenge his dear ones. The poem
goes on:

Then straightway let me die, once I have given the
    wrongdoer
His deserts, less I remain here by the beak-prowed
    ships,
An object of derision, and a burden upon the earth.

Can you suppose that he gave any thought to
death or danger?

You see, here is the truth of the matter, fellow 5
Athenians. Wherever a man has taken up a position
because he considers it best, or has been posted there
by his commander, that is where I believe he should
remain, steadfast in danger, taking no account at all
of death or of anything else rather than dishonour.
I would therefore have been acting absurdly, fellow c
Athenians, if when assigned to a post at Potidaea,
Amphipolis, or Delium by the superiors you had
elected to command me, I remained where I was
posted on those occasions at the risk of death, if ever
any man did; whereas now that the god assigns me,
as I became completely convinced, to the duty of 5
leading the philosophical life by examining myself 29a
and others, I desert that post from fear of death or
anything else. Yes, that would be unthinkable; and
then I truly should deserve to be brought to court
for failing to acknowledge the gods' existence, in
that I was disobedient to the oracle, was afraid of
death, and thought I was wise when I was not.

5 After all, gentlemen, the fear of death amounts simply to thinking one is wise when one is not: it is thinking one knows something one does not know. No one knows, you see, whether death may not in fact prove the greatest of all blessings for mankind; b but people fear it as if they knew it for certain to be the greatest of evils. And yet to think that one knows what one does not know must surely be the kind of folly which is reprehensible.

On this matter especially, gentlemen, that may be the nature of my own advantage over most people. If I really were to claim to be wiser than anyone in any respect, it would consist simply in this: 5 just as I do not possess adequate knowledge of life in Hades, so I also realize that I do not possess it; whereas acting unjustly in disobedience to one's betters, whether god or human being, is something I *know* to be evil and shameful. Hence I shall never fear or flee from something which may indeed be a good for all I know, rather than from things I know to be evils.

c Suppose, therefore, that you pay no heed to Anytus, but are prepared to let me go. He said I need never have been brought to court in the first place; but that once I had been, your only option was to put me to death. He declared before you that, if 5 I got away from you this time, your sons would all be utterly corrupted by practising Socrates' teachings. Suppose, in the face of that, you were to say to me:

"Socrates, we will not listen to Anytus this time. We are prepared to let you go—but only on this condition: you are to pursue that quest of yours and practise philosophy no longer; and if you are caught doing it any more, you shall be put to death."

d Well, as I just said, if you were prepared to let me go on those terms, I should reply to you as follows:

"I have the greatest fondness and affection for you, fellow Athenians, but I will obey my god rather than you; and so long as I draw breath and am able, 5 I shall never give up practising philosophy, or exhorting and showing the way to any of you whom I ever encounter, by giving my usual sort of message. 'Excellent friend,' I shall say; 'You are an Athenian. Your city is the most important and renowned for its wisdom and power; so are you not ashamed that, while you take care to acquire as much wealth as possible, with honour and glory as e well, yet you take no care or thought for understanding or truth, or for the best possible state of your soul?'

"And should any of you dispute that, and claim that he does take such care, I will not let him go straight away nor leave him, but I will question and 5 examine and put him to the test; and if I do not 30a think he has acquired goodness, though he says he has, I shall say, 'Shame on you, for setting the lowest value upon the most precious things, and for rating inferior ones more highly?' That I shall do for anyone I encounter, young or old, alien or fellow citizen; but all the more for the latter, since your kinship with me is closer." 5

Those are my orders from my god, I do assure you. Indeed, I believe that no greater good has ever befallen you in our city than my service to my god; because all I do is to go about persuading you, young and old alike, not to care for your bodies or for your b wealth so intensely as for the greatest possible wellbeing of your souls. "It is not wealth," I tell you, "that produces goodness; rather, it is from goodness that wealth, and all other benefits for human beings, accrue to them in their private and public life."

If, in fact, I am corrupting the young by those as- 5 sertions, you may call them harmful. But if anyone claims that I say anything different, he is talking nonsense. In the face of that I should like to say: "Fellow Athenians, you may listen to Anytus or not, as you please; and you may let me go or not, as you c please, because there is no chance of my acting otherwise, even if I have to die many times over—"

Stop protesting, fellow Athenians! Please abide by my request that you not protest against what I say, but hear me out; in fact, it will be in your in- 5 terest, so I believe, to do so. You see, I am going to say some further things to you which may make you shout out—although I beg you not to.

You may be assured that if you put to death the sort of man I just said I was, you will not harm me more than you harm yourselves. Meletus or Anytus 10 would not harm me at all; nor, in fact, could they d do so, since I believe it is out of the question for a better man to be harmed by his inferior. The latter may, of course, inflict death or banishment or disenfranchisement; and my accuser here, along with others no doubt, believes those to be great evils. But I do not. Rather, I believe it a far greater evil to try to kill a man unjustly, as he does now.

At this point, therefore, fellow Athenians, so far from pleading on my own behalf, as might be supposed, I am pleading on yours, in case by condemning me you should mistreat the gift which God has bestowed upon you—because if you put me to death, you will not easily find another like me. The fact is, if I may put the point in a somewhat comical way, that I have been literally attached by God to our city, as if to a horse—a large thoroughbred, which is a bit sluggish because of its size, and needs to be aroused by some sort of gadfly. Yes, in me, I believe, God has attached to our city just such a creature—the kind which is constantly alighting everywhere on you, all day long, arousing, cajoling, or reproaching each and every one of you. You will not easily acquire another such gadfly, gentlemen; rather, if you take my advice, you will spare my life. I dare say, though, that you will get angry, like people who are awakened from their doze. Perhaps you will heed Anytus, and give me a swat: you could happily finish me off, and then spend the rest of your life asleep—unless God, in his compassion for you, were to send you someone else.

That I am, in fact, just the sort of gift that God would send to our city, you may recognize from this: it would not seem to be in human nature for me to have neglected all my own affairs, and put up with the neglect of my family for all these years, but constantly minded your interests, by visiting each of you in private like a father or an elder brother, urging you to be concerned about goodness. Of course, if I were gaining anything from that, or were being paid to urge that course upon you, my actions could be explained. But in fact you can see for yourselves that my accusers, who so shamelessly level all those other charges against me, could not muster the impudence to call evidence that I ever once obtained payment, or asked for any. It is I who can call evidence sufficient, I think, to show that I am speaking the truth—namely, my poverty.

Now it may perhaps seem peculiar that, as some say, I give this counsel by going around and dealing with others' concerns in private, yet do not venture to appear before the Assembly, and counsel the city about your business in public. But the reason for that is one you have frequently heard me give in many places: it is a certain divine or spiritual sign which comes to me, the very thing to which Meletus made mocking allusion in his indictment. It has been happening to me ever since childhood: a voice of some sort which comes, and which always—whenever it does come—restrains me from what I am about to do, yet never gives positive direction. That is what opposes my engaging in politics—and its opposition is an excellent thing, to my mind; because you may be quite sure, fellow Athenians, that if I had tried to engage in politics, I should have perished long since, and should have been of no use either to you or to myself.

And please do not get angry if I tell you the truth. The fact is that there is no person on earth whose life will be spared by you or by any other majority, if he is genuinely opposed to many injustices and unlawful acts, and tries to prevent their occurrence in our city. Rather, anyone who truly fights for what is just, if he is going to survive for even a short time, must act in a private capacity rather than a public one.

I will offer you conclusive evidence of that—not just words, but the sort of evidence that you respect, namely, actions. Just hear me tell my experiences, so that you may know that I would not submit to a single person for fear of death, contrary to what is just; nor would I do so, even if I were to lose my life on the spot. I shall mention things to you which are vulgar commonplaces of the courts; yet they are true.

Although I have never held any other public office in our city, fellow Athenians, I have served on its Council. My own tribe, Antiochis, happened to be the presiding commission on the occasion when you wanted a collective trial for the ten generals who had failed to rescue the survivors from the naval battle. That was illegal, as you all later recognized. At the time I was the only commissioner opposed to your acting illegally, and I voted against the motion. And though its advocates were prepared to lay information against me and have me arrested, while you were urging them on by shouting, I believed that I should face danger in siding with law and justice, rather than take your side for fear of imprisonment or death, when your proposals were contrary to justice.

Those events took place while our city was still under democratic rule. But on a subsequent occasion, after the oligarchy had come to power, the Thirty summoned me and four others to the round chamber, with orders to arrest Leon the Salaminian, and fetch him from Salamis for execution; they were constantly issuing such orders, of course, to many others, in their wish to implicate as many as possible in their crimes. On that occasion, however, I showed, once again not just by words, but by my actions, that I couldn't care less about death—if that would not be putting it rather crudely—but that my one and only care was to avoid doing anything sinful or unjust. Thus, powerful as it was, that regime did not frighten me into unjust action: when we emerged from the round chamber, the other four went off to Salamis and arrested Leon, whereas I left them and went off home. For that I might easily have been put to death, had the regime not collapsed shortly afterwards. There are many witnesses who will testify before you about those events.

Do you imagine, then, that I would have survived all these years if I had been regularly active in public life, and had championed what was right in a manner worthy of a brave man, and valued that above all else, as was my duty? Far from it, fellow Athenians: I would not, and nor would any other man. But in any public undertaking, that is the sort of person that I, for my part, shall prove to have been throughout my life; and likewise in my private life, because I have never been guilty of unjust association with anyone, including those whom my slanderers allege to have been my students.

I never, in fact, was anyone's instructor at any time. But if a person wanted to hear me talking, while I was engaging in my own business, I never grudged that to anyone, young or old; nor do I hold conversation only when I receive payment, and not otherwise. Rather, I offer myself for questioning to wealthy and poor alike, and to anyone who may wish to answer in response to questions from me. Whether any of those people acquires a good character or not, I cannot fairly be held responsible, when I never at any time promised any of them that

they would learn anything from me, nor gave them instruction. And if anyone claims that he ever learnt anything from me, or has heard privately something that everyone else did not hear as well, you may be sure that what he says is untrue.

Why then, you may ask, do some people enjoy spending so much time in my company? You have already heard, fellow Athenians: I have told you the whole truth—which is that my listeners enjoy the examination of those who think themselves wise but are not, since the process is not unamusing. But for me, I must tell you, it is a mission which I have been bidden to undertake by the god, through oracles and dreams, and through every means whereby a divine injunction to perform any task has ever been laid upon a human being.

That is not only true, fellow Athenians, but is easily verified—because if I do corrupt any of our young people, or have corrupted others in the past, then presumably, when they grew older, should any of them have realized that I had at any time given them bad advice in their youth, they ought now to have appeared here themselves to accuse me and obtain redress. Or else, if they were unwilling to come in person, members of their families—fathers, brothers, or other relations—had their relatives suffered any harm at my hands, ought now to put it on record and obtain redress.

In any case, many of those people are present, whom I can see: first there is Crito, my contemporary and fellow demesman, father of Critobulus here; then Lysanias of Sphettus, father of Aeschines here; next, Epigenes' father, Antiphon from Cephisia, is present; then again, there are others here whose brothers have spent time with me in these studies: Nicostratus, son of Theozotides, brother of Theodotus—Theodotus himself, incidentally, is deceased, so Nicostratus could not have come at his brother's urging; and Paralius here, son of Demodocus, whose brother was Theages; also present is Ariston's son, Adimantus, whose brother is Plato here; and Aeantodorus, whose brother is Apollodorus here.

There are many others I could mention to you, from whom Meletus should surely have called some testimony during his own speech. However, if he forgot to do so then, let him call it now—I yield the floor to him—and if he has any such evidence, let him produce it. But quite the opposite is true, gentlemen: you will find that they are all prepared to support me, their corruptor, the one who is, according to Meletus and Anytus, doing their relatives b mischief. Support for me from the actual victims of corruption might perhaps be explained; but what of the uncorrupted—older men by now, and relatives of my victims? What reason would they have to support me, apart from the right and proper one, which 5 is that they know very well that Meletus is lying, whereas I am telling the truth?

There it is, then, gentlemen. That, and perhaps more of the same, is about all I have to say in my defence. But perhaps, among your number, there c may be someone who will harbour resentment when he recalls a case of his own: he may have faced a less serious trial than this one, yet begged and implored the jury, weeping copiously, and producing his chil-5 dren here, along with many other relatives and loved ones, to gain as much sympathy as possible. By contrast, I shall do none of those things, even though I am running what might be considered the ultimate risk. Perhaps someone with those thoughts will harden his heart against me; and enraged by d those same thoughts, he may cast his vote against me in anger. Well, if any of you are so inclined—not that I expect it of you, but if anyone *should* be—I think it fair to answer him as follows:

"I naturally do have relatives, my excellent friend, because—in Homer's own words—I too was 5 'not born of oak nor of rock,' but of human parents; and so I do have relatives—including my sons, fellow Athenians. There are three of them: one is now a youth, while two are still children. Nevertheless, I shall not produce any of them here, and then entreat you to vote for my acquittal."

10   And why, you may ask, will I do no such thing? e Not out of contempt or disrespect for you, fellow Athenians—whether or not I am facing death boldly is a different issue. The point is that with our reputations in mind—yours and our whole city's, as well as my own—I believe that any such behaviour would be ignominious, at my age and with the rep-5 utation I possess; that reputation may or may not, 35a in fact, be deserved, but at least it is believed that

Socrates stands out in some way from the run of human beings. Well, if those of you who are believed to be pre-eminent in wisdom, courage, or any other form of goodness, are going to behave like that, it would be demeaning.

I have frequently seen such men when they face judgment: they have significant reputations, yet they put on astonishing performances, apparently in the 5 belief that by dying they will suffer something unheard of—as if they would be immune from death, so long as you did not kill them! They seem to me to put our city to shame: they could give any for- b eigner the impression that men preeminent among Athenians in goodness, whom they select from their own number to govern and hold other positions, are no better than women. I say this, fellow Athenians, because none of us who has even the slightest rep- 5 utation should behave like that; nor should you put up with us if we try to do so. Rather, you should make one thing clear: you will be far more inclined to convict one who stages those pathetic charades and makes our city an object of derision, than one who keeps his composure.

But leaving reputation aside, gentlemen, I do not 10 think it right to entreat the jury, nor to win acquit- c tal in that way, instead of by informing and persuading them. A juror does not sit to dispense justice as a favour, but to determine where it lies. And he has sworn, not that he will favour whomever he pleases, but that he will try the case according to law. We should not, then, accustom you to transgress 5 your oath, nor should you become accustomed to doing so: neither of us would be showing respect towards the gods. And therefore, fellow Athenians, do not require behaviour from me toward you d which I consider neither proper nor right nor pious—more especially now, for God's sake, when I stand charged by Meletus here with impiety: because if I tried to persuade and coerce you with entreaties in spite of your oath, I clearly *would* be 5 teaching you not to believe in gods; and I would stand literally self-convicted, by my defence, of failing to acknowledge them. But that is far from the truth: I do acknowledge them, fellow Athenians, as none of my accusers do; and I trust to you, and to God, to judge my case as shall be best for me and for yourselves.

e For many reasons, fellow Athenians, I am not dis-
36a mayed by this outcome[1]—your convicting me, I
mean—and especially because the outcome has
come as no surprise to me. I wonder far more at the
number of votes cast on each side, because I did not
5 think the margin would be so narrow. Yet it seems,
in fact, that if a mere thirty votes had gone the other
way, I should have been acquitted. Or rather, even
as things stand, I consider that I have been cleared
of Meletus' charges. Not only that, but one thing is
obvious to everyone: if Anytus had not come for-
b ward with Lycon to accuse me, Meletus would have
forfeited 1,000 drachmas, since he would not have
gained one-fifth of the votes cast.

But anyhow, this gentleman demands the death
penalty for me. Very well, then: what alternative
penalty shall I suggest to you, fellow Athenians?
5 Clearly, it must be one I deserve. So what do I deserve to incur or to pay, for having taken it into my
head not to lead an inactive life? Instead, I have neglected the things that concern most people—making money, managing an estate, gaining military or
civic honours, or other positions of power, or joining political clubs and parties which have formed in
c our city. I thought myself, in truth, too honest to
survive if I engaged in those things. I did not pursue a course, therefore, in which I would be of no
use to you or to myself. Instead, by going to each individual privately, I tried to render a service for you
5 which is—so I maintain—the highest service of all.
Therefore that was the course I followed: I tried to
persuade each of you not to care for any of his possessions rather than care for himself, striving for the
utmost excellence and understanding; and not to
d care for our city's possessions rather than for the city
itself; and to care about other things in the same way.

So what treatment do I deserve for being such a
benefactor? If I am to make a proposal truly in keeping with my deserts, fellow Athenians, it should be
some benefit; and moreover, the sort of benefit that
5 would be fitting for me. Well then, what *is* fitting
for a poor man who is a benefactor, and who needs
time free for exhorting you? Nothing could be more
fitting, fellow Athenians, than to give such a man
regular free meals in the Prytaneum; indeed, that is
far more fitting for him than for any of you who
may have won an Olympic race with a pair or a team

of horses: that victor brings you only the appearance
of success, whereas I bring you the reality; besides, 10
he is not in want of sustenance, whereas I am. So if, e
as justice demands, I am to make a proposal in keep- 37a
ing with my deserts, that is what I suggest: free
meals in the Prytaneum.

Now, in proposing this, I may seem to you, as
when I talked about appeals for sympathy, to be
speaking from sheer effrontery. But actually I have 5
no such motive, fellow Athenians. My point is rather
this: I am convinced that I do not treat any human
being unjustly, at least intentionally—but I cannot
make you share that conviction, because we have
conversed together so briefly. I say this, because if it
were the law here, as in other jurisdictions, that a 10
capital case must not be tried in a single day, but b
over several, I think you could have been convinced;
but as things stand, it is not easy to clear oneself of
such grave allegations in a short time.

Since, therefore, I am persuaded, for my part,
that I have treated no one unjustly, I have no intention whatever of so treating myself, nor of denouncing myself as deserving ill, or proposing any 5
such treatment for myself. Why should I do that?
For fear of the penalty Meletus demands for me,
when I say that I don't know if that is a good thing
or a bad one? In preference to that, am I then to
choose one of the things I know very well to be bad,
and demand that instead? Imprisonment, for instance? Why should I live in prison, in servitude to c
the annually appointed prison commissioners? Well
then, a fine, with imprisonment until I pay? That
would amount to what I just mentioned, since I
haven't the means to pay it.

Well then, should I propose banishment?
Perhaps that is what you would propose for me. Yet 5
I must surely be obsessed with survival, fellow
Athenians, if I am so illogical as that. You, my fellow citizens, were unable to put up with my dis- d
courses and arguments, but they were so irksome
and odious to you that you now seek to be rid of
them. Could I not draw the inference, in that case,
that others will hardly take kindly to them? Far
from it, fellow Athenians. A fine life it would be for
a person of my age to go into exile, and spend his 5
days continually exchanging one city for another,
and being repeatedly expelled—because I know

very well that wherever I go, the young will come to hear me speaking, as they do here. And if I repel them, they will expel me themselves, by persuading their elders; while if I do not repel them, their fathers and relatives will expel me on their account.

Now, perhaps someone may say: "Socrates, could you not be so kind as to keep quiet and remain inactive, while living in exile?" This is the hardest point of all of which to convince some of you. Why? Because, if I tell you that that would mean disobeying my god, and that is why I cannot remain inactive, you will disbelieve me and think that I am practising a sly evasion. Again, if I said that it really is the greatest benefit for a person to converse every day about goodness, and about the other subjects you have heard me discussing when examining myself and others—and that an unexamined life is no life for a human being to live—then you would believe me still less when I made those assertions. But the facts, gentlemen, are just as I claim them to be, though it is not easy to convince you of them. At the same time, I am not accustomed to think of myself as deserving anything bad. If I had money, I would have proposed a fine of as much as I could afford: that would have done me no harm at all. But the fact is that I have none—unless you wish to fix the penalty at a sum I could pay. I could afford to pay you 1 mina, I suppose, so I suggest a fine of that amount—

One moment, fellow Athenians. Plato here, along with Crito, Critobulus, and Apollodorus, is uring me to propose 30 minas, and they are saying they will stand surety for that sum. So I propose a fine of that amount, and these people shall be your sufficient guarantors of its payment.

For the sake of a slight gain in time, fellow Athenians, you will incur infamy and blame from those who would denigrate our city, for putting Socrates to death[2]—a "wise man"—because those who wish to malign you will say I am wise, even if I am not; in any case, had you waited only a short time, you would have obtained that outcome automatically. You can see, of course, that I am now well advanced in life, and death is not far off. I address that not to all of you, but to those who condemned me to death; and to those same people I would add something further.

Perhaps you imagine, gentlemen, that I have been convicted for lack of arguments of the sort I could have used to convince you, had I believed that I should do or say anything to gain acquittal. But that is far from true. I have been convicted, not for lack of arguments, but for lack of brazen impudence and willingness to address you in such terms as you would most like to be addressed in—that is to say, by weeping and wailing, and doing and saying much else that I claim to be unworthy of me—the sorts of thing that you are so used to hearing from others. But just as I did not think during my defence that I should do anything unworthy of a free man because I was in danger, so now I have no regrets about defending myself as I did; I should far rather present such a defence and die, than live by defending myself in that other fashion.

In court, as in warfare, neither I nor anyone else should contrive to escape death at any cost. On the battlefield too, it often becomes obvious that one could avoid death by throwing down one's arms and flinging oneself upon the mercy of one's pursuers. And in every sort of danger there are many other means of escaping death, if one is shameless enough to do or to say anything. I suggest that it is not death that is hard to avoid, gentlemen, but wickedness is far harder, since it is fleeter of foot than death. Thus, slow and elderly as I am, I have now been overtaken by the slower runner; while my accusers, adroit and quick-witted as they are, have been overtaken by the faster, which is wickedness. And so I take my leave, condemned to death by your judgment, whereas they stand for ever condemned to depravity and injustice as judged by Truth. And just as I accept my penalty, so must they. Things were bound to turn out this way, I suppose, and I imagine it is for the best.

In the next place, to those of you who voted against me, I wish to utter a prophecy. Indeed, I have now reached a point at which people are most given to prophesying—that is, when they are on the point of death. I warn you, my executioners, that as soon as I am dead retribution will come upon you— far more severe, I swear, than the sentence you have passed upon me. You have tried to kill me for now, in the belief that you will be relieved from giving an account of your lives. But in fact, I can tell you, you will face just the opposite outcome. There will be more critics to call you to account, people whom I have restrained for the time being though you were unaware of my doing so. They will be all the harder on you since they are younger, and you will rue it all the more—because if you imagine that by putting 5 people to death you will prevent anyone from reviling you for not living rightly, you are badly mistaken. That way of escape is neither feasible nor honourable. Rather, the most honourable and easiest way is not the silencing of others, but striving to make oneself as good a person as possible. So with that prophecy to those of you who voted against me, 10 I take my leave.

e   As for those who voted for my acquittal, I should like to discuss the outcome of this case while the officials are occupied, and I am not yet on the way to the place where I must die. Please bear with me, gentlemen, just for this short time: there is no rea- 5 son why we should not have a word with one another while that is still permitted.

40a   Since I regard you as my friends, I am willing to show you the significance of what has just befallen me. You see, gentlemen of the jury—and in applying that term to you, I probably use it correctly— something wonderful has just happened to me. 5 Hitherto, the usual prophetic voice from my spiritual sign was continually active, and frequently opposed me even on trivial matters, if I was about to do anything amiss. But now something has befallen me, as you can see for yourselves, which one cer- b tainly might consider—and is generally held—to be the very worst of evils. Yet the sign from God did not oppose me, either when I left home this morning, or when I appeared here in court, or at any point when I was about to say anything during my speech; 5 and yet in other discussions it has very often stopped me in mid-sentence. This time, though, it has not opposed me at any moment in anything I said or did in this whole business.

Now, what do I take to be the explanation for that? I will tell you: I suspect that what has befallen me is a blessing, and that those of us who suppose c death to be an evil cannot be making a correct assumption. I have gained every ground for that suspicion, because my usual sign could not have failed to oppose me, unless I were going to incur some good result.

And let us also reflect upon how good a reason 5 there is to hope that death is a good thing. It is, you see, one or other of two things: either to be dead is to be nonexistent, as it were, and a dead person has no awareness whatever of anything at all; or else, as we are told, the soul undergoes some sort of transformation, or exchanging of this present world 10 for another. Now if there is, in fact, no awareness d in death, but it is like sleep—the kind in which the sleeper does not even dream at all—then death would be a marvellous gain. Why, imagine that someone had to pick the night in which he slept so soundly that he did not even dream, and to compare all the other nights and days of his life with 5 that one; suppose he had to say, upon consideration, how many days or nights in his life he had spent better and more agreeably than that night; in that e case, I think he would find them easy to count compared with his other days and nights—even if he were the Great King of Persia, let alone an ordinary person. Well, if death is like that, then for my part I call it a gain; because on that assumption the whole of time would seem no longer than a single night.

On the other hand, if death is like taking a trip from here to another place, and if it is true, as we are 5 told, that all of the dead do indeed exist in that other place, why then, gentlemen of the jury, what could be a greater blessing than that? If upon arriving in 41a Hades, and being rid of these people who profess to be "jurors," one is going to find those who are truly judges, and who are also said to sit in judgment there—Minos, Rhadamanthys, Aeacus, Triptolemus, and all other demigods who were righteous in their 5 own lives—would that be a disappointing journey?

Or again, what would any of you not give to share the company of Orpheus and Musaeus, of Hesiod and Homer? I say "you," since I personally would be willing to die many times over, if those tales are true. Why? Because my own sojourn there would b be wonderful, if I could meet Palamedes, or Ajax, son of Telamon, or anyone else of old who met their death through an unjust verdict. Whenever I met them, I could compare my own experiences with theirs—which would be not unamusing, I fancy— 5 and best of all, I could spend time questioning and probing people there, just as I do here, to find out who among them is truly wise, and who thinks he is without being so.

What would one not give, gentlemen of the jury, c to be able to question the leader of the great expedition against Troy, or Odysseus, or Sisyphus, or countless other men and women one could mention? Would it not be unspeakable good fortune to converse with them there, to mingle with them and 5 question them? At least that isn't a reason, presumably, for people in that world to put you to death—because amongst other ways in which people there are more fortunate than those in our world, they have become immune from death for the rest of time, if what we are told is actually true.

Moreover, you too, gentlemen of the jury, should be of good hope in the face of death, and fix your d minds upon this single truth: nothing can harm a good man, either in life or in death; nor are his fortunes neglected by the gods. In fact, what has befallen me has come about by no mere accident; 5 rather, it is clear to me that it was better I should die now and be rid of my troubles. That is also the reason why the divine sign at no point turned me back; and for my part, I bear those who condemned me, and my accusers, no ill will at all—though, to

be sure, it was not with that intent that they were condemning and accusing me, but with intent to e harm me—and they are culpable for that. Still, this much I ask of them. When my sons come of age, gentlemen, punish them: give them the same sort of trouble that I used to give you, if you think they care 5 for money or anything else more than for goodness, and if they think highly of themselves when they 42a are of no value. Reprove them, as I reproved you, for failing to care for the things they should, and for thinking highly of themselves when they are worthless. If you will do that, then I shall have received my own just deserts from you, as will my sons.

But enough. It is now time to leave—for me to die, and for you to live—though which of us has the better destiny is unclear to everyone, save only to God.

NOTES

1. The verdict was "Guilty." Socrates here begins his second speech, proposing an alternative to the death penalty demanded by the prosecution.
2. The jury has now voted for the death penalty, and Socrates begins his final speech.

PART II

•

God and Evil

INTRODUCTION

No issues are so likely to lead one into the study of philosophy as those arising from religious practices and beliefs. For most, the central question is the existence of God. All the selections in this part bear on that issue. Saint Anselm, Saint Thomas Aquinas, Blaise Pascal, and the characters Demea and Cleanthes in David Hume's *Dialogues Concerning Natural Religion* provide arguments in favor of the existence of God. Bertrand Russell, the character Philo in Hume's *Dialogues*, and J. L. Mackie all provide arguments against belief in God. All of the skeptics mention the problem posed for believers by the existence of evil; Philo focuses on this problem toward the end of the *Dialogues*, and it is the topic of Mackie's selection. Gottfried Leibniz and Nelson Pike argue that the believer can answer this challenge.

Pascal's essay stands a bit apart from the rest. He does not argue directly for the existence of God. He thinks that if there is a God, He is infinitely incomprehensible to us, and that therefore we cannot expect to know "either what He is or if He is." But this does not spare us from the dilemma of whether to believe or not. If we approach the issue as we would a wager, Pascal argues, it is clear what we should do.

> Let us weigh the gain and the loss in wagering that God is. Let us estimate these two chances. If you gain, you gain all; if you lose, you lose nothing. Wager then, without hesitation that he is. (p. 50)

One might challenge Pascal, on the grounds that he does seem to be assuming that he knows a bit about the nature of God after all. He seems confident that we will be better off if we believe than if we do not. Doesn't that assume that if there is a God, He, She, or It is the sort of being who wants to be believed in? How does Pascal know that, given the incomprehensibility of God?

The other selections consider the issue of God's existence in a more straightforward way, looking for arguments to show that God does or does not exist. Any such arguments presuppose some conception of the nature of God, otherwise it would be unclear what has to be proven. The God at issue in these selections is that of classic Christianity. God is conceived of as perfect; this includes being omnipotent (all-powerful), omniscient (all-knowing), and completely benevolent.

Anselm argues that it would be a contradiction to deny the existence of such a God. He takes it that by "God" we mean *something than which nothing greater can be conceived*. But then, "if that than which a greater cannot be conceived exists just in the understanding, the very thing than which a greater cannot be conceived is something than which a greater *can* be conceived. Without doubt, then, something than which a greater can't be conceived does exist—both in the understanding and in reality."

Anselm's argument may seem to be pulling a large rabbit out of a very small hat—resolving the issue of the existence of God on the basis of a definition and a few deft logical moves. The argument has in fact given rise to a large literature. Descartes defended a version of it. It has been criticized by Aquinas, Immanuel Kant, Bertrand Russell, Gottlob Frege, and others. We include Aquinas's criticism.

Although Aquinas doesn't think the ontological argument works, he does think there are "five ways to prove that God exists." These are the argument from change, the argument from causation, the argument from possibility and necessity, the argument from gradations in things, and the argument from the governance of the world. The first two of these arguments are cosmological arguments. That is, they argue from very general facts about the cosmos to the conclusion that God exists. Demea also puts forward an argument of this type in Hume's *Dialogues*, book Part IX. Philo and Cleanthes both criticize Demea's argument. Aquinas's first two arguments appear to be vulnerable to some of the objections Philo and Cleanthes raise against Demea, as well as the considerations Russell raises in his objections to the First Cause Argument.

Aquinas's Fifth Way, from the governance of the world, is somewhat similar to the argument that Cleanthes raises in the first part of Hume's *Dialogues*, the argument from analogy or design:

> Look round the world: Contemplate the whole and every part of it: You will find it to be nothing but one great machine, subdivided into an infinite number of lesser machines. . . . The curious adapting of means to ends, throughout all nature, resembles exactly, though it much exceeds, the productions of human contrivance; of human design, thought, wisdom and intelligence. Since therefore the effects resemble each other, we are led to infer, by all the rules of analogy, that the causes also resemble; and that the author of nature is somewhat similar to the mind of man; though possessed of much larger faculties, proportioned to the grandeur of the work, which he has executed. By this argument *a posteriori*, and by this argument alone, do we prove at once the existence of the Deity . . . (pp. 59–60)

Cleanthes's argument is the main topic of Hume's *Dialogues*, with Philo shouldering the burden of raising objections to it.

Historically, the most important argument *against* the existence of God—at least against the existence of a perfect God as conceived of in classical Christianity—has been the existence of evil.

> Epicurus' old questions are yet unanswered. Is [God] willing to prevent evil, but not able? then is he impotent. Is he able, but not willing? then is he malevolent. Is he both able and willing? whence then is evil? (p. 80)

This problem is the topic of the second group of selections. We placed Hume's *Dialogues* in this section, somewhat arbitrarily; while Cleanthes's argument from design is the main topic of the book, Philo's powerful statement of the problem of evil in the last three parts has shaped modern discussion of the problem. We include two selections from recent philosophy, by Nelson Pike and J. L. Mackie.

A. Why Believe?

The Ontological Argument

SAINT ANSELM

Saint Anselm of Canterbury (1033–1109) was Archbishop of Canterbury. His works include *Monologion, Proslogion,* and *De Veritate*.

—•—

Chapter I
A Call for the Mind to Contemplate God

. . . I gratefully acknowledge, Lord, that you created your image in me so that I would remember you, conceive of you, and love you. But this image has been so worn away by my corruption, so obscured by the filth of my sins, that it cannot serve its purpose unless you renew and reshape it. I won't try to reach your heights, Lord, since I could never make my understanding reach that high. Yet I still want somehow to understand your truth, which my heart believes and loves. For, rather than seeking to understand so that I can believe, I believe so that I can understand. In fact, one of the things that I believe is that, "unless I believe, I cannot understand" [Isa. 7:9].

Chapter II
God Truly Exists

So Lord—you who reward faith with understanding—let me understand, insofar as you see fit, whether you are as we believe and whether you are what we believe you to be. We believe you to be

something than which nothing greater can be conceived. The question, then, is whether something with this nature exists, since "the fool has said in his heart that there is no God" [Ps. 14:1, 53:1]. But, surely, when the fool hears the words "something than which nothing greater can be conceived," he understands what he hears, and what he understands exists in his understanding—even if he doesn't think that it exists. For it is one thing for an object to exist in someone's understanding, and another for him to think that it exists. When a painter plans out a painting, he has it in his understanding, but—not yet having produced it—he doesn't yet think that it exists. After he has painted it, he has the painting in his understanding, and—having produced it—he thinks that it exists. This should convince even the fool that something than which nothing greater can be conceived exists, if only in the understanding—since the fool understands the phrase "that than which nothing greater can be conceived" when he hears it, and whatever a person understands exists in his understanding. And surely that than which a greater cannot be conceived cannot exist *just* in the understanding. If it were to exist *just* in the understanding, we could conceive it to exist in reality too, in which case it would be greater. Therefore, if that than which a greater cannot be conceived exists just in the understanding, the very thing than which a greater cannot be conceived is something than which a greater *can* be conceived. But surely this cannot be.

From *Proslogion*, translated by Ronald Rubin. Reprinted by permission of the translator.

Without doubt, then, something than which a greater can't be conceived does exist—both in the understanding and in reality.

Chapter III
It Is Impossible to Conceive
That God Doesn't Exist

In fact, this thing so truly exists that it can't be conceived not to exist. For something that can be conceived to exist but can't be conceived not to exist is greater than one which can be conceived not to exist. Hence, if that than which a greater can't be conceived can be conceived not to exist, then that than which a greater can't be conceived is not that than which a greater can't be conceived. But this would be a contradiction. Therefore, something than which a greater can't be conceived so truly exists that it can't be conceived not to exist.

And this thing is you, Lord our God. Therefore, you so truly exist, Lord my God, that you can't be conceived not to exist. And this is as it should be. For, if one's mind could conceive of something better than you, a created thing would rise above its creator and pass judgment on it, which would be completely absurd. Yes, anything other than you can be conceived not to exist. Therefore, you alone have the truest, and hence the greatest, being of all; nothing else has being as true or as great. Then why has the fool said in his heart that there is no God, when it is evident to a rational mind that your being is the greatest of all? Why—unless because he is stupid and a fool!

Chapter IV
How the Fool Can Say in His
Heart That Which Can't
Be Conceived

But how could the fool say in his heart something that he couldn't conceive of? And how could he fail to conceive of what he said in his heart, when saying something in one's heart is the same as conceiving of it? If—or, rather, since—he did conceive (since he spoke his heart) but did not speak in his heart (since he could not conceive), there is more than one way to say something in the heart or to conceive of it. We conceive of something in one way when we conceive of words that signify it, but in another when we understand what the thing itself is. In the first way, we can conceive of God's not existing; in the second way, we cannot. No one who understands what God is can possibly conceive that He doesn't exist—although he can say the "God does not exist" in his heart, if he regards the words as meaningless or takes them in unusual senses. For God is that than which a greater cannot be conceived. He who really understands this correctly understands God so to exist that He can't fail to exist, even in our conception. Therefore, he who understands God to be that than which a greater can't be conceived cannot conceive of His not existing.

I thank you, Lord. I thank you because what I once believed through your generosity I now understand through your enlightenment. If I now wanted not to believe that you exist, I wouldn't be able to prevent myself from understanding that you do.

Chapter XV
God Is Greater Than Can
Be Conceived

Therefore, Lord, you are not only that than which a greater cannot be conceived: you are also something greater than can be conceived. It is possible to conceive that there is something of this sort. And, if you are not this thing, it is possible to conceive of something greater than you—which is impossible.

The Existence of God

SAINT THOMAS AQUINAS

Saint Thomas Aquinas (1225–1274) was the leading Scholastic philosopher whose writings have been deemed authoritative by the Catholic Church. These include *Summa Contra Gentiles* and *Summa Theologica*.

Summa Theologica, Question 2, Article 1

Against the Ontological Argument

. . . Now once we understand the meaning of the word "God" it follows that God exists. For the word means "that than which nothing greater can be meant." Consequently, since existence in thought and fact is greater than existence in thought alone, and since, once we understand the word "God," he exists in thought, he must also exist in fact. It is therefore self-evident that there is a God . . .

Reply. . . . Someone hearing the word "God" may very well not understand it to mean "that than which nothing greater can be thought," indeed, some people have believed God to be a body. And even if the meaning of the word "God" were generally recognized to be "that than which nothing greater can be thought," nothing thus defined would thereby be granted existence in the world of fact, but merely as thought about. Unless one is given that something in fact exists than which nothing greater can be thought—and this nobody denying that existence of God would grant—the conclusion that God in fact exists does not follow . . .

From *Summa Theologica*, translated by Ronald Rubin. Reprinted by permission of the translator.

Summa Theologica, Question 2, Article 3

Whether God Exists

Objection 1. It seems that God does not exist. For, if one of a pair of contraries were infinite, it would completely obliterate the other. But, when we use the word "God," we mean "something infinitely good." Therefore, if God were to exist, nothing would be bad. But there are bad things in the world. Therefore, God does not exist.

Objection 2. Moreover, if we can account for something on the basis of a few original causes [*principia*], we ought not to use many. But it seems that we can account for everything that we find in the world on the basis of various original causes even if we suppose that God does not exist. Nature can be taken as the original cause of natural things, and human reason and will can be taken as the original cause of purposeful acts. There is therefore no need to say that God exists.

On the other hand, the book of *Exodus* depicts God as saying, "I am who am" [*Exodus* 3:14].

Reply. There are five ways to prove that God exists.

The first and clearest way derives from facts about change. Surely, as our senses show, some things in the world do change. But everything that changes is made to change by something else. For a thing only undergoes a change inasmuch as it has a *potentiality* for being that into which it changes, while a thing only causes change inasmuch as it is *actual*. To cause change is just to draw something out of potentiality into actuality, and this can only be done by something that is in actuality. (Thus, something actually hot, like fire, makes wood which is potentially hot become actually hot, thereby changing and altering that wood.) But, while a single thing can simultaneously be in actuality with respect to one property and in potentiality with respect to another, it cannot simultaneously be in actuality and potentiality with respect to the one and the same property. (While that which is actually hot may simultaneously be potentially cold, that which is actually hot cannot simultaneously be potentially hot.) It is therefore impossible for a thing that undergoes a change to cause that change, or for something to change itself. Therefore, whatever undergoes change must be changed by another thing. And, if this other thing undergoes change, it also must be changed by something else, and so on. But this cannot go back to infinity. If it did, there would be no first cause of change and, consequently, no other causes of change—for something can be a secondary cause of change only if it is changed by a primary cause (as a stick moves something only if a hand moves the stick). We must therefore posit a first cause of change which is not itself changed by anything. And this everyone understands to be God.

The second way derives from the nature of efficient causation. In the world that we sense, we find that efficient causes come in series. We do not, and cannot, find that something is its own efficient cause—for, if something were its own efficient cause, it would be prior to itself, which is impossible. But the series of efficient causes cannot possibly go back to infinity. In all such series of causes, a first thing causes one or more intermediaries, and the intermediaries cause the last thing; when a cause is taken out of this series, so is its effect. Therefore, if there were no first efficient cause, there would be no last or intermediary efficient causes. If the series of efficient causes went back to infinity, however, there would be no first efficient cause and, hence, no last or intermediary causes. But there obviously are such causes. We must therefore posit a first efficient cause, which everyone understands to be God.

The third way, which derives from facts about possibility and necessity, is this: In the world, we find some things that can either exist or fail to exist—things which are generated and corrupted and which therefore exist at some times but not at others. It is impossible, however, that everything has being of this sort. If something *can* fail to exist, there must have been a time at which it *has* failed to exist. Therefore, if everything could fail to exist, there would have been a time at which nothing existed. But, if there had been such a time, there would not be anything in the world now—for something can begin to exist only if brought into existence by something that already exists. Therefore, if there once had been nothing in existence, it would have been impossible for anything to come into existence, and there would be nothing now. Therefore, not every entity can fail to exist; there must be something in the world that exists of necessity. But, if something exists of necessity, either this necessity is or is not caused by something else. And the series of necessary beings whose necessity is caused by another cannot possibly go back to infinity. (The reasons are those that were used to show that the series of efficient causes cannot go back to infinity.) We must therefore posit something that is necessary per se—something that does not owe its necessity to anything else but which causes the necessity of other things. And this everyone understands to be God.

The fourth way derives from the gradations to be found in things. Some things are found to be better, truer, or more noble than others. But something is said to have more or less of a quality according to its distance from a maximum. (Thus, the hotter a thing is, the closer it is to that which is maximally hot.) There is therefore something maximally true, good, and noble. And this thing must be the greatest being—for, as Aristotle says in *Metaphysics II* [993b25–30], those things that are greatest in truth are greatest in being. But, as Aristotle says in the same work [993b25], the greatest thing of a kind is the cause of everything of that kind (as fire, the hottest thing is the cause of everything hot). There therefore is something which is the cause of being, of goodness, and of whatever other perfections there may be in things. And this we call God.

The fifth way derives from facts about the governance of the world. We see that even things that lack consciousness, such as physical objects, act for a purpose. They almost always act in the same way, and they tend towards what is best. And this shows that they achieve their ends, not by chance, but on purpose. But something that lacks consciousness can tend towards an end only if directed by something with consciousness and intelligence. (Thus, the arrow must be directed by the archer.) There therefore is some intelligence which directs everything in nature towards an end, and this we call God.

Reply to the First Objection. As Augustine says [in *The Enchiridion*], since God is supremely good, He would allow bad things to exist in the world only if He were so powerful and good that He could even bring good out of bad. It is therefore an indication of God's infinite goodness that He permits bad things to exist and draws good things out of them.

Reply to the Second Objection. Since nature works for a definite end under the direction of a higher agency, we must trace whatever nature does back to God as its first cause. Similarly, we must trace purposeful acts back to a cause higher than human reason and will—for these can change or go out of existence, and, as has been shown, we should trace everything that can change or go out of existence back to an original cause [*principium*] which is unchangeable and necessary per se.

The Wager

BLAISE PASCAL

Blaise Pascal (1623–1662) was a French mathematician, physicist, and theologian. His works include *Pensées* and *Provinciales*.

231

Do you believe it to be impossible that God is infinite, without parts?—Yes. I wish therefore to show you an infinite and indivisible thing. It is a point moving everywhere with an infinite velocity; for it is one in all places, and is all totality in every place.

Let this effect of nature, which previously seemed to you impossible, make you know that there may be others of which you are still ignorant. Do not draw this conclusion from your experiment, that there remains nothing for you to know; but rather that there remains an infinity for you to know.

232

Infinite movement, the point which fills everything, the moment of rest; infinite without quantity, indivisible and infinite.

233

Infinite—nothing.—Our soul is cast into a body, where it finds number, time, dimension. Thereupon it reasons, and calls this nature, necessity, and can believe nothing else.

From *Thoughts*, translated by W. F. Trotter (New York: Collier & Son, 1910).

Unity joined to infinity adds nothing to it, no more than one foot to an infinite measure. The finite is annihilated in the presence of the infinite, and becomes a pure nothing. So our spirit before God, so our justice before divine justice. There is not so great a disproportion between our justice and that of God, as between unity and infinity.

The justice of God must be vast like His compassion. Now justice to the outcast is less vast, and ought less to offend our feelings than mercy towards the elect.

We know that there is an infinite, and are ignorant of its nature. As we know it to be false that numbers are finite, it is therefore true that there is an infinity in number. But we do not know what it is. It is false that it is even, it is false that it is odd; for the addition of a unit can make no change in its nature. Yet it is a number, and every number is odd or even (this is certainly true of every finite number). So we may well know that there is a God without knowing what He is. Is there not one substantial truth, seeing there are so many things which are not the truth itself?

We know then the existence and nature of the finite, because we also are finite and have extension. We know the existence of the infinite, and are ignorant of its nature, because it has extension like us, but not limits like us. But we know neither the existence nor the nature of God, because He has neither extension nor limits.

But by faith we know His existence; in glory we shall know His nature. Now, I have already shown that we may well know the existence of a thing, without knowing its nature.

Let us now speak according to natural lights.

If there is a God, He is infinitely incomprehensible, since, having neither parts nor limits, He has no affinity to us. We are then incapable of knowing either what He is or if He is. This being so, who will dare to undertake the decision of the question? Not we, who have no affinity to Him.

Who then will blame Christians for not being able to give a reason for their belief, since they profess a religion for which they cannot give a reason? They declare, in expounding it to the world, that it is a foolishness, *stultitiam*; and then you complain that they do not prove it! If they proved it, they would not keep their word; it is in lacking proofs, that they are not lacking in sense. "Yes, but although this excuses those who offer it as such, and takes away from them the blame of putting it forward without reason, it does not excuse those who receive it." Let us then examine this point, and say, "God is, or He is not." But to which side shall we incline? Reason can decide nothing here. There is an infinite chaos which separated us. A game is being played at the extremity of this infinite distance where heads or tails will turn up. What will you wager? According to reason, you can do neither the one thing nor the other; according to reason, you can defend neither of the propositions.

Do not then reprove for error those who have made a choice; for you know nothing about it. "No, but I blame them for having made, not this choice, but a choice; for again both he who chooses heads and he who chooses tails are equally at fault, they are both in the wrong. The true course is not to wager at all."

Yes; but you must wager. It is not optional. You are embarked. Which will you choose then? Let us see. Since you must choose, let us see which interests you least. You have two things to lose, the true and the good; and two things to stake, your reason and your will, your knowledge and your happiness; and your nature has two things to shun, error and misery. Your reason is no more shocked in choosing one rather than the other, since you must of necessity choose. This is one point settled. But your happiness? Let us weigh the gain and the loss in wagering that God is. Let us estimate these two chances. If you gain, you gain all; if you lose, you lose nothing. Wager, then, without hesitation that He is.—"That is very fine. Yes, I must wager; but I may perhaps wager too much."—Let us see. Since there is an equal risk of gain and of loss, if you had only to gain two lives, instead of one, you might still wager. But if there were three lives to gain, you would have to play (since you are under the necessity of playing), and you would be imprudent, when you are forced to play, not to chance your life to gain three at a game where there is an equal risk of loss and gain. But there is an eternity of life and happiness. And this being so, if there were an infinity of chances, of which one only would be for you, you would still be right in wagering one to win two, and you would act stupidly, being obliged to play, by refusing to stake one life against three at a game in which out of an infinity of chances there is one for you, if there were an infinity of an infinitely happy life to gain. But there is here an infinity of an infinitely happy life to gain, a chance of gain against a finite number of chances of loss, and what you stake is finite. It is all divided; wherever the infinite is and there is not an infinity of chances of loss against that of gain, there is no time to hesitate, you must give all. And thus, when one is forced to play, he must renounce reason to preserve his life, rather than risk it for infinite gain, as likely to happen as the loss of nothingness.

For it is no use to say it is uncertain if we will gain, and it is certain that we risk, and that the infinite distance between the *certainty* of what is staked and the *uncertainty* of what will be gained, equals the finite good which is certainly staked against the uncertain infinite. It is not so, as every player stakes a certainty to gain an uncertainty, and yet he stakes a finite certainty to gain a finite uncertainty, without transgressing against reason. There is not an infinite distance between the certainty staked and the uncertainty of the gain; that is untrue. In truth, there is an infinity between the certainty of gain and the certainty of loss. But the uncertainty of the gain is proportioned to the certainty of the stake according to the proportion of the chances of gain and loss. Hence it comes that, if there are as many risks on one side as on the other, the course is to play even; and then the certainty of the stake is equal to the uncertainty of the gain, so far is it from fact that there is an infinite distance between them. And so our proposition is of infinite force, when there is the finite to stake in a game where there are equal risks of gain and of loss, and the infinite to gain. This is demonstrable; and if men are capable of any truths, this is one.

"I confess it, I admit it. But, still, is there no means of seeing the faces of the cards?"—Yes, Scripture and the rest, etc. "Yes, but I have my hands tied and my mouth closed; I am forced to wager, and am not free. I am not released, and am so made that I cannot believe. What, then, would you have me do?"

True. But at least learn your inability to believe, since reason brings you to this, and yet you cannot believe. Endeavour then to convince yourself, not by increase of proofs of God, but by the abatement of your passions. You would like to attain faith, and do not know the way; you would like to cure yourself of unbelief, and ask the remedy for it. Learn of those who have been bound like you, and who now stake all their possessions. These are people who know the way which you would follow, and who are cured of an ill of which you would be cured. Follow the way by which they began; by acting as if they believed, taking the holy water, having masses said, etc. Even this will naturally make you believe, and deaden your acuteness.—"But this is what I am afraid of."—And why? What have you to lose?

But to show you this leads you there, it is this which will lessen the passions, which are your stumbling-blocks.

The end of this discourse.—Now, what harm will befall you in taking this side? You will be faithful, honest, humble, grateful, generous, a sincere friend, truthful. Certainly you will not have those poisonous pleasures, glory and luxury; but will you not have others? I will tell you that you will thereby gain in this life, and that, at each step you take on this road, you will see so great certainty of gain, so much nothingness in what you risk, that you will at last recognise that you have wagered for something certain and infinite, for which you have given nothing.

"Ah! This discourse transports me, charms me," etc.

If this discourse pleases you and seems impressive, know that it is made by a man who has knelt, both before and after it, in prayer to that Being, infinite and without parts, before whom he lays all he has, for you also to lay before Him all you have for your own good and for His glory, that so strength may be given to lowliness.

234

If we must not act save on a certainty, we ought not to act on religion, for it is not certain. But how many things we do on an uncertainty, sea voyages, battles!

I say then we must do nothing at all, for nothing is certain, and that there is more certainty in religion than there is as to whether we may see to-morrow; for it is not certain that we may see to-morrow, and it is certainly possible that we may not see it. We cannot say as much about religion. It is not certain that it is; but who will venture to say that it is certainly possible that it is not? Now when we work for to-morrow, and so on an uncertainty, we act reasonably; for we ought to work for an uncertainty according to the doctrine of chance which was demonstrated above.

Saint Augustine has seen that we work for an uncertainty, on sea, in battle, etc. But he has not seen the doctrine of chance which proves that we should do so. Montaigne has seen that we are shocked at a fool, and that habit is all-powerful; but he has not seen the reason of this effect.

All these persons have seen the effects, but they have not seen the causes. They are, in comparison with those who have discovered the causes, as those who have only eyes are in comparison with those who have intellect. For the effects are perceptible by sense, and the causes are visible only to the intellect. And although these effects are seen by the mind, this mind is, in comparison with the mind which sees the causes, as the bodily senses are in comparison with the intellect.

235

*Rem viderunt, causam non viderunt.**

236

According to the doctrine of chance, you ought to put yourself to the trouble of searching for the truth; for if you die without worshipping the True Cause, you are lost.—"But," say you, "if He had wished me to worship Him, He would have left me signs of His will."—He has done so; but you neglect them. Seek them, therefore; it is well worth it.

*[Editors' note: "Things seen, causes unseen."]

237

Chances.—We must live differently in the world, according to these different assumptions: (1) that we could always remain in it; (2) that it is certain that we shall not remain here long, and uncertain if we shall remain here one hour. This last assumption is our condition.

238

What do you then promise me, in addition to certain troubles, but ten years of self-love (for ten years is the chance), to try hard to please without success?

239

Objection.—Those who hope for salvation are so far happy; but they have as a counterpoise the fear of hell.

Reply.—Who has most reason to fear hell: he who is in ignorance whether there is a hell, and who is certain of damnation if there is; or he who certainly believes there is a hell, and hopes to be saved if there is?

240

"I would soon have renounced pleasure," say they, "had I faith." For my part I tell you, "You would soon have faith, if you renounced pleasure." Now, it is for you to begin. If I could, I would give you faith. I cannot do so, nor therefore test the truth of what you say. But you can well renounce pleasure, and test whether what I say is true.

241

Order.—I would have far more fear of being mistaken, and of finding that the Christian religion was true, than of not being mistaken in believing it true.

Why I Am Not a Theist

BERTRAND RUSSELL

—•—

TO COME TO THIS QUESTION OF THE existence of God: it is a large and serious question, and if I were to attempt to deal with it in any adequate manner I should have to keep you here until Kingdom Come, so that you will have to excuse me if I deal with it in a somewhat summary fashion. You know, of course, that the Catholic Church has laid it down as a dogma that the existence of God can be proved by the unaided reason. That is a somewhat curious dogma, but it is one of their dogmas. They had to introduce it because at one time the freethinkers adopted the habit of saying that there were such and such arguments which mere reason might urge against the existence of God, but of course they knew as a matter of faith that God did exist. The arguments and the reasons were set out at great length, and the Catholic Church felt that they must stop it. Therefore they laid it down that the existence of God can be proved by the unaided reason and they had to set up what they considered were arguments to prove it. There are, of course, a number of them, but I shall take only a few.

The First-Cause Argument

Perhaps the simplest and easiest to understand is the argument of the First Cause. (It is maintained that everything we see in this world has a cause, and as you go back in the chain of causes further and further you must come to a First Cause, and to that First Cause you give the name of God.) That argument, I suppose, does not carry very much weight nowadays,

because, in the first place, cause is not quite what it used to be. The philosophers and the men of science have got going on cause, and it has not anything like the vitality it used to have, but, apart from that, you can see that the argument that there must be a First Cause is one that cannot have any validity. I may say that when I was a young man and was debating these questions very seriously in my mind, I for a long time, accepted the argument of the First Cause, until one day, at the age of eighteen, I read John Stuart Mill's Autobiography, and I there found this sentence: "My father taught me that the question 'Who made me?' cannot be answered, since it immediately suggests the further question 'Who made God?' " That very simple sentence showed me, as I still think, the fallacy in the argument of the First Cause. If everything must have a cause, then God must have a cause. If there can be anything without a cause, it may just as well be the world as God, so that there cannot be any validity in that argument. It is exactly of the same nature as the Hindu's view, that the world rested upon an elephant and the elephant rested upon a tortoise; and when they said, "How about the tortoise?" the Indian said, "Suppose we change the subject." The argument is really no better than that. There is no reason why the world could not have come into being without a cause; nor, on the other hand, is there any reason why it should not have always existed. There is no reason to suppose that the world had a beginning at all. The idea that things must have a beginning is really due to the poverty of our imagination. Therefore, perhaps, I need not waste any more time upon the argument about the First Cause.

The Natural-Law Argument

Then there is a very common argument from natural law. That was a favorite argument all through the eighteenth century, especially under the influence of Sir Isaac Newton and his cosmogony. People observed the planets going around the sun according to the law of gravitation, and they thought that God had given a behest to these planets to move in that particular fashion, and that was why they did so. That was, of course, a convenient and simple explanation that saved them the trouble of looking any further for explanations of the law of gravitation. Nowadays we explain the law of gravitation in a somewhat complicated fashion that Einstein has introduced. I do not propose to give you a lecture on the law of gravitation, as interpreted by Einstein, because that again would take some time; at any rate, you no longer have the sort of natural law that you had in the Newtonian system, where, for some reason that nobody could understand, nature behaved in a uniform fashion. We now find that a great many things we thought were natural laws are really human conventions. You know that even in the remotest depths of stellar space there are still three feet to a yard. That is, no doubt, a very remarkable fact, but you would hardly call it a law of nature. And a great many things that have been regarded as laws of nature are of that kind. On the other hand, where you can get down to any knowledge of what atoms actually do, you will find they are much less subject to law than people thought, and that the laws at which you arrive are statistical averages of just the sort that would emerge from chance. There is, as we all know, a law that if you throw dice you will get double sixes only about once in thirty-six times, and we do not regard that as evidence that the fall of the dice is regulated by design; on the contrary, if the double sixes came every time we should think that there was design. The laws of nature are of that sort as regards a great many of them. They are statistical averages such as would emerge from the laws of chance; and that makes this whole business of natural law much less impressive than it formerly was. Quite apart from that, which represents the momentary state of science that may change tomorrow, the whole idea that natural laws imply a lawgiver is due to a confusion between natural and human laws. Human laws are behests commanding you to behave a certain way, in which way you may choose to behave, or you may choose not to behave; but natural laws are a de-

scription of how things do in fact behave, and being a mere description of what they in fact do, you cannot argue that there must be somebody who told them to do that, because even supposing that there were, you are then faced with the question "Why did God issue just those natural laws and no others?" If you say that he did it simply from his own good pleasure, and without any reason, you then find that there is something which is not subject to law, and so your train of natural law is interrupted. If you say, as more orthodox theologians do, that in all the laws which God issues he had a reason for giving those laws rather than others—the reason, of course, being to create the best universe, although you would never think it to look at it—if there were a reason for the laws which God gave, then God himself was subject to law, and therefore you do not get any advantage by introducing God as an intermediary. You have really a law outside and anterior to the divine edicts, and God does not serve your purpose, because he is not the ultimate lawgiver. In short, this whole argument about natural law no longer has anything like the strength that it used to have. I am traveling on in time in my review of the arguments. The arguments that are used for the existence of God change their character as time goes on. They were at first hard intellectual arguments embodying certain quite definite fallacies. As we come to modern times they become less respectable intellectually and more and more affected by a kind of moralizing vagueness.

The Argument from Design

The next step in this process brings us to the argument from design. You all know the argument from design: everything in the world is made just so that we can manage to live in the world, and if the world was ever so little different, we could not manage to live in it. That is the argument from design. It sometimes takes a rather curious form; for instance, it is argued that rabbits have white tails in order to be easy to shoot. I do not know how rabbits would view that application. It is an easy argument to parody. You all know Voltaire's remark, that obviously the nose was designed to be such as to fit spectacles.

That sort of parody has turned out to be not nearly so wide of the mark as it might have seemed in the eighteenth century; because since the time of Darwin we understand much better why living creatures are adapted to their environment. It is not that their environment was made to be suitable to them but that they grew to be suitable to it, and that is the basis of adaptation. There is no evidence of design about it.

When you come to look into this argument from design, it is a most astonishing thing that people can believe that this world, with all the things that are in it, with all its defects, should be the best that omnipotence and omniscience have been able to produce in millions of years. I really cannot believe it. Do you think that, if you were granted omnipotence and omniscience and millions of years in which to perfect your world, you could produce nothing better than the Ku Klux Klan or the Fascists? Moreover, if you accept the ordinary laws of science, you have to suppose that human life and life in general on this planet will die out in due course: it is a stage in the decay of the solar system; at a certain stage of decay you get the sort of conditions of temperature and so forth which are suitable to protoplasm, and there is life for a short time in the life of the whole solar system. You see in the moon the sort of thing to which the earth is tending—something dead, cold, and lifeless.

I am told that that sort of view is depressing, and people will sometimes tell you that if they believed that, they would not be able to go on living. Do not believe it; it is all nonsense. Nobody really worries much about what is going to happen millions of years hence. Even if you think they are worrying much about that, they are really deceiving themselves. They are worried about something much more mundane, or it may merely be a bad digestion; but nobody is really seriously rendered unhappy by the thought of something that is going to happen to this world millions and millions of years hence. Therefore, although it is of course a gloomy view to suppose that life will die out—at least I suppose we may say so, although sometimes when I contemplate the things that people do with their lives I think it is almost a consolation—it is not such as to render life miserable. It merely makes you turn your attention to other things.

The Moral Arguments for Deity

Now we reach one stage further in what I shall call the intellectual descent that the Theists have made in their argumentations, and we come to what we called the moral arguments for the existence of God. You all know, of course, that there used to be in the old days three intellectual arguments for the existence of God, all of which were disposed of by Immanuel Kant in the *Critique of Pure Reason*; but no sooner had he disposed of those arguments than he invented a new one, a moral argument, and that quite convinced him. He was like many people: in intellectual matters he was skeptical, but in moral matters he believed implicitly in the maxims that he had imbibed at his mother's knee. That illustrates what the psychoanalysts so much emphasize—the immensely stronger hold upon us that our very early associations have than those of later times.

Kant, as I say, invented a new moral argument for the existence of God, and that in varying forms was extremely popular during the nineteenth century. It has all sorts of forms. One form is to say that there would be no right or wrong unless God existed. I am not for the moment concerned with whether there is a difference between right and wrong, or whether there is not: that is another question. The point I am concerned with is that, if you are quite sure there is a difference between right and wrong, you are then in this situation: Is that difference due to God's fiat or is it not? If it is due to God's fiat, then for God himself there is no difference between right and wrong, and it is no longer a significant statement to say that God is good. If you are going to say, as theologians do, that God is good, you must then say that right and wrong have some meaning which is independent of God's fiat, because God's fiats are good and not bad independently of the mere fact that he made them. If you are going to say that, you will then have to say that it is not only through God that right and wrong came into being, but that they are in their essence logically anterior to God. You could, of course, if you liked, say that there was a superior deity who gave orders to the God who made this world, or could take up the line that some of the gnostics took up—a line which I often thought was a very plausible one—that as a matter of fact this world that we know was made by the devil at a moment when God was not looking. There is a good deal to be said for that, and I am not concerned to refute it.

The Argument for the Remedying of Injustice

Then there is another very curious form of moral argument, which is this: they say that the existence of God is required in order to bring justice into the world. In the part of this universe that we know there is great injustice, and often the good suffer, and often the wicked prosper, and one hardly knows which of those is the more annoying; but if you are going to have justice in the universe as a whole you have to suppose a future life to redress the balance of life here on earth. So they say that there must be a God, and there must be heaven and hell in order that in the long run there may be justice. That is a very curious argument. If you looked at the matter from a scientific point of view, you would say, "After all, I know only this world. I do not know about the rest of the universe, but so far as one can argue at all on probabilities one would say that prob-

ably this world is a fair sample, and if there is injustice here the odds are that there is injustice elsewhere also." Supposing you got a crate of oranges that you opened, and you found all the top layer of oranges bad, you would not argue, "The underneath ones must be good, so as to redress the balance." You would say, "Probably the whole lot is a bad consignment"; and that is really what a scientific person would argue about the universe. He would say, "Here we find in this world a great deal of injustice, and so far as that goes that is a reason for supposing that justice does not rule in the world; and therefore so far as it goes it affords a moral argument against deity and not in favor of one." Of course I know that the sort of intellectual arguments that I have been talking to you about are not what really moves people. What really moves people to believe in God is not any intellectual argument at all. Most people believe in God because they have been taught from early infancy to do it, and that is the main reason.

Then I think that the next most powerful reason is the wish for safety, a sort of feeling that there is a big brother who will look after you. That plays a very profound part in influencing people's desire for a belief in God.

B. The Problem of Evil

Dialogues Concerning Natural Religion

DAVID HUME

David Hume (1711–1776) is one of the greatest philosophers the world has known. In addition to his *Enquiries* and *Dialogues Concerning Natural Religion*, his writings include *A Treatise of Human Nature* and *History of England*.

David Hume worked on the *Dialogues Concerning Natural Religion* throughout the later part of his life; before his death, in 1776, he left instructions that the *Dialogues* be published posthumously.*

By natural religion, Hume meant the doctrine, popular among intellectuals of his age, that the basic tenets of religion could be discovered and defended by using the same tools that are employed in scientific thought. Natural religion is opposed to revealed religion: the proposition that the doctrines of religion are essentially mysterious and can be known only through divine revelation.

There are three main characters in the *Dialogues*: Philo, Cleanthes, and Demea. Throughout the *Dialogues* Cleanthes defends natural religion, maintaining that we have considerable evidence—of the same sort that we use in science generally—that our universe was created by an intelligent and benevolent deity. In most of the *Dialogues* Philo seems skeptical about all claims of natural religion. However, in Part XII Philo appears willing to accept a guarded version of natural religion: that we have some evidence the cause or causes of the universe possessed something like intelligence but that there is no evidence the cause or causes of the universe were benevolent or had any of the moral attributes usually attributed to God and that form the basis of religious practices (e.g., prayer) and religious doctrines (e.g., an afterlife in which we are rewarded or punished for our actions while alive). Philo and Cleanthes are both represented as able philosophers, each explaining and defending various parts of Hume's philosophy. Demea is represented as being somewhat less clever, but it is his views on religion and how it should be taught that get the discussion started.

*The *Dialogues* were first published in 1779. We have omitted those footnotes in which Kemp-Smith indicates how Hume made various changes in various drafts, and we have used his translations of various passages that were in Latin in the original. Hume's habit was to capitalize proper names. We have preserved the capitalization for the names of the speakers as the dialogues unfold and changed other proper names to lowercase.

The *Dialogues* is in the form of a letter from Pamphilus, the son of a deceased friend of Cleanthes, to his philosophical friend Hermippus. Cleanthes had been charged with the education of Pamphilus, and the *Dialogues* are Pamphilus' account of a conversation between Demea, Cleanthes, and Philo that begins as a discussion of how Cleanthes should instruct Pamphilus about religion.

In Part I, which we omit, Demea asserts that, although religious training should begin early, discussion of the grounds of religious belief should be the last thing in the education plan:

> While they pass through every other science, I still remark the uncertainty of each part, the eternal disputations of men, the obscurity of all philosophy, and the strange, ridiculous conclusions, which some of the greatest geniuses have derived from the principles of mere human reason. Having thus tamed their mind to a proper submission and self-diffidence, I have no longer any scruple of opening to them the greatest mysteries of religion, nor apprehend any danger from that assuming arrogance of philosophy, which may lead them to reject the most established doctrines and opinions.

Philo appears to agree with this:

> Let the errors and deceits of our very senses be set before us; the insuperable difficulties, which attend first principles in all systems; the contradictions, which adhere to the very ideas of matter, cause and effect, extension, space, time motion . . . ; when these familiar objects, I say, are so inexplicable, . . . with what assurance can we decide concerning the origin of worlds, or trace their history from eternity to eternity?

Cleanthes's view of things is quite different. He allows that there are many unsolved intellectual problems of the sort Philo cites. But he thinks that the skepticism to which such problems might lead us does not distinguish between religion and science. In spite of the philosophical puzzles and problems Philo cites, we do know a great deal about how the universe works, and this knowledge is based on complex reasoning. The same sorts of reasoning that led to the Copernican conception of the universe will, Cleanthes thinks, confirm the most important doctrines of religion.

Thus a conversation that began with the question of when Pamphilus should study the basis for belief in religious doctrine has evolved by the beginning of Part II into a debate about whether reasoning—of the same sort that underlies our knowledge in other areas—can be the basis of religion. Part II begins with Demea and Philo, again apparently in agreement, insisting against Cleanthes that, although it is obvious that there is a God, the nature of God is not a fit subject for scientific inquiry, but rather an essentially mysterious subject.

—◆—

Part II

I must own, Cleanthes, said DEMEA, that nothing can more surprise me, than the light, in which you have, all along, put this argument. By the whole tenor of your discourse, one would imagine that you were maintaining the being of a God, against the cavils of atheists and infidels; and were necessitated to become a champion for that fundamental principle of all religion. But this, I hope, is not by any means a question among us. No man; no man, at least, of common sense, I am persuaded, ever entertained a serious doubt with regard to a truth so certain and self-evident. The question is not concerning the *being* but the *nature* of *God*. This, I affirm, from the infirmities of human understanding, to be altogether incomprehensible and unknown to us. The essence of that supreme mind, his attributes, the manner of his existence, the very nature of his duration; these and every particular, which regards so divine a Being, are mysterious to men. Finite, weak, and blind creatures, we ought to humble ourselves in his august presence, and, conscious of our frailties, adore in silence his infinite perfections, which eye hath not seen, ear hath not heard, neither hath it entered into the heart of man to conceive them. They are covered in a deep cloud from human curiosity: It is profaneness to attempt penetrating through these sacred obscurities: And next to the impiety of denying his existence, is the temerity of prying into his nature and essence, decrees and attributes.

But lest you should think, that my *piety* has here got the better of my *philosophy*, I shall support my opinion, if it needs any support, by a very great authority. I might cite all the divines almost, from the foundation of Christianity, who have ever treated of this or any other theological subject: But I shall confine myself, at present, to one equally celebrated for piety and philosophy. It is Father Malebranche, who, I remember, thus expresses himself.[1] "One ought not so much (says he) to call God a spirit, in order to express positively what he is, as in order to signify that he is not matter. He is a Being infinitely perfect: Of this we cannot doubt. But in the same manner as we ought not to imagine, even supposing him corporeal, that he is cloathed with a human body, as the anthropomorphites asserted, under colour that that figure was the most perfect of any; so neither ought we to imagine, that the Spirit of God has human ideas, or bears *any* resemblance to our spirit; under colour that we know nothing more perfect than a human mind. We ought rather to believe, that as he comprehends the perfections of matter without being material . . . he comprehends also the perfections of created spirits, without being spirit, in the manner we conceive spirit: That his true name is, *He that is*, or in other words, Being without restriction, All Being, the Being infinite and universal."

After so great an authority, Demea, replied PHILO, as that which you have produced, and a thousand more, which you might produce, it would appear ridiculous in me to add my sentiment, or express my approbation of your doctrine. But surely, where reasonable men treat these subjects, the question can never be concerning the *being*, but only the *nature* of the Deity. The former truth, as you well observe, is unquestionable and self-evident. Nothing exists without a cause: and the original cause of this universe (whatever it be) we call God; and piously ascribe to him every species of perfection. Whoever scruples this fundamental truth deserves every punishment, which can be inflicted among philosophers, to wit, the greatest ridicule, contempt and disapprobation. But as all perfection is entirely relative, we ought never to imagine, that we comprehend the attributes of this divine Being, or to suppose, that his perfections have any analogy or likeness to the perfections of a human creature. Wisdom, thought, design, knowledge; these we justly ascribe to him; because these words are honourable among men, and we have no other language or other conceptions, by which we can express our adoration of him. But let us beware, lest we think, that our ideas any wise correspond to his perfections, or that his attributes have any resemblance to these qualities among men. He is infinitely superior to our limited view and comprehension; and is more the object of worship in the temple, than of disputation in the schools.

In reality, Cleanthes, continued he, there is no need of having recourse to that affected scepticism, so displeasing to you, in order to come at this determination. Our ideas reach no farther than our experience: We have no experience of divine attributes and operations: I need not conclude my syllogism: You can draw the inference yourself. And it is a pleasure to me (and I hope to you too) that just reasoning and sound piety here concur in the same conclusion, and both of them establish the adorably mysterious and incomprehensible nature of the supreme Being.

Not to lose any time in circumlocutions, said CLEANTHES, addressing himself to Demea, much less in replying to the pious declamations of Philo; I shall briefly explain how I conceive this matter. Look round the world: Contemplate the whole and every part of it: You will find it to be nothing but one great machine, subdivided into an infinite number of lesser machines, which again admit of subdivisions, to a degree beyond what human senses and faculties can trace and explain. All these various machines, and even their most minute parts, are adjusted to each other with an accuracy, which ravishes into admiration all men, who have ever contemplated them. The curious adapting of means to ends, throughout all nature, resembles exactly, though it much exceeds, the productions of human contrivance; of human design, thought, wisdom, and intelligence. Since therefore the effects resemble each other, we are led to infer, by all the rules of analogy, that the causes also resemble; and that the Author of nature is somewhat similar to the mind of man; though possessed of much larger faculties, proportioned to the grandeur of the work, which he has executed. By this argument *a posteriori*, and by this argument alone, do we prove at once the existence of a Deity, and his similarity to human mind and intelligence.

I shall be so free, Cleanthes, said DEMEA, as to tell you, that from the beginning, I could not approve of your conclusion concerning the similarity of the Deity to men; still less can I approve of the mediums, by which you endeavour to establish it. What! No demonstration of the being of a God! No abstract arguments! No proofs *a priori*! Are these, which have hitherto been so much insisted on by philosophers, all fallacy, all sophism? Can we reach no farther in this subject than experience and probability? I will not say, that this is betraying the cause of a Deity: But surely, by this affected candour, you give advantage to atheists, which they never could obtain, by the mere dint of argument and reasoning.

What I chiefly scruple in this subject, said PHILO, is not so much, that all religious arguments are by Cleanthes reduced to experience, as that they appear not to be even the most certain and irrefragable of that inferior kind. That a stone will fall, that fire will burn, that the earth has solidity, we have observed a thousand and a thousand times; and when any new instance of this nature is presented, we draw without hesitation the accustomed inference. The exact similarity of the cases gives us a perfect assurance of a similar event; and a stronger evidence is never desired nor sought after. But wherever you depart, in the least, from the similarity of the cases, you diminish proportionably the evidence; and may at last bring it to a very weak *analogy*, which is confessedly liable to error and uncertainty. After having experienced the circulation of the blood in human creatures, we make no doubt that it takes place in Titius and Maevius: But from its circulation in frogs and fishes, it is only a presumption, though a strong one, from analogy, that it takes place in men and other animals. The analogical reasoning is much weaker, when we infer the circulation of the sap in vegetables from our experience that the blood circulates in animals; and those, who hastily followed that imperfect analogy, are found, by more accurate experiments, to have been mistaken.

If we see a house, Cleanthes, we conclude, with the greatest certainty, that it had an architect or builder; because this is precisely that species of effect, which we have experienced to proceed from that species of cause. But surely you will not affirm, that the universe bears such a resemblance to a house, that we can with the same certainty infer a similar cause, or that the analogy is here entire and perfect. The dissimilitude is so striking, that the utmost you can here pretend to is a guess, a conjecture, a presumption concerning a similar cause; and how that pretension will be received in the world, I leave you to consider.

It would surely be very ill received, replied CLEANTHES; and I should be deservedly blamed and detested, did I allow, that the proofs of a Deity amounted to no more than a guess or conjecture. But is the whole adjustment of means to ends in a house and in the universe so slight a resemblance? The economy of final causes? The order, proportion, and arrangement of every part? Steps of a stair are plainly contrived, that human legs may use them in mounting; and this inference is certain and infallible. Human legs are also contrived for walking and mounting; and this inference, I allow, is not altogether so certain, because of the dissimilarity which you remark; but does it, therefore, deserve the name only of presumption or conjecture?

Good God! cried DEMEA, interrupting him, where are we? Zealous defenders of religion allow, that the proofs of a Deity fall short of perfect evidence! And you, Philo, on whose assistance I depended, in proving the adorable mysteriousness of the divine nature, do you assent to all these extravagant opinions of Cleanthes? For what other name can I give them? Or why spare my censure, when such principles are advanced, supported by such an authority, before so young a man as Pamphilus?

You seem not to apprehend, replied PHILO, that I argue with Cleanthes in his own way; and by showing him the dangerous consequences of his tenets, hope at last to reduce him to our opinion. But what sticks most with you, I observe, is the representation which Cleanthes has made of the argument *a posteriori*; and finding that that argument is likely to escape your hold and vanish into air, you think it so disguised, that you can scarcely believe it to be set in its true light. Now, however much I may dissent, in other respects from the dangerous principles of Cleanthes, I must allow, that he has fairly represented that argument; and I shall endeavour so to state the matter to you, that you will entertain no farther scruples with regard to it.

Were a man to abstract from every thing which he knows or has seen, he would be altogether incapable, merely from his own ideas, to determine what kind of scene the universe must be, or to give the preference to one state or situation of things above another. For as nothing, which he clearly conceives, could be esteemed impossible or implying a contradiction, every chimera of his fancy would be upon an equal footing; nor could he assign any just reason, why he adheres to one idea or system, and rejects the others, which are equally possible.

Again; after he opens his eyes, and contemplates the world, as it really is, it would be impossible for him, at first, to assign the cause of any one event; much less, of the whole of things or of the universe. He might set his fancy a rambling; and she might bring him in an infinite variety of reports and representations. These would all be possible; but being all equally possible, he would never, of himself, give a satisfactory account for his preferring one of them to the rest. Experience alone can point out to him the true cause of any phenomenon.

Now according to this method of reasoning, Demea, it follows (and is, indeed, tacitly allowed by Cleanthes himself) that order, arrangement, or the adjustment of final causes is not, of itself, any proof of design; but only so far as it has been experienced to proceed from that principle. For aught we can know *a priori*, matter may contain the source or spring of order originally, within itself, as well as mind does; and there is no more difficulty in conceiving, that the several elements, from an internal unknown cause, may fall into the most exquisite arrangement, than to conceive that their ideas, in the great, universal mind, from a like internal, unknown cause, fall into that arrangement. The equal possibility of both these suppositions is allowed. But by experience we find (according to Cleanthes), that there is a difference between them. Throw several pieces of steel together, without shape or form; they will never arrange themselves so as to compose a watch: Stone, and mortar, and wood, without an architect, never erect a house. But the ideas in a human mind, we see, by an unknown, inexplicable economy, arrange themselves so as to form the plan of a watch or house. Experience, therefore, proves, that there is an original principle of order in mind, not in matter. From similar effects we infer similar causes. The adjustment of means to ends is alike in the universe, as in a machine of human contrivance. The causes, therefore, must be resembling.

I was from the beginning scandalised, I must own, with this resemblance, which is asserted, between the Deity and human creatures; and must conceive it to imply such a degradation of the supreme Being as no sound theist could endure. With your assistance, therefore, Demea, I shall endeavour to defend what you justly call the adorable mysteriousness of the divine nature, and shall refute this reasoning of Cleanthes; provided he allows, that I have made a fair representation of it.

When Cleanthes had assented, PHILO, after a short pause, proceeded in the following manner.

That all inferences, Cleanthes, concerning fact, are founded on experience, and that all experimental reasonings are founded on the supposition, that similar causes prove similar effects and similar effects similar causes; I shall not, at present, much dispute with you. But observe, I entreat you, with what extreme caution all just reasoners proceed in the transferring of experiments to similar cases. Unless the cases be exactly similar, they repose no perfect confidence in applying their past observation to any particular phenomenon. Every alteration of circumstances occasions a doubt concerning the event; and it requires new experiments to prove certainly, that the new circumstances are of no moment or importance. A change in bulk, situation, arrangement, age, disposition of the air, or surrounding bodies; any of these particulars may be attended with the most unexpected consequences: And unless the objects be quite familiar to us, it is the highest temerity to expect with assurance, after any of these changes, an event similar to that which before fell under our observation. The slow and deliberate steps of philosophers, here, if any where, are distinguished from the precipitate march of the vulgar, who, hurried on by the smallest similitude, are incapable of all discernment or consideration.

But can you think, Cleanthes, that your usual phlegm and philosophy have been preserved in so wide a step as you have taken, when you compared to the universe houses, ships, furniture, machines; and from their similarity in some circumstances inferred a similarity in their causes? Thought, design, intelligence, such as we discover in men and other animals, is no more than one of the springs and principles of the universe, as well as heat or cold, attraction or repulsion, and a hundred others, which fall under daily observation. It is an active cause, by which some particular parts of nature, we find, produce alterations on other parts. But can a conclusion, with any propriety, be transferred from parts to the whole? Does not the great disproportion bar all comparison and inference? From observing the growth of a hair, can we learn any thing concerning the generation of a man? Would the manner of a leaf's blowing, even though perfectly known, afford us any instruction concerning the vegetation of a tree?

But allowing that we were to take the *operations* of one part of nature upon another for the foundation of our judgment concerning the *origin* of the whole (which never can be admitted); yet why select so minute, so weak, so bounded a principle as the reason and design of animals is found to be upon this planet? What peculiar privilege has this little agitation of the brain which we call thought, that we must thus make it the model of the whole universe? Our partiality in our own favour does indeed present it on all occasions: But sound philosophy ought carefully to guard against so natural an illusion.

So far from admitting, continued PHILO, that the operations of a part can afford us any conclusion concerning the origin of the whole, I will not allow any one part to form a rule for another part, if the latter be very remote from the former. Is there any reasonable ground to conclude, that the inhabitants of other planets possess thought, intelligence, reason, or any thing similar to these faculties in men? When nature has so extremely diversified her manner of operation in this small globe; can we imagine, that she incessantly copies herself throughout so immense a universe? And if thought, as we may well suppose, be confined merely to this narrow concern, and has even there so limited a sphere of action; with what propriety can we assign it for the original cause of all things? The narrow views of a peasant, who makes his domestic economy the rule for the government of kingdoms, is in comparison a pardonable sophism.

But were we ever so much assured, that a thought and reason, resembling the human, were to be found throughout the whole universe, and were its activity elsewhere vastly greater and more commanding than it appears in this globe: Yet I cannot see, why the operations of a world, constituted, arranged, adjusted, can with any propriety be extended to a world, which is in its embryo-state, and is advancing towards that constitution and arrangement. By observation, we know somewhat of the economy, action, and nourishment of a finished animal; but we must transfer with great caution that observation to the growth of a foetus in the womb, and still more, to the formation of an animalcule in the loins of its male parent. Nature, we find, even from our limited experience, possesses an infinite number of springs and principles, which incessantly discover themselves on every change of her position and situation. And what new and unknown principles would actuate her in so new and unknown a situation as that of the formation of a universe, we cannot, without the utmost temerity, pretend to determine.

A very small part of this great system, during a very short time, is very imperfectly discovered to us:

And do we thence pronounce decisively concerning the origin of the whole?

Admirable conclusion! Stone, wood, brick, iron, brass, have not, at this time, in this minute globe of earth, an order or arrangement without human art and contrivance: Therefore the universe could not originally attain its order and arrangement, without something similar to human art. But is a part of nature a rule for another part very wide of the former? Is it a rule for the whole? Is a very small part a rule for the universe? Is nature in one situation, a certain rule for nature in another situation, vastly different from the former?

And can you blame me, Cleanthes, if I here imitate the prudent reserve of Simonides, who, according to the noted story,[2] being asked by Hiero, *What God was*? desired a day to think of it, and then two days more; and after that manner continually prolonged the term, without ever bringing in his definition or description? Could you even blame me, if I had answered at first, *that I did not know*, and was sensible that this subject lay vastly beyond the reach of my faculties? You might cry out sceptic and raillier as much as you pleased: But having found, in so many other subjects, much more familiar, the imperfections and even contradictions of human reason, I never should expect any success from its feeble conjectures, in a subject, so sublime, and so remote from the sphere of our observation. When *two species* of objects have always been observed to be conjoined together, I can *infer*, by custom, the existence of one whenever I *see* the existence of the other: And this I call an argument from experience. But how this argument can have place, where the objects, as in the present case, are single, individual, without parallel, or specific resemblance, may be difficult to explain. And will any man tell me with a serious countenance, that an orderly universe must arise from some thought and art, like the human; because we have experience of it? To ascertain this reasoning, it were requisite, that we had experience of this origin of worlds; and it is not sufficient surely, that we have seen ships and cities arise from human art and contrivance.

· · · · · · · ·

Philo was proceeding in this vehement manner, somewhat between jest and earnest, as it appeared to me; when he observed some signs of impatience in Cleanthes, and then immediately stopped short. What I had to suggest, said CLEANTHES, is only that you would not abuse terms, or make use of popular expressions to subvert philosophical reasonings. You know, that the vulgar often distinguish reason from experience, even where the question relates only to matter of fact and existence; though it is found, where that *reason* is properly analysed, that it is nothing but a species of experience. To prove by experience the origin of the universe from mind is not more contrary to common speech than to prove the motion of the earth from the same principle. And a caviller might raise all the same objections to the Copernican system, which you have urged against my reasonings. Have you other earths, might he say, which you have seen to move? Have. . . .

Yes! cried PHILO, interrupting him, we have other earths. Is not the moon another earth, which we see to turn round its centre? Is not Venus another earth, where we observe the same phenomenon? Are not the revolutions of the sun also a confirmation, from analogy, of the same theory? All the planets, are they not earths, which revolve about the sun? Are not the satellites moons, which move round Jupiter and Saturn, and along with these primary planets, round the sun? These analogies and resemblances, with others, which I have not mentioned, are the sole proofs of the Copernican system: And to you it belongs to consider, whether you have any analogies of the same kind to support your theory.

In reality, Cleanthes, continued he, the modern system of astronomy is now so much received by all enquirers, and has become so essential a part even of our earliest education, that we are not commonly very scrupulous in examining the reasons upon which it is founded. It is now become a matter of mere curiosity to study the first writers on that subject, who had the full force of prejudice to encounter, and were obliged to turn their arguments on every side, in order to render them popular and convincing. But if we peruse Galileo's famous Dialogues concerning the system of the world, we shall find, that that great genius, one of the sublimest that ever existed, first bent all his endeavours to prove, that there was no foundation for the distinction commonly made between elementary and celestial substances. The schools, proceeding from the illusions of sense, had carried this distinction very far; and had established the latter substances to be ingenerable, incorruptible, unalterable, impassible; and had assigned all the opposite qualities to the former. But Galileo, beginning with the moon, proved its similarity in every particular to the earth; its convex figure, its natural darkness when not illuminated, its density, its distinction into solid and liquid, the variations of its phases, the mutual illuminations of the earth and moon, their mutual eclipses, the inequalities of the lunar surface, etc. After many instances of this kind, with regard to all the planets, men plainly saw, that these bodies became proper objects of experience; and that the similarity of their nature enabled us to extend the same arguments and phenomena from one to the other.

In this cautious proceeding of the astronomers, you may read your own condemnation, Cleanthes; or rather may see, that the subject in which you are engaged exceeds all human reason and enquiry. Can you pretend to show any such similarity between the fabric of a house, and the generation of a universe? Have you ever seen nature in any such situation as resembles the first arrangement of the elements? Have worlds ever been formed under your eye? and have you had leisure to observe the whole progress of the phenomenon, from the first appearance of order to its final consummation? If you have, then cite your experience, and deliver your theory.

Part III

How the most absurd argument, replied CLEANTHES, in the hands of a man of ingenuity and invention, may acquire an air of probability! Are you now aware, Philo, that it became necessary for Copernicus and his first disciples to prove the similarity of the terrestrial and celestial matter; because several philosophers, blinded by old systems, and supported by some sensible appearances, had denied this similarity? But that it is by no means necessary, that theists should prove the similarity of the works of nature to those of art; because this similarity is self-evident and undeniable? The same matter, a like form: What more

is requisite to show an analogy between their causes, and to ascertain the origin of all things from a divine purpose and intention? Your objections, I must freely tell you, are no better than the abstruse cavils of those philosophers, who denied motion; and ought to be refuted in the same manner, by illustrations, examples, and instances, rather than by serious argument and philosophy.

Suppose, therefore, that an articulate voice were heard in the clouds, much louder and more melodious than any which human art could ever reach: Suppose, that this voice were extended in the same instant over all nations, and spoke to each nation in its own language and dialect: Suppose, that the words delivered not only contain a just sense and meaning, but convey some instruction altogether worthy of a benevolent Being, superior to mankind: Could you possibly hesitate a moment concerning the cause of this voice? And must you not instantly ascribe it to some design or purpose? Yet I cannot see but all the same objections (if they merit that appellation) which lie against the system of theism, may also be produced against this inference.

Might you not say, that all conclusions concerning fact were founded on experience: That when we hear an articulate voice in the dark, and thence infer a man, it is only the resemblance of the effects, which leads us to conclude that there is a like resemblance in the cause: But that this extraordinary voice, by its loudness, extent, and flexibility to all languages, bears so little analogy to any human voice, that we have no reason to suppose any analogy in their causes: And consequently, that a rational, wise, coherent speech proceeded, you knew not whence, from some accidental whistling of the winds, not from any divine reason or intelligence? You see clearly your own objections in these cavils; and I hope too, you see clearly, that they cannot possibly have more force in the one case than in the other.

But to bring the case still nearer the present one of the universe, I shall make two suppositions, which imply not any absurdity or impossibility. Suppose, that there is a natural, universal, invariable language, common to every individual of human race; and that books are natural productions, which perpetuate themselves in the same manner with animals and vegetables, by descent and propagation.

Several expressions of our passions contain a universal language: All brute animals have a natural speech, which, however limited, is very intelligible to their own species. And as there are infinitely fewer parts and less contrivance in the finest composition of eloquence, than in the coarsest organized body, the propagation of an *Iliad* or *Aeneid* is an easier supposition than that of any plant or animal.

Suppose, therefore, that you enter into your library, thus peopled by natural volumes, containing the most refined reason and most exquisite beauty: Could you possibly open one of them, and doubt, that its original cause bore the strongest analogy to mind and intelligence? When it reasons and discourses; when it expostulates, argues, and enforces its views and topics; when it applies sometimes to the pure intellect, sometimes to the affections; when it collects, disposes, and adorns every consideration suited to the subject: could you persist in asserting, that all this, at the bottom, had really no meaning, and that the first formation of this volume in the loins of its original parent proceeded not from thought and design? Your obstinacy, I know, reaches not that degree of firmness: Even your sceptical play and wantonness would be abashed at so glaring an absurdity.

But if there be any difference, Philo, between this supposed case and the real one of the universe, it is all to the advantage of the latter. The anatomy of an animal affords many stronger instances of design than the perusal of Livy or Tacitus: And any objection which you start in the former case, by carrying me back to so unusual and extraordinary a scene as the first formation of worlds, the same objection has placed on the supposition of our vegetating library. Choose, then, your party, Philo, without ambiguity or evasion: Assert either that a rational volume is no proof of a rational cause, or admit of a similar cause to all the works of nature.

Let me here observe too, continued CLEANTHES, that this religious argument, instead of being weakened by that scepticism, so much affected by you, rather acquires force from it, and becomes more firm and undisputed. To exclude all argument or reasoning of every kind is either affectation or madness. The declared profession of every reasonable sceptic is only to reject abstruse, remote and refined arguments; to adhere to common sense and the plain instincts of nature; and to assent, wherever any reasons strike him with so full a force, that he cannot, without the greatest violence, prevent it. Now the arguments for natural religion are plainly of this kind; and nothing but the most perverse, obstinate metaphysics can reject them. Consider, anatomize the eye: Survey its structure and contrivance; and tell me, from your own feeling, if the idea of a contriver does not immediately flow in upon you with a force like that of sensation. The most obvious conclusion surely is in favour of design; and it requires time, reflection and study, to summon up those frivolous, though abstruse, objections, which can support infidelity. Who can behold the male and female of each species, the correspondence of their parts and instincts, their passions and whole course of life before and after generation, but must be sensible, that the propagation of the species is intended by nature? Millions and millions of such instances present themselves through every part of the universe; and no language can convey a more intelligible, irresistible meaning, than the curious adjustment of final causes. To what degree, therefore, of blind dogmatism must one have attained, to reject such natural and such convincing arguments?

Some beauties in writing we may meet with, which seem contrary to rules, and which gain the affections, and animate the imagination, in opposition to all the precepts of criticism, and to the authority of the established masters of art. And if the argument for theism be, as you pretend, contradictory to the principles of logic; its universal, its irresistible influence proves clearly, that there may be arguments of a like irregular nature. Whatever cavils may be urged; an orderly world, as well as a coherent, articulate speech, will still be received as an incontestable proof of design and intention.

It sometimes happens, I own, that the religious arguments have not their due influence on an ignorant savage and barbarian; not because they are obscure and difficult, but because he never asks himself any question with regard to them. Whence arises the curious structure of an animal? From the copulation of its parents. And these whence? From *their* parents. A few removes set the objects at such a distance, that to him they are lost in darkness and confusion; nor is he actuated by any curiosity to trace them farther. But this is neither dogmatism nor scepticism, but stupidity; a state of mind very different from your sifting, inquisitive disposition, my ingenious friend. You can trace causes from effects: You can compare the most distant and remote objects: And your greatest errors proceed not from barrenness of thought and invention, but from too luxuriant a fertility, which suppresses your natural good sense, by a profusion of unnecessary scruples and objections.

Here I could observe, Hermippus, that Philo was a little embarrassed and confounded: But while he hesitated in delivering an answer, luckily for him, DEMEA broke in upon the discourse, and saved his countenance.

Your instance, Cleanthes, said he, drawn from books and language, being familiar, has, I confess, so much more force on that account; but is there not some danger too in this very circumstance, and may it not render us presumptuous, by making us imagine we comprehend the Deity, and have some adequate idea of his nature and attributes? When I read a volume, I enter into the mind and intention of the author: I become him, in a manner, for the instant; and have an immediate feeling and conception of those ideas, which revolved in his imagination, while employed in that composition. But so near an approach we never surely can make to the Deity. His ways are not our ways. His attributes are perfect, but incomprehensible. And this volume of nature contains a great inexplicable riddle, more than any intelligible discourse or reasoning.

The ancient Platonists, you know, were the most religious and devout of all the pagan philosophers: Yet many of them, particularly Plotinus, expressly declare that intellect or understanding is not to be ascribed to the Deity, and that our most perfect worship of him consists, not in acts of veneration, reverence, gratitude or love; but in a certain mysterious self-annihilation or total extinction of all our faculties. These ideas are, perhaps, too far stretched; but still it must be acknowledged, that, by representing the Deity as so intelligible, and comprehensible, and so similar to a human mind, we are guilty of the grossest and most narrow partiality, and make ourselves the model of the whole universe.

All the *sentiments* of the human mind, gratitude, resentment, love, friendship, approbation, blame, pity, emulation, envy, have a plain reference to the state and situation of man, and are calculated for preserving the existence, and promoting the activity of such a being in such circumstances. It seems therefore unreasonable to transfer such sentiments to a supreme existence, or to suppose him actuated by them; and the phenomena, besides, of the universe will not support us in such a theory. All our *ideas*, derived from the senses, are confessedly false and illusive; and cannot, therefore, be supposed to have place in a supreme intelligence: And as the ideas of internal sentiment, added to those of the external senses, compose the whole furniture of human understanding, we may conclude, that none of the *materials* of thought are in any respect similar in the human and in the divine intelligence. Now, as to the *manner* of thinking; how can we make any comparison between them, or suppose them any wise resembling? Our thought is fluctuating, uncertain, fleeting, successive, and compounded; and were we to remove these circumstances, we absolutely annihilate its essence, and it would, in such a case, be an abuse of terms to apply to it the name of thought or reason. At least, if it appear more pious and respectful (as it really is) still to retain these terms, when we mention the supreme Being, we ought to acknowledge, that their meaning, in that case, is totally incomprehensible; and that the infirmities of our nature do not permit us to reach any ideas, which in the least correspond to the ineffable sublimity of the divine attributes.

Part IV

It seems strange to me, said CLEANTHES, that you, Demea, who are so sincere in the cause of religion, should still maintain the mysterious, incomprehensible nature of the Deity, and should insist so strenuously, that he has no manner of likeness or resemblance to human creatures. The Deity, I can readily allow, possesses many powers and attributes, of which we can have no comprehension: But if our ideas, so far as they go, be not just and adequate, and correspondent to his real nature, I know not what there is in this subject worth insisting on. Is the name, without any meaning, of such mighty importance? Or how do you mystics, who maintain the absolute incomprehensibility of the Deity, differ from sceptics or atheists, who assert, that the first cause of All is unknown and unintelligible? Their temerity must be very great, if, after rejecting the production by a mind; I mean, a mind resembling the human (for I know of no other), they pretend to assign, with certainty, any other specific, intelligible cause: And their conscience must be very scrupulous indeed, if they refuse to call the universal, unknown cause a God or Deity; and to bestow on him as many sublime eulogies and unmeaning epithets, as you shall please to require of them.

Who could imagine, replied DEMEA, that Cleanthes, the calm, philosophical Cleanthes, would attempt to refute his antagonists, by affixing a nickname to them; and like the common bigots and inquisitors of the age, have recourse to invective and declamation, instead of reasoning? Or does he not perceive, that these topics are easily retorted, and that *anthropomorphite* is an appellation as invidious, and implies as dangerous consequences, as the epithet of *mystic*, with which he has honoured us? In reality, Cleanthes, consider what it is you assert, when you represent the Deity as similar to a human mind and understanding. What is the soul of man? A composition of various faculties, passions, sentiments, ideas; united, indeed, into one self or person, but still distinct from each other. When it reasons, the ideas, which are the parts of its discourse, arrange themselves in a certain form or order; which is not preserved entire for a moment, but immediately gives place to another arrangement. New opinions, new passions, new affections, new feelings arise, which continually diversify the mental scene, and produce in it the greatest variety, and most rapid succession imaginable. How is this compatible with that perfect immutability and simplicity, which all true theists ascribe to the Deity? By the same act, say they, he sees past, present, and future: His love and his hatred, his mercy and his justice are one individual operation: He is entire in every point of space; and complete in every instant of duration. No succession, no change, no acquisition, no diminution. What he is implies not in it any shadow of distinction or diversity. And what he is, this moment, he ever has been, and ever will be, without any new judgment, sentiment, or operation. He stands fixed in one simple, perfect state; nor can you ever say, with any propriety, that this act of his is different from that other, or that this judgment or idea has been lately formed, and will give place, by succession, to any different judgment or idea.

I can readily allow, said CLEANTHES, that those who maintain the perfect simplicity of the supreme Being, to the extent in which you have explained it, are complete *mystics*, and chargeable with all the consequences which I have drawn from their opinion. They are, in a word, atheists, without knowing it. For though it be allowed, that the Deity possesses attributes, of which we have no comprehension; yet ought we never to ascribe to him any attributes, which are absolutely incompatible with that intelligent nature, essential to him. A mind, whose acts and sentiments and ideas are not distinct and successive; one, that is wholly simple, and totally immutable; is a mind which has no thought, no reason, no will, no sentiment, no love, no hatred; or in a word, is no mind at all. It is an abuse of terms to give it that appellation; and we may as well speak of limited extension without figure, or of number without composition.

Pray consider, said PHILO, whom you are at present inveighing against. You are honouring with the appellation of atheist all the sound, orthodox divines almost, who have treated of this subject; and you will, at last, be, yourself, found, according to your reckoning, the only sound theist in the world. But if idolaters be atheists, as, I think, may justly be asserted, and Christian theologians the same; what becomes of the argument, so much celebrated, derived from the universal consent of mankind?

But because I know you are not much swayed by names and authorities, I shall endeavour to show you, a little more distinctly, the inconveniences of that anthropomorphism, which you have embraced; and shall prove, that there is no ground to suppose a plan of the world to be formed in the divine mind, consisting of distinct ideas, differently arranged; in the same manner as an architect forms in his head the plan of a house which he intends to execute.

It is not easy, I own, to see, what is gained by this

supposition, whether we judge of the matter by *reason* or by *experience*. We are still obliged to mount higher, in order to find the cause of this cause, which you had assigned as satisfactory and conclusive.

If *reason* (I mean abstract reason, derived from enquiries *a priori*) be not alike mute with regard to all questions concerning cause and effect; this sentence at least it will venture to pronounce: That a mental world or universe of ideas requires a cause as much as does a material world or universe of objects; and if similar in its arrangement must require a similar cause. For what is there in this subject, which should occasion a different conclusion or inference? In an abstract view, they are entirely alike; and no difficulty attends the one supposition, which is not common to both of them.

Again, when we will needs force *experience* to pronounce some sentence, even on these subjects, which lie beyond her sphere; neither can she perceive any material difference in this particular, between these two kinds of worlds, but finds them to be governed by similar principles, and to depend upon an equal variety of causes in their operations. We have specimens in miniature of both of them. Our own mind resembles the one: A vegetable or animal body the other. Let experience, therefore, judge from these samples. Nothing seems more delicate with regard to its causes than thought; and as these causes never operate in two persons after the same manner, so we never find two persons, who think exactly alike. Nor indeed does the same person think exactly alike at any two different periods of time. A difference of age, of the disposition of his body, of weather, of food, of company, of books, of passions; any of these particulars or others more minute, are sufficient to alter the curious machinery of thought, and communicate to it very different movements and operations. As far as we can judge, vegetables and animal bodies are not more delicate in their motions, nor depend upon a greater variety or more curious adjustment of springs and principles.

How therefore shall we satisfy ourselves concerning the cause of that Being, whom you suppose the Author of nature, or, according to your system of anthropomorphism, the ideal world, into which you trace the material? Have we not the same reason to trace that ideal world into another ideal world, or new intelligent principle? But if we stop, and go no farther; why go so far? Why not stop at the material world? How can we satisfy ourselves without going on *in infinitum*? And after all, what satisfaction is there in that infinite progression? Let us remember the story of the Indian philosopher and his elephant. It was never more applicable than to the present subject. If the material world rests upon a similar ideal world, this ideal world must rest upon some other; and so on, without end. It were better, therefore, never to look beyond the present material world. By supposing it to contain the principle of its order within itself, we really assert it to be God; and the sooner we arrive at that divine Being so much the better. When you go one step beyond the mundane system, you only excite an inquisitive humour, which it is impossible ever to satisfy.

To say, that the different ideas, which compose the reason of the supreme Being, fall into order, of themselves, and by their own nature, is really to talk without any precise meaning. If it has a meaning, I would fain know, why it is not as good sense to say, that the parts of their material world fall into order, of themselves, and by their own nature? Can the one opinion be intelligible, while the other is not so?

We have, indeed, experience of ideas, which fall into order, of themselves, and without any *known* cause: But, I am sure, we have a much larger experience of matter, which does the same; as in all instances of generation and vegetation, where the accurate analysis of the cause exceeds all human comprehension. We have also experience of particular systems of thought and of matter, which have no order; of the first, in madness, of the second, in corruption. Why then should we think, that order is more essential to one than the other? And if it requires a cause in both, what do we gain by your system, in tracing the universe of objects into a similar universe of ideas? The first step, which we make, leads us on for ever. It were, therefore, wise in us, to limit all our enquiries to the present world, without looking farther. No satisfaction can ever be attained by these speculations, which so far exceed the narrow bounds of human understanding.

It was usual with the Peripatetics, you know, Cleanthes, when the cause of any phenomenon was demanded, to have recourse to their *faculties* or *occult qualities*, and to say, for instance, that bread nourished by its nutritive faculty, and senna purged by its purgative: But it has been discovered, that this subterfuge was nothing but the disguise of ignorance; and that these philosophers, though less ingenuous, really said the same thing with the sceptics or the vulgar, who fairly confessed, that they knew not the cause of these phenomena. In like manner, when it is asked, what cause produces order in the ideas of the supreme Being, can any other reason be assigned by you, anthropomorphites, than that it is a *rational* faculty, and that such is the nature of the Deity? But why a similar answer will not be equally satisfactory in accounting for the order of the world, without having recourse to any such intelligent Creator as you insist on, may be difficult to determine. It is only to say, that *such* is the nature of material objects, and that they are all originally possessed of a *faculty* of order and proportion. These are only more learned and elaborate ways of confessing our ignorance; nor has the one hypothesis any real advantage above the other, except in its greater conformity to vulgar prejudices.

You have displayed this argument with great emphasis, replied CLEANTHES: You seem not sensible, how easy it is to answer it. Even in common life, if I assign a cause for any event; is it any objection, Philo, that I cannot assign the cause of that cause, and answer every new question, which may incessantly be started? And what philosophers could possibly submit to so rigid a rule? philosophers, who confess ultimate causes to be totally unknown, and are sensible, that the most refined principles, into which they trace the phenomena, are still to them as inexplicable as these phenomena themselves are to the vulgar. The order and arrangement of nature, the curious adjustment of final causes, the plain use and intention of every part and organ; all these bespeak in the clearest language an intelligent cause or Author. The heavens and the earth join in the same testimony: The whole chorus of nature raises one hymn to the praises of its Creator: You alone, or almost alone, disturb this general harmony. You start abstruse doubts, cavils, and objections: You ask me, what is the cause of this cause? I know not; I care not; that concerns not me. I have found a Deity; and here I stop my enquiry. Let those go farther, who are wiser or more enterprising.

I pretend to be neither, replied PHILO: And for that very reason, I should never perhaps have attempted to go so far; especially when I am sensible, that I must at last be contented to sit down with the same answer, which, without farther trouble, might have satisfied me from the beginning. If I am still to remain in utter ignorance of causes, and can absolutely give an explication of nothing, I shall never esteem it any advantage to shove off for a moment a difficulty, which, you acknowledge, must immediately, in its full force, recur upon me. Naturalists indeed very justly explain particular effects by more general causes; though these general causes themselves should remain in the end totally inexplicable: But they never surely thought it satisfactory to explain a particular effect by a particular cause, which was no more to be accounted for than the effect itself. An ideal system, arranged of itself, without a precedent design, is not a whit more explicable than a material one, which attains its order in a like manner; nor is there any more difficulty in the latter supposition than in the former.

Part V

But to show you still more inconveniences, continued PHILO, in your anthropomorphism; please to take a new survey of your principles. *Like effects prove like causes.* This is the experimental argument; and this, you say too, is the sole theological argument. Now it is certain, that the liker the effects are, which are seen, and the liker the causes, which are inferred, the stronger is the argument. Every departure on either side diminishes the probability, and renders the experiment less conclusive. You cannot doubt of this principle: Neither ought you to reject its consequences.

All the new discoveries in astronomy, which prove the immense grandeur and magnificence of the works of nature, are so many additional arguments for a Deity, according to the true system of theism: But according to your hypothesis of experimental theism, they become so many objections, by removing the effect still farther from all resemblance to the effects of human art and contrivance. For if Lucretius,[3] even following the old system of the world, could exclaim,

Who can rule the sum, who hold in his hand with controlling force the strong reins, of the immeasurable deep? who can at once make all the different heavens to roll and warm with ethereal fires all the fruitful earths, or be present in all places at all times?

If Tully[4] esteemed this reasoning so natural, as to put it into the mouth of his Epicurean.

For with what eyes of the mind could your Plato have beheld that workshop of such stupendous toil, in which he represents the world as having been put together and built by God? How was so vast an undertaking set about? What tools, what levers, what machines, what servants, were employed in so great a work? How came air, fire, water, and earth to obey and submit to the architect's will?

If this argument, I say, had any force in former ages; how much greater must it have at present; when the bounds of nature are so infinitely enlarged, and such a magnificent scene is opened to us? It is still more unreasonable to form our idea of so unlimited a cause from our experience of the narrow productions of human design and invention.

The discoveries by microscopes, as they open a new universe in miniature, are still objections, according to you; arguments, according to me. The farther we push our researches of this kind, we are still led to infer the universal cause of All to be vastly different from mankind, or from any object of human experience and observation.

And what say you to the discoveries in anatomy, chemistry, botany? ... These surely are no objections, replied CLEANTHES: They only discover new instances of art and contrivance. It is still the image of mind reflected on us from innumerable objects. Add, a mind *like the human*, said PHILO. I know of no other, replied CLEANTHES. And the liker the better, insisted PHILO. To be sure, said CLEANTHES.

Now, Cleanthes, said PHILO, with an air of alacrity and triumph, mark the consequences. *First*, By this method of reasoning, you renounce all claim to infinity in any of the attributes of the Deity. For as the cause ought only to be proportioned to the effect, and the effect, so far as it falls under our cog-

nisance, is not infinite; what pretensions have we, upon your suppositions, to ascribe that attribute to the divine Being? You will still insist, that, by removing him so much from all similarity to human creatures, we give in to the most arbitrary hypothesis, and at the same time weaken all proofs of his existence.

Secondly, You have no reason, on your theory, for ascribing perfection to the Deity, even in his finite capacity; or for supposing him free from every error, mistake, or incoherence in his undertakings. There are many inexplicable difficulties in the works of nature, which, if we allow a perfect Author to be proved *a priori*, are easily solved, and become only seeming difficulties, from the narrow capacity of man, who cannot trace infinite relations. But according to your method of reasoning, these difficulties become all real; and perhaps will be insisted on, as new instances of likeness to human art and contrivance. At least, you must acknowledge, that it is impossible for us to tell, from our limited views, whether this system contains any great faults, or deserves any considerable praise, if compared to other possible, and even real systems. Could a peasant, if the *Aeneid* were read to him, pronounce that poem to be absolutely faultless, or even assign to it its proper rank among the productions of human wit; he, who had never seen any other production?

But were this world ever so perfect a production, it must still remain uncertain, whether all the excellencies of the work can justly be ascribed to the workman. If we survey a ship, what an exalted idea must we form of the ingenuity of the carpenter, who framed so complicated, useful, and beautiful a machine? And what surprise must we entertain, when we find him a stupid mechanic, who imitated others, and copied an art, which, through a long succession of ages, after multiplied trials, mistakes, corrections, deliberations, and controversies, had been gradually improving? Many worlds might have been botched and bungled, throughout an eternity, ere this system was struck out: Much labour lost: Many fruitless trials made: And a slow, but continued improvement carried on during infinite ages in the art of world-making. In such subjects, who can determine, where the truth; nay, who can conjecture where the probability, lies; amidst a great number of hypotheses which may be proposed, and a still greater number which may be imagined?

And what shadow of an argument, continued PHILO, can you produce, from your hypothesis, to prove the unity of the Deity? A great number of men join in building a house or ship, in rearing a city, in framing a commonwealth: Why may not several Deities combine in contriving and framing a world? This is only so much greater similarity to human affairs. By sharing the work among several, we may so much farther limit the attributes of each, and get rid of that extensive power and knowledge, which must be supposed in one Deity, and which, according to you, can only serve to weaken the proof of his existence. And if such foolish, such vicious creatures as man can yet often unite in framing and executing one plan; how much more those Deities or Demons, whom we may suppose several degrees more perfect?

To multiply causes, without necessity, is indeed contrary to true philosophy: But this principle applies not to the present case. Were one Deity antecedently proved by your theory, who were possessed of every attribute requisite to the production of the universe; it would be needless, I own (though not absurd) to suppose any other Deity existent. But while it is still a question, whether all these attributes are united in one subject, or dispersed among several independent Beings: By what phenomena in nature can we pretend to decide the controversy? Where we see a body raised in a scale, we are sure that there is in the opposite scale, however concealed from sight, some counterposing weight equal to it: But it is still allowed to doubt, whether that weight be an aggregate of several distinct bodies, or one uniform united mass. And if the weight requisite very much exceeds any thing which we have ever seen conjoined in any single body, the former supposition becomes still more probable and natural. An intelligent Being of such vast power and capacity, as is necessary to produce the universe, or, to speak in the language of ancient philosophy, so prodigious an animal, exceeds all analogy, and even comprehension.

But farther, Cleanthes; men are mortal, and renew their species by generation; and this is common to all living creatures. The two great sexes of male and female, says Milton, animate the world. Why must this circumstance, so universal, so essential, be excluded from those numerous and limited Deities? Behold then the theogony of ancient times brought back upon us.

And why not become a perfect anthropomorphite? Why not assert the Deity or Deities to be corporeal, and to have eyes, a nose, mouth, ears, etc.? Epicurus maintained, that no man had ever seen reason but in a human figure; therefore the gods must have a human figure. And this argument, which is deservedly so much ridiculed by Cicero, becomes according to you, solid and philosophical.

In a word, Cleanthes, a man, who follows your hypothesis, is able, perhaps, to assert, or conjecture, that the universe, sometime, arose from something like design: But beyond that position he cannot ascertain one single circumstance, and is left afterwards to fix every point of his theology, by the utmost licence of fancy and hypothesis. This world, for aught he knows, is very faulty and imperfect, compared to a superior standard; and was only the first rude essay of some infant Deity, who afterwards abandoned it, ashamed of his lame performance; it is the work only of some dependent, inferior Deity; and is the object of derision to his superiors: it is the production of old age and dotage in some superannuated Deity; and ever since his death, has run on at adventures, from the first impulse and active force, which it received from him. . . . You justly give signs of horror, Demea, at these strange suppositions: But these, and a thousand more of the same kind, are Cleanthes' suppositions, not mine. From the moment the attributes of the Deity are supposed finite, all these have place. And I cannot, for my part, think, that so wild and unsettled a system of theology is, in any respect, preferable to none at all.

These suppositions I absolutely disown, cried CLEANTHES: They strike me, however, with no horror; especially, when proposed in that rambling way in which they drop from you. On the contrary, they give me pleasure, when I see, that, by the utmost indulgence of your imagination, you never get rid of the hypothesis of design in the universe; but are obliged, at every turn, to have recourse to it. To this concession I adhere steadily; and this I regard as a sufficient foundation for religion.

In Parts VI and VII (omitted here) Philo continues his attack on Cleanthes' position. In part VI Philo argues that the hypothesis that the world is an animal, with the Deity as its soul, accounts as well for the evidence Cleanthes has cited as the view that an intelligent Deity created the world:

> . . . if we survey the universe, so far as it falls under our knowledge, it bears a great resemblance to an animal or organized body, and seems actuated with a like principle of life and notion. A continual circulation of matter in it produces no disorder: A continual waste in every part is incessantly repaired: The closest sympathy is perceived throughout the entire system: And each part or member, in performing its proper offices, operates both to its own preservation and to that of the whole. The world, therefore, I infer, is an animal, and the Deity is the Soul of the world, actuating it, and actuated by it.

In Part VII Philo pushes the idea that the world resembles animals—and now vegetables, too,—even further:

> If the universe bears a greater likeness to animal bodies and to vegetables, than to the works of human art, it is more probable that its cause resembles the cause of the former than of the latter, and its origin ought rather to be ascribed to generation or vegetation than to reason or design. Your conclusion, even according to your own principles, is therefore lame and defective.
>
> . . . The world, says [Cleanthes], resembles the works of human contrivance: Therefore its cause must also resemble that of the other . . . the operation of one very small part of nature, to wit man, upon another very small part, to wit that inanimate matter lying within his reach, is the rule by which Cleanthes judges of the origin of the whole; . . . there are other parts of the universe (besides the machines of human invention) which bear still a greater resemblance to the fabric of the world, and which therefore afford a better conjecture concerning the universal origin of this system. . . . The world plainly resembles more an animal or a vegetable, than it does a watch or a knitting loom. Its cause, therefore, it is more probable, resembles the cause of the former. The cause of the former is generation or vegetation. . . .

Demea wonders whether Philo can really make sense of this and can explain the operations of vegetation and generation that he is postulating as the cause of the world. Philo replies:

> As much, at least . . . as Cleanthes can explain the operations of reason. . . . These words *generation*, *reason*, mark only certain powers and energies in nature, whose effects are known, but whose essence is incomprehensible; and one of these principles, more than the other, has no privilege for being made a standard of the whole of nature.
>
> . . . When I enquired concerning the cause of that supreme reason and intelligence, into which [Cleanthes] resolves every thing; he told me, that the impossibility of satisfying such enquiries could never be admitted as an objection in any species of philosophy. *We must stop somewhere*, says he; *nor is it ever within the reach of human capacity to explain ultimate causes, or who the last connections of any objects. It is sufficient, if the steps, so far as we go, are supported by experience and observation.* Now that vegetation and generation, as well as reason, are experienced to be principles of order in nature, is undeniable. If I rest my system of cosmogony on the former, preferably to the latter, it is at my choice. The matter seems entirely arbitrary. . . .

All of this leaves Cleanthes exasperated, but unconvinced:

> I must confess, Philo, . . . that of all men living, the task which you have undertaken, of raising doubts and objections, suits you best, and seems, in a manner, natural and unavoidable to you. So great is your fertility of invention, that I am not ashamed to acknowledge myself unable, on a sudden, to solve regularly such out-of-the-way difficulties as you incessantly start upon me: Though I clearly see, in general, their fallacy and error . . . you must be sensible, that common sense and reason is entirely against you, and that such whimsies, as you have delivered, may puzzle, but never can convince us.

Part VIII

What you ascribe to the fertility of my invention, replied PHILO, is entirely owing to the nature of the subject. In subjects, adapted to the narrow compass of human reason, there is commonly but one determination, which carries probability or conviction with it; and to a man of sound judgment, all other suppositions, but that one, appear entirely absurd and chimerical. But in such questions as the present, a hundred contradictory views may preserve a kind of imperfect analogy; and invention has here full scope to exert itself. Without any great effort of thought, I believe that I could, in an instant, propose other systems of cosmogony, which would have some faint appearance of truth; though it is a thousand, a million to one, if either yours or any one of mine be the true system.

For instance; what if I should revive the old Epicurean hypothesis? This is commonly, and I believe, justly, esteemed the most absurd system, that has yet been proposed; yet, I know not, whether, with a few alterations, it might not be brought to bear a faint appearance of probability. Instead of supposing matter infinite, as Epicurus did; let us suppose it finite. A finite number of particles is only susceptible of finite transpositions: And it must happen, in an eternal duration, that every possible order or position must be tried an infinite number of times. This world, therefore, with all its events, even the most minute, has before been produced and destroyed, and will again be produced and destroyed, without any bounds and limitations. No one, who has a conception of the powers of infinite, in comparison of finite, will ever scruple this determination.

But this supposes, said DEMEA, that matter can acquire motion, without any voluntary agent or first mover.

And where is the difficulty, replied PHILO, of that supposition? Every event, before experience, is equally difficult and incomprehensible; and every event, after experience, is equally easy and intelligible. Motion, in many instances, from gravity, from elasticity, from electricity, begins in matter, without any known voluntary agent; and to suppose always, in these cases, an unknown voluntary agent, is mere hypothesis; and hypothesis attended with no advantages. The beginning of motion in matter itself is as conceivable *a priori* as its communication from the mind and intelligence.

Besides, why may not motion have been propagated by impulse through all eternity, and the same stock of it, or nearly the same, be still upheld in the universe? As much as is lost by the composition of motion, as much is gained by its resolution. And whatever the causes are, the fact is certain, that matter is, and always has been in continual agitation, as far as human experience or tradition reaches. There is not probably, at present, in the whole universe, one particle of matter at absolute rest.

And this very consideration too, continued PHILO, which we have stumbled on in the course of the argument, suggests a new hypothesis of cosmogony, that is not absolutely absurd and improbable. Is there a system, an order, an economy of things, by which matter can preserve that perpetual agitation, which seems essential to it, and yet maintain a constancy in the forms, which it produces? There certainly is such an economy: For this is actually the case with the present world. The continual motion of matter, therefore, in less than infinite transpositions, must produce this economy or order; and by its very nature, that order, when once established, supports itself, for many ages, if not to eternity. But wherever matter is so poised, arranged, and adjusted as to continue in perpetual motion, and yet preserve a constancy in the forms, its situation must, of necessity, have all the same appearance of art and contrivance which we observe at present. All the parts of each form must have a relation to each other, and to the whole: And the whole itself must have a relation to the other parts of the universe; to the element, in which the form subsists; to the materials, with which it repairs its waste and decay; and to every other form, which is hostile or friendly. A defect in any of these particulars destroys the form; and the matter, of which it is composed, is again set loose, and is thrown into irregular motions and fermentations, till it unite itself to some other regular form. If no such form be prepared to receive it, and if there be a great quantity of this corrupted matter in the universe, the universe itself is entirely disordered; whether it be the feeble embryo of a world in its first beginnings, that is thus destroyed, or the rotten carcass of one, languishing in old age and infirmity. In either case, a chaos ensues; till finite, though innumerable revolutions produce at last some forms, whose parts and organs are so adjusted as to support the forms amidst a continued succession of matter.

Suppose (for we shall endeavour to vary the expression), that matter were thrown into any position, by a blind, unguided force; it is evident that this first position must in all probability be the most confused and most disorderly imaginable, without any resemblance to those works of human contrivance, which, along with a symmetry of parts, discover an adjustment of means to ends and a tendency to self-preservation. If the actuating force cease after this operation, matter must remain for ever in disorder, and continue an immense chaos, without any proportion or activity. But suppose, that the actuating force, whatever it be, still continues in matter, this first position will immediately give place to a second, which will likewise in all probability be as disorderly as the first, and so on, through many successions of changes and revolutions. No particular order or position ever continues a mo-

ment unaltered. The original force, still remaining in activity, gives a perpetual restlessness to matter. Every possible situation is produced, and instantly destroyed. If a glimpse or dawn of order appears for a moment, it is instantly hurried away, and confounded, by that never-ceasing force, which actuates every part of matter.

Thus the universe goes on for many ages in a continued succession of chaos and disorder. But is it not possible that it may settle at last, so as not to lose its motion and active force (for that we have supposed inherent in it), yet so as to preserve an uniformity of appearance, amidst the continual motion and fluctuation of its parts? This we find to be the case with the universe at present. Every individual is perpetually changing, and every part of every individual, and yet the whole remains, in appearance, the same. May we not hope for such a position, or rather be assured of it, from the eternal revolutions of unguided matter, and may not this account for all the appearing wisdom and contrivance which is in the universe? Let us contemplate the subject a little, and we shall find, that this adjustment, if attained by matter, of a seeming stability in the forms, with a real and perpetual revolution or motion of parts, affords a plausible, if not a true solution of the difficulty.

It is in vain, therefore, to insist upon the uses of the parts in animals or vegetables, and their curious adjustment to each other. I would fain know how an animal could subsist, unless its parts were so adjusted? Do we not find, that it immediately perishes whenever this adjustment ceases, and that its matter corrupting tries some new form? It happens, indeed, that the parts of the world are so well adjusted, that some regular form immediately lays claim to this corrupted matter: And if it were not so, could the world subsist? Must it not dissolve as well as the animal, and pass through new positions and situations; till in a great, but finite succession, it fall at last into the present or some such order?

It is well, replied CLEANTHES, you told us, that this hypothesis was suggested on a sudden, in the course of the argument. Had you had leisure to examine it, you would soon have perceived the insuperable objections, to which it is exposed. No form, you say, can subsist, unless it possess those powers and organs, requisite for its subsistence: Some new order or economy must be tried, and so on, without intermission; till at last some order, which can support and maintain itself, is fallen upon. But according to this hypothesis, whence arise the many conveniences and advantages which men and all animals possess? Two eyes, two ears, are not absolutely necessary for the subsistence of the species. Human race might have been propagated and preserved, without horses, dogs, cows, sheep, and those innumerable fruits and products which serve to our satisfaction and enjoyment. If no camels had been created for the use of man in the sandy deserts of Africa and Arabia, would the world have been dissolved? If no loadstone had been framed to give that wonderful and useful direction to the needle, would human society and the human kind have been immediately extinguished? Though the maxims of nature be in general very frugal, yet instances of this kind are far from being rare; and any one of them is a sufficient proof of design, and of a benevolent design, which gave rise to the order and arrangement of the universe.

At least, you may safely infer, said PHILO, that the foregoing hypothesis is so far incomplete and imperfect; which I shall not scruple to allow. But can we ever reasonably expect greater success in any attempts of this nature? Or can we ever hope to erect a system of cosmogony, that will be liable to no exceptions, and will contain no circumstance repugnant to our limited and imperfect experience of the analogy of nature? Your theory itself cannot surely pretend to any such advantage; even though you have run into *anthropomorphism*, the better to preserve a conformity to common experience. Let us once more put it to trial. In all instances which we have ever seen, ideas are copied from real objects, and are ectypal, not archetypal, to express myself in learned terms: You reverse this order, and give thought the precedence. In all instances which we have ever seen, thought has no influence upon matter, except where that matter is so conjoined with it, as to have an equal reciprocal influence upon it. No animal can move immediately any thing but the members of its own body; and indeed, the equality of action and re-action seems to be an universal law of nature: But your theory implies a contradiction to this experience. These instances, with many more,

which it were easy to collect (particularly the supposition of a mind or system of thought that is eternal, or in other words, an animal ingenerable and immortal), these instances, I say, may teach, all of us, sobriety in condemning each other, and let us see, that as no system of this kind ought ever to be received from a slight analogy, so neither ought any to be rejected on account of a small incongruity. For that is an inconvenience from which we can justly pronounce no one to be exempted.

All religious systems, it is confessed, are subject to great and insuperable difficulties. Each disputant triumphs in his turn; while he carries on an offensive war, and exposes the absurdities, barbarities, and pernicious tenets of his antagonist. But all of them, on the whole, prepare a complete triumph for the sceptic; who tells them, that no system ought ever to be embraced with regard to such subjects: For this plain reason, that no absurdity ought ever to be assented to with regard to any subject. A total suspense of judgment is here our only reasonable resource. And if every attack, as is commonly observed, and no defence, among theologians, is successful; how complete must be *his* victory, who remains always, with all mankind,[5] on the offensive, and has himself no fixed station or abiding city, which he is ever, on any occasion, obliged to defend?

Part IX

But if so many difficulties attend the argument *a posteriori*, said DEMEA; had we not better adhere to that simple and sublime argument *a priori*, which, by offering to us infallible demonstration, cuts off at once all doubt and difficulty? By this argument, too, we may prove the infinity of the divine attributes, which, I am afraid, can never be ascertained with certainty from any other topic. For how can an effect, which either is finite, or, for aught we know, may be so; how can such an effect, I say, prove an infinite cause? The unity too of the divine nature, it is very difficult, if not absolutely impossible, to deduce merely from contemplating the works of nature; nor will the uniformity alone of the plan, even were it allowed, give us any assurance of that attribute. Whereas the argument *a priori*. . . .

You seem to reason, Demea, interposed CLEAN-THES, as if those advantages and conveniences in the abstract argument were full proofs of its solidity. But it is first proper, in my opinion, to determine what argument of this nature you choose to insist on; and we shall afterwards, from itself, better than from its *useful* consequences, endeavour to determine what value we ought to put upon it.

The argument, replied DEMEA, which I would insist on is the common one. Whatever exists must have a cause or reason of its existence; it being absolutely impossible for any thing to produce itself, or be the cause of its own existence. In mounting up, therefore, from effects to causes, we must either go on in tracing an infinite succession, without any ultimate cause at all, or must at last have recourse to some ultimate cause, that is *necessarily* existent: Now that the first supposition is absurd may be thus proved. In the infinite chain or succession of causes and effects, each single effect is determined to exist by the power and efficacy of that cause which immediately preceded; but the whole eternal chain or succession, taken together, is not determined or caused by any thing: And yet it is evident that it requires a cause or reason, as much as any particular object, which begins to exist in time. The question is still reasonable, why this particular succession of causes existed from eternity, and not any other succession, or no succession at all. If there be no necessarily existent Being, any supposition, which can be formed, is equally possible; nor is there any more absurdity in nothing's having existed from eternity, than there is in that succession of causes, which constitutes the universe. What was it, then, which determined something to exist rather than nothing, and bestowed being on a particular possibility, exclusive of the rest? *External causes*, there are supposed to be none. *Chance* is a word without a meaning. Was it *nothing*? But that can never produce any thing. We must, therefore, have recourse to a necessarily existent Being, who carries the reason of his existence in himself; and who cannot be supposed not to exist without an express contradiction. There is consequently such a Being, that is, there is a Deity.

I shall not leave it to Philo, said CLEANTHES (though I know that the starting objections is his chief delight), to point out the weakness of this metaphysical reasoning. It seems to me so obviously ill-grounded, and at the same time of so little consequence to the cause of true piety and religion, that I shall myself venture to show the fallacy of it.

I shall begin with observing, that there is an evident absurdity in pretending to demonstrate a matter of fact, or to prove it by any arguments *a priori*. Nothing is demonstrable, unless the contrary implies a contradiction. Nothing, that is distinctly conceivable, implies a contradiction. Whatever we conceive as existent, we can also conceive as non-existent. There is no Being, therefore, whose non-existence implies a contradiction. Consequently, there is no Being, whose existence is demonstrable. I propose this argument as entirely decisive, and am willing to rest the whole controversy upon it.

It is pretended that the Deity is a necessarily existent Being; and this necessity of his existence is attempted to be explained by asserting, that, if we knew his whole essence or nature, we should perceive it to be as impossible for him not to exist as for twice two not to be four. But it is evident, that this can never happen, while our faculties remain the same as at present. It will still be possible for us, at any time, to conceive the non-existence of what we formerly conceived to exist; nor can the mind ever lie under a necessity of supposing any object to remain always in being; in the same manner as we lie under a necessity of always conceiving twice two to be four. The words, therefore, *necessary existence*, have no meaning; or, which is the same thing, none that is consistent.

But farther; why may not the material universe be the necessarily existent Being, according to this pretended explication of necessity? We dare not affirm that we know all the qualities of matter; and for aught we can determine, it may contain some qualities, which, were they known, would make its non-existence appear as great a contradiction as that twice two is five. I find only one argument employed to prove, that the material world is not the necessarily existent Being; and this argument is derived from the contingency both of the matter and the form of the world. "Any particle of matter", it is said,[6] "may be *conceived* to be annihilated; and any form may be *conceived* to be altered. Such an annihilation or alteration, therefore, is not impossible."

But it seems a great partiality not to perceive, that the same argument extends equally to the Deity, so far as we have any conception of him; and that the mind can at least imagine him to be non-existent, or his attributes to be altered. It must be some unknown, inconceivable qualities, which can make his non-existence appear impossible, or his attributes unalterable: And no reason can be assigned, why these qualities may not belong to matter. As they are altogether unknown and inconceivable, they can never be proved incompatible with it.

Add to this, that in tracing an eternal succession of objects, it seems absurd to inquire for a general cause or first Author. How can any thing, that exists from eternity, have a cause, since that relation implies a priority in time and a beginning of existence?

In such a chain too, or succession of objects, each part is caused by that which preceded it, and causes that which succeeds it. Where then is the difficulty? But the whole, you say, wants a cause. I answer, that the uniting of these parts into a whole, like the uniting of several distinct counties into one kingdom, or several distinct members into one body, is performed merely by an arbitrary act of the mind, and has no influence on the nature of things. Did I show you the particular causes of each individual in a collection of twenty particles of matter, I should think it very unreasonable, should you afterwards ask me, what was the cause of the whole twenty. This is sufficiently explained in explaining the cause of the parts.

Though the reasonings, which you have urged, Cleanthes, may well excuse me, said PHILO, from starting any farther difficulties; yet I cannot forbear insisting still upon another topic. It is observed by arithmeticians, that the products of 9 compose always either 9 or some lesser product of 9; if you add together all the characters, of which any of the former products is composed. Thus, of 18, 27, 36, which are products of 9, you make 9 by adding 1 to 8, 2 to 7, 3 to 6. Thus 369 is a product also of 9; and if you add 3, 6, and 9, you make 18, a lesser product of 9.[7] To a superficial observer, so wonderful a regularity may be admired as the effect either of chance or design; but a skilful algebraist immediately concludes it to be the work of necessity, and demonstrates, that

it must for ever result from the nature of these numbers. Is it not probable, I ask, that the whole economy of the universe is conducted by a like necessity, though no human algebra can furnish a key which solves the difficulty? And instead of admiring the order of natural beings, may it not happen, that, could we penetrate into the intimate nature of bodies, we should clearly see why it was absolutely impossible, they could ever admit of any other disposition? So dangerous is it to introduce this idea of necessity into the present question! And so naturally does it afford an inference directly opposite to the religious hypothesis!

But dropping all these abstractions, continued PHILO; and confining ourselves to more familiar topics; I shall venture to add an observation, that the argument *a priori* has seldom been found very convincing, except to people of a metaphysical head, who have accustomed themselves to abstract reasoning, and who finding from mathematics, that the understanding frequently leads to truth, through obscurity, and contrary to first appearances, have transferred the same habit of thinking to subjects where it ought not to have place. Other people, even of good sense and the best inclined to religion, feel always some deficiency in such arguments, though they are not perhaps able to explain distinctly where it lies. A certain proof, that men ever did, and ever will, derive their religion from other sources than from this species of reasoning.

Part X

It is my opinion, I own, replied DEMEA, that each man feels, in a manner, the truth of religion within his own breast; and from a consciousness of his imbecility and misery, rather than from any reasoning, is led to seek protection from that Being, on whom he and all nature is dependent. So anxious or so tedious are even the best scenes of life, that futurity is still the object of all our hopes and fears. We incessantly look forward, and endeavour, by prayers, adoration, and sacrifice, to appease those unknown powers, whom we find, by experience, so able to afflict and oppress us. Wretched creatures that we are! What resource for us amidst the innumerable ills of life, did not religion suggest some methods of atonement, and appease those terrors, with which we are incessantly agitated and tormented?

I am indeed persuaded, said PHILO, that the best and indeed the only method of bringing every one to a due sense of religion is by just representations of the misery and wickedness of men. And for that purpose a talent of eloquence and strong imagery is more requisite than that of reasoning and argument. For is it necessary to prove, what every one feels within himself? It is only necessary to make us feel it, if possible, more intimately and sensibly.

The people, indeed, replied DEMEA, are sufficiently convinced of this great and melancholy truth. The miseries of life, the unhappiness of man, the general corruptions of our nature, the unsatisfactory enjoyment of pleasures, riches, honours; these phrases have become almost proverbial in all languages. And who can doubt of what all men declare from their own immediate feeling and experience?

In this point, said PHILO, the learned are perfectly agreed with the vulgar; and in all letters, *sacred* and *profane*, the topic of human misery has been insisted on with the most pathetic eloquence that sorrow and melancholy could inspire. The poets, who speak from sentiment, without a system, and whose testimony has therefore the more authority, abound in images of this nature. From Homer down to Dr. Young, the whole inspired tribe have ever been sensible, that no other representation of things would suit the feeling and observation of each individual.

As to authorities, replied DEMEA, you need not seek them. Look round this library of Cleanthes. I shall venture to affirm, that, except authors of particular sciences, such as chemistry or botany, who have no occasion to treat of human life, there scarce is one of those innumerable writers, from whom the sense of human misery has not, in some passage or other, extorted a complaint and confession of it. At least, the chance is entirely on that side; and no one author has ever, so far as I can recollect, been so extravagant as to deny it.

There you must excuse me, said PHILO: Leibnitz has denied it; and is perhaps the first,[8] who ventured upon so bold and paradoxical an opinion; at least, the first, who made it essential to his philosophical system.

And by being the first, replied DEMEA, might he not have been sensible of his error? For is this a subject in which philosophers can propose to make discoveries, especially in so late an age? And can any man hope by a simple denial (for the subject scarcely admits of reasoning) to bear down the united testimony of mankind, founded on sense and consciousness?

And why should man, added he, pretend to an exemption from the lot of all other animals? The whole earth, believe me, Philo, is cursed and polluted. A perpetual war is kindled amongst all living creatures. Necessity, hunger, want, stimulate the strong and courageous: Fear, anxiety, terror, agitate the weak and infirm. The first entrance into life gives anguish to the new-born infant and to its wretched parent: Weakness, impotence, distress, attend each stage of that life: And it is at last finished in agony and horror.

Observe too, says PHILO, the curious artifices of nature, in order to embitter the life of every living being. The stronger prey upon the weaker, and keep them in perpetual terror and anxiety. The weaker too, in their turn, often prey upon the stronger, and vex and molest them without relaxation. Consider that innumerable race of insects, which either are bred on the body of each animal, or flying about infix their stings in him. These insects have others still less than themselves, which torment them. And thus on each hand, before and behind, above and below, every animal is surrounded with enemies, which incessantly seek his misery and destruction.

Man alone, said DEMEA, seems to be, in part, an exception to this rule. For by combination in society, he can easily master lions, tigers, and bears, whose greater strength and agility naturally enable them to prey upon him.

On the contrary, it is here chiefly, cried PHILO, that the uniform and equal maxims of nature are most apparent. Man, it is true, can, by combination, surmount all his *real* enemies, and become master of the whole animal creation: But does he not immediately raise up to himself *imaginary* enemies, the demons of his fancy, who haunt him with superstitious terrors, and blast every enjoyment of life? His pleasure, as he imagines, becomes, in their eyes, a crime: His food and repose give them umbrage and offence: His very sleep and dreams furnish new materials to anxious fear: And even death, his refuge from every other ill, presents only the dread of endless and innumerable woes. Nor does the wolf molest more the timid flock, than superstition does the anxious breast of wretched mortals.

Besides, consider, Demea; this very society, by which we surmount those wild beasts, our natural enemies; what new enemies does it not raise to us? What woe and misery does it not occasion? Man is the greatest enemy of man. Oppression, injustice, contempt, contumely, violence, sedition, war, calumny, treachery, fraud; by these they mutually torment each other: And they would soon dissolve that society which they had formed, were it not for the dread of still greater ills, which must attend their separation.

But though these external insults, said DEMEA, from animals, from men, from all the elements, which assault us, form a frightful catalogue of woes, they are nothing in comparison of those, which arise within ourselves, from the distempered condition of our mind and body. How many lie under the lingering torment of diseases? Hear the pathetic enumeration of the great poet.

Intestine stone and ulcer, colic-pangs,
Daemoniac frenzy, moping melancholy,
And moon-struck madness, pining atrophy,
Marasmus and wide-wasting pestilence.
Dire was the tossing, deep the groans: DESPAIR
Tended the sick, busiest from couch to couch.
And over them triumphant DEATH his dart
Shook, but delay'd to strike, tho' oft invok'd
With vows, as their chief good and final hope.[9]

The disorders of the mind, continued DEMEA, though more secret, are not perhaps less dismal and vexatious. Remorse, shame, anguish, rage, disappointment, anxiety, fear, dejection, despair; who has ever passed through life without cruel inroads from these tormentors? How many have scarcely ever felt any better sensations? Labour and poverty, so abhorred by every one, are the certain lot of the far greater number: And those few privileged persons, who enjoy ease and opulence, never reach contentment or true felicity. All the goods of life united

would not make a very happy man: But all the ills united would make a wretch indeed; and any one of them almost (and who can be free from every one), nay often the absence of one good (and who can possess all) is sufficient to render life ineligible.

Were a stranger to drop, on a sudden, into this world, I would show him, as a specimen of its ills, an hospital full of diseases, a prison crowded with malefactors and debtors, a field of battle strowed with carcases, a fleet floundering in the ocean, a nation languishing under tyranny, famine, or pestilence. To turn the gay side of life to him, and give him a notion of its pleasures; whither should I conduct him? to a ball, to an opera, to court? He might justly think, that I was only showing him a diversity of distress and sorrow.

There is no evading such striking instances, said PHILO, but by apologies, which still farther aggravate the charge. Why have all men, I ask, in all ages, complained incessantly of the miseries of life? . . . They have no just reason, says one: These complaints proceed only from their discontented, repining, anxious disposition. . . . And can there possibly, I reply, be a more certain foundation of misery, than such a wretched temper?

But if they were really as unhappy as they pretend, says my antagonist, why do they remain in life? . . .

Not satisfied with life, afraid of death.

This is the secret chain, say I, that holds us. We are terrified, not bribed to the continuance of our existence.

It is only a false delicacy, he may insist, which a few refined spirits indulge, and which has spread these complaints among the whole race of mankind. . . . And what is this delicacy, I ask, which you blame? Is it any thing but a greater sensibility to all the pleasures and pains of life? and if the man of a delicate, refined temper, by being so much more alive than the rest of the world, is only so much more unhappy; what judgment must we form in general of human life?

Let men remain at rest, says our adversary; and they will be easy. They are willing artificers of their own misery. . . . No! reply I; an anxious languor follows their repose: Disappointment, vexation, trouble, their activity and ambition.

I can observe something like what you mention in some others, replied CLEANTHES: But I confess, I feel little or nothing of it in myself; and hope that it is not so common as you represent it.

If you feel not human misery yourself, cried DEMEA, I congratulate you on so happy a singularity. Others, seemingly the most prosperous, have not been ashamed to vent their complaints in the most melancholy strains. Let us attend to the great, the fortunate Emperor, Charles V, when, tired with human grandeur, he resigned all his extensive dominions into the hands of his son. In the last harangue, which he made on that memorable occasion, he publicly avowed, *that the greatest prosperities which he had ever enjoyed, had been mixed with so many adversities, that he might truly say he had never enjoyed any satisfaction or contentment.* But did the retired life, in which he sought for shelter, afford him any greater happiness? If we may credit his son's account, his repentence commenced the very day of his resignation.

Cicero's fortune, from small beginnings, rose to the greatest lustre and renown; yet what pathetic complaints of the ills of life do his familiar letters, as well as philosophical discourses, contain? And suitably to his own experience, he introduces Cato, the great, the fortunate Cato, protesting in his old age, that, had he a new life in his offer, he would reject the present.

Ask yourself, ask any of your acquaintance, whether they would live over again the last ten or twenty years of their life. No! but the next twenty, they say, will be better:

And from the dregs of life, hope to receive
What the first sprightly running could not give.[10]

Thus at last they find (such is the greatness of human misery; it reconciles even contradictions) that they complain, at once, of the shortness of life, and of its vanity and sorrow.

And is it possible, Cleanthes, said PHILO, that after all these reflections, and infinitely more, which might be suggested, you can still perserve in your anthropomorphism, and assert the moral attributes of the Deity, his justice, benevolence, mercy, and rectitude, to be of the same nature with these virtues in human creatures? His power we allow infinite: Whatever he wills is executed: But neither man nor any other animal are happy: Therefore he does not will their happiness. His wisdom is infinite: He is never mistaken in choosing the means to any end: But the course of nature tends not to human or animal felicity: Therefore it is not established for that purpose. Through the whole compass of human knowledge, there are no inferences more certain and infallible than these. In what respect, then, do his benevolence and mercy resemble the benevolence and mercy of men?

Epicurus' old questions are yet unanswered. Is he willing to prevent evil, but not able? then is he impotent. Is he able, but not willing? then is he malevolent. Is he both able and willing? whence then is evil?

You ascribe, Cleanthes (and I believe justly) a purpose and intention to nature. But what, I beseech you, is the object of that curious artifice and machinery, which she has displayed in all animals? The preservation alone of individuals and propagation of the species. It seems enough for her purpose, if such a rank be barely upheld in the universe, without any care or concern for the happiness of the members that compose it. No resource for this purpose: No machinery, in order merely to give pleasure or ease: No fund of pure joy and contentment: No indulgence without some want or necessity accompanying it. At least, the few phenomena of this nature are overbalanced by opposite phenomena of still greater importance.

Our sense of music, harmony, and indeed beauty of all kinds, gives satisfaction, without being absolutely necessary to the preservation and propagation of the species. But what racking pains, on the other hand, arise from gouts, gravels, megrims, tooth-aches, rheumatisms; where the injury to the animal-machinery is either small or incurable? Mirth, laughter, play, frolic, seem gratuitous satisfactions which have no farther tendency: Spleen, melancholy, discontent, superstition, are pains of the same nature. How then does the divine benevolence display itself, in the sense of you anthropomorphites? None but we mystics, as you were pleased to call us, can account for this strange mixture of phenomena, by deriving it from attributes, infinitely perfect, but incomprehensible.

And have you at last, said CLEANTHES smiling, betrayed your intentions, Philo? Your long agreement with Demea did indeed a little surprise me; but I find you were all the while erecting a concealed battery against me. And I must confess, that you have now fallen upon a subject worthy of your noble spirit of opposition and controversy. If you can make out the present point, and prove mankind to be unhappy or corrupted, there is an end at once of all religion. For to what purpose establish the natural attributes of the Deity, while the moral are still doubtful and uncertain?

You take umbrage very easily, replied DEMEA, at opinions the most innocent, and the most generally received even amongst the religious and devout themselves: And nothing can be more surprising than to find a topic like this, concerning the wickedness and misery of man, charged with no less than atheism and profaneness. Have not all pious divines and preachers, who have indulged their rhetoric on so fertile a subject; have they not easily, I say, given a solution of any difficulties which may attend it? This world is but a point in comparison of the universe: This life but a moment in comparison of eternity. The present evil phenomena, therefore, are rectified in other regions, and in some future period of existence. And the eyes of men, being then opened to larger views of things, see the whole connection of general laws, and trace, with adoration, the benevolence and rectitude of the Deity, through all the mazes and intricacies of his providence.

No! replied CLEANTHES, No! These arbitrary suppositions can never be admitted, contrary to matter of fact, visible and uncontroverted. Whence can any cause be known but from its known effects? Whence can any hypothesis be proved but from the apparent phenomena? To establish one hypothesis upon another is building entirely in the air; and the utmost we ever attain, by these conjectures and fictions, is to ascertain the bare possibility of our opinion; but never can we, upon such terms, establish its reality.

The only method of supporting divine benevolence (and it is what I willingly embrace) is to deny absolutely the misery and wickedness of man. Your representations are exaggerated: Your melancholy views mostly fictitious: Your inferences contrary to fact and experience. Health is more common than sickness: Pleasure than pain: Happiness than misery. And for one vexation which we meet with, we attain, upon computation, a hundred enjoyments.

Admitting your position, replied PHILO, which yet is extremely doubtful, you must, at the same time, allow, that, if pain be less frequent than pleasure, it is infinitely more violent and durable. One hour of it is often able to outweigh a day, a week, a month of our common insipid enjoyments: And how many days, weeks, and months are passed by several in the most acute torments? Pleasure, scarcely in one instance, is ever able to reach ecstasy and rapture: And in no one instance can it continue for any time at its highest pitch and altitude. The spirits evaporate; the nerves relax; the fabric is disordered; and the enjoyment quickly degenerates into fatigue and uneasiness. But pain often, Good God, how often! rises to torture and agony; and the longer it continues, it becomes still more genuine agony and torture. Patience is exhausted; courage languishes; melancholy seizes us; and nothing terminates our misery but the removal of its cause, or another event, which is the sole cure of all evil, but which, from our natural folly, we regard with still greater horror and consternation.

But not to insist upon these topics, continued PHILO, though most obvious, certain, and important; I must use the freedom to admonish you, Cleanthes, that you have put this controversy upon a most dangerous issue, and are unawares introducing a total scepticism into the most essential articles of natural and revealed theology. What! no method of fixing a just foundation for religion, unless we allow the happiness of human life, and maintain a continued existence even in this world, with all our present pains, infirmities, vexations, and follies, to be eligible and desirable! But this is contrary to every one's feeling and experience: It is contrary to an authority so established as nothing can subvert: No decisive proofs can ever be produced against this authority; nor is it possible for you to compute, estimate, and compare all the pains and all the pleasures in the lives of all men and of all animals: And thus by your resting the whole system of religion on a point, which, from its very nature, must for ever be uncertain, you tacitly confess, that that system is equally uncertain.

But allowing you, what never will be believed; at least, what you never possibly can prove, that animal, or at least, human happiness, in this life, exceeds its misery; you have yet done nothing: For this is not, by any means, what we expect from infinite power, infinite wisdom, and infinite goodness. Why is there any misery at all in the world? Not by chance surely. From some cause then. Is it from the intention of the Deity? But he is perfectly benevolent. Is it contrary to his intention? But he is almighty. Nothing can shake the solidity of this reasoning, so short, so clear, so decisive; except we assert, that these subjects exceed all human capacity, and that our common measures of truth and falsehood are not applicable to them; a topic, which I have all along insisted on, but which you have, from the beginning, rejected with scorn and indignation.

But I will be contented to retire still from this intrenchment: For I deny that you can ever force me in it: I will allow, that pain or misery in man is *compatible* with infinite power and goodness in the Deity, even in your sense of these attributes: What are you advanced by all these concessions? A mere possible compatibility is not sufficient. You must *prove* these pure, unmixed, and uncontrollable attributes from the present mixed and confused phenomena, and from these alone. A hopeful undertaking! Were the phenomena ever so pure and unmixed, yet being finite, they would be insufficient for that purpose. How much more, where they are also so jarring and discordant?

Here, Cleanthes, I find myself at ease in my argument. Here I triumph. Formerly, when we argued concerning the natural attributes of intelligence and design, I needed all my sceptical and metaphysical subtility to elude your grasp. In many views of the universe, and of its parts, particularly the latter, the beauty and fitness of final causes strike us with such irresistible force, that all objections appear (what I believe they really are) mere cavils and sophisms; nor can we then imagine how it was ever possible for us to repose any weight on them. But there is no view of human life, or of the condition of mankind, from

which, without the greatest violence, we can infer the moral attributes, or learn that infinite benevolence, conjoined with infinite power and infinite wisdom, which we must discover by the eyes of faith alone. It is your turn now to tug the labouring oar, and to support your philosophical subtilties against the dictates of plain reason and experience.

Part XI

I scruple not to allow, said CLEANTHES, that I have been apt to suspect the frequent repetition of the word, *infinite*, which we meet with in all theological writers, to savour more of panegyric than of philosophy, and that any purposes of reasoning, and even of religion, would be better served, were we to rest contented with more accurate and more moderate expressions. The terms, *admirable*, *excellent*, *superlatively great*, *wise*, and *holy*; these sufficiently fill the imaginations of men; and any thing beyond, besides that it leads into absurdities, has no influence on the affections or sentiments. Thus, in the present subject, if we abandon all human analogy, as seems your intention, Demea, I am afraid we abandon all religion, and retain no conception of the great object of our adoration. If we preserve human analogy, we must for ever find it impossible to reconcile any mixture of evil in the universe with infinite attributes; much less, can we ever prove the latter from the former. But supposing the Author of nature to be finitely perfect, though far exceeding mankind; a satisfactory account may then be given of natural and moral evil, and every untoward phenomenon be explained and adjusted. A less evil may then be chosen, in order to avoid a greater: Inconveniences be submitted to, in order to reach a desirable end: And in a word, benevolence, regulated by wisdom, and limited by necessity, may produce just such a world as the present. You, Philo, who are so prompt at starting views, and reflections, and analogies; I would gladly hear, at length, without interruption, your opinion of this new theory; and if it deserve our attention, we may afterwards, at more leisure, reduce it into form.

My sentiments, replied PHILO, are not worth being made a mystery of; and therefore, without any ceremony, I shall deliver what occurs to me with regard to the present subject. It must, I think, be allowed, that, if a very limited intelligence, whom we shall suppose utterly unacquainted with the universe, were assured, that it were the production of a very good, wise, and powerful Being, however finite, he would, from his conjectures, form *beforehand* a different notion of it from what we find it to be by experience; nor would he ever imagine, merely from these attributes of the cause, of which he is informed, that the effect could be so full of vice and misery and disorder, as it appears in this life. Supposing now, that this person were brought into the world, still assured, that it was the workmanship of such a sublime and benevolent Being; he might, perhaps, be surprised at the disappointment; but would never retract his former belief, if founded on any very solid argument; since such a limited intelligence must be sensible of his own blindness and ignorance, and must allow, that there may be many solutions of those phenomena, which will for ever escape his comprehension. But supposing, which is the real case with regard to man, that this creature is not antecedently convinced of a supreme intelligence, benevolent, and powerful, but is left to gather such a belief from the appearances of things; this entirely alters the case, nor will he ever find any reason for such a conclusion. He may be fully convinced of the narrow limits of his understanding; but this will not help him in forming an inference concerning the goodness of superior powers, since he must form that inference from what he knows, not from what he is ignorant of. The more you exaggerate his weakness and ignorance, the more diffident you render him, and give him the greater suspicion, that such subjects are beyond the reach of his faculties. You are obliged, therefore, to reason with him merely from the known phenomena, and to drop every arbitrary supposition or conjecture.

Did I show you a house or palace, where there was not one apartment convenient or agreeable; where the windows, doors, fires, passages, stairs, and the whole economy of the building were the source of noise, confusion, fatigue, darkness, and the extremes of heat and cold; you would certainly blame the contrivance, without any farther examination. The architect would in vain display his sub-

tilty, and prove to you, that if this door or that window were altered, greater ills would ensue. What he says, may be strictly true: The alteration of one particular, while the other parts of the building remain, may only augment the inconveniences. But still you would assert in general, that, if the architect had had skill and good intentions, he might have formed such a plan of the whole, and might have adjusted the parts in such a manner, as would have remedied all or most of these inconveniences. His ignorance, or even your own ignorance of such a plan, will never convince you of the impossibility of it. If you find many inconveniences and deformities in the building, you will always, without entering into any detail, condemn the architect.

In short, I repeat the question: Is the world considered in general, and as it appears to us in this life, different from what a man or such a limited being would, *beforehand*, expect from a very powerful, wise, and benevolent Deity? It must be strange prejudice to assert the contrary. And from thence I conclude, that, however consistent the world may be, allowing certain suppositions and conjectures, with the ideal of such a Deity, it can never afford us an inference concerning his existence. The consistence is not absolutely denied, only the inference. Conjectures, especially where infinity is excluded from the divine attributes, may, perhaps, be sufficient to prove a consistence; but can never be foundations for any inference.

There seem to be *four* circumstances, on which depend all, or the greatest part of the ills, that molest sensible creatures; and it is not impossible but all these circumstances may be necessary and unavoidable. We know so little beyond common life, or even of common life, that, with regard to the economy of a universe, there is no conjecture, however wild, which may not be just; nor any one, however plausible, which may not be erroneous. All that belongs to human understanding, in this deep ignorance and obscurity, is to be sceptical, or at least cautious; and not to admit of any hypothesis, whatever; much less, of any which is supported by no appearance of probability. Now this I assert to be the case with regard to all the causes of evil, and the circumstances on which it depends. None of them appear to human reason, in the least degree, necessary or unavoidable; nor can we suppose them such, without the utmost licence of imagination.

The *first* circumstance which introduces evil, is that contrivance or economy of the animal creation, by which pains, as well as pleasures, are employed to excite all creatures to action, and make them vigilant in the great work of self-preservation. Now pleasure alone, in its various degrees, seems to human understanding sufficient for this purpose. All animals might be constantly in a state of enjoyment; but when urged by any of the necessities of nature, such as thirst, hunger, weariness; instead of pain, they might feel a diminution of pleasure, by which they might be prompted to seek that object, which is necessary to their subsistence. Men pursue pleasure as eagerly as they avoid pain; at least, might have been so constituted. It seems, therefore, plainly possible to carry on the business of life without any pain. Why then is any animal ever rendered susceptible of such a sensation? If animals can be free from it an hour, they might enjoy a perpetual exemption from it; and it required as particular a contrivance of their organs to produce that feeling, as to endow them with sight, hearing, or any of the senses. Shall we conjecture, that such a contrivance was necessary, without any appearance of reason? And shall we build on that conjecture as on the most certain truth?

But a capacity of pain would not alone produce pain, were it not for the *second* circumstance, viz. the conducting of the world by general laws; and this seems nowise necessary to a very perfect Being. It is true; if every thing were conducted by particular volitions, the course of nature would be perpetually broken, and no man could employ his reason in the conduct of life. But might not other particular volitions remedy this inconvenience? In short, might not the Deity exterminate all ill, wherever it were to be found; and produce all good, without any preparation or long progress of causes and effects?

Besides, we must consider, that, according to the present economy of the world, the course of nature, though supposed exactly regular, yet to us appears not so, and many events are uncertain, and many disappoint our expectations. Health and sickness, calm and tempest, with an infinite number of other accidents, whose causes are unknown and variable, have a great influence both on the fortunes of particular persons and on the prosperity of public societies: And indeed all human life, in a manner, depends on such accidents. A Being, therefore, who knows the secret springs of the universe, might easily, by particular volitions, turn all these accidents to the good of mankind, and render the whole world happy, without discovering himself in any operation. A fleet, whose purposes were salutary to society, might always meet with a fair wind: Good princes enjoy sound health and long life: Persons born to power and authority, be framed with good tempers and virtuous dispositions. A few such events as these, regularly and wisely conducted, would change the face of the world; and yet would no more seem to disturb the course of nature or confound human conduct, than the present economy of things, where the causes are secret, and variable, and compounded. Some small touches, given to Caligula's brain in his infancy, might have converted him into a Trajan: One wave, a little higher than the rest, by burying Caesar and his fortune in the bottom of the ocean, might have restored liberty to a considerable part of mankind. There may, for aught we know, be good reasons, why providence interposes not in this manner; but they are unknown to us: And though the mere supposition, that such reasons exist, may be sufficient to *save* the conclusion concerning the divine attributes, yet surely it can never be sufficient to *establish* that conclusion.

If every thing in the universe be conducted by general laws, and if animals be rendered susceptible of pain, it scarcely seems possible but some ill must arise in the various shocks of matter, and the various concurrence and opposition of general laws: But this ill would be very rare, were it not for the *third* circumstance, which I proposed to mention, viz. the great frugality with which all powers and faculties are distributed to every particular being. So well adjusted are the organs and capacities of all animals, and so well fitted to their preservation, that, as far as history or tradition reaches, there appears not to be any single species which has yet been extinguished in the universe. Every animal has the requisite endowments; but these endowments are bestowed with so scrupulous an economy, that any considerable diminution must entirely destroy the creature. Wherever one power is increased, there is a proportional abatement in the others. Animals, which excel in swiftness, are commonly defective in force. Those, which possess both, are either imperfect in some of their senses, or are oppressed with the most craving wants. The human species, whose chief excellency is reason and sagacity, is of all others the most necessitous, and the most deficient in bodily advantages; without clothes, without arms, without food, without lodging, without any convenience of life, except what they owe to their own skill and industry. In short, nature seems to have formed an exact calculation of the necessities of her creatures; and like a *rigid master*, has afforded them little more powers or endowments, than what are strictly sufficient to supply those necessities. An *indulgent parent* would have bestowed a large stock, in order to guard against accidents, and secure the happiness and welfare of the creature, in the most unfortunate concurrence of circumstances. Every course of life would not have been so surrounded with precipices, that the least departure from the true path, by mistake or necessity, must involve us in misery and ruin. Some reserve, some fund would have been provided to ensure happiness; nor would the powers and the necessities have been adjusted with so rigid an economy. The Author of nature is inconceivably powerful: His force is supposed great, if not altogether inexhaustible: Nor is there any reason, as far as we can judge, to make him observe this strict frugality in his dealings with his creatures. It would have been better, were his power extremely limited, to have created fewer animals, and to have endowed these with more faculties for their happiness and preservation. A builder is never esteemed prudent, who undertakes a plan, beyond what his stock will enable him to finish.

In order to cure most of the ills of human life, I require not that man should have the wings of the eagle, the swiftness of the stag, the force of the ox, the arms of the lion, the scales of the crocodile or rhinoceros; much less do I demand the sagacity of an angel or cherubim. I am contented to take an increase in one single power or faculty of his soul. Let him be endowed with a greater propensity to industry and labour; a more vigorous spring and activity of mind; a more constant bent to business and application. Let the whole species possess naturally an equal diligence with that which many individuals are able to attain by habit and reflection; and the most beneficial consequences, without any allay of ill, is the immediate and necessary result of this endowment. Almost all the moral, as well as natural evils of human life arise from idleness; and were our species, by the original constitution of their frame, exempt from this vice or infirmity, the perfect cultivation of land, the improvement of arts and manufactures, the exact execution of every office and duty, immediately follow; and men at once may fully reach that state of society, which is so imperfectly attained by the best-regulated government. But as industry is a power, and the most valuable of any, nature seems determined, suitably to her usual maxims, to bestow it on men with a very sparing hand; and rather to punish him severely for his deficiency in it, than to reward him for his attainments. She has so contrived his frame, that nothing but the most violent necessity can oblige him to labour; and she employs all his other wants to overcome, at least in part, the want of diligence, and to endow him with some share of a faculty, of which she has thought fit naturally to bereave him. Here our demands may be allowed very humble, and therefore the more reasonable. If we required the endowments of superior penetration and judgment, of a more delicate taste of beauty, of a nicer sensibility to benevolence and friendship; we might be told, that we impiously pretend to break the order of nature, that we want to exalt ourselves into a higher rank of being, that the presents which we require, not being suitable to our state and condition, would only be pernicious to us. But it is hard; I dare to repeat it, it is hard, that being placed in a world so full of wants and necessities; where almost every being and element is either our foe or refuses us their assistance; we should also have our own temper to struggle with, and should be deprived of that faculty which can alone fence against these multiplied evils.

The *fourth* circumstance, whence arises the misery and ill of the universe, is the inaccurate workmanship of all the springs and principles of the great machine of nature. It must be acknowledged, that there are few parts of the universe, which seem not to serve some purpose, and whose removal would not produce a visible defect and disorder in the whole. The parts hang all together; nor can one be touched without affecting the rest, in a greater or less degree. But at the same time, it must be observed, that none of these parts or principles, however useful, are so accurately adjusted, as to keep precisely within those bounds in which their utility consists; but they are, all of them, apt, on every occasion, to run into the one extreme or the other. One would imagine, that this grand production had not received the last hand of the maker; so little finished is every part, and so coarse are the strokes, with which it is executed. Thus, the winds are requisite to convey the vapours along the surface of the globe, and to assist men in navigation: But how oft, rising up to tempests and hurricanes, do they become pernicious? Rains are necessary to nourish all the plants and animals of the earth: But how often are they defective? how often excessive? Heat is requisite to all life and vegetation; but is not always found in the due proportion. On the mixture and secretion of the humours and juices of the body depend the health and prosperity of the animal: But the parts perform not regularly their proper function. What more useful than all the passions of the mind, ambition, vanity, love, anger? But how oft do they break their bounds, and cause the greatest convulsions in society? There is nothing so advantageous in the universe, but what frequently becomes pernicious, by its excess or defect; nor has nature guarded, with the requisite accuracy, against all disorder or confusion. The irregularity is never, perhaps, so great as to destroy any species; but is often sufficient to involve the individuals in ruin and misery.

On the concurrence, then, of these *four* circumstances does all or the greatest part of natural evil depend. Were all living creatures incapable of pain, or were the world administered by particular volitions, evil never could have found access into the universe: And were animals endowed with a large stock of powers and faculties, beyond what strict necessity requires; or were the several springs and principles of the universe so accurately framed as to preserve always the just temperament and medium; there must have been very little ill in comparison of what we feel at present. What then shall we pro-

nounce on this occasion? Shall we say, that these circumstances are not necessary, and that they might easily have been altered in the contrivance of the universe? This decision seems too presumptuous for creatures so blind and ignorant. Let us be more modest in our conclusions. Let us allow, that, if the goodness of the Deity (I mean a goodness, like the human) could be established on any tolerable reasons *a priori*, these phenomena, however untoward, would not be sufficient to subvert that principle; but might easily, in some unknown manner, be reconcilable to it. But let us still assert, that as this goodness is not antecedently established, but must be inferred from the phenomena, there can be no grounds for such an inference, while there are so many ills in the universe, and while these ills might so easily have been remedied, as far as human understanding can be allowed to judge on such a subject. I am sceptic enough to allow, that the bad appearances, notwithstanding all my reasonings, may be compatible with such attributes as you suppose: But surely they can never prove these attributes. Such a conclusion cannot result from scepticism; but must arise from the phenomena, and from our confidence in the reasonings which we deduce from these phenomena.

Look round this universe. What an immense profusion of beings, animated and organized, sensible and active! You admire this prodigious variety and fecundity. But inspect a little more narrowly these living existences, the only beings worth regarding. How hostile and destructive to each other! How insufficient all of them for their own happiness! How contemptible or odious to the spectator! The whole presents nothing but the idea of a blind nature, impregnated by a great vivifying principle, and pouring forth from her lap, without discernment or parental care, her maimed and abortive children.

Here the Manichean system occurs as a proper hypothesis to solve the difficulty: And no doubt, in some respects, it is very specious, and has more probability than the common hypothesis, by giving a plausible account of the strange mixture of good and ill which appears in life. But if we consider, on the other hand, the perfect uniformity and agreement of the parts of the universe, we shall not discover in it any marks of the combat of a malevolent with a benevolent Being. There is indeed an opposition of pains and pleasures in the feelings of sensible creatures: But are not all the operations of nature carried on by an opposition of principles, of hot and cold, moist and dry, light and heavy? The true conclusion is, that the original source of all things is entirely indifferent to all these principles, and has no more regard to good above ill than to heat above cold, or to drought above moisture, or to light above heavy.

There may *four* hypotheses be framed concerning the first causes of the universe: *that* they are endowed with perfect goodness, *that* they have perfect malice, *that* they are opposite and have both goodness and malice, *that* they have neither goodness nor malice. Mixed phenomena can never prove the two former unmixed principles. And the uniformity and steadiness of general laws seem to oppose the third. The fourth, therefore, seems by far the most probable.

What I have said concerning natural evil will apply to moral, with little or no variation; and we have no more reason to infer, that the rectitude of the supreme Being resembles human rectitude than that his benevolence resembles the human. Nay, it will be thought, that we have still greater cause to exclude from him moral sentiments, such as we feel them; since moral evil, in the opinion of many, is much more predominant above moral good than natural evil above natural good.

But even though this should not be allowed, and though the virtue, which is in mankind, should be acknowledged much superior to the vice; yet so long as there is any vice at all in the universe, it will very much puzzle you anthropomorphites, how to account for it. You must assign a cause for it, without having recourse to the first cause. But as every effect must have a cause, and that cause another; you must either carry on the progression *in infinitum*, or rest on that original principle, who is the ultimate cause of all things. . . .

Hold! Hold! cried DEMEA: Whither does your imagination hurry you? I joined in alliance with you, in order to prove the incomprehensible nature of the divine Being, and refute the principles of Cleanthes, who would measure every thing by a human rule and standard. But I now find you running into all the topics of the greatest libertines and infidels; and betraying that holy cause, which you seemingly espoused. Are you secretly, then, a more dangerous enemy than Cleanthes himself?

And are you so late in perceiving it? replied CLEANTHES. Believe me, Demea; your friend Philo, from the beginning, has been amusing himself at both our expence; and it must be confessed, that the injudicious reasoning of our vulgar theology has given him but too just a handle of ridicule. The total infirmity of human reason, the absolute incomprehensibility of the divine nature, the great and universal misery and still greater wickedness of men; these are strange topics surely to be so fondly cherished by orthodox divines and doctors. In ages of stupidity and ignorance, indeed, these principles may safely be espoused; and perhaps, no views of things are more proper to promote superstition, than such as encourage the blind amazement, the diffidence, and melancholy of mankind. But at present. . . .

Blame not so much, interposed PHILO, the ignorance of these reverend gentlemen. They know how to change their style with the times. Formerly it was a most popular theological topic to maintain, that human life was vanity and misery, and to exaggerate all the ills and pains which are incident to men. But of late years, divines, we find, begin to retract this position, and maintain, though still with some hesitation, that there are more goods than evils, more pleasures than pains, even in this life. When religion stood entirely upon temper and education, it was thought proper to encourage melancholy; as indeed, mankind never have recourse to superior powers so readily as in that disposition. But as men have now learned to form principles, and to draw consequences, it is necessary to change the batteries, and to make use of such arguments as will endure, at least some scrutiny and examination. This variation is the same (and from the same causes) with that which I formerly remarked with regard to scepticism.

Thus Philo continued to the last his spirit of opposition, and his censure of established opinions. But I could observe, that Demea did not at all relish the latter part of the discourse; and he took occasion soon after, on some pretence or other, to leave the company.

Part XII

After Demea's departure, Cleanthes and Philo continued the conversation in the following manner. Our friend, I am afraid, said CLEANTHES, will have little inclination to revive this topic of discourse, while you are in company; and to tell truth, Philo, I should rather wish to reason with either of you apart on a subject so sublime and interesting. Your spirit of controversy, joined to your abhorrence of vulgar superstition, carries you strange lengths, when engaged in an argument; and there is nothing so sacred and venerable, even in your own eyes, which you spare on that occasion.

I must confess, replied PHILO, that I am less cautious on the subject of natural religion than on any other; both because I know that I can never, on that head, corrupt the principles of any man of common sense, and because no one, I am confident, in whose eyes I appear a man of common sense, will ever mistake my intentions. You, in particular, Cleanthes, with whom I live in unreserved intimacy; you are sensible, that, notwithstanding the freedom of my conversation, and my love of singular arguments, no one has a deeper sense of religion impressed on his mind, or pays more profound adoration to the divine Being, as he discovers himself to reason, in the inexplicable contrivance and artifice of nature. A purpose, an intention, a design strikes everywhere the most careless, the most stupid thinker; and no man can be so hardened in absurd systems, as at all times to reject it. *That nature does nothing in vain*, is a maxim established in all the schools, merely from the contemplation of the works of nature, without any religious purpose; and, from a firm conviction of its truth, an *anatomist*, who had observed a new organ or canal, would never be satisfied till he had also discovered its use and intention. One great foundation of the Copernican system is the maxim, *that nature acts by the simplest methods, and chooses the most proper means to any end*; and astronomers often, without thinking of it, lay this strong foundation of piety and religion. The same thing is observable in other parts of philosophy: And thus all the sciences almost lead us insensibly to acknowledge a first intelligent Author; and their authority is often so much the greater, as they do not directly profess that intention.

· · · · · · · ·

So little, replied PHILO, do I esteem this suspense of judgment in the present case to be possible, that I am apt to suspect there enters somewhat of a dispute of words into this controversy, more than is usually imagined. That the works of nature bear a great analogy to the productions of art is evident; and according to all the rules of good reasoning, we ought to infer, if we argue at all concerning them, that their causes have a proportional analogy. But as there are also considerable differences, we have reason to suppose a proportional difference in the causes; and in particular ought to attribute a much higher degree of power and energy to the supreme cause than any we have ever observed in mankind. Here then the existence of a Deity is plainly ascertained by reason; and if we make it a question, whether, on account of these analogies, we can properly call him a *mind* or *intelligence*, notwithstanding the vast difference, which may reasonably be supposed between him and human minds; what is this but a mere verbal controversy? No man can deny the analogies between the effects: To restrain ourselves from enquiring concerning the causes is scarcely possible: From this enquiry, the legitimate conclusion is, that the causes have also an analogy: And if we are not contented with calling the first and supreme cause a God or Deity, but desire to vary the expression; what can we call him but mind or thought, to which he is justly supposed to bear a considerable resemblance?

All men of sound reason are disgusted with verbal disputes, which abound so much in philosophical and theological enquiries; and it is found, that the only remedy for this abuse must arise from clear definitions, from the precision of those ideas which enter into any argument, and from the strict and uniform use of those terms which are employed. But there is a species of controversy, which, from the very nature of language and of human ideas, is involved in perpetual ambiguity, and can never, by any precaution or any definitions, be able to reach a reasonable certainty or precision. These are the controversies concerning the degrees of any quality or circumstance. Men may argue to all eternity, whether Hannibal be a great, or a very great, or a superlatively great man, what degree of beauty Cleopatra possessed, what epithet of praise Livy or Thucydides is entitled to, without bringing the controversy to any determination. The disputants may here agree in their sense and differ in the terms, or *vice versa*; yet never be able to define their terms, so as to enter into each other's meaning: Because the degrees of these qualities are not, like quantity or number, susceptible of any exact mensuration, which may be the standard in the controversy. That the dispute concerning theism is of this nature, and consequently is merely verbal, or perhaps, if possible, still more incurably ambiguous, will appear upon the slightest enquiry. I ask the theist, if he does not allow, that there is a great and immeasurable, because incomprehensible, difference between the *human* and the *divine* mind: The more pious he is, the more readily will he assent to the affirmative, and the more will he be disposed to magnify the difference: He will even assert, that the difference is of a nature which cannot be too much magnified. I next turn to the atheist, who, I assert, is only nominally so, and can never possibly be in earnest; and I ask him, whether, from the coherence and apparent sympathy in all the parts of this world, there be not a certain degree of analogy among all the operations of nature, in every situation and in every age; whether the rotting of a turnip, the generation of an animal, and the structure of human thought be not energies that probably bear some remote analogy to each other: It is impossible he can deny it: He will readily acknowledge it. Having obtained this concession, I push him still farther in his retreat; and I ask him, if it be not probable, that the principle which first arranged, and still maintains, order in this universe, bears not also some remote inconceivable analogy to the other operations of nature, and among the rest to the economy of human mind and thought. However reluctant, he must give his assent. Where then, cry I to both these antagonists, is the subject of your dispute? The theist allows, that the original intelligence is very different from human reason: The atheist allows, that the original

principle of order bears some remote analogy to it. Will you quarrel, Gentlemen, about the degrees, and enter into a controversy, which admits not of any precise meaning, nor consequently of any determination? If you should be so obstinate, I should not be surprised to find you insensibly change sides; while the theist on the one hand exaggerates the dissimilarity between the supreme Being, and frail, imperfect, variable, fleeting, and mortal creatures; and the atheist on the other magnifies the analogy among all the operations of nature, in every period, every situation, and every position. Consider then, where the real point of controversy lies, and if you cannot lay aside your disputes, endeavour, at least, to cure yourselves of your animosity.

And here I must also acknowledge, Cleanthes, that, as the works of nature have a much greater analogy to the effects of *our* art and contrivance, than to those of *our* benevolence and justice; we have reason to infer that the natural attributes of the Deity have a greater resemblance to those of man, than his moral have to human virtues. But what is the consequence? Nothing but this, that the moral qualities of man are more defective in their kind than his natural abilities. For, as the supreme Being is allowed to be absolutely and entirely perfect, whatever differs most from him departs the farthest from the supreme standard of rectitude and perfection.[11]

These, Cleanthes, are my unfeigned sentiments on this subject; and these sentiments, you know, I have ever cherished and maintained. But in proportion to my veneration for true religion, is my abhorrence of vulgar superstitions; and I indulge a peculiar pleasure, I confess, in pushing such principles, sometimes into absurdity, sometimes into impiety. And you are sensible, that all bigots, notwithstanding their great aversion to the latter above the former, are commonly equally guilty of both.

My inclination, replied CLEANTHES, lies, I own, a contrary way. Religion, however corrupted, is still better than no religion at all. The doctrine of a future state is so strong and necessary a security to morals, that we never ought to abandon or neglect it. For if finite and temporary rewards and punishments have so great an effect, as we daily find: How much greater must be expected from such as are infinite and eternal?

How happens it then, said PHILO, if vulgar superstition be so salutary to society, that all history abounds so much with accounts of its pernicious consequences on public affairs? Factions, civil wars, persecutions, subversions of government, oppression, slavery; these are the dismal consequences which always attend its prevalency over the minds of men. If the religious spirit be ever mentioned in any historical narration, we are sure to meet afterwards with a detail of the miseries which attend it. And no period of time can be happier or more prosperous, than those in which it is never regarded, or heard of.

· · · · · · · ·

It is contrary to common sense to entertain apprehensions or terrors, upon account of any opinion whatsoever, or to imagine that we run any risk hereafter, by the freest use of our reason. Such a sentiment implies both an *absurdity* and an *inconsistency*. It is an absurdity to believe that the Deity has human passions, and one of the lowest of human passions, a restless appetite for applause. It is an inconsistency to believe, that, since the Deity has this human passion, he has not others also; and, in particular, a disregard to the opinions of creatures so much inferior.

To know God, says Seneca, *is to worship him.* All other worship is indeed absurd, superstitious, and even impious. It degrades him to the low condition of mankind, who are delighted with entreaty, solicitation, presents, and flattery. Yet is this impiety the smallest of which superstition is guilty. Commonly, it depresses the Deity far below the condition of mankind; and represents him as a capricious Demon, who exercises his power without reason and without humanity! And were that divine Being disposed to be offended at the vices and follies of silly mortals, who are his own workmanship; ill would it surely fare with the votaries of most popular superstitions. Nor would any of human race merit his *favour*, but a very few, the philosophical theists, who entertain, or rather indeed endeavour to entertain, suitable notions of his divine perfections: As the only persons entitled to his *compassion* and *indulgence* would be the philosophical sceptics, a sect almost equally rare, who, from a natural diffidence of their own capacity, suspend, or endeav-our to suspend all judgment with regard to such sublime and such extraordinary subjects.

If the whole of natural theology, as some people seem to maintain, resolves itself into one simple, though somewhat ambiguous, at least undefined proposition, *that the cause or causes of order in the universe probably bear some remote analogy to human intelligence*: If this proposition be not capable of extension, variation, or more particular explication: If it afford no inference that affects human life, or can be the source of any action or forbearance: And if the analogy, imperfect as it is, can be carried no farther than to the human intelligence; and cannot be transferred, with any appearance of probability, to the other qualities of the mind: If this really be the case, what can the most inquisitive, contemplative, and religious man do more than give a plain, philosophical assent to the proposition, as often as it occurs; and believe that the arguments, on which it is established, exceed the objections which lie against it? Some astonishment indeed will naturally arise from the greatness of the object: Some melancholy from its obscurity: Some contempt of human reason, that it can give no solution more satisfactory with regard to so extraordinary and magnificent a question. But believe me, Cleanthes, the most natural sentiment, which a well-disposed mind will feel on this occasion, is a longing desire and expectation, that Heaven would be pleased to dissipate, at least alleviate, this profound ignorance, by affording some more particular revelation to mankind, and making discoveries of the nature, attributes, and operations of the divine object of our Faith. A person, seasoned with a just sense of the imperfections of natural reason, will fly to revealed truth with the greatest avidity: While the haughty dogmatist, persuaded that he can erect a complete system of theology by the mere help of philosophy, disdains any farther aid, and rejects this adventitious instructor. To be a philosophical sceptic is, in a man of letters, the first and most essential step towards being a sound, believing Christian; a proposition which I would willingly recommend to the attention of Pamphilus: And I hope Cleanthes will forgive me for interposing so far in the education and instruction of his pupil.

Cleanthes and Philo pursued not this conversation much farther; and as nothing ever made greater impression on me, than all the reasonings of that day; so I confess, that, upon a serious review of the whole, I cannot but think, that Philo's principles are more probable than Demea's; but that those of Cleanthes approach still nearer to the truth.

NOTES

1. *Recherche de la vérité, liv.* 3, chap. 9.
2. [Cf. Cicero, *De Natura Deorum*, Bk. I, 22.]
3. Lib. II, 1095 [Munro's translation].
4. *De Nat[ura] Deor [um]*, Lib. I, 8.
5. [Hume presumably means *against* all mankind.]
6. Dr. Clarke.
7. *République des Lettres*, Août, 1685.
8. That sentiment had been maintained by Dr. King [*De Origine Mali, 1702*] and some few others, before Leibnitz, though by none of so great fame as that German philosopher.
9. [Milton: *Paradise Lost*, XI.]
10. [Dryden, *Aurengzebe*, Act IV, sc. 1.]
11. It seems evident, that the dispute between the sceptics and dogmatists is entirely verbal, or at least regards only the degrees of doubt and assurance, which we ought to indulge with regard to all reasoning: And such disputes are commonly, at the bottom, verbal, and admit not of any precise determination. No philosophical dogmatist denies, that there are difficulties both with regard to the senses and to all science; and that these difficulties are in a regular, logical method, absolutely insolveable. No sceptic denies, that we lie under an absolute necessity, notwithstanding these difficulties, of thinking, and believing, and reasoning with regard to all kind of subjects, and even of frequently assenting with confidence and security. The only difference, then, between these sects, if they merit that name, is, that the sceptic, from habit, caprice, or inclination, insists most on the difficulties; the dogmatist, for like reasons, on the necessity.

God, Evil and the Best of All Possible Worlds

GOTTFRIED LEIBNIZ

Gottfried Wilhelm Leibniz (1646–1716) was a brilliant philosopher who also discovered the calculus independently of Newton. His main works include *New Essays on the Human Understanding, Theodicy, The Monadology,* and *Discourse on Metaphysics.*

—◆—

SOME INTELLIGENT PERSONS HAVE desired that this supplement be made [to *Theodicy*], and I have the more readily yielded to their wishes as in this way I have an opportunity again to remove certain difficulties and to make some observations which were not sufficiently emphasized in the work itself.

I. *Objection.* Whoever does not choose the best is lacking in power, or in knowledge, or in goodness.

God did not choose the best in creating this world.

Therefore, God has been lacking in power, or in knowledge, or in goodness.

Answer. I deny the minor, that is, the second premise of this syllogism; and our opponent proves it by this:

Prosyllogism. Whoever makes things in which there is evil, which could have been made without any evil, or the making of which could have been omitted, does not choose the best.

God has made a world in which there is evil; a world, I say, which could have been made without any evil, or the making of which could have been omitted altogether.

Therefore, God has not chosen the best.

Answer. I grant the minor of this prosyllogism; for it must be confessed that there is evil in this world which God has made, and that it was possible to make a world without evil, or even not to create a world at all, for its creation has depended on the free will of God; but I deny the major, that is, the first of the two premises of the prosyllogism, and I might content myself with simply demanding its proof; but in order to make the matter clearer, I have wished to justify this denial by showing that the best plan is not always that which seeks to avoid evil, since it may happen that the *evil is accompanied by a greater good.* For example, a general of an army will prefer a great victory with a slight wound to a condition without wound and without victory. We have proved this more fully in the large work by making it clear, by instances taken from mathematics and elsewhere, that an imperfection in the part may be required for a greater perfection in the whole. In this I have followed the opinion of St. Augustine, who has said a hundred times, that God has permitted evil in order to bring about good, that is, a greater good; and that of Thomas Aquinas (in libr. II. sent. dist. 32, qu. I, art. 1), that the permitting of evil tends to the good of the universe. I have shown that the ancients called Adam's fall *felix culpa*, a happy sin, because it had been retrieved with immense advantage by the incarnation of the Son of God, who has given to the universe something nobler than anything that ever would have been among creatures except for it. For the sake of a clearer understanding, I have added, following many good authors, that it was in accordance with order and the general good that God allowed to certain creatures the opportunity of exercising their lib-

erty, even when he foresaw that they would turn to evil, but which he could so well rectify; because it was not fitting that, in order to hinder sin, God should always act in an extraordinary manner. To overthrow this objection, therefore, it is sufficient to show that a world with evil might be better than a world without evil; but I have gone even farther, in the work, and have even proved that this universe must be in reality better than every other possible universe.

II. *Objection.* If there is more evil than good in intelligent creatures, then there is more evil than good in the whole work of God.

Now, there is more evil than good in intelligent creatures.

Therefore, there is more evil than good in the whole work of God.

Answer. I deny the major and the minor of this conditional syllogism. As to the major, I do not admit it at all, because this pretended deduction from a part to the whole, from intelligent creatures to all creatures, supposes tacitly and without proof that creatures destitute of reason cannot enter into comparison nor into account with those which possess it. But why may it not be that the surplus of good in the non-intelligent creatures which fill the world, compensates for, and even incomparably surpasses, the surplus of evil in the rational creatures? It is true that the value of the latter is greater; but, in compensation, the others are beyond comparison the more numerous, and it may be that the proportion of number and quantity surpasses that of value and of quality.

As to the minor, that is no more to be admitted; that is, it is not at all to be admitted that there is more evil than good in the intelligent creatures. There is no need even of granting that there is more evil than good in the human race, because it is possible, and in fact very probable, that the glory and the perfection of the blessed are incomparably greater than the misery and the imperfection of the damned, and that here the excellence of the total good in the smaller number exceeds the total evil in the greater number. The blessed approach the Divinity, by means of a Divine Mediator, as near as may suit these creatures, and make such progress in good as is impossible for the damned to make the evil, approach as nearly as they may to the nature of demons. God is infinite, and the devil is limited; the good may and does go to infinity, while evil has its bounds. It is therefore possible, and is credible, that in the comparison of the blessed and the damned, the contrary of that which I have said might happen in the comparison of intelligent and non-intelligent creatures, takes place; namely, it is possible that in the comparison of the happy and the unhappy, the proportion of degree exceeds that of number, and that in the comparison of intelligent and non-intelligent creatures, the proportion of number is greater than that of value. I have the right to suppose that a thing is possible so long as its impossibility is not proved; and indeed that which I have here advanced is more than a supposition.

But in the second place, if I should admit that there is more evil than good in the human race, I have still good grounds for not admitting that there is more evil than good in all intelligent creatures. For there is an inconceivable number of genii, and perhaps of other rational creatures. And an opponent could not prove that in all the City of God, composed as well of genii as of rational animals without number and of an infinity of kinds, evil exceeds good. And although in order to answer an objection, there is no need of proving that a thing is, when its mere possibility suffices; yet, in this work, I have not omitted to show that it is a consequence of the supreme perfection of the Sovereign of the universe, that the kingdom of God is the most perfect of all possible states or governments, and that consequently the little evil there is, is required for the consummation of the immense good which is found there.

Hume on Evil

NELSON PIKE

Nelson Pike (1930–   ) has pioneered the application of methods of analytical philosophy to traditional problems in the philosophy of religion; his works include *God and Timelessness*.

—•—

In parts X and XI of the *Dialogues Concerning Natural Religion*, Hume sets forth his views on the traditional theological problem of evil. Hume's remarks on this topic seem to me to contain a rich mixture of insight and oversight. It will be my purpose in this paper to disentangle these contrasting elements of his discussion.[1]

Philo's First Position

A. God, according to the traditional Christian view put forward by Cleanthes in the *Dialogues*, is all-powerful, all-knowing, and perfectly good. And it is clear that for Cleanthes, the terms "powerful," "knowing," and "good" apply to God in exactly the same sense in which these terms apply to men. Philo argues as follows: If God is to be all-powerful, all-knowing, and perfectly good (using all key terms in their ordinary sense), then to claim that God exists is to preclude the possibility of admitting that there occur instances of evil; that is, is to preclude the possibility of admitting that there occur instances of suffering, pain, superstition, wickedness, and so forth.[2] The statements "God exists" and "There occur instances of suffering" are logically incompatible. Of course, no one could deny that there occur instances of suffering. Such

From *Philosophical Review* Vol. LXXII, No. 2. Copyright © 1963 by Cornell University. Reprinted by permission of the publisher.

a denial would plainly conflict with common experience.[3] Thus it follows from obvious fact that God (having the attributes assigned to him by Cleanthes) does not exist.

This argument against the existence of God has enjoyed considerable popularity since Hume wrote the *Dialogues*. Concerning the traditional theological problem of evil, F. H. Bradley comments as follows:

> The trouble has come from the idea that the Absolute is a moral person. If you start from that basis, then the relation of evil to the Absolute presents at once an irreducible dilemma. The problem then becomes insoluble, but not because it is obscure or in any way mysterious. To anyone who has the sense and courage to see things as they are, and is resolved not to mystify others or himself, *there is really no question to discuss. The dilemma is plainly insoluble because it is based on a clear self-contradiction.*[4]

John Stuart Mill,[5] J. E. McTaggart,[6] Antony Flew,[7] H. D. Aiken,[8] J. L. Mackie,[9] C. J. Ducasse,[10] and H. J. McCloskey[11] are but a very few of the many others who have echoed Philo's finalistic dismissal of traditional theism after making reference to the logical incompatibility of "God exists" and "There occur instances of suffering." W. T. Stace refers to Hume's discussion of the matter as follows:

> (Assuming that "good" and "powerful" are used in theology as they are used in ordinary discourse), we have to say that Hume was right. The charge has never been answered and never will be. The simultaneous attribution of all-power and all-goodness to the Creator of the whole world is logically incompatible with the existence of evil and pain in the world, for which reason the conception of a finite God, who is not all-powerful . . . has become popular in some quarters.[12]

In the first and second sections of this paper, I shall argue that the argument against the existence of God presented in Part X of the *Dialogues* is quite unconvincing. It is not at all clear that "God exists" and "There occur instances of suffering" are logically incompatible statements.

B. Moving now to the details of the matter, we may, I think, formulate Philo's first challenge to Cleanthes as follows:

1. The world contains instances of suffering.
2. God exists—and is omnipotent and omniscient.
3. God exists—and is perfectly good.

According to the view advanced by Philo, these three statements constitute an "inconsistent triad." Any two of them might be held together. But if any two of them are endorsed, the third must be denied. Philo argues that to say of God that he is omnipotent and omniscient is to say that he *could* prevent suffering if he wanted to. Unless God could prevent suffering, he would not qualify as both omnipotent and omniscient. But, Philo continues, to say of God that he is perfectly good is to say that God *would* prevent suffering if he could. A being who would not prevent suffering when it was within his power to do so would not qualify as perfectly good. Thus, to affirm propositions (2) and (3) is to affirm the existence of a being who both could prevent suffering if he wanted to and who would prevent suffering if he could. This, of course, is to deny the truth of proposition (1). By similar reasoning, Philo would insist, to affirm (1) and (2) is to deny the truth of (3). And to affirm (1) and (3) is to deny the truth of (2). But, as conceived by Cleanthes, God is both omnipotent-omniscient and perfectly good. Thus, as understood by Cleanthes, "God exists" and "There occur instances of suffering" are logically incompatible statements. Since the latter of these statements is obviously true, the former must be false. Philo reflects: "Nothing can shake the solidarity of this reasoning, so short, so clear (and) so decisive."

It seems to me that this argument is deficient. I do not think it follows from the claim that a being is perfectly good that he would prevent suffering if he could.

Consider this case. A parent forces a child to take a spoonful of bitter medicine. The parent thus brings about an instance of discomfort—suffering. The parent could have refrained from administering the medicine; and he knew that the child would suffer discomfort if he did administer it. Yet, when we are assured that the parent acted in the interest of the child's health and happiness, the fact that he knowingly caused discomfort is not sufficient to remove the parent from the class of perfectly good beings. If the parent fails to fit into this class, it is not because he caused *this* instance of suffering.

Given only that the parent knowingly caused an instance of discomfort, we are tempted to *blame* him for his action—that is, to exclude him from the class of perfectly good beings. But when the full circumstances are known, blame becomes inappropriate. In this case, there is what I shall call a "morally sufficient reason" for the parent's action. To say that there is a morally sufficient reason for his action is simply to say that there is a circumstance or condition which, when known, renders *blame* (though, of course, not *responsibility*) for the action inappropriate. As a general statement, a being who permits (or brings about) an instance of suffering might be perfectly good providing only that there is a morally sufficient reason for his action. Thus, it does not follow from the claim that God is perfectly good that he would prevent suffering if he could. God might fail to prevent suffering, or himself bring about suffering, while remaining perfectly good. It is required only that there be a morally sufficient reason for his action.

C. In the light of these reflections, let us now attempt to put Philo's challenge to Cleanthes in sharper form.

4. The world contains instances of suffering.
5. God exists—and is omnipotent, omniscient, and perfectly good.
6. An omnipotent and omniscient being would have no morally sufficient reason for allowing instances of suffering.

This sequence is logically tight. Suppose (6) and (4) true. If an omnipotent and omniscient being would have no morally sufficient reason for allowing instances of suffering, then, in a world containing such instances, either there would be no omnipotent and omniscient being or that being would be blameworthy. On either of these last alternatives, proposition (5) would be false. Thus, if (6) and (4) are true, (5) must be false. In similar fashion, suppose (6) and (5) true. If an omnipotent and omniscient being

would have no morally sufficient reason for allowing suffering, then, if there existed an omnipotent and omniscient being who was also perfectly good, there would occur no suffering. Thus, if (6) and (5) are true, (4) must be false. Lastly, suppose (5) and (4) true. If there existed an omnipotent and omniscient being who was also perfectly good, then if there occurred suffering, the omnipotent and omniscient being (being also perfectly good) would have to have a morally sufficient reason for permitting it. Thus, if (5) and (4) are true, (6) must be false.

Now, according to Philo (and all others concerned), proposition (4) is surely true. And proposition (6)—well, what about proposition (6)? At this point, two observations are needed.

First, it would not serve Philo's purpose were he to argue the truth of proposition (6) by enumerating a number of reasons for permitting suffering (which might be assigned to an omnipotent and omniscient being) and then by showing that in each case the reason offered is not a morally sufficient reason (when assigned to an omnipotent and omniscient being). Philo could never claim to have examined all of the possibilities. And at any given point in the argument, Cleanthes could always claim that God's reason for permitting suffering is one which Philo has not yet considered. A retreat to unexamined reasons would remain open to Cleanthes regardless of how complete the list of examined reasons seemed to be.

Second, the position held by Philo in Part X of the *Dialogues* demands that he affirm proposition (6) as a *necessary truth*. If this is not already clear, consider the following inconsistent triad.

7. All swans are white.
8. Some swans are not large.
9. All white things are large.

Suppose (9) true, but not necessarily true. Either (7) or (8) must be false. But the conjunction of (7) and (8) is not contradictory. If the conjunction of (7) and (8) were contradictory, then (9) would be necessary truth. Thus, unless (9) is a necessary truth, the conjunction of (7) and (8) is not contradictory. Note what happens to this antilogism when "colored" is substituted for "large." Now (9) becomes a necessary truth and, correspondingly, (7) and (8) become logically incompatible. The same holds for the inconsistent triad we are now considering. As already discovered, Philo holds that "There are instances of suffering" (proposition 4) and "God exists" (proposition 5) are logically incompatible. But (4) and (5) will be logically incompatible only if (6) is a necessary truth. Thus, if Philo is to argue that (4) and (5) are logically incompatible, he must be prepared to affirm (6) as a necessary truth.

We may now reconstitute Philo's challenge to the position held by Cleanthes.

Proposition (4) is obviously true. No one could deny that there occur instances of suffering. But proposition (6) is a necessary truth. An omnipotent and omniscient being would have no morally sufficient reason for allowing instances of suffering—just as a bachelor would have no wife. Thus, there exists no being who is, at once, omnipotent, omniscient, and perfectly good. Proposition (5) must be false.

D. This is a formidable challenge to Cleanthes' position. Its strength can best be exposed by reflecting on some of the circumstances or conditions which, in ordinary life, and with respect to ordinary agents, are usually counted as morally sufficient reasons for failing to prevent (or relieve) some given instance of suffering. Let me list five such reasons.

First, consider an agent who lacked physical ability to prevent some instance of suffering. Such an agent could claim to have had a morally sufficient reason for not preventing the instance in question.

Second, consider an agent who lacked knowledge of (or the means of knowing about) a given instance of suffering. Such an agent could claim to have had a morally sufficient reason for not preventing the suffering, even if (on all other counts) he had the ability to prevent it.

Third, consider an agent who knew of an instance of suffering and had the physical ability to prevent it, but did not *realize* that he had this ability. Such an agent could usually claim to have had a morally sufficient reason for not preventing the suffering. Example: if I push the button on the wall, the torment of the man in the next room will cease. I have the physical ability to push the button. I know

that the man in the next room is in pain. But I do not know that pushing the button will relieve the torment. I do not push the button and thus do not relieve the suffering.

Fourth, consider an agent who had the ability to prevent an instance of suffering, knew of the suffering, knew that he had the ability to prevent it, but did not prevent it because he believed (rightly or wrongly) that to do so would be to fail to effect some future good which would outweigh the negative value of the suffering. Such an agent might well claim to have had a morally sufficient reason for not preventing the suffering. Example: go back to the case of the parent causing discomfort by administering bitter medicine to the child.

Fifth, consider an agent who had the ability to prevent an instance of suffering, knew of the suffering, knew that he had the ability to prevent it, but failed to prevent it because to do so would have involved his preventing a prior good which outweighed the negative value of the suffering. Such an agent might claim to have had a morally sufficient reason for not preventing the suffering. Example: a parent permits a child to eat some birthday cake knowing that his eating the cake will result in the child's feeling slightly ill later in the day. The parent estimates that the child's pleasure of the moment outweighs the discomfort which will result.

Up to this point, Philo would insist, we have not hit on a circumstance or condition which could be used by Cleanthes when constructing a "theodicy," that is, when attempting to identify the morally sufficient reason God has for permitting instances of suffering.

The first three entries on the list are obviously not available. Each makes explicit mention of some lack of knowledge or power on the part of the agent. Nothing more need be said about them.

A theologian might, however, be tempted to use a reason for the fourth type when constructing a theodicy. He might propose that suffering *results in goods* which outweigh the negative value of the suffering. Famine (hunger) leads man to industry and progress. Disease (pain) leads man to knowledge and understanding. Philo suggests that no theodicy of this kind can be successful. An omnipotent and omniscient being could find other means of bringing about the same results. The mere fact that evils give rise to goods cannot serve as a morally sufficient reason for an omnipotent and omniscient being to permit suffering.

A theologian might also be tempted to use reasons of the fifth type when constructing a theodicy. He might propose that instances of suffering *result from goods* which outweigh the negative value of the suffering. That the world is run in accordance with natural law is good. But any such regular operation will result in suffering. That men have the ability to make free choices is good. But free choice will sometimes result in wrong choice and suffering. Philo argues that it is not at all clear that a world run in accordance with natural law is better than one not so regulated. And one might issue a similar challenge with respect to free will. But a more general argument has been offered in the contemporary literature on evil which is exactly analogous to the one suggested by Philo above. According to H. J. McCloskey, an omnipotent and omniscient being could devise a law-governed world which would not include suffering.[13] And according to J. L. Mackie, an omnipotent and omniscient being could create a world containing free agents which would include no suffering or wrong-doing.[14] The import of both of these suggestions is that an omnipotent and omniscient being could create a world containing whatever is good (regularity, free will, and so on) without allowing the suffering which (only factually) results from these goods. The mere fact that suffering results from good cannot serve as a morally sufficient reason for an omnipotent and omniscient being to allow suffering.

Though the above reflections may be far from conclusive, let us grant that, of the morally sufficient reasons so far considered, none could be assigned to an omnipotent and omniscient being. This, of course, is not to say that proposition (6) is true—let alone necessarily true. As mentioned earlier, proposition (6) will not be shown true by an enumerative procedure of the above kind. But consider the matter less rigorously. If none of the reasons so far considered could be assigned to an omnipotent and omniscient being, ought this not to raise a suspicion? Might there not be a principle operating in each of these reasons which guarantees that *no* morally suf-

ficient reason for permitting suffering *could* be assigned to an omnipotent and omniscient being? Such a principle immediately suggests itself. Men are sometimes excused for allowing suffering. But in these cases, men are excused only because they lack the knowledge or power to prevent suffering, or because they lack the knowledge or power to bring about goods (which are causally related to suffering) without also bringing about suffering. In other words, men are excusable only because they are limited. Having a morally sufficient reason for permitting suffering *entails* having some lack of knowledge or power. If this principle is sound (and, indeed, it is initially plausible) then proposition (6) must surely be listed as a necessary truth.

Demea's Theodicy

But the issue is not yet decided. Demea has offered a theodicy which does not fit any of the forms outlined above. And Philo must be willing to consider all proposals if he is to claim "decisiveness" for his argument against Cleanthes.

Demea reasons as follows:

This world is but a point in comparison of the universe; this life but a moment in comparison of eternity. The present evil phenomena, therefore, are rectified in other regions, and in some future period of existence. And the eyes of men, being then opened to larger views of things, see the whole connection of general laws, and trace, with adoration, the benevolence and rectitude of the Deity through all mazes and intricacies of his providence.

It might be useful if we had a second statement of this theodicy, one taken from a traditional theological source. In Chapter LXXI of the *Summa Contra Gentiles*, St. Thomas argues as follows:

The good of the whole is of more account than the good of the part. Therefore, it belongs to a prudent governor to overlook a lack of goodness in a part, that there may be an increase of goodness in the whole. Thus, the builder hides the foundation of a house underground, that the whole house may stand firm. Now, if evil were taken away from certain parts of the universe, the perfection of the universe would be much diminished, since its beauty results from the ordered unity of good and evil things, seeing that evil arises from the failure of good, and yet certain goods are occasioned from those very evils through the providence of the governor, even as the silent pause gives sweetness to the chant. Therefore, evil should not be excluded from things by the divine providence.

Neither of these statements seems entirely satisfactory. Demea might be suggesting that the world is good on the whole—that the suffering we discover in our world is, as it were, made up for in other regions of creation. God here appears as the husband who beats his wife on occasion but makes up for it with favors at other times. In St. Thomas' statement, there are unmistakable hints of causal reasoning. Certain goods are "occasioned" by evils, as the foundation of the house permits the house to stand firm. But in both of these statements another theme is at least suggested. Let me state and expand it in my own way without pretense of historical accuracy.

I have a set of ten wooden blocks. There is a T-shaped block, an L-shaped block, an F-shaped block, and so on. No two blocks have the same shape. Let us assign each block a value—say an aesthetic value—making the T-shaped block most valuable and the L-shaped block least valuable. Now the blocks may be fitted together into formations. And let us suppose that the blocks are so shaped that there is one and only one subset of the blocks which will fit together into a square. The L-shaped block is a member of that subset. Further, let us stipulate that any formation of blocks (consisting of two or more blocks fitted together) will have more aesthetic value than any of the blocks taken individually or any subset of the blocks taken as a mere collection. And, as a last assumption, let us say that the square formation has greater aesthetic value than any other logically possible block formation. The L-shaped block is a necessary component of the square formation; that is, the L-shaped block is logically indispensable to the square formation. Thus the L-shaped block is a necessary component of the best of all possible block formations. Hence,

the block with the least aesthetic value is logically indispensable to the best of all possible block formations. Without this very block, it would be logically impossible to create the best of all possible block formations.

Working from this model, let us understand Demea's theodicy as follows. Put aside the claim that instances of suffering are *de facto* causes or consequences of greater goods. God, being a perfectly good, omniscient, and omnipotent being, would create the best of all possible worlds. But the best of all possible worlds must contain instances of suffering: they are logically indispensable components. This is why there are instances of suffering in the world which God created.

What shall we say about this theodicy? Philo expresses no opinion on the subject.

Consider this reply to Demea's reasonings. A world containing instances of suffering as necessary components might be the best of all possible worlds. And if a world containing instances of suffering as necessary components were the best of all possible worlds, an omnipotent and omniscient being would have a morally sufficient reason for permitting instances of suffering. But how are we to know that, in fact, instances of suffering are logically indispensable components of the best of all possible worlds? There would appear to be no way of establishing this claim short of assuming that God does in fact exist and then concluding (as did Leibniz) that the world (containing suffering) which he did in fact create is the best of all possible worlds. But, this procedure assumes that God exists. And this latter is precisely the question now at issue.

It seems to me that this reply to Demea's theodicy has considerable merit. First, my hypothetical objector is probably right in suggesting that the only way one could show that the best of all possible worlds must contain instances of suffering would be via the above argument in which the existence of God is assumed. Second, I think my objector is right in allowing that if instances of suffering were logically indispensable components of the best of all possible worlds, this would provide a morally sufficient reason for an omnipotent and omniscient being to permit instances of suffering. And, third, I think that my objector exhibits considerable discretion in not challenging the claim that the best of all possible worlds *might* contain instances of suffering as necessary components. I know of no argument which will show this claim to be true. But on the other hand, I know of no argument which will show this claim to be false. (I shall elaborate this last point directly.)

Thus, as I have said, the above evaluation of the theodicy advanced by Demea seems to have considerable merit. But this evaluation, *if correct*, seems to be sufficient to refute Philo's claim that "God exists" and "There occur instances of suffering" are logically incompatible statements. If instances of suffering were necessary components of the best of all possible worlds, then an omnipotent and omniscient being would have a morally sufficient reason for permitting instances of suffering. Thus, if it is *possible* that instances of suffering are necessary components of the best of all possible worlds, then there *might be* a morally sufficient reason for an omnipotent and omniscient being to permit instances of suffering. Thus if the statement "Instances of suffering are necessary components of the best of all possible worlds" is not contradictory, then proposition (6) is not a necessary truth. And, as we have seen, if proposition (6) is not a necessary truth, then "God exists" and "There occur instances of suffering" are not logically incompatible statements.

What shall we say? Is the statement "Instances of suffering are logically indispensable components of the best of all possible worlds" contradictory? That it is is simply assumed in Philo's first position. But, surely, this is not a trivial assumption. If it is correct, it must be shown to be so; it is not *obviously* correct. And how shall we argue that it is correct? Shall we, for example, assume that any case of suffering contained in any complex of events detracts from the value of the complex? If this principle were analytic, then a world containing an instance of suffering could not be the best of all possible worlds. But G. E. Moore has taught us to be suspicious of any such principle.[15] And John Wisdom has provided a series of counterexamples which tend to show that this very principle is, in fact, not analytic. Example: if I believe (rightly or wrongly) that you are in pain and become unhappy as a result of that belief, the resulting complex would appear to be better by virtue of my unhappiness (suffering) than it would have been had I believed you to be in pain but had not become unhappy (or had become happy) as a result.[16] Philo's argument against the existence of God is not finished. And it is not at all obvious that it is *capable* of effective completion. It is, I submit, far from clear that God and evil could not exist together in the same universe.

Philo's Second Position

At the end of Part X, Philo agrees to "retire" from his first position. He now concedes that "God exists" and "There occur instances of suffering" are not logically incompatible statements. (It is clear from the context that this adjustment in Philo's thinking is made only for purposes of argument and not because Hume senses any inadequacy in Philo's first position.) Most contemporary philosophers think that Hume's major contribution to the literature on evil was made in Part X of the *Dialogues*. But it seems to me that what is of really lasting value in Hume's reflections on this subject is to be found not in Part X, but in the discussion in Part XI which follows Philo's "retirement" from his first position.

A. Consider, first of all, a theology in which the existence of God is accepted on the basis of what is taken to be a conclusive (a priori) demonstration. (A theology in which the existence of God is taken as an item of faith can be considered here as well.) On this view, that God exists is a settled matter, not subject to review or challenge. It is, as it were, axiomatic to further theological debate. According to Philo, evil in the world presents no special problem for a theology of this sort:

> Let us allow that, if the goodness of the Deity (I mean a goodness like the human) could be established on any tolerable reasons a priori, these (evil) phenomena, however untoward, would not be sufficient to subvert that principle, but might easily, in some unknown manner, be reconcilable to it.

This point, I think, is essentially correct, but it must be put more firmly.

Recalling the remarks advanced when discussing the inconsistent nature of propositions (4) through (6) above, a theologian who accepts the existence of God (either as an item of faith or on the basis of an a priori argument) must conclude either that there is some morally sufficient reason for God's allowing suffering in the world, or that there are no instances of suffering in the world. He will, of course, choose the first alternative. Thus, in a theology of the sort now under consideration, the theologian begins by affirming the existence of God and by acknowledging the occurrence of suffering. It follows *logically* that God has some morally sufficient reason for allowing instances of suffering. The conclusion is not, as Philo suggests, that there *might be* a morally sufficient reason for evil. The conclusion is, rather, that there *must be* such a reason. It *could* not be otherwise.

What then of the traditional theological problem of evil? Within a theology of the above type, the problem of evil can only be the problem of discovering a *specific* theodicy which is adequate—that is, of discovering which, if any, of the specific proposals which might be advanced really describes God's morally sufficient reason for allowing instances of suffering. This problem, of course, is not a major one for the theologian. If the problem of evil is simply the problem of uncovering the specific reason for evil—given assurance that there is (and must be) some such reason—it can hardly be counted as a critical problem. Once it is granted that there is some specific reason for evil, there is a sense in which it is no longer vital to find it. A theologian of the type we are now considering might never arrive at a satisfactory theodicy. (Philo's "unknown" reason might remain forever unknown.) He might condemn as erroneous all existing theodices and might despair of ever discovering the morally sufficient reason in question. A charge of incompleteness would be the worst that could be leveled at his world view.

B. Cleanthes is not, of course, a theologian of the sort just described. He does not accept the existence of God as an item of faith, nor on the basis of an a priori argument. In the *Dialogues*, Cleanthes supports his theological position with an a posteriori ar-

gument from design. He argues that "order" in the universe provides sufficient evidence that the world was created by an omnipotent, omniscient, and perfectly good being.[17] He proposes the existence of God as a quasi-scientific explanatory hypothesis, arguing its truth via the claim that it provides an adequate explanation for observed facts.

Philo has two comments to make regarding the relevance of suffering in the world for a theology of this kind.

The first is a comment with which Philo is obviously well pleased. It is offered at the end of Part X and is repeated no less than three times in Part XI. It is this: even if the existence of God and the occurrence of suffering in the world are logically compatible, one cannot argue from a world containing suffering to the existence of an omnipotent, omniscient, and perfectly good creator. This observation, I think all would agree, is correct. Given only a painting containing vast areas of green, one could not effectively argue that its creator disliked using green. There would be no *logical* conflict in holding that a painter who disliked using green painted a picture containing vast areas of green. But given *only* the picture (and no further information), the hypothesis that its creator disliked using green would be poorly supported indeed.

It is clear that in this first comment Philo has offered a criticism of Cleanthes' *argument* for the existence of God. He explicitly says that this complaint is against Cleanthes' *inference* from a world containing instances of suffering to the existence of an omnipotent, omniscient, and perfectly good creator. Philo's second comment, however, is more forceful than this. It is a challenge of the *truth* of Cleanthes' *hypothesis*.

Philo argues as follows:

Look round this universe. What an immense profusion of beings, animated and organized, sensible and active! You admire this prodigious variety and fecundity. But inspect a little more narrowly these living existences, the only beings worth regarding. How hostile and destructive to each other! How insufficient all of them for their own happiness! . . . There is indeed an opposition of pains and pleasures in the feelings of sensible creatures; but are not all the operations of nature carried on by an opposition of principles, of hot and cold, moist and dry, light and heavy! The true conclusion is that the original Source of all things is entirely indifferent to all these principles, and has no more regard to good above ill than to heat above cold, or to drought above moisture, or to light above heavy.

Philo claims that *there is* an "original Source of all things" and that this source is indifferent with respect to matters of good and evil. He pretends to be inferring this conclusion from observed data. This represents a departure from Philo's much professed skepticism in the *Dialogues*. And, no doubt, many of the criticisms of Cleanthes' position which Philo advanced earlier in the *Dialogues* would apply with equal force to the inference Philo has just offered. But I shall not dwell on this last point. I think the center of Philo's remarks in this passage must be located in their skeptical rather than their metaphysical import. Philo has proposed a hypothesis which is counter to the one offered by Cleanthes. And he claims that his hypothesis is the "true conclusion" to be drawn from the observed data. But the point is not, I think, that Philo's new hypothesis is true, or even probable. The conclusion is, rather, that the hypothesis advanced by Cleanthes is false, or very improbable. When claiming that evil in the world *supports* a hypothesis which is counter to the one offered by Cleanthes, I think Philo simply means to be calling attention to the fact that evil in the world provides *evidence against* Cleanthes' theological position.

Consider the following analogy which, I think, will help expose this point. I am given certain astronomical data. In order to explain the data, I introduce the hypothesis that there exists a planet which has not yet been observed but will be observable at such and such a place in the sky at such and such a time. No other hypothesis seems as good. The anticipated hour arrives and the telescopes are trained on the designated area. No planet appears. Now, either one of two conclusions may be drawn. First, I might conclude that there is no planet there to be seen. This requires either that I reject the original astronomical data or that I admit that what seemed the best explanation of the data is not, in

fact, the true explanation. Second, I might conclude that there is a planet there to be seen, but that something in the observational set-up went amiss. Perhaps the equipment was faulty, perhaps there were clouds, and so on. Which conclusion is correct? The answer is not straightforward. I must check both possibilities.

Suppose I find nothing in the observational setup which is in the least out of order. My equipment is in good working condition, I find no clouds, and so on. To decide to retain the planet hypothesis in the face of the recalcitrant datum (my failure to observe the planet) is, in part, to decide that there is some circumstance (as yet unknown) which explains the datum *other* than the nonexistence of the planet in question. But a decision to retain the planet hypothesis (in the face of my failure to observe the planet and in the absence of an explicit explanation which "squares" this failure with the planet hypothesis) is made correctly *only* when the *evidence for* the planet hypothesis is such as to render its negation less plausible than would be the assumption of a (as yet unknown) circumstance which explains the observation failure. This, I think, is part of the very notion of dealing reasonably with an explanatory hypothesis.

Now Cleanthes has introduced the claim that there exists an omnipotent, omniscient, and perfectly good being as a way of explaining "order" in the world. And Philo, throughout the *Dialogues* (up to and including most of Part XI), has been concerned to show that this procedure provides very little (if any) solid evidence for the existence of God. The inference from the data to the hypothesis is extremely tenuous. Philo is now set for his final thrust at Cleanthes' position. Granting that God and evil are not logically incompatible, the existence of human suffering in the world must still be taken as a recalcitrant datum with respect to Cleanthes' hypothesis. Suffering, as Philo says, is not what we should antecedently expect in a world created by an omnipotent, omniscient, and perfectly good being. Since Cleanthes has offered nothing in the way of an explicit theodicy (that is, an explanation of the recalcitrant datum which would "square" it with his hypothesis) and since the *evidence for* his hypothesis is extremely weak and generally ineffective, there is pretty good reason for thinking that Cleanthes' hypothesis is false.

This, I think, is the skeptical import of Philo's closing remarks in Part XI. On this reading nothing is said about an "original Source of all things" which is indifferent with respect to matters of good and evil. Philo is simply making clear the negative force of the fact of evil in the world for a hypothesis such as the one offered by Cleanthes.

It ought not to go unnoticed that Philo's closing attack on Cleanthes' position has extremely limited application. Evil in the world has central negative importance for theology only when theology is approached as a quasi-scientific subject, as by Cleanthes. That it is seldom approached in this way will be evident to anyone who has studied the history of theology. Within most theological positions, the existence of God is taken as an item of faith or embraced on the basis of an a priori argument. Under these circumstances, where there is nothing to qualify as a "hypothesis" capable of having either negative or positive "evidence," the fact of evil in the world presents no special problem for theology. As Philo himself has suggested, when the existence of God is accepted prior to any rational consideration of the status of evil in the world, the traditional problem of evil reduces to a noncrucial perplexity of relatively minor importance.

NOTES

1. For Parts X and XI of the *Dialogues Concerning Natural Religion*, see pp. 77ff.
2. It is clear that, for Philo, the term "evil" is used simply as a tag for the class containing all instances of suffering, pain and so on. Philo offers no analysis of "evil" nor does his challenge to Cleanthes rest in the least on the particularities of the logic of this term. On page 80, for example, Philo formulates his challenge to Cleanthes without using "evil." Here he speaks only of *misery*. In what is

to follow, I shall (following Hume) make little use of "evil." Also, I shall use "suffering" as short for "suffering pain, superstition, wickedness, and so on."
3. Had Philo been dealing with "evil" (defined in some special way) instead of "suffering," this move in the argument might not have been open to him.
4. *Appearance and Reality* (London: Oxford University Press, 1930), p. 174. Italics mine.
5. *Theism* (New York: The Liberal Arts Press, 1957), p. 40. See also *The Utility of Religion* (New York: The Liberal Arts Press, 1957), pp. 73ff.
6. *Some Dogmas of Religion* (London: Edward Arnold, Ltd., 1906), pp. 212f.
7. "Theology and Falsification," in *New Essays in Philosophical Theology*, A. Flew and A. MacIntyre, eds. (New York: The Macmillan Company, 1955), p. 108.
8. "God and Evil: Some Relations Between Faith and Morals," *Ethics*, Vol. LXVIII (1958), 77ff.
9. "Evil and Omnipotence," in Principia Ethica (London: Macmillan & Co., Ltd., 1903).
10. *A Philosophical Scrutiny of Religion* (New York: The Ronald Press Company, 1953), Chap. 16.
11. "God and Evil," in *Philosophical Quarterly*, Vol. X (1960).
12. *Time and Eternity* (Princeton: Princeton University Press, 1952), p. 56.
13. "God and Evil."
14. "Evil and Omnipotence," pp. 103–110.
15. I refer here to Moore's discussion of "organic unities" in *Principia Ethica*, pp. 28ff.
16. "God and Evil," *Mind*, Vol. XLIV (1935), 13f. I have modified Wisdom's example slightly.
17. It is interesting to notice that, in many cases, theologians who have used an argument from design have not attempted to argue that "order" in the world proves the existence of a perfectly moral being. For example, in St. Thomas' "fifth way" and in William Paley's *Natural Theology*, "order" is used to show only that the creator of the world was *intelligent*. There are, however, historical instances of the argument from design being used to prove the goodness as well as the intelligence of a creator. For example, Bishop Berkeley argues this way in the second of the *Dialogues Between Hylas and Philonous*.

Evil and Omnipotence

J. L. MACKIE

J. L. Mackie (1917–81) taught philosophy at University College, Oxford. His writings were influential in a number of areas of philosophy, including ethics and metaphysics. They include The Cement of the Universe *and* Ethics: Inventing Right and Wrong.

———◆———

THE TRADITIONAL ARGUMENTS for the existence of God have been fairly thoroughly criticized by philosophers. But the theologian can, if he wishes, accept this criticism. He can admit that no rational proof of God's existence is possible. And he can still retain all that is essential to his position, by holding that God's existence is known in some other, nonrational way. I think, however, that a more telling criticism can be made by way of the traditional problem of evil. Here it can be shown, not that religious beliefs lack rational support, but that they are positively irrational, that the several parts of the essential theological doctrine are inconsistent with one another, so that the theologian can maintain his position as a whole only by a much more extreme rejection of reason than in the former case. He must now be prepared to believe, not merely what cannot be proved, but what can be *disproved* from other beliefs that he also holds.

The problem of evil, in the sense in which I shall be using the phrase, is a problem only for someone who believes that there is a God who is both omnipotent and wholly good. And it is a logical problem, the problem of clarifying and reconciling a number of beliefs: it is not a scientific problem that might be solved by further observations, or a practical problem that might be solved by a decision or an action. These points are obvious; I mention them only because they are sometimes ignored by theologians, who sometimes parry a statement of the problem with such remarks as "Well, can you solve the problem yourself?" or "This is a mystery which may be revealed to us later" or "Evil is something to be faced and overcome, not to be merely discussed."

In its simplest form the problem is this: God is omnipotent; God is wholly good; and yet evil exists. There seems to be some contradiction between these three propositions, so that if any two of them were true the third would be false. But at the same time all three are essential parts of most theological positions: the theologian, it seems, at once *must* adhere and *cannot consistently* adhere to all three. (The problem does not arise only for theists, but I shall discuss it in the form in which it presents itself for ordinary theism.)

However, the contradiction does not arise immediately; to show it we need some additional premises, or perhaps some quasi-logical rules connecting the terms "good," "evil," and "omnipotent." These additional principles are that good is opposed to evil, in such a way that a good thing always eliminates evil as far as it can, and that there are no limits to what an omnipotent thing can do. From these it follows that a good omnipotent thing eliminates evil completely, and then the propositions that a good omnipotent thing exists, and that evil exists, are incompatible.

Adequate Solutions

Now once the problem is fully stated it is clear that it can be solved, in the sense that the problem will not arise if one gives up at least one of the propositions that constitute it. If you are prepared to say that God is not wholly good, or not quite omnipotent, or that evil does not exist, or that good is not opposed to the kind of evil that exists, or that there are limits to what an omnipotent thing can do, then the problem of evil will not arise for you.

There are, then, quite a number of adequate solutions of the problem of evil, and some of these have been adopted, or almost adopted, by various thinkers. For example, a few have been prepared to deny God's omnipotence, and rather more have

From *Mind* Vol. LXIV, No. 254. Copyright © 1955 by Oxford University Press. Printed by permission of the publisher.

been prepared to keep the term "omnipotence" but severely to restrict its meaning, recording quite a number of things that an omnipotent being cannot do. Some have said that evil is an illusion, perhaps because they held that the whole world of temporal, changing things is an illusion, and that what we call evil belongs only to this world, or perhaps because they held that although temporal things *are* much as we see them, those that we call evil are not really evil. Some have said that what we call evil is merely the privation of good, that evil in a positive sense, evil that would really be opposed to good, does not exist. Many have agreed with Pope that disorder is harmony not understood, and that partial evil is universal good. Whether any of these views is *true* is, of course, another question. But each of them gives an adequate solution of the problem of evil in the sense that if you accept it this problem does not arise for you, though you may, of course, have *other* problems to face.

But often enough these adequate solutions are only *almost* adopted. The thinkers who restrict God's power, but keep the term "omnipotence," may reasonably be suspected of thinking, in other contexts, that his power is really unlimited. Those who say that evil is an illusion may also be thinking, inconsistently, that this illusion is itself an evil. Those who say that "evil" is merely privation of good may also be thinking, inconsistently, that privation of good is an evil. (The fallacy here is akin to some forms of the "naturalistic fallacy" in ethics, where some think, for example, that "good" is just what contributes to evolutionary progress, and that evolutionary progress is itself good.) If Pope meant what he said in the first line of his couplet, that "disorder" is only harmony not understood, the "partial evil" of the second line must, for consistency, mean "that which, taken in isolation, falsely appears to be evil," but it would more naturally mean "that which, in isolation, really is evil." The second line, in fact, hesitates between two views, that "partial evil" isn't really evil, since only the universal quality is real, and that "partial evil" is really an evil, but only a little one.

In addition, therefore, to adequate solutions, we must recognize unsatisfactory inconsistent solutions, in which there is only a half-hearted or temporary rejection of one of the propositions which together constitute the problem. In these, one of the constituent propositions is explicitly rejected, but it is covertly reasserted or assumed elsewhere in the system.

Fallacious Solutions

Besides these half-hearted solutions, which explicitly reject but implicitly assert one of the constituent propositions, there are definitely fallacious solutions which explicitly maintain all the constituent propositions, but implicitly reject at least one of them in the course of the argument that explains away the problem of evil.

There are, in fact, many so-called solutions which purport to remove the contradiction without abandoning any of its constituent propositions. These must be fallacious, as we can see from the very statement of the problem, but it is not so easy to see in each case precisely where the fallacy lies. I suggest that in all cases the fallacy has the general form suggested above: in order to solve the problem one (or perhaps more) of its constituent propositions is given up, but in such a way that it appears to have been retained, and can therefore be asserted without qualification in other contexts. Sometimes there is a further complication: the supposed solution moves to and fro between, say, two of the constituent propositions, at one point asserting the first of these but covertly abandoning the second, at another point asserting the second but covertly abandoning the first. These fallacious solutions often turn upon some equivocation with the words "good" and "evil," or upon some vagueness about the way in which good and evil are opposed to one another, or about how much is meant by "omnipotence." I propose to examine some of these so-called solutions, and to exhibit their fallacies in detail. Incidentally, I shall also be considering whether an adequate solution could be reached by a minor modification of one or more of the constituent propositions, which would, however, still satisfy all the essential requirements of ordinary theism.

1. "Good cannot exist without evil" or "Evil is necessary as a counterpart to good."

It is sometimes suggested that evil is necessary as a counterpart to good, that if there were no evil there could be no good either, and that this solves the problem of evil. It is true that it points to an answer to the question "Why should there be evil?" But it does so only by qualifying some of the propositions that constitute the problem.

First, it sets a limit to what God can do, saying that God *cannot* create good without simultaneously creating evil, and this means either that God is not omnipotent or that there are *some* limits to what an omnipotent thing can do. It may be replied that these limits are always presupposed, that omnipotence has never meant the power to do what is logically impossible, and on the present view the existence of good without evil would be a logical impossibility. This interpretation of omnipotence may, indeed, be accepted as a modification of our original account which does not reject anything that is essential to theism, and I shall in general assume it in the subsequent discussion. It is, perhaps, the most common theistic view, but I think that some theists at least have maintained that God can do what is logically impossible. Many theists, at any rate, have held that logic itself is created or laid down by God, that logic is the way in which God arbitrarily chooses to think. (This is, of course, parallel to the ethical view that morally right actions are those which God arbitrarily chooses to command, and the two views encounter similar difficulties.) And *this* account of logic is clearly inconsistent with the view that God is bound by logical necessities—unless it is possible for an omnipotent being to bind himself, an issue which we shall consider later, when we come to the Paradox of Omnipotence. This solution of the problem of evil cannot, therefore, be consistently adopted along with the view that logic is itself created by God.

But, secondly, this solution denies that evil is opposed to good in our original sense. If good and evil are counterparts, a good thing will not "eliminate evil as far as it can." Indeed, this view suggests that good and evil are not strictly qualities of things at all. Perhaps the suggestion is that good and evil are related in much the same way as great and small. Certainly, when the term "great" is used relatively as a condensation of "greater than so-and-so," and

"small" is used correspondingly, greatness and smallness are counterparts and cannot exist without each other. But in this sense greatness is not a quality, not an intrinsic feature of anything; and it would be absurd to think of a movement in favor of greatness and against smallness in this sense. Such a movement would be self-defeating, since relative greatness can be promoted only by a simultaneous promotion of relative smallness. I feel sure that no theists would be content to regard God's goodness as analogous to this—as if what he supports were not the *good* but the *better*, and as if he had the paradoxical aim that all things should be better than other things.

This point is obscured by the fact that "great" and "small" seem to have an absolute as well as a relative sense. I cannot discuss here whether there is absolute magnitude or not, but if there is, there could be an absolute sense for "great," it could mean of at least a certain size, and it would make sense to speak of all things getting bigger, of a universe that was expanding all over, and therefore it would make sense to speak of promoting greatness. But in *this* sense great and small are not logically necessary counterparts: either quality could exist without the other. There would be no logical impossibility in everything's being small or in everything's being great.

Neither in the absolute nor in the relative sense, then, of "great" and "small" do these terms provide an analogy of the sort that would be needed to support this solution of the problem of evil. In neither case are greatness and smallness *both* necessary counterparts *and* mutually opposed forces or possible objects for support and attack.

It may be replied that good and evil are necessary counterparts in the same way as any quality and its logical opposite: redness can occur, it is suggested, only if nonredness also occurs. But unless evil is merely the privation of good, they are not logical opposites, and some further argument would be needed to show that they are counterparts in the same way as genuine logical opposites. Let us assume that this could be given. There is still doubt of the correctness of the metaphysical principle that a quality must have a real opposite: I suggest that it is not really impossible that everything should be, say, red, that the truth is merely that if everything were red we should not notice redness, and so we should have no word "red"; we observe and give names to qualities only if they have real opposites. If so, the principle that a term must have an opposite would belong only to our language or to our thought, and would not be an ontological principle, and, correspondingly, the rule that good cannot exist without evil would not state a logical necessity of a sort that God would just have to put up with. God might have made everything good, though *we* should not have noticed it if he had.

But, finally, even if we concede that this *is* an ontological principle, it will provide a solution for the problem of evil only if one is prepared to say, "Evil exists, but only just enough evil to serve as the counterpart of good." I doubt whether any theist will accept this. After all, the *ontological* requirement that nonredness should occur would be satisfied even if all the universe, except for a minute speck, were red, and, if there were a corresponding requirement for evil as a counterpart to good, a minute dose of evil would presumably do. But theists are not usually willing to say, in all contexts, that all the evil that occurs is a minute and necessary dose.

2. "Evil is necessary as a means to good."

It is sometimes suggested that evil is necessary for good not as a counterpart but as a means. In its simple form this has little plausibility as a solution of the problem of evil, since it obviously implies a severe restriction of God's power. It would be a *causal* law that you cannot have a certain end without a certain means, so that if God has to introduce evil as a means to good, he must be subject to at least some causal laws. This certainly conflicts with what a theist normally means by omnipotence. This view of God as limited by causal laws also conflicts with the view that causal laws are themselves made by God, which is more widely held than the corresponding view about the laws of logic. This conflict would, indeed, be resolved if it were possible for an omnipotent being to bind himself, and this possibility has still to be considered. Unless a favorable answer can be given to this question, the suggestion that evil is necessary as a means to good solves the

problem of evil only by denying one of its constituent propositions, either that God is omnipotent or that "omnipotent" means what it says.

3. "The universe is better with some evil in it than it could be if there were no evil."

Much more important is a solution which at first seems to be a mere variant of the previous one, that evil may contribute to the goodness of a whole in which it is found, so that the universe as a whole is better as it is, with some evil in it, than it would be if there were no evil. This solution may be developed in either of two ways. It may be supported by an aesthetic analogy, by the fact that contrasts heighten beauty, that in a musical work, for example, there may occur discords which somehow add to the beauty of the work as a whole. Alternatively, it may be worked out in connection with the notion of progress, that the best possible organization of the universe will not be static, but progressive, that the gradual overcoming of evil by good is really a finer thing than would be the eternal unchallenged supremacy of good.

In either case, this solution usually starts from the assumption that the evil whose existence gives rise to the problem of evil is primarily what is called physical evil, that is to say, pain. In Hume's rather half-hearted presentation of the problem of evil, the evils that he stresses are pain and disease, and those who reply to him argue that the existence of pain and disease makes possible the existence of sympathy, benevolence, heroism, and the gradually successful struggle of doctors and reformers to overcome these evils. In fact, theists often seize the opportunity to accuse those who stress the problem of evil of taking a low, materialistic view of good and evil, equating these with pleasure and pain, and of ignoring the more spiritual goods which can arise in the struggle against evils.

But let us see exactly what is being done here. Let us call pain and misery "first order evil" or "evil (1)." What contrasts with this, namely, pleasure and happiness, will be called "first order good" or "good (1)." Distinct from this is "second order good" or "good (2)" which somehow emerges in a complex situation in which evil (1) is a necessary component—logically, not merely causally, necessary. (Exactly *how* it emerges does not matter: in the crudest version of this solution good [2] is simply the heightening of happiness by the contrast with misery, in other versions it includes sympathy with suffering, heroism in facing danger, and the gradual decrease of first order evil and increase of first order good.) It is also being assumed that second order good is more important than first order good or evil, in particular that it more than outweighs the first order evil it involves.

Now this is a particularly subtle attempt to solve the problem of evil. It defends God's goodness and omnipotence on the ground that (on a sufficiently long view) this is the best of all logically possible worlds, because it includes the important second order goods, and yet it admits that real evils, namely first order evils, exist. But does it still hold that good and evil are opposed? Not, clearly, in the sense that we set out originally: good does not tend to eliminate evil in general. Instead, we have a modified, a more complex pattern. First order good (e.g., happiness) *contrasts with* first order evil (e.g., misery): these two are opposed in a fairly mechanical way; some second order goods (e.g., benevolence) try to maximize first order good and minimize first order evil; but God's goodness is not this, it is rather the will to maximize *second* order good. We might, therefore, call God's goodness an example of a third order goodness, or good (3). While this account is different from our original one, it might well be held to be an improvement on it, to give a more accurate description of the way in which good is opposed to evil, and to be consistent with the essential theist position.

There might, however, be several objections to this solution.

First, some might argue that such qualities as benevolence—and a fortiori the third order goodness which promotes benevolence—have a merely derivative value, that they are not higher sorts of good, but merely means to good (1), that is, to happiness, so that it would be absurd for God to keep misery in existence in order to make possible the virtues of benevolence, heroism, etc. The theist who adopts the present solution must, of course, deny this, but he can do so with some plausibility, so I should not press this objection.

Secondly, it follows from this solution that God is not in our sense benevolent or sympathetic: he is not concerned to minimize evil (1), but only to promote good (2); and this might be a disturbing conclusion for some theists.

But, thirdly, the fatal objection is this. Our analysis shows clearly the possibility of the existence of a *second* order evil, an evil (2) contrasting with good (2) as evil (1) contrasts with good (1). This would include malevolence, cruelty, callousness, cowardice, and states in which good (1) is decreasing and evil (1) increasing. And just as good (2) is held to be the important kind of good, the kind that God is concerned to promote, so evil (2) will, by analogy, be the important kind of evil, the kind which God, if he were wholly good and omnipotent, would eliminate. And yet evil (2) plainly exists, and indeed most theists (in other contexts) stress its existence more than that of evil (1). We should, therefore, state the problem of evil in terms of second order evil, and against this form of the problem the present solution is useless.

An attempt might be made to use this solution again, at a higher level, to explain the occurrence of evil (2): indeed the next main solution that we shall examine does just this, with the help of some new notions. Without any fresh notions, such a solution would have little plausibility: for example, we could hardly say that the really important good was a good (3), such as the increase of benevolence in proportion to cruelty, which logically required for its occurrence the occurrence of some second order evil. But even if evil (2) could be explained in this way, it is fairly clear that there would be third order evils contrasting with this third order good: and we should be well on the way to an infinite regress, where the solution of a problem of evil, stated in terms of evil (*n*), indicated the existence of an evil (*n* + 1), and a further problem to be solved.

4. "Evil is due to human free will."

Perhaps the most important proposed solution of the problem of evil is that evil is not to be ascribed to God at all, but to the independent actions of human beings, supposed to have been endowed by God with freedom of the will. This solution may be combined with the preceding one: first order evil (e.g., pain) may be justified as a logically necessary component in second order good (e.g., sympathy) while second order evil (e.g., cruelty) is not *justified*, but is so ascribed to human beings that God cannot be held responsible for it. This combination evades my third criticism of the preceding solution.

The free-will solution also involves the preceding solution at a higher level. To explain why a wholly good God gave men free will although it would lead to some important evils, it must be argued that it is better on the whole that men should act freely, and sometimes err, than that they should be innocent automata, acting rightly in a wholly determined way. Freedom, that is to say, is now treated as a third order good, and as being more valuable than second order goods (such as sympathy and heroism) would be if they were deterministically produced, and it is being assumed that second order evils, such as cruelty, are logically necessary accompaniments of freedom, just as pain is a logically necessary precondition of sympathy.

I think that this solution is unsatisfactory primarily because of the incoherence of the notion of freedom of the will: but I cannot discuss this topic adequately here, although some of my criticisms will touch upon it.

First I should query the assumption that second order evils are logically necessary accompaniments of freedom. I should ask this: if God has made men such that in their free choices they sometimes prefer what is good and sometimes what is evil, why could he not have made men such that they always freely choose the good? If there is no logical impossibility in a man's freely choosing the good on one, or on several, occasions, there cannot be a logical impossibility in his freely choosing the good on every occasion. God was not, then, faced with a choice between making innocent automata and making beings who, in acting freely, would sometimes go wrong: there was open to him the obviously better possibility of making beings who would act freely but always go right. Clearly, his failure to avail himself of this possibility is inconsistent with his being both omnipotent and wholly good.

If it is replied that this objection is absurd, that the making of some wrong choices is logically nec-

essary for freedom, it would seem that "freedom" must here mean complete randomness or indeterminacy, including randomness with regard to the alternatives good and evil, in other words that men's choices and consequent actions can be "free" only if they are not determined by their characters. Only on this assumption can God escape the responsibility for men's actions; for if he made them as they are, but did not determine their wrong choices, this can only be because the wrong choices are not determined by men as they are. But then if freedom is randomness, how can it be a characteristic of *will*? And, still more, how can it be the most important good? What value or merit would there be in free choices if these were random actions which were not determined by the nature of the agent?

I conclude that to make this solution plausible two different senses of "freedom" must be confused, one sense which will justify the view that freedom is a third order good, more valuable than other goods would be without it, and another sense, sheer randomness, to prevent us from ascribing to God a decision to make men such that they sometimes go wrong when he might have made them such that they would always freely go right.

This criticism is sufficient to dispose of this solution. But besides this there is a fundamental difficulty in the notion of an omnipotent God creating men with free will, for if men's wills are really free this must mean that even God cannot control them, that is, that God is no longer omnipotent. It may be objected that God's gift of freedom to men does not mean that he *cannot* control their wills, but that he always *refrains* from controlling their wills. But why, we may ask, should God refrain from controlling evil wills? Why should he not leave men free to will rightly, but intervene when he sees them beginning to will wrongly? If God could do this, but does not, and if he is wholly good, the only explanation could be that even a wrong free act of will is not really evil, that its freedom is a value which outweighs its wrongness, so that there would be a loss of value if God took away the wrongness and the freedom together. But this is utterly opposed to what theists say about sin in other contexts. The present solution of the problem of evil, then, can be maintained only in the form that God has made men so free that he *cannot* control their wills.

This leads us to what I call the "Paradox of Omnipotence": can an omnipotent being make things which he cannot subsequently control? Or, what is practically equivalent to this, can an omnipotent being make rules which then bind himself? (These are practically equivalent because any such rules could be regarded as setting certain things beyond his control, and vice versa.) The second of these formulations is relevant to the suggestions that we have already met, that an omnipotent God creates the rules of logic or causal laws, and is then bound by them.

It is clear that this is a paradox: the questions cannot be answered satisfactorily either in the affirmative or in the negative. If we answer "Yes," it follows that if God actually makes things which he cannot control, or makes rules which bind himself, he is not omnipotent once he had made them: there are *then* things which he cannot do. But if we answer "No," we are immediately asserting that there are things which he cannot do, that is to say that he is already not omnipotent.

It cannot be replied that the question which sets this paradox is not a proper question. It would make perfectly good sense to say that a human mechanic has made a machine which he cannot control: if there is any difficulty about the question it lies in the notion of omnipotence itself.

This, incidentally, shows that although we have approached this paradox from the free-will theory, it is equally a problem for a theological determinist. No one thinks that machines have free will, yet they may well be beyond the control of their makers. The determinist might reply that anyone who makes anything determines its way of acting, and so determines its subsequent behavior: even the human mechanic does this by his *choice* of materials and structure for his machine, though he does not know all about either of these: the mechanic thus determines, though he may not foresee, his machine's actions. And since God is omniscient, and since his creation of things is total, he both determines and foresees the ways in which his creatures will act. We may grant this, but it is beside the point. The question is not whether God *originally* determined the future actions of his creatures, but whether he can *subsequently* control their actions, or whether he was

able in his original creation to put things beyond his subsequent control. Even on determinist principles the answers "Yes" and "No" are equally irreconcilable with God's omnipotence.

Before suggesting a solution of this paradox, I would point out that there is a parallel Paradox of Sovereignty. Can a legal sovereign make a law restricting its own future legislative power? For example, could the British parliament make a law forbidding any future parliament to socialize banking, and also forbidding the future repeal of this law itself? Or could the British parliament, which was legally sovereign in Australia in, say, 1899, pass a valid law, or series of laws, which made it no longer sovereign in 1933? Again, neither the affirmative nor the negative answer is really satisfactory. If we were to answer "Yes," we should be admitting the validity of a law which, if it were actually made, would mean that parliament was no longer sovereign. If we were to answer "No," we should be admitting that there is a law, not logically absurd, which parliament cannot validly make, that is, that parliament is not now a legal sovereign. This paradox can be solved in the following way. We should distinguish between first order laws, that is laws governing the actions of individuals and bodies other than the legislature, and second order laws, that is laws about laws, laws governing the actions of the legislature itself. Correspondingly, we should distinguish two orders of sovereignty, first order sovereignty (sovereignty [1]) which is unlimited authority to make first order laws, and second order sovereignty (sovereignty [2]) which is unlimited authority to make second order laws. If we say that parliament is sovereign we might mean that any parliament at any time has sovereignty (1), or we might mean that parliament has both sovereignty (1) and sovereignty (2) at present, but we cannot without contradiction mean both that the present parliament has sovereignty (2) and that every parliament at every time has sovereignty (1), for if the present parliament has sovereignty (2) it may use it to take away the sovereignty (1) of later parliaments. What the paradox shows is that we cannot ascribe to any continuing institution legal sovereignty in an inclusive sense.

The analogy between omnipotence and sovereignty shows that the paradox of omnipotence can be solved in a similar way. We must distinguish between first order omnipotence (omnipotence [1]), that is unlimited power to act, and second order omnipotence (omnipotence [2]), that is unlimited power to determine what powers to act things shall have. Then we could consistently say that God all the time has omnipotence (1), but if so no beings at any time have powers to act independently of God. Or we could say that God at one time had omnipotence (2), and used it to assign independent powers to act to certain things, so that God thereafter did not have omnipotence (1). But what the paradox shows is that we cannot consistently ascribe to any continuing being omnipotence in an inclusive sense.

An alternative solution of this paradox would be simply to deny that God is a continuing being, that any times can be assigned to his actions at all. But on this assumption (which also has difficulties of its own) no meaning can be given to the assertion that God made men with wills so free that he could not control them. The paradox of omnipotence can be avoided by putting God outside time, but the free-will solution of the problem of evil cannot be saved

in this way, and equally it remains impossible to hold that an omnipotent God *binds himself* by causal or logical laws.

Conclusion

Of the proposed solutions of the problem of evil which we have examined, none has stood up to criticism. There may be other solutions which require examination, but this study strongly suggests that there is no valid solution of the problem which does not modify at least one of the constituent propositions in a way which would seriously affect the essential core of the theistic position.

Quite apart from the problem of evil, the paradox of omnipotence has shown that God's omnipotence must in any case be restricted in one way or another, that unqualified omnipotence cannot be ascribed to any being that continues through time. And if God and his actions are not in time, can omnipotence, or power of any sort, be meaningfully ascribed to him?

PART III

Knowledge and Reality

INTRODUCTION

There are (at least) three answers to any question: "Yes," "No," and "I don't know." As it stands, the third answer suggests ignorance. But, when we strengthen it and claim not only that knowledge is not at hand, but also that it is impossible for beings like us, we have not admitted ignorance but professed skepticism. We have taken a philosophical position.

There is a long list of questions on which some philosopher or other has come to a skeptical position. During the seventeenth and eighteenth centuries, a very general sort of skepticism that held we could not even know the most basic facts about the external world was a major issue that gave rise to a number of great classics of epistemology—that branch of philosophy that considers the nature and possibility of knowledge. We reprint a number of classics from this Golden Age of Epistemology in Section A of Part III. In two of these, David Hume advocates a moderate skepticism. Two other selections, by René Descartes and George Berkeley, defend theories that are intended to solve problems posed by skeptics. The essay by John Locke, although not directly concerned with skepticism, deals with a central issue in the skeptical controversies: the distinction between ideas in our mind and the objects in the world they are about.

Descartes's Problem

No work in the history of philosophy has had more impact than Descartes's *Meditations on First Philosophy*. This work is a battle with skepticism. Descartes's very trust in reason—the capacity each of us seems to have to learn the truth through careful thought and observation—is thrown into question by skeptical challenges he considers in "Meditation I." Could it be that he is only dreaming? Or worse yet, that an evil demon is devoted to deceiving him in every particular, even those things about which he is most confident? His reason tells Descartes that he should not place his confidence in any belief about which he can have the least doubt. But, unless he can rule out these hypotheses, he seems to have grounds for doubting everything. Reason seems to have rendered itself useless.

The modern student may have little worry about evil demons and be confident that his dreams are too chaotic to be mistaken for waking experience; so, it may be worthwhile to construct a high-tech example to arouse sympathy with Descartes's worry. Suppose that after your last philosophy class, a psychology graduate student shot you with a tranquilizing dart, took you to her dark laboratory in the subbasement of the Psychology Building, and sawed off the top of your skull and removed your brain. Then, she inserted electrodes into your brain. To these electrodes she attached wires through which a computer program could feed electrical charges. The program stimulates the input you would receive from your perceptual system if you had been allowed to go about your business. You are really a brain in a vat in a basement, but the experiences you are having are just the ones you would have had if you were back in your room reading this textbook. Now that you have contemplated this alternative hypothesis to explain the experiences you are having, how can you rule it out? This episode of computer-assisted philosophy should have placed you in the skeptical abyss along with Descartes.

In the rest of the *Meditations*, Descartes ascends step by step out of this abyss. The first steps seem small, but he soon picks up speed; by the end of "Meditation VI," he has vaulted out of the abyss and vindicated most of his earlier beliefs.

Descartes takes his first step (in "Meditation II") when he notes that he cannot doubt that he exists, for he would have to exist to dream or be deceived. And, he cannot doubt that he has ideas either. This is progress, but not much, for the whole physical world still lies within the realm of that which can be doubted.

At the end of "Meditation II" and the beginning of "Meditation III," Descartes develops a conception of what knowledge of the external world would be—to help him determine whether he has any. This conception is known as the theory of representative ideas. (A similar conception is developed by Locke in the selection reprinted from his *An Essay Concerning Human Understanding*). According to this theory, knowledge would consist in a two-way relationship between one's ideas and the objects in the external world. Suppose, for example, that you see a book in front of you. The images you have in your mind could exist, even if there were no book, for you might be dreaming or being deceived by an evil demon or by a psychology graduate student. So, just having those ideas or images does not constitute knowledge that there is a book in front of you. For you to know that, there must be a book there, which is causally responsible for your having the ideas and images you do. To have knowledge, one's ideas must accurately represent the objects that give rise to them.

Given this conception of what it would be to know the external world, can we be sure that we do? It seems that all we can ever be sure of is our own ideas. I might check that there is a book in front of me by reaching out and handling it. Or, I might ask a friend (who is in the room with me) if there is, indeed, a book there. But, what would this show? Suppose, when I reach out, I feel the hard booklike surface and see my hand on the book. And, when I ask my friend, he replies, "Yep, there sure is a book there." But, what do these tests prove? These events could just be additional parts of the dream or of the evil demon's plot.

Once one starts thinking in terms of the theory of representative ideas, one gets the feeling of being trapped in one's own mind. If one is really perceiving an external world, one's ideas must be caused by objects beyond the ideas that these ideas accurately represent. But, how can one ever check this out? One would have to get outside the circle of one's own ideas, and that seems impossible. This epistemological predicament is sometimes called Descartes's Problem.

Descartes believed he had a solution. He thought that one of his ideas, his idea of God, had a very special quality. It is what we might call self-certifying. It could not have been caused by anything other than God. Descartes invoked certain principles—connecting causes and effects—to convince himself of this. He believed that the cause of an idea must be as perfect as that which the idea represents. Given this, he argues that only God could have caused the idea of God in him. Then, Descartes argues that God, being perfect, would not allow him to be deceived when he tries hard to be careful. Thus, Descartes needs God's help to climb back out of the abyss into which he tumbled.

Berkeley and Hume

Many philosophers have followed Descartes's path into the abyss of ignorance, but few have followed his path out of it.

Some have thought that his mistake, and Locke's, was the theory of representative ideas. Berkeley is one such philosopher. In his *Three Dialogues Between Hylas and Philonous* he argues that we should not distinguish between the ideas in our mind and the external objects they represent or else skepticism is unavoidable. Berkeley thought all arguments for such distinctions fallacious. That of which we are directly aware, the ideas in our minds, are what we mean to be speaking of when we talk about tables and chairs in the external world. According to Berkeley, we do not really think there is a nonmental reality behind these ideas. The student may find this notion quite absurd on first encountering it. This was the reaction of Berkeley's character Hylas, when Philonous, the spokesperson for Berkeley's view, first explained it. But Hylas seems powerless to combat the force of Philonous's arguments. Each student should try to lend Hylas a hand and see if Philonous's arguments are actually as powerful as Hylas finally finds them.

Hume's response to Descartes's Problem is different from Berkeley's. Berkeley maintains that the idea of a material object beyond our ideas is a philosopher's confusion and no part of ordinary common sense. Hume, in his "Of Scepticism with Regard to the Senses," argues that, although it is a confusion, it is not just a philosopher's confusion. The way people in general look at chairs and desks and other physical objects—as things that can endure when no one is perceiving them—is a mass of confusion. Should we then revise the way we think about the world? Hume thinks we cannot do this, at least not more than for a moment or two while actively engaged in philosophical reflection. He recommends instead a moderate skepticism. We should be aware of our confusions and limitations while doing philosophy; but, at other times, we should give into our natural inclinations to believe and infer cheerfully, for we really have no choice. And, in his *Enquiry*, Hume argues that only habit or custom, not reason, leads us to expect the future to be like the past: a principle he shows to underlie all of our important beliefs about the world, beyond the most immediate deliverances of sense perception.

Perception

All the philosophers from the Golden Age of Epistemology represented here followed Descartes to a certain point. They all accepted that what were immediately aware of was not a material object outside the mind. There are various arguments for this view. One, the argument from illusion, is implicit in Descartes's worry about whether he is dreaming. Suppose I am in the state I would normally take to be that of seeing a book in front of me. There seems to be something, of which I am directly aware, that could exist, even if I were dreaming (or were in some other way deceived) and there was no book in front of me at all. But this thing, which is common to the cases in which there is a book in front of me and the cases in which there is not a book in front of me, *cannot* be a book. It must, it seems, be an idea in my own mind. Another version of the argument comes from Hume. He pokes a finger in his eye, and he notes that he now sees double. But, what is it of which there are two? Poking oneself in the eye cannot cause there to be two books where there was only one. Again, it seems that of which we are directly aware—that which is doubled when we put pressure on our eye—*cannot* be the material object we might naively take it to be. Finally, all of our authors note that the same material object looks different from various perspectives. The material object does not change, but that of which we are directly aware does change—so, the latter cannot be the former. This last argument, the argument from perceptual relativity, is sometimes considered just a version of the argument from illusion.

All of our seventeenth- and eighteenth-century authors seem to agree that the immediate objects of perception are not material objects; they differ on what to do about it. (There were philosophers of the era, notably Thomas Reid, who did not go along with this view, however.) But in the twentieth century, a great deal of thought has gone into whether the distinction between the material objects and the things we directly perceive can really be sustained. A. J. Ayer argues that the facts of illusion do support a distinction between the direct objects of perception, which he calls "sense data," and the material objects we usually reckon ourselves to be perceiving. Ayer's arguments were subjected to vigorous and influential criticism by J. L. Austin.

Hume's Problems

Abstractly considered, Descartes's Problem is a special case of the following sort of question. Suppose that I know that an event of a certain sort is occurring at one time. How can I, on the basis of this, know of the occurrence of some other event? In Descartes's case, the first event is the occurrence of an idea in my mind; the second is the external existence of a physical world of the sort the idea represents.

Hume considers the general problem in his *Enquiry*. He comes to the conclusion that there is essentially no way that knowledge of one event can give us knowledge of another if knowledge requires immunity from any possible doubt. We are so constituted that, in certain circumstances, we will infer the existence of events of one sort from the occurrence of events of another. Given perception, we will believe in an external world—at least when we do not inhibit our natural inclination to do so by thinking philosophical thoughts. And, if one sort of event has been accompanied in our experience by another sort of event many times in the past, then, when an event of the first sort is perceived by us, we will expect an event of the second sort. If we see lightning, we expect to hear thunder; if we see someone loosen his or her hold on a book, we expect the book to fall. This is the way we are "wired up"; we have no real choice but to follow the natural flow of ideas in our minds. But there is no further guarantee that the world will conform to these inferences and expectations. Our only grounds for supposing it will is that we have no choice. In the "explanation," appeals to reason must give way to appeals to instinct.

Hume thought that these results of his investigation provided a sort of solution to our doubts. If we cannot do better than rely on our natural inclinations to believe, what is there to worry about? But many philosophers have thought that Hume's arguments raised problems rather than solved them.

These philosophers have thought that there *must* be something more to be said in favor of *induction*: the practice of basing our expectations about the future on regularities that have been observed in the past. Even if this practice cannot be guaranteed to work, it has been thought that it must have some favored logical status. Something, beside the brute fact that this is the way our minds work, should mark out this practice as more reasonable than any alternative. This problem has become known as Hume's Problem or the problem of induction. It is a part of the more general inquiry into scientific reasoning that is known as the philosophy of science, for the extrapolation from the observed to the unobserved parts of nature seems essential to the scientific method.

In his selection, "The Problem of Induction," W. C. Salmon surveys the various attempts that have been made to improve on Hume's account of induction, that is, to provide it with some more telling justification than Hume was able to provide. Salmon is unable to accept any of the proposed solutions to Hume's Problem that he considers. Yet, Salmon is convinced that there must be a solution; for, if there is not, science will be just a matter of faith on a par with other faiths. This situation, Salmon says, is "intellectually and socially undesirable. . . . I find it intolerable to suppose that a theory of biological evolution, supported as it is by extensive scientific evidence, has no more rational foundation than has its rejection by ignorant fundamentalists."

The topic of causation is closely related to the problem of induction, and Hume offered us an account of causation in Section VII of his *Enquiry*. Hume thought that the relation of causation (or what we could know of it) amounted to no more than constant conjunction. We say that an event of a certain type E causes an event of type E' if events of type E have been constantly conjoined with those of type E' in our experience. This view has seemed counterintuitive to many philosophers, who feel that Hume has not accounted for the *necessity* that attaches to some causal principles. G. E. M. Anscombe criticizes Hume's position in "Causality and Determination."

The other three essays concern aspects of scientific explanation. Enormous activity has gone on in the philosophy of science since Hume's day. In "Laws and Their Role in Scientific Explanation," Carl G. Hempel explains one of the most important and controversial ideas to emerge in this field, the covering law or deductive nomological model of explanation. This conception is often regarded as a sophisticated version of Hume's treatment of empirical reasoning.

The last two essays provide philosophical criticisms of some assumptions about the institutions of science that often go unquestioned. In "How to Defend Society Against Science," Paul Feyerabend discusses the demarcation between science and religion and the danger of science becoming a government-sponsored orthodoxy. In "Knowledge, Human Interests, and Objectivity in Feminist Epistemology" Elizabeth Anderson investigates the role of social and moral values in scientific and academic inquiry. She discusses the work of Helen Longino, who argues that political and moral values from the social context of science should influence theory and method, and considers criticisms of Longino by Susan Haack.

A. Classics of Epistemology

Meditations on First Philosophy

RENÉ DESCARTES

René Descartes (1596–1650) was one of the greatest philosophers and mathematicians of all time. In addition to the *Meditations*, his works include *Discourse on Method* and *Principles of Philosophy*.

———— • ————

Meditation I
On What Can Be Called
into Doubt

For several years now, I have been aware that I accepted many falsehoods as true in my youth, that what I built on the foundation of those falsehoods was dubious, and therefore that, once in my life, I would need to tear down everything and begin anew from the foundations if I wanted to establish any firm and lasting knowledge. But the task seemed enormous, and I waited until I was so old that no better time for undertaking it would be likely to follow. I have thus delayed so long that it would be wrong for me to waste in indecision the time left for action. Today, then, having rid myself of worries and having arranged for some peace and quiet, I withdraw alone, free at last earnestly and wholeheartedly to overthrow all my beliefs.

To do this, I do not need to show each of my beliefs to be false; I may never be able to do that. But, since reason now convinces me that I ought to withhold my assent just as carefully from what is not obviously certain and indubitable as from what is obviously false, I can justify the rejection of all my beliefs if I can find some ground for doubt in each. And, to do this, I need not take on the endless task of running through my beliefs one by one: since a building collapses when its foundation is cut out from under it, I will go straight to the principles on which all my former beliefs rested.

Of course, whatever I have so far accepted as supremely true I have learned either from the senses or through the senses. But I have occasionally caught the senses deceiving me, and it would be prudent for me never completely to trust those who have cheated me even once.

But, while my senses may deceive me about what is small or far away, there may still be other things taken in by the senses which I cannot possibly doubt—such as that I am here, sitting before the fire, wearing a dressing gown, touching this paper. Indeed, these hands and the rest of my body—on what grounds might I deny that they exist?—unless perhaps I liken myself to madmen whose brains are so rattled by the persistent vapors of melancholy that they are sure they are kings when in fact they are paupers, or that they wear purple robes when in fact they are naked, or that their heads are clay, or that they are gourds, or that they are made of glass. But these people are insane, and I would seem just as crazy if I were to apply what I say about them to myself.

From *Meditations on First Philosophy*, translated from the Latin edition of 1641 by Ronald Rubin. Copyright © 1985 by Arete Press. Reprinted by permission of the translator and publisher.

This would be perfectly obvious—if I weren't a man accustomed to sleeping at night whose experiences while asleep are at least as far-fetched as those that madmen have while awake. How often a dream has convinced me that I was here, sitting before the fire, wearing my dressing gown, when, in fact, I was undressed and between the covers of my bed! But now I am looking at this piece of paper with my eyes wide open; the head that I am shaking has not been lulled to sleep; I put my hand out consciously and deliberately; I feel the paper and see it. None of this would be as distinct if I were asleep. As if I can't remember having been deluded by similar thoughts while asleep! When I think very carefully about this, I see so plainly that there are no reliable signs by which I can distinguish sleeping from waking that I am stupified—and my stupor itself suggests that I am asleep!

Suppose then that I am dreaming. Suppose, in particular, that my eyes are not open, that my head is not moving, and that I have not put out my hand. Suppose that I do not have hands, or even a body. I must still admit that the things I see in sleep are like painted images, which must have been patterned after real things. Hence, things like eyes, heads, hands, and bodies are not imaginary, but real. For, even when painters try to give bizarre shapes to sirens and satyrs, they are unable to give them completely new natures, but can only jumble together the parts of various animals. Even if they were to come up with something so novel that no one had ever seen anything like it before, something entirely fictitious and unreal, there would at least need to be real colors from which they can compose it. By the same reasoning, while things like eyes, heads, and hands may be imaginary, it must be granted that some simpler and more universal things are real—the "real colors" from which the true and the false images in our thoughts are formed. Among things of this sort seem to be general bodily nature and its extension, the shape of extended things, their quantity (that is, their magnitude and number), the place in which they exist, and the time through which they endure.

Perhaps we can correctly infer that, while physics, astronomy, medicine, and other disciplines requiring the study of composites are dubious, disciplines like arithmetic and geometry, which deal only with completely simple and universal things without regard to whether they exist in the world, are somehow certain and indubitable. Whether we are awake or asleep, two plus three is always five, and the square never has more than four sides. It seems impossible even to suspect such obvious truths of falsity.

Nevertheless, the old belief is imprinted on my mind that there is a God who can do anything and by whom I have been made to be as I am. How do I know that He hasn't brought it about that, while there is in fact no earth, no sky, no extended thing, no shape, no magnitude, and no place, all of these things seem to me to exist, just as they now do? Besides, I think that other people sometimes err in what they believe themselves to know perfectly well; mightn't I be deceived when I add two and three, or count the sides of a square, or do even simpler things (if we can even suppose that there is anything simpler)? Maybe God does not want to deceive me; after all, He is said to be supremely good. But, if God's being good is incompatible with His having created me so that I am always deceived, it seems just as out of line with his being good that he sometimes permits me to be deceived—as he undeniably does.

Or maybe some would rather deny that there is an omnipotent God than to believe that everything else is uncertain. Rather than arguing with these people, I will grant that everything I have said about God is fiction. But, however these people think I came to be as I now am (whether they say it is by fate, or by accident, or by a continuous series of events, or in some other way) since it seems that he who errs and is deceived is somehow imperfect, the likelihood that I am constantly deceived increases as the power that they attribute to my original creator decreases. To these arguments, I have no reply; I am forced to admit that nothing that I used to believe is beyond legitimate doubt—not because I have been careless or playful, but because I have valid and well-considered grounds for doubt. I must therefore withhold my assent from my former beliefs as carefully as from obvious falsehoods, if I want to arrive at something certain.

But it is not enough to have noticed this: I must also take care to bear it in mind. For my habitual beliefs constantly return to my mind as if our long-standing, intimate relationship has given them the right to do so, even against my will. I will never break the habit of trusting them and of giving in to them while I see them for what they are—things somewhat dubious (as I have just shown) but nonetheless probable, things that we have much more reason to believe than to deny. That is why I think it will be good deliberately to turn my beliefs around, to allow myself to be deceived, and to suppose that all my previous beliefs are false and imaginary. Eventually, when I have counterbalanced the weight of my prejudices, my bad habits will no longer distort my grasp of things. And I know that there is no danger of error in this and that I won't overindulge in skepticism, since I am now concerned, not with acting, but only with knowing.

I will suppose, then, not that there is a supremely good God who is the source of all truth, but that there is an evil demon, supremely powerful and cunning, who works as hard as he can to deceive me. I will say that sky, air, earth, color, shape, sound, and other external things are just dreamed illusions which the demon uses to ensnare my judgment. I will regard myself as not having hands, eyes, flesh, blood, and senses—but as having the false belief that I have all these things. I will obstinately concentrate on this meditation and will thus ensure by mental resolution that, if I do not really have the ability to know the truth, I will at least withhold assent from what is false and from what a deceiver may try to put over on me, however powerful and cunning he may be. But this plan requires effort, and laziness brings me back to my ordinary life. I am like a prisoner who happens to enjoy the illusion of freedom in his dreams, begins to suspect that he is asleep, fears being awakened, and deliberately lets the enticing illusions slip by unchallenged. Thus, I slide back into my old beliefs; I am afraid that, if I awaken, I will need to spend the waking life which follows my peaceful rest, not in the light, but in the confusing darkness of the problems I have just raised.

Meditation II
On the Nature of the Human Mind, Which Is Better Known Than the Body

Yesterday's meditation has hurled me into doubts so great that I can neither ignore them nor think my way out of them. I am in turmoil, as if I have accidentally fallen into a whirlpool and can neither touch bottom nor swim to the safety of the surface. But I will struggle and try to follow the path that I started on yesterday. That is, I will reject whatever is open to the slightest doubt just as though I have found it to be entirely false, and I will continue until I find something certain—even if it is just that nothing is certain. As Archimedes required only one fixed and immovable point to move the whole earth from its place, I can hope for great things if I can even find one small thing that is certain and unshakable.

I suppose, then, that everything I see is unreal. I believe that none of what my unreliable memory presents to me ever happened. I have no senses. Body, shape, extension, motion, and place are fantasies. What then is true? Perhaps only that nothing is certain.

But how do I know that, in addition to the things I just listed, there isn't something that I do not have the slightest reason to doubt? Isn't there a God, or something like one, who puts my thoughts into me? But why should I say so when I may be the author of those thoughts? Well, isn't it at least the case that I am something? But I now am denying that I have senses and a body. But I stop here. For what follows from these denials? Am I so bound to my body and to my senses that I cannot exist without them? I have convinced myself that there is nothing in the world—no sky, no earth, no minds, no bodies. Doesn't it follow that I don't exist? No; surely I must exist if it's me who is convinced of something. But there is a deceiver, supremely powerful and cunning, whose aim is to see that I am always deceived. Then surely I exist, since I am deceived. Let him deceive me all he can, he will never make it the case that I am nothing while I think that I am something. Thus having fully weighed every consideration, I must finally conclude that the statement "I am, I exist" must be true whenever I state or mentally consider it.

But I do not yet fully understand what this "I" is that must now exist. I must guard against inadvertently taking myself to be something other than I am, thereby going wrong even in the knowledge that I contend is supremely certain and evident. Accordingly, I will think once again about what I believed myself to be before beginning these meditations. From my previous conception of myself, I will subtract everything that can be challenged by the reasons for doubt that I have produced, until nothing remains except what is certain and indubitable.

What, then, did I formerly take myself to be? A man, of course. But what is a man? Should I say a rational animal? No, because then I would need to ask what an animal is and what it is to be rational. Thus, starting from a single question, I would sink into many which are more difficult, and I do not have the time to waste on such subtleties. I would rather pay attention here to the thoughts that occurred to me spontaneously and naturally when I asked what I was. First, it occurred to me that I have a face, hands, arms, and all the other equipment (also found in corpses) which I call a body. Next, it occurred to me that I take nourishment, move myself around, sense, and think—that I do things which I trace back to my soul. I didn't often stop to think about what this soul was, and, when I did, I imagined it to be a rarified air, or fire, or ether permeating the denser parts of my body. On the other hand, I did not have any doubts about physical objects: I thought that I distinctly knew their nature. If I had tried to describe my conception of these objects, I might have said this: "When I call something a physical object, I mean that it is capable of being bounded by a shape and limited to a place; that it can so fill a space as to exclude others from it; that it can be perceived by sight, touch, hearing, taste, and smell; that it cannot move itself but can be moved by something else that touches it." I judged that the powers of self-movement, of sensing, and of thinking did not belong to the nature of physical objects, and, in fact, I marveled that there were some physical objects in which these powers could be found.

But what should I think now, while supposing that a supremely powerful and "evil" deceiver completely devotes himself to seeing to it that I am deceived? Can I say that I have any of the things that I attributed to the nature of physical objects? I concentrate, think, reconsider—but nothing comes to me; I am tired of this pointless repetition. But what about the things that I have assigned to soul? Nutrition and self-movement? Since I have no body, these are merely illusions. Sensing? But I cannot sense without a body, and in sleep I have seemed to sense many things that I did not really sense. Thinking? It comes down to this: There is think-

ing, and thought alone cannot be taken away from me. I am, I exist. That much is certain. For how long? For as long as I think—for it may be that, if I completely stopped thinking, I would also cease to be. I am not now admitting anything unless it must be true, and I am therefore not admitting that I am anything at all other than a thinking thing—that is, a mind, soul, understanding, or reason (terms whose meaning I did not previously know). I know that I am a real, existing thing, but what kind of thing? As I have said, a thing that thinks.

What else? I will draw up mental images. I can't say that I am the collection of organs that we call a human body, or that I am some rarified gas permeating these organs, or that I am air, or fire, or vapor, or breath—for I have supposed that none of these things exist. But I can still say that I am something. It may be, of course, that these things, which I do not yet know and which I am therefore supposing to be nonexistent, are not really distinct from the "I" that I know to exist. I don't know, and I am not going to argue about it now. I can only pass judgment on what I do know. I know that I exist, and I ask what the "I" is that I know to exist. It is obvious that the conception of myself that I derive in *this* way does not depend on anything that I do not yet know to exist and, consequently, that it does not depend on anything of which I can shape a mental image. And the word "shape" points to my mistake. I would truly be creating things if I were to have a mental image of what I am, since to have a mental image is just to contemplate the shape or image of a physical object. I now know with certainty that I exist and at the same time that all images—and, more generally, all things associated with the nature of physical objects—may just be dreams. When I keep this in mind, it seems just as absurd to say "I use mental images to help me understand what I am" as it would be to say "Now, while awake, I see something true—but, since I don't yet see it clearly enough, I'll go to sleep and let my dreams present it to me more clearly and truly." Thus I know that none of the things that I can comprehend with the aid of the mental images bear on my knowledge of myself. I must carefully draw my mind away from such things so that it can gain a distinct knowledge of its own nature.

But what then am I? A thinking thing. And what

is that? Something that doubts, understands, affirms, denies, wills, refuses—and also imagines and senses.

It is no small matter if I do all of these things. But how could it be otherwise? Isn't it me who now doubts nearly everything, understands something, affirms this one thing, refuses to affirm other things, wants to know much more, refuses to be deceived, has mental images (sometimes involuntarily), and is aware of what seems to come from his senses? Even if I am always dreaming, and even if my creator does what he can to deceive me, isn't it just as true that I do all these things as that I exist? Are any of these things distinct from my thought? Can any be said to be separate from me? It's so obvious that it is me who doubts, understands, and wills that I don't see how I could make it more evident. And it is also me who has mental images—for while it may be (as I am supposing) that absolutely nothing of which I have a mental image really exists, the ability to have mental images really does exist and influences my thought. Finally, it is me who senses—or who seems to gain awareness of physical objects through the senses. For example, I now see the light, hear the noise, and feel the heat. These things are unreal, since I am dreaming. But it is still certain that I *seem* to see, to hear, and to feel. This seeming cannot be unreal, but *it* is what is properly called sensing; strictly speaking, sensing is just thinking.

From these considerations, I begin to learn a little about what I am. But I still can't stop thinking that I know physical objects (which I picture in mental images and examine with my senses) much more distinctly than I know this unknown "I" (of which I cannot form a mental image). I think this, even though it would be astounding if it turns out that I comprehend things which I have found to be doubtful, unknown, and alien to me more distinctly than that which I know to be real—namely, my self. But I see what is happening: My mind enjoys wandering, and it won't confine itself to the truth. I will therefore loosen the reins for now so that later, when the time is right, I will be able to control my mind more easily.

Let's consider the things commonly taken to be the most distinctly comprehended: physical objects that we see and touch. Let's not consider the general idea of a physical object, since such general conceptions are very often confused. Rather, let's consider a particular. Take, for example, this piece of wax. It has just been taken from the honeycomb; it hasn't yet completely lost the taste of honey; it still smells of the flowers from which it was gathered; its color, shape, and size are obvious; it is hard, cold, and easy to touch; it makes a sound when rapped. In short, everything required for me to have distinct knowledge of a physical object seems to be present. But, as I speak, I move the wax towards the fire; it loses what was left of its taste; it gives up its smell; it changes color; it loses its shape; it gets bigger; it melts; it heats up; it becomes difficult to touch; it no longer makes a sound when struck. Is it still the same piece of wax? We must say that it is: no one denies it or thinks otherwise. Then what was there in the wax that was so distinctly comprehended? Certainly nothing that I reached with the senses—for, while everything having to do with taste, smell, sight, touch, and hearing has changed, the same piece of wax remains.

Perhaps what I distinctly knew was neither the sweetness of honey, nor the fragrance of flowers, nor a sound, but a physical object that sometimes appeared to me one way and sometimes another. But what exactly is it that I am now imagining? Let's pay careful attention; removing everything that doesn't belong to the wax, let's see what is left. Nothing is left except an extended, flexible, and changeable thing. But what is it for this thing to be flexible and changeable? Is it just that the wax can go from round to square and then to triangular, as I have mentally pictured? Of course not; since I understand that the wax's shape can change in innumerable ways, and since I can't run through all the changes in my imagination, my comprehension of the wax's flexibility and changeability cannot be the product of my ability to have mental images. And what about the thing that is extended? Are we also ignorant of its extension? Since the extension of the wax increases when the wax melts, increases again when the wax boils, and increases still more when the wax gets hotter, I will be mistaken about what the wax is unless I believe that it can undergo more changes in extension than I can ever encompass with mental images. I must therefore admit that I do not have an image of what the wax is—that I grasp what it is with only my mind. (While I am saying this about a particular piece of wax, it is even more clearly true about wax in general.) What then is this piece of wax that I grasp with my mind? It is exactly what I believed it to be at the outset—something that I see, feel, and imagine. It must be noted, however, that my grasp of the wax is not visual, tactile, or pictorial; despite the appearances, I have never had a sensory grasp of what the wax is. Rather, my grasp of the wax is the result of a purely mental inspection, which is imperfect and confused (as it was once) or clear and distinct (as it is now) depending on how much attention I pay to the things of which the wax consists.

But it is surprisingly easy for my mind to be misled. Even when I think to myself nonverbally, language impedes me, and common usage comes close to deceiving me. For, when the wax is present, we say that we see the wax itself, not that we infer its presence from its color and shape. I would leap from this fact about language to the conclusion that I learn about the wax by eyesight rather than by purely mental inspection—except that, if I happen to look out my window and see men walking in the street, it is no less natural to say that I see the men than it is to say that I see the wax. But what do I really see, except hats and coats that could be covering robots? Yet, I judge that there are men in the street. Thus I comprehend with my judgment, which is in my mind, objects that I once believed myself to see with my eyes.

One who aspires to wisdom above that of the common man disgraces himself by deriving doubt from common ways of speaking. Let's go on, then, to ask *when* I most clearly and perfectly grasped what the wax is. Was it when I first looked at the wax and believed my knowledge of it to come from the external senses (or, at any rate from the imagination, the "common sense")? Or is it now, after I have carefully studied what the wax is and how I come to know it? Doubt would be silly here. For what was distinct in my original conception of the wax? How did that conception differ from the one shared by all animals? Of course, when I distinguish the wax from its external forms—when I "undress" it and view it "denuded"—there may still be errors in my judgments about it, but I can't possibly grasp the wax in this way without a human mind.

What should I say about this mind—or, in other words, about myself? (I am not now admitting that there is anything to me but a mind.) What is this "I" that seems to grasp the wax so distinctly? Don't

I know myself much more truly and certainly, and also much more distinctly and plainly, than I know the wax? If I base my judgment that the wax exists on the fact that I see it, my seeing it much more obviously implies that I exist. It is possible that what I see is not really wax, and it is also possible that I don't even have eyes with which to see—but it clearly is *not* possible that, when I see (or, what now amounts to the same thing, when I think I see), the "I" which thinks is not a real thing. Similarly, while I might base my judgment that the wax exists on the fact that I feel it, the same fact makes it obvious that I exist. If I base my judgment that the wax exists on the fact that I have a mental image of it or on some other fact of this sort, the same thing can obviously be said. And what I have said about the wax applies to everything else that is outside me. Moreover, if I seem to grasp the wax more distinctly when I detect it with several senses than when I detect it just with sight or touch, I must know myself even more distinctly—for every consideration that contributes to my grasp of the piece of wax or to my grasp of any other physical object serves better to reveal the nature of my mind. Besides, the mind has so much in it by which it can make its conception of itself distinct that what comes to it from physical objects hardly seems to matter.

And now I have brought myself back to where I wanted to be. I now know that physical objects are not really known through sensation or imagination, but are grasped by the understanding alone. And, from the fact that physical objects are grasped in virtue of their being understandable (rather than tangible or visible), I infer that I can't know anything more easily or plainly than my mind. Since it takes time to break old habits of thought, however, I should pause here to allow the length of contemplation to impress the new thoughts more deeply into my memory.

Meditation III
On God's Existence

I will now close my eyes, plug my ears, and withdraw all my senses. I will even rid my thoughts of the images of physical objects—or, if that is too hard, I will write those images off as empty illusions.

Relying on nothing but myself, I will look more deeply into myself and try gradually to come to know myself better. I am a thinking thing—a thing that doubts, affirms, denies, understands a few things, is ignorant of many things, wills, and refuses. I also imagine and sense—for (as I have noted) I am certain that, even if I do not imagine or sense anything outside me, the modifications of thought that I call sensations and mental images exist in me insofar as they are just modifications of thought.

That is a brief summary of all that I really know—or, at any rate, of all that I have so far noticed that I know. I now will examine more carefully whether there are other things in me which I have not yet discovered. I am certain that I am a thinking thing. Then don't I know what is needed for me to be certain of other things? In this first knowledge, there is nothing but a clear and distinct grasp of what I affirm, and this grasp surely would not suffice to make me certain if it could ever happen that something I grasped so clearly and distinctly was false. Accordingly, I seem to be able to establish the general rule that whatever I clearly and distinctly grasp is true.

But, in the past, I have accepted as completely obvious and certain many thoughts which I later found to be dubious. What were these thoughts about? The earth, the sky, the stars, and other objects of sense. But what did I clearly grasp about these objects? Only that ideas or thoughts of them appeared in my mind. Even now, I do not deny that these ideas occur in me. But there was something else that I used to affirm—something that I used to believe myself to grasp clearly but did not really grasp at all: I affirmed that there were things besides me, that the ideas in me came from these things, and that the ideas perfectly resembled these things. If I didn't err here, I at least reached a true judgment that wasn't justified by the strength of my understanding.

But what follows from this? When I considered very simple and easy points of arithmetic or geometry—such as that two and three together make five—didn't I see them clearly enough to affirm their truth? My only reason for thinking that I ought to doubt these things was the thought that my God-given nature might deceive me, even about what seems most obvious. But, whenever I conceive of this all-powerful God, I am compelled to admit

that, if He wants, he can make it the case that I err even about what I take my mind's eye to see most clearly. On the other hand, when I turn to the things that I believe myself to grasp very clearly, I am so convinced by them that I spontaneously burst forth saying, "Whoever may deceive me, he will never bring it about that I am nothing while I think that I am something, or that I have never been when it is now true that I am, or that two plus three is either more or less than five, or that something else in which I recognize an obvious inconsistency is true." Of course, since I have no reason for thinking that God *is* a deceiver—indeed, since I don't yet know whether God *is*—the grounds for doubt that rest on the supposition that God deceives are very weak and "metaphysical." Still, to rid myself of them I ought to ask as soon as possible whether there is a God and, if so, whether He can be a deceiver. For it seems that, until I know these two things, I can never be completely certain of anything else.

The structure of my project seems to require, however, that I first categorize my thoughts and ask in which of them truth and falsity really reside. Some of my thoughts are like images of things, and only these can properly be called ideas; I have an idea, for example, when I think of a man, of a chimera, of heaven, of an angel, or of God. But other thoughts have other properties: while I always apprehend something as the object of my thought when I will, fear, affirm, or deny, my thought also includes a component in addition to the likeness of that thing. Some of these components are called volitions or emotions; others, judgments.

Now, viewed in themselves and without regard to other things, ideas cannot really be false: if I imagine a chimera and a goat, it is just as true that I imagine the chimera as that I imagine the goat. And I needn't worry about falsehood in volitions or emotions: if I perversely want something that does not exist, it is still true that I want that thing. All that remains, then, are my judgments; it is here that I must be careful not to err. And the first and foremost of the errors that I find in my judgments is that of assuming that the ideas in me have a similarity or conformity to things outside of me. For, if I were to regard ideas merely as modifications of thought, they could hardly lead me wrong.

Of my ideas, some seem to me to be innate, others acquired, and others produced by me. The ideas by which I understand what reality, truth, and thought are seem to have come from my own nature; those by which I hear a noise, see the sun, or feel the fire are ones I formerly judged to come from things outside me; and those of sirens, hippogriffs, and so on are ones that I have formed in myself. Or maybe I can take all of my ideas to be acquired, all innate, or all created by me: I do not yet clearly see where my ideas come from.

For the moment, the central question is about the ideas that I view as derived from objects existing outside me. What reason is there for thinking that these ideas resemble the objects? I seem to have been taught this by nature. Moreover, I find that these ideas are independent of my will (and hence of me) for they often appear when I do not want them to do so. For example, I now feel heat whether I want to or not, and I therefore take the idea or sensation of heat to come from something distinct from me—namely, from the heat of the fire by which I am now sitting. And the obvious thing to think is that what a thing sends to me is its own likeness.

Now, I see whether these reasons are good ones. When I say that nature teaches me something, I mean just that I have a spontaneous impulse to believe it—not that the light of nature reveals the thing's truth to me. There is an important difference. When the light of nature reveals something to me (such as that my thinking implies my existing) that thing is completely beyond doubt, since there is nothing as reliable as the light of nature by means of which I could learn that the thing is not true. As for my natural impulses, however, I have often judged them to have led me astray in practical choices, and I don't see why I should trust them any more on other matters.

Next, while my sensory ideas may not depend on my will, it doesn't follow that they come from outside me. The natural impulses of which I just spoke are in me, but *they* seem to *conflict* with my will. I may therefore have in me an as yet undiscovered ability to produce in myself the ideas that seem to come from outside me. In fact, it has always seemed to me that, while dreaming, I *have* formed such ideas in myself without the aid of external objects.

Finally, even if some of my ideas do come from things distinct from me, it doesn't follow that they are likenesses of things. Indeed, it often seems to me that an idea differs greatly from its cause. For example, I find in myself two different ideas of the sun. One, which I "take in" through the senses and which I ought therefore to view as a typical acquired idea, makes the sun look very small to me. The other, which I derive from astronomical reasoning (that is, which I make, perhaps by composing it from innate ideas), shows the sun to be many times larger than the earth. It is not possible that both of these ideas are accurate likenesses of the sun that exists outside me, and reason convinces me that the one least like the sun is the one that seems to arise most directly from it.

All that I have said shows that, until now, my belief that there are things outside me which implant their ideas or images in me (perhaps through my senses) has rested on blind impulse rather than on certain judgment.

But there may still be a way of telling whether the things which are the sources of my ideas exist outside me. When I regard the ideas of things as mere modifications of thought, I find no inequality among them; all seem to arise from me in the same way. But, inasmuch as different ideas present different things to me, there obviously are great differences among them. The ideas that show me substances are unquestionably greater—or have more "presentational reality"—than those that merely show me modifications or accidents. Similarly, the idea by which I understand the supreme God—eternal, infinite, omniscient, omnipotent, and creator of all things other than Himself—has more presentational reality in it than the ideas which present finite substances.

But the light of nature has revealed that there is at least as much in the complete efficient cause as in its effect. For where could an effect get its reality if not from its cause? And how could a cause give what it did not itself have? It follows both that something cannot come from nothing and that what is more perfect—or, in other words, has more reality in it—cannot come from what is less perfect and has less reality. This obviously holds, not just for those effects whose reality is actual or formal, but also for ideas, whose reality we regard as merely presentational. For example, it's impossible for a nonexistent stone to come into existence unless it is produced by something containing, either formally or eminently, everything in the stone. Similarly, heat can only be induced in something that is not already hot by something having at least the same degree of perfection as heat. Moreover, it is impossible for the idea of heat or of a stone to be in me unless it has been put there by a cause in which there is at least as much reality as in heat or the stone. For, although an idea's cause does not transmit any of its actual or formal reality to the idea, and although an idea does not by its nature require any formal reality other than what it borrows from my thought (of which it is a modification), we should not think that the idea's cause can be less real than the idea. Rather, we should think that each idea contains one particular presentational reality which it must get from a cause having at least as much formal reality as the idea has presentational reality. For, if we suppose that something is in an idea but not in its cause, we must suppose that something has come from nothing. And, however imperfect the existence of a thing that exists presentationally in the understanding through an idea, that thing obviously is *something*, and it therefore cannot come from nothing.

And, although the reality that I am considering in my ideas is just presentational, I ought not to suspect that it need not be in the ideas' cause formally—that it suffices for it to be there presentationally. For, just as the presentational existence of my ideas belongs to the ideas in virtue of their nature, the formal existence of the ideas' causes belongs to those causes—or, at least, to the first and foremost of them—in virtue of their nature. Although one idea may arise from another, this can't go back to infinity; it must eventually arrive at a primary idea whose cause is an "archetype" containing formally all that the idea contains presentationally. Hence, the light of nature makes it clear to me that the ideas in me are like images which may well fall short of the things from which they derive, but which cannot contain anything greater or more perfect.

The more time and care I take in studying all of this, the more clearly and distinctly I know that it is true. But what follows from it? On the one hand, if the presentational reality of one of my ideas is so great that I can be confident that the same degree of reality is not in me either formally or eminently, I can conclude that I cannot be the cause of that idea, that another thing must necessarily exist as its cause, and

consequently that I am not alone in the world. On the other hand, if I can find no such idea in me, I will have no argument at all for the existence of something other than me—for, having diligently searched for another such argument, I have yet to find one.

Besides the idea that shows me to myself (about which there can be no problem here), my ideas include one which presents God, others which present physical objects, others which present angels, others which present animals, and finally others which present men like me.

As to my ideas of other men, of animals, and of angels, it is easy to see that—even if the world contained no men but me, no animals, and no angels—I could have composed these ideas from those that I have of myself, of physical objects, and of God.

And, as to my ideas of physical objects, it seems that nothing in them is so great that it couldn't have come from me. For, if I analyze my ideas of physical objects carefully, taking them one by one as I did yesterday when examining my idea of the piece of wax, I notice that there is very little in them that I grasp clearly and distinctly except magnitude (which is extension in length, breadth, and depth), shape (which arises from extension's limits), position (which the differently shaped things have relative to one another), and motion (which is just change of this relative position). To these I can add substance, duration, and number, but my thoughts of other things in physical objects (such as light and color, sound, odor, taste, heat and cold, and tactile qualities) are so confused and obscure that I can't say whether they are true or false—whether my ideas of these things are of something or of nothing. For, although—as I noted earlier—that which is properly called falsehood (namely, *formal* falsehood) can only be found in judgments, we can still find falsehood of another sort (namely, *material* falsehood) in an idea when it presents what is not a thing as though it were a thing. For example, the ideas that I have of coldness and heat are so unclear and indistinct that I can't tell from them whether coldness is just the absence of heat, or heat just the absence of coldness, or both are real qualities, or neither is. And, since every idea is "of something," the idea that presents coldness to me as something real and positive could justifiably be called false if coldness were just the absence of heat. And the same holds for other similar ideas.

For ideas of this sort, I need not posit a creator other than me. I know by the light of nature that, if one of these ideas is false (that is, if it doesn't present a real thing), it comes from nothing—that is, that the only cause of its being in me is a deficiency of my (obviously imperfect) nature. And, if one of these ideas is true, I still see no reason why I couldn't have produced it—for these ideas present so little reality to me that I can't even distinguish the reality in them from the reality of that which doesn't exist.

Of the things that *are* clear and distinct in my ideas of physical objects, it seems that I may have borrowed some—such as substance, duration, and number—from my idea of myself. Of course, my conception of myself differs from my conception of a stone in that I think of myself as a thinking and unextended thing while I think of the stone as an extended and unthinking thing. But, when I conceive the stone as a substance (that is, as something that can exist by itself), my understanding of substance seems to be the same as when I conceive of myself as a substance. Similarly, when I grasp that I now exist and remember that I have existed in the past, and when I have various thoughts and notice how many of them there are, I get the ideas of duration and number, which I can then apply to other objects of thought. The other components of my ideas of physical objects—namely, extension, shape, place, and motion—can't be in me formally since I am just a thinking thing, but, as they are just modes of substance, and as I am a substance, they can be in me eminently.

All that is left is to consider whether there may be something in my idea of God that couldn't have come from me. By "God" I mean infinite substance, independent, supremely intelligent, and supremely powerful—the thing from which I and everything else that may exist get our existence. The more I consider these attributes, the less it seems that they could have come from me alone. And I must therefore conclude that God necessarily exists.

While I may have the idea of substance in me in virtue of my being a substance, I who am finite would not have the idea of infinite substance in me unless it came from a substance that really was infinite.

And I ought not to say that, rather than having a true idea of infinity, I grasp it merely as the absence of limits—in the way that I grasp rest as the absence of motion and darkness as the absence of light. On the contrary, it's clear to me that there is more reality in an infinite than in a finite substance and, hence, that my grasp of the infinite must somehow be prior to my grasp of the finite—my understanding of God prior to my understanding of myself. For, how could I understand that I doubt and desire, that I am deficient and imperfect, if I don't have the idea of something more perfect to use as a standard of comparison?

And, unlike the ideas of hot and cold which I just discussed, the idea of God cannot be said to be materially false and, hence, to come from nothing. On the contrary, since the idea of God is completely clear and distinct and contains more presentational reality than any other idea, no idea is truer per se and none less open to the suspicion of falsity. The idea of a supremely perfect and infinite entity, I maintain, is completely true. For, while I may be able to suppose that there is no such entity, I cannot even suppose that my idea of God (like the idea of coldness) fails to show me anything real. Yes, this idea is maximally clear and distinct; it contains everything that I grasp clearly and distinctly, everything real and true, everything with any perfection. And it is no ojection that I can't fully comprehend the infinite or that there are innumerable things in God which I can't comprehend fully or even reach with thought. It suffices for me to understand that, being finite, I cannot fully comprehend the infinite and to judge that, if I grasp something clearly and distinctly and know it to have some perfection, it is either formally or eminently present in God (perhaps along with innumerable other things of which I am ignorant). If I do this, my idea of God will be supremely true, and supremely clear and distinct.

But maybe I am greater than I have assumed; maybe all the perfections that I attribute to God are in me potentially, still unreal and unactualized. I have already seen my knowledge gradually increase, and I don't see anything to prevent its becoming greater and greater to infinity. Nor do I see why, by means of such increased knowledge, I couldn't get all the rest of God's perfections. Finally, if the potential for these perfections is in me, I don't see why this potential couldn't by itself produce in me the ideas of these perfections.

None of this is possible. First, while it's true that my knowledge gradually increases and that I have many as yet unactualized potentialities, none of this fits with my idea of God, in whom absolutely nothing is potential; the gradual increase in my knowledge shows that I am *imperfect*, not that I am perfect. Moreover, even if my knowledge were continually to become greater and greater, it would never become actually infinite, since it will never become so great that it couldn't be greater. But I judge that God is actually infinite and that nothing can be added to his perfection. Finally, I see that an idea's presentational being must be produced, not by mere potentiality (which, strictly speaking, is nothing), but by what is actual or formal.

When I pay attention to these things, the light of nature makes all of them obvious. But, when I attend less carefully and the images of sensible things blind my mind's eye, it's hard for me to remember that the idea of an entity more perfect than I am must come from an entity that is more perfect. That's why I want to go on to ask whether I, who have the idea of a perfect entity, could exist if no such entity existed.

From what might I derive my existence if not my God? Either from myself, or from my parents, or from something else less perfect than God (for I can't suppose that anything other than God is His superior, or even His equal, in perfection).

But, if I were to get my existence from myself, I wouldn't doubt, or want, or lack anything; I would have given myself every perfection of which I have an idea and would therefore be God. And I shouldn't think that it might be harder to give myself what I lack than what I already have. On the contrary, it would obviously be much harder to make me (a thinking thing or substance) emerge from nothing than to give me complete knowledge (which is just an attribute of substance). But surely, if I had given myself that which is harder to get, I wouldn't have denied myself complete knowledge, which would have been easier to get. In fact, I wouldn't have denied myself *any* of the perfections that I grasp in the idea of God. None of these perfections seems harder to get than existence, but they would seem harder to get if I had really given myself everything I now have—for in creating myself I would have discovered the limits of my power.

And I can't avoid the force of this argument by supposing that, having always existed as I do now,

I don't have any creator. Since my lifetime can be divided into innumerable, mutually independent parts, the fact that I existed a little while ago does not entail that I exist now, unless a cause "re-creates" me—or, in other words, preserves me—at this moment. Thus, when I keep the nature of time in mind, it becomes obvious that exactly the same power and action is required to preserve a thing at each of the moments at which it exists as would be required to create it anew if it had never existed. Accordingly, one of the things revealed by the light of nature is that preservation and creation differ only in the way we think of them.

I ought to ask myself, then, whether *I* have the power to ensure that I, who now am, will exist a little while from now. Since I am nothing but a thinking thing—or, at any rate, since I am not focusing on the part of me that thinks—I would surely be aware of this power if it were in me. But I find no such power. And this very clearly shows that there is an entity distinct from me on whom I depend.

Maybe this entity isn't God; maybe I am the product of my parents or of some other cause less perfect than God. But, as I just said, there must be at least as much in a cause as in its effect. Therefore, since I am a thinking thing with the idea of God in me, my cause—whatever it is—must be a thinking thing having in it the idea of every perfection that I attribute to God. And I can go on to ask whether this thing gets its existence from itself or from something else. But it's obvious from what I have just said that, if my cause gets its existence from itself, it must *be* God: having the power to exist in itself, it must also have the power actually to give itself every perfection of which it has an idea—including every perfection that I conceive of in God. On the other hand, if my cause gets its existence from some other thing, I can go on to ask whether this other thing gets its existence from itself or from something else. Eventually, I will come to the ultimate cause: God.

It is clear that there can't be an infinite regress here—especially since I am concerned, not so much with the cause that originally produced me, as with the one that preserves me in the present.

But what about the view that several partial causes combined to make me, that I get the ideas of the various perfections I attribute to God from different causes, and that, while each of these perfections can be found somewhere in the universe, there is no God in whom they all come together? I can't suppose that this is true. On the contrary, one of the chief perfections that I understand God to have is unity—that is, simplicity, or inseparability from everything to Him. But, of all God's perfections, unity is the one whose idea could only have been put in me by a cause which gives me the ideas of all the other perfections: I can be made to regard God's perfections as inseparably joined only if I am made aware of what these perfections are.

Finally, it's clear that, even if everything that I used to believe about my parents is true, they do not preserve me. Insofar as I am a thinking thing, they did not even take part in creating me. They simply formed the matter in which I used to think that I resided. (By "I" I mean my mind, which is all that I now grasp of myself.) There can therefore be no problem about my parents, and I am driven to this conclusion: The fact that I exist and have an idea of God as a perfect entity conclusively entails that God does in fact exist.

All that's left is to explain how I have gotten my idea of God from Him. I have not taken it in through my senses; it has never come to me unexpectedly as the ideas of sensible things do when those things affect (or seem to affect) my external organs of sense. Nor have I made the idea myself; I can't subtract from it or add to it. The idea must therefore be innate in me, like my idea of myself.

And it's not at all surprising that in creating me God put this idea into me, impressing it like a craftsman's mark on His work. This mark needn't be distinct from the work itself. Indeed, the very fact that it was God who created me confirms that I have somehow been made in His image or likeness and that I grasp this likeness (which contains the idea of God) in the same way that I grasp myself. For, when I turn my mind's eye on myself, I understand, not only that I am an incomplete, dependent thing which constantly strives for bigger and better things, but also that He on whom I depend, having all these things in Himself as infinite reality rather than just as vague potentiality, must therefore be God. The whole argument comes down to this: I know that I could not exist with my present nature (that is, that I could not exist with the idea of God in me) unless there really were a God—the very God of whom I have an idea, the thing having all of the perfections

that I can't fully comprehend but can somehow reach with thought, the thing that clearly cannot be defective. From this, it is obvious that He can't deceive, for the natural light reveals that fraud and deception arise from defect.

But before examining this more carefully and investigating its consequences, I want to dwell for a moment in the contemplation of God, to ponder His attributes in me, to see, admire, and adore the beauty of His boundless light, insofar as my clouded insight allows. Believing that the supreme happiness of the other life consists wholly of the contemplation of divine greatness, I now find that through less perfect contemplation of the same sort I can gain the greatest joy available in this life.

Meditation IV
On Truth and Falsity

In the last few days, I have gotten used to drawing my mind away from my senses. Having carefully noted that I really grasp very little about physical objects, that I know much more about the human mind, and that I know even more about God, I no longer find it hard to turn my thoughts away from things of which I can have mental images and towards thing which I can only understand—things completely separate from matter. I have a much more distinct idea of the human mind than of physical objects, insofar as the mind is just a thinking thing which isn't extended in length, breadth, or depth and which doesn't have anything in common with physical objects. Moreover, when I observe that I doubt or that I am incomplete and dependent, I have a clear and distinct idea of God, a complete and independent entity. And, from the fact that this idea is in me and that I who have the idea exist, I can infer both that God exists and that I am completely dependent on Him for my existence from moment to moment. This inference is so obvious that I'm sure humans can't know anything more evidently or certainly. And now I think I see a way of moving from the contemplation of the true God, in whom are hidden all treasures of knowledge and wisdom, to knowledge of *other* things.

First, I know it is impossible for Him ever to deceive me. Fraud and deception always contain imperfection, and, while the ability to deceive may seem a sign of cunning and power, the desire to deceive reveals malice or weakness and therefore can't be among God's desires.

Next, I find in myself an ability to judge which, like everything else in me, I have gotten from God. Since He doesn't want to deceive me, He certainly hasn't given me an ability which will lead me wrong when properly used.

There could be no doubt about this—except that it may seem to imply that I *never* err. For, if I have gotten everything in me from God and He hasn't given me the ability to err, it doesn't seem possible for me *ever* to err. Thus, as long as I think only of God and devote all my attention to Him, I can't find any cause for error and falsity. When I turn my attention back to myself, however, I find that I can make innumerable errors. In looking for the cause of these errors, I find before me, not just the real and positive idea of God, but also the negative idea of "nothingness"—the idea of that which is completely devoid of perfection. I find that I am "intermediary" between God and nothingness, between the supreme entity and the nonentity. Insofar as I am the creation of the supreme entity, there is nothing in me that accounts for my being deceived or led into error, but, insofar as I somehow participate in nothingness or the nonentity—that is, insofar as I am not identical to the supreme entity and lack a great many things— it is not surprising that I am deceived. Thus I understand that, in itself, error is a *lack* rather than a real thing dependent on God. And I therefore understand that I can err without God's having given me a special ability to do so: I fall into error because my God-given ability to judge the truth isn't infinite.

But there is still something to be explained. Error is not just an absence, but a deprivation—the lack of knowledge that somehow *ought* to be in me. But, when I attend to God's nature, it seems impossible that He has given me an ability that is an imperfect thing of its kind—an ability lacking a perfection that it ought to have. The greater the craftsman's skill, the more perfect his product. Then how can the supreme creator of all things have made something that isn't absolutely perfect? There is no doubt that God could have made me so that I never err, and there is no doubt that He always wants what is best. Then is it better for me to be deceived than not to be deceived?

When I pay more careful attention, I realize that I should not be surprised at God's doing things that I can't explain and that I should not doubt His existence just because I find that I sometimes can't understand why or how He has made something. For, since I know that my nature is weak and limited while God's is limitless, incomprehensible, and infinite, I also know that He can do innumerable things of whose causes I am ignorant. And, on this ground alone, I regard the common practice of explaining things in terms of their purposes to be useless in physics: I would be foolhardy if I tried to understand God's purposes.

It also seems to me that, rather than looking at a single creation in isolation when asking whether God's works are perfect, I ought to look at all of them together. For a thing that seems imperfect when viewed alone may seem completely perfect when regarded as a part of the world. Of course, since calling everything into doubt, I haven't established that anything exists besides me and God. But, when I consider God's immense power, I can't deny that He has made (or, in any case, that He can make) many other things, and I must therefore regard myself as part of a universe.

Finally, turning to myself and investigating the nature of my errors (which are all that show me to be imperfect), I notice that these errors depend on two concurrent causes: my ability to know and my ability to choose freely—that is, my understanding and my will.

Viewed in itself, the understanding is just the thing by which I grasp the ideas about which I form judgments, and I therefore cannot say that there are errors in the understanding itself. While there may be innumerable things of which I have no idea, I can't say that I am deprived of these ideas, but only that I happen to lack them—for I don't have any reason to think that God ought to have given me a greater ability to know than He has: Although God is a supremely skillful craftsman, I don't think that He ought to endow each of his works with all the perfections that He can put in the others.

On the other hand, I can't complain about the scope or perfection of my God-given freedom of will—for my will doesn't seem to me to be restricted in any way. In fact, it seems well worth noting that nothing in me other than my will is so great and perfect that I couldn't conceivably be bigger or better. When I think about my ability to understand, for example, I immediately realize that it is very small and restricted, and I simultaneously form the idea of something much greater—something supremely perfect and infinite. From the fact that I can form the idea of this perfection, I infer that the perfection is present in God's nature. Similarly, when I consider my other abilities (such as the abilities to remember and to imagine) I clearly see that they all are feeble and limited in me but boundless in God. The only exception is my will or freedom of choice, which cannot conceivably be greater than it is. In fact, it is largely for this reason that I regard myself as an image or likeness of God. God's will is incomparably greater than mine, of course, both in virture of the knowledge and power associated with it (which result in its greater strength and efficacy) and in virtue of the greater range of its objects. Yet, viewed in itself as a will, God's will seems no greater than mine—because having a will just amounts to being able either to do or not to do, to affirm or deny, to seek or avoid. Or better: having a will amounts to being inclined to do or not to do (affirm or deny, seek or shun) what the understanding offers, without an awareness of being forced towards it by external forces. For being free does not require being inclined towards both alternatives. On the contrary, the more I lean towards one alternative—either because I understand the truth or goodness in it or because God has so arranged my deepest thoughts—the more freely I choose it. Thus divine grace and knowledge of nature clearly increase and strengthen rather than diminish my freedom. The indifference that I experience when no consideration impels me towards one alternative rather than the other is freedom of the lowest sort, which reveals a defect or an absence of knowledge rather than a perfection. For, if I always knew what was good or true, I wouldn't ever deliberate about what to do or choose, and consequently, though completely free, I would never be indifferent.

From this I see that my God-given ability to will is not itself the cause of my errors; my will is great, and it is a perfect thing of its kind. Neither is my power of understanding the cause of my errors; whenever I understand something, I understand it correctly and without the possibility of deception,

since my understanding comes from God. Then what *is* the source of my errors? Just that, while my will has a broader scope than my understanding, I don't keep it within the same bounds, but extend it to what I don't understand. Being indifferent to these things, I am easily led away from truth and goodness into error and sin.

For example, when I asked a while ago whether anything exists in the world, I noted that, from the fact that I ask this, it follows that I exist. Since I very clearly understood this, I couldn't fail to believe it to be true. It was not that a force outside me compelled me to believe, but that an intense light in my understanding produced a strong inclination of my will. And, because I wasn't indifferent, my belief was spontaneous and free. However, while I now know that I exist insofar as I am a thinking thing, I still wonder whether the thinking nature that is in me—or, rather, that is me—differs from this bodily nature or is identical to it. Nothing occurs to my reason (I am supposing) to convince me of one alternative rather than the other. Accordingly, I am completely indifferent to affirming either view, to denying either view, and even to suspending judgment.

And indifference of this sort is not limited to things of which the understanding is completely ignorant. It extends to everything about which the will deliberates in the absence of a sufficiently clear understanding. For, however strong the force with which plausible conjectures draw me towards one alternative, the knowledge that they are conjectures rather than assertions backed by certain and indubitable arguments is enough to push my assent the other way. The past few days have provided me with ample experience of this—for I am now supposing each of my former beliefs to be false just because I've found a way to call them into doubt.

If I suspend judgment when I don't clearly and distinctly grasp what's true, I obviously do right and am not deceived. But, if I either affirm or deny in a case of this sort, I misuse my freedom of choice. If I affirm what is false, I clearly err, and, if I stumble onto the truth, I'm still blameworthy since the light of nature reveals that a perception of the understanding should always precede a decision of the will. In these misuses of freedom of choice lies the deprivation which accounts for error. And this deprivation, I maintain, lies in the working of the will insofar as it comes from me—not in my God-given ability to will, or even in the will's operation insofar as it derives from Him.

I have no reason to complain that God hasn't given me a more perfect understanding or a greater natural light than He has. It's in the nature of a finite understanding that there are many things it can't understand, and it's in the nature of created understanding that it's finite. Indeed, I ought to be grateful to Him who owes me absolutely nothing for what He has bestowed, rather than taking myself to be deprived or robbed of what God hasn't given me.

And I have no reason to complain about God's having given me a will whose scope is greater than my understanding's. The will is like a unity made of inseparable parts; its nature apparently will not allow anything to be taken away from it. And, really, the wider the scope of my will, the more grateful I ought to be to Him who gave it to me.

Finally, I ought not to complain that God concurs in bringing about the acts of will and judgment in which I err. Insofar as these acts derive from God, they are completely true and good, and I am more perfect with the ability to perform these acts than I would be without it. And, the deprivation which is the real ground of falsity and error doesn't need God's concurrence, since it's not a thing. When we regard God as its cause, we should say that it is an absence rather than a deprivation. For it clearly is no imperfection in God that He has given me the freedom to assent or not to assent to things of which He hasn't given me a clear and distinct grasp. Rather, it is undoubtedly an imperfection in me that I misuse this freedom by passing judgment on things that I don't properly understand. I see, of course, that God could easily have brought it about that, while I remain free and limited in knowledge, I never err: He could have implanted in me a clear and distinct understanding of everything about which I was ever going to make a choice, or He could have indelibly impressed on my memory that I must never pass judgment on something that I don't clearly and distinctly understand. And I also understand that, regarded in isolation from everything else, I would have been more perfect if God had made me so that I never err. But I can't deny that, because some things are immune to error while others are not, the universe is more perfect than it would have been if all its parts were alike.

And I have no right to complain about God's wanting me to hold a place in the world other than the greatest and most perfect.

Besides, if I can't avoid error by having a clear grasp of every matter on which I make a choice, I can avoid it in the other way, which only requires remembering that I must not pass judgment on matters whose truth isn't apparent. For, although I find myself too weak to fix my attention permanently on this single thought, I can—by careful and frequent meditation—ensure that I call it to mind whenever it's needed and thus that I acquire the habit of avoiding error.

Since the first and foremost perfection of man lies in avoiding error, I've profited from today's meditation, in which I have investigated the cause of error and falsity. Clearly, the only possible cause of error is the one I have described. When I limit my will's range of judgment to the things shown clearly and distinctly to my understanding, I obviously cannot err—for everything that I clearly and distinctly grasp is something and therefore comes, not from nothing, but from God who is supremely perfect and who cannot deceive. What I clearly and distinctly grasp is therefore unquestionably true. Today, then, I have learned what to avoid in order not to err and also what to do to attain the truth: I surely will attain the truth if I attend only to the things that I understand perfectly, distinguishing them from those that I grasp more obscurely and confusedly. And, from now on, I will devote myself to doing just that.

Meditation V
On the Essence of Material Objects and More on God's Existence

Many questions remain about God's attributes and about the nature of my self or mind. I may return to these questions later, but now—having found what to do and what to avoid in order to attain truth—I regard nothing as more pressing than to work my way out of the doubts that I raised the other day and to see whether I can find anything certain about material objects.

Before asking whether any such objects exist outside me, I ought to consider the ideas of these objects as they are in my thoughts and to see which are clear and which confused.

I distinctly imagine that which philosophers commonly call "continuous quantity," of course, and I distinctly imagine the extension of this quantity—or rather of the quantified thing—in length, breadth, and depth. I can distinguish various parts of this extension. I can ascribe at will any size, shape, place, and motion to these parts and any duration to the motions.

And, in addition to having a thorough knowledge of extension in general, I grasp innumerable particulars about shape, number, motion, and so on. The truth of these particulars is so obvious and so consonant with my nature that, when I first think about one of them, I do not seem to be learning anything novel. Rather I seem to be remembering something that I already knew—or noticing something that had been in me for a long time without my having been aware of it.

What is important here, I think, is that I find in myself innumerable ideas of things which, though they may not exist outside me, can't be said to be nothing. While I have some control over my thoughts of these things, I do not make the things up: they have their own real and immutable natures. Suppose, for example, that I imagine a triangle. While it may be that there is not—and never has been—a figure of this sort outside my thought, the figure still has a fixed, immutable, and eternal nature (essence, form) which hasn't been produced by me and which doesn't depend on my mind. The proof is that I can demonstrate various propositions about the triangle, such as that its angles equal two right angles and that its greatest side subtends its greatest angle. Even though I didn't think of these propositions at all when I first imagined the triangle, I now clearly see their truth whether I want to or not, and it follows that I didn't make them up.

It isn't relevant that, having seen triangular physical objects, I may have gotten the idea of the triangle from external objects through my organs of sense. For I can invent innumerable other figures whose ideas I *cannot* have gotten through my senses, and I can demonstrate facts about these other figures just as I can about the triangle. Since I know these facts clearly, they must be true, and they therefore must be something rather than nothing—for it's obvious that everything true is something, and everything that I know clearly and distinctly is true, as I have already shown. But, even if I had not shown this, the nature of my mind would have made it impossible for me to withhold my assent from these things (at least when I clearly and distinctly grasped them). As I recall, I regarded truths about shape and number—truths of arithmetic, geometry, or pure mathematics in general—as more certain than any others, even when I clung most tightly to objects of sense.

But, if anything whose idea I can draw from my thought must in fact have everything that I clearly and distinctly grasp it to have, can't I derive from this a proof of God's existence? Surely, I find the idea of a supremely perfect being in me just as I find the ideas of figures and numbers, and I understand as clearly and distinctly that eternal existence belongs to His nature as that the things that I demonstrate of figures and numbers belong to the natures of those figures and numbers. Accordingly, even if what I have thought up in the past few days hasn't been entirely true, I ought to be at least as certain of God's existence as I have been of the truths of pure mathematics.

At first, this reasoning may seem unclear and fallacious. For, being accustomed to distinguishing existence from essence in other cases, I am easily convinced that I can separate God's existence from His essence and, hence, that I can think of God as nonexistent. But, when I pay more careful attention, it's clear that I can no more separate God's existence from His essence than I can separate the essence of the triangle from its angles equaling two right angles, or the idea of a mountain from the idea of a valley. It is no less a contradiction to think that God (the supremely perfect being) lacks existence (a perfection) than to think that a mountain lacks a valley.

Well, suppose that I can't think of God without existence, just as I can't think of a mountain without a valley. The fact that I can think of a mountain with a valley doesn't entail that a mountain exists in the world, and, similarly, the fact that I can think of God as existing doesn't seem to entail that He exists. For my thought doesn't impose any necessity on things: it may be that I can ascribe existence to God when no God exists, just as I can imagine a winged horse when no such horse exists.

No, there is a fallacy here. From the fact that I can't think of a mountain without a valley it follows, not that the mountain and valley exist, but only that—whether they exist or not—they can't be separated. Similarly, from the fact that I can't think of God without existence, it follows that existence is inseparable from Him and, hence, that he really exists. It's not that my thoughts make things happen or impose a necessity on things. On the contrary, it's the fact that God exists which necessitates my thinking of Him as I do. I am not free to think of God without existence—of the supremely perfect being without supreme perfection—as I am free to think of a horse without wings.

Now someone might say this: "If I take God to have all perfections, and if I take existence to be a perfection, I must take God to exist, but I needn't accept the premise that God has all perfections. Similarly, if I accept the premise that every quadrilateral can be inscribed in a circle, I am forced to the patently false view that every rhombus can be inscribed in a circle, but I need not accept the premise." This is wrong, however. For, while it's not necessary that the idea of God occurs to me, it *is* necessary that I attribute all perfections to Him (even if I don't enumerate them or consider them individually) whenever I think of the primary and supreme entity and bring the idea of Him out of my mind's treasury. And this necessity ensures that, when I do notice that existence is a perfection, I can rightly conclude that the primary and supreme being exists. Similarly, while it's not necessary that I even imagine a triangle, it is necessary that, when I do choose to consider a rectilinear figure having exactly three angles, I attribute to it (perhaps without noticing that I am doing so) properties from which I can rightly infer that its angles are no more than two right angles. But, when I consider the various shapes that can be inscribed in the circle, there's absolutely no necessity for my thinking that all quadrilaterals are among them; in fact, having resolved to accept only what I clearly and distinctly understand, I can't even think that all quadrilaterals are among them. Thus my false suppositions differ greatly from the true ideas implanted in me, the first and foremost of which is my idea of God. In many ways, I see that this idea is not a figment of my thought—that it is the image of a real and immutable nature: First, God is the only thing that I can think of whose existence belongs to its essence. Second, I can't conceive of there being two or more Gods. Third, having supposed that one God now exists, I see that He has necessarily existed from all eternity and will continue to exist into eternity. And there are many other things in God that I can't diminish or alter.

But, whatever proof I offer, it always comes back to the fact that I am only convinced of what I grasp clearly and distinctly. Of the things that I grasp in this way, some are obvious to everyone. Others are discovered only by those who examine things more closely and search more carefully, but, once these things have been discovered, they are regarded as no less certain than the others. That the square on the hypotenuse of a right triangle equals the sum of the squares on the sides is not as readily apparent as that the hypotenuse subtends the greatest angle, but, once it has been seen, it is believed just as firmly. And (when I am not overwhelmed by prejudices and my thoughts are not besieged by images of sensible things) there surely is nothing that I know earlier or more easily than what pertains to God. For what could be more self-evident than there is a supreme entity—that God, the only thing whose existence belongs to His essence, exists?

While I need to pay careful attention in order to grasp this, I am now as certain of it as of any of the things that seem most certain. Moreover, I now see that the certainty of everything else so depends on my being certain that God exists that, if I weren't certain of God's existence, it wouldn't be possible for me to know anything perfectly.

Of course, my nature is such that, when I grasp something clearly and distinctly, I can't fail to believe it. But, since my nature is also such that I can't permanently fix my attention on a single thing so as always to grasp it clearly, the memory of previous judgments often comes to me when I am no longer attending to the grounds on which I originally made them. When this happens, reasons could be produced which would easily overthrow the judgments if I were ignorant of God, and I therefore would not have true and certain knowledge, but only unstable and changing opinion. For example, when I consider the nature of the triangle, it seems plain to me—steeped as I am in the principles of geometry—that its three angles equal two right angles: I can't fail to believe this as long as I pay attention to its demonstration. But, if I were ignorant of God, I might come to doubt its truth as soon as my attention wandered from its demonstration, even if I recalled having mastered the demonstration in the past: I could convince myself that I have been so constructed by nature that I sometimes err about what I believe myself to grasp most plainly—especially if I remembered that, having taken many things to be true and certain, I had later found reasons for judging them false.

But now I grasp that God exists, and I understand both that everything else depends on Him and that He's not a deceiver. From this, I infer that everything I clearly and distinctly grasp must be true. Even if I no longer pay attention to the grounds on which I judged God to exist, my recollection that I once clearly and distinctly knew Him to exist ensures that no contrary ground can be produced to impel me towards doubt. About God's existence, I have true and certain knowledge. And I have such knowledge, not just about this one thing, but about all the other things—such as the theorems of geometry—which I remember having proven. For what can now be said against my believing these things? That I am so constructed that I always err? But I now know that I can't err about what I clearly and distinctly understand. That much of what I took to be true and certain I later found to be false? But I didn't grasp any of these things clearly and distinctly; ignorant of the true standard of truth, I based my belief on grounds that I later found to be unsound. Then what can be said? What about the objection (which I recently used against myself) that I may be dreaming and that the things I am now experiencing may be as unreal as those that occur to me in sleep? No, the point would be irrelevant—for, even if I *am* dreaming, everything that is evident to my understanding *must* be true.

Thus I plainly see that the certainty and truth of all my knowledge derives from my knowledge of the true God. Before I knew Him, I couldn't know anything else perfectly. But now I can plainly and certainly know innumerable things about God, about other mental beings, and (insofar as it is the subject of pure mathematics) about the nature of physical objects.

Meditation VI
On the Existence of Material Objects and the Real Distinction of Mind from Body

It remains for me to examine whether physical objects exist. Insofar as they are the subject of pure mathematics, I now know that they *can* exist, because I grasp them clearly and distinctly. For God can undoubtedly make whatever I can clearly and distinctly grasp, and I never judge that something is impossible for Him to make unless there would be a contradiction in my grasping that thing distinctly. Moreover, the fact that I find myself having mental images when I turn my attention to physical objects seems to imply that these objects really do exist. For, when I pay careful attention to what imagination is, it seems to me that it is just the application of my power of thought to a certain body which is immediately present to my thought and which must therefore exist.

I will begin to clarify this by examining the ways in which having mental images differs from having a pure understanding. When I picture a triangle, for example, I don't just understand that it is a figure bounded by three lines; I also "look at" the lines as though they were present to my mind's eye. And it is this "looking" that I call imagining. In contrast, when I want to think of a chiliagon, I can't imagine the sides or "look" at them as though they were present, but I *understand* that the chiliagon is a figure with a thousand sides as well as I understand that a triangle is a figure with three. Being accustomed to using images when I think about physical objects, I may confusedly picture *some* figure to myself, but—as this figure in no way differs from what I present to myself when thinking about a myriagon or any other many sided figure, and as it does not help me to discern the properties that distinguish chiliagons from the other polygons, it obviously is not a chiliagon. If it's a pentagon that is in question, I can understand its shape (as I can that of the chiliagon) without the aid of mental images. But I can also get a mental image of the pentagon by directing my mind's eye to its five lines and to the areas that they bound. It's obvious to me that getting this mental image requires a special mental effort different from that needed for understanding, and this special effort clearly reveals the difference between imagination and pure understanding.

It also seems to me that my power of imagining, being distinct from my power of understanding, is not essential to myself or, in other words, to my mind—for, if I were to lose this ability, I would surely remain the same thing that I now am. And it seems to follow that this ability depends on something distinct from me. It's easy to understand how my mind might get mental images of physical objects by means of my body, *if* we suppose that there is a body so associated with my mind that the mind can "look into" it at will. If there were such a body, the mode of understanding that we call imagination would only differ from pure understanding in one way: when the mind understood something, it would turn "inward" and view an idea that it found in itself, but, when it imagined, it would turn to the body and look at something there—something resembling an idea that it had understood by itself or had grasped by sense. Thus, as I have said, it is easy to see how imagination works, if we suppose that my body exists. And, since I don't have in mind any other equally plausible explanation of imagination, I conjecture that physical objects probably do exist. But this conjecture is only probable. Despite my careful and thorough investigation, the distinct idea of bodily nature that comes from the imagination does not seem to have anything in it from which I can validly infer that physical objects exist.

Besides having a mental image of the bodily nature that is the subject of pure mathematics, I have mental images of such things as colors, sounds, flavors, and pains—but these images are not very distinct. I seem to grasp these things better by sense, from which they seem to come (with the aid of memory) to the understanding. It therefore seems appropriate to deal with these things in the context of an examination of the senses and to see whether there is something in the mode of awareness that I call *sensation* from which I can draw a conclusive argument for the existence of physical objects.

First, I will remind myself of the things that I believed really to be as I perceived them and of the grounds for my belief. Next, I will set out the grounds on which I later called this belief into doubt. And, finally, I will consider what I ought to think now.

To begin with, I sensed that I had a head, hands, feet, and the other members that make up a human body. I viewed this body as part, or maybe even as all, of me. I sensed that it was influenced by other physical objects whose affects could be either beneficial or harmful—beneficial to the extent that I felt pleasant sensations and harmful to the extent that I

felt pain. In addition to sensations of pain and pleasure, I sensed hunger, thirst, and other such desires—and also bodily inclinations towards cheerfulness, sadness, and other emotions. Outside me, I sensed, not just extension, shape, and motion, but also hardness, hotness, and other qualities detected by touch. I also sensed light, color, odor, taste, and sound—qualities by whose variation I distinguished such things as the sky, earth, and sea from one another.

In view of these ideas of qualities (which presented themselves to my thought and were all that I really sensed directly) I had some reason for believing that I sensed objects distinct from my thought—physical objects from which the ideas came. For I found that these ideas came to me independently of my desires so that, however much I tried, I couldn't sense an object when it wasn't present to an organ to sense or fail to sense one when it was present. And, since the ideas that I grasped by sense were much livelier, more explicit, and (in their own way) more distinct than those I deliberately created or found impressed in my memory, it seemed that these ideas could not have come from me and that they must therefore have come from something else. Having no conception of these things other than the one suggested by my ideas, I could only think that the things resembled the ideas. Indeed, since I remembered using my senses before my reason, since I found the ideas that I created in myself to be less explicit than those grasped by sense, and since I found the ideas that I created to be composed largely of those that I had grasped by sense, I easily convinced myself that I didn't understand anything at all unless I had first sensed it.

I also had some reason for supposing that a certain physical object, which I view as belonging to me in a special way, is related to me more closely than any other. I can't be separated from it as I can from other physical objects; I feel all of my emotions and desires in it and because of it; and I am aware of pains and pleasant feelings in it but nothing else. I don't know *why* sadness goes with the sensation of pain, or *why* joy goes with sensory stimulation. I don't know *why* the stomach twitchings that I call hunger warn me that I need to eat or *why* dryness in my throat warns me that I need to drink. Seeing no connection between stomach twitchings and the desire to eat or between the sensation of a pain-producing thing and the consequent awareness of sadness, I can only say that I have been taught the connection by nature. And nature seems also to have taught me everything else that I knew about the objects of sensation—for I convinced myself that the sensations came to me in a certain way before having found grounds on which to prove that they did.

But, since then, many experiences have shaken my faith in the senses. Towers that seemed round from a distance sometimes looked square from close up, and huge statues on pediments sometimes did not look big when seen from the ground. In innumerable such cases, I found the judgments of the external senses to be wrong. And the same holds for the internal senses. What is felt more inwardly than pain? But I had heard that people with amputated arms and legs sometimes seem to feel pain in the missing limb, and it therefore didn't seem perfectly certain to me that the limb in which *I* feel a pain is always the one that hurts. And, to these grounds for doubt, I have recently added two that are very general: First, since I didn't believe myself to sense anything while awake that I couldn't also take myself to sense in a dream, and since I didn't believe that what I sense in sleep comes from objects outside me, I didn't see why I should believe what I sense while awake comes from such objects. Second, since I didn't yet know my creator (or, rather, since I supposed that I didn't know Him) nothing ruled out my having been so designed by nature that I am deceived even in that which seems most obviously true to me.

And I could easily reply to the reasoning by which I convinced myself of the reality of sensible things. Since my nature seemed to impel me towards many judgments which my reason rejected, I didn't believe that I ought to have much faith in nature's teachings. And, while my will didn't control my sense perceptions, I didn't believe it to follow that these perceptions came from outside me, since I thought that the ability to produce these ideas might have been in me without my being aware of it.

Now that I have begun to know myself and my creator better, I still believe that I oughtn't blindly to accept everything that I seem to get from the senses. But I no longer believe that I ought to call it all into doubt.

In the first place, I know that everything that I clearly and distinctly understand can be made by God to be exactly as I understand it. The fact that I can clearly and distinctly understand one thing apart from another is therefore enough to make me certain that it *is* distinct from the other, since the things could be separated by God if not by something else. (I judge the things to be distinct regardless of the power needed to make them exist separately.) Accordingly, from the fact that I have gained knowledge of my existence without noticing anything about my nature or essence except that I am a thinking thing, I can rightly conclude that my essence consists solely in the fact that I am a thinking thing. It's possible (or, as I will say later, it's certain) that I have a body which is very tightly bound to me. But, on the other hand, I have a clear and distinct idea of myself insofar as I am just a thinking and unextended thing, and, on the other hand, I have a distinct idea of my body insofar as it is just an extended and unthinking thing. It's certain, then, that I am really distinct from my body and can exist without it.

Moreover, I find in myself abilities for special modes of awareness, such as the abilities to have mental images and to sense. I can clearly and distinctly conceive of my whole self as something that lacks these abilities, but I can't conceive of the abilities existing without me, or without an understanding substance in which to reside. Since the conception of these abilities includes the conception of something that understands, I see that these abilities are distinct from me in the way that a thing's properties are distinct from the thing itself.

I recognize other abilities in me, such as the ability to move around and to assume various postures. These abilities can't be understood to exist apart from a substance in which they reside any more than the abilities to imagine and sense, and they therefore cannot exist without such a substance. But it's obvious that, if these abilities do exist, the substance in which they reside must be a body or extended substance rather than an understanding one, for the clear and distinct conceptions of these abilities contain extension but not understanding.

There is also in me, however, a passive ability to sense—to receive and recognize ideas of sensible things. I wouldn't be able to put this ability to use if there weren't—either in me or in something else—an active power to produce or make sensory ideas. But, since this active power does not presuppose understanding, and since it often produces ideas in me without my cooperation and even against my will, it cannot exist in me. Therefore this power must exist in a substance distinct from me. And, for reasons that I have noted, this substance must contain, either formally or eminently, all the reality that is contained presentationally in the ideas that the power produces. Accordingly, this substance must be either a physical object (which contains formally the reality that the idea contains presentationally), or one of God's creations that is higher than physical objects (which contains this reality eminently), or God himself. But, since God isn't a deceiver, it's completely obvious that He doesn't send these ideas to me directly or by means of a creation which contains their reality eminently rather than formally. For, since He has not given me any ability to recognize that these ideas are sent by Him or by creations other than physical objects, and since He has given me a strong inclination to believe that the ideas come from physical objects, there would be no way to avoid the conclusion that He deceives me if the ideas were sent to me by anything other than physical objects. Therefore physical objects exist. These objects may not exist exactly as I comprehend them by sense; in many ways, sensory comprehension is obscure and confused. But these objects must at least have in them everything that I clearly and distinctly understand them to have—every general property within the scope of pure mathematics.

But what about particular properties, such as the size and shape of the sun? And what about things that I understand less clearly than general mathematical properties—things like light, sound, and pain? These are open to doubt. But, since God isn't a deceiver, and since I therefore have the God-given ability to correct any falsity that may be in my beliefs, I have high hopes of finding the truth about even these things. There is undoubtedly some truth in everything I have been taught by nature—for, when I use the term "nature" in its general sense, I refer to God or to the order that He has established in the created world, and, when I apply the term specifically to *my* nature, I refer to the collection of everything that God has given *me*.

Nature teaches me nothing more explicitly, however, than that I have a body which is hurt when I feel pain, which needs food or drink when I experience hunger or thirst, and so on. And, accordingly,

I ought not to doubt that there is some truth to the thought that I have a body.

Nature also teaches me—through sensations like pain, hunger, and thirst—that I am not present in my body in the way that a sailor is present in his ship. Rather, I am very tightly bound to my body and so "mixed up" with it that we form a single thing. If this weren't so, I—who am just a thinking thing—wouldn't feel pain when my body was injured; I would perceive the injury by pure understanding in the way that a sailor sees the leaks in his ship with his eyes. And, when my body needed food or drink, I would explicitly understand that the need existed without having the confused sensations of hunger and thirst. For the sensations of thirst, hunger, and pain are just confused modifications of thought arising from the union and "mixture" of mind and body.

Moreover, nature teaches me that there are other physical objects around my body—some that I ought to seek and others that I ought to avoid. From the fact that I sense colors, sounds, odors, flavors, and temperatures, I correctly infer that sense perceptions come from physical objects which vary as widely (though perhaps not in the same way) as the perceptions do. And, from the fact that some of these perceptions are pleasant while others are unpleasant. I infer with certainty that my body—or, rather, my whole self which consists of a body and a mind—can be benefited and harmed by the physical objects around it.

There are many other things which I *seem* to have been taught by nature, but which I have really accepted out of a habit of thoughtless judgment and which therefore may well be false. Among these things are the judgments that a space is empty if nothing in it happens to affect my senses, that a hot physical object has something in it resembling my idea of heat, that a white or green thing has in it the same whiteness or greenness that I sense, that a bitter or sweet thing has in it the same flavor that I taste, and the stars, towers, and other physical objects have the same size and shape that they show to my senses.

If I am to avoid accepting what is indistinct in these cases, I must more carefully explain my use of the phrase "taught by nature." In particular, I should say that I am now using the term "nature" in a narrower sense than when I took it to refer to the whole complex of what God has given me. This complex includes much having to do with my mind alone (such as my grasp of the fact that what is done cannot be undone and of the rest of what I know by the light of nature) which does not bear on what I am now saying. And the complex also includes much having to do with my body alone (such as its tendency to go downwards) that I also am not now dealing with. I am now using the term "nature" to refer only to what God has given me insofar as I am composite of mind and body. This nature teaches me to avoid that which occasions painful sensations, to seek that which occasions pleasant sensations, and so on, but it seems *not* to teach me to draw conclusions about external objects from sense perceptions without first having examined the matter with my understanding—for true knowledge of external things seems to belong to the mind alone, rather than to the composite of mind and body.

Thus, while a star has no more effect on my eye than a flame does, I do not have a real, positive inclination to believe that the star is as small as the flame; my youthful judgment to the contrary was not based on reason. And, while I feel heat when I approach a fire and pain when I draw nearer, I have absolutely no reason for believing that something in the fire resembles the heat, just as I have no reason for believing that something in the fire resembles the pain; I only have reason for believing that *something* in the fire produces the ideas of heat and pain in me. And, while there may be nothing in a given region of space that affects my senses, it doesn't follow that there are no physical objects in that space. Rather, I now see that, on these matters and others, I used to pervert the natural order of things. For, while nature has given sense perceptions to my mind for the sole purpose of indicating what is beneficial and what harmful to the composite of which my mind is a part, and while the perceptions are sufficiently clear and distinct for this purpose, I used these perceptions as standards for identifying the essence of physical objects—an essence which they only reveal obscurely and confusedly.

I have already explained how it can be that, despite God's goodness, my judgments can be false. But a new difficulty arises here—one having to do with the things that nature presents to me as desirable or undesirable and with the errors that I seem to have found in my internal sensations. One of these

errors seems to be committed, for example, when a man is fooled by some food's pleasant taste into eating poison hidden in that food. But surely, in this case, what the man's nature impels him to eat is the good tasting food, not the poison of which he knows nothing. We can draw no conclusion except that his nature isn't omniscient, and this conclusion isn't surprising: since a man is a limited thing, he can only have limited perfections.

Still, we often err in things towards which nature *does* impel us. This happens, for example, when sick people want food or drink that would quickly harm them. To say that these people err as a result of the corruption of their nature does not solve the problem—for a sick man is no less a creation of God than a well one, and it seems as absurd to suppose that God has given him a deceptive nature. A clock made of wheels and weights follows the natural laws just as precisely when it is poorly made and inaccurate as when it does everything that its maker wants. Thus, if we regard a human body as a machine made up of bones, nerves, muscles, veins, blood, and skin, and if we notice that a body without a mind in it would do just the things that it does now (except for those that require a mind because they are commanded by the will), it is easy to see that what happens to a sick man is no less "natural" than what happens to a well one. For instance, if a body suffers from dropsy, it has a dry throat of the sort that regularly brings the sensation of thirst to the mind, the dryness disposes the nerves and other organs to drink, and the drinking makes the illness worse. But this is just as natural as when a similar dryness of throat moves a person who is perfectly healthy to take a drink that is beneficial.

Bearing in mind my conception of a clock's use, I might say that an inaccurate clock departs from its nature. And, similarly, viewing the machine of the human body as designed for working as it usually does, I can say that it drifts away from its nature if it has a dry throat when drinking will not help to maintain it. I should note, however, that the sense in which I am now using the term "nature" differs from that in which I used it before. For, as I have just used the term, the *nature* of a man (or clock) is something that depends on my thinking of the difference between a sick and a well man (or of the difference between a poorly made and a well-made clock)—something that is regarded as *extrinsic* to the things. But, when I used "nature" before, I referred to something which is *in* things and which therefore has some reality.

It may be that we just offer an extrinsic description of a body suffering from dropsy when, noting that it has a dry throat but doesn't need to drink, we say that its nature is corrupted. Still, the description is not purely extrinsic when we say that a composite or union of mind and body has a corrupted nature: there is a real fault in the composite's nature, for it is thirsty when drinking is harmful to it. It therefore remains to be asked why God's goodness doesn't prevent *this* nature's being deceptive.

To begin the answer, I will note that mind differs importantly from body in that body is by its nature divisible, while mind is indivisible. When I think about my mind—or, in other words, about myself insofar as I am just a thinking thing—I can't distinguish any parts; I understand myself to be a single, unified thing. Although my whole mind seems united to my whole body, I know that cutting off a foot, arm, or other limb would not take anything away from my mind. And the abilities to will, sense, understand can't be called parts, since it is one and the same mind that wills, senses, and understands. On the other hand, whenever I think of a physical or extended thing, I can mentally divide it, and I therefore understand that the object is divisible. This single fact would be enough to teach me that my mind and my body are distinct, if I hadn't already gained that knowledge.

Next, I notice that the mind isn't directly affected by all parts of the body, but only by the brain—or maybe just by the small part of the brain containing the so-called "common sense." Whenever this part of the brain is in a given state, it exhibits the same thing to the mind, regardless of what is happening in the rest of the body (as is shown by innumerable experiments that I need not review here).

Moreover, I notice that the nature of body is such that, if a first part can be moved by a second that is far away, the first part can be moved in exactly the same way by something between the first and second without the second part's being affected. For example, if A, B, C, and D are points on a cord, and if the first point (A) can be moved in a certain way by a pull on the last point (D), then A can be moved in the same way by a pull on one of the middle points (B or C) without D's being moved. Similarly, science teaches me that, when my foot hurts, the sensation of pain is produced by nerves distributed throughout the foot which extend like a cord from there to the brain. When pulled in the foot, these nerves pull the central parts of the brain to which they are attached, moving those parts in ways designated by nature to present the mind with the sensation of a pain "in the foot." Since these nerves pass through the shins, thighs, hips, back, and neck on their way from foot to brain, it can happen that their being touched in the middle, rather than at the end in the foot, produces the same motion in the brain as when the foot is hurt and, consequently, that the mind feels the same pain "in the foot." And the point holds for other sensations as well.

Finally, I notice that, since only one sensation can be produced by a given motion of the part of the brain that directly affects the mind, the best conceivable sensation for it to produce is the one that is most often useful for the maintenance of the healthy man. Experience teaches, however, that all the sensations put in us by nature *are* of this sort and therefore that there is nothing in our sensations which doesn't testify to God's power and goodness. For example, when the nerves in the foot are moved with unusual violence, the motion is communicated through the middle of the spine to the center of the brain, where it signals the mind to sense a pain "in the foot." This urges the mind to view the pain's cause as harmful to the foot and to do what it can to remove the cause. Of course, God could have so designed man's nature that the same motion of the brain showed the mind something else (such as itself as a motion in the brain, or as a motion in the foot, or as a motion somewhere between the brain and foot), but no alternative to the way things are would be as conducive to the maintenance of the body. Similarly, when we need drink, the throat becomes dry, the dryness moves the nerves of the throat thereby moving the center of the brain, and the brain's movements cause the sensation of thirst in the mind. It's the sensation of thirst that is produced, because no information about our condition is more useful to us than that we need to get something to drink in order to remain healthy. And the same is true in other cases.

This makes it completely obvious that, despite

God's immense goodness, the nature of man (whom we now view as a composite of mind and body) cannot fail to be deceptive. For, if something produces the movement usually associated with a bad foot in the nerve running from foot to brain or in the brain itself (rather than in the foot), a pain is felt "in the foot," and the senses are deceived by my nature. Since this motion in the brain must always bring the same sensation to mind, and since the motion's cause more often *is* something hurting the foot than something elsewhere, it is in accordance with reason that the motion always shows the mind a pain in the foot rather than elsewhere. And, if dryness of the throat arises, not (as usual) from drink's being conducive to the body's health, but (as happens in dropsy) from some other cause, it is much better that we are deceived than that we are generally deceived when our bodies are sound. And so on for other sensations.

In addition to helping me to be aware of the errors to which my nature is subject, these reflections help me readily to correct or avoid those errors. I know that sensory indications of what is good for my body are more often true than false; I can almost always examine a given thing with several senses; and I can also use my memory (which connects the present to the past) and my understanding (which has now ascertained all the causes of error). Hence, I need no longer fear that what the senses daily show me is unreal. I should reject the exaggerated doubts of the past few days as ridiculous. This is especially true of the chief ground for these doubts—namely, that I couldn't distinguish dreaming from being awake—for I now notice that dreaming and being awake are importantly different: the events in dreams are not linked by memory to the rest of my life like those that happen while I am awake. If, while I am awake, someone were suddenly to appear and then immediately to disappear without my seeing where he came from or went to (as happens in dreams), I would justifiably judge that he was not a real man, but a ghost—or, better, an apparition created in my brain. But, if I distinctly observe something's source, its place, and the time at which I learn about it, and if I grasp an unbroken connection between it and the rest of my life, I am quite sure that it is something in my waking life rather than in a dream. And I ought not to have the slightest doubt about the reality of such things, if I have examined them with all my senses, my memory, and my understanding without finding any conflicting evidence. For, from the fact that God is not a deceiver, it follows that I am not deceived in any case of this sort. Since the need to act does not always allow time for such a careful examination, however, we must admit the likelihood of men's erring about particular things and acknowledge the weakness of our nature.

Some Further Considerations Concerning Our Simple Ideas of Sensation

JOHN LOCKE

John Locke (1632–1704) was one of the greatest and most influential of English philosophers. His works include *An Essay Concerning Human Understanding* and *Two Treatises on Civil Government*.

———•———

1. Concerning the simple ideas of Sensation, it is to be considered,—that whatsoever is so constituted in nature as to be able, by affecting our senses, to cause any perception in the mind, doth thereby produce in the understanding a simple idea; which, whatever be the external cause of it, when it comes to be taken notice of by our discerning faculty, it is

From *An Essay Concerning Human Understanding* (Oxford: Clarendon Press, 1894), pp. 166–82.

by the mind looked on and considered there to be a real positive idea in the understanding, as much as any other whatsoever; though, perhaps, the cause of it be but a privation of the subject.

2. Thus the ideas of heat and cold, light and darkness, white and black, motion and rest, are equally clear and positive ideas in the mind; though, perhaps, some of the causes which produce them are barely privations, in those subjects from whence our senses derive those ideas. These the understanding, in its view of them, considers all as distinct positive ideas, without taking notice of the causes that produce them: which is an inquiry not belonging to the idea, as it is in the understanding, but to the nature of the things existing without us. These are two very different things, and carefully to be distinguished; it being one thing to perceive and know the idea of white or black, and quite another to examine what kind of particles they must be, and how ranged in the superficies, to make any object appear white or black.

3. A painter or dyer who never inquired into their causes hath the ideas of white and black, and other colours, as clearly, perfectly, and distinctly in his understanding, and perhaps more distinctly, than the philosopher who hath busied himself in considering their natures, and thinks he knows how far either of them is, in its cause, positive or privative; and the idea of black is no less positive in his mind than that of white, however the cause of that colour in the external object may be only a privation.

4. If it were the design of my present undertaking to inquire into the natural causes and manner of perception, I should offer this as a reason why a privative cause might, in some cases at least, produce a positive idea; viz. that all sensation being produced in us only by different degrees and modes of motion in our animal spirits, variously agitated by external objects, the abatement of any former motion must as necessarily produce a new sensation as the variation or increase of it; and so introduce a new idea, which depends only on a different motion of the animal spirits in that organ.

5. But whether this be so or not I will not here determine, but appeal to every one's own experience, whether the shadow of a man, though it con-

sists of nothing but the absence of light (and the more the absence of light is, the more discernible is the shadow) does not, when a man looks on it, cause as clear and positive idea in his mind, as a man himself, though covered over with clear sunshine? And the picture of a shadow is a positive thing. Indeed, we have negative names, which stand not directly for positive ideas, but for their absence, such as *insipid*, *silence*, *nihil*, etc.; which words denote positive ideas, v.g. *taste*, *sound*, *being*, with a signification of their absence.

6. And thus one may truly be said to see darkness. For, supposing a hole perfectly dark, from whence no light is reflected, it is certain one may see the figure of it, or it may be painted; or whether the ink I write with makes any other idea, is a question. The privative causes I have here assigned of positive ideas are according to the common opinion; but, in truth, it will be hard to determine whether there be really any ideas from a privative cause, till it be determined, whether rest be any more a privation than motion.

7. To discover the nature of our *ideas* the better, and to discourse of them intelligibly, it will be convenient to distinguish them *as they are ideas or perceptions in our minds*; and *as they are modifications of matter in the bodies that cause such perceptions in us*: that so we may not think (as perhaps usually is done) that they are exactly the images and resemblances of something inherent in the subject; most of those of sensation being in the mind no more the likeness of something existing without us, than the names that stand for them are the likeness of our ideas, which yet upon hearing they are apt to excite in us.

8. Whatsoever the mind perceives *in itself*, or is the immediate object of perception, thought, or understanding, that I call *idea*; and the power to produce any idea in our mind, I call *quality* of the subject wherein that power is. Thus a snowball having the power to produce in us the ideas of white, cold, and round,—the power to produce those ideas in us, as they are in the snowball, I call qualities; and as they are sensations or perceptions in our understandings, I call them ideas; which *ideas*, if I speak of sometimes as in the things themselves, I would be understood to mean those qualities in the objects which produce them in us.

9. Qualities thus considered in bodies are,

First, such as are utterly inseparable from the body, in what state soever it be; and such as in all the alterations and changes it suffers, all the force can be used upon it, it constantly keeps; and such as sense constantly finds in every particle of matter which has bulk enough to be perceived; and the mind finds inseparable from every particle of matter, though less than to make itself singly be perceived by our senses: v.g. Take a grain of wheat, divide it into two parts; each part has still solidity, extension, figure, and mobility: divide it again, and it retains still the same qualities; and so divide it on, till the parts become insensible; they must retain still each of them all those qualities. For division (which is all that a mill, or pestle, or any other body, does upon another, in reducing it to insensible parts) can never take away either solidity, extension, figure, or mobility from any body, but only makes two or more distinct separate masses of matter, of that which was but one before; all which distinct masses, reckoned as so many distinct bodies, after division, make a certain number. These I call *original* or *primary qualities* of body, which I think we may observe to produce simple ideas in us, viz. solidity, extension, figure, motion or rest, and number.

10. *Secondly*, such qualities which in truth are nothing in the objects themselves but powers to produce various sensations in us by their primary qualities, i.e. by the bulk, figure, texture, and motion of their insensible parts, as colours, sounds, tastes, etc. These I call *secondary qualities*. To these might be added a *third* sort, which are allowed to be barely powers; though they are as much real qualities in the subject as those which I, to comply with the common way of speaking, call qualities, but for distinction, secondary qualities. For the power in fire to produce a new colour, or consistency, in *wax* or *clay*,—by its primary qualities, is as much a quality in fire, as the power it has to produce in *me* a new idea or sensation of warmth or burning, which I felt not before,—by the same primary qualities, viz. the bulk, texture, and motion of its insensible parts.

11. The next thing to be considered is, how bodies produce ideas in us; and that is manifestly by impulse, the only way which we can conceive bodies to operate in.

12. If then external objects be not united to our minds when they produce ideas therein; and yet we perceive these *original* qualities in such of them as singly fall under our senses, it is evident that some motion must be thence continued by our nerves, or animal spirits, by some parts of our bodies, to the brains or the seat of sensation, there to produce in our minds the particular ideas we have of them. And since the extension, figure, number, and motion of bodies of an observable bigness, may be perceived at a distance by the sight, it is evident some singly imperceptible bodies must come from them to the eyes, and thereby convey to the brain some motion; which produces these ideas which we have of them in us.

13. After the same manner that the ideas of these original qualities are produced in us, we may conceive that the ideas of *secondary* qualities are also produced, viz. by the operation of insensible particles on our senses. For, it being manifest that there are bodies and good store of bodies, each whereof are so small, that we cannot by any of our senses discover either their bulk, figure, or motion,—as is evident in the particles of the air and water, and others extremely smaller than those; perhaps as much smaller than the particles of air and water, as the particles of air and water are smaller than peas or hail-stones;— let us suppose at present that the different motions and figures, bulk and number, of such particles, affecting the several organs of our senses, produce in us those different sensations which we have from the colours and smells of bodies; v.g. that a violet, by the impulse of such insensible particles of matter, of peculiar figures and bulks, and in different degrees and modifications of their motions, causes the ideas of the blue colour, and sweet scent of that flower to be produced in our minds. It being no more impossible to conceive that God should annex such ideas to such motions, with which they have no similitude, than that he should annex the idea of pain to the motion of a piece of steel dividing our flesh, with which that idea hath no resemblance.

14. What I have said concerning colours and smells may be understood also of tastes and sounds, and other the like sensible qualities; which, whatever reality we by mistake attribute to them, are in truth nothing in the objects themselves, but powers to produce various sensations in us; and depend on those primary qualities, viz. bulk, figure, texture, and motion of parts as I have said.

15. From whence I think it easy to draw this observation,—that the ideas of primary qualities of bodies are resemblances of them, and their patterns do really exist in the bodies themselves, but the ideas produced in us by these secondary qualities have no resemblance of them at all. There is nothing like our ideas, existing in the bodies themselves. There are, in the bodies we denominate from them, only a power to produce those sensations in us: and what is sweet, blue, or warm in idea, is but the certain bulk, figure, and motion of the insensible parts, in the bodies themselves, which we call so.

16. Flame is denominated hot and light; snow, white and cold; and manna, white and sweet, from the ideas they produce in us. Which qualities are commonly thought to be the same in those bodies that those ideas are in us, the one the perfect resemblance of the other, as they are in a mirror, and it would by most men be judged very extravagant if one should say otherwise. And yet he that will consider that the same fire that, at one distance produces in us the sensation of warmth, does, at a nearer approach, produce in us the far different sensation of pain, ought to bethink himself what reason he has to say—that this idea of warmth, which was produced in him by the fire, is *actually in the fire*; and his idea of pain, which the same fire produced in him the same way, is *not* in the fire. Why are whiteness and coldness in snow, and pain not, when it produces the one and the other idea in us; and can do neither, but by the bulk, figure, number, and motion of its solid parts?

17. The particular bulk, number, figure, and motion of the parts of fire or snow are really in them,—whether any one's senses perceive them or no: and therefore they may be called *real* qualities, because they really exist in those bodies. But light, heat, whiteness, or coldness, are no more really in them than sickness or pain is in manna. Take away the sensation of them; let not the eyes see light or colours, nor the ears hear sounds; let the palate not taste, nor the nose smell, and all colours, tastes, odours, and sounds, *as they are such particular ideas*, vanish and cease, and are reduced to their causes, i.e., bulk, figure, and motion of parts.

18. A piece of manna of a sensible bulk is able to produce in us the idea of a round or square figure; and by being removed from one place to another, the idea of motion. This idea of motion represents it as it really is in manna moving: a circle or square are the same, whether in idea or existence, in the mind or in the manna. And this, both motion and figure, are really in the manna, whether we take notice of them or no: this everybody is ready to agree to. Besides, manna, by the bulk, figure, texture, and motion of its parts, has a power to produce the sensations of sickness, and sometimes of acute pains or gripings in us. That these ideas of sickness and pain are *not* in the manna, but effects of its operations on us, and are nowhere when we feel them not; this also every one readily agrees to. And yet men are hardly to be brought to think that sweetness and whiteness are not really in manna; which are but the effects of the operations of manna, by the motion, size, and figure of its particles, on the eyes and palate: as the pain and sickness caused by manna are confessedly nothing but the effects of its operations on the stomach and guts, by the size, motion, and figure of its insensible parts, (for by nothing else can a body operate, as has been proved): as if it could not operate on the eyes and palate, and thereby produce in the mind particular distinct ideas, which in itself it has not, as well as we allow it can operate on the guts and stomach, and thereby produce distinct ideas, which in itself it has not. These ideas, being all effects of the operations of manna on several parts of our bodies, by the size, figure, number, and motion of its parts;—why those produced by the eyes and palate should rather be thought to be really in the manna, than those produced by the stomach and guts; or why the pain and sickness, ideas that are the effect of manna, should be thought to be nowhere when they are not felt; and yet the sweetness and whiteness, effects of the same manna on other parts of the body, by ways equally as unknown, should be thought to exist in the manna, when they are not seen or tasted, would need some reason to explain.

19. Let us consider red and white colours in porphyry. Hinder light from striking on it, and its colours vanish; it no longer produces any such ideas in us: upon the return of light it produces these appearances on us again. Can any one think any real alterations are made in the prophyry by the presence or absence of light; and that those ideas of whiteness and redness are really in porphyry in the light, when it is plain *it has no colour in the dark?* It has, indeed, such a configuration of particles, both night and day, as are apt, by the rays of light rebounding from some parts of that hard stone, to produce in us the idea of redness, and from others the idea of whiteness; but whiteness or redness are not in it at any time, but such a texture that hath the power to produce such a sensation in us.

20. Pound an almond, and the clear white colour will be altered into a dirty one, and the sweet taste into an oily one. What real alteration can the beating of the pestle make in any body, but an alteration of the texture of it?

21. Ideas being thus distinguished and understood, we may be able to give an account how the same water, at the same time, may produce the idea of cold by one hand and of heat by the other: whereas it is impossible that the same water, if those ideas were really in it, should at the same time be both hot and cold. For, if we imagine *warmth*, as it is in our hands, to be nothing but a certain sort and degree of motion in the minute particles of our nerves or animal spirits, we may understand how it is possible that the same water may, at the same time, produce the sensations of heat in one hand cold in the other; which yet *figure* never does, that never producing the idea of a square by one hand which has produced the idea of a globe by another. But if the sensation of heat and cold be nothing but the increase or diminution of the motion of the minute parts of our bodies, caused by the corpuscles of any other body, it is easy to be understood, that if that motion be greater in one hand than in the other; if a body be applied to the two hands, which has in its minute particles a greater motion than in those of one of the hands, and a less than in those of the other, it will increase the motion of the one hand and lessen it in the other; and so cause the different sensations of heat and cold that depend thereon.

22. I have in what just goes before been engaged in physical inquiries a little further than perhaps I intended. But, it being necessary to make the nature of sensation a little understood; and to make the difference between the *qualities* in bodies, and the *ideas* produced by them in the mind, to be distinctly conceived, without which it were impossible to discourse intelligibly of them;—I hope I shall be pardoned this little excursion into natural philosophy; it being necessary in our present inquiry to distinguish the *primary* and *real* qualities of bodies, which are always in them (viz. solidity, extension, figure, number, and motion, or rest, and are sometimes perceived by us, viz. when the bodies they are in are big enough singly to be discerned), from those *secondary* and *imputed* qualities, which are but the powers of several combinations of those primary ones, when they operate without being distinctly discerned;—whereby we may also come to know what ideas are, and what are not, resemblances of something really existing in the bodies we denominate from them.

23. The qualities, then, that are in bodies, rightly considered, are of three sorts:—

First, The bulk, figure, number, situation, and motion or rest of their solid parts. Those are in them, whether we perceive them or not; and when they are of that size that we can discover them, we have by these an idea of the thing as it is in itself; as is plain in artificial things. These I call *primary qualities.*

Secondly, The power that is in any body, by reason of its insensible primary qualities, to operate after a peculiar manner on any of our senses, and thereby produce in *us* the different ideas of several colours, sounds, smells, tastes, etc. These are usually called *sensible qualities.*

Thirdly, The power that is in any body, by reason of the particular constitution of its primary qualities, to make such a change in the bulk, figure, texture, and motion of *another body*, as to make it operate on our senses differently from what it did before. Thus the sun has a power to make wax white, and fire to make lead fluid. These are usually called *powers.*

The first of these, as has been said, I think may be properly called real, original, or primary qualities; because they are in the things themselves, whether they are perceived or not: and upon their different modifications it is that the secondary qualities depend.

The other two are only powers to act differently

upon other things: which powers result from the different modifications of those primary qualities.

24. But, though the two latter sorts of qualities are powers barely, and nothing but powers, relating to several other bodies, and resulting from the different modifications of the original qualities, yet they are generally otherwise thought of. For the *second* sort, viz. the powers to produce several ideas in us, by our senses, are looked upon as real qualities in the things thus affecting us: but the *third* sort are called and esteemed barely powers. . . . The idea of heat or light, which we receive by our eyes, or touch, from the sun, are commonly thought real qualities existing in the sun, and something more than mere powers in it. But when we consider the sun in reference to wax, which it melts or blanches, we look on the whiteness and softness produced in the wax, not as qualities in the sun, but effects produced by powers in it. Whereas, if rightly considered, these qualities of light and warmth, which are perceptions in me when I am warmed or enlightened by the sun, are no [more] in the sun, than the changes made in the wax, when it is blanched or melted, are in the sun. They are all of them equally *powers in the sun*, *depending on its primary qualities*; whereby it is able, in the one case, so to alter the bulk, figure, texture, or motion of some of the insensible parts of my eyes or hands, as thereby to produce in me the idea of light or heat; and in the other, it is able so to alter the bulk, figure, texture, or motion of the insensible parts of the wax, as to make them fit to produce in me the distinct ideas of white and fluid.

25. The reason why the one are ordinarily taken for real qualities, and the other only for bare powers, seems to be, because the ideas we have of distinct colours, sounds, etc., containing nothing at all in them of bulk, figure, or motion, we are not apt to think them the effects of these primary qualities; which appear not, to our senses, to operate in their production, and with which they have not any apparent congruity or conceivable connexion. Hence it is that we are so forward to imagine, that those ideas are the resemblances of something really existing in the objects themselves: since sensation discovers nothing of bulk, figure, or motion of parts in

their production; nor can reason show how bodies, *by their bulk, figure and motion*, should produce in the mind the ideas of blue or yellow, etc. But, in the other case, in the operations of bodies changing the qualities one of another, we plainly discover that the quality produced hath commonly no resemblance with anything in the thing producing it; wherefore we look on it as a bare effect of power. For, through receiving the idea of heat or light from the sun, we are apt to think *it* is a perception and resemblance of such a quality in the sun; yet when we see wax, or a fair face, receive change of colour from the sun, we cannot imagine *that* to be the reception of resemblance of anything in the sun, because we find not those different colours in the sun itself. For, one senses being able to observe a likeness or unlikeness of sensible qualities in two different external objects, we forwardly enough conclude the production of any sensible quality in any subject to be an effect of bare power, and not the communication of any quality which was really in the efficient, when we find no such sensible quality in the thing that produced it. But our senses, not being able to discover any unlikeness between the idea produced in us, and the quality of the object producing it, we are apt to imagine that our ideas are resemblances of something in the objects, and not the effects of certain powers placed in the modification of the primary qualities, with which primary qualities the ideas produced in us have no resemblance.

26. To conclude. Beside those before-mentioned primary qualities in bodies, viz. bulk, figure, extension, number, and motion of their solid parts; all the rest, whereby we take notice of bodies, and distinguish them one from another, are nothing else but several powers in them, depending on those primary qualities; whereby they are fitted, either by immediately operating on our bodies to produce several different ideas in us; or else, by operating on other bodies, so to change their primary qualities as to render them capable of producing ideas in us different from what before they did. The former of these, I think, may be called secondary qualities *immediately perceivable*: the latter, secondary qualities, *mediately perceivable*.

Three Dialogues Between Hylas and Philonous

GEORGE BERKELEY

The design of which is plainly to demonstrate the reality and perfection of human knowledge, the incorporeal nature of the soul, and the immediate providence of a Deity: in opposition to the Sceptics and Atheists. Also to open a method for rendering the Sciences more easy, useful, and compendious.

George Berkeley (1685–1753) was Bishop of Cloyne. His works are classics of empiricism that have provoked admiration and frustration from generations of philosophy students. He wrote a number of works in addition to the *Three Dialogues*, including *A Treatise Concerning the Principles of Human Knowledge* and *An Essay Towards a New Theory of Vision.*

The First Dialogue

PHILONOUS: Good morrow, Hylas: I did not expect to find you abroad so early.

HYLAS: It is indeed something unusual; but my thoughts were so taken up with a subject I was discoursing of last night, that finding I could not sleep, I resolved to rise and take a turn in the garden.

PHIL: It happened well, to let you see what innocent and agreeable pleasures you lose every morning. Can there be a pleasanter time of the day, or a more delightful season of the year? That purple sky, those wild but sweet notes of birds, the fragrant bloom upon the trees and flowers, the gentle influence of the rising sun, these and a thousand nameless beauties of nature inspire the soul with secret transports; its faculties too being at this time fresh and lively, are fit for those meditations, which the solitude of a garden and tranquillity of the morning naturally dispose us to. But I am afraid I interrupt your thoughts: for you seemed very intent on something.

HYL: It is true, I was, and shall be obliged to you if you will permit me to go on in the same vein; not that I would by any means deprive myself of your company, for my thoughts always flow more easily in conversation with a friend, than when I am alone: but my request is that you would suffer me to impart my reflexions to you.

PHIL: With all my heart, it is what I should have requested myself if you had not prevented me.

HYL: I was considering the odd fate of those men who have in all ages, through an affectation of being distinguished from the vulgar, or some unaccountable turn of thought, pretended either to believe nothing at all, or to believe the most extravagant things in the world. This however might be borne, if their paradoxes and scepticism did not draw after them some consequences of general disadvantage to mankind. But the mischief lieth here; that when men of less leisure see them who are supposed to have spent their whole time in the pursuits of knowledge professing an entire ignorance of all things, or advancing such notions as are repugnant to plain and commonly received principles, they will be tempted to entertain suspicions, concerning the most important truths, which they had hitherto held sacred and unquestionable.

PHIL: I entirely agree with you, as to the ill tendency of the affected doubts of some philoso-

From *The Works of George Berkeley*, edited by A. Campbell Fraser (Oxford: Oxford University Press, 1901), Vol. 1, pp. 379–428, 442–52, 463–70, 480–85.

phers, and fantastical conceits of others. I am even so far gone of late in this way of thinking, that I have quitted several of the sublime notions I had got in their schools for vulgar opinions. And I give it you on my word; since this revolt from metaphysical notions to the plain dictates of nature and common sense, I find my understanding strangely enlightened, so that I can now easily comprehend a great many things which before were all mystery and riddle.

HYL: I am glad to find there was nothing in the accounts I heard of you.

PHIL: Pray, what were those?

HYL: You were represented, in last night's conversation, as one who maintained the most extravagant opinion that ever entered into the mind of man, to wit, that there is no such thing as *material substance* in the world.

PHIL: That there is no such thing as what *philosophers* call *material substance*, I am seriously persuaded: but, if I were made to see anything absurd or sceptical in this, I should then have the same reason to renounce this that I imagine I have now to reject the contrary opinion.

HYL: What! can anything be more fantastical, more repugnant to Common Sense, or a more manifest piece of Scepticism, than to believe there is no such thing as *matter*?

PHIL: Softly, good Hylas. What if it should prove that you, who hold there is, are, by virtue of that opinion, a greater sceptic, and maintain more paradoxes and repugnances to Common Sense, than I who believe no such thing?

HYL: You may as soon persuade me, the part is greater than the whole, as that, in order to avoid absurdity and Scepticism, I should ever be obliged to give up my opinion in this point.

PHIL: Well then, are you content to admit that opinion for true, which upon examination shall appear most agreeable to Common Sense, and remote from Scepticism?

HYL: With all my heart. Since you are for raising disputes about the plainest things in nature, I am content for once to hear what you have to say.

PHIL: Pray, Hylas, what do you mean by a *sceptic*?

HYL: I mean what all men mean—one that doubts of everything.

PHIL: He then who entertains no doubt concerning some particular point, with regard to that point cannot be thought a sceptic.

HYL: I agree with you.

PHIL: Whether doth doubting consist in embracing the affirmative or negative side of a question?

HYL: In neither; for whoever understands English cannot but know that *doubting* signifies a suspense between both.

PHIL: He then that denies any point, can no more be said to doubt of it, than he who affirmeth it with the same degree of assurance.

HYL: True.

PHIL: And, consequently, for such his denial is no more to be esteemed a sceptic than the other.

HYL: I acknowledge it.

PHIL: How cometh it to pass then, Hylas, that you pronounce me a *sceptic*, because I deny what you affirm, to wit, the existence of Matter? Since, for aught you can tell, I am as peremptory in my denial, as you in your affirmation.

HYL: Hold, Philonous, I have been a little out in my definition; but every false step a man makes in discourse is not to be insisted on. I said indeed that a *sceptic* was one who doubted of everything; but I should have added, or who denies the reality and truth of things.

PHIL: What things? Do you mean the principles and theorems of sciences? But these you know are universal intellectual notions, and consequently independent of Matter. The denial therefore of this doth not imply the denying them.

HYL: I grant it. But are there no other things? What think you of distrusting the senses, of denying the real existence of sensible things, or pretending to know nothing of them. Is not this sufficient to denominate a man a *sceptic*?

PHIL: Shall we therefore examine which of us it is that denies the reality of sensible things, or professes the greatest ignorance of them; since, if I take you rightly, he is to be esteemed the greatest *sceptic*?

HYL: That is what I desire.

PHIL: What mean you by Sensible Things?

HYL: Those things which are perceived by the senses. Can you imagine that I mean anything else?

PHIL: Pardon me, Hylas, if I am desirous clearly to apprehend your notions, since this may much shorten our inquiry. Suffer me then to ask you this farther question. Are those things only perceived by the senses which are perceived immediately? Or, may those things properly be said to be *sensible* which are perceived mediately, or not without the intervention of others?

HYL: I do not sufficiently understand you.

PHIL: In reading a book, what I immediately perceive are the letters; but mediately, or by means of these, are suggested to my mind the notions of God, virtue, truth, etc. Now, that the letters are truly sensible things, or perceived by sense, there is no doubt: but I would know whether you take the things suggested by them to be so too.

HYL: No, certainly: it were absurd to think God or *virtue* sensible things; though they may be signified and suggested to the mind by sensible marks, with which they have an arbitrary connexion.

PHIL: It seems then, that by *sensible things* you mean those only which can be perceived *immediately* by sense?

HYL: Right.

PHIL: Doth it not follow from this, that though I see one part of the sky red, and another blue, and that my reason doth thence evidently conclude there must be some cause of that diversity of colours, yet that cause cannot be said to be a sensible thing, or perceived by the sense of seeing?

HYL: It doth.

PHIL: In like manner, though I hear variety of sounds, yet I cannot be said to hear the causes of those sounds?

HYL: You cannot.

PHIL: And when by my touch I perceive a thing to be hot and heavy, I cannot say, with any truth or propriety, that I feel the cause of its heat or weight?

HYL: To prevent any more questions of this kind, I tell you once for all, that by *sensible things* I mean those only which are perceived by sense; and that in truth the senses perceive nothing which they do not perceive *immediately*: for they make no inferences. The deducing therefore of causes or occasions from effects and appearances, which alone are perceived by sense, entirely relates to reason.

PHIL: This point then is agreed between us— That *sensible things are those only which are immediately perceived by sense*. You will farther inform me, whether we immediately perceive by sight anything beside light, and colours, and figures; or by hearing, anything but sounds; by the palate, anything beside tastes; by the smell, beside odours; or by the touch, more than tangible qualities.

HYL: We do not.

PHIL: It seems, therefore, that if you take away all sensible qualities, there remains nothing sensible.

HYL: I grant it.

PHIL: Sensible things therefore are nothing else but so many sensible qualities, or combinations of sensible qualities?

HYL: Nothing else.

PHIL: Heat then is a sensible thing?

HYL: Certainly.

PHIL: Doth the *reality* of sensible things consist in being perceived? or, is it something distinct from their being perceived, and that bears no relation to the mind?

HYL: To *exist* is one thing, and to be *perceived* is another.

PHIL: I speak with regard to sensible things only. And of these I ask, whether by their real existence you mean a subsistence exterior to the mind, and distinct from their being perceived?

HYL: I mean a real absolute being, distinct from, and without any relation to, their being perceived.

PHIL: Heat therefore, if it be allowed a real being, must exist without the mind?

HYL: It must.

PHIL: Tell me, Hylas, is this real existence equally compatible to all degrees of heat, which we perceive; or is there any reason why we should attribute it to some, and deny it to others? And if there be, pray let me know that reason.

HYL: Whatever degree of heat we perceive by sense, we may be sure the same exists in the object that occasions it.

PHIL: What! the greatest as well as the least?

HYL: I tell you, the reason is plainly the same in

respect of both. They are both perceived by sense; nay, the greater degree of heat is more sensibly perceived; and consequently, if there is any difference, we are more certain of its real existence than we can be of the reality of a lesser degree.

PHIL: But is not the most vehement and intense degree of heat a very great pain?

HYL: No one can deny it.

PHIL: And is any unperceiving thing capable of pain or pleasure?

HYL: No, certainly.

PHIL: Is your material substance a senseless being, or a being endowed with sense and perception?

HYL: It is senseless without doubt.

PHIL: It cannot therefore be the subject of pain?

HYL: By no means.

PHIL: Nor consequently of the greatest heat perceived by sense, since you acknowledge this to be no small pain?

HYL: I grant it.

PHIL: What shall we say then of your external object; is it a material Substance, or no?

HYL: It is a material substance with the sensible qualities inhering in it.

PHIL: How then can a great heat exist in it, since you own it cannot in a material substance? I desire you would clear this point.

HYL: Hold, Philonous, I fear I was out in yielding intense heat to be a pain. It should seem rather, that pain is something distinct from heat, and the consequence or effect of it.

PHIL: Upon putting your hand near the fire, do you perceive one simple uniform sensation, or two distinct sensations?

HYL: But one simple sensation.

PHIL: Is not the heat immediately perceived?

HYL: It is.

PHIL: And the pain?

HYL: True.

PHIL: Seeing therefore they are both immediately perceived at the same time, and the fire affects you only with one simple or uncompounded idea, it follows that this same simple idea is both the intense heat immediately perceived, and the pain; and, consequently, that the intense heat immediately perceived is nothing distinct from a particular sort of pain.

HYL: It seems so.

PHIL: Again, try in your thoughts, Hylas, if you can conceive a vehement sensation to be without pain or pleasure.

HYL: I cannot.

PHIL: Or can you frame to yourself an idea of sensible pain or pleasure in general, abstracted from every particular idea of heat, cold, tastes, smells? etc.

HYL: —I do not find that I can.

PHIL: Doth it not therefore follow, that sensible pain is nothing distinct from those sensations or ideas, in an intense degree?

HYL: It is undeniable; and, to speak the truth, I begin to suspect a very great heat cannot exist but in a mind perceiving it.

PHIL: What! are you then in that sceptical state of suspense, between affirming and denying?

HYL: I think I may be positive in the point. A very violent and painful heat cannot exist without the mind.

PHIL: It hath not therefore, according to you, any *real* being?

HYL: I own it.

PHIL: Is it therefore certain, that there is no body in nature really hot?

HYL: I have not denied there is any real heat in bodies. I only say, there is no such thing as an intense real heat.

PHIL: But, did you not say before that all degrees of heat were equally real; or, if there was any difference, that the greater were more undoubtedly real than the lesser?

HYL: True: but it was because I did not then consider the ground there is for distinguishing between them, which I now plainly see. And it is this: because intense heat is nothing else but a particular kind of painful sensation; and pain cannot exist but in a perceiving being; it follows that no intense heat can really exist in an unperceiving corporeal substance. But this is no reason why we should deny heat in an inferior degree to exist in such a substance.

PHIL: But how shall we be able to discern those degrees of heat which exist only in the mind from those which exist without it.

HYL: That is no difficult matter. You know the

least pain cannot exist unperceived; whatever, therefore, degree of heat is a pain exists only in the mind. But, as for all other degrees of heat, nothing obliges us to think the same of them.

PHIL: I think you granted before that no unperceiving being was capable of pleasure, any more than of pain.

HYL: I did.

PHIL: And is not warmth, or a more gentle degree of heat than what causes uneasiness, a pleasure?

HYL: What then?

PHIL: Consequently, it cannot exist without the mind in an unperceiving substance, or body.

HYL: So it seems.

PHIL: Since therefore as well those degrees of heat that are not painful, as those that are, can exist only in a thinking substance; may we not conclude that external bodies are absolutely incapable of any degree of heat whatsoever?

HYL: On second thoughts, I do not think it so evident that warmth is a pleasure as that a great degree of heat is a pain.

PHIL: I do not pretend that warmth is as great pleasure as heat is a pain. But, if you grant it to be even a small pleasure, it serves to make good my conclusion.

HYL: I could rather call it an *indolence*. It seems to be nothing more than a privation of both pain and pleasure. And that such a quality or state as this may agree to an unthinking substance, I hope you will not deny.

PHIL: If you are resolved to maintain that warmth, or a gentle degree of heat, is no pleasure, I know not how to convince you otherwise than by appealing to your own sense. But what think you of cold?

HYL: The same that I do for heat. An intense degree of cold is a pain; for to feel a very great cold, is to perceive a great uneasiness: it cannot therefore exist without the mind; but a lesser degree of cold may, as well as a lesser degree of heat.

PHIL: Those bodies, therefore, upon whose application to our own, we perceive a moderate degree of heat, must be concluded to have a moderate degree of heat or warmth in them; and those, upon whose application we feel a like degree of cold, must be thought to have cold in them.

HYL: They must.

PHIL: Can any doctrine be true that necessarily leads a man into an absurdity?

HYL: Without doubt it cannot.

PHIL: Is it not an absurdity to think that the same thing should be at the same time both cold and warm?

HYL: It is.

PHIL: Suppose now one of your hands hot, and the other cold, and that they are both at once put into the same vessel of water, in an intermediate state; will not the water seem cold to one hand, and warm to the other?

HYL: It will.

PHIL: Ought we not therefore, by your principles, to conclude it is really both cold and warm at the same time, that is, according to your own concession, to believe an absurdity?

HYL: I confess is seems so.

PHIL: Consequently, the principles themselves are false, since you have granted that no true principle leads to an absurdity.

HYL: But, after all, can anything be more absurd than to say, *there is no heat in the fire*?

PHIL: To make the point still clearer; tell me whether, in two cases exactly alike, we ought not to make the same judgment?

HYL: We ought.

PHIL: When a pin pricks your finger, doth it not rend and divide the fibers of your flesh?

HYL: It does.

PHIL: And when a coal burns your finger, doth it any more?

HYL: It doth.

PHIL: Since, therefore, you neither judge the sensation itself occasioned by the pin, nor anything like it to be in the pin; you should not, conformably to what you have now granted, judge the sensation occasioned by the fire, or anything like it, to be in the fire.

HYL: Well, since it must be so, I am content to yield this point, and acknowledge that heat and cold are only sensations existing in our minds. But there still remain qualities enough to secure the reality of external things.

PHIL: But what will you say, Hylas, if it shall appear that this case is the same with regard to all other sensible qualities, and that they can no more be supposed to exist without the mind, than heat and cold?

HYL: Then indeed you will have done something to the purpose; but that is what I despair of seeing proved.

PHIL: Let us examine them in order. What think you of *tastes*—do they exist without the mind, or no?

HYL: Can any man in his senses doubt whether sugar is sweet, or wormwood bitter?

PHIL: Inform me, Hylas. Is a sweet taste a particular kind of pleasure or pleasant sensation, or is it not?

HYL: It is.

PHIL: And is not bitterness some kind of uneasiness or pain?

HYL: I grant it.

PHIL: If therefore sugar and wormwood are unthinking corporeal substances existing without the mind, how can sweetness and bitterness, that is, pleasure and pain, agree to them?

HYL: Hold, Philonous, I now see what it was deluded me all this time. You asked whether heat and cold, sweetness and bitterness, were not particular sorts of pleasure and pain; to which I answered simply, that they were. Whereas I should have thus distinguished:—those qualities, as perceived by us, are pleasures or pains; but not as existing in the external objects. We must not therefore conclude absolutely, that there is no heat in the fire, or sweetness in the sugar, but only that heat or sweetness, as perceived by us, are not in the fire or sugar. What say you to this?

PHIL: I say it is nothing to the purpose. Our discourse proceeded altogether concerning sensible things, which you defined to be, *the things we immediately perceive by our senses*. Whatever other qualities, therefore, you speak of, as distinct from these, I know nothing of them, neither do they all belong to the point in dispute. You may, indeed, pretend to have discovered certain qualities which you do not perceive, and assert those insensible qualities exist in fire and sugar. But what use can be made of this to your present purpose, I am at a loss to conceive. Tell me then once more, do you acknowledge that heat and cold, sweetness and bitterness (meaning those qualities which are perceived by the senses), do not exist without the mind?

HYL: I see it is to no purpose to hold out, so I give up the cause as to those mentioned qualities. Though I profess it sounds oddly, to say that sugar is not sweet.

PHIL: But, for your farther satisfaction, take this along with you: that which at other times seems sweet, shall, to a distempered palate, appear bitter. And, nothing can be plainer than that divers persons perceive different tastes in the same food; since that which one man delights in, another abhors. And how could this be, if the taste was something really inherent in the food?

HYL: I acknowledge I know not how.

PHIL: In the next place, *odours* are to be considered. And, with regard to these, I would fain know whether what hath been said of tastes doth not exactly agree to them? Are they not so many pleasing or displeasing sensations?

HYL: They are.

PHIL: Can you then conceive it possible that they should exist in an unperceiving thing?

HYL: I cannot.

PHIL: Or, can you imagine that filth and ordure affect those brute animals that feed on them out of choice, with the same smells which we perceive in them?

HYL: By no means.

PHIL: May we not therefore conclude of smells, as of the other forementioned qualities, that they cannot exist in any but a perceiving substance or mind?

HYL: I think so.

PHIL: Then as to *sounds*, what must we think of them: are they accidents really inherent in external bodies, or not?

HYL: That they inhere not in the sonorous bodies is plain from hence: because a bell struck in the exhausted receiver of an air-pump sends forth no sound. The air, therefore, must be thought the subject of sound.

PHIL: What reason is there for that, Hylas?

HYL: Because, when any motion is raised in the

air, we perceive a sound greater or lesser, according to the air's motion; but without some motion in the air, we never hear any sound at all.

PHIL: And granting that we never hear a sound but when some motion is produced in the air, yet I do not see how you can infer from thence, that the sound itself is in the air.

HYL: It is this very motion in the external air that produces in the mind the sensation of *sound*. For, striking on the drum of the ear, it causeth a vibration, which by the auditory nerves being communicated to the brain, the soul is thereupon affected with the sensation called *sound*.

PHIL: What! is sound then a sensation?

HYL: I tell you, as perceived by us, it is a particular sensation in the mind.

PHIL: And can any sensation exist without the mind?

HYL: No, certainly.

PHIL: How then can sound, being a sensation, exist in the air, if by the *air* you mean a senseless substance existing without the mind?

HYL: You must distinguish, Philonous, between sound as it is perceived by us, and as it is in itself; or (which is the same thing) between the sound we immediately perceive, and that which exists without us. The former, indeed, is a particular kind of sensation, but the latter is merely a vibrative or undulatory motion in the air.

PHIL: I thought I had already obviated that distinction, by the answer I gave when you were applying it in a like case before. But, to say no more of that, are you sure then that sound is really nothing but motion?

HYL: I am.

PHIL: Whatever therefore agrees to real sound, may with truth be attributed to motion?

HYL: It may.

PHIL: It is then good sense to speak of *motion* as of a thing that is *loud, sweet, acute or grave*.

HYL: I see you are resolved not to understand me. Is it not evident those accidents or modes belong only to sensible sound, or *sound* in the common acceptation of the word, but not to *sound* in the real and philosophic sense; which, as I just now told you, is nothing but a certain motion of the air?

PHIL: It seems then there are two sorts of sound—the one vulgar, or that which is heard, the other philosophical and real?

HYL: Even so.

PHIL: And the latter consists in motion?

HYL: I told you so before.

PHIL: Tell me, Hylas, to which of the senses, think you, the idea of motion belongs? to the hearing?

HYL: No, certainly; but to the sight and touch.

PHIL: It should follow then, that, according to you, real sounds may possibly be *seen* or *felt*, but never *heard*.

HYL: Look you, Philonous, you may, if you please, make a jest of my opinion, but that will not alter the truth of things. I own, indeed, the inferences you draw me into sound something oddly; but common language, you know, is framed by, and for the use of the vulgar: we must not therefore wonder if expressions adapted to exact philosophic notions seem uncouth and out of the way.

PHIL: Is it come to that? I assure you, I imagine myself to have gained no small point, since you make so light of departing from common phrases and opinions; it being a main part of our inquiry, to examine whose notions are widest of the common road, and most repugnant to the general sense of the world. But, can you think it no more than a philosophical paradox, to say that *real sounds are never heard*, and that the idea of them is obtained by some other sense? And is there nothing in this contrary to nature and the truth of things?

HYL: To deal ingenuously, I do not like it. And, after the concessions already made, I had as well grant that sounds too have no real being without the mind.

PHIL: And I hope you will make no difficulty to acknowledge the same of *colours*.

HYL: Pardon me: the case of colours is very different. Can anything be plainer than that we see them on the objects?

PHIL: The objects you speak of are, I suppose, corporeal Substances existing without the mind?

HYL: They are.

PHIL: And have true and real colours inhering in them?

HYL: Each visible object hath that colour which we see in it.

PHIL: How! is there anything visible but what we perceive by sight?

HYL: There is not.

PHIL: And, do we perceive anything by sense which we do not perceive immediately?

HYL: How often must I be obliged to repeat the same thing? I tell you, we do not.

PHIL: Have patience, good Hylas; and tell me once more, whether there is anything immediately perceived by the senses, except sensible qualities. I know you asserted there was not; but I would now be informed, whether you still persist in the same opinion.

HYL: I do.

PHIL: Pray, is your corporeal substance either a sensible quality, or made up of sensible qualities?

HYL: What a question that is! who ever thought it was?

PHIL: My reason for asking was, because in saying, *each visible object hath that colour which we see in it*, you make visible objects to be corporeal substances; which implies either that corporeal substances are sensible qualities, or else that there is something beside sensible qualities perceived by sight: but, as this point was formerly agreed between us, and is still maintained by you, it is a clear consequence, that your *corporeal substance* is nothing distinct from *sensible qualities*.

HYL: You may draw as many absurd consequences as you please, and endeavour to perplex the plainest things; but you shall never persuade me out of my senses. I clearly understand my own meaning.

PHIL: I wish you would make me understand it too. But, since you are unwilling to have your notion of corporeal substance examined, I shall urge that point no farther. Only be pleased to let me know, whether the same colours which we see exist in external bodies, or some other.

HYL: The very same.

PHIL: What! are then the beautiful red and purple we see on yonder clouds really in them? Or do you imagine they have in themselves any other form than that of a dark mist or vapour?

HYL: I must own, Philonous, those colours are not really in the clouds as they seem to be at this distance. They are only apparent colours.

PHIL: *Apparent* call you them? how shall we distinguish these apparent colours from real?

HYL: Very easily. Those are to be thought apparent which, appearing only at a distance, vanish upon a nearer approach.

PHIL: And those, I suppose, are to be thought real which are discovered by the most near and exact survey.

HYL: Right.

PHIL: Is the nearest and exactest survey made by the help of a microscope, or by the naked eye?

HYL: By a microscope, doubtless.

PHIL: But a microscope often discovers colours in an object different from those perceived by the unassisted sight. And, in case we had microscopes magnifying to any assigned degree, it is certain that no object whatsoever, viewed through them, would appear in the same colour which it exhibits to the naked eye.

HYL: And what will you conclude from all this? You cannot argue that there are really and naturally no colours on objects: because by artificial managements they may be altered, or made to vanish.

PHIL: I think it may evidently be concluded from your own concessions, that all the colours we see with our naked eyes are only apparent as those on the clouds, since they vanish upon a more close and accurate inspection which is afforded us by a microscope. Then, as to what you say by way of prevention: I ask you whether the real and natural state of an object is better discovered by a very sharp and piercing sight, or by one which is less sharp?

HYL: By the former without doubt.

PHIL: Is it not plain from *Dioptrics* that microscopes make the sight more penetrating, and represent objects as they would appear to the eye in case it were naturally endowed with a most exquisite sharpness?

HYL: It is.

PHIL: Consequently the microscopical representation is to be thought that which best sets forth the real nature of the thing, or what it is in itself. The colours, therefore, by it perceived are more genuine and real than those perceived otherwise.

HYL: I confess there is something in what you say.

PHIL: Besides, it is not only possible but manifest, that there actually are animals whose eyes are by nature framed to perceive those things which by reason of their minuteness escape our sight. What think you of those inconceivably small animals perceived by glasses? must we suppose they are all stark blind? Or, in case they see, can it be imagined their sight hath not the same use in preserving their bodies from injuries, which appears in that of all other animals? And if it hath, is it not evident they must see particles less than their own bodies; which will present them with a far different view in each object from that which strikes our senses? Even our own eyes do not always represent objects to us after the same manner. In the jaundice every one knows that all things seem yellow. Is it not therefore highly probable those animals in whose eyes we discern a very different texture from that of ours, and whose bodies abound with different humours, do not see the same colours in every object that we do? From all which, should it not seem to follow that all colours are equally apparent, and that none of those which we perceive are really inherent in any outward object?

HYL: It should.

PHIL: The point will be past all doubt, if you consider that, in case colours were real properties or affections inherent in external bodies, they could admit of no alteration without some change wrought in the very bodies themselves: but, is it not evident from what hath been said that, upon the use of microscopes, upon a change happening in the humours of the eye, or a variation of distance, without any manner of real alteration in the thing itself, the colours of any object are either changed, or totally disappear? Nay, all other circumstances remaining the same, change but the situation of some objects, and they shall present different colours to the eye. The same thing happens upon viewing an object in various degrees of light. And what is more known than that the same bodies appear differently coloured by candle-light from what they do in the open day? Add to these the experiment of a prism which, separating the heterogeneous rays of light, alters the colour of any object, and will cause the whitest to appear of a deep blue or red to the naked eye. And now tell me whether you are still of opinion that every body hath its true real colour inhering in it; and, if you think it hath, I would fain know farther from you, what certain distance and position of the object, what peculiar texture and formation of the eye, what degree or kind of light is necessary for ascertaining that true colour, and distinguishing it from apparent ones.

HYL: I own myself entirely satisfied, that they are all equally apparent, and that there is no such thing as colour really inhering in external bodies, but that it is altogether in the light. And what confirms me in this opinion is, that in proportion to the light colours are still more or less vivid; and if there be no light, then are there no colours perceived. Besides, allowing there are colours on external objects, yet, how is it possible for us to perceive them? For no external body affects the mind, unless it acts first on our organs of sense. But the only action of bodies is motion; and motion cannot be communicated otherwise than by impulse. A distant object therefore cannot act on the eye; nor consequently make itself or its properties perceivable to the soul. Whence it plainly follows that it is immediately some contiguous substance, which, operating on the eye, occasions a perception of colours: and such is light.

PHIL: How! is light then a substance?

HYL: I tell you, Philonous, external light is nothing but a thin fluid substance, whose minute particles being agitated with a brisk motion, and in various manners reflected from the different surfaces of outward objects to the eyes, communicate different motions to the optic nerves; which, being propagated to the brain, cause therein various impressions; and these are attended with the sensations of red, blue, yellow, etc.

PHIL: It seems then the light doth no more than shake the optic nerves.

HYL: Nothing else.

PHIL: And consequent to each particular motion of the nerves, the mind is affected with a sensation, which is some particular colour.

HYL: Right.

PHIL: And these sensations have no existence without the mind.

HYL: They have not.

PHIL: How then do you affirm that colours are in the light; since by *light* you understand a corporeal substance external to the mind?

HYL: Light and colours, as immediately perceived by us, I grant cannot exist without the mind. But in themselves they are only the motions and configurations of certain insensible particles of matter.

PHIL: Colours then, in the vulgar sense, or taken for the immediate objects of sight, cannot agree to any but a perceiving substance.

HYL: That is what I say.

PHIL: Well then, since you give up the point as to those sensible qualities which are alone thought colours by all mankind beside, you may hold what you please with regard to those invisible ones of the philosophers. It is not my business to dispute about *them*; only I would advise you to bethink yourself, whether, considering the inquiry we are upon, it be prudent for you to affirm—*the red and blue which we see are not real colours, but certain unknown motions and figures which no man ever did or can see are truly so.* Are not these shocking notions, and are not they subject to as many ridiculous inferences, as those you were obliged to renounce before in the case of sounds?

HYL: I frankly own, Philonous, that it is in vain to stand out any longer. Colours, sounds, tastes, in a word all those termed *secondary qualities*, have certainly no existence without the mind. But by this acknowledgement I must not be supposed to derogate anything from the reality of Matter, or external objects; seeing it is no more than several philosophers maintain, who nevertheless are the farthest imaginable from denying Matter. For the clearer understanding of this, you must know sensible qualities are by philosophers divided into *Primary* and *Secondary*. The former are Extension, Figure, Solidity, Gravity, Motion, and Rest; and these they hold exist really in bodies. The latter are those above enumerated; or, briefly, *all sensible qualities beside the Primary*; which they assert are only so many sensations or ideas existing nowhere but in the mind. But all this, I doubt not, you are apprised of. For my part,

I have been a long time sensible there was such an opinion current among philosophers, but was never thoroughly convinced of its truth until now.

PHIL: You are still then of opinion that *extension* and *figures* are inherent in external unthinking substances?

HYL: I am.

PHIL: But what if the same arguments which are brought against Secondary Qualities will hold good against these also?

HYL: Why then I shall be obliged to think, they too exist only in the mind.

PHIL: Is it your opinion the very figure and extension which you perceive by sense exist in the outward object or material substance?

HYL: It is.

PHIL: Have all other animals as good grounds to think the same of the figure and extension which they see and feel?

HYL: Without doubt, if they have any thought at all.

PHIL: Answer me, Hylas. Think you the senses were bestowed upon all animals for their preservation and well-being in life? or were they given to men alone for this end?

HYL: I make no question but they have the same use in all other animals.

PHIL: If so, is it not necessary they should be enabled by them to perceive their own limbs, and those bodies which are capable of harming them?

HYL: Certainly.

PHIL: A mite therefore must be supposed to see his own foot, and things equal or even less than it, as bodies of some considerable dimension; though at the same time they appear to you scarce discernible, or at best as so many visible points?

HYL: I cannot deny it.

PHIL: And to creatures less than the mite they will seem yet larger?

HYL: They will.

PHIL: Insomuch that what you can hardly discern will to another extremely minute animal appear as some huge mountain?

HYL: All this I grant.

PHIL: Can one and the same thing be the same time in itself of different dimensions?

HYL: That were absurd to imagine.

PHIL: But, from what you have laid down it follows that both the extension by you perceived, and that perceived by the mite itself, as likewise all those perceived by lesser animals, are each of them the true extension of the mite's foot; that is to say, by your own principles you are led into an absurdity.

HYL: There seems to be some difficulty in the point.

PHIL: Again, have you not acknowledged that no real inherent property of any object can be changed without some change in the thing itself?

HYL: I have.

PHIL: But, as we approach to or recede from an object, the visible extension varies, being at one distance ten or a hundred times greater than at another. Doth it not therefore follow from hence likewise that it is not really inherent in the object?

HYL: I own I am at a loss what to think.

PHIL: Your judgment will soon be determined, if you will venture to think as freely concerning this quality as you have done concerning the rest. Was it not admitted as a good argument, that neither heat nor cold was in the water, because it seemed warm to one hand and cold to the other?

HYL: It was.

PHIL: Is it not the very same reasoning to conclude, there is no extension or figure in an object, because to one eye it shall seem little, smooth, and round, when at the same time it appears to the other, great, uneven, and angular?

HYL: The very same. But does this latter fact ever happen?

PHIL: You may at any time make the experiment, by looking with one eye bare, and with the other through a microscope.

HYL: I know not how to maintain it; and yet I am loath to give up *extension*, I see so many odd consequences following upon such a concession.

PHIL: Odd, say you? After the concessions already made, I hope you will stick at nothing for its oddness. But, on the other hand, should it not seem very odd, if the general reasoning which includes all other sensible qualities did not also include extension? If it be allowed that no idea, nor anything like an idea, can exist in an unperceiving substance, then surely it follows that no figure, or mode of extension, which we can either perceive, or imagine, or have any idea of, can be really inherent in Matter; not to mention the peculiar difficulty there must be in conceiving a material substance, prior to and distinct from extension, to be the *substratum* of extension. Be the sensible quality what it will—figure, or sound, or colour, it seems alike impossible it should subsist in that which doth not perceive it.

HYL: I give up the point for the present, reserving still a right to retract my opinion, in case I shall hereafter discover any false step in my progress to it.

PHIL: That is a right you cannot be denied. Figures and extensions being despatched, we proceed next to *motion*. Can a real motion in any external body be at the same time both very swift and very slow?

HYL: It cannot.

PHIL: Is not the motion of a body swift in a reciprocal proportion to the time it takes up in describing any given space? Thus a body that describes a mile in an hour moves three times faster than it would in case it described only a mile in three hours.

HYL: I agree with you.

PHIL: And is not time measured by the succession of ideas in our minds?

HYL: It is.

PHIL: And is it not possible ideas should succeed one another twice as fast in your mind as they do in mine, or in that of some spirit of another kind?

HYL: I own it.

PHIL: Consequently the same body may to another seem to perform its motion over any space in half the time that it doth to you. And the same reasoning will hold as to any other proportion: that is to say, according to your principles (since the motions perceived are both really in the object) it is possible one and the same body shall be really moved the same way at once, both very swift and very slow. How is this consistent either with common sense, or with what you just now granted?

HYL: I have nothing to say to it.

PHIL: Then as for *solidity*; either you do not mean any sensible quality by that word, and so it is beside our inquiry: or if you do, it must be either hardness or resistance. But both the one and the other are plainly relative to our senses: it being evident that what seems hard to one animal may appear soft to another, who hath greater force and firmness of limbs. Nor is it less plain that the resistance I feel is not in the body.

HYL: I own the very *sensation* of resistance, which is all you immediately perceive, is not in the body; but the *cause* of that sensation is.

PHIL: But the causes of our sensations are not things immediately perceived, and therefore are not sensible. This point I thought had been already determined.

HYL: I own it was; but you will pardon me if I seem a little embarrassed: I know not how to quit my old notions.

PHIL: To help you out, do but consider that if *extension* be once acknowledged to have no existence without the mind, the same must necessarily be granted of motion, solidity, and gravity; since they all evidently suppose extension. It is therefore superfluous to inquire particularly concerning each of them. In denying extension, you have denied them all to have any real existence.

HYL: I wonder, Philonous, if what you say be true, why those philosophers who deny the Secondary Qualities any real existence should yet attribute it to the Primary. If there is no difference between them, how can this be accounted for?

PHIL: It is not my business to account for every opinion of the philosophers. But, among other reasons which may be assigned for this, it seems probable that pleasure and pain being rather annexed to the former than the latter may be one. Heat and cold, tastes and smells, have something more vividly pleasing or disagreeable than the ideas of extension, figure, and motion affect us with. And, it being too visibly absurd to hold that pain or pleasure can be in an unperceiving Substance, men are more easily weaned from believing the external existence of the Secondary than the Primary Qualities. You will be satisfied there is something in this, if you recollect the difference you made between an intense and more

moderate degree of heat; allowing the one a real existence, while you denied it to the other. But, after all, there is no rational ground for that distinction; for, surely an indifferent sensation is as truly *a sensation* as one more pleasing or painful; and consequently should not any more than they be supposed to exist in an unthinking subject.

HYL: It is just come into my head, Philonous, that I have somewhere heard of a distinction between absolute and sensible extension. Now, though it be acknowledged that *great* and *small*, consisting merely in the relation which other extended beings have to the parts of our own bodies, do not really inhere in the substances themselves; yet nothing obliges us to hold the same with regard to *absolute extension*, which is something abstracted from *great* and *small*, from this or that particular magnitude or figure. So likewise as to motion; *swift* and *slow* are altogether relative to the succession of ideas in our own minds. But, it doth not follow, because those modifications of motion exist not without the mind, that therefore absolute motion abstracted from them doth not.

PHIL: Pray what is it that distinguishes one motion, or one part of extension, from another? Is it not something sensible, as some degree of swiftness or slowness, some certain magnitude or figure peculiar to each?

HYL: I think so.

PHIL: These qualities, therefore, stripped of all sensible properties, are without all specific and numerical differences, as the schools call them.

HYL: They are.

PHIL: That is to say, they are extension in general, and motion in general.

HYL: Let it be so.

PHIL: But it is a universally received maxim that *Everything which exists is particular*. How then can motion in general, or extension in general, exist in any corporeal substance?

HYL: I will take time to solve your difficulty.

PHIL: But I think the point may be speedily decided. Without doubt you can tell whether you are able to frame this or that idea. Now I am content to put our dispute on this issue. If you can frame in your thoughts a distinct *abstract idea* of motion or extension, divested of all those sensible modes, as swift and slow, great and small, round and square, and the like, which are acknowledged to exist only in the mind, I will then yield the point you contend for. But if you cannot, it will be unreasonable on your side to insist any longer upon what you have no notion of.

HYL: To confess ingenuously, I cannot.

PHIL: Can you even separate the ideas of extension and motion from the ideas of all those qualities which they who make the distinction term *secondary*?

HYL: What! is it not an easy matter to consider extension and motion by themselves, abstracted from all other sensible qualities? Pray how do the mathematicians treat of them?

PHIL: I acknowledge, Hylas, it is not difficult to form general propositions and reasonings about those qualities, without mentioning any other; and, in this sense, to consider or treat of them abstractedly. But, how doth it follow that, because I can pronounce the word *motion* by itself, I can form the idea of it in my mind exclusive of body? or, because theorems may be made of extension and figures, without any mention of *great* or *small*, or any other sensible mode of quality, that therefore it is possible such an abstract idea of extension, without any particular size or figure, or sensible quality, should be distinctly formed, and apprehended by the mind? Mathematicians treat of quantity, without regarding what other sensible qualities it is attended with, as being altogether indifferent to their demonstrations. But, when laying aside the words, they contemplate the bare ideas, I believe you will find, they are not the pure abstracted ideas of extension.

HYL: But what say you to *pure intellect*? May not abstracted ideas be framed by that faculty?

PHIL: Since I cannot frame abstract ideas at all, it is plain I cannot frame them by the help of *pure intellect*; whatsoever faculty you understand by those words. Besides, not to inquire into the nature of pure intellect and its spiritual objects, as *virtue*, *reason*, *God*, or the like, thus much seems manifest—that sensible things are only to be perceived by sense, or represented by the imagination. Figures, therefore, and extension, being

originally perceived by sense, do not belong to pure intellect: but, for your farther satisfaction, try if you can frame the idea of any figure, abstracted from all particularities of size, or even from other sensible qualities.

HYL: Let me think a little—I do not find that I can.

PHIL: And can you think it possible that should really exist in nature which implies a repugnancy in its conception?

HYL: By no means.

PHIL: Since therefore it is impossible even for the mind to disunite the ideas of extension and motion from all other sensible qualities, doth it not follow, that where the one exist there necessarily the other exist likewise?

HYL: It should seem so.

PHIL: Consequently, the very same arguments which you admitted as conclusive against the Secondary Qualities are, without any farther application of force, against the Primary too. Besides, if you will trust your senses, is it not plain all sensible qualities coexist, or to them appear as being in the same place? Do they ever represent a motion, or figure, as being divested of all other visible and tangible qualities?

HYL: You need say no more on this head. I am free to own, if there be no secret error or oversight in our proceedings hitherto, that *all* sensible qualities are alike to be denied existence without the mind. But, my fear is that I have been too liberal in my former concessions, or overlooked some fallacy or other. In short, I did not take time to think.

PHIL: For that matter, Hylas, you may take what time you please in reviewing the progress of our inquiry. You are at liberty to recover any slips you might have made, or offer whatever you have omitted which makes for your first opinion.

HYL: One great oversight I take to be this—that I did not sufficiently distinguish the *object* from the *sensation*. Now, though this latter may not exist without the mind, yet it will not thence follow that the former cannot.

PHIL: What object do you mean? the object of the senses?

HYL: The same.

PHIL: It is then immediately perceived?

HYL: Right.

PHIL: Make me to understand the difference between what is immediately perceived and a sensation.

HYL: The sensation I take to be an act of the mind perceiving; besides which, there is something perceived; and this I call the *object*. For example, there is red and yellow on that tulip. But then the act of perceiving those colours is in me only, and not in the tulip.

PHIL: What tulip do you speak of? Is it that which you see?

HYL: The same.

PHIL: And what do you see beside colour, figure, and extension?

HYL: Nothing.

PHIL: What you would say then is that the red and yellow are coexistent with the extension; is it not?

HYL: That is not all; I would say they have a real existence without the mind, in some unthinking substance.

PHIL: That the colours are really in the tulip which I see is manifest. Neither can it be denied that this tulip may exist independent of your mind or mine; but, that any immediate object of the senses—that is, any idea, or combination of ideas—should exist in an unthinking substance, or exterior to *all* minds, is in itself an evident contradiction. Nor can I imagine how this follows from what you said just now, to wit, that the red and yellow were on the tulip *you saw*, since you do not pretend to *see* that unthinking substance.

HYL: You have an artful way, Philonous, of diverting our inquiry from the subject.

PHIL: I see you have no mind to be pressed that way. To return then to your distinction between *sensation* and *object*; if I take you right, you distinguish in every perception two things, the one an action of the mind, the other not.

HYL: True.

PHIL: And this action cannot exist in, or belong to, any unthinking thing; but, whatever beside is implied in a perception may?

HYL: That is my meaning.

PHIL: So that if there was a perception without any act of the mind, it were possible such a perception should exist in an unthinking substance?

HYL: I grant it. But it is impossible there should be such a perception.

PHIL: When is the mind said to be active?

HYL: When it produces, puts an end to, or changes, anything.

PHIL: Can the mind produce, discontinue, or change anything, but by an act of the will?

HYL: It cannot.

PHIL: The mind therefore is to be accounted *active* in its perceptions so far forth as *volition* is included in them?

HYL: It is.

PHIL: In plucking this flower I am active; because I do it by the motion of my hand, which was consequent upon my volition; so likewise in applying it to my nose. But is either of these smelling?

HYL: No.

PHIL: I act too in drawing the air through my nose; because my breathing so rather than otherwise is the effect of my volition. But neither can this be called *smelling*: for, if it were, I should smell every time I breathed in that manner?

HYL: True.

PHIL: Smelling then is somewhat consequent to all this?

HYL: It is.

PHIL: But I do not find my will concerned any farther. Whatever more there is—as that I perceive such a particular smell, or any smell at all—this is independent of my will, and therein I am altogether passive. Do you find it otherwise with you, Hylas?

HYL: No, the very same.

PHIL: Then, as to seeing, is it not in your power to open your eyes, or keep them shut; to turn them this or that way?

HYL: Without doubt.

PHIL: But, doth it in like manner depend on *your* will that in looking on this flower you perceive *white* rather than any other colour? Or, directing your open eyes towards yonder part of the heaven, can you avoid seeing the sun? Or is light or darkness the effect of your volition?

HYL: No, certainly.

PHIL: You are then in these respects altogether passive?

HYL: I am.

PHIL: Tell me now, whether *seeing* consists in perceiving light and colours, or in opening and turning the eyes?

HYL: Without doubt, in the former.

PHIL: Since therefore you are in the very perception of light and colours altogether passive, what is become of that action you were speaking of as an ingredient in every sensation? And, doth it not follow from your own concessions, that the perception of light and colours, including no action in it, may exist in an unperceiving substance? And is not this a plain contradiction?

HYL: I know not what to think of it.

PHIL: Besides, since you distinguish the *active* and *passive* in every perception, you must do it in that of pain. But how is it possible that pain, be it as little active as you please, should exist in an unperceiving substance? In short, do but consider the point, and then confess ingenuously, whether light and colours, tastes, sounds, etc. are not all equally passions or sensations in the soul. You may indeed call them *external objects*, and give them in words what subsistence you please. But, examine your own thoughts, and then tell me whether it be not as I say?

HYL: I acknowledge, Philonous, that, upon a fair observation of what passes in my mind, I can discover nothing else but that I am a thinking being, affected with variety of sensations; neither is it possible to conceive how a sensation should exist in an unperceiving substance.—But then, on the other hand, when I look on sensible things in a different view, considering them as so many modes and qualities, I find it necessary to suppose a *material substratum*, without which they cannot be conceived to exist.

PHIL: *Material substratum* call you it? Pray, by which of your senses came you acquainted with that being?

HYL: It is not itself sensible; its modes and qualities only being perceived by the senses.

PHIL: I presume then it was by reflexion and reason you obtained the idea of it?

HYL: I do not pretend to any proper positive *idea* of it. However, I conclude it exists, because qualities cannot be conceived to exist without a support.

PHIL: It seems then you have only a relative *notion* of it, or that you conceive it not otherwise than by conceiving the relation it bears to sensible qualities?

HYL: Right.

PHIL: Be pleased therefore to let me know wherein that relation consists.

HYL: Is it not sufficiently expressed in the term *substratum*, or *substance*?

PHIL: If so, the word *substratum* should import that it is spread under the sensible qualities or accidents?

HYL: True.

PHIL: And consequently under extension?

HYL: I own it.

PHIL: It is therefore somewhat in its own nature entirely distinct from extension?

HYL: I tell you, extension is only a mode, and Matter is something that supports modes. And is it not evident the thing supported is different from the thing supporting?

PHIL: So that something distinct from, and exclusive of, extension is supposed to be the *substratum* of extension?

HYL: Just so.

PHIL: Answer me, Hylas. Can a thing be spread without extension? or is not the idea of extension necessarily included in *spreading*?

HYL: It is.

PHIL: Whatsoever therefore you suppose spread under anything must have in itself an extension distinct from the extension of that thing under which it is spread?

HYL: It must.

PHIL: Consequently, every corporeal substance, being the *substratum* of extension, must have in itself another extension, by which it is qualified to be a *substratum*: and so on to infinity? And I ask whether this be not absurd in itself, and repugnant to what you granted just now, to wit, that the *substratum* was something distinct from and exclusive of extension?

HYL: Aye but, Philonous, you take me wrong. I do not mean that Matter is *spread* in a gross literal sense under extension. The word *substratum* is used only to express in general the same thing with *substance*.

PHIL: Well then, let us examine the relation implied in the term *substance*. Is it not that it stands under accidents?

HYL: The very same.

PHIL: But, that one thing may stand under or support another, must it not be extended?

HYL: It must.

PHIL: Is not therefore this supposition liable to the same absurdity with the former?

HYL: You still take things in a strict literal sense. That is not fair, Philonous.

PHIL: I am not for imposing any sense on your words: you are at liberty to explain them as you please. Only, I beseech you, make me understand something by them. You tell me Matter supports or stands under accidents. How! is it as your legs support your body?

HYL: No; that is the literal sense.

PHIL: Pray let me know any sense, literal or not literal, that you understand it in.—How long must I wait for an answer, Hylas?

HYL: I declare I know not what to say. I once thought I understood well enough what was meant by Matter's supporting accidents. But now, the more I think on it the less can I comprehend it: in short I find that I know nothing of it.

PHIL: It seems then you have no idea at all, neither relative nor positive, of Matter; you know neither what it is in itself, nor what relation it bears to accidents?

HYL: I acknowledge it.

PHIL: And yet you asserted that you could not conceive how qualities or accidents should really exist, without conceiving at the same time a material support of them?

HYL: I did.

PHIL: That is to say, when you conceive the *real* existence of qualities, you do withal conceive Something which you cannot conceive?

HYL: It was wrong, I own. But still I fear there is some fallacy or other. Pray what think you of this? It is just come into my head that the ground of all our mistake lies in your treating of each quality by itself. Now, I grant that each quality cannot singly subsist without the mind. Colour cannot without extension, neither can figure without some other sensible quality. But, as the several qualities united or blended together form entire sensible things, nothing hinders why such things may not be supposed to exist without the mind.

PHIL: Either, Hylas, you are jesting, or have a very bad memory. Though indeed we went through all the qualities by name one after another, yet my arguments, or rather your concessions, nowhere tended to prove that the Secondary Qualities did not subsist each alone by itself; but, that they were not *at all* without the mind. Indeed, in treating of figure and motion we concluded they could not exist without the mind, because it was impossible even in thought to separate them from all secondary qualities, so as to conceive them existing by themselves. But then this was not the only argument made use of upon that occasion. But (to pass by all that hath been hitherto said, and reckon it for nothing, if you will have it so) I am content to put the whole upon this issue. If you can conceive it possible for any mixture or combination of qualities, or any sensible object whatever, to exist without the mind, then I will grant it actually to be so.

HYL: If it comes to that the point will soon be decided. What more easy than to conceive a tree or house existing by itself, independent of, and unperceived by, any mind whatsoever? I do at this present time conceive them existing after that manner.

PHIL: How say you, Hylas, can you see a thing which is at the same time unseen?

HYL: No, that were a contradiction.

PHIL: Is it not as great a contradiction to talk of *conceiving* a thing which is *unconceived*?

HYL: It is.

PHIL: The tree or house therefore which you think of is conceived by you?

HYL: How should it be otherwise?

PHIL: And what is conceived is surely in the mind?

HYL: Without question, that which is conceived is in the mind.

PHIL: How then came you to say, you conceived a house or tree existing independent and out of all minds whatsoever?

HYL: That was I own an oversight; but stay, let me consider what led me into it.—It is a pleasant mistake enough. As I was thinking of a tree in a solitary place, where no one was present to see it, methought that was to conceive a tree as existing unperceived or unthought of; not considering that I myself conceived it all the while. But now I plainly see that all I can do is to frame ideas in my own mind. I may indeed conceive in my own thoughts the idea of a tree, or a house, or a mountain, but that is all. And this is far from proving that I can conceive them *existing out of the minds of all Spirits*.

PHIL: You acknowledge then that you cannot possibly conceive how any one corporeal sensible thing should exist otherwise than in a mind?

HYL: I do.

PHIL: And yet you will earnestly contend for the truth of that which you cannot so much as conceive?

HYL: I profess I know not what to think; but still there are some scruples remain with me. Is it not certain I *see things at a distance*? Do we not perceive the stars and moon, for example, to be a great way off? Is not this, I say, manifest to the senses?

PHIL: Do you not in a dream too perceive those or the like objects?

HYL: I do.

PHIL: And have they not then the same appearance of being distant?

IIYL: They have.

PHIL: But you do not thence conclude the apparitions in a dream to be without the mind?

HYL: By no means.

PHIL: You ought not therefore to conclude that sensible objects are without the mind, from their appearance, or manner wherein they are perceived.

HYL: I acknowledge it. But doth not my sense deceive me in those cases?

PHIL: By no means. The idea or thing which you immediately perceive, neither sense nor reason informs you that *it* actually exists without the mind. By sense you only know that you are affected with such certain sensations of light and colours, etc. And these you will not say are without the mind.

HYL: True: but, beside all that, do you not think the sight suggests something of *outness* or *distance*?

PHIL: Upon approaching a distant object, do the visible size and figure change perpetually, or do they appear the same at all distances?

HYL: They are in a continual change.

PHIL: Sight therefore doth not suggest, or any way inform you, that the visible object you immediately perceive exists at a distance, or will be perceived when you advance farther onward; there being a continued series of visible objects succeeding each other during the whole time of your approach.

HYL: It doth not; but still I know, upon seeing an object, what object I shall perceive after having passed over a certain distance: no matter whether it be exactly the same or no: there is still something of distance suggested in the case.

PHIL: Good Hylas, do but reflect a little on the point, and then tell me whether there be any more in it than this: From the ideas you actually perceive by sight, you have by experience learned to collect what other ideas you will (according to the standing order of nature) be affected with, after such a certain succession of time and motion.

HYL: Upon the whole, I take it to be nothing else.

PHIL: Now, is it not plain that if we suppose a man born blind was on a sudden made to see, he could at first have no experience of what may be *suggested* by sight?

HYL: It is.

PHIL: He would not then, according to you, have any notion of distance annexed to the things he saw; but would take them for a new set of sensations, existing only in his mind?

HYL: It is undeniable.

PHIL: But, to make it still more plain: is not *distance* a line turned endwise to the eye?

HYL: It is.

PHIL: And can a line so situated be perceived by sight?

HYL: It cannot.

PHIL: Doth it not therefore follow that distance is not properly and immediately perceived by sight?

HYL: It should seem so.

PHIL: Again, is it your opinion that colours are at a distance?

HYL: It must be acknowledged they are only in the mind.

PHIL: But do not colours appear to the eye as co-existing in the same place with extension and figures?

HYL: They do.

PHIL: How can you then conclude from sight that figures exist without, when you acknowledge colours do not; the sensible appearance being the very same with regard to both?

HYL: I know not what to answer.

PHIL: But, allowing that distance was truly and immediately perceived by the mind, yet it would not thence follow it existed out of the mind. For, whatever is immediately perceived is an idea: and can any idea exist out of the mind?

HYL: To suppose that were absurd: but, inform me, Philonous, can we perceive or know nothing beside our ideas?

PHIL: As for the rational deducing of causes from effects, that is beside our inquiry. And, by the senses you can best tell whether you perceive anything which is not immediately perceived. And I ask you, whether the things immediately perceived are other than your own sensations or ideas? You have indeed more than once, in the course of this conversation, declared yourself on those points; but you seem, by this last question, to have departed from what you then thought.

HYL: To speak the truth, Philonous, I think there are two kinds of objects:—the one perceived immediately, which are likewise called *ideas*; the other are real things or external objects, perceived by the mediation of ideas, which are their images and representations. Now, I own ideas do not exist without the mind; but the latter sort of objects do. I am sorry I did not think of this distinction sooner; it would probably have cut short your discourse.

PHIL: Are those external objects perceived by sense, or by some other faculty?

HYL: They are perceived by sense.

PHIL: How! Is there anything perceived by sense which is not immediately perceived?

HYL: Yes, Philonous, in some sort there is. For example, when I look on a picture or statue of Julius Cæsar, I may be said after a manner to perceive him (though not immediately) by my senses.

PHIL: It seems then you will have our ideas, which alone are immediately perceived, to be pictures of external things: and that these also are perceived by sense, inasmuch as they have a conformity or resemblance to our ideas?

HYL: That is my meaning.

PHIL: And, in the same way that Julius Cæsar, in himself invisible, is nevertheless perceived by sight; real things, in themselves imperceptible, are perceived by sense.

HYL: In the very same.

PHIL: Tell me, Hylas, when you behold the picture of Julius Cæsar, do you see with your eyes any more than some colours and figures, with a certain symmetry and composition of the whole?

HYL: Nothing else.

PHIL: And would not a man who had never known anything of Julius Cæsar see as much?

HYL: He would.

PHIL: Consequently he hath his sight, and the use of it, in as perfect a degree as you?

HYL: I agree with you.

PHIL: Whence comes it then that your thoughts are directed to the Roman emperor, and his are not? This cannot proceed from the sensations or ideas of sense by you then perceived; since you acknowledge you have no advantage over him in that respect. It should seem therefore to proceed from reason and memory: should it not?

HYL: It should.

PHIL: Consequently, it will not follow from that instance that anything is perceived by sense which is not immediately perceived. Though I grant we may, in one acceptation, be said to perceive sensible things mediately by sense: that is, when, from a frequently perceived connexion, the immediate perception of ideas by one sense *suggests* to the mind others, perhaps belonging to another sense, which are wont to be connected with them. For instance, when I hear a coach drive along the streets, immediately I perceive only the sound; but, from the experience I have had that such a sound is connected with a coach, I am said to hear the coach. It is nevertheless evident that, in truth and strictness, nothing can be *heard* but *sound*; and the coach is not then properly perceived by sense, but suggested from experience. So likewise when we are said to see a red-hot bar of iron; the solidity and heat of the iron are not the objects of sight, but suggested to the imagination by the colour and figure which are properly perceived by that sense. In short, those things alone are actually and strictly perceived by any sense, which would have been perceived in case that same sense had then been first conferred on us. As for other things, it is plain they are only suggested to the mind by experience, grounded on former perceptions. But, to return to your comparison of Cæsar's picture, it is plain, if you keep to that, you must hold the real things, or archetypes of our ideas, are not perceived by sense, but by some internal faculty of the soul, as reason or memory. I would therefore fain know what arguments you can draw from reason for the existence of what you call *real things* or *material objects*. Or, whether you remember to have seen them formerly as they are in themselves; or, if you have heard or read of any one that did.

HYL: I see, Philonous, you are disposed to raillery; but that will never convince me.

PHIL: My aim is only to learn from you the way to come at the knowledge of *material beings*. Whatever we perceive is perceived immediately or mediately: by sense, or by reason and reflexion. But, as you have excluded sense, pray shew me what reason you have to believe their existence; or what *medium* you can possibly make use of to prove it, either to mine or your own understanding.

HYL: To deal ingenuously, Philonous, now I consider the point, I do not find I can give you any good reason for it. But, thus much seems pretty plain, that it is at least possible such things may really exist. And, as long as there is no absurdity in supposing them, I am resolved to believe as I did, till you bring good reasons to the contrary.

PHIL: What! Is it come to this, that you only *believe* the existence of material objects, and that your belief is founded barely on the possibility of its being true? Then you will have me bring reasons against it: though another would think it reasonable the proof should lie on him who holds the affirmative. And, after all, this very point which you are now resolved to maintain, without any reason, is in effect what you have more than once during this discourse seen good reason to give up. But, to pass over all this; if I understand you rightly, you say our ideas do not exist without the mind, but that they are copies, images, or representations, of certain originals that do?

HYL: You take me right.

PHIL: They are then like external things?

HYL: They are.

PHIL: Have those things a stable and permanent nature, independent of our senses; or are they in a perpetual change, upon our producing any motions in our bodies—suspending, exerting, or altering, our faculties or organs of sense?

HYL: Real things, it is plain, have a fixed and real nature, which remains the same notwithstanding any change in our senses, or in the posture and motion of our bodies; which indeed may affect the ideas in our minds, but it were absurd to think they had the same effect on things existing without the mind.

PHIL: How then is it possible that things perpetually fleeting and variable as our ideas should be copies or images of anything fixed and constant? Or, in other words, since all sensible qualities, as size, figure, colour, etc., that is, our ideas, are continually changing, upon every alteration in the distance, medium, or instruments of sensation; how can any determinate material objects be properly represented or painted forth by several distinct things, each of which is so different from and unlike the rest? Or, if you say it resembles some one only of our ideas, how shall we be able to distinguish the true copy from all the false ones.

HYL: I profess, Philonous, I am at a loss. I know not what to say to this.

PHIL: But neither is this all. Which are material objects in themselves—perceptible or imperceptible?

HYL: Properly and immediately nothing can be perceived but ideas, All material things, there-

fore, are in themselves insensible, and to be perceived only by our ideas.

PHIL: Ideas then are sensible, and their archetypes
or originals insensible?

HYL: Right.

PHIL: But how can that which is sensible be *like*
that which is insensible? Can a real thing, in itself *invisible*, be like a *colour*; or a real thing,
which is not *audible*, be like a *sound*? In a word,
can anything be like a sensation or idea, but another sensation or idea?

HYL: I must own, I think not.

PHIL: Is it possible there should be any doubt on
the point? Do you not perfectly know your own
· ideas?

HYL: I know them perfectly; since what I do not
perceive or know can be no part of my idea.

PHIL: Consider, therefore, and examine them,
and then tell me if there be anything in them
which can exist without the mind: or if you can
conceive anything like them existing without the
mind.

HYL: Upon inquiry, I find it is impossible for me
to conceive or understand how anything but an
idea can be like an idea. And it is most evident
that *no idea can exist without the mind*.

PHIL: You are therefore, by your principles,
forced to deny the *reality* of sensible things; since
you made it to consist in an absolute existence exterior to the mind. That is to say, you are a down-
right sceptic. So I have gained my point, which
was to shew your principles led to Scepticism.

HYL: For the present I am, if not entirely convinced, at least silenced.

PHIL: I would fain know what more you would
require in order to a perfect conviction. Have you
not had the liberty of explaining yourself all manner of ways? Were any little slips in discourse
laid hold and insisted on? Or were you not allowed to retract or reinforce anything you had
offered, as best served your purpose? Hath not
everything you could say been heard and examined with all the fairness imaginable? In a word,
have you not in every point been convinced out
of your own mouth? And, if you can at present
discover any flaw in any of your former concessions, or think of any remaining subterfuge, any

new distinction, colour, or comment whatsoever,
why do you not produce it?

HYL: A little patience, Philonous. I am at present
so amazed to see myself ensnared, and as it were
imprisoned in the labyrinths you have drawn me
into, that on the sudden it cannot be expected I
should find my way out. You must give me time
to look about me and recollect myself.

PHIL: Hark; is not this the college bell?

HYL: It rings for prayers.

PHIL: We will go in then, if you please, and meet
here again to-morrow morning. In the meantime,
you may employ your thoughts on this morning's
discourse and try if you can find any fallacy in it,
or invent any new means to extricate yourself.

HYL: Agreed.

· · · · · · · ·

The Second Dialogue

PHILONOUS: Well then, are you at length satisfied that no sensible things have a real existence;
and that you are in truth an arrant sceptic?

HYLAS: It is too plain to be denied.

PHIL: Look! are not the fields covered with a delightful verdure? Is there not something in the
woods and groves, in the rivers and clear springs,
that soothes, that delights, that transports the
soul? At the prospect of the wide and deep ocean,
or some huge mountain whose top is lost in the
clouds, or of an old gloomy forest, are not our
minds filled with a pleasing horror? Even in
rocks and deserts is there not an agreeable wildness? How sincere a pleasure is it to behold the
natural beauties of the earth! To preserve and renew our relish for them, is not the veil of night
alternately drawn over her face, and doth she not
change her dress with the seasons? How aptly are
the elements disposed! What variety and use in
the meanest productions of nature! What delicacy, what beauty, what contrivance, in animal
and vegetable bodies! How exquisitely are all
things suited, as well to their particular ends, as
to constitute opposite parts of the whole! And,
while they mutually aid and support, do they not
also set off and illustrate each other? Raise now
your thoughts from this ball of earth to all those

glorious luminaries that adorn the high arch of heaven. The motion and situation of the planets, are they not admirable for use and order? Were those (miscalled *erratic*) globes once known to stray, in their repeated journeys through the pathless void? Do they not measure areas round the sun ever proportioned to the times? So fixed, so immutable are the laws by which the unseen Author of nature actuates the universe. How vivid and radiant is the lustre of the fixed stars! How magnificent and rich that negligent profusion with which they appear to be scattered throughout the whole azure vault! Yet, if you take the telescope, it brings into your sight a new host of stars that escape the naked eye. Here they seem contiguous and minute, but to a nearer view immense orbs of light at various distances, far sunk in the abyss of space. Now you must call imagination to your aid. The feeble narrow sense cannot descry innumerable worlds revolving round the central fires; and in those worlds the energy of an all-perfect Mind displayed in endless forms. But, neither sense nor imagination are big enough to comprehend the boundless extent, with all its glittering furniture. Though the labouring mind exert and strain each power to its utmost reach, there still stands out ungrasped a surplusage immeasurable. Yet all the vast bodies that compose this mighty frame, how distant and remote soever, are by some secret mechanism, some Divine art and force, linked in a mutual dependence and intercourse with each other; even with this earth, which was almost slipt from my thoughts and lost in the crowd of worlds. Is not the whole system immense, beautiful, glorious beyond expression and beyond thought! What treatment, then, do those philosophers deserve, who would deprive these noble and delightful scenes of all *reality*? How should those Principles be entertained that lead us to think all the visible beauty of the creation a false imaginary glare? To be plain, can you expect this Scepticism of yours will not be thought extravagantly absurd by all men of sense?

HYL: Other men may think as they please; but for your part you have nothing to reproach me with. My comfort is, you are as much a sceptic as I am.

PHIL: There, Hylas, I must beg leave to differ from you.

HYL: What! Have you all along agreed to the premises, and do you now deny the conclusion, and leave me to maintain those paradoxes by myself which you led me into? This surely is not fair.

PHIL: I deny that I agreed with you in those notions that led to Scepticism. You indeed said the *reality* of sensible things consisted in an *absolute existence out of the minds of spirits*, or distinct from their being perceived. And pursuant to this notion of reality, *you* are obliged to deny sensible things any real existence: that is, according to your own definition, you profess yourself a sceptic. But I neither said nor thought the reality of sensible things was to be defined after that manner. To me it is evident, for the reasons you allow of, that sensible things cannot exist otherwise than in a mind or spirit. Whence I conclude, not that they have no real existence, but that, seeing they depend not on my thought, and have an existence distinct from being perceived by me, *there must be some other Mind wherein they exist.* As sure, therefore, as the sensible world really exists, so sure is there an infinite omnipresent Spirit who contains and supports it.

HYL: What! This is no more than I and all Christians hold; nay, and all others too who believe there is a God, and that He knows and comprehends all things.

PHIL: Aye, but here lies the difference. Men commonly believe that all things are known or perceived by God, because they believe the being of a God; whereas I, on the other side, immediately and necessarily conclude the being of a God, because all sensible things must be perceived by Him.

HYL: But, so long as we all believe the same thing, what matter is it how we come by that belief?

PHIL: But neither do we agree in the same opinion. For philosophers, though they acknowledge all corporeal beings to be perceived by God, yet they attribute to them an absolute subsistence distinct from their being perceived by any mind whatever; which I do not. Besides, is there no difference between saying, *There is a God, therefore*

He perceives all things; and saying, *Sensible things do really exist; and, if they really exist, they are necessarily perceived by an infinite Mind: therefore there is an infinite Mind, or God?* This furnishes you with a direct and immediate demonstration, from a most evident principle, of the *being of a God.* Divines and philosophers had proved beyond all controversy, from the beauty and usefulness of the several parts of the creation, that it was the workmanship of God. But that—setting aside all help of astronomy and natural philosophy, all contemplation of the contrivance, order, and adjustment of things—an infinite Mind should be necessarily inferred from the bare *existence of the sensible world*, is an advantage to them only who have made this easy reflexion: That the sensible world is that which we perceive by our several senses; and that nothing is perceived by the senses beside ideas; and that no idea or archetype of an idea can exist otherwise than in a mind. You may now, without any laborious search into the sciences, without any subtlety of reason, or tedious length of discourse, oppose and baffle the most strenuous advocate for Atheism. Those miserable refuges, whether in an eternal succession of unthinking causes and effects, or in a fortuitous concourse of atoms; those wild imaginations of Vanini, Hobbes, and Spinoza: in a word, the whole system of Atheism, is it not entirely overthrown, by this single reflexion on the repugnancy included in supposing the whole, or any part, even the most rude and shapeless, of the visible world, to exist without a Mind? Let any one of those abettors of impiety but look into his own thoughts, and there try if he can conceive how so much as a rock, a desert, a chaos, or confused jumble of atoms; how anything at all, either sensible or imaginable, can exist independent of a Mind, and he need go no farther to be convinced of his folly. Can anything be fairer than to put a dispute on such an issue, and leave it to a man himself to see if he can conceive, even in thought, what he holds to be true in fact, and from a notional to allow it a real existence?

. . . .

[PHIL] . . .—It is evident that the things I perceive are my own ideas, and that no idea can exist unless it be in a mind: nor is it less plain that these ideas or things by me perceived, either themselves or their archetypes, exist independently of *my* mind, since I know myself not to be their author, it being out of my power to determine at pleasure what particular ideas I shall be affected with upon opening my eyes or ears: they must therefore exist in some other Mind, whose Will it is they should be exhibited to me. The things, I say, immediately perceived are ideas or sensations, call them which you will. But how can any idea or sensation exist in, or be produced by, anything but a mind or spirit? This indeed is inconceivable. And to assert that which is inconceivable is to talk nonsense: is it not?

HYL: Without doubt.

PHIL: But, on the other hand, it is very conceivable that they should exist in and be produced by a Spirit; since this is no more than I daily experience in myself, inasmuch as I perceive numberless ideas; and, by an act of my will, can form a great variety of them, and raise them up in my imagination: though, it must be confessed, these creatures of the fancy are not altogether so distinct, so strong, vivid, and permanent, as those perceived by my senses—which latter are called *real things.* From all which I conclude, *there is a Mind which affects me every moment with all the sensible impressions I perceive.* And, from the variety, order, and manner of these, I conclude *the Author of them to be wise, powerful, and good, beyond comprehension.* Mark it well; I do not say, I see things by perceiving that which represents them in the intelligible Substance of God. This I do not understand; but I say, the things by me perceived are known by the understanding, and produced by the will of an infinite Spirit. And is not all this most plain and evident? Is there any more in it than what a little observation in our own minds, and that which passeth in them, not only enables us to conceive, but also obliges us to acknowledge?

. . . .

The Third Dialogue

PHILONOUS: Tell me, Hylas, what are the fruits of yesterday's meditation? Has it confirmed you in the same mind you were in at parting? or have you since seen cause to change your opinion?

HYLAS: Truly my opinion is that all our opinions are alike vain and uncertain. What we approve to-day, we condemn to-morrow. We keep a stir about knowledge, and spend our lives in the pursuit of it, when, alas! we know nothing all the while: nor do I think it possible for us ever to know anything in this life. Our faculties are too narrow and too few. Nature certainly never intended us for speculation.

PHIL: What! Say you we can know nothing, Hylas?

HYL: There is not that single thing in the world whereof we can know the real nature, or what it is in itself.

PHIL: Will you tell me I do not really know what fire or water is?

HYL: You may indeed know that fire appears hot, and water fluid; but this is no more than knowing what sensations are produced in your own mind, upon the application of fire and water to your organs of sense. Their internal constitution, their true and real nature, you are utterly in the dark as to *that*.

PHIL: Do I not know this to be a real stone that I stand on, and that which I see before my eyes to be a real tree?

HYL: *Know?* No, it is impossible you or any man alive should know it. All you know is, that you have such a certain idea or appearance in your mind. But what is this to the real tree or stone? I tell you that colour, figure, and hardness, which you perceive, are not the real natures of those things, or in the least like them. The same may be said of all other real things, or corporeal substances, which compose the world. They have none of them anything of themselves, like those sensible qualities by us perceived. We should not therefore pretend to affirm or know anything of them, as they are in their own nature.

PHIL: But surely, Hylas, I can distinguish gold, for example, from iron: and how could this be, if I knew not what either truly was?

HYL: Believe me, Philonous, you can only distinguish between your own ideas. That yellowness, that weight, and other sensible qualities, think you they are really in the gold? They are only relative to the senses, and have no absolute existence in nature. And in pretending to distinguish the species of real things, by the appearances in your mind, you may perhaps act as wisely as he that should conclude two men were of a different species, because their clothes were not of the same colour.

PHIL: It seems, then, we are altogether put off with the appearances of things, and those false ones too. The very meat I eat, and the cloth I wear, have nothing in them like what I see and feel.

HYL: Even so.

PHIL: But is it not strange the whole world should be thus imposed on, and so foolish as to believe their senses? And yet I know not how it is, but men eat, and drink, and sleep, and perform all the offices of life, as comfortably and conveniently as if they really knew the things they are conversant about.

HYL: They do so: but you know ordinary practice does not require a nicety of speculative knowledge. Hence the vulgar retain their mistakes, and for all that make a shift to bustle through the affairs of life. But philosophers know better things.

PHIL: You mean, they *know* that they *know nothing*.

HYL: That is the very top and perfection of human knowledge.

PHIL: But are you all this while in earnest, Hylas; and are you seriously persuaded that you know nothing real in the world? Suppose you are going to write, would you not call for pen, ink, and paper, like another man; and do you not know what it is you call for?

HYL: How often must I tell you, that I know not the real nature of any one thing in the universe? I may indeed upon occasion make use of pen, ink, and paper. But what any one of them is in its own true nature, I declare positively I know not. And the same is true with regard to every other corporeal thing. And, what is more, we are not only ignorant of the true and real nature of things, but even of their existence. It cannot be denied that we perceive such certain appearances or ideas; but it cannot be concluded from thence that bodies really exist. Nay, now I think on it, I must, agreeably to my former concessions, farther declare that it is impossible any *real* corporeal thing should exist in nature.

PHIL: You amaze me. Was ever anything more wild and extravagant than the notions you now maintain: and is it not evident you are led into all these extravagances by the belief of *material substance*? This makes you dream of those unknown natures in everything. It is this occasions your distinguishing between the reality and sensible appearances of things. It is to this you are indebted for being ignorant of what everybody else knows perfectly well. Nor is this all: you are not only ignorant of the true nature of everything, but you know not whether anything really exists, or whether there are any true natures at all; forasmuch as you attribute to your material beings an absolute or external existence, wherein you suppose their reality consists. And, as you are forced in the end to acknowledge such an existence means either a direct repugnancy, or nothing at all, it follows that you are obliged to pull down your own hypothesis of material substance, and positively to deny the real existence of any part of the universe. And so you are plunged into the deepest and most deplorable scepticism that ever man was. Tell me, Hylas, is it not as I say?

HYL: I agree with you. *Material substance* was no more than an hypothesis; and a false and groundless one too. I will no longer spend my breath in defence of it. But whatever hypothesis you advance, or whatsoever scheme of things you introduce in its stead, I doubt not it will appear every whit as false: let me but be allowed to question you upon it. That is, suffer me to serve you in your own kind, and I warrant it shall conduct you through as many perplexities and contradictions, to the very same state of scepticism that I myself am in at present.

PHIL: I assure you, Hylas, I do not pretend to frame any hypothesis at all. I am of a vulgar cast, simple enough to believe my senses, and leave things as I find them. To be plain, it is my opinion that the real things are those very things I see, and feel, and perceive by my senses. These I know; and, finding they answer all the necessities and purposes of life, have no reason to be so-

licitous about any other unknown beings. A piece of sensible bread, for instance, would stay my stomach better than ten thousand times as much of that insensible, unintelligible, real bread you speak of. It is likewise my opinion that colours and other sensible qualities are on the objects. I cannot for my life help thinking that snow is white, and fire hot. You indeed, who by *snow* and *fire* mean certain external, unperceived, unperceiving substances, are in the right to deny whiteness or heat to be affections inherent in *them*. But I, who understand by those words the things I see and feel, am obliged to think like other folks. And, as I am no sceptic with regard to the nature of things, so neither am I as to their existence. That a thing should be really perceived by my senses, and at the same time not really exist, is to me a plain contradiction; since I cannot prescind or abstract, even in thought, the existence of a sensible thing from its being perceived. Wood, stones, fire, water, flesh, iron, and the like things, which I name and discourse of, are things that I know. And I should not have known them but that I perceived them by my senses; and things perceived by the senses are immediately perceived; and things immediately perceived are ideas; and ideas cannot exist without the mind; their existence therefore consists in being perceived; when, therefore, they are actually perceived there can be no doubt of their existence. Away then with all that scepticism, all those ridiculous philosophical doubts. What a jest is it for a philosopher to question the existence of sensible things, till he hath it proved to him from the veracity of God; or to pretend our knowledge in this point falls short of intuition or demonstration! I might as well doubt of my own being, as of the being of those things I actually see and feel.

HYL: Not so fast, Philonous: you say you cannot conceive how sensible things should exist without the mind. Do you not?

PHIL: I do.

HYL: Supposing you were annihilated, cannot you conceive it possible that things perceivable by sense may still exist?

PHIL: I can; but then it must be in another mind. When I deny sensible things an existence out of the mind, I do not mean my mind in particular, but all minds. Now, it is plain they have an existence exterior to my mind; since I find them by experience to be independent of it. There is therefore some other Mind wherein they exist, during the intervals between the times of my perceiving them: as likewise they did before my birth, and would do after my supposed annihilation. And, as the same is true with regard to all other finite created spirits, it necessarily follows there is an *omnipresent eternal Mind*, which knows and comprehends all things, and exhibits them to our view in such a manner, and according to such rules, as He Himself hath ordained, and are by us termed the *laws of nature*.

HYL: Answer me, Philonous. Are all our ideas perfectly inert beings? Or have they any agency included in them?

PHIL: They are altogether passive and inert.

HYL: And is not God an agent, a being purely active?

PHIL: I acknowledge it.

HYL: No idea therefore can be like unto, or represent the nature of God?

PHIL: It cannot.

HYL: Since therefore you have no *idea* of the mind of God, how can you conceive it possible that things should exist in His mind? Or, if you can conceive the mind of God, without having an idea of it, why may not I be allowed to conceive the existence of Matter, notwithstanding I have no idea of it?

PHIL: As to your first question: I own I have properly no *idea*, either of God or any other spirit; for these being active, cannot be represented by things perfectly inert, as our ideas are. I do nevertheless know that I, who am a spirit or thinking substance, exist as certainly as I know my ideas exist. Farther, I know what I mean by the terms *I* and *myself*; and I know this immediately or intuitively, though I do not perceive it as I perceive a triangle, a colour, or a sound. The Mind, Spirit, or Soul is that indivisible unextended thing which thinks, acts, and perceives. I say *indivisible*, because unextended; and *unextended*, because extended, figured, moveable things are ideas; and that which perceives ideas, which

thinks and wills, is plainly itself no idea, nor like an idea. Ideas are things inactive, and perceived. And Spirits a sort of beings altogether different from them. I do not therefore say my soul is an idea, or like an idea. However, taking the word *idea* in a large sense, my soul may be said to furnish me with an idea, that is, an image or likeness of God—though indeed extremely inadequate. For, all the notion I have of God is obtained by reflecting on my own soul, heightening its powers, and removing its imperfections. I have, therefore, though not an inactive idea, yet in *myself* some sort of an active thinking image of the Deity. And, though I perceive Him not by sense, yet I have a notion of Him, or know Him by reflexion and reasoning. My own mind and my own ideas I have an immediate knowledge of; and, by the help of these, do mediately apprehend the possibility of the existence of other spirits and ideas. Farther, from my own being, and from the dependency I find in myself and my ideas, I do, by an act of reason, necessarily infer the existence of a God, and of all created things in the mind of God. So much for your first question. For the second: I suppose by this time you can answer it yourself. For you neither perceive Matter objectively, as you do an inactive being or idea; nor know it, as you do yourself, by a reflex act; neither do you mediately apprehend it by similitude of the one or the other; nor yet collect it by reasoning from that which you know immediately. All which makes the case of *Matter* widely different from that of the *Deity*.

HYL: You say your own soul supplies you with some sort of an idea or image of God. But, at the same time, you acknowledge you have, properly speaking, no *idea* of your own soul. You even affirm that spirits are a sort of beings altogether different from ideas. Consequently that no idea can be like a spirit. We have therefore no idea of any spirit. You admit nevertheless that there is spiritual substance, although you have no idea of it; while you deny there can be such a thing as material substance, because you have no notion or idea of it. Is this fair dealing? To *act* consistently, you must either admit Matter or reject Spirit. What say you to this?

PHIL: I say, in the first place, that I do not deny the existence of material substance, merely because I have no notion of it, but because the notion of it is inconsistent; or, in other words, because it is repugnant that there should be a notion of it. Many things, for aught I know, may exist, whereof neither I nor any other man hath or can have any idea or notion whatsoever. But then those things must be possible, that is, nothing inconsistent must be included in their definition. I say, secondly, that, although we believe things to exist which we do not perceive, yet we may not believe that any particular thing exists, without some reason for such belief: but I have no reason for believing the existence of Matter. I have no immediate intuition thereof: neither can I immediately from my sensations, ideas, notions, actions, or passions, infer an unthinking, unperceiving, inactive substance—either by probable deduction, or necessary consequence. Whereas the being of my Self, that is, my own soul, mind, or thinking principle, I evidently know by reflexion. You will forgive me if I repeat the same things in answer to the same objections. In the very notion or definition of *material substance*, there is included a manifest repugnance and inconsistency. But this cannot be said of the notion of Spirit. That ideas should exist in what doth not perceive, or be produced by what doth not act, is repugnant. But, it is no repugnancy to say that a perceiving thing should be the subject of ideas, or an active thing the cause of them. It is granted we have neither an immediate evidence nor a demonstrative knowledge of the existence of other finite spirits; but it will not hence follow that such spirits are on a foot with material substances: if to suppose the one be inconsistent, and it be not inconsistent to suppose the other; if the one can be inferred by no argument, and there is a probability for the other; if we see signs and effects indicating distinct finite agents like ourselves, and see no sign or symptom whatever that leads to a rational belief of Matter. I say, lastly, that I have a notion of Spirit, though I have not, strictly speaking, an idea of it. I do not perceive it as an idea, or by means of an idea, but know it by reflexion.

HYL: Notwithstanding all you have said, to me it seems that, according to your own way of thinking, and in consequence of your own principles, it should follow that *you* are only a system of floating ideas, without any substance to support them. Words are not to be used without a meaning. And, as there is no more meaning in *spiritual substance* than in *material substance*, the one is to be exploded as well as the other.

PHIL: How often must I repeat, that I know or am conscious of my own being; and that *I myself* am not my ideas, but somewhat else, a thinking, active principle that perceives, knows, wills, and operates about ideas. I know that I, one and the same self, perceive both colours and sounds: that a colour cannot perceive a sound, nor a sound a colour: that I am therefore one individual principle, distinct from colour and sound; and, for the same reason, from all other sensible things and inert ideas. But, I am not in like manner conscious either of the existence or essence of Matter. On the contrary, I know that nothing inconsistent can exist, and that the existence of Matter implies an inconsistency. Farther, I know what I mean when I affirm that there is a spiritual substance or support of ideas, that is, that a spirit knows and perceives ideas. But, I do not know what is meant when it is said that an unperceiving substance hath inherent in it and supports either ideas or the archetypes of ideas. There is therefore upon the whole no parity of case between Spirit and Matter.

. . . .

HYL: But, according to your notions, what difference is there between real things, and chimeras formed by the imagination, or the visions of a dream—since they are all equally in the mind?

PHIL: The ideas formed by the imagination are faint and indistinct: they have, besides, an entire dependence on the will. But the ideas perceived by sense, that is, real things, are more vivid and clear; and, being imprinted on the mind by a spirit distinct from us, have not the like dependence on our will. There is therefore no danger of confounding these with the foregoing; and there is as little of confounding them with the visions of a dream, which are dim, irregular, and confused. And, though they should happen to be never so lively and natural, yet, by their not being connected, and of a piece with the preceding and subsequent transactions of our lives, they might easily be distinguished from realities. In short, by whatever method you distinguish *things* from *chimeras* on your scheme, the same, it is evident, will hold also upon mine. For, it must be, I presume, by some perceived difference; and I am not for depriving you of any one thing that you perceive.

HYL: As for the difficulties other opinions may be liable to, those are out of the question. It is your business to defend your own opinion. Can anything be plainer than that you are for changing all things into ideas? You, I say, who are not ashamed to charge me with *scepticism*. This is so plain, there is no denying it.

PHIL: You mistake me. I am not for changing things into ideas, but rather ideas into things; since those immediate objects of perception, which, according to you, are only appearances of things, I take to be the real things themselves.

HYL: Things! You may pretend what you please; but it is certain you leave us nothing but the empty forms of things, the outside only which strikes the senses.

PHIL: What you call the empty forms and outside of things seem to me the very things themselves. Nor are they empty or incomplete, otherwise than upon your supposition—that Matter is an essential part of all corporeal things. We both, therefore, agree in this, that we perceive only sensible forms: but herein we differ—you will have them to be empty appearances, I real beings. In short, you do not trust your senses, I do.

HYL: You say you believe your senses; and seem to applaud yourself that in this you agree with the vulgar. According to you, therefore, the true nature of a thing is discovered by the senses. If so, whence comes that disagreement: Why is not the same figure, and other sensible qualities, perceived all manner of ways? and why should we use a microscope the better to discover the true nature of a body, if it were discoverable to the naked eye?

PHIL: Strictly speaking, Hylas, we do not see the same object that we feel; neither is the same object perceived by the microscope which was by the naked eye. But, in case every variation was thought sufficient to constitute a new kind or individual, the endless number or confusion of names would render language impracticable. Therefore, to avoid this, as well as other inconveniences which are obvious upon a little thought, men combine together several ideas, apprehended by divers senses, or by the same sense at different times, or in different circumstances, but observed, however, to have some connexion in nature, either with respect to co-existence or succession; all which they refer to one name, and consider as one thing. Hence it follows that when I examine, by my other senses, a thing I have seen, it is not in order to understand better the same object which I had perceived by sight, the object of one sense not being perceived by the other senses. And, when I look through a microscope, it is not that I may perceive more clearly what I perceived already with my bare eyes; the object perceived by the glass being quite different from the former. But, in both cases, my aim is only to know what ideas are connected together; and the more a man knows of the connexion of ideas, the more he is said to know of the nature of things. What, therefore, if our ideas are variable; what if our senses are not in all circumstances affected with the same appearances? It will not thence follow they are not to be trusted; or that they are inconsistent either with themselves or anything else: except it be with your preconceived notion of (I know not what) one single, unchanged, unperceivable, real Nature, marked by each name. Which prejudice seems to have taken its rise from not rightly understanding the common language of men, speaking of several distinct ideas as united into one thing by the mind. And, indeed, there is cause to suspect several erroneous conceits of the philosophers are owing to the same original: while they began to build their schemes not so much on notions as on words, which were framed by the vulgar, merely for conveniency and dispatch in the common actions of life, without any regard to speculation.

HYL: Methinks I apprehend your meaning.

PHIL: It is your opinion the ideas we perceive by our senses are not real things, but images or copies of them. Our knowledge, therefore, is no farther real than as our ideas are the true *representations* of those *originals*. But, as these supposed originals are in themselves unknown, it is impossible to know how far our ideas resemble them; or whether they resemble them at all. We cannot, therefore, be sure we have any real knowledge. Farther, as our ideas are perpetually varied, without any change in the supposed real things, it necessarily follows they cannot all be true copies of them: or, if some are and others are not, it is impossible to distinguish the former from the latter. And this plunges us yet deeper in uncertainty. Again, when we consider the point, we cannot conceive how any idea, or anything like an idea, should have an absolute existence out of a mind: nor consequently, according to you, how there should be any real thing in nature. The result of all which is that we are thrown into the most hopeless and abandoned scepticism. Now, give me leave to ask you, First, Whether your referring ideas to certain absolutely existing unperceived substances, as their originals, be not the source of all this scepticism? Secondly, whether you are informed, either by sense or reason, of the existence of those unknown originals? And, in case you are not, whether it be not absurd to suppose them? Thirdly, Whether, upon inquiry, you find there is anything distinctly conceived or meant by the *absolute or external existence of unperceiving substances*? Lastly, Whether, the premises considered, it be not the wisest way to follow nature, trust your senses, and, laying aside all anxious thought about unknown natures or substances, admit with the vulgar those for real things are perceived by the senses?

HYL: For the present, I have no inclination to the answering part. I would much rather see how you can get over what follows. Pray are not the objects perceived by the *senses* of one, likewise perceivable to others present? If there were a hundred more here, they would all see the garden, the trees, and flowers, as I see them. But they are not in the same manner affected with the ideas I frame in my *imagination*. Does not this make a difference between the former sort of objects and the latter?

PHIL: I grant it does. Nor have I ever denied a difference between the objects of sense and those of imagination. But what would you infer from thence? You cannot say that sensible objects exist unperceived, because they are perceived by many.

HYL: I own I can make nothing of that objection: but it hath led me into another. Is it not your opinion that by our senses we perceive only the ideas existing in our minds?

PHIL: It is.

HYL: But the *same* idea which is in my mind cannot be in yours, or in any other mind. Doth it not therefore follow, from your principles, that no two can see the same thing? And is not this highly absurd?

PHIL: If the term *same* be taken in the vulgar acceptation, it is certain (and not at all repugnant to the principles I maintain) that different persons may perceive the same thing; or the same thing or idea exist in different minds. Words are of arbitrary imposition; and, since men are used to apply the word *same* where no distinction or variety is perceived, and I do not pretend to alter their perceptions, it follows that, as men have said before, *several saw the same thing*, so they may, upon like occasions, still continue to use the same phrase, without any deviation either from propriety or language, or the truth of things. But, if the term *same* be used in the acceptation of philosophers, who pretend to an abstracted notion of identity, then, according to their sundry definitions of this notion (for it is not yet agreed wherein that philosophic identity consists), it may or may not be possible for divers persons to perceive the same thing. But whether philosophers shall think fit to *call* a thing the *same* or no, is, I conceive, of small importance. Let us suppose several men together, all endued with the same faculties, and consequently affected in like sort by their senses, and who had yet never known the use of language; they would, without question, agree in their perceptions. Though perhaps, when they came to the use of speech, some regarding the uniformness of what was perceived, might call it the *same* thing: others, especially regarding the diversity of persons who perceived, might choose the denomination of *different* things. But who sees not that all the dispute is about a word? to wit, whether what is perceived by different persons may yet have the term *same* applied to it? Or, suppose a house, whose walls or outward shell remaining unaltered, the chambers are all pulled down, and new ones built in their place; and that you should call this the *same*, and I should say it was not the *same* house:— would we not, for all this, perfectly agree in our thoughts of the house, considered in itself? And would not all the difference consist in a sound? If you should say, We differed in our notions; for that you superadded to your idea of the house the simple abstracted idea of identity, whereas I did not; I would tell you, I know now what you mean by the *abstracted idea of identity*; and should desire you to look into your own thoughts, and be sure you understood yourself.—Why so silent, Hylas? Are you not yet satisfied men may dispute about identity and diversity, without any real difference in their thoughts and opinions, abstracted from names? Take this farther reflexion with you—that whether Matter be allowed to exist or no, the case is exactly the same as to the point in hand. For the Materialists themselves acknowledge what we immediately perceive by our senses to be our own ideas. Your difficulty, therefore, that no two see the same thing, makes equally against the Materialists and me.

. . . .

HYL: But, what would you say, Philonous, if I should bring the very same reasons against the existence of sensible things *in a mind*, which you have offered against their existing *in a material substratum*?

PHIL: When I see your reasons, you shall hear what I have to say to them.

HYL: Is the mind extended or unextended?

PHIL: Unextended, without doubt.

HYL: Do you say the things you perceive are in your mind?

PHIL: They are.

HYL: Again, have I not heard you speak of sensible impressions?

PHIL: I believe you may.

HYL: Explain to me now, O Philonous! how it is possible there should be room for all those trees and houses to exist in your mind. Can extended things be contained in that which is unextended? Or, are we to imagine impressions made on a thing void of all solidity? You cannot say objects are in your mind, as books in your study: or that things are imprinted on it, as the figure of a seal upon wax. In what sense, therefore, are we to understand those expressions? Explain me this if you can: and I shall then be able to answer all those queries you formerly put to me about my *substratum*.

PHIL: Look you, Hylas, when I speak of objects as existing in the mind, or imprinted on the senses, I would not be understood in the gross literal sense; as when bodies are said to exist in a place, or a seal to make an impression upon wax. My meaning is only that the mind comprehends or perceives them; and that it is affected from without, or by some being distinct from itself. This is my explication of your difficulty; and how it can serve to make your tenet of an unperceiving material *substratum* intelligible, I would fain know.

HYL: Nay, if that be all, I confess I do not see what use can be made of it. But are you not guilty of some abuse of language in this?

PHIL: None at all. It is no more than common custom, which you know is the rule of language, hath authorised: nothing being more usual, than for philosophers to speak of the immediate objects of the understanding as things existing in the mind. Nor is there anything in this but what is conformable to the general analogy of language; most part of the mental operations being signified by words borrowed from sensible things; as is plain in the terms *comprehend, reflect, discourse*, etc., which, being applied to the mind, must not be taken in their gross, original sense.

. . . .

HYL: I agree to all you have now said, and must own that nothing can incline me to embrace your opinion more than the advantages I see it is attended with. I am by nature lazy; and this would be a mighty abridgment in knowledge. What doubts, what hypotheses, what labyrinths of amusement, what fields of disputation, what an ocean of false learning, may be avoided by that single notion of *Immaterialism*!

PHIL: After all, is there anything farther remaining to be done? You may remember you promised to embrace that opinion which upon examination should appear most agreeable to Common Sense and remote from Scepticism. This, by your own confession, is that which denies Matter, or the *absolute* existence of corporeal things. Nor is this all; the same notion has been proved several ways, viewed in different lights, pursued in its consequences, and all objections against it cleared. Can there be a greater evidence of its truth? or is it possible it should have all the marks of a true opinion and yet be false?

HYL: I own myself entirely satisfied for the present in all respects. But, what security can I have that I shall still continue the same full assent to your opinion, and that no unthought-of objection or difficulty will occur hereafter?

PHIL: Pray, Hylas, do you in other cases, when a point is once evidently proved, withhold your consent on account of objections or difficulties it may be liable to? Are the difficulties that attend the doctrine of incommensurable quantities, of the angle of contact, of the asymptotes to curves, or the like, sufficient to make you hold out against mathematical demonstration? Or will you disbelieve the Providence of God, because there may be some particular things which *you* know not how to reconcile with? If there are difficulties attending *Immaterialism*, there are at the same time direct and evident proofs of it. But for the existence of Matter there is not one proof, and far more numerous and insurmountable objections lie against it. But where are those mighty difficulties you insist on? Alas! you know not where or what they are; something which may possibly occur hereafter. If this be a sufficient pretence for withholding your full assent, you should never yield it to any proposition, how free soever from exceptions, how clearly and solidly soever demonstrated.

HYL: You have satisfied me, Philonous.

PHIL: But, to arm you against all future objections, do but consider: That which bears equally hard on two contradictory opinions can be proof against neither. Whenever, therefore, any difficulty occurs, try if you can find a solution for it on the hypothesis of the *Materialists*. Be not deceived by words; but sound your own thoughts. And in case you cannot conceive it easier by the help of *Materialism*, it is plain it can be no objection against *Immaterialism*. Had you proceeded all along by this rule, you would probably have spared yourself abundance of trouble in objecting; since of all your difficulties I challenge you to shew one that is explained by Matter: nay, which is not more unintelligible with than without that supposition; and consequently makes rather *against* than *for* it. You should consider, in each particular, whether the difficulty arises from the *non-existence of Matter*. If it doth not, you might as well argue from the infinite divisibility of extension against the Divine prescience, as from such a difficulty against *Immaterialism*. And yet, upon recollection, I believe you will find this to have been often, if not always, the case. You should likewise take heed not to argue on a *petitio principii*. One is apt to say—The unknown substances ought to be esteemed real things, rather than the ideas in our minds: and who can tell but the unthinking external substance may concur, as a cause or instrument, in the productions of our ideas? But is not this proceeding on a supposition that there are such external substances? And to suppose this, is it not begging the question? But, above all things, you should beware of imposing on yourself by that vulgar sophism which is called *ignoratio elenchi*. You talked often as if you thought I maintained the non-existence of Sensible Things. Whereas in truth no one can be more thoroughly assured of their existence than I am. And it is you who doubt; I should have said, positively deny it. Everything that is seen, felt, heard, or any way perceived by the senses, is, on the principles I embrace, a real being; but not on yours. Remember, the Matter you contend for is an Unknown Somewhat (if indeed it may be termed *somewhat*), which is quite stripped of all sensible qualities, and can neither be perceived by sense, nor apprehended by the mind. Remember, I say, that it is not any object which is hard or soft, hot or cold, blue or white, round or square, etc. For all these things I affirm do exist. Though indeed I deny that they exist out of all minds whatsoever. Think on these points; let them be attentively considered and still kept in view. Otherwise you will not comprehend the state of the question; without which your objections will always be wide of the mark, and, instead of mine, may possibly be directed (as more than once they have been) against your own notions.

HYL: I must needs own, Philonous, nothing seems to have kept me from agreeing with you more than this same *mistaking the question*. In denying Matter, at first glimpse I am tempted to imagine you deny the things we see and feel: but, upon reflexion, find there is no ground for it. What think you, therefore, of retaining the name *Matter*, and applying it to *sensible things*? This may be done without any change in your sentiments: and, believe me, it would be a means of reconciling them to some persons who may be more shocked at an innovation in words than in opinion.

PHIL: With all my heart: retain the word *Matter*, and apply it to the objects of sense, if you please; provided you do not attribute to them any subsistence distinct from their being perceived. I shall never quarrel with you for an expression. *Matter*, or *material substance*, are terms introduced by philosophers; and, as used by them, imply a sort of independency, or a subsistence distinct from being perceived by a mind: but are never used by common people; or, if ever, it is to signify the immediate objects of sense. One would think, therefore, so long as the names of all particular things, with the terms *sensible*, *substance*, *body*, *stuff*, and the like, are retained, the word *Matter* should be never missed in common talk. And in philosophical discourses it seems the best way to leave it quite out: since there is not, perhaps, any one thing that hath more favoured and strengthened the depraved bent of the mind towards Atheism than the use of that general confused term.

HYL: Well but, Philonous, since I am content to give up the notion of an unthinking substance exterior to the mind, I think you ought not to deny me the privilege of using the word *Matter* as I please, and annexing it to a collection of sensible qualities subsisting only in the mind. I freely own there is no other substance, in a strict sense, than *Spirit*. But I have been so long accustomed to the term *Matter* that I know not how to part with it: to say, there is no *Matter* in the world, is still shocking to me. Whereas to say—There is no *Matter*, if by that term be meant an unthinking substance existing without the mind; but if by *Matter* is meant some sensible thing, whose existence consists in being perceived, then there is *Matter*:—this distinction gives it quite another turn; and men will come into your notions with small difficulty, when they are proposed in that manner. For, after all, the controversy about *Matter* in the strict acceptation of it, lies altogether between you and the philosophers: whose principles, I acknowledge, are not near so natural, or so agreeable to the common sense of mankind, and Holy Scripture, as yours. There is nothing we either desire or shun but as it makes, or is apprehended to make, some part of our happiness or misery. But what hath happiness or misery, joy or grief, pleasure or pain, to do with Absolute Existence; or with unknown entities, *abstracted from all relation to us*? It is evident, things regard us only as they are pleasing or displeasing: and they can please or displease only so far forth as they are perceived. Farther, therefore, we are not concerned; and thus far you leave things as you found them. Yet still there is something new in this doctrine. It is plain, I do not now think with the philosophers; nor yet altogether with the vulgar. I would know how the case stands in that respect; precisely, what you have added to, or altered in my former notions.

PHIL: I do not pretend to be a setter-up of new notions. My endeavours tend only to unite, and place in a clearer light, that truth which was before shared between the vulgar and the philosophers:—the former being of opinion, that *those things they immediately perceive are the real things*; and the latter, that *the things immediately perceived are ideas, which exist only in the mind*. Which two notions put together, do, in effect, constitute the substance of what I advance.

HYL: I have been a long time distrusting my senses: methought I saw things by a dim light and through false glasses. Now the glasses are removed and a new light breaks in upon my understanding. I am clearly convinced that I see things in their native forms, and am no longer in pain about their *unknown natures* or *absolute existence*. This is the state I find myself in at present; though, indeed, the course that brought me to it I do not yet thoroughly comprehend. You set out upon the same principles that Academics, Cartesians, and the like sects usually do; and for a long time it looked as if you were advancing

their philosophical Scepticism: but, in the end, your conclusions are directly opposite to theirs.

PHIL: You see, Hylas, the water of yonder fountain, how it is forced upwards, in a round column, to a certain height; at which it breaks, and falls back into the basin from whence it rose: its ascent, as well as descent, proceeding from the same uniform law or principle of gravitation. Just so, the same Principles which, at first view, lead to Scepticism, pursued to a certain point, bring men back to Common Sense.

Of Scepticism with Regard to the Senses

DAVID HUME

———•———

Section II
Of Scepticism with Regard to the Senses

Thus the sceptic still continues to reason and believe, even tho' he asserts, that he cannot defend his reason by reason; and by the same rule he must assent to the principle concerning the existence of body, tho' he cannot pretend by any arguments of philosophy to maintain its veracity. Nature has not left this to his choice, and has doubtless esteem'd it an affair of too great importance to be trusted to our uncertain reasonings and speculations. We may well ask, *What causes induce us to believe in the existence of body?* but 'tis in vain to ask, *Whether there be body or not?* That is a point, which we must take for granted in all our reasonings.

From *A Treatise of Human Nature*, edited by L. A. Selby-Bigge, 2nd edition revised by P. H. Nidditch. Copyright © 1978 by Oxford University Press. Reprinted by permission of the publisher.

The subject, then, of our present enquiry is concerning the *causes* which induce us to believe in the existence of body: And my reasonings on this head I shall begin with a distinction, which at first sight may seem superfluous, but which will contribute very much to the perfect understanding of what follows. We ought to examine apart those two questions, which are commonly confounded together, viz. Why we attribute a CONTINU'D existence to objects, even when they are not present to the senses; and why we suppose them to have an existence DISTINCT from the mind and perception. Under this last head I comprehend their situation as well as relations, their *external* position as well as the *independence* of their existence and operation. These two questions concerning the continu'd and distinct existence of body are intimately connected together. For if the objects of our senses continue to exist, even when they are not perceiv'd, their existence is of course independent of and distinct from the perception; and vice versa, if their existence be independent of the perception and distinct from it, they must continue to exist, even tho' they be not perceiv'd. But tho' the decision of the one question decides the other; yet that we may the more easily discover the principles of human nature, from whence the decision arises, we shall carry along with us this distinction, and shall consider, whether it be the *senses*, *reason*, or the *imagination*, that produces the opinion of a *continu'd* or of a *distinct* existence. These are the only questions, that are intelligible on the present subject. For as to the notion of external existence, when taken for something specifically different from our perceptions,[1] we have already shewn its absurdity.

To begin with the SENSES, 'tis evident these faculties are incapable of giving rise to the notion of the *continu'd* existence of their objects, after they no longer appear to the senses. For that is a contradiction in terms, and supposes that the senses continue to operate, even after they have ceas'd all manner of operation. These faculties, therefore, if they have any influence in the present case, must produce the opinion of a distinct, not of a continu'd existence; and in order to that, must present their impressions either as images and representations, or as these very distinct and external existences.

That our senses offer not their impressions as the images of something *distinct*, or *independent*, and *external*, is evident; because they convey to us nothing but a single perception, and never give us the least intimation of any thing beyond. A single perception can never produce the idea of a double existence, but by some inference either of the reason or imagination. When the mind looks farther than what immediately appears to it, its conclusions can never be put to the account of the senses; and it certainly looks farther, when from a single perception it infers a double existence, and supposes the relations of resemblance and causation betwixt them.

If our senses, therefore, suggest any idea of distinct existences, they must convey the impressions as those very existences, by a kind of fallacy and illusion. Upon this head we may observe, that all sensations are felt by the mind, such as they really are, and that when we doubt, whether they present themselves as distinct objects, or as mere impressions, the difficulty is not concerning their nature, but concerning their relations and situation. Now if

the senses presented our impressions as external to, and independent of ourselves, both the objects and ourselves must be obvious to our senses, otherwise they cou'd not be compar'd by these faculties. The difficulty, then, is how far we are *ourselves* the objects of our senses.

'Tis certain there is no question in philosophy more abstruse than that concerning identity, and the nature of the uniting principle, which constitutes a person. So far from being able by our senses merely to determine this question, we must have recourse to the most profound metaphysics to give a satisfactory answer to it; and in common life 'tis evident these ideas of self and person are never very fix'd nor determinate. 'Tis absurd, therefore, to imagine the senses can ever distinguish betwixt ourselves and external objects.

Add to this, that every impression, external and internal, passions, affections, sensations, pains and pleasures, are originally on the same footing; and that whatever other differences we may observe among them, they appear, all of them, in their true colours, as impressions or perceptions. And indeed, if we consider the matter aright, 'tis scarce possible it shou'd be more capable of deceiving us in the situation and relations, than in the nature of our impressions. For since all actions and sensations of the mind are known to us by consciousness, they must necessarily appear in every particular what they are, and be what they appear. Every thing that enters the mind, being in *reality* as the perception, 'tis impossible any thing shou'd to *feeling* appear different. This were to suppose, that even where we are most intimately conscious, we might be mistaken.

But not to lose time in examining, whether 'tis possible for our senses to deceive us, and represent our perceptions as distinct from ourselves, that is as *external* to and *independent* of us; let us consider whether they really do so, and whether this error proceeds from an immediate sensation, or from some other causes.

To begin with the question concerning *external* existence, it may perhaps be said, that setting aside the metaphysical question of the identity of a thinking substance, our own body evidently belongs to us; and as several impressions appear exterior to the body, we suppose them also exterior to ourselves.

The paper, on which I write at present, is beyond my hand. The table is beyond the paper. The walls of the chamber beyond the table. And in casting my eye towards the window, I perceive a great extent of fields and buildings beyond my chamber. From all this it may be infer'd, that no other faculty is requir'd, beside the senses, to convince us of the external existence of body. But to prevent this inference, we need only weigh the three following considerations. *First,* That, properly speaking, 'tis not our body we perceive, when we regard our limbs and members, but certain impressions, which enter by the senses; so that the ascribing a real and corporeal existence to these impressions, or to their objects, is an act of the mind as difficult to explain, as that which we examine at present. *Secondly*, Sounds, and tastes, and smells, tho' commonly regarded by the mind as continu'd independent quantities, appear not to have any existence in extension, and consequently cannot appear to the senses as situated externally to the body. The reason, why we ascribe a place to them, shall be consider'd[2] afterwards. *Thirdly*, Even our sight informs us not of distance or outness (so to speak) immediately and without a certain reasoning and experience, as is acknowledg'd by the most rational philosophers.

As to the *independency* of our perceptions on ourselves, this can never be an object of the senses; but any opinion we form concerning it, must be deriv'd from experience and observation: And we shall see afterwards, that our conclusions from experience are far from being favourable to the doctrine of the independency of our perceptions. Mean while we may observe that when we talk of real distinct existences, we have commonly more in our eye their independency than external situation in place, and think an object has a sufficient reality, when its Being is uninterrupted, and independent of the incessant revolutions, which we are conscious of in ourselves.

Thus to resume what I have said concerning the senses; they give us no notion of continu'd existence, because they cannot operate beyond the extent, in which they really operate. They as little produce the opinion of a distinct existence, because they neither can offer it to the mind as represented, nor as original. To offer it as represented, they must present both an object and an image. To make it appear as original, they must convey a falshood; and this falshood must lie in the relations and situation: In order to which they must be able to compare the object with ourselves; and even in that case they do not, nor is it possible they shou'd, deceive us. We may, therefore, conclude with certainty, that the opinion of a continu'd and of a distinct existence never arises from the senses.

To confirm this we may observe, that there are three different kinds of impressions convey'd by the senses. The first are those of the figure, bulk, motion and solidity of bodies. The second those of colours, tastes, smells, sounds, heat and cold. The third are the pains and pleasures, that arise from the application of objects to our bodies, as by the cutting of our flesh with steel, and such like. Both philosophers and the vulgar suppose the first of these to have a distinct continu'd existence. The vulgar only regard the second as on the same footing. Both philosophers and the vulgar, again, esteem the third to be merely perceptions; and consequently interrupted and dependent beings.

Now 'tis evident, that, whatever may be our philosophical opinion, colours, sounds, heat and cold, as far as appears to the senses, exist after the same manner with motion and solidity, and that the difference we make betwixt them in this respect, arises not from the mere perception. So strong is the prejudice for the distinct continu'd existence of the former qualities, that when the contrary opinion is advanc'd by modern philosophers, people imagine they can almost refute it from their feeling and experience, and that their very senses contradict this philosophy. 'Tis also evident, that colours, sounds, etc. are originally on the same footing with the pain that arises from steel, and pleasure that proceeds from a fire; and that the difference betwixt them is founded neither on perception nor reason, but on the imagination. For as they are confest to be, both of them, nothing but perceptions arising from the particular configurations and motions of the parts of body, wherein possible can their difference consist? Upon the whole, then, we may conclude, that as far as the senses are judges, all perceptions are the same in the manner of their existence.

We may also observe in this instance of sounds

and colours, that we can attribute a distinct continu'd existence to objects without ever consulting REASON, or weighing our opinions by any philosophical principles. And indeed, whatever convincing arguments philosophers may fancy they can produce to establish the belief of objects independent of the mind, 'tis obvious these arguments are known but to very few, and that 'tis not by them, that children, peasants, and the greatest part of mankind are induc'd to attribute objects to some impressions, and deny them to others. Accordingly we find, that all the conclusions, which the vulgar form on this head, are directly contrary to those, which are confirm'd by philosophy. For philosophy informs us, that every thing, which appears to the mind, is nothing but a perception, and is interrupted, and dependent on the mind; whereas the vulgar confound perceptions and objects, and attribute a distinct continu'd existence to the very things they feel or see. This sentiment, then, as it is entirely unreasonable, must proceed from some other faculty than the understanding. To which we may add, that as long as we take our perceptions and objects to be the same, we can never infer the existence of the one from that of the other, nor form any argument from the relation of cause and effect; which is the only one that can assure us of matter of fact. Even after we distinguish our perceptions from our objects, 'twill appear presently, that we are still incapable of reasoning from the existence of one to that of the other. So that upon the whole our reason neither does, nor is it possible it ever shou'd, upon any supposition, give us an assurance of the continu'd and distinct existence of body. That opinion must be entirely owing to the IMAGINATION: which must now be the subject of our enquiry.

Since all impressions are internal and perishing existences, and appear as such, the notion of their distinct and continu'd existence must arise from a concurrence of some of their qualities with the qualities of the imagination; and since this notion does not extend to all of them, it must arise from certain qualities peculiar to some impressions. 'Twill therefore be easy for us to discover these qualities by a comparison of the impressions, to which we attribute a distinct and continu'd existence, with those, which we regard as internal and perishing.

We may observe, then, that 'tis neither upon account of the involuntariness of certain impressions, as is commonly suppos'd, nor of their superior force and violence, that we attribute to them a reality, and continu'd existence, which we refuse to others, that are voluntary or feeble. For 'tis evident our pains and pleasures, our passions and affections, which we never suppose to have any existence beyond our perception, operate with greater violence, and are equally involuntary, as the impressions of figure and extension, colour and sound, which we suppose to be permanent beings. The heat of a fire, when moderate, is suppos'd to exist in the fire; but the pain, which it causes upon a near approach, is not taken to have any being except in the perception.

These vulgar opinions, then, being rejected, we must search for some other hypothesis, by which we may discover those peculiar qualities in our impressions, which makes us attribute to them a distinct and continu'd existence.

After a little examination, we shall find, that all those objects, to which we attribute a continu'd existence, have a peculiar *constancy*, which distinguishes them from the impressions, whose existence depends upon our perception. Those mountains, and houses, and trees, which lie at present under my eye, have always appear'd to me in the same order; and when I lose sight of them by shutting my eyes or turning my head, I soon after find them return upon me without the least alteration. My bed and table, my books and papers, present themselves in the same uniform manner, and change not upon account of any interruption in my seeing or perceiving them. This is the case with all the impressions, whose objects are suppos'd to have an external existence; and is the case with no other impressions, whether gentle or violent, voluntary or involuntary.

This constancy, however, is not so perfect as not to admit of very considerable exceptions. Bodies often change their position and qualities, and after a little absence or interruption may become hardly knowable. But here 'tis observable, that even in these changes they preserve a *coherence*, and have a regular dependence on each other; which is the foundation of a kind of reasoning from causation, and produces the opinion of their continu'd existence. When I return to my chamber after an hour's absence, I find not my fire in the same situation, in which I left it: But then I am accustom'd in other instances to see a like alteration produc'd in a like time, whether I am present or absent, near or remote. This coherence, therefore, in their changes is one of the characteristics of external objects, as well as their constancy.

Having found that the opinion of the continu'd existence of body depends on the COHERENCE and CONSTANCY of certain impressions, I now proceed to examine after what manner these qualities give rise to so extraordinary an opinion. To begin with the coherence; we may observe, that tho' those internal impressions, which we regard as fleeting and perishing, have also a certain coherence or regularity in their appearances, yet 'tis of somewhat a different nature, from that which we discover in bodies. Our passions are found by experience to have a mutual connexion with and dependance on each other; but on no occasion is it necessary to suppose, that they have existed and operated, when they were not perceiv'd, in order to preserve the same dependance and connexion, of which we have had experience. The case is not the same with relation to external objects. Those require a continu'd existence, or otherwise lose, in a great measure, the regularity of their operation. I am here seated in my chamber with my face to the fire; and all the objects, that strike my senses, are contain'd in a few yards around me. My memory, indeed, informs me of the existence of many objects; but then this information extends not beyond their past existence, nor do either my senses or memory give any testimony to the continuance of their being. When therefore I am thus seated, and revolve over these thoughts, I hear on a sudden a noise as of a door turning upon its hinges; and a little after see a porter, who advances towards me. This gives occasion to many new reflexions and reasonings. First, I never have observ'd, that this noise cou'd proceed from any thing but the motion of a door; and therefore conclude, that the present phenomenon is a contradiction to all past experience, unless the door, which I remember on t'other side the chamber, be still in being. Again, I have always found, that a human body was possest of a quality, which I call gravity, and which hinders it from mounting in the air, as this porter must have

done to arrive at my chamber, unless the stairs I remember be not annihilated by my absence. But this is not all. I receive a letter, which upon opening it I perceive by the hand-writing and subscription to have come from a friend, who says he is two hundred leagues distant. 'Tis evident I can never account for this phenomenon, conformable to my experience in other instances, without spreading out in my mind the whole sea and continent between us, and supposing the effects and continu'd existence of posts and ferries, according to my memory and observation. To consider these phenomena of the porter and letter in a certain light, they are contradictions to common experience, and may be regarded as objections to those maxims, which we form concerning the connexions of causes and effects. I am accustom'd to hear such a sound, and see such an object in motion at the same time. I have not receiv'd in this particular instance both these perceptions. These observations are contrary, unless I suppose that the door still remains, and that it was open'd without my perceiving it: And this supposition, which was at first entirely arbitrary and hypothetical, acquires a force and evidence by its being the only one, upon which I can reconcile these contradictions. There is scarce a moment of my life, wherein there is not a similar instance presented to me, and I have not occasion to suppose the continu'd existence of objects, in order to connect their past and present appearances, and give them such an union with each other, as I have found by experience to be suitable to their particular natures and circumstances. Here then I am naturally led to regard the world, as something real and durable, and as preserving its existence, even when it is no longer present to my perception.

But tho' this conclusion from the coherence of appearances may seem to be of the same nature with our reasonings concerning causes and effects; as being deriv'd from custom, and regulated by past experience; we shall find upon examination, that they are at the bottom considerably different from each other, and that this inference arises from the understanding, and from custom in an indirect and oblique manner. For 'twill readily be allow'd, that since nothing is ever really present to the mind, besides its own perceptions, 'tis not only impossible, that any habit shou'd ever be acquir'd otherwise than by the regular succession of these perceptions, but also that any habit shou'd ever exceed that degree of regularity. Any degree, therefore, of regularity in our perceptions, can never be a foundation for us to infer a greater degree of regularity in some objects, which are not perceiv'd; since this supposes a contradiction, viz. a habit acquir'd by what was never present to the mind. But 'tis evident, that whenever we infer the continu'd existence of the objects of sense from their coherence, and the frequency of their union, 'tis in order to bestow on the objects a greater regularity than what is observ'd in our mere perceptions. We remark a connexion betwixt two kinds of objects in their past appearance to the senses, but are not able to observe this connexion to be perfectly constant, since the turning about of our head, or the shutting of our eyes is able to break it. What then do we suppose in this case, but that these objects still continue their usual connexion, notwithstanding their apparent interruption, and that the irregular appearances are join'd by something, of which we are insensible? But as all reasoning concerning matters of fact arises only from custom, and custom can only be the effect of repeated perceptions, the extending of custom and reasoning beyond the perceptions can never be the direct and natural effect of the constant repetition and connexion, but must arise from the co-operation of some other principles.

I have already[3] observ'd, in examining the foundation of mathematics, that the imagination, when set into any train of thinking, is apt to continue, even when its object fails it, and like a galley put in motion by the oars, carries on its course without any new impulse. This I have assign'd for the reason, why, after considering several loose standards of equality, and correcting them by each other, we proceed to imagine so correct and exact a standard of that relation, as is not liable to the least error or variation. The same principle makes us easily entertain this opinion of the continu'd existence of body. Objects have a certain coherence even as they appear to our senses; but this coherence is much greater and more uniform, if we suppose the objects to have a continu'd existence; and as the mind is once in the train of observing an uniformity among objects, it naturally continues, till it renders the uniformity as compleat as possible. The simple supposition of their continu'd existence suffices for this purpose, and gives us a notion of a much greater regularity among objects, than what they have when we look no farther than our senses.

But whatever force we may ascribe to this principle, I am afraid 'tis too weak to support alone so vast an edifice, as is that of the continu'd existence of all external bodies; and that we must join the *constancy* of their appearance to the *coherence*, in order to give a satisfactory account of that opinion. As the explication of this will lead me into a considerable compass of very profound reasoning; I think it proper, in order to avoid confusion, to give a short sketch or abridgment of my system, and afterwards draw out all its parts in their full compass. This inference from the constancy of our perceptions, like the precedent from their coherence, gives rise to the opinion of the *continu'd* existence of body, which is prior to that of its *distinct* existence, and produces that latter principle.

When we have been accustom'd to observe a constancy in certain impressions, and have found, that the perception of the sun or ocean, for instance, returns upon us after an absence or annihilation with like parts and in a like order, as at its first appearance, we are not apt to regard these interrupted perceptions as different, (which they really are) but on the contrary consider them as individually the same, upon account of their resemblance. But as this interruption of their existence is contrary to their perfect identity, and makes us regard the first impression as annihilated, and the second as newly created, we find ourselves somewhat at a loss, and are involv'd in a kind of contradiction. In order to free ourselves from this difficulty, we disguise, as much as possible, the interruption, or rather remove it entirely, by supposing that these interrupted perceptions are connected by a real existence, of which we are insensible. This supposition, or idea of continu'd existence, acquires a force and vivacity from the memory of these broken impressions, and from that propensity, which they give us, to suppose them the same; and according to the precedent reasoning, the very essence of belief consists in the force and vivacity of the conception.

In order to justify this system, there are four things requisite. *First*, To explain the *principium individuationis*, or principle of identity. *Secondly*, Give a reason, why the resemblance of our broken and interrupted perceptions induces us to attribute an identity to them. *Thirdly*, Account for that propensity, which this illusion gives, to unite these broken appearances by a continu'd existence. *Fourthly* and lastly, Explain that force and vivacity of conception, which arises from the propensity.

First, As to the principle of individuation; we may observe, that the view of any one object is not sufficient to convey the idea of identity. For in that proposition, *an object is the same with itself*, if the idea express'd by the word, *object*, were no ways distinguish'd from that meant by *itself*: we really shou'd mean nothing, nor wou'd the proposition contain a predicate and a subject, which however are imply'd in this affirmation. One single object conveys the idea of unity, not that of identity.

On the other hand, a multiplicity of objects can never convey this idea, however resembling they may be suppos'd. The mind always pronounces the one not to be the other, and considers them as forming two, three, or any determinate number of objects, whose existences are entirely distinct and independent.

Since then both number and unity are incompatible with the relation of identity, it must lie in something that is neither of them. But to tell the truth, at first sight this seems utterly impossible. Betwixt unity and number there can be no medium; no more than betwixt existence and nonexistence. After one object is suppos'd to exist, we must either suppose another also to exist; in which case we have the idea of number: Or we might suppose it not to exist; in which case the first object remains at unity.

To remove this difficulty, let us have recourse to the idea of time or duration. I have already observ'd,[4] that time, in a strict sense, implies succession, and that when we apply its idea to any unchangeable object, 'tis only by a fiction of the imagination, by which the unchangeable object is suppos'd to participate of the changes of the co-existent objects, and in particular of that of our perceptions. This fiction of the imagination almost universally takes place; and 'tis by means of it, that a single object, plac'd before us, and survey'd for any time without our discovering in it any interruption or variation, is able to give us a notion of identity. For when we consider any two points of this time, we may place them in different lights: We may either survey them at the very same instant; in which case they give us the idea of number, both by themselves and by the object; which must be multiply'd, in order to be conceiv'd at once, as existence in these two different points of time: Or on the other hand, we may trace the succession of time by a like succession of ideas, and conceiving first one moment, along with the object then existent, imagine afterwards a change in the time without any *variation* or *interruption* in the object; in which case it gives us the idea of unity. Here then is an idea, which is a medium betwixt unity and number; or more properly speaking, is either of them, according to the view, in which we take it: And this idea we call that of identity. We cannot, in any propriety of speech, say, that an object is the same with itself, unless we mean, that the object existent at one time is the same with itself existent at another. By this means we make a difference, betwixt the idea meant by the word, *object*, and that meant by *itself*, without going the length of number, and at the same time without restraining ourselves to a strict and absolute unity.

Thus the principle of individuation is nothing but the *invariableness* and *uninterruptedness* of any object, thro' a suppos'd variation of time, by which the mind can trace it in the different periods of its existence, without any break of the view, and without being oblig'd to form the idea of multiplicity or number.

I now proceed to explain the *second* part of my system, and show why the constancy of our perceptions makes us ascribe to them a perfect numerical identity, tho' there be very long intervals betwixt their appearance, and they have only one of the essential qualities of identity, viz. *invariableness*. That I may avoid all ambiguity and confusion on this head, I shall observe, that I here account for the opinions and belief of the vulgar with regard to the existence of body; and therefore must entirely conform myself to their manner of thinking and of expressing themselves. Now we have already observ'd, that however philosophers may distinguish betwixt the objects and perceptions of the senses; which they suppose coexistent and resembling; yet this is a distinction, which is not comprehended by the generality of mankind, who as they perceive only one being, can never assent to the opinion of a double existence and representation. Those very sensations, which enter by the eye or ear, are with them the true objects, nor can they readily conceive that this pen or paper, which immediately perceiv'd, represents another, which is different from, but resembling it. In order, therefore, to accommodate myself to their notions, I shall at first suppose; that there is only a single existence, which I shall call indifferently *object* or *perception*, according as it shall seem best to suit my purpose, understanding by both of them what any common man means by a hat, or shoe, or stone, or any other impression, convey'd to him by his senses. I shall be sure to give warning, when I return to a more philosophical way of speaking and thinking.

To enter, therefore, upon the question concerning the source of the error and deception with regard to identity, when we attribute it to our resembling perceptions, notwithstanding their interruption; I must here recall an observation, which I have already prov'd and explain'd.[5] Nothing is more apt to make us mistake one idea for another, than any relation betwixt them, which associates them together in the imagination, and makes it pass with facility from one to the other. Of all relations, that of resemblance is in this respect the most efficacious; and that because it not only causes an association of ideas, but also of dispositions, and makes us conceive the one idea by an act or operation of the mind, similar to that by which we conceive the other. This circumstance I have observ'd to be of great moment; and we may establish it for a general rule, that whatever ideas place the mind in the same disposition or in similar ones, are very apt to be confounded. The mind readily passes from one to the other, and perceives not the change without a strict attention, of which, generally speaking, 'tis wholly incapable.

In order to apply this general maxim, we must first examine the disposition of the mind in viewing any object which preserves a perfect identity, and then find some other object, that is confounded

with it, by causing a similar disposition. When we fix our thought on any object, and suppose it to continue the same for some time; 'tis evident we suppose the change to lie only in the time, and never exert ourselves to produce any new image or idea of the object. The faculties of the mind repose themselves in a manner, and take no more exercise, than what is necessary to continue that idea, of which we were formerly possest, and which subsists without variation or interruption. The passage from one moment to another is scarce felt, and distinguishes not itself by a different perception or idea, which may require a different direction of the spirits, in order to its conception.

Now what other objects, beside identical ones, are capable of placing the mind in the same disposition, when it considers them, and of causing the same uninterrupted passage of the imagination from one idea to another? This question is of the last importance. For if we can find any such objects, we may certainly conclude, from the foregoing principle, that they are very naturally confounded with identical ones, and are taken for them in most of our reasonings. But tho' this question be very important, 'tis not very difficult nor doubtful. For I immediately reply, that a succession of related objects places the mind in this disposition, and is consider'd with the same smooth and uninterrupted progress of the imagination, as attends the view of the same invariable object. The very nature and essence of relation is to connect our ideas with each other, and upon the appearance of the one, to facilitate the transition to its correlative. The passage betwixt related ideas is, therefore, so smooth and easy, that it produces little alteration on the mind, and seems like the continuation of the same action; and as the continuation of the same action is an effect of the continu'd view of the same object, 'tis for this reason we attribute sameness to every succession of related objects. The thought slides along the succession with equal facility, as if it consider'd only one object; and therefore confounds the succession with the identity.

We shall afterwards see many instances of this tendency of relation to make us ascribe an *identity* to *different* objects; but shall here confine ourselves to the present subject. We find by experience, that there is such a *constancy* in almost all the impressions of the senses, that their interruption produces no alteration on them, and hinders them not from returning the same in appearance and in situation as at their first existence. I survey the furniture of my chamber; I shut my eyes, and afterwards open them; and find the new perceptions to resemble perfectly those, which formerly struck my senses. This resemblance is observ'd in a thousand instances, and naturally connects together our ideas of these interrupted perceptions by the strongest relation, and conveys the mind with an easy transition from one to another. An easy transition or passage of the imagination, along the ideas of these different and interrupted perceptions, is almost the same disposition of mind with that in which we consider one constant and uninterrupted perception. 'Tis therefore very natural for us to mistake the one for the other.[6]

The persons, who entertain this opinion concerning the identity of our resembling perceptions, are in general all the unthinking and unphilosophical part of mankind, (that is, all of us, at one time or other) and consequently such as suppose their perceptions to be their only objects, and never think of a double existence internal and external, representing and represented. The very image, which is present to the senses, is with us the real body; and 'tis to these interrupted images we ascribe a perfect identity. But as the interruption of the appearance seems contrary to the identity, and naturally leads us to regard these resembling perceptions as different from each other, we here find ourselves at a loss how to reconcile such opposite opinions. The smooth passage of the imagination along the ideas of the resembling perceptions makes us ascribe to them a perfect identity. The interrupted manner of their appearance makes us consider them as so many resembling, but still distinct beings, which appear after certain intervals. The perplexity arising from this contradiction produces a propension to unite these broken appearances by the fiction of a contin-u'd existence, which is the *third* part of that hypothesis I propos'd to explain.

Nothing is more certain from experience, than that any contradiction either to the sentiments or passions gives a sensible uneasiness, whether it pro-ceeds from without or from within; from the opposition of external objects, or from the combat of internal principles. On the contrary, whatever strikes in with the natural propensities, and either externally forwards their satisfaction, or internally concurs with their movements, is sure to give a sensible pleasure. Now there being here an opposition betwixt the notion of the identity of resembling perceptions, and the interruption of their appearance, the mind must be uneasy in that situation, and will naturally seek relief from the uneasiness. Since the uneasiness arises from the opposition of two contrary principles, it must look for relief by sacrificing the one to the other. But as the smooth passage of our thought along our resembling perceptions makes us ascribe to them an identity, we can never without reluctance yield up that opinion. We must, therefore, turn to the other side, and suppose that our perceptions are no longer interrupted, but preserve a continu'd as well as an invariable existence, and are by that means entirely the same. But here the interruptions in the appearance of these perceptions are so long and frequent, that 'tis impossible to overlook them; and as the *appearance* of a perception in the mind and its *existence* seem at first sight entirely the same, it may be doubted, whether we can ever assent to so palpable a contradiction, and suppose a perception to exist without being present to the mind. In order to clear up this matter, and learn how the interruption in the appearance of a perception implies not necessarily an interruption in its existence, 'twill be proper to touch upon some principles. . . .[7]

We may begin with observing, that the difficulty in the present case is not concerning the matter of fact, or whether the mind forms such a conclusion concerning the continu'd existence of its perceptions, but only concerning the manner in which the conclusion is form'd, and principles from which it is deriv'd. 'Tis certain, that almost all mankind, and even philosophers themselves, for the greatest part of their lives take their perceptions to be their only objects, and suppose, that the very being, which is intimately present to the mind, is the real body or material existence. 'Tis also certain, that this very perception or object is suppos'd to have a continu'd uninterrupted being, and neither to be annihilated by our absence, nor to be brought into existence by our presence. When we are absent from it, we say it still exists, but that we do not feel, we do not see it. When we are present, we say we feel, or see it. Here then may arise two questions; *First*, How can we satisfy ourselves in supposing a perception to be absent from the mind without being annihilated. *Secondly*, After what manner we conceive an object to become present to the mind, without some new creation of a perception or image; and what we mean by this *seeing*, and *feeling*, and *perceiving*.

As to the first question; we may observe, that what we call a *mind*, is nothing but a heap or collection of different perceptions, united together by certain relations, and suppos'd, tho' falsely, to be endow'd with a perfect simplicity and identity. Now as every perception is distinguishable from another, and may be consider'd as separately existent; it evidently follows, that there is no absurdity in separating any particular perception from the mind; that is, in breaking off all its relations, with that connected mass of perceptions, which constitute a thinking being.

The same reasoning affords us an answer to the second question. If the name of *perception* renders not this separation from a mind absurd and contradictory, the name of *object*, standing for the very same thing, can never render their conjunction impossible. External objects are seen, and felt, and become present to the mind; that is, they acquire such a relation to a connected heap of perceptions, as to influence them very considerably in augmenting their number by present reflexions and passions, and in storing the memory with ideas. The same continu'd and uninterrupted Being may, therefore, be sometimes present to the mind, and sometimes absent from it, without any real or essential change in the Being itself. An interrupted appearance to the senses implies not necessarily an interruption in the existence. The supposition of the continu'd existence of sensible objects or perceptions involves no contradiction. We may easily indulge our inclination to that supposition. When the exact resemblance of our perceptions makes us ascribe to them an identity, we may remove the seeming interruption by feigning a continu'd being, which may fill those intervals, and preserve a perfect and entire identity to our perceptions.

But as we here not only *feign* but *believe* this continu'd existence, the question is, *from whence arises such a belief*; and this question leads us to the *fourth* member of this system. It has been prov'd already, that belief in general consists in nothing, but the vivacity of an idea; and that an idea may acquire this vivacity by its relation to some present impression. Impressions are naturally the most vivid perceptions of the mind; and this quality is in part convey'd by the relation to every connected idea. The relation causes a smooth passage from the impression to the idea, and even gives a propensity to that passage. The mind falls so easily from the one perception to the other, that it scarce perceives the change, but retains in the second a considerable share of the vivacity of the first. It is excited by the lively impression; and this vivacity is convey'd to the related idea, without any great diminution in the passage, by reason of the smooth transition and the propensity of the imagination.

But suppose, that this propensity arises from some other principle, besides that of relation; 'tis evident it must still have the same effect, and convey the vivacity from the impression to the idea. Now this is exactly the present case. Our memory presents us with a vast number of instances of perceptions perfectly resembling each other, that return at different distances of time, and after considerable interruptions. This resemblance gives us a propension to consider these interrupted perceptions as the same; and also a propension to connect them by a continu'd existence, in order to justify this identity, and avoid the contradiction, in which the interrupted appearance of these perceptions seems necessarily to involve us. Here then we have a propensity to feign the continu'd existence of all sensible objects; and as this propensity arises from some lively impressions of the memory, it bestows a vivacity on that fiction; or in other words, makes us believe the continu'd existence to objects, which are perfectly new to us, and of whose constancy and coherence we have no experience, 'tis because the manner, in which they present themselves to our senses, resembles that of constant and coherent objects; and this resemblance is a source of reasoning and analogy, and leads us to attribute the same qualities to the similar objects.

I believe an intelligent reader will find less difficulty to assent to this system, than to comprehend it fully and distinctly, and will allow, after a little reflection, that every part carries its own proof along with it. 'Tis indeed evident, that as the vulgar *suppose* their perceptions to be their only objects, and at the same time *believe* the continu'd existence of matter, we must account for the origin of the belief upon that supposition. Now upon that supposition, 'tis a false opinion that any of our objects, or perceptions, are identically the same after an interruption; and consequently the opinion of their identity can never arise from reason, but must arise from the imagination. The imagination is seduc'd into such an opinion only by means of the resemblance of certain perceptions; since we find they are only our resembling perceptions, which we have a propension to suppose the same. This propension to bestow an identity on our resembling perceptions, produces the fiction of a continu'd existence; since that fiction, as well as the identity, is really false, as is acknowledg'd by all philosophers, and has no other effect than to remedy the interruption of our perceptions, which is the only circumstance that is contrary to their identity. In the last place this propension causes belief by means of the present impressions of the memory; since without the remembrance of former sensations, 'tis plain we never shou'd have any belief of the continu'd existence of body. Thus in examining all these parts, we find that each of them is supported by the strongest proofs; and that all of them together form a consistent system, which is perfectly convincing. A strong propensity or inclination alone, without any present impression, will sometimes cause a belief or opinion. How much more when aided by that circumstance?

But tho' we are led after this manner, by the natural propensity of the imagination, to ascribe a continu'd existence to those sensible objects or perceptions, which we find to resemble each other in their interrupted appearance; yet a very little reflection and philosophy is sufficient to make us perceive the fallacy of that opinion. I have already observ'd, that there is an intimate connexion betwixt those two principles, of a *continu'd* and of a *distinct* or *independent* existence, and that we no sooner establish the one than the other follows, as a necessary consequence. 'Tis the opinion of a continu'd existence, which first takes place, and without much study or reflection draws the other along with it, wherever the mind follows its first and most natural tendency. But when we compare experiments, and reason a little upon them, we quickly perceive, that the doctrine of the independent existence of our sensible perceptions is contrary to the plainest experience. This leads us backward upon our footsteps to perceive our error in attributing a continu'd existence to our perceptions, and is the origin of many very curious opinions, which we shall here endeavour to account for.

'Twill first be proper to observe a few of those experiments, which convince us, that our perceptions are not possest of any independent existence. When we press one eye with a finger, we immediately perceive all the objects to become double, and one half of them to be remov'd from their common and natural position. But as we do not attribute a continu'd existence to both these perceptions, and as they are both of the same nature, we clearly perceive, that all our perceptions are dependent on our organs, and the disposition of our nerves and animal spirits. This opinion is confirm'd by the seeming encrease and diminution of objects, according to their distance; by the apparent alterations in their figure; by the changes in their colour and other qualities from our sickness and distempers; and by an infinite number of other experiments of the same kind; from all which we learn, that our sensible perceptions are not possest of any distinct or independent existence.

The natural consequence of this reasoning shou'd be, that our perceptions have no more a continu'd than an independent existence; and indeed philosophers have so far run into this opinion, that they change their system, and distinguish, (as we shall do for the future) betwixt perceptions and objects, of which the former are suppos'd to be interrupted, and perishing, and different at every different return; the latter to be uninterrupted, and to preserve a continu'd existence and identity. But however philosophical this new system may be esteem'd, I assert that 'tis only a palliative remedy, and that it contains all the difficulties of the vulgar system, with some others, that are peculiar to itself. There are no principles either of the understanding or fancy, which lead us directly to embrace this opinion of the double existence of perceptions and objects, nor can we arrive at it but by passing thro' the common hypothesis of the identity and continuance of our interrupted perceptions. Were we not first persuaded, that our perceptions are our only objects, and continue to exist even when they no longer make their appearance to the senses, we shou'd never be led to think that our perceptions and objects are different, and that our objects alone preserve a continu'd existence. 'The latter hypothesis has no primary recommendation either to reason or the imagination, but acquires all its influence on the imagination from the former.' This proposition contains two parts, which we shall endeavour to prove as distinctly and clearly, as such abstruse subjects will permit.

As to the first part of the proposition, *that this philosophical hypothesis has no primary recommendation, either to reason or the imagination*, we may soon satisfy ourselves with regard to *reason* by the following reflections. The only existences, of which we are certain, are perceptions, which being immediately present to us by consciousness, command our strongest assent, and are the first foundation of all our conclusions. The only conclusion we can draw from the existence of one thing to that of another, is by means of the relation of cause and effect, which shows, that there is a connexion betwixt them, and that the existence of one is dependent on that of the other. The idea of this relation is deriv'd from past experience, by which we find, that two beings are constantly conjoin'd together, and are always present at once to the mind. But as no beings are ever present to the mind but perceptions; it follows that we may observe a conjunction or a relation of cause and effect between different perceptions, but can never observe it between perceptions and objects. 'Tis impossible, therefore, that from the existence or any of the qualities of the former, we can ever form any conclusion concerning the existence of the latter, or ever satisfy our reason in this particular.

'Tis no less certain, that this philosophical system has no primary recommendation to the *imagination*, and that the faculty wou'd never, of itself, and by its original tendency, have fallen upon such a prin-

ciple. I confess it will be somewhat difficult to prove this to the full satisfaction of the reader; because it implies a negative, which in many cases will not admit of any positive proof. If any one wou'd take the pains to examine this question, and wou'd invent a system, to account for the direct origin of this opinion from the imagination, we shou'd be able, by the examination of that system, to pronounce a certain judgment in the present subject. Let it be taken for granted, that our perceptions are broken, and interrupted, and however like, are still different from each other; and let any one upon this supposition shew why the fancy, directly and immediately, proceeds to the belief of another existence, resembling these perceptions in their nature, but yet continu'd, and uninterrupted, and identical; and after he has done this to my satisfaction, I promise to renounce my present opinion. Meanwhile I cannot forbear concluding, from the very abstractedness and difficulty of the first supposition, that 'tis an improper subject for the fancy to work upon. Whoever wou'd explain the origin of the *common* opinion concerning the continu'd and distinct existence of body, must take the mind in its *common* situation, and must proceed upon the supposition, that our perceptions are our only objects, and continue to exist even when they are not perceiv'd. Tho' this opinion be false, 'tis the most natural of any, and has alone any primary recommendation to the fancy.

As to the second part of the proposition, *that the philosophical system acquires all its influence on the imagination from the vulgar one*; we may observe, that this is a natural and unavoidable consequence of the foregoing conclusion, *that it has no primary recommendation to reason or the imagination*. For as the philosophical system is found by experience to take hold of many minds, and in particular of all those, who reflect ever so little on this subject, it must derive all its authority from the vulgar system; since it has no original authority of its own. The manner, in which these two systems, tho' directly contrary, are connected together, may be explain'd, as follows.

The imagination naturally runs on in this train of thinking. Our perceptions are our only objects: Resembling perceptions are the same, however broken or uninterrupted in their appearance: This appearing interruption is contrary to the identity: The interruption consequently extends not beyond the appearance, and the perception or object really continues to exist, even when absent from us: Our sensible perceptions have, therefore, a continu'd and uninterrupted existence. But as a little reflection destroys this conclusion, that our perceptions have a continu'd existence, by showing that they have a dependent one, 'twou'd naturally be expected, that we must altogether reject the opinion, that there is such a thing in nature as a continu'd existence, which is preserv'd even when it no longer appears to the senses. The case, however, is otherwise. Philosophers are so far from rejecting the opinion of a continu'd existence upon rejecting that of the independence and continuance of our sensible perceptions, that tho' all sects agree in the latter sentiment, the former, which is, in a manner, its necessary consequence, has been peculiar to a few extravagant sceptics; who after all maintain'd that opinion in words only, and were never able to bring themselves sincerely to believe it.

There is a great difference betwixt such opinions as we form after a calm and profound reflection, and such as we embrace by a kind of instinct or natural impulse, on account of their suitableness and conformity to the mind. If these opinions become contrary, 'tis not difficult to foresee which of them will have the advantage. As long as our attention is bent upon the subject, the philosophical and study'd principle may prevail; but the moment we relax our thoughts, nature will display herself, and draw us back to our former opinion. Nay she has sometimes such an influence, that she can stop our progress, even in the midst of our most profound reflections, and keep us from running on with all the consequences of any philosophical opinion. Thus tho' we clearly perceive the dependence and interruption of our perceptions, we stop short in our career, and never upon that account reject the notion of an independent and continu'd existence. That opinion has taken such deep root in the imagination, that 'tis impossible ever to eradicate it, nor will any strain'd metaphysical conviction of the dependence of our perceptions be sufficient for that purpose.

But tho' our natural and obvious principles here prevail above our study'd reflections, 'tis certain there must be some struggle and opposition in the case; at least so long as these reflections retain any

force or vivacity. In order to set ourselves at ease in this particular, we contrive a new hypothesis, which seems to comprehend both these principles of reason and imagination. This hypothesis is the philosophical one of the double existence of perceptions and objects; which pleases our reason, in allowing, that our dependent perceptions are interrupted and different; and at the same time is agreeable to the imagination in attributing a continu'd existence to something else, which we call *objects*. This philosophical system, therefore, is the monstrous offspring of two principles, which are contrary to each other, which are both at once embrac'd by the mind, and which are unable mutually to destroy each other. The imagination tells us, that our resembling perceptions have a continu'd and uninterrupted existence, and are not annihilated by their absence. Reflection tells us, that even our resembling perceptions are interrupted in their existence, and different from each other. The contradiction betwixt these opinions we elude by a new fiction, which is conformable to the hypotheses both of reflection and fancy, by ascribing these contrary qualities to different existences; the *interruption* to perceptions, and the *continuance* to objects. Nature is obstinate, and will not quit the field, however strongly attack'd by reason; and at the same time reason is so clear in the point, that there is no possibility of disguising her. Not being able to reconcile these two enemies, we endeavor to set ourselves at ease as much as possible, by successively granting to each whatever it demands, and by feigning a double existence, where each may find something, that has all the conditions it desires. Were we fully convinc'd, that our resembling perceptions are continu'd, and identical, and independent, we shou'd never run into this opinion of a double existence; since we shou'd find satisfaction in our first supposition, and wou'd not look beyond. Again, were we fully convinc'd, that our perceptions are dependent, and interrupted, and different, we shou'd be as little inclin'd to embrace the opinion of a double existence; since in that case we shou'd clearly perceive the error of our first supposition of a continu'd existence, and wou'd never regard it any farther. 'Tis therefore from the intermediate situation of the mind, that this opinion arises, and from such an adherence to these two contrary principles, as makes us seek some pretext to justify our receiving both; which happily at last is found in the system of a double existence.

Another advantage of this philosophical system is its similarity to the vulgar one; by which means we can humour our reason for a moment, when it becomes troublesome and solicitous; and yet upon its least negligence or inattention, can easily return to our vulgar and natural notions. Accordingly we find, that philosophers neglect not this advantage; but immediately upon leaving their closets, mingle with the rest of mankind in those exploded opinions, that our perceptions are our only objects, and continue identically and uninterruptedly the same in all their interrupted appearances.

There are other particulars of this system, wherein we may remark its dependence on the fancy, in a very conspicuous manner. Of these, I shall observe the two following. *First*, We suppose external objects to resemble internal perceptions. I have already shewn, that the relation of cause and effect can never afford us any just conclusion from the existence or qualities of our perceptions to the existence of external continu'd objects: And I shall farther add, that even tho' they cou'd afford such a conclusion, we shou'd never have any reason to infer, that our objects resemble our perceptions. That opinion, therefore, is deriv'd from nothing but the quality of the fancy above-explain'd, *that it borrows all its ideas from some precedent perception.* We never can conceive any thing but perceptions, and therefore must make everything resemble them.

Secondly, As we suppose our objects in general to resemble our perceptions, so we take it for granted, that every particular object resembles that perception, which it causes. The relation of cause and effect determines us to join the other of resemblance; and the ideas of these existences being already united together in the fancy but the former relation, we have a strong propensity to compleat every union by joining new relations to those which we have before observ'd betwixt any ideas, as we shall have occasion to observe presently.

Having thus given an account of all the systems both popular and philosophical, with regard to external existence, I cannot forbear giving vent to a certain sentiment, which arises upon reviewing those systems. I begun this subject with premising, that we ought to have an implicit faith in our senses, and that this wou'd be the conclusion, I shou'd draw from the whole of my reasoning. But to be ingenuous, I feel myself *at present* of a quite contrary sentiment, and am more inclin'd to repose no faith at all in my senses, or rather imagination, than to place in it such an implicit confidence. I cannot conceive how such trivial qualities of the fancy, conducted by such false suppositions, can ever lead to any solid and rational system. They are the coherence and constancy of our perceptions, which produce the opinion of their continu'd existence; tho' these qualities of perceptions have no perceivable connexion with such an existence. The constancy of our perceptions has the most considerable effect, and yet is attended with the greatest difficulties. 'Tis a gross illusion to suppose, that our resembling perceptions are numerically the same; and 'tis this illusion, which leads us into the opinion, that these perceptions are uninterrupted, and are still existent, even when they are not present to the senses. This is the case with our popular system. And as to our philosophical one, 'tis liable to the same difficulties; and is over-and-above loaded with this absurdity, that it at once denies and establishes the vulgar supposition. Philosophers deny our resembling perceptions to be identically the same, and uninterrupted; and yet have so great a propensity to believe them such, that they arbitrarily invent a new set of perceptions, to which they attribute these qualities. I say, a new set of perceptions: For we may well suppose in general, but 'tis impossible for us distinctly to conceive, objects to be in their nature any thing but exactly the same with perceptions. What then can we look for from this confusion of groundless and extraordinary opinions but error and falshood? And how can we justify to ourselves any belief we repose in them?

This sceptical doubt, both with respect to reason and the senses, is a malady, which can never be radically cur'd, but must return upon us every moment, however we may chase it away, and sometimes may seem entirely free from it. 'Tis impossible upon any system to defend either our understanding or senses; and we but expose them farther when we endeavour to justify them in that manner. As the sceptical doubt arises naturally from a profound and intense reflection on those subjects, it always encreases, the farther we carry our reflections, whether in opposition or conformity to it. Carelessness and in-atten-

tion alone can afford us any remedy. For this reason I rely entirely upon them; and take it for
granted, whatever may be the reader's opinion at
this present moment, that an hour hence he will be
persuaded there is both an external and internal
world; and going upon that supposition, I intend to
examine some general systems both ancient and
modern, which have been propos'd of both, before
I proceed to a more particular enquiry concerning
our impressions. This will not, perhaps, in the end
be found foreign to our present purpose.

NOTES

1. Part II. sect. 6
2. Sect. 5.
3. Part II. sect. 4.

4. Part II. sect. 5.
5. Part II. sect. 5.
6. This reasoning, it must be confest, is somewhat abstruse, and difficult to be comprehended; but it is
   remarkable, that this very difficulty may be converted into a proof of the reasoning. We may observe, that there are two relations, and both of them
   resemblances, which contribute to our mistaking
   the succession of our interrupted perceptions for an
   identical object. The first is, the resemblance of the
   perceptions: The second is the resemblance, which
   the act of the mind in surveying a succession of resembling objects bears to that in surveying an identical object. Now these resemblances we are apt to
   confound with each other; and 'tis natural we
   shou'd, according to this very reasoning. But let us
   keep them distinct, and we shall find no difficulty
   in conceiving the precedent argument.
7. Sect. 6.

An Enquiry Concerning Human Understanding

DAVID HUME

—•—

Section II
Of the Origin of Ideas

Every one will readily allow, that there is a considerable difference between the perceptions of the
mind, when a man feels the pain of excessive heat,
or the pleasure of moderate warmth, and when he
afterwards recalls to his memory this sensation, or
anticipates it by his imagination. These faculties

From *Enquiries Concerning Human Understanding and
Concerning the Principles of Morals*, edited by L. A. Selby-
Bigge, 3rd edition revised by P. H. Nidditch. Copyright ©
1975 by Oxford University Press. Reprinted by permission
of the publisher.

may mimic or copy the perceptions of the senses; but
they never can entirely reach the force and vivacity
of the original sentiment. The utmost we say of
them, even when they operate with greatest vigour,
is, that they represent their object in so lively a manner, that we could *almost* say we feel or see it: But,
except the mind be disordered by disease or madness, they never can arrive at such a pitch of vivacity, as to render these perceptions altogether undis-
tinguishable. All the colours of poetry, however
splendid, can never paint natural objects in such a
manner as to make the description be taken for a
real landscape. The most lively thought is still inferior to the dullest sensation.

We may observe a like distinction to run through
all the other perceptions of the mind. A man in a fit

of anger, is actuated in a very different manner from one who only thinks of that emotion. If you tell me, that any person is in love, I easily understand your meaning, and form a just conception of his situation; but never can mistake that conception for the real disorders and agitations of the passion. When we reflect on our past sentiments and affections, our thought is a faithful mirror, and copies its objects truly; but the colours which it employs are faint and dull, in comparison of those in which our original perceptions were clothed. It requires no nice discernment or metaphysical head to mark the distinction between them.

Here therefore we may divide all the perceptions of the mind into two classes or species, which are distinguished by their different degrees of force and vivacity. The less forcible and lively are commonly denominated *Thoughts* or *Ideas*. The other species want a name in our language, and in most others; I suppose, because it was not requisite for any, but philosophical purposes, to rank them under a general term or appellation. Let us, therefore, use a little freedom, and call them *Impressions*: employing that word in a sense somewhat different from the usual. By the term *impression*, then, I mean all our more lively perceptions, when we hear, or see, or feel, or love, or hate, or desire, or will. And impressions are distinguished from ideas, which are the less lively perceptions, of which we are conscious, when we reflect on any of those sensations or movements above mentioned.

Nothing, at first view, may seem more unbounded than the thought of man, which not only escapes all human power and authority, but is not even restrained within the limits of nature and reality. To form monsters, and join incongruous shapes and appearances, costs the imagination no more trouble than to conceive the most natural and familiar objects. And while the body is confined to one planet, along which it creeps with pain and difficulty; the thought can in an instant transport us into the most distant regions of the universe; or even beyond the universe, into the unbounded chaos, where nature is supposed to lie in total confusion. What never was seen, or heard of, may yet be conceived; nor is any thing beyond the power of thought, except what implies an absolute contradiction.

But though our thought seems to possess this unbounded liberty, we shall find, upon a nearer examination, that it is really confined within very narrow limits, and that all this creative power of the mind amounts to no more than the faculty of compounding, transposing, augmenting, or diminishing the materials afforded us by the senses and experience. When we think of a golden mountain, we only join two consistent ideas, *gold*, and *mountain*, with which we were formerly acquainted. A virtuous horse we can conceive; because, from our own feeling, we can conceive virtue; and this we may unite to the figure and shape of a horse, which is an animal familiar to us. In short, all the materials of thinking are derived either from our outward or inward sentiment: the mixture and composition of these belongs alone to the mind and will. Or, to express myself in philosophical language, all our ideas or more feeble perceptions are copies of our impressions or more lively ones.

To prove this, the two following arguments will, I hope, be sufficient. First, when we analyze our thoughts or ideas, however compounded or sublime, we always find that they resolve themselves into such simple ideas as were copied from a precedent feeling or sentiment. Even those ideas, which, at first view, seem the most wide of this origin, are found, upon a nearer scrutiny, to be derived from it. The idea of God, as meaning an infinitely intelligent, wise, and good Being, arises from reflecting on the operations of our own mind, and augmenting, without limit, those qualities of goodness and wisdom. We may prosecute this enquiry to what length we please; where we shall always find, that every idea which we examine is copied from a similar impression. Those who would assert that this position is not universally true nor without exception, have only one, and that an easy method of refuting it; by producing that idea, which, in their opinion, is not derived from this source. It will then be incumbent on us, if we would maintain our doctrine, to produce the impression, or lively perception, which corresponds to it.

Secondly. If it happen, from a defect of the organ, that a man is not susceptible of any species of sensation, we always find that he is as little susceptible of the correspondent ideas. A blind man can form no notion of colours; a deaf man of sounds. Restore either of them that sense in which he is deficient; by opening this new inlet for his sensations, you also open an inlet for the ideas; and he finds no difficulty in conceiving these objects. The case is the same, if the object, proper for exciting any sensation, has never been applied to the organ. A Laplander or Negro has no notion of the relish of wine. And though there are a few or no instances of a like deficiency in the mind, where a person has never felt or is wholly incapable of a sentiment or passion that belongs to his species; yet we find the same observation to take place in a less degree. A man of mild manners can form no idea of inveterate revenge or cruelty; nor can a selfish heart easily conceive the heights of friendship and generosity. It is readily allowed, that other beings may possess many senses of which we can have no conception; because the ideas of them have never been introduced to us in the only manner by which an idea can have access to the mind, to wit, by the actual feeling and sensation.

There is, however, one contradictory phenomenon, which may prove that it is not absolutely impossible for ideas to arise, independent of their correspondent impressions. I believe it will readily be allowed, that the several distinct ideas of colour, which enter by the eye, or those of sound, which are conveyed by the ear, are really different from each other; though, at the same time, resembling. Now if this be true of different colours, it must be no less so of the different shades of the same colour; and each shade produces a distinct idea, independent of the rest. For if this should be denied, it is possible, by the continual gradation of shades, to run a colour insensibly into what is most remote from it; and if you will not allow any of the means to be different, you cannot, without absurdity, deny the extremes to be the same. Suppose, therefore, a person to have enjoyed his sight for thirty years, and to have become perfectly acquainted with colours of all kinds except one particular shade of blue, for instance, which it never has been his fortune to meet with. Let all different shades of that colour, except that single one, be placed before him, descending gradually from the deepest to the lightest; it is plain that he will perceive a blank, where that shade is want-

ing, and will be sensible that there is a greater distance in that place between the contiguous colours than in any other. Now I ask, whether it be possible for him, from his own imagination, to supply this deficiency, and raise up to himself the idea of that particular shade, though it had never been conveyed to him by his senses? I believe there are few but will be of opinion that he can: and this may serve as a proof that the simple ideas are not always, in every instance, derived from the correspondent impressions; though this instance is so singular, that it is scarcely worth our observing, and does not merit that for it alone we should alter our general maxim.

Here, therefore, is a proposition, which not only seems, in itself, simple and intelligible; but, if a proper use were made of it, might render every dispute equally intelligible, and banish all that jargon, which has so long taken possession of metaphysical reasonings, and drawn disgrace upon them. All ideas, especially abstract ones, are naturally faint and obscure: the mind has but a slender hold of them: they are apt to be confounded with other resembling ideas; and when we have often employed any term, though without a distinct meaning, we are apt to imagine it has a determinate idea annexed to it. On the contrary, all impressions, that is, all sensations, either outward or inward, are strong and vivid: the limits between them are more exactly determined: nor is it easy to fall into any error or mistake with regard to them. When we entertain, therefore, any suspicion that a philosophical term is employed without any meaning or idea (as is but too frequent), we need but enquire, *from what impression is that supposed idea derived*? And if it be impossible to assign any, this will serve to confirm our suspicion. By bringing ideas into so clear a light we may reasonably hope to remove all dispute, which may arise, concerning their nature and reality.[1]

Section III
Of the Association of Ideas

It is evident that there is a principle connexion between the different thoughts or ideas of the mind, and that, in their appearance to the memory or imagination, they introduce each other with a certain degree of method and regularity. In our more serious thinking or discourse this is so observable that any particular thought, which breaks in upon the regular tract or chain of ideas, is immediately remarked and rejected. And even in our wildest and most wandering reveries, nay in our very dreams, we shall find, if we reflect, that the imagination ran not altogether at adventures, but that there was still a connexion upheld among the different ideas, which succeeded each other. Were the loosest and freest conversation to be transcribed, there would immediately be observed something which connected it in all its transitions. Or where this is wanting, the person who broke the thread of discourse might still inform you, that there had secretly revolved in his mind a succession of thought, which had gradually led him from the subject of conversation. Among different languages, even where we cannot suspect the least connexion or communication, it is found, that the words, expressive of ideas, the most compounded, do yet nearly correspond to each other: a certain proof that the simple ideas, comprehended in the compound ones, were bound together by some universal principle, which had an equal influence on all mankind.

Though it be too obvious to escape observation, that different ideas are connected together; I do not find that any philosopher has attempted to enumerate or class all the principles of association; a subject, however, that seems worthy of curiosity. To me, there appear to be only three principles of connexion among ideas, namely, *Resemblance*, *Contiguity* in time or place, and *Cause* or *Effect*.

That these principles serve to connect ideas will not, I believe, be much doubted. A picture naturally leads our thoughts to the original:[2] the mention of one apartment in a building naturally introduces an enquiry or discourse concerning the others:[3] and if we think of a wound, we can scarcely forbear reflecting on the pain which follows it.[4] But that this enumeration is complete, and that there are no other principles of association except these, may be difficult to prove to the satisfaction of the reader, or even to a man's own satisfaction. All we can do, in such cases, is to run over several instances, and examine carefully the principle which binds the different thoughts to each other, never stopping till we render the principle as general as possible.[5] The more instances we examine, and the more care we employ, the more assurance shall we acquire, that the enumeration, which we form from the whole, is complete and entire.

Section IV
Sceptical Doubts Concerning the Operations of the Understanding

Part I

All the objects of human reason or enquiry may naturally be divided into two kinds, to wit, *Relations of Ideas*, and *Matters of Fact*. Of the first kind are the sciences of Geometry, Algebra, and Arithmetic; and in short, every affirmation which is either intuitively or demonstratively certain. *That the square of the hypotenuse is equal to the square of the two sides*, is a proposition which expresses a relation between these figures. *That three times five is equal to the half of thirty*, expresses a relation between these numbers. Propositions of this kind are discoverable by the mere operation of thought, without dependence on what is anywhere existent in the universe. Though there never were a circle or triangle in nature, the truths demonstrated by Euclid would for ever retain their certainty and evidence.

Matters of fact, which are the second objects of human reason, are not ascertained in the same manner; nor is our evidence of their truth, however great, of a like nature with the foregoing. The contrary of every matter of fact is still possible; because it can never imply a contradiction, and is conceived by the mind with the same facility and distinctness, as if ever so conformable to reality. *That the sun will not rise to-morrow* is no less intelligible a proposition, and implies no more contradiction than the affirmation, *that it will rise*. We should in vain, therefore, attempt to demonstrate its falsehood. Were it demonstratively false, it would imply a contradiction, and could never be distinctly conceived by the mind.

It may, therefore, be a subject worthy of curiosity, to enquire what is the nature of that evidence which assures us of any real existence and matter of fact, beyond the present testimony of our senses, or the records of our memory. This part of philosophy, it is observable, has been little cultivated, either by the ancients or moderns; and therefore our doubts and errors, in the prosecution of so important an enquiry, may be the more excusable; while we march through such difficult paths without any guide or direction. They may even prove useful, by exciting curiosity, and destroying that implicit faith and security, which is the bane of all reasoning and free enquiry. The discovery of defects in the common philosophy, if any such there be, will not, I presume, be a discouragement, but rather an incitement, as is usual, to attempt something more full and satisfactory than has yet been proposed to the public.

All reasonings concerning matter of fact seem to be founded on the relation of *Cause and Effect*. By means of that relation alone we can go beyond the evidence of our memory and senses. If you were to ask a man, why he believes any matter of fact, which is absent; for instance, that his friend is in the country, or in France; he would give you a reason; and this reason would be some other fact; as a letter received from him, or the knowledge of his former resolutions and promises. A man finding a watch or any other machine in a desert island, would conclude that there had once been men in that island. All our reasonings concerning fact are of the same nature. And here it is constantly supposed that there is a connexion between the present fact and that which is inferred from it. Were there nothing to bind them together, the inference would be entirely precarious. The hearing of an articulate voice and rational discourse in the dark assures us of the presence of some person: Why? because these are the effects of the human make and fabric, and closely connected with it. If we anatomize all the other reasonings of this nature, we shall find that they are founded on the relation of cause and effect, and that this relation is either near or remote, direct or collateral. Heat and light are collateral effects of fire, and the one effect may justly be inferred from the other.

If we would satisfy ourselves, therefore, concerning the nature of that evidence, which assures us of matters of fact, we must enquire how we arrive at the knowledge of cause and effect.

I shall venture to affirm, as a general proposition, which admits of no exception, that the knowledge of this relation is not, in any instance, attained by reasonings a priori; but arises entirely from experience, when we find that any particular objects are constantly conjoined with each other. Let an object be presented to a man of ever so strong natural reason and abilities; if that object be entirely new to him, he will not be able, by the most accurate examination of its sensible qualities, to discover any of its causes or effects. Adam, though his rational faculties be supposed, at the very first, entirely perfect, could not have inferred from the fluidity and transparency of water that it would suffocate him, or from the light and warmth of fire that it would consume him. No object ever discovers, by the qualities which appear to the senses, either the causes which produce it, or the effects which will arise from it; nor can our reason, unassisted by experience, ever draw any inference concerning real existence and matter of fact.

This proposition, *that causes and effects are discoverable, not by reason but by experience*, will readily be admitted with regard to such objects, as we remember to have once been altogether unknown to us; since we must be conscious of the utter inability, which we then lay under, of foretelling what would arise from them. Present two smooth pieces of marble to a man who has no tincture of natural philosophy; he will never discover that they will adhere together in such a manner as to require great force to separate them in a direct line, while they make so small a resistance to a lateral pressure. Such events, as bear little analogy to the common course of nature, are also readily confessed to be known only by experience; nor does any man imagine that the explosion of gunpowder, or the attraction of a loadstone, could ever be discovered by arguments a priori. In like manner, when an effect is supposed to depend upon an intricate machinery or secret structure of parts, we make no difficulty in attributing all our knowledge of it to experience. Who will assert that he can give the ultimate reason, why milk or bread is proper nourishment for a man, not for a lion or a tiger?

But the same truth may not appear, at first sight, to have the same evidence with regard to events, which have become familiar to us from our first appearance in the world, which bear a close analogy to the whole course of nature, and which are supposed to depend on the simple qualities of objects, without any secret structure of parts. We are apt to imagine that we could discover these effects by the mere operation of our reason, without experience. We fancy, that were we brought on a sudden into this world, we could at first have inferred that one Billiard-ball would communicate motion to another upon impulse; and that we needed not to have waited for the event, in order to pronounce with certainty concerning it. Such is the influence of custom, that, where it is strongest, it not only covers our natural ignorance, but even conceals itself, and seems not to take place, merely because it is found in the highest degree.

But to convince us that all the laws of nature, and all the operations of bodies without exception, are known only by experience, the following reflections may, perhaps, suffice. Were any object presented to us, and were we required to pronounce concerning the effect, which will result from it, without consulting past observation; after what manner, I beseech you, must the mind proceed in this operation? It must invent or imagine some event, which it ascribes to the object as its effect; and it is plain that this invention must be entirely arbitrary. The mind can never possibly find the effect in the supposed cause, by the most accurate scrutiny and examination. For the effect is totally different from the cause, and consequently can never be discovered in it. Motion in the second Billiard-ball is a quite distinct event from motion in the first; nor is there anything in the one to suggest the smallest hint of the other. A stone or piece of metal raised into the air, and left without any support, immediately falls: but to consider the matter a priori, is there anything we discover in this situation which can beget the idea of a downward, rather than an upward, or any other motion, in the stone or metal?

And as the first imagination or invention of a particular effect, in all natural operations, is arbitrary, where we consult not experience; so must we also esteem the supposed tie or connexion between the cause and effect, which binds them together, and renders it impossible that any other effect could result from the operation of that cause. When I see, for instance, a Billiard-ball moving in a straight line towards another; even suppose motion in the second ball should by accident be suggested to me, as the result of their contact or impulse; may I not conceive, that a hundred different events might as well follow from that cause? May not both these balls remain at absolute rest? May not the first ball return in a straight line, or leap off from the second in any line or direction? All these suppositions are consistent and conceivable. Why then should we give the preference to one, which is no more consistent or conceivable than the rest? All our reasonings a priori will never be able to show us any foundation for this preference.

In a word, then, every effect is a distinct event from its cause. It could not, therefore, be discovered in the cause, and the first invention or conception of it, a priori, must be entirely arbitrary. And even after it is suggested, the conjunction of it with the cause must appear equally arbitrary; since there are always many other effects, which, to reason, must seem fully as consistent and natural. In vain, therefore, should we pretend to determine any single event, or infer any cause of effect, without the assistance of observation and experience.

Hence we may discover the reason why no philosopher, who is rational and modest, has ever pretended to assign the ultimate cause of any natural operation, or to show distinctly the action of that power, which produces any single effect in the universe. It is confessed, that the utmost effort of human reason is to reduce the principles, productive of natural phenomena, to a greater simplicity, and to resolve the many particular effects into a few general causes, by means of reasonings from analogy, experience, and observation. But as to the causes of these general causes, we should in vain attempt their discovery; nor shall we ever be able to satisfy ourselves, by any particular explication of them. These ultimate springs and principles are totally shut up from human curiosity and enquiry. Elasticity, gravity, cohesion of parts, communication of motion by impulse; these are probably the ultimate causes and principles which we shall ever discover in nature; and we may esteem ourselves sufficiently happy, if, by accurate enquiry and reasoning, we can trace up the particular phenomena to, or near to, these general principles. The most perfect philosophy of the natural kind only staves off our ignorance a little longer: as perhaps the most perfect philosophy of the moral or metaphysical kind serves only to discover larger portions of it. Thus the observation of human blindness and weakness is the result of all philosophy, and meets us at every turn, in spite of our endeavours to elude or avoid it.

Nor is geometry, when taken into the assistance of natural philosophy, ever able to remedy this defect, or lead us into the knowledge of ultimate causes, by all that accuracy of reasoning for which it is so justly celebrated. Every part of mixed mathematics proceeds upon the supposition that certain laws are established by nature in her operations; and abstract reasonings are employed, either to assist experience in the discovery of these laws, or to determine their influence in particular instances, where it depends upon any precise degree of distance and quantity. Thus, it is a law of motion, discovered by experience, that the moment or force of any body in motion is in the compound ratio or proportion of its solid contents and its velocity; and consequently, that a small force may remove the greatest obstacle or raise the greatest weight, if, by any contrivance or machinery, we can increase the velocity of that force, so as to make it an overmatch for its antagonist. Geometry assists us in the application of this law, by giving us the just dimensions of all the parts and figures which can enter into any species of machine; but still the discovery of the law itself is owing merely to experience, and all the abstract reasonings in the world could never lead us one step towards the knowledge of it. When we reason a priori, and consider merely any object or cause, as it appears to the mind, independent of all observation, it never could suggest to us the notion of any distinct object, such as its effect; much less, show us the inseparable and inviolable connexion between them. A man must be very sagacious who could discover by reasoning that crystal is the effect of heat, and ice of cold, without being previously acquainted with the operation of these qualities.

Part II

But we have not yet attained any tolerable satisfaction with regard to the question first proposed. Each solution still gives rise to a new question as difficult as the foregoing, and leads us on to farther enquiries. When it is asked, *What is the nature of all our reasonings concerning matter of fact?* the proper answer seems to be, that they are founded on the relation of cause and effect. When again it is asked, *What is the foundation of all our reasonings and conclusions concerning that relation?* it may be replied in one word, Experience. But if we still carry on our sifting humour, and ask, *What is the foundation of all conclusions from experience?* this implies a new question, which may be of more difficult solution and explication. Philosophers, that give themselves airs of superior wisdom and sufficiency, have a hard task when they encounter persons of inquisitive dispositions, who push them from every corner to which they retreat, and who are sure at last to bring them to some dangerous dilemma. The best expedient to prevent this confusion, is to be modest in our pretensions; and even to discover the difficulty ourselves before it is objected to us. By this means, we may make a kind of merit of our very ignorance.

I shall content myself, in this section, with an easy task, and shall pretend only to give a negative answer to the question here proposed. I say then, that, even after we have experience of the operations of cause and effect, our conclusions from that experience are *not* founded on reasoning, or any process of the understanding. This answer we must endeavour both to explain and to defend.

It must certainly be allowed, that nature has kept us at a great distance from all her secrets, and has afforded us only the knowledge of a few superficial qualities of objects; while she conceals from us those powers and principles on which the influence of those objects entirely depends. Our senses inform us of the colour, weight, and consistence of bread; but neither sense nor reason can ever inform us of those qualities which fit it for the nourishment and support of a human body. Sight or feeling conveys an idea of the actual motion of bodies; but as to that wonderful force or power, which would carry on a moving body for ever in a continued change of place, and which bodies never lose but by communicating it to others; of this we cannot form the most distant conception. But notwithstanding this ignorance of natural powers[6] and principles, we always presume, when we see like sensible qualities, that they have like secret powers, and expect that effects, similar to those which we have experienced, will follow from them. If a body of a like colour and consistence with that bread, which we have formerly eat, be presented to us, we make no scruple of repeating the experiment, and foresee, with certainty, like nourishment and support. Now this is a process of the mind or thought, of which I would willingly know the foundation. It is allowed on all hands that there is no known connexion between the sensible qualities and the secret powers; and consequently, that the mind is not led to form such a conclusion concerning their constant and regular conjunction, by anything which it knows of their nature. As to past *Experience*, it can be allowed to give *direct* and *certain* information of those precise objects only, and that precise period of time, which fell under its cognizance: but why this experience should be extended to future times, and to other objects, which for aught we know, may be only in appearance similar; this is the main question on which I would insist. The bread, which I formerly eat, nourished me; that is, a body of such sensible qualities was, at that time, endued with such secret powers: but does it follow, that other bread must also nourish me at another time, and that like sensible qualities must always be attended with like secret powers? The consequence seems nowise necessary. At least, it must be acknowledged that there is here a consequence drawn by the mind; that there is a certain step taken; a process of thought, and an inference, which wants to be explained. These two propositions are far from being the same, *I have found that such an object has always been attended with such an effect*, and *I foresee, that other objects, which are, in appearance, similar, will be attended with similar effects*. I shall allow, if you please, that the one proposition may justly be inferred from the other: I know, in fact, that it always is inferred. But if you insist that the inference is made by a chain of reasoning, I desire you to produce that reasoning. The connexion between these propositions is not intuitive. There is required a medium, which may enable the mind to draw such an inference, if indeed it be drawn by reasoning and argument. What that medium is, I must confess, passes my comprehension; and it is incumbent on those to produce it, who assert that it really exists, and is the origin of all our conclusions concerning matter of fact.

This negative argument must certainly, in process of time, become altogether convincing, if many penetrating and able philosophers shall turn their enquiries this way and no one be ever able to discover any connecting proposition or intermediate step, which supports the understanding in this conclusion. But as the question is yet new, every reader may not trust so far to his own penetration, as to conclude, because an argument escapes his enquiry, that therefore it does not really exist. For this reason it may be requisite to venture upon a more difficult task; and enumerating all the branches of human knowledge, endeavour to show that none of them can afford such an argument.

All reasonings may be divided into two kinds, namely, demonstrative reasoning, or that concerning relations of ideas, and moral reasoning, or that concerning matter of fact and existence. That there are no demonstrative arguments in the case seems evident; since it implies no contradiction that the course of nature may change, and that an object, seemingly like those which we have experienced, may be attended with different or contrary effects. May I not clearly and distinctly conceive that a body, falling from the clouds, and which, in all other respects, resembles snow, has yet the taste of salt or feeling of fire? Is there any more intelligible proposition than to affirm, that all the trees will flourish in December and January, and decay in May and June? Now whatever is intelligible, and can be distinctly conceived, implies no contradiction, and can never be proved false by any demonstrative argument or abstract reasoning a priori.

If we be, therefore, engaged by arguments to put trust in past experience, and make it the standard of our future judgment, these arguments must be probable only, or such as regard matter of fact and real existence, according to the division above mentioned. But that there is no argument of this kind, must appear, if our explication of that species of reasoning be admitted as solid and satisfactory. We have said that all arguments concerning existence are founded on the relation of cause and effect; that our knowledge of that relation is derived entirely from experience; and that all our experimental conclusions proceed upon the supposition that the future will be conformable to the past. To endeavour, therefore, the proof of this last supposition by probable arguments, or arguments regarding existence, must be evidently going in a circle, and taking that for granted, which is the very point in question.

In reality, all arguments from experience are founded on the similarity which we discover among natural objects, and by which we are induced to expect effects similar to those which we have found to follow from such objects. And though none but a fool or madman will ever pretend to dispute the authority of experience, or to reject that great guide of human life, it may surely be allowed a philosopher to have so much curiosity at least as to examine the principle of human nature, which gives this mighty authority to experience, and makes us draw advantage from that similarity which nature has placed among different objects. From causes which appear *similar* we expect similar effects. This is the sum of all our experimental conclusions. Now it seems evident that, if this conclusion were formed by reason, it would be as perfect at first, and upon one instance, as after ever so long a course of experience. But the case is far otherwise. Nothing so like as eggs; yet no one, on account of this appearing similarity, expects the same taste and relish in all of them. It is only after a long course of uniform experiments in any kind, that we attain a firm reliance and security with regard to a particular event. Now where is that process of reasoning which, from one instance, draws a conclusion, so different from that which it infers from a hundred instances that are nowise different from that single one? This question I propose as much for the sake of information, as with an intention of raising difficulties. I cannot find, I cannot imagine any such reasoning. But I keep my mind still open to instruction, if any one will vouchsafe to bestow it on me.

Should it be said that, from a number of uniform experiments, we *infer* a connexion between the sensible qualities and the secret powers; this, I must confess, seems the same difficulty, couched in different terms. The question still recurs, on what process of argument this *inference* is founded? Where is the medium, the interposing ideas, which join propositions so very wide of each other? It is confessed that the colour, consistence, and other sensible qualities of bread appear not, of themselves, to have any connexion with the secret powers of nourishment and support. For otherwise we could infer these secret powers from the first appearance of these sensible qualities, without the aid of experience; contrary to the sentiment of all philosophers, and contrary to plain matter of fact. Here, then, is our natural state of ignorance with regard to the powers and influence of all objects. How is this remedied by experience? It only shows us a number of uniform effects, resulting from certain objects, and teaches us that those particular objects, at that particular time, were endowed with such powers and forces. When a new object, endowed with similar sensible qualities, is produced, we expect similar powers and forces, and look for a like effect. From a body of like colour and consistence with bread we expect like nourishment and support. But this surely is a step or progress of the mind, which wants to be explained. When a man says, *I have found, in all past instances, such sensible qualities conjoined with such secret powers*: And when he says, *Similar sensible qualities will always be conjoined with similar secret powers*, he is not guilty of a tautology, nor are these propositions in any respect the same. You say that the one proposition is an inference from the other. But you must confess that the inference is not intuitive; neither is it demonstrative: Of what nature is it, then? To say it is experimental, is begging the question. For all inferences from experience suppose, as their foundation, that the future will resemble the past, and that similar powers will be conjoined with similar sensible qualities. If there be any suspicion that the course of nature may change, and that the past may be no rule for the future, all experience becomes useless, and can give rise to no inference or conclusion. It is impossible, therefore, that any arguments from experience can prove this resemblance of the past to the future; since all these arguments are founded on the supposition of that resemblance. Let the course of things be allowed hitherto ever so regular; that alone, without some new argument or inference, proves not that, for the future, it will continue so. In vain do you pretend to have learned the nature of bodies from your past experience. The secret nature, and consequently all their effects and influence, may change, without any change in their sensible qualities. This happens sometimes, and with regard to some objects: Why may it not happen always, and with regard to all objects? What logic, what process of argument secures you against this supposition? My practice, you say, refutes my doubts. But you mistake the purport of my question. As an agent, I am quite satisfied in this point; but as a philosopher, who has some share of curiosity, I will not say scepticism. I want to learn the foundation of this inference. No reading, no enquiry has yet been able to remove my difficulty, or give me satisfaction in a matter of such importance. Can I do better than propose the difficulty to the public, even though, perhaps, I have small hopes of obtaining a solution? We shall at least, by this means, be sensible of our ignorance, if we do not augment our knowledge.

I must confess that a man is guilty of unpardonable arrogance who concludes, because an argument has escaped his own investigation, that therefore it does not really exist. I must also confess that, though all the learned, for several ages, should have employed themselves in fruitless search upon any subject, it may still, perhaps, be rash to conclude positively that the subject must, therefore, pass all human comprehension. Even though we examine all the sources of our knowledge, and conclude them unfit for such a subject, there may still remain a suspicion, that the enumeration is not complete, or the examination not accurate. But with regard to the present subject, there are some considerations which seem to remove all this accusation of arrogance or suspicion of mistake.

It is certain that the most ignorant and stupid peasants–nay infants, nay even brute beasts–improve by experience, and learn the qualities of natural objects, by observing the effects which result from them. When a child has felt the sensation of pain from touching the flame of a candle, he will be careful not to put his hand near any candle; but will expect a similar effect from a cause which is similar in its sensible qualities and appearance. If you assert, therefore, that the understanding of the child is led into this conclusion by any process of argument or ratiocination, I may justly require you to produce that argument; nor have you any pretence to refuse so equitable a demand. You cannot say that the argument is abstruse, and may possibly escape your enquiry; since you confess that it is obvious to the capacity of a mere infant. If you hesitate, therefore, a moment, or if, after reflection, you produce any intricate or profound argument, you, in a manner, give up the question, and confess that it is not reasoning which engages us to suppose the past resembling the future, and to expect similar effects from causes which are, to appearance, similar. This is the proposition which I intended to enforce in the present section. If I be right, I pretend not to have made any mighty discovery. And if I be wrong, I must acknowledge myself to be indeed a very backward scholar; since I cannot now discover an argument which, it seems, was perfectly familiar to me long before I was out of my cradle.

Section V
Sceptical Solution of These Doubts

Part I

The passion for philosophy, like that for religion, seems liable to this inconvenience, that, though it aims at the correction of our manners, and extirpation of our vices, it may only serve, by imprudent management, to foster a predominant inclination, and push the mind, with more determined resolution, towards that side which already *draws* too much, by the bias and propensity of the natural temper. It is certain that, while we aspire to the magnanimous firmness of the philosophic sage, and endeavour to confine our pleasures altogether within our own minds, we may, at last, render our philosophy like that of Epictetus, and other *Stoics*, only a more refined system of selfishness, and reason ourselves out of all virtue as well as social enjoyment. While we study with attention the vanity of human life, and turn all our thoughts towards the empty and transitory nature of riches and honours, we are, perhaps, all the while flattering our natural indolence, which, hating the bustle of the world, and drudgery of business, seeks a pretence of reason to give itself a full and uncontrolled indulgence. There is, however, one species of philosophy which seems little liable to this inconvenience, and that because it strikes in with no disorderly passion of the human mind, nor can mingle itself with any natural affection or propensity; and that is the Academic or Sceptical philosophy. The academics always talk of doubt and suspense of judgment, of danger in hasty determinations, of confining to very narrow bounds the enquiries of the understanding, and of renouncing all speculations which lie not within the limits of common life and practice. Nothing, therefore, can be more contrary than such a philosophy to the supine indolence of the mind, its rash arrogance, its lofty pretensions, and its superstitious credulity. Every passion is mortified by it, except the love of truth; and that passion never is, nor can be, carried to too high a degree. It is surprising, therefore, that this philosophy, which, in almost every instance, must be harmless and innocent, should be the subject of so much groundless reproach and obloquy. But, perhaps, the very circumstance which renders it so innocent is what chiefly exposes it to the public hatred and resentment. By flattering no irregular passion, it gains few partizans: By opposing so many vices and follies, it raises to itself abundance of enemies; who stigmatize it as libertine profane, and irreligious.

Nor need we fear that this philosophy, while it endeavours to limit our enquiries to common life, should ever undermine the reasonings of common life, and carry its doubts so far as to destroy all action, as well as speculation. Nature will always maintain her rights, and prevail in the end over any abstract reasoning whatsoever. Though we should conclude, for instance, as in the forgoing section, that, in all reasonings from experience, there is a step taken by the mind which is not supported by any argument or process of the understanding; there is no danger that these reasonings, on which almost all knowledge depends, will ever be affected by such a discovery. If the mind be not engaged by argument to make this step, it must be induced by some other principle of equal weight and authority; and

that principle will preserve its influence as long as human nature remains the same. What that principle is may well be worth the pains of enquiry.

Suppose a person, though endowed with the strongest faculties of reason and reflection, to be brought on a sudden into this world; he would, indeed, immediately observe a continual succession of objects, and one event following another; but he would not be able to discover anything farther. He would not, at first, by any reasoning, be able to reach the idea of cause and effect; since the particular powers, by which all natural operations are performed, never appear to the senses; nor is it reasonable to conclude, merely because one event, in one instance, precedes another, that therefore the one is the cause, the other the effect. Their conjunction may be arbitrary and casual. There may be no reason to infer the existence of one from the appearance of the other. And in a word, such a person, without more experience, could never employ his conjecture or reasoning concerning any matter of fact, or be assured of anything beyond what was immediately present to his memory and senses.

Suppose, again, that he has acquired more experience, and has lived so long in the world as to have observed familiar objects or events to be constantly conjoined together; what is the consequence of this experience? He immediately infers the existence of one object from the appearance of the other. Yet he has not, by all his experience, acquired any idea or knowledge of the secret power by which the one object produces the other; nor is it, by any process of reasoning, he is engaged to draw this inference. But still he finds himself determined to draw it: And though he should be convinced that this understanding has no part in the operation, he would nevertheless continue in the same course of thinking. There is some other principle which determines him to form such a conclusion.

This principle is Custom or Habit. For wherever the repetition of any particular act or operation produces a propensity to renew the same act or operation, without being impelled by any reasoning or process of the understanding, we always say, that this propensity is the effect of *Custom*. By employing that word, we pretend not to have given the ultimate reason of such a propensity. We only point out a principle of human nature, which is universally acknowledged, and which is well known by its effects. Perhaps we can push our enquiries no farther, or pretend to give the cause of this cause; but must rest contented with it as the ultimate principle, which we can assign, of all our conclusions from experience. It is sufficient satisfaction, that we can go so far, without repining at the narrowness of our faculties because they will carry us no farther. And it is certain we here advance a very intelligible proposition at least, if not a true one, when we assert that, after the constant conjunction of two objects—heat and flame, for instance, weight and solidity—we are determined by custom alone to expect the one from the appearance of the other. This hypothesis seems even the only one which explains the difficulty, why we draw, from a thousand instances, an inference which we are not able to draw from one instance, that is, in no respect different from them. Reason is incapable of any such variation. The conclusions which it draws from considering one circle are the same which it would form upon surveying all the circles in the universe. But no man, having seen only one body move after being impelled by another, could infer that every body will move after a like impulse. All inferences from experience, therefore, are effects of custom, not of reasoning.[7]

Custom, then, is the great guide of human life. It is that principle alone which renders our experience useful to us, and makes us expect, for the future, a similar train of events with those which have appeared in the past. Without the influence of custom, we should be entirely ignorant of every matter of fact beyond what is immediately present to the memory and senses. We should never know how to adjust means to ends, or to employ our natural powers in the production of any effect. There would be an end at once of all action, as well as of the chief part of speculation.

But here it may be proper to remark, that though our conclusions from experience carry us beyond our memory and senses, and assure us of matters of fact which happened in the most distant places and most remote ages, yet some fact must always be present to the senses or memory, from which we may first proceed in drawing these conclusions. A man,

who should find in a desert country the remains of pompous buildings, would conclude that the country had, in ancient times, been cultivated by civilized inhabitants; but did nothing of this nature occur to him, he could never form such an inference. We learn the events of former ages from history; but then we must peruse the volumes in which this instruction is contained, and thence carry up our inferences from one testimony to another, till we arrive at the eyewitnesses and spectators of these distant events. In a word, if we proceed not upon some fact, present to the memory or senses, our reasonings would be merely hypothetical; and however the particular links might be connected with each other, the whole chain of inferences would have nothing to support it, nor could we ever, by its means, arrive at the knowledge of any real existence. If I ask why you believe any particular matter of fact, which you relate, you must tell me some reason; and this reason will be some other fact, connected with it. But as you cannot proceed after this manner, *in infinitum*, you must at last terminate in some fact, which is present to your memory or senses; or must allow that your belief is entirely without foundation.

What, then, is the conclusion of the whole matter? A simple one; though, it must be confessed, pretty remote from the common theories of philosophy. All belief of matter of fact or real existence is derived merely from some object, present to the memory or senses, and a customary conjunction between that and some other object. Or in other words, having found, in many instances, that any two kinds of objects—flame and heat, snow and cold—have always been conjoined together; if flame or snow be presented anew to the senses, the mind is carried by custom to expect heat or cold, and to *believe* that such a quality does exist, and will discover itself upon a nearer approach. This belief is the necessary result of placing the mind in such circumstances. It is an operation of the soul, when we are so situated, as unavoidable as to feel the passion of love, when we receive benefits; or hatred, when we meet with injuries. All these operations are a species of natural instincts, which no reasoning or process of the thought and understanding is able either to produce or to prevent.

At this point, it would be very allowable for us to stop our philosophical researches. In most questions we can never make a single step farther; and in all questions we must terminate here at last, after our most restless and curious enquiries. But still our curiosity will be pardonable, perhaps commendable, if it carry us on to still farther researches, and make us examine more accurately the nature of this *belief*, and of the *customary conjunction*, whence it is derived. By this means we may meet with some explications and analogies that will give satisfaction; at least to such as love the abstract sciences, and can be entertained with speculations, which, however accurate, may still retain a degree of doubt and uncertainty. As to readers of a different taste; the remaining part of this section is not calculated for them, and the following enquiries may well be understood, though it be neglected.

Part II

Nothing is more free than the imagination of man; and though it cannot exceed that original stock of ideas furnished by the internal and external senses, it has unlimited power of mixing, compounding, separating, and dividing these ideas, in all the varieties of fiction and vision. It can feign a train of events, with all the appearance of reality, ascribe to them a particular time and place, conceive them as existent, and paint them out to itself with every circumstance, that belongs to any historical fact, which it believes with the greatest certainty. Wherein, therefore, consists the difference between such a fiction and belief? It lies not merely in any peculiar idea, which is annexed to such a conception as commands our assent, and which is wanting to every known fiction. For as the mind has authority over all its ideas, it could voluntarily annex this particular idea to any fiction, and consequently be able to believe whatever it pleases; contrary to what we find by daily experience. We can, in our conception, join the head of a man to the body of a horse; but it is not in our power to believe that such an animal has ever really existed.

It follows, therefore, that the difference between *fiction* and *belief* lies in some sentiment or feeling,

which is annexed to the latter, not to the former, and which depends not on the will, nor can be commanded at pleasure. It must be excited by nature, like all other sentiments; and must arise from the particular situation, in which the mind is placed at any particular juncture. Whenever any object is presented to the memory or sense, it immediately, by the force of custom, carries the imagination to conceive that object, which is usually conjoined to it; and this conception is attended with a feeling or sentiment, different from the loose reveries of the fancy. In this consists the whole nature of belief. For as there is no matter of fact which we believe so firmly that we cannot conceive the contrary, there would be no difference between the conception assented to and that which is rejected, were it not for some sentiment which distinguishes the one from the other. If I see a billiard-ball moving towards another, on a smooth table, I can easily conceive it to stop upon contact. This conception implies no contradiction; but still it feels very differently from that conception by which I represent to myself the impulse and the communication of motion from one ball to another.

Were we to attempt a *definition* of this sentiment, we should perhaps, find it a very difficult, if not an impossible task; in the same manner as if we should endeavour to define the feeling of cold or passion of anger, to a creature who never had any experience of these sentiments. Belief is the true and proper name of this feeling; and no one is ever at a loss to know the meaning of that term; because every man is every moment conscious of the sentiment represented by it. It may not, however, be improper to attempt a *description* of this sentiment; in hopes we may, by that means, arrive at some analogies, which may afford a more perfect explication of it. I say, then, that belief is nothing but a more vivid, lively, forcible, firm, steady conception of an object, than what the imagination alone is ever able to attain. This variety of terms, which may seem so unphilosophical, is intended only to express that act of the mind, which renders realities, or what is taken for such, more present to us than fictions, causes them to weigh more in the thought, and gives them a superior influence on the passions and imagination. Provided we agree about the thing, it is needless to dispute about the terms. The imagination has the command over all its ideas, and can join and mix and vary them, in all the ways possible. It may conceive fictitious objects with all the circumstances of place and time. It may set them, in a manner, before our eyes, in their true colours, just as they might have existed. But as it is impossible that this faculty of imagination can ever, of itself, reach belief, it is evident that belief consists not in the peculiar nature or order of ideas, but in the *manner* of their conception, and in their *feeling* to the mind. I confess, that it is impossible perfectly to explain this feeling or manner of conception. We may make use of words which express something near it. But its true and proper name, as we observed before, is *belief*; which is a term that every one sufficiently understands in common life. And in philosophy, we can go no farther than assert, that *belief* is something felt by the mind, which distinguishes the ideas of the judgement from the fictions of the imagination. It gives them more weight and influence; makes them appear of greater importance; enforces them in the mind; and renders them the governing principle of our actions. I hear at present, for instance, a person's voice, with whom I am acquainted; and the sound comes as from the next room. This impression of my senses immediately conveys my thoughts to the person, together with all the surrounding objects. I paint them out to myself as existing at present, with the same qualities and relations, of which I formerly knew them possessed. These ideas take faster hold of my mind than ideas of an enchanted castle. They are very different to the feeling, and have a much greater influence of every kind, either to give pleasure or pain, joy or sorrow.

Let us, then, take in the whole compass of this doctrine, and allow, that the sentiment of belief is nothing but a conception more intense and steady than what attends the mere fictions of the imagination, and that this *manner* of conception arises from a customary conjunction of the object with something present to the memory or senses: I believe that it will not be difficult, upon these suppositions, to find operations of the mind analogous to it, and to trace up these phenomena to principles still more general.

We have already observed that nature has established connexions among particular ideas, and that

no sooner one idea occurs to our thoughts than it introduces its correlative, and carries our attention towards it, by a gentle and insensible movement. These principles of connexion or association we have reduced to three, namely, *Resemblance, Contiguity* and *Causation*; which are the only bonds that unite our thoughts together, and beget that regular train of reflection or discourse, which, in a greater or less degree, takes place among all mankind. Now here arises a question, on which the solution of the present difficulty will depend. Does it happen, in all these relations, that, when one of the objects is presented to the senses or memory, the mind is not only carried to the conception of the correlative, but reaches a steadier and stronger conception of it than what otherwise it would have been able to attain? This seems to be the case with that belief which arises from the relation of cause and effect. And if the case be the same with the other relations or principles of associations, this may be established as a general law, which takes place in all the operations of the mind.

We may, therefore, observe, as the first experiment to our present purpose, that, upon the appearance of the picture of an absent friend, our idea of him is evidently enlivened by the *resemblance*, and that every passion, which that idea occasions, whether of joy or sorrow, acquires new force and vigour. In producing this effect, there concur both a relation and a present impression. Where the picture bears him no resemblance, at least was not intended for him, it never so much as conveys our thought to him: And where it is absent as well as the person, though the mind may pass from the thought of the one to that of the other, it feels its idea to be rather weakened than enlivened by that transition. We take a pleasure in viewing the picture of a friend, when it is set before us; but when it is removed, rather choose to consider him directly than by reflection in an image, which is equally distant and obscure.

The ceremonies of the Roman Catholic religion may be considered as instances of the same nature. The devotees of that superstition usually plead in excuse for the mummeries, with which they are upbraided, that they feel the good effect of those external motions, and postures, and actions, in enlivening their devotion and quickening their fervour, which otherwise would decay, if directed entirely to distant and immaterial objects. We shadow out the objects of our faith, say they, in sensible types and images, and render them more present to us by the immediate presence of these types, than it is possible for us to do merely by an intellectual view and contemplation. Sensible objects have always a greater influence on the fancy than any other; and this influence they readily convey to those ideas to which they are related, and which they resemble. I shall only infer from these practices, and this reasoning, that the effect of resemblance in enlivening the ideas is very common; and as in every case a resemblance and a present impression must concur, we are abundantly supplied with experiments to prove the reality of the foregoing principle.

We may add force to these experiments by others of a different kind, in considering the effects of *contiguity* as well as of *resemblance*. It is certain that distance diminishes the force of every idea, and that, upon our approach to any object; though it does not discover itself to our senses; it operates upon the mind with an influence, which imitates an immediate impression. The thinking on any object readily transports the mind to what is contiguous; but it is only the actual presence of an object, that transports it with a superior vivacity. When I am a few miles from home, whatever relates to it touches me more nearly than when I am two hundred leagues distant; though even at that distance the reflecting on any thing in the neighbourhood of my friends or family naturally produces an idea of them. But as in this latter case, both the objects of the mind are ideas; notwithstanding there is an easy transition between them; that transition alone is not able to give a superior vivacity to any of the ideas, for want of some immediate impression.[8]

No one can doubt but causation has the same influence as the other two relations of resemblance and contiguity. Superstitious people are fond of the reliques of saints and holy men, for the same reason, that they seek after types or images, in order to enliven their devotion, and give them a more intimate and strong conception of those exemplary lives, which they desire to imitate. Now it is evident, that one of the best reliques, which a devotee could

procure, would be the handywork of a saint; and if his clothes and furniture are ever to be considered in this light, it is because they were once at his disposal, and were moved and affected by him; in which respect they are to be considered as imperfect effects, and as connected with him by a shorter chain of consequences than any of those, by which we learn the reality of his existence.

Suppose, that the son of a friend, who had been long dead or absent, were presented to us; it is evident, that this object would instantly revive its correlative idea, and recall to our thoughts all past intimacies and familiarities, in more lively colours than they would otherwise have appeared to us. This is another phenomenon, which seems to prove the principle above mentioned.

We may observe, that, in these phenomena, the belief of the correlative object is always presupposed; without which the relation could have no effect. The influence of the picture supposes, that we *believe* our friend to have once existed. Contiguity to home can never excite our idea of home, unless we *believe* that it really exists. Now I assert, that this belief, where it reaches beyond the memory or sense, is of a similar nature, and arises from similar causes, with the transition of thought and vivacity of conception here explained. When I throw a piece of dry wood into a fire, my mind is immediately carried to conceive, that it augments, not extinguishes the flame. This transition of thought from the cause to the effect proceeds not from reason. It derives its origin altogether from custom and experience. And as it first begins from an object, present to the senses, it renders the idea or conception of flame more strong and lively than any loose, floating reverie of the imagination. That idea arises immediately. The thought moves instantly towards it, and conveys to it all that force of conception, which is derived from the impression present to the senses. When a sword is levelled at my breast, does not the idea of wound and pain strike me more strongly, than when a glass of wine is presented to me, even though by accident this idea should occur after the appearance of the latter object? But what is there in this whole matter to cause such a strong conception, except only a present object and a customary transition to the idea of another object, which we have been accustomed to conjoin with the former? This is the whole operation of the mind, in all our conclusions concerning matter of fact and existence; and it is a satisfaction to find some analogies, by which it may be explained. The transition from a present object does in all cases give strength and solidity to the related idea.

Here, then, is a kind of pre-established harmony between the course of nature and the succession of our ideas; and though the powers and forces, by which the former is governed, be wholly unknown to us; yet our thoughts and conceptions have still, we find, gone on in the same train with the other works of nature. Custom is that principle, by which this correspondence has been effected; so necessary to the subsistence of our species, and the regulation of our conduct, in every circumstance and occurrence of human life. Had not the presence of an object, instantly excited the idea of those objects, commonly conjoined with it, all our knowledge must have been limited to the narrow sphere of our memory and senses; and we should never have been able to adjust means to ends, or employ our natural powers, either to the producing of good, or avoiding of evil. Those, who delight in the discovery and contemplation of *final causes*, have here ample subject to employ their wonder and admiration.

I shall add, for a further confirmation of the foregoing theory, that, as this operation of the mind, by which we infer like effects from like causes, and vice versa, is so essential to the subsistence of all human creatures, it is not probable, that it could be trusted to the fallacious deductions of our reason, which is slow in its operations; appears not, in any degree, during the first years of infancy; and at best is, in every age and period of human life, extremely liable to error and mistake. It is more conformable to the ordinary wisdom of nature to secure so necessary an act of the mind, by some instinct or mechanical tendency, which may be infallible in its operations, may discover itself at the first appearance of life and thought, and may be independent of all the laboured deductions of the understanding. As nature has taught us the use of our limbs, without giving us the knowledge of the muscles and nerves, by which they are actuated; so has she implanted in us an instinct, which carries forward the thought in a correspondent course to that which she has established among external objects; though we are ignorant of those powers and forces, on which this regular course and succession of objects totally depends.

Section VI
Of Probability[9]

Though there be no such thing as *Chance* in the world; our ignorance of the real cause of any event has the same influence on the understanding, and begets a like species of belief or opinion.

There is certainly a probability, which arises from a superiority of chances on any side; and according as this superiority encreases, and surpasses the opposite chances, the probability receives a proportionable encrease, and begets still a higher degree of belief or assent to that side, in which we discover the superiority. If a dye were marked with one figure or number of spots on four sides, and with another figure or number of spots on the two remaining sides, it would be more probable, that the former would turn up than the latter; though, if it had a thousand sides marked in the same manner, and only one side different, the probability would be much higher, and our belief or expectation of the event more steady and secure. This process of the thought or reasoning may seem trivial and obvious; but to those who consider it more narrowly, it may, perhaps, afford matter for curious speculation.

It seems evident, that, when the mind looks forward to discover the event, which may result from the throw of such a dye, it considers the turning up of each particular side as alike probable; and this is the very nature of chance, to render all the particular events, comprehended in it, entirely equal. But finding a greater number of sides concur in the one event than in the other, the mind is carried more frequently to that event, and meets it oftener, in revolving the various possibilities or chances, on which the ultimate result depends. This concurrence of several views in one particular event begets immediately, by an inexplicable contrivance of nature, the sentiment of belief, and gives that event the advantage over its antagonist, which is supported by a smaller number of views, and recurs less frequently to the mind. If we allow, that belief is nothing but a firmer and stronger conception of an object than what attends the mere fictions of the imagination, this operation may, perhaps, in some measure, be accounted for. The concurrence of these several views or glimpses imprints the idea more strongly on the imagination; gives it superior force and vigour; renders its influence on the passions and affections more sensible; and in a word, begets that reliance or security, which constitutes the nature of belief and opinion.

The case is the same with the probability of causes, as with that of chance. There are some causes, which are entirely uniform and constant in producing a particular effect; and no instance has ever yet been found of any failure or irregularity in their operation. Fire has always burned, and water suffocated every human creature: The production of motion by impulse and gravity is an universal law, which has hitherto admitted of no exception. But there are other causes, which have been found more irregular and uncertain; nor has rhubarb always proved a purge, or opium a soporific to every one, who has taken these medicines. It is true, when any cause fails of producing its usual effect, philosophers ascribe not this to any irregularity in nature; but suppose, that some secret causes, in the particular structure of parts, have prevented the operation. Our reasonings, however, and conclusions concerning the event are the same as if this principle had no place. Being determined by custom to transfer the past to the future, in all our inferences; where the past has been entirely regular and uniform, we expect the event with the greatest assurance, and leave no room for any contrary supposition. But where different effects have been found to follow from causes, which are to *appearance* exactly similar, all these various effects must occur to the mind in transferring the past to the future, and enter into our consideration, when we determine the probability of the event. Though we give the preference to that which has been found most usual, and believe that this effect will exist, we must not overlook the other effects, but must assign to each of them a particular weight and authority, in proportion as we have found it to be more or less frequent. It is more probable, in almost every country of Europe, that there

will be frost sometime in January, than that the weather will continue open throughout that whole month; though this probability varies according to the different climates, and approaches to a certainty in the more northern kingdoms. Here then it seems evident, that, when we transfer the past to the future, in order to determine the effect, which will result from any cause, we transfer all the different events, in the same proportion as they have appeared in the past, and conceive one to have existed a hundred times, for instance, another ten times, and another once. As a great number of views do here concur in one event, they fortify and confirm it to the imagination, beget that sentiment which we call *belief*, and give its object the preference above the contrary event, which is not supported by an equal number of experiments, and recurs not so frequently to the thought in transferring the past to the future. Let any one try to account for this operation of the mind upon any of the received systems of philosophy, and he will be sensible of the difficulty. For my part, I shall think it sufficient, if the present hints excite the curiosity of philosophers, and make them sensible how defective all common theories are in treating of such curious and such sublime subjects.

Section VII
Of the Idea of Necessary Connexion

Part I

The great advantage of the mathematical sciences above the moral consists in this, that the ideas of the former, being sensible, are always clear and determinate, the smallest distinction between them is immediately perceptible, and the same terms are still expressive of the same ideas, without ambiguity or variation. An oval is never mistaken for a circle, nor an hyperbola for an ellipsis. The isosceles and scalenum are distinguished by boundaries more exact than vice and virtue, right and wrong. If any term be defined in geometry, the mind readily, of itself, substitutes, on all occasions, the definition for the term defined: Or even when no definition is employed, the object itself may be presented to the senses, and by that means be steadily and clearly apprehended. But the finer sentiments of the mind, the operations of the understanding, the various agitations of the passions, though really in themselves distinct, easily escape us, when surveyed by reflection; nor is it in our power to recall the original object, as often as we have occasion to contemplate it. Ambiguity, by this means, is gradually introduced into our reasonings: Similar objects are readily taken to be the same: And the conclusion becomes at last very wide of the premises.

One may safely, however, affirm, that, if we consider these sciences in a proper light, their advantages and disadvantages nearly compensate each other, and reduce both of them to a state of equality. If the mind, with greater facility, retains the ideas of geometry clear and determinate, it must carry on a much longer and more intricate chain of reasoning, and compare ideas much wider of each other, in order to reach the abstruser truths of that science. And if moral ideas are apt, without extreme care, to fall into obscurity and confusion, the inferences are always much shorter in these disquisitions, and the intermediate steps, which lead to the conclusion, much fewer than in the sciences which treat of quantity and number. In reality, there is scarcely a proposition in Euclid so simple, as not to consist of more parts, than are to be found in any moral reasoning which runs not into chimera and conceit. Where we trace the principles of the human mind through a few steps, we may be very well satisfied with our progress; considering how soon nature throws a bar to all our inquiries concerning causes, and reduces us to an acknowledgment of our ignorance. The chief obstacle, therefore, to our improvement in the moral or metaphysical sciences is the obscurity of the ideas, and ambiguity of the terms. The principle difficulty in the mathematics is the length of inferences and compass of thought, requisite to the forming of any conclusion. And, perhaps, our progress in natural philosophy is chiefly retarded by the want of proper experiments and phenomena, which are often discovered by chance, and cannot always be found, when requisite even by the most diligent and prudent enquiry. As moral philosophy seems hitherto to have received less improvement than either geometry or physics, we may conclude, that, if there be any difference in this respect among these sciences, the difficulties, which obstruct the progress of the former, require superior care and capacity to be surmounted.

There are no ideas, which occur in metaphysics, more obscure and uncertain, than those of *power, force, energy* or *necessary connexion*, of which it is every moment necessary for us to treat in all our disquisitions. We shall, therefore, endeavour, in this section, to fix, if possible, the precise meaning of these terms, and thereby remove some part of that obscurity, which is so much complained of in this species of philosophy.

It seems a proposition, which will not admit of much dispute, that all our ideas are nothing but copies of our impressions, or, in other words, that it is impossible for us to *think* of any thing, which we have not antecedently *felt*, either by our external or internal senses. I have endeavoured[10] to explain and prove this proposition, and have expressed my hopes, that, by a proper application of it, men may reach a greater clearness and precision in philosophical reasonings, than what they have hitherto been able to attain. Complex ideas may, perhaps, be well known by definition, which is nothing but an enumeration of those parts or simple ideas, that compose them. But when we have pushed up definitions to the most simple ideas, and find still some ambiguity and obscurity; what resource are we then possessed of? By what invention can we throw light upon these ideas, and render them altogether precise and determinate to our intellectual view? Produce the impressions or original sentiments, from which the ideas are copied. These impressions are all strong and sensible. They admit not of ambiguity. They are not only placed in a full light themselves, but may throw light on their correspondent ideas, which lie in obscurity. And by this means, we may, perhaps, attain a new microscope or species of optics, by which, in the moral sciences, the most minute, and most simple ideas may be so enlarged as to fall readily under our apprehension, and be equally known with the grossest and most sensible ideas, that can be the object of our enquiry.

To be fully acquainted, therefore, with the idea of power or necessary connexion, let us examine its impression; and in order to find the impression with greater certainty, let us search for it in all the sources, from which it may possibly be derived.

When we look about us towards external objects, and consider the operation of causes, we are never able, in a single instance, to discover any power or necessary connexion; any quality, which binds the effect to the cause, and renders the one an infallible consequence of the other. We only find, that the one does actually, in fact, follow the other. The impulse of one billiard-ball is attended with motion in the second. This is the whole that appears to the *outward* senses. The mind feels no sentiment or *inward* impression from this succession of objects: Consequently, there is not, in any single, particular instance of cause and effect, any thing which can suggest the idea of power or necessary connexion.

From the first appearance of an object, we never can conjecture what effect will result from it. But were the power or energy of any cause discoverable by the mind, we could foresee the effect, even without experience; and might, at first, pronounce with certainty concerning it, by mere dint of thought and reasoning.

In reality, there is no part of matter, that does ever, by its sensible quantities, discover any power or energy, or give us ground to imagine, that it could produce any thing, or be followed by any other object, which we could denominate its effect. Solidity, extension, motion; these qualities are all complete in themselves, and never point out any other event which may result from them. The scenes of the universe are continually shifting, and one object follows another in an uninterrupted succession; but the power of force, which actuates the whole machine, is entirely concealed from us, and never discovers itself in any of the sensible qualities of body. We know, that, in fact, heat is a constant attendant of flame; but what is the connexion between them, we have no room so much as to conjecture or imagine. It is impossible, therefore, that the idea of power can be derived from the contemplation of bodies, in single instances of their operation; because no bodies ever discover any power, which can be the original of this idea.[11]

Since, therefore, external objects as they appear to the senses, give us no idea of power or necessary connexion, by their operation in particular instances,

let us see, whether this idea be derived from reflection on the operations of our own minds, and be copied from any internal impression. It may be said, that we are every moment conscious of internal power; while we feel, that, by the simple command of our will, we can move the organs of our body, or direct the faculties of our mind. An act of volition produces motions in our limbs, or raises a new idea in our imagination. This influence of the will we know by consciousness. Hence we acquire the idea of power or energy; and are certain, that we ourselves and all other intelligent beings are possessed of power. This idea, then, is an idea of reflection, since it arises from reflecting on the operations of our own mind, and on the command which is exercised by will, both over the organs of the body and faculties of the soul.

We shall proceed to examine this pretension; and first with regard to the influence of volition over the organs of the body. This influence, we may observe, is a fact, which, like all other natural events, can be known only by experience, and can never be foreseen from any apparent energy or power in the cause, which connects it with the effect, and renders the one an infallible consequence of the other. The motion of our body follows upon the command of our will. Of this we are every moment conscious. But the means, by which this is effected: the energy, by which the will performs so extraordinary an operation; of this we are so far from being immediately conscious, that it must for ever escape our most diligent enquiry.

For *first*; is there any principle in all nature more mysterious than the union of the soul with the body; by which a supposed spiritual substance acquires such an influence over a material one, that the most refined thought is able to actuate the grossest matter? Were we empowered, by a secret wish, to remove mountains, or control the planets in their orbit; this extensive authority would not be more extraordinary, nor more beyond our comprehension. But if by consciousness we perceived any power or energy in the will, we must know this power; we must know its connexion with the effect; we must know the secret union of soul and body, and the nature of both these substances; by which the one is able to operate, in so many instances, upon the other.

Secondly, We are not able to move all the organs of the body with a like authority; though we cannot assign any reason besides experience, for so remarkable a difference between one and the other. Why has the will an influence over the tongue and fingers, not over the heart or liver? This question would never embarrass us, were we conscious of a power in the former case, not in the latter. We should then perceive, independent of experience, why the authority of will over the organs of the body is circumscribed within such particular limits. Being in that case fully acquainted with the power or force, by which it operates, we should also know, why its influence reaches precisely to such boundaries, and no farther.

A man, suddenly struck with palsy in the leg or arm, or who had newly lost those members, frequently endeavours, at first to move them, and employ them in their usual offices. Here he is as much conscious of power to command such limbs, as a man in perfect health is conscious of power to actuate any member which remains in its natural state and condition. But consciousness never deceives. Consequently, neither in the one case nor in the other, are we ever conscious of any power. We learn the influence of our will from experience alone. And experience only teaches us, how one event constantly follows another; without instructing us in the secret connexion, which binds them together, and renders them inseparable.

Thirdly, We learn from anatomy, that the immediate object of power in voluntary motion, is not the member itself which is moved, but certain muscles, and nerves, and animal spirits, and, perhaps, something still more minute and more unknown, through which the motion is successively propagated, ere it reach the member itself whose motion is the immediate object of volition. Can there be a more certain proof, that the power, by which this whole operation is performed, so far from being directly and fully known by an inward sentiment or consciousness, is, to the last degree mysterious and unintelligible? Here the mind wills a certain event: Immediately another event, unknown to ourselves, and totally different from the one intended, is produced: This event produces another, equally unknown: Till at last, through a long succession, the desired event is produced. But if the original power were felt, it must

be known: Were it known, its effect also must be known; since all power is relative to its effect. And vice versa, if the effect be not known, the power cannot be known nor felt. How indeed can we be conscious of a power to move our limbs, when we have no such power; but only that to move certain animal spirits, which, though they produce at last the motion of our limbs, yet operate in such a manner as is wholly beyond our comprehension?

We may, therefore, conclude from the whole, I hope, without any temerity, though with assurance; that our idea of power is not copied from any sentiment or consciousness of power within ourselves, when we give rise to animal motion, or apply our limbs to their proper use and office. That this motion follows the command of the will is a matter of common experience, like other natural events: But the power or energy by which this is effected, like that in other natural events, is unknown and inconceivable.[12]

Shall we then assert, that we are conscious of a power or energy in our own minds, when, by an act or command of our will, we raise up a new idea, fix the mind to the contemplation of it, turn it on all sides, and at last dismiss it for some other idea, when we think that we have surveyed it with sufficient accuracy? I believe the same arguments will prove, that even this command of the will gives us no real idea of force or energy.

First, It must be allowed, that, when we know a power, we know that very circumstance in the cause, by which it is enabled to produce the effect: For these are supposed to be synonymous. We must, therefore, know both the cause and effect, and the relation between them. But do we pretend to be acquainted with the nature of the human soul and the nature of an idea, or the aptitude of the one to produce the other? This is a real creation; a production of something out of nothing: Which implies a power so great, that it may seem, at first sight, beyond the reach of any being, less than infinite. At least it must be owned, that such a power is not felt, nor known, nor even conceivable by the mind. We only feel the event, namely, the existence of an idea, consequent to a command of the will: But the manner, in which this operation is performed, the power by which it is produced, is entirely beyond our comprehension.

Secondly, The command of the mind over itself is limited, as well as its command over the body; and these limits are not known by reason, or any acquaintance with the nature of cause and effect, but only by experience and observation, as in all other natural events and in the operation of external objects. Our authority over our sentiments and passions is much weaker than that over our ideas; and even the latter authority is circumscribed within very narrow boundaries. Will any one pretend to assign the ultimate reason of these boundaries, or show why the power is deficient in one case, not in another.

Thirdly, This self-command is very different at different times. A man in health possesses more of it than one languishing with sickness. We are more master of our thoughts in the morning than in the evening: Fasting, than after a full meal. Can we give any reason for these variations, except experience? Where then is the power, of which we pretend to be conscious? Is there not here, either in a spiritual or material substance, or both, some secret mechanism or structure of parts, upon which the effect depends, and which, being entirely unknown to us, renders the power or energy of the will equally unknown and incomprehensible?

Volition is surely an act of the mind, with which we are sufficiently acquainted. Reflect upon it. Consider it on all sides. Do you find anything in it like this creative power, by which it raises from nothing a new idea, and with a kind of *Fiat*, imitates the omnipotence of its Maker, if I may be allowed so to speak, who called forth into existence all the various scenes of nature? So far from being conscious of this energy in the will, it requires as certain experience as that of which we are possessed, to convince us that such extraordinary effects do ever result from a simple act of volition.

The generality of mankind never find any difficulty in accounting for the more common and familiar operations of nature—such as the descent of heavy bodies, the growth of plants, the generation of animals, or the nourishment of bodies by food: But suppose that, in all these cases, they perceive, the very force or energy of the cause, by which it is connected with its effect, and is for ever infallible in

its operation. They acquire, by long habit, such a turn of mind, that upon the appearance of the cause, they immediately expect with assurance its usual attendant, and hardly conceive it possible that any other event could result from it. It is only on the discovery of extraordinary phenomena, such as earthquakes, pestilence, and prodigies of any kind, that they find themselves at a loss to assign a proper cause, and to explain the manner in which the effect is produced by it. It is usual for men, in such difficulties, to have recourse to some invisible intelligent principle[13] as the immediate cause of that event which surprises them, and which, they think, cannot be accounted for from the common powers of nature. But philosophers, who carry their scrutiny a little farther, immediately perceive that, even in the most familiar events, the energy of the cause is as unintelligible as in the most unusual, and that we only learn by experience the frequent *Conjunction* of objects, without being ever able to comprehend anything like *Connexion* between them. Here, then, many philosophers think themselves obliged by reason to have recourse, on all occasions, to the same principle, which the vulgar never appeal to but in cases that appear miraculous and supernatural. They acknowledge mind and intelligence to be, not only the ultimate and original cause of all things, but the immediate and sole cause of every event which appears in nature. They pretend that those objects which are commonly denominated *causes*, are in reality nothing but *occasions*; and that the true and direct principle of every effect is not any power or force in nature, but a volition of the Supreme Being, who wills that such particular objects should for ever be conjoined with each other. Instead of saying that one billiard-ball moves another by force which it has derived from the author of nature, it is the Deity himself, they say, who, by a particular volition, moves the second ball, being determined to this operation by the impulse of the first ball, in consequence of those general laws which he has laid down to himself in the government of the universe. But philosophers advancing still in their inquiries, discover that, as we are totally ignorant of the power on which depends the mutual operation of bodies, we are no less ignorant of that power on which depends the operation of mind on body, or of body on mind; nor are we able, either from our senses or consciousness, to assign the ultimate principle in one case more than in the other. The same ignorance, therefore, reduces them to the same conclusion. They assert that the Deity is the immediate cause of the union between soul and body; and that they are not the organs of sense, which, being agitated by external objects, produce sensations in the mind; but that it is a particular volition of our omnipotent Maker, which excites such a sensation, in consequence of such a motion in the organ. In like manner, it is not any energy in the will that produces local motion in our members: It is God himself, who is pleased to second our will, in itself impotent, and to command that motion which we erroneously attribute to our own power and efficacy. Nor do philosophers stop at this conclusion. They sometimes extend the same inference to the mind itself, in its internal operations. Our mental vision or conception of ideas is nothing but a revelation made to us by our Maker. When we voluntarily turn our thoughts to any object, and raise up its image in the fancy, it is not the will which creates that idea: It is the universal Creator, who discovers it to the mind, and renders it present to us.

Thus, according to these philosophers, every thing is full of God. Not content with the principle, that nothing exists but by his will, that nothing possesses any power but by his concession: They rob nature, and all created beings, of every power, in order to render their dependence on the Deity still more sensible and immediate. They consider not that, by this theory, they diminish, instead of magnifying, the grandeur of those attributes, which they affect so much to celebrate. It argues surely more power in the Deity to delegate a certain degree of power to inferior creatures than to produce every thing by his own immediate volition. It argues more wisdom to contrive at first the fabric of the world with such perfect foresight that, of itself, and by its proper operation, it may serve all the purposes of providence, than if the great Creator were obliged every moment to adjust its parts, and animate by his breath all the wheels of that stupendous machine.

But if we would have a more philosophical confutation of this theory, perhaps the two following reflections may suffice.

First, it seems to me that this theory of the universal energy and operation of the Supreme Being is too bold ever to carry conviction with it to a man, sufficiently apprized of the weakness of human reason, and the narrow limits to which it is confined in all its operations. Though the chain of arguments which conduct to it were ever so logical, there must arise a strong suspicion, if not an absolute assurance, that it has carried us quite beyond the reach of our faculties, when it leads to conclusions so extraordinary, and so remote from common life and experience. We are got into fairy land, long ere we have reached the last steps of our theory; and *there* we have no reason to trust our common methods of argument, or to think that our usual analogies and probabilities have any authority. Our line is too short to fathom such immense abysses. And however we may flatter ourselves that we are guided, in every step which we take, by a kind of verisimilitude and experience, we may be assured that this fancied experience has no authority when we thus apply to it subjects that lie entirely out of the sphere of experience. But on this we shall have occasion to touch afterwards.

Secondly, I cannot perceive any force in the arguments on which this theory is founded. We are ignorant, it is true, of the manner in which bodies operate on each other: Their force or energy is entirely incomprehensible: But are we not equally ignorant of the manner or force by which a mind, even the supreme mind, operates either on itself or on body? Whence, I beseech you, do we acquire any idea of it? We have no sentiment or consciousness of this power in ourselves. We have no idea of the Supreme Being but what we learn from reflection on our own faculties. Were our ignorance, therefore, a good reason for rejecting any thing, we should be led into that principle of denying all energy in the Supreme Being as much as in the grossest matter. We surely comprehend as little the operations of one as of the other. Is it more difficult to conceive that motion may arise from impulse than that it may arise from volition? All we know is our profound ignorance in both cases.[14]

Part II

But to hasten to a conclusion of this argument, which is already drawn out to too great a length: We have sought in vain for an idea of power or necessary connexion in all the sources from which we could suppose it to be derived. It appears that, in single instances of the operation of bodies, we never can, by our utmost scrutiny, discover any thing but one event following another, without being able to comprehend any force or power by which the cause operates, or any connexion between it and its supposed effect. The same difficulty occurs in contemplating the operations of mind on body—where we observe the motion of the latter to follow upon the volition of the former, but are not able to observe or conceive the tie which binds together the motion and volition, or the energy by which the mind produces this effect. The authority of the will over its own faculties and ideas is not a whit more comprehensible: So that, upon the whole, there appears not, throughout all nature, any one instance of connexion which is conceivable by us. All events seem entirely loose and separate. One event follows another; but we never can observe any tie between them. They seem *conjoined*, but never *connected*. And as we can have no idea of any thing which never appeared to our outward sense or inward sentiment, the necessary conclusion *seems* to be that we have no idea of connexion or power at all, and that these words are absolutely without any meaning, when employed either in philosophical reasonings or common life.

But there still remains one method of avoiding this conclusion, and one source which we have not yet examined. When any natural object or event is presented, it is impossible for us, by any sagacity or penetration, to discover, or even conjecture, without experience, what event will result from it, or to carry our foresight beyond that object which is immediately present to the memory and senses. Even after one instance or experiment where we have observed a particular event to follow upon another, we are not entitled to form a general rule, or foretell what will happen in like cases; it being justly esteemed an unpardonable temerity to judge of the whole course of nature from one single experiment, however accurate or certain. But when one particular species of event has always, in all instances, been conjoined with another, we make no longer any scruple of foretelling one upon the appearance of the other, and of employing that reasoning, which can alone assure us of any matter of fact or existence. We then call the one object, *Cause*; the other, *Effect*. We suppose that there is some connexion between them; some power in the one, by which it infallibly produces the other, and operates with the greatest certainty and strongest necessity.

It appears, then, that this idea of a necessary connexion among events arises from a number of similar instances which occur of the constant conjunction of these events; nor can that idea ever be suggested by any one of these instances, surveyed in all possible lights and positions. But there is nothing in a number of instances, different from every single instance, which is supposed to be exactly similar; except only, that after a repetition of similar instances, the mind is carried by habit, upon the appearance of one event, to expect its usual attendant, and to believe that it will exist. This connexion, therefore, which we *feel* in the mind, this customary transition of the imagination from one object to its usual attendant, is the sentiment or impression from which we form the idea of power or necessary connexion. Nothing farther is in the case. Contemplate the subject on all sides; you will never find any other origin of that idea. This is the sole difference between one instance, from which we can never receive the idea of connexion, and a number of similar instances, by which it is suggested. The first time a man saw the communication of motion by impulse, as by the shock of two billiard-balls, he could not pronounce that the one event was *connected*: but only that it was *conjoined* with the other. After he has observed several instances of this nature, he then pronounces them to be *connected*. What alteration has happened to give rise to this new idea of *connexion*? Nothing but that he now *feels* these events to be *connected* in his imagination, and can readily foretell the existence of one from the appearance of the other. When we say, therefore, that one object is connected with another, we mean only that they have acquired a connexion in our thought, and give rise to this inference, by which they become proofs of each other's existence: A conclusion which is somewhat extraordinary, but which seems founded on sufficient evidence. Nor will its evidence be weakened by any general diffidence of the understanding, or sceptical suspicion concerning every conclusion which is new and extraordinary. No conclusions can be more agreeable to scepticism than such as make discoveries concerning the weakness and narrow limits of human reason and capacity.

And what stronger instance can be produced of the surprising ignorance and weakness of the understanding than the present? For surely, if there be any relation among objects which it imports to us to know perfectly, it is that of cause and effect. On this are founded all our reasonings concerning matter of fact or existence. By means of it alone we attain any assurance concerning objects which are removed from the present testimony of our memory and senses. The only immediate utility of all sciences, is to teach us, how to control and regulate future events by their causes. Our thoughts and enquiries are, therefore, every moment, employed about this relation: Yet so imperfect are the ideas which we form concerning it, that it is impossible to give any just definition of cause, except what is drawn from something extraneous and foreign to it. Similar objects are always conjoined with similar. Of this we have experience. Suitably to this experience, therefore, we may define a cause to be *an object, followed by another, and where all the objects similar to the first are followed by objects similar to the second.* Or in other words *where, if the first object had not been, the second never had existed.* The appearance of a cause always conveys the mind, by a customary transition, to the idea of the effect. Of this also we have experience. We may, therefore, suitably to this experience, form another definition of cause, and call it, *an object followed by another, and whose appearance always conveys the thought to that other.* But though both these definitions be drawn from circumstances foreign to the cause, we cannot remedy this inconvenience, or attain any more perfect definition, which may point out that circumstance in the cause, which gives it a connexion with its effect. We have no idea of this connexion, nor even any distinct notion what it is we desire to know, when we endeavour at a conception of it. We say,

for instance, that the vibration of this string is the cause of this particular sound. But what do we mean by that affirmation? We either mean *that this vibration is followed by this sound, and that all similar vibrations have been followed by similar sounds*: Or, *that this vibration is followed by this sound, and that upon the appearance of one the mind anticipates the senses, and forms immediately an idea of the other.* We may consider the relation of cause and effect in either of these two lights; but beyond these, we have no idea of it.[15]

To recapitulate, therefore, the reasonings of this section: Every idea is copied from some preceding impression or sentiment; and where we cannot find any impression, we may be certain that there is no idea. In all single instances of the operation of bodies or minds, there is nothing that produces any impression, nor consequently can suggest any idea of power or necessary connexion. But when many uniform instances appear, and the same object is always followed by the same event; we then begin to entertain the notion of cause and connexion. We then *feel* a new sentiment or impression, to wit, a customary connexion in the thought or imagination between one object and its usual attendant; and this sentiment is the original of that idea which we seek for. For as this idea arises from a number of similar instances, and not from any single instance, it must arise from that circumstance, in which the number of instances differ from every individual instance. But this customary connexion or transition of the imagination is the only circumstance in which they differ. In every other particular they are alike. The first instance which we saw of motion communicated by the shock of two billiard-balls (to return to this obvious illustration) is exactly similar to any instance that may, at present, occur to us; except only, that we could not, at first, *infer* one event from the other; which we are enabled to do at present, after so long a course of uniform experience. I know not whether the reader will readily apprehend this reasoning. I am afraid that, should I multiply words about it, or throw it into a greater variety of lights, it would only become more obscure and intricate. In all abstract reasonings there is one point of view which, if we can happily hit, we shall go farther towards illustrating the subject than by all the eloquence and copious expression in the world. This point of view we should endeavour to reach, and reserve the flowers of rhetoric for subjects which are more adapted to them.

NOTES

1. It is probable that no more was meant by those, who denied innate ideas, than that all ideas were copies of our impressions; though it must be confessed, that the terms, which they employed, were not chosen with such caution, nor so exactly defined, as to prevent all mistakes about their doctrine. For what is meant by *innate*? If innate be equivalent to natural, then all the perceptions and ideas of the mind must be allowed to be innate or natural, in whatever sense we take the latter word, whether in opposition to what is uncommon, artificial, or miraculous. If by innate be meant, contemporary to our birth, the dispute seems to be frivolous; nor is it worth while to enquire at what time thinking begins, whether before, at, or after our birth. Again, the word *idea*, seems to be commonly taken in a very loose sense, by Locke and others; as standing for any of our perceptions, our sensations and passions, as well as thoughts. Now in this sense, I should desire to know, what can be meant by asserting, that self-love, or resentment of injuries, or the passion between the sexes is not innate!

   But admitting these terms, *impressions* and *ideas*, in the sense above explained, and understanding by *innate*, what is original or copied from no precedent perception, then may we assert that all our impressions are innate, and our ideas not innate.

   To be ingenuous, I must own it to be my opinion, that Locke was betrayed into this question by the schoolmen, who, making use of undefined terms, draw out their disputes to a tedious length, without ever touching the point in question. A like ambiguity and circumlocution seems to run through that philosopher's reasonings on this as well as most other subjects.

2. Resemblance.
3. Contiguity.
4. Cause and effect.
5. For instance, Contrast or Contrariety is also a connexion among Ideas: but it may, perhaps, be con-

sidered as a mixture of *Causation* and *Resemblance*. Where two objects are contrary, the one destroys the other; that is, the cause of its annihilation, and the idea of the annihilation of an object, implies the idea of its former existence.

6. The word, Power, is here used in a loose and popular sense. The more accurate explication of it would give additional evidence to this argument. See Section VII.

7. Nothing is more useful than for writers, even, on *moral, political*, or *physical* subjects, to distinguish between *reason* and *experience*, and to suppose, that these species of argumentation are entirely different from each other. The former are taken for the mere result of our intellectual faculties, which, by considering a priori the nature of things, and examining the effects, that must follow from their operation, establish particular principles of science and philosophy. The latter are supposed to be derived entirely from sense and observation, by which we learn what has actually resulted from the operation of particular objects, and are thence able to infer, what will, for the future, result from them. Thus, for instance, the limitations and restraints of civil government, and a legal constitution, may be defended, either from *reason*, which reflecting on the great frailty and corruption of human nature, teaches, that no man can safely be trusted with unlimited authority; or from *experience* and history, which inform us of the enormous abuses, that ambition, in every age and country, has been found to make of so imprudent a confidence.

   The same distinction between reason and experience is maintained in all our deliberations concerning the conduct of life; while the experienced statesman, general, physician, or merchant is trusted and followed; and the unpractised novice, with whatever natural talents endowed, neglected and despised. Though it be allowed, that reason may form very plausible conjectures with regard to the consequences of such a particular conduct in such particular circumstances; it is still supposed imperfect, without the assistance of experience, which is alone able to give stability and certainty to the maxims, derived from study and reflection.

   But notwithstanding that this distinction be thus universally received, both in the active and speculative scenes of life, I shall not scruple to pronounce, that it is, at bottom, erroneous, at least, superficial.

If we examine those arguments, which, in any of the sciences above mentioned, are supposed to be the mere effects of reasoning and reflection, they will be found to terminate, at last, in some general principle or conclusion, for which we can assign no reason but observation and experience. The only difference between them and those maxims, which are vulgarly esteemed the result of pure experience, is, that the former cannot be established without some process of thought, and some reflection on what we have observed, in order to distinguish its circumstances, and trace its consequences: Whereas in the latter, the experienced event is exactly and fully familiar to that which we infer as the result of any particular situation. The history of a TIBERIUS or a NERO makes us dread a like tyranny, were our monarchs freed from the restraints of laws and senates: But the observation of any fraud or cruelty in private life is sufficient, with the aid of a little thought, to give us the same apprehension; while it serves as an instance of the general corruption of human nature, and shows us the danger which we must incur by reposing an entire confidence in mankind. In both cases, it is experience which is ultimately the foundation of our inference and conclusion.

There is no man so young and unexperienced, as not to have formed, from observation, many general and just maxims concerning human affairs and the conduct of life; but it must be confessed, that, when a man comes to put these in practice, he will be extremely liable to error, till time and farther experience both enlarge these maxims, and teach him their proper use and application. In every situation or incident, there are many particular and seemingly minute circumstances, which the man of greatest talent is, at first, apt to overlook, though on them the justness of his conclusions, and consequently the prudence of his conduct, entirely depend. Not to mention, that, to a young beginner, the general observations and maxims occur not always on the proper occasions, nor can be immediately applied with due calmness and distinction. The truth is, an unexperienced reasoner could be no reasoner at all, were he absolutely unexperienced; and when we assign that character to any one, we mean it only in a comparative sense, and suppose him possessed of experience, in a smaller and more imperfect degree.

8. "Whether it is a natural instance or a mere illusion, I can't say; but one's emotions are more strongly aroused by seeing the places that tradition records to have been the favorite resort of men of note in former days, than by hearing about their deeds or reading their writings. My own feelings at the pres-ent moment are a case in point. I am reminded of Plato, the first philosopher, so we are told, that made a practice of holding discussions in this place; and indeed, the garden close at hand, yonder, not only recalls his memory but seems to bring the actual man before my eyes. This was the haunt of Speusippus, of Xenocrates, and of Xenocrates' pupil Polemo, who used to sit on the very seat we see over there. For my own part, even the sight of our senate-house at home (I mean the Curia Hostilia, not the present new building, which looks to my eyes smaller since its enlargement) used to call up to me thoughts of Scipio, Cato, Laelius, and chief of all, my grandfather; such powers of suggestion do places possess. No wonder the scientific training of the memory is based upon locality." Cicero, *De Finibus,* Book V, trans. H. Rackham (Cambridge: Harvard University Press, 1914), pp. 291–92.

9. Mr. Locke divides all arguments into demonstrative and probable. In this view, we must say, that it is only probable all men must die, or that the sun will rise to-morrow. But to conform our language more to common use, we ought to divide arguments into *demonstrations, proofs*, and *probabilities*. By proofs meaning such arguments from experience as leave no room for doubt or opposition.

10. Section II.

11. Mr. Locke, in his chapter of power, says that, finding from experience, that there are several new productions in nature, and concluding that there must somewhere be a power capable of producing them, we arrive at last by this reasoning at the idea of power. But no reasoning can ever give us a new, original, simple idea; as this philosopher himself confesses. This, therefore, can never be the origin of that idea.

12. It may be pretended, that the resistance which we meet with in bodies, obliging us frequently to exert our force, and call up all our power, this gives us the idea of force and power. It is this *nisus*, or strong endeavour, of which we are conscious, that is the original impression from which this idea is copied. But, first, we attribute powers to a vast number of objects, where we never can suppose this resistance or exertion of force to take place; to the Supreme Being, who never meets with any re-

sistance; to the mind in its command over its ideas and limbs, in common thinking and motion, where the effect follows immediately upon the will, without any exertion or summoning up of force; to inanimate matter, which is not capable of this sentiment. *Secondly*, This sentiment of an endeavour to overcome resistance has no known connexion with any event: What follows it, we know by experience; but could not know it a priori. It must, however, be confessed, that the animal *nisus*, which we experience, though it can afford no accurate precise idea of power, enters very much into that vulgar, inaccurate idea, which is formed of it.

13. Θεὸς ἀπὸ μηχανῆς. [In Latin, "*Deus ex machina*." Literally, god from a machine. A thing or person that appears suddenly and unexpectedly in a play to provide a contrived solution to a difficult situation.]

14. I need not examine at length the *vis inertiae* which is so much talked of in the new philosophy, and which is ascribed to matter. We find by experience, that a body at rest or in motion continues for ever in its present state, till put from it by some new cause; and that a body impelled takes as much motion from the impelling body as it acquires itself. These are facts. When we call this a *vis inertiae*, we only mark these facts, without pretending to have any idea of the inert power; in the same manner as, when we talk of gravity, we mean certain effects, without comprehending that active power. It was never the meaning of Sir ISAAC NEWTON to rob second causes of all force or energy; though some of his followers have endeavoured to establish that theory upon his authority. On the contrary, that great philosopher had recourse to an etherial active fluid to explain his universal attraction; though he was so cautious and modest as to allow, that it was a mere hypothesis, not to be insisted on, without more experiments. I must confess, that there is something in the fate of opinions a little extraordinary. DES CARTES insinuated that doctrine of the universal and sole efficacy of the Deity, without insisting on it. MALEBRANCHE and other CARTESIANS made it the foundation of all their philosophy. It had, however, no authority in England. LOCKE, CLARKE,

and CUDWORTH, never so much as take notice of it, but suppose all along, that matter has a real, though subordinate and derived power. By what means has it become so prevalent among our modern metaphysicians?

15. According to these explications and definitions, the idea of *power* is relative as much as that of *cause*; and both have a reference to an effect, or some other event constantly conjoined with the former. When we consider the *unknown* circumstance of an object, by which the degree or quantity of its effect is fixed and determined, we call that its power: And accordingly, it is allowed by all philosophers, that the effect is the measure of the power. But if they had any idea of power, as it is in itself, why could not they Measure it in itself? The dispute whether the force of a body in motion be as its velocity, or the square of its velocity; this dispute, I say, need not be decided by comparing its effects in equal or unequal times; but by a direct mensuration and comparison.

As to the frequency of use of the words, Force, Power, Energy, etc., which every where occur in common conversation, as well as in philosophy; that is no proof, that we are acquainted, in any instance, with the connecting principle between cause and effect, or can account ultimately for the production of one thing to another. These words, as commonly used, have very loose meanings annexed to them; and their ideas are very uncertain and confused. No animal can put external bodies in motion without the sentiment of a *nisus* or endeavour; and every animal has a sentiment or feeling from the stroke or blow of an external object, that is in motion. These sensations, which are merely animal, and from which we can a priori draw no inference, we are apt to transfer to inanimate objects, and to suppose, that they have some such feelings, whenever they transfer or receive motion. With regard to energies, which are exerted, without our annexing to them any idea of communicated motion, we consider only the constant experienced conjunction of the events; and as we *feel* a customary connexion between the ideas, we transfer that feeling to the objects; as nothing is more usual than to apply to external bodies every internal sensation, which they occasion.

B. Perception

The Argument from Illusion

A. J. AYER

A. J. Ayer (1910–90) was one of the most influential philosophers of the twentieth century. His works included *Language, Truth and Logic, Philosophical Essays*, and *Thinking and Meaning*.

—•—

Exposition of the Argument

It does not normally occur to us that there is any need for us to justify our belief in the existence of material things. At the present moment, for example, I have no doubt whatsoever that I really am perceiving the familiar objects, the chairs and table, the pictures and books and flowers with which my room is furnished; and I am therefore satisfied that they exist. I recognize indeed that people are sometimes deceived by their senses, but this does not lead me to suspect that my own sense-perceptions cannot in general be trusted, or even that they may be deceiving me now. And this is not, I believe, an exceptional attitude. I believe that, in practice, most people agree with John Locke that "the certainty of things existing *in rerum natura*, when we have the testimony of our senses for it, is not only as great as our frame can attain to, but as our condition needs."[1]

When, however, one turns to the writings of those philosophers who have recently concerned themselves with the subject of perception, one may begin to wonder whether this matter is quite so simple. It is true that they do, in general, allow that our belief in the existence of material things is well founded; some of them, indeed, would say that there were occasions on which we knew for certain the truth of such propositions as "this is a cigarette" or "this is a pen." But even so they are not, for the most part, prepared to admit that such objects as pens or cigarettes are ever directly perceived. What, in their opinion, we directly perceive is always an object of a different kind from these; one to which it is now customary to give the name of "sense-datum." These sense-data are said to have the "presentative function"[2] of making us conscious of material things. But how they perform this function, and what is their relation to the material things which they present, are questions about which there is much dispute. There is dispute also about the properties of sense-data, apart from their relationship to material things: whether, for example, they are each of them private to a single observer; whether they can appear to have qualities that they do not really have, or have qualities that they do not appear to have; whether they are in any sense "within" the percipient's mind or brain. I shall show later on that these are not empirical questions. They are to be settled by making it clear how the term "sense-datum" is intended to be used. But first I must explain why it is thought necessary to introduce such a term at all. Why may we not say that we are directly aware of material things?

The answer is provided by what is known as the argument from illusion. This argument, as it is ordinarily stated, is based on the fact that material things may present different appearances to different observers, or to the same observer in different conditions, and that the character of these appearances is to some extent causally determined by the state of the conditions and the observer. For instance, it is remarked that a coin which looks circular from one point of view may look elliptical from another; or that a stick which normally appears straight looks bent when it is seen in water; or that to people who take drugs such as mescal, things appear to change their colours. The familiar cases of mirror images, and double vision, and complete hallucinations, such as the mirage, provide further examples. Nor is this a peculiarity of visual appearances. The same thing occurs in the domains of the other senses, including the sense of touch. It may be pointed out, for example, that the taste that a thing appears to have may vary with the condition of the palate; or that a liquid will seem to have a different temperature according as the hand that is feeling it is itself hot or cold; or that a coin seems larger when it is placed on the tongue than when it is held in the palm of the hand; or, to take a case of complete hallucination, that people who have had limbs amputated may still continue to feel pain in them.

Let us now consider one of these examples, say that of the stick which is refracted in water, and see what is to be inferred. For the present it must be assumed that the stick does not really change its shape when it is placed in water. I shall discuss the meaning and validity of this assumption later on. Then it follows that at least one of the visual appearances of the stick is delusive; for it cannot be both crooked and straight. Nevertheless, even in the case where what we see is not the real quality of a material thing, it is supposed that we are still seeing something; and that it is convenient to give this a name. And it is for this purpose that philosophers have recourse to the term "sense-datum." By using it they are able to give what seems to them a satisfactory answer to the question: What is the object of which we are directly aware, in perception, if it is not part of any material thing? Thus, when a man sees a mirage in the desert, he is not thereby perceiving any material thing; for the oasis which he thinks he is perceiving does not exist. At the same time, it is ar-

gued, his experience is not an experience of nothing; it has a definite content. Accordingly, it is said that he is experiencing sense-data, which are similar in character to what he would be experiencing if he were seeing a real oasis, but are delusive in the sense that the material thing which they appear to present is not actually there. Or again, when I look at myself in the glass my body appears to be some distance behind the glass; but other observations indicate that it is in front of it. Since it is impossible for my body to be in both these places at once, these perceptions cannot all be veridical. I believe, in fact, that the ones that are delusive are those in which my body appears to be behind the glass. But can it be denied that when one looks at oneself in the glass one is seeing something? And if, in this case, there really is no such material thing as my body in the place where it appears to be, what is it that I am seeing? Once again the answer we are invited to give is that it is a sense-datum. And the same conclusion may be reached by taking any other of my examples.

If anything is established by this, it can be only that there are some cases in which the character of our perceptions makes it necessary for us to say that what we are directly experiencing is not a material thing but a sense-datum. It has not been shown that this is so in all cases. It has not been denied, but rather assumed, that there are some perceptions that do present material things to us as they really are; and in their case there seems at first sight to be no ground for saying that we directly experience sense-data rather than material things. But, as I have already remarked, there is general agreement among the philosophers who make use of the term "sense-datum," or some equivalent term, that what we immediately experience is always a sense-datum and never a material thing. And for this they give further arguments which I shall now examine.

In the first place it is pointed out that there is no intrinsic difference in kind between those of our perceptions that are veridical in their presentation of material things and those that are delusive.[3] When I look at a straight stick, which is refracted in water and so appears crooked, my experience is qualitatively the same as if I were looking at a stick that really was crooked. When, as the result of my putting on green spectacles, the white walls of my room appear to me to be green, my experience is qualitatively the same as if I were perceiving walls that really were green. When people whose legs have been amputated continue to feel pressure upon them, their experience is qualitatively the same as if pressure really were being exerted upon their legs. But, it is argued, if, when our perceptions were delusive, we were always perceiving something of a different kind from what we perceived when they were veridical, we should expect our experience to be qualitatively different in the two cases. We should expect to be able to tell from the intrinsic character of a perception whether it was a perception of a sense-datum or of a material thing. But this is not possible, as the examples that I have given have shown. In some cases there is indeed a distinction with respect to the beliefs to which the experiences give rise, as can be illustrated by my original example. For when, in normal conditions, we have the experience of seeing a straight stick there; but when the stick appears crooked, through being refracted in water, we do not believe that it really is crooked; we do not regard the fact that it looks crooked in water as evidence against its being really straight. It must, however, be remarked that this difference in the beliefs which accompany our perceptions is not grounded in the nature of the perceptions themselves, but depends upon our past experience. We do not believe that the stick which appears crooked when it stands in water really is crooked because we know from past experience that in normal conditions it looks straight. But a child who had not learned that refraction was a means of distortion would naturally believe that the stick really was crooked as he saw it. The fact, therefore, that there is this distinction between the beliefs that accompany veridical and delusive perceptions does not justify the view that these are perceptions of generically different objects, especially as the distinction by no means applies to all cases. For it sometimes happens that a delusive experience is not only qualitatively indistinguishable from one that is veridical but is also itself believed to be veridical, as in the example of the mirage; and, conversely, there are cases in which experiences that are actually veridical are believed to be delusive, as when we see something

so strange or unexpected that we say to ourselves that we must be dreaming. The fact is that from the character of a perception considered by itself, that is, apart from its relation to further sense-experience, it is not possible to tell whether it is veridical or delusive. But whether we are entitled to infer from this that what we immediately experience is always a sense-datum remains still to be seen.

Another fact which is supposed to show that even in the case of veridical perceptions we are not directly aware of material things is that veridical and delusive perceptions may form a continuous series, both with respect to their qualities and with respect to the conditions in which they are obtained.[4] Thus, if I gradually approach an object from a distance I may begin by having a series of perceptions which are delusive in the sense that the object appears to be smaller than it really is. Let us assume that this series terminates in a veridical perception. Then the difference in quality between this perception and its immediate predecessor will be of the same order as the difference between any two delusive perceptions that are next to one another in the series; and, on the assumption that I am walking at a uniform pace, the same will be true of the difference in the conditions on which the generation of the series depends. A similar example would be that of the continuous alteration in the apparent colour of an object which was seen in a gradually changing light. Here again the relation between a veridical perception and the delusive perception that comes next to it in the series is the same as that which obtains between neighbouring delusive perceptions, both with respect to the difference in quality and with respect to the change in the conditions; and these are differences of degree and not of kind. But this, it is argued, is not what we should expect if the veridical perception were a perception of an object of a different sort, a material thing as opposed to a sense-datum. Does not the fact that veridical and delusive perceptions shade into one another in the way that is indicated by these examples show that the objects that are perceived in either case are generically the same? And from this it would follow, if it was acknowledged that the delusive perceptions were perceptions of sense-data, that what we directly experienced was always a sense-datum and never a material thing.

The final argument that has to be considered in this context is based upon the fact that all our perceptions, whether veridical or delusive, are to some extent causally dependent both upon external conditions, such as the character of the light, and upon our own physiological and psychological states. In the case of perceptions that we take to be delusive this is a fact that we habitually recognize. We say, for example, that the stick looks crooked because it is seen in water; that the white walls appear green to me because I am wearing green spectacles; that the water feels cool because my hand is hot; that the murderer sees the ghost of his victim because of his bad conscience or because he has been taking drugs. In the case of perceptions that we take to be veridical we are apt not to notice such causal dependencies, since as a rule it is only the occurrence of the unexpected or the abnormal that induces us to look for a cause. But in this matter also there is no essential difference between veridical and delusive perceptions. When, for example, I look at the piece of paper on which I am writing, I may claim that I am seeing it as it really is. But I must admit that in order that I should have this experience it is not sufficient that there should actually be such a piece of paper there. Many other factors are necessary, such as the condition of the light, the distance at which I am from the paper, the nature of the background, the state of my nervous system and my eyes. A proof that they are necessary is that if I vary them I find that I have altered the character of my perception. Thus, if I screw up my eyes I see two pieces of paper instead of one; if I grow dizzy the appearance of the paper becomes blurred; if I alter my position sufficiently it appears to have a different shape and size; if the light is extinguished, or another object is interposed, I cease to see it altogether. On the other hand, the converse does not hold. If the paper is removed I shall cease to see it; but the state of the light

or of my nervous system or any other of the factors that were relevant to the occurrence of my perception may still remain the same. From this it may be inferred that the relation between my perception and these accompanying conditions is such that, while they are not causally dependent upon it, it is causally dependent upon them. And the same would apply to any other instance of a veridical perception that one cared to choose.

This point being established, the argument proceeds as follows. It is held to be characteristic of material things that their existence and their essential properties are independent of any particular observer. For they are supposed to continue the same, whether they are observed by one person or another, or not observed at all. But this, it is argued, has been shown not to be true of the objects we immediately experience. And so the conclusion is reached that what we immediately experience is in no case a material thing. According to this way of reasoning, if some perceptions are rightly held to be veridical, and others delusive, it is because of the different relations in which their objects stand to material things, and it is a philosophical problem to discover what these relations are. We may be allowed to have indirect knowledge of the properties of material things. But this knowledge, it is held, must be obtained through the medium of sense-data, since they are the only objects of which, in sense-perception, we are immediately aware.

NOTES

1. *An Essay Concerning Human Understanding*, Book IV, ch. 2, section viii.
2. Cf. H. H. Price, *Perception*, p. 104.
3. Cf. H. H. Price, *Perception*, p. 31.
4. Cf. Price, op. cit. p. 32.

The Argument from Illusion

J. L. AUSTIN

J. L. Austin (1911–1960) taught at Oxford University. He was a leader of the ordinary language movement in philosophy and had a great influence on a generation of British philosophers. His publications include *Sense and Sensibilia*, *Philosophical Papers*, and *How To Do Things with Words*, all published posthumously.

—•—

III

The primary purpose of the argument from illusion is to induce people to accept "sense-data" as the proper and correct answer to the question what they perceive on certain *abnormal, exceptional* occasions; but in fact it is usually followed up with another bit of argument intended to establish that they *always* perceive sense-data. Well, what is the argument?

In Ayer's statement[1] it runs as follows. It is "based on the fact that material things may present different appearances to different observers, or to the same observer in different conditions, and that the character of these appearances is to some extent causally determined by the state of the conditions and the observer." As illustrations of this alleged fact Ayer proceeds to cite perspective ("a coin which looks circular from one point of view may look elliptical from another"); refraction ("a stick which normally appears straight looks bent when it is seen in water"); changes in colour-vision produced by drugs ("such as mescal"); mirror-images; double vision; hallucination; apparent variations in tastes; variations in felt warmth ("according as the hand that is feeling it is itself hot or cold"); variations in felt bulk ("a coin seems larger when it is placed on the tongue than when it is held in the palm of the hand"); and the oft-cited fact that "people who have

had limbs amputated may still continue to feel pain in them."

He then selects three of these instances for detailed treatment. First, refraction—the stick which normally "appears straight" but "looks bent" when seen in water. He makes the "assumptions" (a) that the stick does not *really change its shape* when it is placed in water, and (b) that it *cannot be* both crooked and straight.[2] He then concludes ("it follows") that "at least one of the *visual appearances* of the stick is *delusive*." Nevertheless, even when "what we see is not the *real quality* of a *material thing*, it is supposed that we are still seeing something"—and this something is to be called a "sense-datum." A sense-datum is to be "the object of which we are *directly* aware, in perception, if it is not *part* of any *material thing*." (The italics are mine throughout this and the next two paragraphs.)

Next, mirages. A man who sees a mirage, he says, is "not perceiving any material thing; for the oasis which he thinks he is perceiving *does not exist*." But "his *experience* is not an experience of nothing"; thus "it is said that he is experiencing sense-data, which are similar in character to what he would be experiencing if he were seeing a real oasis, but are delusive in the sense that *the material thing which they appear to present* is not *really there*."

Lastly, reflections. When I look at myself in a mirror "my body *appears to be* some distance behind the glass"; but it cannot actually be in two places at once; thus, my perceptions in this case "cannot all be *veridical*." But I do see *something*; and if "there really is no such material thing as my body in the place where it appears to be, what is it that I am see-

From *Sense and Sensibilia*, edited by G. J. Warnock. Copyright © 1977 by Oxford University Press. Printed by permission of the publisher.

ing?" Answer—a sense-datum. Ayer adds that "the same conclusion may be reached by taking any other of my examples."

Now I want to call attention, first of all, to the name of this argument—the "argument from *illusion*," and to the fact that it is produced as establishing the conclusion that some at least of our "perceptions" are *delusive*. For in this there are two clear implications—(*a*) that all the cases cited in the argument are cases of *illusions*; and (*b*) that *illusion* and *delusion* are the same thing. But both of these implications, of course, are quite wrong; and it is by no means unimportant to point this out, for, as we shall see, the argument trades on confusion at just this point.

What, then, would be some genuine examples of illusion? (The fact is that hardly any of the cases cited by Ayer is, at any rate without stretching things, a case of illusion at all.) Well, first, there are some quite clear cases of *optical* illusion—for instance the case we mentioned earlier in which, of two lines of equal length, one is made to look longer than the other. Then again there are illusions produced by professional "illusionists," conjurors—for instance the Headless Woman on the stage, who is made to look headless, or the ventriloquist's dummy which is made to appear to be talking. Rather different—not (usually) produced on purpose—is the case where wheels rotating rapidly enough in one direction may look as if they were rotating quite slowly in the opposite direction. Delusions, on the other hand, are something altogether different from this. Typical cases would be delusions of persecution, delusions of grandeur. These are primarily a matter of grossly disordered beliefs (and so, probably, behavior) and may well have nothing in particular to do with perception.[3] But I think we might also say that the patient who sees pink rats has (suffers from) delusions—particularly, no doubt, if, as would probably be the case, he is not clearly aware that his pink rats aren't real rats.[4]

The most important differences here are that the term "an illusion" (in a perceptual context) does not suggest that something totally unreal is *conjured up*—on the contrary, there just is the arrangement of lines and arrows on the page, the woman on the stage with her head in a black bag, the rotating wheels; whereas the term "delusion" *does* suggest

something totally unreal, not really there at all. (The convictions of the man who has delusions of persecution can be *completely* without foundation.) For this reason delusions are a much more serious matter—something is really wrong, and what's more, wrong *with* the person who has them. But when I see an optical illusion, however well it comes off, there is nothing wrong with me personally, the illusion is not a little (or a large) peculiarity or idiosyncrasy of my own; it is quite public, anyone can see it, and in many cases standard procedures can be laid down for producing it. Furthermore, if we are not actually to be taken in, we need to be *on our guard*; but it is no use to tell the sufferer from delusions to be on his guard. He needs to be cured.

Why is it that we tend—if we do—to confuse illusions with delusions? Well, partly, no doubt the terms are often used loosely. But there is also the point that people may have, without making this explicit, different views or theories about the facts of some cases. Take the case of seeing a ghost, for example. It is not generally known, or agreed, what seeing ghosts *is*. Some people think of seeing ghosts as a case of something being conjured up, perhaps by the disordered nervous system of the victim; so in their view seeing ghosts is a case of delusion. But other people have the idea that what is called seeing ghosts is a case of being taken in by shadows, perhaps, or reflections, or a trick of the light—that is, they assimilate the case in their minds to illusion. In this way, seeing ghosts, for example, may come to be labelled sometimes as "delusion," sometimes as "illusion"; and it may not be noticed that it makes a difference which label we use. Rather, similarly, there seem to be different doctrines in the field as to what mirages are. Some seem to take a mirage to be a vision conjured up by the crazed brain of the thirsty and exhausted traveller (delusion), while in other accounts it is a case of atmospheric refraction, whereby something below the horizon is made to appear above it (illusion). (Ayer . . . takes the delusion view, although he cites it . . . as a case of illusion. He says not that the oasis appears to be where it is not, but roundly that "it does not exist.")

The way in which the "argument from illusion" positively trades on not distinguishing illusions from delusions is, I think, this. So long as it is being suggested that the cases paraded for our attention are cases of *illusion*, there is the implication (from the ordinary use of the word) that there really is something there that we perceive. But then, when these cases begin to be quietly called delusive, there comes in the very different suggestion of something being conjured up, something unreal or at any rate "immaterial." These two implications taken together may then subtly insinuate that in the cases cited there really is something that we are perceiving, but that this is an immaterial something; and this insinuation, even if not conclusive by itself, is certainly well calculated to edge us a little closer towards just the position where the sense-datum theorist wants to have us.

So much, then—though certainly there could be a good deal more—about the differences between illusions and delusions and the reasons for not obscuring them. Now let us look briefly at some of the other cases Ayer lists. Reflections, for instance. No doubt you *can* produce illusions with mirrors, suitably disposed. But is just *any* case of seeing something in a mirror an illusion, as he implies? Quite obviously not. For seeing things in mirrors is a perfectly *normal* occurrence, completely familiar, and there is usually no question of anyone being taken in. No doubt, if you're an infant or an aborigine and have never come across a mirror before, you may be pretty baffled, and even visibly perturbed, when you do. But is that a reason why the rest of us should speak of illusion here? And just the same goes for the phenomena of perspective—again, one *can* play tricks with perspective, but in the ordinary case there is no question of illusion. That a round coin should "look elliptical" (in one sense) from some points of view is exactly what we expect and what we normally find; indeed, we should be badly put out if we ever found this not to be so. Refraction again—the stick that looks bent in water—is far too familiar a case to be properly called a case of illusion. We may perhaps be prepared to agree that the stick looks bent; but then we can see that it's partly submerged in water, so that is exactly how we should expect it to look.

It is important to realize here how familiarity, so to speak, takes the edge off illusion. Is the cinema a case of illusion? Well, just possibly the first man

who ever saw moving pictures may have felt inclined to say that here was a case of illusion. But in fact it's pretty unlikely that even he, even momentarily, was actually taken in; and by now the whole thing is so ordinary a part of our lives that it never occurs to us even to raise the question. One might as well ask whether producing a photograph is producing an illusion—which would plainly be just silly.

Then we must not overlook, in all this talk about illusions and delusions, that there are plenty of more or less unusual cases, not yet mentioned, which certainly aren't either. Suppose that a proof-reader makes a mistake—he fails to notice that what ought to be "causal" is printed as "casual"; does he have a delusion? Or is there an illusion before him? Neither, of course; he simply *misreads*. Seeing afterimages, too, though not a particularly frequent occurrence and not just an ordinary case of seeing, is neither seeing illusions nor have delusions. And what about dreams? Does the dreamer see illusions? Does he have delusions? Neither; dreams are *dreams*.

Let us turn for a moment to what Price has to say about illusions. He produces,[5] by way of saying "what the term 'illusion' means," the following "provisional definition": "An illusory sense-datum of sight or touch is a sense-datum which is such that we tend to take it to be part of the surface of a material object, but if we take it so we are wrong." It is by no means clear, of course, what this dictum itself means; but still, it seems fairly clear that the definition doesn't actually fit all the cases of illusion. Consider the two lines again. Is there anything here which we tend to take, wrongly, to be part of the surface of a material object? It doesn't seem so. We just see the two lines, we don't think or even tend to think that we see anything else, we aren't even raising the question whether anything is or isn't "part of the surface" of—what, anyway? the lines? the page?—the trouble is just that one line looks longer than the other, though it isn't. Nor surely, in the case of the Headless Woman, is it a question whether anything is or isn't part of her surface; the trouble is just that she looks as if she had no head.

It is noteworthy, of course, that, before he even begins to consider the "argument from illusion,"

Price has already incorporated in this "definition" the idea that in such cases there is something to be seen *in addition to* the ordinary things—which is part of what the argument is commonly used, and not uncommonly taken, to *prove*. But this idea surely has no place in an attempt to say what "illusion" *means*. It comes in again, improperly I think, in his account of perspective (which incidentally he also cites as a species of illusion)—"a distinct hillside which is full of protuberances, and slopes upwards at quite a gentle angle, will appear flat and vertical. . . . This means that the sense-datum, the colour-expanse which we sense, actually *is* flat and vertical." But why should we accept this account of the matter? Why should we say that there is *anything* we see which *is* flat and vertical, though not "part of the surface" of any material object? To speak thus is to assimilate all such cases to cases of delusion, where there *is* something not "part of any material thing." But we have already discussed the undesirability of this assimilation.

Next, let us have a look at the account Ayer himself gives of some at least of the cases he cites. (In fairness we must remember here that Ayer has a number of quite substantial reservations of his own about the merits and efficacy of the argument from illusion, so that it is not easy to tell just how seriously he intends his exposition of it to be taken; but this is a point we shall come back to.)

First, then, the familiar case of the stick in water. Of this case Ayer says (*a*) that since the stick looks bent but is straight, "at least one of the visual appearances of the stick is *delusive*"; and (*b*) that "what we see [directly anyway] is not the real quality of [a few lines later, not part of] a material thing." Well now: does the stick "look bent" to begin with? I think we can agree that it does, we have no better way of describing it. But of course it does *not* look *exactly* like a bent stick, a bent stick out of water— at most, it may be said to look rather like a bent stick partly immersed *in* water. After all, we can't help seeing the water the stick is partly immersed in. So exactly what in this case is supposed to be *delusive*? What is wrong, what is even faintly surprising, in the idea of a stick's being straight but looking bent sometimes? Does anyone suppose that if something is straight, then it jolly well has to *look* straight at

all times and in all circumstances? Obviously no one seriously supposes this. So what mess are we supposed to get into here, what is the difficulty? For of course it has to be suggested that there *is* a difficulty—a difficulty, furthermore, which calls for a pretty radical solution, the introduction of sense-data. But what is the problem we are invited to solve in this way?

Well, we are told, in this case you are seeing *something*; and what is this something "if it is not part of any material thing?" But this question is, really, completely mad. The straight part of the stick, the bit not under water, is presumably part of a material thing; don't we see that? And what about the bit *under* water?—we can see that too. We can see, come to that, the water itself. In fact what we see is *a stick partly immersed in water*; and it is particularly extraordinary that this should appear to be called in question—that a question should be raised about *what* we are seeing—since this, after all, is simply the description of the situation with which we started. It was, that is to say, agreed at the start that we were looking at a stick, a "material thing," part of which was under water. If, to take a rather different case, a church were cunningly camouflaged so that it looked like a barn, how could any serious question be raised about what we see when we look at it? We see, of course, *a church* that now *looks like a barn*. We do *not* see an immaterial barn, an immaterial church, or an immaterial anything else. And what in this case could seriously tempt us to say that we do?

Notice, incidentally, that in Ayer's description of the stick-in-water case, which is supposed to be prior to the drawing of any philosophical conclusions, there has already crept in the unheralded but important expression "visual appearances"—it is, of course, ultimately to be suggested that all we *ever* get when we see is a visual appearance (whatever that may be).

Consider next the case of my reflection in a mirror. My body, Ayer says, "appears to be some distance behind the glass"; but as it's in front, it can't really be behind the glass. So what am I seeing? A sense-datum. What about this? Well, once again, although there is no objection to saying that my body "appears to be some distance behind the glass," in saying this we must remember what sort of situation we are dealing with. It does not "appear to be" there in a way which might tempt me (though it might tempt a baby or a savage) to go round the back and look for it, and be astonished when this enterprise proved a failure. (To say that A is *in* B doesn't always mean that if you open B you will find A, just as to say that A is *on* B doesn't always mean that you could pick it off—consider "I saw my face in the mirror," "There's a pain in my toe," "I heard him on the radio," "I saw the image on the screen," etc. Seeing something in a mirror is not like seeing a bun in a shop-window.) But does it follow that, since my body is not actually located behind the mirror, I am not seeing a material thing? Plainly not. For one thing, I can see the mirror (nearly always anyway). I can see my own body "indirectly," *sc.* in the mirror. I can also see the reflection of my own body or, as some would say, a mirror-image. And a mirror-image (if we choose this answer) is not a "sense-datum"; it can be photographed, seen by any number of people, and so on. (Of course there is no question here of either illusion or delusion.) And if the question is pressed, what actually *is* some distance, five feet say, behind the mirror, the answer is, not a sense-datum, but some region of the adjoining room.

The mirage case—at least if we take the view, as Ayer does, that the oasis the traveler thinks he can see "does not exist"—is significantly more amenable to the treatment it is given. For here we are supposing the man to be genuinely deluded, he is *not* "seeing a material thing."[6] We don't actually have to say, however, even here that he is "experiencing sense-data"; for though, as Ayer says "it is convenient to give a name" to what he is experiencing, the fact is that it already has a name—a *mirage*. Again, we should be wise not to accept too readily the statement that what he is experiencing is "*similar in character* to what he would be experiencing if he were seeing a real oasis." For is it at all likely, really, to be very similar? And, looking ahead, if we were to concede this point we should find the concession being used against us at a later stage—namely, at the stage where we shall be invited to agree that we see sense-data always, in normal cases too.

. . . .

V

I want now to take up again the philosophical argument as it is set out in the texts we are discussing. . . . the argument from illusion is intended primarily to persuade us that, in certain exceptional, abnormal situations, what we perceive—directly anyway—is a sense-datum; but then there comes a second stage, in which we are to be brought to agree that what we (directly) perceive is *always* a sense-datum, even in the normal, unexceptional case. It is this second stage of the argument that we must now examine.

Ayer expounds the argument thus.[7] There is he says, "no intrinsic difference in kind between those of our perceptions that are veridical in their presentation of material things and those that are delusive. When I look at a straight stick, which is refracted in water and so appears crooked, my experience is qualitatively the same as if I were looking at a stick that really was crooked. . . ." If, however, "when our perceptions were delusive, we were always perceiving something of a different kind from what we perceived when they were veridical, we should expect our experience to be qualitatively different in the two cases. We should expect to be able to tell from the intrinsic character of a perception whether it was a perception of a sense datum or of a material thing. But this is not possible. . . ." Price's exposition of this point,[8] to which Ayer refers us, is in fact not perfectly analogous; for Price has already somehow reached the conclusion that we are always aware of sense-data, and here is trying to establish only that we cannot distinguish *normal* sense-data, as "parts of the surfaces of material things," from *abnormal* ones, not "parts of the surfaces of material things." However, the argument used is much the same: "the abnormal crooked sense-datum of a straight stick standing in water is qualitatively indistinguishable from a normal sense-datum of a crooked stick"; but "is it not incredible that two entities so similar in all these qualities should really be so utterly different: that the one should be a real constituent of a material object, wholly independent of the observer's mind and organism, while the other is merely the fleeting product of his cerebral processes?"

It is argued further, both by Ayer and Price, that "even in the case of veridical perceptions we are not directly aware of material things" [or in the work of Price, that our sense-data are not parts of the surfaces of material things] for the reason that "veridical and delusive perceptions may form a continuous series. Thus, if I gradually approach an object from a distance I may begin by having a series of perceptions which are delusive in the sense that the object appears to be smaller than it really is. Let us assume that this series terminates in a veridical perception.[9] Then the difference in quality between this perception and its immediate predecessor will be of the same order as the difference between any two delusive perceptions that are next to one another in the series. . . ." But "these are differences of degree and not of kind. But this, it is argued, is not what we should expect if the veridical perception were a perception of an object of a different sort, a material thing as opposed to a sense-datum. Does not the fact that veridical and delusive perceptions shade into one another in the way that is indicated by these examples show that the objects that are perceived in either case are generically the same? And from this it would follow, if it was acknowledged that the delusive perceptions were perceptions of sense-data, that what we directly experienced was always a sense-datum and never a material thing." As Price puts it, "it seems most extraordinary that there should be a total difference of nature where there is only an infinitesimal difference of quality."[10]

Well, what are we to make of the arguments thus set before us?

1. It is pretty obvious, for a start, that the terms in which the argument is stated by Ayer are grossly tendentious. Price, you remember, is not producing the argument as a proof that we are always aware of sense-data; in his view that question has already been settled, and he conceives himself to be faced here only with the question whether any sense-data are "parts of the surfaces of material objects." But in Ayer's exposition the argument *is* put forward as a ground for the conclusion that what we are (directly) aware of in perception is always a sense-datum; and if so, it seems a rather serious defect that this conclusion is practically assumed from the very first sentence of the statement of the argument itself. In that sentence Ayer uses, not indeed for the first time, the term "perceptions" (which incidentally has never been defined or explained), and takes it for granted, here and throughout, that there is at any rate some kind of entities of which we are aware in absolutely all cases—namely, "perceptions," delusive or veridical. But of course, if one has already been induced to swallow the idea that every case, whether "delusive" or "veridical," supplies us with "perceptions," one is only too easily going to be made to feel that it would be straining at a gnat not to swallow sense-data in an equally comprehensive style. But in fact one has not even been told what "perceptions" *are*: and the assumption of their ubiquity has been slipped in without any explanation or argument whatever. But if those to whom the argument is ostensibly addressed were not thus made to concede the essential point from the beginning, would the statement of the argument be quite such plain sailing?

2. Of course we shall also want to enter a protest against the argument's bland assumption of a simple dichotomy between "veridical and delusive experiences." There is, as we have already seen, *no* justification at all *either* for lumping all so-called "delusive" experiences together, *or* for lumping together all so-called "veridical" experiences. But again, could the argument run quite so smoothly without this assumption? It would certainly—and this, incidentally, would be all to the good—take rather longer to state.

3. But now let us look at what the argument actually says. It begins, you will remember, with an alleged statement of fact—namely, that "there is no intrinsic difference in kind between those of our perceptions that are veridical in their presentation of material things and those that are delusive" (Ayer), that "there is no qualitative difference between normal sense-data as such and abnormal sense-data as such" (Price). Now, waiving so far as possible the numerous obscurities in and objections to this manner of speaking, let us ask whether what is being alleged here is actually true. Is it the case that "delusive and veridical experiences" are not "qualitatively different"? Well, at least it seems perfectly extraordinary to say so in this sweeping way.

Consider a few examples. I may have the experience (dubbed "delusive" presumably) of dreaming that I am being presented to the Pope. Could it be seriously suggested that having this dream is "qualitatively indistinguishable" from *actually being* presented to the Pope? Quite obviously not. After all, we have the phrase "a dream-like quality"; some waking experiences are said to have this dream-like quality, and some artists and writers occasionally try to impart it, usually with scant success, to their works. But of course, if the fact here alleged *were* a fact, the phrase would be perfectly meaningless, because applicable to everything. If dreams were not "qualitatively" different from waking experiences, then *every* waking experience would be like a dream; the dream-like quality would be, not difficult to capture, but impossible to avoid.[11] It is true, to repeat, that dreams are *narrated* in the same terms as waking experiences: these terms, after all, are the best terms we have; but it would be wildly wrong to conclude from this that what is narrated in the two cases is *exactly alike*. When we are hit on the head we sometimes say that we "see stars"; but for all that, seeing stars when you are hit on the head is *not* "qualitatively" indistinguishable from seeing stars when you look at the sky.

Again, it is simply not true to say that seeing a bright green after image against a white wall is exactly like seeing a bright green patch actually on the wall; or that seeing a white wall through blue spectacles is exactly like seeing a blue wall; or that seeing pink rats in D.T.s is exactly like really seeing pink rats; or (once again) that seeing a stick refracted in water is exactly like seeing a bent stick. In all these cases we may *say* the same things ("It looks blue," "It looks bent," etc.), but this is no reason at all for denying the obvious fact that the "experiences" are *different*.

4. Next, one may well wish at least to ask for the credentials of a curious general principle on which both Ayer and Price seem to rely,[12] to the effect that if two things are not "generically the same," the same "in nature," then they can't be alike, or even very nearly alike. If it were true, Ayer says, that from time to time we perceived things of two different kinds, then "we should expect" them to be qualitatively different. But why on earth should

we?—particularly if, as he suggests would be the case, we never actually found such a thing to be true. It is not at all easy to discuss this point sensibly, because of the initial absurdity in the hypothesis that we perceive just *two* kinds of things. But if, for example, I had never seen a mirror, but were told (*a*) that in mirrors one sees reflections of things, and (*b*) that reflections of things are not "generically the same" as things, is there any reason why I should forthwith *expect* there to be some whacking big "qualitative" difference between seeing things and seeing their reflections? Plainly not; if I were prudent, I should simply wait and see what seeing reflections was like. If I am told that a lemon is generically different from a piece of soap, do I "expect" that no piece of soap could look just like a lemon? Why should I?

(It is worth noting that Price helps the argument along at this point by a bold stroke of rhetoric: how *could* two entities be "qualitatively indistinguishable," he asks, if one is a "real constituent of a material object," the other *a fleeting product of his cerebral processes?*" But how in fact are we supposed to have been persuaded that sense-data are *ever* fleeting products of cerebral processes? Does this colourful description fit, for instance, the reflection of my face in a mirror?)

5. Another erroneous principle which the argument here seems to rely on is this: that it *must* be the case that "delusive and veridical experiences" are not (as such) "qualitatively" or "intrinsically" distinguishable—for if they were distinguishable, we should never be "deluded." But of course this is not so. From the fact that I am sometimes "deluded," mistaken, taken in through failing to distinguish A from B, it does not follow at all that A and B must be *indistinguishable*. Perhaps I should have noticed the difference if I had been more careful or attentive; perhaps I am just bad at distinguishing things of this sort (e.g. vintages); perhaps, again, I have never learned to discriminate between them, or haven't had much practice at it. As Ayer observes, probably truly, "a child who had not learned that refraction was a means of distortion would naturally believe that the stick really was crooked as he saw it"; but how is the fact that an uninstructed child probably would not discriminate between *being re-*

fracted and *being crooked* supposed to establish the allegation that there *is* no "qualitative" difference between the two cases? What sort of reception would I be likely to get from a professional tea-taster, if I were to say to him, "But there can't be any difference between the flavours of these two brands of tea, for I regularly fail to distinguish between them?" Again, when "the quickness of the hand deceives the eye," it is not that what the hand is really doing is *exactly like* what we are tricked into thinking it is doing, but simply that it is *impossible to tell* what it is really doing. In this case it may be true that we can't distinguish, and not merely that we don't; but even this doesn't mean that the two cases are exactly alike.

I do not, of course, wish to deny that there may be cases in which "delusive and veridical experiences" really are "qualitatively indistinguishable"; but I certainly do wish to deny (*a*) that such cases are anything like as *common* as both Ayer and Price seem to suppose, and (*b*) that there *have* to be such cases to accommodate the undoubted fact that we are sometimes "deceived by our senses." We are not, after all, quasi-infallible beings, who can be taken in only where the avoidance of mistake is completely impossible. But if we are prepared to admit that there may be, even that there are, *some* cases in which "delusive and veridical perceptions" really are indistinguishable, does this admission require us to drag in, or even to let in, sense-data? No. For even if we were to make the prior admission (which we have so far found no reason to make) that in the "abnormal" cases we perceive sense-data, we should not be obliged to extend this admission to the "normal" cases too. For why on earth should it *not* be the case that, in some few instances, perceiving one sort of thing is exactly like perceiving another?

6. There is a further quite general difficulty in assessing the force of this argument, which we (in common with the authors of our texts) have slurred over so far. The question which Ayer invites us to consider is whether two classes of "perceptions," the veridical and the delusive, are or are not "qualitatively different," "intrinsically different in kind"; but how are we supposed to set about even considering this question, when we are not told what "a perception" *is*? In particular, how many of the cir-

cumstances of a situation, as these would ordinarily be stated, are supposed to be included in "the perception?" For example, to take the stick in water again: it is a feature of this case that part of the stick is under water, and water, of course, is not invisible; is the water, then, part of "the perception?" It is difficult to conceive of any grounds for denying that it is; but *if* it is, surely this is a perfectly obvious respect in which "the perception" differs from, is distinguishable from, the "perception" we have when we look at a bent stick *not* in water. There is a sense, perhaps, in which the presence or absence of water is not the *main thing* in this case—we are supposed to be addressing ourselves primarily to questions about the stick. But in fact, as a great quantity of psychological investigation has shown, discrimination between one thing and another very frequently depends on such more or less extraneous concomitants of the main thing, even when such concomitants are not consciously taken note of. As I said, we are told nothing of what "a perception" is; but could any defensible account, if such an account were offered, completely exclude all these highly significant attendant circumstances? And if they *were* excluded—in some more or less arbitrary way—how much interest or importance would be left in the contention that "delusive" and "veridical" perceptions are indistinguishable? Inevitably, if you rule out the respects in which A and B differ, you may expect to be left with respects in which they are alike.

I conclude, then, that this part of the philosophical argument involves (though not in every case equally essentially) (*a*) acceptance of a quite bogus dichotomy of all "perceptions" into two groups, the "delusive" and the "veridical"—to say nothing of the unexplained introduction of "perceptions" themselves; (*b*) an implicit but grotesque exaggeration of the *frequency* of "delusive perceptions"; (*c*) a further grotesque exaggeration of the *similarity* between "delusive" perceptions and "veridical" ones; (*d*) the erroneous suggestion that there *must* be such similarity, or even qualitative *identity*; (*e*) the acceptance of the pretty gratuitous idea that things "generically different" could not be qualitatively alike; and (*f*)—which is really a corollary of (*c*) and (*a*)—the gratuitous neglect of those more or less subsidiary features which often make possible the discrimination of situations which, in other *broad* respects, may be roughly alike. These seem to be rather serious deficiencies.

NOTES

1. Alfred J. Ayer, *The Foundations of Empirical Knowledge* (London: Macmillan, 1940, 1964).

2. It is not only strange, but also important, that Ayer calls these "assumptions." Later on he is going to take seriously the notion of denying at least one of them, which he could hardly do if he had recognized them here as the plain and incontestable facts that they are.

3. The latter point holds, of course, for *some* uses of "illusion" too; there are the illusions which some people (are said to) lose as they grow older and wiser.

4. Cp. the white rabbit in the play called *Harvey.*

5. H. H. Price, *Perception* (London: Methuen, 1932), p. 27.

6. Not even "indirectly," no such thing is "presented." Doesn't this seem to make the case, though more amenable, a good deal less useful to the philosopher? It's hard to see how normal cases could be said to be *very like* this.

7. Ayer, op. cit., pp. 5–9.

8. Price, op. cit., p. 31.

9. But what, we may ask, does this assumption amount to? From what distance *does* an object, a cricket-ball say, "look the size that it really is?" Six feet? Twenty feet?

10. I omit from consideration a further argument cited by both Price and Ayer, which makes play with the "causal dependence" of our "perceptions" upon the conditions of observation and our own "physiological and psychological states."

11. This is part, no doubt *only* part, of the absurdity in Descartes's toying with the notion that the whole of our experience might be a dream.

12. Ayer in fact expresses qualms later. . . .

C. Induction, Causation, and Scientific Explanation

The Problem of Induction

W. C. SALMON

W. C. Salmon (1925–) is a professor of philosophy at the University of Pittsburgh. His publications include *The Foundations of Scientific Inference* and *Space, Time, and Motion*.

—•—

I. The Problem of Induction

We all believe that we have knowledge of facts extending far beyond those we directly perceive. The scope of our senses is severely limited in space and time; our immediate perceptual knowledge does not reach to events that happened before we were born to events that are happening now in certain other places or to any future events. We believe, nevertheless, that we have some kind of indirect knowledge of such facts. We know that a glacier once covered a large part of North America, that the sun continues to exist at night, and that the tides will rise and fall tomorrow. Science and common sense have at least this one thing in common: Each embodies knowledge of matters of fact that are not open to our direct inspection. Indeed, science purports to establish general laws or theories that apply to all parts of space and time without restriction. A "science" that consisted of no more than a mere summary of the results of direct observation would not deserve the name.

Hume's profound critique of induction begins with a simple and apparently innocent question: How do we acquire knowledge of the unobserved?[1] This question, as posed, may seem to call for an empirical answer. We observe that human beings utilize what may be roughly characterized as inductive or scientific methods of extending knowledge from the observed to the unobserved. The sciences, in fact, embody the most powerful and highly developed methods known, and we may make an empirical investigation of scientific methods much as we might for any other sort of human behavior. We may consider the historical development of science. We may study the psychological, sociological, and political factors relevant to the pursuit of science. We may try to give an exact characterization of the behavior of scientists. In doing all these things, however, important and interesting as they are, we will have ignored the *philosophical* aspect of the problem Hume raised. Putting the matter very simply, these empirical investigations may enable us to describe the ways in which people arrive at *beliefs* about unobserved facts, but they leave open the question of whether beliefs arrived at in this way actually constitute *knowledge*. It is one thing to describe how people go about seeking to extend their knowledge; it is quite another to claim that the methods employed actually do yield knowledge.

One of the basic differences between knowledge and belief is that knowledge must be founded upon evidence—i.e., it must be belief founded upon some rational justification. To say that certain methods yield knowledge of the unobserved is to make a cognitive claim for them. Hume called into question the justification of such cognitive claims. The answer cannot be found entirely within an empirical study of human behavior, for a *logical* problem has been raised. It is the problem of understanding the logical relationship between evidence and conclusion in logically correct inferences. It is the problem of determining whether the inferences by which we attempt to make the transition from knowledge of the observed to knowledge of the unobserved are logically correct. The fact that people do or do not use a certain type of inference is irrelevant to its justifiability. Whether people have confidence in the correctness of a certain type of inference has nothing to do with whether such confidence is justified. If we should adopt a logically incorrect method for inferring one fact from others, these facts would not actually constitute evidence for the conclusion we have drawn. The problem of induction is the problem of explicating the very concept of *inductive evidence*.

There is another possibly misleading feature of the question as I have formulated it. When we ask how we can *acquire* knowledge of the unobserved, it sounds very much as if we are asking for a method for the *discovery* of new knowledge. This is, of course, a vital problem, but it is not the fundamental problem Hume raised. Whether there is or can be any sort of inductive logic of discovery is a controversial question I shall discuss in detail in a later section.[2] Leaving this question aside for now, there remains the problem of *justification* of conclusions concerning unobserved matters of fact. Given some conclusion, however arrived at, regarding unobserved facts, and given some alleged evidence to support that conclusion, the question remains whether that conclusion is, indeed, supported by the evidence offered in support of it.

Consider a simple and highly artificial situation. Suppose a number of balls have been drawn from an urn, and that all of the black ones that have been drawn are licorice-flavored. I am not now concerned with such psychological questions as what makes the observer note the color of these balls, what leads him to taste the black ones, what makes him take note of the fact that licorice flavor is associated with black color in his sample, or what makes him suppose that the black balls not yet drawn will also be licorice-flavored. The problem—Hume's basic *philosophical* problem—is this: Given that all of the observed black balls have been licorice-flavored, and given that somehow the conclusion has been entertained that the unobserved black balls in the urn are also licorice-flavored, do the observed facts constitute sound *evidence* for that conclusion? Would we be *justified* in accepting that conclusion on the basis of the facts alleged to be evidence for it?

As a first answer to this question we may point out that the inference does conform to an accepted inductive principle, a principle saying roughly that observed instances conforming to a generalization constitute evidence for it. It is, however, a very small step to the next question: What grounds have we for accepting this or any other inductive principle? Is there any reason or justification for placing confidence in the conclusions of inferences of this type? Given that the premises of this inference are true, and given that the inference conforms to a certain rule, can we provide any rational justification for accepting its conclusion rather than, for instance, the conclusion that black balls yet to be drawn will taste like quinine?

It is well known that Hume's answer to this problem was essentially skeptical. It was his great merit to have shown that a justification of induction, if possible at all, is by no means easy to provide. In order to appreciate the force of his argument it is first necessary to clarify some terminological points. This is particularly important because the word *induction* has been used in a wide variety of ways.

For purposes of systematic discussion one distinction is fundamental, namely, the distinction between demonstrative and nondemonstrative inference. A *demonstrative* inference is one whose premises necessitate its conclusion; the conclusion cannot be false if the premises are true. All valid deductions are demonstrative inferences. A *nondemonstrative* inference is simply one that fails to be demonstrative. Its conclusion is not necessitated by its premises; the conclusion could be false even if the premises are true. A demonstrative inference is *necessarily truth-preserving*; a nondemonstrative inference is not.

The category of nondemonstrative inferences, as I have characterized it, contains, among other things perhaps, all kinds of fallacious inferences. If, however, there is any kind of inference whose premises, although not necessitating the conclusion, do lend it weight, support it, or make it probable, then such inferences possess a certain kind of logical rectitude. It is not deductive validity, but it is important anyway. Inferences possessing it are *correct inductive inferences*.

Since demonstrative inferences have been characterized in terms of their basic property of necessary truth preservation, it is natural to ask how they achieve this very desirable trait. For a large group of demonstrative inferences, including those discussed under "valid deduction" in most logic texts, the answer is rather easy. Inferences of this type purchase necessary truth preservation by sacrificing any extension of content. The conclusion of such an inference says no more than do the premises—often less.[3] The conclusion cannot be false if the premises are true *because* the conclusion says nothing that was not already stated in the premises. The conclusion is a mere reformulation of all or part of the content of the premises. In some cases the reformulation is unanticipated and therefore psychologically surprising, but the conclusion cannot augment the content of the premises. Such inferences are *nonampliative*; an ampliative inference, then, has a conclusion with content not present either explicitly or implicitly in the premises.

While it is easy to understand why nonampliative inferences are necessarily truth-preserving, the further question arises whether there are any necessarily truth-preserving inferences that are also ampliative. Is there any type of inference whose conclusion must, of necessity, be true if the premises are true, but whose conclusion says something not stated by the premises? Hume believed that the answer is negative and so do I, but it is not easy to produce an adequate defense of this answer. Let us see, however, what an affirmative answer would amount to.

Suppose there were an ampliative inference that is also necessarily truth-preserving. Consider the implication from its premises, $P_1, \ldots, P_k$, to its con-

clusion C. If the inference were an ordinary nonampliative deduction, this implication would be analytic and empty; but since the argument is supposed to be ampliative, the implication must be synthetic. At the same time, because the argument is supposed to be necessarily truth-preserving, this implication must be not only true but necessarily true. Thus, to maintain that there are inferences that are both ampliative and necessarily truth-preserving is tantamount to asserting that there are synthetic a priori truths.[4] This may be seen in another way. Any ampliative inference can be made into a nonampliative one by adding a premise. In particular, if we add to the foregoing ampliative inference the synthetic a priori premise, "If P_1 and P_2 and . . . and P_k, then C," the resulting inference will be an ordinary valid nonampliative deduction. Consider our example once more; this time let us set it out more formally:

1. Some black balls from this urn have been observed.
   All observed black balls from this urn are licorice-flavored.

   All black balls in this urn are licorice-flavored.

This argument is clearly ampliative, for the premise makes a statement about observed balls only, while the conclusion makes a statement about the unobserved as well as the observed balls. It appears to be nondemonstrative as well, for it seems perfectly possible for the conclusion to be false even if the premises are true. We see no reason why someone might not have dropped a black marble in the urn which, when it is drawn, will be found to be tasteless. We could, however, rule out this sort of possibility by adding another premise:

2. Some black balls from this urn have been observed.
   All observed black balls in this urn are licorice-flavored.
   Any two balls in this urn that have the same color also have the same flavor.

   All black balls in this urn are licorice-flavored.

The additional premise has transformed the former nondemonstrative inference into a demonstrative inference, but we must also admit that we have transformed it into a nonampliative inference. If, however, the third premise of 2 were a synthetic a priori truth, the original inference, although ampliative, would have been necessarily truth-preserving and, hence, demonstrative. If the premise that transformed inference 1 into inference 2 were necessarily true, then it would be impossible for the conclusion of inference 1 to be false if the premises were true, for that would contradict the third premise of inference 2.

Hardly anyone would be tempted to say that the statement, "Any two balls in this urn that have the same color also have the same flavor," expresses a synthetic a priori truth. Other propositions have, however, been taken to be synthetic a priori. Hume and many of his successors noticed that typical inductive inferences, such as our example concerning licorice-flavored black balls, would seem perfectly sound if we could have recourse to some sort of principle of uniformity of nature. If we could only prove that the course of nature is uniform, that the future will be like the past, or that uniformities that have existed thus far will continue to hold in the future, then we would seem to be justified in generalizing from past cases to future cases—from the observed to the unobserved. Indeed, Hume suggests that we presuppose in our inductive reasoning a principle from which the third premise of 2 would follow as a special case: "We always presume, when we see like sensible qualities, that they have like secret powers, and expect that effects, similar to those which we have experienced, will follow from them."[5] Again, "From causes which appear *similar* we expect similar effects. This is the sum of all our experimental conclusions."[6]

Hume's searching examination of the principle of uniformity of nature revealed no ground on which it could be taken as a synthetic a priori principle. For all we can know a priori, Hume argued, the course of nature might change, the future might be radically unlike the past, and regularities that have obtained in respect to observed events might prove completely inapplicable to unobserved cases. We have found by experience, of course, that nature has exhibited a high degree of uniformity and regularity so far, and we infer inductively that this will continue, but to use an inductively inferred generalization as a justification for induction, as Hume emphasized, would be flagrantly circular. He concluded, in fact, that there are no synthetic a priori principles in virtue of which we could have demonstrative inferences that are ampliative. Hume recognized two kinds of reasoning: reasoning concerning relations of ideas and reasoning concerning matters of fact and existence. The former is demonstrative but nonampliative while the latter is ampliative but not necessarily truth-preserving.

If we agree that there are no synthetic a priori truths, then we must identify necessarily truth-preserving inference with nonampliative inference. All ampliative inference is nondemonstrative. This leads to an exhaustive trichotomy of inferences: valid deductive inference, correct inductive inference, and assorted fallacies. The first question is, however, whether the second category is empty or whether there are such things as correct inductive inferences. This is Hume's problem of induction. Can we show that any particular type of ampliative inference can be justified in any way? If so, it will qualify as correct induction.

Consider, then, any ampliative inference whatever. The example of the licorice-flavored black balls illustrates the point. We cannot show *deductively* that this inference will have a true conclusion given true premises. If we could, we would have proved that the conclusion must be true if the premises are. That would make it necessarily truth-preserving, hence, demonstrative. This, in turn, would mean that it was nonampliative, contrary to our hypothesis. Thus, if an ampliative inference could be justified deductively it would not be ampliative. It follows that ampliative inference cannot be justified deductively.

At the same time, we cannot justify any sort of ampliative inference *inductively*. To do so would require the use of some sort of nondemonstrative inference. But the question at issue is the justification of nondemonstrative inference, so the procedure would be question begging. Before we can properly employ a nondemonstrative inference in a justifying argument, we must already have justified that nondemonstrative inference.

Hume's position can be summarized succinctly: We cannot justify any kind of ampliative inference. If it could be justified deductively it would not be ampliative. It cannot be justified nondemonstratively because that would be viciously circular. It seems, then, that there is no way in which we can extend our knowledge to the unobserved. We have, to be sure, many beliefs about the unobserved, and in some of them we place great confidence. Nevertheless, they are without rational justification of any kind!

This is a harsh conclusion, yet it seems to be supported by impeccable arguments. It might be called "Hume's paradox," for the conclusion, although ingeniously argued, is utterly repugnant to common sense and our deepest convictions. We *know* ("in our hearts") that we have knowledge of unobserved fact. The challenge is to show how this is possible.

II. Attempted Solutions

It hardly needs remarking that philosophers have attempted to meet Hume's intriguing challenge in a wide variety of ways. There have been direct attacks upon some of Hume's arguments. Attempts to provide inductive arguments to support induction and attempts to supply a synthetic a priori principle of uniformity of nature belong in this category. Some authors have claimed that the whole problem arises out of linguistic confusion, and that careful analysis shows it to be a pseudoproblem. Some have even denied that inductive inference is needed, either in science or in everyday affairs. In this section I shall survey what seem to me to be the most important efforts to deal with the problem.

1. Inductive Justification. If Hume's arguments had never been propounded and we were asked why we accept the methods of science, the most natural answer would be, I think, that these methods have proved themselves by their results. We can point to astonishing technological advances, to vastly increased comprehension, and to impressive predictions. Science has provided us with foresight, control, and understanding. No other method can claim a comparable record of successful accomplishment. If methods are to be judged by their fruits, there is no doubt that the scientific method will come out on top.

Unfortunately, Hume examined this argument

and showed that it is viciously circular. It is an example of an attempt to justify inductive methods inductively. From the premise that science has had considerable predictive success in the past, we conclude that it will continue to have substantial predictive success in the future. Observed cases of the application of scientific method have yielded successful prediction; therefore, as yet unobserved cases of the application of scientific method will yield successful predictions. This argument has the same structure as our black-balls-in-the-urn example; it is precisely the sort of ampliative inference from the observed to the unobserved whose justifiability is in question.

Consider the parallel case for a radically different sort of method. A crystal gazer claims that his method is the appropriate method for making predictions. When we question his claim he says, "Wait a moment; I will find out whether the method of crystal gazing is the best method for making predictions." He looks into his crystal ball and announces that future cases of crystal gazing will yield predictive success. If we should protest that his method has not been especially successful in the past, he might well make certain remarks about parity of reasoning. "Since you have used your method to justify your method, why shouldn't I use my method to justify my method? If you insist upon judging my method by using your method, why shouldn't I use my method to evaluate your method? By the way, I note by gazing into my crystal ball that the scientific method is now in for a very bad run of luck."

The trouble with circular arguments is obvious: with an appropriate circular argument you can prove anything. In recent years, nevertheless, there have been several notable attempts to show how inductive rules can be supported inductively. The authors of such attempts try to show, of course, that their arguments are not circular. Although they argue persuasively, it seems to me that they do not succeed in escaping circularity.

One of the most widely discussed attempts to show that self-supporting inductive inferences are possible without circularity is due to Max Black.[7] Black correctly observes that the traditional fallacy of circular argument (*petitio principii*) involves assuming as a premise, often unwittingly, the conclusion that is to be proved. Thus, for example, a variety of "proofs" of Euclid's fifth postulate offered by mathematicians for about two millennia before the discovery of non-Euclidean geometry are circular in the standard fashion. They fail to show that the fifth postulate follows from the first four postulates alone; instead, they require in addition the assumption of a proposition equivalent to the proposition being demonstrated. The situation is quite different for self-supporting inductive arguments. The conclusion to be proved does not appear as one of the premises. Consider one of Black's examples:[8]

3. In most instances of the use of R_2 in arguments with true premises examined in a wide variety of conditions, R_2 has usually been successful.
   Hence (probably):
   In the next instance to be encountered of the use of R_2 in an argument with true premises, R_2 will be successful.

To say that an argument with true premises is successful is merely to say that it has a true conclusion. The rule R_2 is

To argue from *Most instances of A's examined in a wide variety of conditions have been B* to (probably) *The next A to be encountered will be B.*

Inference 3 can be paraphrased suggestively, although somewhat inaccurately, as:

4. R_2 has usually been successful in the past.
   Hence (probably):
   R_2 will be successful in the next instance.

Inference 3 is governed by R_2, that is, it conforms to the stipulation laid down by R_2. R_2 is *not* a premise, however, nor is any statement to the effect that all, some, or any future instances of R_2 will be successful. As Lewis Carroll showed decisively, there is a fundamental distinction between premises and rules of inference.[9] Any inference, inductive or deductive, must conform to some rule, but neither the rule nor any statement about the rule is to be in-

corporated into the inference as an additional premise. If such additional premises were required, inference would be impossible. Thus, inference 3 is not a standard *petitio principii.*

What, then, are the requirements for a self-supporting argument? At least three are immediately apparent: (1) The argument must have true premises. (2) The argument must conform to a certain rule. (3) The conclusion of that argument must say something about the success or reliability of that rule in unexamined instances of its application. Inference 3 has these characteristics.

It is not difficult to find examples of deductive inferences with the foregoing characteristics.

5. If snow is white, then *modus ponens* is valid.
   Snow is white.

   ―――――――――――――――――――――――

   Modus ponens is valid.

Inference 5 may seem innocuous enough, but the same cannot be said for the following inference:

6. If affirming the consequent is valid, then coal is black.
   Coal is black.

   ―――――――――――――――――――――――

   Affirming the consequent is valid.

Like inference 5, inference 6 has true premises, it conforms to a certain rule, and its conclusion asserts the validity of that rule. Inference 5 did nothing to enhance our confidence in the validity of *modus ponens*, for we have far better grounds for believing it to be valid. Inference 6 does nothing to convince us that affirming the consequent is valid, for we know on other grounds that it is invalid. Arguments like 5 and 6 are, nevertheless, instructive. Both are circular in some sense, though neither assumes *as a premise* the conclusion it purports to establish. In deductive logic the situation is quite straightforward. A deductive inference establishes its conclusion if it has true premises and has a valid form. If either of these features is lacking the conclusion is not established by that argument. If the argument is valid but the premises are not true we need not accept the conclusion. If the premises are true but the argument is invalid we need not accept the conclusion. One way in which an argument can be circular is by adopting as a premise the very conclusion that is to be proved; this is the fallacy of *petitio principii* which I shall call "premise-circularity." Another way in which an argument can be circular is by exhibiting a form whose validity is asserted by the very conclusion that is to be proved; let us call this type of circularity "rule-circularity." Neither type of circular argument establishes its conclusion in any interesting fashion, for in each case the conclusiveness of the argument depends upon the assumption of the conclusion of that argument. Inferences 5 and 6 are not premise-circular; each is rule-circular. They are, nevertheless, completely question begging.

The situation in induction is somewhat more complicated, but basically the same.[10] Consider the following argument:

7. In most instances of the use of R_3 in arguments with true premises examined in a wide variety of conditions, R_3 has usually been *un*successful.
     Hence (probably):
  In the next instance to be encountered of the use of R_3 in an argument with true premises, R_3 will be successful.

The rule R_3 is
  To argue from *Most instances of A's examined in a wide variety of conditions have been non-B to* (probably) *The next A to be encountered will be B.*

Inference 7 can be paraphrased as follows:

8. R_3 has usually been unsuccessful in the past.
     Hence (probably):
  R_3 will be successful in the next instance.

Notice that there is a perfect parallel between R_2, 3, 4 on the one hand and R_3, 7, 8 on the other. Since those instances in which R_2 would be successful are those in which R_3 would be unsuccessful, the premises of 3 and 4 describe the same state of affairs as do the premises of 7 and 8. Thus, the use of R_3 in the next instance seems to be supported in the

same manner and to the same extent as the use of R_2 in the next instance. However, R_2 and R_3 conflict directly with each other. On the evidence that most Italians examined in a wide variety of conditions have been dark-eyed, R_2 allows us to infer that the next Italian to be encountered will be dark-eyed, while R_3 permits us to infer from the same evidence that he will have light-colored eyes. It appears then that we can construct self-supporting arguments for correct and incorrect inductive rules just as we can for valid and invalid deductive rules.

Black would reject self-supporting arguments for the fallacy of affirming the consequent and for a counterinductive rule like R_2, because we know on independent grounds that such rules are faulty. Affirming the consequent is known to be fallacious, and the counterinductive method can be shown to be self-defeating. An additional requirement for a self-supporting argument is that the rule thus supported be one we have no independent reason to reject. Nevertheless, the fact that we can construct self-supporting arguments for such rules should give us pause. What if we had never realized that affirming the consequent is fallacious? What if we had never noticed anything wrong with the counterinductive method? Would arguments like 6, 7, and 8 have to be considered cogent? What about the standard inductive method? Is it as incorrect as the counterinductive method, but for reasons most of us have not yet realized?

It sounds as if a self-supporting argument is applicable only to rules we already know to be correct; as a matter of fact, this is the view Black holds. He has argued in various places that induction is in no need of a general justification.[11] He holds that calling into question of all inductive methods simultaneously results in a hopelessly skeptical position. He is careful to state explicitly at the outset of his discussion of self-supporting inductive arguments that he is not dealing with the view "that *no* inductive argument ought to be regarded as correct until a philosophical justification of induction has been provided."[12] At the conclusion he acknowledges, moreover, that "anybody who thinks he has good grounds for condemning all inductive arguments will also condemn inductive arguments in support of inductive rules."[13] Black is careful to state explicitly that self-supporting inductive arguments provide no answer to the problem of justification of induction as raised by Hume. What good, then, are self-supporting inductive arguments?

In deductive logic, correctness is an all-or-nothing affair. Deductive inferences are either totally valid or totally invalid; there cannot be such a thing as degree of validity. In inductive logic the situation is quite different. Inductive correctness does admit of degrees; one inductive conclusion may be more strongly supported than another. In this situation it is possible, Black claims, to have an inductive rule we know to be correct to some degree, but whose status can be enhanced by self-supporting arguments. We might think a rather standard inductive rule akin to Black's R_2 is pretty good, but through inductive investigation of its application we might find that it is extremely good—much better than we originally thought. Moreover, the inductive inferences we use to draw that conclusion might be governed by precisely the sort of rule we are investigating. It is also possible, of course, to find by inductive investigation that the rule is not as good as we believed beforehand.

It is actually irrelevant to the present discussion to attempt to evaluate Black's view concerning the possibility of increasing the justification of inductive rules by self-supporting arguments. The important point is to emphasize, because of the possibility of constructing self-supporting arguments for counterinductive rules, that the attempt to provide inductive support of inductive rules cannot, without vicious circularity, be applied to the problem of justifying induction from scratch. If there is any way of providing the beginnings of a justification, or if we could show that some inductive rule stands in no need of justification in the first instance, then it would be suitable to return to Black's argument concerning the increase of support. I am not convinced, however, that Black has successfully shown that there is a satisfactory starting place.

I have treated the problem of inductive justification of induction at some length, partly because other authors have not been as cautious as Black in circumscribing the limits of inductive justification of induction.[14] More important, perhaps, is the fact that it is extremely difficult, psychologically speaking, to shake the view that past success of the inductive method constitutes a genuine justification of

induction. Nevertheless, the basic fact remains: Hume showed that inductive justifications of induction are fallacious, and no one has since proved him wrong.

2. The Complexity of Scientific Inference. The idea of a philosopher discussing inductive inference in science is apt to arouse grotesque images in many minds. People are likely to imagine someone earnestly attempting to explain why it is reasonable to conclude that the sun will rise tomorrow morning because it always has done so in the past. There may have been a time when primitive man anticipated the dawn with assurance based only upon the fact that he had seen dawn follow the blackness of night as long as he could remember, but this primitive state of knowledge, if it ever existed, was unquestionably *pre*scientific. This kind of reasoning bears no resemblance to science; in fact, the crude induction exhibits a complete absence of scientific understanding. Our scientific reasons for believing that the sun will rise tomorrow are of an entirely different kind. We understand the functioning of the solar system in terms of the laws of physics. We predict particular astronomical occurrences by means of these laws in conjunction with a knowledge of particular initial conditions that prevail. Scientific laws and theories have the logical form of general statements, but they are seldom, if ever, simple generalizations from experience.

Consider Newton's gravitational theory: Any two bodies are mutually attracted by a force proportional to the product of their masses and inversely proportional to the square of the distance between their centers. Although general in form, this kind of statement is not established by generalization from instances. We do not go around saying, "Here are two bodies—the force between them is such and such; here are two more bodies—the force between them is such and such; etc." Scientific theories are taken quite literally as hypotheses. They are entertained in order that their consequences may be drawn and examined. Their acceptability is judged in terms of these consequences. The consequences are extremely diverse—the greater the variety the better. For Newtonian theory, we look to such consequences as the behavior of Mars, the tides, falling bodies, the pendulum, and the torsion balance. These consequences have no apparent unity among themselves; they do not constitute a basis for inductive generalization. They achieve a kind of unity only by virtue of the fact that they are consequences of a single physical theory.

The type of inference I have been characterizing is very familiar; it is known as the *hypothetico-deductive method*.[15] It stands in sharp contrast to *induction by enumeration*, which consists in simple inductive generalization from instances. Schematically, the hypothetic-deductive method works as follows: From a general hypothesis and particular statements of initial conditions, a particular predictive statement is deduced. The statements of initial conditions, at least for the time, are accepted as true; the hypothesis is the statement whose truth is at issue. By observation we determine whether the predictive statement turned out to be true. If the predictive consequence is false, the hypothesis is disconfirmed. If observation reveals that the predictive statement is true, we say that the hypothesis is confirmed to some extent. A hypothesis is not, of course, conclusively proved by any one or more positively confirming instances, but it may become highly confirmed. A hypothesis that is sufficiently confirmed is accepted, at least tentatively.

It seems undeniable that science uses a type of inference at least loosely akin to the hypothetico-deductive method.[16] This has led some people to conclude that the logic of science is thoroughly deductive in character. According to this view, the only nondeductive aspect of the situation consists in thinking up hypotheses, but this is not a matter of logic and therefore requires no justification. It is a matter of psychological ingenuity of discovery. Once the hypothesis has been discovered, by some entirely nonlogical process, it remains only to *deduce* consequences and check them against observation.

It is, of course, a fallacy to conclude that the premises of an argument must be true if its conclusion is true. This fact seems to be the basis for the quip that a logic text is a book that consists of two parts; in the first part (on deduction) the fallacies are explained, in the second part (on induction) they are committed. The whole trouble with saying that the hypothetico-deductive method renders the logic of science entirely deductive is that we are attempting

to establish a *premise* of the deduction, not the conclusion. Deduction is an indispensible part of the logic of the hypothetic-deductive method, but it is not the only part. There is a fundamental and important sense in which the hypothesis must be regarded as a conclusion instead of a premise. Hypotheses (later perhaps called "theories" or "laws") are among the *results* of scientific investigation; science aims at establishing general statements about the world. Scientific prediction and explanation require such generalizations. While we are concerned with the status of the general hypothesis—whether we should accept it or reject it—the hypothesis must be treated as a conclusion to be supported by evidence, not as a premise lending support to other conclusions. The inference *from* observational evidence *to* hypothesis is surely not deductive. If this point is not already obvious it becomes clear the moment we recall that for any given body of observational data there is, in general, more than one hypothesis compatible with it. These alternative hypotheses differ in factual content and are incompatible with each other. Therefore, they cannot be deductive consequences of any consistent body of observational evidence.

We must grant, then, that science embodies a type of inference resembling the hypothetico-deductive method and fundamentally different from induction by enumeration. Hume, on the other hand, has sometimes been charged with a conception of science according to which the only kind of reasoning is induction by enumeration. His typical examples are cases of simple generalization of observed regularities, something like our example of the licorice-flavored black balls. In the past, water has quenched thirst; in the future, it will as well. In the past, fires have been hot; in the future, they will be hot. In the past, bread has nourished; in the future, it will do so likewise. It might be said that Hume, in failing to see the essential role of the hypothetico-deductive method, was unable to appreciate the complexity of the theoretical science of his own time, to say nothing of subsequent developments. This is typical, some might say, of the misunderstandings engendered by philosophers who undertake to discuss the logic of science without being thoroughly conversant with mathematics and natural science.

This charge against Hume (and other philosophers of induction) is ill-founded. It was part of Hume's genius to have recognized that the arguments he applied to simple enumerative induction apply equally to any kind of ampliative or nondemonstrative inference whatever. Consider the most complex kind of scientific reasoning—the most elaborate example of hypothetico-deductive inference you can imagine. Regardless of subtle features or complications, it is ampliative overall. The conclusion is a statement whose content exceeds the observational evidence upon which it is based. A scientific theory that merely summarized what had already been observed would not deserve to be called a theory. If scientific inference were not ampliative, science would be useless for prediction, postdiction, and explanation. The highly general results that are the pride of theoretical science would be impossible if scientific inference were not ampliative.

In presenting Hume's argument, I was careful to set it up so that it would apply to any kind of ampliative or nondemonstrative inference, no matter how simple or how complex. Furthermore, the distinction between valid deduction and nondemonstrative inference is completely exhaustive. Take any inference whatsoever. It must be deductive or nondemonstrative. Suppose it is nondemonstrative. If we could justify it deductively it would cease to be nondemonstrative. To justify it nondemonstratively would presuppose an already justified type of nondemonstrative inference, which is precisely the problem at issue. Hume's argument does *not* break down when we consider forms more complex than simple enumeration. Although the word "induction" is sometimes used as a synonym for "induction by simple enumeration," I am not using it in that way. Any type of logically correct ampliative inference is induction; the problem of induction is to show that some particular form of ampliative inference is justifiable. It is in this sense that we are concerned with the problem of the justification of inductive inference.

A further misunderstanding is often involved in this type of criticism of Hume. There is a strong inclination to suppose that induction is regarded as the method by which scientific results are discovered.[17] Hume and other philosophers of induction are charged with the view that science has developed historically through patient collection of facts and generalization from them. I know of no philosopher—not even Francis Bacon!—who has held this view, although it is frequently attacked in the contemporary literature.[18] The term "generalization" has an unfortunate ambiguity which fosters the confusion. In one meaning, "generalization" refers to an inferential process in which one makes a sort of mental transition from particulars to a universal proposition; in this sense, generalization is an act of generalizing—a process that yields general results. In another meaning, "generalization" simply refers to a universal type or proposition, without any reference to its source or how it was thought of. It is entirely possible for science to contain many generalizations (in the latter sense) without embodying any generalizations (in the former sense). As I said explicitly at the outset, the problem of induction I am discussing is a problem concerning justification, not discovery. The thesis I am defending—that science does embody induction in a logically indispensable fashion—has nothing to do with the history of science or the psychology of particular scientists. It is simply the claim that scientific inference is ampliative.

3. Deductivism. One of the most interesting and controversial contemporary attempts to provide an account of the logic of science is Karl Popper's deductivism.[19] In the preceding section I discussed the view that the presence of the hypothetico-deductive method in the logic of science makes it possible to dispense with induction in science and, thereby, to avoid the problem of induction. I argued that the hypothetico-deductive method, since it is ampliative and nondemonstrative, is not strictly deductive; it is, in fact, inductive in the relevant sense. As long as the hypothetico-deductive method is regarded as a method for supporting scientific hypotheses, it cannot succeed in making science thoroughly deductive. Popper realizes this, so in arguing that deduction is the sole mode of inference in science he rejects the hypothetico-deductive method as a means for confirming scientific hypotheses. He asserts that induction plays no role whatever in science; indeed, he maintains that there is no such thing as correct inductive inference. Inductive logic is, according to

Popper, a complete delusion. He admits the psychological fact that people (including himself) have faith in the uniformity of nature, but he holds, with Hume, that this can be no more than a matter of psychological fact. He holds, with Hume, that there can be no rational justification of induction, and he thinks Hume proved this point conclusively.

Popper's fundamental thesis is that falsifiability is the mark by which statements of empirical science are distinguished from metaphysical statements and from tautologies. The choice of falsifiability over verifiability as the criterion of demarcation is motivated by a long familiar fact—namely, it is possible to falsify a universal generalization by means of one negative instance, while it is impossible to verify a universal generalization by any limited number of positive instances. This, incidentally, is the meaning of the old saw which is so often made into complete nonsense: "The exception proves the rule." In this context, a rule is a universal generalization, and the term "to prove" means archaically "to test." The exception (i.e., the negative instance) proves (i.e., tests) the rule (i.e., the universal generalization), not by showing it to be true, but by showing it to be false. There is no kind of positive instance to prove (i.e., test) the rule, for positive instances are completely indecisive. Scientific hypotheses, as already noted, are general in form, so they are amenable to falsification but not verification.

Popper thus holds that falsifiability is the hallmark of empirical science. The aim of empirical science is to set forth theories to stand the test of every possible serious attempt at falsification. Scientific theories are hypotheses or conjectures; they are general statements designed to explain the world and make it intelligible, but they are never to be regarded as final truths. Their status is always that of tentative conjecture, and they must continually face the severest possible criticism. The function of the theoretician is to propose scientific conjectures; the function of the experimentalist is to devise every possible way of falsifying these theoretical hypotheses. The attempt to confirm hypotheses is no part of the aim of science.[20]

General hypotheses by themselves do not entail any predictions of particular events, but they do in conjunction with statements of initial conditions.

The laws of planetary motion in conjunction with statements about the relative positions and velocities of the earth, sun, moon, and planets enable us to predict a solar eclipse. The mode of inference is deduction. We have a high degree of intersubjective agreement concerning the initial conditions, and we likewise can obtain intersubjective agreement as to whether the sun's disc was obscured at the predicted time and place. If the predicted fact fails to occur, the theory has suffered falsification. Again, the mode of inference is deduction. If the theory were true, then, given the truth of the statements of initial conditions, the prediction would have to be true. The prediction, as it happens, is false; therefore, the theory is false. This is the familiar principle of *modus tollens*; it is, according to Popper, the only kind of inference available for the acceptance or rejection of hypotheses, and it is clearly suitable for rejection only.

Hypothetico-deductive theorists maintain that we have a confirming instance for the theory if the eclipse occurs as predicted. Confirming instances, they claim, tend to enhance the probability of the hypothesis or give it inductive support. With enough confirming instances of appropriate kinds, the probability of the hypothesis becomes great enough to warrant accepting it as true—not, of course, with finality and certainty, but provisionally. With sufficient inductive support of this kind we are justified in regarding it as well established. Popper, however, rejects the positive account, involving as it does the notion of inductive support. If a hypothesis is tested and the result is negative, we can reject it. If the test is positive, all we can say is that we have failed to falsify it. We cannot say that it has been confirmed or that it is, because of the positive test result, more probable. Popper does admit a notion of *corroboration* of hypotheses, but that is quite distinct from confirmation. We shall come to corroboration presently. For the moment, all we have are successful or unsuccessful attempts at falsification; all we can say about our hypotheses is that they are falsified or unfalsified. This is as far as inference takes us; according to Popper, this is the limit of logic. Popper therefore rejects the hypothetico-deductive method as it is usually characterized and accepts only the completely deductive *modus tollens*.

Popper—quite correctly I believe—denies that there are absolutely basic and incorrigible protocol statements that provide the empirical foundation for all of science. He does believe that there are relatively basic observation statements about macroscopic physical occurrences concerning which we have a high degree of intersubjective agreement. Normally, we can accept as unproblematic such statements as, "There is a wooden table in this room," "The pointer on this meter stands between 325 and 350," and "The rope just broke and the weight fell to the floor." Relatively basic statements of this kind provide the observation base for empirical science. This is the stuff of which empirical tests of scientific theories are made.

Although Popper's basic statements must in the last analysis be considered hypotheses, falsifiable and subject to test like other scientific hypotheses, it is obvious that the kinds of hypotheses that constitute theoretical science are far more general than the basic statements. But now we must face the grim fact that valid deductive inference, although necessarily truth-preserving, is nonampliative.[21] It is impossible to deduce from accepted basic statements any conclusion whose content exceeds that of the basic statements themselves. Observation statements and deductive inference yield nothing that was not stated by the observation statements themselves. If science consists solely of observation statements and deductive inferences, then talk about theories, their falsifiability, and their tests is empty. The content of science is coextensive with the content of the statements used to describe what we directly observe. There are no general theories, there is no predictive content, there are no inferences to the remote past. Science is barren.

Consider a few simple time-honored examples. Suppose that the statement "All ravens are black" has been entertained critically and subjected to every attempt at falsification we can think of. Suppose it has survived all attempts at falsification. What is the scientific content of all this? We can say that "All ravens are black" has not been falsified, which is equivalent to saying that we have not observed a nonblack raven. This statement is even poorer in content than a simple recital of our color observations of ravens. To say that the hypothesis has not been falsified is to say less than is given in a list of

our relevant observation statements. Or, consider the generalization, "All swans are white." What have we said when we say that this hypothesis has been falsified? We have said only that a nonwhite swan has been found. Again, the information conveyed by this remark is less than we would get from a simple account of our observations of swans.

Popper has never claimed that falsification by itself can establish scientific hypotheses. When one particular hypothesis has been falsified, many alternative hypotheses remain unfalsified. Likewise, there is nothing unique about a hypothesis that survives without being falsified. Many other unfalsified hypotheses remain to explain the same facts. Popper readily admits all of this. If science is to amount to more than a mere collection of our observations and various reformulations thereof, it must embody some other methods besides observation and deduction. Popper supplies that additional factor: *corroboration*.[22]

When a hypothesis has been falsified, it is discarded and replaced by another hypothesis which has not yet experienced falsification. Not all unfalsified hypotheses are on a par. There are principles of selection among unfalsified hypotheses. Again, falsifiability is the key. Hypotheses differ from one another with respect to the ease with which they can be falsified, and we can often compare them with respect to degree of falsifiability. Popper directs us to seek hypotheses that are as highly falsifiable as possible. Science, he says, is interested in bold conjectures. These conjectures must be consistent with the known facts, but they must run as great a risk as possible of being controverted by the facts still to be accumulated. Furthermore, the search for additional facts should be guided by the effort to find facts that will falsify the hypothesis.

As Popper characterizes falsifiability, the greater the degree of falsifiability of a hypothesis, the greater its content. Tautologies lack empirical content because they do not exclude any possible state of affairs; they are compatible with any possible world. Empirical statements are not compatible with every possible state of affairs; they are compatible with some and incompatible with others. The greater the number of possible states of affairs excluded by a statement, the greater its content, for the more it does to pin down our actual world by ruling out possible but nonactual states of affairs. At the same time, the greater the range of facts excluded by a statement—the greater the number of situations with which the statement is incompatible—the greater the risk it runs of being false. A statement with high content has more *potential falsifiers* than a statement with low content. For this reason, high content means high falsifiability. At the same time, content varies inversely with probability. The logical probability of a hypothesis is defined in terms of its range—that is, the possible states of affairs with which it is compatible. The greater the logical probability of a hypothesis, the fewer are its potential falsifiers. Thus, high probability means low falsifiability.

Hypothetico-deductive theorists usually recommend selecting, from among those hypotheses that are compatible with the available facts, the most probable hypothesis. Popper recommends the opposite; he suggests selecting the most falsifiable hypothesis. Thus, he recommends selecting a hypothesis with low probability. According to Popper, a highly falsifiable hypothesis which is severely tested becomes highly corroborated. The greater the severity of the tests—the greater their number and variety—the greater the corroboration of the hypothesis that survives them.

Popper makes it very clear that hypotheses are not regarded as true because they are highly corroborated. Hypotheses cannot be firmly and finally established in this or any other way. Furthermore, because of the inverse relation between falsifiability and probability, we cannot regard highly corroborated hypotheses as probable. To be sure, a serious attempt to falsify a hypothesis which fails does add to the corroboration of this hypothesis, so there is some similarity between corroboration and confirmation as hypothetico-deductive theorists think of it, but it would be a misinterpretation to suppose that increasing corroboration is a process of accumulating positive instances to increase the probability of the hypothesis.[23]

Nevertheless, Popper does acknowledge the need for a method of selecting among unfalsified hypotheses. He has been unequivocal in his emphasis upon the indispensability of far-reaching theory in science. Empirical science is not an activity of merely accumulating experiences; it is theoretical through and through. Although we do not regard any hypotheses as certainly true, we do accept them tentatively and provisionally. Highly corroborated hypotheses are required for prediction and explanation. From among the ever-present multiplicity of hypotheses compatible with the available evidence, we select and accept.

There is just one point I wish to make here regarding Popper's theory. It is not properly characterized as *deductivism*. Popper has not succeeded in purging the logic of science of all inductive elements. My reason for saying this is very simple. Popper furnishes a method for selecting hypotheses whose content exceeds that of the relevant available basic statements. Demonstrative inference cannot accomplish this task alone, for valid deductions are nonampliative and their conclusions cannot exceed their premises in content. Furthermore, Popper's theory does not pretend that basic statements plus deduction can give us scientific theory; instead, corroboration is introduced. Corroboration is a nondemonstrative form of inference. It is a way of providing for the acceptance of hypotheses even though the content of these hypotheses goes beyond the content of the basic statements. *Modus tollens* without corroboration is empty; *modus tollens* with corroboration is induction.

When we ask, "Why should we reject a hypothesis when we have accepted one of its potential falsifiers?" the answer is easy. The potential falsifier contradicts the hypothesis, so the hypothesis is false if the potential falsifier holds. That is simple deduction. When we ask, "Why should we accept from among all the unfalsified hypotheses one that is highly corroborated?" we have a right to expect an answer. The answer is some kind of justification for the methodological rule—for the method of corroboration. Popper attempts to answer this question.

Popper makes it clear that his conception of scientific method differs in important respects from the conceptions of many inductivists. I do not want to quibble over a word in claiming that Popper is, himself, a kind of inductivist. The point is not a trivial verbal one. Popper has claimed that scientific inference is exclusively deductive. We have seen, however, that demonstrative inference is not sufficient to the task of providing a reconstruction of the logic of the acceptance—albeit tentative and provisional—of hypotheses. Popper himself realizes this and introduces a mode of nondemonstrative inference. It does not matter whether we call this kind of inference "induction"; whatever we call it, it is ampliative and not necessarily truth-preserving. Using the same force and logic with which Hume raised problems about the justification of induction, we may raise problems about the justification of any kind of nondemonstrative inference. As I argued in the preceding section, Hume's arguments are not peculiar to induction by enumeration or any other special kind of inductive inference; they apply with equal force to any inference whose conclusion can be false, even though it has true premises. Thus, it will not do to dismiss induction by enumeration on grounds of Hume's argument and then accept some other mode of nondemonstrative inference without even considering how Hume's argument might apply to it. I am not arguing that Popper's method is incorrect.[24] I am not even arguing that Popper has failed in his attempt to justify this method. I do claim that Popper is engaged in the same task as many inductivists—namely, the task of providing some sort of justification for a mode of nondemonstrative inference. This enterprise, if successful, *is* a justification of induction.

. . . .

5. The Principle of Uniformity of Nature. A substantial part of Hume's critique of induction rested upon his attack on the principle of the uniformity of nature. He argued definitively that the customary forms of inductive inference cannot be expected to yield correct predictions if nature fails to be uniform—if the future is not like the past—if like sensible qualities are not accompanied by like results.

All inferences from experience suppose, as their foundation, that the future will resemble the past, and that similar powers will be conjoined with similar sensible qualities. If there be any suspicion that the course of nature may change, and that the past may be no rule for the future, all experience becomes useless, and can give rise to no inference or conclusion.[25]

He argued, moreover, that there is no logical contradiction in the supposition that nature is not uniform—that the regularities we have observed up to the present will fail in wholesale fashion in the future.

It implies no contradiction that the course of nature may change, and that an object, seemingly like those which we have experienced, may be attended with different or contrary effects. May I not clearly and distinctly conceive that a body, falling from the clouds, and which, in all other respects resembles snow, has yet the taste of salt or feeling of fire? Is there any more intelligible proposition than to affirm, that all the trees will flourish in December and January, and decay in May and June? Now whatever is intelligible, and can be distinctly conceived, implies no contradiction, and can never be proved false by any demonstrative argument. . . .[26]

He argues, in addition, that the principle of uniformity of nature cannot be established by an inference from experience: "It is impossible, therefore, that any arguments from experience can prove this resemblance of the past to the future; since all these arguments are founded on the supposition of that resemblance."[27] Throughout Hume's discussion there is, however, a strong suggestion that we might have full confidence in the customary inductive methods if nature were known to be uniform.

Kant attempted to deal with the problem of induction in just this way, by establishing a principle of uniformity of nature, in the form of the principle of universal causation, as a synthetic a priori truth. Kant claimed, in other words, that every occurrence is governed by causal regularities, and this general characteristic of the universe can be established by pure reason, without the aid of any empirical evidence. He did not try to show that the principle of universal causation is a principle of logic, for to do so would have been to show that it was analytic—not synthetic—and thus lacking in factual content. He did not reject Hume's claim that there is no logical contradiction in the statement that nature is not uniform; he did not try to prove his principle of universal causation by deducing a contradiction from its denial. He did believe, however, that this principle, while not a proposition of pure logic, is necessarily true nevertheless. Hume, of course, argued against this alternative as well. He maintained not only that the uniformity of nature is not a logical or analytic truth, but also that it cannot be any other kind of a priori truth either. Even before Kant had enunciated the doctrine of synthetic a priori principles, Hume had offered strong arguments against them:

> I shall venture to affirm, as a general proposition, which admits of no exception, that the knowledge of this relation [of cause and effect] is not, in any instance, attained by reasonings a priori.[28]
>
> Adam, though his rational faculties be supposed, at the very first, entirely perfect, could not have inferred from the fluidity and transparency of water that it would suffocate him, or from the light and warmth of fire that it would consume him.[29]
>
> When we reason a priori, and consider merely any object or cause, as it appears to the mind, independent of all observation, it never could suggest to us the notion of any distinct object, such as its effect; much less, show us the inseparable and inviolable connexion between them. A man must be very sagacious who could discover by reasoning that crystal is the effect of heat, and ice of cold, without being previously acquainted with the operation of these qualities.[30]
>
> Now whatever is intelligible, and can be distinctly conceived . . . can never be proved false by any . . . abstract reasoning a priori.[31]

Hume argues, by persuasive example and general principle, that nothing about the causal structure of reality can be established by pure reason. He poses an incisive challenge to those who would claim the ability to establish a priori knowledge of a particular causal relation or of the principle of universal causation. In the foregoing discussion of synthetic a priori statements, I have given reasons for believing that Kant failed to overcome Hume's previous objections.

There is, however, another interesting issue that arises in connection with the principle of uniformity of nature. Suppose it could be established—never mind how—prior to a justification of induction.

Would it then provide an adequate basis for a justification of induction? The answer is, I think, negative.[32]

Even if nature is uniform to some extent, it is not absolutely uniform. The future is something like the past, but it is somewhat different as well. Total and complete uniformity would mean that the state of the universe at any given moment is the same as its state at any other moment. Such a universe would be a changeless, Parmenidean world. Change obviously does occur, so the future is not exactly like the past. There are some uniformities, it appears, but not a complete absence of change. The problem is how to ferret out the genuine uniformities. As a matter of actual fact, there are many uniformities *within experience* that we take to be mere coincidences, and there are others that seem to represent genuine causal regularities. For instance, in every election someone finds a precinct, say in Maryland, which has always voted in favor of the winning presidential candidate. Given enough precincts, one expects this sort of thing by sheer chance, and we classify such regularities as mere coincidences. By contrast, the fact that glass windowpanes break when bricks are hurled at them is more than mere coincidence. Causal regularities provide a foundation for inference from the observed to the unobserved; coincidences do not. We can predict with some confidence that the next glass window pane at which a brick is hurled will break; we take with a grain of salt the prediction of the outcome of a presidential election early on election night when returns from the above-mentioned precinct are in. The most that a principle of uniformity of nature could say is that there are some uniformities that persist into the future; if it stated that every regularity observed to hold within the scope of our experience also holds universally, it would be patently false. We are left with the problem of finding a sound basis for distinguishing between mere coincidence and genuine causal regularity.

Kant's principle of universal causation makes a rather weak and guarded statement. It asserts only that there exist causal regularities: "Everything that happens presupposes something from which it follows according to some rule." For each occurrence it claims only the existence of *some* prior cause and *some* causal regularity. It gives no hint as to how we are to find the prior cause or how we are to identify the causal regularity. It therefore provides no basis upon which to determine whether the inductive inferences we make are correct or incorrect. It would be entirely consistent with Kant's principle for us always to generalize on the basis of observed coincidences and always to fail to generalize on the basis of actual causal relations. It would be entirely consistent with Kant's principle, moreover, for us always to cite a coincidentally preceding event as the cause instead of the event that is the genuine cause. Kant's principle, even if it could be established, would not help us to justify the assertion that our inductive inferences would always or usually be correct. It would provide no criterion to distinguish sound from unsound inductions. Even if Kant's program had succeeded in establishing a synthetic a prior principle of universal causation, it would have failed to produce a justification of induction.

. . . .

7. A Probabilistic Approach. It may seem strange in the extreme that this discussion of the problem of induction has proceeded at such great length without seriously bringing in the concept of probability. It is very tempting to react immediately to Hume's argument with the admission that we do not have *knowledge* of the unobserved. Scientific results are not established with absolute certainty. At best we can make probabilistic statements about unobserved matters of fact, and at best we can claim that scientific generalizations and theories are highly confirmed. We who live in an age of scientific empiricism can accept with perfect equanimity the fact that the quest for certainty is futile; indeed, our thanks go to Hume for helping to destroy false hopes for certainty in science.

Hume's search for a justification of induction, it might be continued, was fundamentally misconceived. He tried to find a way of proving that inductive inferences with true premises would have *true* conclusions. He properly failed to find any such justification precisely because it is the function of *deduction* to prove the truth of conclusions, given true premises. Induction has a different function. An inductive inference with true premises establishes its conclusions as *probable*. No wonder Hume failed to

find a justification of induction. He was trying to make induction into deduction, and he succeeded only in proving the platitude that induction is not deduction.[33] If we want to justify induction, we must show that inductive inferences establish their conclusions as probable, not as true.

The foregoing sort of criticism of Hume's arguments is extremely appealing, and it has given rise to the most popular sort of attempt, currently, to deal with the problem.[34] In order to examine this approach, we must consider, at least superficially, the meaning of the concept of probability. Two basic meanings must be taken into account at present.

One leading probability concept identifies probability with frequency—roughly, the probable is that which happens often, and the improbable is that which happens seldom. Let us see what becomes of Hume's argument under this interpretation of probability. If we were to claim that inductive conclusions are probable in this sense, we would be claiming that inductive inferences with true premises often have true conclusions, although not always. Hume's argument shows, unhappily, that this claim cannot be substantiated. It was recognized long before Hume that inductive inferences cannot be expected always to lead to the truth. Hume's argument shows, not only that we cannot justify the claim that *every* inductive inference with true premises will have a true conclusion, but also, that we cannot justify the claim that *any* inductive inference with true premises will have a true conclusion. Hume's argument shows that, for all we can know, every inductive inference made from now on might have a false conclusion despite true premises. Thus, Hume has proved, we can show neither that inductive inferences establish their conclusions as true nor that they establish their conclusions as probable in the frequency sense. The introduction of the frequency concept of probability gives no help whatever in circumventing the problem of induction, but this is no surprise, for we should not have expected it to be suitable for this purpose.

A more promising probability concept identifies probability with degree of rational belief. To say that a statement is probable in this sense means that one would be rationally justified in believing it; the degree of probability is the degree of assent a person would be rationally justified in giving. We are not, of course, referring to the degree to which anyone *actually* believes in the statement, but rather to the degree to which one could *rationally* believe it. Degree of actual belief is a purely psychological concept, but degree of rational belief is determined objectively by the evidence. To say that a statement is probable in this sense means that it is supported by evidence. But, so the argument goes, if a statement is the conclusion of an inductive inference with true premises, it *is* supported by evidence—by inductive evidence—this is part of what it *means* to be supported by evidence. The very concept of evidence depends upon the nature of induction, and it becomes incoherent if we try to divorce the two. Trivially, then, the conclusion of an inductive inference is probable under this concept of probability. To ask, with Hume, if we should accept inductive conclusions is tantamount to asking if we should fashion our beliefs in terms of the evidence, and this, in turn, is tantamount to asking whether we should be rational. In this way we arrive at an "ordinary language dissolution" of the problem of induction. Once we understand clearly the meanings of such key terms as "rational," "probable," and "evidence," we see that the problem arose out of linguistic confusion and evaporates into the question of whether it is rational to be rational. Such tautological questions, if meaningful at all, demand affirmative answers.

Unfortunately, the dissolution is not satisfactory.[35] Its inadequacy can be exhibited by focusing upon the concept of inductive evidence and seeing how it figures in the foregoing argument. The fundamental difficulty arises from the fact that the very notion of inductive evidence is determined by the rules of inductive inference. If a conclusion is to be supported by inductive evidence, it must be the conclusion of a correct inductive inference with true premises. Whether the inductive inference is correct depends upon whether the rule governing that inference is correct. The relation of inductive evidential support is, therefore, inseparably bound to the correctness of rules of inductive inference. In order to be able to say whether a given statement is supported by inductive evidence we must be able to say which inductive rules are correct.

For example, suppose that a die has been thrown a large number of times, and we have observed that the side two came up in one sixth of the tosses. This is our "evidence" e. Let h be the conclusion that, "in the long run," side two will come up one sixth of the times. Consider the following three rules:

1. (Induction by enumeration.) Given m/n of observed A are B, to infer that the "long run" relative frequency of B among A is m/n.
2. (A priori rule.) Regardless of observed frequencies, to infer that the "long run" relative frequency of B among A is $1/k$, where k is the number of possible outcomes—six in the case of the die.
3. (Counterinductive rule.) Given m/n of observed A are B, to infer that the "long run" relative frequency of B among A is $(n-m)/n$.

Under Rule 1, e is positive evidence for h; under Rule 2, e is irrelevant to h; and under Rule 3, e is negative evidence for h. In order to say which conclusions are supported by what evidence, it is necessary to arrive at a decision as to what inductive rules are acceptable. If Rule 1 is correct, the evidence e supports the conclusion h. If Rule 2 is correct, we are justified in drawing the conclusion h, but this is entirely independent of the observational evidence e; the same conclusions would have been sanctioned by Rule 2 regardless of observational evidence. If Rule 3 is correct, we are not only prohibited from drawing the conclusion h, but also we are permitted to draw a conclusion h' which is logically incompatible with h. Whether a given conclusion is *supported by evidence*—whether it would be *rational to believe* it on the basis of given evidence—whether it is *made probable* by virtue of its relation to given evidence—depends upon selection of the correct rule or rules from among the infinitely many rules we might conceivably adopt.

The problem of induction can now be reformulated as a problem about evidence. What rules ought we to adopt to determine the nature of inductive evidence? What rules provide suitable concepts of inductive evidence? If we take the customary inductive rules to define the concept of inductive evidence, have we adopted a proper concept of evidence?

Would the adoption of some alternative inductive rules provide a more suitable concept of evidence? These are genuine questions which need to be answered.[36]

We find, moreover, that what appeared earlier as a pointless question now becomes significant and difficult. If we take the customary rules of inductive inference to provide a suitable definition of the relation of inductive evidential support, it makes considerable sense to ask whether it is rational to believe on the basis of evidence as thus defined rather than to believe on the basis of evidence as defined according to other rules. For instance, I believe that the a priori rule and the counterinductive rule mentioned above are demonstrably unsatisfactory, and hence, they demonstrably fail to provide a suitable concept of inductive evidence. The important point is that something concerning the selection from among possible rules needs demonstration and is amenable to demonstration.

There is danger of being taken in by an easy equivocation. One meaning we may assign to the concept of inductive evidence is, roughly, the basis on which we ought to fashion our beliefs. Another meaning results from the relation of evidential support determined by whatever rule of inductive inference we adopt. It is only by supposing that these two concepts are the same that we suppose the problem of induction is still there; it is the problem of providing adequate grounds for the selection of inductive rules. We want the relation of evidential support determined by these rules to yield a concept of inductive evidence which is, in fact, the basis on which we ought to fashion our beliefs.[37]

We began this initially promising approach to the problem of the justification of induction by introducing the notion of probability, but we end with a dilemma. If we take "probability" in the frequency sense, it is easy to see why it is advisable to accept probable conclusions in preference to improbable ones. In so doing we shall be right more often. Unfortunately, we cannot show that inferences conducted according to any particular rule establish conclusions that are probable in this sense. If we take "probability" in a nonfrequency sense it may be easy to show that inferences which conform to our accepted inductive rules establish their conclusions as

probable. Unfortunately, we can find no reason to prefer conclusions which are probable in this sense to those that are improbable. As Hume has shown, we have no reason to suppose that probable conclusions will often be true and improbable ones will seldom be true. This dilemma is Hume's problem of induction all over again. We have been led to an interesting reformulation, but it is only a reformulation and not a solution.

8. Pragmatic Justification. Of all the solutions and dissolutions proposed to deal with Hume's problem of induction, Hans Reichenbach's attempt to provide a pragmatic justification seems to me the most fruitful and promising.[38] This approach accepts Hume's arguments up to the point of agreeing that it is impossible to establish, either deductively or inductively, that any inductive inferences will ever again have true conclusions. Nevertheless, Reichenbach claims, the standard method of inductive generalization can be justified. Although its *success* as a method of prediction cannot be established in advance, it can be shown to be superior to any alternative method of prediction.

The argument can be put rather simply. Nature may be sufficiently uniform in suitable respects for us to make successful inductive inferences from the observed to the unobserved. On the other hand, for all we know, she may not. Hume has shown that we cannot prove in advance which case holds. All we can say is that nature may or may not be uniform—if she is, induction works; if she is not, induction fails. Even in the face of our ignorance about the uniformity of nature, we can ask what would happen if we adopted some radically different method of inference. Consider, for instance, the method of the crystal gazer. Since we do not know whether nature is uniform or not, we must consider both possibilities. If nature is uniform, the method of crystal gazing might work successfully, or it might fail. We cannot prove a priori that it will not work. At the same time, we cannot prove a priori that it will work, even if nature exhibits a high degree of uniformity. Thus, in case nature is reasonably uniform, the standard inductive method *must* work while the alternative method of crystal gazing *may or may not* work. In this case, the superiority of the standard inductive method is evident. Now, suppose nature lacks uniformity to such a degree that the standard inductive method is a complete failure. In this case, Reichenbach argues, the alternative method must likewise fail. Suppose it did not fail—suppose, for instance, that the method of crystal gazing worked consistently. This would constitute an important relevant uniformity that could be exploited inductively. If a crystal gazer had consistently predicted future occurrences, we could infer inductively that he has a method of prediction that will enjoy continued success. The inductive method would, in this way, share the success of the method of crystal gazing, and would therefore be, contrary to hypothesis, successful. Hence, Reichenbach concludes, the standard inductive method will be successful *if any other method could succeed*. As a result, we have everything to gain and nothing to lose by adopting the inductive method. If any method works, induction works. If we adopt the inductive method and it fails, we have lost nothing, for any other method we might have adopted would likewise have failed. Reichenbach does not claim to prove that nature is uniform, or that the standard inductive method will be successful. He does not postulate the uniformity of nature. He tries to show that the inductive method is the best method for ampliative inference, whether it turns out to be successful or not.

This ingenious argument, although extremely suggestive, is ultimately unsatisfactory. As I have just presented it, it is impossibly vague. I have not specified the nature of the standard inductive method. I have not stated with any exactness what constitutes success for the inductive method or any other. Moreover, the uniformity of nature is not an all-or-none affair. Nature appears to be uniform to some extent and also to be lacking in uniformity to some degree. As we have already seen, it is not easy to state a principle of uniformity that is strong enough to assure the success of induction inference and weak enough to be plausible. The vagueness of the foregoing argument is not, however, its fundamental drawback. It can be made precise, and I shall do so below in connection with the discussion of the frequency interpretation of probability.[39] When it is made precise, . . . it suffers the serious defect of

equally justifying too wide a variety of rules for ampliative inference.

I have presented Reichenbach's argument rather loosely in order to make intuitively clear its basic strategy. The sense in which it is a pragmatic justification should be clear. Unlike many authors who have sought a justification of induction, Reichenbach does not try to prove the truth of any synthetic proposition. He recognizes that the problem concerns the justification of a rule, and rules are neither true nor false. Hence, he tries to show that the adoption of a standard inductive rule is practically useful in the attempt to learn about and deal with the unobserved. He maintains that this can be shown even though we cannot prove the truth of the assertion that inductive methods will lead to predictive success. This pragmatic aspect is, it seems to me, the source of the fertility of Reichenbach's approach. Even though his argument does not constitute an adequate justification of induction, it seems to me to provide a valid core from which we may attempt to develop a more satisfactory justification.

III. Significance of the Problem

Hume's problem of induction evokes, understandably, a wide variety of reactions. It is not difficult to appreciate the response of the man engaged in active scientific research or practical affairs who says, in effect, "Don't bother me with these silly puzzles; I'm too busy doing science, building bridges, or managing affairs of state." No one, including Hume, seriously suggests any suspension of scientific investigation or practical decision pending a solution of the problem of induction. The problem concerns the *foundations* of science. As Hume eloquently remarks in *Enquiry Concerning Human Understanding*:

Let the course of things be allowed hitherto ever so regular; that alone, without some new argument or inference, proves not that, for the future, it will continue so. In vain do you pretend to have learned the nature of bodies from your past experience. Their secret nature, and consequently all their effects and influence, may change, without any change in their sensible qualities. This happens sometimes, and with regard to some objects: Why may it not happen always, and with regard to all objects? What logic, what process of argument secures you against this supposition? My practice, you say, refutes my doubts. But you mistake the purport of my question. As an agent, I am quite satisfied in the point; but as a philosopher, who has some share of curiosity, I will not say scepticism, I want to learn the foundation of this inference.

We should know by now that the foundations of a subject are usually established long after the subject has been well developed, not before. To suppose otherwise would be a glaring example of "naïve first-things-firstism."[40]

Nevertheless, there is something intellectually disquieting about a serious gap in the foundations of a discipline, and it is especially disquieting when the discipline in question is so broad as to include the whole of empirical science, all of its applications, and indeed, all of common sense. As human beings we pride ourselves on rationality—so much so that for centuries rationality was enshrined as the very essence of humanity and the characteristic that distinguishes man from the lower brutes. Questionable as such pride may be, our intellectual consciences should be troubled by a gaping lacuna in the structure of our knowledge and the foundations of scientific inference. I do not mean to suggest that the structure of empirical science is teetering because of foundational difficulties; the architectural metaphor is really quite inappropriate. I do suggest that intellectual integrity requires that foundational problems not be ignored.

Each of two opposing attitudes has its own immediate appeal. One of these claims that the scientific method is so obviously the correct method that there is no need to waste our time trying to show that this is so. There are two difficulties. First, we have enough painful experience to know that the appeal to obviousness is dangerously likely to be an appeal to prejudice and superstition. What is obvious to one age or culture may well turn out, on closer examination, to be just plain false. Second, if the method of science is so obviously superior to other methods we might adopt, then I should think we

ought to be able to point to those characteristics of the method by which it gains its obvious superiority.

The second tempting attitude is one of pessimism. In the face of Hume's arguments and the failure of many attempts to solve the problem, it is easy to conclude that the problem is hopeless. Whether motivated by Hume's arguments or, as is probably more often the case, by simple impatience with foundational problems, this attitude seems quite widespread. It is often expressed by the formula that science is, at bottom, a matter of faith. While it is no part of my purpose to launch a wholesale attack on faith as such, this attitude toward the foundations of scientific inference is unsatisfactory. The crucial fact is that science makes a *cognitive claim*, and this cognitive claim is a fundamental part of the rationale for doing science at all. Hume has presented us with a serious challenge to that cognitive claim. If we cannot legitimize the cognitive claim, it is difficult to see what reason remains for doing science. Why not turn to voodoo, which would be simpler, cheaper, less time consuming, and more fun?

If science is basically a matter of faith, then the scientific faith exists on a par with other faiths. Although we may be culturally conditioned to accept this faith, others are not. Science has no ground on which to maintain its *cognitive* superiority to any form of irrationalism, however repugnant. This situation is, it seems to me, intellectually and socially undesirable. We have had enough experience with various forms of irrationalism to recognize the importance of being able to distinguish them logically from genuine science. I find it intolerable to suppose that a theory of biological evolution, supported as it is by extensive scientific evidence, has no more rational foundation than has its rejection by ignorant fundamentalists. I, too, have faith that the scientific method is especially well suited for establishing knowledge of the unobserved, but I believe this faith should be justified. It seems to me extremely important that some people should earnestly seek a solution to this problem concerning the foundations of scientific inference.

One cannot say in advance what consequences will follow from a solution to a foundational problem. It would seem to depend largely upon the nature of the solution. But a discipline with well-laid foundations is surely far more satisfactory than one whose foundations are in doubt. We have only to compare the foundationally insecure calculus of the seventeenth and eighteenth centuries with the calculus of the late nineteenth century to appreciate the gains in elegance, simplicity, and rigor. Furthermore, the foundations of calculus provided a basis for a number of other developments, interesting in their own right and *greatly extending the power and fertility of the original theory*. Whether similar extensions will occur as a result of a satisfactory resolution of Hume's problem is a point on which it would be rash to hazard any prediction, but we know from experience that important consequences result from the most unexpected sources. The subsequent discussion of the foundations of probability will indicate directions in which some significant consequences may be found, but for the moment it will suffice to note that a serious concern for the solution of Hume's problem cannot fail to deepen our understanding of the nature of scientific inference. This, after all, is the ultimate goal of the whole enterprise.

NOTES

This book *[The Foundations of Scientific Inference]* is based upon five lectures in the Philosophy of Science Series at the University of Pittsburgh. The first two lectures, *Foundations of Scientific Inference:* I. *The Problem of Induction,* II. *Probability and Induction*, were presented in March 1963. The next two lectures, *Inductive Inference in Science:* I. *Hypothetico-Deductive Arguments,* II. *Plausibility Arguments*, were delivered in October 1964. The final lecture, *A Priori Knowledge*, was given in October 1965. The author wishes to express his gratitude to the National Science Foundation and the Minnesota Center for Philosophy of Science for support of research on inductive logic and probability.

1. David Hume, *Enquiry Concerning Human Understanding*, see IV, I.
2. Ibid.
3. For a more detailed account of the relation between deductive validity and factual content, see p. 24.

4. The problem of the synthetic a priori is discussed earlier, in sec. II, 4, pp. 27–40 [of Salmon's *Foundations of Scientific Inference*, from which this selection is excerpted].
5. Hume, *Human Understanding*.
6. Ibid.
7. Max Black, *Problems of Analysis* (Ithaca: Cornell University Press, 1954), Chap. 11.
8. Ibid., pp. 196–97.
9. Lewis Carroll, "What the Tortoise Said to Achilles," in *The Complete Works of Lewis Carroll* (New York: Random House, n.d.).
10. I presented the following self-supporting argument for the counterinductive method in "Should We Attempt to Justify Induction?" *Philosophical Studies*, 8 (April 1957), pp. 45–47. Max Black in "Self-supporting Inductive Arguments," *Models and Metaphors* (Ithaca: Cornell University Press, 1962), Chap. 12, replies to my criticism, but he does not succeed in shaking the basic point: The counterinductive rule is related to its self-supporting argument in precisely the same way as the standard inductive rule is related to its self-supporting argument. This is the "cash value" of claiming that the self-supporting argument is circular. Peter Achinstein, "The Circularity of a Self-supporting Inductive Argument," *Analysis*, 22 (June 1962), considers neither my formulation nor Black's answer sufficient, so he makes a further attempt to show circularity. Black's reply is found in "Self-Support and Circularity: A Reply to Mr. Achinstein," *Analysis*, 23 (December 1962). Achinstein's rejoinder is "Circularity and Induction," *Analysis*, 23 (June 1963).
11. Max Black, "The Justification of Induction," *Language and Philosophy* (Ithaca: Cornell University Press, 1949), Chap. 3. The view he expresses in this essay, I believe, is closely related to the "probabilistic approach" I discuss in sec. II, 7, pp. 280–82.
12. Max Black, *Problems of Analysis*, p. 191.
13. Ibid., p. 206.
14. Compare Richard Bevan Braithwaite, *Scientific Explanation* (New York: Harper & Row, 1960), Chap. 8. I think the same general view is to be found in A. J. Ayer, *The Problem of Knowledge* (Baltimore: Penguin Books, 1956), p. 75. I have discussed Ayer's view in "The Concept of Inductive Evidence," *American Philosophical Quarterly*, 2 (October 1965).
15. See Braithwaite for a systematic exposition of this conception.

16. Sec. VII, pp. 108–31 [of Salmon's *Foundations of Scientific Inference*]. "The Confirmation of Scientific Hypotheses" is devoted to a detailed analysis of this type of inference.

17. See John Patrick Day, *Inductive Probability* (New York: Humanities Press, 1961), p. 6. The nineteenth-century notion that induction is a process of discovery and the problem of whether there can be a logic of discovery are discussed earlier in sec. VII, pp. 109–14 [of Salmon's *Foundations of Scientific Inference*.]

18. See e.g., Karl R. Popper, *The Logic of Scientific Discovery* (New York: Basic Books, 1959), sec. 30, and Thomas S. Kuhn, *The Structure of Scientific Revolutions* (Chicago: University of Chicago Press, 1962). A fuller discussion of the relations among such concepts as deductive validity and content is given earlier in sec. II, 4, especially p. 33 [of Salmon's *Foundations of Scientific Inference*].

19. The most comprehensive statement of Popper's position is to be found in *The Logic of Scientific Discovery*. This is the English translation, with additions, of Karl R. Popper, *Logik der Forschung* (Vienna, 1934).

20. "I think that we shall have to get accustomed to the idea that we must not look upon science as a 'body of knowledge,' but rather as a system of hypotheses; that is to say, a system of guesses or anticipations which in principle cannot be justified, but with which we work as long as they stand up to tests, and of which we are never justified in saying that we know that they are 'true' or 'more or less certain' or even 'probable.'" *The Logic of Scientific Discovery*, p. 317.

21. I believe Popper openly acknowledges the nonampliative character of deduction. See "Why Are the Calculi of Logic and Arithmetic Applicable to Reality," in Karl R. Popper, *Conjectures and Refutations* (New York: Basic Books, 1962), Chap. 9.

22. See *The Logic of Scientific Discovery*, Chap. 10.

23. Ibid., p. 270.

24. I . . . return to Popper's methodological views in the discussion of confirmation in sec. VII [of *Foundations of Scientific Inference*.] In that context I shall exhibit what I take to be the considerable valid content of Popper's account of the logic of science. See pp. 114–21.

25. David Hume, *Human Understanding*, sec. IV.

26. Ibid.

27. Ibid.

28. Ibid.

29. Ibid.

30. Ibid.

31. Ibid.

32. Wesley C. Salmon, "The Uniformity of Nature," *Philosophy and Phenomenological Research*, 14 (September 1953).

33. Max Black, "The Justification of Induction," in *Language and Philosophy*.

34. Among the authors who subscribe to approaches similar to this are A. J. Ayer, *Language, Truth and Logic* (New York: Dover Publications, 1952); Paul Edwards, "Russell's Doubts about Induction," *Mind*, 58 (1949), p. 141–63; Asher Moore, "The Principle of Induction," *Journal of Philosophy*, 49 (1952), pp. 741–58; Arthur Pap, *Elements of Analytic Philosophy* (New York: Macmillan, 1949), and *An Introduction to the Philosophy of Science*; and P. F. Strawson, *Introduction to Logical Theory* (London: Methuen, 1952).

35. I have criticized this type of argument at some length in "Should We Attempt to Justify Induction?" *Philosophical Studies*, 8 (April 1957), and in "The Concept of Inductive Evidence," *American Philosophical Quarterly*, 2 (October 1965). This latter article is part of a "Symposium on Inductive Evidence" in which Stephen Barker and Henry E. Kyburg, Jr., defend against the attack. See their comments and my rejoinder.

36. This point has enormous import for any attempt to construct an inductive justification of induction. To decide whether the fact that induction has been successful in the past is positive evidence, negative evidence, or no evidence at all begs the very question at issue.

37. As I attempted to show in "Should We Attempt to Justify Induction?" this equivocation seems to arise out of a failure to distinguish *validation* and *vindication*. This crucial distinction is explicated by Herbert Feigl, "De Principiis non Disputandum . . . ?" in *Philosophical Analysis*, ed. Max Black (Ithaca: Cornell University Press, 1950).

38. Hans Reichenbach, *Experience and Prediction* (Chicago: University of Chicago Press, 1938), Chap. 5, and *The Theory of Probability* (Berkeley: University of California Press, 1949), Chap. 11.

39. Sec. V, 5, pp. 83–96 [of Salmon's *Foundations of Scientific Inference*].

40. Leonard J. Savage, *The Foundations of Statistics* (New York: Wiley, 1954), p. 1.

Causality and Determination

G. E. M. ANSCOMBE

G. E. M. Anscombe (1919–   ) is a professor of philosophy at Cambridge University. Her publications include *Intention, An Introduction to Wittgenstein's Tractatus,* and *Three Philosophers* (with Peter Geach).

———•———

I

It is often declared or evidently assumed that causality is some kind of necessary connection, or alternatively, that being caused is—nontrivially—instancing some exceptionless generalization saying that such an event always follows such antecedents. Or the two conceptions are combined.

Obviously there can be, and are, a lot of divergent views covered by this account. Any view that it covers nevertheless manifests one particular doctrine or assumption. Namely:

> If an effect occurs in one case and a similar effect does not occur in an apparently similar case, there must be a relevant further difference.

Any radically different account of causation, then, by contrast with which all those diverse views will be as one, will deny this assumption. Such a radically opposing view can grant that often—though it is difficult to say generally when—the assumption of relevant difference is a sound principle of investigation. It may grant that there are necessitating causes, but will refuse to identify causation as such with necessitation. It can grant there are situations in which, given the initial conditions and no interference, only one result will accord with the laws of nature; but it will not see general reason, in advance of discovery, to suppose that any given course of

things has been so determined. So it may grant that in many cases difference of issue can rightly convince us of a relevant difference of circumstances; but it will deny that, quite generally, this *must* be so.

The first view is common to many philosophers of the past. It is also, usually but not always in a neo-Humeian form, the prevailing received opinion throughout the currently busy and productive philosophical schools of the English-speaking world, and also in some of the European and Latin American schools where philosophy is pursued in at all the same sort of way; nor is it confined to these schools. So firmly rooted is it that for many even outside pure philosophy, it routinely determines the meaning of "cause," when consciously used as a theoretical term: witness the terminology of the contrast between 'causal' and 'statistical' laws, which is drawn by writers on physics—writers, note, who would not conceive themselves to be addicts of any philosophic school when they use this language to express that contrast.

The truth of this conception is hardly debated. It is, indeed, a bit of *Weltanschauung*: it helps to form a cast of mind which is characteristic of our whole culture.

The association between causation and necessity is old; it occurs for example in Aristotle's *Metaphysics*: "When the agent and patient meet suitably to their powers, the one acts and the other is acted on OF NECESSITY." Only with 'rational powers' an extra feature is needed to determine the result: "What has a rational power [e.g. medical knowledge, which can kill *or* cure] OF NECESSITY does what it has the power to do and as it has the power, when it has the desire."[1]

Overleaping the centuries, we find it an axiom in Spinoza, "Given a determinate cause, the effect follows OF NECESSITY, and without its cause, no effect follows."[2] And in the English philosopher Hobbes: "A cause simply, or an entire cause, is the aggregate of all the accidents both of the agents how many soever they be, and of the patients, put together; which when they are supposed to be present, IT CANNOT BE UNDERSTOOD BUT THAT THE EFFECT IS PRODUCED at the same instant; and if any of them be wanting, IT CANNOT BE UNDERSTOOD BUT THAT THE EFFECT IS NOT PRODUCED."[3]

It was this last view, where the connection between cause and effect is evidently seen as *logical* connection of some sort, that was overthrown by Hume, the most influential of all philosophers on this subject in the English-speaking and allied schools. For he made us see that, given any particular cause—or 'total causal situation' for that matter—and its effect, there is not in general any contradiction in supposing the one to occur and the other not to occur. That is to say, we'd know what was being described—what it would be like for it to be true—if it were reported for example that a kettle of water was put, and kept, directly on a hot fire, but the water did not heat up.

Were it not for the preceding philosophers who had made causality out as some species of logical connection, one would wonder at this being called a discovery on Hume's part: for vulgar humanity has always been over-willing to believe in miracles and marvels and *lusus naturae*. Mankind at large saw no contradiction, where Hume worked so hard to show the philosophic world—the Republic of Letters—that there was none.

The discovery was thought to be great. But as touching the equation of causality with necessitation, Hume's thinking did nothing against this but curiously reinforced it. For he himself assumed that NECESSARY CONNECTION is an essential part of the idea of the relation of cause and effect,[4] and he sought for its nature. He thought this could not be found in the situations, objects, or events called "causes" and "effects," but was to be found in the human mind's being determined, by experience of CONSTANT CONJUNCTION, to pass from the sensible impression or memory of one term of the relation to the convinced idea of the other. Thus to say that an event was caused was to say that its occurrence was an instance of some exceptionless generalization connecting such an event with such antecedents as it occurred in. The twist that Hume gave to the topic thus suggested a connection of the notion of causality with that of deterministic laws—i.e. laws such that always, given initial conditions and the laws, a unique result is determined.

The well-known philosophers who lived after Hume may have aimed at following him and developing at least some of his ideas, or they may have put up a resistance; but in no case, so far as I know,[5] has the resistance called in question the equation of causality with necessitation.

Kant, roused by learning of Hume's discovery, laboured to establish causality as an a priori conception and argued that the objective time order consists "in that order of the manifold of appearance according to which, IN CONFORMITY WITH A RULE, the apprehension of that which happens follows upon the apprehension of that which precedes. . . . In conformity with such a rule there must be in that which precedes an event the condition of a rule according to which this event INVARIABLY and NECESSARILY follows."[6] Thus Kant tried to give back to causality the character of a *justified* concept which Hume's considerations had taken away from it. Once again the connection between causation and necessity was reinforced. And this has been the general characteristic of those who have sought to oppose Hume's conception of causality. They have always tried to establish the necessitation that they saw in causality: either a priori, or somehow out of experience.

Since Mill it has been fairly common to explain causation one way or another in terms of 'necessary' and 'sufficient' conditions. Now "sufficient condition" is a term of art whose users may therefore lay down its meaning as they please. So they are in their rights to rule out the query: "May not the sufficient conditions of an event be present, and the event yet not take place?" For "sufficient condition" is so used that if the sufficient conditions for X are there, X occurs. But at the same time, the phrase cozens the understanding into not noticing an assumption. For "sufficient condition" sounds like: "enough." And one certainly *can* ask: "May there not be *enough* to have made something happen—and yet it not have happened?"

Russell wrote of the notion of cause, or at any rate of the 'law of causation' (and he seemed to feel the same way about 'cause' itself), that, like the British monarchy, it had been allowed to survive because it had been erroneously thought to do no harm. In a destructive essay of great brilliance he cast doubt on the notion of necessity involved, unless it is explained in terms of universality, and he argued that upon examination the concepts of determination and of invariable succession of like objects upon like turn out to be empty: they do not differentiate between any conceivable course of things and any other. Thus Russell too assumes that necessity or universality is what is in question, and it never occurs to him that there may be any other conception of causality.[7]

Now it's not difficult to shew it prima facie wrong to associate the notion of cause with necessity or universality in this way. For, it being much easier to trace effects back to causes with certainty than to predict effects from causes, we often know a cause without knowing whether there is an exceptionless generalization of the kind envisaged, or whether there is a necessity.

For example, we have found certain diseases to be contagious. If, then, I have had one and only one contact with someone suffering from such a disease, and I get it myself, we suppose I got it from him. But what if, having had the contact, I ask a doctor whether I will get the disease? He will usually only be able to say, "I don't know—maybe you will, maybe not."

But, it is said, knowledge of causes here is partial; doctors seldom even know any of the conditions under which one invariably gets a disease, let alone all the sets of conditions. This comment betrays the assumption that there is such a thing to know. Suppose there is: still, the question whether there is does not have to be settled before we can know what we mean by speaking of the contact as cause of my getting the disease.

All the same, might it not be like this: knowledge of causes is possible without any satisfactory grasp of what is involved in causation? Compare the possibility of wanting clarification of 'valency' or 'long-run frequency', which yet have been handled by chemists and statisticians without such clarification; and valencies and long-run frequencies, whatever the right way of explaining them, have been known. Thus one of the familiar philosophic analyses of causality, or a new one in the same line, may be correct, though knowledge of it is not necessary for knowledge of causes.

There is something to observe here, that lies under our noses. It is little attended to, and yet still so obvious as to seem trite. It is this: causality consists in the derivativeness of an effect from its causes. This is the core, the common feature, of causality in its various kinds. Effects derive from, arise out of, come of, their causes. For example, everyone will grant that physical parenthood is a causal relation. Here the derivation is material, by fission. Now analysis in terms of necessity or universality does not tell us of this derivedness of the effect; rather it forgets about that. For the necessity will be that of laws of nature; through it *we* shall be able to derive knowledge of the effect from knowledge of the cause, or vice versa, but that does not shew us the cause as source of the effect. Causation, then, is not to be identified with necessitation.

If *A* comes from *B*, this does not imply that every *A*-like thing comes from some *B*-like thing or set-up or that every *B*-like thing or set-up has an *A*-like thing coming from it; or that given *B*, *A* had to come from it, or that given *A*, there had to be *B* for it to come from. Any of these may be true, but if any is, that will be an additional fact, not comprised in *A*'s coming from *B*. If we take "coming from" in the sense of travel, this is perfectly evident.

"But that's because we can observe travel!" The influential Humeian argument at this point is that we can't similarly observe causality in the individual case.[8] So the reason why we connect what we call the cause and what we call the effect as we do must lie elsewhere. It must lie in the fact that the succession of the latter upon the former is of a kind regularly observed.

There are two things for me to say about this. *First*, as to the statement that we can never observe causality in the individual case. Someone who says this is just not going to count anything as 'observation of causality'. This often happens in philosophy; it is argued that 'all we find' is such-and-such, and it turns out that the arguer has excluded from his idea of 'finding' the sort of thing he says we don't 'find'. And when we consider what we are allowed to say we do 'find', we have the right to turn the tables on Hume, and say that neither do we perceive bodies, such as billiard balls, approaching one another. When we "consider the matter with the utmost attention," we find only an impression of travel made by the successive positions of a round white patch in our visual fields . . . etc. Now a 'Humeian' account of causality has to be given in terms of constant conjunction of physical things, events etc., not of experiences of them. If, then, it must be allowed that we "find" bodies in motion, for example, then what theory of perception can justly disallow the perception of a lot of causality? The truthful—though unhelpful—answer to the question: How did we come by our primary knowledge of causality? is that in learning to speak we learned the linguistic representation and application of a host of causal concepts. Very many of them were represented by transitive and other verbs of action used in reporting what is observed. Others—a good example is "infect"—form, not observation statements, but rather expressions of causal hypotheses. The word "cause" itself is highly general. How does someone show that he has the concept *cause*? We may wish to say: only by having such a word in his vocabulary. If so, then the manifest possession of the concept presupposes the mastery of much else in language. I mean: the word "cause" can be *added* to a language in which are already represented many causal concepts. A small selection: *scrape, push, wet, carry, eat, burn, knock over, keep off, squash, make* (e.g. noises, paper boats), *hurt*. But if we care to imagine languages in which no special causal concepts are represented, then no description of the use of a word in such languages will be able to present it as meaning *cause*. Nor will it even contain words for natural kinds of stuff, nor yet words equivalent to "body," "wind," or "fire." For learning to use special causal verbs is part and parcel of learning to apply the concepts answering to these, and many other, substantives. As surely as we learned to call people by name or to report from seeing it that the cat was

on the table, we also learned to report from having observed it that someone drank up the milk or that the dog made a funny noise or that things were cut or broken by whatever we saw cut or break them.

(I will mention, only to set on one side, one of the roots of Hume's argument, the implicit appeal to Cartesian scepticism. He confidently challenges us to "produce some instance, wherein the efficacy is plainly discoverable to the mind, and its operations obvious to our consciousness or sensation."[9] Nothing easier: is cutting, is drinking, is purring not 'efficacy'? But it is true that the apparent perception of such things may be only apparent: we may be deceived by false appearances. Hume presumably wants us to 'produce an instance' in which *efficacy* is related to sensation as *red* is. It is true that we can't do that; it is not *so* related to sensation. He is also helped, in making his argument that we don't perceive 'efficacy', by his curious belief that "efficacy" means much the same thing as "necessary connection"! But as to the Cartesian-sceptical root of the argument, I will not delay upon it, as my present topic is not the philosophy of perception.)

Second, as to that instancing of a universal generalization, which was supposed to supply what could not be observed in the individual case, the causal relation. The needed examples are none too common. "Motion in one body in all past instances that have fallen under our observation, is follow'd upon impulse by motion in another":[10] so Hume. But, as is always a danger in making large generalizations, he was thinking only of the cases where we do observe this—billiard balls against free-standing billiard balls in an ordinary situation; not billiard balls against stone walls. Neo-Humeians are more cautious. They realize that if you take a case of cause and effect, and relevantly describe the cause *A* and the effect *B*, and then construct a universal proposition, "Always, given an *A*, a *B* follows" you usually won't get anything true. You have got to describe the absence of circumstances in which an *A* would not cause a *B*. But the task of excluding all such circumstances can't be carried out. There is, I suppose, a vague association in people's minds between the universal propositions which would be examples of the required type of generalizations, and scientific laws. But there is no similarity.

Suppose we were to call propositions giving the properties of substances 'laws of nature'. Then there will be a law of nature running "The flash-point of such a substance is . . .," and this will be important in explaining why striking matches usually causes them to light. This law of nature has not the form of a generalization running "Always, if a sample of such a substance is raised to such a temperature, it ignites"; nor is it equivalent to such a generalization, but rather to: "If a sample of such a substance is raised to such a temperature and doesn't ignite, there must be a cause of its not doing so." Leaving aside questions connected with the idea of a pure sample, the point here is that 'normal conditions' is quite properly a vague notion. That fact makes generalizations running "Always . . ." merely fraudulent in such cases; it will always be necessary for them to be hedged about with clauses referring to normal conditions; and we may not know in advance whether conditions are normal or not, or what to count as an abnormal condition. In exemplar analytical practice, I suspect, it will simply be a relevant condition in which the generalization, "Always, if such and such, such and such happens . . . ," supplemented with a few obvious conditions that have occurred to the author, turns out to be untrue. Thus the conditional "If it doesn't ignite then there must be some cause" is the better gloss upon the original proposition, for it does not pretend to say specifically or even disjunctively specifically, what *always* happens. It is probably these facts which make one hesitate to call propositions about the action of substances 'laws of nature'. The law of inertia, for example, would hardly be glossed: "If a body accelerates without any force acting on it, there must be some cause of its doing so." (Though I wonder what the author of *Principia* himself would have thought of that.) On the other hand just such 'laws' as that about a substance's flash-point are connected with the match's igniting because struck.

Returning to the medical example, medicine is of course not interested in the hopeless task of constructing lists of all the sets of conditions under each of which people always get a certain disease. It is interested in finding what that is special, if anything, is always the case when people get a particular disease; and, given such a cause or condition (or in any case), in finding circumstances in which people don't get the disease, or tend not to. This is connected with medicine's concern first, and last, with things as they happen in the messy and mixed up conditions of life: only between its first and its last concern can it look for what happens unaffected by uncontrolled and inconstant conditions.

II

Yet my argument lies always open to the charge of appealing to ignorance. I must therefore take a different sort of example.

Here is a ball lying on top of some others in a transparent vertical pipe. I know how it got there: it was forcibly ejected with many others out of a certain aperture into the enclosed space above a row of adjacent pipes. The point of the whole construction is to show how a totality of balls so ejected always build up in rough conformity to the same curve. But I am interested in this one ball. Between its ejection and its getting into this pipe, it kept hitting sides, edges, other balls. If I made a film of it I could run it off in slow motion and tell the impact which produced each stage of the journey. Now was the result necessary? We would probably all have said it was in the time when Newton's mechanics was undisputed for truth. It was the impression made on Hume and later philosophers by that mechanics, that gave them so strong a conviction of the iron necessity with which everything happens, the "absolute fate" by which "Every object is determin'd to a certain degree and direction of its motion."[11]

Yet no one could have deduced the resting place of the ball—because of the indeterminateness that you get even in the Newtonian Mechanics, arising from the finite accuracy of measurements. From exact figures for positions, velocities, directions, spins, and masses you might be able to calculate the result as accurately as you chose. But the minutest inexactitudes will multiply up factor by factor, so that in a short time your information is gone. Assuming a given margin of error in your initial figure, you could assign an associated probability to that ball's falling into each of the pipes. If you want the highest probability you assign to be really high, so that you can take it as practical certainty, it will be a problem to reckon how tiny the permitted margins of inaccuracy must be—analogous to the problem: how small a fraction of a grain of millet must I demand is put on the first square of the chess board, if after doubling up at every square I end up having to pay out only a pound of millet? It would be a figure of such smallness as to have no meaning as a figure for a margin of error.

However, so long as you believed the classical mechanics you might also think there could be no such thing as a figure for a difference that had no meaning. Then you would think that though it was not feasible for us to find the necessary path of the ball because our margins of error are too great, yet there *was* a necessary path, which could be assigned a sufficient probability for firm acceptance of it, by anyone (not one of us) capable of reducing his limits of accuracy in measurement to a sufficiently small compass. Admittedly, so small a compass that he'd be down among the submicroscopic particles and no longer concerned with the measurements, say, of the ball. And now we can say: with certain degrees of smallness we get to a region where Newton's mechanics is no longer believed.

If the classical mechanics can be used to calculate a certain real result, we may give a sense to, and grant, the 'necessity' of the result, given the antecedents. Here, however, you can't use the mechanics to calculate the result, but at most to give yourself a belief in its necessity. For this to be reasonable the system has got to be acknowledged as true. Not, indeed, that that would be enough; but if so much were secured, then it would be worth while to discuss the metaphysics of absolute measures of continuous quantities.

The point needs some labouring precisely because "the system does apply to such bodies"—that is, to moderately massive balls. After all, it's Newton we use to calculate Sputniks! "The system applies to these bodies" is true only in the sense and to the extent that it yields sufficient results of calculations about these bodies. It does not mean: in respect of these bodies the system is the truth, so that it just doesn't matter that we can't use it to calculate such a result in such a case. I am not saying that a deterministic system involves individual predictability: it

evidently does not. But in default of predictability the determinedness declared by the deterministic system has got to be believed because the system itself is believed.

I conclude that we have no ground for calling the path of the ball determined—at least, until it has taken its path—but, it may be objected, is not each state of its path determined, even though we cannot determine it? My argument has partly relied on loss of information through multiplicity of impacts. But from one impact to the next the path is surely determined, and so the whole path is so after all.

It sounds plausible to say: each stage is determined and so the whole is. But what does "determined" mean? The word is a curious one (with a curious history); in this sort of context it is often used as if it *meant* "caused." Or perhaps "caused" is used as if it meant "determined". But there is at any rate one important difference—a thing hasn't been caused until it has happened; but it may be determined before it happens.

(It is important here to distinguish between being *determined* and being *determinate*. In indeterministic physics there is an apparent failure of both. I am concerned only with the former.)

When we call a result determined we are implicitly relating it to an antecedent range of possibilities and saying that all but one of these is disallowed. What disallows them is not the result itself but something antecedent to the result. The antecedences may be logical or temporal or in the order of knowledge. Of the many—antecedent—possibilities, *now* only one is—antecedently—possible.

Mathematical formulae and human decisions are limiting cases; the former because of the obscurity of the notion of antecedent possibilities, and the latter because decisions can be retrieved.

In a chess-game, the antecedent possibilities are, say, the powers of the pieces. By the rules, a certain position excludes all but one of the various moves that were in that sense antecedently possible. This is logical antecedence. The next move is determined.

In the zygote, sex and eye-colour are already determined. Here the antecedent possibilities are the possibilities for sex and eye-colour for a child; or more narrowly: for a child of these parents. *Now*, given the combination of this ovum and this spermatozoon, all but one of these antecedent possibilities is excluded.

It might be said that anything was determined once it had happened. There is now no possibility open: it *has* taken place! It was in this sense that Aristotle said that past and present were necessary. But this does not concern us: what interests us is *pre*-determination.

Then "each stage of the ball's path is determined" must mean "Upon any impact, there is only one path possible for the ball up to the next impact (and assuming no air currents, etc.)." But what ground system could one have for believing this, if one does not believe in some system of which it is a consequence? Consider a steel ball dropping between two pins on a Galton board to hit the pin centred under the gap between them. That it should balance on this pin is not be be expected. It has two possibilities; to go to the right or to the left. If you have a system which forces this on you, you can say: "There has to be a determining factor; otherwise, like Buridan's ass, the ball must balance." But if you have not, then you should say that the ball may be undetermined until it does move to the right or the left. Here the ball had only two significant possibilities and was perhaps unpredetermined between them. This was because it cannot be called determined— no reasonable account can be given of insisting that it is so—within a small range of possibility, actualization within which will lead on to its falling either to the right or to the left. With our flying ball there will also be such a small range of possibility. The further consequences of the path it may take are not tied down to just two significant possibilities, as with one step down the Galton board: the range of further possibility gets wider as we consider the paths it may take. Otherwise, the two cases are similar.

We see that to give content to the idea of something's being determined, we have to have a set of possibilities, which something narrows down to one—before the event.

This accords well with our understanding of part of the dissatisfaction of some physicists with the quantum theory. They did not like the undeterminedness of individual quantum phenomena. Such a physicist might express himself by saying "I believe in causality!" He meant: I believe that the real physical laws and the initial conditions must entail uniqueness of result. Of course, within a range of co-ordinate and mutually exclusive identifiable possible results, only one happens: he means that the result that happens ought to be understood as the only one that was possible before it happened.

Must such a physicist be a 'determinist'? That is, must he believe that the whole universe is a system such that, if its total states at t and t' are thus and so, the laws of nature are such as then to allow only one possibility for its total state at any other time? No. He may not think that the idea of a total state of the universe at a time is one he can do anything with. He may even have no views on the uniqueness of possible results for whatever may be going on in any arbitrary volume of space. For "Our theory should be such that only the actual result was possible for that experiment" doesn't mean "Our theory should have excluded the experiment's being muffed or someone's throwing a boot, so that we didn't get the result," but rather: "Our theory should be such that only this result was possible as *the result of the experiment*." He hates a theory, even if he has to put up with it for the time being, that essentially assigns only probability to a result, essentially allows of a range of possible results, never narrowed down to one until the event itself.

It must be admitted that such dissatisfied physicists very often have been determinists. Witness Schrödinger's account of the 'principle of causality': "The exact physical situation at *any* point P at a given moment t is unambiguously determined by the exact physical situation within a certain surrounding of P at any previous time, say $t - \tau$. If τ is large, that is if that previous time lies far back, it may be necessary to know the previous situation for a wide domain around P."[12] Or Einstein's more modest version of a notorious earlier claim: if you knew all about the contents of a sphere of radius 186,000 miles, and knew the laws, you would be able to know for sure what would happen at the centre for the next second. Schrödinger says: *any* point P; and *a* means *any* sphere of that radius. So their view of causality was not that of my hypothetical physicist, who I said may not have views on the uniqueness of possible results for whatever may be going on in any arbitrary volume of space. My physicist restricts his demand for uniqueness of result to situations in which he has got certain processes going in isolation from inconstant external influences, or where they do not matter, as the weather on a planet does not matter for predicting its course round the sun.

The high success of Newton's astronomy was in one way an intellectual disaster: it produced an illusion from which we tend still to suffer. This illusion was created by the circumstance that Newton's mechanics *had a good model in the solar system*. For this gave the impression that we had here an ideal of scientific explanation; whereas the truth was, it was mere obligingness on the part of the solar system, by having had so peaceful a history in recorded time, to provide such a model. For suppose that some planet had at some time erupted with such violence that its shell was propelled rocket-like out of the solar system. Such an event would not have violated Newton's laws; on the contrary, it would have illustrated them. But also it would not have been calculable as the past and future motions of the planets are presently calculated on the assumption that they can be treated as the simple 'bodies' of his mechanics, with no relevant properties but mass, position, and velocity and no forces mattering except gravity.

Let us pretend that Newton's laws were still to be accepted without qualification: no reserve in applying them in electrodynamics; no restriction to bodies travelling a good deal slower than light; and no quantum phenomena. Newton's mechanics is a deterministic system; but this does not mean that believing them commits us to determinism. We could say: Of course nothing violates those axioms or the laws of the force of gravity. But animals, for example, run about the world in all sorts of paths and no path is dictated for them by those laws, as it is for planets. Thus in relation to the solar system (apart from questions like whether in the past some planet has blown up), the laws are like the rules of an infantile card game: once the cards are dealt we turn them up in turn, and make two piles each, one red, one black; the winner has the biggest pile of red ones. So once the cards are dealt the game is determined, and from any position in it you can derive

all others back to the deal and forward to win or draw. But in relation to what happens on and inside a planet the laws are, rather, like the rules of chess; the play is seldom determined, though nobody breaks the rules.[13]

Why this difference? A natural answer is: the mechanics does not give the special laws of all the forces. Not, for example, for thermal, nuclear, electrical, chemical, muscular forces. And now the Newtonian model suggests the picture: given the laws of all the forces, then there is total coverage of what happens and then the whole game of motion is determined: for, by the first law, any acceleration implies a force of some kind, and must not forces have laws? My hypothetical physicist at least would think so; and would demand that they be deterministic. Nevertheless he still does not have to be a "determinist"; for many forces, unlike gravity, can be switched on and off, are generated, and also shields can be put up against them. It is one thing to hold that in a clear-cut situation—an astronomical or a well-contrived experimental one designed to discover laws—"the result" should be determined: and quite another to say that in the hurly-burly of many crossing contingencies whatever happens next must be determined; or to say that the generation of forces (by human experimental procedures, among other things) is always determined in advance of the generating procedure; or to say that there is always a law of composition, of such a kind that the combined effect of a set of forces is determined in every situation.

Someone who is inclined to say those things, or implicitly to assume them, has almost certainly been affected by the impressive relation between Newton's mechanics and the solar system.

We remember how it was in mechanics. By knowing the position and velocity of a particle at one single instant, by knowing the acting forces, the whole future path of the particle could be foreseen. In Maxwell's theory, if we know the field at one instant only, we can deduce from the equations of the theory how the whole field will change in space and time. Maxwell's equations enable us to follow the history of the field, just as the mechanical equations enabled us to follow the history of material parti-

cles. . . . With the help of Newton's laws we can deduce the motion of the earth from the force acting
between the sun and the earth.[14]

"By knowing the acting forces"—that must of
course include the *future* acting forces, not merely
the present ones. And similarly for the equations
which enable us to follow the history of the field; a
change may be produced by an external influence.
In reading both Newton and later writers one is often led to ponder that word "external." Of course,
to be given 'the acting forces' is to be given the external forces too and any new forces that may later
be introduced into the situation. Thus those first
sentences are true, if true, without the special favour
of fate, being general truths of mechanics and
physics, but the last one is true by favour, by the
brute fact that only the force acting between earth
and sun matters for the desired deductions.

The concept of necessity, as it is connected with
causation, can be explained as follows: a cause C is
a necessitating cause of an effect E *when* (I mean: on
the occasions when) if C occurs it is certain to cause
E unless something prevents it. C and E are to be
understood as general expressions, not singular
terms. If 'certainty' should seem too epistemological a notion: a necessitating cause C of a given kind
of effect E is such that it *is* not possible (on the occasion) that C should occur and should not cause an
E, nor should there be anything that prevents an E
from occurring. A non-necessitating cause is then
one that can fail of its effect without the intervention of anything to frustrate it. We may discover
types of necessitating and non-necessitating cause;
e.g. rabies is a necessitating cause of death, because
it is not possible for one who has rabies to survive
without treatment. We don't have to tie it to the occasion. An example of a non-necessitating cause is
mentioned by Feynman: a bomb is connected with
a Geiger counter, so that it will go off if the Geiger
counter registers a certain reading; whether it will
or not is not determined, for it is so placed near some
radioactive material that it may or may not register
that reading.

There would be no doubt of the cause of the reading or of the explosion if the bomb did go off. Max
Born is one of the people who has been willing to

dissociate causality from determinism: he explicates
cause and effect in terms of dependence of the effect on the cause. It is not quite clear what 'dependence' is supposed to be, but at least it seems to imply that you would not get the effect without the
cause. The trouble about this is that you might—
from some other cause. That this effect was produced by this cause does not at all shew that it could
not, or would not, have been produced by something
else in the absence of this cause.

Indeterminism is not a possibility unconsidered
by philosophers. C. D. Broad, in his inaugural lecture, given in 1934, described it as a possibility; but
added that whatever happened without being determined was accidental. He did not explain what
he meant by being accidental; he must have meant
more than not being necessary. He may have meant
being uncaused; but, if I am right, not being determined does not imply not being caused. Indeed, I
should explain indeterminism as the thesis that not
all physical effects are necessitated by their causes.
But if we think of Feynman's bomb, we get some
idea of what is meant by 'accidental'. It was random:
it 'merely happened' that the radioactive material
emitted particles in such a way as to activate the
Geiger counter enough to set off the bomb.
Certainly the motion of the Geiger counter's needle
is caused; and the actual emission is caused too; it
occurs because there is this mass of radioactive material here. (I have already indicated that, contrary
to the opinion of Hume, there are many different
sorts of causality.) But all the same the *causation* itself is, one could say, *mere hap*. It is difficult to explain this idea any further.

Broad used the idea to argue that indeterminism,
if applied to human action, meant that human actions are 'accidental'. Now he had a picture of
choices as being determining causes, analogous to
determining physical causes, and of choices in their
turn being either determined or accidental. To regard a choice as such—i.e. any case of choice—as a
predetermining causal event, now appears as a naïve
mistake in the philosophy of mind, though that is a
story I cannot tell here.

It was natural that when physics went indeterministic, some thinkers should have seized on this
indeterminism as being just what was wanted for

defending the freedom of the will. They received severe criticism on two counts: one, that this 'mere hap' is the very last thing to be invoked as the physical correlate of 'man's ethical behaviour'; the other, that quantum laws predict statistics of events when situations are repeated; interference with these, by the *will*'s determining individual events which the laws of nature leave undetermined, would be as much a violation of natural law as would have been interference which falsified a deterministic mechanical law.

Ever since Kant it has been a familiar claim among philosophers, that one can believe in both physical determinism and 'ethical' freedom. The reconciliations have always seemed to me to be either so much gobbledegook, or to make the alleged freedom of action quite unreal. My actions are mostly physical movements; if these physical movements are physically predetermined by processes which I do not control, then my freedom is illusory. The truth of physical indeterminism is thus indispensable if we are to make anything of the claim to freedom. But certainly it is insufficient. The physically undetermined is not thereby 'free'. For freedom at least involves the power of acting according to an idea, and no such thing is ascribed to whatever is the subject (what would be the relevant subject?) of unpredetermination in indeterministic physics. Nevertheless, there is nothing unacceptable about the idea that that 'physical haphazard' should be the only physical correlate of human freedom of action; and perhaps also of the voluntariness and intentionalness in the conduct of other animals which we do not call 'free'. The freedom, intentionalness and voluntariness are not to be analysed as the same thing as, or as produced by, the physical haphazard. Different sorts of pattern altogether are being spoken of when we mention them, from those involved in describing elementary processes of physical causality.

The other objection is, I think, more to the point. Certainly if we have a statistical law, but undetermined individual events, and then enough of these are supposed to be pushed by will in one direction to falsify the statistical law, we have again a supposition that puts will into conflict with natural laws. But it is not clear that the same train of minute phys-

ical events should have to be the regular correlate of the same action; in fact, that suggestion looks immensely implausible. It is, however, required by the objection.

Let me construct an analogy to illustrate this point. Suppose that we have a large glass box full of millions of extremely minute coloured particles, and the box is constantly shaken. Study of the box and particles leads to statistical laws, including laws for the random generation of small unit patches of uniform colour. Now the box is remarkable for also presenting the following phenomenon: the word "Coca-Cola" formed like a mosaic, can always be read when one looks at one of the sides. It is not always the same shape in the formation of its letters, not always the same size or in the same position, it varies in its colours; but there it always is. It is not at all clear that those statistical laws concerning the random motion of the particles and their formation of small unit patches of colour would have to be supposed violated by the operation of a cause for this phenomenon which did not derive it from the statistical laws.

It has taken the inventions of indeterministic physics to shake the rather common dogmatic conviction that determinism is a presupposition or perhaps a conclusion, of scientific knowledge. Not that that conviction has been very much shaken even so. Of course, the belief that the laws of nature are deterministic has been shaken. But I believe it has often been supposed that this makes little difference to the assumption of macroscopic determinism: as if undeterminedness were always encapsulated in systems whose internal workings could be described only by statistical laws, but where the total upshot, and in particular the outward effect, was as near as makes no difference always the same. What difference does it make, after all, that the scintillations, whereby my watch dial is luminous, follow only a statistical law—so long as the gross manifest effect is sufficiently guaranteed by the statistical law? Feynman's example of the bomb and Geiger counter smashes this conception; but as far as I can judge it takes time for the lesson to be learned. I find deterministic assumptions more common now among people at large, and among philosophers, than when I was an undergraduate.

The lesson is welcome, but indeterministic physics (if it succeeds in giving the lesson) is only culturally, not logically, required to make the deterministic picture doubtful. For it was always a mere extravagant fancy, encouraged in the 'age of science' by the happy relation of Newtonian mechanics to the solar system. It ought not to have mattered whether the laws of nature were or were not deterministic. For them to be deterministic is for them, together with the description of the situation, to entail unique results in situations defined by certain relevant objects and measures, and where no part is played by inconstant factors external to such definition. If that is right, the law being deterministic does not tell us whether 'determinism' is true. It is the total coverage of every motion that happens, that is a fanciful claim. But I do not mean that any motions lie outside the scope of physical laws, or that one cannot say, in any given context, that certain motions would be violations of physical law. Remember the contrast between chess and the infantile card game.

Meanwhile in non-experimental philosophy it is clear enough what are the dogmatic slumbers of the day. It is over and over again assumed that any singular causal proposition implies a universal statement running "Always when this, then that"; often assumed that true singular causal statements are derived from such 'inductively believed' universalities. Examples indeed are recalcitrant, but that does not seem to disturb. Even a philosopher acute enough to be conscious of this, such as Davidson, will say, without offering any reason at all for saying it, that a singular causal statement implies *that there is* such a true universal proposition[15]—though perhaps we can never have knowledge of it. Such a thesis needs some reason for believing it! "Regularities in nature": that is not a reason. The most neglected of the key topics in this subject are: interference and prevention.

NOTES

1. *Metaphysics*, Book IX, Chapter V.
2. *Ethics*, Book I, Axiom III.
3. *Elements of Philosophy Concerning Body*, Chapter IX.
4. *Treatise of Human Nature*, Book I, Part III, Sections II and VI.
5. My colleague Ian Hacking has pointed out C. S. Peirce to me as an exception to this generalization.
6. *Critique of Pure Reason*, Book II, Chapter II, Section III, Second Analogy.
7. 'The Notion of Cause,' in *Mysticism and Logic*.
8. *Treatise of Human Nature*, Book I, Part III, Section II.
9. Ibid., Book I, Part III, Section XIV.
10. Ibid., Book II, Part III, Section I.
11. Ibid., Book II, Part III, Section I.
12. *Science and Humanism*.
13. I should have made acknowledgements to Gilbert Ryle (*Concept of Mind*, p. 77) for this comparison. But his use of the openness of chess is somewhat ambiguous and is not the same as mine. For the contrast with a closed card game I was indebted to A. J. P. Kenny.
14. Albert Einstein and Leopold Infeld, *The Evolution of Physics*, Simon & Schuster, New York, 1938; (paperback edition, 1967), p. 146.
15. 'Causal Relations,' *Journal of Philosophy*, 64 (November 1967).

Laws and Their Role in Scientific Explanation

CARL G. HEMPEL

Carl G. Hempel (1905–1997) was Emeritus Stuart Professor at Princeton and a professor of philosophy at the University of Pittsburgh. His publications include *Fundamentals of Concept Formation in Empirical Science*, *Aspects of Scientific Explanation*, and *Philosophy of Natural Science*.

—•—

Two Basic Requirements for Scientific Explanations

To explain the phenomena of the physical world is one of the primary objectives of the natural sciences. Indeed, almost all of the scientific investigations that served as illustrations in the preceding chapters were aimed not at ascertaining some particular fact but at achieving some explanatory insight; they were concerned with questions such as how puerperal fever is contracted, why the water-lifting capacity of pumps has its characteristic limitation, why the transmission of light conforms to the laws of geometrical optics, and so forth. In this chapter . . . we will examine in some detail the character of scientific explanations and the kind of insight they afford.

That man has long and persistently been concerned to achieve some understanding of the enormously diverse, often perplexing, and sometimes threatening occurrences in the world around him is shown by the manifold myths and metaphors he has devised in an effort to account for the very existence of the world and of himself, for life and death, for the motions of the heavenly bodies, for the regular sequence of day and night, for the changing seasons, for thunder and lightning, sunshine and rain. Some of these explanatory ideas are based on anthropomorphic conceptions of the forces of nature, others invoke hidden powers or agents, still others refer to God's inscrutable plans or to fate.

Accounts of this kind undeniably may give the questioner a sense of having attained some understanding; they may resolve his perplexity and in this sense "answer" his question. But however satisfactory these answers may be psychologically, they are not adequate for the purposes of science, which, after all, is concerned to develop a conception of the world that has a clear, logical bearing on our experience and is thus capable of objective test. Scientific explanations must, for this reason, meet two systematic requirements, which will be called the requirement of explanatory relevance and the requirement of testability.

The astronomer Francesco Sizi offered the following argument to show why, contrary to what his contemporary, Galileo, claimed to have seen through his telescope, there could be no satellites circling around Jupiter:

There are seven windows in the head, two nostrils, two ears, two eyes and a mouth; so in the heavens there are two favorable stars, two unpropitious, two luminaries, and Mercury alone undecided and indifferent. From which and many other similar phenomena of nature such as the seven metals, etc., which it were tedious to enumerate, we gather that the number of planets is necessarily seven. . . . Moreover, the satellites are invisible to the naked eye and therefore can have no influence on the earth and therefore would be useless and therefore do not exist.[1]

The crucial defect of this argument is evident: the "facts" it adduces, even if accepted without question, are entirely irrelevant to the point at issue; they do not afford the slightest reason for the assumption that Jupiter has no satellites; the claim of relevance suggested by the barrage of words like "therefore", "it follows", and "necessarily" is entirely spurious.

Consider by contrast the physical explanation of a rainbow. It shows that the phenomenon comes about as a result of the reflection and refraction of the white light of the sun in spherical droplets of water such as those that occur in a cloud. By reference to the relevant optical laws, this account shows that the appearance of a rainbow is to be expected whenever a spray or mist of water droplets is illuminated by a strong white light behind the observer. Thus, even if we happened never to have seen a rainbow, the explanatory information provided by the physical account would constitute good grounds for expecting or believing that a rainbow will appear under the specified circumstances. We will refer to this characteristic by saying that the physical explanation meets the *requirement of explanatory relevance*: the explanatory information adduced affords good grounds for believing that the phenomenon to be explained did, or does, indeed occur. This condition must be met if we are to be entitled to say: "That explains it—the phenomenon in question was indeed to be expected under the circumstances!"

The requirement represents a necessary condition for an adequate explanation, but not a sufficient one. For example, a large body of data showing a red-shift in the spectra of distant galaxies provides strong grounds for believing *that* those galaxies recede from our local one at enormous speeds, yet it does not explain *why*.

To introduce the second basic requirement for scientific explanations, let us consider once more the conception of gravitational attraction as manifesting a natural tendency akin to love. As we noted earlier, this conception has no test implications whatever. Hence, no empirical finding could possibly bear it out or disconfirm it. Being thus devoid of empirical content, the conception surely affords no grounds for expecting the characteristic phenomena of gravitational attraction: it lacks objective explanatory power. Similar comments apply to explanations in terms of an inscrutable fate: to invoke such an idea is not to achieve an especially profound insight, but to give up the attempt at explanation altogether. By contrast, the statements on which the physical explanation of a

rainbow is based do have various test implications; these concern, for example, the conditions under which a rainbow will be seen in the sky, and the order of the colors in it; the appearance of rainbow phenomena in the spray of a wave breaking on the rocks and in the mist of a lawn sprinkler; and so forth. These examples illustrate a second condition for scientific explanations, which we will call the *requirement of testability*: the statements constituting a scientific explanation must be capable of empirical test.

It has already been suggested that since the conception of gravitation in terms of an underlying universal affinity has no test implications, it can have no explanatory power: it cannot provide grounds for expecting that universal gravitation will occur, nor that gravitational attraction will show such and such characteristic features; for if it did imply such consequences either deductively or even in a weaker, inductive-probabilistic sense, then it would be testable by reference to those consequences. As this example shows, the two requirements just considered are interrelated: a proposed explanation that meets the requirement of relevance also meets the requirement of testability. (The converse clearly does not hold.)

Now let us see what forms scientific explanations take, and how they meet the two basic requirements.

Deductive-Nomological Explanation

Consider . . . Périer's finding in the Puy-de-Dôme experiment, that the length of the mercury column in a Torricelli barometer decreased with increasing altitude. Torricelli and Pascal's ideas on atmospheric pressure provided an explanation for this phenomenon: somewhat pedantically, it can be spelled out as follows:

(a) At any location, the pressure that the mercury column in the closed branch of the Torricelli apparatus exerts upon the mercury below equals the pressure exerted on the surface of the mercury in the open vessel by the column of air above it.

(b) The pressures exerted by the columns of mercury and of air are proportional to their weights; and the shorter the columns, the smaller their weights.

(c) As Périer carried the apparatus to the top of the mountain, the column of air above the open vessel became steadily shorter.

(d) [Therefore,] the mercury column in the closed vessel grew steadily shorter during the ascent.

Thus formulated, the explanation is an argument to the effect that the phenomenon to be explained, as described by the sentence (d), is just what is to be expected in view of the explanatory facts cited in (a), (b), and (c); and that, indeed, (d) follows deductively from the explanatory statements. The latter are of two kinds; (a) and (b) have the character of general laws expressing uniform empirical connections; whereas (c) describes certain particular facts. Thus, the shortening of the mercury column is here explained by showing that it occurred in accordance with certain laws of nature, as a result of certain particular circumstances. The explanation fits the phenomenon to be explained into a pattern of uniformities and shows that its occurrence was to be expected, given the specified laws and the pertinent particular circumstances.

The phenomenon to be accounted for by an explanation will henceforth also be referred to as the *explanandum phenomenon*; the sentence describing it, as the *explanandum sentence*. When the context shows which is meant, either of them will simply be called the explanandum. The sentences specifying the explanatory information—(a), (b), (c) in our example—will be called the *explanans sentences*; jointly they will be said to form the *explanans*.

As a second example, consider the explanation of a characteristic of image formation by reflection in a spherical mirror; namely, that generally $1/u + 1/v = 2/r$, where u and v are the distances of object-point and image-point from the mirror, and r is the mirror's radius of curvature. In geometrical optics, this uniformity is explained with the help of the basic law of reflection in a plane mirror, by treating the reflection of a beam of light at any one point of a spherical mirror as a case of reflection in a plane tangential to the spherical surface. The resulting explanation can be formulated as a deductive argument whose conclusion is the explanandum sentence, and whose premises include the basic laws of reflection and of rectilinear propagation, as well

as the statement that the surface of the mirror forms a segment of a sphere.[2]

A similar argument, whose premises again include the law for reflection in a plane mirror, offers an explanation of why the light of a small light source placed at the focus of a paraboloidal mirror is reflected in a beam parallel to the axis of the paraboloid (a principle technologically applied in the construction of automobile headlights, searchlights, and other devices).

The explanations just considered may be conceived, then, as deductive arguments whose conclusion is the explanandum sentence, E, and whose premiss-set, the explanans, consists of general laws, $L_1, L_2, \ldots, L_r$ and of other statements, $C_1, C_2, \ldots, C_k$, which make assertions about particular facts. The form of such arguments, which thus constitute one type of scientific explanation, can be represented by the following schema:

$$(\text{D-N}) \quad \left. \begin{array}{c} L_1, L_2, \ldots, L_r \\ \\ C_1, C_2, \ldots, C_k \end{array} \right\} \begin{array}{l} \text{Explanans sentences} \\ \\ \end{array}$$
$$\frac{}{E} \quad \text{Explanandum sentence}$$

Explanatory accounts of this kind will be called explanations by deductive subsumption under general laws, or *deductive-nomological explanations*. (The root of the term 'nomological' is the Greek word 'nomos', for law.) The laws invoked in a scientific explanation will also be called *covering laws* for the explanandum phenomenon, and the explanatory argument will be said to subsume the explanandum under those laws.

The explanandum phenomenon in a deductive-nomological explanation may be an event occurring at a particular place and time, such as the outcome of Périer's experiment. Or it may be some regularity found in nature, such as certain characteristics generally displayed by rainbows; or a uniformity expressed by an empirical law such as Galileo's or Kepler's laws. Deductive explanations of such uniformities will then invoke laws of broader scope, such as the laws of reflection and refraction, or Newton's laws of motion and of gravitation. As this use of Newton's laws illustrates, empirical laws are often explained by means of theoretical principles that refer to structures and processes underlying the uniformities in question. We will return to such explanations in the next chapter.

Deductive-nomological explanations satisfy the requirement of explanatory relevance in the strongest possible sense: the explanatory information they provide implies the explanandum sentence deductively and thus offers logically conclusive grounds why the explanandum phenomenon is to be expected. (We will soon encounter other scientific explanations, which fulfill the requirement only in a weaker, inductive, sense.) And the testability requirement is met as well, since the explanans implies among other things that under the specified conditions, the explanandum phenomenon occurs.

Some scientific explanations conform to the pattern (D-N) quite closely. This is so, particularly, when certain quantitative features of a phenomenon are explained by mathematical derivation from covering general laws, as in the case of reflection in spherical and paraboloidal mirrors. Or take the celebrated explanation, propounded by Leverrier (and independently by Adams), of peculiar irregularities in the motion of the planet Uranus, which on the current Newtonian theory could not be accounted for by the gravitational attraction of the other planets then known. Leverrier conjectured that they resulted from the gravitational pull of an as yet undetected outer planet, and he computed the position, mass, and other characteristics which that planet would have to possess to account in quantitative detail for the observed irregularities. His explanation was strikingly confirmed by the discovery, at the predicted location, of a new planet, Neptune, which had the quantitative characteristics attributed to it by Leverrier. Here again, the explanation has the character of a deductive argument whose premises include general laws—specifically, Newton's laws of gravitation and of motion—as well as statements specifying various quantitative particulars about the disturbing planet.

Not infrequently, however, deductive-nomological explanations are stated in an elliptical form: they omit mention of certain assumptions that are presupposed by the explanation but are simply taken for granted in the given context. Such explanations are sometimes expressed in the form 'E because C', where E is the event to be explained and C is some antecedent or concomitant event or state of affairs. Take, for example, the statement: 'The slush on the sidewalk remained liquid during the frost because it had been sprinkled with salt'. This explanation does not explicitly mention any laws, but it tacitly presupposes at least one: that the freezing point of water is lowered whenever salt is dissolved in it. Indeed, it is precisely by virtue of this law that the sprinkling of salt acquires the explanatory, and specifically causative, role that the elliptical because-statement ascribes to it. That statement, incidentally, is elliptical also in other respects; for example, it tacitly takes for granted, and leaves unmentioned, certain assumptions about the prevailing physical conditions, such as the temperature's not dropping to a very low point. And if nomic and other assumptions thus omitted are added to the statement that salt had been sprinkled on the slush, we obtain the premises for a deductive-nomological explanation of the fact that the slush remained liquid.

Similar comments apply to Semmelweis's explanation that childbed fever was caused by decomposed animal matter introduced into the bloodstream through open wound surfaces. Thus formulated, the explanation makes no mention of general laws; but it presupposes that such contamination of the bloodstream generally leads to blood poisoning attended by the characteristic symptoms of childbed fever, for this is implied by the assertion that the contamination *causes* puerperal fever. The generalization was no doubt taken for granted by Semmelweis, to whom the cause of Kolletschka's fatal illness presented no etiological problem: given that infectious matter was introduced into the bloodstream, blood poisoning would result. (Kolletschka was by no means the first one to die of blood poisoning resulting from a cut with an infected scalpel. And by a tragic irony, Semmelweis himself was to suffer the same fate.) But once the tacit premiss is made explicit, the explanation is seen to involve reference to general laws.

As the preceding examples illustrate, corresponding general laws are always presupposed by an explanatory statement to the effect that a particular event of a certain kind G (e.g., expansion of a gas under constant pressure; flow of a current in a wire loop) was *caused* by an event of another kind, F (e.g., heating of the gas; motion of the loop across a magnetic field). To see this, we need not enter into the complex ramifications of the notion of cause; it suffices to note that the general maxim "Same cause, same effect", when applied to such explanatory statements, yields the implied claim that whenever an event of kind F occurs, it is accompanied by an event of kind G.

To say that an explanation rests on general laws is not to say that its discovery required the discovery of the laws. The crucial new insight achieved by an explanation will sometimes lie in the discovery of some particular fact (e.g., the presence of an undetected outer planet; infectious matter adhering to the hands of examining physicians) which, by virtue of antecedently accepted general laws, accounts for the explanandum phenomenon. In other cases, such as that of the lines in the hydrogen spectrum, the explanatory achievement does lie in the discovery of a covering law (Balmer's) and eventually of an explanatory theory (such as Bohr's); in yet other cases, the major accomplishment of an explanation may lie in showing that, and exactly how, the explanandum phenomenon can be accounted for by reference to laws and data about particular facts that are already available: this is illustrated by the explanatory derivation of the reflection laws for spherical and paraboloidal mirrors from the basic law of geometrical optics in conjunction with statements about the geometrical characteristics of the mirrors.

An explanatory problem does not by itself determine what kind of discovery is required for its solution. Thus, Leverrier discovered deviations from the theoretically expected course also in the motion of the planet Mercury; and as in the case of Uranus, he tried to explain these as resulting from the gravitational pull of an as yet undetected planet, Vulcan, which would have to be a very dense and very small object between the sun and Mercury. But no such planet was found, and a satisfactory explanation was provided only much later by the general theory of relativity, which accounted for the irregularities not by reference to some disturbing particular factor, but by means of a new system of laws.

Universal Laws and Accidental Generalizations

As we have seen, laws play an essential role in deductive-nomological explanations. They provide the link by reason of which particular circumstances (described by $C_1, C_2, \ldots, C_k$) can serve to explain the occurrence of a given event. And when the explanandum is not a particular event, but a uniformity such as those represented by characteristics mentioned earlier of spherical and paraboloidal mirrors, the explanatory laws exhibit a system of more comprehensive uniformities, of which the given one is but a special case.

The laws required for deductive-nomological explanations share a basic characteristic: they are, as we shall say, statements of universal form. Broadly speaking, a statement of this kind asserts a uniform connection between different empirical phenomena or between different aspects of an empirical phenomenon. It is a statement to the effect that whenever and wherever conditions of a specified kind F occur, then so will, always and without exception, certain conditions of another kind, G. (Not all scientific laws are of this type. In the sections that follow, we will encounter laws of probabilistic form, and explanations based on them.)

Here are some examples of statements of universal form: whenever the temperature of a gas increases while its pressure remains constant, its volume increases; whenever a solid is dissolved in a liquid, the boiling point of the liquid is raised; whenever a ray of light is reflected at a plane surface, the angle of reflection equals the angle of incidence; whenever a magnetic iron rod is broken in two, the pieces are magnets again; whenever a body falls freely from rest in a vacuum near the surface of the earth, the distance it covers in t seconds is $16t^2$ feet. Most of the laws of the natural sciences are quantitative: they assert specific mathematical connections between different quantitative characteristics of physical systems (e.g., between volume, temperature, and pressure of a gas) or of processes (e.g., between time and distance in free fall in Galileo's law; between the period of revolution of a planet and its mean distance from the sun, in Kepler's third law; between the angles of incidence and refraction in Snell's law).

Strictly speaking, a statement asserting some uniform connection will be considered a law only if there are reasons to assume it is true: we would not normally speak of false laws of nature. But if this requirement were rigidly observed, then the statements commonly referred to as Galileo's and Kepler's laws would not qualify as laws; for according to current physical knowledge, they hold only approximately; and . . . physical theory explains why this is so. Analogous remarks apply to the laws of geometrical optics. For example, even in a homogeneous medium, light does not move strictly in straight lines: it can bend around corners. We shall therefore use the word 'law' somewhat liberally, applying the term also to certain statements of the kind here referred to, which, on theoretical grounds, are known to hold only approximately and with certain qualifications. . . .

We saw that the laws invoked in deductive-nomological explanations have the basic form: 'In all cases when conditions of kind F are realized, conditions of kind G are realized as well'. But, interestingly, not all statements of this universal form, even if true, can qualify as laws of nature. For example, the sentence 'All rocks in this box contain iron' is of universal form (F is the condition of being a rock in the box, G that of containing iron); yet even if true, it would not be regarded as a law, but as an assertion of something that "happens to be the case," as an "accidental generalization." Or consider the statement: 'All bodies consisting of pure gold have a mass of less than 100,000 kilograms'. No doubt all bodies of gold ever examined by man conform to it; thus, there is considerable confirmatory evidence for it and no disconfirming instances are known. Indeed, it is quite possible that never in the history of the universe has there been or will there be a body of pure gold with a mass of 100,000 kilograms or more. In this case, the proposed generalization would not only be well confirmed, but true. And yet, we would presumably regard its truth as accidental, on the ground that nothing in the basic laws of nature as conceived in contemporary science precludes the possibility of there being—or even the possibility of our producing—a solid gold object with a mass exceeding 100,000 kilograms.

Thus, a scientific law cannot be adequately defined as a true statement of universal form: this characterization expresses a necessary, but not a sufficient, condition for laws of the kind here under discussion.

What distinguishes genuine laws from accidental generalizations? This intriguing problem has been intensively discussed in recent years. Let us look briefly at some of the principal ideas that have emerged from the debate, which is still continuing.

One telling and suggestive difference, noted by Nelson Goodman,[3] is this: a law can, whereas an accidental generalization cannot, serve to support *counterfactual conditionals*, i.e., statements of the form 'If A were (had been) the case, then B would be (would have been) the case', where in fact A is not (has not been) the case. Thus, the assertion 'If this paraffin candle had been put into a kettle of boiling water, it would have melted' could be supported by adducing the law that paraffin is liquid above 60 degrees centigrade (and the fact that the boiling point of water is 100 degrees centigrade). But the statement 'All rocks in this box contain iron' could not be used similarly to support the counterfactual statement 'If this pebble had been put into the box, it would contain iron'. Similarly, a law, in contrast to an accidentally true generalization, can support *subjunctive conditionals*, i.e., sentences of the type 'If A should come to pass, then so would B', where it is left open whether or not A will in fact come to pass. The statement 'If this paraffin candle should be put into boiling water then it would melt' is an example.

Closely related to this difference is another one, which is of special interest to us: a law can, whereas an accidental generalization cannot, serve as a basis for an explanation. Thus, the melting of a particular paraffin candle that was put into boiling water can be explained, in conformity with the schema (D-N), by reference to the particular facts just mentioned and to the law that paraffin melts when its temperature is raised above 60 degrees centigrade. But the fact that a particular rock in the box contains iron cannot be analogously explained by reference to the general statement that all rocks in the box contain iron.

It might seem plausible to say, by way of a further distinction, that the latter statement simply serves as a conveniently brief formulation of a finite conjunction of this kind: 'Rock r_1 contains iron, and the rock r_2 contains iron, . . . , and rock r_{63} contains iron'; whereas the generalization about paraffin refers to a potentially infinite set of particular cases and therefore cannot be paraphrased by a finite conjunction of statements describing individual instances. This distinction is suggestive, but it is overstated. For to begin with, the generalization 'All rocks in this box contain iron' does not in fact tell us how many rocks there are in the box, nor does it name any particular rocks r_1, r_2, etc. Hence, the general sentence is not logically equivalent to a finite conjunction of the kind just mentioned. To formulate a suitable conjunction, we need additional information, which might be obtained by counting and labeling the rocks in the box. Besides, our generalization 'All bodies of pure gold have a mass of less than 100,000 kilograms' would not count as a law even if there were infinitely many bodies of gold in the world. Thus, the criterion we have under consideration fails on several grounds.

Finally, let us note that a statement of universal form may qualify as a law even if it actually has no instances whatever. As an example, consider the sentence: 'On any celestial body that has the same radius as the earth but twice its mass, free fall from rest conforms to the formula $s = 32t^2$'. There might well be no celestial object in the entire universe that has the specified size and mass, and yet the statement has the character of a law. For it (or rather, a close approximation of it, as in the case of Galileo's law) follows from the Newtonian theory of gravitation and of motion in conjunction with the statement that the acceleration of free fall on the earth is 32 feet per second per second; thus, it has strong theoretical support, just like our earlier law for free fall on the moon.

A law, we noted, can support subjunctive and counterfactual conditional statements about potential instances, i.e., about particular cases that might occur, or that might have occurred but did not. In similar fashion, Newton's theory supports our general statement in a subjunctive version that suggests its lawlike status, namely: 'On any celestial body that there may be which has the same size as the earth but twice its mass, free fall would conform to the formula $s = 32t^2$'. By contrast, the generalization about the rocks cannot be paraphrased as asserting that any rock that might be in this box would contain iron, nor of course would this latter claim have any theoretical support.

Similarly, we would not use our generalization about the mass of gold bodies—let us call it H—to support statements such as this: 'Two bodies of pure gold whose individual masses add up to more than 100,000 kilograms cannot be fused to form one body; or if fusion should be possible, then the mass of the resulting body will be less than 100,000 kg', for the basic physical and chemical theories of matter that are currently accepted do not preclude the kind of fusion here considered, and they do not imply that there would be a mass loss of the sort here referred

to. Hence, even if the generalization H should be true, i.e., if no exceptions to it should ever occur, this would constitute a mere accident or coincidence as judged by current theory, which permits the occurrence of exceptions to H.

Thus, whether a statement of universal form counts as a law will depend in part upon the scientific theories accepted at the time. This is not to say that "empirical generalizations"—statements of universal form that are empirically well confirmed but have no basis in theory—never qualify as laws: Galileo's, Kepler's, and Boyle's laws, for example, were accepted as such before they received theoretical grounding. The relevance of theory is rather this: a statement of universal form, whether empirically confirmed or as yet untested, will qualify as a law if it is implied by an accepted theory (statements of this kind are often referred to as theoretical laws); but even if it is empirically well confirmed and presumably true in fact, it will not qualify as a law if it rules out certain hypothetical occurrences (such as the fusion of two gold bodies with a resulting mass of more than 100,000 kilograms, in the case of our generalization H) which an accepted theory qualifies as possible.[4]

Probabilistic Explanation: Fundamentals

Not all scientific explanations are based on laws of strictly universal form. Thus, little Jim's getting the measles might be explained by saying that he caught the disease from his brother, who had a bad case of the measles some days earlier. This account again links the explanandum event to an earlier occurrence, Jim's exposure to the measles; the latter is said to provide an explanation because there is a connection between exposure to the measles and contracting the disease. That connection cannot be expressed by a law of universal form, however; for not every case of exposure to the measles produces contagion. What can be claimed is only that persons exposed to the measles will contract the disease with high probability, i.e., in a high percentage of all cases. General statements of this type, which we shall soon examine more closely, will be called *laws of probabilistic form* or *probabilistic laws*, for short.

In our illustration, then, the explanans consists of the probabilistic law just mentioned and the statement that Jim was exposed to the measles. In contrast to the case of deductive-nomological explanation, these explanans statements do not deductively imply the explanandum statement that Jim got the measles; for in deductive inferences from true premises, the conclusion is invariably true, whereas in our example, it is clearly possible that the explanans statements might be true and yet the explanandum statement false. We will say, for short, that the explanans implies the explanandum, not with "deductive certainty," but only with near-certainty or with high probability.

The resulting explanatory argument may be schematized as follows . . . [:]

> The probability for persons exposed to the measles to catch the disease is high.
>
> Jim was exposed to the measles.
> ════════════════════ [makes highly probable]
> Jim caught the measles.

In the customary presentation of a deductive argument, which was used, for example, in the schema (D-N) above, the conclusion is separated from the premises by a single line, which serves to indicate that the premises logically imply the conclusion. The double line used in our latest schema is meant to indicate analogously that the "premises" (the explanans) make the "conclusion" (the explanandum sentence) more or less probable; the degree of probability is suggested by the notation in brackets.

Arguments of this kind will be called *probabilistic explanations*. As our discussion shows, a probabilistic explanation of a particular event shares certain basic characteristics with the corresponding deductive-nomological type of explanation. In both cases, the given event is explained by reference to others, with which the explanandum event is connected by laws. But in one case, the laws are of universal form; in the other, of probabilistic form. And while a deductive explanation shows that, on the information contained in the explanans, the explanandum was to be expected with "deductive certainty", an inductive explanation shows only that, on the information contained in the explanans, the explanandum was to be expected with high probability, and perhaps with "practical certainty"; it is in this manner that the latter argument meets the requirement of explanatory relevance.

Statistical Probabilities and Probabilistic Laws

We must now consider more closely the two differentiating features of probabilistic explanation that have just been noted: the probabilistic laws they invoke and the peculiar kind of probabilistic implication that connects the explanans with the explanandum.

Suppose that from an urn containing many balls of the same size and mass, but not necessarily of the same color, successive drawings are made. At each drawing, one ball is removed, and its color is noted. Then the ball is returned to the urn, whose contents are thoroughly mixed before the next drawing takes place. This is an example of a so-called random process or random experiment, a concept that will soon be characterized in more detail. Let us refer to the procedure just described as experiment U, to each drawing as one performance of U, and to the color of the ball produced by a given drawing as the result, or the outcome, of that performance.

If all the balls in an urn are white, then a statement of strictly universal form holds true of the results produced by the performance of U: every drawing from the urn yields a white ball, or yields the result W, for short. If only some of the balls—say, 600 of them—are white, whereas the others—say 400—are red, then a general statement of probabilistic form holds true of the experiment: the probability for a performance of U to produce a white ball, or outcome W, is .6; in symbols:

$$P(W,U) = .6 \qquad (5a)$$

Similarly, the probability of obtaining heads as a result of the random experiment C of flipping a fair coin is given by

$$P(H,C) = .5 \qquad (5b)$$

and the probability of obtaining an ace as a result of the random experiment D of rolling a regular die is

$$P(A,D) = 1/6 \qquad (5c)$$

What do such probability statements mean? According to one familiar view, sometimes called the "classical" conception of probability, the statement (5a) would have to be interpreted as follows: each performance of the experiment U effects a choice of one from among 1,000 basic possibilities, or basic alternatives, each represented by one of the balls in the urn; of these possible choices, 600 are "favorable" to the outcome W; and the probability of drawing a white ball is simply the ratio of the number of favorable choices available to the number of all possible choices, i.e., 600/1,000. The classical interpretation of the probability statements (5b) and (5c) follows similar lines.

Yet this characterization is inadequate; for if before each drawing, the 400 red balls in the urn were placed on top of the white ones, then in this new kind of urn experiment—let us call it U'—the ratio of favorable to possible basic alternatives would remain the same, but the probability of drawing a white ball would be smaller than in the experiment U, in which the balls are thoroughly mixed before each drawing. The classical conception takes account of this difficulty by requiring that the basic alternatives referred to in its definition of probability must be "equipossible" or "equiprobable"—a requirement presumably violated in the case of experiment U'.

This added proviso raises the question of how to define equipossibility or equiprobability. We will pass over this notoriously troublesome and controversial issue, because—even assuming that equiprobability can be satisfactorily characterized—the classical conception would still be inadequate, since probabilities are assigned also to the outcomes of random experiments for which no plausible way is known of marking off equiprobable basic alternatives. Thus, for the random experiment D of rolling a regular die, the six faces might be regarded as representing such equiprobable alternatives; but we attribute probabilities to such results as rolling an ace, or an odd number of points, etc., also in the case of a loaded die, even though no equiprobable basic outcomes can be marked off here.

Similarly—and this is particularly important—science assigns probabilities to the outcomes of certain random experiments or random processes encountered in nature, such as the step-by-step decay of the atoms of radioactive substances, or the transition of atoms from one energy state to another. Here again, we find no equiprobable basic alternatives in terms of which such probabilities might be classically defined and computed.

To arrive at a more satisfactory construal of our probability statements, let us consider how one would ascertain the probability of the rolling of an ace with a given die that is not known to be regular. This would obviously be done by making a large number of throws with the die and ascertaining the *relative frequency*, i.e., the proportion, of those cases in which an ace turns up. If, for example, the experiment D' of rolling the given die is performed 300 times and an ace turns up in 62 cases, then the relative frequency, 62/300, would be regarded as an approximate value of the probability $p(A,D')$ of rolling an ace with the given die. Analogous procedures would be used to estimate the probabilities associated with the flipping of a given coin, the spinning of a roulette wheel, and so on. Similarly, the probabilities associated with radioactive decay, with the transitions between different atomic energy states, with genetic processes, etc., are determined by ascertaining the corresponding relative frequencies; however, this is often done in highly indirect ways rather than by simply counting individual atomic or other events of the relevant kinds.

The interpretation in terms of relative frequencies applies also to probability statements such as (5b) and (5c), which concern the results of flipping a fair (i.e., homogeneous and strictly cylindrical) coin or tossing a regular (homogeneous and strictly cubical) die: what the scientist (or the gambler, for that matter) is concerned with in making a probability statement is the relative frequency with which a certain outcome O can be expected in long series of repetitions of some random experiment R. The counting of "equiprobable" basic alternatives and of those among them which are "favorable" to O may be regarded as a heuristic device for guessing at the relative frequency of O. And indeed when a regular die or a fair coin is tossed a large number of times, the different faces tend to come up with equal frequency. One might expect this on the basis of symmetry considerations of the kind frequently used in forming physical hypotheses, for our empirical knowledge affords no grounds on which to expect any of the faces to be favored over any other. But while such considerations often are heuristically useful, they must not be regarded as certain or as self-evident truths: some very plausible symmetry assumptions, such as the principle of parity, have been found not to be generally satisfied at the subatomic level. Assumptions about equiprobabilities are therefore always subject to correction in the light of empirical data concerning the actual relative frequencies of the phenomena in question. This point is illustrated also by the statistical theories of gases developed by Bose and Einstein and by Fermi and Dirac, respectively, which rest on different assumptions concerning what distributions of particles over a phase space are equiprobable.

The probabilities specified in the probabilistic laws, then, represent relative frequencies. They cannot, however, be strictly defined as relative frequencies in long series of repetitions of the relevant random experiment. For the proportion, say, of aces obtained in throwing a given die will change, if perhaps only slightly, as the series of throws is extended; and even in two series of exactly the same length, the number of aces will usually differ. We do find, however, that as the number of throws increases, the relative frequency of each of the different outcomes tends to change less and less, even though the results of successive throws continue to vary in an irregular and practically unpredictable fashion. This is what generally characterizes a random experiment R with outcomes O_1, O_2, O_n: successive performances of R yield one or another of those outcomes in an irregular manner; but the relative frequencies of the outcomes tend to become stable as the number of performances increases. And the probabilities of the outcomes, $p(O_1,R), p(O_2,R), \ldots p(O_{11},R)$, may be regarded as ideal values that the actual frequencies tend to assume as they become increasingly stable. For mathematical convenience, the probabilities are sometimes defined as the mathematical *limits* toward which the relative frequencies converge as the number of performances increases indefinitely. But this definition has certain conceptual shortcomings, and in some more recent mathematical studies of the subject, the intended empirical meaning of the concept of probability is deliberately, and for good reasons, characterized more vaguely by means of the following so-called *statistical interpretation of probability*:[5]

The statement

$$p(O,R) = r$$

means that in a long series of performances of random experiment R, the proportion of cases with outcome O is almost certain to be close to r.

The concept of *statistical probability* thus characterized must be carefully distinguished from the concept of *inductive* or *logical probability*, which we considered [in chapter 4]. Logical probability is a quantitative logical relation between definite *statements*; the sentence

$$c(H,K) = r$$

asserts that the hypothesis H is supported, or made probable, to degree r by the evidence formulated in statement K. Statistical probability is a quantitative relation between repeatable *kinds of events*: a certain kind of outcome, O, and a certain kind of random process, R; it represents, roughly speaking, the relative frequency with which the result O tends to occur in a long series of performances of R.

What the two concepts have in common are their mathematical characteristics: both satisfy the basic principles of mathematical probability theory:

(a) The possible numerical values of both probabilities range from 0 to 1:

$$0 \leq p(O,R) \leq 1$$
$$0 \leq c(H,K) \leq 1$$

(b) The probability for one of two mutually exclusive outcomes of R to occur is the sum of the probabilities of the outcomes taken separately; the probability, on any evidence K, for one or the other of two mutually exclusive hypotheses to hold is the sum of their respective probabilities:

If O_1, O_2 are mutually exclusive, then
$$p(O_1 \text{ or } O_2, R) = p(O_1,R) + p(O_2,R)$$
If H_1, H_2 are logically exclusive hypotheses, then
$$c(H_1 \text{ or } H_2, K) = c(H_1, K) + c(H_2, K)$$

(c) The probability of an outcome that necessarily occurs in all cases—such as O or not O—is 1; the probability, on any evidence, of a hypothesis that is logically (and in this sense necessarily) true, such as H or not H, is 1:

$$p(O \text{ or not } O,R) = 1$$
$$c(H \text{ or not } H,K) = 1$$

Scientific hypotheses in the form of statistical probability statements can be, and are, tested by examining the long-run relative frequencies of the outcomes concerned; and the confirmation of such hypotheses is then judged, broadly speaking, in terms of the closeness of the agreement between hypothetical probabilities and observed frequencies. The logic of such tests, however, presents some intriguing special problems, which call for at least brief examination.

Consider the hypothesis, H, that the probability of rolling an ace with a certain die is .15; or briefly, that $p(A,D) = .15$, where D is the random experiment of rolling the given die. The hypothesis H does not deductively imply any test implications specifying how many aces will occur in a finite series of throws of the die. It does not imply, for example, that exactly 75 among the first 500 throws will yield an ace, nor even that the number of aces will lie between 50 and 100, say. Hence, if the proportion of aces actually obtained in a large number of throws differs considerably from .15, this does not refute H in the sense in which a hypothesis of strictly universal form, such as 'All swans are white', can be refuted, in virtue of the *modus tollens* argument, by reference to one counter-instance, such as a black swan. Similarly, if a long run of throws of the given die yields a proportion of aces very close to .15, this does not confirm H in the sense in which a hypothesis is confirmed by the finding that a test sentence I that it logically implies is in fact true. For in this latter case, the hypothesis asserts I by logical implication, and the test result is thus confirmatory in the sense of showing that a certain part of what the hypothesis asserts is indeed true; but nothing strictly analogous is shown for H by confirmatory frequency data; for H does *not* assert by implication that the frequency of aces in some long run will definitely be very close to .15.

But while H does not logically preclude the possibility that the proportion of aces obtained in a long series of throws of the given die may depart widely from .15, it does logically imply that such departures are highly improbable in the statistical sense; i.e., that if the experiment of performing a long series of throws (say, 1,000 of them per series) is repeated a large number of times, then only a tiny proportion of those long series will yield a proportion of aces that differs considerably from .15. For the case of rolling a die, it is usually assumed that the results of successive throws are "statistically independent"; this means roughly that the probability of obtaining an ace in a throw of the die does not depend on the result of the preceding throw. Mathematical analysis shows that

in conjunction with this independence assumption, our hypothesis H deductively determines the statistical probability for the proportion of aces obtained in n throws to differ from .15 by no more than a specified amount. For example, H implies that for a series of 1,000 throws of the die here considered, the probability is about .976 that the proportion of aces will lie between .125 and .175; and similarly, that for a run of 10,000 throws the probability is about .995 that the proportion of aces will be between .14 and .16. Thus, we may say that if H is true, then it is practically certain that in a long trial run the observed proportion of aces will differ by very little from the hypothetical probability value .15. Hence, if the observed long-run frequency of an outcome is not close to the probability assigned to it by a given probabilistic hypothesis, then that hypothesis is very likely to be false. In this case, the frequency data count as disconfirming the hypothesis, or as reducing its credibility; and if sufficiently strong disconfirming evidence is found, the hypothesis will be considered as practically, though not logically, refuted and will accordingly be rejected. Similarly, close agreement between hypothetical probabilities and observed frequencies will tend to confirm a probabilistic hypothesis and may lead to its acceptance.

If probabilistic hypotheses are to be accepted or rejected on the basis of statistical evidence concerning observed frequencies, then appropriate standards are called for. These will have to determine (*a*) what deviations of observed frequencies from the probability stated by a hypothesis are to count as grounds for rejecting the hypothesis, and (*b*) how close an agreement between observed frequencies and hypothetical probability is to be required as a condition for accepting the hypothesis. The requirements in question can be made more or less strict, and their specification is a matter of choice. The stringency of the chosen standards will normally vary with the context and the objectives of the research in question. Broadly speaking, it will depend on the importance that is attached, in the given context, to avoiding two kinds of error that might be made: rejecting the hypothesis under test although it is true, and accepting it although it is false. The importance of this point is particularly clear when acceptance or rejection of the hypothesis is to serve as a basis for practical action. Thus, if the hypothesis concerns the probable effectiveness and safety of a new vaccine, then the decision about its acceptance will have to take into account not only how well the statistical test results accord with the probabilities specified by the hypothesis, but also how serious would be the consequences of accepting the hypothesis and acting on it (e.g., by inoculating children with the vaccine) when in fact it is false, and of rejecting the hypothesis and acting accordingly (e.g., by destroying the vaccine and modifying or discontinuing the process of manufacture) when in fact the hypothesis is true. The complex problems that arise in this context form the subject matter of the theory of statistical tests and decisions, which has been developed in recent decades on the basis of the mathematical theory of probability and statistics.[6]

Many important laws and theoretical principles in the natural sciences are of probabilistic character, though they are often of more complicated form than the simple probability statements we have discussed. For example, according to current physical theory, radioactive decay is a random phenomenon in which the atoms of each radioactive element possess a characteristic probability of disintegrating during a specified period of time. The corresponding probabilistic laws are usually formulated as statements giving the "half-life" of the element concerned. Thus, the statements that the half-life of radium[226] is 1,620 years and that of polonium[218] is 3.05 minutes are laws to the effect that the probability for a radium[226] atom to decay within 1,620 years, and for an atom of polonium[218] to decay within 3.05 minutes, are both one-half. According to the statistical interpretation cited earlier, these laws imply that of a large number of radium[226] atoms or of polonium[218] atoms given at a certain time, very close to one-half will still exist 1,620 years, or 3.05 minutes, later; the others having disintegrated by radioactive decay.

Again, in the kinetic theory various uniformities in the behavior of gases, including the laws of classical thermodynamics, are explained by means of certain assumptions about the constituent molecules; and some of these are probabilistic hypotheses concerning statistical regularities in the motions and collisions of those molecules.

A few additional remarks concerning the notion of a probabilistic law are indicated. It might seem that all scientific laws should be qualified as probabilistic since the supporting evidence we have for them is always a finite and logically inconclusive

body of findings, which can confer upon them only a more or less high probability. But this argument misses the point that the distinction between laws of universal form and laws of probabilistic form does not refer to the strength of the evidential support for the two kinds of statements, but to their form, which reflects the logical character of the claim they make. A law of universal form is basically a statement to the effect that in *all* cases where conditions of kind F are realized, conditions of kind G are realized as well; a law of probabilistic form asserts, basically, that under certain conditions, constituting the performance of a random experiment R, a certain kind of outcome will occur in a specified percentage of cases. No matter whether true or false, well supported or poorly supported, these two types of claims are of a logically different character, and it is on this difference that our distinction is based.

As we saw earlier, a law of the universal form 'Whenever F then G' is by no means a brief, telescoped equivalent of a report stating for each occurrence of F so far examined that it was associated with an occurrence of G. Rather, it implies assertions also for all unexamined cases of F, past as well as present and future; also, it implies counterfactual and hypothetical conditionals which concern, so to speak "possible occurrences" of F: and it is just this characteristic that gives such laws their explanatory power. Laws of probabilistic form have an analogous status. The law stating that the radioactive decay of radium[226] is a random process with an associated half-life of 1,620 years is plainly not tantamount to a report about decay rates that have been observed in certain samples of radium[226]. It concerns the decaying process of any body of radium[226]—past, present, or future; and it implies subjunctive and counterfactual conditionals, such as: if two particular lumps of radium[226] were to be combined into one, the decay rates would remain the same as if the lumps had remained separate. Again, it is this characteristic that gives probabilistic laws their predictive and their explanatory force.

The Inductive Character of Probabilistic Explanation

One of the simplest kinds of probabilistic explanation is illustrated by our earlier example of Jim's catching the measles. The general form of that explanatory argument may be stated thus:

$$p(O,R) \text{ is close to } 1$$
$$i \text{ is a case of } R$$
$$\overline{\hspace{4cm}} \text{ [makes highly probable]}$$
$$i \text{ is a case of } O$$

Now the high probability which, as indicated in brackets, the explanans confers upon the explanandum is surely not a statistical probability, for it characterizes a relation between sentences, not between (kinds of) events. . . . we might say that the probability in question represents the rational credibility of the explanandum, given the information provided by the explanans; and . . . , in so far as this notion can be construed as a probability, it represents a logical or inductive probability.

In some simple cases, there is a natural and obvious way of expressing that probability in numerical terms. In an argument of the kind just considered, if the numerical value of $p(O,R)$ is specified, then it is reasonable to say that the inductive probability that the explanans confers upon the explanandum has the same numerical value. The resulting probabilistic explanation has the form:

$$p(O,R) = r$$
$$i \text{ is a case of } R$$
$$\overline{\hspace{4cm}} \text{ [r]}$$
$$i \text{ is a case of } O$$

If the explanans is more complex, the determination of corresponding inductive probabilities for the explanandum raises difficult problems, which in part are still unsettled. But whether or not it is possible to assign definite numerical probabilities to all such explanations, the preceding considerations show that when an event is explained by reference to probabilistic laws, the explanans confers upon the explanandum only more or less strong inductive support. Thus, we may distinguish deductive-nomological from probabilistic explanations by saying that the former effect a deductive subsumption under laws of universal form, the latter an inductive subsumption under laws of probabilistic form.

It is sometimes said that precisely because of its inductive character, a probabilistic account does not explain the occurrence of an event, since the explanans does not logically preclude its nonoccurrence. But the important, steadily expanding role that probabilistic laws and theories play in science and its applications, makes it preferable to view accounts based on such principles as affording explanations as well, though of a less stringent kind than those of deductive-nomological form. Take, for example, the radioactive decay of a sample of one milligram of polonium[218]. Suppose that what is left of this initial amount after 3.05 minutes is found to have a mass that falls within the interval from .499 to .501 milligrams. This finding can be explained by the probabilistic law of decay for polonium[218]; for that law, in combination with the principles of mathematical probability, deductively implies that given the huge number of atoms in a milligram of polonium[218], the probability of the specified outcome is overwhelmingly large, so that in a particular case its occurrence may be expected with "practical certainty."

Or consider the explanation offered by the kinetic theory of gases for an empirically established generalization called Graham's law of diffusion. The law states that at fixed temperature and pressure, the rates at which different gases in a container escape, or diffuse, through a thin porous wall are inversely proportional to the square roots of their molecular weights; so that the amount of a gas that diffuses through the wall per second will be the greater, the lighter its molecules. The explanation rests on the consideration that the mass of a given gas that diffuses through the wall per second will be proportional to the average velocity of its molecules, and that Graham's law will therefore have been explained if it can be shown that the average molecular velocities of different pure gases are inversely proportional to the square roots of their molecular weights. To show this, the theory makes certain assumptions broadly to the effect that a gas consists of a very large number of molecules moving in random fashion at different speeds that frequently change as a result of collisions, and that this random behavior shows certain probabilistic uniformities—in particular, that among the molecules of a given gas at specified temperature and pressure, different velocities will occur with definite, and different, probabilities. These assumptions make it possible to compute the probabilistically expected values—or, as we might briefly say, the "most probable" values—that the average velocities of different gases will possess at equal temperatures and pressures.

These most probable average values, the theory shows, are indeed inversely proportional to the square roots of the molecular weights of the gases. But the actual diffusion rates, which are measured experimentally and are the subject of Graham's law, will depend on the actual values that the average velocities have in the large but finite swarms of molecules constituting the given bodies of gas. And the actual average values are related to the corresponding probabilistically estimated, or "most probable," values in a manner that is basically analogous to the relation between the proportion of aces occurring in a large but finite series of tossings of a given die and the corresponding probability of rolling an ace with that die. From the theoretically derived conclusion concerning the probabilistic estimates, it follows only that in view of the very large number of molecules involved, it is overwhelmingly *probable* that at any given time the actual average speeds will have values very close to their probability estimates and that, therefore, it is *practically certain* that they will be, like the latter, inversely proportional to the square roots of their molecular masses, thus satisfying Graham's law.[7]

It seems reasonable to say that this account affords an explanation, even though "only" with very high associated probability, of why gases display the uniformity expressed by Graham's law; and in physical texts and treatises, theoretical accounts of this probabilistic kind are indeed very widely referred to as explanations.

NOTES

1. From Holton and Roller, *Foundations of Modern Physical Science*, p. 160.
2. The derivation of the laws of reflection for the curved surfaces referred to in this example and in the next one is simply and lucidly set forth in Chap. 17 of Morris Kline, *Mathematics and the Physical World* (New York: Thomas Y. Crowell Company, 1959).
3. In his essay, "The Problem of Counterfactual Conditionals," reprinted as the first chapter of his book, *Fact, Fiction, and Forecast*, 2nd ed. (Indianapolis: The Bobbs-Merrill Co., Inc. 1965). This work raises fascinating basic problems concerning laws, counterfactual statements, and inductive reasoning, and examines them from an advanced analytic point of view.
4. For a fuller analysis of the concept of law, and for further bibliographic references, see E. Nagel, *The Structure of Science* (New York: Harcourt, Brace & World, Inc., 1961), Chap. 4.
5. Further details on the concept of statistical probability and on the limit-definition and its shortcomings will be found in E. Nagel's monograph, *Principles of the Theory of Probability* (Chicago: University of Chicago Press, 1939). Our version of the statistical interpretation follows that given by H. Cramer on pp. 148–49 of his book, *Mathematical Methods of Statistics* (Princeton: Princeton University Press, 1946).
6. On this subject, see R. D. Luce and H. Raiffa, *Games and Decisions* (New York: John Wiley & Sons, Inc., 1957).
7. The "average" velocities here referred to are technically defined as root-mean-square velocities. Their values do not differ very much from those of average velocities in the usual sense of the arithmetic mean. A succinct outline of the theoretical explanation of Graham's law can be found in Chapter 25 of Holton and Roller, *Foundations of Modern Physical Science*. The distinction, not explicitly mentioned in that presentation, between the average value of a quantity for some finite number of cases and the probabilistically estimated or expected value of that quantity is briefly discussed in Chapter 6 (especially section 4) of R. P. Feynman, R. B. Leighton, and M. Sands, *The Feynman Lectures on Physics* (Reading, Mass.: Addison-Wesley Publishing Co., 1963).

How to Defend Society Against Science

PAUL FEYERABEND

Paul Feyerabend (1924–1994) was a professor of philosophy at the University of California at Berkeley. His publications include *Against Method* and *Knowledge Without Foundation*.

—◆—

Fairytales

I want to defend society and its inhabitants from all ideologies, science included. All ideologies must be seen in perspective. One must not take them too seriously. One must read them like fairytales which have lots of interesting things to say but which also contain wicked lies, or like ethical prescriptions which may be useful rules of thumb but which are deadly when followed to the letter.

Now—is this not a strange and ridiculous attitude? Science, surely, was always in the forefront of the fight against authoritarianism and superstition. It is to science that we owe our increased intellectual freedom vis-à-vis religious beliefs; it is to science that we owe the liberation of mankind from ancient and rigid forms of thought. Today these forms of thought are nothing but bad dreams—and this we learned from science. Science and enlightenment are one and the same thing—even the most radical critics of society believe this. Kropotkin wants to overthrow all traditional institutions and forms of belief, with the exception of science. Ibsen criticises the most intimate ramifications of nineteenth century bourgeois ideology, but he leaves science untouched. Levi-Strauss has made us realise that Western Thought is not the lonely peak of human achievement it was once believed to be, but he excludes science from his relativization of ideologies. Marx and Engels were convinced that science would aid the workers in their quest for mental and social liberation. Are all these people deceived? Are they all mistaken about the role of science? Are they all the victims of a chimaera?

To these questions my answer is a firm *Yes and No*. Now, let me explain my answer.

My explanation consists of two parts, one more general, one more specific.

The general explanation is simple. Any ideology that breaks the hold a comprehensive system of thought has on the minds of men contributes to the liberation of man. Any ideology that makes man question inherited beliefs is an aid to enlightenment. A truth that reigns without checks and balances is a tyrant who must be overthrown and any falsehood that can aid us in the overthrow of this tyrant is to be welcomed. It follows that seventeenth and eighteenth century science indeed *was* an instrument of liberation and enlightenment. It does not follow that science is bound to *remain* such an instrument. There is nothing inherent in science or in any other ideology that makes it *essentially* liberating. Ideologies can deteriorate and become stupid religions. Look at Marxism. And that the science of today is very different from the science of 1650 is evident at the most superficial glance.

For example, consider the role science now plays in education. Scientific "facts" are taught at a very early age and in the very same manner in which religious "facts" were taught only a century age. There is no attempt to waken the critical abilities of the pupil so that he may be able to see things in perspective. At the universities the situation is even worse, for indoctrination is here carried out in a much more systematic manner. Criticism is not entirely absent. Society, for example, and its institutions, are criticised most severely and often most unfairly and this already at the elementary school level. But science is excepted from the criticism. In society at large the judgement of bishops and cardinals was accepted not too long ago. The move towards "demythologization," example, is largely motivated by the wish to avoid any clash between Christianity and scientific ideas. If such a clash occurs, then science is certainly right and Christianity wrong. Pursue this investigation further and you will see that science has now become as oppressive as the ideologies it had once to fight. Do not be misled by the fact that today hardly anyone gets killed for joining a scientific heresy. This has nothing to do with science. It has something to do with the general quality of our civilization. Heretics in science are still made to suffer from the *most severe* sanctions this relatively tolerant civilization has to offer.

But—is this description not utterly unfair? Have I not presented the matter in a very distorted light by using tendentious and distorting terminology? Must we not describe the situation in a very different way? I have said that science has become rigid, that it has ceased to be an instrument of *change* and *liberation* without adding that it has found the *truth*, or a large part thereof. Considering this additional fact we realise, so the objection goes, that the rigidity of science is not due to human willfulness. It lies in the nature of things. For once we have discovered the truth—what else can we do but follow it?

This trite reply is anything but original. It is used whenever an ideology wants to reinforce the faith of its followers. "Truth" is such a nicely neutral word. Nobody would deny that it is commendable to speak the truth and wicked to tell lies. Nobody would deny that—and yet nobody knows what such an attitude amounts to. So it is easy to twist matters and to change allegiance to truth in one's everyday affairs into allegiance to the Truth of ideology which is nothing but the dogmatic defence of that ideology. And it is of course *not* true we *have* to follow the truth. Human life is guided by many ideas. Truth is one of them. Freedom and mental independence are others. If Truth, as conceived by some ideologists, conflicts with freedom then we have a *choice*. We may abandon freedom. But we may also abandon Truth. (Alternatively, we may adopt a more sophisticated idea of truth that no longer contradicts freedom; that was Hegel's solution.) My criticism of modern science is that it inhibits freedom of thought. If the reason is that it has found the truth and now follows it then I would say that there are better things than first finding, and then following such a monster.

This finishes the general part of my explanation.

There exists a more specific argument to defend the exceptional position science has in society today. Put in a nutshell the argument says (1) that science has finally found the correct *method* for achieving results and (2) that there are many *results* to prove the excellence of the method. The argument is mistaken—but most attempts to show this lead into a dead end. Methodology has by now become so crowded with empty sophistication that it is extremely difficult to perceive the simple errors at the basis. It is like fighting the hydra—cut off one ugly head, and eight formalizations take its place. In this situation the only answer is superficiality: when sophistication loses content then the only way of keeping in touch with reality is to be crude and superficial. This is what I intend to be.

Against Method

There is a method, says part (1) of the argument. What is it? How does it work?

One answer which is no longer as popular as it used to be is that science works by collecting facts and inferring theories from them. The answer is unsatisfactory as theories never *follow* from facts in the strict logical sense. To say that they may yet be *supported* by facts assumes a notion of support that (a) does not show this defect and is (b) sufficiently sophisticated to permit us to say to what extent, say, the theory of relativity is supported by the facts. No such notion exists today nor is it likely that it will ever be found (one of the problems is that we need a notion of support in which grey ravens can be said to support "All Ravens are Black"). This was realised by conventionalists and transcendental idealists who pointed out that theories *shape* and *order* facts and can therefore be retained come what may. They can be retained because the human mind either consciously or unconsciously carried out its ordering function. The trouble with these views is that they assume for the mind what they want to explain for the world, viz. that it works in a regular fashion. There is only one view which overcomes all these difficulties. It was invented twice in the nineteenth century, by Mill, in his immortal essay *On Liberty*, and by some Darwinists who extended Darwinism to the battle of ideas. This view takes the bull by the horns: theories cannot be justified and their excellence cannot be shown without reference to other theories. We may explain the *success* of a theory by reference to a more comprehensive theory (we explain the success of Newton's theory by using the general theory of relativity); and we may explain our *preference* for it by comparing it with other theories. Such a comparison does not establish the intrinsic excellence of the theory we have chosen. As a matter of fact, the theory we have chosen may be pretty lousy. It may contain contradictions, it may conflict with well-known facts, it may be cumbersome, unclear, ad hoc in decisive places and so on. But it may still be better than any other theory that is available at the time. It may in fact be the best lousy theory there is. Nor are the standards of judgement chosen in an absolute manner. Our sophistication increases with every choice we make, and so do our standards. Standards compete just as theories compete and we choose the standards most appropriate to the historical situation in which the choice occurs. The rejected alternatives (theories; standards; "facts") are not eliminated. They serve as correctives (after all, we may have made the wrong choice) and they also explain the content of the preferred views (we understand relativity better when we understand the structure of its competitors; we know the full meaning of freedom only when we have an idea of life in a totalitarian state, of its advantages—and there are many advantages—as well as of its disadvantages). Knowledge so conceived is an ocean of alternatives channelled and subdivided by an ocean of standards. It forces our mind to make imaginative choices and thus makes it grow. It makes our mind capable of choosing, imagining, criticising.

Today this view is often connected with the name of Karl Popper. But there are some very decisive differences between Popper and Mill. To start with, Popper developed his view to solve a special problem of epistemology—he wanted to solve "Hume's problem." Mill, on the other hand, is interested in conditions favourable to human growth. His epistemology is the result of a certain theory of man, and not the other way around. Also Popper, being influenced by the Vienna Circle, improves on the logical form of a theory before discussing it while Mill uses every theory in the form in which it occurs in science. Thirdly, Popper's standards of comparison are rigid and fixed while Mill's standards are permitted to change with the historical situation. Finally, Popper's standards eliminate competitors once and

for all: theories that are either not falsifiable, or falsifiable and falsified have no place in science. Popper's criteria are clear, unambiguous, precisely formulated; Mill's criteria are not. This would be an advantage if science itself were clear, unambiguous, and precisely formulated. Fortunately, it is not.

To start with, no new and revolutionary scientific theory is ever formulated in a manner that permits us to say under what circumstances we must regard it as endangered: many revolutionary theories are unfalsifiable. Falsifiable versions do exist, but they are hardly ever in agreement with accepted basic statements: every moderately interesting theory is falsified. Moreover, theories have formal flaws, many of them contain contradictions, ad hoc adjustments, and so on and so forth. Applied resolutely, Popperian criteria would eliminate science without replacing it by anything comparable. They are useless as an aid to science.

In the past decade this has been realised by various thinkers, Kuhn and Lakatos among them. Kuhn's ideas are interesting but, alas, they are much too vague to give rise to anything but lots of hot air. If you don't believe me, look at the literature. Never before has the literature on the philosophy of science been invaded by so many creeps and incompetents. Kuhn encourages people who have no idea why a stone falls to the ground to talk with assurance about scientific method. Now I have no objection to incompetence but I do object when incompetence is accompanied by boredom and self-righteousness. And this is exactly what happens. We do not get interesting false ideas, we get boring ideas or words connected with no ideas as all. Secondly, wherever one tries to make Kuhn's ideas more definite one finds that they are *false*. Was there ever a period of normal science in the history of thought? No—and I challenge anyone to prove the contrary.

Lakatos is immeasurably more sophisticated than Kuhn. Instead of theories he considers research programmes which are sequences of theories connected by methods of modification, so called heuristics. Each theory in the sequence may be full of faults. It may be beset by anomalies, contradictions, ambiguities. What counts is not the shape of the single theories, but the tendency exhibited by the sequence. We judge historical developments, achievements over a period of time, rather than the situation at a particular time. History and methodology are combined into a single enterprise. A research programme is said to progress if the sequence of theories leads to novel predictions. It is said to degenerate if it is reduced to absorbing facts that have been discovered without its help. A decisive feature of Lakatos's methodology is that such evaluations are no longer tied to methodological rules which tell the scientist to either retain or to abandon a research programme. Scientists may stick to a degenerating programme, they may even succeed in making the programme overtake its rivals and they therefore proceed rationally with whatever they are doing (provided they continue calling degenerating programmes degenerating and progressive programmes progressive). This means that Lakatos offers *words* which *sound* like the elements of a methodology; he does not offer a methodology. This is no method according to the most advanced and sophisticated methodology in existence today. This finishes my reply to part (1) of the specific argument.

Against Results

According to part (2), science deserves a special position because it has produced *results*. This is an argument only if it can be taken for granted that nothing else has ever produced results. Now it may be admitted that almost everyone who discusses the matter makes such an assumption. It may also be admitted that it is not easy to show that the assumption is false. Forms of life different from science have either disappeared or have degenerated to an extent that makes a fair comparison impossible. Still, the situation is not as hopeless as it was only a decade ago. We have become acquainted with methods of medical diagnosis and therapy which are effective (and perhaps even more effective then the corresponding parts of Western medicine) and which are yet based on an ideology that is radically different from the ideology of Western science. We have learned that there are phenomena such as telepathy and telekinesis which are obliterated by a scientific approach and which could be used to do research in an entirely novel way (earlier thinkers such as Agrippa of Nettesheim, John Dee, and even Bacon were aware of these phenomena). And then—is it not the case that the Church saved souls while science often does the very opposite? Of course, nobody now believes in the ontology that underlies this judgement. Why? Because of ideologi-cal pressures identical with those which today make us listen to science to the exclusion of everything else. It is also true that phenomena such as telekinesis and acupuncture may eventually be absorbed into the body of science and may therefore be called "scientific." But note that this happens only *after* a long period of resistance during which a science *not yet* containing the phenomena wants to get the upper hand over forms of life that contain them. And this leads to a further objection against part (2) of the specific argument. The fact that science has results counts in its favour only if these results were achieved by science alone, and without any outside help. A look at history shows that science hardly ever gets its results in this way. When Copernicus introduced a new view of the universe, he did not consult *scientific* predecessors, he consulted a crazy Pythagorean such as Philolaos. He adopted his ideas and he maintained them in the face of all sound rules of scientific method. Mechanics and optics owe a lot to artisans, medicine to midwives and witches. And in our own day we have seen how the interference of the state can advance science: when the Chinese Communists refused to be intimidated by the judgement of experts and ordered traditional medicine back into universities and hospitals there was an outcry all over the world that science would now be ruined in China. The very opposite occurred: Chinese science advanced and Western science learned from it. Wherever we look we see that great scientific advances are due to outside interference which is made to prevail in the face of the most basic and most "rational" methodological rules. The lesson is plain: there does not exist a single argument that could be used to support the exceptional role which science today plays in society. Science has done many things, but so have other ideologies. Science often proceeds systematically, but so do other ideologies (just consult the records of the many doctrinal debates that took place in the Church) and, besides, there are no overriding rules which are adhered to under any circumstances; there is no "scientific methodology" that can be used to separate science from the rest. *Science is just one of the many ideologies that propel society and it should be treated as such* (this statement applies even to the most progressive and most dialectical sections of science). What consequences can we draw from this result?

The most important consequence is that there must be a *formal separation between state and science* just as there is now a formal separation between state and church. Science may influence society but only to the extent to which any political or other pressure group is permitted to influence society. Scientists may be consulted on important projects but the final judgement must be left to the democratically elected consulting bodies. These bodies will consist mainly of laymen. Will the laymen be able to come to a correct judgement? Most certainly, for the competence, the complications and the successes of science are vastly exaggerated. One of the most exhilarating experiences is to see how a lawyer, who is a layman, can find holes in the testimony, the technical testimony of the most advanced expert and thus prepare the jury for its verdict. Science is not a closed book that is understood only after years of training. It is an intellectual discipline that can be examined and criticised by anyone who is interested and that looks difficult and profound only because of a systematic campaign of obfuscation carried out by many scientists (though, I am happy to say, not by all). Organs of the state should never hesitate to reject the judgement of scientists when they have reason for doing so. Such rejection will educate the general public, will make it more confident and it may even lead to improvement. Considering the sizeable chauvinism of the scientific establishment we can say: the more Lysenko affairs the better (it is not the *interference* of the state that is objectionable in the case of Lysenko, but the *totalitarian* interference which kills the opponent rather than just neglecting his advice). Three cheers to the fundamentalists in California who succeeded in having a dogmatic formulation of the theory of evolution removed from the text books and an account of Genesis included (but I know that they would become as chauvinistic and totalitarian as scientists are today when given the chance to run society all by themselves. Ideologies are marvellous when used in the company of other ideologies. They become boring and doctrinaire as soon as their merits lead to the removal of their opponents). The most important change, however, will have to occur in the field of *education*.

Education and Myth

The purpose of education, so one would think, is to introduce the young into life, and that means: into the *society* where they are born and into the *physical universe* that surrounds the society. The method of education often consists in the teaching of some *basic myth*. The myth is available in various versions. More advanced versions may be taught by initiation rites which firmly implant them into the mind. Knowing the myth the grown-up can explain almost everything (or else he can turn to experts for more detailed information). He is the master of Nature and of Society. He understands them both and he knows how to interact with them. However, *he is not the master of the myth that guides his understanding.*

Such further mastery was aimed at, and was partly achieved, by the Pre-Socratics. The Pre-Socratics not only tried to understand the *world.* They also tried to understand, and thus to become the masters of, the *means of understanding the world.* Instead of being content with a single myth they developed many and so diminished the power which a well-told story has over the minds of men. The Sophists introduced still further methods for reducing the debilitating effect of interesting, coherent, "empirically adequate" etc. etc. tales. The achievements of these thinkers were not appreciated and they certainly are not understood today. When teaching a myth we want to increase the chance that it will be understood (i.e. no puzzlement about any feature of the myth), believed, *and accepted.* This does not do any harm when the myth is counterbalanced by other myths: even the most dedicated (i.e. totalitarian) instructor in a certain version of Christianity cannot prevent his pupils from getting in touch with Buddhists, Jews and other disreputable people. It is very different in the case of science, or of rationalism where the field is almost completely dominated by the believers. In this case it is of paramount importance to strengthen the minds of the young and "strengthening the minds of the young" means strengthening them *against* any easy acceptance of comprehensive views. What we need here is an education that makes people *contrary, counter-suggestive without* making them incapable of devoting themselves to the elaboration of any single view. How can this aim be achieved?

It can be achieved by protecting the tremendous imagination which children possess and by developing to the full the spirit of contradiction that exists in them. On the whole children are much more intelligent than their teachers. They succumb, and give up their intelligence because they are bullied, or because their teachers get the better of them by emotional means. Children can learn, understand, and keep separate two to three different languages ("children" and by this I mean 3 to 5 year olds, NOT eight years olds who were experimented upon quite recently and did not come out too well; why? because they were already loused up by incompetent teaching at an earlier age). Of course, the languages must be introduced in a more interesting way than is usually done. There are marvellous writers in all languages who have told marvellous stories—let us begin our language teaching with *them* and not with "der Hund hat einen Schwanz" and similar inanities. Using stories we may of course also introduce "scientific" accounts, say, of the origin of the world and thus make the children acquainted with science as well. But science must not be given any special position except for pointing out that there are lots of people who believe in it. Later on the stories which have been told will be supplemented with "reasons" where by reasons I mean further accounts of the kind found in the tradition to which the story belongs. And, of course, there will also be contrary reasons. Both reasons and contrary reasons will be told by the experts in the fields and so the young generation becomes acquainted with all kinds of sermons and all types of wayfarers. It becomes acquainted with them, it becomes acquainted with their stories and every individual can make up his mind which way to go. By now everyone knows that you can earn a lot of money and respect and perhaps even a Nobel Price by becoming a scientist, so, many will become scientists. They will *become* scientists *without having been taken in by the ideology of science,* they will *be* scientists *because they have made a free choice.* But has not much time been wasted on unscientific subjects and will this not detract from their competence once they have become scientists? Not at all! The progress of science, of good science, depends on novel ideas and on intellectual freedom: science has very often been advanced by outsiders (remember that Bohr and Einstein regarded themselves as outsiders). Will not many people make the wrong choice and end up in a dead end? Well, that depends on what you mean by a "dead end." Most scientists today are devoid of ideas, full of fear, in-

tent on producing some paltry result so that they can add to the flood of inane papers that now constitutes "scientific progress" in many areas. And, besides, what is more important? To lead a life which one has chosen with open eyes, or to spend one's time in the nervous attempt of avoiding what some not so intelligent people call "dead ends"? Will not the number of scientists decrease so that in the end there is nobody to run our precious laboratories? I do not think so. Given a choice many people may choose science, for a science that is run by free agents looks much more attractive than the science of today which is run by slaves, slaves of institutions and slaves of "reason." And if there is a temporary shortage of scientists the situation may always be remedied by various kinds of incentives. Of course, scientists will not play any predominant role in the society I envisage. They will be more than balanced by magicians, or priests, or astrologers. Such a situation is unbearable for many people, old and young, right and left. Almost all of you have the firm belief that at least *some* kind of truth has been found, that it must be preserved, and that the method of teaching I advocate and the form of society I defend will dilute it and make it finally disappear. You have this firm belief; many of you may even have reasons. *But what you have to consider is that the absence of good contrary reasons is due to a historical accident;* it does *not* lie in the nature of things. Build up the kind of society I recommended and the views you now despise (without knowing them, to be sure) will return in such splendour that you will have to work hard to maintain your own position and will perhaps be entirely unable to do so. You do not believe me? Then look at history. Scientific astronomy was firmly founded on Ptolemy and Aristotle, two of the greatest minds in the history of Western Thought. Who upset their well-argued, empirically adequate and precisely formulated system? Philolaos the mad and antediluvian Pythagorean. How was it that Philolaos could stage a comeback; Because he found an able defender: Copernicus. Of course, you may follow your intuitions as I am following mine. But remember that your intuitions are the result of your "scientific" training where by science I also mean the science of Karl Marx. My training, or, rather, my non-training, is that of a journalist who is interested in strange and bizarre events. Finally, is it not utterly irresponsible, in the present world situation, with millions of people starving, others enslaved, downtrodden, in abject misery of body and mind, to think luxurious thoughts such as these? Is not freedom of choice a luxury under such circumstances; Is not the flippancy and the humour I want to see combined with the freedom of choice a luxury under such circumstances? Must we not give up all self-indulgence and *act*? Join together, and *act*? That is the most important objection which today is raised against an approach such as the one recommended by me. It has tremendous appeal, it has the appeal of unselfish dedication. Unselfish dedication—to what? Let us see!

We are supposed to give up our selfish inclinations and dedicate ourselves to the liberation of the oppressed. And selfish inclinations are what? They are our wish for maximum liberty of thought in the society in which we live *now,* maximum liberty not only of an abstract kind, but expressed in appropriate institutions and methods of teaching. This wish for concrete intellectual and physical liberty in our own surroundings is to be put aside, for the time being. This assumes, first, that we do not need this liberty for our task. It assumes that we can carry out our task with a mind that is firmly closed to some alternatives. It assumes that the correct way of liberating others *has already been found* and that all that is needed is to carry it out. I am sorry, I cannot accept such doctrinaire self-assurance in such extremely important matters. Does

this mean that we cannot act at all? It does not. But it means that *while acting we have to try to realise as much of the freedom I have recommended so that our actions may be corrected in the light of the ideas we get while increasing our freedom.* This will slow us down, no doubt, but are we supposed to charge ahead simply because some people tell us that they have found an explanation for all the misery and an excellent way out of it? Also we want to liberate people not to make them succumb to a new kind of slavery, *but to make them realise their own wishes,* however different these wishes may be from our own. Self-righteous and narrow-minded liberators cannot do this. As a rule they soon impose a slavery that is worse, because more systematic, than the very sloppy slavery they have removed. And as regards humour and flippancy the answer should be obvious. Why would anyone want to liberate anyone else? Surely not because of some *abstract* advantage of liberty but because liberty is the best way to free development *and thus to happiness.* We want to liberate people *so that they can smile.* Shall we be able to do this if we ourselves have forgotten how to smile and are frowning on those who still remember? Shall we then not spread another disease, comparable to the one we want to remove, the disease of puritanical self-righteousness? Do not object that dedication and humour do not go together—Socrates is an excellent example to the contrary. *The hardest task needs the lightest hand or else its completion will not lead to freedom but to a tyranny much worse than the one it replaces.*

Knowledge, Human Interests, and Objectivity in Feminist Epistemology

ELIZABETH ANDERSON

Apparatchik (impatiently): How much is 2 + 2?
Mathematician (cautiously): How much do you want it to be?

—Soviet joke

1. Making Room for Values in Feminist Epistemology

This joke from the former Soviet Union aptly captures the dominant view about what happens when social, political, and moral interests shape inquiry: the result is totalitarian thought control, in which those in power force beliefs to conform to their demands and wishes rather than to the facts. No wonder, then, that attempts by feminist epistemologists to legitimate important roles for social and moral values in academic inquiry have been greeted with such alarm in the recent wars over "political correctness." This paper aims to defuse the hysteria over value-laden inquiry by showing how it is based on a misapprehension of the arguments of the most careful advocates of such inquiry, an impoverished understanding of the goals of science, a mistaken model of the interaction of normative and evidential considerations in science, and a singular inattention to the empirical facts about how responsible inquirers go about their business.

Yet, the task of defending value-laden inquiry is a formidable one. For its most careful recent advocates in feminist epistemology have advanced an ambitious agenda. Feminists have long argued that scientific practice[1] should promote women's inter-

ests by removing discriminatory barriers that prevent women from participating in research, by developing technologies that empower women (such as safe, inexpensive birth control), and by paying due regard to women's actual achievements in science and other endeavors. Many who attack the idea of value-laden inquiry are willing to accept such political influences on the conduct of inquiry, because such influences are not thought to touch what they see as the core of scientific integrity: the methods and standards of justification for theoretical claims. These influences affect the context of discovery (where the choice of subjects of investigation and of colleagues is open to influence by the interests of the inquirer or of those who fund the research) or the context of practical application (which, involving action, is always subject to moral scrutiny), not the context of justification. But feminist epistemologists argue that feminist values may properly influence scientific method and theory choice. This ambition challenges the core commitments of many scientists and defenders of the ideal of value-neutral science.

Helen Longino has developed the most careful and closely reasoned recent arguments in favor of using "contexual values"—political, moral, and other values taken from the social context in which science is practiced—to guide scientific method and theory choice.[2] Longino observes that hypotheses are logically underdetermined by the data cited in their support. A particular fact provides evidential support for a given hypothesis only in conjunction with other background assumptions. Thus, two inquirers who accept different background assump-

From *Philosophical Topics* Vol. 23, No. 2. Copyright © 1995 by Elizabeth Anderson. Reprinted by permission of the author.

Note from the author: I would like to thank Sally Haslanger, Hugh Lacey, and the faculty and students at Johns Hopkins University and the University of Toronto for helpful comments and criticisms of the ideas presented in this paper.

tions may take the same fact as evidence for conflicting hypotheses. The failure to observe stellar parallax in the seventeenth century was taken as evidence that the earth did not move around the sun by those who assumed that the stars were not far away. But this same fact was taken as evidence that the stars were very far away by those who believed that the earth did move around the sun. In some cases empirical support, independent of the hypothesis being investigated, can be offered for the background assumptions—although only in conjunction with yet further background assumptions. But in many other cases independent evidence for the background assumptions is not available. Furthermore, as we trace back the sources of support for the interlocking background assumptions of a theory, we find that they do not rest on factual claims alone.

This fact is most dramatically revealed in cases where the available data in conjunction with the shared background assumptions of rival researchers are insufficient to justify the choice of one theory or research program over another. In these cases, dissenting scientists often criticize the background assumptions of their rivals and support their own contested background assumptions by appealing to conceptual, epistemological, methodological, or metaphysical considerations that often rest upon contextually specific norms of inquiry.[3] Thus, Einstein initially appealed to thought experiments grounded in empiricist epistemological norms to argue for the superiority of the theory of relativity over classical Newtonian mechanics. Watson appealed to the methodological norm that we ought to count as evidence only interpersonally accessible observations to argue for the superiority of behaviorism over introspectionist psychology. Functionalist explanation in sociology was discredited partly because it was incompatible with the nonteleological metaphysical framework of modern science: for those who accept this framework, merely pointing out that a social phenomenon promotes social stability does not provide a satisfactory explanation for why it exists. Marginal utility theory in economics triumphed over classical economic theory partly because its hypotheses could be modeled using calculus, which made many economic problems mathematically tractable for the first time. In these cases, normative considerations about the conduct of in-

quiry, normative constraints on the form of acceptable data and of satisfactory explanations, and normative desiderata of calculative ease proved to be powerful arguments for theory choice. Where the data run out, values legitimately step in to take up the "slack" between observation and theory.[4]

These arguments show that values embedded in background assumptions help determine what counts as evidence and an explanation, how the evidence should be represented, and what direction the evidence points to. So values play a legitimate role in guiding science that is not reducible to the prescription to simply follow where the facts lead. But this is not enough to show that any sort of value may permissibly guide science. A prominent branch of mainstream philosophy of science accepts the argument that underdetermination leaves room for values to play a legitimate role in theory choice, but it insists that the admissible values must be epistemic or cognitive, rather than, say, moral, political, or economic. Acceptable values are "internal" to science; unacceptable ones are "contextual," or borrowed from the social context in which science is practiced. Thus, Kuhn argues that the values that properly guide theory choice are accuracy, consistency, fruitfulness, breadth of scope, and simplicity.[5] These cognitive values don't have any obvious moral or political content.

A crucial question for feminist epistemologists, then, is whether the sharp division between epistemic and moral or political values is tenable. Longino argues that this division breaks down once we look beyond the content of the standards for theory choice and focus attention on the grounds for supporting them.[6] Here we see that epistemic, metaphysical, and practical interests may all help support a given standard of theory choice. Empirical adequacy is important not just on epistemic grounds but because an empirically inadequate theory cannot satisfy our practical interests in predicting and controlling phenomena.[7] What's more, the content of our practical interests helps determine what dimensions of empirical adequacy are demanded of science. This is not surprising if we keep in mind that theories do more than represent facts—they organize them for our use. The interest in control puts a premium on theories that accurately track in quantitative terms the behavior of objects in experimental and technological contexts, where background "interfering" conditions are tightly constrained and objects are manipulated by one or very few factors under the control of the knower. The Aristotelian interest in leading a life devoted to contemplating the natures of things (rather than asserting mastery over them) put a premium on accurately accounting for the qualitative characters of objects in unmanipulated contexts, where things can display their "true natures."[8] The interest in self-understanding and successful communication puts a premium on theories that accurately account for subjects' behavior in terms that the subjects themselves can recognize, affirm, and act on.[9]

Consider, in this light, two of the theoretical virtues that Longino identifies as among those that may properly guide theory choice for feminists.[10] One is "ontological heterogeneity." This is a preference for "splitting" over "lumping"—for emphasizing the qualitative diversity and individuality of subjects of study and the distinctions among properties commonly classified together. One purely cognitive motivation for this is to seek fine-grained descriptive accuracy. Barbara McClintock's revolutionary discovery of genetic transposition, which was based on close observation of the cytological differences among individual seeds on corn cobs, demonstrates that such a focus can yield huge theoretical advances.[11] But there are political reasons for emphasizing heterogeneity as well. Ideologies that purport to scientifically demonstrate the inevitability of male dominance often appeal to theories that assimilate disparate phenomena under vague, global classifications. Feminist primatologist Linda Fedigan showed that the common idea that male primates "dominate" females is ill-conceived, by pointing out that the numerous distinct measures of individual dominance (social rank, aggressiveness, winning conflicts, strength, initiating group movement, directing group movement, suppressing conflicts among others, mobilizing cooperation) do not correlate, shift over time and context, and in some cases apply only to within-sex rather than between-sex interactions. There is no global, unitary sense of "dominance" in which the generalization "male primates dominate females" is true.[12] Another political reason for emphasizing heterogeneity is to reinforce the self-critical practices of feminism itself. Feminist theories that focus on gen-

eralizations about "women" all too often have ignored important differences among women. In the U.S. context, this has meant that characteristics common among white, middle-class, heterosexual women have been represented as the norm for women generally, such that other women either are invisible or appear deviant within the theory.[13] What are we to make of the idea that there is something about "women's" cognitive styles that attracts them more to the life sciences then to the physical sciences or mathematics, once we consider that black women scientists are twice as likely as white women scientists to choose a mathematical specialty and only half as likely to choose the life sciences?[14] Emphasizing heterogeneity enables feminist theorists to represent diversity among women and humans generally as a potential resource rather than as deviance.

Both cognitive and political reasons can also be offered in support of a second feminist theoretical virtue: "complexity of relationship." This value supports a preference for dynamic, interactive causal models that emphasize multiple causes of phenomena over single-factor linear or reductionist models. For some theorists, this preference is motivated by a metaphysical conviction that the world is complex, multifaceted, and messy. A cognitive interest in capturing the real causal structure of the world would then concur with this preference. But feminist political interests lend other support to the value of complexity. The preference for complexity encourages historians and social theorists to represent an individual's social power as a feature of context or role supported by others rather than as an individual trait. This representation enables the recognition and appreciation of women's activities, by making "visible the role of private, domestic work in maintaining the activity and institutions of the 'public' sphere.[15] It also opens up opportunities for activists to imagine strategies of resistance to oppression that involve changing the social structure rather than attacking individuals.

Feminists are not the only ones to justify methodological and theoretical standards by appeal to moral or political considerations. Functional explanation in sociology was discredited not just because it didn't offer a satisfactory scheme of explanation but because, by representing phenomena as functional for the social order, it underplayed the significance of social conflict and discouraged criticism of the status quo. A humanist interest in acknowledging and promoting the dignity and freedom of persons has influenced many social scientists. An emerging methodological norm among interpretive anthropologists is to show one's research to the subjects of study and respond to their criticisms. This norm serves the moral interest of respecting the dignity of those one studies. Chomsky argued for the superiority of cognitive psychology over behaviorism on the ground that the behaviorist explanatory framework left no room for representing human creativity in language use, a core ground of our own self-understandings as dignified, free agents.[16] Others have launched a similar critique of behaviorist *methods*, arguing that behaviorism's experimental framework is coercive and demeaning, depriving people of opportunities to express their potentialities for taking initiatives and forging creative solutions to problems.[17]

With all of these moral and political interests shaping methodology and standards of theory choice in so many fields and schools of thought, is there any way to salvage some conception of objectivity in science? Longino argues that there is. In the first place, empirical adequacy is not an optional standard for any research program. Although, as we have seen, moral and political interests may help delineate the domains of evidence which a theory must account for or at least be consistent with, every empirical theory is accountable to some body of evidence.[18] In the second place, all scientists are accountable to other scientists. The evidence to which they appeal must be interpersonally accessible. The methodological standards and criteria of theory choice to which they appeal must be justified to and accepted by others. The entire research community must be open to criticism by others, provide opportunities for such criticism, and respond to it by appropriately modifying its methods, claims, and background assumptions when they fall short of commonly recognized standards. Furthermore, the research community must recognize the equality of inquirers, which is to say that it may not censor or disregard what others say simply on account of their social identity or relative lack of social power.[19] These social aspects of scientific practice—the ways in which it makes each inquirer accountable to oth-

ers' observations and criticism—are what secure the objectivity of science. They are what prevent inquiry from degenerating into a free play of idiosyncratic preference and subjective bias.[20]

2. The Critique of Politically Value-Laden Science

Longino's defense of morally and politically value-laden inquiry strikes at the core self-understandings of many practicing scientists and at the core legitimation stories told about modern science to insulate it from political criticism. Thus it is no surprise that scientists and traditional epistemologists have subjected her work to pointed attacks. Susan Haack's critiques of Longino articulate better than any other the core assumptions behind the ideal of value-neutral inquiry and provide the sharpest response yet to Longino's proposals.[21]

Haack, like other defenders of value-neutral inquiry, sees many great dangers in permitting moral and political values to shape the criteria of theory choice in inquiry. Such a move would allow inquiry to be infected by wishful thinking: people would feel entitled to infer from the fact that they wanted something to be true that it was actually true.[22] It would invite dogmatism: people would feel entitled to attack as pernicious any reasoning or evidence that did not reach a foregone conclusion supported by their political preferences.[23] It would provide a license for dishonest or less than candid research: researchers would be allowed to focus only on evidence that supports "politically correct" conclusions. The result would be the politicization of research along the lines of Nazi science, Lysenkoism, or *1984*, in which disinterested, honest researchers would be hounded out of the academy, which would henceforth be staffed by political propagandists.[24]

Why does Haack think these are the implications of introducing moral and political values into the context of justification? Behind her alarm lies a particular model of the interaction of evidential and political considerations in shaping inquiry. The model supposes that these considerations necessarily *compete* for control of inquiry. Either theory choice is guided by the facts, by observation and evidence, *or* it is guided by moral values and social influences, construed as wishes, desires, or social-political demands. To the extent that moral values and social influences shape theory choice, they *displace* attention to evidence and valid reasoning and hence *interfere* with the discovery of truth. This model depends upon a particular conception of the goals of theoretical inquiry and the nature of the considerations that can justify theory choice. The basic idea is to limit the goals of theory to the articulation of truths, and then to argue that value judgments have no evidential bearing on whether any claim is true. Therefore, value judgments cannot figure in the justification of theoretical claims or in the criteria for theory choice. It is natural to conclude that to the extent that value judgments influence theory choice, they must be diverting attention from the actual evidential support of theories. A simple logical argument supports this model:

1. Significant truth is the sole aim of theoretical inquiry.
2. Whether a theory is justified depends only on features indicative of its truth, not its significance.
3. One shows that a theory is (most probably) true by showing that it is (best) supported by the evidence.
4. A theoretical proposition is supported by the evidence only if there is some valid inference from the evidence (in conjunction with background information) to it.
5. Value judgments take the form "P ought to be the case."
6. There is no valid inference from "P ought to be the case" to "P is the case" (or any other factual truths).
7. There is no valid inference from value judgments to factual truths (5, 6).
8. Value judgments can provide no evidential support for theories (4, 7).
9. Value judgments can play no role in indicating the truth of theories (3, 8).
10. Value judgments can play no role in justifying theories (1, 2, 9).

I believe this argument captures the core assumptions supporting the ideal of value-neutral science.[25] The debate over the value-neutrality of science has traditionally taken (6) as the crux of the argument.

But the argument is not valid as it stands. In fact, it is remarkably hard to find a valid argument against using value judgments to justify theories that hangs on (6). Particular claims are evidence for theories only in conjunction with other background assumptions [premise (4)]. Premise (6), at most, supports the conclusion that value judgments all by themselves cannot provide evidence for theories. In conjunction with background teleological laws of the form "If P ought to be the case, then P is the case," it would be easy to license an inference from value judgments to factual claims. So the argument covertly relies on a background metaphysical assumption that the universe is not governed by tele-ological laws. Furthermore, despite Haack's insistence that no one has ever produced a counterexample to (6), many theorists hold that "ought" implies "can"—that is, that one may validly infer from "M ought to do x" that "M can do x," which is a factual claim about M's capabilities.

These flaws in the argument are not worth pursuing, however. For few contemporary defenders of value-laden inquiry stake their case on the existence of teleological laws or on the inference from "ought" to "can."[26] And no defender of value-laden inquiry has ever suggested that values figure in inquiry by licensing any direct inference from "P ought to be the case" to "P".[27] To focus the debates over values in science on premise (6) is therefore to follow a gigantic red herring. The real contests are over premises (1) and (2): the goals of theory and the relation of justification (criteria of theory choice) to those goals. I shall argue that contextual values properly enter into criteria for theory choice because the constitutive goals of scientific theory-building extend beyond the simple accumulation of bare truths and are themselves properly subject to moral and political evaluation.

But I get ahead of myself. Before we scrutinize Haack's key premises, let us consider whether the alarming conclusions she draws about the implications of contextually value-laden inquiry would follow even if her argument were sound. Haack claims that to allow contextual values to shape theory choice would be to invite wishful thinking, dogmatism, dishonesty, and totalitarianism into science. But the most her argument can so far show is that morally value-laden inquiry will not reliably track the truth. What it *will* track depends on one's further understandings of what value judgments are. Here Haack expresses a remarkable, unexamined cynicism about the nature of value judgments. Her claim that value-laden inquiry leads to wishful thinking makes sense only if value judgments express nothing more than idle wishes or desires: propositions one would like to be true, quite independently of whether they or any other propositions are likely or possible. No serious contemporary theorist accepts such a crude account of value judgments. Even those who believe that value judgments express something more like emotional states than beliefs argue that emotional states can be warranted or not, depending on the facts.[28] So warranted value judgments, too, must be attentive to the facts. Haack's assumption that value-laden inquiry leads to dogmatism makes sense only if value judgments are essentially matters of blind, overbearing assertion, not subject to critical scrutiny or revision in light of arguments and evidence. Again, no serious moral theorist accepts this primitive emotivist view any more. Haack's assumption that value-laden inquiry will be dishonest comes from the thought that morally value-laden inquiry can only be inquiry designed to reach a foregone conclusion, hence inquiry that will neglect, cover up, or misrepresent evidence tending to show that the conclusion is false. Yet, this supposes that honesty is not itself an important moral value that should guide inquiry. Finally, Haack's charge that politically value-laden inquiry will invite totalitarianism supposes that political values are essentially totalitarian. But feminist empiricists, including Longino, are virtually all democrats and aim to extend principles of democracy to scientific practice, notably in insisting on tolerance of diverse value-laden research programs and on the equality of inquirers. Haack's alarm seems based on the nihilistic view that there is no such thing as moral inquiry at all, only arbitrary moral commitment.

Perhaps Haack's worries should be articulated as second-order ones. Her complaint about dishonesty might not be that value-laden research programs will openly embrace lying for political gain. Perhaps the worry is that if political interests are allowed to influence the domain of evidence to which a theory is accountable, then politically oriented researchers will be permitted to simply define that domain to include only those facts that favor conclusions they

would like to reach. But Longino's requirement that research communities be open and responsive to criticism constrains the criteria of theory choice that can claim legitimacy. To restrict the domain of relevant evidence in the way supposed is simply a way to foreclose criticism from dissenters and hence is not permitted within the terms of Longino's defense of value-laden inquiry.

Perhaps Haack's worries about totalitarian control of science express the second-order suspicion that any collective or social values, whether totalitarian or democratic, interfere with truth-seeking by promoting "group-think" over individualistic, autonomous inquiry. This would fit in with the model of inquiry that supposes that social determinants of belief necessarily displace attention to the evidence. It is as if, upon turning our heads to attend to those speaking to us, we necessarily turn our attention away from the world. But Longino is right to insist that the social structure of science, provided that it ensures diversity, equality, openness, and responsiveness to criticism, functions as an essential corrective to individual error and bias. Underdetermination arguments show that individuals, left on their own, can make almost anything out of what they observe, given idiosyncratic enough background assumptions. The history of philosophical skepticism, especially its solipsistic versions, testifies to this. It is the fact that individual inquirers must justify their claims before others that forces them to appeal to evidence that others can check and to standards that others can accept. As we have seen above, the demand that we be accountable to others is what makes us accountable to the world, and thereby forecloses opportunities to tailor criteria of theory choice so that they reach a foregone conclusion or a "politically correct" one.[29]

None of the alarmist implications Haack wishes to draw from Longino's advocacy of value-laden inquiry follow from her arguments. Longino's own normative constraints on research communities guard against them. Nevertheless, Haack's central argument does express a fundamental challenge to Longino's views. Even if Longino's recommendations don't lead to a totalitarian abyss, they may lead to false belief, and that is bad enough. Longino rests her case for value-laden inquiry on a logical analysis of the evidential relation between data and theory. If, as Haack suggests, this evidential relation is something like the relation "supporting the claim to truth," then it is hard to see how value judgments can figure in this relation unless one accepts some kind of inference from "ought" to "is." Thus, Haack reads Longino as arguing that when the choice between rival theories is underdetermined by the available evidence in conjunction with shared background assumptions, then "we should decide which disjunct to accept by asking which would be politically preferable."[30] But surely Haack is right to insist that the fact that the world would be a better place if a theory were true, or the fact that one would like one theory to be true, offers no evidence for the conclusion that it really is true. Haack argues that in such cases of underdetermination one should suspend judgment rather than plump for one side for bad reasons. Even if practical considerations demand that we act on some theory, this does not justify belief in it, merely acceptance of it as if it were true.[31] Longino claims that underdetermination leaves open the permanent possibility that unarticulated moral judgments may be covertly influencing scientists' assessments of the evidence. But Haack argues that even if this is true, it argues for rigorously exposing and expunging these judgments from inquiry, not for allowing them in explicitly.[32]

Longino's arguments thus stand in need of clarification and further defense. We need an account of how value judgments can properly figure in theory choice which does not just come down to choosing a theory because it is politically preferable. Longino argues that criteria of theory choice can be simultaneously supported by epistemic and political considerations. But if epistemic considerations already support the choice of criteria, then aren't the political considerations superfluous?

I shall argue that the key dispute between Haack and Longino concerns the aims of theoretical inquiry. If these aims are broader than the bare accumulation of truths, and the justification of theories is relative to all these aims, then there is an opening for moral, social, and political values to enter into theory choice. In fact, Haack already admits that theoretical inquiry aims for more than a bare accumulation of truths. Idle inquiry has no need for theory to accumulate trivial truths. Theoretical inquiry aims at some *organized* body of truths that can lay

claim to *significance* [premise (1)]. Thus, it is possible for contextual values to figure in determining what counts as significant, even if they don't figure in determining what is true. Haack forestalls this move by claiming that justification is addressed only to the question of truth, not significance [premise (2)]. Against this view, I shall argue in the following section that theoretical justification cannot avoid questions of significance. For not every set of true statements *about* a given phenomenon constitutes an acceptable theory *of* that phenomenon. Some sets offer a distorted, biased representation of the whole. This can make them unworthy representations of a phenomenon even if they contain no falsehoods. But what constitutes an adequate, unbiased representation of the whole is relative to our values, interests, and aims, some of which have moral and political import. Thus, even the project of defining the boundaries of significant phenomena may involve contextual value judgments.

3. Why Being True May Be No Defense of a Theory

If epistemologists took murder mysteries and courtroom dramas as seriously as they take their image of science, they would learn a thing or two about the limitations of truth as a defense of an account of events. Mysteries tease theoretical reason by revealing the facts about crucial events in a sequence designed to turn readers' minds first in one direction, then in another, then in another. Although many characters in mysteries lie, the most interesting characters deceive by telling the truth—but only part of it. It is no accident that in the ritual formula of the courtroom oath one swears not only to tell the truth and nothing but the truth, but the "whole" truth. The significance of most truths can be adequately grasped only in the context of the whole truth. Consider, in this light, the controversy over the role of Jews in the Atlantic slave system, sparked by the Nation of Islam's notorious book *The Secret Relationship between Blacks and Jews*.[33] The book stresses such claims as these: that Jews had considerable investments in the Dutch West India Company, which played a significant role in the seventeenth-century Atlantic slave trade; that Marranos (people forced by the Portuguese to convert from Judaism to Christianity) were among the major slaveowning sugar planters in Northeast Brazil; that Jews were prominent among the white colonists of Dutch Brazil and bought a large share of the slaves traded by the Dutch from the 1630s to the 1650s; and that a larger percentage of Jews living the U.S. South owned slaves than did Southern whites as a whole.[34] These claims are all true. Yet, put together, these and the many other true claims in *The Secret Relationship* do not add up to an acceptable account of the role of Jews in the Atlantic slave system. As the historian David Brion Davis argues, even if every purported fact in the book were true, it would still offer a biased and distorted picture of the role of Jews in Atlantic slavery.[35]

The problem is not so much falsehood (although this is also present in *The Secret Relationship*) as the failure to put the facts into the larger context that would be required to assess their significance. The share of Jewish investment in the Dutch West India Company was small, and the Dutch played a significant role in the Atlantic slave trade only in the seventeenth century, when the trade was small. Slavecowning Marranos were not in Northeast Brazil by choice: Portugal had forced them to colonize the area and take up sugar production. Nor is there any reason to call them Jews, as their forced conversion had long since eliminated whatever connections they once had to Jewish culture and religion. Jews owned slaves in Dutch Brazil for only a few decades and were expelled by the Portuguese in the 1650s.[36] A greater proportion of U.S. Southern Jews owned slaves than other Southern whites only because they were concentrated in urban areas, where rates of slave ownership were higher. Moreover, Jewish slaveowners owned fewer slaves per household than the average slaveowner, because urban slaveowners owned fewer slaves than their rural counterparts. And the vast majority of U.S. Jews lived in the nonslaveholding North. Finally, the absolute numbers of Jews involved in U.S. slavery were vanishingly small: the 1830 census records only 120 Jews among the 45,000 individuals owning 20 or more slaves, and it records only 20 Jews among the 12,000 owning 50 or more slaves.[37] How are we to assess the significance of the facts cited in *The Secret Relationship*? Taken in isolation, they suggest that Jews played a special or disproportionate role

in the Atlantic slave system or that their participation was more intense than that of other ethnic and religious groups. But in the context of additional facts, such as those just cited, they show that Jewish participation in the slave system was minor in absolute terms and was no different in intensity from similarly situated ethnic and religious groups. The larger context exposes a serious bias or distortion in the way *The Secret Relationship* characterizes the significance of Jewish participation in the Atlantic slave system. The characterization is "partial" in the literal sense that it tells only part of the truth needed to assess the significance of the matters at hand. What matters for assessing significance, then, is not just that an account be true but that it in some sense represent the whole truth, that it be unbiased. Furthermore, the fact that an account is biased or distorted is a good reason to reject it, even if it contains only true statements. Haack's premise (2) is therefore false: to justify acceptance of a theory one must defend its significance, not just its truth.

I have argued that significance, bias, and partiality are features of theories, relevant to their justification, that need to be judged in relation to the "whole" truth and that cannot be judged simply by testing the truth-value of each claim a given theory upholds. For in offering T as an adequate theory or an account of a phenomenon, one purports something more than that the constitutive sentences of T are true. Theories don't just state facts; they organize them into patterns that purport to be representative of the phenomenon being theorized, patterns that are adequate to answer some question or satisfy some explanatory demand.[38] But what would be the "whole" historical truth about the Atlantic slave system and about the roles of different ethnic groups in it? What would be an "unbiased" representation of this phenomenon?

One might try to offer a value-neutral account of significance and bias, arguing that an unbiased theory—one that does justice to the whole truth—is one that disregards all contextual values in deciding which facts to represent or how to represent them. But what would such an account look like? The whole truth can't be an account that literally represents every fact about the phenomenon being studied. No theory offers anything close to that. Nor should any theory try. Such a representation would end up burying the significant truths in a mass of irrelevant and trivial detail (e.g., how many waves did each slave ship surmount? how many times did each slave blink?). The whole truth can't be one that rules out in advance all facts that bear on the moral assessment of slavery or of those involved in it, or that describes the phenomenon in terms that evade moral judgment. Such a representation would plainly omit most of the features of slavery that arouse our interest in studying it or else would misrepresent these features by Orwellian euphemism (e.g., by describing whipping as a "labor mobilization technique"). Such a representation would constitute collusion with those who wish to evade moral judgment themselves. I see no contextually value-neutral way to characterize the whole truth, or the significant truths, about slavery.

To get a grip on the notions of significance and wholeness, we need a fuller understanding of the goals and context of theoretical inquiry. Theoretical inquiry does not just seek any random truth. It seeks answers to questions. What counts as a significant truth is any truth that bears on the answer to the question being posed. The whole truth consists of all the truths that bear on the answer, or, more feasibly, it consists of a representative enough sample of such truths that the addition of the rest would not make the answer turn out differently. Many of the questions we ask science to answer are motivated by contextual values and interests—that is, moral, political, cultural, economic, and other concerns drawn from the social context in which science is practiced. When these are the interests that motivate the questions we ask, then what counts as a significant truth, and the whole truth, can only be judged in relation to these interests. Thus, when the question driving inquiry is motivated by concerns with moral content, what counts as a significant truth will be whatever is *morally* relevant to addressing those concerns.

Before we can judge whether a theory is biased, then, we need to specify the question it purports to answer in such a form that we can tell whether the answer satisfactorily addresses the motivations for asking the question in the first place. The question that *The Secret Relationship* purports to answer is thus not adequately specified by such seemingly value-neutral questions as "What was the role of the

Jews in the Atlantic slave system?" or even "How did Jewish roles in the slave system compare with the roles of other ethnic groups?" For these do not specify which roles and which comparisons are of interest. The question that *The Secret Relationship* implicitly purports to answer is rather "Do Jews deserve special moral opprobrium or blame for their roles in the Atlantic slave system or bear special moral responsibility for that system's operations?" The whole truth about the role of Jews in the Atlantic slave system, relative to this question, therefore consists of all the facts morally relevant to answering this question about blame and responsibility, or enough of them that adding the rest would not change the answer. *The Secret Relationship* offers a biased account with respect to this question, because it ignores facts morally relevant to answering it—for instance, facts that show that the Jews behaved no differently, from a moral point of view, than anyone else who had the opportunity to profit from the slave system.

When the questions driving inquiry are motivated by contextual values, judgments of significance and bias can only be made in relation to these values. Since significance and lack of bias are legitimate criteria of theory choice, it follows that contextual values play a legitimate role in justifying theories. It follows, also, that theories of phenomena can be criticized on the ground that the background value judgments that organize the theory's conception of significant facts are themselves unjustified. Thus, if it is a moral mistake to pass judgments of collective guilt or merit on whole ethnic groups, then there is no justification even to make "Jewish" a significant classification in historical studies of the slave trade that are aimed at addressing questions of responsibility. What justification could there be for singling out Jews as a comparison class in such studies, rather than, say, the class of people who have drooping eyelids?

Haack might object that one need not drag in moral judgments to assess questions of the bias and significance of theories. Value-neutral criteria of significance and impartiality can be constructed. Such criteria need not refer to value-laden concepts such as blameworthiness. For example, it might be claimed that an unbiased account of the Jews' roles in the Atlantic slave system is simply one that truthfully represents their roles in their "actual" proportions relative to other ethnic groups. But which roles and proportions are significant? Is it more important that a greater proportion of U.S. Southern Jews owned slaves or that they owned fewer slaves per capita? Purely "factual" criteria may be constructable, against which the significance and impartiality of an account may be judged. But this possibility merely reflects the supervenience of moral judgments on factual judgments: the fact that there can be no moral difference between two states of affairs unless there is some factual difference between them. It remains the case that *what makes a given factual criterion relevant to judging a theory's impartiality or significance is its bearing upon the answer to the contextually value-laden question that motivates the inquiry, and whether it has such a bearing is itself determined by contextual values.*

Haack might object that *The Secret Relationship* is evidence that politically value-laden inquiry is dangerous for all the reasons she cites. Indeed, it does exemplify the vices she warns about: dishonesty, dogmatism, rigging a story to reach a foregone conclusion desired for political reasons, propaganda aimed at collective agitation. But her diagnosis is mistaken. The problem is not that moral and political interests inform the framing of questions, and hence the selection and representation of significant facts in *The Secret Relationship*. The problem is that *The Secret Relationship* doesn't count as inquiry, because it is rigged to reach a foregone conclusion.[39] Inquiry seeks to answer a question. A pragmatic prerequisite to posing a (genuine) question is that one regards the answer as genuinely open (even if one has strong hunches or wishes as to how it will turn out) and that one is prepared to let evidence and arguments guide one to the answer. This implies at least that one must be open and responsive to evidence that tends in different directions, not that one just attend to evidence that supports a conclusion one antecedently favors. There is nothing in this pragmatic requirement that precludes moral and political values from framing the question and hence determining what is to count as a significant fact. If there were, then there could be no such thing as genuine jury deliberation about the guilt of people on trial—jurors could only determine guilt on the basis of prejudice. There could be no such thing as moral inquiry at all.

Historians sometimes contrast biased inquiry with inquiry that does justice to the events being narrated and to the people involved in them. That the virtue of doing justice corrects bias expresses a superior understanding of the demands of inquiry than the ideal of value-neutrality. To adopt a stance of value-neutrality is to disregard contextual values in assessing the merits of theories. We have seen that insofar as science is driven by contextually value-laden questions, the ideal of value-neutrality leaves one incapable of coherently directed inquiry at all, because it leaves one incapable of distinguishing a significant from an insignificant fact, a biased account from one that does justice to the phenomena. One does justice not by adopting a stance of value-neutrality but by being impartial. Impartiality is not a commitment to disregard all evaluative standards but is a commitment to pass judgment in relation to a set of evaluative standards that transcends the competing interests of those who advocate rival answers to a question. These standards include honesty and fairness in judgment. To the extent that significance is judged in relation to highly contested political and moral questions, fairness demands attention to all the facts and arguments that support or undermine each side's value judgments, not a pose of value-neutrality.

4. How Contextual Values Guide Theoretical Classification

I have argued that significance and impartiality are two virtues of theories that are not wholly a function of the truth-values of the claims they contain or explain. They are a function of the relation the theories bear to the background interests that drive inquiry through the way questions are framed. Many of these interests are drawn from the social context of inquiry and have moral and political content. Factual criteria of significance and impartiality are justified in relation to these interests, which in turn stand in need of moral and political justification. These criteria set legitimate standards for theory choice. It follows that moral and political values legitimately figure in the justification of theories.

How might advocates of value-neutral inquiry respond to this argument? I do not believe there is any serious possibility of escaping its implications for the study of subjects, such as history, in which our interests are overwhelmingly of a moral, political, and social character. The best the advocates of value-neutral inquiry can do is to try to limit the scope of the argument. Let us explore the most credible options.

One might try to argue that the scope of my argument is confined to the social sciences, leaving the natural sciences untainted by association with value judgments. Arguing this would require an argument that significance in the natural sciences is purely a function of questions that arise internally to the practice of science, never from the social context in which science operates. Philip Kitcher proposes such a contextually value-neutral account of natural scientific significance. "Significant statements answer significant questions." Significant questions are roughly those that challenge the basic explanatory schemata of a theory—either to show that the schemata can be widely and effectively instantiated or that their presuppositions are true.[40] Kitcher appears to suggest, with Kuhn, that significant questions arise within the internal puzzle-solving activities of science, rather than being posed from the outside by moral and political interests.

We have long since passed the day when this interpretation could offer a complete account of sources of questions in natural science. It hearkens back to the purely contemplative ideal of inquiry that bred Scholasticism in natural science. Bacon correctly foresaw that modern science was not to take this path. Modern natural science is unimaginable apart from technology. To the extent that we call for technological applications of the natural sciences, such a value-neutral explication of scientific significance cannot work. The constitutive goals of many natural sciences include the promotion of particular contextual values. The constitutive aim of medicine is the promotion of health; of horticulture, the advancement of our abilities to grow food and other useful plants; of engineering, the construction and manipulation of useful artifacts. We rightly judge the significance of questions and answers in these fields in relation to these practical interests.

Perhaps, then, the scope of my argument includes the social sciences and "applied" natural sciences but leaves the "pure" natural sciences (and even more

pure mathematics) untouched. This distinction between "pure" and "applied" science has become progressively harder to draw in the material conditions in which we practice modern science. Is physics a "pure" science? In the twentieth century, a highly significant question for physics has been: under what conditions will a mass of fissionable material enter into an uncontrolled nuclear reaction? This question is significant only because states have conceived a political interest in building nuclear weapons and have funded most research in physics with military ends in mind. Is even number theory a "pure" science? A significant question in number theory includes: what algorithms can rapidly factor very large numbers? This question is significant only because states and businesses have political and commercial interests in constructing and decoding encrypted messages. There is no clear way to isolate a special subset of sciences or fields of inquiry in which no such interests play a role in defining significance, and hence in which no such interests play a role in theory choice. Moreover, once we admit that contextual interests play a role in defining significance in such areas as medicine, engineering, and horticulture, the quest for a contextually value-neutral science seems silly. For everyone acknowledges that medicine, engineering, and horticulture yield genuine knowledge. This proves that contextual interests can play a legitimate role in justifying scientific theories without compromising the search for truth.

A second response to my argument about significance is to claim that significance plays a role only in the context of discovery, not in the context of justification. Everyone agrees that contextual values may play a legitimate role in directing scientists' attention to specific subject matters and questions. So perhaps the boundaries of a given scientific inquiry—of what is to count as the "whole" subject matter of interest—are determined by contextual values. But what we subsequently discover about the structure of that whole is purely a matter of the nature of things, not a function of our values. Values may tell us where to cast the spotlight, but nature tells us what the spotlight reveals. Specifically, nature tells us what classifications or descriptive categories theories must deploy. Value judgments therefore do not shape the content of theories even if they delineate their scope.

This argument depends on the view that the classifications and descriptive categories of science track natural kinds. Phenomena may be grouped together into natural kinds if and only if they have common causes or effects—that is, if and only if there exist causal regularities connecting each of the phenomena in the group to phenomena in some other group. These are the classifications with epistemic significance.[41] Since the universe doesn't care about us, the causal regularities of the universe exist independently of human interests. It follows that nature divides itself into kinds independent of human interests. The project of science is to discover the language nature uses to classify itself and thereby the laws nature uses to govern itself. This project can succeed only if we set aside our own anthropocentric classifications and read the book of nature in the language of nature itself.

The scope of this argument is highly limited at best. When contextual values shape the questions posed of science, and hence what counts as a significant fact, they thereby inform the classifications used in science. The classifications are justified because they track particular conceptions of human interests, not because they unify the phenomena conceived in nonanthropocentric terms or out of relation to human interests. Medicine, a branch of applied biology, classifies organisms living in the human body into pathogenic and nonpathogenic. This classification tracks human interests in health.

One might object that there is an independent, nonanthropocentric rationale for this classification in medicine. Organisms that cause disease in humans are grouped together because they reduce human reproductive fitness, and hence have a common causal impact on the course of human evolution. But if our interest is in classifying organisms according to their impact on reproductive fitness, we would not group them exactly the way medicine does. Some nonpathogenic microorganisms cause bad breath. Arguably, these organisms reduce the reproductive fitness of their human hosts because of sexual selection. Some pathogens cause trivial ailments, such as the common cold, that have no impact on survival, fertility, or attractiveness to a sexual partner. Medical and evolutionary classifications of organisms cut across each other, each bearing different causal relations to other phenomena.

This case illustrates the fact that the world is too complex and messy to be organized into a few layers of all-inclusive and mutually exclusive classifications that account for all causal regularities.[42] For each classification that supports some causal regularity, there are likely to be some other crosscutting ones in the neighborhood that bear a causal relation to some other phenomenon. So criteria of epistemic significance alone do not tell us which classifications to base our theory on.

Consider unemployment rates. The unemployed are defined as those people not engaged in work for pay and who are actively seeking such work. Why not also include discouraged workers—those who want such work but have given up looking because search would be futile? The official story is that discouraged workers exert no downward pressure on wage rates. To include them in the unemployment rate would result in a classification that fails to bear a tight causal relationship with wage rates. But if they were included, the unemployment rate would likely bear a closer causal relationship with other variables, such as divorce, poverty, and crime rates. In any event, if the unemployment rate is supposed to capture just those job seekers who actually exert a downward pressure on wage rates, it would have to exclude unskilled, inexperienced workers who are eligible only for minimum-wage jobs, and include part-time workers seeking full-time work. The unemployment rate as currently defined appears to serve a different interest: to delineate the class of jobless people toward which the state expresses some limited concern, either in political rhetoric or actual policy (such as unemployment insurance). In the framework of American individualist ideals, the unemployed as currently defined represent the relatively "deserving unemployed" because they, unlike discouraged workers, are still trying to help themselves.

Unemployment statistics also incorporated a subtle sexist bias until 1994, when the methods for collecting employment information were changed. Employment information is collected through random telephone surveys. Under the pre-1994 interview protocols, if an adult man answered the phone, he would be asked. "What were you doing most of last week—working or something else?" But adult women would be asked, "What were you doing most of last week—keeping house or something else?"[43] For women who spend more hours keeping house than working for pay, the accurate response is "keeping house," even if they are employed part-time. The question suggests to women that the interviewer is interested only in "regular" employment as defined by an androcentric norm: full-time employment that displaces domestic responsibilities. Subsequent questioning, influenced by this suggestion, failed to identify all the women who had, or were seeking, part-time work. The statistics therefore underestimated both women's labor-force participation rates and their unemployment rates.[44] The pre-1994 employment statistics thus reflected (perhaps unexamined) sexist political assumptions about what kind of paid work is significant enough for public policy that the state ought to know about it. The protocol treated some women's part-time work as unimportant, in accord with the once widespread view that such work is a luxury that women and their families don't really need, hence not a proper subject for public concern.

The mere fact that normative political judgments inform the definition of unemployment is not a count against its use in science. It would be absurd to confine economics to studying matters of no political concern. The fact that political norms help define economic classification also does not deprive it of epistemic interest. To the extent that such classifications become incorporated into public policies, the act of delineating a given classification helps produce a system in which the classification becomes causally connected to other events. The Federal Reserve Bank treats the unemployment rate as an inflation barometer and tends to hike interest rates when the unemployment rate as defined by the theory drops below a specified level. So when the Bureau of Labor Statistics revised its interview protocols in 1994 to eliminate sex-differentiated questioning, it thereby made a new causal regularity true of the U.S. economy: one in which women's part-time employment-seeking activities came to have a stronger causal relationship to interest rates. The very act of using a theory to shape public policy endows the theory's classifications with epistemic significance.

The fact that a theoretical classification satisfies a standard of epistemic significance—namely, that its members bear a genuine causal relation to some other phenomenon—is therefore not sufficient to show that the theory that represents the world in terms of that classification is value-neutral. This is so, firstly, because any number of other classifications in the neighborhood could equally well satisfy this standard of epistemic significance. Some further justification is therefore needed for theorizing the world in terms of the classification selected, a justification which may well come from contextual values. Secondly, the political and economic conditions under which modern science is practiced deprive it of the ivory tower defense—that is, the defense of purely contemplative interest, divorced from practical relevance. Modern science is an expensive enterprise, largely funded by the state and business, which produces knowledge that these institutions subsequently use to shape their own policies. When theoretical classifications gain their epistemic significance *because* institutions have subsequently incorporated them into their policies, scientists are hardly in a position to disclaim responsibility for the results. Nor may they claim that their theorizing is neutral among contextual values.

The proper response to this fact is to recognize that theoretical classifications in science that answer questions raised by contextual interests require a dual justification. They must satisfy some standards of epistemic significance: there must be clear empirical criteria for determining when phenomena fall under a classification, some phenomena must actually meet these criteria, the classification must figure in some explanation or some causal or empirical regularity. Such classifications must also pass scrutiny from the standpoint of contextual interests and values. They must track the underlying contextual values accurately; that is, they must group phenomena together that share a common relation to these interests. And the contextual values themselves must be justified from an ethical point of view. Judged from this dual perspective, the 1994 change in the unemployment classification was only vaguely justified on epistemic grounds. The decline in the proportion of full-time, "regular" jobs probably makes a more complete recording of part-time work more important for modeling the impact of employment on variables such as GNP. On the other hand, to the extent that a lower ratio of the newly included women seeking part-time work are eligible for above-minimum-wage jobs than those already included, the new unemployment statistics will bear a weaker relationship to wage rates. From a purely epistemic point of view, there is not much to choose between the two classifications. The better grounds for choice are straightforwardly political: economic theories should prefer the 1994 definitions because women's part-time work is important to themselves and their families, and because economists and public-policy framers should be nonsexist in their treatment of men's and women's employment aspirations.

The need for dual justification of theoretical classifications opens up additional avenues for contextual value-judgments to play a role in theory choice. Two types of contextual criticism are particularly important. The first type broadly accepts the background contextual values that support a given classification but criticizes the theory for misconceiving these values, and thereby misclassifying phenomena. It might lump phenomena together that should be separated in different classes or exclude phenomena that should be included. For example, one might support the value of health that underwrites the classification of some things as diseases but question the inclusion of particular phenomena in the category of disease. Some criticisms of medical theories, particularly in psychiatry, clearly take this form. Is homosexuality a disease, a sin, or a normal variant expression of human sexuality? Is alcoholism a disease or a moral vice? Was Catherine of Siena, the fourteenth-century pus-drinking saint, manifesting symptoms of an atypical form of anorexia or expressing her religious humility? Are people today who are engaged in similarly shocking acts of self-mortification, mentally ill or just very religiously devoted? The answers to these questions depend on ethical inquiry devoted to clarifying the boundaries of health, moral virtue, and reasonable religiosity; inquiry which in turn depends on empirical evidence. In these cases, moral criticisms object to the ways medicine *conceives* of the phenomena, not just to immoral treatment practices, such as the failure to obtain informed consent. They are criticisms of the theory itself, not just of its practical applications.

The second type of contextually value-laden criticism of theories rejects the legitimacy of the background values that underwrite the classification in the first place. Feminist researchers have been particularly active in criticizing theoretical classifications that presuppose the legitimacy of sexist and androcentric values. For example, much research in psychology classifies personality characteristics and personal preferences into "masculine" and "feminine" types. This classification represents as gender-deviant any subjects whose biological sex does not match the gender the theory assigns to their traits and preferences. Thus, Ehrhardt's famous studies of girls prenatally exposed to high levels of androgens describe them as "tomboys" because they exhibit supposedly "masculine" behaviors such as a preference for active, outdoor play.[45] Longino criticizes such gender polarized classifications because they presuppose the legitimacy of the normative judgment that some traits are more appropriate to one gender than another.[46] The classifications thus normalize individuals who rigidly conform to sex-role stereotypes and pathologize individuals who do not. A nonsexist alternative scheme would repudiate such gender polarization and represent such traits and preferences as simply human, equally available to both sexes and belonging to no sex in particular.[47]

The changes in conceptual schemes for psychological research into gender that feminist normative criticism has recommended are not just window dressing. They open up opportunities for exploring human potentialities that were foreclosed under more rigid conceptual schemes. The old Terman-Miles M-F test, a device for measuring "masculine" and "feminine" personality, conceives of these qualities as bipolar opposites on a single continuum. Sandra Bem posed one of the earliest feminist challenges to this scheme in her alternative Bem Sex-Role Inventory, which asks individuals to report how far they identify with various culturally stereotyped masculine and feminine attributes.[48] Unlike the Terman-Miles M-F test, the BSRI does not code low identification with a stereotypically masculine attribute (e.g., liking to hunt) as in itself a feminine attribute (or vice versa). Her conceptual scheme thus made it possible to empirically study two alternative personality orientations that could not even be represented by the old test: androgyny, in which an individual registers high degrees of identification with both masculine and feminine stereotypical attributes, and a gender undifferentiated personality, in which an individual does not see gender-coded attributes as particularly salient in his or her own self-understanding. Feminist critics of Bem's work have pointed out that her challenge to gender-polarized conceptual schemes is incomplete. Although her concept of androgyny enables us to see how individuals can reject rigid gender stereotyping of their own sex without thereby identifying with the "opposite" sex, it still represents androgynous individuals as blending already gender differentiated attributes and so remains conceptually dependent on a gendered classification of attributes.[49]

More recent feminist psychological research challenges a different ontological assumption behind gender classification: the idea that masculinity and femininity are individual personality traits. A trait is something that an individual carries from one social context to another. The trait conception of gender has normative implications. It makes it difficult to imagine how gendered individuals could operate successfully in social contexts that demand expression of the "opposite" gender traits. It therefore suggests that certain social changes desired by feminists, such as getting men more involved in child care, are unachievable, hence foolishly sought. An alternative is to view gender as a dynamic feature of the social context, dependent on the presence and expectations of others, that elicits different behaviors from individuals who have full repertoires of human capabilities, including those that culture labels "masculine" and "feminine."[50] This conception of gender enables an even more expansive representation of human potentialities than Bem's. It allows that even those men and women who express rigidly gender stereotyped behaviors in some social settings, where gendered expectations and sanctions are high, may be able to express themselves more flexibly in other contexts.

5. The Cognitive Value of Feminist Theoretical Virtues: From Classification to Method

These cases of politically motivated feminist conceptual criticism illustrate two of Longino's feminist theoretical virtues in action. Longino's critique

of Ehrhardt's gender stereotyped classifications and Bem's alternative to the Terman-Miles M-F test reflect the virtue of ontological heterogeneity. This virtue involves a commitment both to ensure that a theory's conceptual scheme makes room for the representation of human potentialities that feminists value and to represent these potentialities as normal variations rather than as deviance, defect, or pathology. The contextual conception of gender reflects the virtue of complexity of relationship. This virtue involves a commitment to represent humans' potentialities for flexible behavior in response to altered understandings of themselves and others.

These theoretical virtues are feminist in the sense that they reflect certain contextual values in which feminists take an interest. The virtues are not the exclusive possession of feminist theorists. Indeed, many fields of inquiry not particularly associated with feminism have embraced them. Interpretive anthropology has long favored splitting over lumping—representing cultural differences as normal variations of human potentials rather than neglecting or relegating them to the lower ranks of deviance. Cognitive psychology incorporates complexity by stressing the causal role of agents' internal representations in human behavior, and hence the potential to change behavior by changing agents; self-conceptions. Chomsky in particular has emphasized the advantages cognitive psychology has over behaviorism in providing a model of human behavior with sufficient internal complexity to represent our potential for linguistic creativity.

Critics of contextually value-laden inquiry might agree that it would be nice if we humans really did have the potentialities feminists, cultural anthropologists, and cognitive psychologists prefer to represent us as having. But how can this provide legitimate cognitive grounds for thinking that we do in fact have these potentialities? How can this preference provide legitimate grounds for theory choice? Doesn't appeal to these values in theory choice reflect the very errors of wishful thinking, insistence on a foregone conclusion, and deducing "is" from "ought" that Haack and other critics object to?

No advocate of heterogeneity and complexity argues that the desirability of human flexibility, autonomy, and creativity is evidence that we really are flexible, autonomous, and creative. Rather, advocates argue that because these are valuable potentialities, it is important that our conceptual schemes be able to represent us as having them, if indeed we do. Perhaps it is the case that gender is a fixed, bipolar individual trait. But feminist critique shows that at best this could be an empirical fact about us, not a conceptual truth. Thus, theoretical schemes that leave no conceptual space for representing us otherwise are defective. Bem's scale leaves open the empirical possibility that no one scores as androgynous or undifferentiated. The Terman-Miles M-F test represents an inferior conceptualization of gender, because it does not make room for the empirical possibility that individuals could be androgynes or undifferentiated. The contextual conception of gender as process rather than as trait opens up a further possibility not available in Bem's scheme: that individuals could express rigidly gendered preferences and behaviors in some social settings but not in others. Again, this more expansive, complex conceptualization does not rule out the possibility of discovering that the gendered dispositions displayed by an individual in one setting carry through to all others. But within this framework, discovering this would count as a genuine empirical discovery, not as an artifact of the conceptual scheme of the theory.

Chomsky's critique of Skinner's theory of verbal behavior is on a par with this logic. His argument was not based on a comparison of the empirical adequacy of the two frameworks. For cognitive psychology does no better than behaviorism in explaining why a person utters a specific sequence of words on a particular occasion. The case for the superiority of the cognitive framework is that it at least offers a scheme for *representing* us as potentially free and creative (however inadequately this scheme is presently sketched-in), whereas behaviorism forecloses such representational possibilities in advance.

Theoretical justification, on this view, proceeds on two tracks: normative and evidential. Contextual values determine what phenomena are so significant that a theory ought to represent them when they exist. Evidence indicates when those phenomena are instantiated. There is no question here of making up stories about women's or men's abilities, activities, or achievements, nor of deciding to believe they exist because it would be nice if they did. Nor, where the evidence for rival hypotheses is inconclusive, is

there any question of simply holding that one hypothesis is false because it reaches a politically unpalatable conclusion.[51] Longino does, of course, express a "preference for a neurobiological model that *allows* for agency, for the efficacy of intentionality" (emphasis mine), partly on the political grounds just discussed.[52] But this hardly amounts to rigging a foregone conclusion by calling for "a way of doing science that will negate *any* possibility of biological determinism."[53] Longino expresses a preference for models that *allow* for agency—that is, that preserve the possibility of representing us as agents, if that is what we are. This hardly negates the possibility of determinism. Intentionalist models of human behavior still need to be supported by evidence. If we can't find evidence that people change their behavior in response to changes in the way they conceive of themselves and their circumstances, then intentionalist models will die for failure to produce instantiations of their explanatory schema. Nothing in Longino's expressed preference or in her methodological recommendations guarantees that intentionalist theories will be fruitful. Political interests in preserving representational possibilities also shape methodological preferences. Feminists' political interests in respecting differences among women have been a major spur toward the development of qualitative research methods, often motivating a preference for open-ended, face-to-face interviewing and participant observation over telephone or mail surveys with fixed, researcher-defined responses. Similar concerns for respecting the subjects of study have moved anthropologists to open their work to criticism from their subjects and have moved critics of behaviorism to reject the coercive and demeaning experimental methods of operant conditioning.

Haack's model of cognition, which represents the influence of ethical and cognitive considerations on cognition as necessarily competitive, can at best represent such politically grounded methodological preferences as permissible external ethical constraints on research. Perhaps some of them could be seen as equivalent to the requirement that scientists obtain informed consent before experimenting on subjects. Scientists may be morally required to respect their subjects, but such requirements should still be viewed as constraining rather than enabling the discovery of truth. Thus, cultural anthropologists who share their research with their subjects may be seen as doing a decent thing in treating their subjects with more dignity than lab rats. But sharing research may still compromise the search for truth by giving researchers a motive to soften their representations of their subjects so as not to arouse ill-will.

In contrast with this view, the justice model of unbiased, objective research enables us to see how the expression of certain ethical interests in research can have positive cognitive value. Researchers fulfill the *cognitive* demand to do justice to the subject of study precisely by fulfilling the *ethical* demand to do justice to the individuals being studied. Justice requires that one respect, recognize, and acknowledge the autonomy and valuable potentialities of others. This requirement meshes with the politico-cognitive interest in constructing conceptual space in our theories for the representation of valuable human potentialities. If it is important to represent ourselves in our theories as possessing certain potentialities when we actually have them, then we ought to develop and employ research methods that enable us to find out about them. This requires that research methods enable the subjects of research to express these potentialities, if they do have them. Open-ended interviewing and sharing research with subjects enables subjects to express novel ideas and offer creative interpretations of phenomena that the researcher did not already anticipate. Noncoercive observational settings give subjects opportunities to take initiatives not available in behaviorist experiments. These research methods thus open up opportunities for eliciting, observing, and understanding important phenomena that other methods do not.

One can accept the importance of expressing certain political interests in conducting research and framing research results without descending into dogmatism. Heterogeneity and complexity are feminist theoretical virtues, but they are not unconditional ones. Sometimes it is more important to stress common features of women's condition than to focus on differences. Quantitative research methods inevitably abstract from fine-grained differences and thus homogenize the phenomena to some ex-

tent. But some questions of interest to feminists can only be answered with quantitative methods.[54]

6. A Cooperative Model of the Interaction of Normative and Evidential Considerations in Theory Choice

The critique of contextually value-laden science depends on the assumption that truth is the only goal of science—or at least the only goal relevant to justifying theories. On this assumption, it is practically inevitable that any influence on theory choice other than evidence (considerations that support the claim to truth) must be viewed as *competing* with the evidence for our beliefs. Value judgments, social interests, wishes, and political demands in themselves have no evidentiary status. They do not support claims to truth. Therefore, to the extent that they influence theory choice, they must be seen as displacing attention to the evidence and diverting the search for truth.

I have defended an alternative conception of science, which holds that there are many goals of scientific inquiry. Multiple goals support multiple grounds for criticizing, justifying, and choosing theories besides truth.[55] Because modern science exists in large part to serve human interests, some of these goals and grounds are based on contextual values. I have identified three ways in which contextual values may shape legitimate grounds for theory choice.

First, all inquiry begins with a question. Questions direct inquiry by defining what is to count as a significant fact and what is a complete or adequate account of a phenomenon. A significant fact is one that bears on the answer to the question; an adequate account (one that represents the whole truth) is one that captures enough of the phenomenon that the addition of further detail will not change the answer. Many of the questions we ask science to answer come from the social context of science, not from its internal puzzle-generating activities. The constitutive goals of many sciences, such as engineering, medicine, and economics, are so contextually value-laden that it hardly makes sense to suppose that they have an "internal" source of questions independent from the social context in which they operate. When a theory or account of some phenomenon is taken to address some contextually value-laden question, it is therefore subject to criticism on at least three contextually value-laden grounds. The theory, although it asserts nothing but truths, may be trivial, insignificant, or beside the point: it doesn't address the contextual interests motivating the question. Or, although it asserts nothing but truths, it may be biased: it offers an incomplete account, one that pays disproportionate attention to those pieces of significant evidence that incline toward one answer, ignoring significant facts that support rival answers. When the question which the theory seeks to answer has moral or political import, the charge of bias can only be made relative to an assessment of the moral and political relevance of the evidence the theory cites. Such assessments of course depend upon moral and political value judgments. Finally, the theory may be objectionable for trying to answer a question that has illegitimate normative presuppositions.

Second, questions based on contextual interests require answers expressed in terms that track those interests. Contextual values come to directly inform the content of theories not simply by delineating the body of significant truths but by shaping how we ought to describe them. Purely epistemic criteria of significance are not sufficient to define our theoretical classifications. The world is complex and messy enough that it is all too easy to come up with taxonomies that meet basic standards of epistemic significance. So which classifications should we pick? The interests behind the questions' driving inquiry tell us which classifications to use: ones that group phenomena that bear a common relation to these interests. It follows that theories embodying such classifications can be criticized on at least two normative grounds. They may misconceive the relevant, legitimate interests, and thereby classify together phenomena that should be separated or exclude phenomena that should be included in a class. Or a theoretical classification may be based on illegitimate contextual values and for that reason should be rejected altogether.

Third, questions based on contextual interests can only be answered by methods adequate to reveal the phenomena those interests classify as significant. A theory can therefore be criticized for relying on methods that foreclose the possibility of discovering that we have certain valuable potentialities or that certain important differences or similarities exist among the subjects being studied.

The introduction of multiple goals of inquiry allows us to model the interaction of normative and evidential considerations as cooperative rather than competitive. Contextual values aid empirical inquiry by identifying relevant facts and sources of evidence, shaping conceptual schemes for describing observations, and inspiring methodological innovations that open new avenues for empirical discovery adequate for answering contextually value-laden questions. This cooperative model of inquiry supports a dual-track model of theoretical justification. On this view, theory choice is properly based on both normative and evidential considerations. Contextual values set the standards of significance and completeness (impartiality, lack of bias) for a theory, and evidence determines whether the theory meets the standards. Contextual values help define what counts as a meaningful classification and the empirical criteria for identifying things falling under it, and evidence determines what, if anything meets these criteria. Contextual values help determine what methods are needed to answer a question, and evidence gathered in accordance with those methods helps answer it. In each case, evidential and normative considerations cooperate; neither usurps the role of the other.

The need for dual justification prevents wishful thinking and dogmatic insistence from counting as evidence for belief. Contextual value judgments do not play the same role that evidence does in supporting truth claims. But they do play a role in determining what the evidence means: what it points to, how it should be described. No advocate of value-laden inquiry argues that when the evidence is insufficient to justify belief in one of two rival theories, one may take the desirability of one conclusion as evidence for its truth. But contextual values do provide grounds for preferring theories that leave open the possibility of representing certain claims as true and for methods that leave open the possibility of discovering that we have certain valuable capacities.

My defense of value-laden inquiry suggests that good science is morally value-laden in a more global sense as well: it embodies the virtue of justice. Not value-neutrality, but justice, offers the proper model of objectivity in science. Justice includes the demand to do justice to the subjects of study as well as the demand to do justice to other inquirers: to respect them as equals, to respond to their arguments, evidence, and criticisms, to tolerate the diversity of views needed to secure the objectivity of science as a social practice. The lesson of this defense of value-laden science is not totalitarian, but pluralistic and tolerant.

NOTES

1. I use "science" in the inclusive sense of the German "Wissenschaft," which comprehends not just "science" in the English sense of the natural and social sciences, but all disciplined inquiry found in the academy, including the humanities, mathematics, law, public health, and engineering. I often use "science" rather than the generic "inquiry" to signify that my primary interest is in disciplined, systematic inquiry subject to institutionalized means of quality control (e.g., peer review).
2. Helen Longino, *Science as Social Knowledge* (Princeton, N.J.: Princeton University Press, 1980). See also Lynn Hankinson Nelson, *Who Knows: From Quine to a Feminist Empiricism* (Philadelphia: Temple University Press, 1990).
3. Thomas Kuhn, *The Structure of Scientific Revolutions*, 2d ed. (Chicago: University of Chicago Press, 1970).
4. Nelson, op. cit., 173–4, 248.
5. Thomas Kuhn, "Objectivity, Value Judgment, and Theory Choice," in his *The Essential Tension* (Chicago: University of Chicago Press, 1977), 320–339.
6. Helen Longino, "In Search of Feminist Epistemology," *Monist* 77 (1994): 472–485.
7. Ibid., 481.
8. Mary Tiles, "A Science of Mars or of Venus?" *Philosophy* 62 (1987): 293–306.
9. Jürgen Habermas, *Knowledge and Human Interests*, tr. Jeremy Shapiro (Boston: Beacon Press 1971).
10. Longino, "In Search," 477–478.
11. See Evelyn Fox Keller, *A Feeling for the Organism* (New York: Freeman, 1983).
12. Linda Fedigan, *Primate Paradigms* (Chicago: University of Chicago Press, 1992), ch. 7.
13. bell hooks, *Feminist Theory from Margin to Center* (Boston: South End Press, 1983).
14. Donna Haraway, *Primate Visions* (New York: Routledge, 1989), 296.
15. Longino, "In Search," 478.
16. Noam Chomsky, "Review of B. F. Skinner's *Verbal Behavior*," *Language* 35 (1959): 26–58.
17. Barry Schwartz and Hugh Lacey, *Behaviorism, Science, and Human Nature* (New York: W. W. Norton, 1982).
18. Helen Longino, "Essential Tensions—Phase Two: Feminist, Philosophical, and Social Studies of Science," in Louise M. Antony and Charlotte Witt, eds., *A Mind of One's Own* (Boulder, Colo.: Westview Press, 1993), 261–263.
19. Critics of the equality requirement assume that it tells us to disregard individual differences in expertise and cognitive ability. But the requirement only tells us not to rank the worth of inquirers' contributions on the basis of their social status. For further defense of the equality requirement and its relation to claims of expertise, see Elizabeth Anderson "The Democratic University: The Role of Justice in the Production of Knowledge," *Social Philosophy and Policy* 12(1995): 186–219.
20. Longino, *Science as Social Knowledge*, ch. 4.
21. Susan Haack, "Epistemological Reflections of an Old Feminist," *Reason Papers* 18 (1993): 31–43 (reprinted, without footnotes, as "Knowledge and Propaganda: Reflections of an Old Feminist," *Partisan Review*. 60 [1993]: 556–564); "Science as Social?—Yes and No," in Jack Nelson and Lynn Nelson, eds., *Dialogue on Feminism, Science, and Philosophy of Science* (Netherlands: Kluwer).
22. Haack, "Epistemological Reflections," 35.
23. Haack, "Science as Social?" 9.
24. Haack, "Epistemological Reflections," 38.
25. I am less confident that it accurately represents Haack's views. See Susan Haack, *Evidence and Inquiry* (Oxford: Basil Blackwell, 1993). Haack explicitly endorses premises (1), (2), (3), (5), and (6) [premises (1) and (2): *Evidence and Inquiry*, 199, 203–5; premise (3): ibid., 74, 203–5; premises (5) and (6): "Epistemological Reflections," 35, 42 n. 19]. She seems to think, along with most other defenders of value-neutrality, that (6) is crucial to her case. Premise (6) can play a role in the argument only if something like (4) is accepted. For unless the evidentiary relation can be explicated in logical terms, the lack of any valid logical inference from "ought" to "is" would be irrelevant to the question of whether

"ought" claims can provide evidential support for factual claims. But Haack appears to reject the view that logical inference is the basis of evidential relations. She speaks rather of "fitness" between evidence, background information, and conclusions (See "Science as Social?" 4; *Evidence and Inquiry*, 81–84). Haack might reach (8), not via (4)–(7), but through the assumption that value judgments express something like wishes or desires. Then all she needs for (8) is the claim that the wish or desire that *P* provides no evidential support for *P* or for any other proposition. I render the argument using (4)–(7) because this captures the concerns of those who take (6) to be crucial and because Longino also accepts (4). The argument diverges from Haack's views in a second way. Haack speaks in the idiom of epistemology, Longino in the idiom of philosophy of science. To bring their views into contact, I have cast Haack's premises in terms of "theory," where Haack herself talks of "inquiry" in general. The argument works only if theories are construed in the logical empiricist sense, as sets of propositions which have truth-values. Many theorists, including Longino, construe theories as nonlinguistic models that can't have truth-values. See Longino, "The Fate of Knowledge in Social Theories of Science," in Frederick Schmitt, ed., *Socializing Epistemology* (Lanham, Md.: Rowman and Littlefield, 1994), 146–8. This raises the larger issue, beyond the scope of my paper, of whether truth is an aim of theory-building at all. I set aside this issue and focus on whether truth is the only target of theoretical justification, assuming the logical empiricist picture of theories for the sake of argument.

26. See, however, Peter Railton, "Moral Realism," *Philosophical Review* 95 (1986): 163–207. No one argues any more that teleological laws govern the natural world. But some, like Railton, defend the thought that teleological laws might account for human actions—that is, that sometimes the reason why people do things is just because they are right or good or ought to be done.

27. Why do the critics of value-laden inquiry focus so narrowly on the imagined inference from "*P* ought to be the case" to "*P*"? I think the critics obsess over this single possibility because they imagine only one route by which value judgments could ever influence theory acceptance—via the mechanism of wishful thinking. They therefore overlook the possibility that there could be other routes by which value judgments can influence theory choice.

28. See, for example, Allan Gibbard, *Wise Choices, Apt Feelings* (Cambridge, Mass.: Harvard University Press, 1990).

29. Longino, "Essential Tensions," 260–267.

30. Haack, "Science as Social?" 12.

31. Ibid., 12–13; Haack, "Epistemological Reflections," 35.

32. Haack, "Epistemological Reflections," 36.

33. Historical Research Department, Nation of Islam, *The Secret Relationship between Blacks and Jews* (Chicago: Nation of Islam Press, 1991).

34. Ibid., 23, 20, 28–30, 180.

35. David Brion Davis, "The Slave Trade and the Jews," *The New York Review of Books*, 22 December 1994, 14–16.

36. Ibid.

37. Winthrop Jordon. "Slavery and the Jews," *Atlantic Monthly*, September 1995, 109–112, 114.

38. It follows that one could be justified in believing every sentence of *T* but not justified in accepting *T* as an adequate theory of the phenomenon it purports to be about.

39. The problem is also that the background values presupposed by its inquiry-guiding question are themselves pernicious: They presuppose the legitimacy of blaming ethnic groups for the sins of their ancestors and of ranking whole ethnic groups in a hierarchy of moral worth.

40. Philip Kitcher, *The Advancement of Science* (New York: Oxford University Press, 1993), 95, 112–113.

41. Ibid., 171.

42. For further defense of this view, see John Dupré, *The Disorder of Things* (Cambridge, Mass.: Harvard University Press, 1993). I follow Dupré in arguing that scientific classifications are partly justified by reference to contextual interests.

43. Sharon Cohany, Anne Polivka, and Jennifer Rothgeb, "Revisions in the Current Population Survey Effective January 1994," *Employment and Earnings* 41 (1994): 13–35, 21.

44. Ibid., 17.

45. Anke Ehrhardt and Heino Meyer-Bahlburg, "Effects of Prenatal Sex Hormones on Gender-Related Behavior," *Science* 211 (1981): 1312–1318.

46. Longino, *Science as Social Knowledge*, 131.

47. The conceptual point is, apparently, a subtle one. Paul Gross and Norman Levitt, in their attack on Longino's feminist epistemology, protest that her criticism amounts to a "grossly unfair" ad hominem attack on Ehrhardt and claim to find no sexism in Ehrhardt's "attitudes" (Paul Gross and

Norman Levitt, *Higher Superstition: The Academic Left and Its Quarrels with Science* [Baltimore, Md.: Johns Hopkins University Press, 1994], 145–6). Noting that "tomboy" is not a derogatory term, they also accuse Longino of projecting her own "hypersensitivity" toward sexism onto Ehrhardt's research. Of course, the fact that tomboys are not despised for their gender deviance does not make the term "tomboy" innocent of sexist presumptions. Since sexist societies represent "feminine" traits as contemptible (hence the unmistakably pejorative meaning of "sissy," the boy's counterpart to "tomboy"), it is not surprising that they are likely to pass an ambivalent, even half-admiring judgment on girls who renounce "feminine" traits and exemplify the nobler, "masculine" ones. More importantly, Longino's criticism applies to the background assumptions of Ehrhardt's research, not to her attitudes. What could possibly justify a classification scheme that represents some behaviors, exhibited by both sexes, as belonging more properly to one sex than the other? Empirically observed group differences are simply not sufficient to justify this. African-Americans exhibit considerably lower rates of involvement in higher mathematics and science than whites. But this surely does not justify describing African-Americans who engage in math and science as "acting white." Gross and Levitt exhibit no difficulty recognizing the racism in descriptions like this (ibid., 129), but they fail to recognize the sexist background norms needed to underwrite gender-polarized classifications.

48. Sandra Bem, *The Lenses of Gender* (New Haven: Yale University Press, 1993), 101–127.

49. Ibid., 124.

50. Candace West and Don Zimmerman, "Doing Gender," *Gender and Society* 1 (1987): 125–151; Kay Deaux and Brenda Major, "Putting Gender into Context: An Interactive Model of Gender-Related Behavior," *Psychological Review* 94 (1990): 369–389; Phyllis Rooney, "Methodological Issues in the Construction of Gender as a Meaningful Variable in Scientific Studies of Cognition." *PSA* 2 (1994): 109–119.

51. It is astonishing that Longino's critics have not attended to what Longino actually says about such cases. Haack suggests that between the hypothesis that men's hunting activities caused humans to evolve larger brains and the hypothesis that

women's gathering activities did so, Longino holds that, in the absence of conclusive evidence for either side, "we may legitimately choose to believe whatever theory suits our political purposes" (Haack, "Epistemological Reflections," 35). This is what Longino actually says about the relative merits of these two theories: "As long as both frameworks offer coherent and comprehensive accounts of the relevant data, neither can displace the other." The great virtue of the woman-the-gatherer theory is not its truth but "its revelation of the epistemologically arbitrary character of the man-the-hunter framework" (Longino, *Science as Social Knowledge*, 130). Gross and Levitt suggest that Longino infers from the fact that Ehrhardt's hypothesis—that male hormones cause masculine behavior in "tomboys"—is "unacceptable by feminist lights" that the hypothesis must be erroneous or at least less plausible than an environmental, intentionalist explanation (Gross and Levitt, op. cit., 146). In fact, she concludes her review of the evidence for the two theories by saying that "there is no more reason to assimilate so-called gender role behavior to the hormonal model than to assimilate it to [an intentionalist model]" and that "neither theoretical argument can muster constitutively based arguments sufficient to exclude the other" (Longino, *Science as Social Knowledge*, 161). Longino specifically denies that her account of science can "grant to some form of feminism or to any other social or political program an exclusive grant to truth" (Longino, "Essential Tensions," 270).

52. Longino, "Can There Be a Feminist Science?" in Ann Garry and Marilyn Pearsall, eds., *Women, Knowledge, and Reality* (Boston: Unwin Hyman, 1989), 203–216, 211.

53. Gross and Levitt, op. cit., 147.

54. See Toby Jayaratne and Abigail Stewart, "Quantitative and Qualitative Methods in the Social Sciences: Current Feminist Issues and Practical Strategies," in Mary Fonow and Judith Cook, eds., *Beyond Methodology: Feminist Scholarship as Lived Research* (Bloomington: University of Indiana Press, 1991), 85–106.

55. As Longino also stresses, in her own dual-track model of justification. See her "Subjects, Power, and Knowledge," in Linda Alcoff and Elizabeth Potter, eds., *Feminist Epistemologies* (New York: Routledge, 1993), 101–120, 116.

PART IV

—•—

Minds, Bodies, and Persons

INTRODUCTION

How do we fit into the wider world? Are we simply very complex parts of the physical world? Could a computer be conscious in the way that we are? Are we just things, with the same sort of identity that rocks and buildings have? Or, is there something special about us? Are our actions as subject to the laws of nature and as predictable, at least in theory, as those of other objects? Or, do we have some special sort of freedom? These questions are as old as philosophy. Yet, in spite of the wealth of seemingly relevant knowledge afforded us by contemporary science, discussion of such questions continues unabated.

Descartes's Dualism

René Descartes's *Meditations on First Philosophy* should be considered as relevant to Part IV of this book as it is to Part III. His treatment of the mind-body problem is as important as his attempts to deal with skepticism. Indeed, although his approach to skepticism has not been widely followed, the basic outline of Descartes's treatment of the relation between mind and body was the dominant view among psychologists and others who attempted to deal with the mind specifically until our own century, and remains the view of sophisticated common sense.

Descartes's answer to the second question we asked was a resounding no. The mind is not part of the physical world at all. Physical things are extended: they take up space. And they are not conscious. Our minds, on the other hand, are conscious, and do not take up space. Minds and bodies are as fundamentally different as things could be. Descartes begins to develop this dualistic conception in "Meditation II," where he finds that he cannot doubt the existence of his own mind (that is, of himself), whereas he can doubt the existence of the physical world. In "Meditation VI," after he has resolved his doubts about the physical world and determined that the essence of physical things is extension, Descartes develops his theory of mind and body at greater length and gives arguments for it.

Descartes's view is that we know what the mind is by reflecting on our own thinking or consciousness. We can see that the essence of our minds is this consciousness rather than extension. Thinking about Detroit, wishing for a puce Ferrari, feeling a pain, or having a visual image of a tree are all ways of being conscious, not ways of taking up space. There are no ways of thinking that seem to involve being extended; and there are no ways of being extended—no combination of extended parts, however complex—that carry consciousness with them. To be conscious is not to be of a certain shape or size or to move in a certain way, but a quite different and undefinable property of which we are each intimately aware when we reflect on our own minds.

How, then, are immaterial minds and the material world connected? Descartes's theory is that there is a two-way causal interaction between them (thus, Cartesian dualism is often called interactive dualism). On the one hand, the physical world affects one's mind. This happens, for example, in perception. Light rays bounce off the book in front of me, enter my eye, and cause changes in my nervous system, beginning at the periphery and ending in the brain. The state of the brain (the pineal gland in particular, Descartes thought) directly affects the mind. Thus, my body is not me, but simply the part of the material world that most directly affects me. But, there is also a causal interaction in the other direction. States of my mind affect my body and through it the wider world. The most obvious case is action. The intention to drink from the cup in front of me is a certain sort of mental state that involves ideas of the cup. This has an effect on the brain (through the pineal gland again) that affects the muscles and results in my arm moving in a certain way, and, if things go right, in the cup coming to my lips and my getting a drink. Although Descartes's hypothesis about the role of the pineal gland did not turn out to be correct, his basic conception of immaterial mind linked causally to material bodies proved durable.

Alternatives to Descartes

Descartes's position is not without its problems, however. One such problem, vigorously stated by Gilbert Ryle, is traditionally known as the problem of other minds. If minds are immaterial, then, we cannot see or touch or otherwise perceive any mind but our own mind, of which we seem to be directly aware. But, then, how do we know that other bodies are really, as is our body, animated by minds at all? Perhaps our mind is the only mind in the world, and every other being seemingly like us is just some sort of automaton? Of course, if we remain stuck in the skeptical abyss into which Descartes leads us in "Meditation I," this will only be a small part of a much larger problem: not only other minds, but also other bodies—even our own—are in doubt. The dualist appears to have an additional problem. Even if convinced of a world external to our own minds, how can we know that there are minds lying behind those other human bodies?

In his selection in Section A, "The Argument from Analogy for Other Minds," Bertrand Russell proposes one solution. He claims that our knowledge of other minds is based on a general principle used in scientific reasoning: analogy. Because other bodies behave as our body does, we may postulate other minds as their causal principle. But one may wonder about the strength of such an inference from a single case (my own) to so many other cases.

A second problem is the interaction Descartes assumes between mental and physical events. Many philosophers have found the whole idea of an interaction between two such different realms completely unintelligible. For example, how could an immaterial mind make contact with a material object in order to affect it or to be affected by it?

But what alternatives are there to Descartes's position? George Berkeley has already given us one: there are not minds and bodies, just minds. It is not obvious how this helps with the problem of other minds. Indeed, in the intellectual milieu of the twentieth century, philosophers have sought to solve the problem of interaction in the opposite direction—not to deny the existence of minds, but to argue that minds can, after all, be considered as parts (or aspects) of the physical world. Just as in the eighteenth century Berkeley maintained that talk about tables and chairs only seems to be talk about nonminds but is actually a complex way of talking about minds and their ideas, so, many twentieth-century philosophers claim that talk about beliefs and desires and pains only seems to be talk about a nonphysical realm but is actually just a complicated way of talking about bodies, brains, and behavior.

Five types of theory are represented (or, at least suggested) in Section A. The first theory is *logical behaviorism*. Even with Descartes's view, a strong case can be made for the importance of studying behavior as a way of studying the mind, for the behavior that minds cause is part of the evidence we have about minds. Methodological behaviorism is a movement in psychology that emphasizes the importance of studying behavior as a supplement to (possibly as a replacement for) introspective study of the mind.

But logical behaviorism goes a step further. It claims that our mental language—our talk of beliefs, desires, pains, and so on—is not a way of describing an inner, immaterial cause of behavior, but rather a way of describing behavior itself. An inelegant logical behaviorist might say, for example, that my belief that it is raining out is no more than my behavior of carrying an umbrella and canceling my tennis game. Such a roughcast form of logical behaviorism doesn't seem very plausible. Our representative of this tradition, Gilbert Ryle, would not appreciate being associated with those presenting such an unsophisticated view. Still, we can see his ideas emerging from just such a view, and only in three moves. The first move is from actual behavior to dispositions to behave. Is my belief that it is raining any more than my disposition to carry an umbrella if I want to go out and to cancel my tennis game if I do not want to get wet? The second move is to couch the thesis in a linguistic form. It is not the crude thesis that mental events are behavioral events, but the more perceptive thesis that there are logical connections between behavior descriptions and mental descriptions. Finally, these logical connections are of a complex sort. We should not expect explicit definitions of mental terms in behavioral language. The connections are more subtle. Talk of behavior and talk of the mind are two linguistic systems for describing the same phenomena: they just cut the phenomena up in different ways. But there is not a mind in addition to behavior or action. This would be, Ryle thinks, a category mistake, on a par with taking a university to be an additional group of buildings over and above the buildings of its colleges.

The second theory is represented by David M. Armstrong's essay, "The Nature of Mind." Armstrong thinks that both Descartes and the logical behaviorists have part of the story right. The logical behaviorists are right in thinking that there are logical connections between descriptions of behavior and descriptions of mental states as well as in their rejection of Descartes's idea of an immaterial mind. But Descartes is right in thinking that the mind is an inner cause of behavior, not just behavior redescribed. The key is to see that our mental concepts are simply indirect concepts of brain states. By "pain" we mean something like "that internal state which is apt to produce wincing, crying out, and the like." Our understanding of the causes of such behavior is necessarily indirect, because brains are enormously complex systems enclosed by skulls, which, until recently, could not be examined while still in working condition. Indeed, the concept of pain itself leaves the question open as to whether the cause of pain-behavior is physical or nonphysical. That is what Descartes saw when he noted that mental states are not logically required to be "ways of being extended." But, there is a difference between *not being required to be* a physical state and being required *not to be* a physical state. There is nothing in our concept of mental states, Armstrong argues, that precludes their turning out to be physical states, He thinks the progress of science, which has found physical causes for a wider and wider circle of phenomena, makes it probable that the causes of such behavior are physical. Hence, the mind turns out to be the brain, even though Descartes could conceive of his mind existing without his brain.

Armstrong's view is often called "The Identity Theory," since he holds that mental states are strictly identical with brain states. David Lewis is another advocate of the identity theory. In "Mad Pain and Martian Pain" he defends the theory against two objections. One objection is that someone who is mad might not behave the way we do when they are in pain. Perhaps they do nothing when they are in pain, or perhaps they laugh. In their case, pain wouldn't be the state that caused wincing, crying out, and the like. On the other hand, suppose there turn out to be Martians that behave very much as we do, so that we comfortably ascribe beliefs, desires, pains, and other mental states to them. But then it turned out that their bodies were constituted out of basically different stuff than ours. These beings would not be in the same physical states as we when they "believed that it was raining" or "felt pain." Does the identity theorist then have to deny that these Martians feel pain, or have beliefs? Lewis argues that the identity theory can handle these cases.

Descartes and Armstrong agree that there really are mental states, though they disagree about what they are. In "Intentional Systems" Daniel Dennett suggests a different way of looking at the matter. To have a mind is, at least in part, to be an "intentional system." And something "is an intentional system only in relation to the strategies of someone who is trying to explain and predict its behavior." In treating something as an intentional system we are taking "the intentional stance," but we could also try to take either a "design stance" or a "physical stance." Which strategy, or stance, we pursue, is a pragmatic matter, to be settled by what works best in our pursuit of explanations and predictions. There is no further, deeper, fact of the matter. Finally, Paul Churchland argues for the radical conclusion that our talk of minds, our "folk psychology," should go the way of other "false and radically misleading" theories in the history of science.

Minds, Brains, and Machines

If a Martian could have a mind like ours in spite of being built out of very different stuff, isn't it logically possible that computers could also have minds? Several of the theories of mind seem to leave open this possibility. Surprisingly, Descartes's view is one of them. If God could cause the brain states of humans to be causally connected with states of mind, why should He not do as well for computers? Of course, the problem of other minds arises here, too. If a computer had a Cartesian mind, how would we know?

Armstrong's view seems to dictate that computers could not have minds as long as they are built out of silicon and not living tissue. But the functionalist theory of Hilary Putnam leaves the question open. Why could a computer not have states that were functionally equivalent to ours and, therefore, be in the very same mental states that we are in?

Different points of view on the possibility of a mental life for computers are found in the work of the logician A. M. Turing—whose ideas were important in the development of computer science—and the philosopher John R. Searle. Neither Turing nor Searle is worried about whether any presently existing computer can be said, without metaphor or exaggeration, to think. (Indeed, Turing's selection was written in 1950 when actual computers were primitive by today's standards.) Both authors are not merely interested in whether at some time in the future something we are willing to call a "computer" might be said to think.

Instead, they are interested in whether computers that work on the principles that modern computers do could, if they became sufficiently complex and were programmed sufficiently cleverly, be able to think. Turing argues that insofar as the question has a clear meaning, the answer is probably yes. He sees no reason computers could not be designed to pass the imitation test, that is, the machine could successfully imitate the behavior of humans insofar as such behavior is relevant to assess the intellectual powers of humans. Computers, thus, need not look like humans or feel like humans or sound like humans, but the content of their answers to any conceivable question would have to be just what humans would answer.

Searle writes in 1980, at a time when computers can do things that Turing could only imagine thirty years earlier. Some computer scientists claim that certain mental properties should be attributed to computers on the basis of what they can do. Searle maintains that, if we examine the way that computer programs work, we will see that this claim is nonsense. Although computers may be programmed to do as well as humans on certain tasks, the way they achieve these results does not require the mental properties that humans would typically use if they performed them. Searle's argument for his conclusion is based on his famous Chinese Room example. In that, Searle imagines himself locked in a room following mechanical rules that, unknown to him, result in his writing suitable Chinese answers to Chinese questions, even though he doesn't know a word of Chinese. "I simply behave like a computer; I perform computational operations on formally specified elements. . . . I am simply the instantiation of a computer program." Now, in this case, Searle says, this ability on his part would not mean that he understood Chinese. So why, he asks, should a computer's doing something similar lead us to say that the computer understood Chinese or had any of the numerous mental abilities that a computer can be programmed to imitate?

Consciousness

Armstrong's view would leave Descartes astounded. How can Armstrong suppose that a sensation like pain is just a state of his brain, Descartes might ask. Can Armstrong not reflect and simply note that such sensations are far different than that? Perhaps, Armstrong's theory would be a reasonable conjecture about other people's minds if one did not have the example of one's own mind to show its absurdity. But how can Armstrong think that believing is a brain state when he can tell by introspecting what he believes and has never seen his brain?

Armstrong, one might charge, has traded the problem of other minds for the problem of his own mind. Armstrong devotes a good deal of his article facing up to this objection. A version of this difficulty is pushed by Thomas Nagel in his essay, "What Is It Like to Be a Bat?" Nagel does not defend a full-blown Cartesianism, but he pushes a question Descartes would appreciate. Isn't there something that we can't know about the mental states of bats, even if we know everything there is to know about their brains and how their behavior is caused? It seems in Armstrong's view that there could be nothing left to know—but isn't there? And, isn't there something we do know about our own minds—just by reflecting on what our various experiences are like—that could never be known by someone who couldn't have the same sorts of experiences (no matter how detailed that person's knowledge of our brain states and the connection of those brain states to behavior)?

In "What Mary Didn't Know" Frank Jackson develops this difficulty for the materialist in a simple and elegant argument. Suppose that Mary is raised in a black-and-white room. She isn't color blind, but she never sees colors. She knows there are colors, but she just has never seen one. Then one day she emerges from her room and sees a red object. At this point, Jackson says, she will learn *what it is like* to see a red object. That is a piece of knowledge she didn't have all the years she was in the black-and-white room, even if she read books on color vision while she was in there. This fact that Mary learns, Jackson says, is one that we have to postulate in addition to all the physical facts; it is an irreducible fact about consciousness. David Lewis, however, argues in "Knowing What It's Like" that all that Mary has gained is an ability, and that she poses no significant problem for the materialist.

The Problem of Personal Identity

Many religions believe in survival after death. Usually, such doctrines allow that the survivor does not have the very same body as before death. Suppose a lawyer who leads a faultless life is reincarnated as a philosopher. The lawyer's original body will still be locked in a coffin or, perhaps, will even have rotted away while the philosopher is growing up. Or, suppose our faultless lawyer goes to heaven. Again, it seems the body he will have in heaven—if beings have bodies there at all—will not be the same body that remains behind on earth. These possibilities raise the problem of personal identity. If the very same being can, at different times, have different bodies (or not have a body at all), then, personal identity cannot simply be bodily identity. But, then, what is it?

One possible answer is that of Descartes: personal identity consists of sameness of immaterial mind, not identity of material body. So, there is no problem with survival after death.

It is interesting to see, however, that one might deny that personal identity consisted in bodily identity, even if one were a thoroughgoing materialist about the mind. A high-tech version of our problem will make the point.

In recent years, there have been several books and television shows that have contemplated the possibility of a brain transplant. Suppose Ms. *A*'s brain is put in Ms. *B*'s body. It seems that the survivor of this operation would be mentally like Ms. *A*, not Ms. *B*. That is, if memories, beliefs, desires, and the like are largely dependent on brain states (whether or not they are identical with them), we might expect *that* survivor to remember things that Ms. *A* has done, have Ms. *A*'s beliefs and desires, and, with respect to mental characteristics generally, to be like Ms. *A*, even though she would, of course, look just like Ms. *B* always did.

In this instance, many people would be inclined to say that the survivor is Ms. *A*, not Ms. *B*—in spite of physical appearances and even fingerprints. But, then, we also have a case of a body transplant, not a brain transplant, in which there is sameness of person without sameness of body—without any appeal to an immaterial mind.

Of course, the survivor has a part of Ms. *A*'s body. But, one is inclined to think that it is not just having Ms. *A*'s brain that inclines us to take her to be Ms. *A*. It is not the brain, but what the brain apparently would bring with it, in particular Ms. *A*'s memories—that seems crucial.

So we have three approaches to personal identity: identity of a Cartesian soul, identity of body, and something determined by links of memory.

In John Perry's *A Dialogue on Personal Identity and Immortality* the three characters, Weirob, Miller, and Cohen, discuss the merits of these approaches in the context of Weirob's approaching death. Miller is a religious person, who wants to convince the philosopher Weirob that there is some possibility of survival after death. First he advocates a Cartesian type of theory, and then a memory theory, based on the ideas of John Locke. But Weirob believes that a person is just a live human body, and refuses to grant even the possibility of survival after death. The debate takes a practical turn when the participants consider the possibility of getting Weirob a "body-transplant," but she comes up with ingenious arguments (based on the work of Bernard Williams) to persuade herself that even that would not mean survival.

Freedom and Determinism

Suppose your friend, standing next to you at a party, suddenly lifts her arm and slaps you in the face. You will be inclined to hold her responsible for this action: to blame her for your sore face, resent her for what she did, and think ill of her moral character.

But, suppose you find out that her arm is tied to a fishline, pulled by someone on a balcony above. Your face is still sore, but now you will hardly be inclined to blame her for what happened. Why? Because she wasn't in control of the movement of her arm; once the person in the balcony pulled the line, a sequence of events was put in motion that ended up with your face getting slapped. Given the tug, the rest of the situation, and the laws of nature, your face was going to get slapped. She had no choice. Her movement was the result of a prior, remote event. She was not free to do otherwise. So how can you blame her?

But, if she is not free, are any of us ever free? For the laws of nature do not just concern fishlines, they concern all events inside and outside our bodies. If nature obeys universal laws, then our actions are just the most recent parts of a causal sequence of evermore remote events, the earliest parts of which occurred long before we were born. If the fact that the movement of your friend's arm is explained by the earlier tug on the fishline means she is not free, doesn't the fact that all of our actions can be explained by remote events and the working of general laws mean that none of us are ever free?

But can we really accept such a conclusion? After all, we blame and punish people all the time, and such practices presuppose that these people had a choice in what they did. That we have such choices seems obvious as soon as we reflect on our own actions. Can you doubt that you have the choice right now to lay down this book and to order a pizza?

This is the dilemma of freedom and determinism. Our assumption that people have choices and are, thus, responsible for what they do appears to conflict with the view that everything, even the movements of human agents, has an explanation in terms of universal laws of nature and antecedent conditions.

There are two obvious responses to our dilemma. The first is to accept that, because we are subject to laws of nature, we are not free. C. A. Campbell calls this view determinism, but as we will see, this is misleading. We call it hard determinism for reasons also explained later. The second response to our dilemma is to accept that, because we are free, some of our actions must escape the web of the laws of nature. This is the position of Campbell, which he calls libertarianism.

Given the choice between denying freedom and denying universal causation, most of us would choose the latter. Universal causation may be a useful postulate to guide scientific investigation, but why should we accept it at the cost of giving up a belief so central to our day-to-day lives as our conviction that we are free agents?

But, does giving up universal causation really help? The *absence* of explanation just doesn't seem to add up to the *presence* of freedom. Suppose that instead of being pulled by a fishline, your friend's arm moved as a result of a totally random and unpredictable spasm in her brain. That wouldn't make her action more free or her more responsible. Campbell's response to this challenge is that free actions, though uncaused, are not random. We are forced to "recognize a *third* possibility, as remote from chance as from necessity, that, namely, of *creative activity*, in which . . . nothing determines the act save the agent's doing of it." When we take the "inner standpoint," as Campbell urges us to do, this seems an apt enough description of how things seem. But does an apt description of what freedom feels like to the agent do more than label the problem?

Hume takes a third approach. He refuses to choose between freedom and universal causation (which he calls liberty and necessity), but he accepts them both. How does he think this is possible?

Hume describes himself as reconciling liberty and necessity. This brings us back to the terminological matter we left dangling earlier. Let us call the doctrine of universal causation, determinism. And, let us call the view that freedom and determinism (so defined) are not both possible, incompatibilism; and let us call the opposite view (which Hume held), compatibilism. We call an incompatibilist who accepts determinism a hard determinist. Richard Taylor comes close to accepting such a view. Campbell, in contrast, is an incompatibilist who rejects determinism and accepts freedom; this is what we call (as Campbell does) libertarianism. Of course, incompatibilists like Campbell don't find the distinction between determinism and hard determinism very interesting. Finally, a compatibilist who, like Hume, accepts determinism, we call a soft determinist.

Hume thinks that the appearance of incompatibility is due to confusions about causation. Causes do not compel effects, they are merely regularly followed by them. (Hume, of course, is recalling his own discussion of causation in *An Enquiry Concerning Human Understanding*, from which the selection in Section E is taken. See his discussion—and criticisms by G. E. M. Anscombe—in Part III.) Indeed, Hume claims determinism is just what we want. We want our own desires to determine our actions. The problem with your friend, he would say, was not that her action had a causal explanation, nor even that it had remote causes, but that her own desires were not part of the causal sequence that led to it. Richard Taylor criticizes this compatibilist strategy.

The compatibilist supposes that freedom lies not in the absence of causation, but—at least in part—in one's actions being under the control of the appropriate sorts of causes. For Hume these causes are the agent's desires. But the efficacy of some desires seems to detract from our freedom, not enhance it—consider the desires of a compulsive drug addict. A plausible compatibilism must go beyond Hume in characterizing what Harry G. Frankfurt calls "the structure of a person's will," when that person has the kind of freedom we care about. And that is what Frankfurt tries to do in his essay.

Finally, Peter Strawson focuses on our actual practices of holding people responsible. He suggests that a nuanced conception of these practices supports a compatibilist view. Strawson argues that at the heart of our practices of holding responsible are "participant reactive attitudes" such as gratitude and resentment. These are reactions to "the good or ill will . . . of others towards us." Standard excuses such as ignorance or external compulsion tend to block these reactions because they tend to undermine the assumption that ill will was expressed. If, for example, I learn that you stepped on my foot only because you were blown by the wind I will no longer see your action as expressing ill will; so I will no longer resent you for your action. We also tend to pull back from the reactive attitudes when we think that the other person is incapacitated in ways that preclude "ordinary interpersonal relationships"—one of Strawson's examples is the case of "the mentally deranged." In such cases we tend instead to take an "objective" attitude: we see the person as, perhaps, someone to be treated or trained, but not as a target of resentment or gratitude. This is to refrain from holding him responsible.

Strawson argues, however, that within our framework of reactive attitudes the mere fact that a person's act was determined is not by itself grounds for retreating to an objective attitude. To have such grounds requires a relevant incapacity for interpersonal relations, a sort of incapacity that is not insured by determinism. According to the standards internal to the framework of reactive attitudes, then, a causally determined action may be responsible action. Finally, Strawson challenges the idea that if we came to believe determinism we rationally should abandon the framework of reactive attitudes and take, very generally, the objective attitude.

A. The Traditional Problem of Mind and Body

The Argument from Analogy for Other Minds

BERTRAND RUSSELL

—•—

THE PROBLEM WITH WHICH WE are concerned is the following. We observe in ourselves such occurrences as remembering, reasoning, feeling pleasure, and feeling pain. We think that sticks and stones do not have these experiences, but that other people do. Most of us have no doubt that the higher animals feel pleasure and pain, though I was once assured by a fisherman that "Fish have no sense nor feeling." I failed to find out how he had acquired this knowledge. Most people would disagree with him, but would be doubtful about oysters and starfish. However this may be, common sense admits an increasing doubtfulness as we descend in the animal kingdom, but as regards human beings it admits no doubt.

It is clear that belief in the minds of others requires some postulate that is not required in physics, since physics can be content with a knowledge of structure. My present purpose is to suggest what this further postulate may be.

It is clear that we must appeal to something that may be vaguely called "analogy." The behavior of other people is in many ways analogous to our own, and we suppose that it must have analogous causes. What people say is what we should say if we had certain thoughts, and so we infer that they probably have these thoughts. They give us information which we can sometimes subsequently verify. They behave in ways in which we behave when we are pleased (or displeased) in circumstances in which we should be pleased (or displeased). We may talk over with a friend some incident which we have both experienced, and find that his reminiscences dovetail with our own; this is particularly convincing when he remembers something that we have forgotten but that he recalls to our thoughts. Or again: you set your boy a problem in arithmetic, and with luck he gets the right answer; this persuades you that he is capable of arithmetical reasoning. There are, in short, very many ways in which my responses to stimuli differ from those of "dead" matter, and in all these ways other people resemble me. As it is clear to me that the causal laws governing my behavior have to do with "thoughts," it is natural to infer that the same is true of the analogous behavior of my friends.

The inference with which we are at present concerned is not merely that which takes us beyond solipsism, by maintaining that sensations have causes about which *something* can be known. This kind of inference . . . suffices for physics. . . . We are concerned now with a much more specific kind of inference, the kind that is involved in our knowledge of the thoughts and feelings of others—assuming that we have such knowledge. It is of course obvious that such knowledge is more or less doubtful. There is not only the general argument that we may be dreaming; there is also the possibility of ingenious automata. There are calculating machines that do sums much better than our schoolboy sons; there are gramophone records that remember impeccably what So-and-so said on such-and-such an occasion; there are people in the cinema who, though copies of real people, are not themselves alive. There is no theoretical limit to what ingenuity could achieve in the way of producing the illusion of life where in fact life is absent.

But, you will say, in all such cases it was the thoughts of human beings that produced the ingenious mechanism. Yes, but how do you know this? And how do you know that the gramophone does *not* "think"?

There is, in the first place, a difference in the causal laws of observable behavior. If I say to a student, "Write me a paper on Descartes's reasons for believing in the existence of matter," I shall, if he is industrious, cause a certain response. A gramophone record might be so constructed as to respond to this stimulus, perhaps better than the student, but if so it would be incapable of telling me anything about any other philosopher, even if I threatened to refuse to give it a degree. One of the most notable peculiarities of human behavior is change of response to a given stimulus. An ingenious person could construct an automaton which would always laugh at his jokes, however often it heard them; but a human being, after laughing a few times, will yawn, and end by saying, "How I laughed the first time I heard that joke."

But the differences in observable behavior between living and dead matter do not suffice to prove that there are "thoughts" connected with living bodies other than my own. It is probably possible theoretically to account for the behavior of living bodies by purely physical causal laws, and it is probably impossible to refute materialism by external observation alone. If we are to believe that there are thoughts and feelings other than our own, that must be in virtue of some inference in which our own thoughts and feelings are relevant, and such an inference must go beyond what is needed in physics.

I am, of course, not discussing the history of how we come to believe in other minds. We find ourselves believing in them when we first begin to reflect; the thought that Mother may be angry or pleased is one which arises in early infancy. What I am discussing is the possibility of a postulate which shall establish a rational connection between this belief and data, e.g., between the belief "Mother is angry" and the hearing of a loud voice.

The abstract schema seems to be as follows. We know, from observation of ourselves, a causal law of the form "A causes B," where A is a "thought" and B a physical occurrence. We sometimes observe a B when we cannot observe any A; we then infer an unobserved A. For example: I know that when I say, "I'm thirsty," I say so, usually, because I am thirsty, and therefore, when I hear the sentence "I'm thirsty" at a time when I am not thirsty, I assume that someone else is thirsty. I assume this the more readily if I see before me a hot, drooping body which goes on to say, "I have walked twenty desert miles in this heat with never a drop to drink." It is evident that my confidence in the "inference" is increased by increased complexity in the datum and also by increased certainty of the causal law derived from subjective observation, provided the causal law is such as to account for the complexities of the datum.

It is clear that insofar as plurality of causes is to be suspected, the kind of inference we have been considering is not valid. We are supposed to know "A causes B," and also to know that B has occurred; if this is to justify us in inferring A, we must know that *only* A causes B. Or, if we are content to infer that A is probable, it will suffice if we can know that in most cases it is A that causes B. If you hear thunder without having seen lightning, you confidently infer that there was lightning, because you are convinced that the sort of noise you heard is seldom caused by anything except lightning. As this example shows, our principle is not only employed to establish the existence of other minds but is habitually assumed, though in a less concrete form, in physics. I say "a less concrete form" because unseen lightning is only abstractly similar to seen lightning, whereas we suppose the similarity of other minds to our own to be by no means purely abstract.

Complexity in the observed behavior of another person, when this can all be accounted for by a simple cause such as thirst, increases the probability of the inference by diminishing the probability of some other cause. I think that in ideally favorable circumstances the argument would be formally as follows:

From subjective observation I know that A, which is a thought or feeling, causes B, which is a bodily act, e.g., a statement. I know also that, whenever B is an act of my own body, A is its cause. I now observe an act of the kind B in a body not my own, and I am having no thought or feeling of the kind A. But I still believe, on the basis of self-observation, that only A can cause B; I therefore infer that there was an A which caused B, though it was not an A that I could observe. On this ground I infer that other people's bodies are associated with minds, which resemble mine in proportion as their bodily behavior resembles my own.

In practice, the exactness and certainty of the above statement must be softened. We cannot be sure that, in our subjective experience, A is the only cause of B. And even if A is the only cause of B in our experience, how can we know that this holds outside our experience? It is not necessary that we should know this with any certainty; it is enough if it is highly probable. It is the assumption of probability in such cases that is our postulate. The postulate may therefore be stated as follows:

> If, whenever we can observe whether A and B are present or absent, we find that every case of B has an A as a causal antecedent, then it is probable that most B's have A's as causal antecedents, even in cases where observation does not enable us to know whether A is present or not.

This postulate, if accepted, justifies the inference to other minds, as well as many other inferences that are made unreflectingly by common sense.

Descartes's Myth

GILBERT RYLE

Gilbert Ryle (1900–1976) was Waynflete Professor of Metaphysical Philosophy at Oxford University. A leading ordinary language philosopher, his works include *The Concept of Mind, Dilemmas*, and *Plato's Progress*.

(1) The Official Doctrine

There is a doctrine about the nature and place of minds which is so prevalent among theorists and even among laymen that it deserves to be described as the official theory. Most philosophers, psychologists, and religious teachers subscribe, with minor reservations, to its main articles and, although they admit certain theoretical difficulties in it, they tend to assume that these can be overcome without serious modifications being made to the architecture of the theory. It will be argued here that the central principles of the doctrine are unsound and conflict with the whole body of what we know about minds when we are not speculating about them.

The official doctrine, which hails chiefly from Descartes, is something like this. With the doubtful exceptions of idiots and infants in arms every human being has both a body and a mind. Some would prefer to say that every human being is both a body and a mind. His body and his mind are ordinarily harnessed together, but after the death of the body his mind may continue to exist and function.

Human bodies are in space and are subject to the mechanical laws which govern all other bodies in space. Bodily processes and states can be inspected by external observers. So a man's bodily life is as much a public affair as are the lives of animals and reptiles and even as the careers of trees, crystals, and planets.

But minds are not in space, nor are their operations subject to mechanical laws. The workings of one mind are not witnessable by other observers; its career is private. Only I can take direct cognisance of the states and processes of my own mind. A person therefore lives through two collateral histories, one consisting of what happens in and to his body, the other consisting of what happens in and to his mind. The first is public, the second private. The events in the first history are events in the physical world, those in the second are events in the mental world.

It has been disputed whether a person does or can directly monitor all or only some of the episodes of his own private history; but, according to the official doctrine, of at least some of these episodes he has direct and unchallengeable cognisance. In consciousness, self-consciousness, and introspection he is directly and authentically apprised of the present states and operations of his mind. He may have great or small uncertainties about concurrent and adjacent episodes in the physical world, but he can have none about at least part of what is momentarily occupying his mind.

It is customary to express this bifurcation of his two lives and of his two worlds by saying that the things and events which belong to the physical world, including his own body, are external, while the workings of his own mind are internal. This antithesis of outer and inner is of course meant to be construed as a metaphor, since minds, not being in space, could not be described as being spatially inside anything else, or as having things going on spatially inside themselves. But relapses from this good intention are common and theorists are found speculating how stimuli, the physical sources of which are yards or miles outside a person's skin, can generate mental responses inside his skull, or how decisions framed inside his cranium can set going movements of his extremities.

Even when "inner" and "outer" are construed as metaphors, the problem how a person's mind and body influence one another is notoriously charged with theoretical difficulties. What the mind wills, the legs, arms, and the tongue execute; what affects the ear and the eye has something to do with what the mind perceives; grimaces and smiles betray the mind's moods and bodily castigations lead, it is hoped, to moral improvement. But the actual transactions between the episodes of the private history and those of the public history remain mysterious, since by definition they can belong to neither series. They could not be reported among the happenings described in a person's autobiography of his inner life, but nor could they be reported among those described in some one else's biography of that person's overt career. They can be inspected neither by introspection nor by laboratory experiment. They are theoretical shuttlecocks which are forever being bandied from the physiologist back to the psychologist and from the psychologist back to the physiologist.

Underlying this partly metaphorical representation of the bifurcation of a person's two lives there is a seemingly more profound and philosophical assumption. It is assumed that there are two different kinds of existence or status. What exists or happens may have the status of physical existence, or it may have the status of mental existence. Somewhat as the faces of coins are either heads or tails, or somewhat as living creatures are either male or female, so, it is supposed, some existing is physical existing, other existing is mental existing. It is a necessary feature of what has physical existence that it is in space and time, it is a necessary feature of what has mental existence that it is in time but not in space. What has physical existence is composed of matter, or else is a function of matter; what has mental existence consists of consciousness, or else is a function of consciousness.

There is thus a polar opposition between mind and matter, an opposition which is often brought out as follows. Material objects are situated in a common field, known as "space," and what happens to one body in one part of space is mechanically connected with what happens to other bodies in other parts of space. But mental happenings occur in insulated fields, known as "minds," and there is, apart maybe from telepathy, no direct causal connection between what happens in one mind and what happens in another. Only through the medium of the public physical world can the mind of one person make a difference to the mind of another. The mind is its own place and in his inner life each of us lives the life of a ghostly Robinson Crusoe. People can see, hear, and jolt one another's bodies, but they are irremediably blind and deaf to the workings of one another's minds and inoperative upon them.

What sort of knowledge can be secured of the workings of a mind? On the one side, according to the official theory, a person has direct knowledge of the best imaginable kind of the workings of his own mind. Mental states and processes are (or are normally) conscious states and processes, and the consciousness which irradiates them can engender no illusions and leaves the door open for no doubts. A person's present thinkings, feelings and willings, his perceivings, rememberings, and imaginings are intrinsically "phosphorescent"; their existence and their nature are inevitably betrayed to their owner. The inner life is a stream of consciousness of such a sort that it would be absurd to suggest that the mind whose life is that stream might be unaware of what is passing down it.

True, the evidence adduced recently by Freud seems to show that there exist channels tributary to this stream, which run hidden from their owner. People are actuated by impulses the existence of which they vigorously disavow; some of their thoughts differ from the thoughts which they acknowledge; and some of the actions which they think they will to perform they do not really will. They are thoroughly gulled by some of their own hypocrisies and they successfully ignore facts about their mental lives which on the official theory ought to be patent to them. Holders of the official theory tend, however, to maintain that anyhow in normal circumstances a person must be directly and authentically seized of the present state and workings of his own mind.

Besides being currently supplied with these alleged immediate data of consciousness, a person is also generally supposed to be able to exercise from time to time a special kind of perception, namely inner perception, or introspection. He can take a (non-optical) "look" at what is passing in his mind. Not only can he view and scrutinize a flower through his sense of sight and listen to and discriminate the notes of a bell through his sense of hearing; he can also reflectively or introspectively watch, without any bodily organ of sense, the current episodes of his inner life. This self-observation is also commonly supposed to be immune from illusion, confusion, or doubt. A mind's reports of its own affairs have a certainty superior to the best that is possessed by its reports of matters in the physical world. Sense-perceptions can, but consciousness and introspection cannot, be mistaken or confused.

On the other side, one person has no direct access of any sort to the events of the inner life of another. He cannot do better than make problematic inferences from the observed behaviour of the other person's body to the states of mind which, by analogy from his own conduct, he supposes to be signalised by that behaviour. Direct access to the workings of a mind is the privilege of that mind itself; in default of such privileged access, the workings of one mind are inevitably occult to everyone else. For the supposed arguments from bodily movements similar to their own to mental workings similar to their own would lack any possibility of observational corroboration. Not unnaturally, therefore, an adherent of the official theory finds it difficult to resist this consequence of his premises, that he has no good reason to believe that there do exist minds other than his own. Even if he prefers to believe that to other human bodies there are harnessed minds not unlike his own, he cannot claim to be able to discover their individual characteristics, or the particular things that they undergo and do. Absolute solitude is on this showing the ineluctable destiny of the soul. Only our bodies can meet.

As a necessary corollary of this general scheme there is implicitly prescribed a special way of construing our ordinary concepts of mental powers and operations. The verbs, nouns, and adjectives, with which in ordinary life we describe the wits, characters, and higher-grade performances of the people with whom we have to do, are required to be construed as signifying special episodes in their secret histories, or else as signifying tendencies for such episodes to occur. When someone is described as knowing, believing, or guessing something, as hoping, dreading, intending, or shirking something, as designing this or being amused at that, these verbs are supposed to denote the occurrence of specific modifications in his (to us) occult stream of consciousness. Only his own privileged access to this stream in direct awareness and introspection could provide authentic testimony that these mental-conduct verbs were correctly or incorrectly applied. The onlooker, be he teacher, critic, biographer, or friend, can never assure himself that his comments have any vestige of truth. Yet it was just because we do in fact all know how to make such comments, make them with general correctness and correct them when they turn out to be confused or mistaken, that philosophers found it necessary to construct their theories of the nature and place of minds. Finding mental-conduct concepts being regularly and effectively used, they properly sought to fix their logical geography. But the logical geography officially recommended would entail that there could be no regular or effective use of these mental-conduct concepts in our descriptions of, and prescriptions for, other people's minds.

(2) The Absurdity of the Official Doctrine

Such in outline is the official theory. I shall often speak of it, with deliberate abusiveness, as "the dogma of the Ghost in the Machine." I hope to prove that it is entirely false, and false not in detail but in principle. It is not merely an assemblage of particular mistakes. It is one big mistake and a mistake of a special kind. It is, namely, a category-mistake. It represents the facts of mental life as if they belonged to one logical type or category (or range of types or categories), when they actually belong to another. The dogma is therefore a philosopher's myth. In attempting to explode the myth I shall probably be taken to be denying well-known facts about the mental life of human beings, and my plea

that I aim at doing nothing more than rectify the logic of mental-conduct concepts will probably be disallowed as mere subterfuge.

I must first indicate what is meant by the phrase "Category-mistake." This I do in a series of illustrations.

A foreigner visiting Oxford or Cambridge for the first time is shown a number of colleges, libraries, playing fields, museums, scientific departments and administrative offices. He then asks "But where is the University? I have seen where the members of the Colleges live, where the Registrar works, where the scientists experiment and the rest. But I have not yet seen the University in which reside and work the members of your University." It has then to be explained to him that the University is not another collateral institution, some ulterior counterpart to the colleges, laboratories, and offices which he has seen. The University is just the way in which all that he has already seen is organized. When they are seen and when their coordination is understood, the University has been seen. His mistake lay in his innocent assumption that it was correct to speak of Christ Church, the Bodleian Library, The Ashmolean Museum, *and* the University, to speak, that is, as if "the University" stood for an extra member of the class of which these other units are members. He was mistakenly allocating the University to the same category as that to which the other institutions belong.

The same mistake would be made by a child witnessing the march-past of a division, who, having had pointed out to him such and such battalions, batteries, squadrons, etc., asked when the division was going to appear. He would be supposing that a division was counterpart to the units already seen, partly similar to them and partly unlike them. He would be shown his mistake by being told that in watching the battalions, batteries, and squadrons marching past he had been watching the division marching past. The march-past was not a parade of battalions, batteries, squadrons, *and* a division; it was a parade of the battalions, batteries, and squadrons *of* a division.

One more illustration. A foreigner watching his first game of cricket learns what are the functions of the bowlers, the batsmen, the fielders, the umpires, and the scorers. He than says, "But there is no one left on the field to contribute the famous element of team-spirit. I see who does the bowling, the batting, and the wicket-keeping; but I do not see whose role it is to exercise *esprit de corps.*" Once more, it would have to be explained that he was looking for the wrong type of thing. Team-spirit is not another cricketing-operation supplementary to all of the other special tasks. It is, roughly, the keenness with which each of the special tasks is performed, and performing a task keenly is not performing two tasks. Certainly exhibiting team-spirit is not the same thing as bowling or catching, but nor is it a third thing such that we can say that the bowler first bowls *and* then exhibits team-spirit or that a fielder is at a given moment *either* catching *or* displaying *esprit de corps.*

These illustrations of category-mistakes have a common feature which must be noticed. The mistakes were made by people who did not know how to wield the concepts *University*, *division*, and *team-spirit*. Their puzzles arose from inability to use certain items in the English vocabulary.

The theoretically interesting category-mistakes are those made by people who are perfectly competent to apply concepts, at least in the situations with which they are familiar, but are still liable in their abstract thinking to allocate those concepts to logical types to which they do not belong. An instance of a mistake of this sort would be the following story. A student of politics has learned the main differences between the British, the French, and the American Constitutions, and has learned also the differences and connections between the Cabinet, Parliament, the various Ministries, the Judicature, and the Church of England. But he still becomes embarrassed when asked questions about the connections between the Church of England, the Home Office, and the British Constitution. For while the Church and the Home Office are institutions, the British Constitution is not another institution in the same sense of that noun. So inter-institutional relations which can be asserted or denied to hold between the Church and the Home Office cannot be asserted or denied to hold between either of them and the British Constitution. "The British Constitution" is not a term of the same logical type as "the Home Office" and "the Church of England." In a partially similar way, John Doe may be a relative, a friend,

an enemy, or a stranger to Richard Roe; but he cannot be any of these things to the Average Taxpayer. He knows how to talk sense in certain sorts of discussions about the Average Taxpayer, but he is baffled to say why he could not come across him in the street as he can come across Richard Roe.

It is pertinent to our main subject to notice that, so long as the student of politics continues to think of the British Constitution as a counterpart to the other institutions, he will tend to describe it as a mysteriously occult institution; and so long as John Doe continues to think of the Average Taxpayer as a fellow-citizen, he will tend to think of him as an elusive insubstantial man, a ghost who is everywhere yet nowhere.

My destructive purpose is to show that a family of radical category-mistakes is the source of the double-life theory. The representation of a person as a ghost mysteriously ensconced in a machine derives from this argument. Because, as is true, a person's thinking, feeling, and purposive doing cannot be described solely in the idioms of physics, chemistry, and physiology, therefore they must be described in counterpart idioms. As the human body is a complex organised unit, so the human mind must be another complex organised unit, though one made of a different sort of stuff and with a different sort of structure. Or, again, as the human body, like any other parcel of matter, is a field of causes and effects, so the mind must be another field of causes and effects, though not (Heaven be praised) mechanical causes and effects.

(3) The Origin of the Category-Mistake

One of the chief intellectual origins of what I have yet to prove to be the Cartesian category-mistake seems to be this. When Galileo showed that his methods of scientific discovery were competent to provide a mechanical theory which should cover every occupant of space, Descartes found in himself two conflicting motives. As a man of scientific genius he could not but endorse the claims of mechanics, yet as a religious and moral man he could not accept, as Hobbes accepted, the discouraging rider to those claims, namely that human nature differs only in degree of complexity from clockwork. The mental could not be just a variety of the mechanical.

He and subsequent philosophers naturally but erroneously availed themselves of the following escape-route. Since mental-conduct words are not to be construed as signifying the occurrence of mechanical processes, they must be construed as signifying the occurrence of non-mechanical processes; since mechanical laws explain movements in space as the effects of other movements in space, other laws must explain some of the nonspatial workings of minds as the effects of other non-spatial workings of minds. The difference between the human behaviours which we describe as intelligent and those which we describe as unintelligent must be a difference in their causation; so, while some movements of human tongues and limbs are the effects of mechanical causes, others must be the effects of non-mechanical causes, i.e. some issue from movements of particles of matter, others from workings of the mind.

The differences between the physical and the mental were thus represented as differences inside the common framework of the categories of "thing," "stuff," "attribute," "stage," "process," "change," "cause," and "effect." Minds are things, but different sorts of things from bodies; mental processes are causes and effects but different sorts of causes and effects from bodily movements. And so on. Somewhat as the foreigner expected the University to be an extra edifice, rather like a college but also considerably different, so the repudiators of mechanism represented minds as extra centers of causal processes, rather like machines but also considerably different from them. Their theory was a paramechanical hypothesis.

That this assumption was at the heart of the doctrine is shown by the fact that there was from the beginning felt to be a major theoretical difficulty in explaining how minds can influence and be influenced by bodies. How can a mental process, such as willing, cause spatial movements like the movements of the tongue? How can a physical change in the optic nerve have among its effects a mind's perception of a flash of light? This notorious crux by itself shows the logical mould into which Descartes pressed his theory of the mind. It was the self-same

mould into which he and Galileo set their mechanics. Still unwittingly adhering to the grammar of mechanics, he tried to avert disaster by describing minds in what was merely an obverse vocabulary. The workings of minds had to be described by the mere negatives of the specific descriptions given to bodies; they are not in space, they are not motions, they are not modifications of matter, they are not accessible to public observation. Minds are not bits of clockwork, they are just bits of not-clockwork.

As thus represented, minds are not merely ghosts harnessed to machines, they are themselves just spectral machines. Though the human body is an engine, it is not quite an ordinary engine, since some of its workings are governed by another engine inside it—this interior governor-engine being one of a very special sort. It is invisible, inaudible, and it has no size or weight. It cannot be taken to bits and the laws it obeys are not those known to ordinary engineers. Nothing is known of how it governs the bodily engine.

A second major crux points the same moral. Since, according to the doctrine, minds belong to the same category as bodies and since bodies are rigidly governed by mechanical laws, it seemed to many theorists to follow that minds must be similarly governed by rigid non-mechanical laws. The physical world is a deterministic system, so the mental world must be a deterministic system. Bodies cannot help the modifications that they undergo, so minds cannot help pursuing the careers fixed for them. *Responsibility*, *choice*, *merit* and, *demerit* are therefore inapplicable concepts—unless the compromise solution is adopted of saying that the laws governing mental processes, unlike those governing physical processes, have the congenial attribute of being only rather rigid. The problem of the Freedom of the Will was the problem how to reconcile the hypothesis that minds are to be described in terms drawn from the categories of mechanics with the knowledge that higher-grade human conduct is not of a piece with the behaviour of machines.

It is an historical curiosity that it was not noticed that the entire argument was broken-backed. Theorists correctly assumed that any sane man could already recognise the differences between, say, rational and non-rational utterances or between purposive and automatic behaviour. Else there would have been nothing requiring to be salved from mechanism. Yet the explanation given pre-supposed that one person could in principle never recognise the difference between the rational and the irrational utterances issuing from other human bodies, since he could never get access to the postu-lated immaterial causes of some of their utterances. Save for the doubtful exception of himself, he could never tell the difference between a man and a Robot. It would have to be conceded, for example, that, for all that we can tell, the inner lives of persons who are classed as idiots or lunatics are as rational as those of anyone else. Perhaps only their overt be-haviour is disappointing; that is to say, perhaps "id-iots" are not really idiotic, or "lunatics" lunatic. Perhaps, too, some of those who are classed as sane are really idiots. According to the theory, external observers could never know how the overt behav-iour of others is correlated with their mental pow-ers and processes and so they could never know or even plausibly conjuncture whether their applica-tions of mental-conduct concepts to these other peo-ple were correct or incorrect. It would then be haz-ardous or impossible for a man to claim sanity or logical consistency even for himself, since he would be debarred from comparing his own performances with those of others. In short, our characterisations of per-sons and their performances as intelligent, prudent, and virtuous or as stupid, hypocritical, and cowardly could never have been made, so the problem of pro-viding a special causal hypothesis to serve as the basis of such diagnoses would never have arisen. The ques-tion, "How do persons differ from machines?" arose just because everyone already knew how to apply mental-conduct concepts before the new causal hy-pothesis was introduced. This causal hypothesis could not therefore be the source of the criteria used in those applications. Nor, of course, has the causal hypothesis in any degree improved our handling of those crite-ria. We still distinguish good from bad arithmetic, politic from impolitic conduct, and fertile from infer-tile imaginations in the ways in which Descartes him-self distinguished them before and after he speculated how the applicability of these criteria was compatible with the principle of mechanical causation.

He had mistaken the logic of his problem. Instead of asking by what criteria intelligent be-

haviour is actually distinguished from non-intelli-gent behaviour, he asked, "Given that the principle of mechanical causation does not tell us the differ-ence, what other causal principle will tell it us?" He realised that the problem was not one of mechanics and assumed that it must therefore be one of some counterpart to mechanics. Not unnaturally psychol-ogy is often cast for just this role.

When two terms belong to the same category, it is proper to construct conjunctive propositions em-bodying them. Thus a purchaser may say that he bought a left-hand glove and a right-hand glove, but not that he bought a left-hand glove, a right-hand glove and a pair of gloves. "She came home in a flood of tears and a sedan-chair" is a well-known joke based on the absurdity of conjoining terms of different types. It would have been equally ridicu-lous to construct the disjunction "She came home either in a flood of tears or else in a sedan-chair." Now the dogma of the Ghost in the Machine does just this. It maintains that there exist both bodies and minds; that there occur physical processes and mental processes; that there are mechanical causes of corporeal movements and mental causes of cor-poreal movements. I shall argue that these and other analogous conjunctions are absurd; but, it must be noticed, the argument will not show that either of the illegitimately conjoined propositions is absurd in itself. I am not, for example, denying that there occur mental processes. Doing long division is a mental process and so is making a joke. But I am saying that the phrase "there occur mental processes" does not mean the same sort of thing as "there occur physical processes," and, therefore, that it makes no sense to conjoin or disjoin the two.

If my argument is successful, there will follow some interesting consequences. First, the hallowed contrast between Mind and Matter will be dissi-pated, but dissipated not by either of the equally hal-lowed absorptions of Mind by Matter or of Matter by Mind, but in quite a different way. For the seem-ing contrast of the two will be shown to be as ille-gitimate as would be the contrast of "she came home in a flood of tears" and "she came home in a sedan-chair." The belief that there is a polar opposition be-tween Mind and Matter is the belief that they are terms of the same logical type.

It will also follow that both Idealism and Materialism are answers to an improper question. The "reduction" of the material world to mental states and processes, as well as the "reduction" of mental states and processes to physical states and processes, presuppose the legitimacy of the disjunction "Either there exist minds or there exist bodies (but not both)." It would be like saying, "Either she bought a left-hand and a right-hand glove or she bought a pair of gloves (but not both)."

It is perfectly proper to say, in one logical tone of voice, that there exist minds and to say, in another logical tone of voice, that there exist bodies. But these expressions do not indicate two different species of existence, for "existence" is not a generic word like "coloured" or "sexed." They indicate two different senses of "exist," somewhat as "rising" has different senses in "the tide is rising," "hopes are rising," and "the average age of death is rising." A man would be thought to be making a poor joke who said that three things are now rising, namely the tide, hopes, and the average age of death. It would be just as good or bad a joke to say that there exist prime numbers and Wednesdays and public opinions and navies; or that there exist both minds and bodies. . . .

(4) Historical Note

It would not be true to say that the official theory derives solely from Descartes's theories, or even from a more widespread anxiety about the implications of seventeenth century mechanics. Scholastic and Reformation theology has schooled the intellects of the scientists as well as of the laymen, philosophers, and clerics of that age. Stoic-Augustinian theories of the will were embedded in the Calvinist doctrines of sin and grace; Platonic and Aristotelian theories of the intellect shaped the orthodox doctrines of the immortality of the soul. Descartes was reformulating already prevalent theological doctrines of the soul in the new syntax of Galileo. The theologian's privacy of conscience became the philosopher's privacy of consciousness, and what had been the bogy of Predestination reappeared as the bogy of Determinism.

It would also not be true to say that the two-worlds myth did no theoretical good. Myths often do a lot of theoretical good, while they are still new. One benefit bestowed by the para-mechanical myth was that it partly superannuated the then prevalent para-political myth. Minds and their Faculties had previously been described by analogies with political superiors and political subordinates. The idioms used were those of ruling, obeying, collaborating, and rebelling. They survived and still survive in many ethical and some epistemological discussions. As, in physics, the new myth of occult Forces was a scientific improvement on the old myth of Final Causes, so, in anthropological and psychological theory, the new myth of hidden operations, impulses, and agencies was an improvement on the old myth of dictations, deferences, and disobediences.

The Nature of Mind

DAVID M. ARMSTRONG

David M. Armstrong (1926–   ) is Challis Professor of Philosophy at the University of Sydney. His publications include *Perception and the Physical World, A Materialist Theory of the Mind*, and *Universals and Scientific Realism*.

—◆—

MEN HAVE MINDS, THAT IS TO say, they perceive, they have sensations, emotions, beliefs, thoughts, purposes, and desires.[1] What is it to have a mind? What is it to perceive, to feel emotion, to hold a belief, or to have a purpose? In common with many other modern philosophers, I think that the best clue we have to the nature of mind is furnished by the discoveries and hypotheses of modern science concerning the nature of man.

What does modern science have to say about the nature of man? There are, of course, all sorts of disagreements and divergencies in the views of individual scientists. But I think it is true to say that one view is steadily gaining ground, so that it bids fair to become established scientific doctrine. This is the view that we can give a complete account of man *in purely physico-chemical terms*. This view has received a tremendous impetus in the last decade from the new subject of molecular biology, a subject which promises to unravel the physical and chemical mechanisms which lie at the basis of life. Before that time, it received great encouragement from pioneering work in neurophysiology pointing to the likelihood of a purely electro-chemical account of the working of the brain. I think it is fair to say that those scientists who still reject the physico-chemical account of man do so primarily for philosophical, or moral, or religious reasons, and only secondarily, and halfheartedly, for reasons of scientific detail. This is not to say that in the future new evidence and new problems may not come to light which will force science to reconsider the physico-chemical view of man. But at present the drift of scientific thought is clearly set towards the physico-chemical hypothesis. And we have nothing better to go on than the present.

For me, then, and for many philosophers who think like me, the moral is clear. We must try to work out an account of the nature of mind which is compatible with the view that man is nothing but a physico-chemical mechanism.

And . . . I shall be concerned to do just this: to sketch (in barest outline) what may be called a Materialist or Physicalist account of the mind.

But before doing this I should like to go back and consider a criticism of my position which must inevitably occur to some. What reason have I, it may be asked, for taking my stand on science? Even granting that I am right about what is the currently dominant scientific view of man, why should we concede science a special authority to decide questions about the nature of man? What of the authority of philosophy, of religion, of morality, or even of literature and art? Why do I set the authority of science above all these? Why this "scientism"?

It seems to me that the answer to this question is very simple. If we consider the search for truth, in all its fields, we find that it is only in science that men versed in their subject can, after investigation that is more or less prolonged, and which may in some cases extend beyond a single human lifetime, reach substantial agreement about what is the case. It is only as a result of scientific investigation that we ever seem to reach an intellectual consensus about controversial matters.

In the Epistle Dedicatory to his *De Corpore* Hobbes wrote of William Harvey, the discoverer of the circulation of the blood, that he was "the only man I know, that conquering envy, hath established a new doctrine in his life-time."

Before Copernicus, Galileo and Harvey, Hobbes remarks, "there was nothing certain in natural philosophy." And, we might add, with the exception of mathematics, there was nothing certain in any other learned discipline.

These remarks of Hobbes are incredibly revealing. They show us what a watershed in the intellectual history of the human race the seventeenth century was. Before that time inquiry proceeded, as it were, in the dark. Men could not hope to see their doctrine *established*, that is to say, accepted by the vast majority of those properly versed in the subject under discussion. There was no intellectual consensus. Since that time, it has become a commonplace to see new doctrines, sometimes of the most far-reaching kind, established to the satisfaction of the learned, often within the lifetime of their first proponents. Science has provided us with a method of deciding disputed questions. This is not to say, of course, that the consensus of those who are learned and competent in a subject cannot be mistaken. Of course such a consensus can be mistaken. Sometimes it has been mistaken. But, granting fallibility, what better authority have we than such a consensus?

Now this is of the utmost importance. For in philosophy, in religion, in such disciplines as literary criticism, in moral questions in so far as they are thought to be matters of truth and falsity, there has been a notable failure to achieve an intellectual consensus about disputed questions among the learned. Must we not then attach a peculiar authority to the discipline that can achieve a consensus? And if it presents us with a certain vision of the nature of man, is this not a powerful reason for accepting that vision?

I will not take up here the deeper question *why* it is that the methods of science have enabled us to achieve an intellectual consensus about so many disputed matters. That question, I think, could receive no brief or uncontroversial answer. I am resting my argument on the simple and uncontroversial fact that, as a result of scientific investigation, such a consensus has been achieved.

It may be replied—it often is replied—that while science is all very well in its own sphere—the sphere of the physical, perhaps—there are matters of fact on which it is not competent to pronounce. And among such matters, it may be claimed, is the question what is the whole nature of man. But I cannot see that this reply has much force. Science has provided us with an island of truths, or, perhaps one should say, a raft of truths, to bear us up on the sea of our disputatious ignorance. There may have to be revisions and refinements, new results may set old findings in a new perspective, but what science has given us will not be altogether superseded. Must we not therefore appeal to these relative certainties for guidance when we come to consider uncertainties elsewhere? Perhaps science cannot help us to decide whether or not there is a God, whether or not human beings have immortal souls, or whether or not the will is free. But if science cannot assist us, what can? I conclude that it is the scientific vision of man, and not the philosophical or religious or artistic or moral vision of man, that is the best clue we have to the nature of man. And it is rational to argue from the best evidence we have.

Having in this way attempted to justify my procedure, I turn back to my subject: the attempt to work out an account of mind, or, if you prefer, of mental process, within the framework of the physico-chemical or, as we may call it, the Materialist view of man.

Now there is one account of mental process that is at once attractive to any philosopher sympathetic to a Materialist view of man: this is Behaviourism. Formulated originally by a psychologist, J. B. Watson, it attracted widespread interest and considerable support from scientifically oriented philosophers. Traditional philosophy had tended to think of the mind as a rather mysterious inward arena that lay behind, and was responsible for, the outward or physical behaviour of our bodies. Descartes thought of this inner arena as a *spiritual substance*, and it was this conception of the mind as spiritual object that Gilbert Ryle attacked, apparently in the interest of Behaviourism, in his important book *The Concept of Mind*. He ridiculed the Cartesian view as the dogma of "the ghost in the machine." The mind was not something behind the behaviour of the body, it was simply part of that physical behaviour. My anger with you is not some modification of a spiritual substance which somehow brings about aggressive behaviour; rather it is the aggressive behaviour itself; my addressing strong words to you, striking you, turning my back on you, and so on. Thought is not an inner process that lies behind, and brings about, the words I speak and write: it is my speaking and writing. The mind is not an inner arena, it is outward act.

It is clear that such a view of mind fits in very well with a completely Materialistic or Physicalist view of man. If there is no need to draw a distinction between mental processes and their expression in physical behaviour, but if instead the mental processes are identified with their so-called "expressions," then the existence of mind stands in no conflict with the view that man is nothing but a physico-chemical mechanism.

However, the version of Behaviourism that I have just sketched is a very crude version, and its crudity lays it open to obvious objections. One obvious difficulty is that it is our common experience that there can be mental processes going on although there is no behaviour occurring that could possibly be treated as expressions of these processes. A man may be angry, but give no bodily sign; he may think, but say or do nothing at all.

In my view, the most plausible attempt to refine Behaviourism with a view to meeting this objection was made by introducing the notion of *a disposition to behave*. (Dispositions to behave play a particularly important part in Ryle's account of the mind.) Let us consider the general notion of disposition first. Brittleness is a disposition, a disposition possessed by materials like glass. Brittle materials are those which, when subjected to relatively small forces, break or shatter easily. But breaking and shattering easily is not brittleness, rather it is the *manifestation* of brittleness. Brittleness itself is the tendency or liability of the material to break or shatter easily. A piece of glass may never shatter or break throughout its whole history, but it is still the case that it is brittle: it is liable to shatter or break if dropped quite a small way or hit quite lightly. Now a disposition to *behave* is simply a tendency or liability of a person to behave in a certain way under certain cir-

cumstances. The brittleness of glass is a disposition that the glass retains throughout its history, but clearly there could also be dispositions that come and go. The dispositions to behave that are of interest to the Behaviourist are, for the most part, of this temporary character.

Now how did Ryle and others use the notion of a disposition to behave to meet the obvious objection to Behaviourism that there can be mental processes going on although the subject is engaging in no relevant behaviour? Their strategy was to argue that in such cases, although the subject was not behaving in any relevant way, he or she was *disposed* to behave in some relevant way. The glass does not shatter, but it is still brittle. The man does not behave, but he does have a disposition to behave. We can say he thinks although he does not speak or act because at that time he was disposed to speak or act in a certain way. *If* he had been asked, perhaps, he would have spoken or acted. We can say he is angry although he does not behave angrily, because he is disposed so to behave. *If* only one more word had been addressed to him, he would have burst out. And so on. In this way it was hoped that Behaviourism could be squared with the obvious facts.

It is very important to see just how these thinkers conceived of disposition. I quote from Ryle

> To possess a dispositional property *is not to be in a particular state, or to undergo a particular change*; it is to be bound or liable to be in a particular state, or to undergo a particular change, when a particular condition is realised. (*The Concept of Mind*, p. 43, my italics.)

So to explain the breaking of a lightly struck glass on a particular occasion by saying it was brittle is, on this view of dispositions, simply to say that the glass broke because it is the sort of thing that regularly breaks when quite lightly struck. The breaking was the normal behaviour, or not abnormal behaviour, of such a thing. The brittleness is not to be conceived of as a *cause* for the breakage, or even, more vaguely, a *factor* in bringing about the breaking. Brittleness is just the fact that things of that sort break easily.

But although in this way the Behaviourists did

something to deal with the objection that mental processes can occur in the absence of behaviour, it seems clear, now that the shouting and the dust have died, that they did not do enough. When I think, but my thoughts do not issue in any action, it seems as obvious as anything is obvious that there is something actually going on in me which constitutes my thought. It is not simply that I would speak or act if some conditions that are unfulfilled were to be fulfilled. Something is currently going on, in the strongest and most literal sense of "going on," and this something is my thought. Rylean Behaviourism denies this, and so it is unsatisfactory as a theory of mind. Yet I know of no version of Behaviourism that is more satisfactory. The moral of those of us who wish to take a purely physicalistic view of man is that we must look for some other account of the nature of mind and of mental processes.

But perhaps we need not grieve too deeply about the failure of Behaviourism to produce a satisfactory theory of mind. Behaviourism is a profoundly unnatural account of mental processes. If somebody speaks and acts in certain ways it is natural to speak of this speech and action as the *expression* of his thought. It is not at all natural to speak of his speech and action as identical with his thought. We naturally think of the thought as something quite distinct from the speech and action which, under suitable circumstances, brings the speech and action about. Thoughts are not to be identified with behaviour, we think, they lie behind behaviour. A man's behaviour constitutes the *reason* we have for attributing certain mental processes to him, but the behaviour cannot be identified with the mental processes.

This suggests a very interesting line of thought about the mind. Behaviourism is certainly wrong, but perhaps it is not altogether wrong. Perhaps the Behaviorists are wrong in identifying the mind and mental occurrences with behaviour, but perhaps they are right in thinking that our notion of a mind and of individual mental states is *logically tied to behaviour*. For perhaps what we mean by a mental state is some state of the person which, under suitable circumstances, *brings about* a certain range of behaviour. Perhaps mind can be defined not as behaviour, but rather as the inner *cause* of certain

behaviour. Thought is not speech under suitable circumstances, rather it is something within the person which, in suitable circumstances brings about speech. And, in fact, I believe that this is the true account, or, at any rate, a true first account, of what we mean by a mental state.

How does this line of thought link up with a purely physicalist view of man? The position is, I think, that while it does not make such a physicalist view inevitable, it does make it *possible*. It does not entail, but it is compatible with, a purely physicalist view of man. For if our notion of the mind and mental states is nothing but that of a cause within the person of certain ranges of behaviour, then it becomes a scientific question, and not a question of logical analysis, what in fact the intrinsic nature of that cause is. The cause might be, as Descartes thought it was, a spiritual substance working through the pineal gland to produce the complex bodily behaviour of which men are capable. It might be breath, or specially smooth and mobile atoms dispersed throughout the body; it might be many other things. But in fact the verdict of modern science seems to be that the sole cause of mind-betokening behaviour in man and the higher animals is the physico-chemical workings of the central nervous system. And so, assuming we have correctly characterised our concept of a mental state as nothing but the cause of certain sorts of behaviour, then we can identify these mental states with purely physical states of the central nervous system.

At this point we may stop and go back to the Behaviourists' dispositions. We saw that, according to them, the brittleness of glass or, to take another example, the elasticity of rubber, is not a state of the glass or the rubber, but is simply the fact that things of that sort behave in the way they do. But now let us consider how a scientist would think about brittleness or elasticity. Faced with the phenomenon of breakage under relatively small impacts, or the phenomenon of stretching when a force is applied followed by contraction when the force is removed, he will assume that there is some current *state* of the glass or the rubber which is responsible for the characteristic behaviour of samples of these two materials. At the beginning he will not know what this state is, but he will endeavor to find out, and he may succeed in finding out. And when he has found out he will very likely make remarks of this sort: "We have discovered that the brittleness of glass is in fact a certain sort of pattern in the molecules of the glass." That is to say, he will *identify* brittleness with the state of the glass that is responsible for the liability of the glass to break. For him, a disposition of an object is a state of the object. What makes the state a state of brittleness is the fact that it gives rise to the characteristic manifestations of brittleness. But the disposition itself is distinct from its manifestation: it is the state of the glass that gives rise to these manifestations in suitable circumstances.

You will see that this way of looking at dispositions is very different from that of Ryle and the Behaviourists. The great difference is this: If we treat dispositions as actual states, as I have suggested that scientists do, even if states whose intrinsic nature may yet have to be discovered, then we can say that dispositions are actual *causes*, or causal factors, which, in suitable circumstances, actually bring about those happenings which are the manifestations of the disposition. A certain molecular constitution of glass which constitutes its brittleness is actually *responsible* for the fact that, when the glass is struck, it breaks.

Now I shall not argue the matter here, because the detail of the argument is technical and difficult,[2] but I believe that the view of dispositions as states, which is the view that is natural to science, is the correct one. I believe it can be shown quite strictly that, to the extent that we admit the notion of dispositions at all, we are committed to the view that they are actual *states* of the object that has the disposition. I may add that I think that the same holds for the closely connected notions of capacities and powers. Here I will simply assume this step in my argument.

But perhaps it can be seen that the rejection of the idea that mind is simply a certain range of man's behaviour in favour of the view that mind is rather the inner *cause* of that range of man's behaviour is bound up with the rejection of the Rylean view of dispositions in favour of one that treats dispositions as states of objects and so as having actual causal power. The Behaviourists were wrong to identify the mind with behaviour. They were not so far off the mark when they tried to deal with cases where

mental happenings occur in the absence of behaviour by saying that these are dispositions to behave. But in order to reach a correct view, I am suggesting, they would have to conceive of these dispositions as actual *states* of the person who has the disposition, states that have actual power to bring about behaviour in suitable circumstances. But to do this is to abandon the central inspiration of Behaviourism: that in talking about the mind we do not have to go behind outward behaviour to inner states.

And so two separate but interlocking lines of thought have pushed me in the same direction. The first line of thought is that it goes profoundly against the grain to think of the mind as behaviour. The mind is, rather, that which stands behind and brings about our complex behaviour. The second line of thought is that the Behaviourists' dispositions, properly conceived, are really states that underlie behaviour, and, under suitable circumstances, bring about behaviour. Putting these two together, we reach the conception of a mental state as *a state of the person apt for producing certain ranges of behaviour*. This formula: a mental state is a state of the person apt for producing certain ranges of behaviour, I believe to be a very illuminating way of looking at the concept of a mental state. I have found it very fruitful in the search for detailed logical analyses of the individual mental concepts.

Now, I do not think that Hegel's dialectic has much to tell us about the nature of reality. But I think that human thought often moves in a dialectical way, from thesis to antithesis and then to the synthesis. Perhaps thought about the mind is a case in point. I have already said that classical philosophy tended to think of the mind as an inner arena of some sort. This we may call the Thesis. Behaviourism moved to the opposite extreme: the mind was seen as outward behaviour. This is the Antithesis. My proposed Synthesis is that the mind is properly conceived as an inner principle, but a principle that is identified in terms of the outward behaviour it is apt for bringing about. This way of looking at the mind and mental states does not itself entail a Materialist or Physicalist view of man, for nothing is said in this analysis about the intrinsic nature of these mental states. But is we have, as I have asserted that we do have, general scientific grounds for thinking that man is nothing but a physical mechanism, we can go on to argue that the mental states are in fact nothing but physical states of the central nervous system.

Along these lines, then, I would look for an account of the mind that is compatible with a purely Materialist theory of man. I have tried to carry out this programme in detail in *A Materialist Theory of the Mind*. There are, as may be imagined, all sorts of powerful objections that can be made to this view. But [in what follows] . . . I propose to do only one thing. I will develop one very important objection to my view of the mind—an objection felt by many philosophers—and then try to show how the objection should be met.

The view that our notion of mind is nothing but that of an inner principle apt for bringing about certain sorts of behaviour may be thought to share a certain weakness with Behaviourism. Modern philosophers have put the point about Behaviourism by saying that although Behaviourism may be a satisfactory account of the mind from an *other-person point of view*, it will not do as a *first-person* account. To explain. In our encounters with other people, all we ever observe is their behaviour: their actions, their speech, and so on. And so, if we simply consider other people, Behaviourism might seem to do full justice to the facts. But the trouble about Behaviourism is that it seems so unsatisfactory as applied to our *own* case. In our own case, we seem to be aware of so much more than mere behaviour.

Suppose that now we conceive of the mind as an inner principle apt for bringing about certain sorts of behaviour. This again fits the other-person cases very well. Bodily behaviour of a very sophisticated sort is observed, quite different from the behaviour that ordinary physical objects display. It is inferred that this behaviour must spring from a very special sort of inner cause in the object that exhibits this behaviour. This inner cause is christened "the mind," and those who take a physicalist view of man argue that it is simply the central nervous system of the body observed. Compare this with the case of glass. Certain characteristic behaviour is observed: the breaking and shattering of the material when acted upon by relatively small forces. A special inner state of the glass is postulated to explain this behaviour.

Those who take a purely physicalist view of glass then argue that this state is a *natural* state of the glass. It is, perhaps, an arrangement of its molecules, and not, say, the peculiarly malevolent disposition of the demons that dwell in glass.

But when we turn to our own case, the position may seem less plausible. We are conscious, we have experiences. Now can we say that to be conscious, to have experiences, is simply for something to go on within us apt for the causing of certain sorts of behaviour? Such an account does not seem to do any justice to the phenomena. And so it seems that our account of the mind, like Behaviourism, will fail to do justice to the first-person case.

In order to understand the objection better it may be helpful to consider a particular case. If you have driven for a very long distance without a break, you may have had experience of a curious state of automatism, which can occur in these conditions. One can suddenly "come to" and realise that one has driven for long distances without being aware of what one was doing, or, indeed, without being aware of anything. One has kept the car on the road, used the brake and the clutch perhaps, yet all without any awareness of what one was doing.

Now, if we consider this case it is obvious that *in some sense* mental processes are still going on when one is in such an automatic state. Unless one's will was still operating in some way, and unless one was still perceiving in some way, the car would not still be on the road. Yet, of course, *something* mental is lacking. Now, I think, when it is alleged that an account of mind as an inner principle apt for the production of certain sorts of behaviour leaves out consciousness or experience, what is alleged to have been left out is just whatever is missing in the automatic driving case. It is conceded that an account of mental processes as states of the person apt for the production of certain sorts of behaviour may very possibly be adequate to deal with such cases as that of automatic driving. It may be adequate to deal with most of the mental processes of animals, who perhaps spend a good deal of their lives in this state of automatism. But, it is contended, it cannot deal with the consciousness that we normally enjoy.

I will now try to sketch an answer to this important and powerful objection. Let us begin in an apparently unlikely place, and consider the way that an account of mental processes of the sort I am giving would deal with *sense-perception*.

Now psychologists, in particular, have long realised that there is a very close logical tie between sense-perception and *selective behaviour*. Suppose we want to decide whether an animal can perceive the difference between red and green. We might give the animal a choice between two pathways, over one of which a red light shines and over the other of which a green light shines. If the animal happens by chance to choose the green pathway we reward it; if it happens to choose the other pathway we do not reward it. If, after some trials, the animal systematically takes the green-lighted pathway, and if we become assured that the only relevant differences in the two pathways are the differences in the colour of the lights, we are entitled to say that the animal can see this colour difference. Using its eyes, it selects between red-lighted and green-lighted pathways. So we say it can see the difference between red and green.

Now a Behaviourist would be tempted to say that the animal's regularly selecting the green-lighted pathway *was* its perception of the colour difference. But this is unsatisfactory, because we all want to say that perception is something that goes on within the person or animal—within its mind—although, of course, this mental event is normally *caused* by the operation of the environment upon the organism. Suppose, however, that we speak instead of *capacities* for selective behaviour towards the current environment, and suppose we think of these capacities, like dispositions, as actual inner states of the organism. We can then think of the animal's perception as a state within the animal apt, if the animal is so impelled, for selective behaviour between the red- and green-lighted pathways.

In general, we can think of perceptions as inner states or events apt for the production of certain sorts of selective behaviour towards our environment. To perceive is like acquiring a key to a door. You do not have to use the key: you can put it in your pocket and never bother about the door. But if you do want to open the door the key may be essential. The blind man is a man who does not acquire certain keys, and, as a result, is not able to operate in his environment in the way that somebody who has his sight

can operate. It seems, then, a very promising view to take of perceptions that they are inner states defined by the sorts of selective behaviour that they enable the perceiver to exhibit, if so impelled.

Now how is this discussion of perception related to the question of consciousness of experience, the sort of thing that the driver who is in a state of automatism has not got, but which we normally do have? Simply this. My proposal is that consciousness, in this sense of the word, is nothing but *perception or awareness of the state of our own mind*. The driver in a state of automatism perceives, or is aware of, the road. If he did not, the car would be in a ditch. But he is not currently aware of this awareness of the road. He perceives the road, but he does not perceive his perceiving, or anything else that is going on in his mind. He is not, as we normally are, conscious of what is going on in his mind.

And so I conceive of consciousness or experience, in this sense of the words, in the way that Locke and Kant conceived it, as like perception. Kant, in a striking phrase, spoke of "inner sense." We cannot directly observe the minds of others, but each of us has the power to observe directly our own minds, and "perceive" what is going on there. The driver in the automatic state is one whose "inner eye" is shut: who is not currently aware of what is going on in his own mind.

Now if this account is along the right lines, why should we not give an account of this inner observation along the same lines as we have already given of perception? Why should we not conceive of it as an inner state, a state in this case directed towards other inner states and not to the environment, which enables us, if we are so impelled, to behave in a selective way *towards our own states of mind*? One who is aware, or conscious, of his thoughts or his emotions is one who has the capacity to make discriminations between his different mental states. His capacity might be exhibited in words. He might say that he was in an angry state of mind when, and only when, he *was* in an angry state of mind. But such verbal behaviour would be the mere *expression* or *result* of the awareness. The awareness itself would be an inner state: the sort of inner state that gave the man a capacity for such behavioural expressions.

So I have argued that consciousness of our own

mental state may be assimilated to *perception* of our own mental state, and that, like other perceptions, it may then be conceived of as an inner state or event giving a capacity for selective behaviour, in this case selective behaviour towards our own mental state. All this is meant to be simply a logical analysis of consciousness, and none of it entails, although it does not rule out, a purely physicalist account of what these inner states are. But if we are convinced, on general scientific grounds, that a purely physical account of man is likely to be the true one, then there seems to be no bar to our identifying these inner states with purely physical states of the central nervous system. And so consciousness of our own mental state becomes simply the scanning of one part of our central nervous system by another. Consciousness is a self-scanning mechanism in the central nervous system.

As I have emphasised before, I have done no more than sketch a programme for a philosophy of mind. There are all sorts of expansions and elucidations to be made, and all sorts of doubts and difficulties to be stated and overcome. But I hope I have done enough to show that a purely physicalist theory of the mind is an exciting and plausible intellectual option.

NOTES

1. Inaugural lecture of the Challis Professor of Philosophy at the University of Sydney (1965); slightly amended (1968).
2. It is presented in my book *A Materialist Theory of the Mind* (1968) ch. 6, sec. VI.

Mad Pain and Martian Pain

DAVID LEWIS

David Lewis (1941–   ), professor of philosophy at Princeton University, is a major philosopher of the twentieth century. Among his books are *Convention* and *Counterfactuals*.

—◆—

I

There might be a strange man who sometimes feels pain, just as we do, but whose pain differs greatly from ours in its causes and effects. Our pain is typically caused by cuts, burns, pressure, and the like; his is caused by moderate exercise on an empty stomach. Our pain is generally distracting; his turns his mind to mathematics, facilitating concentration on that but distracting him from anything else.

Intense pain has no tendency whatever to cause him to groan or writhe, but does cause him to cross his legs and snap his fingers. He is not in the least motivated to prevent pain or to get rid of it. In short, he feels pain but his pain does not at all occupy the typical causal role of pain. He would doubtless seem to us to be some sort of madman, and that is what I shall call him, though of course the sort of madness I have imagined may bear little resemblance to the real thing.

I said there might be such a madman. I don't know how to prove that something is possible, but my opinion that this is a possible case seems pretty firm. If I want a credible theory of mind, I need a theory that does not deny the possibility of mad pain. I needn't mind conceding that perhaps the madman is not in pain in *quite* the same sense that the rest of us are, but there had better be some straightforward sense in which he and we are both in pain.

Also, there might be a Martian who sometimes feels pain, just as we do, but whose pain differs greatly from ours in its physical realization. His hydraulic mind contains nothing like our neurons. Rather, there are varying amounts of fluid in many inflatable cavities, and the inflation of any one of these cavities opens some valves and closes others. His mental plumbing pervades most of his body—in fact, all but the heat exchanger inside his head. When you pinch his skin you cause no firing of C-fibers—he has none—but, rather, you cause the inflation of many smallish cavities in his feet. When these cavities are inflated, he is in pain. And the effects of his pain are fitting: his thought and activity are disrupted, he groans and writhes, he is strongly motivated to stop you from pinching him and to see to it that you never do again. In short, he feels pain but lacks the bodily states that either are pain or else accompany it in us.

There might be such a Martian; this opinion too seems pretty firm. A credible theory of mind had better not deny the possibility of Martian pain. I needn't mind conceding that perhaps the Martian is not in pain in *quite* the same sense that we Earthlings are, but there had better be some straightforward sense in which he and we are both in pain.

II

A credible theory of mind needs to make a place both for mad pain and for Martian pain. Prima facie, it seems hard for a materialist theory to pass this twofold test. As philosophers, we would like to characterize pain a priori. (We might settle for less, but let's start by asking for all we want.) As materialists, we want to characterize pain as a physical phenomenon. We can speak of the place of pain in the causal network from stimuli to inner states to behavior. And we can speak of the physical processes that go on when there is pain and that take their place in that causal network. We seem to have no other resources but these. But the lesson of mad pain is that pain is associated only contingently with its causal role, while the lesson of Martian pain is that pain is connected only contingently with its physical realization. How can we characterize pain a priori in terms of causal role and physical realization, and yet respect both kinds of contingency?

A simple identity theory straightforwardly solves the problem of mad pain. It goes just as straightforwardly wrong about Martian pain. A simple behaviorism or functionalism goes the other way: right about the Martian, wrong about the madman. The theories that fail our twofold test so decisively are altogether too simple. (Perhaps they are too simple ever to have had adherents.) It seems that a theory that can pass our test will have to be a mixed theory. It will have to be able to tell us that the madman and the Martian are both in pain, but for different reasons: the madman because he is in the right physical state, the Martian because he is in a state rightly situated in the causal network.

Certainly we can cook up a mixed theory. Here's an easy recipe: First, find a theory to take care of the common man and the madman, disregarding the Martian—presumably an identity theory. Second, find a theory to take care of the common man and the Martian, disregarding the madman—presumably some sort of behaviorism or functionalism. Then disjoin the two: say that to be in pain is to be in pain either according to the first theory or according to the second. Alternatively, claim ambiguity: say that to be in pain in one sense is to be in pain according to the first theory, to be in pain in another sense is to be in pain according to the second theory.

This strategy seems desperate. One wonders why we should have a disjunctive or ambiguous concept of pain, if common men who suffer pain are always in pain according to both disjuncts or both disambiguations. It detracts from the credibility of a theory that it posits a useless complexity in our concept of pain—useless in application to the common man, at least, and therefore useless almost always.

I don't object to the strategy of claiming ambiguity. As you'll see, I shall defend a version of it. But it's not plausible to cook up an ambiguity ad hoc to account for the compossibility of mad pain and Martian pain. It would be better to find a widespread sort of ambiguity, a sort we would believe in no matter what we thought about pain, and show that it will solve our problem. That is my plan.

III

A dozen years or so ago, D. M. Armstrong and I (independently) proposed a materialist theory of mind that joins claims of type-type psychophysical identity with a behaviorist or functionalist way of characterizing mental states such as pain.[1] I believe our theory passes the twofold test. Positing no ambiguity without independent reason, it provides natural senses in which both madman and Martian are in pain. It wriggles through between Scylla and Charybdis.

Our view is that the concept of pain, or indeed of any other experience or mental state, is the concept of a state that occupies a certain causal role, a state with certain typical causes and effects. It is the concept of a state apt for being caused by certain stimuli and apt for causing certain behavior. Or, better, of a state apt for being caused in certain ways by stimuli plus other mental states and apt for combining with certain other mental states to jointly cause certain behavior. It is the concept of a member of a system of states that together more or less realize the pattern of causal generalizations set forth in commonsense psychology. (That system may be characterized as a whole and its members characterized afterward by reference to their place in it.)

If the concept of pain is the concept of a state that occupies a certain causal role, then whatever state does occupy that role is pain. If the state of having neurons hooked up in a certain way and firing in a certain pattern is the state properly apt for causing and being caused, as we materialists think, then that neural state is pain. But the concept of pain is not the concept of that neural state. ("The concept of . . ." is an intensional functor.) The concept of pain, unlike the concept of that neural state which in fact is pain, would have applied to some different state if the relevant causal relations had been different. Pain might have not been pain. The occupant of the role might have not occupied it. Some other state might have occupied it instead. Something that is not pain might have been pain.

This is not to say, of course, that it might have been that pain was not pain and nonpain was pain; that is, that it might have been that the occupant of the role did not occupy it and some nonoccupant did. Compare: "The winner might have lost" (true) versus "It might have been that the winner lost"

(false). No wording is entirely unambiguous, but I trust my meaning is clear.

In short, the concept of pain as Armstrong and I understand it is a *nonrigid* concept. Likewise the word "pain" is a nonrigid designator. It is a contingent matter what state the concept and the word apply to. It depends on what causes what. The same goes for the rest of our concepts and ordinary names of mental states.

Some need hear no more. The notion that mental concepts and names are nonrigid, wherefore what *is* pain might not have been, seems to them just self-evidently false.[2] I cannot tell why they think so. Bracketing my own theoretical commitments, I think I would have no opinion one way or the other. It's not that I don't care about shaping theory to respect naive opinion as well as can be, but in this case I have no naive opinion to respect. If I am not speaking to your condition, so be it.

If pain is identical to a certain neural state, the identity is contingent. Whether it holds is one of the things that varies from one possible world to another. But take care. I do not say that here we have two states, pain and some neural state, that are contingently identical, identical at this world but different at another. Since I'm serious about the identity, we have not two states but one. This one state, this neural state which is pain, is not contingently identical to itself. It does not differ from itself at any world. Nothing does.[3] What's true is, rather, that the concept and name of pain contingently apply to some neural state at this world, but do not apply to it at another. Similarly, it is a contingent truth that Bruce is our cat, but it's wrong to say that Bruce and our cat are contingently identical. Our cat Bruce is necessarily self-identical. What is contingent is that the nonrigid concept of being our cat applies to Bruce rather than to some other cat, or none.

IV

Nonrigidity might begin at home. All actualities are possibilities, so the variety of possibilities includes the variety of actualities. Though some possibilities are thoroughly otherworldly, others may be found on planets within range of our telescopes. One such planet is Mars.

If a nonrigid concept or name applies to different states in different possible cases, it should be no surprise if it also applies to different states in different actual cases. Nonrigidity is to logical space as other relativities are to ordinary space. If the word "pain" designates one state at our actual world and another at a possible world where our counterparts have a different internal structure, then also it may designate one state on Earth and another on Mars. Or, better, since Martians may come here and we may go to Mars, it may designate one state for Earthlings and another for Martians.

We may say that some state *occupies a causal role for a population.* We may say this whether the population is situated entirely at our actual world, or partly at our actual world and partly at other worlds, or entirely at other worlds. If the concept of pain is the concept of a state that occupies that role, then we may say that a state *is pain for a population.* Then we may say that a certain pattern of firing of neurons is pain for the population of actual Earthlings and some but not all of our otherworldly counterparts, whereas the inflation of certain cavities in the feet is pain for the population of actual Martians and some of their otherworldly counterparts. Human pain is the state that occupies the role of pain for humans. Martian pain is the state that occupies the same role for Martians.

A state occupies a causal role for a population, and the concept of occupant of that role applies to it, if and only if, with few exceptions, whenever a member of that population is in that state, his being in that state has the sort of causes and effects given by the role.

The thing to say about Martian pain is that the Martian is in pain because he is in a state that occupies the causal role of pain for Martians, whereas we are in pain because we are in a state that occupies the role of pain for us.

V

Now, what of the madman? He is in pain, but he is not in a state that occupies the causal role of pain for him. He is in a state that occupies that role for most of us, but he is an exception. The causal role of a pattern of firing of neurons depends on one's circuit diagram, and he is hooked up wrong.

His state does not occupy the role of pain for a population comprising himself and his fellow madmen. But it does occupy that role for a more salient population—mankind at large. He is a man, albeit an exceptional one, and a member of that larger population.

We have allowed for exceptions. I spoke of the definitive syndrome of *typical* causes and effects. Armstrong spoke of a state *apt for* having certain causes and effects; that does not mean that it has them invariably. Again, I spoke of a system of states that *comes near* to realizing commonsense psychology. A state may therefore occupy a role for mankind even if it does not at all occupy that role for some mad minority of mankind.

The thing to say about mad pain is that the madman is in pain because he is in the state that occupies the causal role of pain for the population comprising all mankind. He is an exceptional member of that population. The state that occupies the role for the population does not occupy it for him.

VI

We may say that X is in pain simpliciter if and only if X is in the state that occupies the causal role of pain for the *appropriate* population. But what is the appropriate population? Perhaps (1) it should be *us;* after all, it's our concept and our word. On the other hand, if it's X we're talking about, perhaps (2) it should be a population that X himself belongs to, and (3) it should preferably be one in which X is not exceptional. Either way, (4) an appropriate population should be a natural kind—a species, perhaps.

If X is you and I—human and unexceptional—all four considerations pull together. The appropriate population consists of mankind as it actually is, extending into other worlds only to an extent that does not make the actual majority exceptional.

Since the four criteria agree in the case of the common man, which is the case we usually have in mind, there is no reason why we should have made up our minds about their relative importance in cases of conflict. It should be no surprise if ambiguity and uncertainty arise in such cases. Still, some cases do seem reasonably clear.

If X is our Martian, we are inclined to say that he is in pain when the cavities in his feet are inflated; and so says the theory, provided that criterion (1) is outweighed by the other three, so that the appropriate population is taken to be the species of Martians to which X belongs.

If X is our madman, we are inclined to say that he is in pain when he is in the state that occupies the role of pain for the rest of us; and so says the theory, provided that criterion (3) is outweighed by the other three, so that the appropriate population is taken to be mankind.

We might also consider the case of a mad Martian, related to other Martians as the madman is to the rest of us. If X is a mad Martian, I would be inclined to say that he in pain when the cavities in his feet are inflated; and so says our theory provided that criteria (2) and (4) together outweigh either (1) or (3) by itself.

Other cases are less clear-cut. Since the balance is less definitely in favor of one population or another, we may perceive the relativity to population by feeling genuinely undecided. Suppose the state that plays the role of pain for us plays instead the role of thirst for a certain small subpopulation of mankind, and vice versa. When one of them has the state that is pain for us and thirst for him, there may be genuine and irresolvable indecision about whether to call him pained or thirsty—that is, whether to think of him as a madman or as a Martian. Criterion (1) suggests calling his state pain and regarding him as an exception; criteria (2) and (3) suggest shifting to a subpopulation and calling his state thirst. Criterion (4) could go either way, since mankind and the exceptional subpopulation may both be natural kinds. (Perhaps it is relevant to ask whether membership in the subpopulation is hereditary.)

The interchange of pain and thirst parallels the traditional problem of inverted spectra. I have suggested that there is no determinate fact of the matter about whether the victim of interchange undergoes pain or thirst. I think this conclusion accords well with the fact that there seems to be no persuasive solution one way or the other to the old problem of inverted spectra. I would say that there is a good sense in which the alleged victim of inverted spectra sees red when he looks at grass: he is in a state that occupies the role of seeing red for mankind in general. And there is an equally good sense in which he sees green: he is in a state that occupies the role of seeing green for him, and for a small subpopulation of which he is an unexceptional member and which has some claim to be regarded as a natural kind. You are right to say either, though not in the same breath. Need more be said?

To sum up. Armstrong and I claim to give a schema that, if filled in, would characterize pain and other states a priori. If the causal facts are right, then also we characterize pain as a physical phenomenon. By allowing for exceptional members of a population, we associate pain only contingently with its causal role. Therefore we do not deny the possibility of mad pain, provided there is not too much of it. By allowing for variation from one population to another (actual or merely possible) we associate pain only contingently with its physical realization. Therefore we do not deny the possibility of Martian pain. If different ways of filling in the relativity to population may be said to yield different senses of the word "pain," then we plead ambiguity. The madman is in pain in one sense, or relative to one population. The Martian is in pain in another sense, or relative to another population. (So is the mad Martian.)

But we do not posit ambiguity ad hoc. The requisite flexibility is explained simply by supposing that we have not bothered to make up our minds about semantic niceties that would make no difference to any commonplace case. The ambiguity that arises in cases of inverted spectra and the like is simply one instance of a commonplace kind of ambiguity—a kind that may arise whenever we have tacit relativity and criteria of selection that sometimes fail to choose a definite relatum. It is the same kind of ambiguity that arises if someone speaks of relevant studies without making clear whether he means relevance to current affairs, to spiritual well-being, to understanding, or what.

VII

We have a place for commonplace pain, mad pain, Martian pain, and even mad Martian pain. But one case remains problematic. What about pain in a being who is mad, alien, and unique? Have we made a place for that? It seems not. Since he is mad, we may suppose that his alleged state of pain does not occupy the proper causal role for him. Since he is alien, we may also suppose that it does not occupy the proper role for us. And since he is unique, it does not occupy the proper role for others of his species. What is left?

(One thing that might be left is the population consisting of him and his unactualized counterparts at other worlds. If he went mad as a result of some improbable accident, perhaps we can say that he is in pain because he is in the state that occupies the role for most of his alternative possible selves; the state that would have occupied the role for him if he had developed in a more probable way. To make the problem as hard as possible, I must suppose that this solution is unavailable. He did *not* narrowly escape being so constituted that his present state would have occupied the role of pain.)

I think we cannot and need not solve this problem. Our only recourse is to deny that the case is possible. To stipulate that the being in this example is in pain was illegitimate. That seems credible enough. Admittedly, I might have thought offhand that the case was possible. No wonder; it merely combines elements of other cases that are possible. But I am willing to change my mind. Unlike my opinions about the possibility of mad pain and Martian pain, my naive opinions about this case are not firm enough to carry much weight.

VIII

Finally, I would like to try to preempt an objection. I can hear it said that I have been strangely silent about the very center of my topic. *What is it like* to be the madman, the Martian, the mad Martian, the victim of interchange of pain and thirst, or the being who is mad, alien, and unique? What is the *phenomenal character* of his state? If it *feels* to him like pain, then it *is* pain, whatever its causal role or physical nature. If not, it isn't. It's that simple!

Yes. It would indeed be a mistake to consider whether a state is pain while ignoring what it is like to have it. Fortunately, I have not made that mistake. Indeed, it is an impossible mistake to make. It is like the impossible mistake of considering whether

a number is composite while ignoring the question of what factors it has.

Pain is a feeling.[4] Surely that is uncontroversial. To have pain and to feel pain are one and the same. For a state to be pain and for it to feel painful are likewise one and the same. A theory of what it is for a state to be pain is inescapably a theory of what it is like to be in that state, of how that state feels, of the phenomenal character of that state. Far from ignoring questions of how states feel in the odd cases we have been considering, I have been discussing nothing else! Only if you believe on independent grounds that considerations of causal role and physical realization have no bearing on whether a state is pain should you say that they have no bearing on how that state feels.

NOTES

1. D. M. Armstrong, *A Materialist Theory of the Mind* (London: Routledge, 1968); "The Nature of Mind," in C. V. Borst, ed., *The Mind/Brain Identity Theory* (London: Macmillan, 1970), pp. 67–97; "The Causal Theory of the Mind," *Neue Heft für Philosophie*, no. 11 (Vendenhoek & Ruprecht, 1977), pp. 82–95. David Lewis, "An Argument for the Identity Theory," in *Philosophical Papers*, vol. 1 (New York: Oxford University Press, 1983); review of *Art, Mind, and Religion*, *Journal of Philosophy* 66 (1969): 22–27, particularly pp. 23–25; "Psychophysical and Theoretical Identifications," *Australasian Journal of Philosophy* 50 (1972): 249–58; "Radical Interpretation," in *Philosophical Papers*, vol. 1.

2. For instance, see Saul A. Kripke, "Naming and Necessity," in Gilbert Harman and Donald Davidson, eds., *Semantics of Natural Language* (Dordrecht: Reidel, 1972), pp. 253–355, 763–69, particularly pp. 335–36. Note that the sort of identity theory that Kripke opposes by argument, rather than by appeal to self-evidence, is not the sort that Armstrong and I propose.

3. The closest we can come is to have something at one world with twin counterparts at another. See my "Counterpart Theory and Quantified Modal Logic," in *Philosophical Papers*, vol. 1. That possibility is irrelevant to the present case.

4. Occurrent pain, that is. Maybe a disposition that sometimes but not always causes occurrent pain might also be called "pain."

Intentional Systems

DANIEL DENNETT

Daniel Dennett (1942-) is the author of *Content and Consciousness*, *Brainstorms*, *The Intentional Stance*, and *Consciousness Explained*. He is a professor of philosophy at Tufts University.

———•———

I WISH TO EXAMINE THE CONCEPT OF a system whose behavior can be—at least sometimes—explained and predicted by relying on ascriptions to the system of beliefs and desires (and hopes, fears, intentions, hunches, . . .). I will call such systems *intentional systems*, and such explanations and predictions intentional explanations and predictions, in virtue of the intentionality of the idioms of belief and desire (and hope, fear, intention, hunch, . . .).[1]

I used to insist on capitalizing "intentional" wherever I meant to be using Brentano's notion of *intentionality*, in order to distinguish this technical term from its cousin, e.g., "an intentional shove," but the technical term is now in much greater currency, and since almost everyone else who uses the term seems content to risk this confusion, I have decided, with some trepidation, to abandon my typographical eccentricity. But let the uninitiated reader beware: "intentional" as it occurs here is *not* the familiar term of layman's English.[2] For me, as for many recent authors, intentionality is primarily a feature of linguistic entities—idioms, contexts—and for my purposes here we can be satisfied that an idiom is intentional if substitution of codesignative terms do not preserve truth or if the "objects" of the idiom are not capturable in the usual way by quantifiers. I discuss this in more detail in *Content and Consciousness*.[3]

I

The first point to make about intentional systems[4] as I have just defined them is that a particular thing is an intentional system only in relation to the strategies of someone who is trying to explain and predict its behavior. What this amounts to can best be brought out by example. Consider the case of a chess-playing computer, and the different strategies or stances one might adopt as its opponent in trying to predict its moves. There are three different stances of interest to us. First there is the *design stance*. If one knows exactly how the computer is designed (including the impermanent part of its design: its program) one can predict its designed response to any move one makes by following the computation instructions of the program. One's prediction will come true provided only that the computer performs as designed—that is, without breakdown. Different varieties of design-stance predictions can be discerned, but all of them are alike in relying on the notion of *function*, which is purpose-relative or teleological. That is, a design of a system breaks it up into larger or smaller functional parts, and design-stance predictions are generated by assuming that each functional part will function properly. For instance, the radio engineer's schematic wiring diagrams have symbols for each resistor, capacitor, transistor, etc.—*each with its task to perform*—and he can give a design-stance prediction of the behavior of a circuit by assuming that each element performs its task. Thus one can make design-stance predictions of the computer's response at several different levels of abstraction, depending on whether one's design treats as smallest functional elements strategy-generators and consequence-testers, multipliers and dividers, or transistors and switches. (It should be noted that not all diagrams or pictures are designs in this sense, for a diagram may carry no information about the functions—intended or observed—of the elements it depicts.)

We generally adopt the design stance when making predictions about the behavior of mechanical objects, e.g., "As the typewriter carriage approaches the margin, a bell will ring (provided the machine is in working order)," and more simply, "Strike the match and it will light." We also often adopt this stance in predictions involving natural objects: "Heavy pruning will stimulate denser foliage and stronger limbs." The essential feature of the design stance is that we make predictions solely from knowledge or assumptions about the system's functional design, irrespective of the physical constitution or condition of the innards of the particular object.

Second, there is what we may call the *physical stance*. From this stance our predictions are based on the actual physical state of the particular object, and are worked out by applying whatever knowledge we have of the laws of nature. It is from this stance alone that we can predict the malfunction of systems (unless, as sometimes happens these days, a system is *designed* to malfunction after a certain time, in which case malfunctioning in one sense becomes a part of its proper functioning). Instances of predictions from the physical stance are common enough: "If you turn on the switch you'll get a nasty shock," and, "When the snows come that branch will break right off." One seldom adopts the physical stance in dealing with a computer just because the number of critical variables in the physical constitution of a computer would overwhelm the most prodigious calculator. Significantly, the physical stance is generally reserved for instances of breakdown, where the condition preventing normal operation is generalized and easily locatable, e.g., "Nothing will happen when you type in your questions, because it isn't plugged in," or, "It won't work with all that flood water in it." Attempting to give a physical account or prediction of the chess-playing computer would be a pointless and herculean labor, but it would work in principle. One could predict the re-sponse it would make in a chess game by tracing out the effects of the input energies all the way through the computer until once more type was pressed against paper and a response was printed. (Because of the digitial nature of computers, quantum-level indeterminacies, if such there be, will cancel out rather than accumulate, unless of course a radium "randomizer" or other amplifier of quantum effects is built into the computer).

The best chess-playing computers these days are practically inaccessible to prediction from either the design stance or the physical stance; they have become too complex for even their own designers to view from the design stance. A man's best hope of defeating such a machine in a chess match is to predict its responses by figuring out as best he can what the best or most rational move would be, given the rules and goals of chess. That is, one assumes not only (1) that the machine will function as designed, but (2) that the design is optimal as well, that the computer will "choose" the most rational move. Predictions made on these assumptions may well fail if either assumption proves unwarranted in the particular case, but still this *means* of prediction may impress us as the most fruitful one to adopt in dealing with a particular system. Put another way, when one can no longer hope to beat the machine by utilizing one's knowledge of physics or programming to anticipate its responses, one may still be able to avoid defeat by treating the machine rather like an intelligent human opponent.

We must look more closely at this strategy. A prediction relying on the assumption of the system's rationality is relative to a number of things. First, rationality here so far means nothing more than optimal design relative to a goal or optimally weighted hierarchy of goals (checkmate, winning pieces, defense, etc., in the case of chess) and a set of constraints (the rules and starting position). Prediction itself is, moreover, relative to the nature and extent of the information the system has at the time about the field of endeavor. The question one asks in framing a prediction of this sort is: What is the most rational thing for the computer to do, given goals x, $y, z, \ldots$, constraints $a, b, c, \ldots$ and information (including misinformation, if any) about the present state of affairs $p, q, r, \ldots$? In predicting the computer's response to my chess move, my assessment of the computer's most rational move may depend, for instance, not only on my assumption that the computer has information about the present disposition of all the pieces, but also on whether I believe the computer has information about my inability to see four moves ahead, the relative powers of knights and bishops, and my weakness for knight–bishop exchanges. In the end I may not be able to frame a very good prediction, if I am unable to determine with any accuracy what information and goals the computer has, or if the information and goals I take to be given do not dictate any one best move, or if I simply am not so good as the computer is at generating an optimal move from this given. Such predictions then are very precarious; not only are they relative to a set of postulates about goals, constraints, and information, and not only do they hinge on determining an optimal response in situations where we may have no clear criteria for what is optimal, but also they are vulnerable to short-circuit falsifications that are in principle unpredictable from this stance. Just as design-stance predictions are vulnerable to malfunctions (by depending on the assumption of no malfunction), so these predictions are vulnerable to design weaknesses and lapses (by depending on the assumption of optimal design). It is a measure of the success of contemporary program designers that these precarious predictions turn out to be true with enough regularity to make the method useful.

The denouement of this extended example should now be obvious: this third stance, with its assumption of rationality, is the *intentional stance*; the predictions one makes from it are intentional predictions; one is viewing the computer as an intentional system. One predicts behavior in such a case by ascribing to the system *the possession of certain information* and supposing it to be *directed by certain goals*, and then by working out the most reasonable or appropriate action on the basis of these ascriptions and suppositions. It is a small step to calling the information possessed the computer's *beliefs*, its goals and subgoals its *desires*. What I mean by saying that this is a small step, is that the notion of possession of information or misinformation is just as intentional a notion as that of belief. The "possession" at issue is hardly the bland and innocent no-

tion of storage one might suppose; it is, and must be, "epistemic possession"—an analogue of belief. Consider: the Frenchman who possesses the *Encyclopedia Britannica* but knows no English might be said to "possess" the information in it, but if there is such a sense of possession, it is not strong enough to serve as the sort of possession the computer must be supposed to enjoy, relative to the information it *uses* in "choosing" a chess move. In a similar way, the goals of a goal-directed computer must be specified intentionally, just like desires.

Lingering doubts about whether the chess-playing computer *really* has beliefs and desires are misplaced; for the definition of intentional systems I have given does not say that intentional systems *really* have beliefs and desires, but that one can explain and predict their behavior by *ascribing* beliefs and desires to them, and whether one calls what one ascribes to the computer beliefs or belief-analogues or information complexes or intentional whatnots makes no difference to the nature of the calculation one makes on the basis of the ascriptions. One will arrive at the same predictions whether one forthrightly thinks in terms of the computer's beliefs and desires, or in terms of the computer's information-store and goal-specifications. The inescapable and interesting fact is that for the best chess-playing computers of today, intentional explanation and prediction of their behavior is not only common, but works when no other sort of prediction of their behavior is manageable. We do quite successfully treat these computers as intentional systems, and we do this independently of any considerations about what substance they are composed of, their origin, their position or lack of position in the community of moral agents, their consciousness or self-consciousness, or the determinacy or indeterminacy of their operations. The decision to adopt the strategy is pragmatic, and is not intrinsically right or wrong. One can always refuse to adopt the intentional stance toward the computer, and accept its checkmates. One can switch stances at will without involving oneself in any inconsistencies or inhumanities, adopting the intentional stance in one's role as opponent, the design stance in one's role as redesigner, and the physical stance in one's role as repairman.

This celebration of our chess-playing computer is not intended to imply that it is a completely adequate model or simulation of Mind, or intelligent human or animal activity; nor am I saying that the attitude we adopt toward this computer is precisely the same that we adopt toward a creature we deem to be conscious and rational. All that has been claimed is that on occasion, a purely physical system can be so complex, and yet so organized, that we find it convenient, explanatory, pragmatically necessary for prediction, to treat it as if it had beliefs and desires and was rational. The chess-playing computer is just that, a machine for playing chess, which no man or animal is; and hence its "rationality" is pinched and artificial.

Perhaps we could straightforwardly expand the chess-playing computer into a more faithful model of human rationality, and perhaps not. I prefer to pursue a more fundamental line of inquiry first.

When should we expect the tactic of adopting the intentional stance to pay off? Whenever we have reason to suppose the assumption of optimal design is warranted, and doubt the practicality of prediction from the design or physical stance. Suppose we travel to a distant planet and find it inhabited by things moving about its surface, multiplying, decaying, apparently reacting to events in the environment, but otherwise as unlike human beings as you please. Can we make intentional predictions and explanations of their behavior? If we have reason to suppose that a process of natural selection has been in effect, then we can be assured that the populations we observe have been selected in virtue of their design: they will respond to at least some of the more common event-types in this environment in ways that are normally appropriate—that is, conducive to propagation of the species.[5] Once we have tentatively identified the perils and succors of the environment (relative to the constitution of the inhabitants, not ours), we shall be able to estimate which goals and which weighting of goals will be optimal relative to the creatures' *needs* (for survival and propagation), which sorts of information about the environment will be *useful* in guiding goal-directed activity, and which activities will be appropriate given the environmental circumstances. Having doped out these conditions (which will al-

ways be subject to revision) we can proceed at once to ascribe beliefs and desires to the creatures. Their behavior will "manifest" their beliefs by being seen as the actions which, given the creatures' desires, would be appropriate to such beliefs as would be appropriate to the environmental stimulation. Desires, in turn, will be "manifested" in behavior as those appropriate desires (given the needs of the creature) to which the actions of the creature would be appropriate, given the creature's beliefs. The circularity of these interlocking specifications is no accident. Ascriptions of beliefs and desires must be interdependent, and the only point of anchorage are the demonstrable needs for survival, the regularities of behavior, and the assumption, grounded in faith in natural selection, of optimal design. Once one has ascribed beliefs and desires, however, one can at once set about predicting behavior on their basis, and if evolution has done its job—as it must over the long run—our predictions will be reliable enough to be useful.

It might at first seem that this tactic unjustifiably imposes human categories and attributes (belief, desire, and so forth) on these alien entities. It is a sort of anthropomorphizing. We do not have to suppose these creatures share with us any peculiarly human inclinations, attitudes, hopes, foibles, pleasures, or outlooks; their actions may not include running, jumping, hiding, eating, sleeping, listening, or copulating. All we transport from our world to theirs are the categories of rationality, perception (information input by some "sense" modality or modalities—perhaps radar or cosmic radiation), and action. The question of whether we can expect them to share any of our beliefs or desires is tricky, but there are a few points that can be made at this time; in virtue of their rationality they can be supposed to share our belief in logical truths,[6] and we cannot suppose that they normally desire their own destruction, for instance.

II

When one deals with a system—be it man, machine, or alien creature—by explaining and predicting its behavior by citing its beliefs and desires, one has what might be called a "theory of behavior" for the system. Let us see how such intentional theories of behavior relate to other putative theories of behavior.

One fact so obvious that it is easily overlooked is that our "common-sense" explanations and predictions of the behavior of both men and animals are intentional. We start by assuming rationality. We do not *expect* new acquaintances to react irrationally to particular topics or eventualities, but when they do we learn to adjust our strategies accordingly, just as, with a chess-playing computer, one sets out with a high regard for its rationality and adjusts one's estimate downward wherever performance reveals flaws. The presumption of rationality is so strongly entrenched in our inference habits that when our predictions prove false, we at first cast about for adjustments in the information-possession conditions (he must not have heard, he must not know English, he must not have seen x, been aware that y, etc.) or goal weightings, before questioning the rationality of the system as a whole. In extreme cases personalities may prove to be so unpredictable from the intentional stance that we abandon it, and if we have accumulated a lot of evidence in the meanwhile about the nature of response patterns in the individual, we may find that a species of design stance can be effectively adopted. This is the fundamentally different attitude we occasionally adopt toward the insane. To watch an asylum attendant manipulate an obsessively countersuggestive patient, for instance, is to watch something radically unlike normal interpersonal relations.

Our prediction of animal behavior by "common sense" is also intentional. Whether or not sentimental folk go overboard when they talk to their dogs or fill their cats' heads with schemes and worries, even the most hardboiled among us predict animals' behavior intentionally. If we observe a mouse in a situation where it can see a cat waiting at one mousehole and cheese at another, we know which way the mouse will go, providing it is not deranged; our prediction is not based on our familiarity with maze-experiments or any assumptions about the sort of special training the mouse has been through. We suppose the mouse can see the cat and the cheese, and hence has beliefs (belief-analogues, in-tentional whatnots) to the effect that there is a cat to the left, cheese to the right, and we ascribe to the mouse also the desire to eat the cheese and the desire to avoid the cat (subsumed, appropriately enough, under the more general desires to eat and to avoid peril); so we predict that the mouse will do what is appropriate to such beliefs and desires, namely, to go to the right in order to get the cheese and avoid the cat. Whatever academic allegiances or theoretical predilections we may have, we would be astonished if, in the general run, mice and other animals falsified such intentional predictions of their behavior. Indeed, experimental psychologists of every school would have a hard time devising experimental situations to support their various theories without the help of their intentional expectations of how the test animals will respond to circumstances.

Earlier I alleged that even creatures from another planet would share with us our beliefs in logical truths; light can be shed on this claim by asking whether mice and other animals, in virtue of being intentional systems, also believe the truth of logic. There is something bizarre in the picture of a dog or mouse cogitating a list of tautologies, but we can avoid that picture. The assumption that something is an intentional system is the assumption that it is rational; that is, one gets nowhere with the assumption that entity x has beliefs $p, q, r, \ldots$ unless one also supposes that x believes what follows from $p, q, r, \ldots$; otherwise there is no way of ruling out the prediction that x will, in the face of its beliefs $p, q, r, \ldots$ do something utterly stupid, and, if we cannot rule out *that* prediction, we will have acquired no predictive power at all. So whether or not the animal is said to *believe* the *truths* of logic, it must be supposed to *follow* the *rules* of logic. Surely our mouse follows or believes in *modus ponens*, for we ascribed to it the beliefs: (a) *there is a cat to the left*; and (b) *if there is a cat to the left, I had better not go left*, and our prediction relied on the mouse's ability to get to the conclusion. In general there is a trade-off between rules and truths; we can suppose x to have an inference rule taking A to B or we can give x the belief in the "theorem": *if A then B*. As far as our predictions are concerned, we are free to ascribe to the mouse either a few inference rules and belief in many logical propositions, or many inference rules and few if any logical beliefs.[7] We can even take a patently nonlogical belief like (b) and recast it as an inference rule taking (a) to the desired conclusion.

Will all logical truths appear among the beliefs of any intentional system? If the system were ideally or perfectly rational, all logical truths would appear, but any actual intentional system will be imperfect, and so not all logical truths must be ascribed as beliefs to any system. Moreover, not all the inference rules of an actual intentional system may be valid; not all its inference-licensing beliefs may be truths of logic. Experience may indicate where the shortcomings lie in any particular system. If we found an imperfectly rational creature whose allegiance to modus ponens, say, varied with the subject matter, we could characterize that by excluding modus ponens as a rule and ascribing in its stead a set of nonlogical inference rules covering the modus ponens step for each subject matter where the rule was followed. Not surprisingly, as we discover more and more imperfections (as we banish more and more logical truths from the creature's beliefs), our efforts at intentional prediction become more and more cumbersome and undecidable, for we can no longer count on the beliefs, desires, and actions going together that *ought* to go together. Eventually we end up, following this process, by predicting from the design stance; we end up, that is, dropping the assumption of rationality.[8]

This migration from common-sense intentional explanations and predictions to more reliable design-stance explanations and predictions that is forced on us when we discover that our subjects are imperfectly rational is, independently of any such discovery, the proper direction for theory builders to take whenever possible. In the end, we want to be able to explain the intelligence of man, or beast, in terms of his design, and this in turn in terms of the natural selection of this design; so whenever we stop in our explanation at the intentional level we have left over an unexplained instance of intelligence or rationality. This comes out vividly if we look at theory building from the vantage point of economics.

Any time a theory builder proposes to call any event, state, structure, etc., in any system (say the brain of an organism) a *signal* or *message* or *command* or otherwise endows it with content, he *takes out a loan* of intelligence. He implicitly posits along with his signals, messages, or commands, something that can serve as a signal-*reader*, message-*understander*, or *commander*, else his "signals" will be for naught, will decay unreceived, uncomprehended. This loan must be repaid eventually by finding and analyzing away these readers or comprehenders; for, failing this, the theory will have among its elements unanalyzed man-analogues endowed with enough intelligence to read the signals, etc., and thus the theory will *postpone* answering the major question: what makes for intelligence? The intentionality of all such talk of signals and commands reminds us that rationality is being taken for granted, and in this way shows us where a theory is incomplete. It is this feature that, to my mind, puts a premium on the yet unfinished task of devising a rigorous definition of intentionality, for if we can lay claim to a purely formal criterion of intentional discourse, we will have what amounts to a medium of exchange for assessing theories of behavior. Intentionality *abstracts* from the inessential details of the various forms intelligence-loans can take (e.g., signal-readers, volition-emitters, librarians in the corridors of memory, egos and superegos) and serves as a reliable means of detecting exactly where a theory is *in the red* relative to the task of explaining intelligence; wherever a theory relies on a formulation bearing the logical marks of intentionality, there a little man is concealed.

This insufficiency of intentional explanation from the point of view of psychology has been widely felt and as widely misconceived. The most influential misgivings, expressed in the behaviorism of Skinner and Quine, can be succinctly characterized in terms of our economic metaphor. Skinner's and Quine's adamant prohibitions of intentional idioms at all levels of theory is the analogue of rock-ribbed New England conservatism: no deficit spending when building a theory! In Quine's case, the abhorrence of loans is due mainly to his fear that they can never be repaid, whereas Skinner stresses rather that what is borrowed is worthless to begin with. Skinner's suspicion is that intentionally couched claims are empirically vacuous, in the sense that they are altogether too easy to accommodate to the data, like the *virtus dormitiva* Molière's doctor ascribes to the sleeping powder (see Chapter 4 [of Dennett, *Brainstorms*] for a more detailed discussion of these issues). Questions can be begged on a temporary basis, however, permitting a mode of prediction and explanation not totally vacuous. Consider the following intentional prediction: if I were to ask a thousand American mathematicians how much seven times five is, more than nine hundred would respond by saying that it was thirty-five. (I have allowed for a few to mis-hear my question, a few others to be obstreperous, a few to make slips of the tongue.) If you doubt the prediction, you can test it; I would bet good money on it. It seems to have empirical content because it can, in a fashion, be tested, and yet it is unsatisfactory as a prediction of an empirical theory of psychology. It works, of course, because of the contingent, empirical—but evolution-guaranteed—fact that men in general are well enough designed both to get the answer right and to want to get it right. It will hold with as few exceptions for any group of Martians with whom we are able to converse, for it is not a prediction just of *human* psychology, but of the "psychology" of intentional systems generally.

Deciding on the basis of available empirical evidence that something is a piece of copper or a lichen permits one to make predictions based on the empirical theories dealing with copper and lichens, but deciding on the basis of available evidence that something is (may be treated as) an intentional system permits predictions having a normative or logical basis rather than an empirical one, and hence the success of an intentional prediction, based as it is on no particular picture of the system's design, cannot be construed to confirm or disconfirm any particular pictures of the system's design.

Skinner's reaction to this has been to try to frame predictions purely in non-intentional language, by predicting bodily responses to physical stimuli, but to date this has not provided him with the alternative mode of prediction and explanation he has sought, as perhaps an extremely cursory review can indicate. To provide a setting for nonintentional prediction of behavior, he invented the Skinner box, in which the rewarded behavior of the occupant—say, a rat—is a highly restricted and stereotypic bodily motion—usually pressing a bar with the front paws.

The claim that is then made is that once the animal has been trained, a law-like relationship is discovered to hold between non-intentionally characterized events: controlling stimuli and bar-pressing responses. A regularity is discovered to hold, to be sure, but the fact that it is between non-intentionally defined events is due to a property of the Skinner box and not of the occupant. For let us turn our prediction about mathematicians into a Skinnerian prediction: strap a mathematician in a Skinner box so he can move only his head; display in front of him a card on which appear the marks: "How much is seven times five?"; move into the range of his head-motions two buttons, over one of which is the mark "35" and over the other "34"; place electrodes on the soles of his feet and give him a few quick shocks; the controlling stimulus is then to be the sound: "Answer now!" I predict that in a statistically significant number of cases, even *before* training trials to condition the man to press button "35" with his forehead, he will do this when given the controlling stimulus. Is this a satisfactory scientific prediction just because it eschews the intentional vocabulary? No, it is an intentional prediction disguised by so restricting the environment that only one bodily motion is available to fulfill the intentional *action* that anyone would prescribe as appropriate to the circumstances of perception, belief, desire. That it is action, not merely motion, that is predicted can also be seen in the case of subjects less intelligent than mathematicians. Suppose a mouse were trained, in a Skinner box with a food reward, to take exactly four steps forward and press a bar with its nose; if Skinner's laws truly held between stimuli and responses defined in terms of bodily motion, were we to move the bar an inch farther away, so four steps did not reach it, Skinner would have to predict that the mouse would jab its nose into the empty air rather than take a fifth step.

A variation of Skinnerian theory designed to meet this objection acknowledges that the trained response one predicts is not truly captured in a description of skeletal motion alone, but rather in a description of an environmental effect achieved: the bar going down, the "35" button being depressed. This will also not do. Suppose we could in fact train a man or animal to achieve an environmental effect, as this theory proposes. Suppose, for instance, we train a man to push a button under the longer of two displays, such as drawings or simple designs, that is, we reward him when he pushes the button under the longer of two pictures of pencils, or cigars, etc. The miraculous consequence of this theory, were it correct, would be that if, after training him on simple views, we were to present him with the Müller-Lyer arrow-head illusion, he would be immune to it, for *ex hypothesi* he has been trained to achieve an *actual* environmental effect (choosing the display that *is* longer), not a *perceived* or *believed* environmental effect (choosing the display that *seems* longer). The reliable prediction, again, is the intentional one.[9]

Skinner's experimental design is supposed to eliminate the intentional, but it merely masks it. Skinner's non-intentional predictions work to the extent they do, not because Skinner has truly found non-intentional behavioral laws, but because the highly reliable intentional predictions underlying his experimental situations (the rat desires food and believes it will get food by pressing the bar—something for which it has been given good evidence—so it will press the bar) are disguised by leaving virtually no room in the environment for more than one bodily motion to be the appropriate action and by leaving virtually no room in the environment for discrepancy to arise between the subject's beliefs and the reality.

Where, then, should we look for a satisfactory theory of behavior? Intentional theory is vacuous as psychology because it presupposes and does not explain rationality or intelligence. The apparent successes of Skinnerian behaviorism, however, rely on hidden intentional predictions. Skinner is right in recognizing that intentionality can be no *foundation* for psychology, and right also to look for purely mechanistic regularities in the activities of his subjects, but there is little reason to suppose they will lie on the surface in gross behavior—except, as we have seen, when we put an artificial straitjacket on an intentional regularity. Rather, we will find what-

ever mechanistic regularities there are in the functioning of internal systems whose design approaches the optimal (relative to some ends). In seeking knowledge of internal design our most promising tactic is to take out intelligence-loans, endow peripheral and internal events with content, and then look for mechanisms that will function appropriately with such "messages" so that we can pay back the loans. This tactic is hardly untried. Research in artificial intelligence, which has produced, among other things, the chess-playing computer, proceeds by working from an intentionally characterized problem (how to get the computer to consider the right sorts of information, make the right decisions) to a design-stance solution—an approximation of optimal design. Psychophysicists and neurophysiologists who routinely describe events in terms of the transmission of information within the nervous system are similarly borrowing intentional capital—even if they are often inclined to ignore or disavow their debts.

Finally, it should not be supposed that, just because intentional theory is vacuous as psychology, in virtue of its assumption of rationality, it is vacuous from all points of view. Game theory, for example, is inescapably intentional,[10] but as a formal normative theory and not a psychology this is nothing amiss. Game-theoretical predictions applied to human subjects achieve their accuracy in virtue of the evolutionary guarantee that man is well designed as a game player, a special case of rationality. Similarly, economics, the social science of greatest predictive power today, is not a psychological theory and presupposes what psychology must explain. Economic explanation and prediction is intentional (although some is disguised) and succeeds to the extent that it does because individual men are in general good approximations of the optimal operator in the marketplace.

III

The concept of an intentional system is a relatively uncluttered and unmetaphysical notion, abstracted as it is from questions of the composition, constitution, consciousness, morality, or divinity of the entities falling under it. Thus, for example, it is much easier to decide whether a machine can be an intentional system than it is to decide whether a machine can *really* think, or be conscious, or morally responsible. This simplicity makes it ideal as a source of order and organization in philosophical analyses of "mental" concepts. Whatever else a person might be—embodied mind or soul, self-conscious moral agent, "emergent" form of intelligence—he is an intentional system, and whatever follows just from being an intentional system is thus true of a person. It is interesting to see just how much of what we hold to be the case about persons or their minds follows directly from their being intentional systems. To revert for a moment to the economic metaphor, the guiding or challenging question that defines work in the philosophy of mind is this: are there mental treasures that cannot be purchased with intentional coin? If not, a considerable unification of science can be foreseen in outline. Of special importance for such an examination is the subclass of intentional systems that have language, that can communicate; for these provide a framework for a theory of consciousness. In *Content and Consciousness*, part II, and in parts III and IV of [*Brainstorms*] I have attempted to elaborate such a theory; here I would like to consider its implications for the analysis of the concept of belief. What will be true of human believers just in virtue of their being intentional systems with the capacity to communicate?

Just as not all intentional systems currently known to us can fly or swim, so not all intentional systems can talk, but those which can do this raise special problems and opportunities when we come to ascribe beliefs and desires to them. That is a massive understatement; without the talking intentional systems, of course, there would be no ascribing beliefs, no theorizing, no assuming rationality, no predicting. The capacity for language is without doubt the crowning achievement of evolution, an achievement that feeds on itself to produce ever more versatile and subtle rational systems, but still it can be looked at as an adaptation which is subject to the same conditions of environmental utility as any other behavioral talent. When it is looked at in this way several striking facts emerge. One of the most

pervasive features of evolutionary histories is the interdependence of distinct organs and capacities in a species. Advanced eyes and other distance receptors are of no utility to an organism unless it develops advanced means of locomotion; the talents of a predator will not accrue to a species that does not evolve a carnivore's digestive system. The capacities of belief and communication have prerequisites of their own. We have already seen that there is no point in ascribing beliefs to a system unless the beliefs ascribed are in general appropriate to the environment, and the system responds appropriately to the beliefs. An eccentric expression of this would be: the capacity to believe would have no survival value unless it were a capacity to believe truths. What is eccentric and potentially misleading about this is that it hints at the picture of a species "trying on" a faculty giving rise to beliefs most of which were false, having its inutility demonstrated, and abandoning it. A species might "experiment" by mutation in any number of inefficacious systems, but none of these systems would deserve to be called belief systems precisely because of their defects, their nonrationality, and hence a false belief system is a conceptual impossibility. To borrow an example from a short story by MacDonald Harris, a soluble fish is an evolutionary impossibility, but a system for false beliefs cannot even be given a coherent description. The same evolutionary bias in favor of truth prunes the capacity to communicate as it develops; a capacity for false communication would not be a capacity for communication at all, but just an emission proclivity of no systematic value to the species. The faculty of communication would not gain ground in evolution unless it was by and large the faculty of transmitting true beliefs, which means only: the faculty of altering other members of the species in the direction of more optimal design.

This provides a foundation for explaining a feature of belief that philosophers have recently been at some pains to account for.[11] The concept of belief seems to have a normative cast to it that is most difficult to capture. One way of putting it might be that an avowal like "I believe that p" seems to imply in some fashion: "One ought to believe that p." This way of putting it has flaws, however, for we must then account for the fact that "I believe that *p*" seems to have normative force that "He believes that *p*," said of me, does not. Moreover, saying that one ought to believe this or that suggests that belief is voluntary, a view with notorious difficulties.[12] So long as one tries to capture the normative element by expressing it in the form of moral or pragmatic injunctions to believers, such as "one ought to believe the truth" and "one ought to act in accordance with one's beliefs," dilemmas arise. How, for instance, is one to follow the advice to believe the truth? Could one abandon one's sloppy habit of believing falsehoods? If the advice is taken to mean: believe only what you have convincing evidence for, it is the vacuous advice: believe only what you believe to be true. If alternatively it is taken to mean: believe only what is in fact the truth, it is an injunction we are powerless to obey.

The normative element of belief finds its home not in such injunctions but in the preconditions for the ascription of belief, what Phillips Griffiths calls "the general conditions for the possibility of application of the concept." For the concept of belief to find application, two conditions, we have seen, must be met: (1) In general, normally, more often than not, if *x* believes *p*, *p* is true. (2) In general, normally, more often than not, if *x* avows that *p*, he believes *p* [and, by (1), *p* is true]. Were these conditions not met, we would not have rational, communicating systems; we would not have believers or belief-avowers. The norm for belief is evidential well-foundedness (assuring truth in the long run), and the norm for avowal of belief is accuracy (which includes sincerity). These two norms determine pragmatic implications of our utterances. If I assert that *p* (or that I believe that *p*—it makes no difference), I assume the burden of defending my assertion on two fronts. I can be asked for evidence for the truth of *p*, and I can be asked for behavioral evidence that I do in fact believe *p*.[13] I do not need to examine my own behavior in order to be in a position to avow my belief that *p*, but if my sincerity or self-knowledge is challenged, this is where I must turn to defend my assertion. But again, challenges on either point must be the exception rather than the rule if belief is to have a place among our concepts.

Another way of looking at the importance of this predominance of the normal is to consider the well-known circle of implications between beliefs and de-

sires (or intentions) that prevent non-intentional behavioral definitions of international terms. A man's standing under a tree is a behavioral indicator of his belief that it is raining, but only on the assumption that he desires to stay dry, and if we then look for evidence that he wants to stay dry, his standing under the tree will do, but only on the assumption that he believes the tree will shelter him; if we ask him if he believes the tree will shelter him, his positive response is confirming evidence only on the assumption that he desires to tell us the truth, and so forth *ad infinitum*. It is this apparently vicious circle that turned Quine against the intentional (and foiled Tolman's efforts at operational definition of intentional terms), but if it is true that in any particular case a man's saying that *p* is evidence of his belief only conditionally, we can be assured that in the long run and in general the circle is broken; a man's assertions are, unconditionally, indicative of his beliefs, as are his actions in general. We get around the "privacy" of beliefs and desires by recognizing that in general anyone's beliefs and desires must be those he "ought to have" given the circumstances.

These two interdependent norms of belief, one favoring the truth and rationality of belief, the other favoring accuracy of avowal, normally complement each other, but on occasion can give rise to conflict. This is the "problem of incorrigibility." If rationality is the mother of intention, we still must wean intentional systems from the criteria that give them life, and set them up on their own. Less figuratively, if we are to make use of the concept of an intentional system in particular instances, at some point we must cease *testing* the assumption of the system's rationality, adopt the intentional stance, and grant without further ado that the system is qualified for beliefs and desires. For mute animals—and chess-playing computers—this manifests itself in a tolerance for less than optimal performance. We continue to ascribe beliefs to the mouse, and explain its actions in terms of them, after we have tricked it into some stupid belief. This tolerance has its limits of course, and the less felicitous the behavior—especially the less adaptable the behavior—the more hedged are our ascriptions. For instance, we are inclined to say of the duckling that "imprints" on the first moving thing it sees upon emerging from its shell that it "believes" the thing is its mother, whom it follows around, but we emphasize the scare-quotes around "believes." For intentional systems that can communicate—persons for instance—the tolerance takes the form of the convention that a man is incorrigible or a special authority about his own beliefs. This convention is "justified" by the fact that evolution does guarantee that our second norm is followed. What better source could there be of a system's beliefs than its avowals? Conflict arises, however, whenever a person falls short of perfect rationality, and avows beliefs that either are strongly disconfirmed by the available empirical evidence or are self-contradictory or contradict other avowals he has made. If we lean on the myth that a man is perfectly rational, we must find his avowals less than authoritative: "You *can't* mean—understand—what you're saying!"; if we lean on his "right" as a speaking intentional system to have his word accepted, we grant him an irrational set of beliefs. Neither position provides a stable resting place; for, as we saw earlier, intentional explanation and prediction cannot be accommodated either to breakdown or to less than optimal design, so there is no coherent intentional description of such an impasse.[14]

Can any other considerations be brought to bear in such an instance to provide us with justification for one ascription of beliefs rather than another? Where should one look for such considerations? The Phenomenologist will be inclined to suppose that individual introspection will provide us a sort of data not available to the outsider adopting the intentional stance; but how would such data get used? Let the introspector amass as much inside information as you please; he must then communicate it to us, and what are we to make of his communications? We can suppose that they are incorrigible (barring corrigible verbal errors, slips of the tongue, and so forth), but we do not need Phenomenology to give us that option, for it amounts to the decision to lean on the accuracy-of-avowal norm at the expense of the rationality norm. If, alternatively, we demand certain standards of consistency and rationality of his utterances before we accept them as authoritative, what standards will we adopt? If we demand perfect rationality, we have simply flown to the other norm at the expense of the norm of accuracy of avowal. If we try to fix minimum standards

at something less than perfection, what will guide our choice? Not Phenomenological data, for the choice we make will determine what is to count as Phenomenological data. Not neurophysiological data either, for whether we interpret a bit of neural structure to be endowed with a particular belief content hinges on our having granted that the neural system under examination has met the standards of rationality for being an intentional system, an assumption jeopardized by the impasse we are trying to resolve. That is, one might have a theory about an individual's neurology that permitted one to "read off" or predict the propositions to which he would assent, but whether one's theory had uncovered his *beliefs*, or merely a set of assent-inducers, would depend on how consistent, reasonable, true we found the set of propositions.

John Vickers has suggested to me a way of looking at this question. Consider a set T of transformations that take beliefs into beliefs. The problem is to determine the set T_s for each intentional system S, so that if we know that S believes p, we will be able to determine other things that S believes by seeing what the transformations of p are for T_s. If S were ideally rational, every valid transformation would be in T_s; S would believe every logical consequence of every belief (and, ideally, S would have no false beliefs). Now we know that no actual intentional system will be ideally rational; so we must suppose any actual system will have a T with less in it. But we also know that, to qualify as an intentional system at all, S must have a T with some integrity; T cannot be empty. What rationale could we have, however, for fixing some set between the extremes and calling it *the* set for belief (for S, for earthlings, or for ten-year-old girls)? This is another way of asking whether we could replace Hintikka's normative theory of belief with an empirical theory of belief, and, if so, what evidence we would use. "Actually," one is tempted to say, "people do believe contradictions on occasion, as their utterances demonstrate; so any adequate logic of belief or analysis of the concept of belief must accommodate this fact." But any attempt to *legitimize* human fallibility in a theory of belief by fixing a permissible level of error would be like adding one more rule to chess: an Official Tolerance Rule to the effect that any game of chess containing no more than k moves that are illegal relative to the other rules of the game is a legal game of chess. Suppose we discovered that, in a particular large population of poor chess-players, each game on average contained three illegal moves undetected by either opponent. Would we claim that these people *actually* play a different game from ours, a game with an Official Tolerance Rule with k fixed at 3? This would be to confuse the norm they follow with what gets by in their world. We could claim in a similar vein that people *actually* believe, say, all synonymous or intentionally isomorphic consequences of their beliefs, but not all their logical consequences, but of course the occasions when a man resists assenting to a logical consequence of some avowal of his are unstable cases; he comes in for criticism and cannot appeal in his own defense to any canon absolving him from believing nonsynonymous consequences. If one wants to get away from norms and predict and explain the "actual, empirical" behavior of the poor chess-players, one stops talking of their *chess moves* and starts talking of their proclivities to move pieces of wood or ivory about on checkered boards; if one wants to predict and explain the "actual, empirical" behavior of believers, one must similarly cease talking of belief, and descend to the design stance or physical stance for one's account.

The concept of an intentional system explicated in these pages is made to bear a heavy load. It has been used here to form a bridge connecting the intentional domain (which includes our "common-sense" world of persons and actions, game theory, and the "neural signals" of the biologist) to the non-intentional domain of the physical sciences. That is a lot to expect of one concept, but nothing less than Brentano himself expected when, in a day of less fragmented science, he proposed intentionality as the mark that sunders the universe in the most fundamental way: dividing the mental from the physical.

NOTES

1. I am indebted to Peter Woodruff for making extensive improvements in this chapter prior to its initial publication. Since it appeared, I have found anticipations and developments of similar or supporting themes in a variety of writers, most notably Carl Hempel, "Rational Action," *Proceedings and Addresses of the American Philosophical Association*, XXXV (1962), reprinted in N. S. Care and C. Landesman, eds., *Readings in the Theory of Action* (Bloomington: Indiana University Press, 1968); L. Jonathan Cohen, "Teleological Explanation," *Proceedings of the Aristotelian Society* (1950–51), and "Can There be Artificial Minds?" *Analysis* (1954–55); B. A. O. Williams, "Deciding to Believe," in H. E. Kiefer and M. K. Munitz, eds., *Language, Belief, and Metaphysics* (Albany: SUNY Press, 1970); and David Lewis, "Radical Interpretation," *Synthese*, III, IV (1974): 331–44.

2. For a lucid introduction to the concept and its history, see the entry on "intentionality" by Roderick Chisholm in P. Edwards, ed., *The Encyclopedia of Philosophy* (New York: Macmillan, 1967).

3. *Content and Consciousness* (London: Routledge & Kegan Paul, 1969).

4. The term "intentional system" occurs in Charles Taylor's *The Explanation of Behaviour* (London: Routledge & Kegan Paul, 1964), 62, where its use suggests it is co-extensive with the term as I use it, but Taylor does not develop the notion in depth. See, however, his p. 58ff. For an introduction to the concept of an intentional system with fewer philosophical presuppositions, see the first sections of Chapters 12 and 14 of [Daniel Dennett, *Brainstorms* (Montgomery, Vt.: Bradford Books, 1978)].

5. Note that what is *directly* selected, the gene, is a diagram and not a design; it is selected, however, because it happens to ensure that its bearer has a certain (functional) design. This was pointed out to me by Woodruff.

6. Cf. Quine's argument about the necessity of "discovering" our logical connectives in any language we can translate in *Word and Object* (Cambridge, Mass.: MIT, 1960), Section 1.3. More will be said in defense of this below.

7. Accepting the argument of Lewis Carroll, in "What the Tortoise Said to Achilles," *Mind* (1895), reprinted in I. M. Copi and J. A. Gould, *Readings on Logic* (New York: MacMillan, 1964), we cannot allow all the rules for a system to be replaced by beliefs, for this would generate an infinite and unproductive nesting of distinct beliefs about what can be inferred from what.

8. This paragraph owes much to discussion with John Vickers, whose paper "Judgment and

Belief," in K. Lambert, *The Logical Way of Doing Things* (New Haven: Yale, 1969), goes beyond the remarks here by considering the problems of the relative strength or weighing of beliefs and desires.

9. R. L. Gregory, *Eye and Brain* (London: World University Library, 1966), 137, reports that pigeons and fish given just this training are, not surprisingly, susceptible to visual illusions of length.

10. Hintikka notes in passing that game theory is like his epistemic logic in assuming rationality, in *Knowledge and Belief* (Ithaca, N.Y.: Cornell, 1962), 38.

11. I have in mind especially A. Phillips Griffiths' penetrating discussion "On Belief," *Proceedings of the Aristotelian Society*, LXIII (1962/3): 167–86; and Bernard Mayo's "Belief and Constraint," ibid., LXIV (1964): 139–56, Oxford, 1967).

12. See, e.g., H. H. Price, "Belief and Will,"

Proceedings of the Aristotelian Society, suppl. vol. XXVIII (1954), reprinted in S. Hampshire, ed., *Philosophy of Mind* (New York: Harper & Row, 1966).

13. Cf. A. W. Collins, "Unconscious Belief," *Journal of Philosophy*, LXVI, 20 (Oct. 16, 1969): 667–80.

14. Hintikka takes this bull by the horns. His epistemic logic is acknowledged to hold only for the ideally rational believer; were we to apply this logic to persons in the actual world in other than a normative way, thus making its implications *authoritative* about actual belief, the authority of persons would have to go by the board. Thus his rule A.CBB* (*Knowledge and Belief*, pp. 24–26), roughly that if one believes *p* one believes that one believes *p*, cannot be understood, as it is tempting to suppose, as a version of the incorrigibility thesis.

Eliminative Materialism

PAUL M. CHURCHLAND

Paul Churchland (1942–   ) is the author of *Scientific Realism and the Plasticity of Mind, Matter and Consciousness*, and *A Neurocomputational Perspective*. He is a professor of philosophy at the University of California at San Diego.

———•———

THE IDENTITY THEORY WAS CALLED into doubt not because the prospects for a materialist account of our mental capacities were thought to be poor, but because it seemed unlikely that the arrival of an adequate materialist theory would bring with it the nice one-to-one match-ups, between the concepts of folk psychology and the concepts of theoretical neuroscience, that intertheoretic reduction requires. The reason for that

doubt was the great variety of quite different physical systems that could instantiate the required functional organization. *Eliminative materialism* also doubts that the correct neuroscientific account of human capacities will produce a neat reduction of our common-sense framework, but here the doubts arise from a quite different source.

As the eliminative materialists see it, the one-to-one match-ups will not be found, and our common-sense psychological framework is a false and radically misleading conception of the causes of human behavior and the nature of cognitive activity. On this view, folk psychology is not just an incomplete representation of our inner natures; it is an outright *mis*representation of our internal states and activities. Consequently, we cannot expect a truly adequate neuroscientific account of our inner lives to provide theoretical categories that match up nicely with the categories of our common-sense framework. Accordingly, we must expect that the older framework will simply be eliminated, rather than be reduced, by a matured neuroscience.

Historical Parallels

As the identity theorist can point to historical cases of successful intertheoretic reduction, so the eliminative materialist can point to historical cases of the outright elimination of the ontology of an older theory in favor of the ontology of a new and superior theory. For most of the eighteenth and nineteenth centuries, learned people believed that heat was a subtle *fluid* held in bodies, much in the way water is held in a sponge. A fair body of moderately successful theory described the way this fluid substance—called "caloric"—flowed within a body, or from one body to another, and how it produced thermal expansion, melting, boiling, and so forth. But by the end of the last century it had become abundantly clear that the heat was not a substance at all, but just the energy of motion of the trillions of jostling molecules that make up the heated body itself. The new theory—the "corpuscular/kinetic theory of matter and heat"—was much more successful than the old in explaining and predicting the thermal behavior of bodies. And since we were unable to *identify* caloric fluid with kinetic energy (according to the old theory, caloric is a material *substance*; according to the new theory, kinetic energy is a form of *motion*), it was finally agreed that there is *no such thing* as caloric. Caloric was simply eliminated from our accepted ontology.

A second example. It used to be thought that when a piece of wood burns, or a piece of metal rusts, a spiritlike substance called "phlogiston" was being released: briskly, in the former case, slowly in the latter. Once gone, that 'noble' substance left only a base pile of ash or rust. It later came to be appreciated that both processes involve, not the loss of something, but the *gaining* of a substance taken from the atmosphere: oxygen. Phlogiston emerged, not as an incomplete description of what was going on, but as a radical misdescription. Phlogiston was therefore not suitable for reduction to or identification with some notion from within the new oxygen chemistry, and it was simply eliminated from science.

Admittedly, both of these examples concern the elimination of something nonobservable, but our history also includes the elimination of certain widely accepted 'observables.' Before Copernicus's views became available, almost any human who ventured out at night could look up at *the starry sphere of the heavens*, and if he stayed for more than a few minutes he could also see that it *turned*, around an axis through Polaris. What the sphere was made of (crystal?) and what made it turn (the gods?) were theoretical questions that exercised us for over two millennia. But hardly anyone doubted the existence of what everyone could observe with their own eyes. In the end, however, we learned to reinterpret our visual experience of the night sky within a very different conceptual framework, and the turning sphere evaporated.

Witches provide another example. Psychosis is a fairly common affliction among humans, and in earlier centuries its victims were standardly seen as cases of demonic possession, as instances of Satan's spirit itself, glaring malevolently out at us from behind the victims' eyes. That witches exist was not a matter of any controversy. One would occasionally see them, in any city or hamlet, engaged in incoherent, paranoid, or even murderous behavior. But observable or not, we eventually decided that witches simply do not exist. We concluded that the concept of a witch is an element in a conceptual framework that misrepresents so badly the phenomena to which it was standardly applied that literal application of the notion should be permanently withdrawn. Modern theories of mental dysfunction led to the elimination of witches from our serious ontology.

The concepts of folk psychology—belief, desire, fear, sensation, pain, joy, and so on—await a similar fate, according to the view at issue. And when neuroscience has matured to the point where the poverty of our current conceptions is apparent to everyone, and the superiority of the new framework is established, we shall then be able to set about *re*conceiving our internal states and activities, within a truly adequate conceptual framework at last. Our explanations of one another's behavior will appeal to such things as our neuropharmacological states, the neural activity in specialized anatomical areas, and whatever other states are deemed relevant by the new theory. Our private introspection will also be transformed, and may be profoundly enhanced by reason of the more accurate and penetrating framework it will have to work with—just as the astronomer's perception of the night sky is much enhanced by the detailed knowledge of modern astronomical theory that he or she possesses.

The magnitude of the conceptual revolution here suggested should not be minimized: it would be enormous. And the benefits to humanity might be equally great. If each of us possessed an accurate neuroscientific understanding of (what we now conceive dimly as) the varieties and causes of mental illness, the factors involved in learning, the neural basis of emotions, intelligence, and socialization, then the sum total of human misery might be much reduced. The simple increase in mutual understanding that the new framework made possible could contribute substantially toward a more peaceful and humane society. Of course, there would be dangers as well: increased knowledge means increased power, and power can always be misused.

Arguments for Eliminative Materialism

The arguments for eliminative materialism are diffuse and less than decisive, but they are stronger than is widely supposed. The distinguishing feature of this position is its denial that a smooth intertheoretic reduction is to be expected—even a species-specific reduction—of the framework of folk psychology to the framework of a matured neuroscience. The reason for this denial is the eliminative materialist's conviction that folk psychology is a hopelessly primitive and deeply confused conception of our internal activities. But why this low opinion of our commonsense conceptions?

There are at least three reasons. First, the elimi-native materialist will point to the widespread explanatory, predictive, and manipulative failures of folk psychology. So much of what is central and familiar to us remains a complete mystery from within folk psychology. We do not know what *sleep* is, or why we have to have it, despite spending a full third of our lives in that condition. (The answer, "For rest," is mistaken. Even if people are allowed to rest continuously, their need for sleep is undiminished. Apparently, sleep serves some deeper functions, but we do not yet know what they are.) We do not understand how *learning* transforms each of us from a gaping infant to a cunning adult, or how differences in *intelligence* are grounded. We have not the slightest idea how *memory* works, or how we manage to retrieve relevant bits of information instantly from the awesome mass we have stored. We do not know what *mental illness* is, nor how to cure it.

In sum, the most central things about us remain almost entirely mysterious from within folk psychology. And the defects noted cannot be blamed on inadequate time allowed for their correction, for folk psychology has enjoyed no significant changes or advances in well over 2,000 years, despite its manifest failures. Truly successful theories may be expected to reduce, but significantly unsuccessful theories merit no such expectation.

This argument from explanatory poverty has a further aspect. So long as one sticks to normal brains, the poverty of folk psychology is perhaps not strikingly evident. But as soon as one examines the many perplexing behavioral and cognitive deficits suffered by people with *damaged* brains, one's descriptive and explanatory resources start to claw the air (see, for example chapter 7.3 [of *Matter and Consciousness* (Bradford/MIT, 1984)]). As with other humble theories asked to operate successfully in unexplored extensions of their old domain (for example, Newtonian mechanics in the domain of velocities close to the velocity of light, and the classical gas law in the domain of high pressures or temperatures), the descriptive and explanatory inadequacies of folk psychology become starkly evident.

The second argument tries to draw an inductive lesson from our conceptual history. Our early folk theories of motion were profoundly confused, and were eventually displaced entirely by more sophisticated theories. Our early folk theories of the structure and activity of the heavens were wildly off the mark, and survive only as historical lessons in how wrong we can be. Our folk theories of the nature of fire, and the nature of life, were similarly cockeyed. And one could go on, since the vast majority of our past folk conceptions have been similarly exploded. All except folk psychology, which survives to this day and has only recently begun to feel pressure. But the phenomenon of conscious intelligence is surely a more complex and difficult phenomenon than any of those just listed. So far as accurate understanding is concerned, it would be a *miracle* if we had got *that* one right the very first time, when we fell down so badly on all the others. Folk psychology has survived for so very long, presumably, not because it is basically correct in its representations, but because the phenomena addressed are so surpassingly difficult that any useful handle on them, no matter how feeble, is unlikely to be displaced in a hurry.

A third argument attempts to find an a priori advantage for eliminative materialism over the identity theory and functionalism. It attempts to counter the common intuition that eliminative materialism is distantly possible, perhaps, but is much less probable than either the identity theory or functionalism. The focus again is on whether the concepts of folk psychology will find vindicating match-ups in a matured neuroscience. The eliminativist bets no; the other two bet yes. (Even the functionalist bets yes, but expects the match-ups to be only species-specific, or only person-specific. Functionalism, recall, denies the existence only of *universal* type/type identities.)

The eliminativist will point out that the requirements on a reduction are rather demanding. The new theory must entail a set of principles and embedded concepts that mirrors very closely the specific conceptual structure to be reduced. And the fact is, there are vastly many more ways of being an explanatorily successful neuroscience while *not* mirroring the structure of folk psychology. Accordingly, the a priori probability of eliminative materialism is not lower, but substantially *higher* than that of either of its competitors. One's initial intuitions here are simply mistaken.

Granted, this initial a priori advantage could be

reduced if there were a very strong presumption in favor of the truth of folk psychology—true theories are better bets to win reduction. But according to the first two arguments, the presumptions on this point should run in precisely the opposite direction.

Arguments Against Eliminative Materialism

The initial plausibility of this rather radical view is low for almost everyone, since it denies deeply entrenched assumptions. That is at best a question-begging complaint, of course, since those assumptions are precisely what is at issue. But the following line of thought does attempt to mount a real argument.

Eliminative materialism is false, runs the argument, because one's introspection reveals directly the existence of pains, beliefs, desires, fears, and so forth. Their existence is as obvious as anything could be.

The eliminative materialist will reply that this argument makes the same mistake that an ancient or medieval person would be making if he insisted that he could just see with his own eyes that the heavens form a turning sphere, or that witches exist. The fact is, all observation occurs within some system of concepts, and our observation judgments are only as good as the conceptual framework in which they are expressed. In all three cases—the starry sphere, witches, and the familiar mental states—precisely what is challenged is the integrity of the background conceptual frameworks in which the observation judgments are expressed. To insist on the validity of one's experiences, *traditionally interpreted*, is therefore to beg the very question at issue. For in all three cases, the question is whether we should *re*conceive the nature of some familiar observational domain.

A second criticism attempts to find an incoherence in the eliminative materialist's position. The bald statement of eliminative materialism is that the familiar mental states do not really exist. But that statement is meaningful, runs the argument, only if it is the expression of a certain *belief*, and an *intention* to communicate, and a *knowledge* of the language, and so forth. But if the statement is true, then no such mental states exist, and the statement is therefore a meaningless string of marks or noises, and cannot be true. Evidently, the assumption that eliminative materialism is true entails that it cannot be true.

The hole in this argument is the premise concerning the conditions necessary for a statement to be meaningful. It begs the question. If eliminative materialism is true, then meaningfulness must have some different source. To insist on the 'old' source is to insist on the validity of the very framework at issue. Again, an historical parallel may be helpful here. Consider the medieval theory that being biologically *alive* is a matter of being ensouled by an immaterial *vital spirit*. And consider the following response to someone who has expressed disbelief in that theory.

> My learned friend has stated that there is no such thing as vital spirit. But this statement is incoherent. For if it is true, then my friend does not have vital spirit, and must therefore be *dead*. But if he is dead, then his statement is just a string of noises, devoid of meaning or truth. Evidently, the assumption that antivitalism is true entails that it cannot be true! Q.E.D.

This second argument is now a joke, but the first argument begs the question in exactly the same way.

A final criticism draws a much weaker conclusion, but makes a rather stronger case. Eliminative materialism, it has been said, is making mountains out of molehills. It exaggerates the defects in folk psychology, and underplays its real successes. Perhaps the arrival of a matured neuroscience will require the elimination of the occasional folk-psychological concept, continues the criticism, and a minor adjustment in certain folk-psychological principles may have to be endured. But the large-scale elimination forecast by the eliminative materialist is just an alarmist worry or a romantic enthusiasm.

Perhaps this complaint is correct. And perhaps it is merely complacent. Whichever, it does bring out the important point that we do not confront two simple and mutually exclusive possibilities here: pure reduction versus pure elimination. Rather, these are the end points of a smooth spectrum of possible outcomes, between which there are mixed cases of partial elimination and partial reduction. Only empirical research (see chapter 7 [of *Matter and Consciousness*]) can tell us where on that spectrum our own case will fall. Perhaps we should speak here, more liberally, of "revisionary materialism," instead of concentrating on the more radical possibility of an across-the-board elimination. Perhaps we should. But it has been my aim in this [selection] to make it at least intelligible to you that our collective conceptual destiny lies substantially toward the revolutionary end of the spectrum.

B. Minds, Brains, and Machines

Turing Machines

HILARY PUTNAM

Hilary Putnam (1926–   ) is Walter Beverly Pearson Professor of Modern Mathematics and Mathematical Logic at Harvard University. His publications include *Philosophy of Logic* and two volumes of collected papers, *Mathematics, Matter and Method* and *Mind, Language, and Reality*.

—•—

... THE NOTION OF A *TURING MACHINE* ... will now be explained.

Briefly, a Turing machine is a device with a finite number of internal configurations, each of which involves the machine's being in one of a finite number of *states,* and the machine's scanning a tape on which certain symbols appear.

The machine's tape is divided into separate squares, thus:

on each of which a symbol (from a fixed finite alphabet) may be printed. Also the machine has a "scanner" which "scans" one square of the tape at a time. Finally, the machine has a *printing mechanism* which may (a) *erase* the symbol which appears on the square being scanned, and (b) print some other symbol (from the machine's alphabet) on that square.

Any Turing machine is completely described by a *machine table*, which is constructed as follows: the rows of the table correspond to letters of the alphabet (including the "null" letter, i.e. blank space), while the columns correspond to states A, B, C, etc. In each square there appears an "instruction", e.g. "$s_5L\ A$", "$s_7C\ B$", "$s_3R\ C$". These instructions are read as follows: "$s_5L\ A$" means "print the symbol s_5 on the square you are now scanning (after erasing whatever symbol it now contains), and proceed to scan the

square immediately to the left of the one you have just been scanning; also, shift into state A." The other instructions are similarly interpreted ("R" means "scan the square immediately to the *right*," while "C" means "center," i.e. continue scanning the *same* square). The following is a sample machine table:

		A	B	C	D
(s_1)	I	s_1RA	s_1LB	s_3LD	s_1CD
(s_2)	$+$	s_1LB	s_2CD	s_2LD	s_2CD
(s_3)	*blank space*	s_3CD	s_3RC	s_3LD	s_3CD

The machine described by this table is intended to function as follows: the machine is started in state A. On the tape there appears a "sum" (in unary notion) to be "worked out," e.g. "II + III."

The machine is initially scanning the first "I". The machine proceeds to "work out" the sum (essentially by replacing the plus sign by a I, and then going back and erasing the first I). Thus if the "input" was IIII + IIIII the machine would "print out" IIIIIIIII, and then go into the "rest state" (state D).

A "machine table" *describes* a machine if the machine has internal states corresponding to the columns of the table, and if it "obeys" the instruction in the table in the following sense: when it is scanning a square on which a symbol s_1 appears and it is in, say, state B, that it carries out the "instruction" in the appropriate row and column of the table (in this case, column B and row s_1). Any machine that is described by a machine table of the sort just exemplified is a Turing machine.

The notion of a Turing machine is also subject to generalization in various ways—for example, one may suppose that the machine has a second tape (an "input tape") on which additional information may be printed by an operator in the course of a computation. In the sequel we shall make use of this generalization (with electronic "sense organs" taking the place of the "operator").

It should be remarked that Turing machines are able in principle to do anything that any computing machine (of whichever kind) can do.

It has sometimes been contended (e.g. by Nagel and Newman in their book *Gödel's Proof**) that "the theorem [i.e. Gödel's theorem] does indicate that the structure and power of the human mind are far more complex and subtle than any non-living machine yet envisaged" (p. 10), and hence that a Turing machine cannot serve as a model for the human mind, but this is simply a mistake.

*Ernest Nagel and James R. Newman, *Gödel's Proof* (New York: New York University Press, 1958).

Let T be a Turing machine which "represents" me in the sense that T can prove just the mathematical statements I can prove. Then the argument (Nagel and Newman give no argument, but I assume they must have this one in mind) is that by using Gödel's technique I can discover a proposition that T cannot prove, and moreover I can prove this proposition. This refutes the assumption that T "represents" me, hence I am not a Turing machine. The fallacy is a misapplication of Gödel's theorem, pure and simple. Given an arbitrary machine T, all I can do is find a proposition U such that I can prove:

(3) If T is consistent, U is true,

where U in undecidable by T if T is in fact consistent. However, T can perfectly well prove (3) too! And the statement U, which T *cannot* prove (assuming consistency), I cannot prove either (unless I can prove that T is inconsistent, which is unlikely if T is very complicated)!

Computing Machinery and Intelligence

A. M. TURING

A. M. Turing (1912–1954), a Cambridge mathematician, made fundamental contributions to the theory of computation.

---

1. The Imitation Game

I propose to consider the question "Can machines think?" This should begin with definitions of the meaning of the terms "machine" and "think." The

definitions might be framed so as to reflect so far as possible the normal use of the words, but this attitude is dangerous. If the meaning of the words "machine" and "think" are to be found by examining how they are commonly used it is difficult to escape the conclusion that the meaning and the answer to the question, "Can machines think?" is to be sought in a statistical survey such as a Gallup poll. But this is absurd. Instead of attempting such a definition I shall replace the question by another, which is closely related to it and is expressed in relatively unambiguous words.

The new form of the problem can be described in terms of a game which we call the "imitation game." It is played with three people, a man (A), a woman (B), and an interrogator (C) who may be of either sex. The interrogator stays in a room apart from the other two. The object of the game for the interrogator is to determine which of the other two is the man and which is the woman. He knows them by labels X and Y, and at the end of the game he says either "X is A and Y is B" or "X is B and Y is A." The interrogator is allowed to put questions to A and B thus:

C: Will X please tell me the length of his or her hair?

Now suppose X is actually A, then A must answer. It is A's object in the game to try to cause C to make the wrong identification. His answer might therefore be

"My hair is shingled, and the longest strands are about nine inches long."

In order that tones of voice may not help the interrogator the answers should be written, or better still, typewritten. The ideal arrangement is to have a teleprinter communicating between the two rooms. Alternatively the question and answers can be repeated by an intermediary. The object of the game for the third player (B) is to help the interrogator. The best strategy for her is probably to give truthful answers. She can add such things as "I am the woman, don't listen to him!" to her answers, but it will avail nothing as the man can make similar remarks.

We now ask the question, "What will happen when a machine takes the part of A in this game?" Will the interrogator decide wrongly as often when the game is played like this as he does when the game is played between a man and a woman? These questions replace our original, "Can machines think?"

2. Critique of the New Problem

As well as asking, "What is the answer to this new form of the question," one may ask, "Is this new question a worthy one to investigate?" This latter question we investigate without further ado, thereby cutting short an infinite regress.

The new problem has the advantage of drawing a fairly sharp line between the physical and the intellectual capacities of a man. No engineer or chemist claims to be able to produce a material which is indistinguishable from the human skin. It is possible that at some time this might be done, but even supposing this invention available we should feel there was little point in trying to make a "thinking machine" more human by dressing it up in such artificial flesh. The form in which we have set the problem reflects this fact in the condition which prevents the interrogator from seeing or touching the other competitors, or hearing their voices. Some other advantages of the proposed criterion may be shown up by specimen questions and answers. Thus:

Q: Please write me a sonnet on the subject of the Forth Bridge.
A: Count me out on this one. I never could write poetry.
Q: Add 34957 to 70764.
A: (Pause about 30 seconds and then give as answer) 105621.
Q: Do you play chess?
A: Yes.
Q: I have K at my K1, and no other pieces. You have only K at K6 and R at R1. It is your move. What do you play?
A: (After a pause of 15 seconds) R-R8 mate.

The question and answer method seems to be suitable for introducing almost any one of the fields of human endeavor that we wish to include. We do not wish to penalize the machine for its inability to shine in beauty competitions, nor to penalize a man for losing in a race against an airplane. The conditions of our game make these disabilities irrelevant. The "witnesses" can brag, if they consider it advisable, as much as they please about their charms, strength or heroism, but the interrogator cannot demand practical demonstrations.

The game may perhaps be criticized on the ground that the odds are weighted too heavily against the machine. If the man were to try and pretend to be the machine he would clearly make a very poor showing. He would be given away at once by slowness and inaccuracy in arithmetic. May not machines carry out something which ought to be described as thinking but which is very different from what a man does? This objection is a very strong one, but at least we can say that if, nevertheless, a machine can be constructed to play the imitation game satisfactorily, we need not be troubled by this objection.

It might be urged that when playing the "imitation game" the best strategy for the machine may possibly be something other than imitation of the behavior of a man. This may be, but I think it is unlikely that there is any great effect of this kind. In any case there is no intention to investigate here the theory of the game, and it will be assumed that the best strategy is to try to provide answers that would naturally be given by a man.

3. The Machines Concerned in the Game

The question which we put in §1 will not be quite definite until we have specified what we mean by the word "machine." It is natural that we should wish to permit every kind of engineering technique to be used in our machines. We also wish to allow the possibility that an engineer or team of engineers may construct a machine which works, but whose manner of operation cannot be satisfactorily described by its constructors because they have applied a method which is largely experimental. Finally, we wish to exclude from the machines men born in the usual manner. It is difficult to frame the definitions so as to satisfy these three conditions. One might for instance insist that the team of engineers should be all of one sex, but this would not really be satisfactory, for it is probably possible to rear a complete individual from a single cell of the skin (say) of a man. To do so would be a feat of biological technique deserving of the very highest praise, but we would not be inclined to regard it as a case of "constructing a thinking machine." This prompts us to abandon the requirement that every kind of technique should be permitted. We are the more ready to do so in view of the fact that the present interest in "thinking machines" has been aroused by a particular kind of machine, usually called an "electronic computer" or "digital computer." Following this suggestion we only permit digital computers to take part in our game.

This restriction appears af first sight to be a very drastic one. I shall attempt to show that it is not so in reality. To do this necessitates a short account of the nature and properties of these computers.

It may also be said that this identification of machines with digital computers, like our criterion for "thinking," will only be unsatisfactory if (contrary to my belief), it turns out that digital computers are unable to give a good showing in the game.

There are already a number of digital computers in working order, and it may be asked, "Why not try the experiment straight away? It would be easy to satisfy the conditions of the game. A number of interrogators could be used, and statistics compiled to show how often the right identification was given." The short answer is that we are not asking whether all digital computers would do well in the game nor whether the computers at present available would do well, but whether there are imaginable computers which would do well. But this is only the short answer. We shall see this question in a different light later.

4. Digital Computers

The idea behind digital computers may be explained by saying that these machines are intended to carry out any operations which could be done by a human computer. The human computer is supposed to be following fixed rules; he has no authority to deviate from them in any detail. We may suppose that these rules are supplied in a book, which is altered whenever he is put on to a new job. He has also an unlimited supply of paper on which he does his calculations. He may also do his multiplications and additions on a "desk machine," but this is not important.

If we use the above explanation as a definition we shall be in danger of circularity of argument. We avoid this by giving an outline of the means by which the desired effect is achieved. A digital computer can usually be regarded as consisting of three parts:

1. Store.
2. Executive unit.
3. Control.

The store is a store of information, and corresponds to the human computer's paper, whether this is the paper on which he does his calculations or that on which his book of rules is printed. Insofar as the human computer does calculations in his head a part of the store will correspond to his memory.

The executive unit is the part which carries out the various individual operations involved in a calculation. What these individual operations are will vary from machine to machine. Usually fairly lengthy operations can be done such as "Multiply 3540675445 by 7076345687" but in some machines only very simple ones such as "Write down 0" are possible.

We have mentioned that the "book of rules" supplied to the computer is replaced in the machine by a part of the store. It is then called the "table of instructions." It is the duty of the control to see that these instructions are obeyed correctly and in the right order. The control is so constructed that this necessarily happens.

The information in the store is usually broken up into packets of moderately small size. In one machine, for instance, a packet might consist of ten decimal digits. Numbers are assigned to the parts of the store in which the various packets of information are stored, in some systematic manner. A typical instruction might say—

"Add the number stored in position 6809 to that in 4302 and put the result back into the latter storage position."

Needless to say it would not occur in the machine expressed in English. It would more likely be coded in a form such as 6809430217. Here 17 says which of various possible operations is to be performed on the two numbers. In this case the operation is that described above, viz. "Add the number. . . ." It will be noticed that the instruction takes up 10 digits and so forms one packet of information, very conveniently. The control will normally take the instructions to be obeyed in the order of the positions in which they are stored, but occasionally an instruction such as

"Now obey the instruction stored in position 5606, and continue from there" may be encountered, or again

"If position 4505 contains 0 obey next the in-struction stored in 6707, otherwise continue straight on."

Instructions of these latter types are very important because they make it possible for a sequence of operations to be repeated over and over again until some condition is fulfilled, but in doing so to obey, not fresh instructions on each repetition, but the same ones over and over again. To take a domestic analogy. Suppose Mother wants Tommy to call at the cobbler's every morning on his way to school to see if her shoes are done; she can ask him afresh every morning. Alternatively she can stick up a notice once and for all in the hall which he will see when he leaves for school and which tells him to call for the shoes, and also to destroy the notice when he comes back if he has the shoes with him.

The reader must accept it as a fact that digital computers can be constructed, and indeed have been constructed, according to the principles we have described, and that they can in fact mimic the actions of a human computer very closely.

The book of rules which we have described our human computer as using is of course a convenient fiction. Actual human computers really remember what they have got to do. If one wants to make a machine mimic the behavior of the human computer in some complex operation one has to ask him how it is done, and then translate the answer into the form of an instruction table. Constructing instruction tables is usually described as "programing." To "program a machine to carry out the operation A" means to put the appropriate instruction table into the machine so that it will do A.

An interesting variant on the idea of a digital computer is a "digital computer with a random element." These have instructions involving the throwing of a die or some equivalent electronic process; one such instruction might for instance be, "Throw the die and put the resulting number into store 1000." Sometimes such a machine is described as having free will (though I would not use this phrase myself). It is not normally possible to determine from observing a machine whether it has a random element, for a similar effect can be produced by such devices as making the choices depend on the digits of the decimal for π.

Most actual digital computers have only a finite

store. There is no theoretical difficulty in the idea of a computer with an unlimited store. Of course only a finite part can have been used at any one time. Likewise only a finite amount can have been constructed, but we can imagine more and more being added as required. Such computers have special theoretical interest and will be called infinite capacity computers.

The idea of a digital computer is an old one. Charles Babbage, Lucasian Professor of Mathematics at Cambridge from 1828 to 1839, planned such a machine, called the Analytical Engine, but it was never completed. Although Babbage had all the essential ideas, his machine was not at that time such a very attractive prospect. The speed which would have been available would be definitely faster than a human computer but something like 100 times slower than the Manchester machine, itself one of the slower of the modern machines. The storage was to be purely mechanical, using wheels and cards.

The fact that Babbage's Analytical Engine was to be entirely mechanical will help us to rid ourselves of a superstition. Importance is often attached to the fact that modern digital computers are electrical, and that the nervous system also is electrical. Since Babbage's machine was not electrical, and since all digital computers are in a sense equivalent, we see that this use of electricity cannot be of theoretical importance. Of course electricity usually comes in where fast signaling is concerned, so that it is not surprising that we find it in both these connections. In the nervous system chemical phenomena are at least as important as electrical. In certain computers the storage system is mainly acoustic. The feature of using electricity is thus seen to be only a very superficial similarity. If we wish to find such similarities we should look rather for mathematical analogies of function.

5. Universality of Digital Computers

The digital computers considered in the last section may be classified among the "discrete state machines." These are the machines which move by sudden jumps or clicks from one quite definite state to another. These states are sufficiently different for the possibility of confusion between them to be ignored. Strictly speaking there are no such machines. Everything really moves continuously. But there are many kinds of machines which can profitably be *thought of* as being discrete state machines. For instance in considering the switches for a lighting system it is a convenient fiction that each switch must be definitely on or definitely off. There must be intermediate positions, but for most purposes we can forget about them. As an example of a discrete state machine we might consider a wheel which clicks round through 120° once a second, but may be stopped by a lever which can be operated from outside; in addition a lamp is to light in one of the positions of the wheel. This machine could be described abstractly as follows: The internal state of the machine (which is described by the position of the wheel) may be q_1, q_2 or q_3. There is an input signal i_0 or i_1 (position of lever). The internal state at any moment is determined by the last state and input signal according to the table

		Last State		
		q_1	q_2	q_3
	i_0	q_2	q_3	q_1
Input				
	i_1	q_1	q_2	q_3

The output signals, the only externally visible indication of the internal state (the light) are described by the table

State	q_1	q_2	q_3
Output	o_0	o_0	o_1

This example is typical of discrete state machines. They can be described by such tables provided they have only a finite number of possible states.

It will seem that given the initial state of the machine and the input signals it is always possible to predict all future states. This is reminiscent of Laplace's view that from the complete state of the universe at one moment of time, as described by the positions and velocities of all particles, it should be possible to predict all future states. The prediction which we are considering is, however, rather nearer to practicability than that considered by Laplace. The system of the "universe as a whole" is such that quite small errors in the initial conditions can have an overwhelming effect at a later time. The displacement of a single electron by a billionth of a centimeter at one moment might make the difference between a man being killed by an avalanche a year later, or escaping. It is an essential property of the mechanical systems which we have called "discrete state machines" that this phenomenon does not occur. Even when we consider the actual physical machines instead of the idealized machines, reasonably accurate knowledge of the state at one moment yields reasonably accurate knowledge any number of steps later.

As we have mentioned, digital computers fall within the class of discrete state machines. But the number of states of which such a machine is capable is usually enormously large. For instance, the number for the machine now working at Manchester is about $2^{165,000}$, i.e., about $10^{50,000}$. Compare this with our example of the clicking wheel described above, which had three states. It is not difficult to see why the number of states should be so immense. The computer includes a store corresponding to the paper used by a human computer. It must be possible to write into the store any one of the combinations of symbols which might have been written on the paper. For simplicity suppose that only digits from 0 to 9 are used as symbols. Variations in handwriting are ignored. Suppose the computer is allowed 100 sheets of paper each containing 50 lines each with room for 30 digits. Then the number of states is $10^{100 \times 50 \times 30}$, i.e., $10^{150,000}$. This is about the number of states of three Manchester machines put together. The logarithm to the base two of the number of states is usually called the "storage capacity" of the machine. Thus the Manchester machine has a storage capacity of about 165,000 and the wheel machine of our example about $1 \cdot 6$. If two machines are put together their capacities must be added to obtain the capacity of the resultant machine. This leads to the possibility of statements such as "The Manchester machine contains 64 magnetic tracks each with a capacity of 2560, eight electronic tubes with a capacity of 1280. Miscellaneous storage amounts to about 300 making a total of 174,380."

Given the table corresponding to a discrete state

machine it is possible to predict what it will do. There is no reason why this calculation should not be carried out by means of a digital computer. Provided it could be carried out sufficiently quickly the digital computer could mimic the behavior of any discrete state machine. The imitation game could then be played with the machine in question (as B) and the mimicking digital computer (as A) and the interrogator would be unable to distinguish them. Of course the digital computer must have an adequate storage capacity as well as working sufficiently fast. Moreover, it must be programed afresh for each new machine which it is desired to mimic.

This special property of digital computers, that they can mimic any discrete state machine, is described by saying that they are *universal* machines. The existence of machines with this property has the important consequence that, considerations of speed apart, it is unnecessary to design various new machines to do various computing processes. They can all be done with one digital computer, suitably programed for each case. It will be seen that as a consequence of this all digital computers are in a sense equivalent.

We may now consider again the point raised at the end of §3. It was suggested tentatively that the question, "Can machines think?" should be replaced by "Are there imaginable digital computers which would do well in the imitation game?" If we wish we can make this superficially more general and ask "Are there discrete state machines which would do well?" But in view of the universality property we see that either of these questions is equivalent to this, "Let us fix our attention on one particular digital computer C. Is it true that by modifying this computer to have an adequate storage, suitably increasing its speed of action, and providing it with an appropriate program, C can be made to play satisfactorily the part of A in the imitation game, the part of B being taken by a man?"

6. Contrary Views on the Main Question

We may now consider the ground to have been cleared and we are ready to proceed to the debate on our question, "Can machines think?" and the variant of it quoted at the end of the last section. We cannot altogether abandon the original form of the problem, for opinions will differ as to the appropriateness of the substitution and we must at least listen to what has to be said in this connection.

It will simplify matters for the reader if I explain first my own beliefs in the matter. Consider first the more accurate form of the question. I believe that in about fifty years' time it will be possible to program computers, with a storage capacity of about 10^9, to make them play the imitation game so well that an average interrogator will not have more than 70 per cent chance of making the right identification after five minutes of questioning. The original question, "Can machines think?" I believe to be too meaningless to deserve discussion. Nevertheless I believe that at the end of the century the use of words and general educated opinion will have altered so much that one will be able to speak of machines thinking without expecting to be contradicted. I believe further that no useful purpose is served by concealing these beliefs. The popular view that scientists proceed inexorably from well-established fact to well-established fact, never being influenced by any unproved conjecture, is quite mistaken. Provided it is made clear which are proved facts and which are conjectures, no harm can result. Conjectures are of great importance since they suggest useful lines of research.

I now proceed to consider opinions opposed to my own. . . .

(3) *The Mathematical Objection.* There are a number of results of mathematical logic which can be used to show that there are limitations to the powers of discrete state machines. The best known of these results is known as Gödel's theorem, and shows that in any sufficiently powerful logical system statements can be formulated which can neither be proved nor disproved within the system, unless possibly the system itself is inconsistent. There are other, in some respects similar, results due to Church, Kleene, Rosser, and Turing. The latter result is the most convenient to consider, since it refers directly to machines, whereas the others can only be used in a comparatively indirect argument: for instance if Gödel's theorem is to be used we need in addition to have some means of describing logical systems in terms of machines, and machines in terms of logical systems. The result in question refers to a type of machine which is essentially a digital computer with an infinite capacity. It states that there are certain things that such a machine cannot do. If it is rigged up to give answers to questions as in the imitation game, there will be some questions to which it will either give a wrong answer, or fail to give an answer at all however much time is allowed for a reply. There may, of course, be many such questions, and questions which cannot be answered by one machine may be satisfactorily answered by another. We are of course supposing for the present that the questions are of the kind to which an answer "Yes" or "No" is appropriate, rather than questions such as "What do you think of Picasso?" The questions that we know the machines must fail on are of this type, "Consider the machine specified as follows. . . . Will this machine ever answer 'Yes' to any question?" The dots are to be replaced by a description of some machine in a standard form, which could be something like that used in §5. When the machine described bears a certain comparatively simple relation to the machine which is under interrogation, it can be shown that the answer is either wrong or not forthcoming. This is the mathematical result: it is argued that it proves a disability of machines to which the human intellect is not subject.

The short answer to this argument is that although it is established that there are limitations to the powers of any particular machine, it has only been stated, without any sort of proof, that no such limitations apply to the human intellect. But I do not think this view can be dismissed quite so lightly. Whenever one of these machines is asked the appropriate critical question, and gives a definite answer, we know that this answer must be wrong, and this gives us a certain feeling of superiority. Is this feeling illusory? It is no doubt quite genuine, but I do not think too much importance should be attached to it. We too often give wrong answers to questions ourselves to be justified in being very pleased at such evidence of fallibility on the part of the machines. Further, our superiority can only be felt on such an occasion in relation to the one machine over which we have scored our petty triumph. There would be no question of triumphing simultaneously over *all* machines. In short, then, there might be men cleverer than any given machine, but then again there might be other machines cleverer again, and so on.

Those who hold to the mathematical argument would, I think mostly be willing to accept the imitation game as a basis for discussion. . . .

(4) *The Argument from Consciousness.* This argument is very well expressed in Professor Jefferson's Lister Oration for 1949, from which I quote. "Not until a machine can write a sonnet or compose a concerto because of thoughts and emotions felt, and not by the chance fall of symbols, could we agree that machine equals brain—that is, not only write it but know that it had written it. No mechanism could feel (and not merely artificially signal, an easy contrivance) pleasure at its successes, grief when its valves fuse, be warmed by flattery, be made miserable by its mistakes, be charmed by sex, be angry or depressed when it cannot get what it wants."

This argument appears to be a denial of the validity of our test. According to the most extreme form of this view the only way by which one could be sure that a machine thinks is to *be* the machine and to feel oneself thinking. One could then describe these feelings to the world, but of course no one would be justified in taking any notice. Likewise according to this view the only way to know that a *man* thinks is to be that particular man. It is in fact the solipsist point of view. It may be the most logical view to hold but it makes communication of ideas difficult. A is liable to believe "A thinks but B does not" while B believes "B thinks but A does not." Instead of arguing continually over this point it is usual to have the polite convention that every one thinks.

I am sure that Professor Jefferson does not wish to adopt the extreme and solipsist point of view. Probably he would be quite willing to accept the imitation game as a test. The game (with the player B omitted) is frequently used in practice under the name of viva voce to discover whether someone really understands something or has "learned it parrot fashion." Let us listen in to a part of such a viva voce:

INTERROGATOR: In the first line of your sonnet which reads "Shall I compare thee to a summer's day," would not "a spring day" do as well or better?

WITNESS: It wouldn't scan.

INTERROGATOR: How about "a winter's day." That would scan all right.

WITNESS: Yes, but nobody wants to be compared to a winter's day.

INTERROGATOR: Would you say Mr. Pickwick reminded you of Christmas?

WITNESS: In a way.

INTERROGATOR: Yet Christmas is a winter's day, and I do not think Mr. Pickwick would mind the comparison.

WITNESS: I don't think you're serious. By a winter's day one means a typical winter's day, rather than a special one like Christmas.

And so on. What would Professor Jefferson say if the sonnet-writing machine was able to answer like this in the viva voce? I do not know whether he would regard the machine as "merely artificially signaling" these answers, but if the answers were as satisfactory and sustained as in the above passage I do not think he would describe it as "an easy contrivance." This phrase is, I think, intended to cover such devices as the inclusion in the machine of a record of someone reading a sonnet, with appropriate switching to turn it on from time to time.

In short then, I think that most of those who support the argument from consciousness could be persuaded to abandon it rather than be forced into the solipsist position. They will then probably be willing to accept our test.

I do not wish to give the impression that I think there is no mystery about consciousness. There is, for instance, something of a paradox connected with any attempt to localize it. But I do not think these mysteries necessarily need to be solved before we can answer the question with which we are concerned in this paper.

(5) *Arguments from Various Disabilities.* These arguments take the form, "I grant you that you can make machines do all the things you have mentioned but you will never be able to make one to do X." Numerous features X are suggested in this connection. I offer a selection:

Be kind, resourceful, beautiful, friendly . . . have initiative, have a sense of humor, tell right from

wrong, make mistakes . . . fall in love, enjoy strawberries and cream . . . , make someone fall in love
with it, learn from experience . . . , use words properly, be the subject of its own thought . . . , have as
much diversity of behavior as a man, do something
really new. . . .

No support is usually offered for these statements. I believe they are mostly founded on the
principle of scientific induction. A man has seen
thousands of machines in his lifetime. From what
he sees of them he draws a number of general conclusions. They are ugly, each is designed for a very
limited purpose, when required for a minutely different purpose they are useless, the variety of behavior of any one of them is very small, etc., etc.
Naturally he concludes that these are necessary
properties of machines in general. Many of these
limitations are associated with the very small storage capacity of most machines. (I am assuming that
the idea of storage capacity is extended in some way
to cover machines other than discrete state machines. The exact definition does not matter as no
mathematical accuracy is claimed in the present discussion.) A few years ago, when very little had been
heard of digital computers, it was possible to elicit
much incredulity concerning them, if one mentioned their properties without describing their construction. That was presumably due to a similar application of the principle of scientific induction.
These applications of the principle are of course
largely unconscious. When a burned child fears the
fire and shows that he fears it by avoiding it, I should
say that he was applying scientific induction. (I
could of course also describe his behavior in many
other ways.) The works or customs of mankind do
not seem to be very suitable material to which to apply scientific induction. A very large part of space-
time must be investigated if reliable results are to be
obtained. Otherwise we may (as most English children do) decide that everybody speaks English, and
that it is silly to learn French.

There are, however, special remarks to be made
about many of the disabilities that have been mentioned. The inability to enjoy strawberries and
cream may [strike] the reader as frivolous. Possibly
a machine might be made to enjoy this delicious
dish, but any attempt to make one do so would be
idiotic. What is important about this disability is that
it contributes to some of the other disabilities, e.g.,
to the difficulty of the same kind of friendliness occurring between man and machine as between
white man and white man, or between black man
and black man.

The claim that "machines cannot make mistakes" seems a curious one. One is tempted to retort, "Are they any worse for that?" But let us adopt
a more sympathetic attitude, and try to see what is
really meant. I think this criticism can be explained
in terms of the imitation game. It is claimed that the
interrogator could distinguish the machine from the
man simply by setting them a number of problems
in arithmetic. The machine would be unmasked because of its deadly accuracy. The reply to this is simple. The machine (programed for playing the game)
would not attempt to give the *right* answers to the
arithmetic problems. It would deliberately introduce mistakes in a manner calculated to confuse the
interrogator. A mechanical fault would probably
show itself through an unsuitable decision as to what
sort of a mistake to make in the arithmetic. Even
this interpretation of the criticism is not sufficiently
sympathetic. But we cannot afford the space to go
into it much further. It seems to me that this criticism depends on a confusion between two kinds of
mistakes. We may call them "errors of functioning"
and "errors of conclusion." Errors of functioning are
due to some mechanical or electrical fault which
causes the machine to behave otherwise than it was
designed to do. In philosophical discussions one
likes to ignore the possibility of such errors; one is
therefore discussing "abstract machines." These abstract machines are mathematical fictions rather
than physical objects. By definition they are incapable of errors of functioning. In this sense we can
truly say that "machines can never make mistakes."
Errors of conclusion can only arise when some
meaning is attached to the output signals from the
machine. The machine might, for instance, type out
mathematical equations, or sentences in English.
When a false proposition is typed we say that the
machine has committed an error of conclusion.
There is clearly no reason at all for saying that a machine cannot make this kind of mistake. It might do

nothing but type out repeatedly "0 = 1." To take a less perverse example, it might have some method for drawing conclusions by scientific induction. We must expect such a method to lead occasionally to erroneous results.

The claim that a machine cannot be the subject of its own thought can of course only be answered if it can be shown that the machine has *some* thought with *some* matter. Nevertheless, "the subject matter of a machine's operations" does seem to mean something, at least to the people who deal with it. If, for instance, the machine was trying to find a solution of the equation $x^2 - 40x - 11 = 0$ one would be tempted to describe this equation as part of the machine's subject matter at that moment. In this sort of sense a machine undoubtedly can be its own subject matter. It may be used to help in making up its own programs, or to predict the effect of alterations in its own structure. By observing the results of its own behavior it can modify its own programs so as to achieve some purpose more effectively. These are possibilities of the near future, rather than Utopian dreams.

The criticism that a machine cannot have much diversity of behavior is just a way of saying that it cannot have much storage capacity. Until fairly recently a storage capacity of even a thousand digits was very rare.

The criticisms that we are considering here are often disguised forms of the argument from consciousness. Usually if one maintains that a machine *can* do one of these things, and describes the kind of method that the machine could use, one will not make much of an impression. It is thought that the method (whatever it may be, for it must be mechanical) is really rather base. Compare the parenthesis of Jefferson's statement quoted above.

(6) *Lady Lovelace's Objection*. Our most detailed information of Babbage's Analytical Engine comes from a memoir by Lady Lovelace. In it she states, "The Analytical Engine has no pretensions to *originate* anything. It can do *whatever we know how to order it* to perform" (her italics). This statement is quoted by Hartree who adds: "This does not imply that it may not be possible to construct electronic equipment which will 'think for itself,' or in which, in biological terms, one could set up a conditioned

reflex, which would serve as a basis for 'learning.' Whether this is possible in principle or not is a stimulating and exciting question, suggested by some of these recent developments. But it did not seem that the machines constructed or projected at the time had this property."

I am in thorough agreement with Hartree over this. It will be noticed that he does not assert that the machines in question had not got the property, but rather that the evidence available to Lady Lovelace did not encourage her to believe that they had it. It is quite possible that the machines in question had in a sense got this property. For suppose that some discrete state machine has the property. The Analytical Engine was a universal digital computer, so that, if its storage capacity and speed were adequate, it could by suitable programing be made to mimic the machine in question. Probably this argument did not occur to the Countess or to Babbage. In any case there was no obligation on them to claim all that could be claimed.

This whole question will be considered again under the heading of learning machines. . . .

(8) *The Argument from Informality of Behavior*. It is not possible to produce a set of rules purporting to describe what a man should do in every conceivable set of circumstances. One might for instance have a rule that one is to stop when one sees a red traffic light, and to go if one sees a green one, but what if by some fault both appear together? One may perhaps decide that it is safest to stop. But some further difficulty may well arise from this decision later. To attempt to provide rules of conduct to cover every eventuality, even those arising from traffic lights, appears to be impossible. With all this I agree.

From this it is argued that we cannot be machines. I shall try to reproduce the argument, but I fear I shall hardly do it justice. It seems to run something like this. "If each man had a definite set of rules of conduct by which he regulated his life he would be no better than a machine. But there are no such rules, so men cannot be machines." The undistributed middle is glaring. I do not think the argument is ever put quite like this, but I believe this is the argument used nevertheless. There may however be a certain confusion between "rules of conduct" and "laws of behavior" to cloud the issue. By "rules of conduct" I mean precepts such as "Stop if you see red lights," on which one can act, and of which one can be conscious. By "laws of behavior" I mean laws of nature as applied to a man's body such as "if you pinch him he will squeak." If we substitute "laws of behavior which regulate his life" for "laws of conduct by which he regulates his life" in the argument quoted the undistributed middle is no longer insuperable. For we believe that it is not only true that being regulated by laws of behavior implies being some sort of machine (though not necessarily a discrete state machine), but that conversely being such a machine implies being regulated by such laws. However, we cannot so easily convince ourselves of the absence of complete laws of behavior as of complete rules of conduct. The only way we know of for finding such laws is scientific observation, and we certainly know of no circumstances under which we could say, "We have searched enough. There are no such laws."

We can demonstrate more forcibly that any such statement would be unjustified. For suppose we could be sure of finding such laws if they existed. Then given a discrete state machine it should certainly be possible to discover by observation sufficient about it to predict its future behavior, and this within a reasonable time, say a thousand years. But this does not seem to be the case. I have set up on the Manchester computer a small program using only 1000 units of storage, whereby the machine supplied with one sixteen-figure number replies with another within two seconds. I would defy anyone to learn from these replies sufficient about the program to be able to predict any replies to untried values.

(9) *The Argument from Extra-Sensory Perception.* I assume that the reader is familiar with the idea of extra-sensory perception, and the meaning of the four items of it, viz., telepathy, clairvoyance, precognition and psychokinesis. These disturbing phenomena seem to deny all our usual scientific ideas. How we would like to discredit them! Unfortunately the statistical evidence, at least for telepathy, is overwhelming. It is very difficult to rearrange one's ideas so as to fit these new facts in. Once one has accepted them it does not seem a very big step to believe in ghosts and bogies. The idea that our bodies move sim-

ply according to the known laws of physics, together with some others not yet discovered but somewhat similar, would be one of the first to go.

This argument is to my mind quite a strong one. One can say in reply that many scientific theories seem to remain workable in practice, in spite of clashing with E.S.P.; that in fact one can get along very nicely if one forgets about it. This is rather cold comfort, and one fears that thinking is just the kind of phenomenon where E.S.P. may be especially relevant.

A more specific argument based on E.S.P. might run as follows: "Let us play the imitation game, using as witnesses a man who is good as a telepathic receiver, and a digital computer. The interrogator can ask such questions as 'What suit does the card in my right hand belong to?' The man by telepathy or clairvoyance gives the right answer 130 times out of 400 cards. The machine can only guess at random, and perhaps get 104 right, so the interrogator makes the right identification." There is an interesting possibility which opens here. Suppose the digital computer contains a random number generator. Then it will be natural to use this to decide what answer to give. But then the random number generator will be subject to the psychokinetic powers of the interrogator. Perhaps this psychokinesis might cause the machine to guess right more often than would be expected on a probability calculation, so that the interrogator might still be unable to make the right identification. On the other hand, he might be able to guess right without any questioning, by clairvoyance. With E.S.P. anything may happen.

If telepathy is admitted it will be necessary to tighten our test. The situation could be regarded as analogous to that which would occur if the interrogator were talking to himself and one of the competitors was listening with his ear to the wall. To put the competitors into a "telepathy-proof room" would satisfy all requirements.

7. Learning Machines

The reader will have anticipated that I have no very convincing arguments of a positive nature to support my views. If I had I should not have taken such pains to point out the fallacies in contrary views. Such evidence as I have I shall now give.

Let us return for a moment to Lady Lovelace's objection, which stated that the machine can only do what we tell it to do. One could say that a man can "inject" an idea into the machine, and that it will respond to a certain extent and then drop into quiescence, like a piano string struck by a hammer. Another simile would be an atomic pile of less than critical size: an injected idea is to correspond to a neutron entering the pile from without. Each such neutron will cause a certain disturbance which eventually dies away. If, however, the size of the pile is sufficiently increased, the disturbance caused by such an incoming neutron will very likely go on and on increasing until the whole pile is destroyed. Is there a corresponding phenomenon for minds, and is there one for machines? There does seem to be one for the human mind. The majority of them seem to be "subcritical," i.e., to correspond in this analogy to piles of subcritical size. An idea presented to such a mind will on an average give rise to less than one idea in reply. A smallish proportion are supercritical. An idea presented to such a mind may give rise to a whole "theory" consisting of secondary, tertiary and more remote ideas. Animals' minds seem to be very definitely subcritical. Adhering to this analogy we ask, "Can a machine be made to be supercritical?"

The "skin of an onion" analogy is also helpful. In considering the functions of the mind or the brain we find certain operations which we can explain in purely mechanical terms. This we say does not correspond to the real mind: it is a sort of skin which we must strip off if we are to find the real mind. But then in what remains we find a further skin to be stripped off, and so on. Proceeding in this way do we ever come to the "real" mind, or do we eventually come to the skin which has nothing in it? In the latter case the whole mind is mechanical. (It would not be a discrete state machine however. We have discussed this.)

These last two paragraphs do not claim to be convincing arguments. They should rather be described as "recitations tending to produce belief."

The only really satisfactory support that can be given for the view expressed at the beginning of §6,

[p. 360] will be that provided by waiting for the end of the century and then doing the experiment described. But what can we say in the meantime? What steps should be taken now if the experiment is to be successful?

As I have explained, the problem is mainly one of programing. Advances in engineering will have to be made too, but it seems unlikely that these will not be adequate for the requirements. Estimates of the storage capacity of the brain vary from 10^{10} to 10^{15} binary digits. I incline to the lower values and believe that only a very small fraction is used for the higher types of thinking. Most of it is probably used for the retention of visual impressions. I should be surprised if more than 10^9 was required for satisfactory playing of the imitation game, at any rate against a blind man. (Note: The capacity of the *Encyclopaedia Britannica*, eleventh edition, is 2×10^9.) A storage capacity of 10^7 would be a very practicable possibility even by present techniques. It is probably not necessary to increase the speed of operations of the machines at all. Parts of modern machines which can be regarded as analogues of nerve cells work about a thousand times faster than the latter. This should provide a "margin of safety" which could cover losses of speed arising in many ways. Our problem then is to find out how to program these machines to play the game. At my present rate of working I produce about a thousand digits of program a day, so that about sixty workers, working steadily through the fifty years might accomplish the job, if nothing went into the wastepaper basket. Some more expeditious method seems desirable.

In the process of trying to imitate an adult human mind we are bound to think a good deal about the process which has brought it to the state that it is in. We may notice three components,

(a) The initial state of the mind, say at birth,
(b) The education to which it has been subjected,
(c) Other experience, not to be described as education, to which it has been subjected.

Instead of trying to produce a program to simulate the adult mind, why not rather try to produce one which simulates the child's? If this were then subjected to an appropriate course of education one would obtain the adult brain. Presumably the child-brain is something like a notebook as one buys it from the stationers. Rather little mechanism, and lots of blank sheets. (Mechanism and writing are from our point of view almost synonymous.) Our hope is that there is so little mechanism in the child-brain that something like it can be easily programed. The amount of work in the education we can assume, as a first approximation, to be much the same as for the human child.

We have thus divided our problem into two parts—the child-program and the education process. These two remain very closely connected. We cannot expect to find a good child-machine at the first attempt. One must experiment with teaching one such machine and see how well it learns. One can then try another and see if it is better or worse. There is an obvious connection between this process and evolution, by the identifications

$$\frac{\text{Structure of the}}{\text{child-machine}} = \text{Hereditary material}$$

$$\frac{\text{Changes of the}}{\text{child-machine}} = \text{Mutations}$$

$$\frac{\text{Natural selec-}}{\text{tion}} = \frac{\text{Judgment of the}}{\text{experimenter}}$$

One may hope however, that this process will be more expeditious than evolution. The survival of the fittest is a slow method for measuring advantages. The experimenter, by the exercise of intelligence, should be able to speed it up. Equally important is the fact that he is not restricted to random mutations. If he can trace a cause for some weakness he can probably think of the kind of mutation which will improve it. . . .

The idea of a learning machine may appear paradoxical to some readers. How can the rules of operation of the machine change? They should describe completely how the machine will react whatever its history might be, whatever changes it might undergo. The rules are thus quite time-invariant. This is quite true. The explanation of the paradox is that the rules which get changed in the learning process are of a rather less pretentious kind, claiming only an ephemeral validity. The reader may draw a parallel with the Constitution of the United States.

An important feature of a learning machine is that its teacher will often be very largely ignorant of quite what is going on inside, although he may still be able to some extent to predict his pupil's behavior. This should apply most strongly to the later education of a machine arising from a child-machine of well-tried design (or program). This is in clear contrast with normal procedure when using a machine to do computations: one's object is then to have a clear mental picture of the state of the machine at each moment in the computation. This object can only be achieved with a struggle. The view that "the machine can only do what we know how to order it to do,"[1] appears strange in face of this. Most of the programs which we can put into the machine will result in its doing something that we cannot make sense of at all, or which we regard as completely random behavior. Intelligent behavior presumably consists in a departure from the completely disciplined behavior involved in computation, but a rather slight one, which does not give rise to random behavior, or to pointless repetitive loops. Another important result of preparing our machine for its part in the imitation game by a process of teaching and learning is that "human fallibility" is likely to be omitted in a rather natural way, i.e., without special "coaching." Processes that are learned do not produce a hundred per cent certainty of result; if they did they could not be unlearned.

It is probably wise to include a random element in a learning machine. A random element is rather useful when we are searching for a solution of some problem. Suppose for instance we wanted to find a number between 50 and 200 which was equal to the square of the sum of its digits, we might start at 51 then try 52 and go on until we got a number that worked. Alternatively we might choose numbers at random until we got a good one. This method has the advantage that it is unnecessary to keep track of the values that have been tried, but the disadvantage that one may try the same one twice, but this is not very important if there are several solutions. The systematic method has the disadvantage that there may be an enormous block without any solutions in the region which has to be investigated first. Now the learning process may be regarded as a search for a form of behavior which will satisfy the teacher (or some other criterion). Since there is probably a very large number of satisfactory solutions the random method seems to be better than the systematic. It should be noticed that it is used in the analogous process of evolution. But there the systematic method is not possible. How could one keep track of the different genetical combinations that had been tried, so as to avoid trying them again?

We may hope that machines will eventually compete with men in all purely intellectual fields. But which are the best ones to start with? Even this is a difficult decision. Many people think that a very abstract activity, like the playing of chess, would be best. It can also be maintained that it is best to provide the machine with the best sense organs that money can buy, and then teach it to understand and speak English. This process could follow the normal teaching of a child. Things would be pointed out and named, etc. Again I do not know what the right answer is, but I think both approaches should be tried.

We can only see a short distance ahead, but we can see plenty there that needs to be done.

NOTE

1. Compare Lady Lovelace's statement (p. 364), which does not contain the word "only."

Minds, Brains, and Programs

JOHN R. SEARLE

John R. Searle (1932–　) is a professor of philosophy at the University of California at Berkeley. His publications include *Speech Acts* and *Expression and Meaning.*

———•———

WHAT PSYCHOLOGICAL AND PHILosophical significance should we attach to recent efforts at computer simulations of human cognitive capacities? In answering this question, I find it useful to distinguish what I will call "strong" AI from "weak" or "cautious" AI (artificial intelligence). According to weak AI, the principal value of the computer in the study of the mind is that it gives us a very powerful tool. For example, it enables us to formulate and test hypotheses in a more rigorous and precise fashion. But according to strong AI, the computer is not merely a tool in the study of the mind; rather, the appropriately programmed computer really *is* a mind, in the sense that computers given the right programs can be literally said to *understand* and have other cognitive states. In strong AI, because the programmed computer has cognitive states, the programs are not mere tools that enable us to test psychological ex-

From *Behavioral and Brain Sciences.* Copyright © 1980 by Cambridge University Press. Reprinted by permission of the publisher.

I am indebted to a rather large number of people for discussion of these matters and for their patient attempts to overcome my ignorance of artificial intelligence. I would especially like to thank Ned Block, Hubert Dreyfus, John Haugeland, Roger Schank, Robert Wilensky, and Terry Winograd.

planations; rather, the programs are themselves the explanations.

I have no objection to the claims of weak AI, at least as far as this article is concerned. My discussion here will be directed at the claims I have defined as those of strong AI, specifically the claim that the appropriately programmed computer literally has cognitive states and that the programs thereby explain human cognition. When I hereafter refer to AI, I have in mind the strong version, as expressed by these two claims.

I will consider the work of Roger Schank and his colleagues at Yale (Schank and Abelson 1977), because I am more familiar with it than I am with any other similar claims, and because it provides a very clear example of the sort of work I wish to examine. But nothing that follows depends upon the details of Schank's programs. The same arguments would apply to Winograd's SHRDLU (Winograd 1973), Weizenbaum's ELIZA (Weizenbaum 1965), and indeed any Turing machine simulation of human mental phenomena. . . .

Very briefly, and leaving out the various details, one can describe Schank's program as follows: The aim of the program is to simulate the human ability to understand stories. It is characteristic of human beings' story-understanding capacity that they can answer questions about the story even though the information that they give was never explicitly stated in the story. Thus, for example, suppose you are given the following story: "A man went into a restaurant and ordered a hamburger. When the hamburger arrived it was burned to a crisp, and the man stormed out of the restaurant angrily, without paying for the burger or leaving a tip." Now, if you are asked "Did the man eat the hamburger?" you will presumably answer, "No, he did not." Similarly, if you are given the following story: "A man went into a restaurant and ordered a hamburger; when the hamburger came he was very pleased with it; and as he left the restaurant he gave the waitress a large tip before paying his bill," and you are asked the question, "Did the man eat the hamburger?" you will presumably answer, "Yes, he ate the hamburger." Now Schank's machines can similarly answer questions about restaurants in this fashion. To do this, they have a "representation" of the sort of information that human beings have about restaurants, which enables them to answer such questions as those above, given these sorts of stories. When the machine is given the story and then asked the question, the machine will print out answers of the sort that we would expect human beings to give if told similar stories. Partisans of strong AI claim that in this question and answer sequence the machine is not only simulating a human ability but also (1) that the machine can literally be said to *understand* the story and provide the answers to questions, and (2) that what the machine and its program do *explains* the human ability to understand the story and answer questions about it.

Both claims seem to me to be totally unsupported by Schank's work, as I will attempt to show in what follows.[1]

One way to test any theory of the mind is to ask oneself what it would be like if my mind actually worked on the principles that the theory says all minds work on. Let us apply this test to the Schank program with the following *Gedankenexperiment*. Suppose that I'm locked in a room and given a large batch of Chinese writing. Suppose furthermore (as is indeed the case) that I know no Chinese, either written or spoken, and that I'm not even confident that I could recognize Chinese writing as Chinese writing distinct from, say, Japanese writing or meaningless squiggles. To me, Chinese writing is just so many meaningless squiggles. Now suppose further that after this first batch of Chinese writing I am given a second batch of Chinese script together with a set of rules for correlating the second batch with the first batch. The rules are in English, and I understand these rules as well as any other native speaker of English. They enable me to correlate one set of formal symbols with another set of formal symbols, and all that "formal" means here is that I can identify the symbols entirely by their shapes. Now suppose also that I am given a third batch of Chinese symbols together with some instructions, again in English, that enable me to correlate elements of this third batch with the first two batches, and these rules instruct me how to give back certain Chinese symbols with certain sorts of shapes in response to certain sorts of shapes given me in the third batch. Unknown to me, the people who are giving me all of these symbols call the first batch a "script," they call the second batch a "story," and they call the third batch "questions." Furthermore, they call the symbols I give them back in response to the third batch "answers to the questions," and the set of rules in English that they gave me, they call the "program." Now just to complicate the story a little, imagine that these people also give me stories in English, which I understand, and they then ask me questions in English about these stories, and I give them back answers in English. Suppose also that after a while I got so good at following the instructions for manipulating the Chinese symbols and the programmers get so good at writing the programs that from the external point of view—that is, from the point of view of somebody outside the room in which I am locked—my answers to the questions are absolutely indistinguishable from those of native Chinese speakers. Nobody just looking at my answers can tell that I don't speak a word of Chinese. Let us also suppose that my answers to the English questions are, as they no doubt would be, indistinguishable from those of other native English speakers, for the simple reason that I am a native English speaker. From the external point of view—from the point of view of someone reading my "answers"—the answers to the Chinese questions and the English questions are equally good. But in the Chinese case, unlike the English case, I produce the answers by manipulating uninterpreted formal symbols. As far as the Chinese is concerned, I simply behave like a computer; I perform computational operations on formally specified elements. For the purposes of the Chinese, I am simply an instantiation of the computer program.

Now the claims made by strong AI are that the programmed computer understands the stories and that the program in some sense explains human understanding. But we are now in a position to examine these claims in light of our thought experiment.

1. As regards the first claim, it seems to me quite obvious in the example that I do not understand a word of Chinese stories. I have inputs and outputs that are indistinguishable from those of the native Chinese speaker, and I can have any formal program you like, but I still understand nothing. For

the same reasons, Schank's computer understands nothing of any stories, whether in Chinese, English, or whatever, since in the Chinese case the computer is me, and in cases where the computer is not me, the computer has nothing more than I have in the case where I understand nothing.

2. As regards the second claim, that the program explains human understanding, we can see that the computer and its program do not provide sufficient conditions of understanding since the computer and the program are functioning, and there is no understanding. But does it even provide a necessary condition or a significant contribution to understanding? One of the claims made by the supporters of strong AI is that when I understand a story in English, what I am doing is exactly the same—or perhaps more of the same—as what I was doing in manipulating the Chinese symbols. It is simply more formal symbol manipulation that distinguishes the case in English, where I do understand, from the case in Chinese where I don't. I have not demonstrated that this claim is false, but it would certainly appear an incredible claim in the example. Such plausibility as the claim has derives from the supposition that we can construct a program that will have the same inputs and outputs as native speakers, and in addition we assume that speakers have some level of description where they are also instantiations of a program. On the basis of these two assumptions we assume that even if Schank's program isn't the whole story about understanding, it may be part of the story. Well, I suppose that is an empirical possibility, but not the slightest reason has so far been given to believe that it is true, since what is suggested—though certainly not demonstrated—by the example is that the computer program is simply irrelevant to my understanding of the story. In the Chinese case I have everything that artificial intelligence can put into me by way of a program, and I understand nothing; in the English case I understand everything, and there is so far no reason at all to suppose that my understanding has anything to do with computer programs, that is, with computational operations on purely formally specified elements. As long as the program is defined in terms of computational operations on purely formally defined elements, what the example suggests is that these by themselves have no interesting connection with understanding. They are certainly not sufficient conditions, and not the slightest reason has been given to suppose that they are necessary conditions or even that they make a significant contribution to understanding. Notice that the force of the argument is not simply that different machines can have the same input and output while operating on different formal principles—that is not the point at all. Rather, whatever purely formal principles you put into the computer, they will not be sufficient for understanding, since a human will be able to follow the formal principles without understanding anything. No reason whatever has been offered to suppose that such principles are necessary or even contributory, since no reason has been given to suppose that when I understand English I am operating with any formal program at all.

Well, then, what is it that I have in the case of the English sentences that I do not have in the case of the Chinese sentences? The obvious answer is that I know what the former mean, while I haven't the faintest idea what the latter mean. But in what does this consist and why couldn't we give it to a machine, whatever it is? I will return to this question later, but first I want to continue with the example.

I have had the occasions to present this example to several workers in artificial intelligence, and, interestingly, they do not seem to agree on what the proper reply to it is. I get a surprising variety of replies, and in what follows I will consider the most common of these (specified along with their geographic origins).

But first I want to block some common misunderstandings about "understanding": In many of these discussions one finds a lot of fancy footwork about the word "understanding." My critics point out that there are many different degrees of understanding; that "understanding" is not a simple two-place predicate; that there are even different kinds and levels of understanding, and often the law of excluded middle doesn't even apply in a straightforward way to statements of the form "x understands y"; that in many cases it is a matter for decision and not a simple matter of fact whether x understands y; and so on. To all of these points I

want to say: of course, of course. But they have nothing to do with the points at issue. There are clear cases in which "understanding" literally applies and clear cases in which it does not apply; and these two sorts of cases are all I need for this argument.[2] I understand stories in English; to a lesser degree I can understand stories in French; to a still lesser degree, stories in German; and in Chinese, not at all. My car and my adding machine, on the other hand, understand nothing: they are not in that line of business. We often attribute "understanding" and other cognitive predicates by metaphor and analogy to cars, adding machines, and other artifacts, but nothing is proved by such attributions. We say, "The door *knows* when to open because of its photoelectric cell," "The adding machine *knows how* (*understands how*, is *able*) to do addition and subtraction but not division," and "The thermostat *perceives* changes in the temperature." The reason we make these attributions is quite interesting, and it has to do with the fact that in artifacts we extend our own intentionality;[3] our tools are extensions of our purposes, and so we find it natural to make metaphorical attributions of intentionality to them; but I take it no philosophical ice is cut by such examples. The sense in which an automatic door "understands instructions" from its photoelectric cell is not at all the sense in which I understand English. If the sense in which Schank's programmed computers understand stories is supposed to be the metaphorical sense in which the door understands, and not the sense in which I understand English, the issue would not be worth discussing. But Newell and Simon (1963) write that the kind of cognition they claim for computers is exactly the same as for human beings. I like the straightforwardness of this claim, and it is the sort of claim I will be considering. I will argue that in the literal sense the programmed computer understands what the car and the adding machine understand, namely, exactly nothing. The computer understanding is not just (like my understanding of German) partial or incomplete; it is zero.

Now to the replies:

I. The Systems Reply (Berkeley). "While it is true that the individual person who is locked in the room does not understand the story, the fact is that he is merely part of a whole system, and the system does understand the story. The person has a large ledger in front of him in which are written the rules, he has a lot of scratch paper and pencils for doing calculations, he has 'data banks' of sets of Chinese symbols. Now, understanding is not being ascribed to the mere individual; rather it is being ascribed to this whole system of which he is a part."

My response to the systems theory is quite simple: Let the individual internalize all of these elements of the system. He memorizes the rules in the ledger and the data banks of Chinese symbols, and he does all the calculations in his head. The individual then incorporates the entire system. There isn't anything at all to the system that he does not encompass. We can even get rid of the room and suppose he works outdoors. All the same, he understands nothing of the Chinese, and a fortiori neither does the system, because there isn't anything in the system that isn't in him. If he doesn't understand, then there is no way the system could understand because the system is just a part of him.

Actually I feel somewhat embarrassed to give even this answer to the systems theory because the theory seems to me so implausible to start with. The idea is that while a person doesn't understand Chinese, somehow the *conjunction* of that person and bits of paper might understand Chinese. It is not easy for me to imagine how someone who was not in the grip of an ideology would find the idea at all plausible. Still, I think many people who are committed to the ideology of strong AI will in the end be inclined to say something very much like this; so let us pursue it a bit further. According to one version of this view, while the man in the internalized systems example doesn't understand Chinese in the sense that a native Chinese speaker does (because, for example, he doesn't know that the story refers to restaurants and hamburgers, etc.), still "the man as a formal symbol manipulation system" *really does understand Chinese.* The subsystem of the man that is the formal symbol manipulation system for Chinese should not be confused with the subsystem for English.

So there are really two subsystems in the man: one understands English, the other Chinese, and "it's just that the two systems have little to do with each other." But, I want to reply, not only do they have little to do with each other, they are not even remotely alike. The subsystem that understands English (assuming we allow ourselves to talk in this jargon of "subsystems" for a moment) knows that the stories are about restaurants and eating hamburgers, he knows that he is being asked questions about restaurants and that he is answering questions as best he can by making various inferences from the content of the story, and so on. But the Chinese system knows none of this. Whereas the English subsystem knows that "hamburgers" refers to hamburgers, the Chinese subsystem knows only that "squiggle squiggle" is followed by "squoggle squoggle." All he knows is that various formal symbols are being introduced at one end and manipulated according to rules written in English, and other symbols are going out at the other end. The whole point of the original example was to argue that such symbol manipulation by itself couldn't be sufficient for understanding Chinese in any literal sense because the man could write "squoggle squoggle" after "squiggle squiggle" without understanding anything in Chinese. And it doesn't meet that argument to postulate subsystems within the man, because the subsystems are no better off than the man was in the first place: they still don't have anything even remotely like what the English-speaking man (or subsystem) has. Indeed, in the case as described, the Chinese subsystem is simply a part of the English subsystem, a part that engages in meaningless symbol manipulation according to rules in English.

Let us ask ourselves what is supposed to motivate the systems reply in the first place; that is, what *independent* grounds are there supposed to be for saying that the agent must have a subsystem within him that literally understands stories in Chinese? As far as I can tell the only grounds are that in the example I have the same input and output as native Chinese speakers and a program that goes from one to the other. But the whole point of the examples has been to try to show that that couldn't be sufficient for understanding, in the sense in which I understand stories in English, because a person, and hence the set of systems that go to make up a person, could have the right combination of input, output, and program and still not understand anything in the relevant literal sense in which I understand English. The only motivation for saying there *must* be a subsystem in me that understands Chinese is that I have a program and I can pass the Turing test; I can fool native Chinese speakers. But precisely one of the points at issue is the adequacy of the Turing test. The example shows that there could be two "systems," both of which pass the Turing test, but only one of which understands; and it is no argument against this point to say that since they both pass the Turing test they must both understand, since this claim fails to meet the argument that the system in me that understands English has a great deal more than the system that merely processes Chinese. In short, the systems reply simply begs the question by insisting without argument that the system must understand Chinese.

Furthermore, the systems reply would appear to lead to consequences that are independently absurd. If we are to conclude that there must be cognition in me on the grounds that I have a certain sort of input and output and a program in between, then it looks like all sorts of noncognitive subsystems are going to turn out to be cognitive. For example, there is a level of description at which my stomach does information processing, and it instantiates any number of computer programs, but I take it we do not want to say that it has any understanding (cf. Pylyshyn 1980). But if we accept the systems reply, then it is hard to see how we avoid saying that stomach, heart, liver, and so on are all understanding subsystems, since there is no principled way to distinguish the motivation for saying the Chinese subsystem understands from saying that the stomach understands. It is, by the way, not an answer to this point to say that the Chinese system has information as input and output and the stomach has food and food products as input and output, since from the point of view of the agent, from my point of view, there is no information in either the food or the Chinese—the Chinese is just so many meaningless squiggles. The information in the Chinese case is solely in the eyes of the programmers and the interpreters, and there is nothing to prevent them from treating the input and output of my digestive organs as information if they so desire.

This last point bears on some independent problems in strong AI, and it is worth digressing for a moment to explain it. If strong AI is to be a branch of psychology, then it must be able to distinguish those systems that are genuinely mental from those that are not. It must be able to distinguish the principles on which the mind works from those on which nonmental systems work; otherwise it will offer us no explanations of what is specifically mental about the mental. And the mental-nonmental distinction cannot be just in the eye of the beholder but it must be intrinsic to the systems; otherwise it would be up to any beholder to treat people as nonmental and, for example, hurricanes as mental if he likes. But quite often in the AI literature the distinction is blurred in ways that would in the long run prove disastrous to the claim that AI is a cognitive inquiry. McCarthy, for example, writes, "Machines as simple as thermostats can be said to have beliefs, and having beliefs seems to be a characteristic of most machines capable of problem solving performance" (McCarthy 1979). Anyone who thinks strong AI has a chance as a theory of the mind ought to ponder the implications of that remark. We are asked to accept it as a discovery of strong AI that the hunk of metal on the wall that we use to regulate the temperature has beliefs in exactly the same sense that we, our spouses, and our children have beliefs, and furthermore that "most" of the other machines in the room—telephone, tape recorder, adding machine, electric light switch—also have beliefs in this literal sense. It is not the aim of this article to argue against McCarthy's point, so I will simply assert the following without argument. The study of the mind starts with such facts as that humans have beliefs, while thermostats, telephones, and adding machines don't. If you get a theory that denies this point you have produced a counterexample to the theory and the theory is false. One gets the impression that people in the AI who write this sort of thing think they can get away with it because they don't really take it seriously, and they don't think anyone else will either. I propose, for a moment at least, to take it seriously. Think hard for one minute about what would be necessary to establish that the hunk of metal on the wall over there had real beliefs, beliefs with direction of fit, propositional content, and conditions of satisfaction; beliefs that had the possibility of being strong beliefs or weak beliefs; nervous, anxious, or secure beliefs; dogmatic, rational, or superstitious beliefs; blind faiths or hesitant cogitations; any kind of beliefs. The thermostat is not a candidate. Neither is stomach, liver, adding machine, or telephone. However, since we are taking the idea seriously, notice that its truth would be fatal to strong AI's claim to be a science of the mind. For now the mind is everywhere. What we wanted to know is what distinguishes the mind from thermostats and livers. And if McCarthy were right, strong AI wouldn't have a hope of telling us that.

II. The Robot Reply (Yale). "Suppose we wrote a different kind of program from Schank's program. Suppose we put a computer inside a robot, and this computer would not just take in formal symbols as input and give out formal symbols as output, but rather would actually operate the robot in such a way that the robot does something very much like perceiving, walking, moving about, hammering nails, eating, drinking—anything you like. The robot would, for example, have a television camera attached to it that enabled it to see, it would have arms and legs that enabled it to 'act,' and all of this would be controlled by its computer 'brain.' Such a robot would, unlike Schank's computer, have genuine understanding and other mental states."

The first thing to notice about the robot reply is that it tacitly concedes that cognition is not solely a matter of formal symbol manipulation, since this reply adds a set of causal relations with the outside world (cf. Fodor 1980). But the answer to the robot reply is that the addition of such "perceptual" and "motor" capacities adds nothing by way of understanding, in particular, or intentionality, in general, to Schank's original program. To see this, notice that the same thought experiment applies to the robot case. Suppose that instead of the computer inside the robot, you put me inside the room and, as in the original Chinese case, you give me more Chinese symbols with more instructions in English for matching Chinese symbols to Chinese symbols and feeding back Chinese symbols to the outside. Suppose, unknown to me, some of the Chinese sym-

bols that come to me come from a television camera attached to the robot and other Chinese symbols that I am giving out serve to make the motors inside the robot move the robot's legs or arms. It is important to emphasize that all I am doing is manipulating formal symbols: I know none of these other facts, I am receiving "information" from the robot's "perceptual" apparatus, and I am giving out "instructions" to its motor apparatus without knowing either of these facts. I am the robot's homunculus, but unlike the traditional homunculus, I don't know what's going on. I don't understand anything except the rules for symbol manipulation. Now in this case I want to say that the robot has no intentional states at all; it is simply moving about as a result of its electrical wiring and its program. And furthermore, by instantiating the program I have no intentional states of the relevant type. All I do is follow formal instructions about manipulating formal symbols.

III. The Brain Simulator Reply (Berkeley and M.I.T.). "Suppose we design a program that doesn't represent information that we have about the world, such as the information in Schank's scripts, but simulates the actual sequence of neuron firings at the synapses of the brain of a native Chinese speaker when he understands stories in Chinese and gives answers to them. The machine takes in Chinese stories and questions about them as input, it simulates the formal structure of actual Chinese brains in processing these stories, and it gives out Chinese answers as outputs. We can even imagine that the machine operates, not with a single serial program, but with a whole set of programs operating in parallel, in the manner that actual human brains presumably operate when they process natural language. Now surely in such a case we would have to say that the machine understood the stories: and if we refuse to say that, wouldn't we also have to deny that native Chinese speakers understood the stories? At the level of the synapses, what would or could be different about the program of the computer and the program of the Chinese brain?"

Before countering this reply I want to digress to note that it is an odd reply for any partisan of artificial intelligence (or functionalism, etc.) to make: I thought the whole idea of strong AI is that we don't need to know how the brain works to know how the mind works. The basic hypothesis, or so I had supposed, was that there is a level of mental operations consisting of computational processes over formal elements that constitute the essence of the mental and can be realized in all sorts of different brain processes, in the same way that any computer program can be realized in different computer hardwares: On the assumptions of strong AI, the mind is to the brain as the program is to the hardware, and thus we can understand the mind without doing neurophysiology. If we had to know how the brain worked to do AI, we wouldn't bother with AI. However, even getting this close to the operation of the brain is still not sufficient to produce understanding. To see this, image that instead of a monolingual man in a room shuffling symbols we have the man operate an elaborate set of water pipes with valves connecting them. When the man receives the Chinese symbols, he looks up in the program, written in English, which valves he has to turn on and off. Each water connection corresponds to a synapse in the Chinese brain, and the whole system is rigged up so that after doing all the right firings, that is after turning on all the right faucets, the Chinese answers pop out at the output end of the series of pipes.

Now where is the understanding in this system? It takes Chinese as input, it simulates the formal structure of the synapses of the Chinese brain, and it gives Chinese as output. But the man certainly doesn't understand Chinese, and neither do the water pipes, and if we are tempted to adopt what I think is the absurd view that somehow the *conjunction* of man *and* water pipes understands, remember that in principle the man can internalize the formal structure of the water pipes and do all the "neuron firings" in his imagination. The problem with the brain simulator is that it is simulating the wrong things about the brain. As long as it simulates only the formal structure of the sequence of neuron firings at the synapses, it won't have simulated what matters about the brain, namely its causal properties, its ability to produce intentional states. And that the formal properties are not sufficient for the causal properties is shown by the water pipe example: we can have all the formal properties carved off from the relevant neurobiological causal properties.

IV. The Combination Reply (Berkeley and Stanford). "While each of the previous three replies might not be completely convincing by itself as a refutation of the Chinese room counter-example, if you take all three together they are collectively much more convincing and even decisive. Imagine a robot with a brain-shaped computer lodged in its cranial cavity, imagine the computer programmed with all the synapses of a human brain, imagine the whole behavior of the robot is indistinguishable from human behavior, and now think of the whole thing as a unified system and not just as a computer with inputs and outputs. Surely in such a case we would have to ascribe intentionality to the system."

I entirely agree that in such a case we would find it rational and indeed irresistible to accept the hypothesis that the robot had intentionality, as long as we knew nothing more about it. Indeed, besides appearance and behavior, the other elements of the combination are really irrelevant. If we could build a robot whose behavior was indistinguishable over a large range from human behavior, we would attribute intentionality to it, pending some reason not to. We wouldn't need to know in advance that its computer brain was a formal analogue of the human brain.

But I really don't see that this is any help to the claims of strong AI, and here's why: According to strong AI, instantiating a formal program with the right input and output is a sufficient condition of, indeed is constitutive of, intentionality. As Newell (1979) puts it, the essence of the mental is the operation of a physical symbol system. But the attributions of intentionality that we make to the robot in this example have nothing to do with formal programs. They are simply based on the assumption that if the robot looks and behaves sufficiently like us, then we would suppose, until proven otherwise, that it must have mental states like ours that cause and are expressed by its behavior and it must have an inner mechanism capable of producing such mental states. If we knew independently how to account for its behavior without such assumptions we would not attribute intentionality to it, especially if we knew it had a formal program. And this is precisely the point of my earlier reply to objection II.

Suppose we knew that the robot's behavior was entirely accounted for by the fact that a man inside it was receiving uninterpreted formal symbols from the robot's sensory receptors and sending out uninterpreted formal symbols to its motor mechanisms, and the man was doing the symbol manipulation in accordance with a bunch of rules. Furthermore, suppose the man knows none of these facts about the robot, all he knows is which operations to perform on which meaningless symbols. In such a case we would regard the robot as an ingenious mechanical dummy. The hypothesis that the dummy has a mind would now be unwarranted and unnecessary, for there is now no longer any reason to ascribe intentionality to the robot or to the system of which it is a part (except of course for the man's intentionality in manipulating the symbols). The formal symbol manipulations go on, the input and output are correctly matched, but the only real locus of intentionality is the man, and he doesn't know any of the relevant intentional states; he doesn't, for example, *see* what comes into the robot's eyes, he doesn't *intend* to move the robot's arm, and he doesn't *understand* any of the remarks made to or by the robot. Nor, for the reasons stated earlier, does the system of which man and robot are a part.

To see this point, contrast this case with cases in which we find it completely natural to ascribe intentionality to members of certain other primate species such as apes and monkeys and to domestic animals such as dogs. The reasons we find it natural are, roughly, two: We can't make sense of the animal's behavior without the ascription of intentionality, and we can see that the beasts are made of similar stuff to ourselves—that is an eye, that a nose, this is its skin, and so on. Given the coherence of the animal's behavior and the assumption of the same causal stuff underlying it, we assume both that the animal must have mental states underlying its behavior, and that the mental states must be produced by mechanisms made out of the stuff that is like our stuff. We would certainly make similar assumptions about the robot unless we had some reason not to, but as soon as we knew that the behavior was the result of a formal program, and that the actual causal properties of the physical substance were irrelevant we would abandon the assumption of intentionality.

There are two other responses to my example that come up frequently (and so are worth discussing) but really miss the point.

V. The Other Minds Reply (Yale).
"How do you know that other people understand Chinese or anything else? Only by their behavior. Now the computer can pass the behavioral tests as well as they can (in principle), so if you are going to attribute cognition to other people you must in principle also attribute it to computers."

This objection really is only worth a short reply. The problem in this discussion is not about how I know that other people have cognitive states, but rather what it is that I am attributing to them when I attribute cognitive states to them. The thrust of the argument is that it couldn't be just computational processes and their output because the computational processes and their output can exist without the cognitive state. It is no answer to this argument to feign anesthesia. In "cognitive sciences" one presupposes the reality and knowability of the mental in the same way that in physical sciences one has to presuppose the reality and knowability of physical objects.

VI. The Many Mansions Reply (Berkeley).
"Your whole argument presupposes that AI is only about analog and digital computers. But that just happens to be the present state of technology. Whatever these causal processes are that you say are essential for intentionality (assuming you are right), eventually we will be able to build devices that have these causal processes, and that will be artificial intelligence. So your arguments are in no way directed at the ability of artificial intelligence to produce and explain cognition."

I really have no objection to this reply save to say that it in effect trivializes the project of strong AI by redefining it as whatever artificially produces and explains cognition. The interest of the original claim made on behalf of artificial intelligence is that it was a precise, well defined thesis: mental processes are computational processes over formally defined elements. I have been concerned to challenge that thesis. If the claim is redefined so that it is no longer that thesis, my objections no longer apply because there is no longer a testable hypothesis for them to apply to.

Let us now return to the question I promised I would try to answer: Granted that in my original example I understand the English and I do not understand the Chinese, and granted therefore that the machine doesn't understand either English or Chinese, still there must be something about me that makes it the case that I understand English and a corresponding something lacking in me that makes it the case that I fail to understand Chinese. Now why couldn't we give those somethings, whatever they are, to a machine?

I see no reason in principle why we couldn't give a machine the capacity to understand English or Chinese, since in an important sense our bodies with our brains are precisely such machines. But I do see very strong arguments for saying that we could not give such a thing to a machine where the operation of the machine is defined solely in terms of computational processes over formally defined elements; that is, where the operational of the machine is defined as an instantiation of a computer program. It is not because I am the instantiation of a computer program that I am able to understand English and have other forms of intentionality (I am, I suppose, the instantiation of any number of computer programs), but as far as we know it is because I am a certain sort of organism with a certain biological (i.e., chemical and physical) structure, and this structure, under certain conditions, is causally capable of producing perception, action, understanding, learning, and other intentional phenomena. And part of the point of the present argument is that only something that had those causal powers could have that intentionality. Perhaps other physical and chemical processes could produce exactly these effects; perhaps, for example, Martians also have intentionality but their brains are made of different stuff. That is an empirical question, rather like the question whether photosynthesis can be done by something with a chemistry different from that of chlorophyll.

But the main point of the present argument is that no purely formal model will ever be sufficient by itself for intentionality because the formal properties are not by themselves constitutive of intentionality, and they have by themselves no causal powers except the power, when instantiated, to produce the next stage of the formalism when the machine is running. And any other causal properties that particular realizations of the formal model have, are irrelevant to the formal model because we can always put the same formal model in a different realization where those causal properties are obviously absent. Even if, by some miracle, Chinese speakers exactly realize Schank's program, we can put the same program in English speakers, water pipes, or computers, none of which understand Chinese, the program notwithstanding.

What matters about brain operations is not the formal shadow cast by the sequence of synapses but rather the actual properties of the sequences. All the arguments for the strong version of artificial intelligence that I have seen insist on drawing an outline around the shadows cast by cognition and then claiming that the shadows are the real thing.

By way of concluding I want to try to state some of the general philosophical points implicit in the argument. For clarity I will try to do it in a question-and-answer fashion, and I begin with that old chestnut of a question:

"Could a machine think?"

The answer is, obviously, yes. We are precisely such machines.

"Yes, but could an artifact, a man-made machine, think?"

Assuming it is possible to produce artificially a machine with a nervous system, neurons with axons and dendrites, and all the rest of it, sufficiently like ours, again the answer to the question seems to be obviously, yes. If you can exactly duplicate the causes, you could duplicate the effects. And indeed it might be possible to produce consciousness, intentionality, and all the rest of it using some other sorts of chemical principles than those that human beings use. It is, as I said, an empirical question.

"OK, but could a digital computer think?"

If by "digital computer" we mean anything at all

that has a level of description where it can correctly be described as the instantiation of a computer program, then again the answer is, of course, yes, since we are the instantiations of any number of computer programs, and we can think.

"But could something think, understand, and so on *solely* in virtue of being a computer with a right sort of program? Could instantiating a program, the right program of course, by itself be a sufficient condition of understanding?"

This I think is the right question to ask, though it is usually confused with one or more of the earlier questions, and the answer to it is no.

"Why not?"

Because the formal symbol manipulations by themselves don't have any intentionality; they are quite meaningless; they aren't even *symbol* manipulations, since the symbols don't symbolize anything. In the linguistic jargon, they have only a syntax but no semantics. Such intentionality as computers appear to have is solely in the minds of those who program them and those who use them, those who send in the input and those who interpret the output.

The aim of the Chinese room example was to try to show this by showing that as soon as we put something into the system that really does have intentionality (a man), and we program him with the formal program, you can see that the formal program carries no additional intentionality. It adds nothing, for example, to a man's ability to understand Chinese.

Precisely that feature of AI that seemed so appealing—the distinction between the program and the realization—proves fatal to the claim that simulation could be duplication. The distinction between the program and its realization in the hardware seems to be parallel to the distinction between the level of mental operations and the level of brain operations. And if we could describe the level of mental operations as a formal program, then it seems we could describe what was essential about the mind without doing either introspective psychology or neurophysiology of the brain. But the equation "mind is to brain as program is to hardware" breaks down at several points, among them the following three:

First, the distinction between program and real-

ization has the consequence that the same program could have all sorts of crazy realizations that had no form of intentionality. Weizenbaum (1976, Ch. 2), for example, shows in detail how to construct a computer using a roll of toilet paper and a pile of small stones. Similarly, the Chinese story understanding program can be programmed into a sequence of water pipes, a set of wind machines, or a monolingual English speaker, none of which thereby acquires an understanding of Chinese. Stones, toilet paper, wind, and water pipes are the wrong kind of stuff to have intentionality in the first place—only something that has the same causal powers as brains can have intentionality—and though the English speaker has the right kind of stuff for intentionality you can easily see that he doesn't get any extra intentionality by memorizing the program, since memorizing it won't teach him Chinese.

Second, the program is purely formal, but the intentional states are not in that way formal. They are defined in terms of their content, not their form. The belief that it is raining, for example, is not defined as a certain formal shape, but as a certain mental content with conditions of satisfaction, a direction of fit (see Searle 1979), and the like. Indeed the belief as such hasn't even got a formal shape in this syntactic sense, since one and the same belief can be given an indefinite number of different syntactic expressions in different linguistic systems.

Third, as I mentioned before, mental states and events are literally a product of the operation of the brain, but the program is not in that way a product of the computer.

"Well if programs are in no way constitutive of mental processes, why have so many people believed the converse? That at least needs some explanation."

I don't really know the answer to that one. The idea that computer simulations could be the real thing ought to have seemed suspicious in the first place because the computer isn't confined to simulating mental operations, by any means. No one supposes that computer simulations of a five-alarm fire will burn the neighborhood down or that a computer simulation of a rainstorm will leave us all drenched. Why on earth would anyone suppose that a computer simulation of understanding actually understood anything? It is sometimes said that it would be frightfully hard to get computers to feel pain or fall in love, but love and pain are neither harder nor easier than cognition or anything else. For simulation, all you need is the right input and output and a program in the middle that transforms the former into the latter. That is all the computer has for anything it does. To confuse simulation with duplication is the same mistake, whether it is pain, love, cognition, fires, or rainstorms.

Still, there are several reasons why AI must have seemed—and to many people perhaps still does seem—in some way to reproduce and thereby explain mental phenomena, and I believe we will not succeed in removing these illusions until we have fully exposed the reasons that give rise to them.

First, and perhaps the most important, is a confusion about the notion of "information processing": many people in cognitive science believe that the human brain, with its mind, does something called "information processing," and analogously the computer with its program does information processing; but fires and rainstorms, on the other hand, don't do information processing at all. Thus, though the computer can simulate the formal features of any process whatever, it stands in a special relation to the mind and brain because when the computer is properly programmed, ideally with the same program as the brain, the information processing is identical in the two cases, and this information processing is really the essence of the mental. But the trouble with this argument is that it rests on an ambiguity in the notion of "information." In the sense in which people "process information" when they reflect, say, on problems in arithmetic or when they read and answer questions about stories, the programmed computer does not do "information processing." Rather, what it does is manipulate formal symbols. The fact that the programmer and the interpreter of the computer output use the symbols to stand for objects in the world is totally beyond the scope of the computer. The computer, to repeat, has a syntax but no semantics. Thus, if you type into the computer "2 plus 2 equals?" it will type out "4." But it has no idea that "4" means 4 or that it means anything at all. And the point is not that it lacks some second-order information about the interpretation of its first-order symbols, but rather that its first-order symbols don't have any interpretations as far as the computer is concerned. All the computer has is more symbols. The introduction of the notion of "information processing" therefore produces a dilemma: either we construe the notion of "information processing" in such a way that it implies intentionality as part of the process or we don't. If the former, then the programmed computer does not do information processing, it only manipulates formal symbols. If the latter, then, though the computer does information processing, it is only doing so in the sense in which adding machines, typewriters, stomachs, thermostats, rainstorms, and hurricanes do information processing; namely, they have a level of description at which we can describe them as taking information in at one end, transforming it, and producing information as output. But in this case it is up to outside observers to interpret the input and output as information in the ordinary sense. And no similarity is established between the computer and the brain in terms of any similarity of information processing.

Second, in much of AI there is a residual behaviorism or operationalism. Since appropriately programmed computers can have input-output patterns similar to those of human beings, we are tempted to postulate mental states in the computer similar to human mental states. But once we see that it is both conceptually and empirically possible for a system to have human capacities in some realm without having any intentionality at all, we should be able to overcome this impulse. My desk adding machine has calculating capacities, but no intentionality, and in this paper I have tried to show that a system could have input and output capabilities that duplicated those of a native Chinese speaker and still not understand Chinese, regardless of how it was programmed. The Turing test is typical of the tradition in being unashamedly behavioristic and operationalistic, and I believe that if AI workers totally repudiated behaviorism and operationalism much of the confusion between simulation and duplication would be eliminated.

Third, this residual operationalism is joined to a residual form of dualism; indeed strong AI only makes sense given the dualistic assumption that, where the mind is concerned, the brain doesn't matter. In strong AI (and in functionalism, as well) what matters are programs, and programs are independent of their realization in machines; indeed, as far as AI is concerned, the same program could be realized by an electronic machine, a Cartesian mental substance, or a Hegelian world spirit. The single most surprising discovery that I have made in discussing these issues is that many AI workers are quite shocked by my idea that actual human mental phenomena might be dependent on actual physical-chemical properties of actual human brains. But if you think about it a minute you can see that I should not have been surprised; for unless you accept some form of dualism, the strong AI project hasn't got a chance. The project is to reproduce and explain the mental by designing programs, but unless the mind is not only conceptually but empirically independent of the brain you couldn't carry out the project, for the program is completely independent of any realization. Unless you believe that the mind is separable from the brain both conceptually and empirically—dualism in a strong form—you cannot hope to reproduce the mental by writing and running programs since programs must be independent of brains or any other particular forms of instantiation. If mental operations consist in computational operations on formal symbols, then it follows that they have no interesting connection with the brain; the only connection would be that the brain just happens to be one of the indefinitely many types of machines capable of instantiating the program. This form of dualism is not the traditional Cartesian variety that claims there are two sorts of *substances*, but it is Cartesian in the sense that it insists that what is specifically mental about the mind has no intrinsic connection with the actual properties of the brain. This underlying dualism is masked from us by the fact that AI literature contains frequent fulminations against "dualism"; what the authors seem to be unaware of is that their position presupposes a strong version of dualism.

"Could a machine think?" My own view is that *only* a machine could think, and indeed only very special kinds of machines, namely brains and machines that had the same causal powers as brains.

And that is the main reason strong AI has had little to tell us about thinking, since it has nothing to tell us about machines. By its own definition, it is about programs, and programs are not machines. Whatever else intentionality is, it is a biological phenomenon, and it is as likely to be as causally dependent on the specific biochemistry of its origins as lactation, photosynthesis, or any other biological phenomena. No one would suppose that we could produce milk and sugar by running a computer simulation of the formal sequences in lactation and photosynthesis, but where the mind is concerned many people are willing to believe in such a miracle because of a deep and abiding dualism: the mind they suppose is a matter of formal processes and is independent of quite specific material causes in the way that milk and sugar are not.

In defense of this dualism the hope is often expressed that the brain is a digital computer (early computers, by the way, were often called "electronic brains"). But that is no help. Of course the brain is a digital computer. Since everything is a digital computer, brains are too. The point is that the brain's causal capacity to produce intentionality cannot consist in its instantiating a computer program, since for any program you like it is possible for something to instantiate that program and still not have any mental states. Whatever it is that the brain does to produce intentionality, it cannot consist in instantiating a program since no program, by itself, is sufficient for intentionality.

NOTES

1. I am not, of course, saying that Schank himself is committed to these claims.
2. Also, "understanding" implies both the possession of mental (intentional) states and the truth (validity, success) of these states. For the purposes of this discussion we are concerned only with the possession of the states.
3. Intentionality is by definition that feature of certain mental states by which they are directed at or about objects and states of affairs in the world. Thus, beliefs, desires, and intentions are intentional states; undirected forms of anxiety and depression are not.

REFERENCES

Fodor, J. A. 1968. The appeal to tacit knowledge in psychological explanation. *Journal of Philosophy* 65:627–40.

Fodor, J. A. 1980. Methodological solipsism considered as a research strategy in cognitive psychology. *Behavioral and Brain Sciences* 3:1.

McCarthy, J. 1979. Ascribing mental qualities to machines. In: *Philosophical perceptives in artificial intelligence*, ed. M. Ringle. Atlantic Highlands, NJ: Humanities Press.

Newell, A. 1973. Physical symbol systems. Lecture at the La Jolla Conference on Cognitive Science.

Newell, A., and Simon, H. A. 1963. GPS, a program that simulates human thought. In: *Computers and thought.* ed. A. Feigenbaum & V. Feldman, pp. 279–93. New York: McGraw-Hill.

Pylyshyn, Z. W. 1980. Computation and cognition: issues in the foundations of cognitive science. *Behavioral and Brain Sciences* 3.

Schank, R. C., and Abelson, R. P. 1977. *Scripts, plans, goals, and understanding*. Hillsdale, NJ: Lawrence Erlbaum.

Searle, J. R. 1979. The intentionality of intention and action. *Inquiry* 22:253–80.

Weizenbaum, J. 1965. Eliza—a computer program for the study of natural language communication between man and machine. *Communication of the Association for Computing Machinery* 9:36–45.

Weizenbaum, J. 1976. *Computer power and human reason.* San Francisco: W. H. Freeman.

Winograd, T. 1973. A procedural model of language understanding. In: *Computer models of thought and language*, ed. R. Schank & K. Colby. San Francisco: W. H. Freeman.

C. Consciousness

What Is It Like to Be a Bat?

THOMAS NAGEL

—•—

CONSCIOUSNESS IS WHAT MAKES the mind-body problem really intractable. Perhaps that is why current discussions of the problem give it little attention or get it obviously wrong. The recent wave of reductionist euphoria has produced several analyses of mental phenomena and mental concepts designed to explain the possibility of some variety of materialism, psychophysical identification, or reduction.[1] But the problems dealt with are those common to this type of reduction and other types, and what makes the mind-body problem unique, and unlike the water-H_2O problem or the Turing machine-IBM machine problem or the lightning-electrical discharge problem or the gene-DNA problem or the oak tree-hydrocarbon problem, is ignored.

Every reductionist has his favorite analogy from modern science. It is most unlikely that any of these unrelated examples of successful reduction will shed light on the relation of mind to brain. But philosophers share the general human weakness for explanations of what is incomprehensible in terms suited for what is familiar and well understood, though entirely different. This has led to the acceptance of implausible accounts of the mental largely because they would permit familiar kinds of reduction. I shall try to explain why the usual examples do not help us to understand the relation between mind and body—why, indeed, we have at present no con-

ception of what an explanation of the physical nature of a mental phenomenon would be. Without consciousness the mind-body problem would be much less interesting. With consciousness it seems hopeless. The most important and characteristic feature of conscious mental phenomena is very poorly understood. Most reductionist theories do not even try to explain it. And careful examination will show that no currently available concept of reduction is applicable to it. Perhaps a new theoretical form can be devised for the purpose, but such a solution, if it exists, lies in the distant intellectual future.

Conscious experience is a widespread phenomenon. It occurs at many levels of animal life, though we cannot be sure of its presence in the simpler organisms, and it is very difficult to say in general what provides evidence of it. (Some extremists have been prepared to deny it even of mammals other than man.) No doubt it occurs in countless forms totally unimaginable to us, on other planets in other solar systems throughout the universe. But no matter how the form may vary, the fact that an organism has conscious experience *at all* means, basically, that there is something it is like to *be* that organism. There may be further implications about the form of the experience; there may even (though I doubt it) be implications about the behavior of the organism. But fundamentally an organism has conscious mental states if and only if there is something that it is like to *be* that organism—something it is like *for* the organism.

We may call this the subjective character of experience. It is not captured by any of the familiar, recently devised reductive analyses of the mental, for all of them are logically compatible with its absence. It is not analyzable in terms of any explanatory system of functional states, or intentional states, since these could be ascribed to robots or automata that behaved like people though they experienced nothing.[2] It is not analyzable in terms of the causal role of experiences in relation to typical human behavior—for similar reasons.[3] I do not deny that conscious mental states and events cause behavior, nor that they may be given functional characterizations. I deny only that this kind of thing exhausts their analysis. Any reductionist program has to be based on an analysis of what is to be reduced. If the analysis leaves something out, the problem will be falsely posed. It is useless to base the defense of materialism on any analysis of mental phenomena that fails to deal explicitly with their subjective character. For there is no reason to suppose that a reduction which seems plausible when no attempt is made to account for consciousness can be extended to include consciousness. Without some idea, therefore, of what the subjective character of experience is, we cannot know what is required of a physicalist theory.

While an account of the physical basis of mind must explain many things, this appears to be the most difficult. It is impossible to exclude the phenomenological features of experience from a reduction in the same way that one excludes the phenomenal features of an ordinary substance from a physical or chemical reduction of it—namely, by explaining them as effects on the minds of human observers.[4] If physicalism is to be defended, the phenomenological features must themselves be given a physical account. But when we examine their subjective character it seems that such a result is impossible. The reason is that every subjective phenomenon is essentially connected with a single point of view, and it seems inevitable that an objective, physical theory will abandon that point of view.

Let me first try to state the issue somewhat more fully than by referring to the relation between the subjective and the objective, or between the *pour-soi* and the *en-soi*. This is far from easy. Facts about what it is like to be an *X* are very peculiar, so peculiar that some may be inclined to doubt their reality, or the significance of claims about them. To illustrate the connection between subjectivity and a point of view, and to make evident the importance of subjective features, it will help to explore the matter in relation to an example that brings out clearly the divergence between the two types of conception, subjective and objective.

I assume we all believe that bats have experience. After all, they are mammals, and there is no more doubt that they have experience than that mice or pigeons or whales have experience. I have chosen bats instead of wasps or flounders because if one travels too far down the phylogenetic tree, people gradually shed their faith that there is experience there at all. Bats, although more closely related to us than those other species, nevertheless present a range of activity and a sensory apparatus so different from ours that the problem I want to pose is exceptionally vivid (though it certainly could be raised with other species). Even without the benefit of philosophical reflection, anyone who has spent some time in an enclosed space with an excited bat knows what it is to encounter a fundamentally *alien* form of life.

I have said that the essence of the belief that bats have experience is that there is something that it is like to be a bat. Now we know that most bats (the microchiroptera, to be precise) perceive the external world primarily by sonar, or echolocation, detecting the reflections, from objects within range, of their own rapid, subtly modulated, high-frequency shrieks. Their brains are designed to correlate the outgoing impulses with the subsequent echoes, and the information thus acquired enables bats to make precise discriminations of distance, size, shape, motion, and texture comparable to those we make by vision. But bat sonar, though clearly a form of perception, is not similar in its operation to any sense that we possess, and there is no reason to suppose that it is subjectively like anything we can experience or imagine. This appears to create difficulties for the notion of what it is like to be a bat. We must consider whether any method will permit us to extrapolate to the inner life of the bat from our own case,[5] and if not, what alternative methods there may be for understanding the notion.

Our own experience provides the basic material for our imagination, whose range is therefore limited. It will not help to try to imagine that one has webbing on one's arms, which enables one to fly around at dusk and dawn catching insects in one's mouth; that one has very poor vision, and perceives the surrounding world by a system of reflected high-frequency sound signals; and that one spends the day hanging upside down by one's feet in an attic. In so far as I can imagine this (which is not very far), it tells me only what it would be like for *me* to behave as a bat behaves. But that is not the question. I want to know what it is like for a *bat* to be a bat. Yet if I try to imagine this, I am restricted to the resources of my own mind, and those resources are inadequate to the task. I cannot perform it either by imagining additions to my present experience, or by imagining segments gradually subtracted from it, or by imagining some combination of additions, subtractions, and modifications.

To the extent that I could look and behave like a wasp or a bat without changing my fundamental structure, my experiences would not be anything like the experiences of those animals. On the other hand, it is doubtful that any meaning can be attached to the supposition that I should possess the internal neurophysiological constitution of a bat. Even if I could by gradual degrees be transformed into a bat, nothing in my present constitution enables me to imagine what the experiences of such a future stage of myself thus metamorphosed would be like. The best evidence would come from the experiences of bats, if we only knew what they were like.

So if extrapolation from our own case is involved in the idea of what it is like to be a bat, the extrapolation must be incompletable. We cannot form more than a schematic conception of what it *is* like. For example, we may ascribe general *types* of experience on the basis of the animal's structure and behavior. Thus we describe bat sonar as a form of three-dimensional forward perception; we believe that bats feel some versions of pain, fear, hunger, and lust, and that they have other, more familiar types of perception besides sonar. But we believe that these experiences also have in each case a specific subjective character, which it is beyond our ability to conceive. And if there is conscious life elsewhere in the universe, it is likely that some of it will

not be describable even in the most general experiential terms available to us.[6] (The problem is not confined to exotic cases, however, for it exists between one person and another. The subjective character of the experience of a person deaf and blind from birth is not accessible to me, for example, nor presumably is mine to him. This does not prevent us each from believing that the other's experience has such a subjective character.)

If anyone is inclined to deny that we can believe in the existence of facts like this whose exact nature we cannot possibly conceive, he should reflect that in contemplating the bats we are in much the same position that intelligent bats or Martians[7] would occupy if they tried to form a conception of what it was like to be us. The structure of their own minds might make it impossible for them to succeed, but we know they would be wrong to conclude that there is not anything precise that it is like to be us: that only certain general types of mental state could be ascribed to us (perhaps perception and appetite would be concepts common to us both; perhaps not). We know they would be wrong to draw such a skeptical conclusion because we know what it is like to be us. And we know that while it includes an enormous amount of variation and complexity, and while we do not possess the vocabulary to describe it adequately, its subjective character is highly specific, and in some respects describable in terms that can be understood only by creatures like us. The fact that we cannot expect ever to accommodate in our language a detailed description of Martian or bat phenomenology should not lead us to dismiss as meaningless the claim that bats and Martians have experiences fully comparable in richness of detail to our own. It would be fine if someone were to develop concepts and a theory that enabled us to think about those things; but such an understanding may be permanently denied to us by the limits of our nature. And to deny the reality or logical significance of what we can never describe or understand is the crudest form of cognitive dissonance.

This brings us to the edge of a topic that requires much more discussion than I can give it here: namely, the relation between facts on the one hand and conceptual schemes or systems of representation on the other. My realism about the subjective domain in all its forms implies a belief in the existence of facts beyond the reach of human concepts. Certainly it is possible for a human being to believe that there are facts which humans never *will* possess the requisite concepts to represent or comprehend. Indeed, it would be foolish to doubt this, given the finiteness of humanity's expectations. After all, there would have been transfinite numbers even if everyone had been wiped out by the Black Death before Cantor discovered them. But one might also believe that there are facts which *could* not ever be represented or comprehended by human beings, even if the species lasted forever—simply because our structure does not permit us to operate with concepts of the requisite type. This impossibility might even be observed by other beings, but it is not clear that the existence of such beings, or the possibility of their existence, is a precondition of the significance of the hypothesis that there are humanly inaccessible facts. (After all, the nature of beings with access to humanly inaccessible facts is presumably itself a humanly inaccessible fact.) Reflection on what it is like to be a bat seems to lead us, therefore, to the conclusion that there are facts that do not consist in the truth of propositions expressible in a human language. We can be compelled to recognize the existence of such facts without being able to state or comprehend them.

I shall not pursue this subject, however. Its bearing on the topic before us (namely, the mind-body problem) is that it enables us to make a general observation about the subjective character of experience. Whatever may be the status of facts about what it is like to be a human being, or a bat, or a Martian, these appear to be facts that embody a particular point of view.

I am not adverting here to the alleged privacy of experience to its possessor. The point of view in question is not one accessible only to a single individual. Rather it is a *type*. It is often possible to take up a point of view other than one's own, so the comprehension of such facts is not limited to one's own case. There is a sense in which phenomenological facts are perfectly objective: one person can know or say of another what the quality of the other's experience is. They are subjective, however, in the sense that even this objective ascription of experi-

ence is possible only for someone sufficiently similar to the object of ascription to be able to adopt his point of view—to understand the ascription in the first person as well as in the third, so to speak. The more different from oneself the other experiencer is, the less success one can expect with this enterprise. In our own case we occupy the relevant point of view, but we will have as much difficulty understanding our own experience properly if we approach it from another point of view as we would if we tried to understand the experience of another species without taking up *its* point of view.[8]

This bears directly on the mind-body problem. For if the facts of experience—facts about what it is like *for* the experiencing organism—are accessible only from one point of view, then it is a mystery how the true character of experiences could be revealed in the physical operation of that organism. The latter is a domain of objective facts par excellence—the kind that can be observed and understood from many points of view and by individuals with differing perceptual systems. There are no comparable imaginative obstacles to the acquisition of knowledge about bat neurophysiology by human scientists, and intelligent bats or Martians might learn more about the human brain than we ever will.

This is not by itself an argument against reduction. A Martian scientist with no understanding of visual perception could understand the rainbow, or lightning, or clouds as physical phenomena, though he would never be able to understand the human concepts of rainbow, lighting, or cloud, or the place these things occupy in our phenomenal world. The objective nature of the things picked out by these concepts could be apprehended by him because, although the concepts themselves are connected with a particular point of view and a particular visual phenomenology, the things apprehended from that point of view are not: they are observable from the point of view but external to it; hence they can be comprehended from other points of view also, either by the same organisms or by others. Lightning has an objective character that is not exhausted by its visual appearance, and this can be investigated by a Martian without vision. To be precise, it has a *more* objective character than is revealed in its visual appearance. In speaking of the move from subjective to objective characterization, I wish to remain noncommittal about the existence of an end point, the completely objective intrinsic nature of the thing, which one might or might not be able to reach. It may be more accurate to think of objectivity as a direction in which the understanding can travel. And in understanding a phenomenon like lightning, it is legitimate to go as far away as one can from a strictly human viewpoint.[9]

In the case of experience, on the other hand, the connection with a particular point of view seems much closer. It is difficult to understand what could be meant by the *objective* character of an experience, apart from the particular point of view from which its subject apprehends it. After all, what would be left of what it was like to be a bat if one removed the viewpoint of the bat? But if experience does not have, in addition to its subjective character, an objective nature that can be apprehended from many different points of view, then how can it be supposed that a Martian investigating my brain might be observing physical processes which were my mental processes (as he might observe physical processes which were bolts of lightning), only from a different point of view? How, for that matter, could a human physiologist observe them from another point of view?[10]

We appear to be faced with a general difficulty about psychophysical reduction. In other areas the process of reduction is a move in the direction of greater objectivity, toward a more accurate view of the real nature of things. This is accomplished by reducing our dependence on individual or species-specific points of view toward the objective of investigation. We describe it not in terms of the impressions it makes on our senses, but in terms of its more general effects and of properties detectable by means other than the human senses. The less it depends on a specifically human viewpoint, the more objective is our description. It is possible to follow this path because although the concepts and ideas we employ in thinking about the external world are initially applied from a point of view that involves our perceptual apparatus, they are used by us to refer to things beyond themselves—toward which we *have* the phenomenal point of view. Therefore we can abandon it in favor of another, and still be thinking about the same things.

Experience itself, however, does not seem to fit the pattern. The idea of moving from appearance to reality seems to make no sense here. What is the analogue in this case to pursuing a more objective understanding of the same phenomena by abandoning the initial subjective viewpoint toward them in favor of another that is more objective but concerns the same thing? Certainly it *appears* unlikely that we will get closer to the real nature of human experience by leaving behind the particularity of our human point of view and striving for a description in terms accessible to beings that could not imagine what it was like to be us. If the subjective character of experience is fully comprehensible only from one point of view, then any shift to greater objectivity—that is, less attachment to a specific viewpoint—does not take us nearer to the real nature of the phenomenon: it takes us farther away from it.

In a sense, the seeds of this objection to the reducibility of experience are already detectable in successful cases of reduction; for in discovering sound to be, in reality, a wave phenomenon in air or other media, we leave behind one viewpoint to take up another, and the auditory, human or animal viewpoint that we leave behind remains unreduced. Members of radically different species may both understand the same physical events in objective terms, and this does not require that they understand the phenomenal forms in which those events appear to the senses of members of the other species. Thus it is a condition of their referring to a common reality that their more particular viewpoints are not part of the common reality that they both apprehend. The reduction can succeed only if the species-specific viewpoint is omitted from what is to be reduced.

But while we are right to leave this point of view aside in seeking a fuller understanding of the external world, we cannot ignore it permanently, since it is the essence of the internal world, and not merely a point of view on it. Most of the neobehaviorism of recent philosophical psychology results from the effort to substitute an objective concept of mind for the real thing, in order to have nothing left over which cannot be reduced. If we acknowledge that a physical theory of mind must account for the subjective character of experience, we must admit that no presently available conception gives us a clue how this could be done. The problem is unique. If mental processes are indeed physical processes, then there is something it is like, intrinsically,[11] to undergo certain physical processes. What it is for such a thing to be the case remains a mystery.

What moral should be drawn from these reflections, and what should be done next? It would be a mistake to conclude that physicalism must be false. Nothing is proved by the inadequacy of physicalist hypotheses that assume a faulty objective analysis of mind. It would be truer to say that physicalism is a position we cannot understand because we do not at present have any conception of how it might be true. Perhaps it will be thought unreasonable to require such a conception as a condition of understanding. After all, it might be said, the meaning of physicalism is clear enough: mental states are states of the body; mental events are physical events. We do not know *which* physical states and events they are, but that should not prevent us from understanding the hypothesis. What could be clearer than the words "is" and "are"?

But I believe it is precisely this apparent clarity of the word "is" that is deceptive. Usually, when we are told that *X* is *Y* we know *how* it is supposed to be true, but that depends on a conceptual or theoretical background and is not conveyed by the "is" alone. We know how both "*X*" and "*Y*" refer, and the kinds of things to which they refer, and we have a rough idea how the two referential paths might converge on a single thing, be it an object, a person, a process, an event, or whatever. But when the two terms of the identification are very disparate it may not be so clear how it could be true. We may not have even a rough idea of how the two referential paths could converge, or what kind of things they might converge on, and a theoretical framework may have to be supplied to enable us to understand this. Without the framework, an air of mysticism surrounds the identification.

This explains the magical flavor of popular presentations of fundamental scientific discoveries, given out as propositions to which one must subscribe without really understanding them. For example, people are now told at an early age that all matter is really energy. But despite the fact that they know what "is" means, most of them never form a conception of what makes this claim true, because they lack the theoretical background.

At the present time the status of physicalism is similar to that which the hypothesis that matter is energy would have had if uttered by a pre-Socratic philosopher. We do not have the beginnings of a conception of how it might be true. In order to understand the hypothesis that a mental event is a physical event, we require more than an understanding of the word "is." The idea of how a mental and a physical term might refer to the same thing is lacking, and the usual analogies with theoretical identification in other fields fail to supply it. They fail because if we construe the reference of mental terms to physical events on the usual model, we either get a reappearance of separate subjective events as the effects through which mental reference to physical events is secured, or else we get a false account of how mental terms refer (for example, a causal behaviorist one).

Strangely enough, we may have evidence for the truth of something we cannot really understand. Suppose a caterpillar is locked in a sterile safe by someone unfamiliar with insect metamorphosis, and weeks later the safe is reopened, revealing a butterfly. If the person knows that the safe has been shut the whole time, he has reason to believe that the butterfly is or was once the caterpillar, without having any idea in what sense this might be so. (One possibility is that the caterpillar contained a tiny winged parasite that devoured it and grew into the butterfly.)

It is conceivable that we are in such a position with regard to physicalism. Donald Davidson has argued that if mental events have physical causes and effects, they must have physical descriptions. He holds that we have reason to believe this even though we do not—and in fact *could* not—have a general psychophysical theory.[12] His argument applies to intentional mental events, but I think we also have some reason to believe that sensations are physical processes, without being in a position to understand how. Davidson's position is that certain physical events have irreducibly mental properties, and perhaps some view describable in this way is correct. But nothing of which we can now form a conception corresponds to it; nor have we any idea what a theory would be like that enabled us to conceive of it.[13]

Very little work has been done on the basic question (from which mention of the brain can be entirely omitted) whether any sense can be made of experiences having an objective character at all. Does it make sense, in other words, to ask what my experiences are *really* like, as opposed to how they appear to me? We cannot genuinely understand the hypothesis that their nature is captured in a physical description unless we understand the more fundamental idea that they *have* an objective nature (or that objective processes can have a subjective nature).[14]

I should like to close with a speculative proposal. It may be possible to approach the gap between subjective and objective from another direction. Setting aside temporarily the relation between the mind and the brain, we can pursue a more objective understanding of the mental in its own right. At present we are completely unequipped to think about the subjective character of experience without relying on the imagination—without taking up the point of view of the experiential subject. This should be regarded as a challenge to form new concepts and devise a new method—an objective phenomenology not dependent on empathy or the imagination. Though presumably it would not capture everything, its goal would be to describe, at least in part, the subjective character of experiences in a form comprehensible to beings incapable of having those experiences.

We would have to develop such a phenomenology to describe the sonar experiences of bats; but it would also be possible to begin with humans. One might try, for example, to develop concepts that could be used to explain to a person blind from birth what it was like to see. One would reach a blank wall eventually, but it should be possible to devise a method of expressing in objective terms much more than we can at present, and with much greater precision. The loose intermodal analogies—for example, "Red is like the sound of a trumpet"—which crop up in discussions of this subject are of little use. That should be clear to anyone who has both heard a trumpet and seen red. But structural features of perception might be more accessible to objective description, even though something would be left out. And concepts alternative to those we learn in the first person may enable us to arrive at a kind of understanding even of our own experience which is

denied us by the very ease of description and lack of distance that subjective concepts afford.

Apart from its own interest, a phenomenology that is in this sense objective may permit questions about the physical[15] basis of experience to assume a more intelligible form. Aspects of subjective experience that admitted this kind of objective description might be better candidates for objective explanations of a more familiar sort. But whether or not this guess is correct, it seems unlikely that any physical theory of mind can be contemplated until more thought has been given to the general problem of subjective and objective. Otherwise we cannot even pose the mind-body problem without sidestepping it.[16]

NOTES

1. Examples are J. J. C. Smart, *Philosophy and Scientific Realism* (London, 1963); David K. Lewis, "An Argument for the Identity Theory," *Journal of Philosophy*, 63 (1966), reprinted with addenda in David M. Rosenthal, *Materialism and the Mind-Body Problem* (Englewood Cliffs, N.J., 1971); Hilary Putnam, "Psychological Predicates" in Captain and Merrill, *Art, Mind and Religion* (Pittsburgh, 1967), reprinted in Rosenthal, op. cit., as "The Nature of Mental States"; D. M. Armstrong, *A Materialist Theory of the Mind* (London, 1968); D. C. Dennett, *Content and Consciousness* (London, 1969). I have expressed earlier doubts in "Armstrong on the Mind," *Philosophical Review*, 79 (1970), 394–403; "Brain Bisection and the Unity of Consciousness," *Synthese*, 22 (1971); and a review of Dennett, *Journal of Philosophy*, 69 (1972). See also Saul Kripke, "Naming and Necessity" in Davidson and Harman, *Semantics of Natural Language* (Dordrecht, 1972), esp. pp. 334–42; and M. T. Thornton, "Ostensive Terms and Materialism," *Monist*, 56 (1972).

2. Perhaps there could not actually be such robots. Perhaps anything complex enough to behave like a person would have experiences. But that, if true, is a fact which cannot be discovered merely by analyzing the concept of experience.

3. It is not equivalent to that about which we are incorrigible, both because we are not incorrigible about experience and because experience is pres-

ent in animals lacking language and thought, who have no beliefs at all about their experiences.

4. Cf. Richard Rorty, "Mind-Body Identity, Privacy, and Categories," *Review of Metaphysics*, 19 (1965), esp. 37–38.

5. By "our own case" I do not mean just "my own case," but rather the mentalistic ideas that we apply unproblematically to ourselves and other human beings.

6. Therefore the analogical form of the English expression "what it is like" is misleading. It does not mean "what (in our experience) it *resembles*," but rather "how it is for the subject himself."

7. Any intelligent extraterrestrial beings totally different from us.

8. It may be easier than I suppose to transcend interspecies barriers with the aid of the imagination. For example, blind people are able to detect objects near them by a form of sonar, using vocal clicks or taps of a cane. Perhaps if one knew what that was like, one could by extension imagine roughly what it was like to possess the much more refined sonar of a bat. The distance between oneself and other persons and other species can fall anywhere on a continuum. Even for other persons the understanding of what it is like to be them is only partial, and when one moves to species very different from oneself, a lesser degree of partial understanding may still be available. The imagination is remarkably flexible. My point, however, is not that we cannot *know* what it is like to be a bat. I am not raising that epistemological problem. My point is rather that even to form a *conception* of what it is like to be a bat (and a fortiori to know what it is like to be a bat) one must take up the bat's point of view. If one can take it up roughly, or partially, then one's conception will also be rough or partial. Or so it seems in our present state of understanding.

9. The problem I am going to raise can therefore be posed even if the distinction between more subjective and more objective descriptions or viewpoints can itself be made only within a larger human point of view. I do not accept this kind of conceptual relativism, but it need not be refuted to make the point that psychophysical reduction cannot be accommodated by the subjective-to-objective model familiar from other cases.

10. The problem is not just that when I look at the Mona Lisa, my visual experience has a certain quality, no trace of which is to be found by someone looking into my brain. For even if he did observe there a tiny image of the Mona Lisa, he would have no reason to identify it with the experience.

11. The relation would therefore not be a contingent one, like that of a cause and its distinct effect. It would be necessarily true that a certain physical state felt a certain way. Saul Kripke (op. cit.) argues that causal behaviorist and related analyses of the mental fail because they construe, e.g., "pain" as a merely contingent name of pains. The subjective character of an experience ("its immediate phenomenological quality" Kripke calls it [p. 340] is the essential property left out by such analyses, and the one in virtue of which it is, necessarily, the experience it is. My view is closely related to his. Like Kripke, I find the hypothesis that a certain brain state should *necessarily* have a certain subjective character incomprehensible without further explanation. No such explanation emerges from theories which view the mind-brain relation as contingent, but perhaps there are other alternatives, not yet discovered.

A theory that explained how the mind-brain relation was necessary would still leave us with Kripke's problem of explaining why it nevertheless appears contingent. That difficulty seems to me surmountable, in the following way. We may imagine something by representing it to ourselves either perceptually, sympathetically, or symbolically. I shall not try to say how symbolic imagination works, but part of what happens in the other two cases is this. To imagine something perceptually, we put ourselves in a conscious state resembling the state we would be in if we perceived it. To imagine something sympathetically, we put ourselves in a conscious state resembling the thing itself. (This method can be used only to imagine mental events and states—our own or another's.) When we try to imagine a mental state occurring without its associated brain state, we first sympathetically imagine the occurrence of the mental state: that is, we put ourselves into a state that resembles it mentally. At the same time, we attempt to perceptually imagine the non-occurrence of the associated physical state, by putting ourselves into another state unconnected with the first: one resembling that which we would be in if we perceived the non-occurrence of the physical state. Where the imagination of physical features is perceptual and the imagination of mental features is sympathetic, it appears to us that we can imagine any experience occurring without its associated brain state, and vice versa. The relation between them will appear contingent even if it is necessary, because of the independence of the disparate types of imagination.

(Solipsism, incidentally, results if one misinterprets sympathetic imagination as if it worked like perceptual imagination: it then seems impossible to imagine any experience that is not one's own.)

12. See "Mental Events" in Foster and Swanson, *Experience and Theory* (Amherst, 1970); though I don't understand the argument against psychophysical laws.

13. Similar remarks apply to my paper "Physicalism," *Philosophical Review* 74 (1965), 339–56, reprinted with postscript in John O'Connor, *Modern Materialism* (New York, 1969).

14. This question also lies at the heart of the problem of other minds, whose close connection with the mind-body problem is often overlooked. If one understood how subjective experience could have an objective nature, one would understand the existence of subjects other than oneself.

15. I have not defined the term "physical." Obviously it does not apply just to what can be described by the concepts of contemporary physics, since we expect further developments. Some may think there is nothing to prevent mental phenomena from eventually being recognized as physical in their own right. But whatever else may be said of the physical, it has to be objective. So if our idea of the physical ever expands to include mental phenomena, it will have to assign them an objective character—whether or not this is done by analyzing them in terms of other phenomena already regarded as physical. It seems to me more likely, however, that mental-physical relations will eventually be expressed in a theory whose fundamental terms cannot be placed clearly in either category.

16. I have read versions of this paper to a number of audiences, and am indebted to many people for their comments.

What Mary Didn't Know

FRANK JACKSON

MARY IS CONFINED TO A BLACK-and-white room, is educated through black-and-white books and through lectures relayed on black-and-white television. In this way she learns everything there is to know about the physical nature of the world. She knows all the physical facts about us and our environment, in a wide sense of 'physical' which includes everything in *completed* physics, chemistry, and neurophysiology, and all there is to know about the causal and relational factors consequent upon all this, including of course functional roles. If physicalism is true, she knows all there is to know. For to suppose otherwise is to suppose that there is more to know than every physical fact, and that is just what physicalism denies.

Physicalism is not the noncontroversial thesis that the actual world is largely physical, but the challenging thesis that it is entirely physical. This is why physicalists must hold that complete physical knowledge is complete knowledge simpliciter. For

From *The Journal of Philosophy* LXXXIII, No. 5. (May 1986). Copyright © 1986 by Columbia University. Reprinted by permission of the publisher and author.

Note from the author: I am much indebted to discussions with David Lewis and with Robert Pargetter.

suppose it is not complete: then our world must differ from a world, $W(P)$, for which it is complete, and the difference must be in nonphysical facts; for our world and $W(P)$ agree in all matters physical. Hence, physicalism would be false at our world [though contingently so, for it would be true at $W(P)$].[1]

It seems, however, that Mary does not know all there is to know. For when she is let out of the black-and-white room or given a color television, she will learn what it is like to see something red, say. This is rightly described as *learning*—she will not say "ho, hum." Hence, physicalism is false. This is the knowledge argument against physicalism in one of its manifestations.[2] This note is a reply to three objections to it mounted by Paul M. Churchland.*

1. Three Clarifications

The knowledge argument does not rest on the dubious claim that logically you cannot imagine what sensing red is like unless you have sensed red. Powers of imagination are not to the point. The contention about Mary is not that, despite her fantastic grasp of neurophysiology and everything else physical, she *could not imagine* what it is like to sense red; it is that, as a matter of fact, she *would not know*. But if physicalism is true, she would know; and no great powers of imagination would be called for. Imagination is a faculty that those who *lack* knowledge need to fall back on.

Secondly, the intensionality of knowledge is not to the point. The argument does not rest on assuming falsely that, if S knows that a is F and if $a = b$, then S knows that b is F. It is concerned with the nature of Mary's total body of knowledge before she is released: is it complete, or do some facts escape it? What is to the point is that S may know that a is F and *know* that $a = b$, yet arguably not know that b is F, by virtue of not being sufficiently logically alert to follow the consequences through. If Mary's lack of knowledge were at all like this, there would be no threat to physicalism in it. But it is very hard to believe that her lack of knowledge could be reme-

died merely by her explicitly following through enough logical consequences of her vast physical knowledge. Endowing her with great logical acumen and persistence is not in itself enough to fill in the gaps in her knowledge. On being let out, she will not say "I could have worked all this out before by making some more purely logical inferences."

Thirdly, the knowledge Mary lacked which is of particular point for the knowledge argument against physicalism is *knowledge about the experiences of others,* not about her own. When she is let out, she has new experiences, color experiences she has never had before. It is not, therefore, an objection to physicalism that she learns *something* on being let out. Before she was let out, she could not have known facts about her experience of red, for there were no such facts to know. That physicalist and nonphysicalist alike can agree on. After she is let out, things change; and physicalism can happily admit that she learns this; after all, some physical things will change, for instance, her brain states and their functional roles. The trouble for physicalism is that, after Mary sees her first ripe tomato, she will realize how impoverished her conception of the mental life of *others* has been *all along*. She will realize that there was, all the time she was carrying out her laborious investigations into the neurophysiologies of others and into the functional roles of their internal states, something about these people she was quite unaware of. All along their experiences (or many of them, those got from tomatoes, the sky, . . .) had a feature conspicuous to them but until now hidden from her (in fact, not in logic). But she knew all the physical facts about them all along; hence, what she did not know until her release is not a physical fact about their experiences. But it is a fact about them. That is the trouble for physicalism.

II. Churchland's Three Objections

(i) Churchland's first objection is that the knowledge argument contains a defect that "is simplicity itself" (23). The argument equivocates on the sense of 'knows about'. How so? Churchland suggests that the following is "a conveniently tightened version" of the knowledge argument:

* "Reduction, Qualia, and the Direct Introspection of Brain States," this JOURNAL, LXXXII, 1 (January 1985):8–28. Unless otherwise stated, future page references are to this paper.

1. Mary knows everything there is to know about brain states and their properties.
2. It is not the case that Mary knows everything there is to know about sensations and their properties.

Therefore, by Leibniz's law,

3. Sensations and their properties ≠ brain states and their properties (23).

Churchland observes, plausibly enough, that the type or kind of knowledge involved in premise 1 is distinct from the kind of knowledge involved in premise 2. We might follow his lead and tag the first 'knowledge by description', and the second 'knowledge by acquaintance'; but, whatever the tags, he is right that the displayed argument involves a highly dubious use of Leibniz's law.

My reply is that the displayed argument may be convenient, but it is not accurate. It is not the knowledge argument. Take, for instance, premise 1. The whole thrust of the knowledge argument is that Mary (before her release) does *not* know everything there is to know about brain states and their properties, because she does not know about certain qualia associated with them. What is complete, according to the argument, is her knowledge of matters physical. A convenient and accurate way of displaying the argument is:

1.' Mary (before her release) knows everything physical there is to know about other people.
2.' Mary (before her release) does not know everything there is to know about other people (because she *learns* something about them on her release).

Therefore,

3.' There are truths about other people (and herself) which escape the physicalist story.

What is immediately to the point is not the kind, manner, or type of knowledge Mary has, but *what* she knows. What she knows beforehand is ex hypothesi everything physical there is to know, but is it everything there is to know? That is the crucial question.

There is, though, a relevant challenge involving questions about kinds of knowledge. It concerns the *support* for premise 2'. The case for premise 2' is that Mary learns something on her release, she acquires knowledge, and that entails that her knowledge beforehand (*what* she knew, never mind whether by description, acquaintance, or whatever) was incomplete. The challenge, mounted by David Lewis and Laurence Nemirow, is that on her release Mary does *not* learn something or acquire knowledge in the relevant sense. What Mary acquires when she is released is a certain representational or imaginative ability; it is knowledge how rather than knowledge that. Hence, a physicalist can admit that Mary acquires something very significant of a knowledge kind—which can hardly be denied—without admitting that this shows that her earlier factual knowledge is defective. She knew all *that* there was to know about the experiences of others beforehand, but lacked an ability until after her release.[3]

Now it is certainly true that Mary will acquire abilities of various kinds after her release. She will, for instance, be able to imagine what seeing red is like, be able to remember what it is like, and be able to understand why her friends regarded her as so deprived (something which, until her release, had always mystified her). But is it plausible that that is *all* she will acquire? Suppose she received a lecture on skepticism about other minds while she was incarcerated. On her release she sees a ripe tomato in normal conditions, and so has a sensation of red. Her first reaction is to say that she now knows more about the kind of experiences others have when looking at ripe tomatoes. She then remembers the lecture and starts to worry. Does she really know more about what their experiences are like, or is she indulging in a wild generalization from one case? In the end she decides she does know, and that skepticism is mistaken (even if, like so many of us, she is not sure how to demonstrate its errors). What was she to-ing and fro-ing about—her abilities? Surely not; her representational abilities were a known constant throughout. What else then was she agonizing about than whether or not she had gained factual knowledge of others? There would be nothing to agonize about if ability was *all* she acquired on her release.

I grant that I have no *proof* that Mary acquires on her release, as well as abilities, factual knowledge about the experiences of others—and not just because I have no disproof of skepticism. My claim is that the knowledge argument is a valid argument from highly plausible, though admittedly not demonstrable, premises to the conclusion that physicalism is false. And that, after all, is about as good an objection as one could expect in this area of philosophy.

(ii) Churchland's second objection (24/5) is that there must be something wrong with the argument, for it proves too much. Suppose Mary received a special series of lectures over her black-and-white television from a full-blow dualist, explaining the "laws" governing the behavior of "ectoplasm" and telling her about qualia. This would not affect the plausibility of the claim that on her release she learns something. So if the argument works against physicalism, it works against dualism too.

My reply is that lectures about qualia over black-and-white television do not tell Mary all there is to know about qualia. They may tell her some things about qualia, for instance, that they do not appear in the physicalist's story, and that the quale we use 'yellow' for is nearly as different from the one we use 'blue' for as is white from black. But why should it be supposed that they tell her everything about qualia? On the other hand, it is plausible that lectures over black-and-white television might in principle tell Mary everything in the physicalist's story. You do not need color television to learn physics or functionalist psychology. To obtain a good argument against dualism (attribute dualism; ectoplasm is a bit of fun), the premise in the knowledge argument that Mary has the full story according to physicalism before her release, has to be replaced by a premise that she has the full story according to dualism. The former is plausible; the latter is not. Hence, there is no "parity of reasons" trouble for

dualists who use the knowledge argument.

(iii) Churchland's third objection is that the knowledge argument claims "that Mary could not even *imagine* what the relevant experience would be like, despite her exhaustive neuroscientific knowledge, and hence must still be missing certain crucial information" (25), a claim he goes on to argue against.

But, as we emphasized earlier, the knowledge argument claims that Mary would not know what the relevant experience is like. What she could imagine is another matter. If her knowledge is defective, despite being all there is to know according to physicalism, then physicalism is false, whatever her powers of imagination.

NOTES

1. The claim here is not that, if physicalism is true, only what is expressed in explicitly physical language is an item of knowledge. It is that, if physicalism is true, then if you know everything expressed or expressible in explicitly physical language, you know everything. *Pace* Terence Horgan, "Jackson on Physical Information and Qualia," *Philosophical Quarterly,* XXXIV, 135 (April 1984):147–152.
2. Namely, that in my "Epiphenomenal Qualia," *ibid.,* XXXII, 127 (April 1982): 127–136. See also Thomas Nagel, "What Is It Like to Be a Bat?", *Philosophical Review,* LXXXIII, 4 (October 1974): 435–450, and Howard Robinson, *Matter and Sense* (New York: Cambridge, 1982).
3. See Laurence Nemirow, review of Thomas Nagel, *Mortal Questions, Philosophical Review,* LXXXIX, 3 (July 1980):473–477, and David Lewis, "Postscript to 'Mad Pain and Martian Pain'," *Philosophical Papers,* vol. 1 (New York: Oxford, 1983). Churchland mentions both Nemirow and Lewis, and it may be that he intended his objection to be essentially the one I have just given. However, he says quite explicitly (bottom of p. 23) that his objection does not need an "ability" analysis of the relevant knowledge.

Knowing What It's Like

DAVID LEWIS

—•—

THE MOST FORMIDABLE CHAL-
lenge to any sort of materialism and functionalism comes from the friend of
phenomenal qualia. He says we leave out the phenomenal aspect of mental life: we forget that pain is
a feeling, that there is something it is like to hold
one's hand in a flame, that we are aware of something when we suffer pain, that we can recognize
that something when it comes again. . . . So far,
our proper reply is the one sketched in Section VIII
["Mad Pain and Martian Pain"]: we deny none of
that! We say to the friend of qualia that, beneath his
tendentious jargon, he is just talking about pain and
various aspects of its functional role. We have already said what we take pain to be; and we do not
doubt that part of its causal role is to give rise to
judgments that one is in pain, and part is to enable
one to recognize pain (the same realizer of the same
role) when it comes again.

So far, so good. But if he persists, the friend of
qualia can succeed in escaping our unwelcome
agreement; and when he does, we must reverse our
strategy. Suppose he makes his case as follows.[1]

> You have not tasted Vegemite (a celebrated yeast-
> based condiment). So you do not know what it is
> like to taste Vegemite. And you never will, unless
> you taste Vegemite. (Or unless the same experience,
> or counterfeit traces of it, are somehow produced
> in you by artificial means.) No amount of the in-
> formation whereof materialists and functionalists
> speak will help you at all. But if you taste Vegemite,
> *then* you will know what it is like. So you will have
> gained a sort of information that the materialists

and functionalists overlook entirely. Call this *phenomenal information*. By *qualia* I mean the special
subject matter of this phenomenal information.

Now we must turn eliminative. We dare not grant
that there is a sort of information we overlook; or,
in other words, that there are possibilities exactly
alike in the respects we know of, yet different in
some other way. That would be defeat. Neither can
we credibly claim that lessons in physics, physiology, . . . could teach the inexperienced what it is
like to taste Vegemite. Our proper answer, I think,
is that knowing what it's like is not the possession
of information at all. It isn't the elimination of any
hitherto open possibilities. Rather, knowing what
it's like is the possession of abilities: abilities to recognize, abilities to imagine, abilities to predict one's
behavior by means of imaginative experiments.
(Someone who knows what it's like to taste
Vegemite can easily and reliably predict whether he
would eat a second helping of Vegemite ice cream.)
Lessons cannot impart these abilities—who would
have thought they could? There is a state of knowing what it's like, sure enough. And Vegemite has
a special power to produce that state. But phenomenal information and its special subject matter do
not exist.[2]

Imagine a smart data bank. It can be told things,
it can store the information it is given, it can reason with it, it can answer questions on the basis of
its stored information. Now imagine a pattern-
recognizing device that works as follows. When exposed to a pattern it makes a sort of template, which
it then applies to patterns presented to it in future.
Now imagine one device with both faculties, rather
like a clock radio. There is no reason to think that
any such device must have a third faculty: a faculty
of making templates for patterns it has never been
exposed to, using its stored information about these
patterns. If it has a full description about a pattern

but no template for it, it lacks an ability but it doesn't lack information. (Rather, it lacks information in usable form.) When it is shown the pattern it makes a template and gains abilities, but it gains no information. We might be rather like that.

NOTES

1. This is the "knowledge argument" of Frank Jackson, "Epiphenomenal Qualia," *Philosophical Quarterly* 32 (1982): 127–36. It appears also, in less purified form, in Thomas Nagel, "What Is It Like To Be a Bat?" *Philosophical Review* 83 (1974): 435–50, and in Paul Meehl, "The Compleat Autocerebroscopist," in Paul Feyerabend and Grover Maxwell, eds., *Mind, Matter, and Method: Essays in Philosophy and Science in Honor of Herbert Feigl* (Minneapolis: University of Minnesota Press, 1966).

2. This defense against the knowledge argument is presented in detail in Laurence Nemirow, *Functionalism and the Subjective Quality of Experience* (Ph.D. dissertation, Stanford University, 1979), chapter 2; and more briefly in his review of Thomas Nagel's *Mortal Questions, Philosophical Review* 89 (1980): 473–77.

D. Personal Identity

A Dialogue on Personal Identity
and Immortality

JOHN PERRY

This is a record of conversations of Gretchen Weirob, a teacher of philosophy at a small midwestern college, and two of her friends. The conversations took place in her hospital room on the three nights before she died from injuries sustained in a motorcycle accident. Sam Miller is a chaplain and a long-time friend of Weirob's; Dave Cohen is a former student of hers.

———◆———

The First Night

COHEN: I can hardly believe what you say, Gretchen. You are lucid and do not appear to be in great pain. And yet you say things are hopeless?

WEIROB: These devices can keep me alive for another day or two at most. Some of my vital organs have been injured beyond anything the doctors know how to repair, apart from certain rather radical measures I have rejected. I am not in much pain. But as I understand it that is not a particularly good sign. My brain was uninjured and I guess that's why I am as lucid as I ever am.

I wrote this paper while a Guggenheim Fellow and on sabbatical leave from Stanford University. I would like to thank both institutions for their support.

My aim has not been to explain and defend my own views on personal identity, but to introduce and develop positions and arguments that have emerged in the literature on that topic.

The whole situation is a bit depressing, I fear. But here's Sam Miller. perhaps he will know how to cheer me up.

MILLER: Good evening, Gretchen. Hello, Dave. I guess there's not much point in beating around the bush, Gretchen; the medics tell me you're a goner. Is there anything I can do to help?

WEIROB: Crimenetley, Sam! You deal with the dying every day. Don't you have anything more comforting to say than "Sorry to hear you're a goner"?

MILLER: Well, to tell you the truth, I'm a little at a loss for what to say to you. Most people I deal with are believers like I am. We talk of the prospects for survival. I give assurance that God, who is just and merciful, would not permit such a travesty as that our short life on this earth should be the end of things. But you and I have talked about religious and philosophical issues for years. I have never been able to find in you the least inclination to believe in God; indeed, it's a rare day when you are sure that your friends have minds, or that you can see your own hand in front of your face, or that there is any reason to believe that the sun will rise tomorrow. How can I hope to comfort you with the prospect of life after death, when I know you will regard it as having no probability whatsoever?

WEIROB: I would not require so much to be comforted, Sam. Even the possibility of something quite improbable can be comforting, in certain situations. When we used to play tennis, I beat you no more than one time in twenty. But this was enough to establish the possibility of beating you on any given occasion, and by focusing merely on the possibility I remained eager to play. Entombed in a secure prison, thinking our situation quite hopeless, we may find unutterable joy in the information that there is, after all, the slimmest possibility of escape. Hope provides comfort, and hope does not always require probability. But we must believe that what we hope for is at least possible. So I will set an easier task for you. Simply persuade me that my survival after the death of this body, is *possible,* and I promise to be comforted. Whether you succeed or not, your attempts will be a diversion, for you know I like to talk philosophy more than anything else.

MILLER: But what is possibility, if not reasonable probability?

WEIROB: I do not mean possible in the sense of likely, or even in the sense of conforming to the known laws of physics or biology. I mean possible only in the weakest sense—of being conceivable, given the unavoidable facts. Within the next couple of days, this body will die. It will be buried and it will rot away. I ask that, given these facts, you explain to me how it even makes *sense* to talk of me continuing to exist. Just explain to me what it is I am to *imagine,* when I imagine surviving, that is consistent with these facts, and I shall be comforted.

MILLER: But then what is there to do? There are many conceptions of immortality, of survival past the grave, which all seem to make good sense. Surely not the possibility, but only the probability, can be doubted. Take your choice! Christians believe in life, with a body, in some Hereafter—the details vary, of course, from sect to sect. There is the Greek idea of the body as a prison, from which we escape at death—so that we have con-

tinued life without a body. Then there are conceptions in which, so to speak, we merge with the flow of being—

WEIROB: I must cut short your lesson in comparative religion. Survival means surviving, no more, no less. I have no doubts that I shall merge with being; plants will take root in my remains, and the chemicals that I am will continue to make their contribution to life. I am enough of an ecologist to be comforted. But survival, if it is anything, must offer comforts of a different sort, the comforts of *anticipation.* Survival means that tomorrow, or sometime in the future, there will be someone who will experience, who will see and touch and smell—or at the very least, think and reason and remember. And this person will be *me.* This person will be related to me in such a way that it is correct for me to anticipate, to look forward to, those future experiences. And I am related to her in such a way that it will be right for her to remember what I have thought and done, to feel remorse for what I have done wrong, and pride in what I have done right. And the only relation that supports anticipation and memory in this way, is simply *identity.* For it is never correct to anticipate, as happening to oneself, what will happen to someone else, is it? Or to remember, as one's own thoughts and deeds, what someone else did? So don't give me merger with being, or some such nonsense. Give me identity, or let's talk about baseball or fishing—but I'm sorry to get so emotional. I react strongly when words which mean one thing are used for another—when one talks about survival, but does not mean to say that the same person will continue to exist. It's such a sham!

MILLER: I'm sorry. I was just trying to stay in touch with the times, if you want to know the truth, for when I read modern theology or talk to my students who have studied Eastern religions, the notion of survival simply as continued existence of the same person seems out of date. Merger with Being! Merger with Being! That's all I hear. My own beliefs are quite simple, if somewhat vague. I think you will live again—with or without a body, I don't know—*I* draw comfort from my belief that you and I will be together again, after I also die. We will communicate, somehow. We will continue to grow spiritually. That's what I believe, as surely as I believe that I am sitting here. For I don't know how God could be excused, if this small sample of life is all that we are allotted; I don't know why He should have created us, if these few years of toil and torment are the end of it—

WEIROB: Remember our deal, Sam. You don't have to convince me that survival is probable, for we both agree you would not get to first base. You have only to convince me that it is possible. The only condition is that it be real survival we are talking about, not some up-to-date ersatz survival, which simply amounts to what any ordinary person would call totally ceasing to exist.

MILLER: I guess I just miss the problem, then. Of course, it's possible. You just continue to exist, after your body dies. What's to be defended or explained? You want details? Okay. Two people meet a thousand years from now, in a place that may or may not be part of this physical universe. I am one and you are the other. So you must have survived. Surely you can imagine that. What else is there to say?

WEIROB: But in a few days *I* will quit breathing, *I* will be put into a coffin, *I* will be buried. And in a few months or a few years *I* will be reduced to so much humus. That, I take it, is obvious, is given. How then can you say that I am one of these persons a thousand years from now?

Suppose I took this box of Kleenex and lit fire to it. It is reduced to ashes and I smash the ashes and flush them down the john. Then I say to you, go home and on the shelf will be *that very box of Kleenex.* It has survived! Wouldn't that be absurd? What sense could you make of it? And yet that is just what you say to me. I will rot away. And then, a thousand years later, there I will be. What sense does that make?

MILLER: There could be an *identical* box of Kleenex at your home, one just like it in every respect. And, in this sense, there is no difficulty in there being someone identical to you in the Hereafter, though your body has rotted away.

WEIROB: You are playing with words again. There could be an *exactly similar* box of Kleenex on my shelf. We sometimes use "identical" to mean "exactly similar," as when we speak of "identical twins." But I am using "identical" in a way in which *identity* is the condition of memory and correct anticipation. If I am told that tomorrow, though I will be dead, someone else that looks and sounds and thinks just like me will be alive—would that be comforting? Could I correctly *anticipate* having her experiences? Would it make sense for me to fear her pains and look forward to her pleasures? Would it be right for her to feel remorse at the harsh way I am treating you? Of course not. Similarity, however exact, is not identity. I use identity to mean there is but one thing. If I am to survive, there must be one person who lies in this bed now, and who talks to someone in your Hereafter ten or a thousand years from now. After all, what comfort could there be in the notion of a heavenly imposter, walking around getting credit for the few good things I have done?

MILLER: I'm sorry. I see that I was simply confused. Here is what I should have said. If you were merely a live human body—as the Kleenex body is merely cardboard and glue in a certain arrangement—then the death of your body would be the end of you. But surely you are more than that, fundamentally more than that. What is fundamentally you is not your body, but your soul or self or mind.

WEIROB: Do you mean these words, "soul," "self," or "mind" to come to the same thing?

MILLER: Perhaps distinctions could be made, but I shall not pursue them now. I mean the nonphysical and nonmaterial aspects of you, your consciousness. It is this that I get at with these words, and I don't think any further distinction is relevant.

WEIROB: Consciousness? I am conscious, for a while yet. I see, I hear, I think, I remember. But "to be conscious"—that is a verb. What is the subject of the verb, the thing which is conscious? Isn't it just this body, the same object that is overweight, injured, and lying in bed?—and which will be buried and not be conscious in a day or a week at the most?

MILLER: As you are a philosopher, I would expect you to be less muddled about these issues. Did Descartes not draw a clear distinction between the body and the mind, between that which is overweight, and that which is conscious? Your mind or soul is immaterial, lodged in your body while you are on earth. The two are intimately related but not identical. Now clearly, what concerns us in survival is your mind or soul. It is this which must be identical to the person before me now, and to the one I expect to see in a thousand years in heaven.

WEIROB: So I am not really this body, but a soul or mind or spirit? And this soul cannot be seen or felt or touched or smelt? That is implied, I take it, by the fact that it is immaterial?

MILLER: That's right. Your soul sees and smells, but cannot be seen or smelt.

WEIROB: Let me see if I understand you. You would admit that I am the very same person with whom you had lunch last week at Dorsey's?

MILLER: Of course you are.

WEIROB: Now when you say I am the same person, if I understand you, that is not a remark about this body you see and could touch and I fear can smell. Rather it is a remark about a soul, which you cannot see or touch or smell. The fact that the same body that now lies in front of you on the bed was across the table from you at Dorsey's—that would not mean that the same *person* was present on both occasions, if the same soul were not. And if, through some strange turn of events, the same soul were present on both occasions, but lodged in different bodies, then it *would* be the same person. Is that right?

MILLER: You have understood me perfectly. But surely, you understood all of this before!

WEIROB: But wait. I can repeat it, but I'm not sure I understand it. If you cannot see or touch or in any way perceive my soul, what makes you think the one you are confronted with now *is* the very same soul you were confronted with at Dorsey's?

MILLER: But I just explained. To say it is the same soul and to say it is the same person, are the same. And, of course, you are the same person you were before. Who else would you be if not yourself? You *were* Gretchen Weirob, and you *are* Gretchen Weirob.

WEIROB: But how do you know you are talking to Gretchen Weirob at all, and not someone else, say Barbara Walters or even Mark Spitz!

MILLER: Well, it's just obvious. I can see who I am talking to.

WEIROB: But all you can see is my body. You can see, perhaps, that the same body is before you now that was before you last week at Dorsey's. But you have just said that Gretchen Weirob is not a body but a soul. In judging that the same person is before you now as was before you then, you must be making a judgment about souls—which, you said, cannot be seen or touched or smelt or tasted. And so, I repeat, how do you know?

MILLER: Well, I *can* see that it is the same body before me now that was across the table at Dorsey's. And I know that the same soul is connected with the body now that was connected with it before. That's how I know it's you. I see no difficulty in the matter.

WEIROB: You reason on the principle, "Same body, same self."

MILLER: Yes.

WEIROB: And would you reason conversely also? If there were in this bed Barbara Walters' body—that is, the body you see every night on the news—would you infer that it was not me, Gretchen Weirob, in the bed?

MILLER: Of course I would. How would you have come by Barbara Walters' body?

WEIROB: But then merely extend this principle to Heaven, and you will see that your conception of survival is without sense. Surely this very body, which will be buried and as I must so often repeat, *rot away*, will not be in your Hereafter. Different body, different person. Or do you claim that a body can rot away on earth, and then still wind up somewhere else? Must I bring up the Kleenex box again?

MILLER: No, I do not claim that. But I also do not extend a principle, found reliable on earth, to such a different situation as is represented by the Hereafter. That a correlation between bodies and souls has been found on earth does not make it inconceivable or impossible that they should separate. Principles found to work in one circumstance may not be assumed to work in vastly altered circumstances. January and snow go together here, and one would be a fool to expect otherwise. But the principle does not apply in southern California.

WEIROB: So the principle, "same body, same soul," is a well-confirmed regularity, not something you know "a priori."

MILLER: By "a priori" you philosophers mean something which can be known without observing what actually goes on in the world—as I can know that two plus two equals four just by thinking about numbers, and that no bachelors are married, just by thinking about the meaning of "bachelor"?

WEIROB: Yes.

MILLER: Then you are right. If it was part of the meaning of "same body" that wherever we have the same body we have the same soul, it would have to obtain universally, in Heaven as well as on earth. But I just claim it is a generalization we know by observation on earth, and it need not automatically extend to Heaven.

WEIROB: But where do you get this principle? It simply amounts to a correlation between being confronted with the same body and being confronted with the same soul. To establish such a correlation in the first place, surely one must have some *other* means of judging sameness of soul. You do not have such a means; your principle is without foundation; either you really do not know the person before you now is Gretchen Weirob, the very same person you lunched with at Dorsey's, or what you do know has nothing to do with sameness of some immaterial soul.

MILLER: Hold on, hold on. You know I can't follow you when you start spitting out arguments like that. Now what is this terrible fallacy I'm supposed to have committed?

WEIROB: I'm sorry. I get carried away. Here—by way of a peace offering—have one of the chocolates Dave brought.

MILLER: Very tasty. Thank you.

WEIROB: Now why did you choose that one?

MILLER: Because it had a certain swirl on the top which shows that it is a caramel.

WEIROB: That is, a certain sort of swirl is corre-

lated with a certain type of filling—the swirls with caramel, the rosettes with orange, and so forth.

MILLER: Yes. When you put it that way, I see an analogy. Just as I judged that the filling would be the same in this piece as in the last piece that I ate with such a swirl, so I judge that the soul with which I am conversing is the same as the last soul with which I conversed when sitting across from that body. We *see* the outer wrapping and infer what is inside.

WEIROB: But how did you come to realize that swirls of that sort and caramel insides were so associated?

MILLER: Why, from eating a great many of them over the years. Whenever I bit into a candy with that sort of swirl, it was filled with caramel.

WEIROB: Could you have established the correlation had you never been allowed to bite into a candy and never seen what happened when someone else bit into one? You could have formed the hypothesis, "same swirl, same filling." But could you have ever established it?

MILLER: It seems not.

WEIROB: So your inference, in a particular case, to the identity of filling from the identity of swirl would be groundless?

MILLER: Yes, it would. I think I see what is coming.

WEIROB: I'm sure you do. Since you can never, so to speak, bite into my soul, can never see or touch it, you have no way of testing your hypothesis that sameness of body means sameness of self.

MILLER: I daresay you are right. But now I'm a bit lost. What is supposed to follow from all of this?

WEIROB: If, as you claim, identity of persons consisted in identity of immaterial unobservable souls, then judgments of personal identity of the sort we make every day whenever we greet a friend or avoid a pest are really judgments about such souls.

MILLER: Right.

WEIROB: But if such judgments were really about souls, they would all be groundless and without foundation. For we have no direct method of observing sameness of soul, and so—

and this is the point made by the candy example—we can have no indirect method either.

MILLER: That seems fair.

WEIROB: But our judgments about persons are not all simply groundless and silly, so we must not be judging of immaterial souls after all.

MILLER: Your reasoning has some force. But I suspect the problem lies in my defense of my position, and not the position itself. Look here—there *is* a way to test the hypothesis of a correlation after all. When I entered the room, I expected you to react just as you did—argumentatively and skeptically. Had the person with this body reacted completely differently perhaps I would have been forced to conclude it was not you. For example, had she complained about not being able to appear on the six o'clock news, and missing Harry Reasoner, and so forth, I might eventually have been persuaded it *was* Barbara Walters and not you. Similarity of psychological characteristics—a person's attitudes, beliefs, memories, prejudices, and the like—is observable. These are correlated with identity of body on the one side, and of course with sameness of soul on the other. So the correlation between body and soul can be established after all by this intermediate link.

WEIROB: And how do you know that?

MILLER: Know what?

WEIROB: That where we have sameness of psychological characteristics, we have sameness of soul.

MILLER: Well, now you are really being just silly. The soul or mind is just that which is responsible for one's character, memory, belief. These are aspects of the mind, just as one's height, weight, and appearance are aspects of the body.

WEIROB: Let me grant for the sake of argument that belief, character, memory, and so forth are states of mind. That is, I suppose, I grant that what one thinks and feels is due to the states one's mind is in at that time. And I shall even grant that a mind is an immaterial thing—though I harbor the gravest doubts that this is so. I do not see how it follows that similarity of such traits requires, or is evidence to the slightest degree, for identity of the mind or soul.

Let me explain my point with an analogy. If we were to walk out of this room, down past the mill and out towards Wilbur, what would we see?

MILLER: We would come to the Blue River, among other things.

WEIROB: And how would you recognize the Blue River? I mean, of course if you left from here, you would scarcely expect to hit the Platte or Niobrara. But suppose you were actually lost, and came across the Blue River in your wandering, just at that point where an old dam partly blocks the flow. Couldn't you recognize it?

MILLER: Yes, I'm sure as soon as I saw that part of the river I would again know where I was.

WEIROB: And how would you recognize it?

MILLER: Well, the turgid brownness of the water, the sluggish flow, the filth washed up on the banks, and such.

WEIROB: In a word, the states of the water which makes up the river at the time you see it.

MILLER: Right.

WEIROB: If you saw the blue clean water, with bass jumping, you would know it wasn't the Blue River.

MILLER: Of course.

WEIROB: So you expect, each time you see the Blue, to see the water, which makes it up, in similar states—not always exactly the same, for sometimes it's a little dirtier, but by and large similar.

MILLER: Yes, but what do you intend to make of this?

WEIROB: Each time you see the Blue, it consists of *different* water. The water that was in it a month ago may be in Tuttle Creek Reservoir or in the Mississippi or in the Gulf of Mexico by now. So the *similarity* of states of water, by which you judge the sameness of river, does not require *identity* of the water which is in those states at these various times.

MILLER: And?

WEIROB: And so just because you judge as to personal identity by reference to similarity of states of mind, it does not follow that the mind, or soul, is the same in each case. My point is this. For all you know, the immaterial soul which you think is lodged in my body might change from day to day, from hour to hour, from minute to minute, replaced each time by another soul psychologically similar. You cannot see it or touch it, so how would you know?

MILLER: Are you saying I don't really know who you are?

WEIROB: Not at all. *You* are the one who says personal identity consists in sameness of this immaterial, unobservable, invisible, untouchable soul. I merely point out that *if* it did consist in that, you *would* have no idea who I am. Sameness of body would not necessarily mean sameness of person. Sameness of psychological characteristics would not necessarily mean sameness of person. I am saying that if you do know who I am then you are wrong that personal identity consists in sameness of immaterial soul.

MILLER: I see. But wait. I believe my problem is that I simply forgot a main tenet of my theory. The correlation can be established in my own case. I know that *my* soul and my body are intimately and consistently found together. From this one case I can generalize, at least as concerns life in this world, that sameness of body is a reliable sign of sameness of soul. This leaves me free to regard it as intelligible, in the case of death, that the link between the particular soul and the particular body it has been joined with is broken.

WEIROB: This would be quite an extrapolation, wouldn't it, from one case directly observed, to a couple of billion in which only the body is observed? For I take it that we are in the habit of assuming, for every person now on earth, as well as those who have already come and gone, that the principle "one body, one soul" is in effect.

MILLER: This does not seem an insurmountable obstacle. Since there is nothing special about my case, I assume the arrangement I find in it applies universally until given some reason to believe otherwise. And I never have been.

WEIROB: Let's let that pass. I have another problem that is more serious. How is it that you know in your own case that there is a single soul which has been so consistently connected with your body?

MILLER: Now you really cannot be serious, Gretchen. How can I doubt that I am the same person I was? Is there anything more clear and distinct, less susceptible to doubt? How do you expect me to prove anything to you, when you are capable of denying my own continued existence from second to second? Without knowledge of our own identity, everything we think and do would be senseless. How could I think if I did not suppose that the person who begins my thought is the one who completes it? When I act, do I not assume that the person who forms the intention is the very one who performs the action?

WEIROB: But I grant you that a single *person* has been associated with your body since you were born. The question is whether one immaterial soul has been so associated—or more precisely, whether you are in a position to know it. You believe that a judgment that one and the same person has had your body all these many years is a judgment that one and the same immaterial soul has been lodged in it. I say that such judgments concerning the soul are totally mysterious, and that if our knowledge of sameness of persons consisted in knowledge of sameness of immaterial soul, it too would be totally mysterious. To point out, as you do, that it is not mysterious, but perhaps the most secure knowledge we have, the foundation of all reason and action, is simply to make the point that it cannot consist of knowledge of identity of an immaterial soul.

MILLER: You have simply asserted, and not established, that my judgment that a single soul has been lodged in my body these many years is mysterious.

WEIROB: Well, consider these possibilities. One is that a single soul, one and the same, has been with this body I call mine since it was born. The other is that one soul was associated with it until five years ago and then another, psychologically similar, inheriting all the old memories and beliefs, took over. A third hypothesis is that every five years a new soul takes over. A fourth is that every five minutes a new soul takes over. The most radical is that there is a constant flow of souls through this body, each psychologically similar to the preceding, as there is a constant flow of water molecules down the Blue. What evidence do I have that the first hypothesis, the "single soul hypothesis" is true, and not one of the others? Because I am the same person I was five minutes or five years ago? But the issue in question is simply whether from sameness of person, which isn't in doubt, we can infer sameness of soul. Sameness of body? But how do I establish a stable relationship between soul and body? Sameness of thoughts and sensations? But they are in constant flux. By the nature of the case, if the soul cannot be observed, it cannot be observed to be the same. Indeed, no sense has ever been assigned to the phrase "same soul." Nor could any sense be attached to it! One would have to say what a single soul looked like or felt like, how an encounter with a single soul at different times differed from encounters with different souls. But this can hardly be done, since a soul according to your conception doesn't look or feel like *anything* at all. And so of course "souls" can afford no principle of identity. And so they cannot be used to bridge the gulf between my existence now and my existence in the hereafter.

MILLER: Do you doubt the existence of your own soul?

WEIROB: I haven't based my argument on there being no immaterial souls of the sort you describe, but merely on their total irrelevance to questions of personal identity, and so to questions of personal survival. I do indeed harbor grave doubts whether there are any immaterial souls of the sort to which you appeal. Can we have a notion of a soul unless we have a notion of the *same* soul? But I hope you do not think that means I doubt my own existence. I think I lie here, overweight and conscious. I think you can see me, not just some outer wrapping, for I think I am just a live human body. But that is not the basis of my argument. I give you these souls. I merely observe that they can by their nature provide no principle of personal identity.

MILLER: I admit I have no answer.

I'm afraid I do not comfort you, though I have perhaps provided you with some entertainment. Emerson said that a little philosophy turns one away from religion, but that deeper understand-

ing brings one back. I know no one who has thought so long and hard about philosophy as you have. Will it never lead you back to a religious frame of mind?

WEIROB: My former husband used to say that a little philosophy turns one away from religion, and more philosophy makes one a pain in the neck. Perhaps he was closer to the truth than Emerson.

MILLER: Perhaps he was. But perhaps by tomorrow night I will have come up with a better argument.

WEIROB: I hope I live to hear it.

The Second Night

WEIROB: Well, Sam, have you figured out a way to make sense of the identity of immaterial souls?

MILLER: No, I have decided it was a mistake to build my argument on such a dubious notion.

WEIROB: Have you then given up on survival? I think such a position would be a hard one for a clergyman to live with, and would feel bad about having pushed you so far.

MILLER: Don't worry. I'm more convinced than ever. I stayed up late last night thinking and reading, and I'm sure I can convince you now.

WEIROB: Get with it, time is running out.

MILLER: First, let me explain why, independently of my desire to defend survival after death, I am dissatisfied with your view that personal identity is just bodily identity. My argument will be very similar to the one you used to convince me that personal identity could not be identified with identity of an immaterial soul.

Consider a person waking up tomorrow morning, conscious, but not yet ready to open her eyes and look around and, so to speak, let the new day officially begin.

WEIROB: Such a state is familiar enough, I admit.

MILLER: Now couldn't such a person tell who she was? That is, even before opening her eyes and looking around, and in particular before looking at her body or making any judgments about it, wouldn't she be able to say who she was? Surely most of us, in the morning, know who we are before opening our eyes and recognizing our own bodies, do we not?

WEIROB: You seem to be right about that.

MILLER: But such a judgment as this person makes—we shall suppose she judges "I am Gretchen Weirob"—*is* a judgment of personal identity. Suppose she says to herself, "I am the very person who was arguing with Sam Miller last night." This is clearly a statement about her identity with someone who was alive the night before. And she could make this judgment without examining her body at all. You could have made just this judgment this morning, before opening your eyes.

WEIROB: Well, in fact I did so. I remembered our conversation of last night and said to myself, "Could I be the rude person who was so hard on Sam Miller's attempts to comfort me?" And, of course, my answer was that I not only could be but was that very rude person.

MILLER: But then by the same principle you used last night personal identity cannot be bodily identity. For you said that it could not be identity of immaterial soul because we were not judging as to identity of immaterial soul when we judge as to personal identity. But by the same token, as my example shows, we are not judging as to bodily identity when we judge as to personal identity. For we can judge who we are, and that we are the very person who did such and such and so and so, without having to make any judgments at all about the body. So, personal identity, while it may not consist of identity of an immaterial soul, does not consist in identity of material body either.

WEIROB: I did argue as you remember. But I also said that the notion of the identity of an immaterial unobservable unextended soul seemed to make no sense at all. This is one reason that cannot be what we are judging about, when we judge as to personal identity. Bodily identity at least makes sense. Perhaps we are assuming sameness of body, without looking.

MILLER: Granted. But you do admit that we do not in our own cases actually need to make a judgment of bodily identity in order to make a judgment of personal identity?

WEIROB: I don't think I will admit it. I will let it pass, so that we may proceed.

MILLER: Okay. Now it seems to me we are even able to imagine awakening and finding ourselves to have a *different* body than the one we had before. Suppose yourself just as I have described you. And now suppose you finally open your eyes and see, not the body you have grown so familiar with over the years, but one of a fundamentally different shape and size.

WEIROB: Well, I should suppose I had been asleep for a very long time and lost a lot of weight—perhaps I was in a coma for a year or so.

MILLER: But isn't it at least conceivable that it should not be your old body at all? I seem to be able to imagine awakening with a totally new body.

WEIROB: And how would you suppose that this came about?

MILLER: That's beside the point. I'm not saying I can imagine a procedure that would bring this about. I'm saying I can imagine it happening to me. In Kafka's *Metamorpheses,* someone awakens as a cockroach. I can't imagine what would make this happen to me or anyone else, but I can imagine awakening with the body of a cockroach. It is incredible that it should happen—that I do not deny. I simply mean I can imagine experiencing it. It doesn't seem contradictory or incoherent, simply unlikely and inexplicable.

WEIROB: So, if I admit this can be imagined, what follows then?

MILLER: Well, I think it follows that personal identity does not just amount to bodily identity. For I would not, finding that I had a new body, conclude that I was not the very same person I was before. I would be the same *person*, though I did not have the same *body*. So we would have identity of person but not identity of body. So personal identity cannot just amount to bodily identity.

WEIROB: Well suppose—and I emphasize *suppose*—I grant you all of this. Where does it leave you? What do you claim I have recognized as the same, if not my body and not my immaterial soul?

MILLER: I don't claim that you have recognized

anything as the same, except the person involved, that is, you yourself.

WEIROB: I'm not sure what you mean.

MILLER: Let me appeal as you did to the Blue River. Suppose I take a visitor to the stretch of river by the old Mill, and then drive him toward Manhattan. After an hour-or-so drive we see another stretch of river, and I say, "That's the same river we saw this morning." As you pointed out yesterday, I don't thereby imply that the very same molecules of water are seen both times. And the places are different, perhaps a hundred miles apart. And the shape and color and level of pollution might not all be identical. What do I see later in the day that is identical with what I saw earlier in the day?

WEIROB: Nothing except the river itself.

MILLER: Exactly. But now notice that what I see, strictly speaking, is not the whole river but only a part of it. I see different parts of the same river at the two different times. So really, if we restrict ourselves to what I literally see, I do not judge identity at all, but something else.

WEIROB: And what might that be?

MILLER: In saying that the river seen earlier, and the river seen later, are one and the same river, do I mean any more than that the stretch of water seen later and that stretch of water seen earlier are connected by other stretches of water?

WEIROB: That's about right. If the stretches of water are so connected there is but one river of which they are both parts.

MILLER: Yes, that's what I mean. The statement of identity, "This river is the same one we saw this morning," is in a sense about rivers. But in a way it is also about stretches of water or river parts.

WEIROB: So is all of this something special about rivers?

MILLER: Not at all. It is a recurring pattern. After all, we constantly deal with objects extended in space and time. But we are seldom aware of the objects' wholes, but only of their parts or stretches of their histories. When a statement of identity is not just something trivial, like "This bed is this bed," it is usually because we are really judging that different parts fit together, in some appropriate pattern, into a certain kind of whole.

WEIROB: I'm not sure I see just what you mean yet.

MILLER: Let me give you another example. Suppose we are sitting together watching the first game of a double-header. You ask me, "Is this game identical with this game?" This is a perfectly stupid question, though, of course, strictly speaking it makes sense and the answer is "yes."

But now suppose you leave in the sixth inning to go for hot dogs. You are delayed, and return after about forty-five minutes or so. You ask, "Is this the same game I was watching?" Now your question is not stupid, but perfectly appropriate.

WEIROB: Because the first game might still be going on or it might have ended, and the second game begun, by the time I return.

MILLER: Exactly. Which is to say somehow different parts of the game—different innings, or at least different plays—were somehow involved in your question. That's why it wasn't stupid or trivial but significant.

WEIROB: So, you think that judgments as to the identity of an object of a certain kind—rivers or baseball games or whatever—involve judgments as to the *parts* of those things being connected in a certain way, and are significant only when different parts are involved. Is that your point?

MILLER: Yes, and I think it is an important one. How foolish it would be, when we ask a question about the identity of baseball games, to look for something *else*, other than the game as a whole, which had to be the same. It could be the same game, even if different players were involved. It could be the same game, even if it had been moved to a different field. These other things, the innings, the plays, the players, the field, don't have to be the same at the different times for the game to be the same, they just have to be related in certain ways so as to make that complex whole we call a single game.

WEIROB: You think we were going off on a kind of a wild-goose chase when we asked whether it was the identity of soul or body that was involved in the identity of persons?

MILLER: Yes. The answer I should now give is neither. We are wondering about the identity of the person. Of course, if by "soul" we just mean "person," there is no problem. But if we mean, as I did yesterday, some other thing whose identity is already understood, which has to be the same when persons are the same, we are just fooling ourselves with words.

WEIROB: With rivers and baseball games, I can see that they are made up of parts connected in a certain way. The connection is, of course, different in the two cases, as is the sort of "part" involved. River parts must be connected physically with other river parts to form a continuous whole. Baseball innings must be connected so that the score, batting order, and the like are carried over from the earlier inning to the later one according to the rules. Is there something analogous we are to say about persons?

MILLER: Writers who concern themselves with this speak of "person-stages." That is just a stretch of consciousness, such as you and I are aware of now. I am aware of a flow of thoughts and feelings that are mine, you are aware of yours. A person is just a whole composed of such stretches as parts, not some substance that underlies them, as I thought yesterday, and not the body in which they occur, as you seem to think. That is the conception of a person I wish to defend today.

WEIROB: So when I awoke and said to myself, "I am the one who was so rude to Sam Miller last night," I was judging that a certain stretch of consciousness I was then aware of, and an earlier one I remembered having been aware of, from a single whole of the appropriate sort—a single stream of consciousness, we might say.

MILLER: Yes, that's it exactly. You need not worry about whether the same immaterial soul is involved, or even whether that makes sense. Nor need you worry about whether the same body is involved, as indeed you do not since you don't even have to open your eyes and look. Identity is not, so to speak, something under the person-stages, nor in something they are attached to, but something you build from them.

Now survival, you can plainly see, is no problem at all once we have this conception of personal identity. All you need suppose is that there is, in Heaven, a conscious being, and that the per-

son-stages that make her up are in the appropriate relation to those that now make you up, so that they are parts of the same whole—namely, you. If so, you have survived. So will you admit now that survival is at least possible?

WEIROB: Hold on, hold on. Comforting me is not that easy. You will have to show that it is possible that these person-stages or stretches of consciousness be related in the appropriate way. And to do that, won't you have to tell me what that way is?

MILLER: Yes, of course. I was getting ahead of myself. It is right at this point that my reading was particularly helpful. In a chapter of his *Essay On Human Understanding* Locke discusses this very question. He suggests that the relation between two person-stages or stretches of consciousness that makes them stages of a single person is just that the later one contains memories of the earlier one. He doesn't say this in so many words—he talks of "extending our consciousness back in time." But he seems to be thinking of memory.

WEIROB: So, any past thought or feeling or intention or desire that I can remember having is mine?

MILLER: That's right. I can remember only my own past thoughts and feelings, and you only yours. Of course, everyone would readily admit that. Locke's insight is to take this relation as the source of identity and not just its consequence. To remember—or more plausibly, to be able to remember—the thoughts and feelings of a person who was conscious in the past is just what it is to be that person.

Now you can easily see that this solves the problem of the possibility of survival. As I was saying, all you need to do is imagine someone at some future time, not on this earth and not with your present thoughts and feelings, remembering the very conversation we are having now. This does not require sameness of anything else, but it amounts to sameness of person. So, now will you admit it?

WEIROB: No, I don't.

MILLER: Well, what's the problem now?

WEIROB: I admit that if I remember having a certain thought or feeling had by some person in the past, then I must indeed be that person. Though I can remember watching others think, I cannot remember their thinking, any more than I can experience it at the time it occurs if it is theirs and not mine. This is the kernel of Locke's idea, and I don't see that I could deny it.

But we must distinguish—as I'm sure you will agree—between *actually* remembering and merely *seeming* to remember. Many men who think that they are Napoleon claim to remember losing the battle of Waterloo. We may suppose them to be sincere, and to really seem to remember it. But they do not actually remember because they were not at the battle and are not Napoleon.

MILLER: Of course I admit that we must distinguish between actually remembering and only seeming to.

WEIROB: And you will admit too, I trust, that the thought of some person at some far place and some distant time seeming to remember this conversation I am having with you would not give me the sort of comfort that the prospect of survival is supposed to provide. I would have no reason to anticipate future experiences of this person, simply because she is to *seem* to remember my experiences. The experiences of such a deluded imposter are not ones I can look forward to having.

MILLER: I agree.

WEIROB: So the mere possibility of someone in the future seeming to remember this conversation does not show the possibility of my surviving. Only the possibility of someone actually remembering this conversation—or, to be precise, the experiences I am having—would show that.

MILLER: Of course. But what are you driving at? Where is the problem? I can imagine someone being deluded, but also someone actually being you and remembering your present thoughts.

WEIROB: But, what's the difference? How do you know *which* of the two you are imagining, and *what* you have shown possible?

MILLER: Well, I just imagine the one and not the other. I don't see the force of your argument.

WEIROB: Let me try to make it clear with another example. Imagine two persons. One is talking to you, saying certain words, having certain thoughts, and so forth. The other is not talking to you at all, but is in the next room being hypnotized. The hypnotist gives to this person a post-hypnotic suggestion that upon awakening he will remember having had certain thoughts and having uttered certain words to you. The thoughts and words he mentions happen to be just the thoughts and words which the first person actually thinks and says. Do you understand the situation?

MILLER: Yes, continue.

WEIROB: Now, in a while, both of the people are saying sentences which begin, "I remember saying to Sam Miller—" and "I remember thinking as I talked to Sam Miller." And they both report remembering just the same thoughts and utterances. One of these will be remembering and the other only seeming to remember, right?

MILLER: Of course.

WEIROB: Now which one is *actually* remembering?

MILLER: Why, the very one who was in the room talking to me, of course. The other one is just under the influence of the suggestion made by the hypnotist and not remembering talking to me at all.

WEIROB: Now you agree that the difference between them does not consist in the content of what they are now thinking or saying.

MILLER: Agreed. The difference is in the relation to the past thinking and speaking. In the one case the relation of memory obtains. In the other, it does not.

WEIROB: But they both satisfy part of the conditions of remembering, for they both *seem to remember*. So there must be some further condition that the one satisfies and the other does not. I am trying to get you to say what that further condition is.

MILLER: Well, I said that the one who had been in this room talking would be remembering.

WEIROB: In other words, given two putative rememberers of some past thought or action, the real rememberer is the one who, in addition to seeming to remember the past thought or action, actually thought it or did it.

MILLER: Yes.

WEIROB: That is to say, the one who is identical with the person who did the past thinking and uttering.

MILLER: Yes, I admit it.

WEIROB: So, your argument just amounts to this. Survival is possible, because imaginable. It is imaginable, because my identity with some Heavenly person is imaginable. To imagine it, we imagine a person in Heaven who, First, seems to remember my thoughts and actions, and Second, is me.

Surely, there could hardly be a tighter circle. If I have doubts that the Heavenly person is me, I will have doubts as to whether she is really remembering or only seeming to. No one could doubt the possibility of some future person who, after death, seemed to remember the things he thought and did. But that possibility does not resolve the issue about the possibility of survival. Only the possibility of someone *actually* remembering could do that—for that, as we agree, is sufficient for identity. But doubts about survival and identity simply go over without remainder into doubts about whether the memories would be actual or merely apparent. You guarantee me no more than the possibility of a deluded Heavenly imposter.

COHEN: But wait, Gretchen. I think Sam was less than fair to his own idea just now.

WEIROB: You think you can break out of the circle of using real memory to explain identity, and identity to mark the difference between real and apparent memory? Free free to try.

COHEN: Let us return to your case of the hypnotist. You point out that we have two putative rememberers. You ask what marks the difference, and claim the answer must be the circular one—that the real rememberer is the person who actually had the experiences both seem to remember.

But that is not the only possible answer. The experiences themselves cause the later apparent memories in the one case, while the hypnotist causes them in the other. We can say that the rememberer is the one of the two whose memories were *caused in the right way* by the earlier experiences. We thus distinguish between the rememberer and the hypnotic subject, without appeal to identity.

The idea that real memory amounts to apparent memory plus identity is misleading anyway. I seem to remember, as a small child, knocking over the Menorah so the candles fell into and spoiled a tureen of soup. And I did actually perform such a feat. So we have apparent memory and identity. But I do *not* actually remember; I was much too young when I did this to remember it now. I have simply been told the story so often I seem to remember.

Here the suggestion that real memory is apparent memory that was caused in the appropriate way by the past events fares better. Not my experience of pulling over the Menorah, but hearing my parents talk about it later, caused my memory-like impressions.

WEIROB: You analyze personal identity into memory, and memory into apparent memory which is caused in the right way. A person is a certain sort of causal process.

COHEN: Right.

WEIROB: Suppose now for the sake of argument I accept this. How does it help Sam in his defense of the possibility of survival? In ordinary memory, the causal chain from remembered event to memory of it never leads us outside the confines of a single body. Indeed, the normal process of which you speak surely involves storage of information somehow in the brain. How can the states of my brain, when I die, influence in the appropriate way the apparent memories of the Heavenly person Sam takes to be me?

COHEN: Well, I didn't intend to be defending the possibility of survival. That is Sam's problem. I just like the idea that personal identity can be explained in terms of memory, and not just in terms of identity of the body.

MILLER: But surely, this does provide me with the basis for further defense. Your challenge, Gretchen, was to explain the difference between two persons in Heaven, one who actually remembers your experience—and so is you—and one who simply seems to remember it. But can I not just say that the one who is you is the one whose states were caused in the appropriate way?

I do not mean the way they would be in a normal case of earthly memory. But in the case of the Heavenly being who is you, God would have created her with the brain states (or whatever) she has *because* you had the ones you had at death. Surely it is not the exact form of the dependence of my later memories on my earlier perceptions that makes them really memories, but the fact that the process involved has preserved information.

WEIROB: So if God creates a Heavenly person, designing her brain to duplicate the brain I have upon death, that person is me. If, on the other hand, a Heavenly being should come to be with those very same memory-like states by accident (if there are accidents in Heaven) it would not be me.

MILLER: Exactly. Are you satisfied now that survival makes perfectly good sense?

WEIROB: No, I'm still quite unconvinced.

The problem I see is this. If God could create one person in Heaven, and by designing her after me, make her me, why could he not make two such bodies, and cause this transfer of information into both of them? Would both of these Heavenly persons then be me? It seems as clear as anything in philosophy that from

$$A \text{ is } B$$

and

$$C \text{ is } B$$

where by "is" we mean identity, we can infer,

$$A \text{ is } C.$$

So, if each of these Heavenly persons is me, they must be each other. But then they are not two but one. But my assumption was that God creates two, not one. He could create them physically distinct, capable of independent movement, perhaps in widely separated Heavenly locations, each with her own duties to perform, her own circle of Heavenly friends, and the like.

So either God, by creating a Heavenly person with a brain modeled after mine, does not really create someone identical with me but merely someone similar to me, or God is somehow limited to making only one such being. I can see no reason why, if there were a God, He should be so limited. So I take the first option. He could create someone similar to me, but not someone who would *be* me. Either your analysis of memory is wrong, and such a being does not, after all, remember what I am doing or saying, or memory is not sufficient for personal identity. Your theory has gone wrong somewhere, for it leads to absurdity.

COHEN: But wait. Why can't Sam simply say that if God makes one such creature, she is you, while if he makes more, none of them is you? It's possible that he makes only one. So it's possible that you survive. Sam always meant to allow that it's *possible* that you won't survive. He had in mind the case in which there is no God to take the appropriate Heavenly persons, or God exists, but doesn't make even one. You have simply shown that there is another way of not surviving. Instead of making too few Heavenly rememberers, He makes too many. So what? He might make the right number, and then you would survive.

WEIROB: Your remarks really amount to a change in your position. Now you are not claiming that memory alone is enough for personal identity. Now, it is memory *plus* lack of competition, the absence of other rememberers, that is needed for personal identity.

COHEN: It does amount to a change of position. But what of it? Is there anything untenable about the position as changed?

WEIROB: Let's look at this from the point of view of the Heavenly person. She says to herself, "Oh, I must be Gretchen Weirob, for I remember doing what she did and saying what she said." But now that's a pretty tenuous conclusion, isn't it? She is really only entitled to say, "Oh, either I'm Gretchen Weirob, or God has created more than one being like me, and none of us is." Identity has become something dependent on things wholly extrinsic to her. Who she is now turns on not just her states of mind and their relation to my states of mind, but on the existence or nonexistence of other people. Is this really what you want to maintain?

Or look at it from my point of view. God creates one of me in Heaven. Surely I should be glad if convinced this was to happen. Now he creates another, and I should despair again, for this means I won't survive after all. How can doubling a good deed make it worthless?

COHEN: Are you saying that there is some contradiction in my suggestion that only creation of a unique Heavenly Gretchen counts as your survival?

WEIROB: No, it's not contradictory, as far as I can see. But it seems odd in a way that shows that something somewhere is wrong with your theory. Here is a certain relationship I have with a Heavenly person. There being such a person, to whom I am related in this way, is something that is of great importance to me, a source of comfort. It makes it appropriate for me to anticipate having her experiences, since she is just me. Why should my having that relation to another being destroy my relation to this one? You say because then I will not be identical with either of them. But since you have provided a theory about what that identity consists in, we can look and see what it amounts to for me to be or not to be identical. If she is to remember my experience, I can rightly anticipate hers. But then it seems the doubling makes no difference. And yet it must, for one cannot be identical with two. So you add, in a purely *ad hoc* manner, that her memory of me isn't enough to make my anticipation of her experiences appropriate, if there are two rather than one so linked. Isn't it more reasonable to conclude, since memory does not secure identity when there are two Heavenly Gretchens, it also doesn't when there is only one?

COHEN: There is something *ad hoc* about it, I admit. But perhaps that's just the way our concept works. You have not elicited a contradiction—

WEIROB: An infinite pile of absurdities has the same weight as a contradiction. And absurdities can be generated without limit from your account. Suppose God created this Heavenly person before I died. Then He in effect kills me; if He has already created her, then you really are not talking to whom you think, but someone new, created by Gretchen Weirob's strange death

moments ago. Or suppose He first creates one being in Heaven, who is me. Then He creates another. Does the first cease to be me? If God can create such beings in Heaven, surely He can do so in Albuquerque. And there is nothing on your theory to favor this body before you as Gretchen Weirob's, over the one belonging to the person created in Albuquerque. So I am to suppose that if God were to do this, I would suddenly cease to be. I'm tempted to say I would cease to be Gretchen Weirob. But that would be a confused way of putting it. There would be here, in my place, a new person with false memories of having been Gretchen Weirob, who has just died of competition—a strange death if ever there was one. She would have no right to my name, my bank account, or the services of my doctor, who is paid from insurance premiums paid for by deductions from Gretchen Weirob's past salary. Surely this is nonsense; however carefully God should choose to duplicate me, in Heaven or in Albuquerque, I would not cease to be, or cease to be who I am. You may reply that God, being benevolent, would never create an extra Gretchen Weirob. But I do not say that he would, but only that if he did this would not, as your theory implies, mean that I cease to exist. Your theory gives the wrong answer in this possible circumstance, so it must be wrong. I think I have been given no motivation to abandon the most obvious and straightforward view on these matters. I am a live body, and when that body dies, my existence will be at an end.

The Third Night

WEIROB: Well, Sam, are you here for a third attempt to convince me of the possibility of survival?

MILLER: No, I have given up. I suggest we talk about fishing or football or something unrelated to your imminent demise. You will outwit any straightforward attempts to comfort you, but perhaps I can at least divert your mind.

COHEN: But before we start on fishing—although I don't have any particular brief for survival—there is one point in our discussion of the last two evenings that still bothers me. Would you mind discussing for a while the notion of personal identity itself, without worrying about the more difficult case of survival after death?

WEIROB: I would enjoy it. What point bothers you?

COHEN: Your position seems to be that personal identity amounts to identity of a human body, nothing more, nothing less. A person is just a live human body, or more precisely, I suppose, a human body that is alive and has certain capacities—consciousness and perhaps rationality. Is that right?

WEIROB: Yes, it seems that simple to me.

COHEN: But I think there has actually been an episode which disproves that. I am thinking of the strange case of Julia North, which occurred in California a few months ago. Surely you remember it.

WEIROB: Yes, only too well. But you had better explain it to Sam, for I'll wager he has not heard of it.

COHEN: Not heard of Julia North? But the case was all over the headlines.

MILLER: Well, Gretchen is right. I know nothing of it. She knows that I only read the sports page.

COHEN: You only read the sports page!

WEIROB: It's an expression of his unconcern with earthly matters.

MILLER: Well, that's not quite fair, Gretchen. It's a matter of preference. I much prefer to spend what time I have for reading in reading about the eighteenth century, rather than the drab and miserable century into which I had the misfortune to be born. It was really a much more civilized century, you know. But let's not dwell on my peculiar habits. Tell me about Julia North.

COHEN: Very well. Julia North was a young woman who was run over by a streetcar while saving the life of a young child who wandered onto the tracks. The child's mother, one Mary Frances Beaudine, had a stroke while watching the horrible scene. Julia's healthy brain and wasted body, and Mary Frances' healthy body and wasted brain, were transported to a hospital where a brilliant neurosurgeon, Dr. Matthews,

was in residence. He had worked out a procedure for what he called a "body transplant." He removed the brain from Julia's head and placed it in Mary Frances', splicing the nerves, and so forth, using techniques not available until quite recently. The survivor of all of this was obviously Julia, as everyone agreed—except, unfortunately, Mary Frances' husband. His shortsightedness and lack of imagination led to great complications and drama, and made the case more famous in the history of crime than in the history of medicine. I shall not go into the details of this sorry aspect of the case—they are well reported in a book by Barbara Harris called *Who is Julia?*, in case you are interested.

MILLER: Fascinating!

COHEN: Well, the relevance of this case is obvious. Julia North had one body up until the time of the accident, and another body after the operation. So one person had two bodies. So a person cannot be simply *identified* with a human body. So something must be wrong with your view, Gretchen. What do you say to this?

WEIROB: I'll say to you just what I said to Dr. Matthews—

COHEN: You have spoken with Dr. Matthews?

WEIROB: Yes. He contacted me shortly after my accident. My physician had phoned him up about my case. Matthews said he could perform the same operation for me he did for Julia North. I refused.

COHEN: You refused! But Gretchen, why—?

MILLER: Gretchen, I *am* shocked. Your decision practically amounts to suicide? You passed up an opportunity to continue living? Why on earth—

WEIROB: Hold on, hold on. You are both making an assumption I reject. If the case of Julia North amounts to a counterexample to my view that a person is just a live human body, and if my refusal to submit to this procedure amounts to suicide, then the survivor of such an operation must be reckoned as the same person as the brain donor. That is, the survivor of Julia North's operation must have been Julia, and the survivor of the operation on me would have to be me. This is the assumption you both make in criticizing me. But I reject it. I think Jack Beaudine was right. The survivor of the operation involving Julia North's brain was Mary Frances Beaudine, and the survivor of the operation using my brain would not have been me.

MILLER: Gretchen, how on earth can you say that? Will you not give up your view that personal identity is just bodily identity, no matter how clear the counter-example? I really think you simply have an irrational attachment to the lump of material that is your body.

COHEN: Yes, Gretchen, I agree with Sam. You are being preposterous! The survivor of Julia North's operation had no idea who Mary Frances Beaudine was. She remembered being Julia—

WEIROB: She *seemed* to remember being Julia. Have you forgotten so quickly the importance of this distinction? In my opinion, the effect of the operation was that Mary Frances Beaudine survived deluded, thinking she was someone else.

COHEN: But as you know, the case was litigated. It went to the Supreme Court. They said that the survivor was Julia.

WEIROB: That argument is unworthy of you, Dave. Is the Supreme Court infallible?

COHEN: No, it isn't. But I don't think it's such a stupid point.

Look at it this way, Gretchen. This is a case in which two criteria we use to make judgments of identity conflict. Usually we expect personal identity to involve both bodily identity and psychological continuity. That is, we expect that if we have the same body, then the beliefs, memories, character traits, and the like also will be enormously similar. In this case, these two criteria which usually coincide do not. If we choose one criterion, we say that the survivor is Mary Frances Beaudine and she has undergone drastic psychological changes. If we choose the other, we say that Julia has survived with a new body. We have to choose which criterion is more important. It's a matter of choice of how to use our language, how to extend the concept "same person" to a new situation. The overwhelming majority of people involved in the case took the survivor to be Julia. That is, society chose to use the concept one way rather than the other. The Supreme Court is *not* beside the point. One of their func-

tions is to settle just how old concepts shall be applied to new circumstances—how "freedom of the press" is to be understood when applied to movies or television, whose existence was not foreseen when the concept was shaped, or to say whether "murder" is to include the abortion of a fetus. They are fallible on points of fact, but they are the final authority on the development of certain important concepts used in law. The notion of *person* is such a concept.

WEIROB: You think that *who* the survivor was, was a matter of convention, of how we choose to use language?

COHEN: Yes.

WEIROB: I can show the preposterousness of all that with an example.

Let us suppose that I agree to the operation. I lie in bed, expecting my continued existence, anticipating the feelings and thoughts I shall have upon awakening after the operation. Dr. Matthews enters and asks me to take several aspirin, so as not to have a headache when I awake. I protest that aspirin upsets my stomach; he asks whether I would rather have a terrible headache tomorrow or a mild stomachache now, and I agree that it would be reasonable to take them.

Let us suppose that you enter at this point, with bad news. The Supreme Court has changed its mind! So the survivor will not be me. So, I say, "Oh, then I will not take the aspirin, for it's not me that will have a headache, but someone else. Why should I endure a stomachache, however mild, for the comfort of someone else? After all, I am already donating my brain to that person."

Now this is clearly absurd. If I were correct, in the first place, to anticipate having the sensations and thoughts that the survivor is to have the next day, the decision of nine old men a thousand or so miles away wouldn't make me wrong. And if I was wrong to so anticipate, their decision couldn't make me right. How can the correctness of my anticipation of survival be a matter of the way we use our words? If it is not such a matter, then my identity is not either. My identity with the survivor, my survival, is a question of fact, not of convention.

COHEN: Your example is persuasive. I admit I am befuddled. On the one hand, I cannot see how the matter can be other than I have described. When we know all the facts what can remain to be decided but how we are to describe them, how we are to use our language? And yet I can see that it seems absurd to suppose that the correctness or incorrectness of anticipation of future experience is a matter for convention to decide.

MILLER: Well, I didn't think the business about convention was very plausible anyway. But I should like to return you to the main question, Gretchen. Fact or convention, it still remains. Why will you not admit that the survivor of this operation would be you?

WEIROB: Well, *you* tell *me*, why you think she would be me?

MILLER: I can appeal to the theory I developed last night. You argued that the idea that personal identity consists in memory would not guarantee the possibility of survival after death. But you said nothing to shake its plausibility as an account of personal identity. It has the enormous advantage, remember, of making sense of our ability to judge our own identity, without examination of our bodies. I should argue that it is the correctness of this theory that explains the *almost* universal willingness to say that the survivor of Julia's operation was Julia. We need not deliberate over how to extend our concept, we need only apply the concept we already have. Memory is sufficient for identity and bodily identity is *not* necessary for it. The survivor remembered Julia's thoughts and actions, and so was Julia. Would you but submit to the operation, the survivor would remember your thoughts and actions, would remember this very conversation we are now having, and would be you.

COHEN: Yes, I now agree completely with Sam. The theory that personal identity is to be analyzed in terms of memory is correct, and according to it you will survive if you submit to the operation.

Let me add another argument against your view and in favor of the memory theory. You have emphasized that identity is the condition of *anticipation*. That means, among other things,

that we have a particular concern for that person in the future whom we take to be ourselves. If I were told that any of the three of us were to suffer pain tomorrow, I should be sad. But if it were you or Sam that were to be hurt, my concern would be altruistic or unselfish. That is because I would not anticipate having the painful experience myself. Here I do no more than repeat points you have made earlier in our conversations.

Now what is there about mere sameness of body that makes sense of this asymmetry, between the way we look at our own futures, and the way we look at the futures of others? In other words, why is the identity of your body—that mere lump of matter, as Sam put it—of such great importance? Why care so much about it?

WEIROB: You say, and I surely agree, that identity of person is a very special relationship—so special as perhaps not even happily called a relationship at all. And you say that since my theory is that identity of person is identity of body, I should be able to explain the importance of the one in terms of the importance of the other.

I'm not sure I can do that. But does the theory that personal identity consists in memory fare better on this score?

COHEN: Well, I think it does. Those properties of persons which make persons of such great value, and mark their individuality, and make one person so special to his friends and loved ones, are ultimately psychological or mental. One's character, personality, beliefs, attitudes, convictions—they are what make every person so unique and special. A skinny Gretchen would be a shock to us all, but not a Gretchen diminished in any important way. But a Gretchen who was not witty, or not gruff, or not as honest to the path an argument takes as is humanly possible—those would be fundamental changes. Is it any wonder that the survivor of that California fiasco was reckoned as Julia North? Would it make sense to take her to be Mary Jane Beaudine, when she had none of her beliefs or attitudes or memories?

Now if such properties are what is of importance about a person to others, is it not reasonable that they are the basis of one's importance to oneself? And these are just the properties that personal identity preserves when it is taken to consist in links of memory. Do we not have, in this idea, at least the beginning of an explanation of the importance of identity?

WEIROB: So on two counts you two favor the memory theory. First, you say it explains how it is possible to judge as to one's own identity, without having to examine one's body. Second, you say it explains the importance of personal identity.

COHEN: Now surely you must agree the memory theory is correct. Do you agree? There may be still time to contact Dr. Matthews—

WEIROB: Hold on, hold on. Try to relax and enjoy the argument. I am. Quit trying to save my life and worry about saving your theory—for I'm still not persuaded. Granted the survivor will *think* she is me, will *seem* to remember thinking my thoughts. But recall the importance of distinguishing between real and merely apparent memory—

COHEN: But *you* recall that this distinction is to be made on the basis of whether the apparent memories were or were not caused by the prior experiences in the appropriate way. The survivor will not seem to remember your thoughts because of hypnosis or by coincidence or overweening imagination. She will seem to remember them because the traces those experiences left on your brain now activate her mind in the usual way. She will seem to remember them because she does remember them, and will be you.

WEIROB: You are very emphatic, and I'm feeling rather weak. I'm not sure there is time left to untangle all of this. But there is never an advantage to hurrying when doing philosophy. So let's go over this slowly.

We all agree that the fact that the survivor of this strange operation Dr. Matthews proposes would *seem* to remember doing what I have done. Let us even suppose she would take herself to be me, claim to be Gretchen Weirob—and have no idea who else she might be. (We are then assuming that she differs from me in one aspect— her theory of personal identity. But that does not

show her not to be me, for I could change my mind by then.) We all first agree that this much does not make her me. For this could all be true of someone suffering a delusion, or a subject of hypnosis.

COHEN: Yes, this is all agreed.

WEIROB: But now you think that some further condition is satisfied, which makes her apparent memories *real* memories. Now what exactly is this further condition?

COHEN: Well, that the same brain was involved in the perception of the events, and their later *memory*. Thus we have here a causal chain of just the same sort as when only a single body is involved. That is, perceptions when the event occurs leave a trace in the brain, which is later responsible for the content of the memory. And we agreed, did we not, that apparent memory, caused in the right way, is real memory?

WEIROB: Now is it absolutely crucial that the same brain is involved?

COHEN: What do you mean?

WEIROB: Let me explain again by reference to Dr. Matthews. In our conversation he explained a new procedure on which he was working, called a *brain rejuvenation*. By this process, which is not yet available—only the feasibility of developing it is being studied—a new brain could be made which is an exact duplicate of my brain— that is, an exact duplicate in terms of psychologically relevant states. It might not duplicate all the properties of my brain—for example, the blood vessels in the new brain might be stronger than in the old brain.

MILLER: What is the point of developing such a macabre technique?

WEIROB: Dr. Matthews' idea is that when weaknesses which might lead to stroke or other brain injury are noted, a healthy duplicate could be made to replace the original, forestalling the problem.

Now Dave, suppose my problem were not with my liver and kidneys and such, but with my brain. Would you recommend such an operation as to my benefit?

COHEN: You mean, do I think the survivor of such an operation would be you?

WEIROB: Exactly. You may assume that Dr. Matthews' technique works perfectly so the causal process involved is no less reliable than that involved in ordinary memory.

COHEN: Then I would say it was you— No! Wait! No, it wouldn't be you—absolutely not.

MILLER: But why the sudden reversal? It seems to me it would be her. Indeed, I should try such an operation myself, if it would clear up my dizzy spells and leave me otherwise unaffected.

COHEN: No, don't you see, she is leading us into a false trap. If we say it *is* her, then she will say, "then what if he makes two duplicates, or three or ten? They can't all be me, they all have an equal claim, so none will be me." It would be the argument of last night, reapplied on earth. So the answer is no, absolutely not, it wouldn't be you. Duplication of brain does not preserve identity. Identity of the person requires identity of the brain.

MILLER: Quite right.

WEIROB: Now let me see if I have managed to understand your theory, for my powers of concentration seem to be fading. Suppose we have two bodies, A and B. My brain is put into A, a duplicate into B. The survivor of this, call them "A-Gretchen" and "B-Gretchen," both seem to remember giving this very speech. Both are in this state of seeming to remember, as the last stage in an information-preserving causal chain, initiated by my giving this speech. Both have my character, personality, beliefs, and the like. But one is *really* remembering, the other is not. A-Gretchen is really me, B-Gretchen is not.

COHEN: Precisely. Is this incoherent?

WEIROB: No, I guess there is nothing incoherent about it. But look what has happened to the advantages you claimed for the memory theory.

First, you said, it explains how I can know who I am without opening my eyes and recognizing my body. But on your theory Gretchen-A and Gretchen-B cannot know who they are even if they do open their eyes and examine their bodies. How is Gretchen-A to know whether she has the original brain and is who she seems to be, or has the duplicate and is a new person, only a few minutes old, and with no memories but mere

delusions? If the hospital kept careless records, or the surgeon thought it was of no great importance to keep track of who got the original and who got the duplicate, she might never know who she was. By making identity of person turn into identity of brain, your theory makes the ease with which I can determine who I am not less but more mysterious than my theory.

Second, you said, your theory explains why my concern for Gretchen-A, who is me whether she knows it or not, would be selfish, and my anticipation of her experience correct while my concern for Gretchen-B with her duplicated brain would be unselfish, and my anticipation of having her experiences incorrect. And it explains this, you said, because by insisting on the links of memory, we preserve in personal identity more psychological characteristics which are the most important features of a person.

But Gretchen-A and Gretchen-B are psychologically indiscernible. Though they will go their separate ways, at the moment of awakening they could well be exactly similar in every psychological respect. In terms of character and belief and the contents of their minds, Gretchen-A is no more like me than Gretchen-B. So there is nothing in your theory after all to explain why anticipation is appropriate when we have identity and not otherwise.

You said, Sam, that I had an irrational attachment for this unworthy material object, my body. But you too are as irrationally attached to your brain. I have never seen my brain. I should have easily given it up for a rejuvenated version, had that been the choice with which I was faced. I have never seen it, never felt it, and have no attachment to it. But my body? That seems to me all that I am. I see no point in trying to evade its fate, even if there were still time.

But perhaps I miss the merit of your arguments. I am tired, and perhaps my poor brain, feeling slighted, has begun to desert me—

COHEN: Oh, don't worry, Gretchen, you are still clever. Again you have left me befuddled. I don't know what to say. But answer me this. Suppose you are right and we are wrong. But suppose these arguments had not occurred to you, and, sharing in our error, you had agreed to the operation. You anticipate the operation until it happens, thinking you will survive. You are happy. The survivor takes herself to be you, and thinks she made a decision before the operation which has now turned out to be right. She is happy. Your friends are happy. Who would be worse off, either before or after the operation?

Suppose even that you realize identity would not be preserved by such an operation, but have it done anyway, and as the time for the operation approaches, you go ahead and anticipate the experiences of the survivor. Where exactly is the mistake? Do you really have any less reason to care for the survivor than for yourself? Can mere identity of body, the lack of which alone keeps you from being her, mean that much? Perhaps we were wrong, after all, in focusing on identity as the necessary condition of anticipation—

MILLER: Dave, it's too late.

NOTES

THE FIRST NIGHT: The arguments against the position that personal identity consists in identity of an immaterial soul are similar to those found in John Locke, "Of Identity and Diversity," chapter 27 of Book II of the *Essay Concerning Human Understanding.* This chapter first appeared in the second edition of 1694.
THE SECOND NIGHT: The arguments against the view that personal identity consists in bodily identity are also suggested by Locke, as is the theory that memory is crucial. The argument that the memory theory is circular was made by Joseph Butler in "Of Personal Identity," an Appendix to his *Analogy of Religion,* first published in 1736. Locke's memory theory has been developed by a number of modern authors, including H. P. Grice, A. M. Quinton and, in a different direction, Sydney Shoemaker. The possibility of circumventing Butler's charge of circularity by an appeal to

causation is noted by Shoemaker in his article "Persons and Their Pasts" (*American Philosophical Quarterly,* 1970) and by David Wiggins in *Identity and Spatial Temporal Continuity.* The "duplication argument" was apparently first used by Samuel Clarke, arguing against the eighteenth-century freethinker, Antony Collins. Collins assumed that something like Locke's theory of personal identity was correct. Clarke assumed immortality made sense, and used the duplication argument to raise problems for Collins's Lockean theory.
THE THIRD NIGHT: *Who Is Julia?*, by Barbara Harris, is an engaging novel published in 1972. (Dr. Matthews had not yet thought of brain rejuvenations.)

Locke considers the possibility of the "consciousness" of a prince being transferred to the body of a cobbler. The idea of using the removal of a brain to suggest how this might happen comes from Sydney Shoemaker's seminal book, *Self-Knowledge and Self-Identity* (1963). In a number of important articles which are collected in his book *Problems of the Self* (1973), Bernard Williams has cleverly and articulately resisted the memory theory and the view that such a brain removal would amount to a body transplant. In particular, Williams has stressed the relevance of the duplication argument even in questions of terrestrial personal identity. Weirob's position in this essay is more inspired by Williams than anyone else. I have discussed Williams' arguments and related topics in "Can the Self Divide?" (*Journal of Philosophy,* 1972) and in a review of his book (*Journal of Philosophy,* 1976).

An important article on the themes which emerge toward the end of the dialogue is Derek Parfit's "Personal Identity" (*Philosophical Review,* 1971). This article, along with Locke's chapter and a number of other important chapters and articles by Hume, Shoemaker, Williams, and others are collected in my anthology *Personal Identity* (1975). A number of articles on personal identity appear in Amelie Rorty (ed.), *The Identities of Persons* (1976), including my "The Importance of Being Identical," which addresses the questions raised by Cohen at the end.

E. Freedom, Determinism, and Responsibility

Has the Self "Free Will"?

C. A. CAMPBELL

C. A. Campbell (1897–1974) was a professor of philosophy at the University of Glasgow. His publications include *On Selfhood and Godhood*.

❧—•—☙

1. . . . It is something of a truism that in philosophic enquiry the exact formulation of a problem often takes one a long way on the road to its solution. In the case of the Free Will problem I think there is a rather special need of careful formulation. For there are many sorts of human freedom; and it can easily happen that one wastes a great deal of labour in proving or disproving a freedom which has almost nothing to do with the freedom which is at issue in the traditional problem of Free Will. The abortiveness of so much of the argument for and against Free Will in contemporary philosophical literature seems to me due in the main to insufficient pains being taken over the preliminary definition of the problem. . . .

Fortunately we can at least make a beginning with a certain amount of confidence. It is not seriously disputable that the kind of freedom in question is the freedom which is commonly recognised to be in some sense a precondition of moral responsibility. Clearly, it is on account of this integral connection with moral responsibility that such exceptional importance has always been felt to attach to the Free Will problem. But in what precise sense is

free will a precondition of moral responsibility, and thus a postulate of the moral life in general? This is an exceedingly troublesome question; but until we have satisfied ourselves about the answer to it, we are not in a position to state, let alone decide, the question whether "Free Will" in its traditional, ethical, significance is a reality.

Our first business, then, is to ask, exactly what kind of freedom is it which is required for moral responsibility? And as to method of procedure in this inquiry, there seems to me to be no real choice. I know of only one method that carries with it any hope of success; viz. the critical comparison of those acts for which, on due reflection, we deem it proper to attribute moral praise or blame to the agents, with those acts for which, on due reflection, we deem such judgments to be improper. The ultimate touchstone, as I see it, can only be our moral consciousness as it manifests itself in our more critical and considered moral judgments. . . .

2. The first point to note is that the freedom at issue (as indeed the very name "Free *Will* Problem" indicates) pertains primarily not to overt acts but to inner acts. The nature of things has decreed that, save in the case of one's self, it is only overt acts which one can directly observe. But a very little reflection serves to show that in our moral judgments upon others their overt acts are regarded as significant only in so far as they are the expression of inner acts. We do not consider the acts of a robot to be morally responsible acts; nor do we consider the acts of a man to be so save insofar as they are distinguishable from those of a robot by reflecting an inner life of choice. Similarly, from the other side, if we are satisfied (as we may on occasion be, at least in the case of ourselves) that a person has definitely elected to follow a course which he believes to be wrong, but has been prevented by external circumstances from translating his inner choice into an overt act, we still regard him as morally blameworthy. Moral freedom, then, pertains to *inner* acts.

The next point seems at first sight equally obvious and non-controversial; but, as we shall see, it has awkward implications if we are in real earnest with it (as almost nobody is). It is the simple point that the act must be one of which the person judged can be regarded as the *sole* author. It seems plain enough that if there are any *other* determinants of the act, external to the self, to that extent the act is not an act which the *self* determines, and to that extent not an act for which the self can be held morally responsible. The self is only part-author of the act, and his moral responsibility can logically extend only to those elements within the act (assuming for the moment that these can be isolated) of which he is the *sole* author.

The awkward implications of this apparent truism will be readily appreciated. For, if we are mindful of the influences exerted by heredity and environment, we may well feel some doubt whether there is any act of will at all of which one can truly say that the self is sole author, sole determinant. No man has a voice in determining the raw material of impulses and capacities that constitute his hereditary endowment, and no man has more than a very partial control of the material and social environment in which he is destined to live his life. Yet it would be manifestly absurd to deny that these two factors do constantly and profoundly affect the nature of a man's choices. That this is so we all of us recognise in our moral judgments when we "make allowances," as we say, for a bad heredity or a vicious environment, and acknowledge in the victim of them a diminished moral responsibility for evil courses. Evidently we do *try*, in our moral judgments, however crudely, to praise or blame a man

only in respect of that of which we can regard him as *wholly* the author. And evidently we do recognise that, for a man to be the author of an act in the full sense required for moral responsibility, it is not enough merely that he "wills" or "chooses" the act: since even the most unfortunate victim of heredity or environment does, as a rule, "will" what he does. It is significant, however, that the ordinary man, though well enough aware of the influence upon choices of heredity and environment, does not feel obliged thereby to give up his assumption that moral predicates *are* somehow applicable. Plainly he still believes that there is *something* for which a man is morally responsible, something of which we can fairly say that he is the sole author. *What is this something?* To that question common-sense is not ready with an explicit answer—though an answer is, I think, implicit in the line which its moral judgments take. I shall do what I can to give an explicit answer later in this lecture. Meantime it must suffice to observe that, if we are to be true to the deliverances of our moral consciousness, it is very difficult to deny that *sole* authorship is a necessary condition of the morally responsible act.

Thirdly we come to a point over which much recent controversy has raged. We may approach it by raising the following question. Granted an act of which the agent is sole author, does this "sole authorship" suffice to make the act a morally free act? We may be inclined to think that it does, until we contemplate the possibility that an act of which the agent is sole author might conceivably occur as a necessary expression of the agent's nature; the way in which, e.g. some philosophers have supposed the Divine act of creation to occur. This consideration excites a legitimate doubt, for it is far from easy to see how a person can be regarded as a proper subject for moral praise or blame in respect of an act which he *cannot help* performing—even if it be his own "nature" which necessitates it. Must we not recognise it as a condition of the morally free act that the agent "could have acted otherwise" than he in fact did? It is true, indeed, that we sometimes praise or blame a man for an act about which we are prepared to say, in the light of our knowledge of his established character, that he "could no other." But I think that a little reflection shows that in such cases we are not praising or blaming the man strictly for what he does *now* (or at any rate we ought not to be), but rather for those past acts of his which have generated the firm habit of mind from which his *present* act follows "necessarily." In other words, our praise and blame, so far as justified, are really retrospective, being directed not to the agent *qua* performing *this* act, but to the agent *qua* performing those past acts which have built up his present character, and in respect to which we presume that he *could* have acted otherwise, that there really *were* open possibilities before him. These cases, therefore, seem to me to constitute no valid exception to what I must take to be the rule, viz. that a man can be morally praised or blamed for an act only if he could have acted otherwise.

Now philosophers today are fairly well agreed that it is a postulate of the morally responsible act that the agent "could have acted otherwise" in *some* sense of that phrase. But sharp differences of opinion have arisen over the way in which the phrase ought to be interpreted. There is a strong disposition to water down its apparent meaning by insisting that it is not (as a postulate of moral responsibility) to be understood as a straightforward categorical proposition, but rather as a disguised hypothetical proposition. All that we really require to be assured of, in order to justify our holding X morally responsible for an act, is, we are told, that X could have acted otherwise *if* he had *chosen* otherwise (Moore, Stevenson); or perhaps that X could have acted otherwise *if* he had had a different character, or *if* he had been placed in different circumstances.

I think it is easy to understand, and even, in a measure, to sympathise with, the motives which induce philosophers to offer these counter-interpretations. It is not just the fact that "X could have acted otherwise," as a bald categorical statement, is incompatible with the universal sway of causal law—though this is, to some philosophers, a serious stone of stumbling. The more widespread objection is that it at least looks as though it were incompatible with that causal continuity of an agent's character with his conduct which is implied when we believe (surely with justice) that we can often tell the sort of thing a man will do from our knowledge of the sort of man he is.

We shall have to make our accounts with that

particular difficulty later. At this stage I wish merely to show that neither of the hypothetical propositions suggested—and I think the same could be shown for *any* hypothetical alternative—is an acceptable substitute for the categorical proposition "X could have acted otherwise" as the presupposition of moral responsibility.

Let us look first at the earlier suggestion—"X could have acted otherwise *if* he had chosen otherwise." Now clearly there are a great many acts with regard to which we are entirely satisfied that the agent is thus situated. We are often perfectly sure that—for this is all it amounts to—if X had chosen otherwise, the circumstances presented no external obstacle to the translation of that choice into action. For example, we often have no doubt at all that X, who in point of fact told a lie, could have told the truth *if* he had so chosen. But does our confidence on this score allay all legitimate doubts about whether X is really blameworthy? Does it entail that X is free in the sense required for moral responsibility? Surely not. The obvious question immediately arises: "But *could* X have *chosen* otherwise than he did?" It is doubt about the true answer to *that* question which leads most people to doubt the reality of moral responsibility. Yet on this crucial question the hypothetical proposition which is offered as a sufficient statement of the condition justifying the ascription of moral responsibility gives us no information whatsoever.

Indeed this hypothetical substitute for the categorical "X could have acted otherwise" seems to me to lack all plausibility unless one contrives to forget why it is, after all, that we ever come to feel fundamental doubts about man's moral responsibility. Such doubts are born, surely, when one becomes aware of certain reputable worldviews in religion or philosophy, or of certain reputable scientific beliefs, which in their several ways imply that man's actions are necessitated, and thus could not be otherwise than they in fact are. But clearly a doubt so based is not even touched by the recognition that a man could very often act otherwise *if* he so chose. That proposition is entirely compatible with the necessitarian theories which generate our doubt: indeed it is this very compatibility that has recommended it to some philosophers, who are reluctant to give up either moral responsibility or Determinism. The proposition which we *must* be able to affirm if moral praise or blame of X is to be justified is the categorical proposition that X could have acted otherwise because—not if—he could have chosen otherwise; or, since it is essentially the inner side of the act that matters, the proposition simply that X could have chosen otherwise.

For the second of the alternative formulae suggested we cannot spare more than a few moments. But its inability to meet the demands it is required to meet is almost transparent. "X could have acted otherwise," as a statement of a precondition of X's moral responsibility, really means (we are told) "X could have acted otherwise *if* he were differently constituted, or *if* he had been placed in different circumstances." It seems a sufficient reply to this to point out that the person whose moral responsibility is at issue is *X*; a specific individual, in a specific set of circumstances. It is totally irrelevant to *X*'s moral responsibility that we should be able to say that some person differently constituted from X, or X in a different set of circumstances, could have done something different from what X did.

3. Let me, then, briefly sum up the answer at which we have arrived to our question about the kind of freedom required to justify moral responsibility. It is that a man can be said to exercise free will in a morally significant sense only insofar as his chosen act is one of which he is the sole cause or author, and only if—in the straightforward, categorical sense of the phrase—he "could have chosen otherwise."

I confess that this answer is in some ways a disconcerting one. Disconcerting, because most of us, however objective we are in the actual conduct of our thinking, would *like* to be able to believe that moral responsibility is real: whereas the freedom required for moral responsibility, on the analysis we have given, is certainly far more difficult to establish than the freedom required on the analyses we found ourselves obliged to reject. If, e.g. moral freedom entails only that I could have acted otherwise *if* I had chosen otherwise, there is no real "problem" about it at all. I am "free" in the normal case where there is no external obstacle to prevent my translating the alternative choice into action, and not free in other cases. Still less is there a problem if all that moral freedom entails is that I could have acted oth-

erwise *if* I had been a differently constituted person, or been in different circumstances. Clearly I am *always* free in *this* sense of freedom. But, as I have argued, these so-called "freedoms" fail to give us the pre-conditions of moral responsibility, and hence leave the freedom of the traditional free-will problem, the freedom that people are really concerned about, precisely where it was.

. . . .

5. That brings me to the second, and more constructive, part of this lecture. From now on I shall be considering whether it is reasonable to believe that man does in fact possess a free will of the kind specified in the first part of the lecture. If so, just how and where within the complex fabric of the volitional life are we to locate it?—for although free will must presumably belong (if anywhere) to the volitional side of human experience, it is pretty clear from the way in which we have been forced to define it that it does not pertain simply to volition as such; not even to all volitions that are commonly dignified with the name of "choices". It has been, I think, one of the more serious impediments to profitable discussion of the Free Will problem that Libertarians and Determinists alike have so often failed to appreciate the comparatively narrow area within which the free will that is necessary to "save" morality is required to operate. It goes without saying that this failure has been gravely prejudicial to the case for Libertarianism. I attach a good deal of importance, therefore, to the problem of locating free will correctly within the volitional orbit. Its solution forestalls and annuls, I believe, some of the more tiresome clichés of Determinist criticism.

We saw earlier that Common Sense's practice of "making allowances" in its moral judgments for the influence of heredity and environment indicates Common Sense's conviction, both that a just moral judgment must discount determinants of choice over which the agent has no control, and also (since it still accepts moral judgments as legitimate) that *something* of moral relevance survives which can be regarded as genuinely self-originated. We are now to try to discover what this "something" is. And I think we may still usefully take Common Sense as our guide. Suppose one asks the ordinary intelligent citizen *why* he deems it proper to make allowances for X, whose heredity and/or environment are unfortunate. He will tend to reply, I think, in some such terms as these: that X has more and stronger temptations to deviate from what is right than Y or Z, who are normally circumstanced, so that he must put forth a *stronger moral effort* if he is to achieve the same level of external conduct. The intended implication seems to be that X is just as morally praiseworthy as Y or Z *if* he exerts an equivalent moral effort, even though he may not thereby achieve an equal success in conforming his will to the "concrete" demands of duty. And this implies, again, Common Sense's belief that *in moral effort* we have something for which a man is responsible *without qualification,* something that is *not* affected by heredity and environment but depends *solely* upon the self itself.

Now in my opinion Common Sense has here, in principle, hit upon the one and only defensible answer. Here, and here alone, so far as I can see, in the act of deciding whether to put forth or withhold the moral effort required to resist temptation and rise to duty, is to be found an act which is free in the sense required for moral responsibility; an act of which the self is sole author, and of which it is true to say that "it could be" (or, after the event, "could have been") "otherwise." Such is the thesis which we shall now try to establish.

6. The species of argument appropriate to the establishment of a thesis of this sort should fall, I think, into two phases. First, there should be a consideration of the evidence of the moral agent's own inner experience. What *is* the act of moral decision, and what does it imply, from the standpoint of the actual participant? Since there is no way of knowing the act of moral decision—or for that matter any other form of activity—except by actual participation in it, the evidence of the subject, or agent, is on an issue of this kind of primary importance. It can hardly, however, be taken as in itself conclusive. For even if that evidence should be overwhelmingly to the effect that moral decision does have the characteristics required by moral freedom, the question is bound to be raised—and in view of considerations from other quarters pointing in a contrary direction is *rightly* raised—Can we *trust* the evidence in inner experience? That brings us to what will be the second phase of the argument. We shall have to go on to show, if we are to make good our case, that the

extraneous considerations so often supposed to be fatal to the belief in moral freedom are in fact innocuous to it.

In the light of what was said [previously] about the self's experience of moral decision as a *creative* activity, we may perhaps be absolved from developing the first phase of the argument at any great length. The appeal is throughout to one's own experience in the actual taking of the moral decision in the situation of moral temptation. "Is it possible," we must ask, "for anyone so circumstanced to *dis*believe that he could be deciding otherwise?" The answer is surely not in doubt. When we decide to exert moral effort to resist a temptation, we feel quite certain that we *could* withhold the effort; just as, if we decide to withhold the effort and yield to our desires, we feel quite certain that we *could* exert it—otherwise we should not blame ourselves afterwards for having succumbed. It may be, indeed, that this conviction is mere self-delusion. But that is not at the moment our concern. It is enough at present to establish that the act of deciding to exert or to withhold moral effort, as we know it from the inside in actual moral living, belongs to the category of acts which "could have been otherwise."

Mutatis mutandis, the same reply is forthcoming if we ask, "Is it possible for the moral agent in the taking of his decision to *dis*believe that he is the *sole* author of that decision?" Clearly he cannot disbelieve that it is *he* who takes the decision. That, however, is not in itself sufficient to enable him, on reflection, to regard himself as *solely* responsible for the act. For his "character" as so far formed might conceivably be a factor in determining it, and no one can suppose that the constitution of his "character" is uninfluenced by circumstances of heredity and environment with which *he* has nothing to do. But as we pointed out . . . , the very essence of the moral decision as it is experienced is that it is a decision whether or not to *oppose* our character. I think we are entitled to say, therefore, that the act of moral decision is one in which the self is for itself not merely "author" but "sole author."

7. We may pass on, then, to the second phase of our constructive argument; and this will demand more elaborate treatment. Even if a moral agent *qua* making a moral decision in the situation of "temptation" cannot help believing that he has free will in the sense at issue—a moral freedom between real alternatives, between genuinely open possibilities— are there, nevertheless, objections to a freedom of this kind so cogent that we are bound to distrust the evidence of "inner experience"?

I begin by drawing attention to a simple point whose significance tends, I think, to be underestimated. If the phenomenological analysis we have offered is substantially correct, no one while functioning as a moral agent can help believing that he enjoys free will. Theoretically he may be completely convinced by Determinist arguments, but when actually confronted with a personal situation of conflict between duty and desire he is quite certain that it lies with him here and now whether or not he will rise to duty. It follows that if Determinists could produce convincing theoretical arguments against a free will of this kind, the awkward predicament would ensue that man has to deny as a theoretical being what he had to assert as a practical being. Now I think the Determinist ought to be a good deal more worried about this than he usually is. He seems to imagine that a strong case on general theoretical grounds is enough to prove that the "practical" belief in free will, even if inescapable for us as practical beings, is mere illusion. But in fact it proves nothing of the sort. There is no reason whatever why a belief that we find ourselves obliged to hold *qua* practical beings should be required to give way before a belief which we find ourselves obliged to hold *qua* theoretical beings; or, for that matter, vice versa. All that the theoretical arguments of Determinism can prove, unless they are reinforced by a refutation of the phenomenological analysis that supports Libertarianism, is that there is a radical conflict between the theoretical and the practical sides of man's nature, an antinomy at the very heart of the self. And this is a state of affairs with which no one can easily rest satisfied. I think therefore that the Determinist ought to concern himself a great deal more than he does with phenomenological analysis, in order to show, if he can, that the assurance of free will is not really an inexpungable element in man's practical consciousness. There is just as much obligation upon him, convinced though he may be of the soundness of his theoretical arguments, to expose the errors of the Libertarian's phenomenological

analysis, as there is upon us, convinced though we may be of the soundness of the Libertarian's phenomenological analysis, to expose the errors of the Determinist's theoretical arguments.

8. However, we must at once begin the discharge of our own obligation. The rest of this lecture will be devoted to trying to show that the arguments which seem to carry most weight with Determinists are, to say the least of it, very far from compulsive.

Fortunately a good many of the arguments which at an earlier time in the history of philosophy would have been strongly urged against us make almost no appeal to the bulk of philosophers today, and we may here pass them by. That applies to any criticism of "open possibilities" based on a metaphysical theory about the nature of the universe as a whole. Nobody today *has* a metaphysical theory about the nature of the universe as a whole! It applies also, with almost equal force, to criticisms based upon the universality of causal law as a supposed postulate of science. There have always been, in my opinion, sound philosophic reasons for doubting the validity, as distinct from the convenience, of the causal postulate in its universal form, but at the present time, when scientists themselves are deeply divided about the need for postulating causality even within their own special field, we shall do better to concentrate our attention upon criticisms which are more confidently advanced. I propose to ignore also, on different grounds, the type of criticism of free will that is sometimes advanced from the side of religion, based upon religious postulates of Divine Omnipotence and Omniscience. So far as I can see, a postulate of human freedom is every bit as necessary to meet certain religious demands (e.g. to make sense of the "conviction of sin"), as postulates of Divine Omniscience and Omnipotence are to meet certain other religious demands. If so, then it can hardly be argued that religious experience as such tells more strongly against than for the position we are defending; and we may be satisfied, in the present context, to leave the matter there. It will be more profitable to discuss certain arguments which contemporary philosophers do think important, and which recur with a somewhat monotonous regularity in the literature of anti-Libertarianism.

These arguments can, I think, be reduced in

principle to no more than two: first, the argument from "predictability"; second, the argument from the alleged meaninglessness of an act supposed to be the self's act and yet not an expression of the self's character. Contemporary criticism of free will seems to me to consist almost exclusively of variations on these two themes. I shall deal with each in turn.

9. On the first we touched in passing at an earlier stage. Surely it is beyond question (the critic urges) that when we know a person intimately we can foretell with a high degree of accuracy how he will respond to at least a large number of practical situations. One feels safe in predicting that one's dog-loving friend will not use his boot to repel the little mongrel that comes yapping at his heels; or again that one's wife will not pass with incurious eyes (or indeed pass at all) the new hat-shop in the city. So to behave would not be (as we say) "in character." But, so the criticism runs, you with your doctrine of "genuinely open possibilities," of a free will by which the self can diverge from its own character, remove all rational basis from such prediction. You require us to make the absurd supposition that the success of countless predictions of the sort in the past has been mere matter of chance. If you *really* believed in your theory, you would not be surprised if tomorrow your friend with the notorious horror of strong drink should suddenly exhibit a passion for whisky and soda, or if your friend whose taste for reading has hitherto been satisfied with the sporting columns of the newspapers should be discovered on a fine Saturday afternoon poring over the works of Hegel. But of course you *would* be surprised. Social life would be sheer chaos if there were not well-grounded social expectations; and social life is not sheer chaos. Your theory is hopelessly wrecked upon obvious facts.

Now whether or not this criticism holds good against some versions of Libertarian theory I need not here discuss. It is sufficient if I can make it clear that against the version advanced in this lecture according to which free will is localised in a relatively narrow field of operation, the criticism has no relevance whatsoever.

Let us remind ourselves briefly of the setting within which, on our view, free will functions. There is X, the course which we believe we ought to follow, and Y, the course towards which we feel our desire is strongest. The freedom which we ascribe to the agent is the freedom to put forth or refrain from putting forth the moral effort required to resist the pressure of desire and do what he thinks he ought to do.

But then there is surely an immense range of practical situations—covering by far the greater part of life—in which there is no question of a conflict within the self between what he most desires to do and what he thinks he ought to do? Indeed such conflict is a comparatively rare phenomenon for the majority of men. Yet over that whole vast range there is nothing whatever in our version of Libertarianism to prevent our agreeing that character determines conduct. In the absence, real or supposed, of any "moral" issue, what a man chooses will be simply that course which, after such reflection as seems called for, he deems most likely to bring him what he most strongly desires; and that is the same as to say the course to which his present character inclines him.

Over by far the greater area of human choices, then, our theory offers no more barrier to successful prediction on the basis of character than any other theory. For where there is no clash of strongest desire with duty, the free will we are defending has no business. There is just nothing for it to do.

But what about the situations—rare enough though they may be—in which there *is* this clash and in which free will does therefore operate? Does our theory entail that there at any rate, as the critic seems to suppose, "anything may happen"?

Not by any manner of means. In the first place, and by the very nature of the case, the range of the agent's possible choices is bounded by what he thinks he ought to do on the one hand, and what he most strongly desires on the other. The freedom claimed for him is a freedom of decision to make or withhold the effort required to do what he thinks he ought to do. There is no question of a freedom to act in some "wild" fashion, out of all relation to his characteristic beliefs and desires. This so-called "freedom of caprice," so often charged against the Libertarian, is, to put it bluntly, a sheer figment of the critic's imagination, with no *habitat* in serious Libertarian theory. Even in situations where free will does come into play it is perfectly possible, on a view like ours, given the appropriate knowledge of a man's character, to predict within certain limits how he will respond.

But "probable" prediction in such situations can, I think, go further than this. It is obvious that where desire and duty are at odds, the felt "gap" (as it were) between the two may vary enormously in breadth in different cases. The moderate drinker and the chronic tippler may each want another glass, and each deem it his duty to abstain, but the felt gap between desire and duty in the case of the former is trivial beside the great gulf which is felt to separate them in the case of the latter. Hence it will take a far harder moral effort for the tippler than for the moderate drinker to achieve the same external result of abstention. So much is matter of common agreement. And we are entitled, I think, to take it into account in prediction, on the simple principle that the harder the moral effort required to resist desire the less likely it is to occur. Thus in the example taken, most people would predict that the tippler will very probably succumb to his desires, whereas there is a reasonable likelihood that the moderate drinker will make the comparatively slight effort needed to resist them. So long as the prediction does not pretend to more than a measure of probability, there is nothing in our theory which would disallow it.

I claim, therefore, that the view of free will I have been putting forward is consistent with predictability of conduct on the basis of character over a very wide field indeed. And I make the further claim that the field will cover all the situations of life concerning which there is any empirical evidence that successful prediction is possible.

10. Let us pass on to consider the second main line of criticism. This is, I think, much the more illuminating of the two, if only because it compels the Libertarian to make explicit certain concepts which are indispensable to him, but which, being desperately hard to state clearly, are apt not to be stated at all. The critic's fundamental point might be stated somewhat as follows:

"Free will as you describe it is completely unintelligible. On your own showing no *reason* can be given, because there just *is* no reason, why a man decides to exert rather than to withhold moral effort, or vice versa. But such an act—or more properly, such an 'occurrence'—it is nonsense to speak of as an act of a *self*. If there is nothing in the self's

character to which it is, even in principle, in any way traceable, the self has nothing to do with it. Your so-called 'freedom,' therefore, so far from supporting the self's moral responsibility, destroys it as surely as the crudest Determinism could do."

If we are to discuss this criticism usefully, it is important, I think, to begin by getting clear about two different senses of the word "intelligible".

If, in the first place, we mean by an "intelligible" act one whose occurrence is in principle capable of being inferred, since it follows necessarily from something (though we may not know in fact from what), then it is certainly true that the Libertarian's free will is unintelligible. But that is only saying, is it not, that the Libertarian's "free" act is not an act which follows necessarily from something! This can hardly rank as a *criticism* of Libertarianism. It is just a description of it. That there can be nothing unintelligible in *this* sense is precisely what the Determinist has got to *prove*.

Yet it is surprising how often the critic of Libertarianism involves himself in this circular mode of argument. Repeatedly it is urged against the Libertarian, with a great air of triumph, that on his view he can't say *why* I now decide to rise to duty, or now decide to follow my strongest desire in defiance of duty. Of course he can't. If he could he wouldn't *be* a Libertarian. To "account for" a "free" act is a contradiction in terms. A free will is *ex hypothesi* the sort of thing of which the request for an *explanation* is absurd. The assumption that an explanation must be in principle possible for the act of moral decision deserves to rank as a classic example of the ancient fallacy of "begging the question."

But the critic usually has in mind another sense of the word "unintelligible". He is apt to take it for granted that an act which is unintelligible in the *above* sense (as the morally free act of the Libertarian undoubtedly is) is unintelligible in the *further* sense that we can attach no meaning to it. And this is an altogether more serious matter. If it could really be shown that the Libertarian's "free will" were unintelligible in this sense of being meaningless, that, for myself at any rate, would be the end of the affair. Libertarianism would have been conclusively refuted.

But it seems to me manifest that this can *not* be shown. The critic has allowed himself, I submit, to become the victim of a widely accepted but fundamentally vicious assumption. He has assumed that whatever is meaningful must exhibit its meaningfulness to those who view it from the standpoint of external observation. Now if one chooses thus to limit one's self to the rôle of external observer, it is, I think, perfectly true that one can attach no meaning to an act which is the act of something we call a "self" and yet follows from nothing in that self's character. But then *why should we* so limit ourselves, when what is under consideration is a subjective activity? For the apprehension of subjective acts there is *another* standpoint available, that of *inner experience*, of the practical consciousness in its actual functioning. If our free will should turn out to be something to which we can attach a meaning from *this* standpoint, no more is required. And no more ought to be expected. For I must repeat that only from the inner standpoint of living experience *could* anything of the nature of "activity" be directly grasped. Observation from without is in the nature of the case impotent to apprehend the active *qua* active. We can from without observe sequences of states. If into these we read activity (as we sometimes do), this can only be on the basis of what we discern in ourselves from the inner standpoint. It follows that if anyone insists upon taking his criterion of the meaningful simply from the standpoint of external observation, he is really deciding in advance of the evidence that the notion of activity, and a fortiori the notion of a free will, is "meaningless." He looks for the free act through a medium which is in the nature of the case incapable of revealing it, and then, because inevitably he doesn't find it, he declares that it doesn't exist!

But if, as we surely ought in this context, we adopt the inner standpoint, then (I am suggesting) things appear in a totally different light. From the inner standpoint, it seems to me plain, there is no difficulty whatever in attaching meaning to an act which is the self's act and which nevertheless does not follow from the self's character. So much I claim has been established by the phenomenological analysis . . . of the act of moral decision in face of moral temptation. It is thrown into particularly clear relief where the moral decision is to make the moral effort required to rise to duty. For the very function of moral effort, as it appears to the agent engaged in the act, is to enable the self to act against the line of least resistance, against the line to which his character as so far formed most strongly inclines him.

But if the self is thus conscious here of *combating* his formed character, he surely cannot possibly suppose that the act, although his own act, *issues from* his formed character? I submit, therefore, that the self knows very well indeed—from the inner standpoint—what is meant by an act which is the *self's* act and which nevertheless does not follow from the self's *character*.

What this implies—and it seems to me to be an implication of cardinal importance for any theory of the self that aims at being more than superficial—is that the nature of the self is for itself something more than just its character as so far formed. The "nature" of the self and what we commonly call the "character" of the self are by no means the same thing, and it is utterly vital that they should not be confused. The "nature" of the self comprehends, but is not without remainder reducible to, its "character"; it must, if we are to be true to the testimony of our experience of it, be taken as including *also* the authentic creative power of fashioning and re-fashioning "character."

The misguided, and as a rule quite uncritical, belittlement, of the evidence offered by inner experience has, I am convinced, been responsible for more bad argument by the opponents of Free Will than has any other single factor. How often, for example, do we find the Determinist critic saying, in effect, "*Either* the act follows necessarily upon precedent states, *or* it is a mere matter of chance and accordingly of no moral significance." The disjunction is invalid, for it does not exhaust the possible alternatives. It seems to the critic to do so only because he *will* limit himself to the standpoint which is proper, and indeed alone possible, in dealing with the physical world, the standpoint of the external observer. If only he would allow himself to assume the standpoint which is not merely proper for, but necessary to, the apprehension of subjective activity, the inner standpoint of the practical consciousness in its actual functioning, he would find himself obliged to recognise the falsity of his disjunction. Reflection upon the act of moral decision as apprehended from the inner standpoint would force him to recognise a *third* possibility, as remote from chance as from necessity, that, namely, of *creative activity*, in which (as I have ventured to express it) nothing determines the act save the agent's doing of it.

11. There we must leave the matter. But as this lecture has been, I know, somewhat densely packed, it may be helpful if I conclude by reminding you, in bald summary, of the main things I have been trying to say. Let me set them out in so many successive theses.

   (1) The freedom which is at issue in the traditional Free Will problem is the freedom which is presupposed in moral responsibility.

   (2) Critical reflection upon carefully considered attributions of moral responsibility reveals that the only freedom that will do is a freedom which permits to inner acts of choice, and that these acts must be acts (*a*) of which the self is *sole* author, and (*b*) which the self could have performed otherwise.

   (3) From phenomenological analysis of the situation of moral temptation we find that the self as engaged in this situation is inescapably convinced that it possesses a freedom of precisely the specified kind, located in the decision to exert or withhold the moral effort needed to rise to duty where the pressure of its desiring nature is felt to urge it in a contrary direction.

   (4) Of the two types of Determinist criticism which seem to have most influence today, that based on the predictability of much human behaviour fails to touch a Libertarianism which confines the area of free will as above indicated. Libertarianism so understood is compatible with all the predictability that the empirical facts warrant. And:

   (5) The second main type of criticism, which alleges the "meaninglessness" of an act which is the self's act and which is yet not determined by the self's character, is based on a failure to appreciate that the standpoint of inner experience is not only legitimate but indispensable where what is at issue is the reality and nature of a subjective activity. The creative act of moral decision is inevitably meaningless to the mere external observer; but from the inner standpoint it is as real, and as significant, as anything in human experience.

Of Liberty and Necessity

DAVID HUME

—•—

Part I

It might reasonably be expected in questions which have been canvassed and disputed with great eagerness, since the first origin of science and philosophy, that the meaning of all the terms, at least, should have been agreed upon among the disputants; and our enquiries, in the course of two thousand years, been able to pass from words to the true and real subject of the controversy. For how easy may it seem to give exact definitions of the terms employed in reasoning, and make these definitions, not the mere sound of words, the object of future scrutiny and examination? But if we consider the matter more narrowly, we shall be apt to draw a quite opposite conclusion. From this circumstance

From *A Treatise of Human Nature*, edited by L.A. Selby-Bigge, 2nd edition revised by P. H. Nidditch. Copyright © 1978 by Oxford University Press. Reprinted by permission of the publisher.

alone, that a controversy has been long kept on foot, and remains still undecided, we may presume that there is some ambiguity in the expression, and that the disputants affix different ideas to the terms employed in the controversy. For as the faculties of the mind are supposed to be naturally alike in every individual; otherwise nothing could be more fruitless than to reason or dispute together; it were impossible, if men affix the same ideas to their terms, that they could so long form different opinions of the same subject; especially when they communicate their views, and each party turn themselves on all sides, in search of arguments which may give them the victory over their antagonists. It is true, if men attempt the discussion of questions which lie entirely beyond the reach of human capacity, such as those concerning the origin of worlds, or the economy of the intellectual system or region of spirits, they may long beat the air in their fruitless contests, and never arrive at any determinate conclusion. But if the question regard any subject of common life and experience, nothing, one would think, could preserve the dispute so long undecided but some ambiguous expressions, which keep the antagonists still at a distance, and hinder them from grappling with each other.

This has been the case in the long disputed question concerning liberty and necessity; and to so remarkable a degree that, if I be not much mistaken, we shall find, that all mankind, both learned and ignorant, have always been of the same opinion with regard to this subject, and that a few intelligible definitions would immediately have put an end to the whole controversy. I own that this dispute has been so much canvassed on all hands, and has led philosophers into such a labyrinth of obscure sophistry, that it is no wonder, if a sensible reader indulge his ease so far as to turn a deaf ear to the proposal of such a question, from which he can expect neither instruction nor entertainment. But the state of the argument here proposed may, perhaps, serve to renew his attention; as it has more novelty, promises at least some decision of the controversy, and will not much disturb his ease by any intricate or obscure reasoning.

I hope, therefore, to make it appear that all men have ever agreed in the doctrine both of necessity and of liberty, according to any reasonable sense, which can be put on these terms; and that the whole controversy has hitherto turned merely upon words. We shall begin with examining the doctrine of necessity.

It is universally allowed that matter, in all its operations, is actuated by a necessary force, and that every natural effect is so precisely determined by the energy of its cause that no other effect, in such particular circumstances, could possibly have resulted from it. The degree and direction of every motion is, by the laws of nature, prescribed with such exactness that a living creature may as soon arise from the shock of two bodies as motion in any other degree or direction than what is actually produced by it. Would we, therefore, form a just and precise idea of *necessity*, we must consider whence that idea arises when we apply it to the question of bodies.

It seems evident that, if all the scenes of nature were continually shifted in such a manner that no two events bore any resemblance to each other, but every object was entirely new, without any similitude to whatever had been seen before, we should never, in that case, have attained the least idea of necessity, or of a connexion among these objects. We might say, upon such a supposition, that one object or event has followed another; not that one was produced by the other. The relation of cause and effect must be utterly unknown to mankind. Inference and reasoning concerning the operations of nature would, from that moment, be at an end; and the memory and senses remain the only canals, by which the knowledge of any real existence could possibly have access to the mind. Our idea, therefore, of necessity and causation arises entirely from the uniformity observable in the operations of nature, where similar objects are constantly conjoined together, and the mind is determined by custom to infer the one from the appearance of the other. These two circumstances form the whole of that necessity, which we ascribe to matter. Beyond the constant *conjunction* of similar objects, and the consequent *inference* from one to the other, we have no notion of any necessity or connexion.

If it appear, therefore, that all mankind have ever allowed, without any doubt or hesitation, that these two circumstances take place in the voluntary actions of men, and in the operations of mind; it must follow, that all mankind have ever agreed in the doctrine of necessity, and that they have hitherto disputed, merely for not understanding each other.

As to the first circumstance, the constant and regular conjunction of similar events, we may possibly satisfy ourselves by the following considerations. It is universally acknowledged that there is a great uniformity among the actions of men, in all nations and ages, and that human nature remains still the same, in its principles and operations. The same motives always produce the same actions. The same events follow from the same causes. Ambition, avarice, self-love, vanity, friendship, generosity, public spirit: these passions, mixed in various degrees, and distributed through society, have been, from the beginning of the world, and still are, the source of all the actions and enterprises, which have ever been observed among mankind. Would you know the sentiments, inclinations, and course of life of the Greeks and Romans? Study well the temper and actions of the French and English: You cannot be much mistaken in transferring to the former *most* of the observations which you have made with regard to the latter. Mankind are so much the same, in all times and places, that history informs us of nothing new or strange in this particular. Its chief use is only to discover the constant and universal principles of human nature, by showing men in all varieties of circumstances and situations, and furnishing us with materials from which we may form our observations and become acquainted with the regular springs of human action and behaviour. These records or wars, intrigues, factions, and revolutions, are so many collections of experiments, by which the political or moral philosopher fixes the principles of his science, in the same manner as the physician or natural philosopher becomes acquainted with the nature of plants, minerals, and other external objects, by the experiments which he forms concerning them. Nor are the earth, water, and other elements, examined by Aristotle, and Hippocrates, more like to those which at present lie under our observation than the men described by Polybius and Tacitus are to those who now govern the world.

Should a traveller, returning from a far country, bring us an account of men, wholly different from any with whom we were ever acquainted; men, who were entirely divested of avarice, ambition, or revenge; who knew no pleasure but friendship, generosity, and public spirit; we should immediately, from these circumstances, detect the falsehood, and prove him a liar, with the same certainty as if he had stuffed his narration with stories of centaurs and dragons, miracles and prodigies. And if we would explode any forgery in history, we cannot make use of a more convincing argument, than to prove, that the actions ascribed to any person are directly contrary to the course of nature, and that no human motives, in such circumstances, could ever induce him to such a conduct. The veracity of Quintus Curtius is as much to be suspected, when he describes the supernatural courage of Alexander, by which he was hurried on singly to attack multitudes, as when he describes his supernatural force and activity, by which he was able to resist them. So readily and universally do we acknowledge a uniformity in human motives and actions as well as in the operations of body.

Hence likewise the benefit of that experience, acquired by long life and a variety of business and company, in order to instruct us in the principles of human nature, and regulate our future conduct, as well as speculation. By means of this guide, we mount up to the knowledge of men's inclinations and motives, from their actions, expressions, and even gestures; and again descend to the interpretation of their actions from our knowledge of their motives and inclinations. The general observations treasured up by a course of experience, give us the clue of human nature, and teach us to unravel all its intricacies. Pretexts and appearances no longer deceive us. Public declarations pass for the specious colouring of a cause. And though virtue and honour be allowed their proper weight and authority, that perfect disinterestedness, so often pretended to, is never expected in multitudes and parties; seldom in their leaders; and scarcely even in individuals of any rank or station. But were there no uniformity in human actions, and were every experiment which we could form of this kind irregular and anomalous, it were impossible to collect any general observations concerning mankind; and no experience, however accurately digested by reflection, would ever serve to any purpose. Why is the aged husbandman more skilful in his calling than the young beginner but because there is a certain uniformity in the operation of the sun, rain, and earth towards the production of vegetables; and experience teaches the old practitioner the rules by which this operation is governed and directed.

We must not, however, expect that this uniformity of human actions should be carried to such a length as that all men, in the same circumstances, will always act precisely in the same manner, without making any allowance for the diversity of characters, prejudices, and opinions. Such a uniformity in every particular, is found in no part of nature. On the contrary, from observing the variety of conduct in different men, we are enabled to form a greater variety of maxims, which still suppose a degree of uniformity and regularity.

Are the manners of men different in different ages and countries? We learn thence the great force of custom and education, which mould the human mind from its infancy and form it into a fixed and established character. Is the behaviour and conduct of the one sex very unlike that of the other? Is it thence we become acquainted with the different characters which nature has impressed upon the sexes, and which she preserves with constancy and regularity? Are the actions of the same person much diversified in the different periods of his life, from infancy to old age? This affords room for many general observations concerning the gradual change of our sentiments and inclinations, and the different maxims which prevail in the different ages of human creatures. Even the characters, which are peculiar to each individual, have a uniformity in their influence; otherwise our acquaintance with the persons and our observation of their conduct could never teach us their dispositions, or serve to direct our behaviour with regard to them.

I grant it possible to find some actions, which seem to have no regular connexion with any known motives, and are exceptions to all the measures of conduct which have ever been established for the government of men. But if we would willingly know what judgment should be formed of such irregular and extraordinary actions, we may consider the sentiments commonly entertained with regard to those irregular events which appear in the course of nature, and the operations of external objects. All causes are not conjoined to their usual effects with like uniformity. An artificer, who handles only dead matter, may be disappointed of his aim, as well as the politician, who directs the conduct of sensible and intelligent agents.

The vulgar, who take things according to their first appearance, attribute the uncertainty of events to such an uncertainty in the causes as makes the latter often fail of their usual influence; though they meet with no impediment in their operation. But philosophers, observing that, almost in every part of nature, there is contained a vast variety of springs and principles, which are hid, by reason of their minuteness or remoteness, find, that it is at least possible the contrariety of events may not proceed from any contingency in the cause, but from the secret operation of contrary causes. This possibility is converted into certainty by farther observation, when they remark that, upon an exact scrutiny, a contrariety of effects always betrays a contrariety of causes, and proceeds from their mutual opposition. A peasant can give no better reason for the stopping of any clock or watch than to say that it does not commonly go right: But an artist easily perceives that the same force in the spring or pendulum has always the same influence on the wheels; but fails of its usual effect, perhaps by reason of a grain of dust, which puts a stop to the whole movement. From the observation of several parallel instances, philosophers form a maxim that the connexion between all causes and effects is equally necessary, and that its seeming uncertainty in some instances proceeds from the secret opposition of contrary causes.

Thus, for instance, in the human body, when the usual symptoms of health or sickness disappoint our expectation; when medicines operate not with their wonted powers; when irregular events follow from any particular cause; the philosopher and physician are not surprised at the matter, nor are even tempted to deny, in general, the necessity and uniformity of those principles by which the animal economy is conducted. They know that a human body is a mighty complicated machine: That many secret powers lurk in it, which are altogether beyond our comprehension: That to us it must often appear very uncertain in its operations: And that therefore the irregular events, which outwardly discover themselves, can be no proof that the laws of nature are not observed with the greatest regularity in its internal operations and government.

The philosopher, if he be consistent, must apply the same reasoning to the actions and volitions of intelligent agents. The most irregular and unexpected resolutions of men may frequently be accounted for by those who know every particular circumstance of their character and situation. A person of an obliging disposition gives a peevish answer: But he has the toothache, or has not dined. A stupid fellow discovers an uncommon alacrity in his carriage: But he has met with a sudden piece of good fortune. Or even when an action, as sometimes happens, cannot be particularly accounted for, either by the person himself or by others; we know, in general, that the characters of men are, to a certain degree, inconstant and irregular. This is, in a manner, the constant character of human nature; though it be applicable, in a more particular manner, to some persons who have no fixed rule for their conduct, but proceed in a continued course of caprice and inconstancy. The internal principles and motives may operate in a uniform manner, notwithstanding these seeming irregularities; in the same manner as the winds, rain, clouds, and other variations of the weather are supposed to be governed by steady principles; though not easily discoverable by human sagacity and enquiry.

Thus it appears, not only that the conjunction between motives and voluntary actions is as regular and uniform as that between the cause and effect in any part of nature; but also that this regular conjunction has been universally acknowledged among mankind, and has never been the subject of dispute, either in philosophy or common life. Now, as it is from past experience that we draw all inferences concerning the future, and as we conclude that objects will always be conjoined together which we find to have always been conjoined; it may seem superfluous to prove that this experienced uniformity in human actions is a source whence we draw *inferences* concerning them. But in order to throw the argument into a greater variety of lights we shall also insist, though briefly, on this latter topic.

The mutual dependence of men is so great in all societies that scarce any human action is entirely complete in itself, or is performed without some reference to the actions of others, which are requisite to make it answer fully the intention of the agent. The poorest artificer, who labours alone, expects at least the protection of the magistrate, to ensure him the enjoyment of the fruits of his labour. He also expects that, when he carries his goods to market, and offers them at a reasonable price, he shall find purchasers, and shall be able, by the money he acquires, to engage others to supply him with those commodities which are requisite for his subsistence. In proportion as men extend their dealings, and render their intercourse with others more complicated, they always comprehend, in their schemes of life, a greater variety of voluntary actions, which they expect, from the proper motives, to co-operate with their own. In all these conclusions they take their measures from past experience, in the same manner as in their reasonings concerning external objects; and firmly believe that men, as well as all the elements, are to continue, in their operations, the same that they have ever found them. A manufacturer reckons upon the labour of his servants for the execution of any work as much as upon the tools which he employs, and would be equally surprised were his expectations disappointed. In short, this experimental inference and reasoning concerning the actions of others enters so much into human life that no man, while awake, is ever a moment without employing it. Have we not reason, therefore, to affirm that all mankind have always agreed in the doctrine of necessity according to the foregoing definition and explication of it?

Nor have philosophers ever entertained a different opinion from the people in this particular. For, not to mention that almost every action of their life supposes that opinion, there are even few of the speculative parts of learning to which it is not essential. What would become of *history*, had we not a dependence on the veracity of the historian according to the experience which we have had of mankind? How could *politics* be a science, if laws and forms of government had not a uniform influence upon society? Where would be the foundation of *morals*, if particular characters had no certain or determinate power to produce particular sentiments, and if these sentiments had no constant operation on actions? And with what pretence could we employ our *criticism* upon any poet or polite author, if we could not pronounce the conduct and sentiments of his actors either natural or unnatural to such characters, and in such circumstances? It seems almost impossible, therefore, to engage either in science or action of any kind without acknowledging the doctrine of necessity, and this *inference* from motive to voluntary actions, from characters to conduct.

And indeed, when we consider how aptly *natural* and *moral* evidence link together, and form only one chain of argument, we shall make no scruple to allow that they are of the same nature, and derived from the same principles. A prisoner who has neither money nor interest, discovers the impossibility of his escape, as well when he considers the obstinacy of the gaoler, as the walls and bars with which he is surrounded; and, in all attempts for his freedom, chooses rather to work upon the stone and iron of the one, than upon the inflexible nature of the other. The same prisoner, when conducted to the scaffold, foresees his death as certainly from the constancy and fidelity of his guards, as from the operation of the axe or wheel. His mind runs along a certain train of ideas: The refusal of the soldiers to consent to his escape; the action of the executioner; the separation of the head and body; bleeding, convulsive motions, and death. Here is a connected chain of natural causes and voluntary actions; but the mind feels no difference between them in passing from one link to another: Nor is less certain of the future event than if it were connected with the objects present to the memory or senses, by a train of causes, cemented together by what we are pleased to call a *physical* necessity. The same experienced union has the same effect on the mind, whether the united objects be motives, volition, and actions; or figure and motion. We may change the name of things; but their nature and their operation on the understanding never change.

Were a man, whom I know to be honest and opulent, and with whom I live in intimate friendship, to come into my house, where I am surrounded with my servants, I rest assured that he is not to stab me before he leaves it in order to rob me of my silver standish; and I no more suspect this event than the falling of the house itself, which is new, and solidly built and founded—*But he may have been seized with a sudden and unknown frenzy.*—So may a sudden earthquake arise, and shake and tumble my house about my ears. I shall therefore change the suppositions. I shall say that I know with certainty that he is not to put his hand into the fire and hold it there till it be consumed: And this event, I think I can foretell with the same assurance, as that, if he throw himself out at the window, and meet with no obstruction, he will not remain a moment suspended in the air. No suspicion of an unknown frenzy can give the least possibility to the former event, which is so contrary to all the known principles of human nature. A man who at noon leaves his purse full of gold on the pavement at Charing-Cross, may as well expect that it will fly away like a feather, as that he will find it untouched an hour after. Above one half of human reasonings contain inferences of a similar nature, attended with more or less degrees of certainty proportioned to our experience of the usual conduct of mankind in such particular situations.

I have frequently considered, what could possibly be the reason why all mankind, though they have ever, without hesitation, acknowledged the doctrine of necessity in their whole practice and reasoning, have yet discovered such a reluctance to acknowledge it in words, and have rather shown a propensity, in all ages, to profess the contrary opinion. The matter, I think, may be accounted for after the following manner. If we examine the operations of body, and the production of effects from their causes, we shall find that all our faculties can never carry us farther in our knowledge of this relation than barely to observe that particular objects are *constantly conjoined* together, and that the mind is carried, by a *customary transition*, from the appearance of one to the belief of the other. But though this conclusion concerning human ignorance be the result of the strictest scrutiny of this subject, men still entertain a strong propensity to believe that they penetrate farther into the powers of nature, and perceive something like a necessary connexion between the cause and the effect. When again they turn their reflections towards the operations of their own minds, and *feel* no such connexion of the motive and the action; they are thence apt to suppose, that there is a difference between the effects which result from material force, and those which arise from thought and intelligence. But being once convinced that we know nothing farther of causation of any kind than merely the *constant conjunction* of objects, and the consequent *inference* of the mind from one to another, and finding that these two circumstances are universally allowed to have place in voluntary actions; we may be more easily led to own the same necessity common to all causes. And though this reasoning may contradict the systems of many philosophers, in ascribing necessity to the determinations of the will, we shall find, upon reflection, that they dissent from it in words only, not in their real sentiment. Necessity, according to the sense in which it is here taken, has never yet been rejected, nor can ever, I think, be rejected by any philosopher. It may only, perhaps, be pretended that the mind can perceive, in the operations of matter, some farther connexion between the cause and effect; and connexion that has not place in voluntary actions of intelligent beings. Now whether it be so or not, can only appear upon examination; and it is incumbent on these philosophers to make good their assertion, by defining or describing that necessity, and pointing it out to us in the operations of material causes.

It would seem, indeed, that men begin at the wrong end of this question concerning liberty and necessity, when they enter upon it by examining the faculties of the soul, the influence of the understanding, and the operations of the will. Let them first discuss a more simple question, namely, the operations of body and of brute unintelligent matter; and try whether they can there form any idea of causation and necessity, except that of a constant conjunction of objects, and subsequent inference of the mind from one to another. If these circumstances form, in reality, the whole of that necessity, which we conceive in matter, and if these circumstances be also universally acknowledged to take place in the operations of the mind, the dispute is at an end; at least, must be owned to be thenceforth merely verbal. But as long as we will rashly suppose, that we have some farther idea of necessity and causation in the operations of external objects; at the same time, that we can find nothing farther in the voluntary

actions of the mind; there is no possibility of bringing the question to any determinate issue, while we proceed upon so erroneous a supposition. The only method of undeceiving us is to mount up higher; to examine the narrow extent of science when applied to material causes; and to convince ourselves that all we know of them is the constant conjunction and inference above mentioned. We may, perhaps, find that it is with difficulty we are induced to fix such narrow limits to human understanding: But we can afterwards find no difficulty when we come to apply this doctrine to the actions of the will. For as it is evident that these have a higher regular conjunction with motives and circumstances and characters, and as we always draw inferences from one to the other, we must be obliged to acknowledge in words that necessity, which we have already avowed, in every deliberation of our lives, and in every step of our conduct and behaviour.[1]

But to proceed in this reconciling project with regard to the question of liberty and necessity; the most contentious question of metaphysics, the most contentious science; it will not require many words to prove, that all mankind have ever agreed in the doctrine of liberty as well as in that of necessity, and that the whole dispute, in this respect also, has been hitherto merely verbal. For what is meant by liberty, when applied to voluntary actions? We cannot surely mean that actions have so little connexion with motives, inclinations, and circumstances, that one does not follow with a certain degree of uniformity from the other, and that one affords no inference by which we can conclude the existence of the other. For these are plain and acknowledged matters of fact. By liberty, then, we can only mean *a power of acting or not acting, according to the determinations of the will*; that is, if we choose to remain at rest, we may; if we choose to move, we also may. Now this hypothetical liberty is universally allowed to belong to every one who is not a prisoner and in chains. Here, then, is no subject of dispute.

Whatever definition we may give of liberty, we should be careful to observe two requisite circumstances; *first*, that it be consistent with plain matter of fact; *secondly*, that it be consistent with itself. If we observe these circumstances, and render our definition intelligible, I am persuaded that all mankind will be found of one opinion with regard to it.

It is universally allowed that nothing exists without a cause of its existence, and that chance, when strictly examined, is a mere negative word, and means not any real power which has anywhere a being in nature. But it is pretended that some causes are necessary, some not necessary. Here then is the advantage of definitions. Let any one *define* a cause, without comprehending, as a part of the definition, a *necessary connexion* with its effect; and let him show distinctly the origin of the idea, expressed by the definition; and I shall readily give up the whole controversy. But if the foregoing explication of the matter be received, this must be absolutely impracticable. Had not objects a regular conjunction with each other, we should never have entertained any notion of cause and effect; and this regular conjunction produces that inference of the understanding, which is the only connexion, that we can have any comprehension of. Whoever attempts a definition of cause, exclusive of these circumstances, will be obliged either to employ unintelligible terms or such as are synonymous to the term which he endeavours to define.[2] And if the definition above mentioned be admitted; liberty, when opposed to necessity, not to constraint, is the same thing with chance; which is universally allowed to have no existence.

Part II

There is no method of reasoning more common, and yet none more blameable, than, in philosophical disputes, to endeavour the refutation of any hypothesis, by a pretence of its dangerous consequences to religion and morality. When any opinion leads to absurdities, it is certainly false; but it is not certain that an opinion is false, because it is of dangerous consequence. Such topics, therefore, ought entirely to be forborne; as serving nothing to the discovery of truth, but only to make the person of an antagonist odious. This I observe in general, without pretending to draw any advantage from it. I frankly submit to an examination of this kind, and shall venture to affirm that the doctrines, both of

necessity and of liberty, as above explained, are not only consistent with morality, but are absolutely essential to its support.

Necessity may be defined two ways, conformably to the two definitions of *cause*, of which it makes an essential part. It consists either in the constant conjunction of like objects, or in the inference of the understanding from one object to another. Now necessity, in both these senses, (which, indeed, are at bottom the same) has universally, though tacitly, in the schools, in the pulpit, and in common life, been allowed to belong to the will of man; and no one has ever pretended to deny that we can draw inferences concerning human actions, and that those inferences are founded on the experienced union of like actions, with like motives, inclinations, and circumstances. The only particular in which any one can differ, is, that either, perhaps, he will refuse to give the name of necessity to this property of human actions: But as long as the meaning is understood, I hope the word can do no harm: Or that he will maintain it possible to discover something farther in the operations of matter. But this, it must be acknowledged, can be of no consequence to morality or religion, whatever it may be to natural philosophy or metaphysics. We may here be mistaken in asserting that there is no idea of any other necessity of connexion in the actions of the mind, but what everyone does, and must readily allow of. We change no circumstance in the received orthodox system with regard to the will, but only in that with regard to material objects and causes. Nothing, therefore, can be more innocent, at least, than this doctrine.

All laws being founded on rewards and punishments, it is supposed as a fundamental principle, that these motives have a regular and uniform influence on the mind, and both produce the good and prevent the evil actions. We may give to this influence what name we please; but, as it is usually conjoined with the action, it must be esteemed a *cause*, and be looked upon as an instance of that necessity, which we would here establish.

The only proper object of hatred or vengeance is a person or creature, endowed with thought and consciousness; and when any criminal or injurious actions excite that passion, it is only by their relation to the person, or connexion with him. Actions are, by their very nature, temporary and perishing; and where they proceed not from some *cause* in the character and disposition of the person who performed them, they can neither redound to his honour, if good; nor infamy, if evil. The actions themselves may be blameable; they may be contrary to all the rules of morality and religion: But the person is not answerable for them; and as they proceed from nothing in him that is durable and constant, and leave nothing of that nature behind them, it is impossible he can, upon their account, become the object of punishment or vengeance. According to the principle, therefore, which denies necessity, and consequently causes, a man is as pure and untainted, after having committed the most horrid crime, as at the first moment of his birth, nor is his character anywise concerned in his actions, since they are not derived from it, and the wickedness of the one can never be used as a proof of the depravity of the other.

Men are not blamed for such actions as they perform ignorantly and casually, whatever may be the consequences. Why? but because the principles of these actions are only momentary, and terminate in them alone. Men are less blamed for such actions as they perform hastily and unpremeditately than for such as proceed from deliberation. For what reason? but because a hasty temper, though a constant cause or principle in the mind, operates only by intervals, and infects not the whole character. Again, repentance wipes off every crime, if attended with a reformation of life and manners. How is this to be accounted for? but by asserting that actions render a person criminal merely as they are proofs of criminal principles in the mind; and when, by an alteration of these principles, they cease to be just proofs, they likewise cease to be criminal. But, except upon the doctrine of necessity, they never were just proofs, and consequently never were criminal.

It will be equally easy to prove, and from the same arguments, that *liberty*, according to that definition above mentioned, in which all men agree, is also essential to morality, and that no human actions, where it is wanting, are susceptible of any moral qualities, or can be the objects either of approbation or dislike. For as actions are objects of our moral sentiment, so far only as they are indications of the internal character, passions, and affections; it is impossible that they can give rise either to praise or blame, where they proceed not from these principles, but are derived altogether from external violence.

I pretend not to have obviated or removed all objections to this theory, with regard to necessity and liberty. I can foresee other objections, derived from topics which have not here been treated of. It may be said, for instance, that, if voluntary actions be subjected to the same laws of necessity with the operations of matter, there is a continued chain of necessary causes, pre-ordained and pre-determined, reaching from the original cause of all to every single volition of every human creature. No contingency anywhere in the universe; no indifference; no liberty. While we act, we are, at the same time, acted upon. The ultimate Author of all our volitions is the Creator of the world, who first bestowed motion on this immense machine, and placed all beings in that particular position, whence every subsequent event, by an inevitable necessity, must result. Human actions, therefore, either can have no moral turpitude at all, as proceeding from so good a cause; or if they have any turpitude, they must involve our Creator in the same guilt, while he is acknowledged to be their ultimate cause and author. For as a man, who fired a mine, is answerable for all the consequences whether the train he employed be long or short; so wherever a continued chain of necessary causes is fixed, that Being, either finite or infinite, who produces the first, is likewise the author of all the rest, and must both bear the blame and acquire the praise which belong to them. Our clear and unalterable ideas of morality establish this rule, upon unquestionable reasons, when we examine the consequences of any human action; and these reasons must still have greater force when applied to the volitions and intentions of a Being infinitely wise and powerful. Ignorance or impotence may be pleaded for so limited a creature as man; but those imperfections have no place in our Creator. He foresaw, he ordained, he intended all those actions of men, which we so rashly pronounce criminal. And we must therefore conclude, either that they are not criminal, or that the Deity, not man, is accountable for them. But as either of these positions is absurd and impious, it follows, that the doctrine from which they are deduced cannot possibly be true, as being liable to all the same objections. An absurd consequence, if necessary, proves the original doctrine to be absurd; in the same manner as criminal actions render criminal the original cause, if the connexion between them be necessary and evitable.

This objection consists of two parts, which we shall examine separately; *First*, that, if human actions can be traced up, by a necessary chain, to the Deity, they can never be criminal; on account of the infinite perfection of that Being from whom they are derived, and who can intend nothing but what is altogether good and laudable. Or, *Secondly*, if they be criminal, we must retract the attribute of perfection, which we ascribe to the Deity, and must acknowledge him to be the ultimate author of guilt and moral turpitude in all his creatures.

The answer to the first objection seems obvious and convincing. There are many philosophers who, after an exact scrutiny of all the phenomena of nature, conclude, that the WHOLE, considered as one system, is, in every period of its existence, ordered with perfect benevolence; and that the utmost possible happiness will, in the end, result to all created beings, without any mixture of positive or absolute ill or misery. Every physical ill, say they, makes an essential part of this benevolent system, and could not possibly be removed, even by the Deity himself, considered as a wise agent, without giving entrance to greater ill, or excluding greater good, which will result from it. From this theory, some philosophers, and the ancient *Stoics* among the rest, derived a topic of consolation under all afflictions, while they taught their pupils that those ills under which they laboured were, in reality, goods to the universe; and that to an enlarged view, which could comprehend the whole system of nature, every event became an object of joy and exultation. But though this topic be specious and sublime, it was soon found in practice weak and ineffectual. You would surely more irritate than appease a man lying under the racking pains of the gout by preaching up to him the rectitude of those general laws, which produced the malignant humours in his body, and led them through the proper canals, to the sinews and nerves, where they now excite such acute torments. These en-

larged views may, for a moment, please the imagination of a speculative man, who is placed in ease and security; but neither can they dwell with constancy on his mind, even though undisturbed by the emotions of pain or passion; much less can they maintain their ground when attacked by such powerful antagonists. The affections take a narrower and more natural survey of their object; and by an economy, more suitable to the infirmity of human minds, regard alone the beings around us, and are actuated by such events as appear good or ill to the private system.

The case is the same with *moral* as with *physical* ill. It cannot reasonably be supposed, that those remote considerations, which are found of so little efficacy with regard to one, will have a more powerful influence with regard to the other. The mind of man is so formed by nature that, upon the appearance of certain characters, dispositions, and actions, it immediately feels the sentiment of approbation or blame; nor are there any emotions more essential to its frame and constitution. The characters which engage our approbation are chiefly such as contribute to the peace and security of human society; as the characters which excite blame are chiefly such as tend to public detriment and disturbance: Whence it may reasonably be presumed, that the moral sentiments arise, either mediately or immediately, from a reflection of these opposite interests. What though philosophical meditations establish a different opinion or conjecture; that everything is right with regard to the WHOLE, and that the qualities, which disturb society, are, in the main, as beneficial, and are as suitable to the primary intention of nature as those which more directly promote its happiness and welfare? Are such remote and uncertain speculations able to counterbalance the sentiments which arise from the natural and immediate view of the objects? A man who is robbed of a considerable sum; does he find his vexation for the loss anywise diminished by these sublime reflections? Why then should his moral resentment against the crime be supposed incompatible with them? Or why should not the acknowledgment of a real distinction between vice and virtue be reconcilable to all speculative systems of philosophy, as well as that of a real distinction between personal beauty and deformity? Both these distinctions are founded in the natural sentiments of the human mind: And these sentiments are not to be controlled or altered by any philosophical theory or speculation whatsoever.

The *second* objection admits not of so easy and satisfactory an answer; nor is it possible to explain distinctly, how the Deity can be the mediate cause of all the actions of men, without being the author of sin and moral turpitude. These are mysteries, which mere natural and unassisted reason is very unfit to handle; and whatever system she embraces, she must find herself involved in inextricable difficulties, and even contradictions, at every step which she takes with regard to such subjects. To reconcile the indifference and contingency of human actions with prescience; or to defend absolute decrees, and yet free the Deity from being the author of sin, has been found hitherto to exceed all the power of philosophy. Happy, if she be thence sensible of her temerity, when she pries into these sublime mysteries; and leaving a scene so full of obscurities and perplexities, return, with suitable modesty, to her true and proper province, the examination of common life; where she will find difficulties enough to employ her enquiries, without launching into so boundless an ocean of doubt, uncertainty, and contradiction!

NOTES

1. The prevalence of the doctrine of liberty may be accounted for, from another cause, viz, a false sensation or seeming experience which we have, or may have, of liberty or indifference, in many of our actions. The necessity of any action, whether of matter or of mind, is not, properly speaking, a quality in the agent, but in any thinking or intelligent being, who may consider the action; and it consists chiefly in the determination of his thoughts to infer the existence of that action from some preceding objects; as liberty, when opposed to necessity, is nothing but the want of that determination, and a certain looseness or indifference, which we feel, in passing, or not passing, from the idea of one object to that of any succeeding one. Now we may observe, that though, in *reflecting* on human actions, we seldom feel such a looseness, or indifference, but are commonly able to infer them with considerable certainty from their motives, and from the dispositions of the agent; yet it frequently happens, that, in *performing* the actions themselves, we are sensible of something like it: And as all resembling objects are readily taken for each other, this has been employed as a demonstrative and even intuitive proof of human liberty. We feel, that our actions are subject to our will, on most occasions; and imagine we feel, that the will itself is subject to nothing, because, when by a denial of it we are provoked to try, we feel, that it moves easily every way, and produces an image of itself (or a *Velleïty*, as it is called in the schools) even on that side, on which it did not settle. This image, or faint motion, we persuade ourselves, could, at that time, have been compleated into the thing itself; because, should that be denied, we find, upon a second trial, that, at present, it can. We consider not, that the fantastical desire of shewing liberty, is here the motive of our actions. And it seems certain, that, however we may imagine we feel a liberty within ourselves, a spectator can commonly infer our actions from our motives and character; and even where he cannot, he concludes in general, that he might, were he perfectly acquainted with every circumstance of our situation and temper, and the most secret springs of our complexion and disposition. Now this is the very essence of necessity, according to the foregoing doctrine.

2. Thus, if a cause be defined, *that which produces any thing*; it is easy to observe, that *producing* is synonimous to *causing*. In like manner, if a cause be defined, *that by which any thing exists*; this is liable to the same objection. For what is meant by these words, *by which*? Had it been said, that a cause is *that* after which *any thing constantly exists*; we should have understood the terms. For this is, indeed, all we know of the matter. And this constancy forms the very essence of necessity, nor have we any other idea of it.

Freedom and Determinism

RICHARD TAYLOR

Richard Taylor (1919–   ) is the author of *Metaphysics*, and *Freedom*, *Anarchy and the Law* and other works on problems in metaphysics and ethics.

—•—

IF I CONSIDER THE WORLD OR ANY part of it at any particular moment, it seems certain that it is perfectly determinate in every detail. There is no vagueness, looseness, or ambiguity. There is, indeed, vagueness, and even error, in my conceptions of reality, but not in reality itself. A lilac bush, which surely has a certain exact number of blossoms, appears to me only to have many blossoms, and I do not know how many. Things seen in the distance appear of indefinite form, and often of a color and size which in fact they have not. Things near the border of my visual field seem to me vague and amorphous, and I can never even say exactly where that border itself is, it is so indefinite and vague. But all such indeterminateness resides solely in my conceptions and ideas; the world itself shares none of it. The sea, at any exact time and place, has exactly a certain salinity and temperature, and every grain of sand on its shore is exactly disposed with respect to all the others. The wind at any point in space has at any moment a certain direction and force, not more nor less. It matters not whether these properties and relations are known to anyone. A field of wheat at any moment contains just an exact number of ripening grains, each having reached just the ripeness it exhibits, each presenting a determinate color and shade, an exact shape and mass. A man, too, at any given point in his life, is perfectly determinate to the minutest cells of his body. My own brain, nerves—even my thoughts, intentions, and feelings—are at any moment just what they then specifically are. These thoughts might, to be

sure, be vague and even false as representations, but as thoughts they are not, and even a false idea is no less an exact and determinate idea than a true one.

Nothing seems more obvious. But if I now ask *why* the world and all its larger or smaller parts are this moment just what they are, the answer comes to mind: Because the world, the moment before, was precisely what it then was. Given exactly what went before, the world, it seems, could now be none other than it is. And what it was a moment before, in all its larger and minuter parts, was the consequence of what had gone just before then, and so on, back to the very beginning of the world, if it had a beginning, or through an infinite past time, in case it had not. In any case, the world as it now is, and every part of it, and every detail of every part, would seem to be the only world that now could be, given just what it has been.

Determinism

Reflections such as these suggest that, in the case of everything that exists, there are antecedent conditions, known or unknown, given which that thing could not be other than it is. This is an exact statement of the metaphysical thesis of determinism. More loosely, it says that everything, including every cause, is the effect of some cause or causes; or that everything is not only determinate but causally determined. The statement, moreover, makes no allowance for time, for past, or for future. Hence, if true, it holds not only for all things that have existed but for all things that do or ever will exist.

Of course men rarely think of such a principle, and hardly one in a thousand will ever formulate it to himself in words. Yet all men do seem to assume it in their daily affairs, so much so that some philosophers have declared it an a priori principle of the understanding, that is, something that is known independently of experience, while others have deemed it to be at least a part of the common sense of mankind. Thus, when I hear a noise I look up to see where it came from. I never suppose that it was just a noise that came from nowhere and had no cause. All men do the same—even animals, though they have never once thought about metaphysics or the principle of universal determinism. Men believe, or at least act as though they believed, that things have causes, without exception. When a child or animal touches a hot stove for the first time, it unhesitatingly believes that the pain then felt was caused by that stove, and so firm and immediate is that belief that hot stoves are avoided ever after. We all use our metaphysical principles, whether we think of them or not, or are even capable of thinking of them. If I have a bodily or other disorder— a rash, for instance, or a fever or a phobia—I consult a physician for a diagnosis and explanation, in the hope that the cause of it might be found and removed or moderated. I am never tempted to suppose that such things just have no causes, arising from nowhere, else I would take no steps to remove the causes. The principle of determinism is here, as in everything else, simply assumed, without being thought about.

Determinism and Human Behavior

I am a part of the world. So is each of the cells and minute parts of which I am composed. The principle of determinism, then, in case it is true, applies to me and to each of those minute parts, no less than to the sand, wheat, winds, and waters of which we have spoken. There is no particular difficulty in thinking so, as long as I consider only what are sometimes called the "purely physiological" changes of my body, like growth, the pulse, glandular secretions, and the like. But what of my thoughts and ideals? And what of my behavior that is supposed to be deliberate, purposeful, and perhaps morally

significant? These are all changes of my own being, changes that I undergo, and if these are all but the consequences of the conditions under which they occur, and these conditions are the only ones that could have obtained, given the state of the world just before and when they arose, what now becomes of my responsibility for my behavior and of the control over my conduct that I fancy myself to possess? What am I but a helpless product of nature, destined by her to do whatever I do and to become whatever I become?

There is no moral blame nor merit in any man who cannot help what he does. It matters not whether the explanation for his behavior is found within him or without, whether it is expressed in terms of ordinary physical causes or allegedly "mental" ones, or whether the causes be proximate or remote. I am not responsible for being a man rather than a woman, nor for having the temperament, desires, purposes, and ideals characteristic of that sex. I was never asked whether these should be given to me. The kleptomaniac, similarly, steals from compulsion, the chronic alcoholic drinks from compulsion, and sometimes even the hero dies from compulsive courage. Though these causes are within them, they compel no less for that, and their victims never chose to have them inflicted upon themselves. To say they are compulsions is to say only that they compel. But to say they compel is only to say that they cause; for the cause of a thing being given, the effect cannot fail to follow. By the thesis of determinism, however, everything whatever is caused, and not one single thing could ever be other than exactly what it is. Perhaps one thinks that the kleptomaniac and the drunkard did not have to become what they are, that they could have done better at another time and thereby ended up better than they are now, or that the hero could have done worse and then ended up a coward. But this shows only an unwillingness to understand what made them become as they are. Having found that their behavior is caused from within them, we can hardly avoid asking what caused these inner springs of action, and then asking what were the causes of these causes, and so on through the infinite past. We shall not, certainly, with our small understanding and our fragmentary knowledge of the past ever know why the world should at just this time and place have produced just this thief, this drunkard, and this hero, but the vagueness and smatteringness of our knowledge should not tempt us to imagine a similar vagueness in nature herself. Everything in nature is and always has been determinate, with no loose edges at all, and she was forever destined to bring forth just what she has produced, however slight may be our understanding of the origins of these works. Ultimate responsibility for anything that exists, and hence for any man and his deeds, can thus only rest with the first cause of all things, if there is such a cause, or nowhere at all, in case there is not. Such at least seems to be the unavoidable implication of determinism.

Determinism and Morals

Some philosophers, faced with all this, which seems quite clear to the ordinary understanding, have tried to cling to determinism while modifying traditional conceptions of morals. They continue to *use* such words as "merit," "blame," "praise," and "desert," but they so divest them of their meanings as to finish by talking about things entirely different, sometimes without themselves realizing that they are no longer on the subject. An ordinary man will hardly understand that anyone can possess merit or vice and be deserving of moral praise or blame, as a result of traits that he has or of behavior arising from those traits, once it is well understood that he could never have avoided being just what he is and doing just what he does.

We are happily spared going into all this, however, for the question whether determinism is true of human nature is not a question of ethics at all but of metaphysics. There is accordingly no hope of answering it within the context of ethics. One can, to be sure, simply *assume* an answer to it—assume that determinism is true, for instance—and then see what are the implications of this answer for ethics; but that does not answer the question. Or one can *assume* some theory or other of ethics—assume some version of "the greatest happiness" principle, for instance—and then see whether that theory is consistent with determinism. But such confrontations of theories with theories likewise make us no wiser, so far as any fundamental question is concerned. We can suppose at once that determinism is consistent with some conceptions of morals, and inconsistent with others, and that the same holds for indeterminism. We shall still not know what theories are true; we shall only know which are consistent with each other.

We shall, then, eschew all considerations of ethics, as having no real bearing on our problem. We want to learn, if we can, whether determinism is true, and this is a question of metaphysics. It can, like all good questions of philosophy, be answered only on the basis of certain data; that is, by seeing whether or not it squares with certain things which every man knows, or believes himself to know, or things of which every man is at least more sure than the answer to the question at issue.

Now I could, of course, simply affirm that I am a morally responsible being, in the sense in which my responsibility for my behavior implies that I could have avoided that behavior. But this would take us into the nebulous realm of ethics, and it is, in fact, far from obvious that I am responsible in that sense. Many have doubted that they are responsible in that sense, and it is in any case not difficult to doubt it, however strongly one might feel about it.

There are, however, two things about myself of which I feel quite certain and which have no necessary connection with morals. The first is that I sometimes deliberate, with the view to making a decision; a decision, namely, to do this thing or that. And the second is that whether or not I deliberate about what to do, it is sometimes up to me what I do. This might all be an illusion, of course; but so also any philosophical theory, such as the theory of determinism, might be false. The point remains that it is far more difficult for me to doubt that I sometimes deliberate, and that it is sometimes up to me what to do, than to doubt any philosophical theory whatever, including the theory of determinism. We must, accordingly, if we ever hope to be wiser, adjust our theories to our data and not try to adjust our data to our theories.

Let us, then, get these two data quite clearly before us so we can see what they are, what they presuppose, and what they do and do not entail.

Deliberation

Deliberation is an activity, or at least a kind of experience, that cannot be defined, or even described without metaphors. We speak of weighing this and that in our minds, of trying to anticipate consequences of various possible courses of action, and so on, but such descriptions do not convey to us what deliberation is unless we already know.

Whenever I deliberate, however, I find that I make certain presuppositions, whether I actually think of them or not. That is, I assume that certain things are true, certain things which are such that, if I thought they were not true, it would be impossible for me to deliberate at all. Some of these can be listed as follows.

First, I find that I can deliberate only about my own behavior and never about the behavior of another. I can try to guess, speculate, or figure out what another person is going to do; I can read certain signs and sometimes infer what he will do; but I cannot deliberate about it. When I deliberate I try to decide something, to make up my mind, and this is as remote as anything could be from speculating, trying to guess, or to infer from signs. Sometimes one *does* speculate on what he is going to do, by trying to draw conclusions from certain signs or omens—he might infer that he is going to sneeze, for instance, or speculate that he is going to become a grandfather—but he is not then deliberating whether to do these things or not. One does, to be sure, sometimes deliberate about whether another person will do a certain act, when that other person is subject to his command or otherwise under his control; but then he is not really deliberating about another person's acts at all, but about his own— namely, whether or not to have that other person carry out the order.

Second, I find that I can deliberate only about future things, never things past or present. I may not know what I did at a certain time in the past, in case I have forgotten, but I can no longer deliberate whether to do it then or not. I can, again, only speculate, guess, try to infer, or perhaps try to remember. Similarly, I cannot deliberate whether or not to be doing something now; I can only ascertain whether or not I am in fact doing it. If I am sitting I cannot deliberate about whether or not to be sit-

ting. I can only deliberate about whether to remain sitting—and this has to do with the future.

Third, I cannot deliberate about what I shall do, in case I already know what I am going to do. If I were to say, for example, "I know that I am going to be married tomorrow and in the meantime I am going to deliberate about whether to get married," I would contradict myself. There are only two ways that I could know now what I am going to do tomorrow; namely, either by inferring this from certain signs and omens or by having already decided what I am going to do. But if I have inferred from signs and omens what I am going to do, I cannot deliberate about it— there is just nothing for me to decide; and similarly, if I have already decided. If, on the other hand, I can still deliberate about what I am going to do, to that extent I must regard the signs and omens as unreliable, and the inference uncertain, and I do not therefore know what I am going to do after all.

And finally, I cannot deliberate about what to do, even though I may not know what I am going to do, unless I believe that it is up to me what I am going to do. If I am within the power of another person, or at the mercy of circumstances over which I have no control, then, although I may have no idea what I am going to do, I cannot deliberate about it. I can only wait and see. If, for instance, I am a conscript, and regulations regarding uniforms are posted each day by my commanding officer and are strictly enforced by him, then I shall not know what uniforms I shall be wearing from time to time, but I cannot deliberate about it. I can only wait and see what regulations are posted; it is not up to me. Similarly, a woman who is about to give birth to a child cannot deliberate whether to have a boy or a girl, even though she may not know. She can only wait and see; it is not up to her. Such examples can be generalized to cover any case wherein one does not know what he is going to do, but believes that it is not up to him, and hence no matter for his decision and hence none for his deliberation.

"It Is Up to Me"

I sometimes feel certain that it is, at least to some extent, up to me what I am going to do; indeed, I must believe this if I am to deliberate about what to do. But what does this mean? It is, again, hard to say, but the idea can be illustrated, and we can fairly easily see what it does not mean.

Let us consider the simplest possible sort of situation in which this belief might be involved. At this moment, for instance, it seems quite certain to me that, holding my finger before me, I can move it either to the left or to the right, that each of these motions is possible for me. This does not mean merely that my finger can move either way, although it entails that, for this would be true in case nothing obstructed it, even if I had no control over it at all. I can say of a distant, fluttering leaf that it can move either way, but not that I can move it, since I have no control over it. How it moves is not up to me. Nor does it mean merely that my finger can be moved either way, although it entails this too. If the motions of my finger are under the control of some other person or of some machine, then it might be true that the finger can be moved either way, by that person or machine, though false that I can move it at all.

If I say, then, that it is up to me how I move my finger, I mean that I can move it in this way and I can move it in that way, and not merely that it can move or be moved in this way and that. I mean that the motion of my finger is within my direct control. If someone were to ask me to move it to the right, I could do that, and if he were to ask me to move it to the left, I could do that too. Further, I could do these simple acts without being asked at all, and, having been asked, I could move it in a manner the exact opposite of what was requested, since I can ignore the request. There are, to be sure, some motions of my finger that I cannot make, so it is not *entirely* up to me how it moves. I cannot bend it backward, for instance, or bend it into a knot, for these motions are obstructed by the very anatomical construction of the finger itself; and to say that I can move any finger at all means at least that nothing obstructs such a motion, though it does not mean merely this. There is, however, at this moment, no obstruction, anatomical or otherwise, to my moving it to the right, and none to my moving it to the left.

This datum, it should be noted, is properly expressed as a conjunction and not as a disjunction. That is, my belief is that I can move my finger in one way, *and* that I can also move it another way;

and it does not do justice to this belief to say that I can move it one way *or* the other. It is fairly easy to see the truth of this, for the latter claim, that I can move it one way or the other, would be satisfied in case there were only one way I could move it, and *that* is not what I believe. Suppose, for instance, my hand were strapped to a device in such a fashion that I could move my finger to the right but not to the left. Then it would still be entirely true that I could move it either to the left *or* to the right—since it would be true that I could move it to the right. But that is not what I now believe. My finger is not strapped to anything, and nothing obstructs its motion in either direction. And what I believe, in this situation, is that I can move it to the right *and* I can move it to the left.

We must note further that the belief expressed in our datum is not a belief in what is logically impossible. It is the belief that I now *can* move my finger in different ways but not that I can move it in different ways at once. What I believe is that I am now able to move my finger one way and that I am now equally able to move it another way, but I do not claim to be able now or any other time to move it both ways simultaneously. The situation here is analogous to one in which I might, for instance, be offered a choice of either of two apples but forbidden to take both. Each apple is such that I may select it, but neither is such that I may select it together with the other.

Now are these two data—the belief that I do sometimes deliberate, and the belief that it is sometimes up to me what I do—consistent with the metaphysical theory of determinism? We do not know yet. We intend to find out. It is fairly clear, however, that they are going to present difficulties to that theory. But let us not, in any case, try to avoid those difficulties by just denying the data themselves. If we eventually deny the data, we shall do so for better reasons than this. Virtually all men are convinced that beliefs such as are expressed in our data are sometimes true. They cannot be simply dismissed as false just because they might appear to conflict with a metaphysical theory that hardly any men have ever really thought much about at all. Almost any man, unless his fingers are paralyzed, bound, or otherwise incapable of movement, believes sometimes that the motions of his fingers are within his control, in exactly the sense expressed by our data. If consequences of considerable importance to him depend on how he moves his fingers, he sometimes deliberates before moving them, or at least, he is convinced that he does, or that he can. Philosophers might have different notions of just what things are implied by such data, but there is in any case no more, and in fact considerably less, reason for denying the data than for denying some philosophical theory.

Causal vs. Logical Necessity

Philosophers have long since pointed out that causal connections involve no logical necessity, that the denial of a particular causal connection is never self-contradictory, and this is undoubtedly true. But neither does the assertion or the denial of determinism involve any concept of what is and what is not logically necessary. If determinism is true, then anything that happens is, given the conditions under which it occurs, the only thing possible, the thing that is necessitated by those conditions. But it is not the only thing that is logically possible, nor do those conditions logically necessitate it. Similarly, if one denies the thesis of determinism, by asserting, for instance, that each of two bodily motions is possible for him under identical conditions, he is asserting much more than that each is logically possible, for that would be a trivial claim.

This distinction, between logical necessity and the sort of necessity involved in determinism, can be illustrated with examples. If, for instance, a man is beheaded, we can surely say that it is impossible for him to go on living, that his being beheaded necessitates his death, and so on; but there are no logical necessities or impossibilities involved here. It is not logically impossible for a man to live without his head. Yet no one will deny that a man cannot live under conditions that include his being headless, that such a state of affairs is in a perfectly clear sense impossible. Similarly, if my finger is in a tight and fairly strong cast, then it is impossible for me to move it in any way at all, though this is not logically impossible. It is logically possible that I should be vastly stronger than I am, and that I should move it

and, in doing so, break the cast, though this would ordinarily not be possible in the sense that concerns us. Again, it is not logically impossible that I should bend my finger backward, or into a knot, though it is, in fact, impossible for me to do either or, what means the same thing, necessary that I should do neither. Certain conditions prohibit my doing such things, though they impose no logical barrier. And finally, if someone—a physican, for example—should ask me whether I can move my finger, and I should reply truly that I can, I would not merely be telling him that it is logically possible for me to move it, for this he already knows. I would be telling him that I am able to move it, that it is within my power to do so, that there are no conditions, such as paralysis or whatnot, that prevent my moving it.

It follows that not all necessity is logical necessity, nor all impossibility logical impossibility, and that to say that something is possible is sometimes to say much more than that it is logically possible. The kind of necessity involved in the thesis of determinism is quite obviously the nonlogical kind, as is also the kind of possibility involved in its denial. If we needed a *name* for these nonlogical modalities, we could call them *causal* necessity, impossibility, and possibility, but the concepts are clear enough without making a great deal of the name.

Freedom

To say that it is, in a given instance, up to me what I do, is to say that I am in that instance *free* with respect to what I then do. Thus, I am sometimes free to move my finger this way and that, but not, certainly, to bend it backward or into a knot. But what does this mean?

It means, first, that there is no *obstacle* or *impediment* to my activity. Thus, there is sometimes no obstacle to my moving my finger this way and that, though there are obvious obstacles to my moving it far backward or into a knot. Those things, accordingly, that pose obstacles to my motions limit my freedom. If my hand were strapped in such a way as to permit only a leftward motion of my finger, I would not then be free to move it to the right. If it were encased in a tight cast that permitted no motion, I would not be free to move it at all. Freedom of motion, then, is limited by obstacles.

Further, to say that it is, in a given instance, up to me what I do, means that nothing *constrains* or *forces* me to do one thing rather than another. Constraints are like obstacles, except that while the latter prevent, the former enforce. Thus, if my finger is being forcibly bent to the left—by a machine, for instance, or by another person, or by any force that I cannot overcome—then I am not free to move it this way and that. I cannot, in fact, move it at all; I can only watch to see how it is moved, and perhaps vainly resist. Its motions are not up to me, or within my control, but in the control of some other thing or person.

Obstacles and constraints, then, both obviously limit my freedom. To say I am free to perform some action thus means at least that there is no obstacle to my doing it, and that nothing constrains me to do otherwise.

Now if we rest content with this observation, as many have, and construe free activity simply as activity that is unimpeded and unconstrained, there is evidently no inconsistency between affirming both the thesis of determinism and the claim that I am sometimes free. For to say that some action of mine is neither impeded nor constrained does not by itself imply that it is not causally determined. The absence of obstacles and constraints are mere negative conditions, and do not by themselves rule out the presence of positive causes. It might seem, then, that we can say of some of my actions that there are conditions antecedent to their performance so that no other actions were possible, and also that these actions were unobstructed and unconstrained. And to say that would logically entail that such actions were both causally determined, and free.

Soft Determinism

It is this kind of consideration that has led many philosophers to embrace what is sometimes called "soft determinism." All versions of this theory have in common three claims, by means of which, it is naively supposed, a reconciliation is achieved between determinism and freedom. Freedom being, furthermore, a condition of moral responsibility and the only condition that metaphysics seriously questions, it is supposed by the partisans of this view that determinism is perfectly compatible with such responsibility. This, no doubt, accounts for its great appeal and wide acceptance, even by some men of considerable learning.

The three claims of soft determinism are (1) that the thesis of determinism is true, and that accordingly all human behavior, voluntary or other, like the behavior of all other things, arises from antecedent conditions, given which no other behavior is possible—in short, that all human behavior is caused and determined; (2) that voluntary behavior is nonetheless free to the extent that it is not externally constrained or impeded; and (3) that, in the absence of such obstacles and constraints, the causes of voluntary behavior are certain states, events, or conditions within the agent himself; namely, his own acts of will or volitions, choices, decisions, desires, and so on.

Thus, on this view, I am free, and therefore sometimes responsible for what I do, provided nothing prevents me from acting according to my own choice, desire or volition, or constrains me to act otherwise. There may, to be sure, be other conditions for my responsibility—such as, for example, an understanding of the probable consequences of my behavior, and that sort of thing—but absence of constraint or impediment is, at least, one such condition. And, it is claimed, it is a condition that is compatible with the supposition that my behavior is caused—for it is, by hypothesis, caused by my own inner choices, desires, and volitions.

The Refutation of This

The theory of soft determinism looks good at first—so good that it has for generations been solemnly taught from numberless philosophical chairs and implanted in the minds of students as sound philosophy—but no great acumen is needed to discover that far from solving any problem, it only camouflages it.

My free actions are those unimpeded and unconstrained motions that arise from my own inner desires, choices, and volitions; let us grant this provisionally. But now, whence arise those inner states that determine what my body shall do? Are they within my control or not? Having made my choice or decision and acted upon it, could I have chosen otherwise or not?

Here the determinist, hoping to surrender nothing and yet to avoid the problem implied in that question, bids us not to ask it; the question itself, he announces, is without meaning. For to say that I could have done otherwise, he says, means only that I *would* have done otherwise *if* those inner states that determined my action had been different; if, that is, I had decided or chosen differently. To ask, accordingly, whether I could have chosen or decided differently is only to ask whether, had I decided to decide differently or chosen to choose differently, or willed to will differently, I would have decided or chosen or willed differently. And this, of course, *is* unintelligible nonsense.

But it is not nonsense to ask whether the causes of my actions—my own inner choices, decisions, and desires—are themselves caused. And of course they are, if determinism is true, for on that thesis everything is caused and determined. And if they are, then we cannot avoid concluding that, given the causal conditions of those inner states, I could not have decided, willed, chosen, or desired otherwise than I in fact did, for this is a logical consequence of the very definition of determinism. Of course we can still say that, *if* the causes of those inner states, whatever they were, had been different, then their effects, those inner states themselves, would have been different, and that in this hypothetical sense I could have decided, chosen, willed, or desired differently—but that only pushes our problem back still another step. For we will then want to know whether the causes of those inner states were within my control; and so on, *ad infinitum*. We are, at each step, permitted to say "could have been otherwise" only in a provisional sense—provided, that is, something else had been different—but must then retract it and replace it with "could not have been otherwise" as soon as we discover, as we must at each step, that whatever would have to have been different could not have been different.

Examples

Such is the dialectic of the problem. The easiest way to see the shadowy quality of soft determinism, however, is by means of examples.

Let us suppose that my body is moving in various ways, that these motions are not externally constrained or impeded, and that they are all exactly in accordance with my own desires, choices, or acts of will and what not. When I will that my arm should move in a certain way, I find it moving in that way, unobstructed and unconstrained. When I will to speak, my lips and tongue move, unobstructed and unconstrained, in a manner suitable to the formation of the words I choose to utter. Now given that this is a correct description of my behavior, namely, that it consists of the unconstrained and unimpeded motions of my body in response to my own volitions, then it follows that my behavior is free, on the soft determinist's defintion of "free." It follows further that I am responsible for that behavior; or at least, that if I am not, it is not from any lack of freedom on my part.

But if the fulfillment of these conditions renders my behavior free—that is to say, if my behavior satisfies the conditions of free action set forth in the theory of soft determinism—then my behavior will be no less free if we assume further conditions that are perfectly consistent with those already satisfied.

We suppose further, accordingly, that while my behavior is entirely in accordance with my own volitions, and thus "free" in terms of the conception of freedom we are examining, my volitions themselves are caused. To make this graphic, we can suppose that an ingenious physiologist can induce in me any volition he pleases, simply by pushing various buttons on an instrument to which, let us suppose, I am attached by numerous wires. All the volitions I have in that situation are, accordingly, precisely the ones he gives me. By pushing one button, he evokes in me the volition to raise my hand; and my hand, being unimpeded, rises in response to that volition. By pushing another, he induces the volition in me to kick, and my foot, being unimpeded, kicks in response to that volition. We can even suppose that the physiologist puts a rifle in my hands, aims it at some passer-by, and then, by pushing the proper button, evokes in me the volition to squeeze my finger against the trigger, whereupon the passer-by falls dead of a bullet wound.

This is the description of a man who is acting in accordance with his inner volitions, a man whose body is unimpeded and unconstrained in its motions, these motions being the effects of those inner states. It is hardly the description of a free and responsible agent. It is the perfect description of a puppet. To render a man your puppet, it is not necessary forcibly to constrain the motions of his limbs, after the fashion that real puppets are moved. A subtler but no less effective means of making a man your puppet would be to gain complete control of his inner states, and ensuring, as the theory of soft determinism does ensure, that his body will move in accordance with them.

The example is somewhat unusual, but it is no worse for that. It is perfectly intelligible, and it does appear to refute the soft determinist's conception of freedom. One might think that, in such a case, the agent should not have allowed himself to be so rigged in the first place, but this is irrelevant; we can suppose that he was not aware that he was, and was hence unaware of the source of those inner states that prompted his bodily motions. The example can, moreover, be modified in perfectly realistic ways, so as to coincide with actual and familiar cases. One can, for instance, be given a compulsive desire for certain drugs, simply by having them administered to him over a course of time. Suppose, then, that I do, with neither my knowledge or consent, thus become a victim of such a desire and act upon it. Do I act freely, merely by virtue of the fact that I am unimpeded in my quest for drugs? In a sense I do, surely, but I am hardly free with respect to whether or not I shall use drugs. I never chose to have the desire for them inflicted upon me.

Nor does it, of course, matter whether the inner states which allegedly prompt all my "free" activity are evoked in me by another agent or by perfectly impersonal forces. Whether a desire which causes my body to behave in a certain way is inflicted upon me by another person, for instance, or derived from hereditary factors, or indeed from anything at all, matters not the least. In any case, if it is in fact the cause of my bodily behavior, I cannot but act in ac-

cordance with it. Wherever it came from, whether from personal or impersonal origins, it was entirely caused or determined, and not within my control. Indeed, if determinism is true, as the theory of soft determinism holds it to be, all those inner states which cause my body to behave in whatever ways it behaves must arise from circumstances that existed before I was born; for the chain of causes and effects is infinite, and none could have been the least different, given those that preceded.

Simple Indeterminism

We might at first now seem warranted in simply denying determinism, and saying that, insofar as they are free, my actions are not caused; or that, if they are caused by my own inner states—my own desires, impulses, choices, volitions, and whatnot—then these, in any case, are not caused. This is a perfectly clear sense in which a man's action, assuming that it was free, could have been otherwise. If it was uncaused, then, even given the conditions under which it occurred and all that preceded, some other act was nonetheless possible, and he did not have to do what he did. Or if his action was the inevitable consequence of his own inner states, and could not have been otherwise given these, we can nevertheless say that these inner states, being uncaused, could have been otherwise, and could thereby have produced different actions.

Only the slightest consideration will show, however, that this simple denial of determinism has not the slightest plausibility. For let us suppose it is true, and that some of my bodily motions—namely, those that I regard as my free acts—are not caused at all or, if caused by my own inner states, that these are not caused. We shall thereby avoid picturing a puppet, to be sure—but only by substituting something even less like a man; for the conception that now emerges is not that of a free man, but of an erratic and jerking phantom, without any rhyme or reason at all.

Suppose that my right arm is free, according to this conception; that is, that its motions are uncaused. It moves this way and that from time to time, but nothing causes these motions. Sometimes it moves forth vigorously, sometimes up, sometimes down, sometimes it just drifts vaguely about—these motions all being wholly free and uncaused. Manifestly I have nothing to do with them at all; they just happen, and neither I nor anyone can ever tell what this arm will be doing next. It might seize a club and lay it on the head of the nearest bystander, no less to my astonishment than his. There will never be any point in asking why these motions occur, or in seeking any explanation of them, for under the conditions assumed there is no explanation. They just happen, from no causes at all.

This is no description of free, voluntary, or responsible behavior. Indeed, so far as the motions of my body or its parts are entirely uncaused, such motions cannot even be ascribed to me as my behavior in the first place, since I have nothing to do with them. The behavior of my arm is just the random motion of a foreign object. Behavior that is mine must be behavior that is within my control, but motions that occur from no causes are without the control of anyone. I can have no more to do with, and no more control over, the uncaused motions of my limbs than a gambler has over the motions of an honest roulette wheel. I can only, like him, idly wait to see what happens.

Nor does it improve things to suppose that my bodily motions are caused by my own inner states, so long as we suppose these to be wholly uncaused. The result will be the same as before. My arm, for example, will move this way and that, sometimes up and sometimes down, sometimes vigorously and sometimes just drifting about, always in response to certain inner states, to be sure. But since these are supposed to be wholly uncaused, it follows that I have no control over them and hence none over their effects. If my hand lays a club forcefully on the nearest bystander, we can indeed say that this motion resulted from an inner club-wielding desire of mine; but we must add that I had nothing to do with that desire, and that it arose, to be followed by its inevitable effect, no less to my astonishment than to his. Things like this do, alas, sometimes happen. We are all sometimes seized by compulsive impulses that arise we know not whither, and we do sometimes act upon these. But since they are far from being examples of free, voluntary, and responsible be-

havior, we need only to learn that behavior was of this sort to conclude that it was not free, voluntary, nor responsible. It was erratic, impulsive, and irresponsible.

Determinism and Simple Indeterminism as Theories

Both determinism and simple indeterminism are loaded with difficulties, and no one who has thought much on them can affirm either of them without some embarrassment. Simple indeterminism has nothing whatever to be said for it, except that it appears to remove the grossest difficulties of determinism, only, however, to imply perfect absurdities of its own. Determinism, on the other hand, is at least initially plausible. Men seem to have a natural inclination to believe in it; it is, indeed, almost required for the very exercise of practical intelligence. And beyond this, our experience appears always to confirm it, so long as we are dealing with everyday facts of common experience, as distinguished from the esoteric researches of theoretical physics. But determinism, as applied to human behavior, has implications which few men can casually accept, and they appear to be implications which no modification of the theory can efface.

Both theories, moreover, appear logically irreconcilable to the two items of data that we set forth at the outset; namely, (1) that my behavior is sometimes the outcome of my deliberation, and (2) that in these and other cases it is sometimes up to me what I do. Since these were our data, it is important to see, as must already be quite clear, that these theories cannot be reconciled to them.

I can deliberate only about my own future actions, and then only if I do not already know what I am going to do. If a certain nasal tickle warns me that I am about to sneeze, for instance, then I cannot deliberate whether to sneeze or not; I can only prepare for the impending convulsion. But if determinism is true, then there are always conditions existing antecedently to everything I do, sufficient for my doing just that, and such as to render it inevitable. If I can know what those conditions are and what behavior they are sufficient to produce, then I can in every such case know what I am going to do and cannot then deliberate about it.

By itself this only shows, of course, that I can deliberate only in ignorance of the causal conditions of my behavior; it does not show that such conditions cannot exist. It is odd, however, to suppose that deliberation should be a mere substitute for clear knowledge. Ignorance is a condition of speculation, inference, and guesswork, which have nothing whatever to do with deliberation. A prisoner awaiting execution may not know when he is going to die, and he may even entertain the hope of reprieve, but he cannot deliberate about this. He can only speculate, guess—and wait.

Worse yet, however, it now becomes clear that I cannot deliberate about what I am going to do, if it is even possible for me to find out in advance, whether I do in fact find out in advance or not. I can deliberate only with the view to deciding what to do, to making up my mind; and this is impossible if I believe that it could be inferred what I am going to do, from conditions already existing, even though I have not made that inference myself. If I believe that what I am going to do has been rendered inevitable by conditions already existing, and could be inferred by anyone having the requisite sagacity, then I cannot try to decide whether to do it or not, for there is simply nothing left to decide. I can at best only guess or try to figure it out myself or, all prognostics failing, I can wait and see; but I cannot deliberate. I deliberate in order to *decide* what *to* do, not to *discover* what it is that I am *going* to do. But if determinism is true, then there are always antecedent conditions sufficient for everything that I do, and this can always be inferred by anyone having the requisite sagacity; that is, by anyone having a knowledge of what those conditions are and what behavior they are sufficient to produce.

This suggests what in fact seems quite clear, that determinism cannot be reconciled with our second datum either, to the effect that it is sometimes up to me what I am going to do. For if it is ever really up to me whether to do this thing or that, then, as we have seen, each alternative course of action must be such that I can do it; not that I can do it in some abstruse or hypothetical sense of "can"; not that I could do it if only something were true that is not true;

but in the sense that it is then and there within my power to do it. But this is never so, if determinism is true, for on the very formulation of that theory whatever happens at any time is the only thing that can then happen, given all that precedes it. It is simply a logical consequence of this that whatever I do at any time is the only thing I can then do, given the conditions that precede my doing it. Nor does it help in the least to interpose, among the causal antecedents of my behavior, my own inner states, such as my desires, choices, acts of will, and so on. For even supposing these to be always involved in voluntary behavior—which is highly doubtful in itself—it is a consequence of determinism that these, whatever they are at any time, can never be other than what they then are. Every chain of causes and effects, if determinism is true, is infinite. This is why it is not now up to me whether I shall a moment hence be male or female. The conditions determining my sex have existed through my whole life, and even prior to my life. But if determinism is true, the same holds of anything that I ever am, ever become, or ever do. It matters not whether we are speaking of the most patent facts of my being, such as my sex; or the most subtle, such as my feelings, thoughts, desires, or choices. Nothing could be other than it is, given what was; and while we may indeed say, quite idly, that something—some inner state of mine, for instance—*could* have been different, had only something *else* been different, any consolation of this thought evaporates as soon as we add that whatever would have to have been different could not have been different.

It is even more obvious that our data cannot be reconciled to the theory of simple indeterminism. I can deliberate only about my own actions; this is obvious. But the random, uncaused motion of any body whatever, whether it be a part of my body or not, is no action of mine and nothing that is within my power. I might try to guess what these motions will be, just as I might try to guess how a roulette wheel will behave, but I cannot deliberate about them or try to decide what they shall be, simply because these things are not up to me. Whatever is not caused by anything is not caused by me, and nothing could be more plainly inconsistent with saying that it is nevertheless up to me what it shall be.

The Theory of Agency

The only conception of action that accords with our data is one according to which men—and perhaps some other things too—are sometimes, but of course not always, self-determining beings; that is, beings which are sometimes the causes of their own behavior. In the case of an action that is free, it must be such that it is caused by the agent who performs it, but such that no antecedent conditions were sufficient for his performing just that action. In the case of an action that is both free and rational, it must be such that the agent who performed it did so for some reason, but this reason cannot have been the cause of it.

Now this conception fits what men take themselves to be; namely, beings who act, or who are agents, rather than things that are merely acted upon, and whose behavior is simply the causal consequence of conditions which they have not wrought. When I believe that I have done something, I do believe that it was I who caused it to be done, I who made something happen, and not merely something within me, such as one of my own subjective states, which is not identical with myself. If I believe that something not identical with myself was the cause of my behavior—some event wholly external to myself, for instance, or even one internal to myself, such as a nerve impulse, volition, or whatnot—then I cannot regard that behavior as being an act of mine, unless I further believe that I was the cause of that external or internal event. My pulse, for example, is caused and regulated by certain conditions existing within me, and not by myself. I do not, accordingly, regard this activity of my body as my action, and would be no more tempted to do so if I became suddenly conscious within myself of those conditions or impulses that produce it. This is behavior with which *I* have nothing to do, behavior that is not within my immediate control, behavior that is not only not free activity, but not even the activity of an agent to begin with; it is nothing but a mechanical reflex. Had I never learned that my very life depends on this pulse beat, I would regard it with complete indifference, as something foreign to me, like the oscillations of a clock pendulum that I idly contemplate.

Now this conception of activity, and of an agent who is the cause of it, involves two rather strange metaphysical notions that are never applied elsewhere in nature. The first is that of a *self* or *person*—for example, a man—who is not merely a collection of things or events, but a substance and a self-moving being. For on this view it is a man himself, and not merely some part of him or something within him, that is the cause of his own activity. Now we certainly do not know that a man is anything more than an assemblage of physical things and processes, which act in accordance with those laws that describe the behavior of all other physical things and processes. Even though a man is a living being, of enormous complexity, there is nothing, apart from the requirements of this theory, to suggest that his behavior is so radically different in its origin from that of other physical objects, or that an understanding of it must be sought in some metaphysical realm wholly different from that appropriate to the understanding of nonliving things.

Second, this conception of activity involves an extraordinary conception of causation, according to which an agent, which is a substance and not an event, can nevertheless be the cause of an event. Indeed, if he is a free agent then he can, on this conception, cause an event to occur—namely, some act of his own—without anything else causing him to do so. This means that an agent is sometimes a cause, without being an antecedent sufficient condition; for if I affirm that I am the cause of some act of mine, then I am plainly not saying that my very existence is sufficient for its occurrence, which would be absurd. If I say that my hand causes my pencil to move, then I am saying that the motion of my hand is, under the other conditions then prevailing, sufficient for the motion of the pencil. But if I then say that I cause my hand to move, I am not saying anything remotely like this, and surely not that the motion of my self is sufficient for the motion of my arm and hand, since these are only things about me that are moving.

This conception of the causation of events by beings or substances that are not events is, in fact, so different from the usual philosophical conception of a cause that it should not even bear the same name, for "being a cause" ordinarily just means "being an antecedent sufficient condition or set of conditions."

Instead, then, of speaking of agents as *causing* their own acts, it would perhaps be better to use another word entirely, and say, for instance, that they *originate* them, *initiate* them, or simply that they *perform* them.

Now this is on the face of it a dubious conception of what a man is. Yet it is consistent with our data, reflecting the presuppositions of deliberation, and appears to be the only conception that is consistent with them, as determinism and simple indeterminism are not. The theory of agency avoids the absurdities of simple indeterminism by conceding that human behavior is caused, while at the same time avoiding the difficulties of determinism by denying that every chain of causes and effects is infinite. Some such causal chains, on this view, have beginnings, and they begin with agents themselves. Moreover, if we are to suppose that it is sometimes up to me what I do, and understand this in a sense which is not consistent with determinism, we must suppose that I am an agent or a being who initiates his own actions, sometimes under conditions which do not determine what action he shall perform. Deliberation becomes, on this view, something that is not only possible but quite rational, for it does make sense to deliberate about activity that is truly my own and that depends in its outcome upon me as its author, and not merely upon something more or less esoteric that is supposed to be intimately associated with me, such as my thoughts, volitions, choices, or whatnot.

One can hardly affirm such a theory of agency with complete comfort, however, and wholly without embarrassment, for the conception of men and their powers which is involved in it is strange indeed, if not positively mysterious. In fact, one can hardly be blamed here for simply denying our data outright, rather than embracing this theory to which they do most certainly point. Our data—to the effect that men do sometimes deliberate before acting, and that when they do, they presuppose among other things that it is up to them what they are going to do—rest upon nothing more than fairly common consent. These data might simply be illusions. It might in fact be that no man ever deliberates, but only imagines that he does, that from pure conceit he supposes himself to be the master of his behavior and the author of his acts. Spinoza has suggested that if a stone, having been thrown into the air, were suddenly to become conscious, it would suppose itself to be the source of its own motion, being then conscious of what it was doing but not aware of the real cause of its behavior. Certainly men are *sometimes* mistaken in believing that they are behaving as a result of choice deliberately arrived at. A man might, for example, easily imagine that his embarking upon matrimony is the result of the most careful and rational deliberation, when in fact the causes, perfectly sufficient for that behavior, might be of an entirely physiological, unconscious origin. If it is sometimes false that we deliberate and then act as the result of a decision deliberately arrived at, even when we suppose it to be true, it might always be false. No one seems able, as we have noted, to describe deliberation without metaphors, and the conception of a thing's being "within one's power" or "up to him" seems to defy analysis or definition altogether, if taken in a sense which the theory of agency appears to require.

These are, then, dubitable conceptions, despite their being so well implanted in the commonsense of mankind. Indeed, when we turn to the theory of fatalism, we shall find formidable metaphysical considerations which appear to rule them out altogether. Perhaps here, as elsewhere in metaphysics, we should be content with discovering difficulties, with seeing what is and what is not consistent with such convictions as we happen to have, and then drawing such satisfaction as we can from the realization that, no matter where we begin, the world is mysterious and the men who try to understand it are even more so. This realization can, with some justification, make one feel wise, even in the full realization of his ignorance.

Freedom of the Will and the Concept of a Person

HARRY G. FRANKFURT

Harry Frankfurt (1922–) is the author of a number of important works on freedom of the will, other topics in metaphysics and ethics and the history of philosophy including *Demons, Dreamers and Madmen* and *The Importance of What We Care About*. He has been a Professor of Philosophy at Rockefeller, Yale, and Princeton Universities.

———•———

WHAT PHILOSOPHERS HAVE lately come to accept as analysis of the concept of a person is not actually analysis of *that* concept at all. Strawson, whose usage represents the current standard, identifies the concept of a person as "the concept of a type of entity such that *both* predicates ascribing states of consciousness *and* predicates ascribing corporeal characteristics . . . are equally applicable to a single individual of that single type.[1] But there are many entities besides persons that have both mental and physical properties. As it happens—though it seems extraordinary that this should be so—there is no common English word for the type of entity Strawson has in mind, a type that includes not only human beings but animals of various lesser species as well. Still, this hardly justifies the misappropriation of a valuable philosophical term.

Whether the members of some animal species are persons is surely not to be settled merely by determining whether it is correct to apply to them, in addition to predicates ascribing corporeal characteristics, predicates that ascribe states of consciousness. It does violence to our language to endorse the application of the term "person" to those numerous creatures which do have both psychological and material properties but which are manifestly not persons in any normal sense of the word. This misuse of language is doubtless innocent of any theoretical

error. But although the offence is "merely verbal," it does significant harm. For it gratuitously diminishes our philosophical vocabulary, and it increases the likelihood that we will overlook the important area of inquiry with which the term "person" is most naturally associated. It might have been expected that no problem would be of more central and persistent concern to philosophers than that of understanding what we ourselves essentially are. Yet this problem is so generally neglected that it has been possible to make off with its very name almost without being noticed and, evidently, without evoking any widespread feeling of loss.

There is a sense in which the word "person" is merely the singular form of "people" and in which both terms connote no more than membership in a certain biological species. In those senses of the word which are of greater philosophical interest, however, the criteria for being a person do not serve primarily to distinguish the members of our own species from the members of other species. Rather, they are designed to capture those attributes which are the subject of our most humane concern with ourselves and the source of what we regard as most important and most problematical in our lives. Now these attributes would be of equal significance to us even if they were not in fact peculiar and common to the members of our own species. What interests us most in the human condition would not interest us less if it were also a feature of the condition of other creatures as well.

Our concept of ourselves as persons is not to be understood, therefore, as a concept of attributes that are necessarily species-specific. It is conceptually

From *Journal of Philosophy*, LXVIII, No. 1 (Jan. 1971). Copyright © 1971 by Columbia University. Reprinted by permission of the publisher and author.

possible that members of novel or even of familiar non-human species should be persons; and it is also conceptually possible that some members of the human species are not persons. We do in fact assume, on the other hand, that no member of another species is a person. Accordingly, there is a presumption that what is essential to persons is a set of characteristics that we generally suppose—whether rightly or wrongly—to be uniquely human.

It is my view that one essential difference between persons and other creatures is to be found in the structure of a person's will. Human beings are not alone in having desires and motives, or in making choices. They share these things with the members of certain other species, some of whom even appear to engage in deliberation and to make decisions based upon prior thought. It seems to be peculiarly characteristic of humans, however, that they are able to form what I shall call "second-order desires" or "desires of the second order."

Besides wanting and choosing and being moved *to do* this or that, men may also want to have (or not to have) certain desires and motives. They are capable of wanting to be different, in their preferences and purposes, from what they are. Many animals appear to have the capacity for what I shall call "first-order desires" or "desires of the first order," which are simply desires to do or not to do one thing or another. No animal other than man, however, appears to have the capacity for reflective self-evaluation that is manifested in the formation of second-order desires.[2]

I

The concept designated by the verb "to want" is extraordinarily elusive. A statement of the form "A wants to X"—taken by itself, apart from a context that serves to amplify or to specify its meaning—conveys remarkably little information. Such a statement may be consistent, for example, with each of the following statements: (a) the prospect of doing X elicits no sensation or introspectible emotional response in A; (b) A is unaware that he wants to X; (c) A believes that he does not want to X; (d) A wants to refrain from X-ing; (e) A wants to Y and believes

that it is impossible for him both to Y and to X; (f) A does not "really" want to X; (g) *A would rather die than X*; and so on. It is therefore hardly sufficient to formulate the distinction between first-order and second-order desires, as I have done, by suggesting merely that someone has a first-order desire when he wants to do or not to do such-and-such, and that he has a second-order desire when he wants to have or not to have a certain desire of the first order.

As I shall understand them, statements of the form "A wants to X" cover a rather broad range of possibilities.[3] They may be true even when statements like (a) through (g) are true: when A is unaware of any feelings concerning X-ing, when he is unaware that he wants to X, when he deceives himself about what he wants and believes falsely that he does not want to X, when he also has other desires that conflict with his desire to X, or when he is ambivalent. The desires in question may be conscious or unconscious, they need not be univocal, and A may be mistaken about them. There is a further source of uncertainty with regard to statements that identify someone's desires, however, and here it is important for my purposes to be less permissive.

Consider first those statements of the form "A wants to X" which identify first-order desires—that is, statements in which the term "to X" refers to an action. A statement of this kind does not, by itself, indicate the relative strength of A's desire to X. It does not make it clear whether this desire is at all likely to play a decisive role in what A actually does or tries to do. For it may correctly be said that A wants to X even when his desire to X is only one among his desires and when it is far from being paramount among them. Thus, it may be true that A wants to X when he strongly prefers to do something else instead; and it may be true that he wants to X despite the fact that, when he acts, it is not the desire to X that motivates him to do what he does. On the other hand, someone who states that A wants to X may mean to convey that it is this desire that is motivating or moving A to do what he is actually doing or that A will in fact be moved by this desire (unless he changes his mind) when he acts.

It is only when it is used in the second of these ways that, given the special usage of "will" that I propose to adopt, the statement identifies A's will.

To identify an agent's will is either to identify the desire (or desires) by which he is motivated in some action he performs or to identify the desire (or desires) by which he will or would be motivated when or if he acts. An agent's will, then, is identical with one or more of his first-order desires. But the notion of the will, as I am employing it, is not coextensive with the notion of first-order desires. It is not the notion of something that merely inclines an agent in some degree to act in a certain way. Rather, it is the notion of an *effective* desire—one that moves (or will or would move) a person all the way to action. Thus the notion of the will is not coextensive with the notion of what an agent intends to do. For even though someone may have a settled intention to do X, he may nonetheless do something else instead of doing X because, despite his intention, his desire to do X proves to be weaker or less effective than some conflicting desire.

Now consider those statements of the form "*A* wants to *X*" which identify second-order desires—that is, statements in which the term "to *X*" refers to a desire of the first order. There are also two kinds of situation in which it may be true that *A* wants to want to *X*. In the first place, it might be true of *A* that he wants to have a desire to *X* despite the fact that he has a univocal desire, altogether free of conflict and ambivalence, to refrain from *X*-ing. Someone might want to have a certain desire, in other words, but univocally want that desire to be unsatisfied.

Suppose that a physician engaged in psychotherapy with narcotics addicts believes that his ability to help his patients would be enhanced if he understood better what it is like for them to desire the drug to which they are addicted. Suppose that he is led in this way to want to have a desire for the drug. If it is a genuine desire that he wants, then what he wants is not merely to feel the sensations that addicts characteristically feel when they are gripped by their desires for the drug. What the physician wants, in so far as he wants to have a desire, is to be inclined or moved to some extent to take the drug.

It is entirely possible, however, that, although he wants to be moved by a desire to take the drug, he does not want this desire to be effective. He may not want it to move him all the way to action. He need

not be interested in finding out what it is like to take the drug. And in so far as he now wants only to *want* to take it, and not to *take* it, there is nothing in what he now wants that would be satisfied by the drug itself. He may now have, in fact, an altogether univocal desire *not* to take the drug; and he may prudently arrange to make it impossible for him to satisfy the desire he would have if his desire to want the drug should in time be satisfied.

It would thus be incorrect to infer, from the fact that the physician now wants to desire to take the drug, that he already does desire to take it. His second-order desire to be moved to take the drug does not entail that he has a first-order desire to take it. If the drug were now to be administered to him, this might satisfy no desire that is implicit in his desire to want to take it. While he wants to take the drug, he may have *no* desire to take it; it may be that *all* he wants is to taste the desire for it. That is, his desire to have a certain desire that he does not have may not be a desire that his will should be at all different than it is.

Someone who wants only in this truncated way to want to *X* stands at the margin of preciosity, and the fact that he wants to want to *X* is not pertinent to the identification of his will. There is, however, a second kind of situation that may be described by "*A* wants to *X*"; and when the statement is used to describe a situation of this second kind, then it does pertain to what *A* wants his will to be. In such cases the statement means that *A* wants the desire to *X* to be the desire that moves him effectively to act. It is not merely that he wants the desire to *X* to be among the desires by which, to one degree or another, he is moved or inclined to act. He wants this desire to be effective—that is, to provide the motive in what he actually does. Now when the statement that *A* wants to want to *X* is used in this way, it does entail that *A* already has a desire to *X*. It could not be true both that *A* wants the desire to *X* to move him into action and that he does not want to *X*. It is only if he does want to *X* that he can coherently want the desire to *X* not merely to be one of his desires but, more decisively, to be his will.[4]

Suppose a man wants to be motivated in what he does by the desire to concentrate on his work. It is necessarily true, if this supposition is correct, that he already wants to concentrate on his work. This desire is now among his desires. But the question of whether or not his second-order desire is fulfilled does not turn merely on whether the desire he wants is one of his desires. It turns on whether this desire is, as he wants it to be, his effective desire or will. If, when the chips are down, it is his desire to concentrate on his work that moves him to do what he does, then what he wants at that time is indeed (in the relevant sense) what he wants to want. If it is some other desire that actually moves him when he acts, on the other hand, then what he wants at that time is not (in the relevant sense) what he wants to want. This will be so despite the fact that the desire to concentrate on his work continues to be among his desires.

II

Someone has a desire of the second order either when he wants simply to have a certain desire or when he wants a certain desire to be his will. In situations of the latter kind, I shall call his second-order desires "second-order volitions" or "volitions of the second order." Now it is having second-order volitions, and not having second-order desires generally, that I regard as essential to being a person. It is logically possible, however unlikely, that there should be an agent with second-order desires but with no volitions of the second order. Such a creature, in my view, would not be a person. I shall use the term "wanton" to refer to agents who have first-order desires but who are not persons because, whether or not they have desires of the second order, they have no second-order volitions.[5]

The essential characteristic of a wanton is that he does not care about his will. His desires move him to do certain things, without its being true of him either that he wants to be moved by those desires or that he prefers to be moved by other desires. The class of wantons includes all non-human animals that have desires and all very young children. Perhaps it also includes some adult human beings as well. In any case, adult humans may be more or less wanton; they may act wantonly, in response to first-order desires concerning which they have no volitions of the second order, or less frequently.

The fact that a wanton has no second-order volitions does not mean that each of his first-order desires is translated heedlessly and at once into action. He may have no opportunity to act in accordance with some of his desires. Moreover, the translation of his desires into action may be delayed or precluded either by conflicting desires of the first order or by the intervention of deliberation. For a wanton may possess and employ rational faculties of a high order. Nothing in the concept of a wanton implies that he cannot reason or that he cannot deliberate concerning how to do what he wants to do. What distinguishes the rational wanton from other rational agents is that he is not concerned with the desirability of his desires themselves. He ignores the question of what his will is to be. Not only does he pursue whatever course of action he is most strongly inclined to pursue, but he does not care which of his inclinations is the strongest.

Thus a rational creature, who reflects upon the suitability to his desires of one course of action or another, may nonetheless be a wanton. In maintaining that the essence of being a person lies not in reason but in will, I am far from suggesting that a creature without reason may be a person. For it is only in virtue of his rational capabilities that a person is capable of becoming critically aware of his own will and of forming volitions of the second order. The structure of a person's will presupposes, accordingly, that he is a rational being.

The distinction between a person and a wanton may be illustrated by the difference between two narcotics addicts. Let us suppose that the physiological condition accounting for the addiction is the same in both men, and that both succumb inevitably to their periodic desires for the drug to which they are addicted. One of the addicts hates his addiction and always struggles desperately, although to no avail, against its thrust. He tries everything that he thinks might enable him to overcome his desires for the drug. But these desires are too powerful for him to withstand, and invariably, in the end, they conquer him. He is an unwilling addict, helplessly violated by his own desires.

The unwilling addict has conflicting first-order desires: he wants to take the drug, and he also wants to refrain from taking it. In addition to these first-order desires, however, he has a volition of the second order. He is not a neutral with regard to the conflict between his desire to take the drug and his desire to refrain from taking it. It is the latter desire, and not the former, that he wants to constitute his will; it is the latter desire, rather than the former, that he wants to be effective and to provide the purpose that he will seek to realize in what he actually does.

The other addict is a wanton. His actions reflect the economy of his first-order desires, without his being concerned whether the desires that move him to act are desires by which he wants to be moved to act. If he encounters problems in obtaining the drug or in administering it to himself, his responses to his urges to take it may involve deliberation. But it never occurs to him to consider whether he wants the relation among his desires to result in his having the will he has. The wanton addict may be an animal, and thus incapable of being concerned about his will. In any event he is, in respect of his wanton lack of concern, no different from an animal.

The second of these addicts may suffer a first-order conflict similar to the first-order conflict suffered by the first. Whether he is human or not, the wanton may (perhaps due to conditioning) both want to take the drug and want to refrain from taking it. Unlike the unwilling addict, however, he does not prefer that one of his conflicting desires should be paramount over the other; he does not prefer that one first-order desire rather than the other should constitute his will. It would be misleading to say that he is neutral as to the conflict between his desires, since this would suggest that he regards them as equally acceptable. Since he has no identity apart from his first-order desires, it is true neither that he prefers one to the other nor that he prefers not to take sides.

It makes a difference to the unwilling addict, who is a person, which of his conflicting first-order desires wins out. Both desires are his, to be sure; and whether he finally takes the drug or finally succeeds in refraining from taking it, he acts to satisfy what is in a literal sense his own desire. In either case he does something he himself wants to do, and he does it not because of some external influence whose aim happens to coincide with his own but because of his

desire to do it. The unwilling addict identifies himself, however, through the formation of a second-order volition, with one rather than with the other of his conflicting first-order desires. He makes one of them more truly his own and, in so doing, he withdraws himself from the other. It is in virtue of this identification and withdrawal, accomplished through the formation of a second-order volition, that the unwilling addict may meaningfully make the analytically puzzling statements that the force moving him to take the drug is a force other than his own, and that it is not of his own free will but rather against his will that this force moves him to take it.

The wanton addict cannot or does not care which of his conflicting first-order desires wins out. His lack of concern is not due to his inability to find a convincing basis for preference. It is due either to his lack of the capacity for reflection or to his mindless indifference to the enterprise of evaluating his own desires and motives.[6] There is only one issue in the struggle to which his first-order conflict may lead: whether the one or the other of his conflicting desires is the stronger. Since he is moved by both desires, he will not be altogether satisfied by what he does no matter which of them is effective. But it makes no difference to *him* whether his craving or his aversion gets the upper hand. He has no stake in the conflict between them and so, unlike the unwilling addict, he can neither win nor lose the struggle in which he is engaged. When a *person* acts, the desire by which he is moved is either the will he wants or a will he wants to be without. When a *wanton* acts, it is neither.

III

There is a very close relationship between the capacity for forming second-order volitions and another capacity that is essential to persons—one that has often been considered a distinguishing mark of the human condition. It is only because a person has volitions of the second order that he is capable both of enjoying and of lacking freedom of will. The concept of a person is not only, then, the concept of a type of entity that has both first-order desires and volitions of the second order. It can also be construed as the concept of a type of entity for whom the freedom of its will may be a problem. This concept excludes all wantons, both infrahuman and human, since they fail to satisfy an essential condition for the enjoyment of freedom of the will. And it excludes those suprahuman beings, if any, whose wills are necessarily free.

Just what kind of freedom is the freedom of the will? This question calls for an identification of the special area of human experience to which the concept of freedom of the will, as distinct from the concepts of other sorts of freedom, is particularly germane. In dealing with it, my aim will be primarily to locate the problem with which a person is most immediately concerned when he is concerned with the freedom of his will.

According to one familiar philosophical tradition, being free is fundamentally a matter of doing what one wants to do. Now the notion of an agent who does what he wants to do is by no means an altogether clear one: both the doing and the wanting, and the appropriate relation between them as well, require elucidation. But although its focus needs to be sharpened and its formulation refined, I believe that this notion does capture at least part of what is implicit in the idea of an agent who *acts* freely. It misses entirely, however, the peculiar content of the quite different idea of an agent whose *will* is free.

We do not suppose that animals enjoy freedom of the will, although we recognize that an animal may be free to run in whatever direction it wants. Thus, having the freedom to do what one wants to do is not a sufficient condition of having a free will. It is not a necessary condition either. For to deprive someone of his freedom of action is not necessarily to undermine the freedom of his will. When an agent is aware that there are certain things he is not free to do, this doubtless affects his desires and limits the range of choices he can make. But suppose that someone, without being aware of it, has in fact lost or been deprived of his freedom of action. Even though he is no longer free to do what he wants to do, his will may remain as free as it was before. Despite the fact that he is not free to translate his desires into actions or to act according to the determinations of his will, he may still form those desires

and make those determinations as freely as if his freedom of action had not been impaired.

When we ask whether a person's will is free we are not asking whether he is in a position to translate his first-order desires into actions. That is the question of whether he is free to do as he pleases. The question of the freedom of his will does not concern the relation between what he does and what he wants to do. Rather, it concerns his desires themselves. But what question about them is it?

It seems to me both natural and useful to construe the question of whether a person's will is free in close analogy to the question of whether an agent enjoys freedom of action. Now freedom of action is (roughly, at least) the freedom to do what one wants to do. Analogously, then, the statement that a person enjoys freedom of the will means (also roughly) that he is free to want what he wants to want. More precisely, it means that he is free to will what he wants to will, or to have the will he wants. Just as the question about the freedom of an agent's action has to do with whether it is the action he wants to perform, so the question about the freedom of his will has to do with whether it is the will he wants to have.

It is in securing the conformity of his will to his second-order volitions, then, that a person exercises freedom of the will. And it is in the discrepancy between his will and his second-order volitions, or in his awareness that their coincidence is not his own doing but only a happy chance, that a person who does not have this freedom feels its lack. The unwilling addict's will is not free. This is shown by the fact that it is not the will he wants. It is also true, though in a different way, that the will of the wanton addict is not free. The wanton addict neither has the will he wants nor has a will that differs from the will he wants. Since he has no volitions of the second order, the freedom of his will cannot be a problem for him. He lacks it, so to speak, by default.

People are generally far more complicated than my sketchy account of the structure of a person's will may suggest. There is as much opportunity for ambivalence, conflict, and self-deception with regard to desires of the second order, for example, as there is with regard to first-order desires. If there is an unresolved conflict among someone's second-or-

der desires, then he is in danger of having no second-order volition; for unless this conflict is resolved, he has no preference concerning which of
his first-order desires is to be his will. This condition, if it is so severe that it prevents him from identifying himself in a sufficiently decisive way with
any of his conflicting first-order desires, destroys
him as a person. For it either tends to paralyse his
will and to keep him from acting at all, or it tends
to remove him from his will so that his will operates without his participation. In both cases he becomes, like the unwilling addict though in a different way, a helpless bystander to the forces that move
him.

Another complexity is that a person may have, especially if his second-order desires are in conflict, desires and volitions of a higher order than the second.
There is no theoretical limit to the length of the series of desires of higher and higher orders; nothing
except common sense and, perhaps, a saving fatigue
prevents an individual from obsessively refusing to
identify himself with any of his desires until he forms
a desire of the next higher order. The tendency to
generate such a series of acts of forming desires,
which would be a case of humanization run wild, also
leads toward the destruction of a person.

It is possible, however, to terminate such a series
of acts without cutting it off arbitrarily. When a person identifies himself *decisively* with one of his first-
order desires, this commitment "resounds" throughout the potentially endless array of higher orders.
Consider a person who, without reservation or conflict, wants to be motivated by the desire to concentrate on his work. The fact that his second-order
volition to be moved by this desire is a decisive one
means that there is no room for questions concerning the pertinence of desires or volitions of higher
orders. Suppose the person is asked whether he
wants to want to want to concentrate on his work.
He can properly insist that this question concerning a third-order desire does not arise. It would be
a mistake to claim that, because he has not considered whether he wants the second-order volition he
has formed, he is indifferent to the question of
whether it is with this volition or with some other
that he wants his will to accord. The decisiveness
of the commitment he has made means that he has

decided that no further question about his second-
order volition, or any higher order, remains to be
asked. It is relatively unimportant whether we explain this by saying that this commitment implicitly generates an endless series of confirming desires of higher orders, or by saying that the
commitment is tantamount to a dissolution of the
pointedness of all questions concerning higher orders of desire.

Examples such as the one concerning the unwilling addict may suggest that volitions of the second
order, or of higher orders, must be formed deliberately and that a person characteristically struggles to
ensure that they are satisfied. But the conformity of
a person's will to his higher-order volitions may be
far more thoughtless and spontaneous than this.
Some people are naturally moved by kindness when
they want to be kind, and by nastiness when they
want to be nasty, without any explicit forethought
and without any need for energetic self-control.
Others are moved by nastiness when they want to be
kind and by kindness when they intend to be nasty,
equally without forethought and without active resistance to these violations of their higher-order desires. The enjoyment of freedom comes easily to
some. Others must struggle to achieve it.

IV

My theory concerning the freedom of the will accounts easily for our disinclination to allow that this
freedom is enjoyed by the members of any species
inferior to our own. It also satisfies another condition that must be met by any such theory, by making it apparent why the freedom of the will should
be regarded as desirable. The enjoyment of a free
will means the satisfaction of certain desires—desires of the second or of higher orders—whereas its
absence means their frustration. The satisfactions at
stake are those which accrue to a person of whom
it may be said that his will is his own. The corresponding frustrations are those suffered by a person
of whom it may be said that he is estranged from
himself, or that he finds himself a helpless or a passive bystander to the forces that move him.

A person who is free to do what he wants to do

may yet not be in a position to have the will he wants. Suppose, however, that he enjoys both freedom of action and freedom of the will. Then he is not only free to do what he wants to do; he is also free to want what he wants to want. It seems to me that he has, in that case, all the freedom it is possible to desire or to conceive. There are other good things in life, and he may not possess some of them. But there is nothing in the way of freedom that he lacks.

It is far from clear that certain other theories of the freedom of the will meet these elementary but essential conditions: that it be understandable why we desire this freedom and why we refuse to ascribe it to animals. Consider, for example, Roderick Chisholm's quaint version of the doctrine that human freedom entails an absence of causal determination.[7] Whenever a person performs a free action, according to Chisholm, it's a miracle. The motion of a person's hand, when the person moves it, is the outcome of a series of physical causes; but some event in this series, "and presumably one of those that took place within the brain, was caused by the agent and not by any other events" (18). A free agent has, therefore, "a prerogative which some would attribute only to God: each of us, when we act, is a prime mover unmoved" (23).

This account fails to provide any basis for doubting that animals of subhuman species enjoy the freedom it defines. Chisholm says nothing that makes it seem less likely that a rabbit performs a miracle when it moves its leg than that a man does so when he moves his hand. But why, in any case, should anyone *care* whether he can interrupt the natural order of causes in the way Chisholm describes? Chisholm offers no reason for believing that there is a discernible difference between the experience of a man who miraculously initiates a series of causes when he moves his hand and a man who moves his hand without any such breach of the normal causal sequence. There appears to be no concrete basis for preferring to be involved in the one state of affairs rather than in the other.[8]

It is generally supposed that, in addition to satisfying the two conditions I have mentioned, a satisfactory theory of the freedom of the will necessarily provides an analysis of one of the conditions of moral responsibility. The most common recent approach to the problem of understanding the freedom of the will has been, indeed, to inquire what is entailed by the assumption that someone is morally responsible for what he has done. In my view, however, the relation between moral responsibility and the freedom of the will has been very widely misunderstood. It is not true that a person is morally responsible for what he has done only if his will was free when he did it. He may be morally responsible for having done it even though his will was not free at all.

A person's will is free only if he is free to have the will he wants. This means that, with regard to any of his first-order desires, he is free either to make that desire his will or to make some other first-order desire his will instead. Whatever his will, then, the will of the person whose will is free could have been otherwise; he could have done otherwise than to constitute his will as he did. It is a vexed question just how "he could have done otherwise" is to be understood in contexts such as this one. But although this question is important to the theory of freedom, it has no bearing on the theory of moral responsibility. For the assumption that a person is morally responsible for what he has done does not entail that the person was in a position to have whatever will he wanted.

This assumption *does* entail that the person did what he did freely, or that he did it of his own free will. It is a mistake, however, to believe that someone acts freely only when he is free to do whatever he wants or that he acts of his own free will only if his will is free. Suppose that a person has done what he wanted to do, that he did it because he wanted to do it, and that the will by which he was moved when he did it was his will because it was the will he wanted. Then he did it freely and of his own free will. Even supposing that he could have done otherwise, he would not have done otherwise; and even supposing that he could have had a different will, he would not have wanted his will to differ from what it was. Moreover, since the will that moved him when he acted was his will because he wanted it to be, he cannot claim that his will was forced upon him or that he was a passive bystander to its constitution. Under these conditions, it is quite irrelevant to the evaluation of his moral responsibility to inquire whether the alternatives that he opted against were actually available to him.[9]

In illustration, consider a third kind of addict. Suppose that his addiction has the same physiological basis and the same irresistible thrust as the addictions of the unwilling and wanton addicts, but that he is altogether delighted with his condition. He is a willing addict, who would not have things any other way. If the grip of his addiction should somehow weaken, he would do whatever he could to reinstate it; if his desire for the drug should begin to fade, he would take steps to renew its intensity.

The willing addict's will is not free, for his desire to take the drug will be effective regardless of whether or not he wants this desire to constitute his will. But when he takes the drug, he takes it freely and of his own free will. I am inclined to understand his situation as involving the overdetermination of his first-order desire to take the drug. This desire is his effective desire because he is physiologically addicted. But it is his effective desire also because he wants it to be. His will is outside his control, but, by his second-order desire that his desire for the drug should be effective, he has made this will his own. Given that it is therefore not only because of his addiction that his desire for the drug is effective, he may be morally responsible for taking the drug.

My conception of the freedom of the will appears to be neutral with regard to the problem of determinism. It seems conceivable that it should be causally determined that a person is free to want what he wants to want. If this is conceivable, then it might be causally determined that a person enjoys a free will. There is no more than an innocuous appearance of paradox in the proposition that it is determined, ineluctably and by forces beyond their control, that certain people have free wills and that others do not. There is no incoherence in the proposition that some agency other than a person's own is responsible (even *morally* responsible) for the fact that he enjoys or fails to enjoy freedom of the will. It is possible that a person should be morally responsible for what he does of his own free will and that some other person should also be morally responsible for his having done it.[10]

On the other hand, it seems conceivable that it should come about by chance that a person is free to have the will he wants. If this is conceivable, then it might be a matter of chance that certain people enjoy freedom of the will and that certain others do not. Perhaps it is also conceivable, as a number of philosophers believe, for states of affairs to come about in a way other than by chance or as the outcome of a sequence of natural causes. If it is indeed conceivable for the relevant states of affairs to come about in some third way, then it is also possible that a person should in that third way come to enjoy the freedom of the will.

NOTES

1. P. F. Strawson, *Individuals* (London: Methuen, 1959), pp. 101–2. Ayer's usage of "person" is similar: "it is characteristic of persons in this sense that besides having various physical properties . . . they are also credited with various forms of consciousness" (A. J. Ayer, *The Concept of a Person* [New York: St. Martin's, 1963], p. 82). What concerns Strawson and Ayer is the problem of understanding the relation between mind and body, rather than the quite different problem of understanding what it is to be a creature that not only has a mind and a body but is also a person.

2. For the sake of simplicity, I shall deal only with what someone wants or desires, neglecting related phenomena such as choices and decisions. I propose to use the verbs "to want" and "to desire" interchangeably, although they are by no means perfect synonyms. My motive in forsaking the established nuances of these words arises from the fact that the verb "to want," which suits my purposes better so far as its meaning is concerned, does not lend itself so readily to the formation of nouns as does the verb "to desire." It is perhaps acceptable, albeit graceless, to speak in the plural of someone's "wants." But to speak in the singular of someone's "want" would be an abomination.

3. What I say in this paragraph applies not only to cases in which "to X" refers to a possible action or inaction. It also applies to cases in which "to X" refers to a first-order desire and in which the statement that "A wants to X" is therefore a shortened version of a statement—"A wants to want X"—that identifies a desire of the second order.

4. It is not so clear that the entailment relation described here holds in certain kinds of cases, which I think may fairly be regarded as non-standard, where the essential difference between the standard and the non-standard cases lies in the kind of description by which the first-order desire in question is identified. Thus, suppose that *A* admires *B* so fulsomely that, even though he does not know what *B* wants to do, he wants to be effectively moved by whatever desire effectively moves *B*; without knowing what *B*'s will is, in other words, *A* wants his own will to be the same. It certainly does not follow that *A* already has, among his desires, a desire like the one that constitutes *B*'s will. I shall not pursue here the questions of whether there are genuine counterexamples to the claim made in the text or of how, if there are, that claim should be altered.

5. Creatures with second-order desires but no second-order volitions differ significantly from brute animals, and, for some purposes, it would be desirable to regard them as persons. My usage, which withholds the designation "person" from them, is thus somewhat arbitrary. I adopt it largely because it facilitates the formulation of some of the points I wish to make. Hereafter, whenever I consider statements of the form "*A* wants to want to *X*," I shall have in mind statements identifying second-order volitions and not statements identifying second-order desires that are not second-order volitions.

6. In speaking of the evaluation of his own desires and motives as being characteristic of a person, I do not mean to suggest that a person's second-order volitions necessarily manifest a *moral* stance on his part toward his first-order desires. It may not be from the point of view of morality that the person evaluates his first-order desires. Moreover, a person may be capricious and irresponsible in forming his second-order volitions and give no serious consideration to what is at stake. Second-order volitions express evaluations only in the sense that they are preferences. There is no essential restriction on the kind of basis, if any, upon which they are formed.

7. "Freedom and Action," in *Freedom and Determinism*, ed. Keith Lehrer (New York: Random House, 1966), pp. 11–44.

8. I am not suggesting that the alleged difference between these two states of affairs is unverifiable. On the contrary, physiologists might well be able to show that Chisholm's conditions for a free action are not satisfied, by establishing that there is no relevant brain event for which a sufficient physical cause cannot be found.

9. For another discussion of the considerations that cast doubt on the principle that a person is morally responsible for what he has done only if he could have done otherwise, see my "Alternate Possibilities and Moral Responsibility," *Journal of Philosophy* (1969): 829–39.

10. There is a difference between being *fully* responsible and being *solely* responsible. Suppose that the willing addict has been made an addict by the deliberate and calculated work of another. Then it may be that both the addict and this other person are fully responsible for the addict's taking the drug, while neither of them is solely responsible for it. That there is a distinction between full moral responsibility and sole moral responsibility is apparent in the following example. A certain light can be turned on or off by flicking either of two switches, and each of these switches is simultaneously flicked to the "on" position by a different person, neither of whom is aware of the other. Neither person is solely responsible for the light's going on, nor do they share the responsibility in the sense that each is partially responsible; rather, each of them is fully responsible.

Freedom and Resentment

PETER STRAWSON

Peter Strawson (1919–) is Professor Emeritus at Magdalen College, Oxford. He is a major contributor to twentieth-century philosophy. His books include *Individuals* and *The Bounds of Sense*.

———•———

SOME PHILOSOPHERS SAY THEY DO not know what the thesis of determinism is. Others say, or imply, that they do know what it is. Of these, some—the pessimists perhaps—hold that if the thesis is true, then the concepts of moral obligation and responsibility really have no application, and the practices of punishing and blaming, of expressing moral condemnation and approval, are really unjustified. Others—the optimists perhaps—hold that these concepts and practices in no way lose their *raison d'être* if the thesis of determinism is true. Some hold even that the justification of these concepts and practices requires the truth of the thesis. There is another opinion which is less frequently voiced: the opinion, it might be said, of the genuine moral sceptic. This is that the notions of moral guilt, of blame, of moral responsibility are inherently confused and that we can see this to be so if we consider the consequences either of the truth of determinism or of its falsity. The holders of this opinion agree with the pessimists that these notions lack application if determinism is true, and add simply that they also lack it if determinism is false. If I am asked which of these parties I belong to, I must say it is the first of all, the party of those who do not know what the thesis of determinism is. But this does not stop me from having some sympathy with the others, and a wish to reconcile them. Should not ignorance, rationally, inhibit such sympathies? Well, of course, though darkling, one has some inkling—some notion of what sort of thing is being talked about. This lecture is intended as a move towards reconciliation; so is likely to seem wrongheaded to everyone.

But can there be any possibility of reconciliation between such clearly opposed positions as those of pessimists and optimists about determinism? Well, there might be a formal withdrawal on one side in return for a substantial concession on the other. Thus, suppose the optimist's position were put like this: (1) the facts as we know them do not show determinism to be false; (2) the facts as we know them supply an adequate basis for the concepts and practices which the pessimist feels to be imperilled by the possibility of determinism's truth. Now it might be that the optimist is right in this, but is apt to give an inadequate account of the facts as we know them, and of how they constitute an adequate basis for the problematic concepts and practices; that the reasons he gives for the adequacy of the basis are themselves inadequate and leave out something vital. It might be that the pessimist is rightly anxious to get this vital thing back and, in the grip of his anxiety, feels he has to go beyond the facts as we know them; feels that the vital thing can be secure only if, beyond the facts as we know them, there is the further fact that determinism is false. Might *he* not be brought to make a formal withdrawal in return for a vital concession?

2. Let me enlarge very briefly on this, by way of preliminary only. Some optimists about determinism point to the efficacy of the practices of punishment, and of moral condemnation and approval, in regulating behaviour in socially desirable ways.[1] In the fact of their efficacy, they suggest, is an adequate basis for these practices; and this fact certainly does not show determinism to be false. To this the pessimists reply, all in a rush, that *just* punishment and *moral* condemnation imply moral guilt and guilt implies moral responsibility and moral responsibility implies freedom and freedom implies the falsity of determinism. And to this the optimists are wont to reply in turn that it is true that these practices require freedom in a sense, and the existence of free-

From *Proceedings of the British Academy* Vol. XLVII. Copyright © 1962 by The British Academy. Reprinted by permission of the publisher.

dom in this sense is one of the facts as we know them. But what "freedom" means here is nothing but the absence of certain conditions the presence of which would make moral condemnation or punishment inappropriate. They have in mind conditions like compulsion by another, or innate incapacity, or insanity, or other less extreme forms of psychological disorder, or the existence of circumstances in which the making of any other choice would be morally inadmissible or would be too much to expect of any man. To this list they are constrained to add other factors which, without exactly being limitations of freedom, may also make moral condemnation or punishment inappropriate or mitigate their force: as some forms of ignorance, mistake, or accident. And the general reason why moral condemnation or punishment is inappropriate when these factors or conditions are present is held to be that the practices in question will be generally efficacious means of regulating behaviour in desirable ways only in cases where these factors are *not* present. Now the pessimist admits that the facts as we know them include the existence of freedom, the occurrence of cases of free action, in the negative sense which the optimist concedes; and admits, or rather insists, that the existence of freedom in this sense is compatible with the truth of determinism. Then what does the pessimist find missing? When he tries to answer this question, his language is apt to alternate between the very familiar and the very unfamiliar.[2] Thus he may say, familiarly enough, that the man who is the subject of justified punishment, blame or moral condemnation must really *deserve* it; and then add, perhaps, that in the case at least where he is blamed for a positive act rather than an omission, the condition of his really deserving blame is something that goes beyond the negative freedoms that the optimist concedes. It is, say, a genuinely free identification of the will with the act. And this is the condition that is incompatible with the truth of determinism.

The conventional, but conciliatory, optimist need not give up yet. He may say: Well, people often decide to do things, really intend to do what they do, know just what they're doing in doing it; the reasons they think they have for doing what they do, often really are their reasons and not their rational-

izations. These facts, too, are included in the facts as we know them. If this is what you mean by freedom—by the identification of the will with the act—then freedom may again be conceded. But again the concession is compatible with the truth of the determinist thesis. For it would not follow from that thesis that nobody decides to do anything; that nobody ever does anything intentionally; that it is false that people sometimes know perfectly well what they are doing. I tried to define freedom negatively. You want to give it a more positive look. But it comes to the same thing. Nobody denies freedom in this sense, or these senses, and nobody claims that the existence of freedom in these senses shows determinism to be false.

But it is here that the lacuna in the optimistic story can be made to show. For the pessimist may be supposed to ask: But *why* does freedom in this sense justify blame, &c.? You turn towards me first the negative, and then the positive, faces of a freedom which nobody challenges. But the only reason you have given for the practices of moral condemnation and punishment in cases where this freedom is present is the efficacy of these practices in regulating behaviour in socially desirable ways. But this is not a sufficient basis, it is not even the right *sort* of basis, for these practices as we understand them.

Now my optimist, being the sort of man he is, is not likely to invoke an intuition of fittingness at this point. So he really has no more to say. And my pessimist, being the sort of man he is, has only one more thing to say; and that is that the admissibility of these practices, as we understand them, demands another kind of freedom, the kind that in turn demands the falsity of the thesis of determinism. But might we not induce the pessimist to give up saying this by giving the optimist something more to say?

3. I have mentioned punishing and moral condemnation and approval; and it is in connexion with these practices or attitudes that the issue between optimists and pessimists—or, if one is a pessimist, the issue between determinists and libertarians—is felt to be particularly important. But it is not of these practices and attitudes that I propose, at first, to speak. These practices or attitudes permit, where they do not imply, a certain detachment from the actions or agents which are their objects. I want to

speak, at least at first, of something else: of the non-detached attitudes and reactions of people directly involved in transactions with each other; of the attitudes and reactions of offended parties and beneficiaries; of such things as gratitude, resentment, forgiveness, love, and hurt feelings. Perhaps something like the issue between optimists and pessimists arises in this neighbouring field too; and since this field is less crowded with disputants, the issue might here be easier to settle; and if it is settled here, then it might become easier to settle it in the disputant-crowded field.

What I have to say consists largely of commonplaces. So my language, like that of commonplaces generally, will be quite unscientific and imprecise. The central commonplace that I want to insist on is the very great importance that we attach to the attitudes and intentions towards us of other human beings, and the great extent to which our personal feelings and reactions depend upon, or involve, our beliefs about these attitudes and intentions. I can give no simple description of the field of phenomena at the centre of which stands this commonplace truth; for the field is too complex. Much imaginative literature is devoted to exploring its complexities; and we have a large vocabulary for the purpose. There are simplifying styles of handling it in a general way. Thus we may, like La Rochefoucauld, put self-love or self-esteem or vanity at the centre of the picture and point out how it may be caressed by the esteem, or wounded by the indifference or contempt, of others. We might speak, in another jargon, of the need for love, and the loss of security which results from its withdrawal; or, in another, of human self-respect and its connexion with the recognition of the individual's dignity. These simplifications are of use to me only if they help to emphasize how much we actually mind, how much it matters to us, whether the actions of other people—and particularly of *some* other people—reflect attitudes towards us of goodwill, affection, or esteem on the one hand or contempt, indifference, or malevolence on the other. If someone treads on my hand accidentally, while trying to help me, the pain may be no less acute than if he treads on it in contemptuous disregard of my existence or with a

malevolent wish to injure me. But I shall generally feel in the second case a kind and degree of resentment that I shall not feel in the first. If someone's actions help me to some benefit I desire, then I am benefited in any case; but if he intended them so to benefit me because of his general goodwill towards me, I shall reasonably feel a gratitude which I should not feel at all if the benefit was an incidental consequence, unintended or even regretted by him, of some plan of action with a different aim.

These examples are of actions which confer benefits or inflict injuries over and above any conferred or inflicted by the mere manifestation of attitude and intention themselves. We should consider also in how much of our behaviour the benefit or injury resides mainly or entirely in the manifestation of attitude itself. So it is with good manners, and much of what we call kindness, on the one hand; with deliberate rudeness, studied indifference, or insult on the other.

Besides resentment and gratitude, I mentioned just now forgiveness. This is a rather unfashionable subject in moral philosophy at present; but to be forgiven is something we sometimes ask, and forgiving is something we sometimes say we do. To ask to be forgiven is in part to acknowledge that the attitude displayed in our actions was such as might properly be resented and in part to repudiate that attitude for the future (or at least for the immediate future); and to forgive is to accept the repudiation and to forswear the resentment.

We should think of the many different kinds of relationship which we can have with other people—as sharers of a common interest; as members of the same family; as colleagues; as friends; as lovers; as chance parties to an enormous range of transactions and encounters. Then we should think, in each of these connexions in turn, and in others, of the kind of importance we attach to the attitudes and intentions towards us of those who stand in these relationships to us, and of the kinds of *reactive* attitudes and feelings to which we ourselves are prone. In general, we demand some degree of goodwill or regard on the part of those who stand in these relationships to us, though the forms we require it to take vary widely in different connexions. The range and intensity of our *reactive* attitudes towards good-will, its absence or its opposite vary no less widely. I have mentioned, specifically, resentment and gratitude; and they are a usefully opposed pair. But, of course, there is a whole continuum of reactive attitude and feeling stretching on both sides of these and—the most comfortable area—in between them.

The object of these commonplaces is to try to keep before our minds something it is easy to forget when we are engaged in philosophy, especially in our cool, contemporary style, viz. what it is actually like to be involved in ordinary inter-personal relationships, ranging from the most intimate to the most casual.

4. It is one thing to ask about the general causes of these reactive attitudes I have alluded to; it is another to ask about the variations to which they are subject, the particular conditions in which they do or do not seem natural or reasonable or appropriate; and it is a third thing to ask what it would be like, what it *is* like, not to suffer them. I am not much concerned with the first question; but I am with the second; and perhaps even more with the third.

Let us consider, then, occasions for resentment: situations in which one person is offended or injured by the action of another and in which—in the absence of special considerations—the offended person might naturally or normally be expected to feel resentment. Then let us consider what sorts of special considerations might be expected to modify or mollify this feeling or remove it altogether. It needs no saying now how multifarious these considerations are. But, for my purpose, I think they can be roughly divided into two kinds. To the first group belong all those which might give occasion for the employment of such expressions as "He didn't mean to," "He hadn't realized," "He didn't know"; and also all those which might give occasion for the use of the phrase "He couldn't help it," when this is supported by such phrases as "He was pushed," "He had to do it," "It was the only way," "They left him no alternative," &c. Obviously these various pleas, and the kinds of situations in which they would be appropriate, differ from each other in striking and important ways. But for my present purpose they have something still more important in common.

None of them invites us to suspend towards the agent, either at the time of his action or in general, our ordinary reactive attitudes. They do not invite us to view the *agent* as one in respect of whom these attitudes are in any way inappropriate. They invite us to view the *injury* as one in respect of which a particular one of these attitudes is inappropriate. They do not invite us to see *agent* as other than a fully responsible agent. They invite us to see the *injury* as one for which he was not fully, or at all, responsible. They do not suggest that the agent is in any way an inappropriate object of that kind of demand for goodwill or regard which is reflected in our ordinary reactive attitudes. They suggest instead that the fact of injury was not in this case incompatible with that demand's being fulfilled, that the fact of injury was quite consistent with the agent's attitude and intentions being just what we demand they should be.[3] The agent was just ignorant of the injury he was causing, or had lost his balance through being pushed or had reluctantly to cause the injury for reasons which acceptably override his reluctance. The offering of such pleas by the agent and their acceptance by the sufferer is something in no way opposed to, or outside the context of, ordinary inter-personal relationships and the manifestation of ordinary reactive attitudes. Since things go wrong and situations are complicated, it is an essential and integral element in the transactions which are the life of these relationships.

The second group of considerations is very different. I shall take them in two subgroups of which the first is far less important than the second. In connexion with the first subgroup we may think of such statements as "He wasn't himself," "He has been under very great strain recently," "He was acting under posthypnotic suggestion"; in connexion with the second, we may think of "He's only a child," "He's a hopeless schizophrenic," "His mind has been systematically perverted," "That's purely compulsive behaviour on his part." Such pleas as these do, as pleas of my first general group do not, invite us to suspend our ordinary reactive attitudes towards the agent, either at the time of his action or all the time. They do not invite us to see the agent's action in a way consistent with the full retention of ordinary inter-personal attitudes and merely inconsistent with one particular attitude. They invite us to view the agent himself in a different light from the light in which we should normally view one who has acted as he has acted. I shall not linger over the first subgroup of cases. Though they perhaps raise, in the short term, questions akin to those raised, in the long term, by the second subgroup, we may dismiss them without considering those questions by taking that admirably suggestive phrase, "He wasn't himself," with the seriousness that—for all its being logically comic—it deserves. We shall not feel resentment against the man he is for the action done by the man he is not; or at least we shall feel less. We normally have to deal with him under normal stresses; so we shall not feel towards him, when he acts as he does under abnormal stresses, as we should have felt towards him had he acted as he did under normal stresses.

The second and more important subgroup of cases allows that the circumstances were normal, but presents the agent as psychologically abnormal—or as morally undeveloped. The agent was himself; but he is warped or deranged, neurotic or just a child. When we see someone in such a light as this, all our reactive attitudes tend to be profoundly modified. I must deal here in crude dichotomies and ignore the ever-interesting and ever-illuminating varieties of case. What I want to contrast is the attitude (or range of attitudes) of involvement or participation in a human relationship, on the one hand, and what might be called the objective attitude (or range of attitudes) to another human being, on the other. Even in the same situation, I must add, they are not altogether *exclusive* of each other; but they are, profoundly, *opposed* to each other. To adopt the objective attitude to another human being is to see him, perhaps, as an object of social policy; as a subject for what, in a wide range of sense, might be called treatment; as something certainly to be taken account, perhaps precautionary account, of; to be managed or handled or cured or trained; perhaps simply to be avoided, though *this* gerundive is not peculiar to cases of objectivity of attitude. The objective attitude may be emotionally toned in many ways, but not in all ways; it may include repulsion or fear, it may include pity or even love, though not all kinds

of love. But it cannot include the range of reactive feelings and attitudes which belong to involvement or participation with others in inter-personal human relationships; it cannot include resentment, gratitude, forgiveness, anger, or the sort of love which two adults can sometimes be said to feel reciprocally, for each other. If your attitude towards someone is wholly objective, then though you may fight him, you cannot quarrel with him, and though you may talk to him, even negotiate with him, you cannot reason with him. You can at most pretend to quarrel, or to reason, with him.

Seeing someone, then, as warped or deranged or compulsive in behaviour or peculiarly unfortunate in his formative circumstances—seeing someone so tends, at least to some extent, to set him apart from normal participant reactive attitudes on the part of one who so sees him, tends to promote, at least in the civilized, objective attitudes. But there is something curious to add to this. The objective attitude is not only something we naturally tend to fall into in cases like these, where participant attitudes are partially or wholly inhibited by abnormalities or by immaturity. It is also something which is available as a resource in other cases too. We look with an objective eye on the compulsive behaviour of the neurotic or the tiresome behaviour of a very young child, thinking in terms of treatment or training. But we *can* sometimes look with something like the same eye on the behaviour of the normal and the mature. We *have* this resource and can sometimes use it: as a refuge, say, from the strains of involvement; or as an aid to policy; or simply out of intellectual curiosity. Being human, we cannot, in the normal case, do this for long, or altogether. If the strains of involvement, say, continue to be too great, then we have to do something else—like severing a relationship. But what is above all interesting is the tension there is, in us, between the participant attitude and the objective attitude. One is tempted to say: between our humanity and our intelligence. But to say this would be to distort both notions.

What I have called the participant reactive attitudes are essentially natural human reactions to the good or ill will or indifference of others towards us, as displayed in *their* attitudes and actions. The question we have to ask is: What effect would, or should, the acceptance of the truth of a general thesis of determinism have upon these reactive attitudes? More specifically, would, or should, the acceptance of the truth of the thesis lead to the decay or the repudiation of all such attitudes? Would, or should, it mean the end of gratitude, resentment, and forgiveness; of all reciprocated adult loves; of all the essentially *personal* antagonisms?

But how can I answer, or even pose, this question without knowing *exactly* what the thesis of determinism is? Well, there is one thing we do know: that if there is a coherent thesis of determinism, then there must be a sense of "determined" such that, if that thesis is true, then all behaviour whatever is determined in that sense. Remembering this, we can consider at least what possibilities lie formally open; and then perhaps we shall see that the question can be answered *without* knowing exactly what the thesis of determinism is. We can consider what possibilities lie open because we have already before us an account of the ways in which particular reactive attitudes, or reactive attitudes in general, may be, and, sometimes, we judge, should be, inhibited. Thus I considered earlier a group of considerations which tend to inhibit, and, we judge, should inhibit, resentment, in particular cases of an agent causing an injury, without inhibiting reactive attitudes in general towards that agent. Obviously this group of considerations cannot strictly bear upon our question; for that question concerns reactive attitudes in general. But resentment has a particular interest; so it is worth adding that it has never been claimed as a consequence of the truth of determinism that one or another of *these* considerations was operative in every case of an injury being caused by an agent; that it would follow from the truth of determinism that anyone who caused an injury *either* was quite simply ignorant of causing it *or* had acceptably overriding reasons for acquiescing reluctantly in causing it *or* . . . , & c. The prevalence of this happy state of affairs would not be a consequence of the reign of universal determinism, but of the reign of universal goodwill. We cannot, then, find here the possibility of an affirmative answer to our question, even for the particular case of resentment.

Next, I remarked that the participant attitude, and the personal reactive attitudes in general, tend to give place, and it is judged by the civilized should give place, to objective attitudes, just in so far as the agent is seen as excluded from ordinary adult human relationships by deep-rooted psychological abnormality—or simply by being a child. But it cannot be a consequence of any thesis which is not itself self-contradictory that abnormality is the universal condition.

Now this dismissal might seem altogether too facile; and so, in a sense, it is. But whatever is too quickly dismissed in this dismissal is allowed for in the only possible form of affirmative answer that remains. We can sometimes, and in part, I have remarked, look on the normal (those we rate as "normal") in the objective way in which we have learned to look on certain classified cases of abnormality. And our question reduces to this: could, or should, the acceptance of the determinist thesis lead us always to look on everyone exclusively in this way? For this is the only condition worth considering under which the acceptance of determinism could lead to the decay or repudiation of participant reactive attitudes.

It does not seem to be self-contradictory to suppose that this might happen. So I suppose we must say that it is not absolutely inconceivable that it should happen. But I am strongly inclined to think that it is, for us as we are, practically inconceivable. The human commitment to participation in ordinary inter-personal relationships is, I think, too thoroughgoing and deeply rooted for us to take seriously the thought that a general theoretical conviction might so change our world that, in it, there were no longer any such things as inter-personal relationships as we normally understand them; and being involved in inter-personal relationships as we normally understand them precisely is being exposed to the range of reactive attitudes and feelings that is in question.

This, then, is a part of the reply to our question. A sustained objectivity of inter-personal attitude, and the human isolation which that would entail, does not seem to be something of which human beings would be capable, even if some general truth were a theoretical ground for it. But this is not all. There is a further point, implicit in the foregoing, which must be made explicit. Exceptionally, I have said, we can have direct dealings with human beings without any degree of personal involvement, treating them simply as creatures to be handled in our own interest, or our side's, or society's—or even theirs. In the extreme case of the mentally deranged, it is easy to see the connexion between the possibility of a wholly objective attitude and the impossibility of what we understand by ordinary inter-personal relationships. Given this latter impossibility, no other civilized attitude is available than that of viewing the deranged person simply as something to be understood and controlled in the most desirable fashion. To view him as outside the reach of personal relationships is already, for the civilized, to view him in this way. For reasons of policy or self-protection we may have occasion, perhaps temporary, to adopt a fundamentally similar attitude to a "normal" human being; to concentrate, that is, on understanding "how he works," with a view to determining our policy accordingly, or to finding in that very understanding a relief from the strains of involvement. Now it is certainly true that in the case of the abnormal, though not in the case of the normal, our adoption of the objective attitude is a consequence of our viewing the agent as *incapacitated* in some or all respects for ordinary inter-personal relationships. He is thus incapacitated, perhaps, by the fact that his picture of reality is pure fantasy, that he does not, in a sense, live in the real world at all; or by the fact that his behaviour is, in part, an unrealistic acting out of unconscious purposes; or by the fact that he is an idiot, or a moral idiot. But there is something else which, *because* this is true, is equally certainly *not* true. And that is that there is a sense of 'determined' such that (1) if determinism is true, all behaviour is determined in this sense, and (2) determinism might be true, i.e. it is not inconsistent with the facts as we know them to suppose that all behaviour might be determined in this sense, and (3) our adoption of the objective attitude towards the abnormal is the result of a prior embracing of the belief that the behaviour, or the relevant stretch of behaviour, of the human being in question *is* determined in this sense. Neither in the case

of the normal, then, nor in the case of the abnormal is it true that, when we adopt an objective attitude, we do so *because* we hold such a belief. So my answer has two parts. The first is that we cannot, as we are, seriously envisage ourselves adopting a thoroughgoing objectivity of attitude to others as a result of theoretical conviction of the truth of determinism; and the second is that when we do in fact adopt such an attitude in a particular case, our doing so is not the consequence of a theoretical conviction which might be expressed as 'Determinism in this case', but is a consequence of our abandoning, for different reasons in different cases, the ordinary inter-personal attitudes.

It might be said that all this leaves the real question unanswered, and that we cannot hope to answer it without knowing exactly what the thesis of determinism is. For the real question is not a question about what we actually do, or why we do it. It is not even a question about what we would *in fact* do if a certain theoretical conviction gained general acceptance. It is a question about what it would be *rational* to do if determinism were true, a question about the rational justification of ordinary inter-personal attitudes in general. To this I shall reply, first, that such a question could seem real only to one who had utterly failed to grasp the purport of the preceding answer, the fact of our natural human commitment to ordinary inter-personal attitudes. This commitment is part of the general framework of human life, not something that can come up for review as particular cases can come up for review within this general framework. And I shall reply, second, that if we could imagine what we cannot have, viz. a choice in this matter, then we could choose rationally only in the light of an assessment of the gains and losses to human life, its enrichment or impoverishment; and the truth or falsity of a general thesis of determinism would not bear on the rationality of *this* choice.[4]

5. The point of this discussion of the reactive attitudes in their relation—or lack of it—to the thesis of determinism was to bring us, if possible, nearer to a position of compromise in a more usual area of debate. We are not now to discuss reactive attitudes which are essentially those of offended parties or beneficiaries. We are to discuss reactive attitudes which are essentially not those, or only incidentally are those, of offended parties or beneficiaries, but are nevertheless, I shall claim, kindred attitudes to those I have discussed. I put resentment in the centre of the previous discussion. I shall put moral indignation—or, more weakly, moral disapprobation—in the centre of this one.

The reactive attitudes I have so far discussed are essentially reactions to the quality of others' wills towards us, as manifested in their behaviour: to their good or ill will or indifference or lack of concern. Thus resentment, or what I have called resentment, is a reaction to injury or indifference. The reactive attitudes I have now to discuss might be described as the sympathetic or vicarious or impersonal or disinterested or generalized analogues of the reactive attitudes I have already discussed. They are reactions to the qualities of others' wills, not towards ourselves, but towards others. Because of this impersonal or vicarious character, we give them different names. Thus one who experiences the vicarious analogue of resentment is said to be indignant or disapproving, or morally indignant or disapproving. What we have here is, as it were, resentment on behalf of another, where one's own interest and dignity are not involved; and it is this impersonal or vicarious character of the attitude, added to its others, which entitle it to the qualification 'moral'. Both my description of, and my name for, these attitudes are, in one important respect, a little misleading. It is not that these attitudes are essentially vicarious—one can feel indignation on one's own account—but that they are essentially capable of being vicarious. But I shall retain the name for the sake of its suggestiveness; and I hope that what is misleading about it will be corrected in what follows.

The personal reactive attitudes rest on, and reflect, an expectation of, and demand for, the manifestation of a certain degree of goodwill or regard on the part of other human beings towards ourselves; or at least on the expectation of, and demand for, an absence of the manifestation of active ill will or indifferent disregard. (What will, in particular cases, *count* as manifestations of good or ill will or disregard will vary in accordance with the particular relationship in which we stand to another human being.) The generalized or vicarious analogues of the personal reactive attitudes rest on, and reflect, exactly the same expectation or demand in a generalized form; they rest on, or reflect, that is, the demand for the manifestation of a reasonable degree of goodwill or regard, on the part of others, not simply towards oneself, but towards all those on whose behalf moral indignation may be felt, i.e. as we now think, towards all men. The generalized and nongeneralized forms of demand, and the vicarious and personal reactive attitudes which rest upon, and reflect, them are connected not merely logically. They are connected humanly; and not merely with each other. They are connected also with yet another set of attitudes which I must mention now in order to complete the picture. I have considered from two points of view the demands we make on others and our reactions to their possibly injurious actions. These were the points of view of one whose interest was directly involved (who suffers, say, the injury) and of others whose interest was not directly involved (who do not themselves suffer the injury). Thus I have spoken of personal reactive attitudes in the first connexion and of their vicarious analogues in the second. But the picture is not complete unless we consider also the correlates of these attitudes on the part of those on whom the demands are made, on the part of the agents. Just as there are personal and vicarious reactive attitudes associated with demands on others for oneself and demands on others for others, so there are self-reactive attitudes associated with demands on oneself for others. And here we have to mention such phenomena as feeling bound or obliged (the "sense of obligation"); feeling compunction; feeling guilty or remorseful or at least responsible; and the more complicated phenomenon of shame.

All these three types of attitude are humanly connected. One who manifested the personal reactive attitudes in a high degree but showed no inclination at all to their vicarious analogues would appear as an abnormal case of moral egocentricity, as a kind of moral solipsist. Let him be supposed fully to acknowledge the claims to regard that others had on him, to be susceptible of the whole range of self-reactive attitudes. He would then see himself as unique both as one (*the* one) who had a general claim on human regard and as one (*the* one) on whom human beings in general had such a claim. This would be a kind of moral solipsism. But is barely more than a conceptual possibility; if it is that. In general, though within varying limits, we demand of others for others, as well as of ourselves for others, something of the regard which we demand of others for ourselves. Can we imagine, besides that of the moral solipsist, any other case of one or two of these three types of attitude being fully developed, but quite unaccompanied by any trace, however slight, of the remaining two or one? If we can, then we imagine something far below or far above the level of our common humanity—a moral idiot or a saint. For all these types of attitude alike have common roots in our human nature and our membership of human communities.

Now, as of the personal reactive attitudes, so of their vicarious analogues, we must ask in what ways, and by what considerations, they tend to be inhibited. Both types of attitude involve, or express, a certain sort of demand for inter-personal regard. The fact of injury constitutes a prima facie appearance of this demand's being flouted or unfulfilled. We saw, in the case of resentment, how one class of considerations may show this appearance to be mere appearance, and hence inhibit resentment, *without* inhibiting, or displacing, the sort of demand of which resentment can be an expression, without in any way tending to make us suspend our ordinary inter-personal attitudes to the agent. Considerations of this class operate in just the same way, for just the same reasons, in connexion with moral disapprobation or indignation; they inhibit indignation without in any way inhibiting the sort of demand on the agent of which indignation can be an expression, the range of attitudes towards him to which it belongs. But in this connexion we may express the facts with a new emphasis. We may say, stressing the moral, the generalized aspect of the demand: considerations of this group have no tendency to make us see the agent as other than a morally responsible agent; they simply make us see the injury as one for which he was not morally responsible. The offering and acceptance of such exculpatory pleas as are here in question in no way detracts in our eyes from the agent's status as a term of moral relationships. On the contrary, since

things go wrong and situations are complicated, it is an essential part of the life of such relationships.

But suppose we see the agent in a different light: as one whose picture of the world is an insane delusion; or as one whose behaviour, or a part of whose behaviour, is unintelligible to us, perhaps even to him, in terms of conscious purposes, and intelligible only in terms of unconscious purposes; or even, perhaps, as one wholly impervious to the self-reactive attitudes I spoke of, wholly lacking, as we say, in moral sense. Seeing an agent in such a light as this tends, I said, to inhibit resentment in a wholly different way. It tends to inhibit resentment because it tends to inhibit ordinary inter-personal attitudes in general, and the kind of demand and expectation which those attitudes involve; and tends to promote instead the purely objective view of the agent as one posing problems simply of intellectual understanding, management, treatment, and control. Again the parallel holds for those generalized or moral attitudes towards the agent which we are now concerned with. The same abnormal light which shows the agent to us as one in respect of whom the personal attitudes, the personal demand, are to be suspended, shows him to us also as one in respect of whom the impersonal attitudes, the generalized demand, are to be suspended. Only, abstracting now from direct personal interest, we may express the facts with a new emphasis. We may say: to the extent to which the agent is seen in this light, he is not seen as one on whom demands and expectations lie in that particular way in which we think of them as lying when we speak of moral obligation; he is not, to that extent, seen as a morally responsible agent, as a term of moral relationships, as a member of the moral community.

I remarked also that the suspension of ordinary inter-personal attitudes and the cultivation of a purely objective view is sometimes possible even when we have no such reasons for it as I have just mentioned. Is this possible also in the case of the moral reactive attitudes? I think so; and perhaps it is easier. But the motives for a total suspension of moral reactive attitudes are fewer, and perhaps weaker: fewer, because only where there is antecedent personal involvement can there be the motive of seeking refuge from the strains of such involvement; perhaps weaker, because the tension between objectivity of view and the moral reactive attitudes is perhaps less than the tension between objectivity of view and the personal reactive attitudes, so that we can in the case of the moral reactive attitudes more easily secure the speculative or political gains of objectivity of view by a kind of setting on one side, rather than a total suspension, of those attitudes.

These last remarks are uncertain; but also, for the present purpose, unimportant. What concerns us now is to inquire, as previously in connexion with the personal reactive attitudes, what relevance any general thesis of determinism might have to their vicarious analogues. The answers once more are parallel; though I shall take them in a slightly different order. First, we must note, as before, that when the suspension of such an attitude or such attitudes occurs in a particular case, it is *never* the consequence of the belief that the piece of behaviour in question was determined in a sense such that all behaviour *might be*, and, if determinism is true, all behaviour *is*, determined in that sense. For it is not a consequence of any general thesis of determinism which might be true that nobody knows what he's doing or that everybody's behaviour is unintelligible in terms of conscious purposes or that everybody lives in a world of delusion or that nobody has a moral sense, i.e. is susceptible of self-reactive attitudes, &c. In fact no such sense of "determined" as would be required for a general thesis of determinism is ever relevant to our actual suspensions of moral reactive attitudes. Second, suppose it granted, as I have already argued, that we cannot take seriously the thought that theoretical conviction of such a general thesis would lead to the total decay of the personal reactive attitudes. Can we then take seriously the thought that such a conviction—a conviction, after all, that many have held or said they held—would nevertheless lead to the total decay or repudiation of the vicarious analogues of these attitudes? I think that the change in our social world which would leave us exposed to the personal reactive attitudes but not at all to their vicarious analogues, the generalization of abnormal egocentricity which this would entail, is perhaps even harder for us to envisage as a real possibility than the de-

cay of both kinds of attitude together. Though there are some necessary and some contingent differences between the ways and cases in which these two kinds of attitudes operate or are inhibited in their operation, yet, as general human capacities or pronenesses, they stand or lapse together. Finally, to the further question whether it would not be *rational*, given a general theoretical conviction of the truth of determinism, so to change our world that in it all those attitudes were wholly suspended, I must answer, as before, that one who presses this question has wholly failed to grasp the import of the preceding answer, the nature of the human commitment that is here involved: it is *useless* to ask whether it would not be rational for us to do what it is not in our nature to (be able to) do. To this I must add, as before, that if there were, say, for a moment open to us the possibility of such a god-like choice, the rationality of making or refusing it would be determined by quite other considerations than the truth or falsity of the general theoretical doctrine in question. The latter would be simply irrelevant; and this becomes ironically clear when we remember that for those convinced that the truth of determinism nevertheless really would make the one choice rational, there has always been the insuperable difficulty of explaining in intelligible terms how its falsity would make the opposite choice rational.

I am aware that in presenting the argument as I have done, neglecting the ever-interesting varieties of case, I have presented nothing more than a schema, using sometimes a crude opposition of phrase where we have a great intricacy of phenomena. In particular the simple opposition of objective attitudes on the one hand and the various contrasted attitudes which I have opposed to them must seem as grossly crude as it is central. Let me pause to mitigate this crudity a little, and also to strengthen one of my central contentions, by mentioning some things which straddle these contrasted kinds of attitude. Thus parents and others concerned with the care and upbringing of young children cannot have to their charges either kind of attitude in a pure or unqualified form. They are dealing with creatures who are potentially and increasingly capable both of holding, and being objects of, the full range of human and moral attitudes, but are not yet truly capable of either. The treatment of such creatures must therefore represent a kind of compromise, constantly shifting in one direction, between objectivity of attitude and developed human attitudes. Rehearsals insensibly modulate towards true performances. The punishment of a child is both like and unlike the punishment of an adult. Suppose we try to relate this progressive emergence of the child as a responsible being, as an object of non-objective attitudes, to that sense of "determined" in which, if determinism is a possibly true thesis, all behaviour *may* be determined, and in which, if it is a true thesis, all behaviour *is* determined. What bearing *could* such a sense of "determined" have upon the progressive modification of attitudes towards the child? Would it not be grotesque to think of the development of the child as a progressive or patchy emergence from an area in which its behaviour is in this sense determined into an area in which it isn't? Whatever sense of "determined" is required for stating the thesis of determinism, it can scarcely be such as to allow of compromise, border-line-style answers to the question, "Is this bit of behaviour determined or isn't it?" But in this matter of young children, it is essentially a border-line, penumbral area that we move in. Again, consider—a very different matter—the strain in the attitude of a psychoanalyst to his patient. His objectivity of attitude, *his* suspension of ordinary moral reactive attitudes, is profoundly modified by the fact that the aim of the enterprise is to make such suspension unnecessary or less necessary. Here we may and do naturally speak of restoring the agent's freedom. But here the restoring of freedom means bringing it about that the agent's behaviour shall be intelligible in terms of conscious purposes rather than in terms only of unconscious purposes. *This* is the object of the enterprise; and it is in so far as *this* object is attained that the suspension, or half-suspension, of ordinary moral attitudes is deemed no longer necessary or appropriate. And in this we see once again the *irrelevance* of that concept of "being determined" which must be the central concept of determinism. For we cannot both agree that this object is attainable and that its attainment has this consequence and yet hold (1) that neurotic behaviour is determined in a sense in which, it may be, all behaviour is determined, and

(2) that it is because neurotic behaviour is determined in this sense that objective attitudes are deemed appropriate to neurotic behaviour. Not, at least, without accusing ourselves of incoherence in our attitude to psycho-analytic treatment.

6. And now we can try to fill in the lacuna which the pessimist finds in the optimist's account of the concept of moral responsibility, and of the bases of moral condemnation and punishment; and to fill it in from the facts as we know them. For, as I have already remarked, when the pessimist himself seeks to fill it in, he rushes beyond the facts as we know them and proclaims that it cannot be filled in at all unless determinism is false.

Yet a partial sense of the facts as we know them is certainly present to the pessimist's mind. When his opponent, the optimist, undertakes to show that the truth of determinism would not shake the foundations of the concept of moral responsibility and of the practices of moral condemnation and punishment, he typically refers, in a more or less elaborated way, to the efficacy of these practices in regulating behaviour in socially desirable ways. These practices are represented solely as instruments of policy, as methods of individual treatment and social control. The pessimist recoils from this picture; and in his recoil there is, typically, an element of emotional shock. He is apt to say, among much else, that the humanity of the offender himself is offended by *this* picture of his condemnation and punishment.

The reasons for this recoil—the explanation of the sense of an emotional, as well as a conceptual, shock—we have already before us. The picture painted by the optimists is painted in a style appropriate to a situation envisaged as wholly dominated by objectivity of attitude. The only operative notions invoked in this picture are such as those of policy, treatment, control. But a thoroughgoing objectivity of attitude, excluding as it does the moral reactive attitudes, excludes at the same time essential elements in the concepts of *moral* condemnation and *moral* responsibility. This is the reason for the conceptual shock. The deeper emotional shock is a reaction, not simply to an inadequate conceptual analysis, but to the suggestion of a change in our world. I have remarked that it is possible to cultivate an exclusive objectivity of attitude in some cases, and for some reasons, where the object of the attitude is not set aside from developed inter-personal and moral attitudes by immaturity or abnormality. And the suggestion which seems to be contained in the optimist's account is that such an attitude should be universally adopted to all offenders. This is shocking enough in the pessimist's eyes. But, sharpened by shock, his eyes see further. It would be hard to make *this* division in our natures. If to all offenders, then to all mankind. Moreover, to whom could this recommendation be, in any real sense, addressed? Only to the powerful, the authorities. So abysses seem to open.[5]

But we will confine our attention to the case of the offenders. The concepts we are concerned with are those of responsibility and guilt, qualified as "moral," on the one hand—together with that of membership of a moral community; of demand, indignation, disapprobation and condemnation, qualified as "moral," on the other hand—together with that of punishment. Indignation, disapprobation, like resentment, tend to inhibit or at least to limit our goodwill towards the object of these attitudes, tend to promote an at least partial and temporary withdrawal of goodwill; they do so in proportion as they are strong; and their strength is in general proportioned to what is felt to be the magnitude of the injury and to the degree to which the agent's will is identified with, or indifferent to, it. (These, of course, are not contingent connexions.) But these attitudes of disapprobation and indignation are precisely the correlates of the moral demand in the case where the demand is felt to be disregarded. The making of the demand *is* the proneness to such attitudes. The holding of them does not, as the holding of objective attitudes does, involve as a part of itself viewing their object other than as a member of the moral community. The partial withdrawal of goodwill which *these* attitudes entail, the modification *they* entail of the general demand that another should, if possible, be spared suffering, is, rather, the consequence of *continuing* to view him as a member of the moral community; only as one who has offended against its demands. So the preparedness to acquiesce in that infliction of suffering on the offender which is an essential part of punishment is all of a piece with this whole range of attitudes of which I have been speaking. It is not only moral re-

active attitudes towards the offender which are in question here. We must mention also the self-reactive attitudes of offenders themselves. Just as the other-reactive attitudes are associated with a readiness to acquiesce in the infliction of suffering on an offender, within the "institution" of punishment, so the self-reactive attitudes are associated with a readiness on the part of the offender to acquiesce in such infliction *without* developing the reactions (e.g. of resentment) which he would normally develop to the infliction of injury upon him; i.e. with a readiness, as we say, to accept punishment[6] as "his due" or as "just."

I am not in the least suggesting that these readinesses to acquiesce, either on the part of the offender himself or on the part of others, are always or commonly accompanied or preceded by indignant boilings or remorseful pangs; only that we have here a continuum of attitudes and feelings to which these readinesses to acquiesce themselves belong. Nor am I in the least suggesting that it belongs to this continuum of attitudes that we should be ready to acquiesce in the infliction of injury on offenders in a fashion which we saw to be quite indiscriminate or in accordance with procedures which we knew to be wholly useless. On the contrary, savage or civilized, we have some belief in the utility of practices of condemnation and punishment. But the social utility of these practices, on which the optimist lays such exclusive stress, is not what is now in question. What is in question is the pessimist's justified sense that to speak in terms of social utility alone is to leave out something vital in our conception of these practices. The vital thing can be restored by attending to that complicated web of attitudes and feelings which form an essential part of the moral life as we know it, and which are quite opposed to objectivity of attitude. Only by attending to this range of attitudes can we recover from the facts as we know them a sense of what we mean, i.e. of *all* we mean, when, speaking the language of morals, we speak of desert, responsibility, guilt, condemnation, and justice. But we *do* recover it from the facts as we know them. We do not have to go beyond them. Because the optimist neglects or misconstrues these attitudes, the pessimist rightly claims to find a lacuna in his account. We can fill the lacuna for him. But in return we must demand of the pessimist a surrender of his metaphysics.

Optimist and pessimist misconstrue the facts in very different styles. But in a profound sense there is something in common to their misunderstandings. Both seek, in different ways, to over-intellectualize the facts. Inside the general structure or web of human attitudes and feelings of which I have been speaking, there is endless room for modification, redirection, criticism, and justification. But questions of justification are internal to the structure or relate to modifications internal to it. The existence of the general framework of attitudes itself is something we are given with the fact of human society. As a whole, it neither calls for, nor permits, an external "rational" justification. Pessimist and optimist alike show themselves, in different ways, unable to accept this.[7] The optimist's style of over-intellectualizing the facts is that of a characteristically incomplete empiricism, a one-eyed utilitarianism. He seeks to find an adequate basis for certain social practices in calculated consequences, and loses sight (perhaps wishes to lose sight) of the human attitudes of which these practices are, in part, the expression. The pessimist does not lose sight of these attitudes, but is unable to accept the fact that it is just these attitudes themselves which fill the gap in the optimist's account. Because of this, he thinks the gap can be filled only if some general metaphysical proposition is repeatedly verified, verified in all cases where it is appropriate to attribute moral responsibility. This proposition he finds it as difficult to state coherently and with intelligible relevance as its determinist contradictory. Even when a formula has been found ("contra-casual freedom" or something of the kind) there still seems to remain a gap between its applicability in particular cases and its supposed moral consequences. Sometimes he plugs this gap with an intuition of fittingness—a pitiful intellectualist trinket for a philosopher to wear as a charm against the recognition of his own humanity.

Even the moral sceptic is not immune from his own form of the wish to over-intellectualize such notions as those of moral responsibility, guilt, and blame. He sees that the optimist's account is inadequate and the pessimist's libertarian alternative inane; and finds no resource except to declare that the notions in question are inherently confused, that "blame is metaphysical." But the metaphysics was in the eye of the metaphysician. It is a pity that talk of the moral sentiments has fallen out of favour. The phrase would be quite a good name for that network of human attitudes in acknowledging the character and place of which we find, I suggest, the only possibility of reconciling these disputants to each other and the facts.

There are, at present, factors which add, in a slightly paradoxical way, to the difficulty of making this acknowledgement. These human attitudes themselves, in their development and in the variety of their manifestations, have to an increasing extent become objects of study in the social and psychological sciences; and this growth of human self-consciousness, which we might expect to reduce the difficulty of acceptance, in fact increases it in several ways. One factor of comparatively minor importance is an increased historical and anthropological awareness of the great variety of forms which these human attitudes may take at different times and in different cultures. This makes one rightly chary of claiming as essential features of the concept of morality in general, forms of these attitudes which may have a local and temporary prominence. No doubt to some extent my own descriptions of human attitudes have reflected local and temporary features of our own culture. But an awareness of variety of forms should not prevent us from acknowledging also that in the absence of *any* forms of these attitudes it is doubtful whether we should have anything that *we* could find intelligible as a system of human relationships, as human society. A quite different factor of greater importance is that psychological studies have made us rightly mistrustful of many particular manifestations of the attitudes I have spoken of. They are a prime realm of self-deception, of the ambiguous and the shady, of guilt-transference, unconscious sadism and the rest. But it is an exaggerated horror, itself suspect, which would make us unable to acknowledge the facts because of the seamy side of the facts. Finally, perhaps the most important factor of all is the prestige of these theoretical studies themselves. That prestige is great and is apt to make us forget that in philosophy, though it also is a theoretical study, we have to take account of the facts in *all* their bearings; we are not to suppose that we are required, or permitted, as philosophers, to regard ourselves, as human beings, as detached from the attitudes which, as scientists, we study with detachment. This is in no way to deny the possibility and desirability of redirection and modification of our human attitudes in the light of these studies. But we may reasonably think it unlikely that our progressively greater understanding of certain aspects of ourselves will lead to the total disappearance of those aspects. Perhaps it is not inconceivable that it should; and perhaps, then, the dreams of some philosophers will be realized.

If we sufficiently, that is *radically*, modify the view of the optimist, his view is the right one. It is far from wrong to emphasize the efficacy of all those practices which express or manifest our moral attitudes, in regulating behaviour in ways considered desirable; or to add that when certain of our beliefs about the efficacy of some of these practices turn out to be false, then we may have good reason for dropping or modifying those practices. What *is* wrong is to forget that these practices, and their reception, the reactions to them, really *are* expressions of our moral attitudes and not merely devices we calculatingly employ for regulative purposes. Our practices do not merely exploit our natures, they express them. Indeed the very understanding of the kind of efficacy these expressions of our attitudes have turns on our remembering this. When we do remember this, and modify the optimist's position accordingly, we simultaneously correct its conceptual deficiencies and ward off the dangers it seems to entail, without recourse to the obscure and panicky metaphysics of libertarianism.

NOTES

1. Cf. P. H. Nowell-Smith, 'Freewill and Moral Responsibility', *Mind*, 1948.
2. As Nowell-Smith pointed out in a later article: 'Determinists and Libertarians', *Mind*, 1954.
3. Perhaps not in every case *just* what we demand they should be, but in any case *not* just what we demand they should not be. For my present purpose these differences do not matter.
4. The question, then, of the connexion between rationality and the adoption of the objective attitude to others is misposed when it is made to seem dependent on the issue of determinism. But there is another question which should be raised, if only to distinguish it from the misposed question. Quite apart from the issue of determinism, might it not be said that we should be nearer to being purely rational creatures in proportion as our relation to others was in fact dominated by the objective attitude? I think this might be said; only it would have to be added, once more, that if such a choice were possible, it would not neccessarily be rational to choose to be more purely rational than we are.
5. Peered into by Mr. J. D. Mabbott, in his article 'Freewill and Punishment', published in *Contemporary British Philosophy*, 3rd ser., 1956.
6. Of course not *any* punishment for *anything* deemed an offense.
7. Compare the question of the justification of induction. The human commitment to inductive belief-formation is original, natural, non-rational (not *irrational*), in no way something we choose or could give up. Yet rational criticism and reflection can refine standards and their application, supply "rules for judging of cause and effect." Ever since the facts were made clear by Hume, people have been resisting acceptance of them.

PART V

——•——

Ethics and Society

INTRODUCTION

Almost all of us hold a wide range of moral views. We have views about when it is wrong to lie, cheat, steal, betray a friend, have an abortion, break a law or a promise, kill an adult human being, or threaten to kill one. And we have views about why such acts are wrong when they are. We assess lives, our own and others, as going more or less well or badly. We have views about the contribution to a good life of material well-being, artistic accomplishment, athletic prowess, intellectual curiosity, friendship and love, sex, courage, and so on. We also assess social institutions from a moral perspective. Most of us think that the slavery practiced in the United States in the nineteenth century was unjust. And one has only to pick up the daily newspaper to find views expressed about the fairness or unfairness of the federal tax code.

These views are at many different levels of generality. You may think that your friend was wrong to have cheated on yesterday's exam; and you may also think that if you are faced with saving one life or many, you ought always to save the larger number of lives. Some of these views you may hold with a great deal of confidence, for example, that wanton killing of an adult human being is wrong. Other views you may hold less confidently: this may be true of your assessment of the moral permissibility of abortion. Yet, despite uncertainty, you sometimes must act one way or another. Our moral views are significant to our lives in part because they frequently guide our action.

Moral philosophy begins with reflection on such views. It aims at detecting unsuspected inconsistencies; at articulating and assessing central arguments; at determining the extent to which such views have a defensible, underlying rationale; at articulating and defending systematic approaches to moral issues; and, in general, at understanding the nature of morality.

A. UTILITARIANISM

Begin by distinguishing two general questions: What makes acts right (or wrong)? What things are good (bad)? *Consequentialist* moral theories treat the second question as basic. Such theories begin by determining what things are good and what things bad. They then see the rightness of an action as determined by the goodness or badness of relevant consequences.

The most common consequentialist theories are *utilitarian* theories. Such theories suppose that the only thing that has nonderivative value is the *welfare* or *happiness* of sentient beings.

It is granted that other things—courage, knowledge, love, and money, for example—have value. But their value is derivative from their contribution to happiness. Jeremy Bentham and John Stuart Mill defend different versions of such a utilitarian perspective. Bentham identifies happiness with pleasure and the absence of pain, and he proceeds to develop a calculus to measure the relative value of different pleasures and pains. He supposes that what makes an act right (or wrong) is the extent to which it increases pleasure or decreases pain. His theory can be called *hedonistic act utilitarianism: hedonistic* because it sees pleasure and pain as the only things with nonderivative value; *act* utilitarianism because, in answering our question about what makes acts right, it applies the test of utility directly to actions.

On one common interpretation, Mill also accepts a version of act utilitarianism. But he differs from Bentham in his view that some pleasures are "higher" than others. Bentham saw happiness as depending only on the felt pleasures and pains of the organism. Mill's emphasis on the "quality" of pleasure seems to make happiness depend also on the satisfaction of certain ideals, for example, those satisfied by a discontented Socrates but not by a contented but unreflective person.

E. F. Carritt argues that such utilitarian theories make "no room for justice." For example, they seem to have the consequence that a prosecutor should frame an innocent person if that is the only way she can prevent a disastrous riot. Act utilitarianism makes the rightness of an action depend solely on *forward-looking* considerations; but the demand that punishment be of the guilty is a *backward-looking* consideration with no clear place in such a theory. A similar point could be made about breaking a solemn promise. Again, cases of lying or even intentionally killing an innocent person as ways in particular circumstances of increasing overall happiness raise similar worries. In such cases the utilitarian requirement to increase happiness as much as possible seems in conflict with common-sense prohibitions on certain ways of treating individuals in the pursuit of overall good. (Such problems are explored further in Thomas Nagel's "War and Massacre").

Some philosophers (e.g., J. O. Urmson) have argued that Mill is better seen as a *rule* rather than an *act* utilitarian: the utilitarian test is to be applied directly only to general rules. A moral rule is shown to be correct by showing that its recognition promotes happiness. An act is right as long as it does not violate some correct moral rule, wrong if it does. The suggestion is that among the correct moral rules will be, for example, a rule generally prohibiting the intentional punishment of innocents; and this is why criticisms along Carritt's lines do not work so easily against Mill's theory.

Rule utilitarianism (which J. J. C. Smart calls "restricted utilitarianism") is a two-tier theory: it sanctions utilitarian reasoning at the level of rules, but not at the level of particular acts. This may seem arbitrary. After all, if happiness is so important, why shouldn't I be able to justify my action by saying that *it* best promotes happiness? As Smart argues, once we accept the main outlines of the utilitarian framework, refusal to allow this form of moral justification may seem like a case of "rule worship."

Carritt's objections to act utilitarianism focus on prohibitions on ways of treating others. Bernard Williams argues that there is another problem, one posed by the value we place on integrity. In section D John Rawls objects to utilitarianism that it "does not take seriously the distinction between persons." Finally, Peter Singer shows just how powerful even a weak version of a theory in the spirit of utilitarianism can be by arguing that we are subject to fairly strong moral demands to aid those who are suffering from famine in distant lands.

B. KANTIAN ETHICS

Utilitarianism supposes that we can determine what things are good independently of an account of what actions are right and then go on to see the rightness of actions as depending on the goodness of consequences. Immanuel Kant argues, in contrast, that the rightness of an action does not depend in this way solely on the goodness of consequences; for the rightness of an action depends on the principle (the "maxim") on which the agent acts.

Kant begins his *Groundwork of the Metaphysic of Morals* with a discussion of "the good will." A person of good will is a morally conscientious person, one who is firmly committed to doing her or his moral duty, come what may. Kant argues that only such a good will is "good without qualification." A person's intelligence, wit, or charm may be a good or a bad thing, depending on other circumstances, or the use to which it is put. But moral conscientiousness "shine[s] like a jewel" in any context, independently of its actual consequences.

In chapter 2 Kant tries to determine "the supreme principle of morality." Kant supposes there are objective principles concerning what it is rational to do under certain circumstances. For beings like us who are sometimes tempted to act contrary to reason, these principles are seen as "imperatives." Some imperatives only tell us what to do on the assumption that we have a certain end. These are *hypothetical* imperatives. For example, "you ought to wear a coat outside today" normally expresses only a hypothetical imperative since it tells you what to do on the assumption (let us suppose) that you want to stay warm. You could escape from this imperative by not caring about staying warm. Kant supposes that there are also *categorical* imperatives that tell us what to do without assuming that we have a particular end we could rationally give up. Moral oughts, Kant supposes, must be categorical and not merely hypothetical imperatives. Otherwise we could escape from the demands of morality, just by giving up certain ends. (For challenges to this view of morality, see the selections by David Hume and J. L. Mackie in section E, "Challenges to Morality.")

Kant supposes that all moral demands on our conduct are grounded in a single basic imperative: The Categorical Imperative. Kant offers three main formulations of this principle (although he argues that these are formulations of the same principle): The Formula of Universal Law (which itself has two different versions); The Formula of the End in Itself; and The Formula of the Kingdom of Ends (which is preceded by a closely related Formula of Autonomy). The first is related to, but importantly different from, the Golden Rule. Kwame Anthony Appiah appeals to related pleas in his criticisms of intrinsic racism in section D. The second is developed by Onora O'Neill in her discussion of famine problems. And the third can usefully be compared to the framework developed by John Rawls in *A Theory of Justice*. (See the selection in Section D.)

Kant's theory prohibits my treating a person merely as a means, even when that is necessary to avoid terrible results. In "War and Massacre," Thomas Nagel calls such a theory *absolutist* and explores its nonutilitarian perspective on what we may do in pursuit of wartime objectives.

C. ARISTOTELIAN ETHICS

Aristotle turns our attention away from questions of the rightness of particular acts to the question of what we should aim at in trying to live a good human life. His initial answer is that it is *eudaimonia*—here translated as happiness, but sometimes translated as flourishing.

In contrast with Bentham, Aristotle does not see human happiness as just a matter of more pleasure and less pain. To say more about what human happiness is, he tries to determine the characteristic function (*ergon*) of human beings. As Nagel puts it in his essay, "the *ergon* of a thing, in general, is what it does that makes it what it is." We are complex organisms with many different capacities, capacities that constitute our "soul." Some of these capacities are merely nutritive—for example, capacities for digestion and breathing—and are shared with other animals. But our capacities for rational deliberation and reflection are peculiar to us; their active exercise, Aristotle thought, is our *ergon*. *Eudaimonia*—happiness, flourishing—consists in the active exercise of these rational capacities in accordance with their characteristic virtues or excellences (*arete*).

Some of our rational activities are theoretical (e.g., the study of mathematics), some concern our day-to-day lives in a world with material needs and social complexities. The virtues (excellences) involved in the first sort of activity Aristole calls intellectual; the latter virtues he calls moral (or practical). Aristotle's Doctrine of the Mean is his theory of what the moral virtues are. Nagel discusses Aristotle's ambivalence concerning the relative importance of theoretical and practical activities to human flourishing.

Aristotle's theory is frequently cited as an important example of "virtue ethics." (Hume's theory of what character traits are virtues—section E—can also be seen as part of this tradition.) Theories in the tradition of virtue ethics are commonly contrasted with utilitarian theories in the spirit of Bentham and Mill, and with "deontological" theories in the spirit of Kant. Rosalind Hursthouse aims to clarify these contrasts and then to deepen our understanding of virtue ethics. She aims to do this in part by seeing how a virtue-based ethics can reasonably be applied to difficult moral issues raised by abortion.

D. JUSTICE AND EQUALITY

When you criticize slavery or a certain tax system as unjust or unfair, you are assessing certain social institutions, not just certain individuals and their actions. Such social institutions have a deep impact on the ways in which various goods are distributed among the members of a society. When does this impact satisfy the demands of justice?

In the selection from his book, *A Theory of Justice*, John Rawls tries to answer this question for those institutions that constitute the "basic structure" of a society. The main idea is that the public principles of justice for this basic structure are those that we would choose in a hypothetical situation that is fair. Thus the label "Justice as Fairness."

Rawls calls his specification of such a fair-choice situation "the original position." He supposes that the parties in the situation are rational but are behind a "veil of ignorance" that blocks from their view any knowledge that would give its possessor an unfair advantage in choosing basic principles of justice. The parties do not know whether they are rich or poor, male or female. They do not know their racial or ethnic background or their particular talents. They do not even know exactly what in the real world they deem most important. What they do care about, in the original position, is their share of "primary goods," goods that are assumed to have a use whatever a person's particular goals and abilities are. Rawls supposes that among the chief primary goods whose distribution is shaped by the basic structure are various basic liberties (e.g., freedom of speech and association), opportunities (e.g., educational opportunities), and income and wealth. The parties in the original position are to decide on principles that will publicly govern the ways in which the basic structure shapes the distribution of such primary goods.

Rawls argues that the parties in the original position would unanimously choose two principles: a principle of maximum, equal basic liberties and a principle that requires that inequalities in the distribution of other social primary goods be to *everyone's* advantage (e.g., not merely to the advantage of the majority) and provide for equality of opportunity. Both principles depart from the utilitarian's overriding concern with maximizing overall happiness.

Robert Nozick would classify Rawls's principles as nonhistorical, end-state principles: they attempt to assess the justice of the social distributions of goods without looking at the actual history of how these distributions came about. Or so it might seem. Nozick argues that no end-state principle of justice can be continuously realized without serious restrictions on people's liberties. This is the point of his Wilt Chamberlain example. Nozick's alternative is his historical, entitlement theory. This theory aims at three kinds of principles: principles that say when an original acquisition of some good is just; principles that say when the transfer of some good is just; and principles that say what is to be done to rectify past violations of the first two principles. The first principle will involve the Lockean proviso that the apropriation of a previously unowned object must not worsen the situation of others. According to this theory, I am entitled to those goods I possess either through a just original acquisition or through a series of just transfers that begin with a just original acquisition.

Rawls's argument for his principles of justice begins with a "benchmark of initial equality." Rawls then argues that parties in the original position would allow inequalities in the distribution of primary goods like income and wealth, so long as those inequalities would make the members of the "least fortunate group in society" better off than they otherwise would be. This is Rawls's "difference principle." This principle might, for example, permit inequalities that result from a structure of incentives that encourages production that promotes the interest of all. Rawls applies this principle to the basic structure of society, not to the motivation of individuals making choices within that structure—not, for example, to the motivation of an individual who aims at maximizing her profits. G. A. Cohen argues that this is a mistake, that the choices and motivations of individual agents—including "high-flying marketeers"—are also subject to a version of the difference principle. This leads, Cohen argues, to the equalitarian conclusion that "affirmation of the difference principle implies that justice requires (virtually) unqualified equality."

Samuel Scheffler poses a different challenge to Rawls's theory of justice (as well as to a number of other theories of justice)—a challenge that returns us to issues about responsible agency discussed in Part IV. (See, in particular, the essay by Strawson.) Scheffler notes that these theories of justice avoid "an independent standard of desert by reference to which the justice of institutional arrangements is to be measured." They do this, it seems, because they rest on "an attenuated conception of personal responsibility." Scheffler worries that this may be a basis for a fundamental challenge to these theories.

Inequalities associated with differences of race or gender can raise pressing issues of justice. In his "The Subjection of Women," published in 1869, John Stuart Mill considered, in a critical light, what he called "the arrangements which place women in social and political subjection to men." More than a century later Debra Satz also focuses on "conditions of pervasive gender inequality in our society." She argues that these conditions are at the heart of the best account of why we should limit the use of markets in women's reproductive labor. Finally, Kwame Anthony Appiah seeks an analysis of different kinds of racism. Elsewhere Appiah argues against "racialism"—the view that "there are heritable characteristics, possessed by members of our species, that allow us to divide them into a small set of races, in such a way that all members of these races share certain traits and tendencies with each other that they do not share with members of any other race." In this essay Appiah distinguishes different varieties of racism, all of which presuppose racialism. He argues that even if racialism were true none of these forms of racism would be defensible. His criticism of "intrinsic" racism, in particular, returns us to Kantian themes explored in section B.

E. CHALLENGES TO MORALITY

Morality and Self-interest

Suppose you discovered a way to gain access to the files of any computer system in the country and could change those files at will. Suppose you knew you could do this with no chance of being caught. You could change the grades of anyone at any university. You could change the totals in bank accounts. And so on. You think it would be wrong to do this. But, you still wonder whether you should let that stop you. Why should you let moral considerations prevent you from pursuing what seems to be in your self-interest? Why should you be moral?

Your problem is a high-tech version of Glaucon's problem of the ring of Gyges, posed in Plato's *Republic*. Since Gyges can treat others unjustly with impunity, wouldn't he live a better life by acting unjustly rather than justly? In the selections reprinted here from Books I through IV of the *Republic*, Socrates argues that it is in a person's interest to be just and against his interest to be unjust. Properly understood, morality and self-interest are not in conflict. Socrates's argument proceeds by way of a famous parallel between the state and an individual and an analysis of the structure of human motivation that leads Socrates to talk of three "parts" of the soul.

We next have excerpts from David Hume's *An Enquiry Concerning the Principles of Morals*. Hume's discussion touches on many issues. His two main questions are: How far do reason and sentiment enter into moral judgment? What character traits are virtues, and why? Hume sees character traits as virtues insofar as they are "useful or agreeable to the person himself or to others." We look at his answer to the former question later. We include Hume's *Enquiry* in this section because of its discussions of the relation between morality and self-interest.

Hume's explicit discussion of this issue occurs in Section IX, Part II. Here, he extols the contribution of the moral virtues to the life of their possessor—although, "[t]reating vice with the greatest candour," he does worry that his remarks may not be convincing for the case of justice (which, for Hume, is a virtue primarily concerned with property, honesty, and promise-keeping). But Hume does not think that it is solely because of their contribution to our own interests that we approve of the moral virtues. Rather, Hume argues that as a matter of fact we are all to some extent directly concerned with the interests of others—this is the point of his example of avoiding another's gouty toes. This universal principle of benevolence accounts in large part for our approval of the virtues and is the basis of our moral judgments.

Hume sketches a complex account of the relation between benevolence and self-love. "It is requisite," he says, "that there be an original propensity of some kind, in order to be a basis to self-love, by giving a relish to the objects of its pursuit." Benevolence is itself one such original propensity. Self-love is a "secondary passion," whose concern is with the satisfaction of various original propensities, and these include benevolence, the basis of morality.

In the Prisoner's Dilemma, discussed in Part VI, "Puzzles and Paradoxes," it is in each prisoner's individual interest to confess, even though both prisoners do better if both remain silent than they do if both confess. Prisoners guided solely by a concern with their individual self-interest will each end up worse off than if they were able to cooperate and maintain joint silence. There is a useful analogy here with morality. Consider the moral demand to be truthful. Each person may on occasion be in a situation in which it is in his or her individual interest to lie. Yet, we all do better if everyone is always truthful—even when this conflicts with one's self-interest—than if everyone were to lie whenever this was in one's own interest. A group of people who are guided solely by individual self-interest will each end up worse off than each would have been if they had all been guided by a commitment to honesty. This suggests that there are reasons of self-interest to be moral. In "Morality and Advantage" David Gauthier explores this suggestion, but he concludes that in the end it provides a more limited rationale for being moral than may have been thought. (Gauthier develops an importantly different line of argument in his 1986 book, *Morals by Agreement*.)

Finally, J. L. Mackie explores what Richard Dawkins has called "the biology of selfishness and altruism." Mackie suggests that there may be evolutionary reasons to expect the emergence of tendencies toward "reciprocal altruism"—a strategy of tit for tat. Insofar as morality is the expression of such reciprocal altruism, it may be possible to see morality as itself a product of natural selection.

Subjectivism, Relativism, and Skepticism

I believe that wanton torture of an innocent child is wrong; and (I hope) you do, too. Is there some objective fact here—the fact that such conduct is wrong—that is what both of us know? Or, is this merely a case in which we share similar negative attitudes?

In Appendix I of his *An Enquiry Concerning the Principles of Morals* Hume argues that our moral attitudes could not consist merely in the knowledge of facts about the world. Knowledge of facts is not itself sufficient to move us to act. Yet, Hume assumes, our moral views can themselves move us to act. To reach a moral conclusion, then, it is not enough to know that certain acts or character traits have certain effects. We must also have appropriate pro or con attitudes—what Hume calls sentiments—toward those effects. Given our benevolence, we react negatively to torture. But, if (contrary to fact) we were rational but nonbenevolent beings, we could grasp all the facts about torture and yet not react in these ways.

Although there is, for Hume, neither moral knowledge nor moral facts, there is a clear and powerful point of view of morality: the point of view of informed benevolence, which he describes in Section IX, Part I. Hume thinks that his skepticism about the objectivity of morality leaves untouched the importance of this moral point of view for us.

J. L. Mackie develops similar views, and usefully contrasts them with the views of Aristotle and Kant. (See the selections from Aristotle and Kant in sections B and C.) Mackie distinguishes three levels of investigation: descriptive ethics, first-order normative ethics, and second-order theories about what moral valuing and moral values are. At the level of descriptive ethics we are only concerned to describe what moral views certain people in fact endorse. At the level of first-order normative ethics we are interested in ourselves making judgments about what is right and what is good. Mackie's main concerns are at the second-order level. He argues that there are no moral facts and no moral knowledge; although he thinks his arguments still allow us to make serious first-order judgments of right and wrong, good and bad, as long as these judgments have been purged of a claim to objectivity.

Mackie thinks that the idea that values are "part of the fabric of the world" is deeply embedded in our common-sense thought. But he offers two main reasons for rejecting such objectivism: the argument from relativity and the argument from queerness. The first begins with a premise from descriptive ethics, but it aims at a second-order conclusion; the second is an extension of Hume's argument from the connection between morality and motivation. Our tendency, nevertheless, to see values as objective is a tendency to project our subjective attitudes and desires onto the objective world.

Can we test and confirm our moral beliefs by way of observation in the ways in which we offer observational support for conjectures in the sciences? Gilbert Harman argues that the answer is No. He thinks this poses a basic problem if we want to avoid skepticism about the possibility of moral knowledge. Nicholas L. Sturgeon takes issue with this line of argument for skepticism about moral knowledge; though he grants that a main argument for moral skepticism—the argument from "relativity" or "the apparent difficulty of *settling* moral dis-agreements"—poses a further, and as-yet-unanswered, challenge.

A. Utilitarianism

The Principle of Utility

JEREMY BENTHAM

Jeremy Bentham (1748–1832) was the founder of utilitarianism. His best-known work is *An Introduction to the Principles of Morals and Legislation*.

—•—

Chapter 1 Of the Principle of Utility

I. Nature has placed mankind under the governance of two sovereign masters, *pain* and *pleasure*. It is for them alone to point out what we ought to do, as well as to determine what we shall do. On the one hand the standard of right and wrong, on the other the chain of causes and effects, are fastened to their throne. They govern us in all we do, in all we say, in all we think: every effort we can make to throw off our subjection, will serve but to demonstrate and confirm it. In words a man may pretend to abjure their empire: but in reality he will remain subject to it all the while. The *principle of utility*[*] recognises this subjection, and assumes it for the foundation of that system, the object of which is to rear the fabric of felicity by the hands of reason and law. Systems which attempt to question it, deal in sounds instead of sense, in caprice instead of reason, in darkness instead of light.

But enough of metaphor and declamation: it is not by such means that moral science is to be improved.

II. The principle of utility is the foundation of the present work: it will be proper therefore at the outset to give an explicit and determinate account of what is meant by it. By the principle of utility is meant that principle which approves or disapproves of every action whatsoever, according to the tendency which it appears to have to augment or diminish the happiness of the party whose interest is in question: or, what is the same thing in other

---

From *An Introduction to the Principles of Morals and Legislation* (New York: Hafner, 1948), pp. 1–4, 29–32.

[*]Note by the Author, July 1822.

To this denomination has of late been added, or substituted, the *greatest happiness* or *greatest felicity* principle: this for shortness, instead of saying at length *that principle* which states the greatest happiness of all those whose interest is in question, as being the right and proper, and only right and proper and universally desirable, end of human action: of human action in every situation, and in particular in that of a functionary or set of functionaries exercising the powers of Government. The word *utility* does not so clearly point to the ideas of *pleasure* and *pain* as the words *happiness* and *felicity* do: nor does it lead us to the consideration of the *number*, of the interests affected; to the *number*, as being the circumstance, which contributes, in the largest proportion, to the formation of the standard here in question; the *standard of right and wrong*, by which alone the propriety of human conduct, in every situation, can with propriety be tried. This want of a sufficiently manifest connexion between the ideas of *happiness* and *pleasure* on the one hand, and the idea of *utility* on the other, I have every now and then found operating, and with but too much efficiency, as a bar to the acceptance, that might otherwise have been given, to this principle.—BENTHAM

483

words, to promote or to oppose that happiness. I say of every action whatsoever; and therefore not only of every action of a private individual, but of every measure of government.

III. By utility is meant that property in any object, whereby it tends to produce benefit, advantage, pleasure, good, or happiness, (all this in the present case comes to the same thing) or (what comes again to the same thing) to prevent the happening of mischief, pain, evil, or unhappiness to the party whose interest is considered: if that party be the community in general, then the happiness of the community: if a particular individual, then the happiness of that individual.

IV. The interest of the community is one of the most general expressions that can occur in the phraseology of morals: no wonder that the meaning of it is often lost. When it has a meaning, it is this. The community is a fictitious *body*, composed of the individual persons who are considered as constituting as it were its *members*. The interest of the community then is, what?—the sum of the interests of the several members who compose it.

V. It is in vain to talk of the interest of the community without understanding what is the interest of the individual.* A thing is said to promote the interest, or to be *for* the interest, of an individual, when it tends to add to the sum total of his pleasures: or, what comes to the same thing, to diminish the sum total of his pains.

VI. An action then may be said to be conformable to the principle of utility, or, for shortness sake, to utility, (meaning with respect to the community at large) when the tendency it has to augment the happiness of the community is greater than any it has to diminish it.

VII. A measure of government (which is but a particular kind of action, performed by a particular person or persons) may be said to be conformable to or dictated by the principle of utility, when in like manner the tendency which it has to augment the happiness of the community is greater than any which it has to diminish it.

*Interest is one of those words, which not having any superior *genus*, cannot in the ordinary way be defined.

VIII. When an action, or in particular a measure of government, is supposed by a man to be conformable to the principle of utility, it may be convenient, for the purposes of discourse, to imagine a kind of law or dictate, called a law or dictate of utility: and to speak of the action in question, as being conformable to such law or dictate.

IX. A man may be said to be a partizan of the principle of utility, when the approbation or disapprobation he annexes to any action, or to any measure, is determined by and proportioned to the tendency which he conceives it to have to augment or to diminish the happiness of the community: or in other words, to its conformity or unconformity to the laws or dictates of utility.

X. Of an action that is conformable to the principle of utility one may always say either that it is one that ought to be done, or at least that it is not one that ought not to be done. One may say also, that it is right it should be done; at least that it is not wrong it should be done; that it is a right action; at least that it is not a wrong action. When thus interpreted, the words *ought*, and *right* and *wrong*, and others of that stamp, have a meaning: when otherwise, they have none.

XI. Has the rectitude of this principle been ever formally contested? It should seem that it had, by those who have not known what they have been meaning. Is it susceptible of any direct proof? it should seem not: for that which is used to prove every thing else, cannot itself be proved: a chain of proofs must have their commencement somewhere. To give such proof is as impossible as it is needless.

XII. Not that there is or ever has been that human creature breathing, however stupid or perverse, who has not on many, perhaps on most occasions of his life, deferred to it. By the natural constitution of the human frame, on most occasions of their lives men in general embrace this principle, without thinking of it: if not for the ordering of their own actions, yet for the trying of their own actions, as well as of those of other men. There have been, at the same time, not many, perhaps, even of the most intelligent, who have been disposed to embrace it purely and without reserve. There are even few who have not taken some occasion or other to quarrel with it, either on account of their not understanding always how to apply it, or on account of some prejudice or other which they were afraid to examine into, or could not bear to part with. For such is the stuff that man is made of: in principle and in practice, in a right track and in a wrong one, the rarest of all human qualities is consistency.

Chapter IV Value of a Lot of Pleasure or Pain, How to Be Measured

I. Pleasures then, and the avoidance of pains, are the *ends* which the legislator has in view: it behoves him therefore to understand their *value*. Pleasures and pains are the *instruments* he has to work with: it behoves him therefore to understand their force, which is again, in other words, their value.

II. To a person considered *by himself*, the value of a pleasure or pain considered *by itself*, will be greater or less, according to the four following circumstances:

1. Its *intensity*.
2. Its *duration*.
3. Its *certainty* or *uncertainty*.
4. Its *propinquity* or *remoteness*.

III. These are the circumstances which are to be considered in estimating a pleasure or a pain considered each of them by itself. But when the value of any pleasure or pain is considered for the purpose of estimating the tendency of any *act* by which it is produced, there are two other circumstances to be taken into the account; these are,

5. Its *fecundity*, or the chance it has of being followed by sensations of the *same* kind: that is, pleasures, if it be a pleasure: pains, if it be a pain.

6. Its *purity*, or the chance it has of *not* being followed by sensations of the *opposite* kind: that is, pains, if it be a pleasure: pleasures, if it be a pain.

These two last, however, are in strictness scarcely to be deemed properties of the pleasure or the pain itself; they are not, therefore, in strictness to be taken into the account of the value of that pleasure or that pain. They are in strictness to be deemed properties only of the act, or other event, by which such pleasure or pain has been produced; and accordingly are

only to be taken into the account of the tendency of such act or such event.

IV. To a *number* of persons, with reference to each of whom the value of a pleasure or a pain is considered, it will be greater or less, according to seven circumstances: to wit, the six preceding ones; viz.

1. Its *intensity*.
2. Its *duration*.
3. Its *certainty* or *uncertainty*.
4. Its *propinquity* or *remoteness*.
5. Its *fecundity*.
6. Its *purity*.

And one other; to wit:

7. Its *extent*; that is, the number of persons to whom it *extends*; or (in other words) who are affected by it.

V. To take an exact account then of the general tendency of any act, by which the interests of a community are affected, proceed as follows. Begin with any one person of those whose interests seem most immediately to be affected by it: and take an account.

1. Of the value of each distinguishable *pleasure* which appears to be produced by it in the *first* instance.

2. Of the value of each *pain* which appears to be produced by it in the *first* instance.

3. Of the value of each pleasure which appears to be produced by it *after* the first. This constitutes the *fecundity* of the first *pleasure* and the *impurity* of the first *pain*.

4. Of the value of each *pain* which appears to be produced by it after the first. This constitutes the *fecundity* of the first *pain*, and the *impurity* of the first pleasure.

5. Sum up all the values of all the *pleasures* on the one side, and those of all the pains on the other. The balance, if it be on the side of pleasure, will give the *good* tendency of the act upon the whole, with respect to the interests of that *individual* person; if on the side of pain, the *bad* tendency of it upon the whole.

6. Take an account of the *number* of persons whose interests appear to be concerned; and repeat the above process with respect to each. *Sum up* the numbers expressive of the degrees of *good* tendency, which the act has, with respect to each individual, in regard to whom the tendency of it is *good* upon the whole: do this again with respect to each individual, in regard to whom the tendency of it is *bad* upon the whole. Take the *balance*; which, if on the side of *pleasure*, will give the general *good tendency* of the act, with respect to the total number or community of individuals concerned; if on the side of pain, the general *evil tendency*, with respect to the same community.

VI. It is not to be expected that this process should be strictly pursued previously to every moral judgment, or to every legislative or judicial operation. It may, however, be always kept in view: and

as near as the process actually pursued on these occasions approaches to it, so near will such process approach to the character of an exact one.

VII. The same process is alike applicable to pleasure and pain, in whatever shape they appear: and by whatever denomination they are distinguished: to pleasure, whether it be called *good* (which is properly the cause or instrument of pleasure) or *profit* (which is distant pleasure, or the cause or instrument of distant pleasure) or *convenience*, or *advantage, benefit, emolument, happiness*, and so forth; to pain, whether it be called *evil*, (which corresponds to *good*) or *mischief*, or *inconvenience*, or *disadvantage*, or *loss*, or *unhappiness*, and so forth.

Utilitarianism

JOHN STUART MILL

John Stuart Mill (1806–1873) was a leading exponent of utilitarianism and empiricist philosophy. In addition to *Utilitarianism*, his works include *A System of Logic, Examination of Sir William Hamilton's Philosophy, Principles of Political Economy*, and *On Liberty*.

—•—

Chapter 1 General Remarks

There are few circumstances among those which make up the present condition of human knowledge, more unlike what might have been expected, or more significant of the backward state in which speculation on the most important subjects still lingers, than the little progress which has been made in the decision of the controversy respecting the criterion of right and wrong. From the dawn of philosophy, the question concerning the *summum bonum*, or,

what is the same thing, concerning the foundation of morality, has been accounted the main problem in speculative thought, has occupied the most gifted intellects, and divided them into sects and schools, carrying on a vigorous warfare against one another. And after more than two thousand years the same discussions continue, philosophers are still ranged under the same contending banners, and neither thinkers nor mankind at large seem nearer to being unanimous on the subject, than when the youth Socrates listened to the old Protagoras, and asserted (if Plato's dialogue be grounded on a real conversation) the theory of utilitarianism against the popular morality of the so-called sophist.

. . . .

On the present occasion, I shall, without further discussion of the other theories, attempt to contribute something towards the understanding and appreciation of the Utilitarian or Happiness theory, and towards such proof as it is susceptible of. It is evident that this cannot be proof in the ordinary and popular meaning of the term. Questions of ultimate ends are not amenable to direct proof. Whatever can be proved to be good, must be so by being shown to be a means to something admitted to be good without proof. The medical art is proved to be good by its conducing to health; but how is it possible to prove that health is good? The art of music is good, for the reason, among others, that it produces pleasure; but what proof is it possible to give that pleasure is good? If, then, it is asserted that there is a comprehensive formula, including all things which are in themselves good, and that whatever else is good, is not so as an end, but as a mean, the formula may be accepted or rejected, but is not a subject of what is commonly understood by proof. We are not, however, to infer that its acceptance or rejection must depend on blind impulse, or arbitrary choice. There is a larger meaning of the word proof, in which this question is as amenable to it as any other of the disputed questions of philosophy. The subject is within the cognisance of the rational faculty; and neither does that faculty deal with it solely in the way of intuition. Considerations may be presented capable of determining the intellect either to give or withhold its assent to the doctrine; and this is equivalent to proof.

We shall examine presently of what nature are these considerations; in what manner they apply to the case, and what rational grounds, therefore, can be given for accepting or rejecting the utilitarian formula. But it is a preliminary condition of rational acceptance or rejection, that the formula should be correctly understood. I believe that the very imperfect notion ordinarily formed of its meaning, is the chief obstacle which impedes its reception; and that could it be cleared, even from only the grosser misconceptions, the question would be greatly simplified, and a large proportion of its difficulties removed. Before, therefore, I attempt to enter into the philosophical grounds which can be given for assenting to the utilitarian standard, I shall offer some illustrations of the doctrine itself; with the view of showing more clearly what it is, distinguishing it from what it is not, and disposing of such of the practical objections to it as either originate in, or are closely connected with, mistaken interpretations of its meaning. Having thus prepared the ground, I shall afterwards endeavour to throw such light as I can upon the question, considered as one of philosophical theory.

Chapter 2 What Utilitarianism Is

. . . The creed which accepts as the foundation of morals, Utility, or the Greatest Happiness Principle, holds that actions are right in proportion as they tend to promote happiness, wrong as they tend to produce the reverse of happiness. By happiness is intended pleasure, and the absence of pain; by unhappiness, pain, and the privation of pleasure. To give a clear view of the moral standard set up by the theory, much more requires to be said; in particular, what things it includes in the ideas of pain and pleasure; and to what extent this is left an open question. But these supplementary explanations do not affect the theory of life on which this theory of morality is grounded—namely, that pleasure, and freedom from pain, are the only things desirable as ends; and that all desirable things (which are as numerous in the utilitarian as in any other scheme) are desirable either for the pleasure inherent in themselves, or as means to the promotion of pleasure and the prevention of pain.

Now, such a theory of life excites in many minds, and among them in some of the most estimable in feeling and purpose, inveterate dislike. To suppose that life has (as they express it) no higher end than pleasure—no better and nobler object of desire and pursuit—they designate as utterly mean and grovelling; as a doctrine worthy only of swine, to whom the followers of Epicurus were, at a very early period, contemptuously likened; and modern holders of the doctrine are occasionally made the subject of equally polite comparisons by its German, French, and English assailants.

When thus attacked, the Epicureans have always answered, that it is not they, but their accusers, who represent human nature in a degrading light; since the accusation supposes human beings to be capable of no pleasures except those of which swine are capable. If this supposition were true, the charge could not be gainsaid, but would then be no longer an imputation; for if the sources of pleasure were precisely the same to human beings and to swine, the rule of life which is good enough for the one would be good enough for the other. The comparison of the Epicurean life to that of beasts is felt as degrading, precisely because a beast's pleasures do not satisfy a human being's conceptions of happiness. Human beings have faculties more elevated than the animal appetites, and when once made conscious of them, do not regard anything as happiness which does not include their gratification. I do not, indeed, consider the Epicureans to have been by any means faultless in drawing out their scheme of consequences from the utilitarian principle. To do this in any sufficient manner, many Stoic, as well as Christian elements require to be included. But there is no known Epicurean theory of life which does not assign to the pleasures of the intellect, of the feelings and imagination, and of the moral sentiments, a much higher value as pleasures than to those of mere sensation. It must be admitted, however, that utilitarian writers in general have placed the superiority of mental over bodily pleasures chiefly in the greater permanency, safety, uncostliness, etc., of the former—that is, in their circumstantial advantages rather than in their intrinsic nature. And on all these points utilitarians have fully proved their case; but they might have taken the other, and, as it may be called, higher ground, with entire consistency. It is quite compatible with the principle of utility to recognise the fact, that some *kinds* of pleasure are more desirable and more valuable than others. It would be absurd that while, in estimating all other things, quality is considered as well as quantity, the estimation of pleasures should be supposed to depend on quantity alone.

If I am asked, what I mean by difference of quality in pleasures, or what makes one pleasure more valuable than another, merely as a pleasure, except its being greater in amount, there is but one possible answer. Of two pleasures, if there be one to which all or almost all who have experience of both

give a decided preference, irrespective of any feeling of moral obligation to prefer it, that is the more desirable pleasure. If one of the two is, by those who are competently acquainted with both, placed so far above the other that they prefer it, even though knowing it to be attended with a greater amount of discontent, and would not resign it for any quantity of the other pleasure which their nature is capable of, we are justified in ascribing to the preferred enjoyment a superiority in quality, so far outweighing quantity as to render it, in comparison, of small account.

Now it is an unquestionable fact that those who are equally acquainted with, and equally capable of appreciating and enjoying, both, do give a most marked preference to the manner of existence which employs their higher faculties. Few human creatures would consent to be changed into any of the lower animals, for a promise of the fullest allowance of a beast's pleasures; no intelligent human being would consent to be a fool, no instructed person would be an ignoramus, no person of feeling and conscience would be selfish and base, even though they should be persuaded that the fool, the dunce, or the rascal is better satisfied with his lot than they are with theirs. They would not resign what they possess more than he for the most complete satisfaction of all the desires which they have in common with him. If they ever fancy they would, it is only in cases of unhappiness so extreme, that to escape from it they would exchange their lot for almost any other, however undesirable in their own eyes. A being of higher faculties requires more to make him happy, is capable probably of more acute suffering, and certainly accessible to it at more points, than one of an inferior type; but in spite of these liabilities, he can never really wish to sink into what he feels to be a lower grade of existence. We may give what explanation we please of this unwillingness; we may attribute to it pride, a name which is given indiscriminately to some of the most and to some of the least estimable feelings of which mankind are capable: we may refer it to the love of liberty and personal independence, an appeal to which was with the Stoics one of the most effective means for the inculcation of it; to the love of power, or to the love of excitement, both of which do really enter into and contribute to it: but its most appropriate appellation is a sense of dignity, which all human beings possess in one form or other, and in some, though by no means in exact, proportion to their higher faculties, and which is so essential a part of the happiness of those in whom it is strong, that nothing which conflicts with it could be, otherwise than momentarily, an object of desire to them. Whoever supposes that this preference takes place at a sacrifice of happiness—that the superior being, in anything like equal circumstances, is not happier than the inferior—confounds the two very different ideas, of happiness, and content. It is indisputable that the being whose capacities of enjoyment are low, has the greatest chance of having them fully satisfied; and a highly endowed being will always feel that any happiness which he can look for, as the world is constituted, is imperfect. But he can learn to bear its imperfections, if they are at all bearable; and they will not make him envy the being who is indeed unconscious of the imperfections, but only because he feels not at all the good which those imperfections qualify. It is better to be a human being dissatisfied than a pig satisfied; better to be Socrates dissatisfied than a fool satisfied. And if the fool, or the pig, are of a different opinion, it is because they only know their own side of the question. The other party to the comparison knows both sides.

It may be objected, that many who are capable of the higher pleasures, occasionally, under the influence of temptation, postpone them to the lower. But this is quite compatible with a full appreciation of the intrinsic superiority of the higher. Men often, from infirmity of character, make their election for the nearer good, though they know it to be the less valuable; and this no less when the choice is between two bodily pleasures, than when it is between bodily and mental. They pursue sensual indulgences to the injury of health, though perfectly aware that health is the greater good. It may be further objected, that many who begin with youthful enthusiasm for everything noble, as they advance in years sink into indolence and selfishness. But I do not believe that those who undergo this very common change, voluntarily choose the lower description of pleasures in preference to the higher. I believe that before they devote themselves exclusively to the one,

they have already become incapable of the other. Capacity for the nobler feelings is in most natures a very tender plant, easily killed, not only by hostile influences, but by mere want of sustenance; and in the majority of young persons it speedily dies away if the occupations to which their position in life has devoted them, and the society into which it has thrown them, are not favourable to keeping that higher capacity in exercise. Men lose their high aspirations as they lose their intellectual tastes, because they have not time or opportunity for indulging them; and they addict themselves to inferior pleasures, not because they deliberately prefer them, but because they are either the only ones to which they have access, or the only ones which they are any longer capable of enjoying. It may be questioned whether any one who has remained equally susceptible to both classes of pleasures, ever knowingly and calmly preferred the lower; though many, in all ages, have broken down in an ineffectual attempt to combine both.

From this verdict of the only competent judges, I apprehend there can be no appeal. On a question which is the best worth having of two pleasures, or which of two modes of existence is the most grateful to the feelings, apart from its moral attributes and from its consequences, the judgment of those who are qualified by knowledge of both, or, if they differ, that of the majority among them, must be admitted as final. And there needs be the less hesitation to accept this judgment respecting the quality of pleasures, since there is no other tribunal to be referred to even on the question of quantity. What means are there of determining which is the acutest of two pains, or the intensest of two pleasurable sensations, except the general suffrage of those who are familiar with both? Neither pains nor pleasures are homogeneous, and pain is always heterogeneous with pleasure. What is there to decide whether a particular pleasure is worth purchasing at the cost of a particular pain, except the feelings and judgment of the experienced? When, therefore, those feelings and judgment declare the pleasures derived from the higher faculties to be preferable *in kind*, apart from the question of intensity, to those of which the animal nature, disjoined from the higher faculties, is susceptible, they are entitled on this subject to the same regard.

I have dwelt on this point, as being a necessary part of a perfectly just conception of Utility or Happiness, considered as the directive rule of human conduct. But it is by no means an indispensable condition to the acceptance of the utilitarian standard; for that standard is not the agent's own greatest happiness, but the greatest amount of happiness altogether; and if it may possibly be doubted whether a noble character is always the happier for its nobleness, there can be no doubt that it makes other people happier, and that the world in general is immensely a gainer by it. Utilitarianism, therefore, could only attain its end by the general cultivation of nobleness of character, even if each individual were only benefited by the nobleness of others, and his own, so far as happiness is concerned, were a sheer deduction from the benefit. But the bare enunciation of such an absurdity as this last, renders refutation superfluous.

According to the Greatest Happiness Principle, as above explained, the ultimate end, with reference to and for the sake of which all other things are desirable (whether we are considering our own good or that of other people), is an existence exempt as far as possible from pain, and as rich as possible in enjoyments, both in point of quantity and quality; the test of quality, and the rule for measuring it against quantity, being the preference felt by those who in their opportunities of experience, to which must be added their habits of self-consciousness and self-observation, are best furnished with the means of comparison. This, being, according to the utilitarian opinion, the end of human action, is necessarily also the standard of morality; which may accordingly be defined, the rules and precepts for human conduct, by the observance of which an existence such as has been described might be, to the greatest extent possible, secured to all mankind; and not to them only, but, so far as the nature of things admits, to the whole sentient creation.

. . . .

I must again repeat, what the assailants of utilitarianism seldom have the justice to acknowledge, that the happiness which forms the utilitarian standard of what is right in conduct, is not the agent's own happiness, but that of all concerned. As between his own happiness and that of others, utilitarianism requires him to be as strictly impartial as a disinterested and benevolent spectator. In the golden rule of Jesus of Nazareth, we read the complete spirit of the ethics of utility. To do as you would be done by, and to love your neighbour as yourself, constitute the ideal perfection of utilitarian morality. As the means of making the nearest approach to this ideal, utility would enjoin, first, that laws and social arrangements should place the happiness, or (as speaking practically it may be called) the interest, of every individual, as nearly as possible in harmony with the interest of the whole; and secondly, that education and opinion, which have so vast a power over human character, should so use that power as to establish in the mind of every individual an indissoluble association between his own happiness and the good of the whole; especially between his own happiness and the practice of such modes of conduct, negative and positive, as regard for the universal happiness prescribes; so that not only he may be unable to conceive the possibility of happiness to himself, consistently with conduct opposed to the general good, but also that a direct impulse to promote the general good may be in every individual one of the habitual motives of action, and the sentiments connected therewith may fill a large and prominent place in every human being's sentient existence. If the impugners of the utilitarian morality represented it to their own minds in this its true character, I know not what recommendation possessed by any other morality they could possibly affirm to be wanting to it; what more beautiful or more exalted developments of human nature any other ethical system can be supposed to foster, or what springs of action, not accessible to the utilitarian, such systems rely on for giving effect to their mandates.

The objectors to utilitarianism cannot always be charged with representing it in a discreditable light. On the contrary, those among them who entertain anything like a just idea of its disinterested character, sometimes find fault with its standard as being too high for humanity. They say it is exacting too much to require that people shall always act from the inducement of promoting the general interests of society. But this is to mistake the very meaning of a standard of morals, and confound the rule of action with the motive of it. It is the business of ethics to tell us what are our duties, or by what test we may know them; but no system of ethics requires that the sole motive of all we do shall be a feeling of duty; on the contrary, ninety-nine hundredths of all our actions are done from other motives, and rightly so done, if the rule of duty does not condemn them. It is the most unjust to utilitarianism that this particular misapprehension should be made a ground of objection to it, inasmuch as utilitarian moralists have gone beyond almost all others in affirming that the motive has nothing to do with the morality of the action, though much with the worth of the agent. He who saves a fellow creature from drowning does what is morally right, whether his motive be duty, or the hope of being paid for his trouble; he who betrays the friend that trusts him, is guilty of a crime, even if his object be to serve another friend to whom he is under greater obligations. But to speak only of actions done from the motive of duty, and in direct obedience to principle: it is a misapprehension of the utilitarian mode of thought, to conceive it as implying that people should fix their minds upon so wide a generality as the world, or society at large. The great majority of good actions are intended not for the benefit of the world, but for that of individuals, of which the good of the world is made up; and the thoughts of the most virtuous man need not on these occasions travel beyond the particular persons concerned, except so far as is necessary to assure himself that in benefiting them he is not violating the rights, that is, the legitimate and authorised expectations, of any one else. The multiplication of happiness is, according to the utilitarian ethics, the object of virtue: the occasions on which any person (except one in a thousand) has it in his power to do this on an extended scale, in other words to be a public benefactor, are but exceptional; and on these occasions alone is he called on to consider public utility; in every other case, private utility, the interest or happiness of some few persons, is all he has to attend to. Those alone the influence of whose actions extends to society in general, need concern themselves habitually about so large an object. In the case of abstinences indeed—of things which people forbear to do from moral considerations, though the consequences in the particular case might be beneficial—it would be unworthy of an intelligent agent not to be consciously aware that the action is of a class which, if practised generally, would be generally injurious, and that this is the ground of the obligation to abstain from it. The amount of regard for the public interest implied in this recognition, is no greater than is demanded by every system of morals, for they all enjoin to abstain from whatever is manifestly pernicious to society.

The same considerations dispose of another reproach against the doctrine of utility, founded on a still grosser misconception of the purpose of a standard of morality, and of the very meaning of the words right and wrong. It is often affirmed that utilitarianism renders men cold and unsympathising; that it chills their moral feelings towards individuals; that it makes them regard only the dry and hard consideration of the consequences of actions, not taking into their moral estimate the qualities from which those actions emanate. If the assertion means that they do not allow their judgment respecting the rightness or wrongness of an action to be influenced by their opinion of the qualities of the person who does it, this is a complaint not against utilitarianism, but against having any standard of morality at all; for certainly no known ethical standard decides an action to be good or bad because it is done by a good or a bad man, still less because done by an amiable, a brave, or a benevolent man, or the contrary. These considerations are relevant, not to the estimation of actions, but of persons; and there is nothing in the utilitarian theory inconsistent with the fact that there are other things which interest us in persons besides the rightness and wrongness of their actions. The Stoics, indeed, with the paradoxical misuse of language which was part of their system, and by which they strove to raise themselves above all concern about anything but virtue, were fond of saying, that he who has that has everything; that he, and only he, is rich, is beautiful, is a king. But no claim of this description is made for the virtuous man by the utilitarian doctrine. Utilitarians are quite aware that there are other desirable possessions and qualities besides virtue, and are perfectly willing to allow to all of them their full worth. They are also aware that a right action does not necessarily indicate a virtuous character, and that actions which are blamable, often proceed from qualities entitled to praise. When this is apparent in any particular case, it modifies their estimation, not certainly of the act, but of the agent. I grant that they are, notwithstanding, of opinion, that in the long run the best proof of a good character is good actions; and resolutely refuse to consider any mental disposition as good, of which the predominant tendency is to produce bad conduct. This makes them unpopular with many people; but it is an unpopularity which they must share with every one who regards the distinction between right and wrong in a serious light; and the reproach is not one which a conscientious utilitarian need be anxious to repel.

If no more be meant by the objection than that many utilitarians look on the morality of actions, as measured by the utilitarian standard, with too exclusive a regard, and do not lay sufficient stress upon the other beauties of character which go toward making a human being lovable or admirable, this may be admitted. Utilitarians who have cultivated their moral feelings, but not their sympathies nor their artistic perceptions, do fall into this mistake; and so do all other moralists under the same conditions. What can be said in excuse for other moralists is equally available for them, namely, that, if there is to be any error, it is better that it should be on that side. As a matter of fact, we may affirm that among utilitarians as among adherents of other systems, there is every imaginable degree of rigidity and of laxity in the application of their standard: some are even puritanically rigorous, while others are as indulgent as can possibly be desired by sinner or by sentimentalist. But on the whole, a doctrine which brings prominently forward the interest that mankind have in the repression and prevention of conduct which violates the moral law, is likely to be inferior to no other in turning the sanctions of opinion against such violations. It is true, the question, What does violate the moral law? is one on which those who recognise different standards of morality are likely now and then to differ. But difference of opinion on moral questions was not first introduced into the world by utilitarianism, while that doctrine does supply, if not always an easy, at all events a tangible and intelligible mode of deciding such differences.

It may not be superfluous to notice a few more of the common misapprehensions of utilitarian ethics, even those which are so obvious and gross that it might appear impossible for any person of candour and intelligence to fall into them; since persons, even of considerable mental endowments, often give themselves so little trouble to understand the bearings of any opinion against which they entertain a prejudice, and men are in general so little conscious of this voluntary ignorance as a defect, that the vulgarest misunderstandings of ethical doctrines are continually met with in the deliberate writings of persons of the greatest pretensions both to high principle and to philosophy. We not uncommonly hear the doctrine of utility inveighed against as a *godless* doctrine. If it be necessary to say anything at all against so mere an assumption, we may say that the question depends upon what idea we have formed of the moral character of the Deity. If it be a true belief that God desires, above all things, the happiness of his creatures, and that this was his purpose in their creation, utility is not only not a godless doctrine, but more profoundly religious than any other. If it be meant that utilitarianism does not recognise the revealed will of God as the supreme law of morals, I answer, that a utilitarian who believes in the perfect goodness and wisdom of God, necessarily believes that whatever God has thought fit to reveal on the subject of morals, must fulfil the requirements of utility in a supreme degree. But others besides utilitarians have been of opinion that the Christian revelation was intended, and is fitted, to inform the hearts and minds of mankind with a spirit which should enable them to find for themselves what is right, and incline them to do it when found, rather than to tell them, except in a very general way, what it is; and that we need a doctrine of ethics, carefully followed out, to *interpret* to us the will of God. Whether this opinion is correct or not, it is superfluous here to discuss; since whatever aid religion, either natural or revealed, can afford to ethical investigation, is as open to the utilitarian moralist as to any other. He can use it as the testimony of God to the usefulness or hurtfulness of any given course of action, by as good a right as others can use it for the indication of a transcendental law, having no connexion with usefulness or with happiness.

Again, Utility is often summarily stigmatised as an immoral doctrine by giving it the name of Expediency, and taking advantage of the popular use of that term to contrast it with Principle. But the Expedient, in the sense in which it is opposed to the Right, generally means that which is expedient for the particular interest of the agent himself; as when a minister sacrifices the interests of his country to keep himself in place. When it means anything better than this, it means that which is expedient for some immediate object, some temporary purpose, but which violates a rule whose observance is expedient in a much higher degree. The Expedient, in this sense, instead of being the same thing with the useful, is a branch of the hurtful. Thus, it would often be expedient, for the purpose of getting over some momentary embarrassment, or attaining some object immediately useful to ourselves or others, to tell a lie. But inasmuch as the cultivation in ourselves of a sensitive feeling on the subject of veracity, is one of the most useful, and the enfeeblement of that feeling one of the most hurtful, things to which our conduct can be instrumental; and inasmuch as any, even unintentional, deviation from truth, does that much towards weakening the trustworthiness of human assertion, which is not only the principal support of all present social well-being, but the insufficiency of which does more than any one thing that can be named to keep back civilisation, virtue, everything on which human happiness on the largest scale depends: we feel that the violation, for a present advantage, of a rule of such transcendent expediency, is not expedient, and that he who, for the sake of a convenience to himself or to some other individual, does what depends on him to deprive mankind of the good, and inflict upon them the evil, involved in the greater or less reliance which they can place in each other's word, acts the part of one of their worst enemies. Yet that even this rule, sacred as it is, admits of possible exceptions, is acknowledged by all moralists; the chief of which is when the withholding of some fact (as of information from a malefactor, or of bad news from a person dangerously ill) would save an individual (especially an individual other than oneself) from great and unmerited evil, and when the withholding can only be effected by denial. But in order that the exception may not extend itself beyond the need, and may have the least possible ef-

fect in weakening reliance on veracity, it ought to be recognised, and, if possible, its limits defined; and if the principle of utility is good for anything, it must be good for weighing these conflicting utilities against one another, and marking out the region within which one or the other preponderates.

Again, defenders of utility often find themselves called upon to reply to such objections as this—that there is not time, previous to action, for calculating and weighing the effects of any line of conduct on the general happiness. This is exactly as if any one were to say that it is impossible to guide our conduct by Christianity, because there is not time, on every occasion on which anything has to be done, to read through the Old and New Testaments. The answer to the objection is, that there has been ample time, namely, the whole past duration of the human species. During all that time, mankind have been learning by experience the tendencies of actions; on which experience all the prudence, as well as all the morality of life, are dependent. People talk as if the commencement of this course of experience had hitherto been put off, and as if, at the moment when some man feels tempted to meddle with the property or life of another, he had to begin considering for the first time whether murder and theft are injurious to human happiness. Even then I do not think that he would find the question very puzzling; but, at all events, the matter is now done to his hand. It is truly a whimsical supposition that, if mankind were agreed in considering utility to be the test of morality, they would remain without any agreement as to what *is* useful, and would take no measures for having their notions on the subject taught to the young, and enforced by law and opinion. There is no difficulty in proving any ethical standard whatever to work ill, if we suppose universal idiocy to be conjoined with it; but on any hypothesis short of that, mankind must by this time have acquired positive beliefs as to the effects of some actions on their happiness; and the beliefs which have thus come down are the rules of morality for the multitude, and for the philosopher until he has succeeded in finding better. That philosophers might easily do this, even now, on many subjects; that the received code of ethics is by no means of divine right; and that mankind have still much to learn as to the effects of actions on the general happiness, I admit, or rather, earnestly maintain. The corollaries from the principle of utility, like the precepts of every practical art, admit of indefinite improvement, and, in a progressive state of the human mind, their improvement is perpetually going on. But to consider the rules of morality as improvable, is one thing; to pass over the intermediate generalisations entirely, and endeavour to test each individual action directly by the first principle, is another. It is a strange notion that the acknowledgment of a first principle is inconsistent with the admission of secondary ones. To inform a traveller respecting the place of his ultimate destination, is not to forbid the use of landmarks and direction-posts on the way. The proposition that happiness is the end and aim of morality does not mean that no road ought to be laid down to that goal, or that persons going thither should not be advised to take one direction rather than another. Men really ought to leave off talking a kind of nonsense on this subject, which they would neither talk nor listen to on other matters of practical concernment. Nobody argues that the art of navigation is not founded on astronomy, because sailors cannot wait to calculate the Nautical Almanack. Being rational creatures, they go to sea with it ready calculated; and all rational creatures go out upon the sea of life with their minds made up on the common questions of right and wrong, as well as on many of the far more difficult questions of wise and foolish. And this, as long as foresight is a human quality, it is to be presumed they will continue to do. Whatever we adopt as the fundamental principle of morality, we require subordinate principles to apply it by; the impossibility of doing without them, being common to all systems, can afford no argument against any one in particular; but gravely to argue as if no such secondary principles could be had, and as if mankind had remained till now, and always must remain, without drawing any general conclusions from the experience of human life, is as high a pitch, I think, as absurdity has ever reached in philosophical controversy.

The remainder of the stock arguments against utilitarianism mostly consist in laying to its charge the common infirmities of human nature, and the general difficulties which embarrass conscientious persons in shaping their course through life. We are told that a utilitarian will be apt to make his own particular case an exception to moral rules, and, when under temptation, will see a utility in the breach of a rule, greater than he will see in its observance. But is utility the only creed which is able to furnish us with excuses for evil doing, and means of cheating our own conscience? They are afforded in abundance by all doctrines which recognise as a fact in morals the existence of conflicting considerations; which all doctrines do, that have been believed by sane persons. It is not the fault of any creed, but of the complicated nature of human affairs, that rules of conduct cannot be so framed as to require no exceptions, and that hardly any kind of action can safely be laid down as either always obligatory or always condemnable. There is no ethical creed which does not temper the rigidity of its laws, by giving a certain latitude, under the moral responsibility of the agent, for accommodation to peculiarities of circumstances; and under every creed, at the opening thus made, self-deception and dishonest casuistry get in. There exists no moral system under which there do not arise unequivocal cases of conflicting obligations. These are the real difficulties, the knotty points both in the theory of ethics, and in the conscientious guidance of personal conduct. They are overcome practically, with greater or with less success, according to the intellect and virtue of the individual; but it can hardly be pretended that any one will be the less qualified for dealing with them, from possessing an ultimate standard to which conflicting rights and duties can be referred. If utility is the ultimate source of moral obligations, utility may be invoked to decide between them when their demands are incompatible. Though the application of the standard may be difficult, it is better than none at all; while in other systems, the moral laws all claiming independent authority, there is no common umpire entitled to interfere between them; their claims to precedence one over another rest on little better than sophistry, and unless determined, as they generally are, by the unacknowledged influence of considerations of utility, afford a free scope for the action of personal desires and partialities. We must remember that only in these cases of conflict between secondary principles is it requisite that first principles should be appealed to. There is no case of moral obligation in which some secondary principle is not involved; and if only one, there can seldom by any real doubt which one it is, in the mind of any person by whom the principle itself is recognised.

Chapter 3 Of the Ultimate Sanction of the Principle of Utility

The question is often asked, and properly so, in regard to any supposed moral standard—What is its sanction? what are the motives to obey it? or more specifically, what is the source of its obligation? whence does it derive its binding force? It is a necessary part of moral philosophy to provide the answer to this question; which, though frequently assuming the shape of an objection to the utilitarian morality, as if it had some special applicability to that above others, really arises in regard to all standards. It arises, in fact, whenever a person is called on to *adopt* a standard, or refer morality to any basis on which he has not been accustomed to rest it. For the customary morality, that which education and opinion have consecrated, is the only one which presents itself to the mind with the feeling of being *in itself* obligatory; and when a person is asked to believe that this morality *derives* its obligation from some general principle round which custom has not thrown the same halo, the assertion is to him a paradox; the supposed corollaries seem to have a more binding force than the original theorem; the superstructure seems to stand better without, than with, what is represented as its foundation. He says to himself, I feel that I am bound not to rob or murder, betray or deceive; but why am I bound to promote the general happiness? If my own happiness lies in something else, why may I not give that the preference?

If the view adopted by the utilitarian philosophy of the nature of the moral sense be correct, this difficulty will always present itself, until the influences which form moral character have taken the same hold of the principle which they have taken of some of the consequences—until, by the improvement of education, the feeling of unity with our fellow-creatures shall be (what it cannot be denied that Christ intended it to be) as deeply rooted in our character, and to our own consciousness as completely a part of our nature, as the horror of crime is in an ordinarily well brought up young person. In the meantime, however, the difficulty has no peculiar application to the doctrine of utility, but is inherent in every attempt to analyse morality and reduce it to principles; which, unless the principle is already in men's minds invested with as much sacredness as any of its applications, always seems to divest them of a part of their sanctity.

The principle of utility either has, or there is no reason why it might not have, all the sanctions which belong to any other system of morals. Those sanctions are either external or internal. Of the external sanctions it is not necessary to speak at any length. They are, the hope of favour and the fear of displeasure, from our fellow-creatures or from the Ruler of the Universe along with whatever we may have of sympathy or affection for them, or of love and awe of Him, inclining us to do His will independently of selfish consequences. There is evidently no reason why all these motives for observance should not attach themselves to the utilitarian morality, as completely and as powerfully as to any other. Indeed, those of them which refer to our fellow-creatures are sure to do so, in proportion to the amount of general intelligence; for whether there be any other ground of moral obligation than the general happiness or not, men do desire happiness; and however imperfect may be their own practice, they desire and commend all conduct in others towards themselves, by which they think their happiness is promoted. With regard to the religious motive, if men believe, as most profess to do, in the goodness of God, those who think that conduciveness to the general happiness is the essence, or even only the criterion of good, must necessarily believe that it is also that which God approves. The whole force therefore of external reward and punishment, whether physical or moral, and whether proceeding from God or from our fellow men, together with all that the capacities of human nature admit of disinterested devotion to either, become available to enforce the utilitarian morality, in proportion as that morality is recognised; and the more powerfully, the more the appliances of education and general cultivation are bent to the purpose.

So far as to external sanctions. The internal sanction of duty, whatever our standard of duty may be, is one and the same—a feeling in our own mind; a pain, more or less intense, attendant on violation of duty, which in properly cultivated moral natures rises, in the more serious cases, into shrinking from it as an impossibility. This feeling, when disinterested, and connecting itself with the pure idea of duty, and not with some particular form of it, or with any of the merely accessory circumstances, is the essence of Conscience; though in that complex phenomenon as it actually exists, the simple fact is in general all encrusted over with collateral associations, derived from sympathy, from love, and still more from fear; from all the forms of religious feeling; from the recollections of childhood and of all our past life; from self-esteem, desire of the esteem of others, and occasionally even self-abasement. This extreme complication is, I apprehend, the origin of the sort of mystical character which, by a tendency of the human mind of which there are many other examples, is apt to be attributed to the idea of moral obligation, and which leads people to believe that the idea cannot possibly attach itself to any other objects than those which, by a supposed mysterious law, are found in our present experience to excite it. Its binding force, however, consists in the existence of a mass of feeling which must be broken through in order to do what violates our standard of right, and which, if we do nevertheless violate that standard, will probably have to be encountered afterwards in the form of remorse. Whatever theory we have of the nature of origin of conscience, this is what essentially constitutes it.

The ultimate sanction, therefore, of all morality (external motives apart) being a subjective feeling in our own minds, I see nothing embarrassing to those whose standard is utility, in the question, what is the sanction of that particular standard? We may answer, the same as of all other moral standards— the conscientious feelings of mankind. Undoubtedly this sanction has no binding efficacy on those who do not possess the feelings it appeals to; but neither will these persons be more obedient to any other

moral principle than to the utilitarian one. On them morality of any kind has no hold but through the external sanctions. Meanwhile the feelings exist, a fact in human nature, the reality of which, and the great power with which they are capable of acting on those in whom they have been duly cultivated, are proved by experience. No reason has ever been shown why they may not be cultivated to as great intensity in connexion with the utilitarian, as with any other rule of morals.

There is, I am aware, a disposition to believe that a person who sees in moral obligation a transcendental fact, an objective reality belonging to the province of "Things in themselves," is likely to be more obedient to it than one who believes it to be entirely subjective, having its seat in human consciousness only. But whatever a person's opinion may be on this point of Ontology, the force he is really urged by is his own subjective feeling, and is exactly measured by its strength. No one's belief that duty is an objective reality is stronger than the belief that God is so; yet the belief in God, apart from the expectation of actual reward and punishment, only operates on conduct through, and in proportion to, the subjective religious feeling. The sanction, so far as it is disinterested, is always in the mind itself; and the notion therefore of the transcendental moralists must be, that this sanction will not exist *in* the mind unless it is believed to have its root out of the mind; and that if a person is able to say to himself, This which is restraining me, and which is called my conscience, is only a feeling in my own mind, he may possibly draw the conclusion that when the feeling ceases the obligation ceases, and that if he find the feeling inconvenient, he may disregard it, and endeavour to get rid of it. But is this danger confined to the utilitarian morality? Does the belief that moral obligation has its seat outside the mind make the feeling of it too strong to be got rid of? The fact is so far otherwise, that all moralists admit and lament the ease with which, in the generality of minds, conscience can be silenced or stifled. The question, Need I obey my conscience? is quite as often put to themselves by persons who never heard of the principle of utility, as by its adherents. Those whose conscientious feelings are so weak as to allow of their asking this question, if they answer it affirmatively, will not do so because they believe in the transcendental theory, but because of the external sanctions.

It is not necessary, for the present purpose, to decide whether the feeling of duty is innate or implanted. Assuming it to be innate, it is an open question to what objects it naturally attaches itself; for the philosophic supporters of that theory are now agreed that the intuitive perception is of principles of morality and not of the details. If there be anything innate in the matter, I see no reason why the feeling which is innate should not be that of regard to the pleasures and pains of others. If there is any principle of morals which is intuitively obligatory, I should say it must be that. If so, the intuitive ethics would coincide with the utilitarian, and there would be no further quarrel between them. Even as it is, the intuitive moralists, though they believe that there are other intuitive moral obligations, do already believe this to be one; for they unanimously hold that a large *portion* of morality turns upon the consideration due to the interests of our fellow-creatures. Therefore, if the belief in the transcendental origin of moral obligation gives any additional efficacy to the internal sanction, it appears to me that the utilitarian principle has already the benefit of it.

On the other hand, if, as is my own belief, the moral feelings are not innate, but acquired, they are not for that reason the less natural. It is natural to man to speak, to reason, to build cities, to cultivate the ground, though these are acquired faculties. The moral feelings are not indeed a part of our nature, in the sense of being in any perceptible degree present in all of us; but this, unhappily, is a fact admitted by those who believe the most strenuously in their transcendental origin. Like the other acquired capacities above referred to, the moral faculty, if not a part of our nature, is a natural outgrowth from it; capable, like them, in a certain small degree, of springing up spontaneously; and susceptible of being brought by cultivation to a high degree of development. Unhappily it is also susceptible, by a sufficient use of the external sanctions and of the force of early impressions, of being cultivated in almost any direction: so that there is hardly anything so absurd or so mischievous that it may not, by means of these influences, be made to act on the human mind

with all the authority of conscience. To doubt that the same potency might be given by the same means to the principle of utility, even if it had no foundation in human nature, would be flying in the face of all experience.

But moral associations which are wholly of artificial creation, when intellectual culture goes on, yield by degrees to the dissolving force of analysis: and if the feeling of duty, when associated with utility, would appear equally arbitrary; if there were no leading department of our nature, no powerful class of sentiments, with which that association would harmonise, which would make us feel it congenial, and incline us not only to foster it in others (for which we have abundant interested motives), but also to cherish it in ourselves; if there were not, in short, a natural basis of sentiment for utilitarian morality, it might well happen that this association also, even after it had been implanted by education, might be analysed away.

But there *is* this basis of powerful natural sentiment; and this it is which, when once the general happiness is recognised as the ethical standard, will constitute the strength of the utilitarian morality. This firm foundation is that of the social feelings of mankind; the desire to be in unity with our fellow creatures, which is already a powerful principle in human nature, and happily one of those which tend to become stronger, even without express inculcation, from the influences of advancing civilisation. The social state is at once so natural, so necessary, and so habitual to man, that, except in some unusual circumstances or by an effort of voluntary abstraction, he never conceives himself otherwise than as a member of a body; and this association is riveted more and more, as mankind are further removed from the stage of savage independence. Any condition, therefore, which is essential to a state of society, becomes more and more an inseparable part of every person's conception of the state of things which he is born into, and which is the destiny of a human being. Now, society between human beings, except in the relation of master and slave, is manifestly impossible on any other footing than that the interests of all are to be consulted. Society between equals can only exist on the understanding that the interests of all are to be regarded equally. And since in all states of civilisation, every person, except an absolute monarch, has equals, every one is obliged to live on these terms with somebody; and in every age some advance is made towards a state in which it will be impossible to live permanently on other terms with anybody. In this way people grow up unable to conceive as possible to them a state of total disregard of other people's interests. They are under a necessity of conceiving themselves as at least abstaining from all the grosser injuries, and (if only for their own protection) living in a state of constant protest against them. They are also familiar with the fact of co-operating with others, and proposing to themselves a collective, not an individual interest as the aim (at least for the time being) of their actions. So long as they are co-operating, their ends are identified with those of others; there is at least a temporary feeling that the interests of others are their own interests. Not only does all strengthening of social ties, and all healthy growth of society, give to each individual a stronger personal interest in practically consulting the welfare of others; it also leads him to identify his *feelings* more and more with their good, or at least with an even greater degree of practical consideration for it. He comes, as though instinctively, to be conscious of himself as a being who *of course* pays regard to others. The good of others becomes to him a thing naturally and necessarily to be attended to, like any of the physical conditions of our existence. Now, whatever amount of this feeling a person has, he is urged by the strongest motives both of interest and of sympathy to demonstrate it, and to the utmost of his power encourage it in others; and even if he has none of it himself, he is as greatly interested as any one else that others should have it. Consequently the smallest germs of the feeling are laid hold of and nourished by the contagion of sympathy and the influences of education; and a complete web of corroborative association is woven round it, by the powerful agency of the external sanctions. This mode of conceiving ourselves and human life, as civilisation goes on, is felt to be more and more natural. Every step in political improvement renders it more so, by removing the sources of opposition of interest, and levelling those inequalities of legal privilege between individuals or classes, owing to which there are large portions of mankind whose happiness it is still practicable to disregard. In an improving state of the human mind, the influences are constantly on the increase, which tend to generate in each individual a feeling of unity with all the rest; which, if perfect, would make him never think of, or desire, any beneficial condition for himself, in the benefits of which they are not included. If we now suppose this feeling of unity to be taught as a religion, and the whole force of education, of institutions, and of opinion, directed, as it once was in the case of religion, to make every person grow up from infancy surrounded on all sides both by the profession and the practice of it, I think that no one, who can realise this conception, will feel any misgiving about the sufficiency of the ultimate sanction for the Happiness morality. To any ethical student who finds the realisation difficult, I recommend, as a means of facilitating it, the second of M. Comte's two principal works, the *Traité de politique positive*. I entertain the strongest objections to the system of politics and morals set forth in that treatise; but I think it has superabundantly shown the possibility of giving to the service of humanity, even without the aid of belief in a Providence, both the psychological power and the social efficacy of a religion; making it take hold of human life, and colour all thought, feeling, and action, in a manner of which the greatest ascendancy ever exercised by any religion may be but a type and foretaste; and of which the danger is, not that it should be insufficient, but that it should be so excessive as to interfere unduly with human freedom and individuality.

Neither is it necessary to the feeling which constitutes the binding force of the utilitarian morality on those who recognise it, to wait for those social influences which would make its obligation felt by mankind at large. In the comparatively early state of human advancement in which we now live, a person cannot indeed feel that entireness of sympathy with all others, which would make any real discordance in the general direction of their conduct in life impossible; but already a person in whom the social feeling is at all developed, cannot bring himself to think of the rest of his fellow-creatures as struggling rivals with him for the means of happiness, whom he must desire to see defeated in their object in order that he may succeed in his. The deeply rooted conception which every individual even now has of himself as a social being, tends to make him feel it one of his natural wants that there should be harmony between his feelings and aims and those of his fellow-creatures. If differences of opinion and of mental culture make it impossible for him to share many of their actual feelings—perhaps make him denounce and defy those feelings—he still needs to be conscious that his real aim and theirs do not conflict; that he is not opposing himself to what they really wish for, namely their own good, but is, on the contrary, promoting it. This feeling in most individuals is much inferior in strength to their selfish feelings, and is often wanting altogether. But to those who have it, it possesses all the characters of a natural feeling. It does not present itself to their minds as a superstition of education, or a law despotically imposed by the power of society, but as an attribute which it would not be well for them to be without. This conviction is the ultimate sanction of the greatest happiness morality. This it is which makes any mind, of well-developed feelings, work with, and not against, the outward motives to care for others, afforded by what I have called the external sanctions; and when those sanctions are wanting, or act in an opposite direction, constitutes in itself a powerful internal binding force, in proportion to the sensitiveness and thoughtfulness of the character; since few but those whose mind is a moral blank, could bear to lay out their course of life on the plan of paying no regard to others except so far as their own private interest compels.

Chapter 4 Of What Sort of Proof the Principle of Utility is Susceptible

It has already been remarked, that questions of ultimate ends do not admit of proof, in the ordinary acceptation of the term. To be incapable of proof by reasoning is common to all first principles; to the first premises of our knowledge, as well as to those of our conduct. But the former, being matters of fact, may be the subject of a direct appeal to the faculties which judge of fact—namely, our senses, and our internal consciousness. Can an appeal be made to the same faculties on questions of practical ends? Or by what other faculty is cognisance taken of them?

Questions about ends are, in other words questions about what things are desirable. The utilitarian doctrine is, that happiness is desirable, and the only thing desirable, as an end; all other things being only desirable as means to that end. What ought to be required of this doctrine—what conditions is it requisite that the doctrine should fulfil—to make good its claim to be believed?

The only proof capable of being given that an object is visible, is that people actually see it. The only proof that a sound is audible, is that people hear it: and so of the other sources of our experience. In like manner, I apprehend, the sole evidence it is possible to produce that anything is desirable, is that people do actually desire it. If the end which the utilitarian doctrine proposes to itself were not, in theory and in practice, acknowledged to be an end, nothing could ever convince any person that it was so. No reason can be given why the general happiness is desirable, except that each person, so far as he believes it to be attainable, desires his own happiness. This, however, being a fact, we have not only all the proof which the case admits of, but all which it is possible to require, that happiness is a good: that each person's happiness is a good to that person, and the general happiness, therefore, a good to the aggregate of all persons. Happiness has made out its title as *one* of the ends of conduct, and consequently one of the criteria of morality.

But it has not, by this alone, proved itself to be the sole criterion. To do that, it would seem, by the same rule, necessary to show, not only that people desire happiness, but that they never desire anything else. Now it is palpable that they do desire things which, in common language, are decidedly distinguished from happiness. They desire, for example, virtue, and the absence of vice, no less really than pleasure and the absence of pain. The desire of virtue is not as universal, but it is as authentic a fact, as the desire of happiness. And hence the opponents of the utilitarian standard deem that they have a right to infer that there are other ends of human action besides happiness, and that happiness is not the standard of approbation and disapprobation.

But does the utilitarian doctrine deny that people desire virtue, or maintain that virtue is not a thing to be desired? The very reverse. It maintains not only that virtue is to be desired, but that it is to be desired disinterestedly, for itself. Whatever may be the opinion of utilitarian moralists as to the original conditions by which virtue is made virtue; however they may believe (as they do) that actions and dispositions are only virtuous because they promote another end than virtue; yet this being granted, and it having been decided, from considerations of this description, what *is* virtuous, they not only place virtue at the very head of the things which are good as means to the ultimate end, but they also recognize as a psychological fact the possibility of its being, to the individual, a good in itself, without looking to any end beyond it; and, hold, that the mind is not in a right state, not a state conformable to Utility, not in the state most conducive to the general happiness, unless it does love virtue in this manner—as a thing desirable in itself, even although, in the individual instance, it should not produce those other desirable consequences which it tends to produce, and on account of which it is held to be virtue. This opinion is not, in the smallest degree, a departure from the Happiness principle. The ingredients of happiness are very various, and each of them is desirable in itself, and not merely when considered as swelling an aggregate. The principle of utility does not mean that any given pleasure, as music, for instance, or any given exemption from pain, as for example health, is to be looked upon as means to a collective something termed happiness, and to be desired on that account. They are desired and desirable in and for themselves; besides being means, they are a part of the end. Virtue, according to the utilitarian doctrine, is not naturally and originally part of the end, but it is capable of becoming so; and in those who love it disinterestedly it has become so, and is desired and cherished, not as a means to happiness, but as a part of their happiness.

To illustrate this farther, we may remember that virtue is not the only thing, originally a means, and which if it were not a means to anything else, would be and remain indifferent, but which by association with what it is a means to, comes to be desired for itself, and that too with the utmost intensity. What, for example, shall we say of the love of money? There is nothing originally more desirable about money than about any heap of glittering pebbles. Its worth is solely that of the things which it will buy; the desires for other things than itself, which it is a means of gratifying. Yet the love of money is not only one of the strongest moving forces of human life, but money is, in many cases, desired in and for itself; the desire to possess it is often stronger than the desire to use it, and goes on increasing when all the desires which point to ends beyond it, to be compassed by it, are falling off. It may, then, be said truly, that money is desired not for the sake of an end, but as part of the end. From being a means to happiness, it has come to be itself a principal ingredient of the individual's conception of happiness. The same may be said of the majority of the great objects of human life—power, for example, or fame; except that to each of these there is a certain amount of immediate pleasure annexed, which has at least the semblance of being naturally inherent in them; a thing which cannot be said of money. Still, however, the strongest natural attraction, both of power and of fame, is the immense aid they give to the attainment of our other wishes; and it is the strong association thus generated between them and all our objects of desire, which gives to the direct desire of them the intensity it often assumes, so as in some characters to surpass in strength all other desires. In these cases the means have become a part of the end, and a more important part of it than any of the things which they are means to. What was once desired as an instrument for the attainment of happiness, has come to be desired for its own sake. In being desired for its own sake it is, however, desired as *part* of happiness. The person is made, or thinks he would be made, happy by its mere possession; and is made unhappy by failure to obtain it. The desire of it is not a different thing from the desire of happiness, any more than the love of music, or the desire of health. They are included in happiness. They are some of the elements of which the desire of happiness is made up. Happiness is not an abstract idea, but a concrete whole; and these are some of its parts. And the utilitarian standard sanctions and approves their being so. Life would be a poor thing, very ill provided with sources of happiness, if there were not this provision of nature, by which things originally indifferent, but conducive to, or otherwise associated with, the satisfaction of our primitive desires, become in themselves sources of pleasure more valuable than the primitive pleasures, both in permanency, in the space of human existence that they are capable of covering, and even in intensity.

Virtue, according to the utilitarian conception, is a good of this description. There was no original desire of it, or motive to it, save its conduciveness to pleasure, and especially to protection from pain. But through the association thus formed, it may be felt a good in itself, and desired as such with as great intensity as any other good; and with this difference between it and the love of money, of power, or of fame, that all of these may, and often do, render the individual noxious to the other members of society to which he belongs, whereas there is nothing which makes him so much a blessing to them as the cultivation of the disinterested love of virtue. And consequently, the utilitarian standard, while it tolerates and approves those other acquired desires, up to the point beyond which they would be more injurious to the general happiness than promotive of it, enjoins and requires the cultivation of the love of virtue up to the greatest strength possible, as being above all things important to the general happiness.

It results from the preceding considerations, that there is in reality nothing desired except happiness. Whatever is desired otherwise than as a means to some end beyond itself, and ultimately to happiness, is desired as itself a part of happiness, and is not desired for itself until it has become so. Those who desire virtue for its own sake, desire it either because the consciousness of it is a pleasure, or because the consciousness of being without it is a pain, or for both reasons united; as in truth the pleasure and pain seldom exist separately, but almost always together, the same person feeling pleasure in degree of virtue attained, and pain in not having attained more. If one of these give him no pleasure, and the other no pain, he would not love or desire virtue, or would desire it only for the other benefits which it might produce to himself or to persons whom he cared for.

We have now, then, an answer to the question, of what sort of proof the principle of utility is susceptible. If the opinion which I have now stated is psychologically true—if human nature is so constituted as to desire nothing which is not either a part of happiness or a means of happiness, we can have no other proof, and we require no other, that these are the only things desirable. If so, happiness is the sole end of human action, and the promotion of it the test by which to judge of all human conduct; from whence it necessarily follows that it must be the criterion of morality, since a part is included in the whole.

And now to decide whether this is really so; whether mankind do desire nothing for itself but that which is a pleasure to them or of which the absence is a pain; we have evidently arrived at a question of fact and experience, dependent, like all similar questions, upon evidence. It can only be determined by practised self-consciousness and self-observation, assisted by observation of others. I believe that these sources of evidence, impartially consulted, will declare that desiring a thing and finding it pleasant, aversion to it and thinking of it as painful, are phenomena entirely inseparable, or rather two parts of the same phenomenon; in strictness of language, two different modes of naming the same psychological fact: that to think of an object as desirable (unless for the sake of its consequences), and to think of it as pleasant, are one and the same thing; and that to desire anything, except in proportion as the idea of it is pleasant, is a physical and metaphysical impossibility.

So obvious does this appear to me, that I expect it will hardly be disputed: and the objection made will be, not that desire can possibly be directed to anything ultimately except pleasure and exemption from pain, but that the will is a different thing from desire; that a person of confirmed virtue, or any other person whose purposes are fixed, carries out his purposes without any thought of the pleasure he has in contemplating them, or expects to derive from their fulfilment; and persists in acting on them, enough though these pleasures are much diminished, by changes in his character or decay of his passive sensibilities, or are outweighed by the pains which the pursuit of the purposes may bring upon him. All this I fully admit, and have stated it elsewhere, as positively and emphatically as any one. Will, the active phenomenon, is a different thing from desire, the state of passive sensibility, and though originally an offshoot from it, may in time take root and detach itself from the parent stock; so much so, that in the case of an habitual purpose, instead of willing the thing because we desire it, we often desire it only because we will it. This, however, is but an instance of that familiar fact, the power of habit, and is nowise confined to the case of virtuous actions. Many indifferent things, which men originally did from a motive of some sort, they continue to do from habit. Sometimes this is done unconsciously, the consciousness coming only after the action; at other times with conscious volition, but volition which has become habitual, and is put in operation by the force of habit, in opposition perhaps to the deliberate preference, as often happens with those who have contracted habits of vicious or hurtful indulgence. Third and last comes the case in which the habitual act of will in the individual instance is not in contradiction to the general intention prevailing at other times, but in fulfilment of it; as in the case of the person of confirmed virtue, and of all who pursue deliberately and consistently any determinate end. The distinction between will and desire thus understood is an authentic and highly important psychological fact; but the fact consists solely in this—that will, like all other parts of our constitution, is amenable to habit, and that we may will from habit what we no longer desire for itself, or desire only because we will it. It is not the less true that will, in the beginning, is entirely produced by desire; including in that term the repelling influence of pain as well as the attractive one of pleasure. Let us take into consideration, no longer the person who has a confirmed will to do right, but him in whom that virtuous will is still feeble, con-

querable by temptation, and not to be fully relied on; by what means can it be strengthened? How can the will to be virtuous, where it does not exist in sufficient force, be implanted or awakened? Only by making the person *desire* virtue—by making him think of it in a pleasurable light, or of its absence in a painful one. It is by associating the doing right with pleasure, or the doing wrong with pain, or by eliciting and impressing and bringing home to the person's experience the pleasure naturally involved in the one or the pain in the other, that it is possible to call forth that will to be virtuous, which, when confirmed, acts without any thought of either pleasure or pain. Will is the child of desire, and passes out of the dominion of its parent only to come under that of habit. That which is the result of habit affords no presumption of being intrinsically good; and there would be no reason for wishing that the purpose of virtue should become independent of pleasure and pain, were it not that the influence of the pleasurable and painful associations which prompt to virtue is not sufficiently to be depended on for unerring constancy of action until it has acquired the support of habit. Both in feeling and in conduct, habit is the only thing which imparts certainty; and it is because of the importance to others of being able to rely absolutely on one's feelings and conduct, and to oneself of being able to rely on one's own, that the will to do right ought to be cultivated into this habitual independence. In other words, this state of the will is a means to good, not intrinsically a good; and does not contradict the doctrine that nothing is a good to human beings but in so far as it is either itself pleasurable, or a means of attaining pleasure or averting pain.

But if this doctrine be true, the principle of utility is proved. Whether it is so or not, must now be left to the consideration of the thoughtful reader.

Criticisms of Utilitarianism

E. F. CARRITT

E. F. Carritt (1876–1964) was a Fellow of University College, Oxford. His publications include *The Theory of Morals: An Introduction to Ethical Philosophy.*

—•—

1. One criticism frequently brought against utilitarianism seems to me invalid. It is said that pleasures and pains cannot be measured or weighed like proteins or money and therefore cannot be compared, so that I can never tell whether I shall produce an overbalance of pleasure in this way or in that. I cannot weigh the pleasure of a starving man whom I feed on bread against my own in eating strawberries and say that his is twice as great as mine. Such an argument might seem hardly worth serious discussion had it not been used in defence of applying to conduct a theory of abstract economics: "There is no scientific criterion which would enable us to compare or assess the relative importance of needs of different persons . . . illegitimate inter-personal comparison,"[1] and "There is no means of testing the magnitude of Λ's satisfaction as compared with B's."[2]

But this argument, though those who use it are not ready to admit so much, really should apply against any comparison of my own desires and needs. I cannot say that two glasses of beer will give me twice as much pleasure as one, and still less that hearing a concert will give me three times or half as much: yet I may know very well indeed which will give me *more*, and may act upon the knowledge, since the two things though not measurable are comparable. It is true that, not being measurable, they are less easy to discriminate precisely, where the difference is not great, than physical objects; I may be unable to say whether the smell of roasting coffee or of bacon fried gives me the greater pleasure (mixed with some pain of appetite) even at two successive moments. It is no doubt often easier to read off the luminosity of two very similar surfaces on a pointer than to say which looks brighter, though in the end I have to trust my eyes for the pointer. As we have admitted, the mere existence of other minds is not demonstrable, still less is the intensity of their desires. But if in self-regarding acts I am sometimes prepared to spend my money in the belief that I shall desire to-morrow's bread more than to-morrow's jam, the utilitarian is justified, on his principles, in believing that it is his duty to provide bread for the starving sooner than jam for the well fed.

In fact it would be no commendation of an ethical theory if, on its showing, moral or even beneficent choice were always clear, since in practice we know that it is not. We often wonder if we can do more for the happiness, even the immediate happiness, of our parents or of our children; the former seem more in need of enjoyments, the latter have a keener capacity but a quicker recovery from disappointment. Utilitarianism has no need to stake its case on the possibility of an accurate "hedonistic (or agathistic) calculus." We have a well-founded belief that starvation hurts most people more than a shortage of grape-fruit, and *no knowledge how much* more it will hurt even ourselves to-morrow; and it is on such beliefs that we have to act; we can never know either our objective duty or our objective long-run interest.

2. The second objection to the utilitarians is serious and indeed fatal. They make no room for justice. Most of them really admitted this when they found it hard on their principle to allow for the admitted obligation to distribute happiness "fairly," that is either equally or in proportion to desert. This led them to qualify their definition of duty as "promoting the greatest amount of happiness," by adding "of the greatest number," and to emphasize this by the proviso "every one count for one and no more." They can hardly have meant by this merely that it did not matter to whom I gave the happiness so long as I produced the most possible, for this they had already implied. They must at least have meant that if I could produce the same amount either in equal shares or in unequal I ought to prefer the former; and this means that I ought to be just as well as generous. The other demand of justice, that we should take account of past merit in our distribution, I think they would have denied, or rather explained away by the argument that to reward beneficence was to encourage such behaviour by example, and therefore a likely way to increase the total of happiness.

3. A third criticism, incurred by some utilitarians[3] in the attempt to accommodate their theory to our moral judgements, was that of inconsistency in considering differences of quality or kind, as well as of amount, among pleasures when determining what we ought to do. It seems clear that people do not feel the same obligation to endow the art of cookery or pot-boiling as that of poetry or music, and this not because they are convinced that the one causes keener and more constant pleasure to a greater number than the other. Yet the recognition of a stronger obligation to promote "higher" or "better" pleasures implies that we think something good, say musical or poetic experience, not merely in proportion to its general pleasantness but by its own nature. The attempt to unite this "qualification of pleasures" with hedonistic utilitarianism is like saying 'I care about nothing but money, but I would not come by it dishonestly.' The fundamental fact is that we do not think some pleasures, such as that of cruelty, good at all.

4. Though the inconsistency of modifying their theory in these two ways seems to have escaped the notice of most utilitarians, they could not help seeing that they were bound to meet a fourth criticism by giving some account of the universal belief that we have obligations to keep our promises. It is obvi-

ous that the payment of money to a rich creditor may not immediately result in so much satisfaction as the keeping of it by a poor debtor or the giving of it to a useful charity, and that yet it may, under most circumstances, be judged a duty and always an obligation. The argument of utilitarians to explain this has usually been as follows: It is true that a particular instance of justice may not directly increase the sum of human happiness but quite the contrary, and yet we often approve such an instance. This is because the *general* practice of such good faith, with the consequent possibility of credit and contract, is supremely conducive to happiness, and therefore so far as any violation of a bargain impairs this confidence, it is, indirectly and in the long run, pernicious.

Such an attempt to bring promise-keeping under the utilitarian formula breaks down because it only applies where the promise and its performance or neglect would be public and therefore serve as an example to others.

Suppose the two explorers in the Arctic have only enough food to keep one alive till he can reach the base, and one offers to die if the other will promise to educate his children. No other person can know that such a promise was made, and the breaking or keeping of it cannot influence the future keeping of promises. On the utilitarian theory, then, its the duty of the returned traveller to act precisely as he ought to have acted if no bargain had been made: to consider how he can spend his money most expediently for the happiness of mankind, and, if he thinks his own child is a genius, to spend it upon him.

Or, to take a different kind of justice, the utilitarian must hold that we are justified in inflicting pain always and only in order to prevent worse pain or bring about greater happiness. This, then, is all we need consider in so-called punishment, which must be purely preventive. But if some kind of very cruel crime becomes common, and none of the criminals can be caught, it might be highly expedient, as an example, to hang an innocent man, if a charge against him could be so framed that he were universally thought guilty; indeed this would only fail to be an ideal instance of utilitarian "punishment" because the victim himself would not have been so likely as a real felon to commit such a crime in the future, in all other respects it would be perfectly deterrent and therefore felicific.

In short, utilitarianism has forgotten rights; it allows no right to a man because he is innocent or because he has worked hard or has been promised or injured, or because he stands in any other special relation to us. It thinks only of duties or rather of a single duty, to dump happiness wherever we most conveniently can. If it speaks of rights at all it could only say all men have one and the same right, namely that all men should try to increase the total happiness. And this is a manifest misuse of language.

NOTES

1. Hayek, *Collectivist Economic Planning*, p. 25.
2. Robbins, *Nature and Significance of Economic Science*, pp. 122–4. Cf. Jay, *The Socialist Case*, ch. 2.
3. E.g., J. S. Mill. Bentham more consistently held that "the pleasure of push-pin is as good as the pleasure of poetry."

Extreme and Restricted Utilitarianism

J. J. C. SMART

I

Utilitarianism is the doctrine that the rightness of actions is to be judged by their consequences. What do we mean by "actions" here? Do we mean particular actions or do we mean classes of actions? According to which way we interpret the word "actions" we get two different theories, both of which merit the appellation "utilitarian."

1. If by "actions" we mean particular individual actions we get the sort of doctrine held by Bentham, Sidgwick, and Moore. According to this doctrine we test individual actions by their consequences, and general rules, like "keep promises," are mere rules of thumb which we use only to avoid the necessity of estimating the probable consequences of our actions at every step. The rightness or wrongness of keeping a promise on a particular occasion depends only on the goodness or badness of the consequences of keeping or of breaking the promise on that particular occasion. Of course part of the consequences of breaking the promise, and a part to which we will normally ascribe decisive importance, will be the weakening of faith in the institution of promising. However, if the goodness of the consequences of breaking the rule is *in toto* greater than the goodness of the consequences of keeping it, then we must break the rule, irrespective of whether the goodness of the consequences of *everybody's* obeying the rule is or is not greater than the consequences of *everybody's* breaking it. To put it shortly, rules do not matter, save *per accidens* as rules of thumb and as *de facto* social institutions with which the utilitarian has to reckon when estimating consequences. I shall call this doctrine "extreme utilitarianism."

From *Theories of Ethics*, ed. Philippa Foot (Oxford: Oxford University Press, 1967), pp. 171–83.

Based on a paper read to the Victorian Branch of the Australasian Association of Psychology and Philosophy, October 1955. [The article is discussed in J. H. McCloskey, "An Examination of Restricted Utilitarianism" *Philosophical Review* (1957); also by D. Lyons, *Forms and Limits of Utilitarianism* (Clarendon Press, Oxford, 1965). Ed. *(in original)*]

2. A more modest form of utilitarianism has recently become fashionable. The doctrine is to be found in Toulmin's book *The Place of Reason in Ethics*, in Nowell-Smith's *Ethics* (though I think Nowell-Smith has qualms), in John Austin's *Lectures on Jurisprudence* (Lecture II), and even in J. S. Mill, if Urmson's interpretation of him is correct (*Philosophical Quarterly*, Vol. 3, pp. 3–39, 1953). Part of its charm is that it appears to resolve the dispute in moral philosophy between intuitionists and utilitarians in a way which is very neat. The above philosophers hold, or seem to hold, that moral rules are more than rules of thumb. In general the rightness of an action is *not* to be tested by evaluating its consequences but only by considering whether or not it falls under a certain rule. Whether the rule is to be considered an acceptable moral rule, is, however, to be decided by considering the consequences of adopting the rule. Broadly, then, actions are to be tested by rules and rules by consequences. The only cases in which we must test an individual action directly by its consequences are (*a*) when the action comes under two different rules, one of which enjoins it and one of which forbids it, and (*b*) when there is no rule whatever that governs the given case. I shall call this doctrine "restricted utilitarianism."

It should be noticed that the distinction I am making cuts across, and is quite different from, the distinction commonly made between hedonistic and ideal utilitarianism. Bentham was an extreme hedonistic utilitarian and Moore an extreme ideal utilitarian, and Toulmin (perhaps) could be classified as a restricted ideal utilitarian. A hedonistic utilitarian holds that the goodness of the consequences of an action is a function only of their pleasurableness and an ideal utilitarian, like Moore, holds that pleasurableness is not even a necessary condition of goodness. Mill seems, if we are to take his remarks about higher and lower pleasures seriously, to be neither a pure hedonistic nor a pure ideal utilitarian. He seems to hold that pleasurableness is a necessary condition for goodness, but that goodness is a function of other qualities of mind as well. Perhaps we can call him a quasi-ideal utilitarian. When we say that a state of mind is good I take it that we are expressing some sort of *rational preference*. When we say that it is pleasurable I take it that we are saying

that it is enjoyable, and when we say that something is a higher pleasure I take it that we are saying that it is more truly, or more deeply, enjoyable. I am doubtful whether "more deeply enjoyable" does not just mean "more enjoyable, even though not more enjoyable on a first look," and so I am doubtful whether quasi-ideal utilitarianism, and possibly ideal utilitarianism too, would not collapse into hedonistic utilitarianism on a closer scrutiny of the logic of words like "preference," "pleasure," "enjoy," "deeply enjoy," and so on. However, it is beside the point of the present paper to go into these questions. I am here concerned only with the issue between extreme and restricted utilitarianism and am ready to concede that both forms of utilitarianism can be either hedonistic or non-hedonistic.

The issue between extreme and restricted utilitarianism can be illustrated by considering the remark "But suppose everyone did the same." (Cf. A. K. Stout's article in *The Australasian Journal of Philosophy*, Vol. 32, pp. 1–29.) Stout distinguishes two forms of the universalization principle, the causal form and the hypothetical form. To say that you ought not to do an action A because it would have bad results if everyone (or many people) did action A may be merely to point out that while the action A would otherwise be the optimific one, nevertheless when you take into account that doing A will probably cause other people to do A too, you can see that A is not, on a broad view, really optimific. If this causal influence could be avoided (as may happen in the case of a secret desert island promise) then we would disregard the universalization principle. This is the causal form of the principle. A person who accepted the universalization principle in its hypothetical form would be one who was concerned only with what would happen *if* everyone did the action A: he would be totally unconcerned with the question of whether in fact everyone would do the action A. That is, he might say that it would be wrong not to vote because it would have bad results if everyone took this attitude, and he would be totally unmoved by arguments purporting to show that my refusing to vote has no effect whatever on other people's propensity to vote. Making use of Stout's distinction, we can say that an extreme utilitarian would apply the universalization principle in the causal form, while a restricted utilitarian would apply it in the hypothetical form.

How are we to decide the issue between extreme and restricted utilitarianism? I wish to repudiate at the outset that milk and water approach which describes itself sometimes as "investigating what is implicit in the common moral consciousness" and sometimes as "investigating how people ordinarily talk about morality." We have only to read the newspaper correspondence about capital punishment or about what should be done with Formosa to realize that the common moral consciousness is in part made up of superstitious elements, of morally bad elements, and of logically confused elements. I address myself to good hearted and benevolent people and so I hope that if we rid ourselves of the logical confusion the superstitious and morally bad elements will largely fall away. For even among good hearted and benevolent people it is possible to find superstitious and morally bad reasons for moral beliefs. These superstitious and morally bad reasons hide behind the protective screen of logical confusion. With people who are not logically confused but who are openly superstitious or morally bad I can of course do nothing. That is, our ultimate pro-attitudes may be different. Nevertheless I propose to rely on *my own* moral consciousness and to appeal to *your* moral consciousness and to forget about what people ordinarily say. "The obligation to obey a rule," says Nowell-Smith (*Ethics*, p. 239), "does not, *in the opinion of ordinary men*," (my italics), "rest on the beneficial consequences of obeying it in a particular case." What does this prove? Surely it is more than likely that ordinary men are confused here. Philosophers should be able to examine the question more rationally.

II

For an extreme utilitarian moral rules are rules of thumb. In practice the extreme utilitarian will mostly guide his conduct by appealing to the rules ("do not lie," "do not break promises," etc.) of common-sense morality. This is not because there is anything sacrosanct in the rules themselves but because he can argue that probably he will most often act in an extreme utilitarian way if he does not think as a utilitarian.

For one thing, actions have frequently to be done in a hurry. Imagine a man seeing a person drowning. He jumps in and rescues him. There is no time to reason the matter out, but usually this will be the course of action which an extreme utilitarian would recommend if he did reason the matter out. If, however, the man drowning had been drowning in a river near Berchtesgaden in 1938, and if he had had the well-known black forelock and moustache of Adolf Hitler, an extreme utilitarian would, if he had time, work out the probability of the man's being the villainous dictator, and if the probability were high enough he would, on extreme utilitarian grounds, leave him to drown. The rescuer, however, has not time. He trusts to his instincts and dives in and rescues the man. And this trusting to instincts and to moral rules can be justified on extreme utilitarian grounds. Furthermore, an extreme utilitarian who knew that the drowning man was Hitler would nevertheless praise the rescuer, not condemn him. For by praising the man he is strengthening a courageous and benevolent disposition of mind, and in general this disposition has great positive utility. (Next time, perhaps, it will be Winston Churchill that the man saves!) We must never forget that an extreme utilitarian may praise actions which he knows to be wrong. Saving Hitler was wrong, but it was a member of a class of actions which are generally right, and the motive to do actions of this class is in general an optimific one. In considering questions of praise and blame it is not the expediency of the praised or blamed action that is at issue, but the expediency of the praise. It can be expedient to praise an inexpedient action and inexpedient to praise an expedient one.

Lack of time is not the only reason why an extreme utilitarian may, on extreme utilitarian principles, trust to rules of common-sense morality. He knows that in particular cases where his own interests are involved his calculations are likely to be biased in his own favour. Suppose that he is unhappily married and is deciding whether to get divorced. He will in all probability greatly exaggerate his own unhappiness (and possibly his wife's) and greatly underestimate the harm done to his children by the break up of the family. He will probably also underestimate the likely harm done by the weakening of the general faith in marriage vows. So probably he will come to the correct extreme utilitarian conclusion if he does not in this instance think as an extreme utilitarian but trusts to common-sense morality.

There are many more and subtle points that could be made in connexion with the relation between extreme utilitarianism and the morality of common sense. All those that I have just made and many more will be found in Book IV Chapters 3–5 of Sidgwick's *Methods of Ethics*. I think that this book is the best book ever written on ethics, and that these chapters are the best chapters of the book. As they occur so near the end of a very long book they are unduly neglected. I refer the reader, then, to Sidgwick for the classical exposition of the relation between (extreme) utilitarianism and the morality of common sense. One further point raised by Sidgwick in this connexion is whether an (extreme) utilitarian ought on (extreme) utilitarian principles to propagate (extreme) utilitarianism among the public. As most people are not very philosophical and not good at empirical calculations, it is probable that they will most often act in an extreme utilitarian way if they do not try to think as extreme utilitarians. We have seen how easily it would be to misapply the extreme utilitarian criterion in the case of divorce. Sidgwick seems to think it quite probable that an extreme utilitarian should not propagate his doctrine too widely. However, the great danger to humanity comes nowadays on the plane of public morality—not private morality. There is a greater danger to humanity from the hydrogen bomb than from an increase of the divorce rate, regrettable though that might be, and there seems no doubt that extreme utilitarianism makes for good sense in international relations. When France walked out of the United Nations because she did not wish Morocco discussed, she said that she was within her rights because Morocco and Algiers are part of her metropolitan territory and nothing to do with U.N. This was clearly a legalistic if not superstitious argument. We should not be concerned with the so-called "rights" of France or any other country but with whether the cause of humanity would best be served by discussing Morocco in U.N. (I am not saying that the answer to this is "Yes." There are good grounds for supposing that more harm than good would have come by such a discussion.) I myself have no hesitation in saying that on extreme utilitarian principles we ought to propagate extreme utilitarianism as widely as possible. But Sidgwick had respectable reasons for suspecting the opposite.

The extreme utilitarian, then, regards moral rules as rules of thumb and as sociological facts that have to be taken into account when deciding what to do, just as facts of any other sort have to be taken into account. But in themselves they do not justify any action.

III

The restricted utilitarian regards moral rules as more than rules of thumb for short-circuiting calculations of consequences. Generally, he argues, consequences are not relevant at all when we are deciding what to do in a particular case. In general, they are relevant only to deciding what rules are good reasons for acting in a certain way in particular cases. This doctrine is possibly a good account of how the modern unreflective twentieth century Englishman often thinks about morality, but surely it is monstrous as an account of how it is most rational to think about morality. Suppose that there is a rule R and that in 99 percent of cases the best possible results are obtained by acting in accordance with R. Then clearly R is a useful rule of thumb; if we have not time or are not impartial enough to assess the consequences of an action it is an extremely good bet that the thing to do is to act in accordance with R. But is it not monstrous to suppose that if we *have* worked out the consequences and if we have perfect faith in the impartiality of our calculations, and if we *know* that in this instance to break R will have better results than to keep it, we should nevertheless obey the rule? Is it not to erect R into a sort of idol if we keep it when breaking it will prevent, say, some avoidable misery? Is not this a form of superstitious rule-worship (easily explicable psychologically) and not the rational thought of a philosopher?

The point may be made more clearly if we consider Mill's comparison of moral rules to the tables in the nautical almanack. (*Utilitarianism*, Everyman

Edition, pp. 22–23). This comparison of Mill's is adduced by Urmson as evidence that Mill was a restricted utilitarian, but I do not think that it will bear this interpretation at all. (Though I quite agree with Urmson that many other things said by Mill are in harmony with restricted rather than extreme utilitarianism. Probably Mill had never thought very much about the distinction and was arguing for utilitarianism, restricted or extreme, against other and quite non-utilitarian forms of moral argument.) Mill says: "Nobody argues that the art of navigation is not founded on astronomy, because sailors cannot wait to calculate the Nautical Almanack. Being rational creatures, they go out upon the sea of life with their minds made up on the common questions of right and wrong, as well as on many of the far more difficult questions of wise and foolish. . . . Whatever we adopt as the fundamental principle of morality, we require subordinate principles to apply it." Notice that this is, as it stands, only an argument for subordinate principles as rules of thumb. The example of the nautical almanack is misleading because the information given in the almanack is in all cases the same as the information one would get if one made a long and laborious calculation from the original astronomical data on which the almanack is founded. Suppose, however, that astronomy were different. Suppose that the behaviour of the sun, moon and planets was very nearly as it is now, but that on rare occasions there were peculiar irregularities and discontinuities, so that the almanack gave us rules of the form "in 99 percent of cases where the observations are such and such you can deduce that your position is so and so." Furthermore, let us suppose that there were methods which enabled us, by direct and laborious calculation from the original astronomical data, not using the rough and ready tables of the almanack, to get our correct position in 100 percent of cases. Seafarers might use the almanack because they never had time for the long calculations and they were content with the 99 percent chance of success in calculating their positions. Would it not be absurd, however, if they *did* make the direct calculation, and finding that it disagreed with the almanack calculation, nevertheless they ignored it and stuck to the almanack conclusion? Of course the

case would be altered if there were a high enough probability of making slips in the direct calculation: then we might stick to the almanack result, liable to error though we knew it to be, simply because the direct calculation would be open to error for a different reason, the fallibility of the computer. This would be analogous to the case of the extreme utilitarian who abides by the conventional rule against the dictates of his utilitarian calculations simply because he thinks that his calculations are probably affected by personal bias. But if the navigator were sure of his direct calculations would he not be foolish to abide by his almanack? I conclude, then, that if we change our suppositions about astronomy and the almanack (to which there are no exceptions) to bring the case into line with that of morality (to whose rules there are exceptions), Mill's example loses its appearance of supporting the restricted form of utilitarianism. Let me say once more that I am not here concerned with how ordinary men think about morality but with how they ought to think. We could quite well imagine a race of sailors who acquired a superstitious reverence for their almanack, even though it was only right in 99 percent of cases, and who indignantly threw overboard any man who mentioned the possibility of a direct calculation. But would this behaviour of the sailors be rational?

Let us consider a much discussed sort of case in which the extreme utilitarian might go against the conventional moral rule. I have promised to a friend, dying on a desert island from which I am subsequently rescued, that I will see that his fortune (over which I have control) is given to a jockey club. However, when I am rescued I decide that it would be better to give the money to a hospital, which can do more good with it. It may be argued that I am wrong to give the money to the hospital. But why? (*a*) The hospital can do more good with the money than the jockey club can. (*b*) The present case is unlike most cases of promising in that no one except me knows about the promise. In breaking the promise I am doing so with complete secrecy and am doing nothing to weaken the general faith in promises. That is, a factor, which would normally keep the extreme utilitarian from promise breaking even in otherwise unoptimific cases, does not at present operate. (*c*) There is no doubt a slight weakening in my own character as an habitual promise keeper, and moreover psychological tensions will be set up in me every time I am asked what the man made me promise him to do. For clearly I shall have to say that he made me promise to give the money to the hospital, and, since I am an habitual truth teller, this will go very much against the grain with me. Indeed I am pretty sure that in practice I myself would keep the promise. But we are not discussing what my moral habits would probably make me do; we are discussing what I ought to do. Moreover, we must not forget that even if it would be most rational of me to give the money to the hospital it would also be most rational of you to punish or condemn me if you did, most improbably, find out the truth (e.g. by finding a note washed ashore in a bottle). Furthermore, I would agree that though it was most rational of me to give the money to the hospital it would be most rational of you to condemn me for it. We revert again to Sidgwick's distinction between the utility of the action and the utility of the praise of it.

Many such issues are discussed by A. K. Stout in the article to which I have already referred. I do not wish to go over the same ground again, especially as I think that Stout's arguments support my own point of view. It will be useful, however, to consider one other example that he gives. Suppose that during hot weather there is an edict that no water must be used for watering gardens. I have a garden and I reason that most people are sure to obey the edict, and that as the amount of water that I use will be by itself negligible no harm will be done if I use the water secretly. So I do use the water, thus producing some lovely flowers which give happiness to various people. Still, you may say, though the action was perhaps optimific, it was unfair and wrong.

There are several matters to consider. Certainly my action should be condemned. We revert once more to Sidgwick's distinction. A right action may be rationally condemned. Furthermore, this sort of offence is normally found out. If I have a wonderful garden when everybody else's is dry and brown there is only one explanation. So if I water my garden I am weakening my respect for law and order, and as this leads to bad results an extreme utilitar-

ian would agree that I was wrong to water the garden. Suppose now that the case is altered and that I can keep the thing secret: there is a secluded part of the garden where I grow flowers which I give away anonymously to a home for old ladies. Are you still so sure that I did the wrong thing by watering my garden? However, this is still a weaker case than that of the hospital and the jockey club. There will be tensions set up within myself: my secret knowledge that I have broken the rule will make it hard for me to exhort others to keep the rule. These psychological ill effects in myself may not be inconsiderable: directly and indirectly they may lead to harm which is at least of the same order as the happiness that the old ladies get from the flowers. You can see that on an extreme utilitarian view there are two sides to the question.

So far I have been considering the duty of an extreme utilitarian in a predominantly non-utilitarian society. The case is altered if we consider the extreme utilitarian who lives in a society every member, or most members, of which can be expected to reason as he does. Should he water his flowers now? (Granting, what is doubtful, that in the case already considered he would have been right to water his flowers.) As a first approximation, the answer is that he should not do so. For since the situation is a completely symmetrical one, what is rational for him is rational for others. Hence, by a *reductio ad absurdum* argument, it would seem that watering his garden would be rational for none. Nevertheless, a more refined analysis shows that the above argument is not quite correct, though it is correct enough for practical purposes. The argument considers each person as confronted with the choice either of watering his garden or of not watering it. However there is a third possibility, which is that each person should, with the aid of a suitable randomizing device, such as throwing dice, give himself a certain probability of watering his garden. This would be to adopt what in the theory of games is called "a mixed strategy." If we could give numerical values to the private benefit of garden watering and to the public harm done by 1, 2, 3, etc., persons using the water in this way, we could work out a value of the probability of watering his garden that each extreme utilitarian should given himself. Let *a* be the value which each extreme utilitarian gets from watering his garden, and let $f(1), f(2), f(3)$, etc., be the public harm done by exactly 1, 2, 3, etc., persons respectively watering their gardens. Suppose that p is the probability that each person gives himself of watering his garden. Then we can easily calculate, as functions of p, the probabilities that exactly 1, 2, 3, etc., persons will water their gardens. Let these probabilities be p_1, $p_2, \ldots p_n$. Then the total net probable benefit can be expressed as

$$V = p_1(a - f(1)) + p_2(2a - f(2)) \\ + \ldots p_n(na - f(n))$$

Then if we know the function of $f(x)$ we can calculate the value of p for which $(dV/dp) = 0$. This gives the value of p which it would be rational for each extreme utilitarian to adopt. The present argument does not of course depend on a perhaps unjustified assumption that the values in question are measurable, and in a practical case such as that of the garden watering we can doubtless assume that p will be so small that we can take it near enough as equal to zero. However the argument is of interest for the theoretical underpinning of extreme utilitarianism, since the possibility of a mixed strategy is usually neglected by critics of utilitarianism, who wrongly assume that the only relevant and symmetrical alternatives are of the form "everybody does X" and "nobody does X."[1]

I now pass on to a type of case which may be thought to be the trump card of restricted utilitarianism. Consider the rule of the road. It may be said that since all that matters is that everyone should do the same it is indifferent which rule we have, "go on the left-hand side" or "go on the right-hand side." Hence the only *reason* for going on the left-hand side in British countries is that this is the rule. Here the rule does seem to be a reason, in itself, for acting in a certain way. I wish to argue against this. The rule in itself is not a reason for our actions. We would be perfectly justified in going on the right-hand side if (*a*) we knew that the rule was to go on the left-hand side, and (*b*) we were in a country peopled by superanarchists who always on principle did the opposite of what they were told. This shows that the rule does not give us a reason for acting so much as

an indication of the probable actions of others, which helps us to find out what would be our own most rational course of action. If we are in a country not peopled by anarchists, but by nonanarchist extreme Utilitarians, we expect, other things being equal, that they will keep rules laid down for them. Knowledge of the rule enables us to predict their behaviour and to harmonize our own actions with theirs. The rule "keep to the left-hand side," then, is not a logical *reason* for action but an anthropological *datum* for planning actions.

I conclude that in every case if there is a rule R the keeping of which is in general optimific, but such that in a special sort of circumstances the optimific behaviour is to break R, then in these circumstances we should break R. Of course we must consider all the less obvious effects of breaking R, such as reducing people's faith in the moral order, before coming to the conclusion that to break R is right: in fact we shall rarely come to such a conclusion. Moral rules, on the extreme utilitarian view, are rules of thumb only, but they are not bad rules of thumb. But if we *do* come to the conclusion that we should break the rule and if we have weighed in the balance of our own fallibility and liability to personal bias, what good reason remains for keeping the rule? I can understand "it is optimific" as a reason for action, but why should "it is a member of a class of actions which are usually optimific" or "it is a member of a class of actions which as a class are more optimific than any alternative general class" be a good reason? You might as well say that a person ought to be picked to play for Australia just because all his brothers have been, or that the Australian team should be compose entirely of the Harvey family because this would be better than composing it entirely of any other family. The extreme utilitarian does not appeal to artificial feelings, but only to our feelings of benevolence, and what better feelings can there be to appeal to? Admittedly we can have a pro-attitude to anything, even to rules, but such artificially begotten pro-attitudes smack of superstition. Let us get down to realities, human happiness and misery, and make these the objects of our pro-attitudes and anti-attitudes.

The restricted utilitarian might say that he is

talking only of *morality*, not of such things as rules of the road. I am not sure how far this objection, if valid, would affect my argument, but in any case I would reply that as a philosopher I conceive of ethics as the study of how it would be *most rational* to act. If my opponent wishes to restrict the word "morality" to a narrower use he can have the word. The fundamental question is the question of rationality of action *in general*. Similarly if the restricted utilitarian were to appeal to ordinary usage and say "it might be most rational to leave Hitler to drown but it would surely not be *wrong* to rescue him," I should again let him have the words "right" and "wrong" and should stick to "rational" and "irrational." We already saw that it would be rational to praise Hitler's rescuer, even though it would have been most rational not to have rescued Hitler. In ordinary language, no doubt, "right" and "wrong" have not only the meaning "most rational to do" and "not most rational to do" but also have the meaning "praiseworthy" and "not praiseworthy." Usually to the utility of an action corresponds utility of praise of it, but as we saw, this is not always so. Moral language could thus do with tidying up, for example by reserving "right" for "most rational" and "good" as an epithet of praise for the motive from which the action sprang. It would be more becoming in a philosopher to try to iron out illogicalities in moral language and to make suggestions for its reform than to use it as a court of appeal whereby to perpetuate confusions.

One last defence of restricted utilitarianism might be as follows. "Act optimifically" might be regarded as itself one of the rules of our system (though it would be odd to say that this rule was justified by its optimificality). According to Toulmin (*The Place of Reason in Ethics*, pp. 146–8) if "keep promises," say, conflicts with another rule we are allowed to argue the case on its merits, as if we were extreme utilitarians. If "act optimifically" is itself one of our rules then there will always be a conflict of rules whenever to keep a rule is not itself optimific. If this is so, restricted utilitarianism collapses into extreme utilitarianism. And no one could read Toulmin's book or Urmson's article on Mill without thinking that Toulmin and Urmson are of the opinion that they have thought of a doctrine which does *not* collapse into extreme utilitarianism, but which is, on the contrary, an improvement on it.

NOTE

1. [This paragraph has been substantially emended by the author. Ed. *(in original)*]

Utilitarianism and Integrity

BERNARD WILLIAMS

—●—

[L]ET US LOOK MORE CONcretely at two examples, to see what utilitarianism might say about them,

From J. J. C. Smart and Bernard Williams *Utilitarianism: For and Against*. Copyright © 1973 by Cambridge University Press. Reprinted by permission of the publisher.

what we might say about utilitarianism and, most importantly of all, what would be implied by certain ways of thinking about the situations. The examples are inevitably schematized, and they are open to the objection that they beg as many questions as they illuminate. There are two ways in particular in which examples in moral philosophy tend to beg important questions. One is that, as presented, they arbitrarily cut off and restrict the range of alternative courses of action—this objection might particularly be made against the first of my two examples. The second is that they inevitably present one with the situation as a going concern, and cut off questions about how the agent got into it, and correspondingly about moral considerations which might flow from that: this objection might perhaps specially arise with regard to the second of my two situations. These difficulties, however, just have to be accepted, and if anyone finds these examples cripplingly defective in this sort of respect, then he must in his own thought rework them in richer and less question-begging form. If he feels that no presentation of any imagined situation can ever be other than misleading in morality, and that there can never be any substitute for the concrete experienced complexity of actual moral situations, then this discussion, with him, must certainly grind to a halt: but then one may legitimately wonder whether every discussion with him about conduct will not grind to a halt, including any discussion about the actual situations, since discussion about how one would think and feel about situations somewhat different from the actual (that is to say, situations to that extent imaginary) plays an important role in discussion of the actual.

I. George, who has just taken his Ph.D. in chemistry, finds it extremely difficult to get a job. He is not very robust in health, which cuts down the number of jobs he might be able to do satisfactorily. His wife has to go out to work to keep them, which itself causes a great deal of strain, since they have small children and there are severe problems about looking after them. The results of all this, especially on the children, are damaging. An older chemist, who knows about this situation, says that he can get George a decently paid job in a certain laboratory, which pursues research into chemical and biological warfare. George says that he cannot accept this, since he is opposed to chemical and biological warfare. The older man replies that he is not too keen on it himself, come to that, but after all George's refusal is not going to make the job or the laboratory go away; what is more, he happens to know that if George refuses the job, it will certainly go to a contemporary of George's who is not inhibited by any

such scruples and is likely if appointed to push along the research with greater zeal than George would. Indeed, it is not merely concern for George and his family, but (to speak frankly and in confidence) some alarm about this other man's excess of zeal, which had led the older man to offer to use his influence to get George the job. . . . George's wife, to whom he is deeply attached, has views (the details of which need not concern us) from which it follows that at least there is nothing particularly wrong with research into CBW. What should he do?

II. Jim finds himself in the central square of a small South American town. Tied up against the wall are a row of twenty Indians, most terrified, a few defiant, in front of them several armed men in uniform. A heavy man in a sweat-stained khaki shirt turns out to be the captain in charge and, after a good deal of questioning of Jim which establishes that he got there by accident while on a botanical expedition, explains that the Indians are a random group of the inhabitants who, after recent acts of protest against the government, are just about to be killed to remind other possible protestors of the advantages of not protesting. However, since Jim is an honoured visitor from another land, the captain is happy to offer him a guest's privilege of killing one of the Indians himself. If Jim accepts, then as a special mark of the occasion, the other Indians will be let off. Of course, if Jim refuses, then there is no special occasion, and Pedro here will do what he was about to do when Jim arrived, and kill them all. Jim, with some desperate recollection of schoolboy fiction, wonders whether if he got hold of a gun, he could hold the captain, Pedro and the rest of the soldiers to threat, but it is quite clear from the set-up that nothing of that kind is going to work: any attempt at that sort of thing will mean that all the Indians will be killed, and himself. The men against the wall, and the other villagers, understand the situation, and are obviously begging him to accept. What should he do?

To these dilemmas, it seems to me that utilitarianism replies, in the first case, that George should accept the job, and in the second, that Jim should kill the Indian. Not only does utilitarianism give these answers but, if the situations are essentially as described and there are no further special factors, it regards them, it seems to me, as *obviously* the right answers. But many of us would certainly wonder whether, in (I), that could possibly be the right answer at all; and in the case of (II), even one who came to think that perhaps that was the answer, might well wonder whether it was obviously the answer. Nor is it just a question of the rightness or obviousness of these answers. It is also a question of what sort of considerations come into finding the answer. A feature of utilitarianism is that it cuts out a kind of consideration which for some others makes a difference to what they feel about such cases: a consideration involving the idea, as we might first and very simply put it, that each of us is specially responsible for what *he* does, rather than for what other people do. This is an idea closely connected with the value of integrity. It is often suspected that utilitarianism, at least in its direct forms, makes integrity as a value more or less unintelligible. I shall try to show that this suspicion is correct. Of course, even if that is correct, it would not necessarily follow that we should reject utilitarianism; perhaps, as utilitarians sometimes suggest, we should just forget about integrity, in favour of such things as a concern for the general good. However, if I am right, we cannot merely do that, since the reason why utilitarianism cannot understand integrity is that it cannot coherently describe the relations between a man's projects and his actions.

Two Kinds of Remoter Effect

A lot of what we have to say about this question will be about the relations between my projects and other people's projects. But before we get on to that, we should ask first whether we are assuming too hastily what the utilitarian answers to the dilemmas will be. In terms of more direct effects of the possible decisions, there does not indeed seem much doubt about the answer in either case; but it might be said that in terms of more remote or less evident effects counterweights might be found to enter the utilitarian scales. Thus the effect on George of a decision to take the job might be invoked, or its effect on others who might know of his decision. The possibility of there being more beneficent labours in the future from which he might be barred or disquali-

fied, might be mentioned; and so forth. Such effects—in particular, possible effects on the agent's character, and effects on the public at large—are often invoked by utilitarian writers dealing with problems about lying or promise-breaking, and some similar considerations might be invoked here.

There is one very general remark that is worth making about arguments of this sort. The certainty that attaches to these hypotheses about possible effects is usually pretty low; in some cases, indeed, the hypothesis invoked is so implausible that it would scarcely pass if it were not being used to deliver the respectable moral answer, as in the standard fantasy that one of the effects of one's telling a particular lie is to weaken the disposition of the world at large to tell the truth. The demands on the certainty or probability of these beliefs as beliefs about particular actions are much milder than they would be on beliefs favouring the unconventional course. It may be said that this is as it should be, since the presumption must be in favour of the conventional course: but that scarcely seems a *utilitarian* answer, unless utilitarianism has already taken off in the direction of not applying the consequences to the particular act at all.

Leaving aside that very general point, I want to consider now two types of effect that are often invoked by utilitarians, and which might be invoked in connexion with these imaginary cases. The attitude or tone involved in invoking these effects may sometimes seem peculiar; but that sort of peculiarity soon becomes familiar in utilitarian discussions, and indeed it can be something of an achievement to retain a sense of it.

First, there is the psychological effect on the agent. Our descriptions of these situations have not so far taken account of how George or Jim will be after they have taken the one course or the other; and it might be said that if they take the course which seemed at first the utilitarian one, the effects on them will be in fact bad enough and extensive enough to cancel out the initial utilitarian advantages of that course. Now there is one version of this effect in which, for a utilitarian, some confusion must be involved, namely that in which the agent feels bad, his subsequent conduct and relations are crippled and so on, *because he thinks that he has done the wrong thing*—for if the balance of outcomes was as it appeared to be *before* invoking this effect, then he has not (from the utilitarian point of view) done the wrong thing. So that version of the effect, for a rational and utilitarian agent, could not possibly make any difference to the assessment of right and wrong. However, perhaps he is not a thoroughly rational agent, and is disposed to have bad feelings, whichever he decided to do. Now such feelings, which are from a strictly utilitarian point of view irrational—nothing, a utilitarian can point out, is advanced by having them—cannot, consistently, have any great weight in a utilitarian calculation. I shall consider in a moment an argument to suggest that they should have no weight at all in it. But short of that, the utilitarian could reasonably say that such feelings should not be encouraged, even if we accept their existence, and that to give them a lot of weight is to encourage them. Or, at the very best, even if they are straightforwardly and without any discount to be put into the calculation, their weight must be small: they are after all (and at best) one man's feelings.

That consideration might seem to have particular force in Jim's case. In George's case, his feelings represent a larger proportion of what is to be weighed, and are more commensurate in character with other items in the calculation. In Jim's case, however, his feelings might seem to be of very little weight compared with other things that are at stake. There is a powerful and recognizable appeal that can be made on this point: as that a refusal by Jim to do what he has been invited to do would be a kind of self-indulgent squeamishness. That is an appeal which can be made by other than utilitarians—indeed, there are some uses of it which cannot be consistently made by utilitarians, as when it essentially involves the idea that there is something dishonourable about such self-indulgence. But in some versions it is a familiar, and it must be said a powerful, weapon of utilitarianism. One must be clear, though, about what it can and cannot accomplish. The most it can do, so far as I can see, is to invite one to consider how seriously, and for what reasons, one feels that what one is invited to do is (in these circumstances) wrong, and in particular, to consider that question from the utilitarian point of

view. When the agent is not seeing the situation from a utilitarian point of view, the appeal cannot force him to do so; and if he does come round to seeing it from a utilitarian point of view, there is virtually nothing left for the appeal to do. If he does not see it from a utilitarian point of view, he will not see his resistance to the invitation, and the unpleasant feelings he associates with accepting it, *just* as disagreeable experiences of his; they figure rather as emotional expressions of a thought that to accept would be wrong. He may be asked, as by the appeal, to consider whether he is right, and indeed whether he is fully serious, in thinking that. But the assertion of the appeal, that he is being self-indulgently squeamish, will not itself answer that question, or even help to answer it, since it essentially tells him to regard his feelings just as unpleasant experiences of his, and he cannot, by doing that, answer the question they pose when they are precisely not so regarded, but are regarded as indications of what he thinks is right and wrong. If he does come round fully to the utilitarian point of view then of course he will regard these feelings just as unpleasant experiences of his. And once Jim—at least—has come to see them in that light, there is nothing left for the appeal to do, since *of course* his feelings so regarded, are of virtually no weight at all in relation to the other things at stake. The "squeamishness" appeal is not an argument which adds in a hitherto neglected consideration. Rather, it is an invitation to consider the situation, and one's own feelings, from a utilitarian point of view.

The reason why the squeamishness appeal can be very unsettling, and one can be unnerved by the suggestion of self-indulgence in going against utilitarian considerations, is not that we are utilitarians who are uncertain what utilitarian value to attach to our moral feelings, but that we are partially at least not utilitarians, and cannot regard our moral feelings merely as objects of utilitarian value. Because our moral relation to the world is partly given by such feelings, and by a sense of what we can or cannot "live with," to come to regard those feelings from a purely utilitarian point of view, that is to say, as happenings outside one's moral self, is to lose a sense of one's moral identity; to lose, in the most literal way, one's integrity. At this point utilitarianism alienates one from one's moral feelings; we shall see a little later how, more basically, it alienates one from one's actions as well.

If, then, one is really going to regard one's feelings from a strictly utilitarian point of view, Jim should give very little weight at all to his; it seems almost indecent, in fact, once one has taken that point of view, to suppose that he should give any at all. In George's case one might feel that things were slightly different. It is interesting, though, that one reason why one might think that—namely that one person principally affected is his wife—is very dubiously available to a utilitarian. George's wife has some reason to be interested in George's integrity and his sense of it; the Indians, quite properly, have no interest in Jim's. But it is not at all clear how utilitarianism would describe that difference.

There is an argument, and a strong one, that a strict utilitarian should give not merely small extra weight, in calculations of right and wrong, to feelings of this kind, but that he should give absolutely no weight to them at all. This is based on the point, which we have already seen, that if a course of action is, before taking these sorts of feelings into account, utilitarianly preferable, then bad feelings about that kind of action will be from a utilitarian point of view irrational. Now it might be thought that even if that is so, it would not mean that in a utilitarian calculation such feelings should not be taken into account; it is after all a well-known boast of utilitarianism that it is a realistic outlook which seeks the best in the world as it is, and takes any form of happiness or unhappiness into account. While a utilitarian will no doubt seek to diminish the incidence of feelings which are utilitarianly irrational—or at least of disagreeable feelings which are so—he might be expected to take them into account while they exist. This is without doubt classical utilitarian doctrine, but there is good reason to think that utilitarianism cannot stick to it without embracing results which are startlingly unacceptable and perhaps self-defeating.

Suppose that there is in a certain society a racial minority. Considering merely the ordinary interests of the other citizens, as opposed to their sentiments, this minority does no particular harm; we may suppose that it does not confer any very great benefits either. Its presence is in those terms neutral or mildly beneficial. However, the other citizens have such prejudices that they find the sight of this group, even the knowledge of its presence, very disagreeable. Proposals are made for removing in some way this minority. If we assume various quite plausible things (as that programmes to change the majority sentiment are likely to be protracted and ineffective) then even if the removal would be unpleasant for the minority, a utilitarian calculation might well end up favouring this step, especially if the minority were a rather small minority and the majority were very severely prejudiced, that is to say, were made very severely uncomfortable by the presence of the minority.

A utilitarian might find that conclusion embarrassing; and not merely because of its nature, but because of the grounds on which it is reached. While a utilitarian might be expected to take into account certain other sorts of consequences of the prejudice, as that a majority prejudice is likely to be displayed in conduct disagreeable to the minority, and so forth, he might be made to wonder whether the unpleasant experiences of the prejudiced people should be allowed, *merely as such*, to count. If he does count them, merely as such, then he has once more separated himself from a body of ordinary moral thought which he might have hoped to accommodate; he may also have started on the path of defeating his own view of things. For one feature of these sentiments is that they are from the utilitarian point of view itself irrational, and a thoroughly utilitarian person would either not have them, or if he found that he did tend to have them, would himself seek to discount them. Since the sentiments in question are such that a rational utilitarian would discount them in himself, it is reasonable to suppose that he should discount them in his calculations about society; it does seem quite unreasonable for him to give just as much weight to feelings—considered just in themselves, one must recall, as experiences of those that have them—which are essentially based on views which are from a utilitarian point of view irrational, as to those which accord with utilitarian principles. Granted this idea, it seems reasonable for him to rejoin a body of moral thought in other respects congenial to him, and discount those sentiments, just considered in themselves, totally, on the principle that no pains or discomforts are to count in the utilitarian sum which their subjects have just because they hold views which are by utilitarian standards irrational. But if he accepts that, then in the cases we are at present considering no extra weight at all can be put in for bad feelings of George or Jim about their choices, if those choices are, leaving out those feelings, on the first round utilitarianly rational.

The psychological effect on the agent was the first of two general effects considered by utilitarians, which had to be discussed. The second is in general a more substantial item, but it need not take so long, since it is both clearer and has little application to the present cases. This is the *precedent effect*. As Burke rightly emphasized, this effect can be important: that one morally *can* do what someone has actually done, is a psychologically effective principle, if not a deontically valid one. For the effect to operate, obviously some conditions must hold on the publicity of the act and on such things as the status of the agent (such considerations weighed importantly with Sir Thomas More); what these may be will vary evidently with circumstances.

In order for the precedent effect to make a difference to a utilitarian calculation, it must be based upon a confusion. For suppose that there is an act which would be the best in the circumstances, except that doing it will encourage by precedent other people to do things which will not be the best things to do. Then the situation of those other people must be relevantly different from that of the original agent; if it were not, then in doing the same as what would be the best course for the original agent, they would necessarily do the best thing themselves. But if the situations are in this way relevantly different, it must be a confused perception which takes the first situation, and the agent's course in it, as an adequate precedent for the second.

However, the fact that the precedent effect, if it really makes a difference, is in this sense based on a confusion, does not mean that it is not perfectly real, nor that it is to be discounted: social effects are by their nature confused in this sort of way. What it does emphasize is that calculations of the precedent effect have got to be realistic, involving considera-

tions of how people are actually likely to be influenced. In the present examples, however, it is very implausible to think that the precedent effect could be invoked to make any difference to the calculation. Jim's case is extraordinary enough, and it is hard to imagine who the recipients of the effect might be supposed to be; while George is not in a sufficiently public situation or role for the question to arise in that form, and in any case one might suppose that the motivations of others on such an issue were quite likely to be fixed one way or another already.

No appeal, then, to these other effects is going to make a difference to what the utilitarian will decide about our examples. Let us now look more closely at the structure of those decisions.

Integrity

The situations have in common that if the agent does not do a certain disagreeable thing, someone else will, and in Jim's situation at least the result, the state of affairs after the other man has acted, if he does, will be worse than after Jim has acted, if Jim does. The same, on a smaller scale, is true of George's case. I have already suggested that it is inherent in consequentialism that it offers a strong doctrine of negative responsibility: if I know that if I do X, O_1 will eventuate, and if I refrain from doing X, O_2 will, and that O_2 is worse than O_1, then I am responsible for O_2 if I refrain voluntarily from doing X. "You could have prevented it," as will be said, and truly, to Jim, if he refuses, by the relatives of the other Indians. . . .

In the present cases, the situation of O_2 includes another agent bringing about results worse than O_1. So far as O_2 has been identified up to this point—merely as the worse outcome which will eventuate if I refrain from doing X—we might equally have said that what that other brings about is O_2; but that would be to underdescribe the situation. For what occurs if Jim refrains from action is not solely twenty Indians dead, but *Pedro's killing twenty Indians*, and that is not a result which Pedro brings about, though the death of the Indians is. We can say: what one does is not included in the outcome of what one does, while what another does can be included in the outcome of what one does. For that to be so, as the terms are now being used, only a very weak condition has to be satisfied: for Pedro's killing the Indians to be the outcome of Jim's refusal, it only has to be causally true that if Jim had not refused, Pedro would not have done it.

That may be enough for us to speak, in some sense, of Jim's responsibility for that outcome, if it occurs; but it is certainly not enough, it is worth noticing, for us to speak of Jim's *making* those things happen. For granted this way of their coming about, he could have made them happen only by making Pedro shoot, and there is no acceptable sense in which his refusal makes Pedro shoot. If the captain had said on Jim's refusal, "you leave me with no alternative," he would have been lying, like most who use that phrase. While the deaths, and the killing, may be the outcome of Jim's refusal, it is misleading to think, in such a case, of Jim having an *effect* on the world through the medium (as it happens) of Pedro's acts; for this is to leave Pedro out of the picture in his essential role of one who has intentions and projects, projects for realizing which Jim's refusal would leave an opportunity. Instead of thinking in terms of supposed effects of Jim's projects on Pedro, it is more revealing to think in terms of the effects of Pedro's projects on Jim's decision. This is the direction from which I want to criticize the notion of negative responsibility.

. . . .

What projects does a utilitarian agent have? As a utilitarian, he has the general project of bringing about maximally desirable outcomes; how he is to do this at any given moment is a question of what causal levers, so to speak, are at that moment within reach. The desirable outcomes, however, do not just consist of agents carrying out *that* project; there must be other more basic or lower-order projects which he and other agents have, and the desirable outcomes are going to consist, in part, of the maximally harmonious realization of those projects ("in part," because one component of a utilitarily desirable outcome may be the occurrence of agreeable experiences which are not the satisfaction of anybody's projects). Unless there were first-order projects, the general utilitarian project would have

nothing to work on, and would be vacuous. What do the more basic or lower-order projects comprise? Many will be the obvious kinds of desires for things for oneself, one's family, one's friends, including basic necessities of life, and in more relaxed circumstances, objects of taste. Or there may be pursuits and interests of an intellectual, cultural or creative character. I introduce those as a separate class not because the objects of them lie in a separate class, and provide—as some utilitarians, in their churchy way, are fond of saying—"higher" pleasure. In introduce them separately because the agent's identification with them may be of a different order. It does not have to be: cultural and aesthetic interests just belong, for many, along with any other taste; but some people's commitment to these kinds of interests just is at once more thoroughgoing and serious than their pursuit of various objects of taste, while it is more individual and permeated with character than the desire for the necessities of life.

Beyond these, someone may have projects connected with his support of some cause: Zionism, for instance, or the abolition of chemical and biological warfare. Or there may be projects which flow from some more general disposition toward human conduct and character, such as a hatred of injustice, or of cruelty, or of killing.

It may be said that this last sort of disposition and its associated project do not count as (logically) "lower-order" relative to the higher-order project of maximizing desirable outcomes; rather, it may be said, it is itself a "higher-order" project. The vital question is not, however, how it is to be classified, but whether it and similar projects are to count among the projects whose satisfaction is to be included in the maximizing sum, and, correspondingly, as contributing to the agent's happiness. If the utilitarian says "no" to that, then he is almost certainly committed to a version of utilitarianism as absurdly superficial and shallow as Benthamite versions have often been accused of being. For this project will be discounted, presumably, on the ground that it involves, in the specification of its object, the mention of other people's happiness or interests: thus it is the kind of project which (unlike the pursuit of food for myself) presupposes a reference to other people's projects. But that criterion would eliminate any desire at all which was not blankly and in the most straight-forward sense egoistic.[1] Thus we should be reduced to frankly egoistic first-order projects, and—for all essential purposes—the one second-order utilitarian project of maximally satisfying first-order projects. Utilitarianism has a tendency to slide in this direction, and to leave a vast hole in the range of human desires, between egoistic inclinations and necessities at one end, and impersonally benevolent happiness-management at the other. But the utilitarianism which has to leave this hole is the most primitive form, which offers a quite rudimentary account of desire. Modern versions of the theory are supposed to be neutral with regard to what sorts of things make people happy or what their projects are. Utilitarianism would do well then to acknowledge the evident fact that among the things that make people happy is not only making other people happy, but being taken up or involved in any of a vast range of projects, or—if we waive the evangelical and moralizing associations of the word—commitments. One can be committed to such things as a person, a cause, an institution, a career, one's own genius, or the pursuit of danger.

Now none of these is itself the *pursuit of happiness*: by an exceedingly ancient platitude, it is not at all clear that there could be anything which was just that, or at least anything that had the slightest chance of being successful. Happiness, rather, requires being involved in, or at least content with, something else.[2] It is not impossible for utilitarianism to accept that point: it does not have to be saddled with a naïve and absurd philosophy of mind about the relation between desire and happiness. What it does have to say is that if such commitments are worth while, then pursuing the projects that flow from them, and realizing some of those projects, will make the person for whom they are worthwhile, happy. It may be that to claim that is still wrong: it may well be that a commitment can make sense to a man (can make sense of his life) without his supposing that it will make him *happy*. But that is not the present point; let us grant to utilitarianism that all worthwhile human projects must conduce, one way or another, to happiness. The point is that even if that is true, it does not follow, nor could it possibly be true, that those projects are

themselves projects of pursuing happiness. One has to believe in, or at least want, or quite minimally, be content with, other things, for there to be anywhere that happiness can come from.

Utilitarianism, then, should be willing to agree that its general aim of maximizing happiness does not imply that what everyone is doing is just pursuing happiness. On the contrary, people have to be pursuing other things. What those other things may be, utilitarianism, sticking to its professed empirical stance, should be prepared just to find out. No doubt some possible projects it will want to discourage, on the grounds that their being pursued involves a negative balance of happiness to others: though even there, the unblinking accountant's eye of the strict utilitarian will have something to put in the positive column, the satisfactions of the destructive agent. Beyond that, there will be a vast variety of generally beneficent or at least harmless projects; and some no doubt, will take the form not just of tastes or fancies, but of what I have called "commitments." It may even be that the utilitarian researcher will find that many of those with commitments, who have really identified themselves with objects outside themselves, who are thoroughly involved with other persons, or institutions, or activities or causes, are actually happier than those whose projects and wants are not like that. If so, that is an important piece of utilitarian empirical lore.

. . . .

Let us now go back to the agent as utilitarian, and his higher-order project of maximizing desirable outcomes. At this level, he is committed only to that: what the outcome will actually consist of will depend entirely on the facts, on what persons with what projects and what potential satisfactions there are within calculable reach of the causal levers near which he finds himself. His own substantial projects and commitments come into it, but only as one lot among others—they potentially provide one set of satisfactions among those which he may be able to assist from where he happens to be. He is the agent of the satisfaction system who happens to be at a particular point at a particular time: in Jim's case, our man in South America. His own decisions as a utilitarian agent are a function of all the satisfactions which he can affect from where he is: and this means that the projects of others, to an indeterminately great extent, determine his decision.

This may be so either positively or negatively. It will be so positively if agents within the causal field of his decision have projects which are at any rate harmless, and so should be assisted. It will equally be so, but negatively, if there is an agent within the causal field whose projects are harmful, and have to be frustrated to maximize desirable outcomes. So it is with Jim and the soldier Pedro. On the utilitarian view, the undesirable projects of other people as much determine, in this negative way, one's decisions as the desirable ones do positively: if those people were not there, or had different projects, the causal nexus would be different, and it is the actual state of the causal nexus which determines the decision. The determination to an indefinite degree of my decisions by other people's projects is just another aspect of my unlimited responsibility to act for the best in a causal framework formed to a considerable extent by their projects.

The decision so determined is, for utilitarianism, the right decision. But what if it conflicts with some project of mine? This, the utilitarian will say, has already been dealt with: the satisfaction to you of fulfilling your project, and any satisfactions to others of your so doing, have already been through the calculating device and have been found inadequate. Now in the case of many sorts of projects, that is a perfectly reasonable sort of answer. But in the case of projects of the sort I have called "commitments," those with which one is more deeply and extensively involved and identified, this cannot just by itself be an adequate answer, and there may be no adequate answer at all. For, to take the extreme sort of case, how can a man, as a utilitarian agent, come to regard as one satisfaction among others, and a dispensable one, a project or attitude round which he has built his life, just because someone else's projects have so structured the causal scene that that is how the utilitarian sum comes out?

The point here is not, as utilitarians may hasten to say, that if the project or attitude is that central to his life, then to abandon it will be very disagreeable to him and great loss of utility will be involved. I have already argued [earlier] that it is not like that; on the contrary, once he is prepared to look at it like that, the argument in any serious case is over anyway. The point is that he is identified with his actions as flowing from projects and attitudes which in some cases he takes seriously at the deepest level, as what his life is about (or, in some cases, this section of his life—seriousness is not necessarily the same as persistence). It is absurd to demand of such a man, when the sums come in from the utility network which the projects of others have in part determined, that he should just step aside from his own project and decision and acknowledge the decision which utilitarian calculation requires. It is to alienate him in a real sense from his actions and the source of his action in his own convictions. It is to make him into a channel between the input of everyone's projects, including his own, and an output of optimific decision; but this is to neglect the extent to which *his* actions and *his* decisions have to be seen as the actions and decisions which flow from the projects and attitudes with which he is most closely identified. It is thus, in the most literal sense, an attack on his integrity.

NOTES

1. On the subject of egoistic and non-egoistic desires, see 'Egoism and altruism', in *Problems of the Self* (Cambridge University Press, London, 1973).
2. This does not imply that there is no such thing as the project of pursuing pleasure. Some writers who have correctly resisted the view that all desires are desires for pleasure, have given an account of pleasure so thoroughly adverbial as to leave it quite unclear how there could be a distinctively hedonist way of life at all. Some room has to be left for that, though there are important difficulties both in defining it and living it. Thus (particularly in the case of the very rich) it often has highly ritual aspects, apparently part of a strategy to counter boredom.

Famine, Affluence, and Morality

PETER SINGER

Peter Singer (1946–   ) is a professor of philosophy at Monash University. His publications include *Democracy and Disobedience*, *Animal Liberation*, and *Practical Ethics*.

———•———

AS I WRITE THIS, IN NOVEMBER 1971, people are dying in East Bengal from lack of food, shelter, and medical care. The suffering and death that are occurring there now are not inevitable, not unavoidable in any fatalistic sense of the term. Constant poverty, a cyclone, a civil war have turned at least nine million people into destitute refugees; nevertheless, it is not beyond the capacity of the richer nations to give enough assistance to reduce any further suffering to very small proportions. The decisions and actions of human beings can prevent this kind of suffering. Unfortunately, human beings have not made the necessary decisions. At the individual level, people have, with very few exceptions, not responded to the situation in any significant way. Generally speaking, people have not given large sums to relief funds; they have not written to their parliamentary representatives demanding increased government assistance; they have not demonstrated in the streets, held symbolic fasts, or done anything else directed toward providing the refugees with the means to satisfy their essential needs. At the government level, no government has given the sort of massive aid that would enable the refugees to survive for more than a few days. Britain, for instance, has given rather more than most countries. It has, to date, given £14,750,000. For comparative purposes, Britain's share of the nonrecoverable development costs of the Anglo-French Concorde project is already in excess of £275,000,000, and on present estimates will reach £440,000,000. The im-plication is that the British government values a supersonic transport more than thirty times as highly as it values the lives of the nine million refugees. Australia is another country which, on a per capita basis, is well up in the "aid to Bengal" table. Australia's aid, however, amounts to less than one-twelfth of the cost of Sydney's new opera house. The total amount given, from all sources, now stands at about £65,000,000. The estimated cost of keeping the refugees alive for one year is £464,000,000. Most of the refugees have now been in the camps for more than six months. The World Bank has said that India needs a minimum of £300,000,000 in assistance from other countries before the end of the year. It seems obvious that assistance on this scale will not be forthcoming. India will be forced to choose between letting the refugees starve or diverting funds from her own development program, which will mean that more of her own people will starve in the future.[1]

These are the essential facts about the present situation in Bengal. So far as it concerns us here, there is nothing unique about this situation except its magnitude. The Bengal emergency is just the latest and most acute of a series of major emergencies in various parts of the world, arising both from natural and from man-made causes. There are also many parts of the world in which people die from malnutrition and lack of food independent of any special emergency. I take Bengal as my example only because it is the present concern, and because the size of the problem has ensured that it has been given adequate publicity. Neither individuals nor governments can claim to be unaware of what is happening there.

What are the moral implications of a situation like this? In what follows, I shall argue that the way

From *Philosophy and Public Affairs* 1, no. 3. Copyright © 1972 Princeton University Press. Reprinted by permission of the publisher.

people in relatively affluent countries react to a situation like that in Bengal cannot be justified; indeed, the whole way we look at moral issues—our moral conceptual scheme—needs to be altered, and with it, the way of life that has come to be taken for granted in our society.

In arguing for this conclusion I will not, of course, claim to be morally neutral. I shall, however, try to argue for the moral position that I take, so that anyone who accepts certain assumptions, to be made explicit, will, I hope, accept my conclusion.

I begin with the assumption that suffering and death from lack of food, shelter, and medical care are bad. I think most people will agree about this, although one may reach the same view by different routes. I shall not argue for this view. People can hold all sorts of eccentric positions, and perhaps from some of them it would not follow that death by starvation is in itself bad. It is difficult, perhaps impossible, to refute such positions, and so for brevity I will henceforth take this assumption as accepted. Those who disagree need read no further.

My next point is this: if it is in our power to prevent something bad from happening, without thereby sacrificing anything of comparable moral importance, we ought, morally, to do it. By "without sacrificing anything of comparable moral importance" I mean without causing anything else comparably bad to happen, or doing something that is wrong in itself, or failing to promote some moral good, comparable in significance to the bad thing that we can prevent. This principle seems almost as uncontroversial as the last one. It requires us only to prevent what is bad, and not to promote what is good, and it requires this of us only when we can do it without sacrificing anything that is, from the moral point of view, comparably important. I could even, as far as the application of my argument to the Bengal emergency is concerned, qualify the point so as to make it: if it is in our power to prevent something very bad from happening, without thereby sacrificing anything morally significant, we ought, morally, to do it. An application of this principle would be as follows: if I am walking past a shallow pond and see a child drowning in it, I ought to wade in and pull the child out. This will mean getting my

clothes muddy, but this is insignificant, while the death of the child would presumably be a very bad thing.

The uncontroversial appearance of the principle just stated is deceptive. If it were acted upon, even in its qualified form, our lives, our society, and our world would be fundamentally changed. For the principle takes, firstly, no account of proximity or distance. It makes no moral difference whether the person I can help is a neighbor's child ten yards from me or a Bengali whose name I shall never know, ten thousand miles away. Secondly, the principle makes no distinction between cases in which I am the only person who could possibly do anything and cases in which I am just one among millions in the same position.

I do not think I need to say much in defense of the refusal to take proximity and distance into account. The fact that a person is physically near to us, so that we have personal contact with him, may make it more likely that we *shall* assist him, but this does not show that we *ought* to help him rather than another who happens to be further away. If we accept any principle of impartiality, universalizability, equality, or whatever, we cannot discriminate against someone merely because he is far away from us (or we are far away from him). Admittedly, it is possible that we are in a better position to judge what needs to be done to help a person near to us than one far away, and perhaps also to provide the assistance we judge to be necessary. If this were the case, it would be a reason for helping those near to us first. This may once have been a justification for being more concerned with the poor in one's own town than with famine victims in India. Unfortunately for those who like to keep their moral responsibilities limited, instant communication and swift transportation have changed the situation. From the moral point of view, the development of the world into a "global village" has made an important, though still unrecognized, difference to our moral situation. Expert observers and supervisors, sent out by famine relief organizations or permanently stationed in famine-prone areas, can direct our aid to a refugee in Bengal almost as effectively as we could get it to someone in our own block. There would seem, therefore, to be no possible justification for discriminating on geographical grounds.

There may be a greater need to defend the second implication of my principle—that the fact there are millions of other people in the same position, in respect to the Bengali refugees, as I am, does not make the situation significantly different from a situation in which I am the only person who can prevent something very bad from occurring. Again, of course, I admit that there is a psychological difference between the cases; one feels less guilty about doing nothing if one can point to others, similarly placed, who have also done nothing. Yet this can make no real difference to our moral obligations.[2] Should I consider that I am less obliged to pull the drowning child out of the pond if on looking around I see other people, no further away than I am, who have also noticed the child but are doing nothing? One has only to ask this question to see the absurdity of the view that numbers lessen obligation. It is a view that is an ideal excuse for inactivity; unfortunately most of the major evils—poverty, overpopulation, pollution—are problems in which everyone is almost equally involved.

The view that numbers do make a difference can be made plausible if stated in this way: if everyone in circumstances like mine gave £5 to the Bengal Relief Fund, there would be enough to provide food, shelter, and medical care for the refugees; there is no reason why I should give more than anyone else in the same circumstances as I am; therefore I have no obligation to give more than £5. Each premise in this argument is true, and the argument looks sound. It may convince us, unless we notice that it is based on a hypothetical premise, although the conclusion is not stated hypothetically. The argument would be sound if the conclusion were: if everyone in circumstances like mine were to give £5, I would have no obligation to give more than £5. If the conclusion were so stated, however, it would be obvious that the argument has no bearing on a situation in which it is not the case that everyone else gives £5. This, of course, is the actual situation. It is more or less certain that not everyone in circumstances like mine will give £5. So there will not be enough to provide the needed food, shelter, and medical care. Therefore by giving more than £5 I will prevent more suffering than I would if I gave just £5.

It might be thought that this argument has an absurd consequence. Since the situation appears to be that very few people are likely to give substantial amounts, it follows that I and everyone else in similar circumstances ought to give as much as possible, that is, at least up to the point at which by giving more one would begin to cause serious suffering for oneself and one's dependents—perhaps even beyond this point to the point of marginal utility, at which by giving more one would cause oneself and one's dependents as much suffering as one would prevent in Bengal. If everyone does this, however, there will be more than can be used for the benefit of the refugees, and some of the sacrifice will have been unnecessary. Thus, if everyone does what he ought to do, the result will not be as good as it would be if everyone did a little less than he ought to do, or if only some do all that they ought to do.

The paradox here arises only if we assume that the actions in question—sending money to the relief funds—are performed more or less simultaneously, and are also unexpected. For if it is to be expected that everyone is going to contribute something, then clearly each is not obliged to give as much as he would have been obliged to had others not been giving too. And if everyone is not acting more or less simultaneously, then those giving later will know how much more is needed, and will have no obligation to give more than is necessary to reach this amount. To say this is not to deny the principle that people in the same circumstances have the same obligations, but to point out that the fact that others have given, or may be expected to give, is a relevant circumstance: those giving after it has become known that many others are giving and those giving before are not in the same circumstances. So the seemingly absurd consequence of the principle I have put forward can occur only if people are in error about the actual circumstances—that is, if they think they are giving when others are not, but in fact they are giving when others are. The result of everyone doing what he really ought to do cannot be worse than the result of everyone doing less than he ought to do, although the result of everyone doing what he reasonably believes he ought to do could be.

If my argument so far has been sound, neither our distance from a preventable evil nor the number of other people who, in respect to that evil, are in the same situation as we are, lessens our obligation to mitigate or prevent that evil. I shall therefore take as established the principle I asserted earlier. As I have already said, I need to assert it only in its qualified form: if it is in our power to prevent something very bad from happening, without thereby sacrificing anything else morally significant, we ought, morally, to do it.

The outcome of this argument is that our traditional moral categories are upset. The traditional distinction between duty and charity cannot be drawn, or at least, not in the place we normally draw it. Giving money to the Bengal Relief Fund is regarded as an act of charity in our society. The bodies which collect money are known as "charities." These organizations see themselves in this way—if you send them a check, you will be thanked for your "generosity." Because giving money is regarded as an act of charity, it is not thought that there is anything wrong with not giving. The charitable man may be praised, but the man who is not charitable is not condemned. People do not feel in any way ashamed or guilty about spending money on new clothes or a new car instead of giving it to famine relief. (Indeed, the alternative does not occur to them.) This way of looking at the matter cannot be justified. When we buy new clothes not to keep ourselves warm but to look "well-dressed" we are not providing for any important need. We would not be sacrificing anything significant if we were to continue to wear our old clothes, and give the money to famine relief. By doing so, we would be preventing another person from starving. It follows from what I have said earlier that we ought to give money away, rather than spend it on clothes which we do not need to keep us warm. To do so is not charitable, or generous. Nor is it the kind of act which philosophers and theologians have called "supererogatory"—an act which it would be good to do, but not wrong not to do. On the contrary, we ought to give the money away, and it is wrong not to do so.

I am not maintaining that there are no acts which are charitable, or that there are no acts which it would be good to do but not wrong not to do. It may be possible to redraw the distinction between duty and charity in some other place. All I am arguing here is that the present way of drawing the distinction, which makes it an act of charity for a man living at the level of affluence which most people in the "developed nations" enjoy to give money to save someone else from starvation, cannot be supported. It is beyond the scope of my argument to consider whether the distinction should be redrawn or abolished altogether. There would be many other possible ways of drawing the distinction—for instance, one might decide that it is good to make other people as happy as possible, but not wrong not to do so.

Despite the limited nature of the revision in our moral conceptual scheme which I am proposing, the revision would, given the extent of both affluence and famine in the world today, have radical implications. These implications may lead to further objections, distinct from those I have already considered. I shall discuss two of these.

One objection to the position I have taken might be simply that it is too drastic a revision of our moral scheme. People do not ordinarily judge in the way I have suggested they should. Most people reserve their moral condemnation for those who violate some moral norm, such as the norm against taking another person's property. They do not condemn those who indulge in luxury instead of giving to famine relief. But given that I did not set out to present a morally neutral description of the way people make moral judgments, the way people do in fact judge has nothing to do with the validity of my conclusion. My conclusion follows from the principle which I advanced earlier, and unless that principle is rejected, or the arguments shown to be unsound, I think the conclusion must stand, however strange it appears.

It might, nevertheless, be interesting to consider why our society, and most other societies, do judge differently from the way I have suggested they should. In a well-known article, J. O. Urmson suggests that the imperatives of duty, which tell us what we must do, as distinct from what it would be good to do but not wrong not to do, function so as to prohibit behavior that is intolerable if men are to live together in society.[3] This may explain the origin and continued existence of the present division between acts of duty and acts of charity. Moral attitudes are shaped by the needs of society, and no doubt society needs people who will observe the rules that make social existence tolerable. From the point of view of a particular society, it is essential to prevent violations of norms against killing, stealing, and so on. It is quite inessential, however, to help people outside one's own society.

If this is an explanation of our common distinction between duty and supererogation, however, it is not a justification of it. The moral point of view requires us to look beyond the interests of our own society. Previously, as I have already mentioned, this may hardly have been feasible, but it is quite feasible now. From the moral point of view, the prevention of the starvation of millions of people outside our society must be considered at least as pressing as the upholding of property norms within our society.

It has been argued by some writers, among them Sidgwick and Urmson, that we need to have a basic moral code which is not too far beyond the capacities of the ordinary man, for otherwise there will be a general breakdown of compliance with the moral code. Crudely stated, this argument suggests that if we tell people that they ought to refrain from murder and give everything they do not really need to famine relief, they will do neither, whereas if we tell them that they ought to refrain from murder and that it is good to give to famine relief but not wrong not to do so, they will at least refrain from murder. The issue here is: Where should we draw the line between conduct that is required and conduct that is good although not required, so as to get the best possible result? This would seem to be an empirical question, although a very difficult one. One objection to the Sidgwick–Urmson line of argument is that it takes insufficient account of the effect that moral standards can have on the decisions we make. Given a society in which a wealthy man who gives five percent of his income to famine relief is regarded as most generous, it is not surprising that a proposal that we all ought to give away half our incomes will be thought to be absurdly unrealistic. In a society which held that no man should have more than enough while others have less than they need, such a proposal might seem narrowminded. What it is possible for a man to do and what he is likely to do are both, I think, very greatly

influenced by what people around him are doing and expecting him to do. In any case, the possibility that by spreading the idea that we ought to be doing very much more than we are to relieve famine we shall bring about a general breakdown of moral behavior seems remote. If the stakes are an end to widespread starvation, it is worth the risk. Finally, it should be emphasized that these considerations are relevant only to the issue of what we should require from others, and not to what we ourselves ought to do.

The second objection to my attack on the present distinction between duty and charity is one which has from time to time been made against utilitarianism. It follows from some forms of utilitarian theory that we all ought, morally, to be working full time to increase the balance of happiness over misery. The position I have taken here would not lead to this conclusion in all circumstances, for if there were no bad occurrences that we could prevent without sacrificing something of comparable moral importance, my argument would have no application. Given the present conditions in many parts of the world, however, it does follow from my argument that we ought, morally, to be working full time to relieve great suffering of the sort that occurs as a result of famine or other disasters. Of course, mitigating circumstances can be adduced—for instance, that if we wear ourselves out through overwork, we shall be less effective than we would otherwise have been. Nevertheless, when all considerations of this sort have been taken into account, the conclusion remains: we ought to be preventing as much suffering as we can without sacrificing something else of comparable moral importance. This conclusion is one which we may be reluctant to face. I cannot see, though, why it should be regarded as a criticism of the position for which I have argued, rather than a criticism of our ordinary standards of behavior. Since most people are self-interested to some degree, very few of us are likely to do everything that we ought to do. It would, however, hardly be honest to take this as evidence that it is not the case that we ought to do it.

It may still be thought that my conclusions are so wildly out of line with what everyone else thinks and has always thought that there must be something wrong with the argument somewhere. In order to show that my conclusions, while certainly contrary to contemporary Western moral standards, would not have seemed so extraordinary at other times and in other places, I would like to quote a passage from a writer not normally thought of as a way-out radical, Thomas Aquinas.

> Now, according to the natural order instituted by divine providence, material goods are provided for the satisfaction of human needs. Therefore the division and appropriation of property, which proceeds from human law, must not hinder the satisfaction of man's necessity from such goods. Equally, whatever a man has in superabundance is owed, of natural right, to the poor for their sustenance. So Ambrosius says, and it is also to be found in the *Decretum Gratiani*: "The bread which you withhold belongs to the hungry; the clothing you shut away, to the naked; and the money you bury in the earth is the redemption and freedom of the penniless."[4]

I now want to consider a number of points, more practical than philosophical, which are relevant to the application of the moral conclusion we have reached. These points challenge not the idea that we ought to be doing all we can to prevent starvation, but the idea that giving away a great deal of money is the best means to this end.

It is sometimes said that overseas aid should be a government responsibility, and that therefore one ought not to give to privately run charities. Giving privately, it is said, allows the government and the noncontributing members of society to escape their responsibilities.

This argument seems to assume that the more people there are who give to privately organized famine relief funds, the less likely it is that the government will take over full responsibility for such aid. This assumption is unsupported, and does not strike me as at all plausible. The opposite view—that if no one gives voluntarily, a government will assume that its citizens are uninterested in famine relief and would not wish to be forced into giving aid—seems more plausible. In any case, unless there were a definite probability that by refusing to give one would be helping to bring about massive gov-

ernment assistance, people who do refuse to make voluntary contributions are refusing to prevent a certain amount of suffering without being able to point to any tangible beneficial consequence of their refusal. So the onus of showing how their refusal will bring about government action is on those who refuse to give.

I do not, of course, want to dispute the contention that governments of affluent nations should be giving many times the amount of genuine, no-strings-attached aid that they are giving now. I agree, too, that giving privately is not enough, and that we ought to be compaigning actively for entirely new standards for both public and private contributions to famine relief. Indeed, I would sympathize with someone who thought that compaigning was more important than giving oneself, although I doubt whether preaching what one does not practice would be very effective. Unfortunately, for many people the idea that "it's the government's responsibility" is a reason for not giving which does not appear to entail any political action either.

Another, more serious reason for not giving to famine relief funds is that until there is effective population control, relieving famine merely postpones starvation, If we save the Bengal refugees now, others, perhaps the children of these refugees, will face starvation in a few years' time. In support of this, one may cite the now well-known facts about the population explosion and the relatively limited scope for expanded production.

This point, like the previous one, is an argument against relieving suffering that is happening now, because of a belief about what might happen in the future; it is unlike the previous point in that very good evidence can be adduced in support of this belief about the future. I will not go into the evidence here. I accept that the earth cannot support indefinitely a population rising at the present rate. This certainly poses a problem for anyone who thinks it important to prevent famine. Again, however, one could accept the argument without drawing the conclusion that it absolves one from any obligation to do anything to prevent famine. The conclusion that should be drawn is that the best means of preventing famine, in the long run, is population control. It would then follow from the position reached earlier that one ought to be doing all one can to promote population control (unless one held that all forms of population control were wrong in themselves, or would have significantly bad consequences). Since there are organizations working specifically for population control, one would then support them rather than more orthodox methods of preventing famine.

A third point raised by the conclusion reached earlier relates to the question of just how much we all ought to be giving away. One possibility, which has already been mentioned, is that we ought to give until we reach the level of marginal utility—that is, the level at which, by giving more, I would cause as much suffering to myself or my dependents as I would relieve by my gift. This would mean, of course, that one would reduce oneself to very near the material circumstances of a Bengali refugee. It will be recalled that earlier I put forward both a strong and a moderate version of the principle of preventing bad occurrences. The strong version, which required us to prevent bad things from happening unless in doing so we would be sacrificing something of comparable moral significance, does seem to require reducing ourselves to the level of marginal utility. I should also say that the strong version seems to me to be the correct one. I proposed the more moderate version—that we should prevent bad occurrences unless, to do so, we had to sacrifice something morally significant—only in order to show that even on this surely undeniable principle a great change in our way of life is required. On the more moderate principle, it may not follow that we ought to reduce ourselves to the level of marginal utility, for one might hold that to reduce oneself and one's family to this level is to cause something significantly bad to happen. Whether this is so I shall not discuss, since, as I have said, I can see no good reason for holding the moderate version of the principle rather than the strong version. Even if we accepted the principle only in its moderate form, however, it should be clear that we would have to give away enough to ensure that the consumer society, dependent as it is on people spending on trivia rather than giving to famine relief, would slow down and perhaps disappear entirely. There are several reasons why this would be desirable in itself. The value

and necessity of economic growth are now being questioned not only by conservationists, but by economists as well.[5] There is no doubt, too, that the consumer society has had a distorting effect on the goals and purposes of its members. Yet looking at the matter purely from the point of view of overseas aid, there must be a limit to the extent to which we should deliberately slow down our economy; for it might be the case that if we gave away, say, forty percent of our Gross National Product, we would slow down the economy so much that in absolute terms we would be giving less than if we gave twenty-five percent of the much larger GNP that we would have if we limited our contribution to this smaller percentage.

I mention this only as an indication of the sort of factor that one would have to take into account in working out an ideal. Since Western societies generally consider one percent of the GNP an acceptable level for overseas aid, the matter is entirely academic. Nor does it affect the question of how much an individual should give in a society in which very few are giving substantial amounts.

It is sometimes said, though less often now than it used to be, that philosophers have no special role to play in public affairs, since most public issues depend primarily on an assessment of facts. On questions of fact, it is said, philosophers as such have no special expertise, and so it has been possible to engage in philosophy without committing oneself to any position on major public issues. No doubt there are some issues of social policy and foreign policy about which it can truly be said that a really expert assessment of the facts is required before taking sides or acting, but the issue of famine is surely not one of these. The facts about the existence of suffering are beyond dispute. Nor, I think, is it disputed that we can do something about it, either through orthodox methods of famine relief or through population control or both. This is therefore an issue on which philosophers are competent to take a position. The issue is one which faces everyone who has more money than he needs to support himself and his dependents, or who is in a position to take some sort of political action. These categories must include practically every teacher and student of philosophy in the universities of the Western world. If philosophy is to deal with matters that are relevant to both teachers and students, this is an issue that philosophers should discuss.

Discussion, though, is not enough. What is the point of relating philosophy to public (and personal) affairs if we do not take our conclusions seriously? In this instance, taking our conclusion seriously means acting upon it. The philosopher will not find it any easier than anyone else to alter his attitudes and way of life to the extent that, if I am right, is involved in doing everything that we ought to be doing. At the very least, though, one can make a start. The philosopher who does so will have to sacrifice some of the benefits of the consumer society, but he can find compensation in the satisfaction of a way of life in which theory and practice, if not yet in harmony, are at least coming together.

NOTES

1. There was also a third possibility: that India would go to war to enable the refugees to return to their lands. Since I wrote this paper, India has taken this way out. The situation is no longer that described above, but this does not affect my argument, as the next paragraph indicates.

2. In view of the special sense philosophers often give to the term, I should say that I use "obligation" simply as the abstract noun derived from "ought," so that "I have an obligation to" means no more, and no less, than "I ought to." This usage is in accordance with the definition of "ought" given by the *Shorter Oxford English Dictionary*: "the general verb to express duty or obligation." I do not think any issue of substance hangs on the way the term is used; sentences in which I use "obligation" could all be rewritten, although somewhat clumsily, as sentences in which a clause containing "ought" replaces the term "obligation."

3. J. O. Urmson, "Saints and Heroes," in *Essays in Moral Philosophy*, ed. Abraham I. Melden (Seattle and London, 1958), p. 214. For a related but significantly different view see also Henry Sidgwick, *The Methods of Ethics*, 7th ed. (London, 1907), pp. 220–1, 492–3.

4. *Summa Theologica*, II–II, Question 66, Article 7, in *Aquinas, Selected Political Writings*, ed. A. P. d'Entreves, trans. J. G. Dawson (Oxford, 1948), p. 171.

5. See, for instance, John Kenneth Galbraith, *The New Industrial State* (Boston, 1967); and E. J. Mishan, *The Costs of Economic Growth* (London, 1967).

B. KANTIAN ETHICS

Groundwork of the Metaphysic of Morals

IMMANUEL KANT

Immanuel Kant (1724–1804) was one of the most important philosophers in the history of Western thought. His major works include *The Critique of Pure Reason* (1781), *The Critique of Practical Reason* (1788), and *Groundwork of the Metaphysic of Morals* (1785).

——•——

Chapter 1
Passage from Ordinary
Rational Knowledge of
Morality to Philosophical

The Good Will

It is impossible to conceive anything at all in the world, or even out of it, which can be taken as good without qualification, except a **good will.** Intelligence, wit, judgement, and any other *talents* of the mind we may care to name, or courage, resolution, and constancy of purpose, as qualities of *temperament*, are without doubt good and desirable in many respects; but they can also be extremely bad and hurtful when the will is not good which has to make use of these gifts of nature, and which for this reason has the term "*character*" applied to its peculiar quality. It is exactly the same with *gifts of fortune.* Power, wealth, honour, even health and that complete well-being and contentment with one's state which goes by the name of "*happiness*," produce boldness, and as a consequence

From *Groundwork of the Metaphysic of Morals*, selections from chapters 1 and 2, translated by H. J. Paton. Copyright © by Hutchinson Publishing Group Limited. Reprinted by permission of the publisher.

often overboldness as well, unless a good will is present by which their influence on the mind—and so too the whole principle of action—may be corrected and adjusted to universal ends; not to mention that a rational and impartial spectator can never feel approval in contemplating the uninterrupted prosperity of a being graced by no touch of a pure and good will, and that consequently a good will seems to constitute the indispensable condition of our very worthiness to be happy.

Some qualities are even helpful to this good will itself and can make its task very much easier. They have none the less no inner unconditioned worth, but rather presuppose a good will which sets a limit to the esteem in which they are rightly held and does not permit us to regard them as absolutely good. Moderation in affections and passions, self-control, and sober reflexion are not only good in many respects: they may even seem to constitute part of the *inner* worth of a person. Yet they are far from being properly described as good without qualification (however unconditionally they have been commended by the ancients). For without the principles of a good will they may become exceedingly bad; and the very coolness of a scoundrel makes him, not merely more dangerous, but also immediately more abominable in our eyes than we should have taken him to be without it.

The Good Will and Its Results

A good will is not good because of what it effects or accomplishes—because of its fitness for attaining some proposed end: it is good through its willing alone—that is, good in itself. Considered in itself it is to be esteemed beyond comparison as far higher than anything it could ever bring about merely in order to favour some inclination or, if you like, the sum total of inclinations. Even if, by some special disfavour of destiny or by the niggardly endowment of step-motherly nature, this will is entirely lacking in power to carry out its intentions; if by its utmost effort it still accomplishes nothing, and only good will is left (not, admittedly, as a mere wish, but as the straining of every means so far as they are in our control); even then it would still shine like a jewel for its own sake as something which has its full value in itself. Its use-fulness or fruitlessness can neither add to, nor sub-tract from, this value. Its usefulness would be merely, as it were, the setting which enables us to handle it better in our ordinary dealings or to attract the at-tention of those not yet sufficiently expert, but not to commend it to experts or to determine its value.

. . . .

The Good Will and Duty

We have now to elucidate the concept of a will es-timable in itself and good apart from any further end. This concept, which is already present in a naturally sound understanding and requires not so much to be taught as merely to be clarified, always holds the high-est place in estimating the total worth of our actions and constitutes the condition of all the rest. We will therefore take up the concept of **duty**, which includes that of a good will, exposed, however, to certain sub-jective limitations and obstacles. These, so far from hiding a good will or disguising it, rather bring it out by contrast and make it shine forth more brightly.

The Motive of Duty

I will here pass over all actions already recognized as contrary to duty, however useful they may be with a view to this or that end; for about these the question does not even arise whether they could have been done *for the sake of duty* inasmuch as they are directly opposed to it. I will also set aside actions which in fact accord with duty, yet for which men have *no immediate inclination*, but perform them be-cause impelled to do so by some other inclination. For there it is easy to decide whether the action which accords with duty has been done *from duty* or from some purpose of self-interest. This distinction is far more difficult to perceive when the action ac-cords with duty and the subject has in addition an *immediate* inclination to the action. For example, it certainly accords with duty that a grocer should not overcharge his inexperienced customer; and where there is much competition a sensible shopkeeper re-frains from so doing and keeps to a fixed and gen-eral price for everybody so that a child can buy from him just as well as anyone else. Thus people are served *honestly*; but this is not nearly enough to jus-tify us in believing that the shopkeeper has acted in this way from duty or from principles of fair deal-ing; his interests required him to do so. We cannot assume him to have in addition an immediate in-clination towards his customers, leading him, as it were out of love, to give no man preference over an-other in the matter of price. Thus the action was done neither from duty nor from immediate incli-nation, but solely from purposes of self-interest.

On the other hand, to preserve one's life is a duty, and besides this every one has also an immediate in-clination to do so. But on account of this the often anxious precautions taken by the greater part of mankind for this purpose have no inner worth, and the maxim of their action is without moral content. They do protect their lives *in conformity with duty*, but not *from the motive of duty*. When, on the con-trary, disappointments and hopeless misery have quite taken away the taste for life; when a wretched man, strong in soul and more angered at his fate than faint-hearted or cast down, longs for death and still preserves his life without loving it—not from inclination or fear but from duty; then indeed his maxim has a moral content.

To help others where one can is a duty, and be-sides this there are many spirits of so sympathetic a temper that, without any further motive of vanity or self-interest, they find an inner pleasure in spread-ing happiness around them and can take delight in the contentment of others as their own work. Yet I maintain that in such a case an action of this kind, however right and however amiable it may be, has still no genuinely moral worth. It stands on the same footing as other inclinations—for example, the inclination for honour, which if fortunate enough to hit on something beneficial and right and consequently honourable, deserves praise and encouragement, but not esteem; for its maxim lacks moral content, namely, the performance of such actions, not from inclination, but *from duty*. Suppose then that the mind of this friend of man was overclouded by sorrows of his own which extinguished all sympathy with the fate of others, but that he still had power to help those in distress, though no longer stirred by the need of others because sufficiently occupied with his own; and suppose that, when no longer moved by any inclination, he tears himself out of this deadly insensibility and does the action without any inclination for the sake of duty alone; then for the first time his action has its genuine moral worth. Still further: if nature had implanted little sympathy in this or that man's heart; if (being in other respects an honest fellow) he were cold in temperament and indifferent to the sufferings of others—perhaps because, being endowed with the special gift of patience and robust endurance in his own sufferings, he assumed the like in others or even demanded it; if such a man (who would in truth not be the worst product of nature) were not exactly fashioned by her to be a philanthropist, would he not still find in himself a source from which he might draw a worth far higher than any that a good-natured temperament can have? Assuredly he would. It is precisely in this that the worth of character begins to show—a moral worth and beyond all comparison the highest—namely that he does good, not from inclination, but from duty.

To assure one's own happiness is a duty (at least indirectly); for discontent with one's state, in a press of cares and amidst unsatisfied wants, might easily become a great *temptation to the transgression of duty*. But here also, apart from regard to duty, all men have already of themselves the strongest and deepest inclination toward happiness, because precisely in this Idea of happiness there is combined the sum total of inclinations. The prescription for happiness is, however, often so constituted as greatly to interfere with some inclinations, and yet men cannot form under the name of "happiness" any determinate and assured conception of the satisfaction of all inclinations as a sum. Hence it is not to be wondered at that a single inclination which is determinate as to what it promises and as to the time of its satisfaction may outweigh a wavering Idea; and that a man, for example, a sufferer from gout, may choose to enjoy what he fancies and put up with what he can—on the ground that on balance he has here at least not killed the enjoyment of the present moment because of some possibly groundless expectations of the good fortune supposed to attach to soundness of health. But in this case also, when the universal inclination towards happiness has failed to determine his will, when good health, at least for him, has not entered into his calculations as so necessary, what remains over, here as in other cases, is a law—the law of furthering his happiness, not from inclination, but from duty—and in this for the first time his conduct has a real moral worth.

It is doubtless in this sense that we should understand too the passages from Scripture in which we are commanded to love our neighbor and even our enemy. For love out of inclination cannot be commanded; but kindness done from duty—although no inclination impels us, and even although natural and unconquerable disinclination stands in our way—is *practical*, and not *pathological*, love, residing in the will and not in the propensions of feeling, in principles of action and not of melting compassion; and it is this practical love alone which can be an object of command.

. . . .

Chapter II
Passage from Popular Moral Philosophy to a Metaphysic of Morals

. . . .

Imperatives in General

Everything in nature works in accordance with laws. Only a rational being has the power to act *in accordance with his idea* of laws—that is, in accordance with principles—and only so has he a *will*.

Since *reason* is required in order to derive actions from laws, the will is nothing but practical reason. If reason infallibly determines the will, then in a being of this kind the actions which are recognized to be objectively necessary are also subjectively necessary—that is to say, the will is then a power to choose *only that* which reason independently of inclination recognizes to be practically necessary, that is, to be good. But if reason solely by itself is not sufficient to determine the will; if the will is exposed also to subjective conditions (certain impulsions) which do not always harmonize with the objective ones; if, in a word, the will is not *in itself* completely in accord with reason (as actually happens in the case of men); then actions which are recognized to be objectively necessary are subjectively contingent, and the determining of such a will in accordance with objective laws is *necessitation*. That is to say, the relation of objective laws to a will not good through and through is conceived as one in which the will of a rational being, although it is determined by principles of reason, does not necessarily follow these principles in virtue of its own nature.

The conception of an objective principle so far as this principle is necessitating for a will is called a command (of reason), and the formula of this command is called an **Imperative.**

All imperatives are expressed by an *"ought"* (*Sollen*). By this they mark the relation of an objective law of reason to a will which is not necessarily determined by this law in virtue of its subjective constitution (the relation of necessitation). They say that something would be good to do or to leave undone; only they say it to a will which does not always do a thing because it has been informed that this is a good thing to do. The practically *good* is that which determines the will by concepts of reason, and therefore not by subjective causes, but objectively—that is, on grounds valid for every rational being as such. It is distinguished from the *pleasant* as that which influences the will, not as a principle of reason valid for every one, but solely through the medium of sensation by purely subjective causes valid only for the senses of this person or that.[1]

A perfectly good will would thus stand quite as much under objective laws (laws of the good), but it could not on this account be conceived as *necessi-*

tated to act in conformity with law, since of itself, in accordance with its subjective constitution, it can be determined only by the concept of the good. Hence for the *divine* will, and in general for a *holy* will, there are no imperatives: "*I ought*" is here out of place, because "*I will*" is already of itself necessarily in harmony with the law. Imperatives are in consequence only formulae for expressing the relation of objective laws of willing to the subjective imperfection of the will of this or that rational being—for example, of the human will.

Classification of Imperatives

All *imperatives* command either *hypothetically* or *categorically.* Hypothetical imperatives declare a possible action to be practically necessary as a means to the attainment of something else that one wills (or that one may will). A categorical imperative would be one which represented an action as objectively necessary in itself apart from its relation to a further end.

Every practical law represents a possible action as good and therefore as necessary for a subject whose actions are determined by reason. Hence all imperatives are formulae for determining an action which is necessary in accordance with the principle of a will in some sense good. If the action would be good solely as a means *to something else*, the imperative is *hypothetical*; if the action is represented as good *in itself* and therefore as necessary, in virtue of its principle, for a will which of itself accords with reason, then the imperative is *categorical*.

An imperative therefore tells me which of my possible actions would be good; and it formulates a practical rule for a will that does not perform an action straight away because the action is good—whether because the subject does not always know that it is good or because, even if he did know this, he might still act on maxims contrary to the objective principles of practical reason.

A hypothetical imperative thus says only that an action is good for some purpose or other, either *possible* or *actual*. In the first case it is a **problematic** practical principle; in the second case an **assertoric** practical principle. A categorical imperative, which declares an action to be objectively necessary in itself without reference to some purpose—that is, even without any further end—ranks as an **apodeictic** practical principle.

Everything that is possible only through the efforts of some rational being can be conceived as a possible purpose of some will; and consequently there are in fact innumerable principles of action so far as action is thought necessary in order to achieve some possible purpose which can be effected by it. All sciences have a practical part consisting of problems which suppose that some end is possible for us and of imperatives which tell us how it is to be attained. Hence the latter can in general be called imperatives of **skill.** Here there is absolutely no question about the rationality or goodness of the end, but only about what must be done to attain it. A prescription required by a doctor in order to cure his man completely and one required by a poisoner in order to make sure of killing him are of equal value so far as each serves to effect its purpose perfectly. Since in early youth we do not know what ends may present themselves to us in the course of life, parents seek above all to make their children learn things *of many kinds;* they provide carefully for *skill* in the use of means to all sorts of *arbitrary* ends, of none of which can they be certain that it could not in the future become an actual purpose of their ward, while it is always *possible* that he might adopt it. Their care in this matter is so great that they commonly neglect on this account to form and correct the judgement of their children about the worth of things which they might possibly adopt as ends.

There is, however, *one* end that can be presupposed as actual in all rational beings (so far as they are dependent beings to whom imperatives apply); and thus there is one purpose which they not only *can* have, but which we can assume with certainty that they all *do* have by a natural necessity—the purpose, namely, of *happiness.* A hypothetical imperative which affirms the practical necessity of an action as a means to the furtherance of happiness is **assertoric.** We may represent it, not simply as necessary to an uncertain, merely possible purpose, but as necessary to a purpose which we can presuppose a priori and with certainty to be present in every man because it belongs to his very being. Now skill in the choice of means to one's own greatest well-

being can be called *prudence*[2] in the narrowest sense. Thus an imperative concerned with the choice of means to one's own happiness—that is, a precept of prudence—still remains *hypothetical:* an action is commanded, not absolutely, but only as a means to a further purpose.

Finally, there is an imperative which, without being based on, and conditioned by, any further purpose to be attained by a certain line of conduct, enjoins this conduct immediately. This imperative is **categorical.** It is concerned, not with the matter of the action and its presumed results, but with its form and with the principle from which it follows; and what is essentially good in the action consists in the mental disposition, let the consequences be what they may. This imperative may be called the imperative of **morality.**

Willing in accordance with these three kinds of principle is also sharply distinguished by a *dissimilarity* in the necessitation of the will. To make this dissimilarity obvious we should, I think, name these kinds of principle most appropriately in their order if we said they were either *rules* of skill or *counsels* of prudence or *commands (laws)* of morality. For only *law* carries with it the concept of an *unconditioned,* and yet objective and so universally valid, *necessity*; and commands are laws which must be obeyed—that is, must be followed even against inclination. *Counsel* does indeed involve necessity, but necessity valid only under a subjective and contingent condition—namely, if this or that man counts this or that as belonging to his happiness. As against this, a categorical imperative is limited by no condition and can quite precisely be called a command, as being absolutely, although practically, necessary. We could also call imperatives of the first kind *technical* (concerned with art); of the second kind *pragmatic*[3] (concerned with well-being); of the third kind *moral* (concerned with free conduct as such—that is—with morals).

How Are Imperatives Possible?

The question now arises "How are all these imperatives possible?" This question does not ask how we can conceive the execution of an action commanded by the imperative, but merely how we can conceive the necessitation of the will expressed by the imperative in setting us a task. How an imperative of skill is possible requires no special discussion. Who wills the end, wills (so far as reason has decisive influence on his actions) also the means which are indispensably necessary and in his power. So far as willing is concerned, this proposition is analytic: for in my willing of an object as an effect there is already conceived the causality of myself as an acting cause—that is, the use of means; and from the concept of willing an end the imperative merely extracts the concept of actions necessary to this end. (Synthetic propositions are required in order to determine the means to a proposed end, but these are concerned, not with the reason for performing the act of will, but with the cause which produces the object.) That in order to divide a line into two equal parts on a sure principle I must from its ends describe two intersecting arcs—this is admittedly taught by mathematics only in synthetic propositions; but when I know that the aforesaid effect can be produced only by such an action, the proposition "If I fully will the effect, I also will the action required for it" is analytic; for it is one and the same thing to conceive something as an effect possible in a certain way through me and to conceive myself as acting in the same way with respect to it.

If it were only as easy to find a determinate concept of happiness, the imperatives of prudence would agree entirely with those of skill and would be equally analytic. For here as there it could alike be said "Who wills the end, wills also (necessarily, if he accords with reason) the sole means which are in his power." Unfortunately, however, the concept of happiness is so indeterminate a concept that although every man wants to attain happiness, he can never say definitely and in unison with himself what it really is that he wants and wills. The reason for this is that all the elements which belong to the concept of happiness are without exception empirical— that is, they must be borrowed from experience; but that none the less there is required for the Idea of happiness an absolute whole, a maximum of well-being in my present, and in every future, state. Now it is impossible for the most intelligent, and at the same time most powerful, but nevertheless finite,

being to form here a determinate concept of what he really wills. Is it riches that he wants? How much anxiety, envy, and pestering might he not bring in this way on his own head! Is it knowledge and insight? This might perhaps merely give him an eye so sharp that it would make evils at present hidden from him and yet unavoidable seem all the more frightful, or would add a load of still further needs to the desires which already give him trouble enough. Is it long life? Who will guarantee that it would not be a long misery? Is it at least health? How often has infirmity of body kept a man from excesses into which perfect health would have let him fall!—and so on. In short, he has no principle by which he is able to decide with complete certainty what will make him truly happy, since for this he would require omniscience. Thus we cannot act on determinate principles in order to be happy, but only on empirical counsels, for example, of diet, frugality, politeness, reserve, and so on—things which experience shows contribute most to well-being on the average. From this it follows that imperatives of prudence, speaking strictly, do not command at all—that is, cannot exhibit actions objectively as practically *necessary*; that they are rather to be taken as recommendations (*consilia*), than as commands (*praecepta*), of reason; that the problem of determining certainly and universally what action will promote the happiness of a rational being is completely insoluble; and consequently that in regard to this there is no imperative possible which in the strictest sense could command us to do what will make us happy, since happiness is an Ideal, not of reason, but of imagination—an Ideal resting merely on empirical grounds, of which it is vain to expect that they should determine an action by which we could attain the totality of a series of consequences which is in fact infinite. Nevertheless, if we assume that the means to happiness could be discovered with certainty, this imperative of prudence would be an analytic practical proposition; for it differs from the imperative of skill only in this—that in the latter the end is merely possible, while in the former the end is given. In spite of this difference, since both command solely the means to something assumed to be willed as an end, the imperative which commands him who wills the end to will the means is in both cases analytic. Thus there is likewise no difficulty in regard to the possibility of an imperative of prudence.

As against this, the question "How is the imperative of *morality* possible?" is the only one in need of a solution; for it is in no way hypothetical, and consequently we cannot base the objective necessity which it affirms on any presupposition, as we can with hypothetical imperatives. Only we must never forget here that it is impossible to settle *by an example*, and so empirically, whether there is any imperative of this kind at all: we must rather suspect that all imperatives which seem to be categorical may none the less be covertly hypothetical. Take, for example, the saying "Thou shalt make no false promises." Let us assume that the necessity for this abstention is no mere advice for the avoidance of some further evil—as it might be said "You ought not to make a lying promise lest, when this comes to light, you destroy your credit." Let us hold, on the contrary, that an action of this kind must be considered as bad in itself, and that the imperative of prohibition is therefore categorical. Even so, we cannot with any certainty show by an example that the will is determined here solely by the law without any further motive, although it may appear to be so; for it is always possible that fear of disgrace, perhaps also hidden dread of other risks, may unconsciously influence the will. Who can prove by experience that a cause is not present? Experience shows only that it is not perceived. In such a case, however, the so-called moral imperative, which as such appears to be categorical and unconditioned, would in fact be only a pragmatic prescription calling attention to our advantage and merely bidding us take this into account.

We shall thus have to investigate the possibility of a *categorical* imperative entirely a priori, since here we do not enjoy the advantage of having its reality given in experience and so of being obliged merely to explain, and not to establish, its possibility. So much, however, can be seen provisionally—that the categorical imperative alone purports to be a practical **law**, while all the rest may be called *principles* of the will but not laws; for an action necessary merely in order to achieve an arbitrary purpose can be considered as in itself contingent, and we can

always escape from the precept if we abandon the purpose; whereas an unconditioned command does not leave it open to the will to do the opposite at its discretion and therefore alone carries with it that necessity which we demand from a law.

In the second place, with this categorical imperative or law of morality the reason for our difficulty (in comprehending its possibility) is a very serious one. We have here a synthetic a priori practical proposition;[4] and since in theoretical knowledge there is so much difficulty in comprehending the possibility of propositions of this kind, it may readily be gathered that in practical knowledge the difficulty will be no less.

The Formula of Universal Law

In this task we wish first to enquire whether perhaps the mere concept of a categorical imperative may not also provide us with the formula containing the only proposition that can be a categorical imperative; for even when we know the purport of such an absolute command, the question of its possibility will still require a special and troublesome effort, which we postpone to the final chapter.

When I conceive a *hypothetical* imperative in general, I do not know beforehand what it will contain—until its condition is given. But if I conceive a *categorical* imperative, I know at once what it contains. For since besides the law this imperative contains only the necessity that our maxim[5] should conform to this law, while the law, as we have seen, contains no condition to limit it, there remains nothing over to which the maxim has to conform except the universality of a law as such; and it is this conformity alone that the imperative properly asserts to be necessary.

There is therefore only a single categorical imperative and it is this: "*Act only on that maxim through which you can at the same time will that it should become a universal law.*"

Now if all imperatives of duty can be derived from this one imperative as their principle, then even although we leave it unsettled whether what we call duty may not be an empty concept, we shall still be able to show at least what we understand by it and what the concept means.

The Formula of the Law of Nature

Since the universality of the law governing the production of effects constitutes what is properly called *nature* in its most general sense (nature as regards its form)—that is, the existence of things so far as determined by universal laws—the universal imperative of duty may also run as follows: "*Act as if the maxim of your action were to become through your will a* UNIVERSAL LAW OF NATURE."

Illustrations

We will now enumerate a few duties, following their customary division into duties towards self and duties towards others and into perfect and imperfect duties.[6]

1. A man feels sick of life as the result of a series of misfortunes that has mounted to the point of despair, but he is still so far in possession of his reason as to ask himself whether taking his own life may not be contrary to his duty to himself. He now applies the test "Can the maxim of my action really become a universal law of nature?" His maxim is "From self-love I make it my principle to shorten my life if its continuance threatens more evil than it promises pleasure." The only further question to ask is whether this principle of self-love can become a universal law of nature. It is then seen at once that a system of nature by whose law the very same feeling whose function (*Bestimmung*) is to stimulate the furtherance of life should actually destroy life would contradict itself and consequently could not subsist as a system of nature. Hence this maxim cannot possibly hold as a universal law of nature and is therefore entirely opposed to the supreme principle of all duty.

2. Another finds himself driven to borrowing money because of need. He well knows that he will not be able to pay it back; but he sees too that he will get no loan unless he gives a firm promise to pay it back within a fixed time. He is inclined to make such a promise; but he has still enough conscience to ask "Is it not unlawful and contrary to duty to get out of difficulties in this way?" Supposing, however, he did resolve to do so, the maxim of his action would run thus: "Whenever I believe myself short of money, I will borrow money and promise to pay it back, though I know that this will never be done." Now this principle of self-love or personal advantage is perhaps quite compatible with my own entire future welfare; only there remains the question "Is it right?" I therefore transform the demand of self-love into a universal law and frame my question thus: "How would things stand if my maxim became a universal law?" I then see straight away that this maxim can never rank as a universal law and be self-consistent, but must necessarily contradict itself. For the universality of a law that every one believing himself to be in need may make any promise he pleases with the intention not to keep it would make promising, and the very purpose of promising, itself impossible, since no one would believe he was being promised anything, but would laugh at utterances of this kind as empty shams.

3. A third finds in himself a talent whose cultivation would make him a useful man for all sorts of purposes. But he sees himself in comfortable circumstances, and he prefers to give himself up to pleasure rather than to bother about increasing and improving his fortunate natural aptitudes. Yet he asks himself further "Does my maxim of neglecting my natural gifts, besides agreeing in itself with my tendency to indulgence, agree also with what is called duty?" He then sees that a system of nature could indeed always subsist under such a universal law, although (like the South Sea Islanders) every man should let his talents rust and should be bent on devoting his life solely to idleness, indulgence, procreation, and, in a word, to enjoyment. Only he cannot possibly **will** that this should become a universal law of nature or should be implanted in us as such a law by a natural instinct. For as a rational being he necessarily wills that all his powers should be developed, since they serve him, and are given him, for all sorts of possible ends.

4. Yet a *fourth* is himself flourishing, but he sees others who have to struggle with great hardships (and whom he could easily help); and he thinks "What does it matter to me? Let every one be as happy as Heaven wills or as he can make himself; I won't deprive him of anything; I won't even envy him; only I have no wish to contribute anything to his well-being or to his support in distress!" Now admittedly if such an attitude were a universal law of nature, mankind could get on perfectly well—better no doubt than if everybody prates about sympathy and good will, and even takes pains, on occasion, to practise them, but on the other hand cheats where he can, traffics in human rights, or violates them in other ways. But although it is possible that a universal law of nature could subsist in harmony with this maxim, yet it is impossible to **will** that such a principle should hold everywhere as a law of nature. For a will which decided in this way would be at variance with itself, since many a situation might arise in which the man needed love and sympathy from others, and in which, by such a law of nature sprung from his own will, he would rob himself of all hope of the help he wants for himself.

The Canon of Moral Judgment

These are some of the many actual duties—or at least of what we take to be such—whose derivation from the single principle cited above leaps to the eye. We must *be able to will* that a maxim of our action should become a universal law—this is the general canon for all moral judgement of action. Some actions are so constituted that their maxim cannot even be *conceived* as a universal law of nature without contradiction, let alone be *willed* as what *ought* to become one. In the case of others we do not find this inner impossibility, but it is still impossible to *will* that their maxim should be raised to the universality of a law of nature, because such a will would contradict itself. It is easily seen that the first kind of action is opposed to strict or narrow (rigorous) duty, the second only to wider (meritorious) duty; and thus that by these examples all duties—so far as the type of obligation is concerned (not the object of dutiful action)—are fully set out in their dependence on our single principle.

If we now attend to ourselves whenever we transgress a duty, we find that we in fact do not will that our maxim should become a universal law—since this is impossible for us—but rather that its opposite should remain a law universally: we only take the liberty of making an *exception* to it for ourselves (or even just for this once) to the advantage of our inclination. Consequently if we weighed it all up from one and the same point of view—that of reason—we should find a contradiction in our own will, the contradiction that a certain principle should be objectively necessary as a universal law and yet subjectively should not hold universally but should admit of exceptions. Since, however, we first consider our action from the point of view of a will wholly in accord with reason, and then consider precisely the same action from the point of view of a will affected by inclination, there is here actually no contradiction, but rather an opposition of inclination to the precept of reason (*antagonismus*), whereby the universality of the principle (*universalitas*) is turned into a mere generality (*generalitas*) so that the practical principle of reason may meet our maxim half-way. This procedure, though in our own impartial judgement it cannot be justified, proves none the less that we in fact recognize the validity of the categorical imperative and (with all respect for it) merely permit ourselves a few exceptions which are, as we pretend, inconsiderable and apparently forced upon us.

We have thus at least shown this much—that if duty is a concept which is to have meaning and real legislative authority for our actions, this can be expressed only in categorical imperatives and by no means in hypothetical ones. At the same time—and this is already a great deal—we have set forth distinctly, and determinately for every type of application, the content of the categorical imperative, which must contain the principle of all duty (if there is to be such a thing at all). But we are still not so far advanced as to prove a priori that there actually is an imperative of this kind—that there is a practical law which by itself commands absolutely and without any further motives, and that the following of this law is duty.

. . . .

The Formula of the End in Itself

The will is conceived as a power of determining oneself to action *in accordance with the idea of certain laws*. And such a power can be found only in rational beings. Now what serves the will as a subjective ground of its self-determination is an *end*; and this, if it is given by reason alone, must be equally valid for all rational beings. What, on the other hand, contains merely the ground of the possibility of an action whose effect is an end is called a *means*. The subjective ground of a desire is an *impulsion (Triebfeder)*; the objective ground of a volition is a *motive (Bewegungsgrund)*. Hence the difference between subjective ends, which are based on impulsions, and objective ends, which depend on motives valid for every rational being. Practical principles are *formal* if they abstract from all subjective ends; they are *material*, on the other hand, if they are based on such ends and consequently on certain impulsions. Ends that a rational being adopts arbitrarily as *effects* of his action (material ends) are in every case only relative; for it is solely their relation to special characteristics in the subject's power of appetition which gives them their value. Hence this value can provide no universal principles, no principles valid and necessary for all rational beings and also for every volition—that is, no practical laws. Consequently all these relative ends can be the ground only of hypothetical imperatives.

Suppose, however, there were something *whose existence* has *in itself* an absolute value, something which as *an end in itself* could be a ground of determinate laws; then in it, and in it alone, would there be the ground of a possible categorical imperative—that is, of a practical law.

Now I say that man, and in general every rational being, *exists* as an end in himself, *not merely as a means* for arbitrary use by this or that will: he must in all his actions, whether they are directed to himself or to other rational beings, always be viewed *at the same time as an end*. All the objects of inclination have only a conditioned value; for if there were not these inclinations and the needs grounded on them, their object would be valueless. Inclinations themselves, as sources of needs, are so far from having an absolute value to make them desirable for their own sake that it must rather be the universal wish of every rational being to be wholly free from them. Thus the value of all objects that can *be produced* by our action is always conditioned. Beings whose existence depends, not on our will, but on nature, have

none the less, if they are non-rational beings, only a relative value as means and are consequently called *things*. Rational beings, on the other hand, are called *persons* because their nature already marks them out as ends in themselves—that is, as something which ought not to be used merely as a means—and consequently imposes to that extent a limit on all arbitrary treatment of them (and is an object of reverence). Persons, therefore, are not merely subjective ends whose existence as an effect of our actions has a value *for us*: they are *objective ends*—that is, things whose existence is in itself an end, and indeed an end such that in its place we can put no other end to which they should serve *simply* as means; for unless this is so, nothing at all of *absolute* value would be found anywhere. But if all value were conditioned—that is, contingent—then no supreme principle could be found for reason at all.

If then there is to be a supreme practical principle and—so far as the human will is concerned—a categorical imperative, it must be such that from the idea of something which is necessarily an end for every one because it is an *end in itself* it forms an *objective* principle of the will and consequently can serve as a practical law. The ground of this principle is: *Rational nature exists as an end in itself.* This is the way in which a man necessarily conceives his own existence: it is therefore so far a *subjective* principle of human actions. But it is also the way in which every other rational being conceives his existence on the same rational ground which is valid also for me;[7] hence it is at the same time an *objective* principle, from which, as a supreme practical ground, it must be possible to derive all laws for the will. The practical imperative will therefore be as follows: *Act in such a way that you always treat humanity, whether in your own person or in the person of any other, never simply as a means, but always at the same time as an end.* We will now consider whether this can be carried out in practice.

Illustrations

Let us keep to our previous examples.

First, as regards the concept of necessary duty to oneself, the man who contemplates suicide will ask

"Can my action be compatible with the Idea of humanity *as an end in itself*?" If he does away with himself in order to escape from a painful situation, he is making use of a person merely as a *means* to maintain a tolerable state of affairs till the end of his life. But man is not a thing—not something to be used *merely* as a means: he must always in all his actions be regarded as an end in himself. Hence I cannot dispose of man in my person by maiming, spoiling, or killing. (A more precise determination of this principle in order to avoid all misunderstanding—for example, about having limbs amputated to save myself or about exposing my life to danger in order to preserve it, and so on—I must here forego: this question belongs to morals proper.)

Secondly, so far as necessary or strict duty to others is concerned, the man who has a mind to make a false promise to others will see at once that he is intending to make use of another man *merely as a means* to an end he does not share. For the man whom I seek to use for my own purposes by such a promise cannot possibly agree with my way of behaving to him, and so cannot himself share the end of the action. This incompatibility with the principle of duty to others leaps to the eye more obviously when we bring in examples of attempts on the freedom and property of others. For then it is manifest that a violator of the rights of man intends to use the person of others merely as a means without taking into consideration that, as rational beings, they ought always at the same time to be rated as ends—that is, only as beings who must themselves be able to share in the end of the very same action.[8]

Thirdly, in regard to contingent (meritorious) duty to oneself, it is not enough that an action should refrain from conflicting with humanity in our own person as an end in itself: it must also *harmonize with this end*. Now there are in humanity capacities for greater perfection which form part of nature's purpose for humanity in our person. To neglect these can admittedly be compatible with the *maintenance* of humanity as an end in itself, but not with the *promotion* of this end.

Fourthly, as regards meritorious duties to others, the natural end which all men seek is their own happiness. Now humanity could no doubt subsist if everybody contributed nothing to the happiness of others but at the same time refrained from deliberately impairing their happiness. This is, however, merely to agree negatively and not positively with *humanity as an end in itself* unless every one endeavours also, so far as in him lies, to further the ends of others. For the ends of a subject who is an end in himself must, if this conception is to have its *full* effect in me, be also, as far as possible, *my* ends.

The Formula of Autonomy

This principle of humanity, and in general of every rational agent, *as an end in itself* (a principle which is the supreme limiting condition of every man's freedom of action) is not borrowed from experience; firstly, because it is universal, applying as it does to all rational beings as such, and no experience is adequate to determine universality; secondly, because in it humanity is conceived, not as an end of man (subjectively)—that is, as an object which, as a matter of fact, happens to be made an end—but as an objective end—one which, be our ends what they may, must, as a law, constitute the supreme limiting condition of all subjective ends and so must spring from pure reason. That is to say, the ground for every enactment of practical law lies *objectively in the rule* and in the form of universality which (according to our first principle) makes the rule capable of being a law (and indeed a law of nature); *subjectively,* however, it lies in the *end*; but (according to our second principle) the subject of all ends is to be found in every rational being as an end in himself. From this there now follows our third practical principle for the will—as the supreme condition of the will's conformity with universal practical reason—namely, the Idea *of the will of every rational being as a will which makes universal law*.

By this principle all maxims are repudiated which cannot accord with the will's own enactment of universal law. The will is therefore not merely subject to the law, but is so subject that it must be considered as also *making the law* for itself and preciseley on this account as first of all subject to the law (of which it can regard itself as the author).

The Exclusion of Interest

Imperatives as formulated above—namely, the imperative enjoining conformity of actions to universal law on the analogy of a *natural order* and that enjoining the universal *supremacy* of rational beings in themselves *as ends*—did, by the mere fact that they were represented as categorical, exclude from their sovereign authority every admixture of interest as a motive. They were, however, merely *assumed* to be categorical because we were bound to make this assumption if we wished to explain the concept of duty. That there were practical propositions which commanded categorically could not itself be proved, any more than it can be proved in this chapter generally; but one thing could have been done— namely, to show that in willing for the sake of duty renunciation of all interest, as the specific mark distinguishing a categorical from a hypothetical imperative, was expressed in the very imperative itself by means of some determination inherent in it. This is what is done in the present third formulation of the principle—namely, in the Idea of the will of every rational being as *a will which makes universal law*.

Once we conceive a will of this kind, it becomes clear that while a will *which is subject to law* may be bound to this law by some interest, nevertheless a will which is itself a supreme law-giver cannot possibly as such depend on any interest; for a will which is dependent in this way would itself require yet a further law in order to restrict the interest of self-love to the condition that this interest should itself be valid as a universal law.

Thus the *principle* that every human will is *a will which by all its maxims enacts universal law*[9]—provided only that it were right in other ways—would be *well suited* to be a categorical imperative in this respect: that precisely because of the Idea of making universal law it is *based on no interest* and consequently can alone among all possible imperatives be *unconditioned*. Or better still—to convert the proposition—if there is a categorical imperative (that is, a law for the will of every rational being), it can command us only to act always on the maxim of such a will in us as can at the same time look upon itself as making universl law; for only then is the practical principle and the imperative which we obey unconditioned, since it is wholly impossible for it to be based on any interest.

We need not now wonder, when we look back upon all the previous efforts that have been made to discover the principle of morality, why they have one and all been bound to fail. Their authors saw man as tied to laws by his duty, but it never occurred to them that he is subject only to *laws which are made by himself* and yet are *universal*, and that he is bound only to act in accordance with a will which is his own but has for its natural purpose the function of making universal law. For when they thought of man merely as subject to a law (whatever it might be), the law had to carry with it some interest in order to attract or compel, because it did not spring as a law from *his own* will: in order to conform with the law his will had to be necessitated by *something else* to act in a ceratin way. This absolutely inevitable conclusion meant that all the labour spent in trying to find a supreme principle of duty was lost beyond recall; for what they discovered was never duty, but only the necessity of acting from a certain interest. This interest might be one's own or another's; but on such a view the imperative was bound to be always a conditioned one and could not possibly serve as a moral law. I will therefore call my principle the principle of the **Autonomy** of the will in contrast with all others, which I consequently class under **Heteronomy**.

The Formula of the Kingdom of Ends

The concept of every rational being as one who must regard himself as making universal law by all the maxims of his will, and must seek to judge himself and his actions from this point of view, leads to a closely connected and very fruitful concept— namely, that of *a kingdom of ends*.

I understand by a *"kingdom"* a systematic union of different rational beings under common laws. Now since laws determine ends as regards their universal validity, we shall be able—if we abstract from the personal differences between rational beings, and also from all the content of their private ends— to conceive a whole of all ends in systematic conjunction (a whole both of rational beings as ends in themselves and also of the personal ends which each may set before himself); that is, we shall be able to concieve a kingdom of ends which is possible in accordance with the above principles.

For rational beings all stand under the *law* that each of them should treat himself and all others, *never merely as a means*, but always *at the same time as an end in himself*. But by so doing there arises a systematic union of rational beings under common objective laws—that is, a kingdom. Since these laws are directed precisely to the relation of such beings to one another as ends and means, this kingdom can be called a kingdom of ends (which is admittedly only an Ideal).

A rational being belongs to the kingdom of ends as a *member*, when, although he makes its universal laws, he is also himself subject to these laws. He belongs to it as its *head*, when as the maker of laws he is himself subject to the will of no other.

A rational being must always regard himself as making laws in a kingdom of ends which is possible through freedom of the will—whether it be as member or as head. The position of the latter he can maintain, not in virtue of the maxim of his will alone, but only if he is a completely independent being, without needs and with an unlimited power adequate to his will.

Thus morality consists in the relation of all action to the making of laws whereby alone a kingdom ends is possible. This making of laws must be found in every rational being himself and must be able to spring from his will. The principle of his will is therefore never to perform an action except on a maxim such as can also be a universal law, and consequently such *that the will can regard itself as at the same time making universal law by means of its maxim*. Where maxims are not already by their very nature in harmony with this objective principle of rational beings as makers of universal law, the necessity of acting on this principle is pracitcal necessitation—that is, *duty*. Duty does not apply to the head in a kingdom of ends, but it does apply to every member and to all members in equal measure.

The practical necessity of acting on this principle—that is, duty—is in no way based on feelings, impulses, and inclincations, but only on the relation of rational beings to one another, a relation in which the will of a rational being must always be regarded as *making universal law*, because otherwise he could not be conceived as *an end in himself*. Reason thus relates every maxim of the will, considered as making universal law, to every other will and also to every action towards oneself: it does so, not because of any further motive or future advantage, but from the Idea of the *dignity* of a rational being who obeys no law other than that which he at the same time enacts himself.

The Dignity of Virtue

In the kingdom of ends everything has either a *price* or a *dignity*. If it has a price, something else can be put in its place as an *equivalent*: if it is exalted above all price and so admits of no equivalent, then it has a dignity.

What is relative to universal human inclinations and needs has a *market price*; what, even without presupposing a need, accords with a certain taste—that is, with satisfaction in the mere purposeless play of our mental powers—has a *fancy price (Affektionspreis)*; but that which constitutes the sole condition under which anything can be an end in itself has not merely a relative value—that is, a price—but has an intrinsic value—that is, *dignity*.

Now morality is the only condition under which a rational being can be an end in himself; for only through this is it possible to be a law-making member in a kingdom of ends. Therefore morality, and humanity so far as it is capable of morality, is the only thing which has dignity. Skill and diligence in work have a market price; wit, lively imagination, and humour have a fancy price; but fidelity to promises and kindness based on principle (not on instinct) have an intrinsic worth. In default of these, nature and art alike contain nothing to put in their place; for their worth consists, not in the effects which result from them, not in the advantage or profit they produce, but in the attitudes of mind—that is, in the maxims of the will—which are ready in this way to manifest themselves in action even if they are not favoured by success. Such actions too need no recommendation from any subjective disposition or taste in order to meet with immediate favour and approval; they need no immediate propensity or feeling for themselves; they exhibit the will which performs them as an object of immediate reverence; nor is anything other than reason required to *impose* them upon the will, not to *coax* them from the will—which last would anyhow be a contradiction in the case of duties. This assessment reveals as dignity the value of such a mental attitude and puts it infinitely above all price, with which it cannot be brought into reckoning or comparison without, as it were, a profanation of its sanctity.

What is it then that entitles a morally good attitude of mind—or virtue—to make claims so high? It is nothing less than the *share* which it affords to a rational being *in the making of universal law*, and which therefore fits him to be a member in a possible kingdom of ends. For this he was already marked out in virtue of his own proper nature as an end in himself and consequently as a maker of laws in the kingdom of ends—as free in respect of all laws of nature, obeying only those laws which he makes himself and in virtue of which his maxims can have their part in the making of universal law (to which he at the same time subjects himself). For nothing can have a value other than that determined for it by the law. But the law-making which determines all value must for this reason have a dignity—that is, an unconditioned and incomparable worth—for the appreciation of which, as necessarily given by a rational being, the word "*reverence*" is the only becoming expression. *Autonomy* is therefore the ground of the dignity of human nature and of every rational nature.

Review of the Formulae

The aforesaid three ways of representing the principle of morality are at bottom merely so many formulations of precisely the same law, one of them by itself containing a combination of the other two. There is nevertheless a difference between them, which, however, is subjectively rather than objectively practical: that is to say, its purpose is to bring an Idea of reason nearer to intuition (in accordance with a certain analogy) and so nearer to feeling. All maxims have, in short,

1. a *form*, which consists in their universality; and in this respect the formula of the moral imperative is expressed thus: "Maxims must be chosen as if they had to hold as universal laws of nature";

2. a *matter*—that is, an end; and in this respect the formula says: "A rational being, as by his very nature an end and consequently an end in himself, must serve for every maxim as a condition limiting all merely relative and arbitrary ends";

3. a *complete determination* of all maxims by the following formula, namely: "All maxims as proceeding from our own making of law ought to harmonize with a possible kingdom of ends as a kingdom of nature."[10] This progression may be said to take place through the categories of the *unity* of the form of will (its universality); of the *multiplicity* of its matter (its objects—that is, its ends); and of the *totality* or completeness of its systems of ends. It is, however, better if in moral *judgement* we proceed always in accordance with the strictest method and take as our basis the universal formula of the categorical imperative: *Act on the maxim which can at the same time be made a universal law.*" If, however, we wish also to secure acceptance for the moral law, it is very useful to bring one and the same action under the above-mentioned three concepts and so, as far as we can, to bring the universal formula nearer to intuition.

Review of the Whole Argument

We can now end at the point from which we started out at the beginning—namely, the concept of an unconditionally good will. The *will* is *absolutely good* if it cannot be evil—that is, if its maxim, when made into a universal law, can never be at variance with itself. This principle is therefore also its supreme law: "Act always on that maxim whose universality as a law you can at the same time will." This is the one principle on which a will can never be at variance with itself, and such an imperative is categorical. Because the validity of the will as a universal law for possible actions is analogous to the universal interconnexion of existent things in accordance with universal laws—which constitutes the formal aspect of nature as such—we can also express the categorical imperative as follows: "*Act on that maxim which can at the same time have for its object itself as a universal law of nature.*" In this way we provide the formula for an absolutely good will.

Rational nature separates itself out from all other things by the fact that it sets itself an end. An end would thus be the matter of every good will. But in the Idea of a will which is absolutely good—good without any qualifying condition (namely, that it should attain this or that end)—there must be complete abstraction from every end that has to be *produced* (as something which would make every will only relatively good). Hence the end must here be conceived, not as an end to be produced, *but as a self-existent* end. It must therefore be conceived only negatively—that is, as an end against which we should never act, and consequently as one which in all our willing we must never rate *merely* as a means, but always at the same time as an end. Now this end can be nothing other than the subject of all possible ends himself, because this subject is also the subject of a will that may be absolutely good; for such a will cannot without contradiction be subordinated to any other object. The principle "So act in relation to every rational being (both to yourself and to others) that he may at the same time count in your maxim as an end in himself" is thus at bottom the same as the principle "Act on a maxim which at the same time contains in itself its own universal validity for every rational being." For to say that in using means to every end I ought to restrict my maxim by the condition that it should also be universally valid as a law for every subject is just the same as to say this—that a subject of ends, namely, a rational being himself, must be made the ground for all maxims of action, never *merely* as a means, but as a supreme condition restricting the use of every means—that is, always also as an end.

Now from this it unquestionably follows that every rational being, as an end in himself, must be able to regard himself as also the maker of universal law in respect of any law whatever to which he may be subjected; for it is precisely the fitness of his maxims to make universal law that marks him out as an end in himself. It follows equally that this dignity (or prerogative) of his above all the mere things of nature carries with it the necessity of always

choosing his maxims from the point of view of himself—and also of every other rational being—as a maker of law (and this is why they are called persons). It is in this way that a world of rational beings (*mundus intelligibilis*) is possible as a kingdom of ends—possible, that is, through the making of their own laws by all persons as its members. Accordingly every rational being must so act as if he were through his maxims always a law-making member in the universal kingdom of ends. The formal principle of such maxims is "So act as if your maxims had to serve at the same time as a universal law (for all rational beings)." Thus a kingdom of ends is possible only on the analogy of a kingdom of nature; yet the kingdom of ends is possible only through maxims—that is, self-imposed rules—while nature is possible only through laws concerned with causes whose action is necessitated from without. In spite of this difference, we give to nature as a whole, even although it is regarded as a machine, the name of a "kingdom of nature" so far as—and for the reason that—it stands in a relation to rational beings as its ends. Now a kingdom of ends would actually come into existence through maxims which the categorical imperative prescribes as a rule for all rational beings, *if these maxims were universally followed*. Yet even if a rational being were himself to follow such a maxim strictly, he cannot count on everybody else being faithful to it on this ground, nor can he be confident that the kingdom of nature and its purposive order will work in harmony with him, as a fitting member, towards a kingdom of ends made possible by himself—or, in other words, that it will favour his expectation of happiness. But in spite of this the law "Act on the maxims of a member who makes universal laws for a merely possible kingdom of ends" remains in full force, since its command is categorical. And precisely here we encounter the paradox that without any further end or advantage to be attained the mere dignity of humanity, that is, of rational nature in man—and consequently that reverence for a mere Idea—should function as an inflexible precept for the will; and that it is just this freedom from dependence on interested motives which constitutes the sublimity of a maxim and the worthiness of every rational subject to be a law-making member in the kingdom of ends; for otherwise he would have to be regarded as subject only to the law of nature—the law of his own needs. Even if it were thought that both the kingdom of nature and the kingdom of ends were united under one head and that thus the latter kingdom ceased to be a mere Idea and achieved genuine reality, the Idea would indeed gain by this the addition of a strong motive, but never any increase in its intrinsic worth; for, even if this were so, it would still be necessary to conceive the unique and absolute lawgiver himself as judging the worth of rational beings solely by the disinterested behaviour they prescribed to themselves in virtue of this Idea alone. The essence of things does not vary with their external relations; and where there is something which, without regard to such relations, constitutes by itself the absolute worth of man, it is by this that man must also be judged by everyone whatsoever—even by the Supreme Being. Thus *morality* lies in the relation of actions to the autonomy of the will—that is, to a possible making of universal law by means of its maxims. An action which is compatible with the autonomy of the will is *permitted*; one which does not harmonize with it is *forbidden*. A will whose maxims necessarily accord with the laws of autonomy is a *holy*, or absolutely good, will. The dependence of a will not absolutely good on the principle of autonomy (that is, moral necessitation) is *obligation*. Obligation can thus have no reference to a holy being. The objective necessity to act from obligation is called *duty*.

From what was said a little time ago we can now easily explain how it comes about that, although in the concept of duty we think of subjection to the law, yet we also at the same time attribute to the person who fulfils all his duties a certain sublimity and *dignity*. For it is not in so far as he is *subject* to the law that he has sublimity, but rather in so far as, in regard to this very same law, he is at the same time its *author* and is subordinated to it only on this ground. We have also shown above how neither fear nor inclination, but solely reverence for the law, is the motive which can give an action moral worth. Our own will, provided it were to act only under the condition of being able to make universal law by means of its maxims—this ideal will which can be ours is the proper object of reverence; and the

dignity of man consists precisely in his capacity to make universal law, although only on condition of being himself also subject to the law he makes.

NOTES

1. The dependence of the power of appetition on sensations is called an inclination, and thus an inclination always indicates a *need*. The dependence of a contingently determinable will on principles of reason is called an *interest*. Hence an interest is found only where there is a dependent will which in itself is not always in accord with reason: to a divine will we cannot ascribe any interest. But even the human will can *take an interest* in something without therefore *acting from interest*. The first expression signifies *practical* interest in the action; the second *pathological* interest in the object of the action. The first indicates only dependence of the will on principles of reason by itself; the second its dependence on principles of reason at the service of inclination—that is to say, where reason merely supplies a practical rule for meeting the need of inclination. In the first case what interests me is the action; in the second case what interests me is the object of the action (so far as this object is pleasant to me). We have seen in Chapter 1 that in an action done for the sake of duty we must have regard, not to interest in the object, but to interest in the action itself and in its rational principle (namely, the law).

2. The word "prudence" (*Klugheit*) is used in a double sense: in one sense it can have the name of "worldly wisdom" (*Weltklugheit*): in a second sense that of "personal wisdom" (*Privatklugheit*). The first is the skill of a man in influencing others in order to use them for his own ends. The second is sagacity in combining all these ends to his own lasting advantage. The latter is properly that to which the value of the former can itself be traced; and of him who is prudent in the first sense, but not in the second, we might better say that he is clever and astute, but on the whole imprudent.

3. It seems to me that the proper meaning of the word "*pragmatic*" can be defined most accurately in this way. For those *Sanctions* are called Pragmatic which, properly speaking, do not spring as necessary laws from the Natural Right of States, but from *forethought* in regard to the general welfare. A *his-*

tory is written pragmatically when it teaches *prudence*—that is, when it instructs the world of to-day how to provide for its own advantage better than, or at least as well as, the world of other times.

4. Without presupposing a condition taken from some inclination I connect an action with the will a priori and therefore necessarily (although only objectively so—that is, only subject to the Idea of a reason having full power over all subjective impulses to action). Here we have a practical proposition in which the willing of an action is not derived analytically from some other willing already presupposed (for we do not possess any such perfect will), but is on the contrary connected immediately with the concept of the will of a rational being as something which is not contained in this concept.

5. A *maxim* is a subjective principle of action and must be distinguished from an *objective principle*—namely, a practical law. The former contains a practical rule determined by reason in accordance with the conditions of the subject (often his ignorance or again his inclinations): it is thus a principle on which the subject *acts*. A law, on the other hand, is an objective principle valid for every rational being; and it is a principle on which he *ought to act*—that is, an imperative.

6. It should be noted that I reserve my division of duties entirely for a future *Metaphysic of Morals* and that my present division is therefore put forward as arbitrary (merely for the purpose of arranging my examples). Further, I undersatnd here by a perfect duty one which allows no exception in the interests of inclination, and so I recognize among *perfect duties*, not only outer ones, but also inner. This is contrary to the accepted usage of the schools, but I do not intend to justify it here, since for my purpose it is all one whether this point is conceded or not.

7. This proposition I put forward here as a postulate. The grounds for it will be found in the final chapter. [Editors' note: This final chapter is omitted here.]

8. Let no one think that here the trivial "*quod tibi non vis fieri, etc.*" can serve as a standard or principle. For it is merely derivative from our principle, although subject to various qualifications: it cannot be a universal law since it contains the ground neither of duties to oneself nor of duties of kindness to others (for many a man would readily agree that others should not help him if only he could be dispensed from affording help to them), nor finally of strict duties towards others; for on this basis the criminal would be able to dispute with the judges who punish him, and so on.

9. I may be excused from bringing forward examples to illustrate this principle, since those which were first used as illustrations of the categorical imperative and its formula can all serve this purpose here.

10. Teleology views nature as a kingdom of ends; ethics views a possible kingdom of ends as a kingdom of nature. In the first case the kingdom of ends is a theoretical Idea used to explain what exists. In the second case it is a practical Idea used to bring into existence what does not exist but can be made actual by our conduct—and indeed to bring it into existence in conformity with this Idea.

Kantian Approaches to Some Famine Problems

ONORA O'NEILL

Onora O'Neill (1941–) is a professor of philosophy at the University of Essex. Her works include *Acting on Principle* and *Faces of Hunger*.

——•——

§22 A Simplified Account of Kant's Ethics

Kant's moral theory has acquired the reputation of being forbiddingly difficult to understand and, once understood, excessively demanding in its requirements. I don't believe that this reputation has been wholly earned, and I am going to try to undermine it. In §§23–26 I shall try to reduce some of the difficulties, and in §§27–[29] I shall try to show the implications of a Kantian moral theory for action toward those who do or may suffer famine. Finally, I shall compare Kantian and utilitarian approaches and assess their strengths and weaknesses.

The main method by which I propose to avoid some of the difficulties of Kant's moral theory is by explaining only one part of the theory. This does not seem to me to be an irresponsible approach in this case. One of the things that makes Kant's moral theory hard to understand is that he gives a number of different versions of the principle that he calls the Supreme Principle of Morality, and these different versions don't look at all like one another. They also don't look at all like the utilitarians' Greatest Happiness Principle. But the Kantian principle is supposed to play a similar role in arguments about what to do.

Kant calls his Supreme Principle the *Categorical Imperative*: its various versions also have sonorous names. One is called the Formula of Universal Law; another is the Formula of the Kingdom of Ends. The

From *Matters of Life and Death*, ed. T. Regan. Copyright © 1980 by McGraw-Hill Companies. Reprinted by permission of the publisher.

one on which I shall concentrate is known as the *Formula of the End in Itself*. To understand why Kant thinks that these picturesquely named principles are equivalent to one another takes quite a lot of close and detailed analysis of Kant's philosophy. I shall avoid this and concentrate on showing the implications of this version of the Categorical Imperative.

§23 The Formula of the End in Itself

Kant states the Formula of the End in Itself as follows:

> Act in such a way that you always treat humanity, whether in your own person or in the person of any other, never simply as a means but always at the same time as an end.[1]

To understand this we need to know what it is to treat a person as a means or as an end. According to Kant, each of our acts reflects one or more *maxims*. The maxim of the act is the principle on which one sees oneself as acting. A maxim expresses a person's policy, or if he or she has no settled policy, the principle underlying the particular intention or decision on which he or she acts. Thus, a person who decides "This year I'll give 10 percent of my income to famine relief" has as a maxim the principle of tithing his or her income for famine relief. In practice, the difference between intentions and maxims is of little importance, for given any intention, we can formulate the corresponding maxim by deleting references to particular times, places, and persons. In what follows I shall take the terms "maxim" and "intention" as equivalent.

Whenever we act intentionally, we have at least one maxim and can, if we reflect, state what it is. (There is of course room for self-deception here—"I'm only keeping the wolf from the door" we may claim as we wolf down enough to keep ourselves overweight, or, more to the point, enough to feed someone else who hasn't enough food.)

When we want to work out whether an act we propose to do is right or wrong, according to Kant, we should look at our maxims and not at how much misery or happiness the act is likely to produce, and whether it does better at increasing happiness than other available acts. We just have to check that the act we have in mind will not use anyone as a mere means, and, if possible, that it will treat other persons as ends in themselves.

§24 Using Persons as Mere Means

To use someone as a *mere means* is to involve them in a scheme of action *to which they could not in principle consent.* Kant does not say that there is anything wrong about using someone as a means. Evidently we have to do so in any cooperative scheme of action. If I cash a check I use the teller as a means, without whom I could not lay my hands on the cash; the teller in turn uses me as a means to earn his or her living. But in this case, each party consents to her or his part in the transaction. Kant would say that though they use one another as means, they do not use one another as *mere* means. Each person assumes that the other has maxims of his or her own and is not just a thing or a prop to be manipulated.

But there are other situations where one person uses another in a way to which the other could not in principle consent. For example, one person may make a promise to another with every intention of breaking it. If the promise is accepted, then the person to whom it was given must be ignorant of what the promisor's intention (maxim) really is. If one knew that the promisor did not intend to do what he or she was promising, one would, after all, not

accept or rely on the promise. It would be as though there had been no promise made. Successful false promising depends on deceiving the person to whom the promise is made about what one's real maxim is. And since the person who is deceived doesn't know that real maxim, he or she can't in principle consent to his or her part in the proposed scheme of action. The person who is deceived is, as it were, a prop or a tool—a mere means—in the false promisor's scheme. A person who promises falsely treats the acceptor of the promise as a prop or a thing and not as a person. In Kant's view, it is this that makes false promising wrong.

One standard way of using others as mere means is by deceiving them. By getting someone involved in a business scheme or a criminal activity on false pretenses, or by giving a misleading account of what one is about, or by making a false promise or a fraudulent contract, one involves another in something to which he or she in principle cannot consent, since the scheme requires that he or she doesn't know what is going on. Another standard way of using others as mere means is by coercing them. If a rich or powerful person threatens a debtor with bankruptcy unless he or she joins in some scheme, then the creditor's intention is to coerce; and the debtor, if coerced, cannot consent to his or her part in the creditor's scheme. To make the example more specific: If a moneylender in an Indian village threatens not to renew a vital loan unless he is given the debtor's land, then he uses the debtor as a mere means. He coerces the debtor, who cannot truly consent to this "offer he can't refuse." (Of course the outward form of such transactions may look like ordinary commercial dealings, but we know very well that some offers and demands couched in that form are coercive.)

In Kant's view, acts that are done on maxims that require deception or coercion of others, and so cannot have the consent of those others (for consent precludes both deception and coercion), are wrong. When we act on such maxims, we treat others as mere means, as things rather than as ends in themselves. If we act on such maxims, our acts are not only wrong but unjust: such acts wrong the particular others who are deceived or coerced.

§25 Treating Persons as Ends in Themselves

Duties of justice are, in Kant's view (as in many others'), the most important of our duties. When we fail in these duties, we have used some other or others as mere means. But there are also cases where, though we do not use others as mere means, still we fail to use them as ends in themselves in the fullest possible way. To treat someone as an end in him or herself requires in the first place that one not use him or her as mere means, that one respect each as a rational person with his or her own maxims. But beyond that, one may also seek to foster others' plans and maxims by sharing some of their ends. To act beneficently is to seek others' happiness, therefore to intend to achieve some of the things that those others aim at with their maxims. If I want to make others happy, I will adopt maxims that not merely do not manipulate them but that foster some of their plans and activities. Beneficent acts try to achieve what others want. However, we cannot seek everything that others want; their wants are too numerous and diverse, and, of course, sometimes incompatible. It follows that beneficence has to be selective.

There is then quite a sharp distinction between the requirements of justice and of beneficence in Kantian ethics. Justice requires that we act on *no* maxims that use others as mere means. Beneficence requires that we act on *some* maxims that foster others' ends, though it is a matter for judgment and discretion which of their ends we foster. Some maxims no doubt ought not to be fostered because it would be unjust to do so. Kantians are not committed to working interminably through a list of happiness-producing and misery-reducing acts; but there are some acts whose obligatoriness utilitarians may need to debate as they try to compare total outcomes of different choices, to which Kantians are stringently bound. Kantians will claim that they have done nothing wrong if none of their acts is unjust, and that their duty is complete if in addition their life plans have in the circumstances been reasonably beneficent.

In making sure that they meet all the demands of justice, Kantians do not try to compare all available acts and see which has the best effects. They consider only the proposals for action that occur to them and check that these proposals use no other as mere means. If they do not, the act is permissible; if omitting the

act would use another as mere means, the act is obligatory. Kant's theory has less scope than utilitarianism. Kantians do not claim to discover whether acts whose maxims they don't know fully are just. They may be reluctant to judge others' acts or policies that cannot be regarded as the maxim of any person or institution. They cannot rank acts in order of merit. Yet, the theory offers more precision than utilitarianism when data are scarce. One can usually tell whether one's act would use others as mere means, even when its impact on human happiness is thoroughly obscure.

§26 Kantian Deliberations on Famine Problems

The theory I have just sketched may seem to have little to say about famine problems. For it is a theory that forbids us to use others as mere means but does not require us to direct our benevolence first to those who suffer most. A conscientious Kantian, it seems, has only to avoid being unjust to those who suffer famine and can then be beneficent to those nearer home. He or she would not be obliged to help the starving, even if no others were equally distressed.

Kant's moral theory does make less massive demands on moral agents than utilitarian moral theory. On the other hand, it is somewhat clearer just what the more stringent demands are, and they are not negligible. We have here a contrast between a theory that makes massive but often indeterminate demands and a theory that makes fewer but less unambiguous demands and leaves other questions, in particular the allocation of beneficence, unresolved. We have also a contrast between a theory whose scope is comprehensive and one that is applicable only to persons acting intentionally and to those institutions that adopt policies, and so maxims. Kantian ethics is silent about the moral status of unintentional action; utilitarians seek to assess all consequences regardless of the intentions that led to them.

§27 Kantian Duties of Justice in Times of Famine

In famine situations, Kantian moral theory requires unambiguously that we do no injustice. We should not act on any maxim that uses another as mere means, so we should neither deceive nor coerce others. Such a requirement can become quite exacting when the means of life are scarce, when persons can more easily be coerced, and when the advantage of gaining more than what is justly due to one is great. I shall give a list of acts that on Kantian principles it would be unjust to do, but that one might be strongly tempted to do in famine conditions.

I will begin with a list of acts that one might be tempted to do as a member of a famine-stricken population. First, where there is a rationing scheme, one ought not to cheat and seek to get more than one's share—any scheme of cheating will use someone as mere means. Nor may one take advantage of others' desperation to profiteer or divert goods onto the black market or to accumulate a fortune out of others' misfortunes. Transactions that are outwardly sales and purchases can be coercive when one party is desperate. All the forms of corruption that deceive or put pressure on others are also wrong: hoarding unallocated food, diverting relief supplies for private use, corruptly using one's influence to others' disadvantage. Such requirements are far from trivial and frequently violated in hard times. In severe famines, refraining from coercing and deceiving may risk one's own life and require the greatest courage.

Second, justice requires that in famine situations one still try to fulfill one's duties to particular others. For example, even in times of famine, a person has duties to try to provide for dependents. These duties may, tragically, be unfulfillable. If they are, Kantian ethical theory would not judge wrong the acts of a person who had done her or his best. There have no doubt been times in human history where there was nothing to be done except abandon the weak and old or to leave children to fend for themselves as best they might. But providing the supporter of dependents acts on maxims of attempting to meet their claims, he or she uses no others as mere means to his or her own survival and is not unjust. A conscientious attempt to meet the particular obligations one has undertaken may also require of one many further maxims of self-restraint and of endeavor—for example, it may require a conscientious attempt to avoid having (further) children; it may require contributing one's time and effort to programs of economic development. Where there is

no other means to fulfill particular obligations, Kantian principles may require a generation of sacrifice. They will not, however, require one to seek to maximize the happiness of later generations but only to establish the modest security and prosperity needed for meeting present obligations.

The obligations of those who live with or near famine are undoubtedly stringent and exacting; for those who live further off it is rather harder to see what a Kantian moral theory demands. Might it not, for example, be permissible to do nothing at all about those suffering famine? Might one not ensure that one does nothing unjust to the victims of famine by adopting no maxims whatsoever that mention them? To do so would, at the least, require one to refrain from certain deceptive and coercive practices frequently employed during the European exploration and economic penetration of the now underdeveloped world and still not unknown. For example, it would be unjust to "purchase" valuable lands and resources from persons who don't understand commercial transactions or exclusive property rights or mineral rights, so do not understand that their acceptance of trinkets destroys their traditional economic pattern and way of life. The old adage "trade follows the flag" reminds us to how great an extent the economic penetration of the less-developed countries involved elements of coercion and deception, so was on Kantian principles unjust (regardless of whether or not the net effect has benefited the citizens of those countries).

Few persons in the developed world today find themselves faced with the possibility of adopting on a grand scale maxims of deceiving or coercing persons living in poverty. But at least some people find that their jobs require them to make decisions about investment and aid policies that enormously affect the lives of those nearest to famine. What does a commitment to Kantian moral theory demand of such persons?

It has become common in writings in ethics and social policy to distinguish between one's *personal responsibilities* and one's *role responsibilities*. So a person may say, "As an individual I sympathize, but in my official capacity I can do nothing"; or we may excuse persons' acts of coercion because they are acting in some particular capacity—e.g., as a soldier or a jailer. On the other hand, this distinction isn't made or accepted by everyone. At the Nuremberg trials of war criminals, the defense "I was only doing my job" was disallowed, at least for those whose command position meant that they had some discretion in what they did. Kantians generally would play down any distinction between a person's own responsibilities and his or her role responsibilities. They would not deny that in any capacity one is accountable for certain things for which as a private person one is not accountable. For example, the treasurer of an organization is accountable to the board and has to present periodic reports and to keep specified records. But if she fails to do one of these things for which she is held accountable she will be held responsible for that failure—it will be imputable to her as an individual. When we take on positions, we *add* to our responsibilities those that the job requires; but we do not lose those that are already required of us. Our social role or job gives us, on Kant's view, no license to use others as mere means; even business executives and aid officials and social revolutionaries will act unjustly, so wrongly, if they deceive or coerce—however benevolent their motives.

If persons are responsible for all their acts, it follows that it would be unjust for aid officials to coerce persons into accepting sterilization, wrong for them to use coercive power to achieve political advantages (such as military bases) or commercial advantages (such as trade agreements that will harm the other country). It would be wrong for the executives of large corporations to extort too high a price for continued operation employment and normal trading. Where a less-developed country is pushed to exempt a multinational corporation from tax laws, or to construct out of its meager tax revenues the infrastructure of roads, harbors, or airports (not to mention executive mansions) that the corporation—but perhaps not the country—needs, then one suspects that some coercion has been involved.

The problem with such judgments—and it is an immense problem—is that it is hard to identify coercion and deception in complicated institutional settings. It is not hard to understand what is coercive about one person threatening another with serious injury if he won't comply with the first person's suggestion. But it is not at all easy to tell where

the outward forms of political and commercial negotiation—which often involve an element of threat—have become coercive. I can't here explore this fascinating question. But I think it is at least fairly clear that the preservation of the outward forms of negotiation, bargaining, and voluntary consent do *not* demonstrate that there is no coercion, especially when one party is vastly more powerful or the other in dire need. Just as our judiciary has a long tradition of voiding contracts and agreements on grounds of duress or incompetence of one of the parties, so one can imagine a tribunal of an analogous sort rejecting at least some treaties and agreements as coercive, despite the fact that they were negotiated between "sovereign" powers or their representatives. In particular, where such agreements were negotiated with some of the cruder deceptions and coercion of the early days of European economic expansion or the subtler coercions and deceptions of contemporary superpowers, it seems doubtful that the justice of the agreement could be sustained.

Justice, of course, is not everything, even for Kantians. But its demands are ones that they can reasonably strive to fulfill. They may have some uncertain moments—for example, does advocating cheap raw materials mean advocating an international trade system in which the less developed will continue to suffer the pressures of the developed world—or is it a benevolent policy that will maximize world trade and benefit all parties, while doing no one an injustice? But for Kantians, the important moral choices are above all those in which one acts directly, not those in which one decides which patterns of actions to encourage in others or in those institutions that one can influence. And such moral decisions include decisions about the benevolent acts that one will or will not do.

§28 Kantian Duties of Beneficence in Times of Famine

The grounds of duties of beneficence are that such acts not merely don't use others as mere means but are acts that develop or promote others' ends and that, in particular, foster others' capacities to pursue ends, to be autonomous beings.

Clearly there are many opportunities for beneficence. But one area in which the *primary* task of developing others' capacity to pursue their own ends is particularly needed is in the parts of the world where extreme poverty and hunger leave people unable to pursue *any* of their other ends. Beneficence directed at putting people in a position to pursue whatever ends they may have has, for Kant, a stronger claim on us than beneficence directed at sharing ends with those who are already in a position to pursue varieties of ends. It would be nice if I bought a tennis racquet to play with my friend who is tennis mad and never has enough partners; but it is more important to make people able to plan their own lives to a minimal extent. It is nice to walk a second mile with someone who requests one's company; better to share a cloak with someone who may otherwise be too cold to make any journey. Though these suggestions are not a detailed set of instructions for the allocation of beneficence by Kantians, they show that relief of famine must stand very high among duties of beneficence.

§29 The Limits of Kantian Ethics: Intentions and Results

Kantian ethics differs from utilitarian ethics both in its scope and in the precision with which it guides action. Every action, whether of a person or of an agency, can be assessed by utilitarian methods, provided only that information is available about all the consequences of the act. The theory has unlimited scope, but, owing to a lack of data, often lacks precision. Kantian ethics has a more restricted scope. Since it assesses actions by looking at the maxims of agents, it can only assess intentional acts. This means that it is most at home in assessing individuals' acts; but it can be extended to assess acts of agencies that (like corporations and governments and student unions) have decision-making procedures. It can do nothing to assess patterns of action that reflect no intention or policy, hence it cannot assess the acts of groups lacking decision-making procedures, such as the student movement, the women's movement, or the consumer movement.

It may seem a great limitation of Kantian ethics that it concentrates on intentions to the neglect of results. It might seem that all conscientious Kantians have to do is to make sure that they never intend to use others as mere means, and that they sometimes intend to foster others' ends. And, as we all know, good intentions sometimes lead to bad results, and correspondingly, bad intentions sometimes do no harm, or even produce good. If Hardin is right, the good intentions of those who feed the starving lead to dreadful results in the long run. If some traditional arguments in favor of capitalism are right, the greed and selfishness of the profit motive have produced unparalleled prosperity for many.

But such discrepancies between intentions and results are the exception and not the rule. For we cannot just *claim* that our intentions are good and do what we will. Our intentions reflect what we expect the immediate results of our action to be. Nobody credits the "intentions" of a couple who practice neither celibacy nor contraception but still insist "we never meant to have (more) children." Conception is likely (and known to be likely) in such cases. Where people's expressed intentions ignore the normal and predictable results of what they do, we infer that (if they are not amazingly ignorant) their words do not express their true intentions. The Formula of the End in Itself applies to the intentions on which one acts—not to some prettified version that one may avow. Provided this intention—the agent's real intention—uses no other as mere means, he or she does nothing unjust. If some of his or her intentions foster others' ends, then he or she is sometimes beneficent. It is therefore possible for people to test their proposals by Kantian arguments even when they lack the comprehensive causal knowledge that utilitarianism requires. Conscientious Kantians can work out whether they will be doing wrong by some act even though they know that their foresight is limited and that they may cause some harm or fail to cause some benefit. But they will not cause harms that they can foresee without this being reflected in their intentions.

NOTE

1. I. Kant, *Groundwork of the Metaphysic of Morals*, trans. H. J. Paton (New York: Harper Torchbooks, 1964), p. 96.

War and Massacre

THOMAS NAGEL

—•—

FROM THE APATHETIC REACTION to atrocities committed in Vietnam by the United States and its allies, one may conclude that moral restrictions on the conduct of war command almost as little sympathy among the general public as they do among those charged with the formation of U.S. military policy.[1] Even when restrictions on the conduct of warfare are defended, it is usually on legal grounds alone: their moral basis is often poorly understood. I wish to argue that certain restrictions are neither arbitrary nor merely conventional, and that their validity does not depend simply on their usefulness. There is, in other words, a moral basis for the rules of war, even though the conventions now officially in force are far from giving it perfect expression.

I

No elaborate moral theory is required to account for what is wrong in cases like the Mylai massacre, since it did not serve, and was not intended to serve, any strategic purpose. Moreover, if the participation of the United States in the Indo-Chinese war is entirely wrong to begin with, then that engagement is incapable of providing a justification for *any* measures taken in its pursuit—not only for the measures which are atrocities in every way, however just its aims.

But this war has revealed attitudes of a more general kind, which influenced the conduct of earlier wars as well. After it has ended, we shall still be faced with the problem of how warfare may be con-

ducted, and the attitudes that have resulted in the specific conduct of this war will not have disappeared. Moreover, similar problems can arise in wars or rebellions fought for very different reasons, and against very different opponents. It is not easy to keep a firm grip on the idea of what is not permissible in warfare, because while some military actions are obvious atrocities, other cases are more difficult to assess, and the general principles underlying these judgments remain obscure. Such obscurity can lead to the abandonment of sound intuitions in favor of criteria whose rationale may be more obvious. If such a tendency is to be resisted, it will require a better understanding of the restrictions than we now have.

I propose to discuss the most general moral problem raised by the conduct of warfare: the problem of means and ends. In one view, there are limits on what may be done even in the service of an end worth pursuing—and even when adherence to the restriction may be very costly. A person who acknowledges the force of such restrictions can find himself in acute moral dilemmas. He may believe, for example, that by torturing a prisoner he can obtain information necessary to prevent a disaster, or that by obliterating one village with bombs he can halt a campaign of terrorism. If he believes that the gains from a certain measure will clearly outweigh its costs, yet still suspects that he ought not to adopt it, then he is in a dilemma produced by the conflict between two disparate categories of moral reason: categories that may be called *utilitarian* and *absolutist*.

Utilitarianism gives primacy to a concern with what will *happen*. Absolutism gives primacy to a concern with what one is *doing*. The conflict between them arises because the alternatives we face are rarely just choices between *total outcomes*: they are also choices between alternative pathways or measures to be taken. When one of the choices is to do terrible things to another person, the problem is altered fundamentally; it is no longer merely a question of which outcome would be worse.

Few of us are completely immune to either of these types of moral intuition, though in some people, either naturally or for doctrinal reasons, one type will be dominant and the other suppressed or weak. But it is perfectly possible to feel the force of both types of reason very strongly; in that case the moral dilemma in certain situations of crisis will be acute, and it may appear that every possible course of action or inaction is unacceptable for one reason or another.

II

Although it is this dilemma that I propose to explore, most of the discussion will be devoted to its absolutist component. The utilitarian component is straightforward by comparison, and has a natural appeal to anyone who is not a complete skeptic about ethics. Utilitarianism says that one should try, either individually or through institutions, to maximize good and minimize evil (the definition of these categories need not enter into the schematic formulation of the view), and that if faced with the possibility of preventing a great evil by producing a lesser, one should choose the lesser evil. There are certainly problems about the formulation of utilitarianism, and much has been written about it, but its intent is morally transparent. Nevertheless, despite the additions and refinements, it continues to leave large portions of ethics unaccounted for. I do not suggest that some form of absolutism can account for them all, only that an examination of absolutism will lead us to see the complexity, and perhaps the incoherence, of our moral ideas.

Utilitarianism certainly justifies *some* restrictions on the conduct of warfare. There are strong utilitarian reasons for adhering to any limitation which seems natural to most people—particularly if the limitation is widely accepted already. An exceptional measure which seems to be justified by its results in a particular conflict may create a precedent with disastrous long-term effects.[2] It may even be

argued that war involves violence on such a scale that it is never justified on utilitarian grounds—the consequences of refusing to go to war will never be as bad as the war itself would be, even if atrocities were not committed. Or in a more sophisticated vein it might be claimed that a uniform policy of never resorting to military force would do less harm in the long run, if followed consistently, than a policy of deciding each case on utilitarian grounds (even though on occasion particular applications of the pacifist policy might have worse results than a specific utilitarian decision). But I shall not consider these arguments, for my concern is with reasons of a different kind, which may remain when reasons of utility and interest fail.[3]

In the final analysis, I believe that the dilemma cannot always be resolved. While not every conflict between absolutism and utilitarianism creates an insoluble dilemma, and while it seems to me certainly right to adhere to absolutist restrictions unless the utilitarian considerations favoring violation are overpoweringly weighty and extremely certain—nevertheless, when that special condition is met, it may become impossible to adhere to an absolutist position. What I shall offer, therefore, is a somewhat qualified defense of absolutism. I believe it underlies a valid and fundamental type of moral judgment—which cannot be reduced to or overridden by other principles. And while there may be other principles just as fundamental, it is particularly important not to lose confidence in our absolutist intuitions, for they are often the only barrier before the abyss of utilitarian apologetics for large-scale murder.

III

One absolutist position that creates no problems of interpretation is pacifism: the view that one may not kill another person under any circumstances, no matter what good would be achieved or evil averted thereby. The type of absolutist position that I am going to discuss is different. Pacifism draws the conflict with utilitarian considerations very starkly. But there are other views according to which violence may be undertaken, even on a large scale, in a clearly just cause, so long as certain absolute restrictions on the character and direction of that violence are observed. The line is drawn somewhat closer to the bone, but it exists.

The philosopher who has done most to advance contemporary philosophical discussion of such a view, and to explain it to those unfamiliar with its extensive treatment in Roman Catholic moral theology, is G. E. M. Anscombe. In 1958 Miss Anscombe published a pamphlet entitled *Mr. Truman's Degree*,[4] on the occasion of the award by Oxford University of an honorary doctorate to Harry Truman. The pamphlet explained why she had opposed the decision to award that degree, recounted the story of her unsuccessful opposition, and offered some reflections on the history of Truman's decision to drop atom bombs on Hiroshima and Nagasaki, and on the difference between murder and allowable killing in warfare. She pointed out that the policy of deliberately killing large numbers of civilians either as a means or as an end in itself did not originate with Truman, and was common practice among all parties during World War II for some time before Hiroshima. The Allied area bombings of German cities by conventional explosives included raids which killed more civilians than did the atomic attacks; the same is true of certain fire-bomb raids on Japan.

The policy of attacking the civilian population in order to induce an enemy to surrender, or to damage his morale, seems to have been widely accepted in the civilized world, and seems to be accepted still, at least if the stakes are high enough. It gives evidence of a moral conviction that the deliberate killing of noncombatants—women, children, old people—is permissible if enough can be gained by it. This follows from the more general position that any means can in principle be justified if it leads to a sufficiently worthy end. Such an attitude is evident not only in the more spectacular current weapons systems but also in the day-to-day conduct of the non-global war in Indo-China: the indiscriminate destructiveness of antipersonnel weapons, napalm, and aerial bombardment; cruelty to prisoners; massive relocation of civilians; destruction of crops; and so forth. An absolutist position opposes to this the view that certain acts cannot be justified

no matter what the consequences. Among those acts is murder—the deliberate killing of the harmless: civilians, prisoners of war, and medical personnel.

In the present war such measures are sometimes said to be regrettable, but they are generally defended by reference to military necessity and the importance of the long-term consequences of success or failure in the war. I shall pass over the inadequacy of this consequentialist defense in its own terms. (That is the dominant form of moral criticism of the war, for it is part of what people mean when they ask, "Is it worth it?") I am concerned rather to account for the inappropriateness of offering any defense of that kind for such actions.

Many people feel, without being able to say much more about it, that something has gone seriously wrong when certain measures are admitted into consideration in the first place. The fundamental mistake is made there, rather than at the point where the overall benefit of some monstrous measure is judged to outweigh its disadvantages, and it is adopted. An account of absolutism might help us to understand this. If it is not allowable to *do* certain things, such as killing unarmed prisoners or civilians, then no argument about what will happen if one does not do them can show that doing them would be all right.

Absolutism does not, of course, require one to ignore the consequences of one's acts. It operates as a limitation on utilitarian reasoning, not as a substitute for it. An absolutist can be expected to try to maximize good and minimize evil, so long as this does not require him to transgress an absolute prohibition like that against murder. But when such a conflict occurs, the prohibition takes complete precedence over any consideration of consequences. Some of the results of this view are clear enough. It requires us to forgo certain potentially useful military measures, such as the slaughter of hostages and prisoners or indiscriminate attempts to reduce the enemy civilian population by starvation, epidemic infectious diseases like anthrax and bubonic plague, or mass incineration. It means that we cannot deliberate on whether such measures are justified by the fact that they will avert still greater evils, for as intentional measures they cannot be justified in terms of any consequences whatever.

Someone unfamiliar with the events of this century might imagine that utilitarian arguments, or arguments of national interest, would suffice to deter measures of this sort. But it has become evident that such considerations are insufficient to prevent the adoption and employment of enormous antipopulation weapons once their use is considered a serious moral possibility. The same is true of the piecemeal wiping out of rural civilian populations in airborne antiguerrilla warfare. Once the door is opened to calculations of utility and national interest, the usual speculations about the future of freedom, peace, and economic prosperity can be brought to bear to ease the consciences of those responsible for a certain number of charred babies.

For this reason alone it is important to decide what is wrong with the frame of mind which allows such arguments to begin. But it is also important to understand absolutism in the cases where it genuinely conflicts with utility. Despite its appeal, it is a paradoxical position, for it can require that one refrain from choosing the lesser of two evils when that is the only choice one has. And it is additionally paradoxical because, unlike pacifism, it permits one to do horrible things to people in some circumstances but not in others.

IV

Before going on to say what, if anything, lies behind the position, there remain a few relatively technical matters which are best discussed at this point.

First, it is important to specify as clearly as possible the kind of thing to which absolutist prohibitions can apply. We must take seriously the proviso that they concern what we deliberately do to people. There could not, for example, without incoherence, be an absolute prohibition against *bringing about* the death of an innocent person. For one may find oneself in a situation in which, no matter what one does, some innocent people will die as a result. I do not mean just that there are cases in which someone will die no matter what one does, because one is not in a position to affect the outcome one way or the other. That, it is to be hoped, is one's relation to the deaths of most innocent people. I have

in mind, rather, a case in which someone is bound to die, but who it is will depend on what one does. Sometimes these situations have natural causes, as when too few resources (medicine, lifeboats) are available to rescue everyone threatened with a certain catastrophe. Sometimes the situations are manmade, as when the only way to control a campaign of terrorism is to employ terrorist tactics against the community from which it has arisen. Whatever one does in cases such as these, some innocent people will die as a result. If the absolutist prohibition forbade doing what would result in the deaths of innocent people, it would have the consequence that in such cases nothing one could do would be morally permissible.

This problem is avoided, however, because what absolutism forbids is *doing* certain things to people, rather than bringing about certain *results*. Not everything that happens to others as a result of what one does is something that one has *done* to them. Catholic moral theology seeks to make this distinction precise in a doctrine known as the law of double effect, which asserts that there is a morally relevant distinction between bringing about or permitting the death of an innocent person deliberately, either as an end in itself or as a means, and bringing it about or permitting it as a side effect of something else one does deliberately. In the latter case, even if the outcome is foreseen, it is not murder, and does not fall under the absolute prohibition, though of course it may still be wrong for other reasons (reasons of utility, for example). Briefly, the principle states that one is sometimes permitted knowingly to bring about or permit as a side-effect of one's actions something which it would be absolutely impermissible to bring about or permit deliberately as an end or as a means. In application to war or revolution, the law of double effect permits a certain amount of civilian carnage as a side-effect of bombing munitions plants or attacking enemy soldiers. And even this is permissible only if the cost is not too great to be justified by one's objectives.

However, despite its importance and its usefulness in accounting for certain plausible moral judgments, I do not believe that the law of double effect is a generally applicable test for the consequences of an absolutist position. Its own application is not always clear, so that it introduces uncertainty where there need not be uncertainty.

In Indo-China, for example, there is a great deal of aerial bombardment, strafing, spraying of napalm, and employment of pellet- or needle-spraying antipersonnel weapons against rural villages in which guerrillas are suspected to be hiding, or from which small-arms fire has been received. The majority of those killed and wounded in these aerial attacks are reported to be women and children, even when some combatants are caught as well. However, the government regards these civilian casualties as a regrettable side-effect of what is a legitimate attack against an armed enemy.

It might be thought easy to dismiss this as sophistry: if one bombs, burns, or strafes a village containing a hundred people, twenty of whom one believes to be guerrillas, so that by killing most of them one will be statistically likely to kill most of the guerrillas, then is not one's attack on the group of one hundred a *means* of destroying the guerrillas, pure and simple? If one makes no attempt to discriminate between guerrillas and civilians, as is impossible in an aerial attack on a small village, then one cannot regard as a mere side-effect the deaths of those in the group that one would not have bothered to kill if more selective means had been available.

The difficulty is that this argument depends on one particular description of the act, and the reply might be that the means used against the guerrillas is not: killing everybody in the village—but rather: obliteration bombing of the *area* in which the twenty guerrillas are known to be located. If there are civilians in the area as well, they will be killed as a side-effect of such action.[5]

Because of casuistical problems like this, I prefer to stay with the original, unanalyzed distinction between what one does to people and what merely happens to them as a result of what one does. The law of double effect provides an approximation to that distinction in many cases, and perhaps it can be sharpened to the point where it does better than that. Certainly the original distinction itself needs clarification, particularly since some of the things we do to people involve things happening to them as a result of other things we do. In a case like the one discussed, however, it is clear that by bombing the village one slaughters and maims the civilians in it. Whereas by giving the only available medicine to one of the two sufferers from a disease, one does not kill the other or deliberately allow him to die, even if he dies as a result.

The second technical point is this. The absolutist focus on actions rather than outcomes does not merely introduce a new, outstanding item into the catalogue of evils. That is, it does not say that the worst thing in the world is the deliberate murder of an innocent person. For if that were all, then one could presumably justify one such murder on the ground that it would prevent several others, or ten thousand on the ground that they would prevent a hundred thousand more. That is a familiar argument. But if this is allowable, then there is no absolute prohibition against murder after all. Absolutism requires that we *avoid* murder at all costs, not that we *prevent* it at all costs.

It would also be possible to adopt a deontological position less stringent than absolutism, without falling into utilitarianism. There are two ways in which someone might acknowledge the moral relevance of the distinction between deliberate and nondeliberate killing, without being an absolutist. One would be to count murder as a specially bad item in the catalogue of evils, much worse than accidental death or nondeliberate killing. But the other would be to say that deliberately killing an innocent is impermissible unless it is the only way to prevent some very large evil (say the deaths of fifty innocent people). Call this the *threshold* at which the prohibition against murder is overridden. The position is not absolutist, obviously, but it is also not equivalent to an assignment of utilitarian disvalue to murder equal to the disvalue of the threshold. This is easily seen. If a murder had the disvalue of fifty accidental deaths, it would still be permissible on utilitarian grounds to commit a murder to prevent one other murder, plus some lesser evil like a broken arm. Worse still, we would be required on utilitarian grounds to prevent one murder even at the cost of forty-nine accidental deaths that we could otherwise have prevented. These are not in fact consequences of a deontological prohibition against murder with a threshold, because it does not say that the occurrence of a certain kind of act is a bad thing, and therefore to be prevented, but rather tells everyone to *refrain* from such acts, except under certain conditions. In fact, it is perfectly compatible with a deontological prohibition against murder to hold that, considered as an outcome, a murder has *no* more disvalue than an accidental death. While the admission of thresholds would reduce the starkness of the conflicts discussed here, I do not think it would make them disappear, or change their basic character. They would persist in the clash between any deontological requirement and utilitarian values somewhat lower than its threshold.

Finally, let me remark on a frequent criticism of absolutism that depends on a misunderstanding. It is sometimes suggested that such prohibitions depend on a kind of moral self-interest, a primary obligation to preserve one's own moral purity, to keep one's hands clean no matter what happens to the rest of the world. If this were the position, it might be exposed to the charge of self-indulgence. After all, what gives one man a right to put the purity of his soul or the cleanness of his hands above the lives or welfare of large numbers of other people? It might be argued that a public servant like Truman has no right to put himself first in that way; therefore if he is convinced that the alternatives would be worse, he must give the order to drop the bombs, and take the burden of those deaths on himself, as he must do other distasteful things for the general good.

But there are two confusions behind the view that moral self-interest underlies moral absolutism. First, it is a confusion to suggest that the need to preserve one's moral purity might be the *source* of an obligation. For if by committing murder one sacrifices one's moral purity or integrity, that can only be because there is *already* something wrong with murder. The general reason against committing murder cannot therefore be merely that it makes one an immoral person. Secondly, the notion that one might sacrifice one's moral integrity justifiably, in the service of a sufficiently worthy end, is an incoherent notion. For if one were justified in making such a sacrifice (or even morally required to make it), then one would not be sacrificing one's moral integrity by adopting that course: one would be preserving it.

Moral absolutism is not unique among moral theories in requiring each person to do what will preserve his own moral purity in all circumstances. This is equally true of utilitarianism, or of any other theory which distinguishes between right and wrong. Any theory which defines the right course of action in various circumstances and asserts that one should adopt that course, ipso facto asserts that one should do what will preserve one's moral purity, simply because the right course of action *is* what will preserve one's moral purity in those circumstances. Of course utilitarianism does not assert that this is *why* one should adopt that course, but we have seen that the same is true of absolutism.

V

It is easier to dispose of false explanations of absolutism than to produce a true one. A positive account of the matter must begin with the observation that war, conflict, and aggression are relations between persons. The view that it can be wrong to consider merely the overall effect of one's actions on the general welfare comes into prominence when those actions involve relations with others. A man's acts usually affect more people than he deals with directly, and those effects must naturally be considered in his decisions. But if there are special principles governing the manner in which he should *treat* people, that will require special attention to the particular persons toward whom the act is directed, rather than just to its total effect.

Absolutist restrictions in warfare appear to be of two types: restrictions on the class of persons at whom aggression or violence may be directed and restrictions on the manner of attack, given that the object falls within that class. These can be combined, however, under the principle that hostile treatment of any person must be justified in terms of something *about that person* which makes the treatment appropriate. Hostility is a personal relation, and it must be suited to its target. One consequence of this condition will be that certain persons may not be subjected to hostile treatment in war at all, since nothing about them justifies such treatment. Others will be proper objects of hostility only in certain circumstances, or when they are engaged in certain pursuits. And the appropriate manner and extent of hostile treatment will depend on what is justified by the particular case.

A coherent view of this type will hold that extremely hostile behavior toward another is compatible with treating him as a person—even perhaps as an end in himself. This is possible only if one has not automatically stopped treating him as a person as soon as one starts to fight with him. If hostile, aggressive, or combative treatment of others always violated the condition that they be treated as human beings, it would be difficult to make further distinctions on that score *within* the class of hostile actions. That point of view, on the level of international relations, leads to the position that if complete pacifism is not accepted, no holds need be barred at all, and we may slaughter and massacre to our hearts' content, if it seems advisable. Such a position is often expressed in discussions of war crimes.

But the fact is that ordinary people do not believe this about conflicts, physical or otherwise, between individuals, and there is no more reason why it should be true of conflicts between nations. There seems to be a perfectly natural conception of the distinction between fighting clean and fighting dirty. To fight dirty is to direct one's hostility or aggression not at its proper object, but at a peripheral target which may be more vulnerable, and through which the proper object can be attacked indirectly. This applies in a fist fight, an election campaign, a duel, or a philosophical argument. If the concept is general enough to apply to all these matters, it should apply to war—both to the conduct of individual soldiers and to the conduct of nations.

Suppose that you are a candidate for public office, convinced that the election of your opponent would be a disaster, that he is an unscrupulous demagogue who will serve a narrow range of interests and seriously infringe the rights of those who disagree with him; and suppose you are convinced that you cannot defeat him by conventional means. Now imagine that various unconventional means present themselves as possibilities: you possess information about his sex life which would scandalize the electorate if made public; or you learn that his wife is an alcoholic or that in his youth he was associated for a brief period with a proscribed political party, and you believe that this information could be used to blackmail him into withdrawing his candidacy; or you can have a team of your supporters flatten the tires of a crucial subset of his supporters on election day; or you are in a position to stuff the ballot boxes; or, more simply, you can have him assassinated. What is wrong with these methods, given that they will achieve an overwhelmingly desirable result?

There are, of course, many things wrong with them: some are against the law; some infringe the procedures of an electoral process to which you are presumably committed by taking part in it; very importantly, some may backfire, and it is in the interest of all political candidates to adhere to an unspoken agreement not to allow certain personal matters to intrude into a campaign. But that is not all. We have in addition the feeling that these measures, these methods of attack, are *irrelevant* to the issue between you and your opponent, that in taking them up you would not be directing yourself to that which makes him an object of your opposition. You would be directing your attack not at the true target of your hostility, but at peripheral targets that happen to be vulnerable.

The same is true of a fight or argument outside the framework of any system of regulations or law. In an altercation with a taxi driver over an excessive fare, it is inappropriate to taunt him about his accent, flatten one of his tires, or smear chewing gum on his windshield; and it remains inappropriate even if he casts aspersions on your race, politics, or religion, or dumps the contents of your suitcase into the street.[6]

The importance of such restrictions may vary with the seriousness of the case; and what is unjustifiable in one case may be justified in a more extreme one. But they all derive from a single principle: that hostility or aggression should be directed at its true object. This means both that it should be directed at the person or persons who provoke it and that it should aim more specifically at what is provocative about them. The second condition will determine what form the hostility may appropriately take.

It is evident that some idea of the relation in which one should stand to other people underlies this principle, but the idea is difficult to state. I believe it is roughly this: whatever one does to another person intentionally must be aimed at him as a subject, with the intention that he receive it as a subject. It should manifest an attitude to *him* rather than just to the situation, and he should be able to recognize it and identify himself as its object. The procedures by which such an attitude is manifested need not be addressed to the person directly. Surgery, for example, is not a form of personal confrontation but part of a medical treatment that can be offered to a patient face to face and received by him as a response to his needs and the natural outcome of an attitude toward *him*.

Hostile treatment, unlike surgery, is already addressed *to* a person, and does not take its interpersonal meaning from a wider context. But hostile acts can serve as the expression or implementation of only a limited range of attitudes to the person who is attacked. Those attitudes in turn have as objects certain real or presumed characteristics or activities of the person which are thought to justify them. When this background is absent, hostile or aggressive behavior can no longer be intended for the reception of the victim as a subject. Instead it takes on the character of a purely bureaucratic operation. This occurs when one attacks someone who is not the true object of one's hostility—the true object may be someone else, who can be attacked through the victim; or one may not be manifesting a hostile attitude toward anyone, but merely using the easiest available path to some desired goal. One finds oneself not facing or addressing the victim at all, but operating on him—without the larger context of personal interaction that surrounds a surgical operation.

If absolutism is to defend its claim to priority over considerations of utility, it must hold that the maintenance of a direct interpersonal response to the people one deals with is a requirement which no advantages can justify one in abandoning. The requirement is absolute only if it rules out any calculation of what would justify its violation. I have said earlier that there may be circumstances so extreme that they render an absolutist position untenable. One may find then that one has no choice but to do something terrible. Nevertheless, even in such cases absolutism re-

tains its force in that one cannot claim *justification* for the violation. It does not become *all right*.

As a tentative effort to explain this, let me try to connect absolutist limitations with the possibility of justifying *to the victim* what is being done to him. If one abandons a person in the course of rescuing several others from a fire or a sinking ship, one *could* say to him, "You understand, I have to leave you to save the others." Similarly, if one subjects an unwilling child to a painful surgical procedure, one can say to him, "If you could understand, you would realize that I am doing this to help you." One could *even* say, as one bayonets an enemy soldier, "It's either you or me." But one cannot really say while torturing a prisoner, "You understand, I have to pull out your finger-nails because it is absolutely essential that we have the names of your confederates"; nor can one say to the victims of Hiroshima, "You understand, we have to incinerate you to provide the Japanese government with an incentive to surrender."

This does not take us very far, of course, since a utilitarian would presumably be willing to offer justifications of the latter sort to his victims, in cases where he thought they were sufficient. They are really justifications to the world at large, which the victim, as a reasonable man, would be expected to appreciate. However, there seems to me something wrong with this view, for it ignores the possibility that to treat someone else horribly puts you in a special relation to him, which may have to be defended in terms of other features of your relation to him. The suggestion needs much more development; but it may help us to understand how there may be requirements which are absolute in the sense that there can be no justification for violating them. If the justification for what one did to another person had to be such that it could be offered to him specifically, rather than just to the world at large, that would be a significant source of restraint.

If the account is to be deepened, I would hope for some results along the following lines. Absolutism is associated with a view of oneself as a small being interacting with others in a large world. The justifications it requires are primarily interpersonal. Utilitarianism is associated with a view of oneself as a benevolent bureaucrat distributing such benefits as one can control to countless other beings, with whom one may have various relations or none. The justifications it requires are primarily administrative. The argument between the two moral attitudes may depend on the relative priority of these two conceptions.[7]

VI

Some of the restrictions on methods of warfare which have been adhered to from time to time are to be explained by the mutual interests of the involved parties: restrictions on weaponry, treatment of prisoners, etc. But that is not all there is to it. The conditions of directness and relevance which I have argued apply to relations of conflict and aggression apply to war as well. I have said that there are two types of absolutist restrictions on the conduct of war: those that limit the legitimate targets of hostility and those that limit its character, even when the target is acceptable. I shall say something about each of these. As will become clear, the principle I have sketched does not yield an unambiguous answer in every case.

First let us see how it implies that attacks on some people are allowed, but not attacks on others. It may seem paradoxical to assert that to fire a machine gun at someone who is throwing hand grenades at your emplacement is to treat him as a human being. Yet the relation with him is direct and straightforward.[8] The attack is aimed specifically against the threat presented by a dangerous adversary, and not against a peripheral target through which he happens to be vulnerable but which has nothing to do with that threat. For example, you might stop him by machine-gunning his wife and children, who are standing nearby, thus distracting him from his aim of blowing you up and enabling you to capture him. But if his wife and children are not threatening your life, that would be to treat them as means with a vengeance.

This, however, is just Hiroshima on a smaller scale. One objection to weapons of mass annihilation—nuclear, thermonuclear, biological, or chemical—is that their indiscriminateness disqualifies them as direct instruments for the expression of hostile relations. In attacking the civilian population, one treats neither the military enemy nor the civilians with that minimal respect which is owed to them as human beings. This is clearly true of the direct attack on people who present no threat at all. But it is also true of the character of the attack on those who *are* threatening you, i.e., the government and military forces of the enemy. Your aggression is directed against an area of vulnerability quite distinct from any threat presented by them which you may be justified in meeting. You are taking aim at them through the mundane life and survival of their countryman, instead of aiming at the destruction of their military capacity. And of course it does not require hydrogen bombs to commit such crimes.

This way of looking at the matter also helps us to understand the importance of the distinction between combatants and noncombatants, and the irrelevance of much of the criticism offered against its intelligibility and moral significance. According to an absolutist position, deliberate killing of the innocent is murder, and in warfare the role of the innocent is filled by noncombatants. This has been thought to raise two sorts of problems: first, the widely imagined difficulty of making a division, in modern warfare, between combatants and noncombatants; second, problems deriving from the connotation of the word "innocence."

Let me take up the latter question first.[9] In the absolutist position, the operative notion of innocence is not moral innocence, and it is not opposed to moral guilt. If it were, then we would be justified in killing a wicked but noncombatant hairdresser in an enemy city who supported the evil policies of his government, and unjustified in killing a morally pure conscript who was driving a tank toward us with the profoundest regrets and nothing but love in his heart. But moral innocence has very little to do with it, for in the definition of murder "innocent" means "currently harmless", and it is opposed not to "guilty" but to "doing harm." It should be noted that such an analysis has the consequence that in war we may often be justified in killing people who do not deserve to die, and unjustified in killing people who do deserve to die, if anyone does.

So we must distinguish combatants from noncombatants on the basis of their immediate threat or harmfulness. I do not claim that the line is a sharp one, but it is not so difficult as is often supposed to place individuals on one side of it or the other. Children are not combatants even though they may join the armed forces if they are allowed to grow up. Women are not combatants just because they bear children or offer comfort to the soldiers. More problematic are the supporting personnel, whether in or out of uniform, from drivers of munitions trucks and army cooks to civilian munitions workers and farmers. I believe they can be plausibly classified by applying the condition that the prosecution of conflict must direct itself to the cause of danger, and not to what is peripheral. The threat presented by an army and its members does not consist merely in the fact that they are men, but in the fact that they are armed and are using their arms in the pursuit of certain objectives. Contributions to their arms and logistics are contributions to this threat; contributions to their mere existence as men are not. It is therefore wrong to direct an attack against those who merely serve the combatants' needs as human beings, such as farmers and food suppliers, even though survival as a human being is a necessary condition of efficient functioning as a soldier.

This brings us to the second group of restrictions: those that limit what may be done even to combatants. These limits are harder to explain clearly. Some of them may be arbitrary or conventional, and some may have to be derived from other sources; but I believe that the condition of directness and relevance in hostile relations accounts for them to a considerable extent.

Consider first a case which involves both a protected class of noncombatants and a restriction of the measures that may be used against combatants. One provision of the rules of war which is universally recognized, though it seems to be turning into a dead letter in Vietnam, is the special status of medical personnel and the wounded in warfare. It might be more efficient to shoot medical officers on sight and to let the enemy wounded die rather than be patched up to fight another day. But someone with medical insignia is supposed to be left alone and permitted to tend and retrieve the wounded. I believe this is because medical attention is a species of attention to completely general human needs, not specifically the needs of a combat soldier, and our conflict with the soldier is not with his existence as a human being.

By extending the application of this idea, one can justify prohibitions against certain particularly cruel weapons: starvation, poisoning, infectious diseases (supposing they could be inflicted on combatants only), weapons designed to maim or disfigure or torture the opponent rather than merely to stop him. It is not, I think, mere casuistry to claim that such weapons attack the men, not the soldiers. The effect of dum-dum bullets, for example, is much more extended than necessary to cope with the combat situation in which they are used. They abandon any attempt to discriminate in their effects between the combatant and the human being. For this reason the use of flamethrowers and napalm is an atrocity in all circumstances that I can imagine, whoever the target may be. Burns are both extremely painful and extremely disfiguring—far more than any other category of wound. That this well-known fact plays no (inhibiting) part in the determination of U.S. weapons policy suggests that moral sensitivity among public officials has not increased markedly since the Spanish Inquisition.[10]

Finally, the same condition of appropriateness to the true object of hostility should limit the scope of attacks on an enemy country: its economy, agriculture, transportation system, and so forth. Even if the parties to a military conflict are considered to be not armies or governments but entire nations (which is usually a grave error), that does not justify one nation in warring against every aspect or element of another nation. That is not justified in a conflict between individuals, and nations are even more complex than individuals, so the same reasons apply. Like a human being, a nation is engaged in countless other pursuits while waging war, and it is not in those respects that it is an enemy.

The burden of the argument has been that absolutism about murder has a foundation in principles governing all one's relations to other persons, whether aggressive or amiable, and that these principles and that absolutism, apply to warfare as well, with the result that certain measures are impermissible no matter what the consequences.[11] I do not mean to romanticize war. It is sufficiently utopian to suggest that when nations conflict they might rise to the level of limited barbarity that typically characterizes violent conflict between individuals, rather than wallowing in the moral pit where they appear to have settled, surrounded by enormous arsenals.

VI

Having described the elements of the absolutist position, we must now return to the conflict between it and utilitarianism. Even if certain types of dirty tactics become acceptable when the stakes are high enough, the most serious of the prohibited acts, like murder and torture, are not just supposed to require unusually strong justification. They are supposed *never* to be done, because no quantity of resulting benefit is thought capable of *justifying* such treatment of a person.

The fact remains that when an absolutist knows or believes that the utilitarian cost of refusing to adopt a prohibited course will be very high, he may hold to his refusal to adopt it, but he will find it difficult to feel that a moral dilemma has been satisfactorily resolved. The same may be true of someone who rejects an absolutist requirement and adopts instead the course yielding the most acceptable consequences. In either case, it is possible to feel that one has acted for reasons insufficient to justify violation of the opposing principle. In situations of deadly conflict, particularly where a weaker party is threatened with annihilation or enslavement by a stronger one, the argument for resorting to atrocities can be powerful, and the dilemma acute.

There may exist principles, not yet codified, which would enable us to resolve such dilemmas. But then again there may not. We must face the pessimistic alternative that these two forms of moral intuition are not capable of being brought together into a single, coherent moral system, and that the world can present us with situations in which there is no honorable or moral course for a man to take, no course free of guilt and responsibility for evil.[12]

The idea of a moral blind alley is a perfectly intelligible one. It is possible to get into such a situation by one's own fault, and people do it all the time. If, for example, one makes two incompatible promises or commitments—becomes engaged to two people,

for example—then there is no course one can take which is not wrong, for one must break one's promise to at least one of them. Making a clean breast of the whole thing will not be enough to remove one's reprehensibility. The existence of such cases is not morally disturbing, however, because we feel that the situation was not unavoidable: one had to do something wrong in the first place to get into it. But what if the world itself, or someone else's actions, could face a previously innocent person with a choice between morally abominable courses of action, and leave him no way to escape with his honor? Our intuitions rebel at the idea, for we feel that the constructibility of such a case must show a contradiction in our moral views. But it is not in itself a contradiction to say that someone can do X or not do X, and that for him to take either course would be wrong. It merely contradicts the supposition that *ought* implies *can*—since presumably one ought to refrain from what is wrong, and in such a case it is impossible to do so.[13] Given the limitations on human action, it is näive to suppose that there is a solution to every moral problem with which the world can face us. We have always known that the world is a bad place. It appears that it may be an evil place as well.

NOTES

1. This essay was completed in 1971. Direct U.S. military involvement in the Vietnam War lasted from 1961 to 1973. Hence the present tense.
2. Straightforward considerations of national interest often tend in the same direction: the inadvisability of using nuclear weapons seems to be overdetermined in this way.
3. These reasons, moreover, have special importance in that they are available even to one who denies the appropriateness of utilitarian considerations in international matters. He may acknowledge limitations on what may be done to the soldiers and civilians of other countries in pursuit of his nation's military objectives, while denying that one country should in general consider the interests of nationals of other countries in determining its policies.
4. (Privately printed.) See also her essay "War and

Murder," in *Nuclear Weapons and Christian Conscience*, ed. Walter Stein (London: The Merlin Press, 1961). The present paper is much indebted to these two essays throughout. These and related subjects are extensively treated by Paul Ramsey in *The Just War* (New York: Scribners, 1968). Among recent writings that bear on the moral problem are Jonathan Bennett, "Whatever the Consequences," *Analysis*, 26, no. 3 (1966), 83–102; and Philippa Foot, "The Problem of Abortion and the Doctrine of the Double Effect," *Oxford Review*, 5 (1967), 5–15. Miss Anscombe's replies are "A Note on Mr. Bennett," *Analysis*, 26, no. 3 (1966), 208 and "Who Is Wronged?" *Oxford Review*, 5 (1967), 16–17.

5. This counter-argument was suggested by Rogers Albritton.

6. Why, on the other hand, does it seem appropriate, rather than irrelevant, to punch someone in the mouth if he insults you? The answer is that in our culture it is an insult to punch someone in the mouth, and not just an injury. This reveals, by the way, a perfectly unobjectionable sense in which convention may play a part in determining exactly what falls under an absolutist restriction and what does not. I am indebted to Robert Fogelin for this point.

7. Finally, I should mention a different possibility, suggested by Robert Nozick: that there is a strong general presumption against benefiting from the calamity of another, whether or not it has been deliberately inflicted for that or any other reason. This broader principle may well lend its force to the absolutist position.

8. Marshall Cohen once remarked that, according to my view, shooting at someone establishes an I–thou relationship.

9. What I say on this subject derives from Anscombe.

10. Beyond this I feel uncertain. Ordinary bullets, after all, can cause death, and nothing is more permanent than that. I am not at all sure why we are justified in trying to kill those who are trying to kill us (rather than merely in trying to stop them with force which may also result in their deaths). It is often argued that incapacitating gases are a relatively humane weapon (when not used, as in Vietnam, merely to make people easier to shoot). Perhaps the legitimacy of restrictions against them must depend on the dangers of escalation, and the great utility of maintaining *any* conventional category of restriction so long as nations are willing to adhere to it.

Let me make clear that I do not regard my argument as a defense of the moral immutability of the Hague and Geneva Conventions. Rather, I believe that they rest partly on a moral foundation, and that modifications of them should also be assessed on moral grounds.

11. It is possible to draw a more radical conclusion, which I shall not pursue here. Perhaps the technology and organization of modern war are such as to make it impossible to wage as an acceptable form of interpersonal or even international hostility. Perhaps it is too impersonal and large-scale for that. If so, then absolutism would in practice imply pacifism, given the present state of things. On the other hand, I am skeptical about the unstated assumption that a technology dictates its own use.

12. In his reply to this essay ("Rules of War and Moral Reasoning," *Philosophy & Public Affairs*, I, no. 2 [Winter, 1972], 167), R. M. Hare pointed out the apparent discrepancy between my acceptance of such a possibility here and my earlier claim in section IV that absolutism must be formulated so as to avoid the consequence that in certain cases nothing one could do would be morally permissible. The difference is that in those cases the moral incoherence would result from the application of a single principle, whereas the dilemmas described here result from a conflict between two fundamentally different types of principle.

13. This was first pointed out to me by Christopher Boorse. The point is also made in E. J. Lemmon's "Moral Dilemmas," *Philosophical Review*, 71 (April, 1962), 150.

C. Aristotelian Ethics

Nicomachean Ethics

ARISTOTLE

Aristotle (384–322 B.C.) was a student of Plato's who, some think, surpassed his teacher to become the greatest philosopher of all. His works include *Metaphysics, Categories, Physics*, and many others in addition to the *Nicomachean Ethics*.

———◆———

Book I

1 Every art and every inquiry, and similarly every ac-
1094ª tion and pursuit, is thought to aim at some good; and for this reason the good has rightly been declared to be that at which all things aim. But a certain difference is found among ends; some are activities, others are products apart from the activities that produce them. Where there are ends apart from the actions, it is the nature of the products to be better than the activities. Now, as there are many actions, arts, and sciences, their ends also are many; the end of the medical art is health, that of shipbuilding a vessel, that of strategy victory, that of economics wealth. But where such arts fall under a single capacity—as bridlemaking and the other arts concerned with the equipment of horses fall under the art of riding, and this and every military action under strategy, in the same way other arts fall under yet others—in all of these the ends of the master arts are to be preferred to all the subordinate ends; for it is for the sake of the former that the latter are pursued. It makes no difference whether the activities themselves are the ends of the actions, or something else apart from the activities, as in the case of the sciences just mentioned.

If, then, there is some end of the things we do, 2 which we desire for its own sake (everything else being desired for the sake of this), and if we do not choose everything for the sake of something else (for at that rate the process would go on to infinity, so that our desire would be empty and vain), clearly this must be the good and the chief good. Will not the knowledge of it, then, have a great influence on life? Shall we not, like archers who have a mark to aim at, be more likely to hit upon what is right? If so, we must try, in outline at least, to determine what it is, and of which of the sciences or capacities it is the object. It would seem to belong to the most authoritative art and that which is most truly the master art. And politics appears to be of this nature; for it is this that ordains which of the sciences should 1094ᵇ be studied in a state, and which each class of citizens should learn and up to what point they should learn them; and we see even the most highly esteemed of capacities to fall under this, e.g. strategy, economics, rhetoric; now, since politics uses the rest of the sciences, and since, again, it legislates as to what we are to do and what we are to abstain from, the end of this science must include those of the others, so that this end must be the good for man. For even if the end is the same for a single man and for a state, that of the state seems at all events something greater and more complete whether to attain or to preserve; though it is worth while to attain the end merely for one man, it is finer and more god-like to attain it for a nation or for city-states. These, then, are the ends at which our inquiry aims, since it is political science, in one sense of that term.

3   Our discussion will be adequate if it has as much clearness as the subject-matter admits of, for precision is not to be sought for alike in all discussions, any more than in all the products of the crafts. Now fine and just actions, which political science investigates, admit of much variety and fluctuation of opinion, so that they may be thought to exist only by convention, and not by nature. And goods also give rise to a similar fluctuation because they bring harm to many people; for before now men have been undone by reason of their wealth, and others by reason of their courage. We must be content, then, in speaking of such subjects and with such premisses to indicate the truth roughly and in outline, and in speaking about things which are only for the most part true and with premisses of the same kind to reach conclusions that are no better. In the same spirit, therefore, should each type of statement be *received*; for it is the mark of an educated man to look for precision in each class of things just so far as the nature of the subject admits; it is evidently equally foolish to accept probable reasoning from a mathematician and to demand from a rhetorician scientific proofs.

1095ª   Now each man judges well the things he knows, and of these he is a good judge. And so the man who has been educated in a subject is a good judge of that subject, and the man who has received an all-round education is a good judge in general. Hence a young man is not a proper hearer of lectures on political science; for he is inexperienced in the actions that occur in life, but its discussions start from these and are about these; and, further, since he tends to follow his passions, his study will be vain and unprofitable, because the end aimed at is not knowledge but action. And it makes no difference whether he is young in years or youthful in character; the defect does not depend on time, but on his living, and pursuing each successive object, as passion directs. For to such persons, as to the incontinent, knowledge brings no profit; but to those who desire and act in accordance

with a rational principle knowledge about such matters will be of great benefit.

These remarks about the student, the sort of treatment to be expected, and the purpose of the inquiry, may be taken as our preface.

Let us resume our inquiry and state, in view of the 4 fact that all knowledge and every pursuit aims at some good, what it is that we say political science aims at and what is the highest of all goods achievable by action. Verbally there is very general agreement; for both the general run of men and people of superior refinement say that it is happiness, and identify living well and doing well with being happy; but with regard to what happiness is they differ, and the many do not give the same account as the wise. For the former think it is some plain and obvious thing, like pleasure, wealth, or honour; they differ, however, from one another—and often even the same man identifies it with different things, with health when he is ill, with wealth when he is poor; but, conscious of their ignorance, they admire those who proclaim some great ideal that is above their comprehension. Now some thought that apart from these many goods there is another which is self-subsistent and causes the goodness of all these as well. To examine all the opinions that have been held were perhaps somewhat fruitless; enough to examine those that are most prevalent or that seem to be arguable.

Let us not fail to notice, however, that there is a difference between arguments from and those to the first principles. For Plato, too, was right in raising this question and asking, as he used to do, "are we on the way from or to the first principles?" There is a difference, as there is in a racecourse between the course from the judges to the turning-point and the way back. For, while we must begin with what is known, 1095ᵇ things are objects of knowledge in two senses—some to us, some without qualification. Presumably, then, *we* must begin with things known to *us*. Hence any one who is to listen intelligently to lectures about what is noble and just and, generally, about the subjects of political science must have been brought up in good habits. For the fact is the starting-point, and if this is sufficiently plain to him, he will not at the start need the reason as well; and the man who has been well brought up has or can easily get starting-points. And as for him who neither has nor can get them, let him hear the words of Hesiod:

Far best is he who knows all things himself;
Good, he that hearkens when men counsel right;
But he who neither knows, nor lays to heart
Another's wisdom, is a useless wight.

5   Let us, however, resume our discussion from the point at which we digressed. To judge from the lives that men lead, most men, and men of the most vulgar type, seem (not without some ground) to identify the good, or happiness, with pleasure; which is the reason why they love the life of enjoyment. For there are, we may say, three prominent types of life—that just mentioned, the political, and thirdly the contemplative life. Now the mass of mankind are evidently quite slavish in their tastes, preferring a life suitable to beasts, but they get some ground for their view from the fact that many of those in high places share the tastes of Sardanapallus. A consideration of the prominent types of life shows that people of superior refinement and of active disposition identify happiness with honour; for this is, roughly speaking, the end of the political life. But it seems too superficial to be what we are looking for, since it is thought to depend on those who bestow honour rather than on him who receives it, but the good we divine to be something proper to a man and not easily taken from him. Further, men seem to pursue honour in order that they may be assured of their goodness; at least it is by men of practical wisdom that they seek to be honoured, and among those who know them, and on the ground of their virtue; clearly, then, according to them, at any rate, virtue is better. And perhaps one might even suppose this to be, rather than honour, the end of the political life. But even this appears somewhat incomplete; for possession of virtue seems actually compatible with being asleep, or with lifelong inactivity, and, further, with the greatest sufferings and misfortunes; but a man who was living so no one would call happy, unless he were maintaining a thesis at all costs. Third comes the contemplative life, which we shall consider later. But enough of this; for the subject has been sufficiently treated even in the current discussions.

1096ᵃ

The life of money-making is one undertaken under compulsion, and wealth is evidently not the good we are seeking; for it is merely useful and for the sake of something else. And so one might rather take the aforenamed objects to be ends; for they are loved for themselves. But it is evident that not even these are ends; yet many arguments have been thrown away in support of them. Let us leave this subject, then.

. . . .

Let us again return to the good we are seeking, and 7 ask what it can be. It seems different in different actions and arts; it is different in medicine, in strategy, and in the other arts likewise. What then is the good of each? Surely that for whose sake everything else is done. In medicine this is health, in strategy victory, in architecture a house, in any other sphere something else, and in every action and pursuit the end; for it is for the sake of this that all men do whatever else they do. Therefore, if there is an end for all that we do, this will be the good achievable by action, and if there are more than one, these will be the goods achievable by action.

So the argument has by a different course reached the same point; but we must try to state this even more clearly. Since there are evidently more than one end, and we choose some of these (e.g. wealth, flutes, and in general instruments) for the sake of something else, clearly not all ends are final ends; but the chief good is evidently something final. Therefore, if there is only one final end, this will be what we are seeking, and if there are more than one, the most final of these will be what we are seeking. Now we call that which is in itself worthy of pursuit more final than that which is worthy of pursuit for the sake of something else, and that which is never desirable for the sake of something else more final than the things that are desirable both in themselves and for the sake of that other thing, and therefore we call final without qualification that which is always desirable in itself and never for the sake of something else.

Now such a thing happiness, above all else, is 1097ᵇ held to be; for this we choose always for itself and never for the sake of something else, but honour, pleasure, reason, and every virtue we choose indeed for themselves (for if nothing resulted from them we should still choose each of them), but we choose them also for the sake of happiness, judging that by means of them we shall be happy. Happiness, on the other hand, no one chooses for the sake of these, nor, in general, for anything other than itself.

From the point of view of self-sufficiency the same result seems to follow; for the final good is thought to be self-sufficient. Now by self-sufficient we do not mean that which is sufficient for a man by himself, for one who lives a solitary life, but also for parents, children, wife, and in general for his friends and fellow citizens, since man is born for citizenship. But some limit must be set to this; for if we extend our requirement to ancestors and descendants and friends' friends we are in for an infinite series. Let us examine this question, however, on another occasion; the self-sufficient we now define as that which when isolated makes life desirable and lacking in nothing; and such we think happiness to be; and further we think it most desirable of all things, without being counted as one good thing among others—if it were so counted it would clearly be made more desirable by the addition of even the least of goods; for that which is added becomes an excess of goods, and of goods the greater is always more desirable. Happiness, then, is something final and self-sufficient, and is the end of action.

Presumably, however, to say that happiness is the chief good seems a platitude, and a clearer account of what it is is still desired. This might perhaps be given, if we could first ascertain the function of man. For just as for a flute-player, a sculptor, or any artist, and, in general, for all things that have a function or activity, the good and the "well" is thought to reside in the function, so would it seem to be for man, if he has a function. Have the carpenter, then, and the tanner certain functions or activities, and has man none? Is he born without a function? Or as eye, hand, foot, and in general each of the parts evidently has a function, may one lay it down that man similarly has a function apart from all these? What then can this be? Life seems to be common even to plants, but we are seeking what is peculiar to man. Let us 1098ᵃ exclude, therefore, the life of nutrition and growth. Next there would be a life of perception, but *it* also seems to be common even to the horse, the ox, and every animal. There remains, then, an active life of the element that has a rational principle; of this, one part has such a principle in the sense of being obe-

dient to one, the other in the sense of possessing one and exercising thought. And, as "life of the rational element" also has two meanings, we must state that life in the sense of activity is what we mean; for this seems to be the more proper sense of the term. Now if the function of man is an activity of soul which follows or implies a rational principle, and if we say "a so-and-so" and "a good so-and-so" have a function which is the same in kind, e.g. a lyre-player and a good lyre-player, and so without qualification in all cases, eminence in respect of goodness being added to the name of the function (for the function of a lyre-player is to play the lyre, and that of a good lyre-player is to do so well): if this is the case, [and we state the function of man to be a certain kind of life, and this to be an activity or actions of the soul implying a rational principle, and the function of a good man to be the good and noble performance of these, and if any action is well performed when it is performed in accordance with the appropriate excellence: if this is the case,] human good turns out to be activity of soul in accordance with virtue, and if there are more than one virtue, in accordance with the best and most complete.

But we must add "in a complete life." For one swallow does not make a summer, nor does one day; and so too one day, or a short time, does not make a man blessed and happy.

Let this serve as an outline of the good; for we must presumably first sketch it roughly, and then later fill in the details. But it would seem that any one is capable of carrying on and articulating what has once been well outlined, and that time is a good discoverer or partner in such a work; to which facts the advances of the arts are due; for any one can add what is lacking. And we must also remember what has been said before, and not look for precision in all things alike, but in each class of things such precision as accords with the subject-matter, and so much as is appropriate to the inquiry. For a carpenter and a geometer investigate the right angle in different ways; the former does so in so far as the right angle is useful for his work, while the latter inquires what it is or what sort of thing it is; for he is a spectator of the truth. We must act in the same way, then, in all other matters as well, that our main task may not be subordinated to minor questions. Nor must we demand the cause in all matters alike;

1098^b it is enough in some cases that the *fact* be well established, as in the case of the first principles; the fact is the primary thing or first principle. Now of first principles we see some by induction, some by perception, some by a certain habituation, and others too in other ways. But each set of principles we must try to investigate in the natural way, and we must take pains to state them definitely, since they have a great influence on what follows. For the beginning is thought to be more than half of the whole, and many of the questions we ask are cleared up by it.

8   We must consider it, however, in the light not only of our conclusion and our premises, but also of what is commonly said about it; for with a true view all the data harmonize, but with a false one the facts soon clash. Now goods have been divided into three classes, and some are described as external, others as relating to soul or to body; we call those that relate to soul most properly and truly goods, and psychical actions and activities we class as relating to soul. Therefore our account must be sound, at least according to this view, which is an old one and agreed on by philosophers. It is correct also in that we identify the end with certain actions and activities; for thus it falls among goods of the soul and not among external goods. Another belief which harmonizes with our account is that the happy man lives well and does well; for we have practically defined happiness as a sort of good life and good action. The characteristics that are looked for in happiness seem also, all of them, to belong to what we have defined happiness as being. For some identify happiness with virtue, some with practical wisdom, others with a kind of philosophic wisdom, others with these, or one of these, accompanied by pleasure or not without pleasure; while others include also external prosperity. Now some of these views have been held by many men and men of old, others by a few eminent persons; and it is not probable that either of these should be entirely mistaken, but rather that they should be right in at least some one respect or even in most respects.

With those who identify happiness with virtue or some one virtue our account is in harmony; for to virtue belongs virtuous activity. But it makes, perhaps, no small difference whether we place the chief good in possession or in use, in state of mind or in activity. For the state of mind may exist without pro- 1099^a ducing any good result, as in a man who is asleep or in some other way quite inactive, but the activity cannot; for one who has the activity will of necessity be acting, and acting well. And as in the Olympic Games it is not the most beautiful and the strongest that are crowned but those who compete (for it is some of these that are victorious), so those who act win, and rightly win, the noble and good things in life.

Their life is also in itself pleasant. For pleasure is a state of *soul*, and to each man that which he is said to be a lover of is pleasant; e.g. not only is a horse pleasant to the lover of horses, and a spectacle to the lover of sights, but also in the same way just acts are pleasant to the lover of justice and in general virtuous acts to the lover of virtue. Now for most men their pleasures are in conflict with one another because these are not by nature pleasant, but the lovers of what is noble find pleasant the things that are by nature pleasant; and virtuous actions are such, so that these are pleasant for such men as well as in their own nature. Their life, therefore, has no further need of pleasure as a sort of adventitious charm, but has its pleasure in itself. For, besides what we have said, the man who does not rejoice in noble actions is not even good; since no one would call a man just who did not enjoy acting justly, nor any man liberal who did not enjoy liberal actions; and similarly in all other cases. If this is so, virtuous actions must be in themselves pleasant. But they are also *good* and *noble*, and have each of these attributes in the highest degree, since the good man judges well about these attributes; his judgement is such as we have described. Happiness then is the best, noblest, and most pleasant thing in the world, and these attributes are not severed as in the inscription at Delos—

Most noble is that which is justest, and best is health;
But pleasantest is it to win what we love.

For all these properties belong to the best activities; and these, or one—the best—of these, we identify with happiness.

Yet evidently, as we said, it needs the external 1099^b

goods as well; for it is impossible, or not easy, to do noble acts without the proper equipment. In many actions we use friends and riches and political power as instruments; and there are some things the lack of which takes the lustre from happiness, as good birth, goodly children, beauty; for the man who is very ugly in appearance or ill-born or solitary and childless is not very likely to be happy, and perhaps a man would be still less likely if he had thoroughly bad children or friends or had lost good children or friends by death. As we said, then, happiness seems to need this sort of prosperity in addition; for which reason some identify happiness with good fortune, though others identify it with virtue.

. . . .

13 Since happiness is an activity of soul in accordance with perfect virtue, we must consider the nature of virtue; for perhaps we shall thus see better the nature of happiness. The true student of politics, too, is thought to have studied virtue above all things; for he wishes to make his fellow citizens good and obedient to the laws. As an example of this we have the lawgivers of the Cretans and the Spartans, and any others of the kind that there may have been. And if this inquiry belongs to political science, clearly the pursuit of it will be in accordance with our original plan. But clearly the virtue we must study is human virtue; for the good we were seeking was human good and the happiness human happiness. By human virtue we mean not that of the body but that of the soul; and happiness also we call an activity of soul. But if this is so, clearly the student of politics must know somehow the facts about soul, as the man who is to heal the eyes or the body as a whole must know about the eyes or the body; and all the more since politics is more prized and better than medicine; but even among doctors the best educated spend much labour on acquiring knowledge of the body. The student of politics, then, must study the soul, and must study it with these objects in view, and do so just to the extent which is sufficient for the questions we are discussing; for further precision is perhaps something more laborious than our purposes require.

Some things are said about it, adequately enough, even in the discussions outside our school, and we must use these; e.g. that one element in the soul is

irrational and one has a rational principle. Whether these are separated as the parts of the body or of anything divisible are, or are distinct by definition but by nature inseparable, like convex and concave in the circumference of a circle, does not affect the present question.

Of the irrational element one division seems to be widely distributed, and vegetative in its nature, I mean that which causes nutrition and growth; for it is this kind of power of the soul that one must assign to all nurslings and to embryos, and this same power 1102^b to full-grown creatures; this is more reasonable than to assign some different power to them. Now the excellence of this seems to be common to all species and not specifically human; for this part or faculty seems to function most in sleep, while goodness and badness are least manifest in sleep (whence comes the saying that the happy are no better off than the wretched for half their lives; and this happens naturally enough, since sleep is an inactivity of the soul in that respect in which it is called good or bad), unless perhaps to a small extent some of the movements actually penetrate to the soul, and in this respect the dreams of good men are better than those of ordinary people. Enough of this subject, however; let us leave the nutritive faculty, alone, since it has by its nature no share in human excellence.

There seems to be also another irrational element in the soul—one which in a sense, however, shares in a rational principle. For we praise the rational principle of the continent man and of the incontinent, and the part of their soul that has such a principle, since it urges them aright and towards the best objects; but there is found in them also another element naturally opposed to the rational principle, which fights against and resists that principle. For exactly as paralysed limbs when we intend to move them to the right turn on the contrary to the left, so is it with the soul; the impulses of incontinent people move in contrary directions. But while in the body we see that which moves astray, in the soul we do not. No doubt, however, we must none the less suppose that in the soul too there is something contrary to the rational principle, resisting and opposing it. In what sense it is distinct from the other elements does not concern us. Now even this seems to have a share in a rational principle, as we said; at any rate in the continent man it obeys the rational principle—and presumably in the temperate and brave man it is still more obedient; for in him it speaks, on all matters, with the same voice as the rational principle.

Therefore the irrational element also appears to be twofold. For the vegetative element in no way shares in a rational principle, but the appetitive and in general the desiring element in a sense shares in it, in so far as it listens to and obeys it; this is the sense in which we speak of "taking account" of one's father or one's friends, not that in which we speak of "accounting" for a mathematical property. That the irrational element is in some sense persuaded by a rational principle is indicated also by the giving of 1103ᵃ advice and by all reproof and exhortation. And if this element also must be said to have a rational principle, that which has a rational principle (as well as that which has not) will be twofold, one subdivision having it in the strict sense and in itself, and the other having a tendency to obey as one does one's father.

Virtue too is distinguished into kinds in accordance with this difference; for we say that some of the virtues are intellectual and others moral, philosophic wisdom and understanding and practical wisdom being intellectual, liberality and temperance moral. For in speaking about a man's character we do not say that he is wise or has understanding but that he is good-tempered or temperate; yet we praise the wise man also with respect to his state of mind; and of states of mind we call those which merit praise virtues.

Book II

1 Virtue, then, being of two kinds, intellectual and moral, intellectual virtue in the main owes both its birth and its growth to teaching (for which reason it requires experience and time), while moral virtue comes about as a result of habit, whence also its name ($\mathring{\eta}\theta\iota\kappa\mathring{\eta}$) is one that is formed by a slight variation from the word $\check{\epsilon}\theta o\varsigma$ (habit). From this it is also plain that none of the moral virtues arises in us by nature; for nothing that exists by nature can form a habit contrary to its nature. For instance the stone

which by nature moves downwards cannot be habituated to move upwards, not even if one tries to train it by throwing it up ten thousand times; nor can fire be habituated to move downwards, nor can anything else that by nature behaves in one way be trained to behave in another. Neither by nature, then, nor contrary to nature do the virtues arise in us; rather we are adapted by nature to receive them, and are made perfect by habit.

Again, of all the things that come to us by nature we first acquire the potentiality and later exhibit the activity (this is plain in the case of the senses; for it was not by often seeing or often hearing that we got these senses, but on the contrary we had them before we used them, and did not come to have them by using them); but the virtues we get by first exercising them, as also happens in the case of the arts as well. For the things we have to learn before we can do them, we learn by doing them, e.g. men become builders by building and lyre-players by playing the lyre; so too we become just by doing just acts, temperate by doing temperate acts, brave by doing brave acts.

This is confirmed by what happens in states; for 1103ᵇ legislators make the citizens good by forming habits in them, and this is the wish of every legislator, and those who do not effect it miss their mark, and it is in this that a good constitution differs from a bad one.

Again, it is from the same causes and by the same means that every virtue is both produced and destroyed, and similarly every art; for it is from playing the lyre that both good and bad lyre-players are produced. And the corresponding statement is true of builders and of all the rest; men will be good or bad builders as a result of building well or badly. For if this were not so, there would have been no need of a teacher, but all men would have been born good or bad at their craft. This, then, is the case with the virtues also; by doing the acts that we do in our transactions with other men we become just or unjust, and by doing the acts that we do in the presence of danger, and being habituated to feel fear or confidence, we become brave or cowardly. The same is true of appetites and feelings of anger; some men become temperature and good-tempered, others self-indulgent and irascible, by behaving in one way or the other in the appropriate circumstances. Thus, in one word, states of character arise out of like activities. This is why the activities we exhibit must be of a certain kind; it is because the states of character correspond to the differences between these. It makes no small difference, then, whether we form habits of one kind or of another from our very youth; it makes a very great difference, or rather *all* the difference.

2   Since, then, the present inquiry does not aim at theoretical knowledge like the others (for we are inquiring not in order to know what virtue is, but in order to become good, since otherwise our inquiry would have been of no use), we must examine the nature of actions, namely how we ought to do them; for these determine also the nature of the states of character that are produced, as we have said. Now, that we must act according to the right rule is a common principle and must be assumed—it will be discussed later, i.e. both what the right rule is, and how it is re-

1104ᵃ lated to the other virtues. But this must be agreed upon beforehand, that the whole account of matters of conduct must be given in outline and not precisely, as we said at the very beginning that the accounts we demand must be in accordance with the subject-matter; matters concerned with conduct and questions of what is good for us have no fixity, any more than matters of health. The general account being of this nature, the account of particular cases is yet more lacking in exactness; for they do not fall under any art or precept but the agents themselves must in each case consider what is appropriate to the occasion, as happens also in the art of medicine or of navigation.

But though our present account is of this nature we must give what help we can. First, then, let us consider this, that it is the nature of such things to be destroyed by defect and excess, as we see in the case of strength and of health (for to gain light on things imperceptible we must use the evidence of sensible things); both excessive and defective exercise destroys the strength, and similarly drink or food which is above or below a certain amount destroys the health, while that which is proportionate both produces and increases and preserves it. So too is it, then, in the case of temperance and courage and the other virtues. For the man who flies from and fears everything and does not stand his ground against anything becomes a coward, and the man who fears nothing at all but goes to meet every danger becomes rash; and similarly the man who indulges in every pleasure and abstains from none becomes self-indulgent, while the man who shuns every pleasure, as boors do, becomes in a way insensible; temperance and courage, then, are destroyed by excess and defect, and preserved by the mean.

But not only are the sources and causes of their origination and growth the same as those of their destruction, but also the sphere of their actualization will be the same; for this is also true of the things which are more evident to sense, e.g. of strength; it is produced by taking much food and undergoing much exertion, and it is the strong man that will be most able to do these things. So too is it with the virtues; by abstaining from pleasures we become temperate, and it is when we have become so that we are most able to abstain from them; and similarly too in the case of courage; for by being habit- 1104ᵇ uated to despise things that are terrible and to stand our ground against them we become brave, and it is when we have become so that we shall be most able to stand our ground against them.

We must take as a sign of states of character the 3 pleasure or pain that ensues on acts; for the man who abstains from bodily pleasures and delights in this very fact is temperate, while the man who is annoyed at it is self-indulgent, and he who stands his ground against things that are terrible and delights in this or at least is not pained is brave, while the man who is pained is a coward. For moral excellence is concerned with pleasures and pains; it is on account of the pain that we abstain from noble ones. Hence we ought to have been brought up in a particular way from our very youth, as Plato says, so as both to delight in and to be pained by the things that we ought; for this is the right education.

Again, if the virtues are concerned with actions and passions, every passion and every action is accompanied by pleasure and pain, for this reason also virtue will be concerned with pleasures and pains. This is indicated also by the fact that punishment is inflicted by these means; for it is a kind of cure, and it is the nature of cures to be effected by contraries.

Again, as we said but lately, every state of soul has a nature relative to and concerned with the kind of things by which it tends to be made worse or better; but it is by reason of pleasures and pains that men become bad, by pursuing and avoiding these—either the pleasures and pains they ought not or when they ought not or as they ought not, or by going wrong in one of the other similar ways that may be distinguished. Hence men even define the virtues as certain states of impassivity and rest; not well, however, because they speak absolutely, and do not say "as one ought" and "as one ought not" and "when one ought or ought not," and the other things that may be added. We assume, then, that this kind of excellence tends to do what is best with regard to pleasures and pains, and vice does the contrary.

The following facts also may show us that virtue and vice are concerned with these same things. There being three objects of choice and three of avoidance, the noble, the advantageous, the pleasant, and their contraries, the base, the injurious, the painful, about all of these the good man tends to go right and the bad man to go wrong, and especially about pleasure; for this is common to the animals, and also it accompanies all objects of choice; for even the noble and the advantageous appear pleasant.

1105ᵃ Again, it has grown up with us all from our infancy; this is why it is difficult to rub off this passion, engrained as it is in our life. And we measure even our actions, some of us more and others less, by the rule of pleasure and pain. For this reason, then, our whole inquiry must be about these; for to feel delight and pain rightly or wrongly has no small effect on our actions.

Again, it is harder to fight with pleasure than with anger, to use Heraclitus' phrase, but both art and virtue are always concerned with what is harder; for even the good is better when it is harder. Therefore for this reason also the whole concern both of virtue and of political science is with pleasures and pains; for the man who uses these well will be good, he who uses them badly bad.

That virtue, then, is concerned with pleasures and pains, and that by the acts from which it arises it is both increased and, if they are done differently, destroyed, and that the acts from which it arose are those in which it actualizes itself—let this be taken as said.

The question might be asked, what we mean by 4 saying that we must become just by doing just acts, and temperate by doing temperate acts; for if men do just and temperate acts, they are already just and temperate, exactly as, if they do what is in accordance with the laws of grammar and of music, they are grammarians and musicians.

Or is this not true even of the arts? It is possible to do something that is in accordance with the laws of grammar, either by chance or at the suggestion of another. A man will be a grammarian, then, only when he has both done something grammatical and done it grammatically; and this means doing it in accordance with the grammatical knowledge in himself.

Again, the case of the arts and that of the virtues are not similar; for the products of the arts have their goodness in themselves, so that it is enough that they should have a certain character, but if the acts that are in accordance with the virtues have themselves a certain character it does not follow that they are done justly or temperately. The agent also must be in a certain condition when he does them; if the first place he must have knowledge, secondly he must choose the acts, and choose them for their own sakes, and thirdly his action must proceed from a firm and unchangeable character. These are not reckoned in 1105ᵇ as conditions of the possession of the arts, except the bare knowledge; but as a condition on the possession of the virtues knowledge has little or no weight, while the other conditions count not for a little but for everything, i.e. the very conditions which result from often doing just and temperate acts.

Actions, then, are called just and temperate when they are such as the just or the temperate man would do; but it is not the man who does these that is just and temperate, but the man who also does them *as* just and temperate men do them. It is well said, then, that it is by doing just acts that the just man is produced, and by doing temperate acts the temperate man; without doing these no one would have even a prospect of becoming good.

But most people do not do these, but take refuge in theory and think they are being philosophers and will become good in this way, behaving somewhat like patients who listen attentively to their doctors, but do none of the things they are ordered to do. As the latter will not be made well in body by such a course of treatment, the former will not be made well in soul by such a course of philosophy.

5   Next we must consider what virtue is. Since things that are found in the soul are of three kinds—passions, faculties, states of character, virtue must be one of these. By passions I mean appetite, anger, fear, confidence, envy, joy, friendly feeling, hatred, longing, emulation, pity, and in general the feelings that are accompanied by pleasure or pain; by faculties the things in virtue of which we are said to be capable of feeling these, e.g. of becoming angry or being pained or feeling pity; by states of character the things in virtue of which we stand well or badly with reference to the passions, e.g. with reference to anger we stand badly if we feel it violently or too weakly, and well if we feel it moderately; and similarly with reference to the other passions.

Now neither the virtues nor the vices are *passions*, because we are not called good or bad on the ground of our passions, but are so called on the ground of our virtues and our vices, and because we are neither praised nor blamed for our passions (for the man who feels fear or anger is not praised, nor is the man who simply feels anger blamed, but the man who feels it in a certain way), but for our virtues and our vices we *are* praised or blamed.

1106ᵃ   Again, we feel anger and fear without choice, but the virtues are modes of choice or involve choice. Further, in respect of the passions we are said to be moved, but in respect of the virtues and the vices we are said not to be moved but to be disposed in a particular way.

For these reasons also they are not *faculties*: for we are neither called good nor bad, nor praised nor blamed, for the simple capacity of feeling the passions; again, we have the faculties by nature, but we are not made good or bad by nature; we have spoken of this before.

If, then, the virtues are neither passions nor faculties, all that remains is that they should be *states of character*.

Thus we have stated what virtue is in respect of its genus.

6   We must, however, not only describe virtue as a state of character, but also say what sort of state it is. We may remark, then, that every virtue or excellence both brings into good condition the thing of which it is the excellence and makes the work of that thing be done well; e.g. the excellence of the eye makes both the eye and its work good; for it is by the excellence of the eye that we see well. Similarly the excellence of the horse makes a horse both good in itself and good at running and at carrying its rider and at awaiting the attack of the enemy. Therefore, if this is true in every case, the virtue of man also will be the state of character which makes a man good and which makes him do his own work well.

How this is to happen we have stated already, but it will be made plain also by the following consideration of the specific nature of virtue. In everything that is continuous and divisible it is possible to take more, less, or an equal amount, and that either in terms of the thing itself or relatively to us; and the equal is an intermediate between excess and defect. By the intermediate in the object I mean that which is equidistant from each of the extremes, which is one and the same for all men; by the intermediate relatively to us that which is neither too much nor too little—and this is not one, nor the same for all. For instance, if ten is many and two is few, six is the intermediate, taken in terms of the object; for it exceeds and is exceeded by an equal amount; this is intermediate according to arithmetical proportion. But the intermediate relatively to us is not to be taken so; if ten pounds are too much 1106ᵇ for a particular person to eat and two too little, it does not follow that the trainer will order six pounds; for this also is perhaps too much for the person who is to take it, or too little—too little for Milo, too much for the beginner in athletic exercises. The same is true of running and wrestling. Thus a master of any art avoids excess and defect, but seeks the intermediate and chooses this—the intermediate not in the object but relatively to us.

If it is thus, then, that every art does its work well—by looking to the intermediate and judging its works by this standard (so that we often say of good works of art that it is not possible either to take away or to add anything, implying that excess and defect destroy the goodness of works of art, while the mean preserves it; and good artists, as we say, look to this in their work), and if, further, virtue is more exact and better than any art, as nature also is, then virtue must have the quality of aiming at the intermediate. I mean moral virtue; for it is this that is concerned with passions and actions, and in these there is excess, defect, and the intermediate. For instance, both fear and confidence and appetite and anger and pity and in general pleasure and pain may be felt both too much and too little, and in both cases not well; but to feel them at the right times, with reference to the right objects, towards the right people, with the right motive, and in the right way, is what is both intermediate and best, and this is characteristic of virtue. Similarly with regard to actions also there is excess, defect, and the intermediate. Now virtue is concerned with passions and actions, in which excess is a form of failure, and so is defect, while the intermediate is praised and is a form of success; and being praised and being successful are both characteristics of virtue. Therefore virtue is a kind of mean, since, as we have seen, it aims at what is intermediate.

Again, it is possible to fail in many ways (for evil belongs to the class of the unlimited, as the Pythagoreans conjectured, and good to that of the limited), while to succeed is possible only in one way (for which reason also one is easy and the other difficult—to miss the mark easy, to hit it difficult); for these reasons also, then, excess and defect are characteristic of vice, and the mean of virtue;

For men are good in but one way, but bad in many.

1107ª   Virtue, then, is a state of character concerned with choice, lying in a mean, i.e., the mean relative to us, this being determined by a rational principle, and by that principle by which the man of practical wisdom would determine it. Now it is a mean between two vices, that which depends on excess and that which depends on defect; and again it is a mean because the vices respectively fall short of or exceed what is right in both passions and actions, while virtue both finds and chooses that which is intermediate. Hence in respect of its substance and the definition which states its essence virtue is a mean, with regard to what is best and right an extreme.

But not every action nor every passion admits of a mean; for some have names that already imply badness, e.g. spite, shamelessness, envy, and in the case of actions adultery, theft, murder; for all of these and suchlike things imply by their names that they are themselves bad, and not the excesses or deficiencies of them. It is not possible, then, ever to be right with regard to them; one must always be wrong. Nor does goodness or badness with regard to such things depend on committing adultery with the right woman, at the right time, and in the right way, but simply to do any of them is to go wrong. It would be equally absurd, then, to expect that in unjust, cowardly, and voluptuous action there should be a mean, an excess, and a deficiency; for at that rate there would be a mean of excess and of deficiency, an excess of excess, and a deficiency of deficiency. But as there is no excess and deficiency of temperance and courage because what is intermediate is in a sense an extreme, so too of the actions we have mentioned there is no mean nor any excess and deficiency, but however they are done they are wrong; for in general there is neither a mean of excess and deficiency, nor excess and deficiency of a mean.

We must, however, not only make this general 7 statement, but also apply it to the individual facts. For among statements about conduct those which are general apply more widely, but those which are particular are more genuine, since conduct has to do with individual cases, and our statements must harmonize with the facts in these cases. We may take these cases from our table. With regard to feelings 1107ᵇ of fear and confidence courage is the mean; of the people who exceed, he who exceeds in fearlessness has no name (many of the states have no name), while the man who exceeds in confidence is rash, and he who exceeds in fear and falls short in confidence is a coward. With regard to pleasures and pains—not all of them, and not so much with regard to the pains—the mean is temperance, the excess self-indulgence. Persons deficient with regard to the pleasures are not often found; hence such persons also have received no name. But let us call them "insensible."

With regard to giving and taking of money the mean is liberality, the excess and the defect prodigality and meanness. In these actions people exceed and fall short in contrary ways; the prodigal exceeds in spending and falls short in taking, while the mean man exceeds in taking and falls short in spending. . . . With regard to money there are also other dispositions—a mean, magnificence (for the magnificent man differs from the liberal man; the former deals with large sums, the latter with small ones), an excess, tastelessness and vulgarity, and a deficiency, niggardliness; these differ from the states opposed to liberality. . . .

With regard to honour and dishonor the mean is proper pride, the excess is known as a sort of "empty vanity," and the deficiency is undue humility; and as we said liberality was related to magnificence, differing from it by dealing with small sums, so there is a state similarly related to proper pride, being concerned with small honours while that is concerned with great. For it is possible to desire honour as one ought, and more than one ought, and less, and the man who exceeds in his desires is called ambitious, the man who falls short unambitious, while the intermediate person has no name. The dispositions also are nameless, except that that of the ambitious man is called ambition. Hence the people who are at the extremes lay claim to the middle place; and we ourselves sometimes call the intermediate person ambitious and sometimes unambitious, and sometimes praise the ambitious man and sometimes the unambitious. . . . [N]ow let us speak of the remaining states according to the method which has been indicated.

1108ᵃ With regard to anger also there is an excess, a deficiency, and a mean. Although they can scarcely be said to have names, yet since we call the intermediate person good-tempered let us call the mean good temper; of the persons at the extremes let the one who exceeds be called irascible, and his vice irascibility, and the man who falls short an inirascible sort of person, and the deficiency inirascibility.

There are also three other means, which have a certain likeness to one another, but differ from one another: for they are all concerned with intercourse in words and actions, but differ in that one is concerned with truth in this sphere, the other two with pleasantness; and of this one kind is exhibited in giving amusement, the other in all the circumstances of life. We must therefore speak of these too, that we may the better see that in all things the mean is praiseworthy, and the extremes neither praiseworthy nor right, but worthy of blame. Now most of these states also have no names, but we must try, as in the other cases, to invent names ourselves so that we may be clear and easy to follow. With regard to truth, then, the intermediate is a truthful sort of person and the mean may be called truthfulness, while the pretence which exaggerates is boastfulness and the person characterized by it a boaster, and that which understates is mock modesty and the person characterized by it mock-modest. With regard to pleasantness in the giving of amusement the intermediate person is ready-witted and the disposition ready wit, the excess is buffoonery and the person characterized by it a buffoon, while the man who falls short is a sort of boor and his state is boorishness. With regard to the remaining kind of pleasantness, that which is exhibited in life in general, the man who is pleasant in the right way is friendly and the mean is friendliness, while the man who exceeds is an obsequious person if he has no end in view, a flatterer if he is aiming at his own advantage, and the man who falls short and is unpleasant in all circumstances is a quarrelsome and surly sort of person.

There are also means in the passions and concerned with the passions; since shame is not a virtue, and yet praise is extended to the modest man. For even in these matters one man is said to be intermediate, and another to exceed, as for instance the bashful man who is ashamed of everything; while he who falls short or is not ashamed of anything at all is shameless, and the intermediate person is modest. Righteous indignation is a mean between envy and spite, and these states are concerned 1108ᵇ with the pain and pleasure that are felt at the fortunes of our neighbours; the man who is characterized by righteous indignation is pained at undeserved good fortune, the envious man, going beyond him, is pained at all good fortune, and the spiteful man falls so far short of being pained that he even rejoices. . . .

There are three kinds of disposition, then, two of 8 them vices, involving excess and deficiency respectively, and one a virtue, viz. the mean, and all are in a sense opposed to all; for the extreme states are contrary both to the intermediate state and to each other, and the intermediate to the extremes; as the equal is greater relatively to the less, less relatively to the greater, so the middle states are excessive relatively to the deficiencies, deficient relatively to the excesses, both in passions and in actions. For the brave man appears rash relatively to the coward, and cowardly relatively to the rash man; and similarly the temperate man appears self-indulgent relatively to the insensible man, insensible relatively to the self-indulgent, and the liberal man prodigal relatively to the mean man, mean relatively to the prodigal. Hence also the people at the extremes push the intermediate man each over to the other, and the brave man is called rash by the coward, cowardly by the rash man, and correspondingly in the other cases.

These states being thus opposed to one another, the greatest contrariety is that of the extremes to each other, rather than to the intermediate; for these are further from each other than from the intermediate, as the great is further from the small and the small from the great than both are from the equal. Again, to the intermediate some extremes show a certain likeness, as that of rashness to courage and that of prodigality to liberality; but the extremes show the greatest unlikeness to each other; now contraries are defined as the things that are furthest from each other, so that things that are further apart are more contrary.

1109ᵃ   To the mean in some cases the deficiency, in some the excess is more opposed; e.g. it is not rashness, which is an excess, but cowardice, which is a deficiency, that is more opposed to courage, and not insensibility, which is a deficiency, but self-indulgence, which is an excess, that is more opposed to temperance. This happens from two reasons, one being drawn from the thing itself; for because one extreme is nearer and liker to the intermediate, we oppose not this but rather its contrary to the intermediate. E.g., since rashness is thought liker and nearer to courage, and cowardice more unlike, we oppose rather the latter to courage; for things that are further from the intermediate are thought more contrary to it. This, then, is one cause, drawn from the thing itself; another is drawn from ourselves; for the things to which we ourselves more naturally tend seem more contrary to the intermediate. For instance, we ourselves tend more naturally to pleasures, and hence are more easily carried towards self-indulgence than toward propriety. We describe as contrary to the mean, then, rather the directions in which we more often go to great lengths; and therefore self-indulgence, which is an excess, is the more contrary to temperance.

That moral virtue is a mean, then, and in what 9 sense it is so, and that it is a mean between two vices, the one involving excess, the other deficiency, and that it is such because its character is to aim at what is intermediate in passions and in actions, has been sufficiently stated. Hence also it is no easy task to be good. For in everything it is no easy task to find the middle, e.g. to find the middle of a circle is not for every one but for him who knows; so, too, any one can get angry—that is easy—or to give or spend money; but to do this to the right person, to the right extent, at the right time, with the right motive, and in the right way, *that* is not for every one, nor is it easy; wherefore goodness is both rare and laudable and noble.

Hence he who aims at the intermediate must first depart from what is the more contrary to it, as Calypso advises—

Hold the ship out beyond that surf and spray.

For of the extremes one is more erroneous, one less so; therefore, since to hit the mean is hard in the extreme, we must as a second best, as people say, take the least of the evils; and this will be done best in the way we describe.

But we must consider the things towards which 1109ᵇ we ourselves also are easily carried away; for some of us tend to one thing, some to another; and this will be recognizable from the pleasure and the pain we feel. We must drag ourselves away to the contrary extreme; for we shall get into the intermediate state by drawing well away from error, as people do in straightening sticks that are bent.

Now in everything the pleasant or pleasure is most to be guarded against; for we do not judge it impartially. We ought, then, to feel towards pleasure as the elders of the people felt towards Helen, and in all circumstances repeat their saying; for if we dismiss pleasure thus we are less likely to go astray. It is by doing this, then, (to sum the matter up) that we shall best be able to hit the mean.

But this is no doubt difficult, and especially in individual cases; for it is not easy to determine both how and with whom and on what provocation and how long one should be angry; for we too sometimes praise those who fall short and call them good-tempered, but sometimes we praise those who get angry and call them manly. The man, however, who deviates little from goodness is not blamed, whether he do so in the direction of the more or of the less, but only the man who deviates more widely; for *he* does not fail to be noticed. But up to what point and to what extent a man must deviate before he becomes blameworthy it is not easy to determine by reasoning, any more than anything else that is perceived by the senses; such things depend on particular facts, and the decision rests with perception. So much, then, is plain, that the intermediate state is in all things to be praised, but that we must incline sometimes towards the excess, sometimes towards the deficiency; for so shall we most easily hit the mean and what is right.

· · · · · · · ·

Book X

7 If happiness is activity in accordance with virtue, it is reasonable that it should be in accordance with the highest virtue; and this will be that of the best thing in us. Whether it be reason or something else that is this element which is thought to be our natural ruler and guide and to take thought of things noble and divine, whether it be itself also divine or only the most divine element in us, the activity of this in accordance with its proper virtue will be perfect happiness. That this activity is contemplative we have already said.

Now this would seem to be in agreement both with what we said before and with the truth. For, firstly, this activity is the best (since not only is reason the best thing in us, but the objects of reason are the best of knowable objects); and, secondly, it is the most continuous, since we can contemplate truth more continuously than we can *do* anything. And we think happiness has pleasure mingled with it, but the activity of philosophic wisdom is admittedly the pleasantest of virtuous activities; at all events the pursuit of it is thought to offer pleasures marvellous

for their purity and their enduringness, and it is to be expected that those who know will pass their time more pleasantly than those who inquire. And the self-sufficiency that is spoken of must belong most to the contemplative activity. For while a philosopher, as well as a just man or one possessing any other virtue, needs the necessaries of life, when they are sufficiently equipped with things of that sort the just man needs people towards whom and with whom he shall act justly, and the temperate man, the brave man, and each of the others is in the same case, but the philosopher, even when by himself, can contemplate truth, and the better the wiser he is; he can perhaps do so better if he has fellow-workers, but still he is the most self-sufficient. And this activity alone would seem to be loved for its own sake; for nothing arises from it apart from the contemplating, while from practical activities we gain more or less apart from the action. And happiness is thought to depend on leisure; for we are busy that we may have leisure, and make war that we may live in peace. Now the activity of the practical virtues is exhibited in political or military affairs, but the actions concerned with these seem to be unleisurely. Warlike actions are completely so (for no one chooses to be at war, or provokes war, for the sake of being at war; any one would seem absolutely murderous if he were to make enemies of his friends in order to bring about battle and slaughter); but the action of the statesman is also unleisurely, and—apart from the political action itself—aims at despotic power and honours, or at all events happiness, for him and his fellow citizens—a happiness different from political action, and evidently sought as being different. So if among virtuous actions political and military actions are distinguished by nobility and greatness, and these are unleisurely and aim at an end and are not desirable for their own sake, but the activity of reason, which is contemplative, seems both to be superior in serious worth and to aim at no end beyond itself, and to have its pleasure proper to itself (and this augments the activity), and the self-sufficiency, leisureliness, unweariedness (so far as this is possible for man), and all the other attributes ascribed to the supremely happy man are evidently those connected with this activity, it follows that this will be the complete happiness of man,

1177^b

if it be allowed a complete term of life (for none of the attributes of happiness is *in*complete).

But such a life would be too high for man; for it is not in so far as he is man that he will live so, but in so far as something divine is present in him; and by so much as this is superior to our composite nature is its activity superior to that which is the exercise of the other kind of virtue. If reason is divine, then, in comparison with man, the life according to it is divine in comparison with human life. But we must not follow those who advise us, being men, to think of human things, and, being mortal, of mortal things, but must, so far as we can, make ourselves immortal, and strain every nerve to live in accordance with the best thing in us; for even if it be small 1178ᵃ in bulk, much more does it in power and worth surpass everything. This would seem, too, to be each man himself, since it is the authoritative and better part of him. It would be strange, then, if he were to choose not the life of his self but that of something else . . . [T]hat which is proper to each thing is by nature best and most pleasant for each thing; for man, therefore, the life according to reason is best and pleasantest, since reason more than anything else *is* man. This life therefore is also the happiest.

8   But in a secondary degree the life in accordance with the other kind of virtue is happy; for the activities in accordance with this befit our human estate. Just and brave acts, and other virtuous acts, we do in relation to each other, observing our respective duties with regard to contracts and services and all manner of actions and with regard to passions; and all of these seem to be typically human. Some of them seem even to arise from the body, and virtue of character to be in many ways bound up with the passions. Practical wisdom, too, is linked to virtue of character, and this to practical wisdom, since the principles of practical wisdom are in accordance with the moral virtues and rightness in morals is in accordance with practical wisdom. Being connected with the passions also, the moral virtues must belong to our composite nature; and the virtues of our composite nature are human; so, therefore, are the life and the happiness which correspond to these. The excellence of the reason is a thing apart; we must be content to say this much about it, for to describe it precisely is a task

greater than our purpose requires. It would seem, however, also to need external equipment but little, or less than moral virtue does. Grant that both need the necessaries, and do so equally, even if the statesman's work is the more concerned with the body and things of that sort; for there will be little difference there; but in what they need for the exercise of their activities there will be much difference. The liberal man will need money for the doing of his liberal deeds, and the just man too will need it for the returning of services (for wishes are hard to discern, and even people who are not just pretend to wish to act justly); and the brave man will need power if he is to accomplish any of the acts that correspond to his virtue, and the temperate man will need opportunity; for how else is either he or any of the others to be recognized? It is debated, too, whether the will or the deed is more essential to virtue, which is assumed to involve both; it is surely clear that its perfection involves both; but for deeds many things are 1178ᵇ needed, and more, the greater and nobler the deeds are. But the man who is contemplating the truth needs no such thing, at least with a view to the exercise of his activity; indeed they are, one may say, even hindrances, at all events to his contemplation; but in so far as he is a man and lives with a number of people, he chooses to do virtuous acts; he will therefore need such aids to living a human life.

But that perfect happiness is a contemplative activity will appear from the following consideration as well. We assume the gods to be above all other beings blessed and happy; but what sort of actions must we assign to them? Acts of justice? Will not the gods seem absurd if they make contracts and return deposits, and so on? Acts of a brave man, then, confronting dangers and running risks because it is noble to do so? Or liberal acts? To whom will they give? It will be strange if they are really to have money or anything of the kind. And what would their temperate acts be? Is not such praise tasteless, since they have no bad appetites? If we were to run through them all, the circumstances of action would be found trivial and unworthy of gods. Still, every one supposes that they *live* and therefore that they are active; we cannot suppose them to sleep like Endymion. Now if you take away from a living being action, and still more production, what is left but contemplation? Therefore the activity of God, which surpasses all others in blessedness, must be contemplative; and of human activities, therefore, that which is most akin to this must be most of the nature of happiness.

This is indicated, too, by the fact that the other animals have no share in happiness, being completely deprived of such activity. For while the whole life of the gods is blessed, and that of men too in so far as some likeness of such activity belongs to them, none of the other animals is happy, since they in no way share in contemplation. Happiness extends, then, just so far as contemplation does, and those to whom contemplation more fully belongs are more truly happy, not as a mere concomitant but in virtue of the contemplation; for this is in itself precious. Happiness, therefore, must be some form of contemplation.

But, being a man, one will also need external prosperity; for our nature is not self-sufficient for the purpose of contemplation, but our body also 1179ᵃ must be healthy and must have food and other attention. Still, we must not think that the man who is to be happy will need many things or great things, merely because he cannot be supremely happy without external goods; for self-sufficiency and action do not involve excess, and we can do noble acts without ruling earth and sea; for even with moderate advantages one can act virtuously (this is manifest enough; for private persons are thought to do worthy acts no less than despots—indeed even more); and it is enough that we should have so much as that; for the life of the man who is active in accor-

dance with virtue will be happy. Solon, too, was perhaps sketching well the happy man when he described him as moderately furnished with externals but as having done (as Solon thought) the noblest acts, and lived temperately; for one can with but moderate possessions do what one ought. Anaxagoras also seems to have supposed the happy man not to be rich nor a despot, when he said that he would not be surprised if the happy man were to seem to most people a strange person; for they judge by externals, since these are all they perceive. The opinions of the wise seem, then, to harmonize with our arguments. But while even such things carry some conviction, the truth in practical matters is discerned from the facts of life; for these are the decisive factor. We must therefore survey what we have already said, bringing it to the test of the facts of life, and if it harmonizes with the facts we must accept it, but if it clashes with them we must suppose it to be mere theory. Now he who exercises his reason and cultivates it seems to be both in the best state of mind and most dear to the gods. For if the gods have any care for human affairs, as they are thought to have, it would be reasonable both that they should delight in that which was best and most akin to them (i.e. reason) and that they should reward those who love and honour this most, as caring for the things that are dear to them and acting both rightly and nobly. And that all these attributes belong most of all to the philosopher is manifest. He, therefore, is the dearest to the gods. And he who is that will presumably be also the happiest; so that in this way too the philosopher will more than any other be happy.

Aristotle on Eudaimonia

THOMAS NAGEL

—•—

THE *NICOMACHEAN ETHICS* EX-
hibits indecision between two accounts of *eudaimonia*—a comprehensive and an intellectualist account. According to the intellectualist
account, stated in Book X Chap. 7, *eudaimonia* is realized in the activity of the most divine part of man,
functioning in accordance with its proper excellence. This is the activity of theoretical contemplation. According to the comprehensive account (described as "secondary" at 1178 a 9), *eudaimonia*
essentially involves not just the activity of the theoretical intellect, but the full range of human life and
action, in accordance with the broader excellences
of moral virtue and practical wisdom. This view
connects *eudaimonia* with the conception of human
nature as composite, i.e. as involving the interaction
of reason, emotion, perception, and action in an ensouled body.

The *Eudemian Ethics* exhibits a similar indecision, less elaborately expressed. Most of the work expounds a comprehensive account, but the following
passage appears at its close:

> Therefore whatever mode of choosing and of ac-
> quiring things good by nature—whether goods of
> body or wealth or friends or the other goods—will
> best promote the contemplation of God, that is the
> best mode, and that standard is the finest; and any
> mode of choice and acquisition that either through
> deficiency or excess hinders us from serving and

from contemplating God—that is a bad one. This
is how it is for the soul, and this is the soul's best
standard—to be as far as possible unconscious of
the irrational part of the soul, as such. (1249 b 17–24)

Although this passage is admittedly somewhat isolated, it seems to support the conclusion that
Aristotle was tempted by an intellectualist (or perhaps spiritualist) account of the ends of life in the
Eudemian Ethics. In fact, considering the emphasis
on the divine element in our nature at the end of
the *Nicomachean Ethics* (1178 b 7–33), it does not
seem out of line to bring God into the matter at the
end of the *Eudemian*. "Intellectualist" may be rather
too dry a term for the almost Augustinian sentiments which can be detected in both works.

Since the philosophical issue between these two
positions arises in virtue of the ambivalence of the
Nicomachean Ethics alone, I shall discuss it largely
in that setting. I shall also comment on the relation of this issue to the psychology of the *De
Anima*. There is a connection between intellectualist tendencies in the *Ethics* and Aristotle's view
of the relation between *nous* and the rest of the
soul. But the latter view appears to me to contain
as much indecision as the former. It is because he
is not sure who we are that Aristotle finds it difficult to say unequivocally in what our *eudaimonia* consists, and how the line is to be drawn between its constituents and its necessary conditions.
Moreover I shall argue that intellectualism has
strong defenses even without a two-substance theory of human beings.

Aristotle's program is compactly set out in NE I
7, beginning at 1097 b 22. If we are not to stop with
the truism that the supreme human good is *eudaimonia*, we must inquire into the *ergon* of man, since
if something has an *ergon*, that thing's good is a function of its *ergon*. The *ergon* of a thing, in general, is
what it does that makes it what it is. Not everything

From *Phronesis* 17. Copyright © 1972 by *Phronesis*. Reprinted
by permission of the publisher.

These remarks derive from comments on a paper by John M.
Cooper, "Intellectualism and Practical Reasoning in Aristotle's
Moral Philosophy," presented at a meeting of the Society for Ancient
Greek Philosophy, in New York, December 28, 1969. My research
was supported in part by the National Science Foundation.

has an *ergon*, for there are things to be which is not to do anything. But when something has an *ergon*, that thing's good is specified by it. The proper *ergon* of man, by which human excellence is measured, is that which makes him a man rather than anything else. Humans do a great many things, but since some are done equally well, or better, by plants, fish, and animals, they are not among the things to do which is to be human.

This lands us immediately in difficulty, for the inference seems unsound. If the feature of life unique to humans could exist in the absence of those features which humans share with the beasts, the result would be not a human being but something else. And why should we take the highest good of a rarefied individual like that as the ultimate end for complicated and messy individuals like ourselves? One would expect at the very least that the *interaction* between the function that differentiates us from animals, and the functions that we share with them, would play a role in the definition of *eudaimonia*. This would mean including the *practical* exercise of the rational faculty as well as the contemplative.

Suppose we pursue this line of criticism further, however, by asking whether we should not demand the inclusion of still more functions in the definition of human *ergon* and hence of human good. What about health, for example, or fertility? It will be objected that these fail to meet an essential condition for inclusion: the condition of autonomy.[1] This condition states that the fundamental elements of human good cannot be due simply to luck. And health, for example, can be the result of sheer good fortune, rather than a man's own efforts.

But the basis of this objection must be examined. It stems, presumably, from the condition that good is tied to *ergon* or functioning, and what simply *befalls* a thing, whether that thing be a man or a plant, is not an instance of its functioning or malfunctioning. Therefore if I contract cholera, the intrusion of the hostile bacilli is a calamity, but not a malfunction of mine, hence not to be weighed in counting me *eudaimon* or not. Its *effect* on me, however, is certainly a malfunction. And why should this purely physical malfunction not be *in itself* a deviation from my human well-being (rather than just because of its deleterious effects on the life of reason)? if it is

excluded on the ground that sweating, throwing up, and shuddering with fever are not things that *I do*, then the question has been begged. For the issue is precisely whether the account of what a person is and does should include or exclude the bodily functions that he shares with animals and even plants. If digesting, for instance, is something a clam does, why is it not something a human does as well—and something to do which is part of being human, even though it does not require *effort*?

In neither the *De Anima* nor the *Nicomachean Ethics* is the nutritive element excluded from the human soul, yet it is not one of the aspects of human functioning that Aristotle is willing to regard as a measure of *eudaimonia*. This position has considerable intuitive appeal. If we could see why nutrition is assigned such a low status, we might have a clue to the train of thought which tempts Aristotle to pare away everything except the intellect, till the only thing which intrinsically bears on *eudaimonia* is the quality of contemplative activity.[2]

Let me introduce a homely example. A combination corkscrew and bottle-opener has the function of removing corks and caps from bottles. This is a simple *ergon*, which allows us to evaluate the implement in terms of its capacity for successful performance. However, it does not seem simple enough to escape the question Aristotle has raised. It removes bottle-caps, to be sure. But since it has that function in common with any mere bottle-opener, *that* cannot be the special *ergon* (*to idion*) of our implement—the *ergon* by which its excellence is judged. So, by elimination, to idion must be removing corks. Unfortunately that is a capacity it shares with mere corkscrews, so that can't be part of its special *ergon* either. Obviously this argument is no good. The thing must have a simple conjunctive *ergon*, and its excellence is a function of both conjuncts.

Why won't such a reduction work for the case of the human soul and *eudaimonia*? We have dispensed with digestion and procreation on the ground that clams do it too. Sensation and desire are common to dogs. So we are left with reason. But the gods have reason without having these other capacities, so *that* isn't the peculiar *ergon* of man, either. Therefore we must abandon this method of arguing by elimination, and acknowledge that man has a conjunctive *ergon* which overlaps the *erga* of gods and dogs, as a combination corkscrew and bottle-opener combines the functions of corkscrews and bottle-openers. They just happen to find themselves in the same *ergon* box.

If this argument were correct, it would support not just a comprehensive position extending to non-intellectual areas of consciousness and activity, but the inclusion of all the lower life functions in the measure of human excellence. But in fact the conjunctive picture of the component capacities of the human soul is absurd, and if we can say why it is absurd, we may be able to understand why Aristotle accords to reason the title of *ergon idion* of man, despite the fact that it, like digestion, might be shared by other beings as well.

The operative idea is evidently that of a hierarchy of capacities. The life capacities of a complex organism are not all on a level: some serve to support others. This is not so easy to account for clearly. Take for example the prima facie subservience of nutrition to perception and locomotion. That might be a ground for denying that nutrition was part of the special *ergon* of a higher animal. But perception and locomotion e.g. in a giraffe, largely serve the ends of nutrition and reproduction, so the case is unclear. What is the point of being a giraffe? A giraffe leads a certain type of active life, supported by complex metabolic, digestive, and circulatory processes, and ordered in such a way as to permit those processes to proceed efficiently. One thing is clear: its walking and seeing and digesting are not simply three separate activities going on side by side in the same individual, like a doll that wets, cries, and closes its eyes. A giraffe is one organism and its functions are coherently organized. Its proper excellence is not just the conjunction of the special excellences of its component functions, but the optimal functioning of the total system in the giraffe's *life*. And the highest-level account of this will be concerned not with blood pressure and peristalsis but with activity—some of which, admittedly, helps to control blood pressure and provide material for peristalsis.

The main difference between a human being and a giraffe is that a human being has reason, and that his entire complex of organic functions supports rational as well as irrational activity. There is of course feedback as well: in humans, not only perception and locomotion, but also reason, is employed in the service of nutrition and reproduction. Reason is also involved in the control of perception, locomotion, and desire. Nevertheless the highest-level account of a human life puts all the other functions into a supportive position in relation to rational activity. And although reason helps us to get enough to eat and move around, it is not subservient to those lower functions. Occasionally it may have to serve as the janitor or pimp of the passions, but that is not basically what it is *for*. On one plausible view reason, despite its continual service to the lower functions, is what human life is all about. The lower functions serve it, provide it with a setting, and are to some extent under its control, but the dominant characterization of a human being must refer to his reason. This is why intellectualism tempts Aristotle, and why a conjunctive position, which lets various other aspects of life into the measure of good, is less plausible. Neither a conjunctive nor a disjunctive view about *eudaimonia* is adequate to these facts. The supreme good for man must be measured in terms of that around which all other human functions are organized.

But at this point it is essential to recall that much of the practical employment of reason is in the service of lower functions. Is this a proper exercise of that faculty, or does it have a point beyond the uses of cleverness, prudence, and courage, beyond the rational calculation of the most sensible way to spend one's time and money, or to organize society? This question prompts Aristotle to pass from the vague characterization that human life, as opposed to other life, is rational, to a consideration of the *objects* best suited for the exercise of this capacity. This is a peculiar question, which did not arise about giraffes. The nonrational activity of giraffes and its feedback on the metabolic functions seems at first sight a perfectly satisfactory model, and we might be tempted to apply it to humans. Why can't we reach a parallel account of proper human functioning by just adding reason to the top of the class of capacities that cooperate in an organized fashion to further the life of the individual? Why should there be any doubt that the use of reason to earn a living or procure food should belong to the central function of man?

The answer is as follows. Human possibilities reveal that reason has a use beyond the ordering of practical life. The circle of mutual support between reason, activity, and nutrition is not completely closed. In fact all of it, including the practical employment of reason, serves to support the individual for an activity that completely transcends these wordly concerns. The model of feedback does not work for the *ergon* of humans, because the best and purest employment of reason has nothing to do with daily life. Aristotle believes, in short, that human life is not important enough for humans to spend their lives on. A person should seek to transcend not only his individual practical concerns, but also those of society or humanity as a whole.

In *NE* VI 7, while arguing that *sophia* is the highest type of knowledge, and knowledge of the highest objects, he says (1141 a 21–23): "For it is absurd to think that Political Science or Prudence is the loftiest kind of knowledge, inasmuch as man is not the highest thing in the universe." Theoretical and practical matters must compete for the attention of the rational faculty; and the capacity which enables humans to concentrate on subjects more elevated than themselves at the same time spoils them for lowlier concerns. The imperfection of applications of reason to practical matters is that these applications make human life the primary object of rational attention, whereas with reason man has become the only creature capable of concentrating on what is higher than himself and thereby sharing in it to some extent. His time is, so to speak, too valuable to waste on anything so insignificant as human life.

This does not mean that there is no distinction between excellence and depravity in the practical domain. It is certainly better to exercise reason well in providing for one's needs and in dealing with others—i.e. to have moral virtue—than to exercise it badly. But this is essentially a caretaker function of reason, in which it is occupied with matters—i.e. the sordid details of the life of a complex person—far below those which it might be considering if it had more time and were less called upon merely to *manage*.

It is this point of view, I believe, which domi-nates Chapters 7 and 8 of Book X, where the intellectualist account of *eudaimonia* receives its strongest endorsement. Even there the possibility of doubt is acknowledged. Aristotle appears uncertain whether the result is to be described as a strictly human good. Having argued the claims of the contemplative life on a variety of grounds, he breaks in at 1177 b 27 with the remark that such a life would be higher than human. It is achieved not in virtue simply of being a man, but in virtue of something divine of which men partake. Nevertheless this divine element, which gives us the capacity to think about things higher than ourselves, is the highest aspect of our souls, and we are not justified in foregoing its activities to concentrate on lowlier matters, viz. our own lives, unless the demands in the latter area threaten to make contemplation impossible. As he says at 1177 b 33, we should not listen to those who urge that a human should think human thoughts and a mortal mortal ones. Rather we should cultivate that portion of our nature that promises to transcend the rest. If anyone insists that the rest belongs to a complete account of human life, then the view might be put, somewhat paradoxically, by saying that comprehensive human good isn't everything, and should not be the main human goal. We must identify with the highest part of ourselves rather than with the whole. The other functions, including the practical employment of reason itself, provide support for the highest form of activity, but do not enter into our proper excellence as primary component factors. This is because men are not simply the most complex species of animal, but possess as their essential nature a capacity to transcend themselves and become like gods. It is in virtue of this capacity that they are capable of *eudaimonia*, whereas animals are incapable of it, children have not achieved it, and certain adults, e.g. slaves, are prevented from reaching it.

Perhaps this is an unsatisfactory view of human nature and hence an unsatisfactory view of what it is for a human being to flourish. I believe it is a compelling position, however, and one that does not have to depend on a denial of the hylomorphic doctrine of the soul. It might be challenged in either of two ways. One might simply deny that the *ergon* of man is single, and allege that it is a collection of sub-

erga without orderings of priority and support—like those of a manybladed knife. This leaves us uncertain how to draw the line against good digestion as a component of *eudaimonia* (rather than just as a contribution to it.) A second method would be to preserve the assumption that the *ergon* of man is one, but to offer a different account of its organization, according to which the highest-level specification of human capacities was not just intellectual but involved both theoretical and practical concerns. While this seems to me the most promising line of attack, I shall not pursue it here.

NOTES

1. Cooper is responsible for pointing out the importance of this condition. His paper cites three textual statements of it: *EE* 1215 a 12–19, *NE* 1099 b 18–25, and most explicitly *Politics* 1323 b 24–29.
2. This conclusion would require explanation even if a two-substance reading of the *Ethics* were correct. That is, even if the psychology of the *Nicomachean Ethics* included a soul composed of both a form or

primary actuality of the body and a pure intellect which was distinct from this, we would still have to ask why the proper function of the hylomorphic section was not counted in the assessment of *eudaimonia*. And I suspect that any account which made sense of the restriction in light of the two-substance theory, could be applied with equal success to justify corresponding restrictions on what counts toward *eudaimonia* on a purely hylomorphic theory of persons, where *nous*, instead of being another soul, was just the highest type of first-order actuality in the complex—distinguishable only in thought from the other parts of the soul, and not really *distinct* from them. That Aristotle shares this view is shown by a parenthetical remark in *NE* I 13, where he is considering which part of the soul possesses the excellence which is to be identified with *eudaimonia*.

> Whether these two parts are really distinct in the sense that the parts of the body or of any other divisible whole are distinct, or whether though distinguishable in thought as two they are inseparable in reality, like the convex and concave sides of a curve, is a question of no importance for the matter in hand. (1102 a 30–34).

Virtue Theory and Abortion

ROSALIND HURSTHOUSE

Rosalind Hursthouse (1943–   ) is a professor of philosophy at Open University in the United Kingdom. She is the author of *Beginning Lives*.

—◆—

THE SORT OF ETHICAL THEORY DErived from Aristotle, variously described as virtue ethics, virtue-based ethics, or neo-Aristotelianism, is becoming better known, and is now quite widely recognized as at least a possible rival to deontological and utilitarian theories. With recognition has come criticism, of varying quality.

From *Philosophy and Public Affairs*, 20. Copyright © 1991 by Princeton University Press. Reprinted by permission of the publisher.

In this article I shall discuss nine separate criticisms that I have frequently encountered, most of which seem to me to betray an inadequate grasp either of the structure of virtue theory or of what would be involved in thinking about a real moral issue in its terms. In the first half I aim particularly to secure an understanding which will reveal that many of these criticisms are simply misplaced, and to articulate what I take to be the major criticism of virtue theory. I reject this criticism, but do not claim that it is necessarily misplaced. In the second half I aim to deepen that understanding and highlight the issues raised by the criticisms by illustrating what the theory looks like when it is applied to a particular issue, in this case, abortion.

Virtue Theory

Virtue theory can be laid out in a framework that reveals clearly some of the essential similarities and differences between it and some versions of deontological and utilitarian theories. I begin with a rough sketch of familiar versions of the latter two sorts of theory, not, of course, with the intention of suggesting that they exhaust the field, but on the assumption that their very familiarity will provide a helpful contrast with virtue theory. Suppose a deontological theory has basically the following framework. We begin with a premiss providing a specification of right action:

> P.1. An action is right if it is in accordance with a moral rule or principle.

This is a purely formal specification, forging a link between the concepts of *right action* and *moral rule*, and gives one no guidance until one knows what a moral rule is. So the next thing the theory needs is a premiss about that:

> P.2. A moral rule is one that . . .

Historically, an acceptable completion of P.2 would have been

> i. is laid on us by God

or

> ii. is required by natural law.

In secular versions (not, of course, unconnected to God's being pure reason, and the universality of natural law) we get such completions as

> iii. is laid on us by reason

or

> iv. is required by rationality

or

> v. would command universal rational acceptance

or

> vi. would be the object of choice of all rational beings

and so on. Such a specification forges a second conceptual link, between the concepts of *moral rule* and *rationality*.

We have here the skeleton of a familiar version of a deontological theory, a skeleton which reveals that what is essential to any such version is the links between *right action*, *moral rule*, and *rationality*. That these form the basic structure can be seen particularly vividly if we lay out the familiar act-utilitarianism in such a way as to bring out the contrasts.

Act-utilitarianism begins with a premiss that provides a specification of right action:

> P.1. An action is right if it promotes the best consequences.

It thereby forges the link between the concepts of *right action* and *consequences*. It goes on to specify what the best consequences are in its second premiss:

> P.2. The best consequences are those in which happiness is maximized.

It thereby forges the link between *consequences* and *happiness*.

Now let us consider what a skeletal virtue theory looks like. It begins with a specification of right action:

> P.1. An action is right if it is what a virtuous agent would do in the circumstances.[1]

This, like the first premisses of the other two sorts of theory, is a purely formal principle, giving one no guidance as to what to do, which forges the conceptual link between *right action* and *virtuous agent*. Like the other theories, it must, of course, go on to specify what the latter is. The first step towards this may appear quite trivial, but is needed to correct a prevailing tendency among many critics to define the virtuous agent as one who is disposed to act in accordance with a deontologist's moral rules.

> P.1a. A virtuous agent is one who acts virtuously, that is, one who has and exercises the virtues.

This subsidiary premiss lays bare the fact that virtue theory aims to provide a non-trivial specification of the virtuous agent *via* a non-trivial specification of the virtues, which is given in its second premiss:

P.2. A virtue is a character trait a human being needs to flourish or live well.

This premiss forges a conceptual link between *virtue* and *flourishing* (or *living well* or *eudaimonia*). And, just as deontology, in theory, then goes on to argue that each favoured rule meets its specification, so virtue ethics, in theory, goes on to argue that each favoured character trait meets its.

There are the bare bones of virtue theory: here follow five brief comments directed to some misconceived criticisms which should be cleared out of the way.

First, the theory does not have a peculiar weakness or problem in virtue of the fact that it involves the concept of *eudaimonia* (a standard criticism being that this concept is hopelessly obscure). Now no virtue theorist will pretend that the concept of human flourishing is an easy one to grasp. I will not even claim here (though I would elsewhere) that it is no more obscure than the concepts of *rationality* and *happiness*, since, if our vocabulary were more limited, we might, *faute de mieux*, call it (human) *rational happiness*, and thereby reveal that it has at least some of the difficulties of both. But virtue theory has never, so far as I know, been dismissed on the grounds of the *comparative* obscurity of this central concept; rather, the popular view is that it has a problem with this which deontology and utilitarianism in no way share. This, I think, is clearly false. Both *rationality* and *happiness*, as they figure in their respective theories, are rich and difficult concepts—hence all the disputes about the various tests for a rule's being an object of rational choice, and the disputes, dating back to Mill's introduction of the higher and lower pleasures, about what constitutes happiness.

Secondly, the theory is not trivially circular; it does not specify right action in terms of the virtuous agent and then immediately specify the virtuous agent in terms of right action. Rather, it specifies her in terms of the virtues, and then specifies these, not merely as dispositions to right action, but as the character traits (which are dispositions to feel and react as well as act in certain ways) required for *eudaimonia*.[2]

Thirdly, it does answer the question "What should I do?" as well as the question "What sort of person should I be?" (That is, it is not, as one of the catchphrases has it, concerned only with Being and not with Doing.)

Fourthly, the theory does, to a certain extent, answer this question by coming up with rules or principles (contrary to the common claim that it does not come up with any rules or principles). Every virtue generates a positive instruction (act justly, kindly, courageously, honestly, etc.) and every vice a prohibition (do not act unjustly, cruelly, like a coward, dishonestly, etc.). So trying to decide what to do within the framework of virtue theory is not, as some people seem to imagine, necessarily a matter of taking one's favoured candidate for a virtuous person and asking oneself, "What would they do in these circumstances?" (as if the raped 15-year-old girl might be supposed to say to herself, "Now would Socrates have an abortion if he were in my circumstances?" and as if someone who had never known or heard of anyone very virtuous were going to be left, according to the theory, with no way to decide what to do at all). The agent may instead ask herself, "If I were to do such and such now, would I be acting justly or unjustly (or neither), kindly or unkindly [and so on]?" I shall consider below the problem created by cases in which such a question apparently does not yield an answer to "What should I do?" (because, say, the alternatives are being unkind or being unjust; here my claim is only that it sometimes does—the agent may employ her concepts of the virtues and vices directly, rather than imagining what some hypothetical exemplar would do.

Fifthly, (a point that is implicit but should be made explicit), virtue theory is not committed to any sort of reductionism which involves defining all our moral concepts in terms of the virtuous agent. On the contrary, it relies on a lot of very significant moral concepts. Charity or benevolence, for instance, is the virtue whose concern is the *good* of others; that concept of *good* is related to the concept of *evil* or *harm*, and they are both related to the concepts of the *worthwhile*, the *advantageous*, and the *pleasant*. If I have the wrong conception of what is worthwhile and advantageous and pleasant, then I shall have the wrong conception of what is good for, and harmful to, myself and others, and, even with the best will in the world, will lack the virtue of charity, which involves getting all this right. (This point will be illustrated at some length in the second half of this article; I mention it here only in support of the fact that no virtue theorist who takes her inspiration from Aristotle would even contemplate aiming at reductionism.[3])

Let me now, with equal brevity, run through two more standard criticisms of virtue theory (the sixth and seventh of my nine) to show that, though not entirely misplaced, they do not highlight problems peculiar to that theory but, rather, problems that are shared by familiar versions of deontology.

One common criticism is that we do not know which character traits are the virtues, or that this is open to much dispute, or particularly subject to the threat of moral scepticism or "pluralism"[4] or cultural relativism. But the parallel roles played by the second premises of both deontological and virtue theories reveal the way in which both sorts of theory share this problem. It is at the stage at which one tries to get the right conclusions to drop out of the bottom of one's theory that, *theoretically*, all the work has to be done. Rule deontologists know that they want to get "don't kill," "keep promises," "cherish your children," and so on as the rules that meet their specification, whatever it may be. They also know that any of these can be disputed, that some philosopher may claim, of any one of them, that it is reasonable to reject it, and that at least people claim that there has been, for each rule, some culture which rejected it. Similarly, the virtue theorists know that they want to get justice, charity, fidelity, courage, and so on as the character traits needed for *eudaimonia*; and they also know that any of these can be disputed, that some philosopher will say of any one of them that it is reasonable to reject it as a virtue, and that there is said to be, for each character trait, some culture that has thus rejected it.

This is a problem for both theories, and the virtue theorist certainly does not find it any harder to argue against moral scepticism, 'pluralism', or cultural relativism than the deontologist. Each theory has to stick out its neck and say, in some cases, "This person/these people/other cultures are (or would be) in error," and find some grounds for saying this.

Another criticism (the seventh) often made is that virtue ethics has unresolvable conflict built into it. "It is common knowledge," it is said, "that the requirements of the virtues can conflict; charity may prompt me to end the frightful suffering of the person in my care by killing him, but justice bids me to stay my hand. To tell my brother that his wife is being unfaithful to him would be honest and loyal, but it would be kinder to keep quiet about it. So which should I do? In such cases, virtue ethics has nothing helpful to say." (This is one version of the problem, mentioned above, that considering whether a proposed action falls under a virtue or vice term does not always yield an answer to "What should I do?")

The obvious reply to this criticism is that rule deontology notoriously suffers from the same problem, arising not only from the fact that its rules can apparently conflict, but also from the fact that, at first blush, it appears that one and the same rule (e.g., preserve life) can yield contrary instructions in a particular case.[5] As before, I agree that this is a problem for virtue theory, but deny that it is a problem peculiar to it.

Finally, I want to articulate, and reject, what I take to be the major criticism of virtue theory. Perhaps because it is *the* major criticism, the reflection of a very general sort of disquiet about the theory, it is hard to state clearly—especially for someone who does not accept it—but it goes something like this.[6] My interlocutor says:

> Virtue theory can't *get* us anywhere in real moral issues because it's bound to be all assertion and no argument. You admit that the best it can come up with in the way of action-guiding rules are the ones that rely on the virtue and vice concepts, such as 'act charitably', 'don't act cruelly', and so on; and, as if that weren't bad enough, you admit that these virtue concepts, such as charity, presuppose concepts such as the *good*, and the *worthwhile*, and so on. But that means that any virtue theorist who writes about real moral issues must rely on her audience's agreeing with her application of all these concepts, and hence accepting all the premises in which those applications are enshrined. But some other virtue theorist might take different premises about these matters, and come up with very different conclusions, and, within the terms of the

theory, there is no way to distinguish between the two. While there is agreement, virtue theory can repeat conventional wisdom, preserve the status quo, but it can't get us anywhere in the way that a normative ethical theory is supposed to, namely, by providing rational grounds for acceptance of its practical conclusions.

My strategy will be to split this criticism into two: one (the eighth) addressed to the virtue theorist's employment of the virtue and vice concepts enshrined in her rules—act charitably, honestly, and so on—and the other (the ninth) addressed to her employment of concepts such as that of the *worthwhile*. Each objection, I shall maintain, implicitly appeals to a certain *condition of adequacy* on a normative moral theory, and in each case, I shall claim, the condition of adequacy, once made explicit, is utterly implausible.

Yes, it is true that when she discusses real moral issues, the virtue theorist has to assert that certain actions are honest, dishonest, or neither; charitable, uncharitable, or neither. And it is true that this is often a very difficult matter to decide; her rules are not always easy to apply. But this counts as a criticism of the theory only if we assume, as a condition of adequacy, that any adequate action-guiding theory must make the difficult business of knowing what to do if one is to act well easy, that it must provide clear guidance about what ought not to be done which any reasonably clever adolescent could follow if she chose. But such a condition of adequacy is implausible. Acting rightly *is* difficult, and *does* call for much moral wisdom, and the relevant condition of adequacy, which virtue theory meets, is that it should have built into it an explanation of a truth expressed by Aristotle,[7] namely, that moral knowledge—unlike mathematical knowledge—cannot be acquired merely by attending lectures and is not characteristically to be found in people too young to have had much experience of life. There are youthful mathematical geniuses, but rarely, if ever, youthful moral geniuses, and this shows us something significant about the sort of knowledge that moral knowledge is. Virtue ethics builds this in straight off precisely by couching its rules in terms whose application may indeed call for the most delicate and sensitive judgement.

Here we may discern a slightly different version of the problem that there are cases in which applying the virtue and vice terms does not yield an answer to "What should I do?" Suppose someone "youthful in character," as Aristotle puts it, having applied the relevant terms, finds herself landed with what is, unbeknownst to her, a case not of real but of apparent conflict, arising from a misapplication of those terms. Then she will not be able to decide what to do unless she knows of a virtuous agent to look to for guidance. But her quandary is (*ex hypothesi*) the result of her lack of wisdom, and just what virtue theory expects. Someone hesitating over whether to reveal a hurtful truth, for example, thinking it would be kind but dishonest or unjust to lie, may need to realize, with respect to these particular circumstances, not that kindness is more (or less) important than honesty or justice, and not that honesty or justice sometimes requires one to act unkindly or cruelly, but that one does people no kindness by concealing this sort of truth from them, hurtful as it may be. This is the *type* of thing (I use it only as an example) that people with moral wisdom know about, involving the correct application of *kind*, and that people without such wisdom find difficult.

What about the virtue theorist's reliance on concepts such as that of the *worthwhile*? If such reliance is to count as a fault in the theory, what condition of adequacy is implicitly in play? It must be that any good normative theory should provide answers to questions about real moral issues whose truth is in no way determined by truths about what is worthwhile, or what really matters in human life. Now although people are initially inclined to reject out of hand the claim that the practical conclusions of a normative moral theory have to be based on premisses about what is truly worthwhile, the alternative, once it is made explicit, may look even more unacceptable. Consider what the condition of adequacy entails. If truths about what is worthwhile (or truly good, or serious, or about what matters in human life) do *not* have to be appealed to in order to answer questions about real moral issues, then I might sensibly seek guidance about what I ought to do from someone who had declared in advance that she knew nothing about such matters, or from someone who said that, although she had opinions about them, these were quite likely to be wrong but that this did not matter, because they would play no determining role in the advice she gave me.

I should emphasize that we are talking about real moral issues and real guidance; I want to know whether I should have an abortion, take my mother off the life-support machine, leave academic life and become a doctor in the Third World, give up my job with the firm that is using animals in its experiments, tell my father he has cancer. Would I go to someone who says she has *no* views about what is worthwhile in life? Or to someone who says that, as a matter of fact, she tends to think that the only thing that matters is having a good time, but has a normative theory that is consistent both with this view and with my own rather more puritanical one, which will yield the guidance I need?

I take it as a premiss that this is absurd. The relevant condition of adequacy should be that the practical conclusions of a good normative theory *must* be in part determined by premises about what is worthwhile, important, and so on. Thus I reject this 'major criticism' of virtue theory, that it cannot get us anywhere in the way that a normative moral theory is supposed to. According to my response, a normative theory which any clever adolescent can apply, or which reaches practical conclusions that are in no way determined by premises about what is truly worthwhile, serious, and so on, is guaranteed to be an inadequate theory.

Although I reject this criticism, I have not argued that it is misplaced and that it necessarily manifests a failure to understand what virtue theory is. My rejection is based on premises about what an adequate normative theory must be like—what sorts of concepts it must contain, and what sort of account it must give of moral knowledge—and thereby claims, implicitly, that the "major criticism" manifests a failure to understand what an *adequate normative theory* is. But, as a matter of fact, I think the criticism is often made by people who have no idea of what virtue theory looks like when applied to a real moral issue; they drastically underestimate the variety of ways in which the virtue and vice concepts, and the others, such as that of the *worthwhile*, figure in such discussion.

As promised, I now turn to an illustration of such discussion, applying virtue theory to abortion. Before I embark on this tendentious business, I should remind the reader of the aim of this discussion. I am not, in this article, trying to solve the problem of abortion; I am illustrating how virtue theory directs one to think about it. It might indeed be said that thinking about the problem in this way "solves" it by *dis*solving it, in so far as it leads one to the conclusion that there is no single right answer, but a variety of particular answers, and in what follows I am certainly trying to make that conclusion seem plausible. But, that granted, it should still be said that I am not trying to "solve the problem" in the practical sense of telling people that they should, or should not, do this or that if they are pregnant and contemplating abortion in these or those particular circumstances.

I do not assume, or expect, that all of my readers will agree with everything I am about to say. On the contrary, given the plausible assumption that some are morally wiser than I am, and some less so, the theory has built into it that we are bound to disagree on some points. For instance, we may well disagree about the particular application of some of the virtue and vice terms; and we may disagree about what is worthwhile or serious, worthless or trivial. But my aim is to make clear how these concepts figure in a discussion conducted in terms of virtue theory. What is at issue is whether these concepts are indeed the ones that should come in, that is, whether virtue theory should be criticized for employing them. The problem of abortion highlights this issue dramatically, since virtue theory quite transforms the discussion of it.

Abortion

As everyone knows, the morality of abortion is commonly discussed in relation to just two considerations: first, and predominantly, the status of the foetus and whether or not it is the sort of thing that may or may not be innocuously or justifiably killed; secondly, and less predominantly (when, that is, the discussion concerns the *morality* of abortion rather than the question of permissible legislation in a just society), women's rights. If one thinks within this familiar framework, one may well be puzzled about what virtue theory, as such, could contribute. Some people assume the discussion will be conducted solely in terms of what the virtuous agent would or would not do (cf. the third, fourth, and fifth criticisms above). Others assume that only justice, or at most justice and charity,[8] will be applied to the issue, generating a discussion very similar to Judith Jarvis Thomson's.[9]

Now if this is the way the virtue theorist's discussion of abortion is imagined to be, no wonder people think little of it. It seems obvious in advance that in any such discussion there must be either a great deal of extremely tendentious application of the virtue terms *just*, *charitable*, and so on or a lot of rhetorical appeal to "this is what only the virtuous agent knows." But these are caricatures; they fail to appreciate the way in which virtue theory quite transforms the discussion of abortion by dismissing the two familiar dominating considerations as, in a way, fundamentally irrelevant. In what way or ways, I hope to make both clear and plausible.

Let us first consider women's rights. Let me emphasize again that we are discussing the *morality* of abortion, not the rights and wrongs of laws prohibiting or permitting it. If we suppose that women do have a moral right to do as they choose with their own bodies, or, more particularly, to terminate their pregnancies, then it may well follow that a *law* forbidding abortion would be unjust. Indeed, even if they have no such right, such a law might be, as things stand at the moment, unjust, or impractical, or inhumane: on this issue I have nothing to say in this article. But, putting all questions about the justice or injustice of laws to one side, and supposing only that women have such a moral right, *nothing* follows from this supposition about the morality of abortion, according to virtue theory, once it is noted (quite generally, not with particular reference to abortion) that in exercising a moral right I can do something cruel, or callous, or selfish, light-minded, self-righteous, stupid, inconsiderate, disloyal, dishonest—that is, act viciously.[10] Love and friendship do not survive their parties' constantly insisting on their rights, nor do people live well when they think that getting what they have a right to is of pre-eminent importance; they harm others, and they harm themselves. So whether women have a moral right to terminate their pregnancies is irrelevant within virtue theory, for it is irrelevant to the question "In

having an abortion in these circumstances, would the agent be acting virtuously or viciously or neither?"

What about the consideration of the status of the foetus—what can virtue theory say about that? One might say that this issue is not in the province of *any* moral theory; it is a metaphysical question, and an extremely difficult one at that. Must virtue theory then wait upon metaphysics to come up with the answer?

At first sight it might seem so. For virtue is said to involve knowledge, and part of this knowledge consists in having the *right* attitude to things. "Right" here does not just mean "morally right" or "proper" or "nice" in the modern sense; it means "accurate, true." One cannot have the right or correct attitude to something if the attitude is based on or involves false beliefs. And this suggests that if the status of the foetus is relevant to the rightness or wrongness of abortion, its status must be known, as a truth, to the fully wise and virtuous person.

But the sort of wisdom that the fully virtuous person has is not supposed to be recondite: it does not call for fancy philosophical sophistication, and it does not depend upon, let alone wait upon, the discoveries of academic philosophers.[11] And this entails the following, rather startling, conclusion: that the status of the foetus—that issue over which so much ink has been spilt—is, according to virtue theory, simply not relevant to the rightness or wrongness of abortion (within, that is, a secular morality).

Or rather, since that is clearly too radical a conclusion, it is in a sense relevant, but only in the sense that the familiar biological facts are relevant. By 'the familiar biological facts' I mean the facts that most human societies are and have been familiar with—that, standardly (but not invariably), pregnancy occurs as the result of sexual intercourse, that it lasts about nine months, during which time the foetus grows and develops, that standardly it terminates in the birth of a living baby, and that this is how we all come to be.

It might be thought that this distinction—between the familiar biological facts and the status of the foetus—is a distinction without a difference. But this is not so. To attach relevance to the status of the foetus, in the sense in which virtue theory claims it is not relevant, is to be gripped by the conviction that we must go beyond the familiar biological facts, deriving some sort of conclusion from them, such as that the foetus has rights, or is not a person, or something similar. It is also to believe that this exhausts the relevance of the familiar biological facts, that all they are relevant to is the status of the foetus and whether or not it is the sort of thing that may or may not be killed.

These convictions, I suspect, are rooted in the desire to solve the problem of abortion by getting it to fall under some general rule such as "You ought not to kill anything with the right to life but may kill anything else." But they have resulted in what should surely strike any non-philosopher as a most bizarre aspect of nearly all the current philosophical literature on abortion, namely, that, far from treating abortion as a unique moral problem, markedly unlike any other, nearly everything written on the status of the foetus and its bearing on the abortion issue would be consistent with the facts of human reproduction (to say nothing of family life) being totally different from what they are. Imagine that you are an alien extraterrestrial anthropologist who does not know that the human race is roughly 50 per cent female and 50 per cent male, or that our only (natural) form of reproduction involves heterosexual intercourse, viviparous birth, and the female's (and only the female's) being pregnant for nine months, or that females are capable of childbearing from late childhood to late middle age, or that childbearing is painful, dangerous, and emotionally involving—do you think you would pick up these facts from the hundreds of articles written on the status of the foetus? I am quite sure you would not. And that, I think, shows that the current philosophical literature on abortion has got badly out of touch with reality.

Now if we are using virtue theory, our first question is not "What do the familiar biological facts show—what can be derived from them about the status of the foetus?" but "How do these facts figure in the practical reasoning, actions and passions, thoughts and reactions, of the virtuous and the nonvirtuous? What is the mark of having the right attitude to these facts and what manifests having the wrong attitude to them?" This immediately makes essentially relevant not only all the facts about human reproduction I mentioned above, but a whole range of facts about or emotions in relation to them as well. I mean such facts as that human parents, both male and female, tend to care passionately about their offspring, and that family relationships are among the deepest and strongest in our lives—and, significantly, among the longest-lasting.

These facts make it obvious that pregnancy is not just one among many other physical conditions; and hence that anyone who genuinely believes that an abortion is comparable to a haircut or an appendectomy is mistaken.[12] The fact that the premature termination of a pregnancy is, in some sense, the cutting-off of a new human life, and thereby, like the procreation of a new human life, connects with all our thoughts about human life and death, parenthood, and family relationships, must make it a serious matter. To disregard this fact about it, to think of abortion as nothing but the killing of something that does not matter, or as nothing but the exercise of some right or rights one has, or as the incidental means to some desirable state of affairs, is to do something callous and light-minded, the sort of thing that no virtuous and wise person would do. It is to have the wrong attitude not only to foetuses, but more generally to human life and death, parenthood, and family relationships.

Although I say that the facts make this obvious, I know that this is one of my tendentious points. In partial support of it I note that even the most dedicated proponents of the view that deliberate abortion is just like an appendectomy or haircut rarely hold the same view of spontaneous abortion, that is, miscarriage. It is not so tendentious of me to claim that to react to people's grief over miscarriage by saying, or even thinking, "What a fuss about nothing!" would be callous and light-minded, whereas to try to laugh someone out of grief over an appendectomy scar or a botched haircut would not be. It is hard to give this point due prominence within act-centred theories, for the inconsistency is an inconsistency in attitude about the seriousness of loss of life, not in beliefs about which acts are right or wrong. Moreover, an act-centred theorist may say, "Well, there is nothing wrong with *thinking* 'What a fuss about nothing!' as long as you do not say it and hurt the person who is grieving. And besides, we cannot be held responsible for our thoughts, only for the intentional actions they give rise to." But the character traits that virtue theory emphasizes are not simply dispositions to intentional actions, but a seamless disposition to certain actions and passions, thoughts and reactions.

To say that the cutting-off of a human life is always a matter of some seriousness, at any stage, is not to deny the relevance of gradual foetal development. Notwithstanding the well-worn point that clear boundary lines cannot be drawn, our emotions and attitudes regarding the foetus do change as it develops, and again when it is born, and indeed further as the baby grows. Abortion for shallow reasons in the later stages is much more shocking than abortion for the same reasons in the early stages in a way that matches the fact that deep grief over miscarriage in the later stages is more appropriate than it is over miscarriage in the earlier stages (when, that is, the grief is solely about the loss of *this* child, not about as might be the case, the loss of one's only hope of having a child or of having one's husband's child). Imagine (or recall) a women who already has children; she has not intended to have more, but finds herself unexpectedly pregnant. Though contrary to her plans, the pregnancy, once established as a fact, is welcomed—and then she loses the embryo almost immediately. If this were bemoaned as a tragedy, it would, I think, be a misapplication of the concept of what is tragic. But it may still properly be mourned as a loss. The grief is expressed in such terms as "I shall always wonder how she or he would have turned out" or 'When I look at the others, I shall think, "How different their lives would have been if this other one had been part of them.'" It would, I take it, be callous and light-minded to say, or think, "Well, she has already *got* four children; what's the problem?"; it would be neither, nor arrogantly intrusive in the case of a close friend, to try to correct prolonged mourning by saying, "I know it's sad, but it's not a tragedy: rejoice in the ones you have." The application of *tragic* becomes more appropriate as the foetus grows, for the mere fact that one has lived with it for longer, conscious of its existence, makes a difference. To shrug off an early abortion is understandable just because it is very

hard to be fully conscious of the foetus's existence in the early stages and hence hard to appreciate that an early abortion is the destruction of life. It is particularly hard for the young and inexperienced to appreciate this, because appreciation of it usually comes only with experience.

I do not mean "with the experience of having an abortion" (though that may be part of it) but, quite generally, "with the experience of life." Many women who have borne children contrast their later pregnancies with their first successful one, saying that in the later ones they were conscious of a new life growing in them from very early on. And, more generally, as one reaches the age at which the next generation is coming up close behind one, the counterfactuals "If I, or she, had had an abortion, Alice, or Bob, would not have been born" acquire a significant application, which casts a new light on the conditionals "If I or Alice have an abortion then some Caroline or Bill will not be born."

The fact that pregnancy is not just one among many physical conditions does not mean that one can never regard it in that light without manifesting a vice. When women are in very poor physical health, or worn out from childbearing, or forced to do very physically demanding jobs, then they cannot be described as self-indulgent, callous, irresponsible, or light-minded if they seek abortions mainly with a view to avoiding pregnancy as the physical condition that it is. To go through with a pregnancy when one is utterly exhausted, or when one's job consists of crawling along tunnels hauling coal, as many women in the nineteenth century were obliged to do, is perhaps heroic, but people who do not achieve heroism are not necessarily vicious. That they can view the pregnancy only as eight months of misery, followed by hours if not days of agony and exhaustion, and abortion only as the blessed escape from this prospect, is entirely understandable and does not manifest any lack of serious respect for human life or a shallow attitude to motherhood. What it does show is that something is terribly amiss in the conditions of their lives, which makes it so hard to recognize pregnancy and childbearing as the good that they can be.

In relation to this last point I should draw attention to the way in which virtue theory has a sort of built-in indexicality. Philosophers arguing against anything remotely resembling a belief in the sanctity of life (which the above claims clearly embody) frequently appeal to the existence of other communities in which abortion and infanticide are practised. We should not automatically assume that it is impossible that some other communities could be morally inferior to our own; maybe some are, or have been, precisely in so far as their members are, typically, callous or light-minded or unjust. But in communities in which life is a great deal tougher for everyone than it is in ours, having the right attitude to human life and death, parenthood, and family relationships might well manifest itself in ways that are unlike ours. When it is essential to survival that most members of the community fend for themselves at a very young age or work during most of their waking hours, selective abortion or infanticide might be practised either as a form of genuine euthanasia or for the sake of the community and not, I think, be thought callous or light-minded. But this does not make everything all right; as before, it shows that there is something amiss with the conditions of their lives, which are making it impossible for them to live really well.[13]

The foregoing discussion, in so far as it emphasizes the right attitude to human life and death, parallels to a certain extent those standard discussions of abortion that concentrate on it solely as an issue of killing. But it does not, as those discussions do, gloss over the fact, emphasized by those who discuss the morality of abortion in terms of women's rights, that abortion, wildly unlike any other form of killing, is the termination of a pregnancy, which is a condition of a woman's body and results in *her* having a child if it is not aborted. This fact is given due recognition not by appeal to women's rights but by emphasizing the relevance of the familiar biological and psychological facts and their connection with having the right attitude to parenthood and family relationships. But it may well be thought that failing to bring in women's rights still leaves some important aspects of the problem of abortion untouched.

Speaking in terms of women's rights, people sometimes say things like, "Well, it's her life you're talking about too, you know; she's got a right to her own life, her own happiness." And the discussion stops there. But in the context of virtue theory, given that we are particularly concerned with what constitutes a good human life, with what true happiness or *eudaimonia* is, this is no place to stop. We go on to ask, "And is this life of hers a good one? Is she living well?"

If we are to go on to talk about good human lives, in the context of abortion, we have to bring in our thoughts about the value of love and family life, and our proper emotional development through a natural life cycle. The familiar facts support the view that parenthood in general, and motherhood and childbearing in particular, are intrinsically worthwhile, are among the things that can be correctly thought to be partially constitutive of a flourishing human life.[14] If this is right, then a woman who opts for not being a mother (at all, or again, or now) by opting for abortion may thereby be manifesting a flawed grasp of what her life should be, and be about—a grasp that is childish, or grossly materialistic, or shortsighted, or shallow.

I said "*may* thereby": this *need* not be so. Consider, for instance, a woman who has already had several children and fears that to have another will seriously affect her capacity to be a good mother to the ones she has—she does not show a lack of appreciation of the intrinsic value of being a parent by opting for abortion. Nor does a woman who has been a good mother and is approaching the age at which she may be looking forward to being a good grandmother. Nor does a woman who discovers that her pregnancy may well kill her, and opts for abortion and adoption. Nor, necessarily, does a woman who has decided to lead a life centred around some other worthwhile activity or activities with which motherhood would compete.

People who are childless by choice are sometimes described as "irresponsible," or "selfish," or "refusing to grow up," or "not knowing what life is about." But one can hold that having children is intrinsically worthwhile without endorsing this, for we are, after all, in the happy position of there being more worthwhile things to do than can be fitted into one lifetime. Parenthood, and motherhood in particular, even if granted to be intrinsically worthwhile, undoubtedly take up a lot of one's adult life, leaving no room for some other worthwhile pursuits. But

some women who choose abortion rather than having their first child, and some men who encourage
their partners to choose abortion, are not avoiding
parenthood for the sake of other worthwhile pursuits, but for the worthless one of 'having a good
time', or for the pursuit of some false vision of the
ideals of freedom or self-realization. And some others who say "I am not ready for parenthood yet" are
making a mistake about the extent to which one can
manipulate the circumstances of one's life so as to
make it fulfil some dream that one has. Perhaps
one's dream is of having two perfect children, a girl
and a boy, within a perfect marriage, in financially
secure circumstances, with an interesting job of
one's own. But to care too much about that dream,
to demand of life that it give it to one and to act accordingly, may be both greedy and foolish, and is to
run the risk of missing out on happiness entirely.
Not only may fate make the dream impossible, or
destroy it, but one's own attachment to it may make
it impossible. Good marriages, and the most promising children, can be destroyed by just one adult's excessive demand for perfection.

Once again, this is not to deny that girls may
quite properly say "I am not ready for motherhood
yet," especially in our society, and, far from manifesting irresponsibility or light-mindedness, show
an appropriate modesty or humility, or a fearfulness
that does not amount to cowardice. However, even
when the decision to have an abortion is the right
decision—one that does not itself fall under a vice-
related term and thereby one that the perfectly virtuous could recommend—it does not follow that
there is no sense in which having the abortion is
wrong, or guilt appropriate. For, by virtue of the
fact that a human life has been cut short, some evil
has probably been brought about,[15] and that circumstances make the decision to bring about some
evil the right decision will be a ground for guilt if
getting into those circumstances in the first place itself manifested a flaw in character.

What "gets one into those circumstances" in the
case of abortion is, except in the case of rape, one's
sexual activity and one's choices, or the lack of them,
about one's sexual partner and about contraception.
The virtuous woman (which here of course does not
mean simply "chaste woman" but "woman with the

virtues") has such character traits as strength, independence, resoluteness, decisiveness, self-confi-
dence, responsibility, serious-mindedness, and self-
determination—and no one, I think, could deny
that many women become pregnant in circumstances in which they cannot welcome or cannot face
the thought of having *this* child precisely because
they lack one or some of these character traits. So
even in the cases where the decision to have an abortion is the right one, it can still be the reflection of
a moral failing—not because the decision itself is
weak or cowardly or irresolute or irresponsible or
light-minded, but because lack of the requisite opposite of these failings landed one in the circumstances in the first place. Hence the common uni-
versalized claim that guilt and remorse are never
appropriate emotions about an abortion is denied.
They may be appropriate, and appropriately inculcated, even when the decision was the right one.

Another motivation for bringing women's rights
into the discussion may be to attempt to correct the
implication, carried by the killing-centred approach,
that in so far as abortion is wrong, it is a wrong that
only women do, or at least (given the preponder-
ance of male doctors) that only women instigate. I
do not myself believe that we can thus escape the
fact that nature bears harder on women than it does
on men,[16] but virtue theory can certainly correct
many of the injustices that the emphasis on women's
rights is rightly concerned about. With very little
amendment, everything that has been said above applies to boys and men too. Although the abortion
decision is, in a natural sense, the woman's decision,
proper to her, boys and men are often party to it,
for well or ill, and even when they are not, they are
bound to have been party to the circumstances that
brought it up. No less than girls and women, boys
and men can, in their actions, manifest self-cen-
tredness, callousness, and light-mindedness about
life and parenthood in relation to abortion. They can
be self-centred or courageous about the possibility
of disability in their offspring; they need to reflect
on their sexual activity and their choices, or the lack
of them, about their sexual partner and contraception; they need to grow up and take responsibility
for their own actions and life in relation to fatherhood. If it is true, as I maintain, that in so far as moth-

erhood is intrinsically worthwhile, being a mother is an important purpose in women's lives, being a father (rather than a mere generator) is an important purpose in men's lives too, and it is adolescent of men to turn a blind eye to this and pretend that they have many more important things to do.

Conclusion

Much more might be said, but I shall end the actual discussion of the problem of abortion here, and conclude by highlighting what I take to be its significant features. These hark back to many of the criticisms of virtue theory discussed earlier.

The discussion does not proceed simply by our trying to answer the question "Would a perfectly virtuous agent ever have an abortion and, if so, when?"; virtue theory is not limited to considering "Would Socrates have had an abortion if he were a raped, pregnant 15-year-old?" nor automatically stumped when we are considering circumstances into which no virtuous agent would have got herself. Instead, much of the discussion proceeds in the virtue- and vice-related terms whose application, in several cases, yields practical conclusions (cf. the third and fourth criticisms above). These terms are difficult to apply correctly, and anyone might challenge my application of any one of them. So, for example, I have claimed that some abortions, done for certain reasons, would be callous or light-minded; that others might indicate an appropriate modesty or humility; that others would reflect a greedy and foolish attitude to what one could expect out of life. Any of these examples may be disputed, but what is at issue is, should these difficult terms be there, or should the discussion be couched in terms that all clever adolescents can apply correctly? (Cf. the first half of the "major objection" above.)

Proceeding as it does in the virtue- and vice-related terms, the discussion thereby, inevitably, also contains claims about what is worthwhile, serious and important, good and evil, in our lives. So, for example, I claimed that parenthood is intrinsically worthwhile, and that having a good time was a worthless end (in life, not on individual occasions); that losing a foetus is always a serious matter (albeit

not a tragedy in itself in the first trimester) whereas acquiring an appendectomy scar is a trivial one; that (human) death is an evil. Once again, these are difficult matters, and anyone might challenge any one of my claims. But what is at issue is, as before, should those difficult claims be there or can one reach practical conclusions about real moral issues that are in no way determined by premises about such matters? (Cf. the fifth criticism, and the second half of the "major criticism.")

The discussion also thereby, inevitably, contains claims about what life is like (e.g., my claim that love and friendship do not survive their parties' constantly insisting on their rights; or the claim that to demand perfection of life is to run the risk of missing out on happiness entirely). What is at issue is, should those disputable claims be there, or is our knowledge (or are our false opinions) about what life is like irrelevant to our understanding of real moral issues? (Cf. both halves of the "major criticism.")

Naturally, my own view is that all these concepts should be there in any discussion of real moral issues, and that virtue theory, which uses all of them, is the right theory to apply to them. I do not pretend to have shown this. I realize that proponents of rival theories may say that, now that they have understood how virtue theory uses the range of concepts it draws on, they are more convinced than ever that such concepts should not figure in an adequate normative theory, because they are sectarian, or vague, or too particular, or improperly anthropocentric, and reinstate what I called the 'major criticism'. Or, finding many of the details of the discussion appropriate, they may agree that many, perhaps even all, of the concepts should figure, but argue that virtue theory gives an inaccurate account of the way the concepts fit together (and indeed of the concepts themselves) and that another theory provides a better account; that would be interesting to see. Moreover, I admitted that there were at least two problems for virtue theory: that it has to argue against moral scepticism, 'pluralism', and cultural relativism, and that it has to find something to say about conflicting requirements of different virtues. Proponents of rival theories might argue that their favoured theory provides better solutions to these problems than virtue theory can. Indeed, they might criticize virtue theory for finding problems here at all. Anyone who argued for at least one of moral scepticism, "pluralism," or cultural relativism could presumably do so (provided their favoured theory does not find a similar problem); and a utilitarian might say that benevolence is the only virtue and hence that virtue theory errs when it discusses even apparent conflicts between the requirements of benevolence and some other character trait such as honesty.

Defending virtue theory against all possible, or even likely, criticisms of it would be a lifelong task. As I said at the outset, in this article I aimed to defend the theory against some criticisms which I thought arose from an inadequate understanding of it, and to improve that understanding. If I have succeeded, we may hope for more comprehending criticisms of virtue theory than have appeared hitherto.[17]

NOTES

1. It should be noted that this premiss intentionally allows for the possibility that two virtuous agents, faced with the same choice in the same circumstances, may act differently. For example, one might opt for taking her father off the life-support machine and the other for leaving her father on it. The theory requires that neither agent thinks that what the other does is wrong (see n. 4 below), but it explicitly allows that no action is uniquely right in such a case—both are right. It also intentionally allows for the possibility that in some circumstances—those into which no virtuous agent could have got herself—no action is right. I explore this premiss at greater length in 'Applying Virtue Ethics', in *Virtues and Reasons*, ed. Rosalind Hursthouse, Gavin Lawrence, and Warren Quinn (Oxford, 1995).

2. There is, of course, the further question of whether the theory eventually describes a larger circle and winds up relying on the concept of right action in its interpretation of *eudaimonia*. In denying that the theory is trivially circular, I do not pretend to answer this intricate question. It is certainly true that virtue theory does not claim that the correct conception of *eudaimonia* can be got from 'an independent "value-free" investigation of

human nature' (John McDowell, 'The Role of *Eudaimonia* in Aristotle's Ethics', Amélie O. Rorty (ed.), *Essays on Aristotle's Ethics* (Berkeley and Los Angeles, 1980)). The sort of training that is required for acquiring the correct conception no doubt involves being taught from early on such things as "Decent people do this sort of thing, not that" and "To do such and such is the mark of a depraved character" (cf. *Nicomachean Ethics* 1110ª22). But whether this counts as relying on the concept of right (or wrong) action seems to me very unclear and requiring much discussion.

3. Cf. Bernard Williams's point in *Ethics and the Limits of Philosophy* (London, 1985) that we need an enriched ethical vocabulary, not a cut-down one.

4. I put *pluralism* in scare quotes to serve as a warning that virtue theory is not incompatible with all forms of it. It allows for "competing conceptions" of *eudaimonia* and the worthwhile, for instance, in the sense that it allows for a plurality of flourishing lives—the theory need not follow Aristotle in specifying the life of contemplation as the only one that truly constitutes *eudaimonia* (if he does). But the conceptions "compete" only in the sense that, within a single flourishing life, not everything worthwhile can be fitted in; the theory does not allow that two people with a correct conception of *eudaimonia* can disagree over whether the way the other is living constitutes flourishing. Moreover, the theory is committed to the strong thesis that the same set of character traits is needed for *any* flourishing life; it will not allow that, for instance, soldiers need courage but wives and mothers do not, or that judges need justice but can live well despite lacking kindness. (This obviously is related to the point made in n. 1 above.) For an interesting discussion of pluralism (different interpretations thereof) and virtue theory, see Douglas B. Rasmussen, 'Liberalism and Natural End Ethics', *American Philosophical Quarterly*, 27 (1990), 153–61.

5. e.g., in Williams's Jim and Pedro case in J. J. C. Smart and Bernard Williams, *Utilitarianism: For and Against* (London, 1973).

6. Intimations of this criticism constantly come up in discussion; the clearest statement of it I have found is by Onora O'Neill, in her review of Stephen Clark's *The Moral Status of Animals*, in *Journal of Philosophy*, 77 (1980), 440–6. For a response I am much in sympathy with, see Cora Diamond, 'Anything But Argument?', *Philosophical Investigations*, 5 (1982), 23–41.

7. Aristotle, *Nicomachean Ethics* 1142ª12–16.

8. It seems likely that some people have been misled by Foot's discussion of euthanasia (through no fault of hers) into thinking that a virtue theorist's discussion of terminating human life will be conducted exclusively in terms of justice and charity (and the corresponding vice terms) (Philippa Foot, 'Euthanasia', *Philosophy and Public Affairs*, 6/2 (Winter 1977), 85–112). But the act-category *euthanasia* is a very special one, at least as defined in her article, since such an act must be done 'for the sake of the one who is to die'. Building a virtuous motivation into the specification of the act in this way immediately rules out the application of many other vice terms.

9. Judith Jarvis Thomson, 'A Defense of Abortion', *Philosophy and Public Affairs*, 1/1 (Fall 1971), 47–66. One could indeed regard this article as proto-virtue theory (no doubt to the surprise of the author) if the concepts of callousness and kindness were allowed more weight.

10. One possible qualification: if one ties the concept of justice very closely to rights, then if women do have a moral right to terminate their pregnancies it *may* follow that in doing so they do not act unjustly. (Cf. Thomson, 'A Defense of Abortion'.) But it is debatable whether even that much follows.

11. This is an assumption of virtue theory, and I do not attempt to defend it here. An adequate discussion of it would require a separate article, since, although most moral philosophers would be chary of claiming that intellectual sophistication is a necessary condition of moral wisdom or virtue, most of us, from Plato onwards, tend to write as if this were so. Sorting out which claims about moral knowledge are committed to this kind of élitism and which can, albeit with difficulty, be reconciled with the idea that moral knowledge can be acquired by anyone who really wants it would be a major task.

12. Mary Anne Warren, in 'On the Moral and Legal Status of Abortion', *Monist*, 57 (1973), sect. 1, says of the opponents of restrictive laws governing abortion that "their conviction (for the most part) is that abortion is not a *morally* serious and extremely unfortunate, even though sometimes justified, act, comparable to killing in self-defense or to letting the violinist die, but rather is closer to being a *morally neutral* act, like cutting one's hair" (emphasis added). I would like to think that no one *genuinely* believes this. But certainly in discussion, particularly when arguing against restrictive laws or the suggestion that remorse over abortion might be appropriate, I have found that some people *say* they believe it (and often cite Warren's article, albeit inaccurately, despite its age). Those who allow that it is morally serious, and far from morally neutral, have to argue against restrictive laws, or the appropriateness of remorse, on a very different ground from that laid down by the premiss "The foetus is just part of the woman's body (and she has a right to determine what happens to her body and should not feel guilt about anything she does to it)."

13. For another example of the way in which "tough conditions" can make a difference to what is involved in having the right attitude to human life and death and family relationships, see the concluding sentences of Foot, 'Euthanasia'.

14. I take this as a premiss here, but argue for it in some detail in my *Beginning Lives* (Oxford, 1987). In this connection I also discuss adoption and the sense in which it may be regarded as 'second best', and the difficult question of whether the good of parenthood may properly be sought, or indeed bought, by surrogacy.

15. I say "some evil has probably been brought about" on the ground that (human) life is (usually) a good and hence (human) death usually an evil. The exceptions would be (*a*) where death is actually a good or a benefit, because the baby that would come to be if the life were not cut short would be better off dead than alive, and (*b*) where death, though not a good, is not an evil either, because the life that would be led (e.g., in a state of permanent coma) would not be a good. (see Foot, 'Euthanasia'.)

16. I discuss this point at greater length in *Beginning Lives*.

17. Versions of this article have been read to philosophy societies at University College, London, Rutgers University, and the Universities of Dundee, Edinburgh, Oxford, Swansea, and California–San Diego; at a conference of the Polish and British Academies in Cracow in 1988 on 'Life, Death and the Law', and as a symposium paper at the Pacific Division of the American Philosophical Association in 1989. I am grateful to the many people who contributed to the discussions of it on these occasions, and particularly to Philippa Foot and Anne Jaap Jacobson for private discussion.

D. Justice and Equality

A Theory of Justice

JOHN RAWLS

John Rawls (1921–   ) is Professor Emeritus of Philosophy at Harvard University. His book *A Theory of Justice* is one of the most influential twentieth-century works on ethics and political philosophy. He is also the author of *Political Liberalism*.

———◆———

Chapter I. Justice as Fairness

. . . .

1. The Role of Justice

Justice is the first virtue of social institutions, as truth is of systems of thought. A theory however elegant and economical must be rejected or revised if it is untrue; likewise laws and institutions no matter how efficient and well arranged must be reformed or abolished if they are unjust. Each person possesses an inviolability founded on justice that even the welfare of society as a whole cannot override. For this reason justice denies that the loss of freedom for some is made right by a greater good shared by others. It does not allow that the sacrifices imposed on a few are outweighed by the larger sum of advantages enjoyed by many. Therefore in a just society, the liberties of equal citizenship are taken as settled; the rights secured by justice are not subject to political bargaining or to the calculus of social interests. The only thing that permits us to acquiesce in an erroneous theory is the lack of a better one; analogously, an injustice is tolerable only when it is necessary to avoid an even greater in-

justice. Being first virtues of human activities, truth and justice are uncompromising.

These propositions seem to express our intuitive conviction of the primacy of justice. No doubt they are expressed too strongly. In any event I wish to inquire whether these contentions or others similar to them are sound, and if so how they can be accounted for. To this end it is necessary to work out a theory of justice in the light of which these assertions can be interpreted and assessed. I shall begin by considering the role of the principles of justice. Let us assume, to fix ideas, that a society is a more or less self-sufficient association of persons who in their relations to one another recognize certain rules of conduct as binding and who for the most part act in accordance with them. Suppose further that these rules specify a system of cooperation designed to advance the good of those taking part in it. Then, although a society is a cooperative venture for mutual advantage, it is typically marked by a conflict as well as by an identity of interests. There is an identity of interests since social cooperation makes possible a better life for all than any would have if each were to live solely by his own efforts. There is a conflict of interests since persons are not indifferent as to how the greater benefits produced by their collaboration are distributed, for in order to pursue their ends they each prefer a larger to a lesser share. A set of principles is required for choosing among the various social arrangements which determine this division of advantages and for underwriting an agreement on the proper distributive shares. These principles are the principles of social justice: they provide a way of assigning rights and duties in the basic institutions of society and they define the appropriate distribution of the benefits and burdens of social cooperation.

Now let us say that a society is well ordered when it is not only designed to advance the good of its members but when it is also effectively regulated by a public conception of justice. That is, it is a society in which (1) everyone accepts and knows that the others accept the same principles of justice, and (2) the basic social institutions generally satisfy and are generally known to satisfy these principles. In this case while men may put forth excessive demands on one another, they nevertheless acknowledge a common point of view from which their claims may be adjudicated. If men's inclination to self-interest makes their vigilance against one another necessary, their public sense of justice makes their secure association together possible. Among individuals with disparate aims and purposes a shared conception of justice establishes the bonds of civic friendship; the general desire for justice limits the pursuit of other ends. One may think of a public conception of justice as constituting the fundamental charter of a well-ordered human association.

. . . .

2. The Subject of Justice

Many different kinds of things are said to be just and unjust: not only laws, institutions, and social systems, but also particular actions of many kinds, including decisions, judgments, and imputations. We also call the attitudes and dispositions of persons, and persons themselves, just and unjust. Our topic, however, is that of social justice. For us the primary subject of justice is the basic structure of society, or more exactly, the way in which the major social institutions distribute fundamental rights and duties and determine the division of advantages from social cooperation. By major institutions I understand the political constitution and the principal economic and social arrangements. Thus the legal

protection of freedom of thought and liberty of conscience, competitive markets, private property in the means of production, and the monogamous family are examples of major social institutions. Taken together as one scheme, the major institutions define men's rights and duties and influence their life-prospects, what they can expect to be and how well they can hope to do. The basic structure is the primary subject of justice because its effects are so profound and present from the start. The intuitive notion here is that this structure contains various social positions and that men born into different positions have different expectations of life determined, in part, by the political system as well as by economic and social circumstances. In this way the institutions of society favor certain starting places over others. These are especially deep inequalities. Not only are they pervasive, but they affect men's initial chances in life; yet they cannot possibly be justified by an appeal to the notions of merit or desert. It is these inequalities, presumably inevitable in the basic structure of any society, to which the principles of social justice must in the first instance apply. These principles, then, regulate the choice of a political constitution and the main elements of the economic and social system. The justice of a social scheme depends essentially on how fundamental rights and duties are assigned and on the economic opportunities and social conditions in the various sectors of society.

. . . .

3. The Main Idea of the Theory of Justice

My aim is to present a conception of justice which generalizes and carries to a higher level of abstraction the familiar theory of the social contract as found, say, in Locke, Rousseau, and Kant. In order to do this we are not to think of the original contract as one to enter a particular society or to set up a particular form of government. Rather, the guiding idea is that the principles of justice for the basic structure of society are the object of the original agreement. They are the principles that free and rational persons concerned to further their own interests would accept in an initial position of equality as defining the fundamental terms of their association. These principles are to regulate all further agreements; they specify the kinds of social cooperation that can be entered into and the forms of government that can be established. This way of regarding the principles of justice I shall call justice as fairness.

Thus we are to imagine that those who engage in social cooperation choose together, in one joint act, the principles which are to assign basic rights and duties and to determine the division of social benefits. Men are to decide in advance how they are to regulate their claims against one another and what is to be the foundation charter of their society. Just as each person must decide by rational reflection what constitutes his good, that is, the system of ends which it is rational for him to pursue, so a group of persons must decide once and for all what is to count among them as just and unjust. The choice which rational men would make in this hypothetical situation of equal liberty, assuming for the present that this choice problem has a solution, determines the principles of justice.

In justice as fairness the original position of equality corresponds to the state of nature in the traditional theory of the social contract. This original position is not, of course, thought of as an actual historical state of affairs, much less as a primitive condition of culture. It is understood as a purely hypothetical situation characterized so as to lead to a certain conception of justice. Among the essential features of this situation is that no one knows his place in society, his class position or social status, nor does any one know his fortune in the distribution of natural assets and abilities, his intelligence, strength, and the like. I shall even assume that the parties do not know their conceptions of the good or their special psychological propensities. The principles of justice are chosen behind a veil of ignorance. This ensures that no one is advantaged or disadvantaged in the choice of principles by the outcome of natural chance or the contingency of social circumstances. Since all are similarly situated and no one is able to design principles to favor his particular condition, the principles of justice are the result of a fair agreement or bargain. For given the circumstances of the original position, the symmetry of everyone's relations to each other, this initial

situation is fair between individuals as moral persons, that is, as rational beings with their own ends and capable, I shall assume, of a sense of justice. The original position is, one might say, the appropriate initial status quo, and thus the fundamental agreements reached in it are fair. This explains the propriety of the name "justice as fairness"; it conveys the idea that the principles of justice are agreed to in an initial situation that is fair. The name does not mean that the concepts of justice and fairness are the same, any more than the phrase "poetry as metaphor" means that the concepts of poetry and metaphor are the same.

Justice as fairness begins, as I have said, with one of the most general of all choices which persons might make together, namely, with the choice of the first principles of a conception of justice which is to regulate all subsequent criticism and reform of institutions. Then, having chosen a conception of justice, we can suppose that they are to choose a constitution and a legislature to enact laws, and so on, all in accordance with the principles of justice initially agreed upon. Our social situation is just if it is such that by this sequence of hypothetical agreements we would have contracted into the general system of rules which defines it. Moreover, assuming that the original position does determine a set of principles (that is, that a particular conception of justice would be chosen), it will then be true that whenever social institutions satisfy these principles those engaged in them can say to one another that they are cooperating on terms to which they would agree if they were free and equal persons whose relations with respect to one another were fair. They could all view their arrangements as meeting the stipulations which they would acknowledge in an initial situation that embodies widely accepted and reasonable constraints on the choice of principles. The general recognition of this fact would provide the basis for a public acceptance of the corresponding principles of justice. No society can, of course, be a scheme of cooperation which men enter voluntarily in a literal sense; each person finds himself placed at birth in some particular position in some particular society, and the nature of this position materially affects his life prospects. Yet a society satisfying the principles of justice as fairness comes as close as a society can to being a voluntary scheme, for it meets the principles which free and equal persons would assent to under circumstances that are fair. In this sense its members are autonomous and the obligations they recognize self-imposed.

One feature of justice as fairness is to think of the parties in the initial situation as rational and mutually disinterested. This does not mean that the parties are egoists, that is, individuals with only certain kinds of interests, say in wealth, prestige, and domination. But they are conceived as not taking an interest in one another's interests. They are to presume that even their spiritual aims may be opposed, in the way that the aims of those of different religions may be opposed. Moreover, the concept of rationality must be interpreted as far as possible in the narrow sense, standard in economic theory, of taking the most effective means to given ends. . . . [O]ne must try to avoid introducing into it any controversial ethical elements. The initial situation must be characterized by stipulations that are widely accepted.

In working out the conception of justice as fairness one main task clearly is to determine which principles of justice would be chosen in the original position. To do this we must describe this situation in some detail and formulate with care the problem of choice which it presents. . . . It may be observed, however, that once the principles of justice are thought of as arising from an original agreement in a situation of equality, it is an open question whether the principle of utility would be acknowledged. Offhand it hardly seems likely that persons who view themselves as equals, entitled to press their claims upon one another, would agree to a principle which may require lesser life prospects for some simply for the sake of a greater sum of advantages enjoyed by others. Since each desires to protect his interests, his capacity to advance his conception of the good, no one has a reason to acquiesce in an enduring loss for himself in order to bring about a greater net balance of satisfaction. In the absence of strong and lasting benevolent impulses, a rational man would not accept a basic structure merely because it maximized the algebraic sum of advantages irrespective of its permanent effects on his own basic rights and interests. Thus it seems that the principle of utility is incompatible with the conception of social cooperation among equals for mutual advantage. It appears to be inconsistent with the idea

of reciprocity implicit in the notion of a well-ordered society. Or, at any rate, so I shall argue.

I shall maintain instead that the persons in the initial situation would choose two rather different principles: the first requires equality in the assignment of basic rights and duties, while the second holds that social and economic inequalities, for example inequalities of wealth and authority, are just only if they result in compensating benefits for everyone, and in particular for the least advantaged members of society. These principles rule out justifying institutions on the grounds that the hardships of some are offset by a greater good in the aggregate. It may be expedient but it is not just that some should have less in order that others may prosper. But there is no injustice in the greater benefits earned by a few provided that the situation of persons not so fortunate is thereby improved. The intuitive idea is that since everyone's well-being depends upon a scheme of cooperation without which no one could have a satisfactory life, the division of advantages should be such as to draw forth the willing cooperation of everyone taking part in it, including those less well situated. Yet this can be expected only if reasonable terms are proposed. The two principles mentioned seem to be a fair agreement on the basis of which those better endowed, or more fortunate in their social position, neither of which we can be said to deserve, could expect the willing cooperation of others when some workable scheme is a necessary condition of the welfare of all. Once we decide to look for a conception of justice that nullifies the accidents of natural endowment and the contingencies of social circumstance as counters in quest for political and economic advantage, we are led to these principles. They express the result of leaving aside those aspects of the social world that seem arbitrary from a moral point of view.

. . . .

4. The Original Position and Justification

I have said that the original position is the appropriate initial status quo which insures that the fundamental agreements reached in it are fair. This fact yields the name "justice as fairness." It is clear, then, that I want to say that one conception of justice is more reasonable than another, or justifiable with respect to it, if rational persons in the initial situation would choose its principles over those of the other for the role of justice. Conceptions of justice are to be ranked by their acceptability to persons so circumstanced. Understood in this way the question of justification is settled by working out a problem of deliberation: we have to ascertain which principles it would be rational to adopt given the contractual situation. This connects the theory of justice with the theory of rational choice.

If this view of the problem of justification is to succeed, we must, of course, describe in some detail the nature of this choice problem. A problem of rational decision has a definite answer only if we know the beliefs and interests of the parties, their relations with respect to one another, the alternatives between which they are to choose, the procedure whereby they make up their minds, and so on. As the circumstances are presented in different ways, correspondingly different principles are accepted. The concept of the original position, as I shall refer to it, is that of the most philosophically favored interpretation of this initial choice situation for the purposes of a theory of justice.

But how are we to decide what is the most favored interpretation? I assume, for one thing, that there is a broad measure of agreement that principles of justice should be chosen under certain conditions. To justify a particular description of the initial situation one shows that it incorporates these commonly shared presumptions. One argues from widely accepted but weak premises to more specific conclusions. Each of the presumptions should by itself be natural and plausible; some of them may seem innocuous or even trivial. The aim of the contract approach is to establish that taken together they impose significant bounds on acceptable principles of justice. The ideal outcome would be that these conditions determine a unique set of principles; but I shall be satisfied if they suffice to rank the main traditional conceptions of social justice.

One should not be misled, then, by the somewhat unusual conditions which characterize the original position. The idea here is simply to make vivid to ourselves the restrictions that it seems reasonable to impose on arguments for principles of justice, and therefore on these principles themselves. Thus it seems reasonable and generally acceptable that no one should be advantaged or disadvantaged by natural fortune or social circumstances in the choice of principles. It also seems widely agreed that it should be impossible to tailor principles to the circumstances of one's own case. We should insure further that particular inclinations and aspirations, and persons' conceptions of their good do not affect the principles adopted. The aim is to rule out those principles that it would be rational to propose for acceptance, however little the chance of success, only if one knew certain things that are irrelevant from the standpoint of justice. For example, if a man knew that he was wealthy, he might find it rational to advance the principle that various taxes for welfare measures be counted unjust; if he knew that he was poor, he would most likely propose the contrary principle. To represent the desired restrictions one imagines a situation in which everyone is deprived of this sort of information. One excludes the knowledge of those contingencies which sets men at odds and allows them to be guided by their prejudices. In this manner the veil of ignorance is arrived at in a natural way. This concept should cause no difficulty if we keep in mind the constraints on arguments that it is meant to express. At any time we can enter the original position, so to speak, simply by following a certain procedure, namely, by arguing for principles of justice in accordance with these restrictions.

It seems reasonable to suppose that the parties in the original position are equal. That is, all have the same rights in the procedure for choosing principles; each can make proposals, submit reasons for their acceptance, and so on. Obviously the purpose of these conditions is to represent equality between human beings as moral persons, as creatures having a conception of their good and capable of a sense of justice. The basis of equality is taken to be similarity in these two respects. Systems of ends are not ranked in value; and each man is presumed to have the requisite ability to understand and to act upon whatever principles are adopted. Together with the veil of ignorance, these conditions define the principles of justice as those which rational persons concerned to advance their interests would consent to as equals when none are known to be advantaged or disadvantaged by social and natural contingencies.

There is, however, another side to justifying a particular description of the original position. This is to see if the principles which would be chosen match our considered convictions of justice or extend them in an acceptable way. We can note whether applying these principles would lead us to make the same judgments about the basic structure of society which we now make intuitively and in which we have the greatest confidence; or whether, in cases where our present judgments are in doubt and given with hesitation, these principles offer a resolution which we can affirm on reflection. There are questions which we feel sure must be answered in a certain way. For example, we are confident that religious intolerance and racial discrimination are unjust. We think that we have examined these things with care and have reached what we believe is an impartial judgment not likely to be distorted by an excessive attention to our own interests. These convictions are provisional fixed points which we presume any conception of justice must fit. But we have much less assurance as to what is the correct distribution of wealth and authority. Here we may be looking for a way to remove our doubts. We can check an interpretation of the initial situation, then, by the capacity of its principles to accommodate our firmest convictions and to provide guidance where guidance is needed.

In searching for the most favored description of this situation we work from both ends. We begin by describing it so that it represents generally shared and preferably weak conditions. We then see if these conditions are strong enough to yield a significant set of principles. If not, we look for further premises equally reasonable. But if so, and these principles match our considered convictions of justice, then so far well and good. But presumably there will be discrepancies. In this case we have a choice. We can either modify the account of the initial situation or we can revise our existing judgments, for even the judgments we take provisionally as fixed points are liable to revision. By going back and forth, sometimes altering the conditions of the contractual circum-

stances, at others withdrawing our judgments and conforming them to principle, I assume that eventually we shall find a description of the initial situation that both expresses reasonable conditions and yields principles which match our considered judgments duly pruned and adjusted. This state of affairs I refer to as reflective equilibrium.[1] It is an equilibrium because at last our principles and judgments coincide; and it is reflective since we know to what principles our judgments conform and the premises of their derivation. At the moment everything is in order. But this equilibrium is not necessarily stable. It is liable to be upset by further examination of the conditions which should be imposed on the contractual situation and by particular cases which may lead us to revise our judgments. Yet for the time being we have done what we can to render coherent and to justify our convictions of social justice. We have reached a conception of the original position.

I shall not, of course, actually work through this process. Still, we may think of the interpretation of the original position that I shall present as the result of such a hypothetical course of reflection. It represents the attempt to accommodate within one scheme both reasonable philosophical conditions on principles as well as our considered judgments of justice. In arriving at the favored interpretation of the initial situation there is no point at which an appeal is made to self-evidence in the traditional sense either of general conceptions or particular convictions. I do not claim for the principles of justice proposed that they are necessary truths or derivable from such truths. A conception of justice cannot be deduced from self-evident premises or conditions on principles; instead, its justification is a matter of the mutual support of many considerations, of everything fitting together into one coherent view.

A final comment. We shall want to say that certain principles of justice are justified because they would be agreed to in an initial situation of equality. I have emphasized that this original position is purely hypothetical. It is natural to ask why, if this agreement is never actually entered into, we should take any interest in these principles, moral or otherwise. The answer is that the conditions embodied in the description of the original position are ones that we do in fact accept. Or if we do not, then perhaps we can be persuaded to do so by philosophical reflection. Each aspect of the contractual situation can be given supporting grounds. Thus what we shall do is to collect together into one conception a number of conditions on principles that we are ready upon due consideration to recognize as reasonable. These constraints express what we are prepared to regard as limits on fair terms of social cooperation. One way to look at the idea of the original position, therefore, is to see it as an expository device which sums up the meaning of these conditions and helps us to extract their consequences. On the other hand, this conception is also an intuitive notion that suggests its own elaboration, so that led on by it we are drawn to define more clearly the standpoint from which we can best interpret moral relationships. We need a conception that enables us to envision our objective from afar: the intuitive notion of the original position is to do this for us.

5. Classical Utilitarianism

. . . [T]he kind of utilitarianism I shall describe here is the strict classical doctrine which receives perhaps its clearest and most accessible formulation in Sidgwick. The main idea is that society is rightly ordered, and therefore just, when its major institutions are arranged so as to achieve the greatest net balance of satisfaction summed over all the individuals belonging to it.

We may note first that there is, indeed, a way of thinking of society which makes it easy to suppose that the most rational conception of justice is utilitarian. For consider: each man in realizing his own interests is certainly free to balance his own losses against his own gains. We may impose a sacrifice on ourselves now for the sake of a greater advantage later. A person quite properly acts, at least when others are not affected, to achieve his own greatest good, to advance his rational ends as far as possible. Now why should not a society act on precisely the same principle applied to the group and therefore regard that which is rational for one man as right for an association of men? Just as the well-being of a person is constructed from the series of satisfactions that

are experienced at different moments in the course of his life, so in very much the same way the well-being of society is to be constructed from the fulfillment of the systems of desires of the many individuals who belong to it. Since the principle for an individual is to advance as far as possible his own welfare, his own system of desires, the principle for society is to advance as far as possible the welfare of the group, to realize to the greatest extent the comprehensive system of desire arrived at from the desires of its members. Just as an individual balances present and future gains against present and future losses, so a society may balance satisfactions and dissatisfactions between different individuals. And so by these reflections one reaches the principle of utility in a natural way: a society is properly arranged when its institutions maximize the net balance of satisfaction. The principle of choice for an association of men is interpreted as an extension of the principle of choice for one man. Social justice is the principle of rational prudence applied to an aggregative conception of the welfare of the group. . . .

This idea is made all the more attractive by a further consideration. The two main concepts of ethics are those of the right and the good; the concept of a morally worthy person is, I believe, derived from them. The structure of an ethical theory is, then, largely determined by how it defines and connects these two basic notions. Now it seems that the simplest way of relating them is taken by teleological theories: the good is defined independently from the right, and then the right is defined as that which maximizes the good. More precisely, those institutions and acts are right which of the available alternatives produce the most good, or at least as much good as any of the other institutions and acts open as real possibilities (a rider needed when the maximal class is not a singleton). Teleological theories have a deep intuitive appeal since they seem to embody the idea of rationality. It is natural to think that rationality is maximizing something and that in morals it must be maximizing the good. Indeed, it is tempting to suppose that it is self-evident that things should be arranged so as to lead to the most good.

It is essential to keep in mind that in a teleological theory the good is defined independently from the right. This means two things. First, the theory accounts for our considered judgments as to which things are good (our judgments of value) as a separate class of judgments intuitively distinguishable by common sense, and then proposes the hypothesis that the right is maximizing the good as already specified. Second, the theory enables one to judge the goodness of things without referring to what is right. For example, if pleasure is said to be the sole good, then presumably pleasures can be recognized and ranked in value by criteria that do not presuppose any standards of right, or what we would normally think of as such. Whereas if the distribution of goods is also counted as a good, perhaps a higher order one, and the theory directs us to produce the most good (including the good of distribution among others), we no longer have a teleological view in the classical sense. The problem of distribution falls under the concept of right as one intuitively understands it, and so the theory lacks an independent definition of the good. The clarity and simplicity of classical teleological theories derives largely from the fact that they factor our moral judgments into two classes, the one being characterized separately while the other is then connected with it by a maximizing principle.

Teleological doctrines differ, pretty clearly, according to how the conception of the good is specified. If it is taken as the realization of human excellence in the various forms of culture, we have what may be called perfectionism. This notion is found in Aristotle and Nietzsche, among others. If the good is defined as pleasure, we have hedonism; if as happiness, eudaimonism, and so on. I shall understand the principle of utility in its classical form as defining the good as the satisfaction of desire, or perhaps better, as the satisfaction of rational desire. This accords with the view in all essentials and provides, I believe, a fair interpretation of it. The appropriate terms of social cooperation are settled by whatever in the circumstances will achieve the greatest sum of satisfaction of the rational desires of individuals. It is impossible to deny the initial plausibility and attractiveness of this conception.

The striking feature of the utilitarian view of justice is that it does not matter, except indirectly, how this sum of satisfactions is distributed among individuals any more than it matters, except indirectly, how one man distributes his satisfactions over time. The correct distribution in either case is that which yields the maximum fulfillment. Society must allocate its means of satisfaction whatever these are, rights and duties, opportunities and privileges, and various forms of wealth, so as to achieve this maximum if it can. But in itself no distribution of satisfaction is better than another except that the more equal distribution is to be preferred to break ties. It is true that certain common-sense precepts of justice, particularly those which concern the protection of liberties and rights, or which express the claims of desert, seem to contradict this contention. But from a utilitarian standpoint the explanation of these precepts and of their seemingly stringent character is that they are those precepts which experience shows should be strictly respected and departed from only under exceptional circumstances if the sum of advantages is to be maximized. Yet, as with all other precepts, those of justice are derivative from the one end of attaining the greatest balance of satisfaction. Thus there is no reason in principle why the greater gains of some should not compensate for the lesser losses of others; or more importantly, why the violation of the liberty of a few might not be made right by the greater good shared by many. It simply happens that under most conditions, at least in a reasonably advanced stage of civilization, the greatest sum of advantages is not attained in this way. No doubt the strictness of common-sense precepts of justice has a certain usefulness in limiting men's propensities to injustice and to socially injurious actions, but the utilitarian believes that to affirm this strictness as a first principle of morals is a mistake. For just as it is rational for one man to maximize the fulfillment of his system of desires, it is right for a society to maximize the net balance of satisfaction taken over all of its members.

The most natural way, then, of arriving at utilitarianism (although not, of course, the only way of doing so) is to adopt for society as a whole the principle of rational choice for one man. Once this is recognized, the place of the impartial spectator and the emphasis on sympathy in the history of utilitarian thought is readily understood. For it is by the conception of the impartial spectator and the use of sympathetic identification in guiding our imagination that the principle for one man is applied to society. It is this spectator who is conceived as carrying out the required organization of the desires of all persons into one coherent system of desire; it is by this construction that many persons are fused into one. Endowed with ideal powers of sympathy and imagination, the impartial spectator is the perfectly rational individual who identifies with and experiences the desires of others as if these desires were his own. In this way he ascertains the intensity of these desires and assigns them their appropriate weight in the one system of desire the satisfaction of which the ideal legislator then tries to maximize by adjusting the rules of the social system. On this conception of society separate individuals are thought of as so many different lines along which rights and duties are to be assigned and scarce means of satisfaction allocated in accordance with rules so as to give the greatest fulfillment of wants. The nature of the decision made by the ideal legislator is not, therefore, materially different from that of an entrepreneur deciding how to maximize his profit by producing this or that commodity, or that of a consumer deciding how to maximize his satisfaction by the purchase of this or that collection of goods. In each case there is a single person whose system of desires determines the best allocation of limited means. The correct decision is essentially a question of efficient administration. This view of social cooperation is the consequence of extending to society the principle of choice for one man, and then, to make this extension work, conflating all persons into one through the imaginative acts of the impartial sympathetic spectator. Utilitarianism does not take seriously the distinction between persons.

. . . .

11. Two Principles of Justice

I shall now state in a provisional form the two principles of justice that I believe would be chosen in the original position. . . .

The first statement of the two principles reads as follows.

First: each person is to have an equal right to the most extensive basic liberty compatible with a similar liberty for others.

Second: social and economic inequalities are to be arranged so that they are both (a) reasonably expected to be to everyone's advantage, and (b) attached to positions and offices open to all.

. . . .

By way of general comment, these principles primarily apply, as I have said, to the basic structure of society. They are to govern the assignment of rights and duties and to regulate the distribution of social and economic advantages. As their formulation suggests, these principles presuppose that the social structure can be divided into two more or less distinct parts, the first principle applying to the one, the second to the other. They distinguish between those aspects of the social system that define and secure the equal liberties of citizenship and those that specify and establish social and economic inequalities. The basic liberties of citizens are, roughly speaking, political liberty (the right to vote and to be eligible for public office) together with freedom of speech and assembly; liberty of conscience and freedom of thought; freedom of the person along with the right to hold (personal) property; and freedom from arbitrary arrest and seizure as defined by the concept of the rule of law. These liberties are all required to be equal by the first principle, since citizens of a just society are to have the same basic rights.

The second principle applies, in the first approximation, to the distribution of income and wealth and to the design of organizations that make use of differences in authority and responsibility, or chains of command. While the distribution of wealth and income need not be equal, it must be to everyone's advantage, and at the same time, positions of authority and offices of command must be accessible to all. One applies the second principle by holding positions open, and then, subject to this constraint, arranges social and economic inequalities so that everyone benefits.

These principles are to be arranged in a serial order with the first principle prior to the second. This ordering means that a departure from the institutions of equal liberty required by the first principle cannot be justified by, or compensated for, by greater social and economic advantages. The distribution of wealth and income, and the hierarchies of authority, must be consistent with both the liberties of equal citizenship and equality of opportunity.

It is clear that these principles are rather specific in their content, and their acceptance rests on certain assumptions that I must eventually try to explain and justify. A theory of justice depends upon a theory of society in ways that will become evident as we proceed. For the present, it should be observed that the two principles (and this holds for all formulations) are a special case of a more general conception of justice that can be expressed as follows.

All social values—liberty and opportunity, income and wealth, and the bases of self-respect—are to be distributed equally unless an unequal distribution of any, or all, of these values is to everyone's advantage.

Injustice, then, is simply inequalities that are not to the benefit of all. Of course, this conception is extremely vague and requires interpretation.

As a first step, suppose that the basic structure of society distributes certain primary goods, that is, things that every rational man is presumed to want. These goods normally have a use whatever a person's rational plan of life. For simplicity, assume that the chief primary goods at the disposition of society are rights and liberties, powers and opportunities, income and wealth. (Later on in Part Three the primary good of self-respect has a central place.) These are the social primary goods. Other primary goods such as health and vigor, intelligence and imagination, are natural goods; although their possession is influenced by the basic structure, they are not so directly under its control. Imagine, then, a hypothetical initial arrangement in which all the social primary goods are equally distributed: everyone has similar rights and duties, and income and wealth are evenly shared. This state of affairs provides a benchmark for judging improvements. If certain inequalities of wealth and organizational powers would make everyone better off than in this hypothetical starting situation, then they accord with the general conception.

Now it is possible, at least theoretically, that by giving up some of their fundamental liberties men are sufficiently compensated by the resulting social and economic gains. The general conception of justice imposes no restrictions on what sort of inequalities are permissible; it only requires that everyone's position be improved. We need not suppose anything so drastic as consenting to a condition of slavery. Imagine instead that men forego certain political rights when the economic returns are significant and their capacity to influence the course of policy by the exercise of these rights would be marginal in any case. It is this kind of exchange which the two principles as stated rule out; being arranged in serial order they do not permit exchanges between basic liberties and economic and social gains. The serial ordering of principles expresses an underlying preference among primary social goods. When this preference is rational so likewise is the choice of these principles in this order.

· · · · · · · ·

Now the second principle insists that each person benefit from permissible inequalities in the basic structure. This means that it must be reasonable for each relevant representative man defined by this structure, when he views it as a going concern, to prefer his prospects with the inequality to his prospects without it. One is not allowed to justify differences in income or organizational powers on the ground that the disadvantages of those in one position are outweighed by the greater advantages of those in another. Much less can infringements of liberty be counterbalanced in this way. Applied to the basic structure, the principle of utility would have us maximize the sum of expectations of representative men (weighted by the number of persons they represent, on the classical view); and this would permit us to compensate for the losses of some by the gains of others. Instead, the two principles require that everyone benefit from economic and social inequalities.

· · · · · · · ·

26. The Reasoning Leading to the Two Principles of Justice

In this [section] I take up the choice between the two principles of justice and the principle of average utility. Determining the rational preference between these two options is perhaps the central problem in developing the conception of justice as fairness as a viable alternative to the utilitarian tradition. I shall begin in this section by presenting some intuitive remarks favoring the two principles. I shall also discuss briefly the qualitative structure of the argument that needs to be made if the case for these principles is to be conclusive.

It will be recalled that the general conception of justice as fairness requires that all primary social goods be distributed equally unless an unequal distribution would be to everyone's advantage. No restrictions are placed on exchanges of these goods and therefore a lesser liberty can be compensated for by greater social and economic benefits. Now looking at the situation from the standpoint of one person selected arbitrarily, there is no way for him to win special advantages for himself. Nor, on the other hand, are there grounds for his acquiescing in special disadvantages. Since it is not reasonable for him to expect more than an equal share in the division of social goods, and since it is not rational for him to agree to less, the sensible thing for him to do is to acknowledge as the first principle of justice one requiring an equal distribution. Indeed, this principle is so obvious that we would expect it to occur to anyone immediately.

Thus, the parties start with a principle establishing equal liberty for all, including equality of opportunity, as well as an equal distribution of income and wealth. But there is no reason why this acknowledgment should be final. If there are inequalities in the basic structure that work to make everyone better off in comparison with the benchmark of initial equality, why not permit them? The immediate gain which a greater equality might allow can be regarded as intelligently invested in view of its future return. If, for example, these inequalities set up various incentives which succeed in eliciting more productive efforts, a person in the original position may look upon them as necessary to cover the costs of training and to encourage effective performance. One might think that ideally individuals should want to serve one another. But since the parties are assumed not to take an interest in one another's interests, their acceptance of these

inequalities is only the acceptance of the relations in which men stand in the circumstances of justice. They have no grounds for complaining of one another's motives. A person in the original position would, therefore, concede the justice of these inequalities. Indeed, it would be shortsighted of him not to do so. He would hesitate to agree to these regularities only if he would be dejected by the bare knowledge or perception that others were better situated; and I have assumed that the parties decide as if they are not moved by envy. In order to make the principle regulating inequalities determinate, one looks at the system from the standpoint of the least advantaged representative man. Inequalities are permissible when they maximize, or at least all contribute to, the long-term expectations of the least fortunate group in society.

Now this general conception imposes no constraints on what sorts of inequalities are allowed, whereas the special conception, by putting the two principles in serial order (with the necessary adjustments in meaning) forbids exchanges between basic liberties and economic and social benefits. I shall not try to justify this ordering here. . . . But roughly, the idea underlying this ordering is that if the parties assume that their basic liberties can be effectively exercised, they will not exchange a lesser liberty for an improvement in economic well-being. It is only when social conditions do not allow the effective establishment of these rights that one can concede their limitation; and these restrictions can be granted only to the extent that they are necessary to prepare the way for a free society. The denial of equal liberty can be defended only if it is necessary to raise the level of civilization so that in due course these freedoms can be enjoyed. Thus in adopting a serial order we are in effect making a special assumption in the original position, namely, that the parties know that the conditions of their society, whatever they are, admit the effective realization of the equal liberties. The serial ordering of the two principles of justice eventually comes to be reasonable if the general conception is consistently followed. This lexical ranking is the long-run tendency of the general view. For the most part I shall assume that the requisite circumstances for the serial order obtain.

It seems clear from these remarks that the two principles are at least a plausible conception of justice. The question, though, is how one is to argue for them more systematically. Now there are several things to do. One can work out their consequences for institutions and note their implications for fundamental social policy. In this way they are tested by a comparison with our considered judgments of justice. . . . But one can also try to find arguments in their favor that are decisive from the standpoint of the original position. In order to see how this might be done, it is useful as a heuristic device to think of the two principles as the maximin solution to the problem of social justice. There is an analogy between the two principles and the maximin rule for choice under uncertainty. This is evident from the fact that the two principles are those a person would choose for the design of a society in which his enemy is to assign him his place. The maximin rule tells us to rank alternatives by their worst possible outcomes: we are to adopt the alternative the worst outcome of which is superior to the worst outcomes of the others. The persons in the original position do not, of course, assume that their initial place in society is decided by a malevolent opponent. As I note below, they should not reason from false premises. The veil of ignorance does not violate this idea, since an absence of information is not misinformation. But that the two principles of justice would be chosen if the parties were forced to protect themselves against such a contingency explains the sense in which this conception is the maximin solution. And this analogy suggests that if the original position has been described so that it is rational for the parties to adopt the conservative attitude expressed by this rule, a conclusive argument can indeed be constructed for these principles. Clearly the maximin rule is not, in general, a suitable guide for choices under uncertainty. But it is attractive in situations marked by certain special features. My aim, then, is to show that a good case can be made for the two principles based on the fact that the original position manifests these features to the fullest possible degree, carrying them to the limit, so to speak.

Consider the gain-and-loss table below. It represents the gains and losses for a situation which is not a game of strategy. There is no one playing against the person making the decision; instead he is faced with several possible circumstances which may or may not obtain. Which circumstances happen to exist does not depend upon what the person choosing decides or whether he announces his moves in advance. The numbers in the table are monetary values (in hundreds of dollars) in comparison with some initial situation. The gain (g) depends upon the individual's decision (d) and the circumstances (c). Thus $g = f(d, c)$. Assuming that there are three possible decisions and three possible circumstances, we might have this gain-and-loss table.

Decisions	Circumstances		
	C_1	C_2	C_3
d_1	-7	8	12
d_2	-8	7	14
d_3	5	6	8

The maximin rule requires that we make the third decision. For in this case the worst that can happen is that one gains five hundred dollars, which is better than the worst for the other actions. If we adopt one of these we may lose either eight or seven hundred dollars. Thus, the choice of d_3 maximizes $f(d,c)$ for that value of c, which for a given d, minimizes f. The term "maximin" means the *maximum minimorum*; and the rule directs our attention to the worst that can happen under any proposed course of action, and to decide in the light of that.

Now there appear to be three chief features of situations that give plausibility to this unusual rule. First, since the rule takes no account of the likelihoods of the possible circumstances, there must be some reason for sharply discounting estimates of these probabilities. Offhand, the most natural rule of choice would seem to be to compute the expectation of monetary gain for each decision and then to adopt the course of action with the highest prospect. (This expectation is defined as follows: let us suppose that g_{ij} represent the numbers in the gain-and-loss table, where i is the row index and j is the column index; and let p_j, $j = 1, 2, 3$, be the likelihoods of the circumstances, with $\Sigma p_j = 1$. Then the expectation for the ith decision is equal to $\Sigma p_j g_{ij}$.) Thus it must be, for example, that the situation is one in which a knowledge of likelihoods is impossible, or at best extremely insecure. In this case it is unreasonable not to be skeptical of probabilistic calculations unless there is no other way out, particularly if the decision is a fundamental one that needs to be justified to others.

The second feature that suggests the maximin rule is the following: the person choosing has a conception of the good such that he cares very little, if anything, for what he might gain above the minimum stipend that he can, in fact, be sure of by following the maximin rule. It is not worthwhile for him to take a chance for the sake of a further advantage, especially when it may turn out that he loses much that is important to him. This last provision brings in the third feature, namely, that the rejected alternatives have outcomes that one can hardly accept. The situation involves grave risks. Of course these features work most effectively in combination. The paradigm situation for following the maximin rule is when all three features are realized to the highest degree. This rule does not, then, generally apply, nor of course is it self-evident. Rather, it is a maxim, a rule of thumb, that comes into its own in special circumstances. Its application depends upon the qualitative structure of the possible gains and losses in relation to one's conception of the good, all this against a background in which it is reasonable to discount conjectural estimates of likelihoods.

It should be noted, as the comments on the gain-and-loss table say, that the entries in the table represent monetary values and not utilities. This difference is significant since for one thing computing expectations on the basis of such objective values is not the same thing as computing expected utility and may lead to different results. The essential point though is that in justice as fairness the parties do not know their conception of the good and cannot estimate their utility in the ordinary sense. In any case, we want to go behind de facto preferences generated by given conditions. Therefore expectations are based upon an index of primary goods and the parties make their choice accordingly. The entries in the example are in terms of money and not utility to indicate this aspect of the contract doctrine.

Now, as I have suggested, the original position has been defined so that it is a situation in which the maximin rule applies. In order to see this, let us review briefly the nature of this situation with these three special features in mind. To begin with, the veil of ignorance excludes all but the vaguest knowledge of likelihoods. The parties have no basis for determining the probable nature of their society, or their place in it. Thus they have strong reasons for being wary of probability calculations if any other course is open to them. They must also take in account the fact that their choice of principles should seem reasonable to others, in particular their descendants, whose rights will be deeply affected by it. There are further grounds for discounting that I shall mention as we go along. For the present it suffices to note that these considerations are strengthened by the fact that the parties know very little about the gain-and-loss table. Not only are they unable to conjecture the likelihoods of the various possible circumstances, they cannot say much about what the possible circumstances are, much less enumerate them and foresee the outcome of each alternative available. Those deciding are much more in the dark than the illustration by a numerical table suggests. It is for this reason that I have spoken of an analogy with the maximin rule.

Several kinds of arguments for the two principles of justice illustrate the second feature. Thus, if we can maintain that these principles provide a workable theory of social justice, and that they are compatible with reasonable demands of efficiency, then this conception guarantees a satisfactory minimum. There may be, on reflection, little reason for trying to do better. . . .

Finally, the third feature holds if we can assume that other conceptions of justice may lead to institutions that the parties would find intolerable. For example, it has sometimes been held that under some conditions the utility principle (in either form) justifies, if not slavery or serfdom, at any rate serious infractions of liberty for the sake of greater social benefits. We need not consider here the truth of this claim, or the likelihood that the requisite conditions obtain. For the moment, this contention is only to illustrate the way in which conceptions of justice may allow for outcomes which the parties may not be able to accept. And having the ready alternative of the two principles of justice which secure a satisfactory minimum, it seems unwise, if not irrational, for them to take a chance that these outcomes are not realized.

NOTE

1. The process of mutual adjustment of principles and considered judgments is not peculiar to moral philosophy. See Nelson Goodman, *Fact, Fiction, and Forecast* (Cambridge, Mass.: Harvard University Press, 1955), pp. 65–68, for parallel remarks concerning the justification of the principles of deductive and inductive inference.

Justice and Entitlement

ROBERT NOZICK

Robert Nozick (1938–) is a professor of philosophy at Harvard University. His publications include *Philosophical Explanations* and *The Nature of Rationality*.

———•———

Chapter 7
Distributive Justice

. . . .

The term "distributive justice" is not a neutral one. Hearing the term "distribution," most people presume that some thing or mechanism uses some principle or criterion to give out a supply of things. Into this process of distributing shares some error may have crept. So it is an open question, at least, whether *re*distribution should take place; whether we should do again what has already been done once, though poorly. However, we are not in the position of children who have been given portions of pie by someone who now makes last minute adjustments to rectify careless cutting. There is no *central* distribution, no person or group entitled to control all the resources,

jointly deciding how they are to be doled out. What each person gets, he gets from others who give to him in exchange for something, or as a gift. In a free society, diverse persons control different resources, and new holdings arise out of the voluntary exchanges and actions of persons. There is no more a distributing or distribution of shares than there is a distributing of mates in a society in which persons choose whom they shall marry. The total result is the product of many individual decisions which the different individuals involved are entitled to make. . . . We shall speak of people's holdings; a principle of justice in holdings describes (part of) what justice tells us (requires) about holdings. I shall state first what I take to be the correct view about justice in holdings, and then turn to the discussion of alternate views.

The Entitlement Theory

The subject of justice in holdings consists of three major topics. The first is the *original acquisition of holdings*, the appropriation of unheld things. This includes the issues of how unheld things may come to be held, the process, or processes, by which unheld things may come to be held, the things that may come to be held by these processes, the extent of what comes to be held by a particular process, and so on. We shall refer to the complicated truth about this topic, which we shall not formulate here, as the principle of justice in acquisition. The second topic concerns the *transfer of holdings* from one person to another. By what processes may a person transfer holdings to another? How may a person acquire a holding from another who holds it? Under this topic come general descriptions of voluntary exchange, and gift and (on the other hand) fraud, as well as reference to particular conventional details fixed upon in a given society. The complicated truth about this subject (with placeholders for conventional details) we shall call the principle of justice in transfer. (And we shall suppose it also includes principles governing how a person may divest himself of a holding, passing it into an unheld state.)

If the world were wholly just, the following inductive definition would exhaustively cover the subject of justice in holdings.

1. A person who acquires a holding in accordance with the principle of justice in acquisition is entitled to that holding.
2. A person who acquires a holding in accordance with the principle of justice in transfer, from someone else entitled to the holding, is entitled to the holding.
3. No one is entitled to a holding except by (repeated) applications of 1 and 2.

The complete principle of distributive justice would say simply that a distribution is just if everyone is entitled to the holdings they possess under the distribution.

A distribution is just if it arises from another just distribution by legitimate means. The legitimate means of moving from one distribution to another are specified by the principle of justice in transfer. The legitimate first "moves" are specified by the principle of justice in acquisition.[1] Whatever arises from a just situation by just steps is itself just. The means of change specified by the principle of justice in transfer preserve justice. As correct rules of in-

ference are truth preserving, and any conclusion deduced via repeated application of such rules from only true premises is itself true, so the means of transition from one situation to another specified by the principle of justice in transfer are justice preserving, and any situation actually arising from repeated transitions in accordance with the principle from a just situation is itself just. The parallel between justice-preserving transformations and truth-preserving transformations illuminates where it fails as well as where it holds. That a conclusion could have been deduced by truth-preserving means from premises that are true suffices to show its truth. That from a just situation a situation *could* have arisen via justice-preserving means does *not* suffice to show its justice. The fact that a thief's victims voluntarily *could* have presented him with gifts does not entitle the thief to his ill-gotten gains. Justice in holdings is historical; it depends upon what actually has happened. We shall return to this point later.

Not all actual situations are generated in accordance with the two principles of justice in holdings: the principle of justice in acquisition and the principle of justice in transfer. Some people steal from others, or defraud them, or enslave them, seizing their product and preventing them from living as they choose, or forcibly exclude others from competing in exchanges. None of these are permissible modes of transition from one situation to another. And some persons acquire holdings by means not sanctioned by the principle of justice in acquisition. The existence of past injustice (previous violations of the first two principles of justice in holdings) raises the third major topic under justice in holdings: the rectification of injustice in holdings. If past injustice has shaped present holdings in various ways, some identifiable and some not, what now, if anything, ought to be done to rectify these injustices? What obligations do the performers of injustice have toward those whose position is worse than it would have been had the injustice not been done? Or, than it would have been had compensation been paid promptly? How, if at all, do things change if the beneficiaries and those made worse off are not the direct parties in the act of injustice, but, for example, their descendants? Is an injustice done to someone whose holding was itself based upon an unrectified injustice? How far back must one go in wiping clean the historical slate of injustices? What may victims of injustice permissibly do in order to rectify the injustices being done to them, including the many injustices done by persons acting through their government? I do not know of a thorough or theoretically sophisticated treatment of such issues. Idealizing greatly, let us suppose theoretical investigation will produce a principle of rectification. This principle uses historical information about previous situations and injustices done in them (as defined by the first two principles of justice and rights against interference), and information about the actual course of events that flowed from these injustices, until the present, and it yields a description (or descriptions) of holdings in the society. The principle of rectification presumably will make use of its best estimate of subjunctive information about what would have occurred (or a probability distribution over what might have occurred, using the expected value) if the injustice had not taken place. If the actual description of holdings turns out not to be one of the descriptions yielded by the principle, then one of the descriptions yielded must be realized.[2]

The general outlines of the theory of justice in holdings are that the holdings of a person are just if he is entitled to them by the principles of justice in acquisition and transfer, or by the principle of rectification of injustice (as specified by the first two principles). If each person's holdings are just, then the total set (distribution) of holdings is just. To turn these general outlines into a specific theory we would have to specify the details of each of the three principles of justice in holdings: the principle of acquisition of holdings, the principle of transfer of holdings, and the principle of rectification of violations of the first two principles. I shall not attempt that task here. (Locke's principle of justice in acquisition is discussed below.)

Historical Principles and End-result Principles

The general outlines of the entitlement theory illuminate the nature and defects of other conceptions of distributive justice. The entitlement theory of justice in distribution is *historical*; whether a distribution is just depends upon how it came about. In contrast, *current time-slice principles* of justice hold that the justice of a distribution is determined by how things are distributed (who has what) as judged by some *structural* principle(s) of just distribution. A utilitarian who judges between any two distributions by seeing which has the greater sum of utility and, if the sums tie, applies some fixed equality criterion to choose the more equal distribution, would hold a current time-slice principle of justice. As would someone who had a fixed schedule of trade-offs between the sum of happiness and equality. According to a current time-slice principle, all that needs to be looked at, in judging the justice of a distribution, is who ends up with what; in comparing any two distributions one need look only at the matrix presenting the distributions. No further information need be fed into a principle of justice. It is a consequence of such principles of justice that any two structurally identical distributions are equally just. (Two distributions are structurally identical if they present the same profile, but perhaps have different persons occupying the particular slots. My having ten and your having five, and my having five and your having ten are structurally identical distributions.) Welfare economics is the theory of current time-slice principles of justice. The subject is conceived as operating on matrices representing only current information about distribution. This, as well as some of the usual conditions (for example, the choice of distribution is invariant under relabeling of columns), guarantees that welfare economics will be a current time-slice theory, with all of its inadequacies.

Most persons do not accept current time-slice principles as constituting the whole story about distributive shares. They think it relevant in assessing the justice of a situation to consider not only the distribution it embodies, but also how that distribution came about. If some persons are in prison for murder or war crimes, we do not say that to assess the justice of the distribution in the society we must look only at what this person has, and that person has, and that person has, . . . at the current time. We think it relevant to ask whether someone did something so that he *deserved* to be punished, deserved to have a lower share. Most will agree to the relevance of further information with regard to punishments and penalties. Consider also desired things. One traditional socialist view is that workers are entitled to the product and full fruits of their labor; they have earned it; a distribution is unjust if it does not give the workers what they are entitled to. Such entitlements are based upon some past history. No socialist holding this view would find it comforting to be told that because the actual distribution A happens to coincide structurally with the one he desires D, A therefore is no less just that D; it differs only in that the "parasitic" owners of capital receive under A what the workers are entitled to under D, and the workers receive under A what the owners are entitled to under D, namely very little. This socialist rightly, in my view, holds onto the notions of earning, producing, entitlement, desert, and so forth, and he rejects current time-slice principles that look only to the structure of the resulting set of holdings. (The set of holdings resulting from what? Isn't is implausible that how holdings are produced and come to exist has no effect at all on who should hold what?) His mistake lies in his view of what entitlements arise out of what sorts of productive processes.

We construe the position we discuss too narrowly by speaking of *current* time-slice principles. Nothing is changed if structural principles operate upon a time sequence of current time-slice profiles and, for example, give someone more now to counterbalance the less he has had earlier. A utilitarian or an egalitarian or any mixture of the two over time will inherit the difficulties of his more myopic comrades. He is not helped by the fact that *some* of the information others consider relevant in assessing a distribution is reflected, unrecoverably, in past matrices. Henceforth, we shall refer to such unhistorical principles of distributive justice, including the current time-slice principles, as *end-result principles* or *end-state principles*.

In contrast to end-result principles of justice, *historical principles* of justice hold that past circumstances or actions of people can create differential entitlement or differential deserts to things. An injustice can be worked by moving from one distribution to another structurally identical one, for the second, in profile the same, may violate people's entitlements or deserts; it may not fit the actual history.

Patterning

The entitlement principles of justice in holdings that we have sketched are historical principles of justice. To better understand their precise character, we shall distinguish them from another subclass of the historical principles. Consider, as an example, the principle of distribution according to moral merit. This principle requires that total distributive shares vary directly with moral merit; no person should have a greater share than anyone whose moral merit is greater. (If moral merit could be not merely ordered but measured on an interval or ratio scale, stronger principles could be formulated.) Or consider the principle that results by substituting "usefulness to society" for "moral merit" in the previous principle. Or instead of "distribute according to moral merit," or "distribute according to usefulness to society," we might consider "distribute according to the weighted sum of moral merit, usefulness to society, and need," with the weights of the different dimensions equal. Let us call a principle of distribution *patterned* if it specifies that a distribution is to vary along with some natural dimension, weighted sum of natural dimensions, or lexicographic ordering of natural dimensions. And let us say a distribution is patterned if it accords with some patterned principle. (I speak of natural dimensions, admittedly without a general criterion for them, because for any set of holdings some artificial dimensions can be gimmicked up to vary along with the distribution of the set.) The principle of distribution in accordance with moral merit is a patterned historical principle, which specifies a patterned distribution. "Distribute according to I.Q." is a patterned principle that looks to information not contained in distributional matrices. It is not historical, however, in that it does not look to any past actions creating differential entitlements to evaluate a distribution; it requires only distributional matrices whose columns are labeled by I.Q. scores. The distribution in a society, however, may be composed of such simple patterned distributions, without itself being simply patterned. Different sectors may operate different patterns, or some combination of patterns may operate in different proportions across a society. A distribution composed in this manner, from a small number of patterned distributions, we also shall term "patterned." And we extend the use of "pattern" to include the overall designs put forth by combinations of end-state principles.

Almost every suggested principle of distributive justice is patterned: to each according to his moral merit, or needs, or marginal product, or how hard he tries, or the weighted sum of the foregoing, and so on. The principle of entitlement we have sketched is *not* patterned. There is no one natural dimension or weighted sum or combination of a small number of natural dimensions that yields the distributions generated in accordance with the principle of entitlement. The set of holdings that results when some persons receive their marginal products, others win at gambling, others receive a share of their mate's income, others receive gifts from foundations, others receive interest on loans, others receive gifts from admirers, others receive returns on investment, others make for themselves much of what they have, others find things, and so on, will not be patterned.

. . . .

How Liberty Upsets Patterns

It is not clear how those holding alternative conceptions of distributive justice can reject the entitlement conception of justice in holdings. For suppose a distribution favored by one of these nonentitlement conceptions is realized. Let us suppose it is your favorite one and let us call this distribution D_1; perhaps everyone has an equal share, perhaps shares vary in accordance with some dimension you treasure. Now suppose that Wilt Chamberlain is greatly in demand by basketball teams, being a great gate attraction. (Also suppose contracts run only for a year, with players being free agents.) He signs the following sort of contract with a team: In each home game, twenty-five cents from the price of each ticket of admission goes to him. (We ignore the question of whether this is "gouging" the owners, letting them look out for themselves.) The season starts, and people cheerfully attend his team's games; they buy their tickets, each time dropping a separate twenty-five cents of their admission price into a special box with Chamberlain's name on it. They are excited about seeing him play; it is worth the total

admission price to them. Let us suppose that in one season one million persons attend his home games, and Wilt Chamberlain winds up with $250,000, a much larger sum than the average income and larger even than anyone else has. Is he entitled to this income? Is this new distribution D_2, unjust? If so, why? There is *no* question about whether each of the people was entitled to the control over the resources they held in D_1; because that was the distribution (your favorite) that (for the purposes of argument) we assumed was acceptable. Each of these persons *chose* to give twenty-five cents of their money to Chamberlain. They could have spent it on going to the movies, or on candy bars, or on copies of *Dissent* magazine, or of *Monthly Review*. But they all, at least one million of them, converged on giving it to Wilt Chamberlain in exchange for watching him play basketball. If D_1 was a just distribution, and people voluntarily moved from it to D_2, transferring parts of their shares they were given under D_1 (what was it for if not to do something with?), isn't D_2 also just? If the people were entitled to dispose of the resources to which they were entitled (under D_1), didn't this include their being entitled to give it to, or exchange it with, Wilt Chamberlain? Can anyone else complain on grounds of justice? Each other person already has his legitimate share under D_1. Under D_1, there is nothing that anyone has that anyone else has a claim of justice against. After someone transfers something to Wilt Chamberlain, third parties *still* have their legitimate shares; *their* shares are not changed. By what process could such a transfer among two persons give rise to a legitimate claim of distributive justice on a portion of what was transferred, by a third party who had no claim of justice on any holding of the others *before* the transfer?

. . . .

The general point illustrated by the Wilt Chamberlain example . . . is that no end-state principle or distributional-patterned principle of justice can be continuously realized without continuous interference with people's lives. Any favored pattern would be transformed into one unfavored by the principle, by people choosing to act in various ways; for example, by people exchanging goods and services with other people, or giving things to other people, things the transferrers are entitled to under the favored distributional pattern. To maintain a pattern one must either continually interfere to stop people from transferring resources as they wish to, or continually (or periodically) interfere to take from some persons resources that others for some reason chose to transfer to them.

. . . .

Locke's Theory of Acquisition

. . . [W]e must introduce an additional bit of complexity into the structure of the entitlement theory. This is best approached by considering Locke's attempt to specify a principle of justice in acquisition. Locke views property rights in an unowned object as originating through someone's mixing his labor with it. This gives rise to many questions. What are the boundaries of what labor is mixed with? If a private astronaut clears a place on Mars, has he mixed his labor with (so that he comes to own) the whole planet, the whole uninhabited universe, or just a particular plot? Which plot does an act bring under ownership? The minimal (possibly disconnected) area such that an act decreases entropy in that area, and not elsewhere? Can virgin land (for the purposes of ecological investigation by high-flying airplane) come under ownership by a Lockean process? Building a fence around a territory presumably would make one the owner of only the fence (and the land immediately underneath it).

Why does mixing one's labor with something make one the owner of it? Perhaps because one owns one's labor, and so one comes to own a previously unowned thing that becomes permeated with what one owns. Ownership seeps over into the rest. But why isn't mixing what I own with what I don't own a way of losing what I own rather than a way of gaining what I don't? If I own a can of tomato juice and spill it in the sea so that its molecules (made radioactive, so I can check this) mingle evenly throughout the sea, do I thereby come to own the sea, or have I foolishly dissipated my tomato juice? Perhaps the idea, instead, is that laboring on something improves it and makes it more valuable; and anyone is entitled to own a thing whose value he has

created. (Reinforcing this, perhaps, is the view that laboring is unpleasant. If some people made things effortlessly, as the cartoon characters in *The Yellow Submarine* trail flowers in their wake, would they have lesser claim to their own products whose making didn't *cost* them anything?) Ignore the fact that laboring on something may make it less valuable (spraying pink enamel paint on a piece of driftwood that you have found). Why should one's entitlement extend to the whole object rather than just to the *added value* one's labor has produced? (Such reference to value might also serve to delimit the extent of ownership; for example, substitute "increases the value of" for "decreases entropy in" in the above entropy criterion.) No workable or coherent value-added property scheme has yet been devised, and any such scheme presumably would fall to objections (similar to those) that fell the theory of Henry George.

It will be implausible to view improving an object as giving full ownership to it, if the stock of unowned objects that might be improved is limited. For an object's coming under one person's ownership changes the situation of all others. Whereas previously they were at liberty (in Hohfeld's sense) to use the object, they now no longer are. This change in the situation of others (by removing their liberty to act on a previously unowned object) need not worsen their situation. If I appropriate a grain of sand from Coney Island, no one else may now do as they will with *that* grain of sand. But there are plenty of other grains of sand left for them to do the same with. Or if not grains of sand, then other things. Alternatively, the things I do with the grain of sand I appropriate might improve the position of others, counterbalancing their loss of the liberty to use that grain. The crucial point is whether appropriation of an unowned object worsens the situation of others.

Locke's proviso that there be "enough and as good left in common for others" (sect. 27) is meant to ensure that the situation of others is not worsened.

. . . .

Is the situation of persons who are unable to appropriate (there being no more accessible and useful unowned objects) worsened by a system allowing appropriation and permanent property? Here enter the various familiar social considerations favoring private property: it increases the social product by putting means of production in the hands of those who can use them most efficiently (profitably); experimentation is encouraged, because with separate persons controlling resources, there is no one person or small group whom someone with a new idea must convince to try it out; private property enables people to decide on the pattern and types of risks they wish to bear, leading to specialized types of risk bearing; private property protects future persons by leading some to hold back resources from current consumption for future markets; it provides alternate sources of employment for unpopular persons who don't have to convince any one person or small group to hire them, and so on. These considerations enter a Lockean theory to support the claim that appropriation of private property satisfies the intent behind the "enough and as good left over" proviso, *not* as a utilitarian justification of property. They enter to rebut the claim that because the proviso is violated no natural right to private property can arise by a Lockean process. The difficulty in working such an argument to show that the proviso is satisfied is in fixing the appropriate baseline for comparison. Lockean appropriation makes people no worse off than they would be *how?* This question of fixing the baseline needs more detailed investigation than we are able to give it here.

. . . .

The Proviso

Whether or not Locke's particular theory of appropriation can be spelled out so as to handle various difficulties, I assume that any adequate theory of justice in acquisition will contain a proviso similar to the weaker of the ones we have attributed to Locke. A process normally giving rise to a permanent bequeathable property right in a previously unowned thing will not do so if the position of others no longer at liberty to use the thing is thereby worsened. It is important to specify *this* particular mode of worsening the situation of others, for the proviso does not encompass other modes. It does not include the worsening due to more limited opportunities to

appropriate . . . , and it does not include how I "worsen" a seller's position if I appropriate materials to make some of what he is selling, and then enter into competition with him. Someone whose appropriation otherwise would violate the proviso still may appropriate provided he compensates the others so that their situation is not thereby worsened; unless he does compensate the others, his appropriation will violate the proviso of the principle of justice in acquisition and will be an illegitimate one. A theory of appropriation incorporating this Lockean proviso will handle correctly the cases (objections to the theory lacking the proviso) where someone appropriates the total supply of something necessary for life.

A theory which includes this proviso in its principle of justice in acquisition must also contain a more complex principle of justice in transfer. Some reflection of the proviso about appropriation constrains later actions. If my appropriating all of a certain substance violates the Lockean proviso, then so does my appropriating some and purchasing all the rest from others who obtained it without otherwise violating the Lockean proviso. If the proviso excludes someone's appropriating all the drinkable water in the world, it also excludes his purchasing it all. (More weakly, and messily, it may exclude his charging certain prices for some of his supply.) This proviso (almost?) never will come into effect; the more someone acquires of a scarce substance which others want, the higher the price of the rest will go, and the more difficult it will become for him to acquire it all. But still, we can imagine, at least, that something like this occurs: someone makes simultaneous secret bids to the separate owners of a substance, each of whom sells assuming he can easily purchase more from the other owners; or some natural catastrophe destroys all of the supply of something except that in one person's possession. The total supply could not be permissibly appropriated by one person at the beginning. His later acquisition of it all does not show that the original appropriation violated the proviso. . . . Rather, it is the combination of the original appropriation *plus* all the later transfers and actions that violates the Lockean proviso.

Each owner's title to his holding includes the historical shadow of the Lockean proviso on appropriation. This excludes his transferring it into an agglomeration that does violate the Lockean proviso and excludes his using it in a way, in coordination with others or independently of them, so as to violate the proviso by making the situation of others worse than their baseline situation. Once it is known that someone's ownership runs afoul of the Lockean proviso, there are stringent limits on what he may do with (what it is difficult any longer unreservedly to call) "his property." Thus a person may not appropriate the only water hole in a desert and charge what he will. Nor may he charge what he will if he possesses one, and unfortunately it happens that all the water holes in the desert dry up, except for his. This unfortunate circumstance, admittedly no fault of his, brings into operation the Lockean proviso and limits his property rights. Similarly, an owner's property right in the only island in an area does not allow him to order a castaway from a shipwreck off his island as a trespasser, for this would violate the Lockean proviso.

. . . .

The fact that someone owns the total supply of something necessary for others to stay alive does *not* entail that his (or anyone's) appropriation of anything left some people (immediately or later) in a situation worse than the baseline one. A medical researcher who synthesizes a new substance that effectively treats a certain disease and who refuses to sell except on his terms does not worsen the situation of others by depriving them of whatever he has appropriated. The others easily can possess the same materials he appropriated; the researcher's appropriation or purchase of chemicals didn't make those chemicals scarce in a way so as to violate the Lockean proviso. Nor would someone else's purchasing the total supply of the synthesized substance from the medical researcher. The fact that the medical researcher uses easily available chemicals to synthesize the drug no more violates the Lockean proviso than does the fact that the only surgeon able to perform a particular operation eats easily obtainable food in order to stay alive and to have the energy to work. This shows that the Lockean proviso is not an "end-state principle"; it focuses on a particular way that appropriative actions affect others, and not on the structure of the situation that results.

Intermediate between someone who takes all of

the public supply and someone who makes the total supply out of easily obtainable substances is someone who appropriates the total supply of something in a way that does not deprive the others of it. For example, someone finds a new substance in an out-of-the-way place. He discovers that it effectively treats a certain disease and appropriates the total supply. He does not worsen the situation of others; if he did not stumble upon the substance no one else would have, and the others would remain without it. However, as time passes, the likelihood increases that others would have come across the substance; upon this fact might be based a limit to his property right in the substance so that others are not below their baseline position; for example, its bequest might be limited. The theme of someone worsening another's situation by depriving him of something he otherwise would possess may also illuminate the example of patents. An inventor's patent does not deprive others of an object which would not exist if not for the inventor. Yet patents would have this effect on others who independently invent the object. Therefore, these independent inventors, upon whom the burden of proving independent discovery may rest, should not be excluded from utilizing their own invention as they wish (including selling it to others). Furthermore, a known inventor drastically lessens the chances of actual independent invention. For persons who know of an invention usually will not try to reinvent it, and the notion of independent discovery here would be murky at best. Yet we may assume that in the absence of the original invention, sometime later someone else would have come up with it. This suggests placing a time limit on patents, as a rough rule of thumb to approximate how long it would have taken, in the absence of knowledge of the invention, for independent discovery.

I believe that the free operation of a market system will not actually run afoul of the Lockean proviso. . . .

NOTES

1. Applications of the principle of justice in acquisition may also occur as part of the move from one distribution to another. You may find an unheld thing now and appropriate it. Acquisitions also are

to be understood as included when, to simplify, I speak only of transitions by transfers.

2. If the principle of rectification of violations of the first two principles yields more than one description of holdings, then some choice must be made as to which of these is to be realized. Perhaps the sort of considerations about distributive justice and equality that I argue against play a legitimate role in *this* subsidiary choice. Similarly, there may be room for such considerations in deciding which otherwise arbitrary features a statute will embody, when such features are unavoidable because other considerations do not specify a precise line; yet a line must be drawn.

Where the Action Is: On the Site of Distributive Justice

G. A. COHEN

G.A. Cohen (1941–   ) is professor of philosophy at All Souls College, Oxford. He is the author of *Self-ownership, Freedom, and Equality*.

—•—

I

In this paper I defend a claim which can be expressed in the words of a now familiar slogan: the personal is political. That slogan, as it stands, is vague, but I shall mean something reasonably precise by it here, to wit, that principles of distributive justice, principles, that is, about the just distribution of benefits and burdens in society, apply, wherever else they do, to people's legally unconstrained choices. Those principles, so I claim, apply to the choices that people make *within* the legally coercive structures to which, so everyone would agree, principles of justice (also) apply. In speaking of the choices that people make *within* coercive structures, I do not include the choice whether or not to comply with the rules of such structures (to which choice, once again, so everyone would agree, principles of justice [also] apply), but the choices left open by those rules because neither enjoined nor forbidden by them.

The slogan that I have appropriated here is widely used by feminists.[1] More importantly, however, the idea itself, which I have here used the slogan to formulate, and which I have tried to explicate above, is a feminist idea. Notice, however, that, in briefly explaining the idea that I shall defend, I have not mentioned relations between men and women in particular, or the issue of sexism. We can distinguish between the substance and the form of the feminist critique of standard ideas about justice, and it is the form of it which is of prime concern to me here,[2] even though I also endorse its substance.

The substance of the feminist critique is that standard liberal theory of justice, and the theory of Rawls in particular, unjustifiably ignore an unjust division of labor, and unjust power relations, within families (whose legal structure *may* show no sexism at all). That is the key point of the feminist critique, from a political point of view. But the (often merely implicit) form of the feminist critique, which we get when we

From *Philosophy and Public Affairs*, 26. Copyright © 1997 by Princeton University Press. Reprinted by permission of the publisher.

For comments that influenced the final version of this paper, I thank Gerald Barnes, Diemut Bubeck, Joshua Cohen, Margaret Gilbert, Susan Hurley, John McMurtry, Derek Parfit, Thomas Pogge, John Roemer, Amelie Rorty, Hillel Steiner, Andrew Williams, Erik Wright, and Arnold Zuboff.

abstract from its gender-centered content, is that choices not regulated by the law fall within the primary purview of justice, and that is the key lesson of the critique, from a theoretical point of view.

In defending the claim that the personal is political, the view that I oppose is the Rawlsian one that principles of justice apply only to what Rawls calls the "basic structure" of society. Feminists have noticed that Rawls wobbles, across the course of his writings, on the matter of whether or not the family belongs to the basic structure and is therefore, in his view, a site at which principles of justice apply. I shall argue that Rawls's wobble on this matter is not a case of mere indecision, which could readily be resolved in favor of inclusion of the family within the basic structure: that is the view of Susan Okin,[3] and, in my opinion, she is wrong about that. I shall show (in Section V below) that Rawls cannot admit the family into the basic structure of society without abandoning his insistence that it is to the basic structure only that principles of distributive justice apply. In supposing that he could include family relations, Okin shows failure to grasp the *form* of the feminist critique of Rawls.

II

I reach the conclusion announced above at the end of a trail of argument that runs as follows. Here, in Section II, I restate a criticism that I have made elsewhere of John Rawls's application of his difference principle,[4] to wit, that he does not apply it in censure of the self-seeking choices of high-flying marketeers, which induce an inequality that, so I claim, is harmful to the badly off. In Section III, I present an objection to my criticism of Rawls. The objection says that the difference principle is, by stipulation and design, a principle that applies only to social institutions (to those, in particular, which compose the basic structure of society), and, therefore, not one that applies to the choices, such as those of self-seeking high fliers, that people make *within* such institutions. Sections IV and V offer independent replies to that *basic structure objection*. I show, in Section IV, that the objection is inconsistent with many statements by Rawls about the role of princi-

ples of justice in a just society. I then allow that the discordant statements may be dropped from the Rawlsian canon, and, in Section V, I reply afresh to the basic structure objection, by showing that no defensible account of what the basic structure *is* allows Rawls to insist that the principles which apply to it do not apply to choices within it. I conclude that my original criticism of Rawls rests vindicated, against the particular objection in issue here. (Section VI comments on the implications of my position for the moral blamability of individuals whose choices violate principles of justice. The Endnote explores the distinction between coercive and noncoercive institutions, which plays a key role in the argument of Section V).

My criticism of Rawls is of his application of the difference principle. That principle says, in one of its formulations,[5] that inequalities are just if and only if they are necessary to make the worst off people in society better off than they would otherwise be. I have no quarrel here with the difference principle itself,[6] but I disagree sharply with Rawls on the matter of *which* inequalities pass the test for justifying inequality that it sets and, therefore, about how *much* inequality passes that test. In my view, there is hardly any serious inequality that satisfies the requirement set by the difference principle, when it is conceived, as Rawls himself proposes to conceive it,[7] as regulating the affairs of a society whose members themselves accept that principle. If I am right, affirmation of the difference principle implies that justice requires (virtually) unqualified equality itself, as opposed to the "deep inequalities" in initial life chances with which Rawls thinks justice to be consistent.[8]

It is commonly thought, for example by Rawls, that the difference principle licenses an argument for inequality which centers on the device of material incentives. The idea is that talented people will produce more than they otherwise would if, and only if, they are paid more than an ordinary wage, and some of the extra which they will then produce can be recruited on behalf of the worse off.[9] The inequality consequent on differential material incentives is said to be justified within the terms of the difference principle, for, so it is said, that inequality benefits the worst off people: the inequality is necessary for them to be positioned as well as they are, however paltry their position may nevertheless be.

Now, before I mount my criticism of this argument, a *caveat* is necessary with respect to the terms in which it is expressed. The argument focuses on a *choice* enjoyed by well-placed people who command a high salary in a market economy: they can choose to work more or less hard, and also to work at this occupation rather than that one, and for this employer rather than that one, in accordance with how well they are remunerated. These well-placed people, in the foregoing standard presentation of the argument, are designated as "the talented," and, for reasons to be given presently, I shall so designate them throughout my criticism of the argument. Even so, these fortunate people need not be thought to be talented, in any sense of that word which implies something more than a capacity for high market earnings, for the argument to possess whatever force it has. All that need be true of them is that *they are so positioned that, happily, for them, they do command a high salary and they can vary their productivity according to exactly how high it is.* But, as far as the incentives argument is concerned, their happy position could be due to circumstances that are entirely accidental, relative to whatever kind of natural or even socially induced endowment they possess. One need not think that the average dishwasher's endowment of strength, flair, ingenuity, and so forth falls below that of the average chief executive to accept the argument's message. One no doubt does need to think some such thing to agree with the different argument which justifies rewards to well-placed people in whole or in part as a fair return to exercise of unusual ability, but Rawls's theory is built around his rejection of such desert considerations. Nor are the enhanced rewards justified because extra contribution warrants extra reward on grounds of proper reciprocity. They are justified purely because they elicit more productive performance.

I nevertheless persist in designating the relevant individuals as "the talented," because to object that they are not actually especially talented *anyway* is to enter an empirical claim which is both contentious and, in context, misleading, since it would give the impression that it should matter to our assessment of the incentives argument whether or not well-placed people merit the contestable designation. The particular criticism of the incentives argument that I shall develop is best understood in its specificity when the apparently concessive word "talented" is used: it does not indicate a concession on the factual question of how top people in a market society get to be where they are. My use of the argument's own terms shows the strength of my critique of it: that critique stands even if we make generous assumptions about how well-placed people secured their powerful market positions. It is, moreover, especially appropriate to make such assumptions here, since the Rawlsian difference principle is lexically secondary to his principle that fair equality of opportunity has been enforced with respect to the attainment of desired positions: if anything ensures that those who occupy them possess superior creative endowment, that does. (Which is not to say that it indeed ensures that: it is consistent with fair equality of opportunity that what principally distinguishes top people is superior cunning and/or prodigious aggressivity, and nothing more admirable.)

Now, for the following reasons, I believe that the incentives argument for inequality represents a distorted application of the difference principle, even though it is its most familiar and perhaps even its most persuasive application. Either the relevant talented people themselves affirm the difference principle or they do not. That is: either they themselves believe that inequalities are unjust if they are not necessary to make the badly off better off, or they do not believe that to be a dictate of justice. If they do not believe it, then their society is not just in the appropriate Rawlsian sense, for a society is just, according to Rawls, only if its members themselves affirm and uphold the correct principles of justice. The difference principle might be appealed to in justification of a government's toleration, or promotion, of inequality in a society in which the talented do not themselves accept it, but it then justifies a public policy of inequality in a society some members of which—the talented—do not share community with the rest:[10] their behavior is then taken as fixed or parametric, a datum vis-à-vis a principle applied to it from without, rather than as itself answerable to that principle. That is not how principles of justice operate in a just society, as Rawls specifies that concept: within his terms, one may distinguish between a just society and a just government, one, that is, which applies just principles to a society whose members may not themselves accept those principles.

So we turn to the second and only remaining possibility, which is that the talented people do affirm the difference principle, that, as Rawls says, they apply the principles of justice *in their daily life* and achieve a sense of their own justice in doing so.[11] But they can then be asked why, in the light of their own belief in the principle, they require more pay than the untalented get, for work that may indeed demand special talent, but which is not specially unpleasant (for no such consideration enters the Rawlsian justification of incentives-derived inequality). The talented can be asked whether the extra they get is *necessary* to enhance the position of the worst off, which is the only thing, according to the difference principle, that could justify it. Is it necessary *tout court*, that is, independently of human will, so that, with all the will in the world removal of inequality would make everyone worse off? Or is it necessary only insofar as the talented would *decide* to produce less than they now do, or not to take up posts where they are in special demand, if inequality were removed (by, for example, income taxation which redistributes to fully egalitarian effect)?[12]

Talented people who affirm the difference principle would find those questions hard to handle. For they could not claim, *in self-justification*, at the bar of the difference principle, that their high rewards are necessary to enhance the position of the worst off, since, in the standard case,[13] it is they themselves who *make* those rewards necessary, through their own unwillingness to work for ordinary rewards as productively as they do for exceptionally high ones, an unwillingness which ensures that the untalented get less than they otherwise would. Those rewards are, therefore, necessary only because the choices of talented people are not appropriately informed by the difference principle.

Apart, then, from the very special cases in which the talented literally *could* not, as opposed to the normal case where they (merely) would not, perform as

productively as they do without superior remuneration, the difference principle can justify inequality only in a society where not everyone accepts that very principle. It therefore cannot justify inequality in the appropriate Rawlsian way.

Now, this conclusion about what it means to accept and implement the difference principle implies that the justice of a society is not exclusively a function of its legislative structure, of its legally imperative rules, but also of the choices people make within those rules. The standard (and, in my view, misguided) Rawlsian application of the difference principle can be modeled as follows. There is a market economy all agents in which seek to maximize their own gains, and there is a Rawlsian state that selects a tax function on income that maximizes the income return to the worst off people, within the constraint that, because of the self-seeking motivation of the talented, a fully equalizing taxation system would make everyone worse off than one which is less than fully equalizing. But this double-minded modeling of the implementation of the difference principle, with citizens inspired by justice endorsing a state policy which plays a tax game against (some of) them in their manifestation as self-seeking economic agents, is wholly out of accord with the (sound) Rawlsian requirement on a just society that its citizens themselves willingly submit to the standard of justice embodied in the difference principle. A society that is just within the terms of the difference principle, so we may conclude, requires not simply just coercive *rules*, but also an *ethos* of justice that informs individual choices. In the absence of such an ethos, inequalities will obtain that are not necessary to enhance the condition of the worst off: the required ethos promotes a distribution more than what the rules of the economic game by themselves can secure.

To be sure, one might imagine, in the abstract, a set of coercive rules so finely tuned that universally self-interested choices within them would raise the worst off to as high a position as any other pattern of choices would produce. Where coercive rules had and were known to have such a character, agents could choose self-interestedly in confidence that the results of their choices would satisfy an appropriately uncompromising interpretation of the difference principle. In that (imaginary) case, the only ethos necessary for difference principle justice would be willing obedience to the relevant rules, an ethos which Rawls expressly requires. But the vast economics literature on incentive compatibility teaches that rules of the contemplated perfect kind cannot be designed. Accordingly, as things actually are, the required ethos must, as I have argued, guide choice within the rules, and not merely direct agents to obey them. (I should emphasize that this is not so because it is *in general* true that the point of the rules governing an activity must be aimed at when agents pursue that activity in good faith: every competitive sport represents a counterexample to that generalization. But my argument for the conclusion stated above did not rest on that false generalization.)

III

There is an objection which friends of Rawls's *Theory of Justice* would press against my argument in criticism of his application of the difference principle. The objection is that my focus on the posture of talented producers in daily economic life is inappropriate, since their behavior occurs within, and does not determine, *the basic structure* of society, and it is only to the latter that the difference principle applies.[14] Whatever people's choices within it may be, the basic structure is just provided that it satisfies the two principles of justice. To be sure, so Rawls acknowledges, people's choices can themselves be assessed as just or unjust, from a number of points of view. Thus, for example, appointment to a given job of candidate A rather than candidate B might be judged unjust, even though it occurs within the rules of a just basic structure.[15] But injustice in such a choice is not the sort of injustice that the Rawlsian principles are designed to condemn. For, *ex hypothesi*, that choice occurs within an established basic structure: it therefore cannot affect the justice of the basic structure itself, which is what, according to Rawls, the two principles govern. Nor, similarly, should the choices with respect to work and remuneration that talented people make be submitted for judgment at the bar of the difference principle. So to judge those choices is to

apply that principle at the wrong point. The difference principle is a "principle of justice for institutions."[16] It governs the choice of institutions, not the choices made within them. The development of the second horn of the dilemma argument at p. 622 above misconstrues the Rawlsian requirement that citizens in a just society uphold the principles that make it just: by virtue of the stipulated scope of the difference principle, talented people do count as faithfully upholding it, as long as they conform to the prevailing economic rules *because* that principle requires those rules.

Call that "the basic structure objection." Now, before I develop it further, and then reply to it, I want to point out that there is an important ambiguity in the concept of the basic structure, as that is wielded by Rawlsians. The ambiguity turns on whether the Rawlsian basic structure includes only coercive aspects of the social order or, also, conventions and usages that are deeply entrenched but not legally or literally coercive. I shall return to that ambiguity in Section V below, and I shall show that it shipwrecks not only the basic structure objection but also the whole approach to justice that Rawls has taught so many to pursue. But, for the time being, I shall ignore the fatal ambiguity, and I shall take the phrase "basic structure," as it appears in the basic structure objection, as denoting *some* sort of structure, be it legally coercive or not, but whose key feature, for the purposes of the objection, is that it is indeed a structure, that is, a framework of rules within which choices are made, as opposed to a set of choices and/or actions.[17] Accordingly, my Rawlsian critic would say, whatever structure, precisely, the basic structure is, the objection stands that my criticism of the incentives argument misapplies principles devised for a structure to individual choices and actions.

In further clarification of the polemical position, let me make a background point about the difference between Rawls and me with respect to the site or sites at which principles of justice apply. My own fundamental concern is neither the basic structure of society, in any sense, nor people's individual choices, but the pattern of benefits and burdens in society: that is neither a structure in which choice occurs nor a set of choices, but the upshot of structure and choices alike. My concern is *distributive justice*, by which I uneccentrically mean justice (and its lack) in the distribution of benefits and burdens to individuals. My root belief is that there is injustice in distribution when inequality of goods reflects not such things as differences in the arduousness of different people's labors, or people's different preferences and choices with respect to income and leisure, but myriad forms of lucky and unlucky circumstance. Such differences of advantage are a function of the structure *and* of people's choices within it, so I am concerned, secondarily, with *both* of those.

Now Rawls could say that his concern, too, is distributive justice, in the specified sense, but that, for him, distributive justice obtains just in case the allocation of benefits and burdens in society results from actions which display full conformity with the rules of a just basic structure.[18] When full compliance with the rules of a just basic structure obtains, it follows, on Rawls's view, that there is no scope for (further) personal justice and injustice which affects *distributive* justice, whether it be by enhancing it or by reducing it. There is, Rawls would, of course, readily agree, scope, within a just structure, for distribution-affecting meanness and generosity,[19] but generosity, though it would alter the distribution, and might make it more equal than it would otherwise be, could not make it more *just* than it would otherwise be, for it would then be doing the impossible, to wit, enhancing the justice of what is already established as a (perfectly) just distribution by virtue merely of the just structure in conformity with which it is produced. But, as I have indicated, I believe that there is scope for relevant (relevant, that is, because it affects justice in distribution) personal justice and injustice *within* a just structure, and, indeed, that it is not possible to achieve distributive justice by purely structural means.

In discussion of my claim (see p. 622 above) that social justice requires a social *ethos* that inspires uncoerced equality-supporting choice, Ronald Dworkin suggested[20] that a Rawlsian government might be thought to be charged with a duty, under the difference principle, of promoting such an ethos. Dworkin's suggestion was intended to support Rawls, against me, by diminishing the difference between Rawls's position and my own, and thereby reducing the reach of my criticism of him. I do not

know what Rawls's response to Dworkin's proposal would be, but one thing is clear: Rawls could not say that, to the extent that the indicated policy failed, society would, as a result, be less just than if the policy had been more successful. Accordingly, if Dworkin is right that Rawlsian justice requires government to promote an ethos friendly to equality, it could not be for the sake of making society more distributively just that it was doing so, *even* though it would be for the sake of making its distribution more *equal*. The following threefold conjunction, which is an inescapable consequence of Rawls's position, on Dworkin's not unnatural interpretation of it, is strikingly incongruous: (1) the difference principle is an egalitarian principle of distributive justice; (2) it imposes on government a duty to promote an egalitarian ethos; (3) it is not for the sake of enhancing distributive justice in society that it is required to promote that ethos. Dworkin's attempt to reduce the distance between Rawls's position and my own threatens to render the former incoherent.

Now, before I mount my two replies to the basic structure objection, a brief conceptual digression is required, in clarification of the relationship between a just *society*, in Rawls's (and my own) understanding of that idea and a just *distribution*, in my (non-Rawlsian) understanding of that different idea. A just society, here, is one whose citizens affirm and act upon the correct principles of justice, but justice in distribution, as here defined, consists in a certain egalitarian profile of rewards. It follows that, as a matter of logical possibility, a just distribution might obtain in a society that is not itself just.

To illustrate this possibility, imagine a society whose ethos, though not inspired by a belief in equality, nevertheless induces an equal distribution. An example of such an ethos would be an intense Protestant ethic, which is indifferent to equality (on earth) as such, but whose stress on self-denial, hard work, and investment of assets surplus to needs somehow (despite the asceticism in it) makes the worst off as well off as is possible. Such an ethos achieves difference principle justice in distribution, but agents informed by it would not be motivated by the difference principle, and they could not, therefore, themselves be accounted just, within the terms of that principle. Under the specifications that were introduced here, this Protestant society would not be just, despite the fact that it displays a just distribution. We might say of the society that it is accidentally, but not constitutively, just. But, whatever phrasings we may prefer, the important thing is to distinguish "society" and "distribution" as candidate subjects of the predicate "just." (And it bears mentioning that, in contemporary practice, an ethos that achieves difference principle equality would almost certainly have to be equality-inspired: the accident of a non-equality-inspired ethos producing the right result is, at least in modern times, highly unlikely. The Protestantism described here is utterly fantastic, at least for our day.)

Less arresting is the opposite case, in which people strive to govern their behavior by (what are in fact) just principles, but ignorance, or the obduracy of wholly external circumstance, or collective action problems, or self-defeatingness of the kinds studied by Derek Parfit,[21] or something else which I have not thought of, frustrates their intention, so that the distribution remains unjust. It would perhaps be peculiar to call such a society *just*, and neither Rawls nor I need do so: justice in citizens was put, above, as a *necessary* condition of a just society.

However we resolve the secondary, and largely verbal, complications raised in this digression, the point will stand[22] that an ethos informing choice within just rules is necessary in a society that is committed to the difference principle. My argument for that conclusion did not rely on aspects of my conception of justice which distinguish it from Rawls's, but on our shared conception of what a just society is. The fact that distributive justice, as I conceive it, causally requires an ethos (be it merely equality-promoting, such as our imaginary Protestantism, or also equality-inspired) that goes beyond conformity to just rules, was not a premise in my argument against Rawls. The argument of Section II turned essentially on my understanding of Rawls's well-considered requirement that the citizens of a just society are themselves just. The basic structure objection challenges that understanding.

IV

I now present a preliminary reply to the basic structure objection. It is preliminary in that it precedes

my interrogation, in Section V, of what the phrase "basic structure" denotes, and also in that, by contrast with the fundamental reply that will follow that interrogation, there is a certain way out for Rawls, in face of the preliminary reply. That way out is not costless for him, but it does exist.

Although Rawls says often enough that the two principles of justice govern only justice in basic structure, he also says three things that tell against that restriction. This means that, in each case, he must either uphold the restriction and repudiate the comment in question, or maintain the comment and drop the restriction.[23]

First, Rawls says that, when the difference principle is satisfied, society displays *fraternity*, in a particularly strong sense: its citizens do not want

> to have greater advantages unless this is to the benefit of others who are less well off. . . . Members of a family commonly do not wish to gain unless they can do so in ways that further the interests of the rest. Now wanting to act on the difference principle has precisely this consequence.[24]

But fraternity of that strong kind is not realized when all the justice delivered by that principle comes from the basic structure, and, therefore, whatever people's motivations may be. Wanting not "to gain unless they can do so in ways that further the interests of the rest" is incompatible with the self-interested motivation of market maximizers, which the difference principle, in its purely structural interpretation, does not condemn.[25]

Second, Rawls says that the worst off in a society governed by the difference principle can bear their inferior position with dignity, since they know that no improvement of it is possible, that they would lose under any less unequal dispensation. Yet that is false, if justice relates to structure alone, since it might then be necessary for the worst off to occupy their relatively low place only because the choices of the better off tend strongly against equality. Why should the fact that no purely structurally induced improvement in their position is possible suffice to guarantee the dignity of the worst off, when their position might be very inferior indeed, because of unlimited self-seekingness in the economic choices of well-placed people?[26] Suppose, for example, that, as many politicians claim, raising rates of income taxation with a view to enhancing benefits for the badly off would be counterproductive, since the higher rates would induce severe disincentive effects on the productivity of the better off. Would awareness of that truth contribute to a sense of dignity on the part of the badly off?

Third, Rawls says that people in a just society act with a sense of justice *from* the principles of justice in their daily lives: they strive to apply those principles in their own choices. And they do so because they

> have a desire to express their nature as free and equal moral persons, and this they do most adequately by acting *from* the principles that they would acknowledge in the original position. When all strive to comply with these principles and each succeeds, then individually and collectively their nature as moral persons is most fully realized, and with it their individual and collective good.[27]

But why do they have to act *from* the principles of justice, and "apply" them "as their circumstances require"[28] if just behavior consists in choosing as one pleases within, and without disturbing, a structure designed to effect an implementation of those principles? And how can they, without a redolence of hypocrisy, celebrate the full realization of their natures as moral persons, when they know that they are out for the most that they can get in the market?

Now, as I said, these inconsistencies are not decisive against Rawls. For, in each case, he could stand pat on his restriction of justice to basic structure, and give up, or weaken, the remark that produces the inconsistency. And that is indeed what he is disposed to do at least with respect to the third inconsistency that I have noted. He said[29] that *A Theory of Justice* erred by in some respects treating the two principles as defining a *comprehensive* conception of justice:[30] he would, accordingly, now drop the high-pitched homily which constitutes the text to footnote 27. But this accommodation carries a cost: it means that the ideals of dignity, fraternity, and full realization of people's moral natures can no longer be said to be delivered by Rawlsian justice.[31]

V

I now provide a more fundamental reply to the basic structure objection. It is more fundamental in that it shows, decisively, that justice requires an ethos governing daily choice that goes beyond one of obedience to just rules,[32] on grounds which do not, as the preliminary reply did, exploit things that Rawls says in apparent contradiction of his stipulation that justice applies to the basic structure of society alone. The fundamental reply interrogates, and refutes, that stipulation itself.

A major fault line in the Rawlsian architectonic not only wrecks the basic structure objection but also produces a dilemma for Rawls's view of the subject[33] of justice from which I can imagine no way out. The fault line exposes itself when we ask the apparently simple question: what (exactly) *is* the basic structure? For there is a fatal ambiguity in Rawls's specification of the basic structure, and an associated discrepancy between his criterion for what justice judges and his desire to exclude the effects of structure-consistent personal choice from the purview of its judgment.

The basic structure, the primary subject of justice, is always said by Rawls to be a set of institutions, and, so he infers, the principles of justice do not judge the actions of people within (just) institutions whose rules they observe. But it is seriously unclear *which* institutions are supposed to qualify as part of the basic structure. Sometimes it appears that coercive (in the legal sense) institutions exhaust it, or, better, that institutions belong to it only insofar as they are (legally) coercive.[34] In this widespread interpretation of what Rawls intends by the "basic structure" of a society, that structure is legible in the provisions of its constitution, in such specific legislation as may be required to implement those provisions, and in further legislation and policy which are of central importance but which resist formulation in the constitution itself.[35] The basic structure, in this first understanding of it, is, so one might say, the *broad coercive outline* of society, which determines in a relatively fixed and general way what people may and must do, in advance of legislation that is optional, relative to the principles of justice, and irrespective of the constraints and opportunities created and destroyed by the choices that people make within the given basic structure, so understood.

Yet it is quite unclear that the basic structure is *always* thus defined, in exclusively coercive terms, within the Rawlsian text. For Rawls often says that the basic structure consists of the *major* social institutions, and he does not put a particular accent on coercion when he announces *that* specification of the basic structure.[36] In this second reading of what it is, institutions belong to the basic structure whose structuring can depend far less on law than on convention, usage, and expectation: a signal example is the family, which Rawls sometimes includes in the basic structure and sometimes does not.[37] But once the line is crossed, from coercive ordering to the non-coercive ordering of society by rules and conventions of accepted practice, then the ambit of justice can no longer exclude chosen behavior, since the usages which constitute informal structure (think, again, of the family) are bound up with the customary actions of people.

"Bound up with" is vague, so let me explain how I mean it, here. One can certainly speak of the structure of the family, and it is not identical with the choices that people customarily make within it; but it is nevertheless impossible to claim that the principles of justice which apply to family structure do not apply to day-to-day choices within it. For consider the following contrast. The *coercive* structure arises independently of people's quotidian choices: it is formed by those specialized choices which legislate the law of the land. By contrast, the non-coercive structure of the family has the character it does only because of the choices that its members routinely make. The constraints and pressures that sustain the non-coercive structure reside in the dispositions of agents which are actualized as and when those agents choose to act in a constraining or pressuring way. With respect to coercive structure, one may fairly readily distinguish the choices which institute and sustain a structure from the choices that occur within it.[38] But with respect to informal structure, that distinction, though conceptually intelligible, collapses extensionally: when A chooses to conform to the prevailing usages, the pressure on B to do so is reinforced, and no such pressure exists, the

very usages themselves do not exist, in the absence of conformity to them.

Now, since that is so, since behavior is *constitutive* of *non*-coercive structure, it follows that the only way of protecting the basic structure objection against my claim that the difference principle condemns maximizing economic behavior (and, more generally, of protecting the restriction of justice to the basic structure against the insistence that the personal, too, is political) is by holding fast to a purely coercive specification of the basic structure. But that way out is not open to Rawls, because of a further characterization that he offers of the basic structure: this is where the discrepancy adverted to in the second paragraph of this section appears. For Rawls says that "the basic structure is the primary subject of justice because its effects are so profound and present from the start."[39] Nor is that further characterization of the basic structure optional: it is needed to explain why it *is* primary, as far as justice is concerned. Yet it is false that only the *coercive* structure causes profound effects, as the example of the family once again reminds us.[40] Accordingly, if Rawls retreats to coercive structure, he contradicts his own criterion for what justice judges, and he lands himself with an arbitrarily narrow definition of his subject matter. So he must let other structure in, and that means, as we have seen, letting chosen behavior in. What is more, even if behavior were not, as I claim it is, constitutive of non-coercive structure, it will come in by direct appeal to the profundity-of-effect criterion for what justice governs. So, for example, we need not decide whether or not a regular practice of favoring sons over daughters in the matter of providing higher education forms part of the *structure* of the family to condemn it as unjust, under that criterion.[41]

Given, then, his stated rationale[42] for exclusive focus on the basic structure—and what *other* rational could there be for calling it the *primary* subject of justice?—Rawls is in a dilemma. For he must either admit application of the principles of justice to (legally optional) social practices, and, indeed, to patterns of personal choice that are not legally prescribed, *both* because they are the substance of those practices, *and* because they are similarly profound in effect, in which case the restriction of justice to structure, in any sense, collapses; or, if he restricts his concern to the coercive structure only, then he saddles himself with a purely arbitrary delineation of his subject matter. I now illustrate this dilemma by reference to the two contexts that have figured most in this paper: the family, and the market economy.

Family structure is fateful for the benefits and burdens that redound to different people, and, in particular, to people of different sexes, where "family structure" includes the socially constructed expectations which lie on husband and wife. And such expectations are sexist and unjust if, for example, they direct the woman in a family where both spouses work outside the home to carry a greater burden of domestic tasks. Yet such expectations need not be supported by the law for them to possess informal coercive force: sexist family structure is consistent with sex-neutral family law. Here, then, is a circumstance, outwith the basic structure, as that would be coercively defined, which profoundly affects people's life-chances, *through the choices people make in response to the stated expectations, which are, in turn, sustained by those choices.*[43] Yet Rawls must say, on pain of giving up the basic structure objection, that (legally uncoerced) family structure and behavior have no implications for justice in the sense of "justice" in which the basic structure has implications for justice, since they are not a consequence of the formal coercive order. But that implication of the stated position is perfectly incredible: no such differentiating sense is available.

John Stuart Mill taught us to recognize that informal social pressure can restrict liberty as much as formal coercive law does. And the family example shows that informal pressure is as relevant to distributive justice as it is to liberty. One reason why the rules of the basic structure, when it is coercively defined, do not by themselves determine the justice of the distributive upshot is that, by virtue of circumstances that are relevantly independent of coercive rules, some people have much more power than others to determine what happens *within* those rules.

The second illustration of discrepancy between what coercive structure commands and what profoundly affects the distribution of benefits and burdens is my own point about incentives. Maximizing

legislation,[44] and, hence, a coercive basic structure that is just as far as the difference principle is concerned, are consistent with a maximizing ethos across society which, under many conditions, will produce severe inequalities and a meager level of provision for the worst off, yet both have to be declared just by Rawls, if he stays with a coercive conception of what justice judges. And that implication is, surely, perfectly incredible.

Rawls cannot deny the difference between the coercively defined basic structure and that which produces major distributive consequences: the coercively defined basic structure is only an instance of the latter. Yet he must, to retain his position on justice and personal choice, restrict the ambit of justice to what a coercive basic structure produces. But, so I have (by implication) asked: why should we *care* so disproportionately about the coercive basic structure, when the major reason for caring about it, its impact on people's lives, is *also* a reason for caring about informal structure and patterns of personal choice? To the extent that we care about coercive structure because it is fateful with regard to benefits and burdens, we must care equally about the ethi that sustain gender inequality, and inegalitarian incentives. And the similarity of our reasons for caring about these matters will make it lame to say: ah, but only the caring about coercive structure is a caring about *justice,* in a certain distinguishable sense. That thought is, I submit, incapable of coherent elaboration.

My response to the basic structure objection is now fully laid out, but before proceeding, in the sections that remain, to matters arising, it will be useful to rehearse, in compressed form, the arguments that were presented in Sections II through V.

My original criticism of the incentives argument ran, in brief, as follows:

1. Citizens in a just society adhere to its principles of justice.

But

2. They do not adhere to the difference principle if they are acquisitive maximizers in daily life.

∴3. In a society that is governed by the difference principle, citizens lack the acquisitiveness that the incentives argument attributes to them.

The basic structure objection to that criticism is of this form:

4. The principles of justice govern only the basic structure of a just society.

∴5. Citizens in a just society may adhere to the difference principle whatever their choices may be within the structure it determines, and, in particular, even if their economic choices are entirely acquisitive.

∴6. Proposition 2. lacks justification.

My preliminary reply to the basic structure objection says:

7. Proposition 5. is inconsistent with many Rawlsian statements about the relationship between citizens and principles of justice in a just society.

And my fundamental reply to the basic structure objection says:

8. Proposition 4. is unsustainable.

VI

So the personal is indeed political: personal choices to which the writ of the law is indifferent are fateful for social justice.

But that raises a huge question, with respect to *blame*. The injustice in distribution that reflects personal choices within a just coercive structure can plainly not be blamed on that structure itself, nor, therefore, on whoever legislated that structure. Must it, then, be blamed, in our two examples, on men[45] and on acquisitive people, respectively?

I shall presently address, and answer, that question about blame, but, before I do so, I wish to explain why I could remain silent in the face of it, why, that is, my argument in criticism of Rawls's restricted application of the principles of justice re-

quires no judgment about blaming individual choosers. The conclusion of my argument is that the principles of justice apply not only to coercive rules but also to the pattern in people's (legally) uncoerced choices. Now, if we judge a certain set of rules to be just or unjust, we need not add, as pendant to that judgment, that those who legislated the rules in question should be praised or blamed for what they did.[46] And something analogous applies when we come to see that the ambit of justice covers the pattern of choices in a society. We can believe whatever we are inclined to do about how responsible and/or culpable people are for their choices, and that includes believing that they are not responsible and/or culpable for them at all, while holding that on which I insist: that the pattern in such choices is relevant to how just or unjust a society is.

That said, I return to the question of how blamable individuals are. It would be inappropriate to answer it, here, by first declaring my position, if, indeed, I have one, on the philosophical problem of the freedom of the will. Instead, I shall answer the question about blame on the prephilosophical assumptions which inform our ordinary judgments about when, and how much, blame is appropriate. On such assumptions, we should avoid two opposite mistakes about how culpable chauvinistic men and self-seeking high fliers are. One is the mistake of saying: there is no ground for blaming these people as *individuals*, for they simply participate in an accepted social practice, however tawdry or awful that practice may be. That is a mistake, since people do have choices: it is, indeed, *only* their choices that reproduce social practices; and some, moreover, choose *against* the grain of nurture, habit, and self-interest. But one also must not say: look how each of these people shamefully decides to behave so badly. That, too, is unbalanced, since, although there exists personal choice, there is heavy social conditioning behind it and there can be heavy costs in deviating from the prescribed and/or permitted ways. If we care about social justice, we have to look at four things: the coercive structure, other structures, the social ethos, and the choices of individuals, and judgment on the last of those must be informed by awareness of the power of the others. So, for example, a properly sensitive appreciation of these matters allows one to hold that an acquisitive ethos is profoundly unjust in its effects, without holding that those who are gripped by it are commensurately unjust. It is essential to apply principles of justice to dominant patterns in social behavior— that, as it were, is where the action is—but it doesn't follow that we should have a persecuting attitude to the people who emit that behavior. We might have good reason to exonerate the perpetrators of injustice, but we should not deny, or apologize for, the injustice itself.[47]

On an extreme view, which I do not accept but need not reject, a typical husband in a thoroughly sexist society, one, that is, in which families in their overwhelming majority display an unjust division of domestic labor, is literally incapable of revising his behavior, or capable of revising it only at the cost of cracking up, to nobody's benefit. But even if that is true of typical husbands, we know it to be false of husbands in general. It is a plain empirical fact that some husbands are capable of revising their behavior, since some husbands have done so, in response to feminist criticism. These husbands, we could say, were moral pioneers. They made a path which becomes easier and easier to follow as more and more people follow it, until social pressures are so altered that it becomes harder to stick to sexist ways than to abandon them. That is a central way in which a social ethos changes. Or, for another example, consider the recent rise in ecological consciousness. At first, only people that appear to be freaky because they do so bother to save and recycle their paper, plastic, and so forth. Then, more do that, and, finally, it becomes not only difficult not to do it but easy to do it. It is pretty easy to discharge burdens that have become part of the normal round of everybody's life. Expectations determine behavior, behavior determines expectations, which determine behavior, and so on.

Are there circumstances in which a similar incremental process could occur with respect to economic behavior? I do not know. But I do know that universal maximizing is by no means a necessary feature of a market economy. For all that much of its industry was state-owned, the United Kingdom from 1945 to 1951 had a market economy. But salary differentials were nothing like as great as they were

to become, or as they were then in the United States. Yet, so I hazard, when British executives making five times what their workers did met American counterparts making fifteen times what their (anyhow better paid) workers did, many of the British executives would *not* have felt: *we* should press for more. For there was a social ethos of reconstruction after war, an ethos of common project, that restrained desire for personal gain. It is not for a philosopher to delimit the conditions under which such, and even more egalitarian ethi, can prevail. But a philosopher can say that a maximizing ethos is not a necessary feature of society, even of market society, and that, to the extent that such an ethos prevails, satisfaction of the difference principle is prejudiced.

In 1988, the ratio of top executive salaries to production worker wages was 6.5 to 1 in West Germany and 17.5 to 1 in the United States.[48] Since it is not plausible to think that Germany's lesser inequality was a disincentive to productivity, since it is plausible to think that an ethos that was relatively friendly to equality[49] protected German productivity in the face of relatively modest material incentives, we can conclude that the said ethos caused the worst paid to be better paid than they would have been under a different culture of reward. It follows, on my view of things, that the difference principle was better realized in Germany in 1988 than it would have been if its culture of reward had been more similar to that of the United States. But Rawls cannot say that, since the smaller inequality that benefited the less well off in Germany was not a matter of law but of ethos. I think that Rawls's inability to regard Germany as having done comparatively well with respect to the difference principle is a grave defect in his conception of the site of distributive justice.

Endnote on Coercive and Other Structure

The legally coercive structure of society functions in two ways. It *prevents* people from doing things by erecting insurmountable barriers (fences, police lines, prison walls, etc.), and it *deters* people from doing things by ensuring that certain forms of unprevented behavior carry an (appreciable risk of) penalty.[50] The second (deterrent) aspect of coercive structure may be described counterfactually, in terms of what would or might happen to someone who elects the forbidden behavior: knowledge of the relevant counterfactual truths motivates the complying citizen's choices.

Not much pure prevention goes on within the informal structure of society: not none, but not much. (Locking an errant teenager in her room would represent an instance of pure prevention, which, if predictable for determinate behavior, would count as part of a society's informal structure: it would be a rule in accordance with which that society operates.) That being set aside, informal structure manifests itself in predictable sanctions such as criticism, disapproval, anger, refusal of future cooperation, ostracism, beating (of, for example, wives who refuse sexual service) and so on.

Finally, to complete this conceptual review, the ethos of a society is the set of sentiments and attitudes in virtue of which its normal practices, and informal pressures, are what they are.

Now, the pressures that sustain the informal structure lack force save insofar as there is a normal practice of compliance with the rules they enforce. That is especially true of that great majority of those pressures (beating does not belong to that majority) which carry a moral coloring: criticism and disapproval are ineffective when they come from the mouths of those who ask others not to do what they do themselves. To be sure, that is not a conceptual truth, but a social-psychological one. Even so, it enables us to say that what people ordinarily do supports and partly constitutes (again, not conceptually, but in effect) the informal structure of society, in such a way that it makes no sense to pass judgments of justice on that structure while withholding such judgment from the behavior that supports and constitutes it: that point is crucial to the anti-Rawlsian inference at p. 627 above.[51] Informal structure is not a behavior pattern, but a set of rules, yet the two are so closely related that, so one might say, they are *merely* categorically different. Accordingly, so I argued, to include (as one must) informal structure within the basic structure is to countenance behavior, too, as a primary subject of judgments of justice.

Now, two truths about legally coercive structure might be thought to cast doubt on the contrast I drew between it and informal structure in Section V above. First, although the legally coercive structure of society is indeed discernible in the ordinances of its constitution and law, those ordinances count as delineating it only on condition that they enjoy a broad measure of compliance.[52] And, second, legally coercive structure achieves its intended social effect only in and through the actions which constitute compliance with its rules. To be more accurate, those propositions are true provided that we exclude from consideration "1984" states in which centralized brute force prevails against nonconformity even, if necessary, at the cost of half the population being in jail. But it is appropriate to ignore 1984 scenarios here.[53]

In light of those truths, it might be objected that the dilemma that I posed for Rawls (see pp. 627–628) and by means of which I sought to defeat his claim that justice judges structure *as opposed to* the actions of agents, was critically misframed. For I said, against that claim, that the required opposition between structure and actions works for coercive structure only, with respect to which a relevantly strong distinction can be drawn between structure-sustaining and structure-conforming action, but that coercive structure could not reasonably be thought to exhaust the structure falling within the purview of justice: accordingly, so I concluded, justice must also judge everyday actions.

The truths rehearsed two paragraphs back challenge my articulation of the distinction between coercive structure and action within it. They thereby also challenge the contrast that I drew between two relationships, that between coercive structure and action, and that between informal structure and action.

This problem needs more thought than I have to date spent on it. For the moment I shall say this: even if coercive structure counts as such only if appropriate compliance obtains, that structure may nevertheless be *identified* with a set of laws which are not themselves patterns of behavior. And one can distinguish sharply between behavior forbidden and directed by those laws, and behavior that is optional under them, however systematic and widespread it may be. By contrast, the identity of informal structure is less separable from practice: no distinction is sustainable between widespread practices which do not.

If the would-be saving contrast which I there essay is an unrealistic idealization, then the distinction, vis-à-vis action, between coercive and informal structure, may be more blurred than I have been disposed to allow. Yet that would not be because informal structure is more separable from action than I claimed, but because coercive structure is less separable from it. Therefore, even if the dilemma constructed on pp. 627–628 was for the stated reasons misframed, the upshot would hardly be congenial to Rawls's position, that justice judges structure rather than actions, but, if anything, congenial to my own rejection of it, if not, indeed, to the terms in which some of the argument for that rejection was cast.

NOTES

1. But it was, apparently, used by Christian liberation theologians before it was used by feminists: see Denys Turner, "Religion: Illusions and Liberation," in Terrel Carver, ed., *The Cambridge Companion to Marx* (Cambridge: Cambridge University Press, 1991), p. 334.

2. Or, more precisely, that which *distinguishes* its form. (Insofar as the feminist critique targets government legislation and policy, there is nothing distinctive about its form.)

3. Okin is singularly alive to Rawls's ambivalence about admitting or excluding the family from the basic structure: see, e.g. her "*Political Liberalism*, Justice and Gender," *Ethics* 105, no. 1 (Oct. 1994): 23–24, and, more generally, her *Justice, Gender and the Family* (New York: Basic Books, 1989), Chapter 5. But, so far as I can tell, she is unaware of the wider consequences, for Rawls's view of justice in general, of the set of ambiguities of which this one is an instance.

4. See "Incentives, Inequality, and Community," in Grethe Peterson, ed., *The Tanner Lectures on Human Values*, Vol. 13 (Salt Lake City: University of Utah Press, 1992), and "The Pareto Argument for Inequality," *Social Philosophy and Policy*, 12 (Winter 1995). These articles are henceforth referred to as "Incentives" and "Pareto," respectively.

5. See "Incentives," p. 266, n. 6, for four possible formulations of the difference principle, all of which, arguably, find support in *A Theory of Justice* (Cambridge, Mass.: Harvard University Press, 1971). The argument of the present paper is, I believe, robust across those variant formulations of the principle.

6. I do have some reservations about the principle, but they are irrelevant to this paper. I agree, for example, with Ronald Dworkin's criticism of the "ambition-insensitivity" of the difference principle: see his "What Is Equality? Part 2: Equality of Resources," *Philosophy & Public Affairs*, 10, no. 4 (Fall 1981): 343

7. "Proposes to conceive it": I use that somewhat precious phrase because part of the present criticism of Rawls is that he does not succeed in so conceiving it—he does not, that is, recognize the implications of so conceiving it.

8. *A Theory of Justice*, p. 7.

9. This is just the crudest causal story connecting superior payment to the better off with benefit to the worst off. I adopt it here for simplicity of exposition.

10. They do not, more precisely, share *justificatory community* with the rest, in the sense of the italicized phrase that I specified at p. 282 of "Incentives."

11. "Citizens in everyday life affirm and act from the first principles of justice." They act "from these principles as their sense of justice dictates" and thereby "their nature as moral persons is most fully realized." (Quotations drawn from, respectively, "Kantian Constructivism in Moral Theory," *The Journal of Philosophy*, 77, no. 9 (Sept. 1980): 521, 528, and *A Theory of Justice*, p. 528.)

12. That way of achieving equality preserves the information function of the market while extinguishing its motivational function: see Joseph Carens, *Equality, Moral Incentives, and the Market* (Chicago: University of Chicago Press, 1981).

13. See "Incentives," p. 298 *et circa*, for precisely what I mean by "the standard case."

14. For a typical statement of this restriction, see, John Rawls, *Political Liberalism* (New York: Columbia University Press, 1993), pp. 282–83.

15. See the first sentence of Sec. 2 of *A Theory of Justice* ("The Subject of Justice"): "Many different kinds of things are said to be just and unjust: not only laws, institutions, and social systems, but also particular actions of many kinds, including decisions, judgments, and imputations" (*ibid.*, p. 7). But

Rawls excludes examples such as the one given in the text above from his purview, because "our topic . . . is that of social justice. For us the primary subject of justice is the basic structure of society" (*ibid.*).

16. *A Theory of Justice*, p. 303.

17. The contrast between structure and action is further explained, though also, as it were, put in its place, in the Endnote to this article.

18. *A Theory of Justice*, pp. 274–75: "The principles of justice apply to the basic structure. . . . The social system is to be designed so that the resulting distribution is just however things turn out." Cf. *ibid.*, p. 545: ". . . the distribution of material means is left to take care of itself in accordance with the idea of pure procedural justice."

19. This is a different point from the one made at p. 623 above, to wit, that there is scope within a just structure for justice and injustice in choice in a "nonprimary" sense of "justice."

20. At a seminar in Oxford, in Hilary Term of 1994.

21. See his *Reasons and Persons* (Oxford: Oxford University Press, 1984), Chapter 4.

22. If, that is, my argument survives the basic structure objection, to which I reply in Secs. IV and V.

23. Because of these tensions in Rawls, people have resisted my incentives critique of him in two opposite ways. Those convinced that his primary concern is the basic structure object in the fashion set out in Sec. III. But others do not realize how important that commitment is to him: they accept my (as I see it, anti-Rawlsian) view that the difference principle should condemn incentives, but they believe that Rawls would also accept it, since they think his commitment to that principle is relevantly uncompromising. They therefore do not regard what I say about incentives as a *criticism* of Rawls.

Those who respond in that second fashion seem not to realize that Rawls's liberalism is jeopardized if he takes the route that they think open to him. He then becomes a radical egalitarian socialist, whose outlook is very different from that of a liberal who holds that "deep inequalities" are "inevitable in the basic structure of any society" (*A Theory of Justice*, p. 7).

24. *A Theory of Justice*, p. 105.

25. See, further, "Incentives," pp. 321–22, "Pareto," pp. 178–79.

26. See, further, "Incentives," pp. 320–21.

27. *A Theory of Justice*, p. 528, my emphasis. See, further, footnote 11 above, and "Incentives," pp. 316–20.

28. John Rawls, "Justice as Fairness: A Briefer Restatement," Harvard University, 1989, typescript, p. 154.

29. In reply to a lecture that I gave at Harvard in March of 1993.

30. That is, as (part of) a complete moral theory, as opposed to a purely political one: see, for explication of that distinction, *Political Liberalism*, *passim*, and, in particular, pp. xv–xvii.

31. See "Incentives," p. 322.

32. Though not necessarily an ethos embodying the very principles that the rules formulate: see the last four paragraphs of Sec. III above. Justice will be shown to require an ethos, and the basic structure objection will thereby be refuted, but it will be a contingent question whether the ethos required by justice can be read off the content of the just rules themselves. Still, the answer to that question is almost certainly "Yes."

33. That is, the subject matter that principles of justice judge. I follow Rawls's usage here (e.g. in the title of Lecture VII of *Political Liberalism*: "The Basic Structure as Subject"; and cf. n. 15 above)

34. Henceforth, unless I indicate otherwise, I shall use "coercive," "coercion," etc. to mean "legally coercive," etc.

35. Thus, the difference principle, though pursued through (coercively sustained) state policy, cannot, so Rawls thinks, be aptly inscribed in a society's constitution: see *Political Liberalism*, pp. 227–30.

36. Consider, for example, the passage at pp. 7–8 of *A Theory of Justice* in which the concept of the basic structure is introduced:

> Our topic . . . is that of social justice. For us the primary subject of justice is the basic structure of society, or more exactly, the way in which the major social institutions distribute fundamental rights and duties and determine the division of advantages from social cooperation. By major institutions I understand the political constitution and the principal economic and social arrangements. Thus the legal protection of freedom of thought and liberty of conscience, competitive markets, private property in the means of production, and the monogamous family are examples of major social institutions. . . . I shall not consider the justice of institutions and social practices generally. . . . [The two principles of justice] may not work for the rules and practices of private associations or for those of less comprehensive social groups. They may be irrelevant for the various informal conventions and customs of everyday life; they may not elucidate the justice, or perhaps better, the fairness of voluntary cooperative arrangements or procedures for making contractual agreements.

I cannot tell, from those statements, what is to be included in, and what excluded from, the basic structure, nor, more particularly, whether coercion is the touchstone of inclusion. Take, for example, the case of the monogamous family. Is it simply its "legal protection" that is a major social institution, in line with a coercive definition of the basic structure (if not, perhaps, with the syntax of the relevant sentence)? Or is the monogamous family itself part of that structure? And, in that case, are its typical usages part of it? They certainly constitute a "principal social arrangement," yet they may also count as "practices of private associations or . . . of less comprehensive social groups," and they are heavily informed by the "conventions and customs of everyday life."

Puzzlement with respect to the bounds of the basic structure is not relieved by examination of the relevant pages of *Political Liberalism*, to wit, 11, 68, 201–202, 229, 258, 268, 271–72, 282–83, and 301. Some formulations on those pages lean toward a coercive specification of the basic structure. Others do not.

37. See the final paragraph of Sec. I of this paper.

38. For more on structure and choice, see the Endnote to this article. Among other things, I there entertain a doubt about the strength of the distinction drawn in the above sentence, but, as I indicate, if that doubt is sound, then my case against Rawls is not weakened.

39. *A Theory of Justice*, p. 7.

40. Or consider access to that primary good which Rawls calls "the social basis of self-respect." While the law may play a large role in securing that good to people vulnerable to racism, legally unregulable racist attitudes also have an enormous negative impact on how much of that primary good they get.

But are the profound effects of the family, or of racism, "present from the start" (see the text to n. 39)? I am not sure how to answer that question, because I am unclear about the intended import, here, of the quoted phrase. Rawls probably means "present from the start of each person's life": the surrounding text at *Theory*, p. 7 supports this interpretation. If so, the family, and racial attitudes, certainly qualify. If not, then I do not know how to construe the phrase. But what matters, surely, is the asserted profundity of effect, not whether it is "present from the start," whatever may be the sense which attaches, here, to that phrase.

41. Note that one can condemn the said practice without condemning those who engage in it. For there might be a collective action problem here, which weighs heavily on poor families in particular. If, in addition to discrimination in education, there is discrimination in employment, then a poor family might sacrifice a great deal through choosing evenhandedly across the sexes with whatever resources it can devote to its children's education. This illustrates the important distinction between condemning injustice and condemning the people whose actions perpetuate it: see, further, Sec. VI below.

42. See the text to n. 39 above.

43. Hugo Adam Bedau noticed that the family falls outside the basic structure, under the coercive specification of it often favored by Rawls, though he did not notice the connection between noncoercive structure and choice that I emphasize in the above sentence: see his "Social Justice and Social Institutions," *Midwest Studies in Philosophy*, 3 (1978):171.

44. That is, legislation which maximizes the size of the primary goods bundle held by the worst off people, given whatever is correctly expected to be the pattern in the choices made by economic agents.

45. We can here set aside the fact that women often subscribe to, and inculcate, male-dominative practices.

46. We can distinguish between how unjust past practices (e.g. slavery) were and how unjust those who protected and benefited from those unjust practices were. Most of us (rightly) do not condemn Lincoln for his (conditional) willingness to tolerate slavery as strongly as we would a statesman who did the same in 1997, but the institution of slavery itself was as unjust in Lincoln's time as it would be today.

What made slavery unjust in, say, Greece, is exactly what would make slavery (with, of course, the very same rules of subordination) unjust today, to wit, the content of its rules. But sound judgments about the justice and injustice of people are much more contextual: they must take into account the institutions under which they live, the prevailing level of intellectual and oral development, collective action problems such as the one delineated in n. 41 above, and so forth. The morally best slaveholder might deserve admiration. The morally best form of slavery would not.

47. See the preceding note.

48. See Lawrence Mishel and David M. Frankel, *The State of Working America*, 1990–1991 (Armonk, N.Y.: M. E. Sharpe, 1991), p. 122.

49. That ethos need not have been an egalitarian one. For present purposes, it could have been an ethos which disendorses acquisitiveness as such (see n. 32, and the digression at the end of Sec. III), other than on *Behalf of* the worst off.

50. The distinction given above corresponds to that between the difficulty and the cost of actions: see my *Karl Marx's Theory of History* (Oxford: Oxford University Press, and Princeton: Princeton University Press, 1978), pp. 238–39.

51. See the sentence beginning "But once" on the top of that page.

52. It does not follow that they are not *laws* unless they enjoy such compliance: perhaps they are nevertheless laws, if they "satisfy a test set out in a Hartian rule of recognition, even if they are themselves neither complied with nor accepted" (Joshua Cohen, in comment on an earlier draft of this paper). But such laws (or "laws") are not plausibly represented as part of the basic structure of society, so the statement in the text can stand as it is.

53. That is because of Rawls's reasonable stipulation that, in a just society, the threat of coercion is necessary for assurance game reasons only: each is disposed to comply provided that others do, and coercion is needed not because, in the absence of its threat *to me*, I might not comply, but because in the absence of its threat to others I cannot be sure that *they* will comply (see *A Theory of Justice*, p. 315). This stipulation makes formal law less *essentially* coercive than one might otherwise suppose and therefore less contrastable with custom than I have supposed.

Responsibility, Reactive Attitudes, and Liberalism in Philosophy and Politics

SAMUEL SCHEFFLER

Samuel Scheffler (1951–) is professor of philosophy at University of California, Berkeley. He is the author of *Human Morality* and *The Rejection of Consequentialism*.

HISTORY WILL RECORD THAT, during the 1980s, liberalism came under sustained and politically devastating attack in the United States.[1] The bearing of this attack, if any, on contemporary liberal philosophical theories, such as those advanced by John Rawls and others, is not obvious. In part, this is because the relation between American political liberalism and contemporary philosophical liberalism is not a simple one.[2] On the one hand, nobody would wish seriously to suggest that the United States, during the period that began when Franklin Roosevelt became president and ended when Ronald Reagan did, was a well-ordered Rawlsian society, or that the social

From *Philosophy and Public Affairs*, 21. Copyright © 1992 by Princeton University Press. Reprinted by permission of the publisher.

Earlier versions of this article were presented to audiences at the University of Arizona, the University of California at Davis, the University of California at Santa Barbara, the University of Washington, and the Boalt Hall School of Law and the University of California at Berkeley. I am grateful to all of these audiences for valuable discussion, which prompted numerous improvements. In addition, I received enormously helpful written comments, for which I am greatly indebted, from G. A. Cohen, Eric Rakowski, T. M. Scanlon, and the Editors of *Philosophy & Public Affairs*.

welfare programs implemented during that period gave full expression to the difference principle. Yet, at the same time, Rawls's work is naturally understood as providing a theoretical justification for many of the sorts of programs advocated by political liberals, and it would surely be a mistake to think of liberalism in the philosophical context as entirely unrelated to the liberal politics of the day. Thus it is reasonable to wonder about the philosophical relevance of the political repudiation of liberalism represented by the "Reagan revolution."

The conservatives who came to power during the 1980s are standardly interpreted as having tapped into two different sources of dissatisfaction with political liberalism. The first was primarily economic, and focused on liberal taxation and social welfare policies. The second was primarily social, and focused on liberal policies with respect to issues like abortion, pornography, and the role of religion in society. To the extent that social conservatives emphasized traditional values of family and community, their concerns had something in common with the opposition by communitarian philosophers to the purportedly excessive individualism of liberalism. At the same time, however, much of the dissatisfaction with political liberalism in the 1980s was due not to the belief that it was excessively individualistic but rather to the belief that it was, in an important respect, not individualistic enough. In saying this, I do not mean merely that liberalism was perceived as insufficiently individualistic in economic terms. It is certainly true, as everyone agrees and as I have said, that the overwhelming success of the political right was due to its capacity to appeal both to social conservatives and to economic conservatives. It is also true, and it has been widely noted, that the alliance between these two groups was sometimes an uneasy one, precisely because of the tension between the libertarian spirit of laissez-faire capitalism and the broadly communitarian tendency of much social conservatism. But when I say that liberalism came under attack partly because it was perceived as insufficiently individualistic, I am not just alluding to the conservative criticism of liberal economic policies. Rather, I mean that a more general conception of individual responsibility, a conception whose appeal cuts across political lines,

was perceived as under threat both from liberal programs of economic redistribution and from liberal policies on certain social issues. Both types of liberal position were perceived, in effect, as resting on a reduced conception of individual agency and responsibility. And so resistance to this diminished conception of responsibility helped to fuel opposition to both parts of the liberal agenda.

Of course, many liberals would vigorously deny that the programs and policies they favor rely on a reduced conception of responsibility, as opposed to a proper understanding of the standard conception. These liberals might expect that support for their position could be found in contemporary liberal philosophical theories. I will argue in this article, however, that the reason various liberal programs may appear incompatible with ordinary thinking about responsibility is that they assign important benefits and burdens on the basis of considerations other than individual desert.[3] And, I will argue, it is noteworthy that none of the most prominent contemporary versions of philosophical liberalism assigns a significant role to desert at the level of fundamental principle. Moreover, contemporary philosophical defenses of liberalism appear to underestimate the importance of the human attitudes and emotions that find expression through our practices with respect to desert. If these claims are correct, then contemporary philosophical liberalism may provide little support for the view that liberal policies can be reconciled with ordinary notions of responsibility. Indeed, if these claims are correct, then there are deeply entrenched ideas about responsibility that have contributed to the political repudiation of liberalism, and that leading contemporary versions of philosophical liberalism simply do not accept. This suggests that, far from helping political liberals to rebut the charge of incompatibility with ordinary notions of responsibility, contemporary philosophical liberalism may itself be vulnerable to such a charge.

I

There are a variety of liberal political positions that have been perceived as incompatible with ordinary beliefs about the responsibility of an individual agent for his or her actions. For example, liberals have long been accused of responding to crime by advocating policies that emphasize the social causes of criminal behavior while neglecting the responsibility of the individual who engages in such behavior. In the area of criminal justice in particular, this emphasis is said to have manifested itself in interpretations of the insanity defense and related pleas that treat an excessively broad range of conditions and circumstances as nullifying an individual's responsibility for his or her criminal conduct. Liberalism has also been blamed, relatedly, for the growing tendency in our culture to reinterpret what were previously viewed as vices—excessive drinking or gambling, for example—as diseases or addictions, thus relocating them outside the ambit of personal responsibility. Liberal social welfare programs, meanwhile, have been accused of undermining individual responsibility by making society bear the cost of meeting its poorest members' most urgent needs. This is said to provide the poor with strong incentives to avoid making efforts to support themselves, thus producing a permanent class of dependent citizens who view social welfare programs as "entitlements," and who see no need to take responsibility for improving their own material position. Finally, liberal affirmative action programs have been perceived as implying a reduced conception of individual responsibility insofar as they award social positions and opportunities on the basis of membership in targeted social groups rather than on the basis of individual effort, merit, or achievement. Thus, on some of the most important and intensely controversial social issues of the day, the liberal position has met with resistance at least in part because of the perception that it rests on an attenuated conception of personal responsibility.

To avoid misunderstanding, let me emphasize that I am not endorsing the criticisms of liberalism that I have mentioned. I am merely calling attention to the range of liberal positions and policies that have been subject to political attack on the grounds of their supposed incompatibility with ordinary principles of personal responsibility. In so doing, I am trying to focus attention on an important question that arises for liberals about the form that their response to such criticisms should take. Should lib-

erals dispute the charge that the policies they advocate are incompatible with the standard conception of personal responsibility, or should they instead concede that the alleged incompatibility is genuine, but argue that this reveals a flaw in the standard conception rather than in liberalism?

As a matter of political strategy, liberals may well be reluctant to present their position as resting on a reduced conception of responsibility. For any such conception would appear to run counter to the dominant ethos of American society. The extraordinary litigiousness of modern-day America has been widely commented upon. In combination with other features of the prevailing cultural climate, it has led some observers to conclude that Americans no longer believe in simple bad luck, but think instead that any misfortune that befalls a person must be somebody's fault. Offhand, this would not seem to be a promising climate in which to argue the virtues of a reduced conception of responsibility. Admittedly, it may be argued that much of the litigiousness of American society has been made possible by developments in tort law that have themselves been taken to illustrate the erosion of traditional standards of responsibility. Yet the erosion of those standards cannot plausibly be said to explain the prevalence of the underlying litigious impulse, still less the wider impulse to blame and find fault. It is true, as earlier noted, that there has been a growing tendency in our society to extend the concept of *disease* to certain patterns of behavior that were previously regarded as vices, thus narrowing the scope of individual responsibility in some areas. Yet, at the same time, countervailing tendencies have also developed, including, interestingly enough, a sharply increased level of moralizing about personal health itself: with the individual's habits of diet and exercise, for example, treated increasingly as appropriate objects of moral approval or disapproval. Thus, in short, although the perceived boundaries of individual responsibility are to some extent in flux, and although, as the political controversies we are discussing indicate, there is a widespread sense that traditional notions of responsibility are under attack and that their influence is eroding, there is no evidence that the impulse to employ the concepts and categories of responsibility is disappearing or even diminishing significantly in strength.

In view of these considerations, it would seem that the more promising political strategy for liberals would be to present the policies they advocate as compatible with traditional notions of responsibility. This would presumably mean arguing that any appearance of incompatibility is due to a failure properly to interpret the implications of those notions. The question, however, is whether this argument can be successfully made. In the case of each of the liberal policies I have mentioned, the appearance of incompatibility arises, as I have said, from the fact that the policy in question assigns important benefits or burdens on the basis of considerations other than those of individual desert. In order to reconcile these policies with ordinary notions of responsibility, what liberals would need to argue is not that we should, in general, be skeptics about desert, but rather that ordinary principles of desert, properly understood, do not have the policy implications in these cases that critics of liberalism suppose them to have. Many liberals would undoubtedly say that they are fully prepared to offer such arguments. As I shall attempt to show, however, it is a striking fact that, according to the dominant philosophical defenses of liberalism that are current today, desert has no role whatsoever to play in the fundamental normative principles that apply to the basic social, political, and economic institutions of society. This suggests that political liberals can expect to receive little assistance from contemporary liberal philosophers as they attempt to demonstrate the compatibility of their agenda with ordinary notions of desert and responsibility. And this cannot but raise the question of whether there is any theoretically defensible interpretation of liberalism that would support such a demonstration.

Of course, philosophical defenses of liberalism continue to be offered, as they always have been, from a variety of importantly different perspectives. My claim, however, is that none of the major strands in contemporary liberal philosophy assigns a significant role to desert at the level of fundamental principle. This is most obvious in the case of the utilitarian strand. Although Rawlsian liberalism explicitly defines itself in opposition to utilitarianism, there is of course an important tradition of utilitarian support for liberal institutions that extends from Mill to the present day. Yet there is no form of utilitarianism that treats desert as a basic moral concept. Indeed, utilitarianism as it is most naturally interpreted presents a radical challenge to ordinary notions of responsibility. On the one hand, utilitarianism greatly widens the scope of individual responsibility, insofar as it treats the outcomes that one fails to prevent as no less important in determining the rightness or wrongness of one's actions than the outcomes that one directly brings about. On the other hand, the responsibility whose scope is thus widened is also quite shallow, on the utilitarian view, for assignments of responsibility carry no direct implications of blame or desert, and amount to little more in themselves than judgments about the optimality of acts. The shallowness of utilitarian responsibility is reflected in J.J.C. Smart's well-known comment that "the notion of *the* responsibility [for an outcome] is a piece of metaphysical nonsense."[4] This does not mean that utilitarians are incapable of recognizing that, in order to function efficiently, a social institution or cooperative scheme may need to assign distinct functions and roles to different individuals, thus producing a clear division of responsibility among the participants in that institution or scheme. Nor need utilitarians deny that there are often sound reasons for social institutions to distribute benefits and burdens of certain types in accordance with publicly acknowledged standards of individual merit or demerit, or that when they do so, individuals who meet the relevant criteria or standards may be said to deserve the benefit or burden in question. But here desert is understood as an institutional artifact rather than as one of the normative bases of institutional design.

For the purposes of my argument, it is an important fact that the most influential contemporary proponent of a purely institutional view of desert is not a utilitarian at all, but is rather Rawls himself. As is well known, Rawls maintains in *A Theory of Justice* that it is "one of the fixed points of our considered judgments that no one deserves his place in the distribution of native endowments any more than one deserves one's initial starting point in society."[5] He takes this uncontroversial judgment to imply that the better endowed also do not deserve the greater economic advantages that their endowments might enable them to amass under certain possible institutional arrangements. According to Rawls, the "principles of justice that regulate the basic structure [of society] and specify the duties and obligations of individuals do not mention moral desert," or desert of any other kind for that matter.[6] Nevertheless, he says:

> It is perfectly true that given a just system of cooperation as a scheme of public rules and the expectations set up by it, those who, with the prospect of improving their condition, have done what the system announces that it will reward are entitled to their advantages. In this sense the more fortunate have a claim to their better situation; their claims are legitimate expectations established by social institutions, and the community is obligated to meet them. But this sense of desert presupposes the existence of the cooperative scheme; it is irrelevant to the question . . . [of how] in the first place the scheme is to be designed.[7]

On this way of understanding desert, the idea that social institutions should be designed in such a way as to ensure that people get what they deserve makes about as much sense as the idea that universities were created so that professors would have somewhere to turn in their grades, or that baseball was invented in order to ensure that batters with three strikes would always be out.

The fact that Rawlsian and utilitarian liberals agree about the derivative status of desert suffices to establish this view as the prevailing liberal orthodoxy in philosophy. This does not mean, however, that it has attracted no opposition. The best-known criticism of Rawls's position on desert is the one developed by Robert Nozick in *Anarchy, State, and Utopia*.[8] Nozick is especially critical of the way Rawls moves from the premise that people do not deserve their "natural assets" to the conclusion that they do not deserve the advantages that those assets may enable them to amass. "It needn't be," Nozick writes, "that the foundations underlying desert are themselves deserved, *all the way down*."[9] Yet when Nozick develops his own conception of distributive

justice, the concept of desert once again plays no role. Instead, he argues that individuals are "entitled" to their natural assets whether or not they can be said to deserve them, and that they are also entitled, within limits, to the "holdings" that those assets enable them to acquire.

Although Nozick's libertarian conception of justice is not a liberal position in the sense we are discussing, it does of course belong to the older tradition of Lockean liberalism, to which the version of liberalism that we are considering stands in a complex relationship both historically and conceptually. And if there is any position capable of laying claim to the term *liberal* that might be expected to assign an important role to the concept of desert, it is surely this type of Lockean libertarianism. It is therefore a remarkable fact that the most conspicuous contemporary proponent of such a position makes no more use of the notion of desert in elaborating his own view of distributive justice than do the Rawlsian and utilitarian positions he so severely criticizes. It is even more remarkable when one considers that these three positions—Nozick's, Rawls's, and the utilitarian's—represent three of the four viewpoints that, taken together, have dominated American political philosophy for the last twenty years.

Nor do things look very different when we consider the fourth position, communitarianism. Readers of Michael Sandel's influential book *Liberalism and the Limits of Justice*[10] might be tempted to think otherwise. In that book, Sandel provides an extended critique of Rawlsian liberalism from a communitarian perspective, and he devotes considerable attention both to Rawls's treatment of desert and to Nozick's criticism of that treatment. The main thrust of Sandel's argument is that Rawls's treatment of desert is an outgrowth of his reliance on an unsatisfactory conception of the self: a conception that leaves the self "too thin to be capable of desert."[11] In Sandel's view, the Rawlsian self is a "pure subject of possession," whose identity is fixed independently of the aims, attributes, and attachments that it happens to have.[12] Conceived of in this way, the self is said to lack any features by virtue of which it could be thought to deserve anything; it is a mere "condition of agency standing beyond the objects of its possession."[13] "Claims of desert," by contrast, "presuppose thickly-constituted selves," whose very identity is in part determined by their particular aims, attachments, and loyalties.[14]

Since Sandel thinks that we "cannot coherently regard ourselves"[15] in the way that he believes Rawls requires us to do, but must instead regard ourselves as "thickly-constituted," one might expect that he would then go on to assign a more important role to desert than Rawls does. Yet that is just what he does not do. In the course of a discussion of affirmative action, he considers the "meritocratic" position "that the individual possesses his attributes in some unproblematic sense and therefore deserves the benefits that flow from them, and that part of what it means for an institution or distributive scheme to be just is that it rewards individuals antecedently worthy of reward."[16] Rather than endorsing these propositions, Sandel says that "Rawls and Dworkin present powerful arguments against these assumptions which defenders of meritocracy would be hard-pressed to meet."[17] And although Sandel reiterates his claim that the liberal vision provided by philosophers like Rawls and Dworkin nevertheless depends on unsatisfactory notions of community and the self, nowhere does he actually argue that a proper understanding of community and self would vindicate the conception of desert that Rawls and Dworkin reject.[18]

Not only, then, do the main lines of contemporary philosophical liberalism agree in avoiding any appeal to a preinstitutional conception of desert— any appeal, that is, to an independent standard of desert by reference to which the justice of institutional arrangements is to be measured—but, moreover, some of the most prominent critics of contemporary liberalism also shy away from such appeals. And they do so even when, like Sandel, they see the liberal rejection of preinstitutional desert as associated with an unsatisfactory conception of the self, and even when, like Nozick, they are clearly sympathetic to the idea of preinstitutional desert. How is this surprising degree of convergence to be explained? Doubtless there are a number of factors at work, no single one of which will suffice to explain the thinking of each and every philosopher. However, I believe that there is one factor that any adequate explanation of the general phenomenon

will need to cite, and that is the influence of naturalism. The widespread reluctance among political philosophers to defend a robust notion of preinstitutional desert is due in part to the power in contemporary philosophy of the idea that human thought and action may be wholly subsumable within a broadly naturalistic view of the world. The reticence of these philosophers—their disinclination to draw on any preinstitutional notion of desert in their theorizing about justice—testifies in part to the prevalence of the often unstated conviction that a thoroughgoing naturalism leaves no room for a conception of individual agency substantial enough to sustain such a notion. This problem, the problem of the relation between naturalism and individual agency, is of course a descendant of the problem of determinism and free will. Or, more accurately perhaps, it is the variant of that problem that seems most urgent from a contemporary standpoint. Thus my suggestion is that the reluctance of many contemporary political philosophers to rely on a preinstitutional notion of desert results in part from a widespread though often implicit skepticism about individual agency, a form of skepticism that is the contemporary descendant of skepticism about freedom of the will.

It might be thought an objection to this diagnosis that the same contemporary philosophers who avoid any reliance on desert nevertheless make heavy use of other moral notions, including notions of rights, justice, equality, and the like. As in the case of free will and determinism, however, the moral notions that seem most directly threatened by modern naturalistic outlooks are the notions of desert and responsibility. That is because the threat to morality posed by such outlooks proceeds via their threat to individual agency, and of all moral notions, the notions of desert and responsibility are the ones that depend most obviously and immediately on an understanding of what human agency involves. Thus if the internalization of a broadly naturalistic outlook were going to produce skepticism about any single aspect of morality, this would surely be the one. Of course, it might be argued that, in the end, naturalism supports skepticism about desert only if it also supports skepticism about moral thought more generally, so that it is ultimately inconsistent to forswear any reliance on desert while continuing to use other moral notions as before. Even if this is correct, however, it does not impugn the diagnosis I have offered. For, as I have said, desert and responsibility are the moral notions that are most conspicuously threatened by a thoroughgoing naturalism. So whether or not their position is ultimately consistent, it is not implausible that political philosophers whose justificatory ambitions give them every reason to resist skepticism about morality in general, but who have also absorbed a broadly naturalistic view of the place of human beings in the world, should register their uneasiness about the implications of naturalism through a reluctance to rely on any preinstitutional notion of desert.

II

If the diagnosis just offered is correct, then the project of reconciling the policies advocated by political liberals with traditional ideas about individual responsibility is one that contemporary philosophical liberals are poorly equipped to undertake. For they reject the preinstitutional notion of desert on which the traditional ideas rely, and, if I am right, they do so, at least in part, out of a sense that, given our best current understanding of how the world works, that preinstitutional notion can no longer be taken seriously. The defense of political liberalism would therefore appear to require either a liberal theory unlike those that dominate contemporary political philosophy or a frank repudiation of traditional ideas about responsibility, at least insofar as those ideas rely on a preinstitutional notion of desert. I have already argued that such a repudiation is unlikely to be popular politically. However, this invites a further question. If indeed the repudiation of traditional ideas about responsibility would be politically unpopular, is that owing to contingent features of the present political climate, or do these ideas have a deeper and more securely entrenched hold on our thought?

There is at least some reason to think that the latter may be the case. This can be seen most readily by considering the relation between the conception of desert advocated by contemporary philosophical liberals and some of the attitudes recommended by

a familiar form of "compatibilism" about free will and determinism. As against those who believe that the truth of determinism would leave no room for traditional notions of desert and responsibility, and would, therefore, undermine our existing practices of moral praise and blame, one standard version of compatibilism holds that even if determinism were true, such practices would continue to be justified by virtue of their social efficacy or utility. As P. F. Strawson has noted,[19] however, far from reassuring those "pessimists" who see determinism as posing a threat to our practices of praise and blame, this compatibilist argument seems to them not to provide "a sufficient basis, . . . or even the right *sort* of basis, for these practices as we understand them."[20] For the argument represents the practices in question "as instruments of policy, as methods of individual treatment and social control."[21] And, Strawson says, pessimists react to this representation with both conceptual and emotional shock: conceptual shock, because the compatibilist construal omits an important feature of our actual concepts of praise and blame, and emotional shock, because this omission suggests that compatibilism, if accepted, would require a drastic change in human attitudes and personal relations. What the compatibilist construal leaves out is an acknowledgment of the fact that our actual practices of moral praise and blame, in addition to having social utility, serve to express a variety of feelings and attitudes, such as gratitude, resentment, and indignation, liability to which is essential to participation in most of the types of human relationship that we value most deeply.[22] Strawson refers to these emotions as "reactive attitudes," because, he says, they are reactions to the attitudes and intentions of others, either toward ourselves or toward third parties. When we do not regard an individual as capable of participating in ordinary human relationships, because, for example, of some extreme psychological abnormality, then the reactive attitudes tend to be inhibited and replaced by an "objective attitude" in which the person is viewed, in a clinical spirit, as someone to be managed or treated or controlled. The compatibilist construal of our practices of moral praise and blame is unnerving because the exclusively instrumental role that it assigns to those practices would be appropriate only in a relationship in which the reactive attitudes were absent and a thoroughgoing objectivity of attitude prevailed. Thus the effect of that construal is to convince pessimists that determinism may threaten not only our existing practices of praise and blame but also the wide range of ordinary human relationships that could not exist if, as this version of compatibilism appears to require, the reactive attitudes were systematically suspended.

Strawson himself believes that, in the end, such pessimism is unwarranted, for the reactive attitudes as a whole neither need nor admit of any justification, and so no thesis of determinism could possibly give us a reason to suspend them, still less "require" us to do so. If certain influential compatibilist formulations treat our practices of praise and blame in isolation from their connections to the reactive attitudes, that is just a defect in those formulations. It does not testify to any genuine incompatibility between determinism and the attitudes themselves.

Much as I admire Strawson's article, I find myself more persuaded by his diagnosis of what troubles pessimists about the form of compatibilism he discusses than by his conclusion that pessimism is in the end unwarranted. My aim here, however, is not to argue against that conclusion. It is rather to call attention to the way in which the issues Strawson raises are relevant to debates about liberalism. What makes them relevant is the close connection between the compatibilist construal of praise and blame to which Strawson objects and the purely institutional conception of desert favored by liberal philosophers. Strawson's compatibilist seeks to justify the practices whereby we hold people responsible or accountable for their actions by reference to the social utility of such practices. Liberal philosophers, meanwhile, regard the defensibility of the practices whereby we treat individuals who behave in certain ways as deserving certain rewards or penalties as entirely dependent on the prior defensibility of the social institutions that are said to give rise to those practices.[23] In each case, the assignment of benefits and burdens in accordance with the conception of merit or desert is seen as requiring justification by reference to something putatively more fundamental: either to the utility of such assignments or to their placement within a larger institutional framework that is

thought of as independently justifiable. In neither case is a conception of merit or desert treated as morally fundamental or as an independent normative constraint on the design of social institutions.

It is true that liberal philosophers, or at least those liberal philosophers whose orientation is not utilitarian, need not conceive of our practices with respect to merit and desert in the narrowly instrumental way that is characteristic of what Strawson calls "the objective attitude." In this respect, their position differs from the type of compatibilist position that Strawson criticizes. Yet it resembles that position in the ways that I have described, and this is sufficient to raise the question of whether it too is insufficiently sensitive to the role of the relevant practices in giving expression to our reactive attitudes. Admittedly, some liberal philosophers who reject the idea of preinstitutional desert in favor of the notion of legitimate institutional expectations would nevertheless agree that punishment, at least, has an important "expressive function."[24] Yet these philosophers need to show that the reactive attitudes whose expression through the institution of punishment they acknowledge do not rest on just the sorts of assumptions about preinstitutional desert that they reject. Offhand, it would seem that if the punishment of a murderer or a rapist, say, serves to express the community's outrage and indignation, it does so by answering to the thought that the perpetrator *deserves* a severe penalty, where this does not mean merely that he has reason to expect one. Furthermore, the liberal philosophers I am discussing do not treat desert-based judgments about the assignment of social and economic benefits as serving to express significant interpersonal reactions at all. Yet it is clear that judgments to the effect that certain individuals do or do not deserve certain benefits have an important expressive function in many contexts. This might not present a problem for liberals if the reactive attitudes were sufficiently plastic that they were capable of finding full expression via whatever system of institutional expectations and entitlements happened to be in place. To the extent that those attitudes are less than fully flexible, however, any purely institutional conception of desert runs the risk of conflicting with them, and hence of presenting itself as incompatible with a web of fundamental interpersonal responses. Thus, if liberalism proposes to replace our ordinary notion of desert with the idea of legitimate institutional expectations, and if that proposal meets with political resistance, the possibility cannot be excluded that such resistance is responsive in part to an underlying tension between liberalism and the reactive attitudes, rather than stemming exclusively from contingent features of the prevailing political climate.

The upshot of the discussion to this point may be summarized as follows. Political liberalism has come under heavy attack in this country owing in part to a perception that many of the programs and policies advocated by liberals rest on a reduced conception of individual responsibility. Although some liberals might wish to reject this perception as erroneous, it is a striking fact that the dominant contemporary philosophical defenses of liberalism, by virtue of their reliance on a purely institutional notion of desert, do indeed advocate a reduced conception of responsibility. And in so doing, they may to some extent be underestimating the significance of the human attitudes and emotions that find expression through our practices with respect to desert and responsibility. If so, then two conclusions seem to follow. The first is that contemporary philosophical liberalism may be vulnerable to a criticism not unlike the one that has been directed at contemporary political liberalism. The second is that the prospects of political liberalism might best be served, not by additional arguments in favor of a purely institutional conception of desert, but rather by a demonstration that liberal programs and policies do not in fact require such a conception.

As I have indicated, these conclusions could perhaps be avoided, at least in the case of liberal principles of distributive justice, if it could be shown that the reactive attitudes were sufficiently plastic as to render them fully compatible with an institutional system of economic expectations that was insensitive to any independent considerations of desert. It is unclear whether a convincing argument to this effect is available. To the best of my knowledge, the closest thing to such an argument that one finds in contemporary liberal theory is Rawls's argument for the stability of his conception of justice.[25] That argument turns on the claim that citizens in a well-

ordered society regulated by Rawlsian principles would acquire a more effective sense of justice than would citizens in societies ordered by other conceptions of justice, most notably utilitarianism. In order to establish this claim, Rawls sketches an account of the development of the moral sentiments with the aim of demonstrating that an effective sense of justice would be the normal outcome of the processes of moral development in a Rawlsian society. Rawls's account emphasizes the intimate relation between the sense of justice and reactive attitudes like shame, guilt, and resentment, and he takes pains to argue that these attitudes would tend to develop in a well-ordered society in such a way that, in their mature form, they would naturally come to be regimented by the Rawlsian principles of justice. That is, people would feel guilty if they violated those principles, they would feel resentful of violations committed by others, and so on. Rawls takes the psychological plausibility of his account to depend on the idea that his principles of justice embody an ideal of reciprocity or mutuality, and it is therefore natural that he should contrast his account primarily with the moral psychology of utilitarianism. For the ideas of reciprocity and mutuality have no fundamental ethical significance for utilitarianism, and as a result utilitarian moral psychology seems forced to make implausibly heavy demands on the human capacity for sympathetic identification. In so doing, utilitarianism seems to underestimate the psychological constraints on the design of stable social and political institutions, and Rawls's account has great force by comparison. Yet Rawls never explicitly addresses the question whether his own repudiation of preinstitutional desert may not itself involve such an underestimation, albeit one of a less extreme sort. In other words, he never explicitly considers, and thus never convincingly rules out, the possibility, first, that our judgments about the proper distribution of benefits and burdens in society may, in addition to regimenting our reactive attitudes, serve as a vehicle for expressing those attitudes; and, second, that the attitudes in question may rest on an assumption that individuals are responsible agents in a sense that implies that their distributive shares ought to be influenced in certain ways by their behavior.[26] Here it seems relevant to note that, whereas Strawson says that resentment and other reactive attitudes are "essentially reactions to the quality of others' wills toward us,"[27] resentment in political contexts—whether it arises on the left or on the right—is more often a reaction to (what are perceived as) the *undeserved advantages* of others, and not to the quality of their wills at all.

III

There is some irony in the fact that the difficulty to which I have been calling attention arises for nonutilitarian versions of contemporary liberal theory. For such theories tend to appeal to people who regard utilitarianism's aggregative character as rendering it incapable of providing a tolerably secure foundation for individual rights, and who regard its instrumental, goal-oriented structure as rendering it incapable of attaching sufficient weight, or the right kind of weight, to those features of human life and personal relations about which we care most. Many such people would view the failure of familiar forms of compatibilism to appreciate either the role of our practices of praise and blame in giving expression to our reactive attitudes or the role of the reactive attitudes in human interpersonal relations as an unsurprising consequence of the instrumental, utilitarian character of those compatibilist formulations. In this way, they would see the failings of such formulations as serving to illustrate the very sorts of considerations that make nonutilitarian versions of liberal theory look attractive. Hence the irony in the fact that those versions of liberalism may themselves be insufficiently sensitive to the significance of the reactive attitudes in relation to our notions of desert and responsibility.

Even if this is granted, of course, it may be thought to reveal nothing more important than the existence of an internal tension in the views of a certain group of people. However, I believe that the tension between philosophical liberalism and ordinary notions of desert and responsibility has wider significance, for three main reasons. The first reason, which I have already emphasized, is that the prospects of political liberalism may depend in part on how this tension is resolved. This will be so,

at any rate, at least insofar as it is contemporary philosophical liberalism, with its disavowal of pre-institutional desert, that is seen as providing the theoretical foundation for the positions and policies advocated by political liberals.

The second reason is that an appreciation of the tension between liberalism and desert helps to illuminate the intense philosophical controversy surrounding liberalism's alleged "neutrality" among competing "conceptions of the good." Liberalism's claims to neutrality have always struck critics of varying persuasions as involving a certain degree of bad faith. There are a number of reasons for this, but one of the most important is that liberalism seems to many of its critics to presuppose a conception of human life and an understanding of the place of human beings in the world that is itself in conflict with many conceptions of the good. To these critics, the difficulty is not that liberalism directly endorses some particular conception of the good or directly condemns some other conception. The fundamental problem arises much earlier, at the stage at which liberalism defines the "individuals" among whose conceptions of the good it purports to be neutral. To its critics, the liberal framework itself seems to incorporate an understanding of what it is to be a human individual that is highly contentious, and that leads inevitably to the design of institutions and the creation of conditions that are far more hospitable to some ways of life than to others. The argument I have been developing in this article reveals one of the bases for this criticism. For, as I have said, the unwillingness of liberal philosophers to rely on any preinstitutional conception of desert is due in part to their internalization of a broadly naturalistic outlook, and to their skeptical understanding of how robust a notion of individual agency is compatible with such an outlook. Yet a purely naturalistic understanding of human life *is* contentious. The modern world is deeply divided in its attempt to come to terms with the power of naturalism, and one of the defining features of modern life is a deep uneasiness about what place there may be for our selves and our values in the world that science is in the process of discovering. It is clear, moreover, that different conceptions of the good respond to this uneasiness in very different ways. Thus if liberalism does presuppose a naturalistically based skepticism about individual agency, it is hardly surprising that its claims to neutrality among diverse conceptions of the good should seem suspect. Moreover, although the political prospects of liberalism might be improved if liberal policies could be defended by appeal to a more robust conception of agency and responsibility, there would be no gain in neutrality if liberalism were seen to rest upon such a conception. For as long as a purely naturalistic understanding of human life remains controversial—as long as the place of human beings in the world of science is subject to debate—*no* conception of agency and responsibility can claim to be neutral among conceptions of the good. This may seem to imply that, in order to preserve its neutrality, liberalism should refrain from endorsing any conception of individual agency or responsibility. However, even if such abstinence were a conceptual possibility, as it almost certainly is not,[28] it would have the peculiar effect of reducing liberalism to silence on the very subject that was supposed to be its specialty, namely, the nature and moral importance of the individual human agent.

The third reason why the tension between philosophical liberalism and ordinary notions of desert and responsibility is significant is that it raises a philosophically and politically important question about the moral psychology of liberalism. I have already argued that the question of the plasticity of the reactive attitudes assumes great importance for liberal philosophers in view of their reliance on a purely institutional conception of desert. However, this is really but an instance of a more general challenge facing liberalism. The more general challenge is to allay the suspicion that the interpersonal attitudes that liberals value in the private sphere may be psychologically continuous with social and political attitudes whose implications are uncongenial to liberalism. The suggestion that our reactive attitudes may presuppose a preinstitutional notion of desert that is incompatible with liberal principles of justice represents one way in which this suspicion can arise. Another way in which it can arise is via the suggestion that the very same psychological proclivities that lead people to develop personal loyalties and attachments may also lead them to develop forms of group identification and allegiance that lib-

eralism cannot easily accommodate. The suggestion, in other words, is that the psychology of friendship and close personal relations is also the psychology of communal solidarity and partiality. This suggestion receives support from communitarianism in the domain of theory, and from the rise of nationalism and multiculturalism in the domain of political practice. Indeed, it is at this point that the communitarian criticism of liberalism and the desert-based criticism begin to converge. For each sees liberalism as demanding, at the level of political interaction, an individual psychology of bland impartiality: a psychology that is thoroughly unrealistic, and that would be incapable, even if it *were* realistic, of sustaining the rich interpersonal relations that liberals are prepared to celebrate in the realm of private life.[29]

IV

I should emphasize that my aim in this article has not been to defend the preinstitutional notion of desert that is embedded in traditional conceptions of responsibility. Indeed, liberals (among whom I number myself) may well be right to be skeptical of this notion, and, hence, of the traditional conceptions that rely on it. My aim has merely been to call attention to the extent of such skepticism among liberals, and to its significance. Before concluding, however, let me address two objections to my argument that will long since have occurred to the reader. The first objection is that my characterization of contemporary liberal philosophy as having internalized a naturalistically based skepticism about individual agency and responsibility cannot possibly be correct, at least as applied to the liberalism of Rawls. For, especially in those writings that postdate *A Theory of Justice*, Rawls takes pains to emphasize the Kantian roots of his theory, and to highlight the role played in that theory by a conception of citizens as "free and equal moral persons." Moreover, he says it is a feature of that conception that citizens "are regarded as taking responsibility for their ends and [that] this affects how their various claims are assessed."[30] Thus it may seem clearly inaccurate to represent Rawls as relying on an attenuated conception of agency and responsibility.

In response, however, I would make two points. First, the doctrine of "responsibility for ends," as Rawls presents it, does not involve any preinstitutional conception of desert, nor is it intended as an independent constraint on the design of just institutions. Instead, it simply amounts to the claim that

> given just background institutions and the provision for all of a fair index of primary goods (as required by the principles of justice), citizens are capable of adjusting their aims and ambitions in the light of what they can reasonably expect and of restricting their claims in matters of justice to certain kinds of things. They recognize that the weight of their claims is not given by the strength or intensity of their wants and desires, even when they are rational.[31]

Rawls's argument in this passage is that people have the capacity to adjust their aims and aspirations in light of their institutional expectations, provided that the institutions in question are just. The purpose of this argument is to explain why a reliance on primary goods as an index of well-being is not inappropriate, despite the fact that someone with unusually expensive tastes and preferences may derive less satisfaction from a given bundle of those goods than someone with more modest tastes and preferences. Rawls's claim is that just institutions need make no special provision for expensive preferences, not because individuals are responsible in some preinstitutional sense for their own preferences, but rather because people living in a just society have the capacity to adjust their preferences in light of the resources they can expect to have at their command. To be sure, this capacity may itself be preinstitutional in some sense. However, there is an important difference between the claim that people possess preinstitutional capacities that would enable them to adapt to a certain institutional assignment of responsibility and the claim that the assignment of responsibility is itself preinstitutional. Thus, whatever one thinks of Rawls's argument, there is, as far as I can see, nothing in it that has any tendency to vindicate traditional notions of responsibility or desert.[32]

A similar conclusion applies, incidentally, to Ronald Dworkin's treatment of expensive tastes. Dworkin appears at one point to express sympathy for the position that people do not *deserve* compensation for expensive tastes, or at least for those expensive tastes that they have deliberately cultivated. However, it quickly emerges that, for Dworkin, the claim that some individual does not deserve compensation for his expensive tastes may be legitimate only insofar as it is based on a judgment that the individual in question has already received what has independently been identified as his fair share of social resources.[33] For Dworkin, in other words, there is no prior standard of desert that determines what counts as a fair share or as a just institutional arrangement. Thus Dworkin does not appeal to a preinstitutional conception of desert any more than do the other liberal theorists we have discussed.[34]

Returning to Rawls, the other point I want to make is simply that, although his broadly Kantian conception of the person may well be incompatible with the attenuated notion of individual agency to which I have referred, explicit endorsement of the former is compatible with tacit reliance on the latter. Insofar as Rawls's unwillingness to accept preinstitutional desert gives rise to a reduced conception of individual responsibility, any tension between such a conception and Rawls's Kantian ideal of the person must be viewed as a tension internal to his theory. Moreover, a tension of this sort seems likely to afflict any form of liberalism that defers at crucial points to the authority of a naturalistic outlook, while seeking simultaneously to situate itself within the philosophical tradition of Kant.[35]

The second objection that I wish very briefly to address may be put as follows. If, as I have argued, there is a surprising degree of agreement among contemporary philosophical liberals and their critics about the advisability of avoiding any appeal to preinstitutional desert, then why should it be a special problem for political liberalism if it too avoids any such appeal? The answer is that although liberalism's most prominent philosophical critics may be reluctant to appeal to preinstitutional desert, its most prominent political critics certainly are not. On the contrary, conservative politicians do not hesitate to invoke traditional notions of desert and responsibility in attacking liberal positions. Thus if political liberalism does require the rejection of preinstitutional desert, then although it will be in tune with the prevailing philosophical consensus, that may not suffice to prevent its political isolation. Indeed, if one takes the view that our reactive attitudes require a preinstitutional conception of desert that is incompatible with a broadly naturalistic outlook, then, to the extent that political liberalism reflects the prevailing philosophical consensus, pessimism about the philosophical implications of naturalism may translate into pessimism about the political prospects of liberalism.

NOTES

1. Similar developments also occurred, to one degree or another, in some of the other western democracies, most notably Great Britain. But I will limit my discussion to the United States, which is where the philosophical debate about liberalism was most active during the period in question.

2. In recent work Rawls has distinguished between "political liberalism," which is said not to depend on any "comprehensive moral doctrine," and "comprehensive liberalism," which does so depend. See "Justice as Fairness: Political Not Metaphysical," *Philosophy & Public Affairs* 14, no. 3 (Summer 1985): 223–51, and "The Idea of an Overlapping Consensus," *Oxford Journal of Legal Studies* 7 (1987): 1–25. His own view is said to be an instance of the former, while those of Kant and Mill are cited as examples of the latter. The distinction I am drawing is, as should be evident, a different one. I am concerned with the relations between liberalism as a position in American political life and liberalism as a view in contemporary political philosophy. In this sense, Rawls's view is an example of philosophical liberalism.

3. For illuminating discussion of many issues concerning desert, see Joel Feinberg, "Justice and Personal Desert," in his *Doing and Deserving* (Princeton: Princeton University Press, 1970), pp. 55–94; and George Sher, *Desert* (Princeton: Princeton University Press, 1987).

4. J.C.C. Smart, "An Outline of a System of Utilitarian Ethics," in J.C.C. Smart and Bernard Williams, *Utilitarianism: For and Against* (Cambridge: Cambridge University Press, 1973), p. 54.

5. John Rawls, *A Theory of Justice* (Cambridge, Mass.: Harvard University Press, 1971), p. 104.

6. Ibid., p. 311.

7. Ibid., p. 103. Curiously, Rawls appears to suggest (on pp. 314–15) that reliance on a preinstitutional conception of desert *is* appropriate in the case of retributive justice, despite the fact that it is inappropriate in the case of distributive justice. As Michael Sandel argues (in *Liberalism and the Limits of Justice* [Cambridge: Cambridge University Press, 1982], pp. 89–92), it is very difficult to see what basis Rawls has for making this distinction, since the considerations that lead him to reject preinstitutional desert in the case of distributive justice seem to apply with equal force to the case of retributive justice. And, as T. M. Scanlon observes, "Rawls' theory of distributive justice" employs "a general philosophical strategy" that is equally available in the retributive case:

> In approaching the problems of justifying both penal and economic institutions we begin with strong theoretical intuitions about the significance of choice: voluntary and intentional commission of a criminal act is a necessary condition of just punishment, and voluntary economic contribution can make an economic reward just and its denial unjust. One way to account for those intuitions is by appeal to a preinstitutional notion of desert: certain acts deserve punishment, certain contributions merit rewards, and institutions are just if they distribute benefits and burdens in accord with these forms of desert.
>
> The strategy I am describing makes a point of avoiding any such appeal. The only notions of desert which it recognizes are internal to institutions and dependent upon a prior notion of justice: if institutions are just then people deserve the rewards and punishments which those institutions assign them. In the justification of institutions, the notion of desert is replaced by an independent notion of justice; in the justification of specific actions and outcomes it is replaced by the idea of legitimate (institutional) expectations. ("The Significance of Choice," in *The Tanner Lectures on Human Values VIII*, ed. Sterling McMurrin [Salt Lake City: University of Utah Press, 1988], p. 188)

Scanlon himself is generally sympathetic to the strategy he describes, and his own account of the "significance of choice" also avoids any reliance on a preinstitutional notion of desert. Because Rawls's view of retributive justice is not developed at any length and plays virtually no role in the overall argument of his book, and because it is dubiously consistent with his account of distributive justice, I will not devote any further attention to it. I regard it as a small and insufficiently motivated departure from the general attitude toward desert that dominates his work and the work of the other liberal theorists with whom I am concerned.

8. Robert Nozick, *Anarchy, State, and Utopia* (New York: Basic Books, 1974).

9. Ibid., p. 225.

10. Cited in note 7.

11. Sandel, *Liberalism and the Limits of Justice*, p. 178.

12. Ibid., p. 85.

13. Ibid., p. 93.

14. Ibid., p. 178.

15. Ibid., p. 65.

16. Ibid., p. 139.

17. Ibid.

18. Alasdair MacIntyre may be cited as a critic of liberalism who endorses a robust notion of desert and who does so within the context of a broadly communitarian framework. It is certainly true that MacIntyre calls attention to the absence in contemporary theories of justice, especially those of Rawls and Nozick, of any significant role for desert, and that he attaches great significance to this omission. However, it cannot be said that MacIntyre develops a rival theory of justice for our society that does assign a fundamental role to desert. He is more concerned to persuade us of how far-reaching a repudiation of modern political thought would be necessary in order to embrace such a conception. Indeed, he believes that the tradition of thought in which the concept of desert is most securely situated requires "a rejection of the modern political order" altogether (*After Virtue*, 2d ed. [Notre Dame, Ind.: University of Notre Dame Press, 1984], p. 237). His argument therefore provides not a counterexample to, but rather additional support for, my thesis about the extent of skepticism within contemporary political philosophy about the concept of desert.

19. In "Freedom and Resentment," *Proceedings and Addresses of the British Academy* 48 (1962): 1–25, reprinted in *Free Will*, ed. Gary Watson (Oxford University Press, 1982), pp. 59–80. References to Strawson's essay will be to the reprinting in Watson's volume.

20. Ibid., p. 62.

21. Ibid., p. 76.

22. Feinberg makes some closely related points in "Justice and Personal Desert" and in "The Expressive Function of Punishment" (in his *Doing and Deserving*, pp. 95–118), although he is not con-

cerned in those essays with questions about freedom of the will.

23. As noted earlier, Rawls would apparently take this view only of our practices with respect to distributive justice, and not of our practices with respect to retributive justice. Other liberal philosophers would take the same view of both. Although I doubt that Rawls can consistently restrict his rejection of preinstitutional desert to the distributive case alone, the problem I am describing arises even on the assumption that he can.

24. An example is Scanlon in "The Significance of Choice."

25. In chapter 8 of *A Theory of Justice*.

26. In an unpublished manuscript ("Justice as Fairness: A Restatement" [Cambridge, Mass., 1990], pp. 58–64), Rawls says that he does not reject preinstitutional desert altogether; he merely denies that it can play any role in a "political" conception of justice designed for a modern, pluralistic democracy, and believes that it must be replaced for the purposes of such a conception by the idea of legitimate expectations. This seems to me to represent a significant departure from the views expressed in *A Theory of Justice*, at (for example) pp. 312–13. And, in any case, it leaves the question I have raised in the text unanswered.

27. Strawson, "Freedom and Resentment," p. 70.

28. The "almost" is a mark of my respect for the "method of avoidance" employed by Rawls in "Justice as Fairness: Political Not Metaphysical" and subsequent writings. The "certainly" is a measure of my skepticism about whether that method can successfully be extended to the issue at hand.

29. In "Foundations of Liberal Equality" (in *The Tanner Lectures on Human Values XI*, ed. Grethe Peterson [Salt Lake City: University of Utah Press, 1990], pp. 3–119, esp. sec. 2), Ronald Dworkin addresses the apparent discontinuity between what he calls the "personal" and "political" perspectives in liberal thought.

30. Rawls, "Justice as Fairness: Political Not Metaphysical," p. 243.

31. John Rawls, "Kantian Constructivism in Moral Theory: The Dewey Lectures 1980," *Journal of Philosophy* 77 (1980): 545. See also his "Fairness to Goodness," *Philosophical Review* 84 (1975): 551–54; "A Kantian Conception of Equality," *Cambridge Review* 96 (1975): 96–97; "Social Unity and Primary Goods," in *Utilitarianism and Beyond*, ed. Amartya Sen and Bernard Williams (Cambridge: Cambridge

University Press, 1982), pp. 167–70; and "Justice as Fairness: Political Not Metaphysical," pp. 243-44.

32. For a discussion of Rawls's argument that I take to support this conclusion, see Scanlon, "The Significance of Choice," pp. 197–201. (See also Scanlon's "Preference and Urgency," *Journal of Philosophy* 72 [1975]: 655–69.) G. A. Cohen would apparently disagree with my reading of Rawls, for he says, in commenting on a passage similar to the one I have quoted in the text, that Rawls's "picture of the individual as responsibly guiding his own taste formation is hard to reconcile with . . . the skepticism which he expresses about extra reward for extra benefit" ("On the Currency of Egalitarian Justice," *Ethics* 99 [1989]: 914). If, as I believe, Rawls's doctrine of responsibility for ends does not rely on a preinstitutional conception of desert or responsibility, then it need not conflict with his refusal to reward effort per se.

33. Ronald Dworkin, "What Is Equality? Part I: Equality of Welfare," *Philosophy & Public Affairs* 10, no. 3 (Summer 1981): 237–40.

34. G. A. Cohen argues that we should "distinguish among expensive tastes according to whether or not their bearer can reasonably be held responsible for them" ("On the Currency of Egalitarian Justice," p. 923). He also argues that although Dworkin's solution to the problem of expensive tastes rests explicitly on a distinction between preferences and resources, nevertheless Dworkin's position owes what plausibility it has to the fact that the notions of choice and responsibility lie in the background of his discussion, "doing a good deal of unacknowledged work" (ibid., p. 928). Indeed, Cohen concludes that, despite his reliance on the preferences/resources distinction, "Dworkin has, in effect, performed for egalitarianism the consider-able service of incorporating within it the most powerful idea in the arsenal of the anti-egalitarian right: the idea of choice and responsibility. But that supreme effect of his contribution needs to be rendered more explicit" (ibid., p. 933). In my view, Dworkin's avoidance of preinstitutional desert, especially when combined with his explicit reliance on the preferences/resources distinction, casts serious doubt on the idea that he has incorporated the same conception of responsibility relied on by the "anti-egalitarian right." Of course, this is compatible with Cohen's claim that, "insofar as [Dworkin] succeeds in making his cut [between preferences and resources] plausible, it is by obscuring . . . the differences between it" and a distinction that emphasizes the importance of responsibility (ibid., p. 922).

35. Rawls's recent assertion (see note 26) that he does not *reject* preinstitutional desert, but merely believes that it is too controversial to play any role in a political conception of justice designed for a modern pluralistic democracy, may seem to provide another reason for thinking that my claim about the influence of naturalism cannot be correct. As I indicated in note 26, however, I believe that Rawls's recent discussion understates the extent of the skepticism about preinstitutional desert that is expressed in *A Theory of Justice*. Nor is there any hint in *A Theory of Justice* that Rawls's reason for avoiding preinstitutional desert is that he believes the notion to be too controversial to play a role in a political conception of justice. In any event, my claim about the influence of naturalism is not a claim about the explicit premises of liberal arguments, nor does it purport to be an exhaustive statement of the factors responsible for the liberal aversion to preinstitutional desert.

The Subjection of Women

JOHN STUART MILL

—◆—

THE OBJECT OF THIS ESSAY IS TO explain as clearly as I am able, the grounds of an opinion which I have held from the very earliest period when I had formed any opinions at all on social or political matters, and which, instead of being weakened or modified, has been constantly growing stronger by the progress of reflection and the experience of life: That the principle which regulates the existing social relations between the two sexes—the legal subordination of one sex to the other—is wrong in itself, and now one of the chief hindrances to human improvement; and that it ought to be replaced by a principle of perfect equality, admitting no power or privilege on the one side, nor disability on the other.

. . .

The preceding considerations are amply sufficient to show that custom, however universal it may be, affords in this case no presumption and ought not to create any prejudice, in favour of the arrangements which place women in social and political subjection to men. But I may go farther, and maintain that the course of history, and the tendencies of progressive human society, afford not only no presumption in favour of this system of inequality of rights, but a strong one against it; and that, so far as the whole course of human improvement up to this time, the whole stream of modern tendencies, warrants any inference on the subject, it is, that this relic of the past is discordant with the future, and must necessarily disappear.

For, what is the peculiar character of the modern world—the difference which chiefly distinguishes modern institutions, modern social ideas, modern life itself, from those of times long past? It is, that human beings are no longer born to their place in life, and chained down by an inexorable bond to the place they are born to, but are free to employ their faculties, and such favourable chances as offer, to achieve the lot which may appear to them most desirable. Human society of old was constituted on a very different principle. All were born to a fixed social position, and were mostly kept in it by law, or interdicted from any means by which they could emerge from it. As some men are born white and others black, so some were born slaves and others freemen and citizens; some were born patricians, other plebeians; some were born feudal nobles, others commoners and *roturiers*. A slave or serf could never make himself free, nor, except by the will of his master, become so. In most European countries it was not till towards the close of the middle ages, and as a consequence of the growth of regal power, that commoners could be ennobled. Even among nobles, the eldest son was born the exclusive heir to the paternal possessions, and a long time elapsed before it was fully established that the father could disinherit him. Among the industrious classes, only those who were born members of a guild, or were admitted into it by its members, could lawfully practise their calling within its local limits; and nobody could practise any calling deemed important, in any but the legal manner—by processes authoritatively prescribed. Manufacturers have stood in the pillory for presuming to carry on their business by new and improved methods. In modern Europe, and most in those parts of it which have participated most largely in all other modern improvements, diametrically opposite doctrines now prevail. Law and government do not undertake to prescribe by whom any social or industrial operation shall or shall not be conducted, or what modes of conducting them shall be lawful. These things are left to the unfettered choice of individuals. Even the laws which required that workmen should serve an apprenticeship, have

From *The Subjection of Women* (Indianapolis: Hackett, 1988). pp. 1, 17–24.

in this country been repealed: there being ample assurance that in all cases in which an apprenticeship is necessary, its necessity will suffice to enforce it. The old theory was, that the least possible should be left to the choice of the individual agent; that all he had to do should, as far as practicable, be laid down for him by superior wisdom. Left to himself he was sure to go wrong. The modern conviction, the fruit of a thousand years of experience, is, that things in which the individual is the person directly interested, never go right but as they are left to his own discretion; and that any regulation of them by authority, except to protect the rights of others, is sure to be mischievous. This conclusion, slowly arrived at, and not adopted until almost every possible application of the contrary theory had been made with disastrous result, now (in the industrial department) prevails universally in the most advanced countries, almost universally in all that have pretensions to any sort of advancement. It is not that all processes are supposed to be equally good, or all persons to be equally qualified for everything; but that freedom of individual choice is now known to be the only thing which procures the adoption of the best processes, and throws each operation into the hands of those who are best qualified for it. Nobody thinks it necessary to make a law that only a strong-armed man shall be a blacksmith. Freedom and competition suffice to make blacksmiths strong-armed men, because the weak-armed can earn more by engaging in occupations for which they are more fit. In consonance with this doctrine, it is felt to be an overstepping of the proper bounds of authority to fix beforehand, on some general presumption, that certain persons are not fit to do certain things. It is now thoroughly known and admitted that if some such presumptions exist, no such presumption is infallible. Even if it be well grounded in a majority of cases, which it is very likely not to be, there will be a minority of exceptional cases in which it does not hold: and in those it is both an injustice to the individuals, and a detriment to society, to place barriers in the way of their using their faculties for their own benefit and for that of others. In the cases, on the other hand, in which the unfitness is real, the ordinary motives of human conduct will on the whole

suffice to prevent the incompetent person from making, or from persisting in, the attempt.

If this general principle of social and economical science is not true; if individuals, with such help as they can derive from the opinion of those who know them, are not better judges than the law and the government, of their own capacities and vocation; the world cannot too soon abandon this principle, and return to the old system of regulations and disabilities. But if the principle is true, we ought to act as if we believed it, and not to ordain that to be born a girl instead of a boy, any more than to be born black instead of white, or a commoner instead of a nobleman, shall decide the person's position through all life— shall interdict people from all the more elevated social positions, and from all, except a few, respectable occupations. Even were we to admit the utmost that is ever pretended as to the superior fitness of men for all the functions now reserved to them, the same argument applies which forbids a legal qualification for members of Parliament. If only once in a dozen years the conditions of eligibility exclude a fit person, there is a real loss, while the exclusion of thousands of unfit persons is no gain; for if the constitution of the electoral body disposes them to choose unfit persons, there are always plenty of such persons to choose from. In all things of any difficulty and importance, those who can do them well are fewer than the need, even with the most unrestricted latitude of choice: and any limitation of the field of selection deprives society of some chances of being served by the competent, without ever saving it from the incompetent.

At present, in the more improved countries, the disabilities of women are the only case, save one, in which laws and institutions take persons at their birth, and ordain that they shall never in all their lives be allowed to compete for certain things. The one exception is that of royalty. Persons still are born to the throne; no one, not of the reigning family, can ever occupy it, and no one even of that family can, by any means but the course of hereditary succession, attain it. All other dignities and social advantages are open to the whole male sex: many indeed are only attainable by wealth, but wealth may be striven for by any one, and is actually obtained by many men of the very humblest origin. The difficulties, to the majority, are indeed insuperable without the aid of fortunate accidents; but no male human being is under any legal ban: neither law nor opinion superadd artificial obstacles to the natural ones. Royalty, as I have said, is excepted: but in this case every one feels it to be an exception—an anomaly in the modern world, in marked opposition to its customs and principles, and to be justified only by extraordinary special expediencies, which, though individuals and nations differ in estimating their weight, unquestionably do in fact exist. But in this exceptional case, in which a high social function is, for important reasons, bestowed on birth instead of being put up to competition, all free nations contrive to adhere in substance to the principle from which they nominally derogate; for they circumscribe this high function by conditions avowedly intended to prevent the person to whom it ostensibly belongs from really performing it; while the person by whom it is performed, the responsible minister, does obtain the post by a competition from which no full-grown citizen of the male sex is legally excluded. The disabilities, therefore, to which women are subject from the mere fact of their birth, are the solitary examples of the kind in modern legislation. In no instance except this, which comprehends half the human race, are the higher social functions closed against any one by a fatality of birth which no exertions, and no change of circumstances, can overcome; for even religious disabilities (besides that in England and in Europe they have practically almost ceased to exist) do not close any career to the disqualified person in case of conversion.

The social subordination of women thus stands out an isolated fact in modern social institutions; a solitary breach of what has become their fundamental law; a single relic of an old world of thought and practice exploded in everything else, but retained in the one thing of most universal interest; as if a gigantic dolmen, or a vast temple of Jupiter Olympius, occupied the site of St. Paul's and received daily worship, while the surrounding Christian churches were only resorted to on fasts and festivals. This entire discrepancy between one social fact and all those which accompany it, and the radical opposition between its nature and the progressive movement which is the boast of the modern world, and which has successively swept away everything else of an analogous character, surely affords, to a conscientious observer of human tendencies, serious matter for reflection. It raises a prima facie presumption on the unfavourable side, far outweighing any which custom and usage could in such circumstances create on the favourable; and should at least suffice to make this, like the choice between republicanism and royalty, a balanced question.

The least that can be demanded is, that the question should not be considered as prejudged by existing act and existing opinion, but open to discussion on its merits, as a question of justice and expediency: the decision on this, as on any of the other social arrangements of mankind, depending on what an enlightened estimate of tendencies and consequences may show to be most advantageous to humanity in general, without distinction of sex. And the discussion must be a real discussion, descending to foundations, and not resting satisfied with vague and general assertions. It will not do, for instance, to assert in general terms, that the experience of mankind has pronounced in favour of the existing system. Experience cannot possibly have decided between two courses, so long as there has only been experience of one. If it be said that the doctrine of the equality of the sexes rests only on theory, it must be remembered that the contrary doctrine also has only theory to rest upon. All that is proved in its favour by direct experience, is that mankind have been able to exist under it, and to attain the degree of improvement and prosperity which we now see; but whether that prosperity has been attained sooner, or is now greater, than it would have been under the other system, experience does not say. On the other hand, experience does say, that every step in improvement has been so invariably accompanied by a step made in raising the social position of women, that historians and philosophers have been led to adopt their elevation or debasement as on the whole the surest test and most correct measure of the civilization of a people or an age.[1] Through all the progessive period of human history, the condition of women has been approaching nearer to equality with men. This does not of itself prove that the assimilation must go on to complete equality;

but it assuredly affords some presumption that such is the case.

Neither does it avail anything to say that the *nature* of the two sexes adapts them to their present functions and position, and renders these appropriate to them. Standing on the ground of common sense and the constitution of the human mind, I deny that any one knows, or can know, the nature of the two sexes, as long as they have only been seen in their present relation to one another. If men had ever been found in society without women, or women without men, or if there had been a society of men and women in which the women were not under the control of the men, something might have been positively known about the mental and moral differences which may be inherent in the nature of each. What is now called the nature of women is an eminently artificial thing—the result of forced repression in some directions, unnatural stimulation in others. It may be asserted without scruple, that no other class of dependents have had their character so entirely distorted from its natural proportions by their relation with their masters; for, if conquered and slave races have been, in some respects, more forcibly repressed, whatever in them has not been crushed down by an iron heel has generally been let alone, and if left with any liberty of development, it has developed itself according to its own laws; but in the case of women, a hot-house and stove cultivation has always been carried on of some of the capabilities of their nature, for the benefit and pleasure of their masters. Then, because certain products of the general vital force sprout luxuriantly and reach a great development in this heated atmosphere and under this active nurture and watering, while other shoots from the same root, which are left outside in the wintry air, with ice purposely heaped all around them, have a stunted growth, and some are burnt off with fire and disappear; men, with that inability to recognise their own work which distinguishes the unanalytic mind, indolently believe that the tree grows of itself in the way they have made it grow, and that it would die if one half of it were not kept in a vapour bath and the other half in the snow.

Of all difficulties which impede the progress of thought, and the formation of well-grounded opinions on life and social arrangements, the greatest is now the unspeakable ignorance and inattention of mankind in respect to the influences which form human character. Whatever any portion of the human species now are, or seem to be, such, it is supposed, they have a natural tendency to be: even when the most elementary knowledge of the circumstances in which they have been placed, clearly points out the causes that made them what they are. Because a cottier deeply in arrears to his landlord is not industrious, there are people who think that the Irish are naturally idle. Because constitutions can be overthrown when the authorities appointed to execute them turn their arms against them, there are people who think the French incapable of free government. Because the Greeks cheated the Turks, and the Turks only plundered the Greeks, there are persons who think that the Turks are naturally more sincere: and because women, as is often said, care nothing about politics except their personalities, it is supposed that the general good is naturally less interesting to women than to men. History, which is now so much better understood than formerly, teaches another lesson: if only by showing the extraordinary susceptibility of human nature to external influences, and the extreme variableness of those of its manifestations which are supposed to be most universal and uniform. But in history, as in travelling, men usually see only what they already had in their own minds; and few learn much from history, who do not bring much with them to its study.

Hence, in regard to that most difficult question, what are the natural differences between the two sexes—a subject on which it is impossible in the present state of society to obtain complete and correct knowledge—while almost everybody dogmatizes upon it, almost all neglect and make light of the only means by which any partial insight can be obtained into it. This is, an analytic study of the most important department of psychology, the laws of the influence of circumstances on character. For, however great and apparently ineradicable the moral and intellectual differences between men and women might be, the evidence of their being natural differences could only be negative. Those only could be inferred to be natural which could not possibly be artificial—the residuum, after deducting every characteristic of either sex which can admit of being explained from education or external circumstances. The profoundest knowledge of the laws of the formation of character is indispensable to entitle any one to affirm even that there is any difference, much more what the difference is, between the two sexes considered as moral and rational beings; and since no one, as yet, has that knowledge, (for there is hardly any subject which, in proportion to its importance, has been so little studied), no one is thus far entitled to any positive opin-

ion on the subject. Conjectures are all that can at present be made; conjectures more or less probable, according as more or less authorized by such knowledge as we yet have of the laws of psychology, as applied to the formation of character.

NOTE

1. Charles Fourier and Karl Marx were two such philosophers.

Markets in Women's Reproductive Labor

DEBRA SATZ

Debra Satz (1956–   ) is a professor of philosophy at Stanford University. She is the author of numerous articles in political philosophy and the philosophy of social science.

—•—

MUCH OF THE EVOLUTION OF social policy in the twentieth century has occurred around conflicts over the scope of markets. To what extent, under what conditions, and for what reasons should we limit the use of markets?[1] Recently, American society has begun to experiment with markets in women's reproductive labor. Many people believe that markets in women's reproductive labor, as exemplified by contract pregnancy,[2] are more problematic than other currently accepted labor markets. I will call this the asymmetry thesis because its proponents believe that there ought to be an asymmetry between our treatment of reproductive labor and our treatment of other

forms of labor. Advocates of the asymmetry thesis hold that treating reproductive labor as a commodity, as something subject to the supply-and-demand principles that govern economic markets, is worse than treating other types of human labor as commodities. Is the asymmetry thesis true? And, if so, what are the reasons for thinking that it is true?

My aims in this article are to criticize several popular ways of defending the asymmetry thesis[3] and to offer an alternative defense. Other foundations for an argument against contract pregnancy are, of course, possible. For example, several of the arguments that I examine in this article have sometimes been raised in the context of more general anti-

From *Philosophy and Public Affairs*, 21. Copyright © 1992 by Princeton University Press. Reprinted by permission of the publisher.

Many people were helpful during the "gestation" of this essay. I especially wish to thank Elizabeth Anderson, Richard Arneson, Michael Bratman, Jiwei Ci, Rachel Cohon, John Dupre, Howard Eilberg-Schwartz, John Ferejohn, Geoff Garrett, Margo Horn, Andrew Levine, Susan Okin, Margaret Jane Radin, Richard Terdiman, Mark Tunick, Jacob Weiner, Elisabeth Wood, and the Editors of *Philosophy & Public Affairs* for their detailed comments. Versions of this article were read at a Stanford Political Theory Seminar and the Stanford Feminist Theory Seminar; I am grateful for discussions with all of the participants. Research on this article was supported by a Stanford University Humanities Center Fellowship and an NEH Summer Grant.

commodification arguments. I do not examine such general arguments here. Instead, I focus my discussion on those arguments against contract pregnancy that *depend* on the asymmetry thesis. I believe that the asymmetry thesis both captures strong intuitions that exist in our society and provides a plausible argument against contract pregnancy.

Many feminists hold that the asymmetry thesis is true because women's reproductive labor is a special kind of labor that should not be treated according to market norms. They draw a sharp dividing line between women's reproductive labor and human labor in general: while human labor may be bought and sold, women's reproductive labor is intrinsically not a commodity. According to these views, contract pregnancy allows for the extension of the market into the "private" sphere of sexuality and reproduction. This intrusion of the economic into the personal is seen as improper: it fails to respect the intrinsic, special nature of reproductive labor. As one writer has put it, "When women's labor is treated as a commodity, the women who perform it are degraded."[4]

Below, I argue that this is the wrong way to defend the asymmetry thesis. While I agree with the intuition that markets in women's reproductive labor are more troubling than other labor markets, in this article I develop an alternative account of why this should be so. My analysis has four parts. In the first part, I criticize the arguments against the commodification of women's reproductive labor that turn on the assumption that reproductive labor is a special form of labor, part of a separate realm of sexuality. I argue that there is no distinction between women's reproductive labor and human labor generally, which is relevant to the debate about contract pregnancy. Moreover, I argue that the sale of women's reproductive labor is not *ipso facto* degrading. Rather, it becomes "degrading" only in a particular political and social context.[5] In the second part, I criticize arguments in support of the asymmetry thesis that appeal to norms of parental love. Here, the asymmetry between reproductive labor and labor in general is taken to derive from a special bond between mothers and children: the bond between a mother and her child is different from the bond between a worker and his product. In re-

sponse, I argue that the bond between mothers and children is more complicated than critics of contract pregnancy have assumed and that, moreover, contract pregnancy does not cause parents to view children as commodities. The third part of the article examines an argument that stresses the potential negative consequences of contract pregnancy for children. While this argument has some merit, I argue that it is unpersuasive.

The first three parts of the article argue that the various reasons given in the literature for banning contract pregnancy on the basis of its asymmetry with other forms of labor are inadequate. Nonetheless, most people think that there should be some limits to commodification, and there does seem to be something more problematic about pregnancy contracts than other types of labor contract. The question is, what is the basis for and the significance of these intuitions? And what, apart from its agreement with these particular intuitions, can be said in favor of the asymmetry thesis?

In the fourth part of my article, I argue that the asymmetry thesis is true, but that the reason it is true has not been properly understood. The asymmetry thesis should be defended on external and not intrinsic or essentialist grounds. The conditions of pervasive gender inequality in our society are primary to the explanation of what is wrong with contract pregnancy. I claim that the most compelling objection to contract pregnancy concerns the background conditions of gender inequality that characterize our society. Markets in women's reproductive labor are especially troubling because they reinforce gender hierarchies in a way that other accepted labor markets do not. My defense of the asymmetry thesis thus rests on the way that contract pregnancy reinforces asymmetrical social relations of gender domination in American society. However, not all of the features of contract pregnancy that make it troubling concern gender inequality. Contract pregnancy may also heighten racial inequalities[6] and have harmful effects on the other children of the gestational mother.[7] In addition, the background conditions of economic inequality that characterize our society raise questions about the equal status of the contracting parties. I do not address these points in detail here. However, these latter considerations would have to be addressed in order to generate a complete argument against contract pregnancy.

I. The Special Nature of Reproductive Labor

A wide range of attacks on contract pregnancy turn out to share a single premise, viz., that the intrinsic nature of reproductive labor is different from that of other kinds of labor. Critics claim that reproductive labor is not just another kind of work; they argue that unlike other forms of labor, reproductive labor is not properly regarded as a commodity. I will refer to this thesis as the essentialist thesis, since it holds that reproductive labor is *essentially* something that should not be bought and sold.

In contrast to the essentialist thesis, modern economic theories tend to treat the market as "theoretically all encompassing."[8] Such theories tend to treat all goods and capacities as exchangeable commodities, at least in principle.[9] Economists generally base their defense of markets as distributive mechanisms on three distinct ideas.

First, there is the idea that markets are good for social welfare. Indeed, the fundamental theorem of welfare economics states that every competitive (market) equilibrium is Pareto optimal.[10] A Pareto optimum is a distribution point at which, given the initial distribution of resources, no individual can become better off (in view of her preferences) without at least one other individual becoming worse off. The so-called converse theorem of welfare economics states that every Pareto optimum is a competitive equilibrium.

Second, there is the idea that markets promote freedom. The agent of economic theory is a free, autonomous chooser.[11] Markets enhance her capacities for choosing by decentralizing decision-making, decentralizing information, and providing opportunities for experimentation. Markets also place limits on the viability of unjust social relationships by providing avenues for individual exit, thereby making the threat of defection a credible bargaining device.

Third, there is the idea that excluding a free exchange of some good, as a matter of principle, is incompatible with liberal neutrality. Liberalism re-

quires state neutrality among conceptions of value. This neutrality constrains liberals from banning free exchanges: liberals cannot mandate that individuals accept certain values as having "intrinsic" or ultimate worth.[12] Liberals can, of course, seek to regulate exchanges so that they fall within the bounds of justice. But any argument prohibiting rather than regulating market activity is claimed to violate liberal neutrality.[13]

If we accept the logic of the economic approach to human behavior, we seem led to endorse a world in which everything is potentially for sale: body parts, reproductive labor, children, even persons.[14] Many people are repulsed by such a world. But what exactly is the problem with it? Defenders of the essentialist thesis provide the starting point for a counterattack: not all human goods are commodities. In particular, human reproductive labor is improperly treated as a commodity. When reproductive labor is purchased on the market, it is inappropriately valued.

The essentialist thesis provides support for the asymmetry thesis. The nature of reproductive labor is taken to be fundamentally different from that of labor in general. In particular, proponents of the essentialist thesis hold that women's reproductive labor should be respected and not used.[15] What is it about women's reproductive labor that singles it out for a type of respect that precludes market use?

Some versions of the essentialist thesis focus on the biological or naturalistic features of women's reproductive labor: (1) Women's reproductive labor has both a genetic and a gestational component.[16] Other forms of labor do not involve a genetic relationship between the worker and her product. (2) While much human labor is voluntary at virtually every step, many of the phases of the reproductive process are involuntary. Ovulation, conception, gestation, and birth occur without the conscious direction of the mother. (3) Reproductive labor extends over a period of approximately nine months; other types of labor do not typically necessitate a long-term commitment. (4) Reproductive labor involves significant restrictions of a woman's behavior during pregnancy; other forms of labor are less invasive with respect to the worker's body.

These characteristics of reproductive labor do not, however, establish the asymmetry thesis: (1)

With respect to the genetic relationship between the reproductive worker and her product, most critics object to contract pregnancy even where the "surrogate" is not the genetic mother. In fact, many critics consider "gestational surrogacy"—in which a woman is implanted with a preembryo formed in vitro from donated gametes—more pernicious than those cases in which the "surrogate" is also the genetic mother.[17] In addition, men also have a genetic tie to their offspring, yet many proponents of the asymmetry thesis would not oppose the selling of sperm. (2) With respect to the degree to which reproductive labor is involuntary, there are many forms of work in which workers do not have control over the work process; for example, mass-production workers cannot generally control the speed of the assembly line, and they have no involvement in the overall purpose of their activity. (3) With regard to the length of the contract's duration, some forms of labor involve contracts of even longer duration, for example, book contracts. Like pregnancy contracts, these are not contracts in which one can quit at the end of the day. Yet, presumably, most proponents of the essentialist thesis would not find commercial publishing contracts objectionable. (4) With regard to invasions into the woman's body, nonreproductive labor can also involve incursions into the body of the worker. To take an obvious example, athletes sign contracts that give team owners considerable control over their diet and behavior, allowing owners to conduct periodic tests for drug use. Yet there is little controversy over the sale of athletic capacities.[18] Sales of blood also run afoul of a noninvasiveness condition. In fact, leaving aside the genetic component of reproductive labor, voluntary military service involves features 2 through 4; do we really want to object to such military service on *essentialist* grounds?

Carole Pateman suggests a different way of defending the asymmetry thesis as the basis for an argument against contract pregnancy. Rather than focusing on the naturalistic, biological properties of reproductive labor, she argues that a woman's reproductive labor is more "integral" to her identity than her other productive capacities. Pateman first sketches this argument with respect to prostitution: "Womanhood, too, is confirmed in sexual activity, and when a prostitute contracts out use of her body she is thus selling herself in a very real sense. Women's selves are involved in prostitution in a different manner from the involvement of the self in other occupations. Workers of all kinds may be more or less 'bound up in their work,' but the integral connection between sexuality and sense of the self means that, for self-protection, a prostitute must distance herself from her sexual use."[19]

Pateman's objection to prostitution rests on a claim about the intimate relation between a woman's sexuality and her identity. It is by virtue of this tie, Pateman believes, that sex should not be treated as an alienable commodity. Is her claim true? How do we decide which of a woman's attributes or capacities are essential to her identity and which are not? In particular, why should we consider sexuality more integral to self than friendship, family, religion, nationality, and work?[20] Yet we allow commodification in each of these spheres. For example, rabbis or priests may view their religion as central to their identity, but they often accept payment for performing religious services, and hardly anyone objects to their doing so. Does Pateman think that *all* activities that fall within these spheres and that bear an intimate relationship to a person's identity should be inalienable?

Pateman's argument in the above passage appears to support the asymmetry thesis, by suggesting that a woman's sexuality is *more* intimately related to her identity than her other capacities. Yet she provides no explicit argument for this suggestion. Indeed, at times, her argument seems intended not so much to support the asymmetry thesis as to support a more general thesis against alienating those activities that are closely tied to the identity of persons. But this more general argument is implausible. It would not allow individuals to sell their homes or their paintings or their book manuscripts or their copyrights.

A similar argument about the close connection between sexuality and identity underlies the objection to contract pregnancy raised by the British government–commissioned Warnock Report on Human Fertilisation and Embryology. The Warnock Report links reproductive labor to a person's dignity, claiming that "it is inconsistent with human dignity that a woman should use her uterus for financial profit."[21] But why is selling the use of a woman's uterus "undignified" while selling the use of images of her body in a television commercial is not?

The Warnock Report's argument implicitly rests on the assumption that women's sexuality and reproduction belong to a sacred, special realm. In the words of another author, it is a realm "worthy of respect."[22] Even if this is so, however, the idea of respect alone cannot guarantee the conclusion that reproductive labor should not be treated as a commodity. We sometimes sell things that we also respect. As Margaret Radin puts it, "we can both know the price of something and know that it is priceless."[23] For example, I think that my teaching talents should be respected, but I don't object to being paid for teaching on such grounds. Giving my teaching a price does not diminish the other ways in which my teaching has value.

This point undermines Pateman's argument as well. For although Pateman would not endorse the idea that sexuality is part of a private realm, she does believe that it bears a special relationship to our identities and that by virtue of that relationship it should be inalienable. But we sometimes sell things intimately tied to our identities, without ceasing to be the people that we are. For example, as I suggested above, a person's home may be intimately tied to her identity, but she can also sell it without losing her sense of self.[24]

Finally, I believe that it is a mistake to focus, as does the Warnock Report, on maintaining certain cultural values without examining critically the specific social circumstances from which those values emerge. Thus, the view that selling sexual or reproductive capacities is "degrading" may reflect society's attempts to control women and their sexuality. At the very least, the relations between particular views of sexuality and the maintenance of gender inequality must be taken into account. This is especially important insofar as one powerful defense of contract pregnancy rests on its alleged consequence of empowering poor women.[25] Indeed, there is something hypocritical in the objection to contract pregnancy as "degrading," when the fundamental background conditions of social inequality—many of which are at least "degrading"—are ignored.

II. The Special Bonds of Motherhood

Sometimes what critics of pregnancy contracts have in mind is not the effect of such contracts on the relationship between reproductive labor and a woman's sense of self or her dignity, but its effect on her views (and ours) of the mother-fetus and mother-child bond. On this view, what is wrong with commodifying reproductive labor is that by relying on a mistaken picture of the nature of these relationships, it degrades them. Further, it leads to a view of children as fungible objects. In part I of this section I examine arguments against contract pregnancy based on its portrayal of the mother-fetus bond; in part 2 I examine arguments based on contract pregnancy's portrayal of the mother-child bond.

1. Mothers and Fetuses

Some critics of contract pregnancy contend that the relationship between a mother and a fetus is not simply a biochemical relationship or a matter of contingent physical connection. They claim that the relationship between a mother and a fetus is essentially different from that between a worker and her material product. The long months of pregnancy and the experience of childbirth are part of forming a relationship with the child-to-be. Elizabeth Anderson makes an argument along these lines. She suggests that the commodification of reproductive labor makes pregnancy an alienated form of labor for the women who perform it: selling her reproductive labor alienates a woman from her "normal" and justified emotions.[26] Rather than viewing pregnancy as an evolving relationship with a child-to-be, contract pregnancy reinforces a vision of the pregnant woman as a mere "home" or an "environment."[27] The commodification of reproductive labor thus distorts the nature of the bond between the mother and fetus by misrepresenting the nature of a woman's reproductive labor. What should we make of this argument?

Surely there is truth in the claim that pregnancy contracts may reinforce a vision of women as baby machines or mere "wombs." Recent court rulings with respect to contract pregnancy have tended to acknowledge women's contribution to reproduction only insofar as it is identical to men's: the donation of genetic material. The gestational labor involved in reproduction is explicitly ignored in such rulings. Thus, Mary Beth Whitehead won back her parental rights in the "Baby M" case because the New Jersey Supreme Court acknowledged her genetic contribution.[28]

However, as I will argue in Section IV below, the concern about the discounting of women's reproductive labor is best posed in terms of the principle of equal treatment. By treating women's reproductive labor as identical to men's when it is not, women are not in fact being treated equally. But those who conceptualize the problem with pregnancy contracts in terms of the degradation of the mother-fetus relationship rather than in terms of the equality of men and women tend to interpret the social practice of pregnancy in terms of a maternal "instinct," a sacrosanct bonding that takes place between a mother and her child-to-be. However, not all women "bond" with their fetuses. Some women abort them.

Indeed, there is a dilemma for those who wish to use the mother-fetus bond to condemn pregnancy contracts while endorsing a woman's right to choose abortion. They must hold that it is acceptable to abort a fetus, but not to sell it. While the Warnock Report takes no stand on the issue of abortion, it uses present abortion law as a term of reference in considering contract pregnancy. Since abortion is currently legal in England, the Report's position has this paradoxical consequence: one can kill a fetus, but one cannot contract to sell it.[29] One possible response to this objection would be to claim that women do not bond with their fetuses in the first trimester. But the fact remains that some women never bond with their fetuses; some women even fail to bond with their babies after they deliver them.

Additionally, are we really sure that we know which emotions pregnancy "normally" involves? While married women are portrayed as nurturing and altruistic, society has historically stigmatized the unwed mother as selfish, neurotic, and unconcerned with the welfare of her child. Until quite recently, social pressure was directed at unwed mothers to surrender their children after birth. Thus, married

women who gave up their children were seen as "abnormal" and unfeeling, while unwed mothers who failed to surrender their children were seen as selfish.[30] Such views of the mother-fetus bonding relationship reinforce this traditional view of the family and a woman's proper role within it.

2. Mothers and Children

A somewhat different argument against contract pregnancy contends that the commodification of women's reproductive labor entails the commodification of children. Once again, the special nature of reproduction is used to support the asymmetry thesis: the special nature of maternal love is held to be incompatible with market relations. Children should be loved by their mothers, yet commercial surrogacy responds to and promotes other motivations. Critics argue that markets in reproductive labor give people the opportunity to "shop" for children. Prospective womb-infertile couples will seek out arrangements that "maximize" the value of their babies: sex, eye color, and race will be assessed in terms of market considerations.[31] Having children on the basis of such preferences reflects an inferior conception of persons. It brings commercial attitudes into a sphere that is thought to be properly governed by love.

What are the reasons that people seek to enter into contract pregnancy arrangements? Most couples or single people who make use of "surrogates' want simply to have a child that is "theirs," that is, genetically related to them. In fact, given the clogged adoption system, some of them may simply want to have a child. Furthermore, the adoption system itself is responsive to people's individual preferences: it is much easier, for example, to adopt an older black child than a white infant. Such preferences may be objectionable, but no one seriously argues that parents should have no choice in the child they adopt nor that adoption be prohibited because it gives rein to such preferences. Instead, we regulate adoption to forbid the differential payment of fees to agencies on the basis of a child's ascribed characteristics. Why couldn't contract pregnancy be regulated in the same way?

Critics who wish to make an argument for the asymmetry thesis based on the nature of maternal love must defend a strong claim about the relationship between markets and love. In particular, they must claim that even regulated markets in reproductive services will lead parents to love their children for the wrong reasons: love will be conditional on the child's having the "right" set of physical characteristics. While I share the view that there is something wrong with the "shopping" attitude in the sphere of personal relations, I wonder if it has the adverse effects that the critics imagine. Individuals in our society seek partners with attributes ranging from a specified race and height to a musical taste for Chopin. Should such singles' advertisements in magazines be illegal? Should we ban dating services that cater to such preferences? Isn't it true that people who meet on such problematic grounds may grow to love each other? I suspect that most parents who receive their child through a contract pregnancy arrangement will love their child as well.

Even if contract pregnancy does not distort our conception of personhood per se, critics can still associate contract pregnancy with baby-selling. One popular argument runs: In contract pregnancy women not only sell their reproductive services, but also their babies. Because baby-selling is taken to be intrinsically wrong, this type of argument attempts to use an analogy to support the following syllogism: If baby-selling is wrong, and contract pregnancy is a form of baby-selling, then contract pregnancy is wrong. The Warnock Report, for example, makes this charge.[32] Suppose that we grant, as seems plausible, that baby-selling is wrong (perhaps on essentialist grounds). Is this argument successful?

It is important to keep in mind that pregnancy contracts do not enable fathers (or prospective "mothers," women who are infertile or otherwise unable to conceive) to acquire children as property. Even where there has been a financial motivation for conceiving a child, and whatever the status of the labor that produced it, the *child* cannot be treated as a commodity. The father cannot, for example, destroy, transfer, or abandon the child. He is bound by the same norms and laws that govern the behavior of a child's biological or adoptive parents. Allowing women to contract for their reproductive

services does not entail baby-selling, if we mean by that a proxy for slavery.

Anderson has argued that what makes contract pregnancy a form of baby-selling is the way such contracts treat the "mother's rights over her child."[33] Such contracts mandate that the mother relinquish her parental rights to the child. Furthermore, such contracts can be enforced against the mother's wishes. Anderson argues that forcing a woman to part with her child and to cede her parental rights by sale entails treating the child as a mere commodity, as something that can be sold. Even if this is true, it does not necessarily lead to the conclusion that pregnancy contracts should be banned. There are many similarities between contract pregnancy and adoption. Like adoption, pregnancy contracts could be regulated to respect a change of mind of the "surrogate" within some specified time period; to accord more with an "open" model in which all the parties to the contract retain contact with the child; or by making pregnancy contracts analogous to contracts that require informed consent, as in the case of medical experiments. Pregnancy contracts could be required to provide detailed information about the emotional risks and costs associated with giving up a child.[34]

Finally, some writers have objected to pregnancy contracts on the ground that they must, by their nature, exploit women. They point to the fact that the compensation is very low, and that many of the women who agree to sell their reproductive labor have altruistic motivations. Anderson writes, "A kind of exploitation occurs when one party to a transaction is oriented toward the exchange of 'gift' values, while the other party operates in accordance with the norms of the market exchange of commodities."[35]

Two responses are possible to this line of argument. First, even if it is the case that all or most of the women who sell their reproductive labor are altruistically motivated,[36] it is unfair to argue that the other parties to the contract are motivated solely in accord with market values. The couples who use contract pregnancy are not seeking to make a profit, but to have a child. Some of them might even be willing to maintain an "extended family" relationship with the "surrogate" after the child's birth.

Second, even if an asymmetry in motivation is established, it is also present in many types of service work: teaching, health care, and social work are all liable to result in "exploitation" of this sort. In all of these areas, the problem is at least partially addressed by regulating compensation. Why is contract pregnancy different?

III. The Consequences of Contract Pregnancy for Children

Susan Okin makes an argument against contract pregnancy that is based on its direct consequences for children, and not on the intrinsic features of reproductive labor or the bonds of motherhood. She argues that the problem with pregnancy contracts is that they do not consider the interests of the child.[37] Okin thus focuses on a different aspect of the concern that contract pregnancy leads us to adopt an inferior understanding of children. She points not to the conception itself, but to its consequences for children. The asymmetry, then, between reproductive labor and other forms of labor is based on the fact that only in the former are the child's interests directly at stake.

Putting aside the difficult question of what actually constitutes the child's best interests,[38] it is not certain that such interests will always be served by the child's remaining with its biological parents. Some children may be better off separated from their biological parents when such parents are abusive. No one would claim that children should always remain with their biological parents. Nevertheless, I agree with Okin that one problem with pregnancy contracts lies in their potential for weakening the biological ties that give children a secure place in the world.[39] If it can be shown that pregnancy contracts make children more vulnerable, for example, by encouraging parental exit, then such a consideration might contribute to calls for restricting or prohibiting such contracts.[40] Such an argument will have nothing to do with the special nature of reproductive labor, nor will it have to do with the special biological relationship between a parent and a child. It will remain valid even where the child bears no genetic relation to its parents.

Children are vulnerable and dependent, and this vulnerability justifies the moral obligations parents have toward them. While this objection can be used to support the asymmetry thesis, it is important to note that asymmetrical vulnerabilities are found throughout the social world; they are not unique to the spheres of the family, sex, and reproduction. The same principles that will mandate against pregnancy contracts will also mandate against the use of child labor and argue for helping the disabled and the aged.

Nonetheless, this objection does point out an asymmetry between reproductive labor and other forms of labor. Can it be used to justify prohibiting contract pregnancy? One of the difficulties with evaluating pregnancy contracts in terms of their effects on children is that we have very little empirical evidence of these effects. The first reported case of a pregnancy contract in the United States occurred in 1976.[41] Even with the more established practice of artificial insemination, no research is available on the effects of donor anonymity on the child. Nor do we know how different family structures, including single-parent and alternative families and adoption, affect children. We should be wary of prematurely making abstract arguments based on the child's best interests without any empirical evidence. Moreover, in the case of families whose life situation may be disapproved of by their community, we may have moral reasons for overriding the best interests of an individual child.[42] For example, if the child of a single or lesbian mother were to suffer discrimination, I do not think that this would justify removal of the child from the mother. Thus, while pregnancy contracts may threaten the interests of children, this is not yet established; nor is this consideration by itself a sufficient reason for forbidding such contracts.

IV. Reproductive Labor and Equality

In the preceding three sections I have argued that the asymmetry thesis cannot be defended by claiming that there is something "essential" about reproductive labor that singles it out for different treatment from other forms of labor; nor by arguing that contract pregnancy distorts the nature of the bonds of motherhood; nor by the appeal to the best interests of the child. The arguments I have examined ignore the existing background conditions that underlie pregnancy contracts, many of which are objectionable. In addition, some of the arguments tend to accept uncritically the traditional picture of the family. Such arguments take current views of the maternal bond and the institution of motherhood as the baseline for judging pregnancy contracts—as if such views were not contested.

If we reject these arguments for the asymmetry thesis, are we forced back to the view that the market is indeed theoretically all-encompassing? Can we reject contract pregnancy, and defend the asymmetry thesis, without claiming either that reproductive labor is essentially not a commodity, or that it necessarily degrades the bonds between mothers and children, or that it is harmful to children?

I think that the strongest argument against contract pregnancy that depends upon the asymmetry thesis is derived from considerations of gender equality. It is this consideration that I believe is tacitly driving many of the arguments; for example, it is the background gender inequality that makes the commodification of women's and children's attributes especially objectionable. My criticism of contract pregnancy centers on the hypothesis that in our society such contracts will turn women's labor into something that is used and controlled by others[43] and will reinforce gender stereotypes that have been used to justify the unequal treatment of women.

Contrary to the democratic ideal, gender inequality is pervasive in our society. This inequality includes the unequal distribution of housework and child care that considerably restricts married women's opportunities in the work force; the fact that the ratio between an average full-time working woman's earnings and those of her average male counterpart is 59.3:100,[44] and the fact that divorce is an economically devastating experience for women (during the 1970s, the standard of living of young divorced mothers fell 73%, while men's standard of living following divorce rose 42%).[45] These circumstances consti-

tute the baseline from which women form their preferences and make their "choices." Thus, even a woman's choice to engage in commercial surrogacy must be viewed against a background of unequal opportunity. Most work done by women in our society remains in a "female ghetto": service and clerical work, secretarial work, cleaning, domestic labor, nursing, elementary school teaching, and waitressing.

I assume that there is something deeply objectionable about gender inequality. My argument is that contract pregnancy's reinforcing of this inequality lies at the heart of what is wrong with it. In particular, reproduction is a sphere that historically has been marked by inequality: women and men have not had equal influence over the institutions and practices involved in human reproduction. In its current form and context, contract pregnancy contributes to gender inequality in three ways:

1. Contract pregnancy gives others increased access to and control over women's bodies and sexuality. In a provocative book, Carmel Shalev argues that it is wrong to forbid a woman to sell her reproductive capacities when we already allow men to sell their sperm.[46] But Shalev ignores a crucial difference between artificial insemination by donor (AID) and a pregnancy contract. AID does not give anyone control over men's bodies and sexuality. A man who elects AID simply sells a product of his body or his sexuality; he does not sell control over his body itself. The current practices of AID and pregnancy contracts are remarkably different in the scope of intervention and control they allow the "buyer." Pregnancy contracts involve substantial control over women's bodies.[47]

What makes this control objectionable, however, is not the intrinsic features of women's reproductive labor, but rather the ways in which such control reinforces a long history of unequal treatment. Consider an analogous case that has no such consequence: voluntary (paid) military service, where men sell their fighting capacities. Military service, like contract pregnancy, involves significant invasions into the body of the seller; soldiers' bodies are controlled to a large extent by their commanding officers under conditions in which the stakes are often life and death. But military service does not *directly* serve to perpetuate traditional gender inequalities.[48] The fact that pregnancy contracts, like military contracts, give someone control over someone else's body is not the issue. Rather, the issue is that in contract pregnancy the body that is controlled belongs to a woman, in a society that historically has subordinated women's interests to those of men, primarily through its control over her sexuality and reproduction.

Market theorists might retort that contract pregnancy could be regulated to protect women's autonomy, in the same way that we regulate other labor contracts. However, it will be difficult, given the nature of the interests involved, for such contracts not to be very intrusive with respect to women's bodies in spite of formal agreements. The purpose of such contracts is, after all, to produce a healthy child. In order to help guarantee a healthy baby, a woman's behavior must be highly controlled.[49]

Moreover, if the pregnancy contract is a contract for reproductive labor, then, as in other types of labor contracts, compliance—what the law terms "specific performance"—cannot be enforced. For example, if I contract to paint your house, and I default on my agreement, you can sue me for breaking the contract, but even if you win, the courts will not require me to paint your house. Indeed, this is the salient difference between even poorly paid wage labor and indentured servitude. Thus, by analogy, if the woman in a pregnancy contract defaults on her agreement and decides to keep the child, the other parties should not be able to demand performance (that is, surrender of the child); rather, they can demand monetary compensation.[50]

This inability to enforce performance in pregnancy contracts may have consequences for the *content* of such contracts that will make them especially objectionable. Recall that such contracts occur over a long period of time, during which a woman may undergo fundamental changes in her willingness to give up the child. The other parties will need some mechanism to ensure her compliance. There are two mechanisms that are likely to produce compliance, but both are objectionable: (a) The contract could be set up so that payment is delivered to the woman only after the child is born. But this structure of compensation closely resembles baby-selling; it now looks as if what is being bought is not the woman's services, but the child itself. Thus, if baby-selling is wrong, then we should be very troubled by the fact that, in order to be self-enforcing, contract pregnancy must use incentives that make it resemble baby-selling. (b) The contract could mandate legal and psychological counseling for a woman who is tempted to change her mind. Given that it is hard to imagine in advance what it means to surrender a child, such counseling could involve a great deal of manipulation and coercion of the woman's emotions.[51]

2. Contract pregnancy reinforces stereotypes about the proper role of women in the reproductive division of labor. At a time when women have made strides in labor force participation, moving out of the family into other social spheres, pregnancy contracts provide a monetary incentive for women to remain in the home.[52] And, while some women may "prefer" to say at home, we need to pay attention to the limited range of economic opportunities available to these women, and to the ways in which these opportunities have shaped their preferences. Under present conditions, pregnancy contracts entrench a traditional division of labor—men at work, women in the home—based on gender.

Additionally, pregnancy contracts will affect the way society views women: they will tend to reinforce the view of women as "baby machines."[53] It is also likely that they will affect the way women see themselves. Insofar as the sale of women's reproductive capacities contributes to the social subordination of women, and only of women, there are antidiscrimination grounds for banning it.

3. Contract pregnancy raises the danger, manifested in several recent court rulings, that "motherhood" will be defined in terms of genetic material, in the same way as "fatherhood." Mary Beth Whitehead won back parental rights to Baby M on the basis of her being the genetic "mother." On the other hand, Anna Johnson, a "gestational" surrogate, lost such rights because she bore no genetic relationship to the child.[54] These court rulings estab-

lish the principle of motherhood on the basis of ge-netic contribution. In such cases, women's contri-bution to reproduction is recognized only insofar as it is identical to that of men. Genes alone are taken to define natural and biological motherhood. By not taking women's actual gestational contributions into account, the courts reinforce an old stereotype of women as merely the incubators of men's seeds.[55] In fact, the court's inattention to women's unique labor contribution is itself a form of unequal treat-ment. By defining women's rights and contributions in terms of those of men, when they are different, the courts fail to recognize an adequate basis for women's rights and needs. These rulings place an additional burden on women.[56]

Given its consequences for gender inequality, I think that the asymmetry thesis is true, and that pregnancy contracts are especially troubling. Current gender inequality lies at the heart of what is wrong with pregnancy contracts. The problem with commodifying women's reproductive labor is not that it "degrades" the special nature of repro-ductive labor, or "alienates" women from a core part of their identities, but that it reinforces a traditional gender-hierarchical division of labor. A conse-quence of my argument is that under very different background conditions, in which men and women had equal power and had an equal range of choices, such contracts would be less objectionable.[57] For ex-ample, in a society in which women's work was val-ued as much as men's and in which child care was shared equally, pregnancy contracts might serve pri-marily as a way for single persons, disabled persons, and same-sex families to have children. Indeed, pregnancy contracts and similar practices have the potential to transform the nuclear family. We know too little about possible new forms of family life to restrict such experiments on a priori grounds; but in our society, I have argued that there are conse-quentialist reasons for making this restriction.

At the same time, there are potential caveats to the acceptability of a regulated form of pregnancy contract even under conditions of gender equality: (1) the importance of background economic in-equality;[58] (2) the effect of the practice on race equality; (3) the need to ensure the woman's par-ticipation in the overall purpose of the activity; (4)

the need to ensure that the vulnerable—children—are protected. We know very little about the pre-requisites for psychologically healthy children. We know very little about the effects of pregnancy con-tracts on parental exit or on the other children of the birth mother.[59] For this reason, even under more ideal circumstances, there is reason to be cau-tious about the potential use of such contracts. For the time being, I believe that pregnancy contracts should be discouraged. This can be done by mak-ing such contracts unenforceable in the courts. Furthermore, in contested cases, the courts should recognize no distinction between genetic and ges-tational "surrogates" with respect to parental rights. Finally, brokerage of pregnancy contracts should be illegal. These proposals aim to discourage con-tract pregnancy and to strengthen the position of the "surrogate," who is the most economically and emotionally vulnerable party in any such arrange-ment.

V. Conclusion: Wage Labor, Reproductive Labor, and Equality

In this article, I have analyzed various grounds for forbidding markets in women's reproductive labor. While I rejected most of these grounds, including the essentialist thesis, the opposing approach of mar-ket theorists misses the point that there are noneco-nomic values that should constrain social policy. Market theorists, in representing all of human be-havior as if it were a product of voluntary choice, ignore the fact of unequal power in the family and in the wider society.

While market theorists often defend their ap-proach in terms of the values of liberty, welfare, and neutrality, they abstract away from the inegalitar-ian social context in which an individual's prefer-ences are formed. But how preferences are formed, and in the light of what range of choices,[60] has a great deal to do with whether or not acting on those preferences is liberty- and welfare-enhancing.[61] Under some circumstances, for example, it could be welfare-enhancing to sell oneself into slavery.[62]

What about liberal neutrality? Market theorists may claim that the asymmetry thesis is a violation of liberal neutrality: it imposes a standard of gender equality on free exchanges. Furthermore, it may seem biased—distinguishing activities that harm women from those that harm everyone. The issue of neutrality is a difficult matter to assess, for there are many interpretations of neutrality. At the very least, however, two considerations seem relevant. First, why should existing distributions serve as the standard against which neutrality is measured? I have argued that it is a mistake to assume that the realm of reproduction and sexuality is "neutral"; it is a product (at least in part) of the unequal social, political, and economic power of men and women. Second, most liberals draw the line at social practices such as slavery, indentured servitude, labor at slave wages, and the selling of votes or political liberties. Each of these practices undermines a framework of free deliberation among equals. If such restrictions violate viewpoint "neutrality," then the mere violation of neutrality does not seem objectionable.

Contract pregnancy places women's bodies under the control of others and serves to perpetuate gender inequality. The asymmetries of gender—the fact of social relations of gender domination—provide the best foundation for the asymmetry thesis. However, not all of the negative consequences of contract pregnancy involve its effects on gender inequality. I have also referred to its possible effects on children, and to the problematic form that such contracts will have to take to be self-enforcing. In addition, a full assessment of the practice would have to consider both its potential for deepening racial inequality and the unequal bargaining power of the parties to the contract. Some of these features of pregnancy contracts are shared with other labor contracts. Indeed, there is an important tradition in social philosophy that argues that it is precisely these shared features that make wage labor itself unacceptable. This tradition emphasizes that wage labor, like contract pregnancy, places the productive capacities of one group of citizens at the service and under the control of another. Unfortunately, there has been little attention in political philosophy to the effects of gender and class inequality on the development of women's and workers' deliberative capacities or on the formation of their preferences. We

have to ask: What kinds of work and family relations and environments best promote the development of the deliberative capacities needed to support democratic institutions?

NOTES

1. See Karl Polanyi, *The Great Transformation* (Boston: Beacon Press, 1970); Gosta Esping-Anderson, *Politics Against Markets: The Social Democratic Road to Power* (Princeton: Princeton University Press, 1985); Michael Walzer, *Spheres of Justice: A Defense of Pluralism and Equality* (New York: Basic Books, 1983); Richard M. Titmuss, *The Gift Relationship: From Human Blood to Social Policy* (New York: Pantheon Books, 1971); Margaret Jane Radin, "Market-Inalienability," *Harvard Law Review* 100 (1987): 1849–1937; Viviana A. Zelizer, "Human Values and the Market: The Case of Life Insurance and Death in Nineteenth Century America," *American Journal of Sociology* 84 (1978): 591–610.

2. I will use the terms *contract pregnancy* and *pregnancy contract* in place of the misleading term *surrogacy*. The so-called surrogate mother is not a surrogate; she is the biological and/or gestational mother. In this article, I do not make any assumptions about who is and who is not a "real" mother.

3. See Elizabeth S. Anderson, "Is Women's Labor a Commodity?" *Philosophy & Public Affairs* 19, no. 1 (Winter 1990): 71–92; Christine Overall, *Ethics and Human Reproduction: A Feminist Analysis* (Boston: Allen and Unwin, 1987); Mary Warnock, *A Question of Life: The Warnock Report on Human Fertilisation and Embryology* (Oxford: Basil Blackwell, 1985); Martha Field, *Surrogate Motherhood: The Legal and Human Issues* (Cambridge, Mass.: Harvard University Press, 1988); Gena Corea, *The Mother Machine* (New York: Harper and Row, 1985); Carole Pateman, *The Sexual Contract* (Stanford: Stanford University Press, 1988). Not all of the arguments against contract pregnancy in these texts depend on the asymmetry thesis.

4. Anderson, "Women's Labor," p. 75.

5. I believe that my argument can also be applied to the case of prostitution, but I do not pursue that point in this article.

6. See Anita Allen, "Surrogacy, Slavery and the

Ownership of Life," *Harvard Journal of Law and Public Policy* 13 (1990): 139–49.

7. See Amy Z. Overvold, *Surrogate Parenting* (New York: Pharos, 1988); Elizabeth Kane, *Birth Mother* (San Diego: Harcourt Brace Jovanovich, 1988).

8. Radin, "Market-Inalienability," p. 1859. Radin refers to this view as "universal commodification."

9. The theoretical assumption that everything is commodifiable characterizes a range of modern economic theories. It is found in both liberal welfare economics and in the conservative economics of the Chicago School. In welfare economics, there are technical reasons for this assumption: Walrasian equilibrium theory, as generalized by Arrow and Debreu, depends on there being markets in everything, including futures, uncertainty, and public goods. In order to demonstrate the existence of a general equilibrium, all goods must be included in the equations.

   The economists of the Chicago School argue that most things should be treated as commodities. They start with the assumption that rational human beings make their choices according to economic principles. Gary Becker, for example, has claimed that all human behavior can be understood in terms of maximizing efficiency, market equilibrium, and stable preferences. Becker's work uses these assumptions to explain criminal punishment, marriage, childbearing, education, and racial discrimination. See Becker, *The Economic Approach to Human Behavior* (Chicago: University of Chicago Press, 1976). (For criticisms of the application of Walrasian equilibrium theory to certain domains, see Joseph Stiglitz, "The Causes and Consequences of the Dependence of Quality on Price," *Journal of Economic Literature* 25 [1987]: 1-48; Louis Putterman. "On Some Recent Explanations of Why Capital Hires Wage Labor," in *The Economic Nature of the Firm*, ed. Putterman [Cambridge: Cambridge University Press, 1986]; Samuel Bowles and Herbert Gintis, "Contested Exchange: New Microfoundations for the Political Economy of Capitalism," *Politics and Society* 18 [1990]: 165–222.)

10. The first welfare theorem holds only under specific conditions, for example, where external economies and diseconomies are absent.

11. See Milton Friedman, *Capitalism and Freedom* (Chicago: University of Chicago Press, 1962).

12. See Will Kymlicka, "Rethinking the Family," *Philosophy & Public Affairs* 20, no. 1 (Winter 1991): 95–96.

13. In *Birthpower* (New Haven: Yale University Press, 1989) Carmel Shalev develops a powerful defense of contract pregnancy that draws on considerations of liberty, welfare, and liberal neutrality. She argues that it is a matter of the "constitutional privacy" of individuals to define legal parenthood in terms of their prior-to-conception intentions; that contract pregnancy will empower women and improve their welfare by unleashing a new source of economic wealth; and that the market is neutral between competing conceptions of human relationships.

14. See Robert Nozick, *Anarchy, State and Utopia* (New York: Basic Books, 1974), p. 331.

15. See Anderson, "Women's Labor," p. 72.

16. In cases of in vitro fertilization, reproductive labor is divided between two women.

17. See Katha Pollitt, "When Is a Mother Not a Mother?" *The Nation*, 31 December 1990, p. 843.

18. See Orlando Patterson, *Slavery and Social Death* (Cambridge, Mass.: Harvard University Press, 1982) for comparisons between slaves and athletes.

19. Pateman. *The Sexual Contract*, p. 207.

20. Freudian theory, with its emphasis on "natural" drives, might give us such reasons, but Pateman does not explicitly endorse such a theory.

21. Warnock. *A Question of Life*, p. 45.

22. See Anderson, "Women's Labor," p. 72.

23. Margaret Jane Radin, "Justice and the Market Domain," in *Markets and Justice*, ed. John W. Chapman and J. R. Pennock (New York: New York University Press, 1989), p. 175.

24. However, I believe that there should be limits on the sale of housing: poor people should not be displaced from their homes for someone else's profit. But in this case, as in contract pregnancy, I think that markets should be limited by considerations of equality. For an interesting alternative approach, see Margaret Jane Radin, "Residential Rent Control," *Philosophy & Public Affairs* 15, no. 4 (Fall 1986): 350–80.

25. Radin calls our attention to the problem of the "double bind": under current conditions of inequality, there are negative external effects of both banning and allowing pregnancy contracts. See Radin, "Market-Inalienability," p. 1917.

26. Anderson, "Women's Labor," p. 81.

27. See Orange County Superior Court Judge Richard Parslow's ruling in which he referred to birth mother Anna Johnson as a "home" for an embryo and not a "mother." *New York Times*, 23 October 1990.

28. *In the Matter of Baby M*, 537 A.2d 1227 (N.J. 1988).

29. Michael Bratman has suggested that the analogy between abortion and contract pregnancy breaks down in the following way. In contract pregnancy, a woman gets pregnant with the intention of giving up the child. There is presumably no analogous intention in the case of abortion: few women, if any, intentionally get pregnant in order to have an abortion. Critics of contract pregnancy might claim that intentionally conceiving a child either to give it up for money or to abort it is immoral. I am not persuaded by such arguments. If abortion is murder, then it is so regardless of the intentions involved. My own view is that the best argument in favor of the right to abortion makes no reference to intentions, but concerns the consequences of abortion restrictions for women, restrictions that, moreover, directly burden only women.

30. See Adrienne Rich, *Of Women Born: Motherhood as Experience and Institution* (New York: Norton, 1976).

31. See Radin, "Market-Inalienability," p. 1927.

32. Warnock, *A Question of Life*, p. 45.

33. Anderson, "Women's Labor," p. 78.

34. I owe this suggestion to Rachel Cohon.

35. Anderson, "Women's Labor," p. 84.

36. Philip Parker, "Motivation of Surrogate Mothers: Initial Findings," *American Journal of Psychiatry* 140 (1983): 117–18. I am grateful to Elizabeth Anderson for bringing this article to my attention.

37. Susan Okin, "A Critique of Pregnancy Contracts: Comments on Articles by Hill, Merrick, Shevory, and Woliver," *Politics and the Life Sciences* 8 (1990): 205–10.

38. See Jon Elster, *Solomonic Judgements* (Cambridge: Cambridge University Press, 1989) for a discussion of the difficulties of ascertaining the best interests of the child. Elster is also skeptical of the idea that the best interests of the child should necessarily prevail in custody disputes.

39. Anderson raises this point as well. See "Women's Labor," p. 80.

40. We must be careful in considering the scope of this argument. Divorce and adoption, for example, may weaken the ties between children and parents, but very few people would be willing to give the state the right to forbid divorce or adoption on such grounds.

41. D. Gelman and E. Shapiro, "Infertility: Babies by Contract," *Newsweek*, 4 November 1985.

42. See Elster, *Solomonic Judgements*, pp. 148ff.

43. Of course, pregnancy contracts also give another woman, the adoptive mother, control over the body of the surrogate mother. The important point here is that in a society characterized by gender inequalities, such contracts put women's bodies at the disposal of others.

44. This figure compares the earnings of white women and white men. In 1980, black and Hispanic women earned, respectively, 55.3% and 40.1% of white men's earnings. See Sara M. Evans and Barbara Nelson, *Wage Justice: Comparable Worth and the Paradox of Technocratic Reform* (Chicago: University of Chicago Press, 1989).

45. Lenore J. Weitzman, *The Divorce Revolution: The Unexpected Social and Economic Consequences for Women and Children in America* (New York: The Free Press, 1985), p. 323.

46. Shalev, *Birthpower*.

47. A man who buys women's reproductive labor can choose his "surrogate"; he does not legally require his wife's permission; pregnancy contracts include substantial provisions regulating the surrogate's behavior. Such provisions include agreements concerning medical treatment, the conditions under which the surrogate agrees to undergo an abortion, and regulation of the surrogate's emotions. Thus, in the case of Baby M, Mary Beth Whitehead consented to refrain from forming or attempting to form any relationship with the child she would conceive. She agreed not to smoke cigarettes, drink alcoholic beverages, or take medications without written consent from her physician. She also agreed to undergo amniocentesis and to abort the fetus "upon demand of William Stern, natural father" if tests found genetic or congenital defects. See "Appendix: Baby M Contract," *Beyond Baby M*, ed. Dianne Bartels (Clifton, N.J.: Humana Press, 1990).

48. This is not to imply that voluntary military service is not objectionable on other grounds, a question that I cannot discuss here.

49. There is already legal precedent for regulating women's behavior in the "best interests" of the fetus. A Massachusetts woman was charged with vehicular homicide when her fetus was delivered stillborn following a car accident. See Eileen McNamara, "Fetal Endangerment Cases on the Rise," *Boston Globe*, 3 October 1989; cited in Lawrence Tribe, *Abortion: The Clash of Absolutes* (New York: Norton, 1990).

50. This analogy may be complicated by the fact that the other parties to the contract may have at least some biological relationship to the child.

51. Anderson also makes this point. See "Women's Labor," pp. 84ff.
52. This is not to imply that the current sexual division of labor, in which women are disproportionately involved in unpaid domestic work, is just.
53. See Corea, *The Mother Machine*.
54. Anita Allen, in "Ownership of Life," has pointed to the disturbing possibilities contract pregnancy poses for racial equality. In cases like *Johnson v. Calvert*, where the gestator (surrogate), Johnson, was a black woman and the Calverts were white and Filipina, it is difficult to imagine a judge awarding the baby to Johnson. For example, there are almost no adoption cases in which a healthy white infant is placed with black parents. In his ruling in *Johnson v. Calvert*, Judge Parslow referred to Johnson as the baby's "wet nurse." Any full assessment of contract pregnancy must consider the implications of the practice for women of color.
55. The medieval church held that the male implanted into the female body a fully formed homunculus (complete with a soul). See Barbara Ehrenreich and Deidre English, *Witches, Midwives and Nurses: A History of Women Healers* (Old Westbury, N.Y.: Feminist Press, 1973).
56. For a perceptive discussion of the ways in which the social treatment of difference has been used to perpetuate inequalities, see Martha Minow, *Making All the Difference* (Ithaca, N.Y.: Cornell University Press, 1990).
57. Of course, under different conditions, the importance of genetically based ties between parents and children might decline.
58. According to a 1987 study by the U.S. Office of Technology Assessment, the typical clients of surrogate parenting agencies are white: 64% have annual incomes of over $50,000. By contrast, 66% of the "surrogates" reported annual incomes of less than $30,000.
59. See n. 7 above.
60. I am indebted to Elisabeth Wood for many discussions about the importance of the "range of choice" in evaluating social practices.
61. Cass Sunstein has criticized the tendency of a wide range of political views to take preferences as given, without attention to the background conditions that shaped them. See his "Preferences and Politics," *Philosophy & Public Affairs* 20, no. 1 (Winter 1991): 3–34.
62. See Patterson, *Slavery and Social Death*, for a discussion of such circumstances.

Racisms

KWAME ANTHONY APPIAH

Kwame Anthony Appiah (1954–   ) is Professor of Afro-American Studies and Philosophy at Harvard University. He is the author of *Assertions and Conditionals* and, with Amy Gutmann, *Color Conscious: The Political Morality of Race*.

———◆———

IF THE PEOPLE I TALK TO AND THE newspapers I read are representative and reliable, there is a good deal of racism about. People and policies in the United States, in Eastern and Western Europe, in Asia and Africa and Latin America are regularly described as "racist." Australia had, until recently, a racist immigration policy; Britain still has one; racism is on the rise in France; many Israelis support Meir Kahane, an anti-Arab racist; many Arabs, according to a leading authority, are anti-Semitic racists;[1] and the movement to establish English as the "official language" of the United States is motivated by racism. Or, at least, so many of the people I talk to and many of the journalists with the newspapers I read believe.

But visitors from Mars—or from Malawi—unfamiliar with the Western concept of racism could be excused if they had some difficulty in identifying what exactly racism was. We see it everywhere, but rarely does anyone stop to say what it is, or to explain what is wrong with it. Our visitors from Mars would soon grasp that it had become at least conventional in recent years to express abhorrence for racism. They might even notice that those most often accused of it—members of the South African Nationalist party, for example—may officially abhor it also. But if they sought in the popular media of our day—in newspapers and magazines, on television or radio, in novels or films—for an explicit definition of this thing "we" all abhor, they would very likely be disappointed.

Now, of course, this would be true of many of our most familiar concepts. *Sister, chair, tomato*—none of these gets defined in the course of our daily business. But the concept of racism is in worse shape than these. For much of what we say about it is, on the face of it, inconsistent.

It is, for example, held by many to be racist to refuse entry to a university to an otherwise qualified "Negro" candidate, but not to be so to refuse entry to an equally qualified "Caucasian" one. But "Negro" and "Caucasian" are both alleged to be names of races, and invidious discrimination on the basis of race is usually held to be a paradigm case of racism. Or, to take another example, it is widely believed to be evidence of unacceptable racism to exclude people from clubs on the basis of race; yet most people, even those who think of "Jewish" as a racial term, seem to think that there is nothing wrong with Jewish clubs, whose members do not share any particular religious beliefs, or Afro-American societies, whose members share the juridical characteristic of American citizenship and the "racial" characteristic of being black.

I say that these are inconsistencies "on the face of it," because, for example, affirmative action in university admissions is importantly different from the earlier refusal to admit blacks or Jews (or other "Others") that it is meant, in part, to correct. Deep enough analysis may reveal it to be quite consistent with the abhorrence of racism; even a shallow analysis suggests that it is intended to be so. Similarly,

justifications can be offered for "racial" associations in a plural society that are not available for the racial exclusivisms of the country club. But if we take racism seriously we ought to be concerned about the adequacy of these justifications.

In this essay, then, I propose to take our ordinary ways of thinking about race and racism and point up some of their presuppositions. And since popular concepts are, of course, usually fairly fuzzily and untheoretically conceived, much of what I have to say will seem to be both more theoretically and more precisely committed than the talk of racism and racists in our newspapers and on television. My claim is that these theoretical claims are required to make sense of racism as the practice of reasoning human beings. If anyone were to suggest that much, perhaps most, of what goes under the name "racism" in our world cannot be given such a rationalized foundation, I should not disagree: but to the extent that a practice cannot be rationally reconstructed it ought, surely, to be given up by reasonable people. The right tactic with racism, if you really want to oppose it, is to object to it rationally in the form in which it stands the best chance of meeting objections. The doctrines I want to discuss can be rationally articulated: and they are worth articulating rationally in order that we can rationally say what we object to in them.

Racist Propositions

There are at least three distinct doctrines that might be held to express the theoretical content of what we call "racism." One is the view—which I shall call *racialism*[2]—that there are heritable characteristics, possessed by members of our species, that allow us to divide them into a small set of races, in such a way that all the members of these races share certain traits and tendencies with each other that they do not share with members of any other race. These traits and tendencies characteristic of a race constitute, on the racialist view, a sort of racial essence; and it is part of the content of racialism that the essential heritable characteristics of what the nineteenth century called the "Races of Man" account for more than the visible morphological characteristics—skin color, hair type, facial features—on the basis of which we make our informal classifications. Racialism is at the heart of nineteenth-century Western attempts to develop a science of racial difference; but it appears to have been believed by others—for example, Hegel, before then, and many in other parts of the non-Western world since—who have had no interest in developing scientific theories.

Racialism is not, in itself, a doctrine that must be dangerous, even if the racial essence is thought to entail moral and intellectual dispositions. Provided positive moral qualities are distributed across the races, each can be respected, can have its "separate but equal" place. Unlike most Western-educated people, I believe—and I have argued elsewhere[3]—that racialism is false; but by itself, it seems to be a cognitive rather than a moral problem. The issue is how the world is, not how we would want it to be.

Racialism is, however, a presupposition of other doctrines that have been called "racism," and these other doctrines have been, in the last few centuries, the basis of a great deal of human suffering and the source of a great deal of moral error.

One such doctrine we might call "extrinsic racism": extrinsic racists make moral distinctions between members of different races because they believe that the racial essence entails certain morally relevant qualities. The basis for the extrinsic racists' discrimination between people is their belief that members of different races differ in respects that *warrant* the differential treatment, respects—such as honesty or courage or intelligence—that are uncontroversially held (at least in most contemporary cultures) to be acceptable as a basis for treating people differently. Evidence that there are no such differences in morally relevant characteristics—that Negroes do not necessarily lack intellectual capacities, that Jews are not especially avaricious—should thus lead people out of their racism if it is purely extrinsic. As we know, such evidence often fails to change an extrinsic racist's attitudes substantially, for some of the extrinsic racist's best friends have always been Jewish. But at this point—if the racist is sincere—what we have is no longer a false doctrine but a cognitive incapacity, one whose significance I shall discuss later in this essay.

I say that the *sincere* extrinsic racist may suffer from a cognitive incapacity. But some who espouse extrinsic racist doctrines are simply insincere intrinsic racists. For *intrinsic racists*, on my definition, are people who differentiate morally between members of different races because they believe that each race has a different moral status, quite independent of the moral characteristics entailed by its racial essence. Just as, for example, many people assume that the fact that they are biologically related to another person—a brother, an aunt, a cousin—gives them a moral interest in that person,[4] so an intrinsic racist holds that the bare fact of being of the same race is a reason for preferring one person to another. (I shall return to this parallel later as well.)

For an intrinsic racist, no amount of evidence that a member of another race is capable of great moral, intellectual, or cultural achievements, or has characteristics that, in members of one's own race, would make them admirable or attractive, offers any ground for treating that person as he or she would treat similarly endowed members of his or her own race. Just so, some sexists are "intrinsic sexists," holding that the bare fact that someone is a woman (or man) is a reason for treating her (or him) in certain ways.

There are interesting possibilities for complicating these distinctions: some racists, for example, claim, as the Mormons once did, that they discriminate between people because they believe that God requires them to do so. Is this an extrinsic racism, predicated on the combination of God's being an intrinsic racist and the belief that it is right to do what God wills? Or is it intrinsic racism because it is based on the belief that God requires these discriminations because they are right? (Is an act pious because the gods love it, or do they love it because it is pious?) Nevertheless, the distinctions between racialism and racism and between two potentially overlapping kinds of racism provide us with the skeleton of an anatomy of the propositional contents of racial attitudes.

Racist Dispositions

Most people will want to object already that this discussion of the propositional content of racist moral and factual beliefs misses something absolutely crucial to the character of the psychological and sociological reality of racism, something I touched on when I mentioned that extrinsic racist utterances are often made by people who suffer from what I called a "cognitive incapacity." Part of the standard force of accusations of racism is that their objects are in some way *irrational*. The objection to Professor Shockley's claims about the intelligence of blacks is not just that they are false; it is rather that Professor Shockley seems, like many people we call "racist," to be unable to see that the evidence does not support his factual claims and that the connection between his factual claims and his policy prescriptions involves a series of non sequiturs.

What makes these cognitive incapacities especially troubling—something we should respond to with more than a recommendation that the individual, Professor Shockley, be offered psychotherapy—is that they conform to a certain pattern: namely, that it is especially where beliefs and policies are to the disadvantage of nonwhite people that he shows the sorts of disturbing failure that have made his views both notorious and notoriously unreliable. Indeed, Professor Shockley's reasoning works extremely well in some other areas: that he is a Nobel Laureate in physics is part of what makes him so interesting an example.

This cognitive incapacity is not, of course, a rare one. Many of us are unable to give up beliefs that play a part in justifying the special advantages we gain (or hope to gain) from our positions in the social order—in particular, beliefs about the positive characters of the class of people who share that position. Many people who express extrinsic racist beliefs—many white South Africans, for example—are beneficiaries of social orders that deliver advantages to them by virtue of their "race," so that their disinclination to accept evidence that would deprive them of a justification for those advantages is just an instance of this general phenomenon.

So too, evidence that access to higher education is as largely determined by the quality of our earlier educations as by our own innate talents, does not, on the whole, undermine the confidence of college entrants from private schools in England or the United States or Ghana. Many of them continue to believe in the face of this evidence that their acceptance at "good" universities shows them to be intel-

lectually better endowed (and not just better prepared) than those who are rejected. It is facts such as these that give sense to the notion of false consciousness, the idea that an ideology can prevent us from acknowledging facts that would threaten our position.

The most interesting cases of this sort of ideological resistance to the truth are not, perhaps, the ones I have just mentioned. On the whole, it is less surprising, once we accept the admittedly problematic notion of self-deception, that people who think that certain attitudes or beliefs advantage them or those they care about should be able, as we say, to "persuade" themselves to ignore evidence that undermines those beliefs or attitudes. What is more interesting is the existence of people who resist the truth of a proposition while thinking that its wider acceptance would in no way disadvantage them or those individuals about whom they care—this might be thought to describe Professor Shockley; or who resist the truth when they recognize that its acceptance would actually advantage them—this might be the case with some black people who have internalized negative racist stereotypes; or who fail, by virtue of their ideological attachments, to recognize what is in their own best interests at all.

My business here is not with the psychological or social processes by which these forms of ideological resistance operate, but it is important, I think, to see the refusal on the part of some extrinsic racists to accept evidence against the beliefs as an instance of a widespread phenomenon in human affairs. It is a plain fact, to which theories of ideology must address themselves, that our species is prone both morally and intellectually to such distortions of judgment, in particular to distortions of judgment that reflect partiality. An inability to change your mind in the face of appropriate[5] evidence is a cognitive incapacity; but it is one that all of us surely suffer from in some areas of belief; especially in areas where our own interests or self-images are (or seem to be) at stake.

It is not, however, as some have held, a tendency that we are powerless to resist. No one, no doubt, can be impartial about everything—even about everything to which the notion of partiality applies; but there is no subject matter about which most sane people cannot, in the end, be persuaded to avoid partiality in judgment. And it may help to shake the convictions of those whose incapacity derives from this sort of ideological defense if we show them how their reaction fits into this general pattern. It is, indeed, because it generally *does* fit this pattern that we call such views "racism"—the suffix "-ism" indicating that what we have in mind is not simply a theory but an ideology. It would be odd to call someone brought up in a remote corner of the world with false and demeaning views about white people a "racist" if that person gave up these beliefs quite easily in the face of appropriate evidence.

Real live racists, then, exhibit a systematically distorted rationality, the kind of systematically distorted rationality that we are likely to call "ideological." And it is a distortion that is especially striking in the cognitive domain: extrinsic racists, as I said earlier, however intelligent or otherwise well informed, often fail to treat evidence against the theoretical propositions of extrinsic racism dispassionately. Like extrinsic racism, intrinsic racism can also often be seen as ideological; but since scientific evidence is not going to settle the issue, a failure to see that it is wrong represents a cognitive incapacity only on controversially realist views about morality. What makes intrinsic racism similarly ideological is not so much the failure of inductive or deductive rationality that is so striking in someone like Professor Shockley but rather the connection that it, like extrinsic racism, has with the interests—real or perceived—of the dominant group.[6] Shockley's racism is in a certain sense directed *against* nonwhite people: many believe that his views would, if accepted, operate against their objective interests, and he certainly presents the black "race" in a less than flattering light.

I propose to use the old-fashioned term "racial prejudice" in the rest of this essay to refer to the deformation of rationality in judgment that characterizes those whose racism is more than a theoretical attachment to certain propositions about race.

Racial Prejudice

It is hardly necessary to raise objections to what I am calling "racial prejudice"; someone who exhibits such deformations of rationality is plainly in trou-

ble. But it is important to remember that propositional racists in a racist culture have false moral beliefs but may not suffer from racial prejudice. Once we show them how society has enforced extrinsic racist stereotypes, once we ask them whether they really believe that race in itself, independently of those extrinsic racist beliefs, justifies differential treatment, many will come to give up racist propositions, although we must remember how powerful a weight of authority our arguments have to overcome. Reasonable people may insist on substantial evidence if they are to give up beliefs that are central to their cultures.

Still, in the end, many will resist such reasoning; and to the extent that their prejudices are really not subject to any kind of rational control, we may wonder whether it is right to treat such people as morally responsible for the acts their racial prejudice motivates, or morally reprehensible for holding the views to which their prejudice leads them. It is a bad thing that such people exist; they are, in a certain sense, bad people. But it is not clear to me that they are responsible for the fact that they are bad. Racial prejudice, like prejudice generally, may threaten an agent's autonomy, making it appropriate to treat or train rather than to reason with them.

But once someone has been offered evidence both (1) that their reasoning in a certain domain is distorted by prejudice, and (2) that the distortions conform to a pattern that suggests a lack of impartiality, they ought to take special care in articulating views and proposing policies in that domain. They ought to do so because, as I have already said, the phenomenon of partiality in judgment is well attested in human affairs. Even if you are not immediately persuaded that you are yourself a victim of such a distorted rationality in a certain domain, you should keep in mind always that this is the usual position of those who suffer from such prejudices. To the extent that this line of thought is not one that itself falls within the domain in question, one can be held responsible for not subjecting judgments that *are* within that domain to an especially extended scrutiny; and this is a fortiori true if the policies one is recommending are plainly of enormous consequence.

If it is clear that racial prejudice is regrettable, it

is also clear in the nature of the case that providing even a superabundance of reasons and evidence will often not be a successful way of removing it. Nevertheless, the racist's prejudice will be articulated through the sorts of theoretical propositions I dubbed extrinsic and intrinsic racism. And we should certainly be able to say something reasonable about why these theoretical propositions should be rejected.

Part of the reason that this is worth doing is precisely the fact that many of those who assent to the propositional content of racism do not suffer from racial prejudice. In a country like the United States, where racist propositions were once part of the national ideology, there will be many who assent to racist propositions simply because they were raised to do so. Rational objection to racist propositions has a fair chance of changing such people's beliefs.

Extrinsic and Intrinsic Racism

It is not always clear whether someone's theoretical racism is intrinsic or extrinsic, and there is certainly no reason why we should expect to be able to settle the question. Since the issue probably never occurs to most people in these terms, we cannot suppose that they must have an answer. In fact, given the definition of the terms I offered, there is nothing barring someone from being both an intrinsic and an extrinsic racist, holding both that the bare fact of race provides a basis for treating members of his or her own race differently from others and that there are morally relevant characteristics that are differentially distributed among the races. Indeed, for reasons I shall discuss in a moment, *most* intrinsic racists are likely to express extrinsic racist beliefs, so that we should not be surprised that many people seem, in fact, to be committed to both forms of racism.

The Holocaust made unreservedly clear the threat that racism poses to human decency. But it also blurred our thinking because in focusing our attention on the racist character of the Nazi atrocities, it obscured their character as atrocities. What is appalling about Nazi racism is not just that it presupposes, as all racism does, false (racialist) beliefs—not simply that it involves a moral incapacity (the

inability to extend our moral sentiments to all our fellow creatures) and a moral failing (the making of moral distinctions without moral differences)—but that it leads, first, to oppression and then to mass slaughter. In recent years, South African racism has had a similar distorting effect. For although South African racism has not led to killings on the scale of the Holocaust—even if it has both left South Africa judicially executing more (mostly black) people per head of population than most other countries and led to massive differences between the life chances of white and nonwhite South Africans—it *has* led to the systematic oppression and economic exploitation of people who are not classified as "white," and to the infliction of suffering on citizens of all racial classifications, not least by the police state that is required to maintain that exploitation and oppression.

Part of our resistance, therefore, to calling the racial ideas of those, such as the Black Nationalists of the 1960s, who advocate racial solidarity, by the same term that we use to describe the attitudes of Nazis or of members of the South African Nationalist party, surely resides in the fact that they largely did not contemplate using race as a basis for inflicting harm. Indeed, it seems to me that there is a significant pattern in the modern rhetoric of race, such that the discourse of racial solidarity is usually expressed through the language of *intrinsic* racism, while those who have used race as the basis for oppression and hatred have appealed to *extrinsic* racist ideas. This point is important for understanding the character of contemporary racial attitudes.

The two major uses of race as a basis for moral solidarity that are most familiar in the West are varieties of Pan-Africanism and Zionism. In each case it is presupposed that a "people," Negroes or Jews, has the basis for shared political life in the fact of being of the same race. There are varieties of each form of "nationalism" that make the basis lie in shared traditions; but however plausible this may be in the case of Zionism, which has in Judaism, the religion, a realistic candidate for a common and nonracial focus for nationality, the peoples of Africa have a good deal less in common culturally than is usually assumed. I discuss this issue at length in *In My Father's House: Essays in the Philosophy of African Culture*, but let me say here that I believe the central fact is this: what blacks in the

West, like secularized Jews, have mostly in common is that they are perceived—both by themselves and by others—as belonging to the same race, and that this common race is used by others as the basis for discriminating against them. "If you ever forget you're a Jew, a goy will remind you." The Black Nationalists, like some Zionists, responded to their experience of racial discrimination by accepting the racialism it presupposed.[7]

Although race is indeed at the heart of Black Nationalism, however, it seems that it is the fact of a shared race, not the fact of a shared racial character, that provides the basis for solidarity. Where racism is implicated in the basis for national solidarity, it is intrinsic, not (or not only) extrinsic. It is this that makes the idea of fraternity one that is naturally applied in nationalist discourse. For, as I have already observed, the moral status of close family members is not normally thought of in most cultures as depending on qualities of character; we are supposed to love our brothers and sisters in spite of their faults and not because of their virtues. Alexander Crummell, one of the founding fathers of Black Nationalism, literalizes the metaphor of family in these startling words:

> Races, like families, are the organisms and ordinances of God; and race feeling, like family feeling, is of divine origin. The extinction of race feeling is just as possible as the extinction of family feeling. Indeed, a race *is* a family.[8]

It is the assimilation of "race feeling" to "family feeling" that makes intrinsic racism seem so much less objectionable than extrinsic racism. For this metaphorical identification reflects the fact that, in the modern world (unlike the nineteenth century), intrinsic racism is acknowledged almost exclusively as the basis of feelings of community. We can surely, then, share a sense of what Crummell's friend and co-worker Edward Blyden called "the poetry of politics," that is, "the feeling of race," the feeling of "people with whom we are connected."[9] The racism here is the basis of acts of supererogation, the treatment of others better than we otherwise might, better than moral duty demands of us.

This is a contingent fact. There is no logical im-

possibility in the idea of racialists whose moral beliefs lead them to feelings of hatred for other races while leaving no room for love of members of their own. Nevertheless most racial hatred is in fact expressed through extrinsic racism: most people who have used race as the basis for causing harm to others have felt the need to see the others as independently morally flawed. It is one thing to espouse fraternity without claiming that your brothers and sisters have any special qualities that deserve recognition, and another to espouse hatred of others who have done nothing to deserve it.[10]

Many Afrikaners—like many in the American South until recently—have a long list of extrinsic racist answers to the question why blacks should not have full civil rights. Extrinsic racism has usually been the basis for treating people worse than we otherwise might, for giving them less than their humanity entitles them to. But this too is a contingent fact. Indeed, Crummell's guarded respect for white people derived from a belief in the superior moral qualities of the Anglo-Saxon race.

Intrinsic racism is, in my view, a moral error. Even if racialism were correct, the bare fact that someone was of another race would be no reason to treat them worse—or better—than someone of my race. In our public lives, people are owed treatment independently of their biological characters: if they are to be differently treated there must be some morally relevant difference between them. In our private lives, we are morally free to have aesthetic preferences between people, but once our treatment of people raises moral issues, we may not make arbitrary distinctions. Using race in itself as a morally relevant distinction strikes most of us as obviously arbitrary. Without associated moral characteristics, why should race provide a better basis than hair color or height or timbre of voice? And if two people share all the properties morally relevant to some action we ought to do, it will be an error—a failure to apply the Kantian injunction to universalize our moral judgments—to use the bare facts of race as the basis for treating them differently. No one should deny that a common ancestry might, in particular cases, account for similarities in moral character. But then it would be the moral similarities that justified the different treatment.

It is presumably because most people—outside the South African Nationalist party and the Ku Klux Klan—share the sense that intrinsic racism requires arbitrary distinctions that they are largely unwilling to express it in situations that invite moral criticism. But I do not know how I would argue with someone who was willing to announce an intrinsic racism as a basic moral idea; the best one can do, perhaps, is to provide objections to possible lines of defense of it.

De Gustibus

It might be thought that intrinsic racism should be regarded not so much as an adherence to a (moral) proposition as the expression of a taste, analogous, say, to the food prejudice that makes most English people unwilling to eat horse meat, and most Westerners unwilling to eat the insect grubs that the !Kung people find so appetizing. The analogy does at least this much for us, namely, to provide a model of the way the *extrinsic* racist propositions can be a reflection of an underlying prejudice. For, of course, in most cultures food prejudices are rationalized: we say insects are unhygienic and cats taste horrible. Yet a cooked insect is no more health-threatening than a cooked carrot, and the unpleasant taste of cat meat, far from justifying our prejudice against it, probably derives from that prejudice.

But there the usefulness of the analogy ends. For intrinsic racism, as I have defined it, is not simply a taste for the company of one's "own kind," but a moral doctrine, one that is supposed to underlie differences in the treatment of people in contexts where moral evaluation is appropriate. And for moral distinctions we cannot accept that "de gustibus non est disputandum." We do not need the full apparatus of Kantian ethics to require that public morality be constrained by reason.

A proper analogy would be with someone who thought that we could continue to kill cattle for beef, even if cattle exercised all the complex cultural skills of human beings. I think it is obvious that creatures that shared our capacity for understanding as well as our capacity for pain should not be treated the way we actually treat cattle—that "intrinsic speciesism"

would be as wrong as racism. And the fact that most people think it is worse to be cruel to chimpanzees than to frogs suggests that they may agree with me. The distinction in attitudes surely reflects a belief in the greater richness of the mental life of chimps. Still, I do not know how I would *argue* against someone who could not see this; someone who continued to act on the contrary belief might, in the end, simply have to be locked up.

The Family Model

I have suggested that intrinsic racism is, at least sometimes, a metaphorical extension of the moral priority of one's family; it might, therefore, be suggested that a defense of intrinsic racism could proceed along the same lines as a defense of the family as a center of moral interest. The possibility of a defense of family relations as morally relevant—or, more precisely, of the claim that one may be morally entitled (or even obliged) to make distinctions between two otherwise morally indistinguishable people because one is related to one and not to the other—is theoretically important for the prospects of a philosophical defense of intrinsic racism. This is because such a defense of the family involves—like intrinsic racism—a denial of the basic claim, expressed so clearly by Kant, that from the perspective of morality, it is as rational agents *simpliciter* that we are to assess and be assessed. For anyone who follows Kant in this, what matters, as we might say, is not who you are but how you try to live. Intrinsic racism denies this fundamental claim also. And, in so doing, as I have argued elsewhere, it runs against the mainstream of the history of Western moral theory.[11]

The importance of drawing attention to the similarities between the defense of the family and the defense of the race, then, is not merely that the metaphor of family is often invoked by racism; it is that each of them offers the same general challenge to the Kantian stream of our moral thought. And the parallel with the defense of the family should be especially appealing to an intrinsic racist, since many of us who have little time for racism would hope that the family is susceptible to some such defense.

The problem in generalizing the defense of the family, however, is that such defenses standardly begin at a point that makes the argument for intrinsic racism immediately implausible: namely, with the family as the unit through which we live what is most intimate, as the center of private life. If we distinguish, with Bernard Williams, between ethical thought, which takes seriously "the demands, needs, claims, desires, and generally, the lives of other people,"[12] and morality, which focuses more narrowly on obligation, it may will be that private life matters to us precisely because it is altogether unsuited to the universalizing tendencies of morality.

The functioning family unit has contracted substantially with industrialization, the disappearance of the family as the unit of production, and the increasing mobility of labor, but there remains that irreducible minimum: the parent or parents with the child or children. In this "nuclear" family, there is, of course, a substantial body of shared experience, shared attitudes, shared knowledge and beliefs; and the mutual psychological investment that exists within this group is, for most of us, one of the things that gives meaning to our lives. It is a natural enough confusion—which we find again and again in discussions of adoption in the popular media—that identifies the relevant group with the biological unit of *genitor*, *genetrix*, and *offspring* rather than with the social unit of those who share a common domestic life.

The relations of parents and their biological children are of moral importance, of course, in part because children are standardly the product of behavior voluntarily undertaken by their biological parents. But the moral relations between biological siblings and half-siblings cannot, as I have already pointed out, be accounted for in such terms. A rational defense of the family ought to appeal to the causal responsibility of the biological parent and the common life of the domestic unit, and not to the brute fact of biological relatedness, even if the former pair of considerations defines groups that are often coextensive with the groups generated by the latter. For brute biological relatedness bears no necessary connection to the sorts of human purposes that seem likely to be relevant at the most basic level of ethical thought.

An argument that such a central group is bound to be crucially important in the lives of most human beings in societies like ours is not, of course, an argument for any specific mode of organization of the "family": feminism and the gay liberation movement have offered candidate groups that could (and sometimes do) occupy the same sort of role in the lives of those whose sexualities or whose dispositions otherwise make the nuclear family uncongenial; and these candidates have been offered specifically in the course of defenses of a move toward societies that are agreeably beyond patriarchy and homophobia. The central thought of these feminist and gay critiques of the nuclear family is that we cannot continue to view any one organization of private life as "natural," once we have seen even the broadest outlines of the archaeology of the family concept.

If that is right, then the argument for the family must be an argument for a mode of organization of life and feeling that subserves certain positive functions; and however the details of such an argument would proceed it is highly unlikely that the same functions could be served by groups on the scale of races, simply because, as I say, the family is attractive in part exactly for reasons of its personal scale.

I need hardly say that rational defenses of intrinsic racism along the lines I have been considering are not easily found. In the absence of detailed defenses to consider, I can only offer these general reasons for doubting that they can succeed: the generally Kantian tenor of much of our moral thought threatens the project from the start; and the essentially unintimate nature of relations within "races" suggests that there is little prospect that the defense of the family—which seems an attractive and plausible project that extends ethical life beyond the narrow range of a universalizing morality—can be applied to a defense of races.

Conclusions

I have suggested that what we call "racism" involves both propositions and dispositions.

The propositions were, first, that there are races (this was *racialism*) and, second, that these races are morally significant either (a) because they are contingently correlated with morally relevant properties (this was *extrinsic racism*) or (b) because they are intrinsically morally significant (this was *intrinsic racism*).

The disposition was a tendency to assent to false propositions, both moral and theoretical, about races—propositions that support policies or beliefs that are to the disadvantage of some race (or races) as opposed to others, and to do so even in the face of evidence and argument that should appropriately lead to giving those propositions up. This disposition I called "racial prejudice."

I suggested that intrinsic racism had tended in our own time to be the natural expression of feelings of community, and this is, of course, one of the reasons why we are not inclined to call it racist. For, to the extent that a theoretical position is not associated with irrationally held beliefs that tend to the *dis*advantage of some group, it fails to display the *directedness* of the distortions of rationality characteristic of racial prejudice. Intrinsic racism may be as irrationally held as any other view, but it does not *have* to be directed *against* anyone.

So far as theory is concerned I believe racialism to be false: since theoretical racism of both kinds presupposes racialism, I could not logically support racism of either variety. But even if racialism were true, both forms of theoretical racism would be incorrect. Extrinsic racism is false because the genes that account for the gross morphological differences that underlie our standard racial categories are not linked to those genes that determine, to whatever degree such matters are determined genetically, our moral and intellectual characters. Intrinsic racism is mistaken because it breaches the Kantian imperative to make moral distinctions only on morally relevant grounds—granted that there is no reason to believe that race, *in se*, is morally relevant, and also no reason to suppose that races are like families in providing a sphere of ethical life that legitimately escapes the demands of a universalizing morality.

NOTES

1. Bernard Lewis, *Semites and Anti-Semites* (New York: Norton, 1986).

2. I shall be using the words "racism" and "racialism" with the meanings I stipulate: in some dialects of English they are synonyms, and in most dialects their definition is less than precise. For discussion of recent biological evidence see M. Nei and A. K. Roychoudhury, "Genetic Relationship and Evolution of Human Races," *Evolutionary Biology*, vol. 14 (New York: Plenum, 1983), pp. 1–59; for useful background see also M. Nei and A. K. Roychoudhury, "Gene Differences between Caucasian, Negro, and Japanese Populations," *Science*, 177 (August 1972), pp. 434–35.

3. See my "The Uncompleted Argument: Du Bois and the Illusion of Race," *Critical Inquiry*, 12 (Autumn 1985); reprinted in Henry Louis Gates (ed.), *"Race, Writing, and Difference* (Chicago: University of Chicago Press, 1986), pp. 21–37.

4. This fact shows up most obviously in the assumption that adopted children intelligibly make claims against their natural siblings: natural parents are, of course, causally responsible for their child's existence and that could be the basis of moral claims, without any sense that biological relatedness entailed rights or responsibilities. But no such basis exists for an interest in natural *siblings*; my sisters are not causally responsible for my existence. See "The Family Model," later in this essay.

5. Obviously what evidence should *appropriately* change your beliefs is not independent of your social or historical situation. In mid-nineteenth-century America, in New England quite as much as in the heart of Dixie, the pervasiveness of the institutional support for the prevailing system of racist belief—the fact that it was reinforced by religion and state, and defended by people in the universities and colleges, who had the greatest cognitive authority—meant that it would have been appropriate to insist on a substantial body of evidence and argument before giving up assent to racist propositions. In California in the 1980s, of course, matters stand rather differently. To acknowledge this is not to admit to a cognitive relativism; rather, it is to hold that, at least in some domains, the fact that a belief is widely held—and especially by people in positions of cognitive authority—may be a good prima facie reason for believing it.

6. Ideologies, as most theorists of ideology have admitted, standardly outlive the period in which they conform to the objective interests of the dominant group in a society; so even someone who thinks the dominant group in our society no longer needs

racism to buttress its position can see racism as the persisting ideology of an earlier phase of society. (I say "group" to keep the claim appropriately general; it seems to me a substantial further claim that the dominant group whose interests an ideology serves is always a class.) I have argued, however, in "The Conservation of 'Race'" that racism continues to serve the interests of the ruling classes in the West; in *Black American Literature Forum*, 23 (Spring 1989), pp. 37–60.

7. As I argued in "The Uncompleted Argument: Du Bois and the Illusion of Race." The reactive (or dialectical) character of this move explains why Sartre calls its manifestations in Négritude an "antiracist racism"; see "Orphée Noir," his preface to Senghor's *Anthologie de la nouvelle poésie négre et malagache de langue française* (Paris: PUF, 1948). Sartre believed, of course, that the synthesis of this dialectic would be the transcendence of racism; and it was his view of it as a stage—the antithesis—in that process that allowed him to see it as a positive advance over the original "thesis" of European racism. I suspect that the reactive character of antiracist racism accounts for the tolerance that it regularly extended to it in liberal circles; but this tolerance is surely hard to justify unless one shares Sartre's optimistic interpretation of it as a stage in a process that leads to the end of all racisms. (And unless your view of this dialectic is deterministic, you should in any case want to play an argumentative role in moving to this next stage.)

For a similar Zionist response see Horace Kallen's "The Ethics of Zionism," *Maccabaean*, August 1906.

8. "The Race Problem in America," in Brotz's *Negro Social and Political Thought* (New York: Basic Books, 1966), p. 184.

9. *Christianity, Islam and the Negro Race* (1887; reprinted Edinburgh: Edinburgh University Press, 1967), p. 197.

10. This is in part a reflection of an important asymmetry: loathing, unlike love, needs justifying; and this, I would argue, is because loathing usually leads to acts that are *in se* undesirable, whereas love leads to acts that are largely *in se* desirable—indeed, supererogatorily so.

11. See my "Racism and Moral Pollution," *Philosophical Forum*, 18 (Winter-Spring 1986–87), pp. 185–202.

12. *Ethics and the Limits of Philosophy* (Cambridge, Mass.: Harvard University Press, 1985), p. 12. I do not, as is obvious, share Williams's skepticism about morality.

E. Challenges to Morality

1. MORALITY AND SELF–INTEREST

The Republic

PLATO

—•—

Part I
(Book I)
Some Current Views of Justice

Chapter I
(I. 327–331 D)
Cephalus: Justice as Honesty
in Word and Deed

The whole imaginary conversation is narrated by Socrates to an unspecified audience. The company who will take part in it assemble at the house of Cephalus, a retired manufacturer living at the Piraeus, the harbour town about five miles from Athens. It includes, besides Plato's elder brothers, Glaucon and Adeimantus, Cephalus' sons, Polemarchus, Lysias, well known as a writer of speeches, and Euthydemus; Thrasymachus of Chalcedon, a noted teacher of rhetoric, who may have formulated the definition of justice as 'the interest of the stronger,' though hardly any evidence about his opinions exists outside the

From *The Republic*, translated by F. MacDonald Cornford. Copyright © 1974 by Oxford University Press. Reprinted by permission of the publisher.

Republic; and a number of Socrates' young friends. The occasion is the festival of Bendis, a goddess whose cult had been imported from Thrace. Cephalus embodies the wisdom of a long life honourably spent in business. He is well-to-do, but values money as a means to that peace of mind which comes of honesty and the ability to render to gods and men their due. This is what he understands by 'right' conduct or justice.

SOCRATES. I walked down to the Piraeus yesterday with Glaucon, the son of Ariston, to make my prayers to the goddess. As this was the first celebration of her festival, I wished also to see how the ceremony would be conducted. The Thracians, I thought, made as fine a show in the procession as our own people, though they did well enough. The prayers and the spectacle were over, and we were leaving to go back to the city, when from some way off Polemarchus, the son of Cephalus, caught sight of us starting homewards and sent his slave running to ask us to wait for him. The boy caught my garment from behind and gave me the message.

I turned round and asked where his master was.

There, he answered; coming up behind. Please wait.

Very well, said Glaucon; we will.

A minute later Polemarchus joined us, with Glaucon's brother, Adeimantus, and Niceratus, the son of Nicias, and some others who must have been at the procession.

Socrates, said Polemarchus, I do believe you are starting back to town and leaving us.

You have guessed right, I answered.

Well, he said, you see what a large party we are? I do.

Unless you are more than a match for us, then, you must stay here.

Isn't there another alternative? said I; we might convince you that you must let us go.

How will you convince us, if we refuse to listen? We cannot, said Glaucon.

Well, we shall refuse; make up your minds to that.

Here Adeimantus interposed: Don't you even know that in the evening there is going to be a torch-race on horseback in honour of the goddess?

On horseback! I exclaimed; that is something new. How will they do it? Are the riders going to race with torches and hand them on to one another?

Just so, said Polemarchus. Besides, there will be a festival lasting all night, which will be worth seeing. We will go out after dinner and look on. We shall find plenty of young men there and we can have a talk. So please stay, and don't disappoint us.

It looks as if we had better stay, said Glaucon.

Well, said I, if you think so, we will.

Accordingly, we went home with Polemarchus; and there we found his brothers, Lysias and Euthydemus, as well as Thrasymachus of Chalcedon, Charmantides of Paeania, and Cleitophon, the son of Aristonymus. Polemarchus' father, Cephalus, was at home too. I had not seen him for some time, and it struck me that he had aged a good deal. He was sitting in a cushioned chair, wearing a garland, as he had just been conducting a sacrifice in the courtyard. There were some chairs standing round, and we sat down beside him.

As soon as he saw me, Cephalus greeted me. You don't often come down to the Piraeus to visit us, Socrates, he said. But you ought to. If I still had the strength to walk to town easily, you would not have to come here; we would come to you. But, as things are, you really ought to come here oftener. I find, I

can assure you, that in proportion as bodily pleasures lose their savour, my appetite for the things of the mind grows keener and I enjoy discussing them more than ever. So you must not disappoint me. Treat us like old friends, and come here often to have a talk with these young men.

To tell the truth, Cephalus, I answered, I enjoy talking with very old people. They have gone before us on a road by which we too may have to travel, and I think we do well to learn from them what it is like, easy or difficult, rough or smooth. And now that you have reached an age when your foot, as the poets say, is on the threshold, I should like to hear what report you can give and whether you find it a painful time of life.

I will tell you by all means what it seems like to me, Socrates. Some of us old men often meet, true to the old saying that people of the same age like to be together. Most of our company are very sorry for themselves, looking back with regret to the pleasures of their young days, all the delights connected with love affairs and merry-making. They are vexed at being deprived of what seems to them so important; life was good in those days, they think, and now they have no life at all. Some complain that their families have no respect for their years, and make that a reason for harping on all the miseries old age has brought. But to my mind, Socrates, they are laying the blame on the wrong shoulders. If the fault were in old age, so far as that goes, I and all who have ever reached my time of life would have the same experience; but in point of fact, I have met many who felt quite differently. For instance, I remember someone asking Sophocles, the poet, whether he was still capable of enjoying a woman. "Don't talk that way," he answered; "I am only too glad to be free of all that; it is like escaping from bondage to a raging madman." I thought that a good answer at the time, and I still think so; for certainly a great peace comes when age sets us free from passions of that sort. When they weaken and relax their hold, most certainly it means, as Sophocles said, a release from servitude to many forms of madness. All these troubles, Socrates, including the complaints about not being respected, have only one cause; and that is not old age, but a man's character. If you have a contented mind at peace with itself, age is no intolerable burden; without that, Socrates, age and youth will be equally painful.

I was charmed with these words and wanted him to go on talking; so I tried to draw him out. I fancy, Cephalus, said I, most people will not accept that account; they imagine that it is not character that makes your burden light, but your wealth. The rich, they say, have many consolations.

That is true, he replied; they do not believe me; and there is something in their suggestion, though not so much as they suppose. When a man from Seriphus taunted Themistocles and told him that his fame was due not to himself but to his country, Themistocles made a good retort: "Certainly, if I had been born a Seriphian, I should not be famous; but no more would you, if you had been born at Athens." And so one might say to men who are not rich and feel old age burdensome: If it is true that a good man will not find it easy to bear old age and poverty combined, no more will riches ever make a bad man contented and cheerful.

And was your wealth, Cephalus, mostly inherited or have you made your own fortune?

Made my fortune, Socrates? As a man of business I stand somewhere between my grandfather and my father. My grandfather, who was my namesake, inherited about as much property as I have now and more than doubled it; whereas my father Lysanias reduced it below its present level. I shall be content if I can leave these sons of mine not less than I inherited, and perhaps a little more.

I asked, said I, because you strike me as not caring overmuch about money; and that is generally so with men who have not made their own fortune. Those who have are twice as fond of their possessions as other people. They have the same affection for the money they have earned that poets have for their poems, or fathers for their children: they not merely find it useful, as we all do, but it means much to them as being of their own creation. That makes them disagreeable company; they have not a good word for anything but riches.

That is quite true.

It is indeed, I said; but one more question: what do you take to be the greatest advantage you have got from being wealthy?

One that perhaps not many people would take

my word for. I can tell you, Socrates, that, when the prospect of dying is near at hand, a man begins to feel some alarm about things that never troubled him before. He may have laughed at those stories they tell of another world and of punishments there for wrongdoing in this life; but now the soul is tormented by a doubt whether they may not be true. Maybe from the weakness of old age, or perhaps because, now that he is nearer to what lies beyond, he begins to get some glimpse of it himself—at any rate he is beset with fear and misgiving; he begins thinking over the past: is there anyone he has wronged? If he finds that his life has been full of wrongdoing, he starts up from his sleep in terror like a child, and his life is haunted by dark forebodings; whereas, if his conscience is clear, that "sweet Hope" that Pindar speaks of is always with him to tend his age. Indeed, Socrates, there is great charm in those lines describing the man who has led a life of righteousness:

Hope is his sweet companion, she who guides
Man's wandering purpose, warms his heart
And nurses tenderly his age.

That is admirably expressed, admirably. Now in this, as I believe, lies the chief value of wealth, not for everyone, perhaps, but for the right-thinking man. It can do much to save us from going to that other world in fear of having cheated or deceived anyone even unintentionally or of being in debt to some god for sacrifice or to some man for money. Wealth has many other uses, of course; but, taking one with another, I should regard this as the best use that can be made of it by a man of sense.

You put your case admirably, Cephalus, said I. But take this matter of doing right: can we say that it really consists in nothing more nor less than telling the truth and paying back anything we may have received? Are not these very actions sometimes right and sometimes wrong? Suppose, for example, a friend who had lent us a weapon were to go mad and then ask for it back, surely anyone would say we ought not to return it. It would not be "right" to do so; nor yet to tell the truth without reserve to a madman.

No, it would not.

Right conduct, then, cannot be defined as telling the truth and restoring anything we have been trusted with.

Yes, it can, Polemarchus broke in, at least if we are to believe Simonides.

Well, well, said Cephalus, I will bequeath the argument to you. It is time for me to attend to the sacrifice.

Your part, then, said Polemarchus, will fall to me as your heir.

By all means, said Cephalus with a smile; and with that he left us, to see to the sacrifice.

Chapter II (I. 331 E–336 A)
Polemarchus: Justice as Helping
Friends and Harming Enemies

. . . .

Then, said I, if you are to inherit this discussion, tell me, what is this saying of Simonides about right conduct which you approve?

That is just to render every man his due. That seems to me a fair statement.

It is certainly hard to question the inspired wisdom of a poet like Simonides; but what this saying means you may know, Polemarchus, but I do not. Obviously it does not mean what we were speaking of just now—returning something we have been entrusted with to the owner even when he has gone out of his mind. And yet surely it is his due, if he asks for it back?

Yes.

But it is out of the question to give it back when he has gone mad?

True.

Simonides, then, must have meant something different from that when he said it was just to render a man his due.

Certainly he did; his idea was that, as between friends, what one owes to another is to do him good, not harm.

I see, said I; to repay money entrusted to one is not to render what is due, if the two parties are friends and the repayment proves harmful to the lender. That is what you say Simonides meant?

Yes, certainly.

And what about enemies? Are we to render whatever is their due to them?

Yes certainly, what really is due to them; which means, I suppose, what is appropriate to an enemy—some sort of injury.

It seems, then, that Simonides was using words with a hidden meaning, as poets will. He really meant to define justice as rendering to everyone what is appropriate to him; only he called that his "due."

Well, why not?

But look here, said I. Suppose we could question Simonides about the art of medicine—whether a physician can be described as rendering to some object what is due or appropriate to it; how do you think he would answer?

That the physician administers the appropriate diet or remedies to the body.

And the art of cookery—can that be described in the same way?

Yes; the cook gives the appropriate seasoning to his dishes.

Good. And the practice of justice?

If we are to follow those analogies, Socrates, justice would be rendering services or injuries to friends or enemies.

So Simonides means by justice doing good to friends and harm to enemies?

I think so.

And in matters of health who would be the most competent to treat friends and enemies in that way?

A physician.

And on a voyage, as regards the dangers of the sea?

A ship's captain.

In what sphere of action, then, will the just man be the most competent to do good or harm?

In war, I should imagine; when he is fighting on the side of his friends and against his enemies.

I see. But when we are well and staying on shore, the doctor and the ship's captain are of no use to us.

True.

Is it also true that the just man is useless when we are not at war?

I should not say that.

So justice has its uses in peace-time too?

Yes.

Like farming, which is useful for producing crops, or shoemaking, which is useful for providing us with shoes. Can you tell me for what purposes justice is useful or profitable in time of peace?

For matters of business, Socrates.

In a partnership, you mean?

Yes.

But if we are playing draughts, or laying bricks, or making music, will the just man be as good and helpful a partner as an expert draught-player, or a builder, or a musician?

No.

Then in what kind of partnership will he be more helpful?

Where money is involved, I suppose.

Except, perhaps, Polemarchus, when we are putting our money to some use. If we are buying or selling a horse, a judge of horses would be a better partner; or if we are dealing in ships, a shipwright or a sea-captain.

I suppose so.

Well, when will the just man be especially useful in handling our money?

When we want to deposit it for safe-keeping.

When the money is to lie idle, in fact?

Yes.

So justice begins to be useful only when our money is out of use?

Perhaps so.

And in the same way, I suppose, if a pruning-knife is to be used, or a shield, or a lyre, then a vine-dresser, or a soldier, or a musician will be of service; but justice is helpful only when these things are to be kept safe. In fact justice is never of any use in using things; it becomes useful when they are useless.

That seems to follow.

If that is so, my friend, justice can hardly be a thing of much value. And here is another point. In boxing or fighting of any sort skill in dealing blows goes with skill in keeping them off; and the same doctor that can keep us from disease would also be clever at producing it by stealth; or again, a general will be good at keeping his army safe, if he can also cheat the enemy and steal his plans and dispositions. So a man who is expert in keeping things will always make an expert thief.

Apparently.

The just man, then, being good at keeping money safe, will also be good at stealing it.

That seems to be the conclusion, at any rate.

So the just man turns out to be a kind of thief. You must have learnt that from Homer, who showed his predilection for Odysseus' grandfather Autolycus by remarking that he surpassed all men in cheating and perjury. Justice, according to you and Homer and Simonides, turns out to be a form of skill in cheating, provided it be to help a friend or harm an enemy. That was what you meant?

Good God, no, he protested; but I have forgotten now what I did mean. All the same, I do still believe that justice consists in helping one's friends and harming one's enemies.

. . . .

Which do you mean by a man's friends and enemies—those whom he believes to be good honest people and the reverse, or those who really are, though they may not seem so?

Naturally, his loves and hates depend on what he believes.

But don't people often mistake an honest man for a rogue, or a rogue for an honest man; in which case they regard good people as enemies and bad people as friends?

No doubt.

But all the same, it will then be right for them to help the rogue and to injure the good man?

Apparently.

And yet a good man is one who is not given to doing wrong.

True.

According to your account, then, it is right to ill-treat a man who does no wrong.

No, no, Socrates; that can't be sound doctrine.

It must be the wrongdoers, then, that it is right to injure, and the honest that are to be helped.

That sounds better.

Then, Polemarchus, the conclusion will be that for a bad judge of character it will often be right to injure his friends, when they really are rogues, and to help his enemies, when they really are honest men—the exact opposite of what we took Simonides to mean.

That certainly does follow, he said. We must shift our ground. Perhaps our definition of friend and enemy was wrong.

What definition, Polemarchus?

We said a friend was one whom we believe to be an honest man.

And how are we to define him now?

As one who really is honest as well as seeming so. If he merely seems so, he will be only a seeming friend. And the same will apply to enemies.

On this showing, then, it is the good people that will be our friends, the wicked our enemies.

Yes.

You would have us, in fact, add something to our original definition of justice: it will not mean merely doing good to friends and harm to enemies, but doing good to friends who are good, and harm to enemies who are wicked.

Yes, I think that is all right.

Can it really be a just man's business to harm any human being?

Certainly; it is right for him to harm bad men who are his enemies.

But does not harming a horse or a dog mean making it a worse horse or dog, so that each will be a less perfect creature in its own special way?

Yes.

Isn't that also true of human beings—that to harm them means making them worse men by the standard of human excellence?

Yes.

And is not justice a peculiarly human excellence?

Undoubtedly.

To harm a man, then, must mean making him less just.

I suppose so.

But a musician or a riding-master cannot be exercising his special skill, if he makes his pupils unmusical or bad riders.

No.

Whereas the just man is to exercise his justice by making men unjust? Or, in more general terms, the good are to make men bad by exercising their virtue? Can that be so?

No, it cannot.

It can no more be the function of goodness to do harm than of heat to cool or of drought to produce moisture. So if the just man is good, the business of harming people, whether friends or not, must belong to his opposite, the unjust.

I think that is perfectly true, Socrates.

So it was not a wise saying that justice is giving every man his due, if that means that harm is due from the just man to his enemies, as well as help to his friends. That is not true; because we have found that it is never right to harm anyone.

I agree.

Then you and I will make common cause against anyone who attributes that doctrine to Simonides or to any of the old canonical sages, like Bias or Pittacus.

Yes, he said, I am prepared to support you.

Do you know, I think that account of justice, as helping friends and harming enemies, must be due to some despot, so rich and powerful that he thought he could do as he liked—someone like Periander, or Perdiccas, or Xerxes, or Ismenias of Thebes.

That is extremely probable.

Very good, said I; and now that we have disposed of that definition of justice, can anyone suggest another?

Chapter III (I. 336 B–347 E)
Thrasymachus: Justice as the Interest of the Stronger

. . . .

All this time Thrasymachus had been trying more than once to break in upon our conversation; but his neighbours had restrained him, wishing to hear the argument to the end. In the pause after my last words he could keep quiet no longer; but gathering himself up like a wild beast he sprang at us as if he would tear us in pieces. Polemarchus and I were frightened out of our wits, when he burst out to the whole company:

What is the matter with you two, Socrates? Why do you go on in this imbecile way, politely deferring to each other's nonsense? If you really want to know what justice means, stop asking questions and scoring off the answers you get. You know very well it is easier to ask questions than to answer them. Answer yourself, and tell us what you think justice means. I won't have you telling us it is the same as what is obligatory or useful or advantageous or profitable or expedient; I want a clear and precise statement; I won't put up with that sort of verbiage.

I was amazed by this onslaught and looked at him in terror. If I had not seen this wolf before he saw me, I really believe I should have been struck dumb; but fortunately I had looked at him earlier, when he was beginning to get exasperated with our argument; so I was able to reply, though rather tremulously:

Don't be hard on us, Thrasymachus. If Polemarchus and I have gone astray in our search, you may be quite sure the mistake was not intentional. If we had been looking for a piece of gold, we should never have deliberately allowed politeness to spoil our chance of finding it; and now when we are looking for justice, a thing much more precious than gold, you cannot imagine we should defer to each other in that foolish way and not do our best to bring it to light. You must believe we are in earnest, my friend; but I am afraid the task is beyond our powers, and we might expect a man of your ability to pity us instead of being so severe.

Thrasymachus replied with a burst of sardonic laughter.

Good Lord, he said; Socrates at his old trick of shamming ignorance! I knew it; I told the others you would refuse to commit yourself and do anything sooner than answer a question.

Yes, Thrasymachus, I replied; because you are clever enough to know that if you asked someone what are the factors of the number twelve, and at the same time warned him: "Look here, you are not to tell me that 12 is twice 6, or 3 times 4, or 6 times 2, or 4 times 3; I won't put up with any such nonsense"—you must surely see that no one would answer a question put like that. He would say: "What do you mean, Thrasymachus? Am I forbidden to give any of these answers, even if one happens to be right? Do you want me to give a wrong one?" What would you say to that?

Humph! said he. As if that were a fair analogy!

I don't see why it is not, said I; but in any case, do you suppose our barring a certain answer would prevent the man from giving it, if he thought it was the truth?

Do you mean that you are going to give me one of those answers I barred?

I should not be surprised, if it seemed to me true, on reflection.

And what if I give you another definition of justice, better than any of those? What penalty are you prepared to pay?[1]

The penalty deserved by ignorance, which must surely be to receive instruction from the wise. So I would suggest that as a suitable punishment.

I like your notion of a penalty! he said; but you must pay the costs as well.

I will, when I have any money.

That will be all right, said Glaucon; we will all subscribe for Socrates. So let us have your definition, Thrasymachus.

Oh yes, he said; so that Socrates may play the old game of questioning and refuting someone else, instead of giving an answer himself!

But really, I protested, what can you expect from a man who does not know the answer or profess to know it, and, besides that, has been forbidden by no mean authority to put forward any notions he may have? Surely the definition should naturally come from you, who say you do know the answer and can tell it us. Please do not disappoint us. I should take it as a kindness, and I hope you will not be chary of giving Glaucon and the rest of us the advantage of your instruction.

Glaucon and the others added their entreaties to mine. Thrasymachus was evidently longing to win credit, for he was sure he had an admirable answer ready, though he made a show of insisting that I should be the one to reply. In the end he gave way and exclaimed:

So this is what Socrates' wisdom comes to! He refuses to teach, and goes about learning from others without offering so much as thanks in return.

I do learn from others, Thrasymachus; that is quite true; but you are wrong to call me ungrateful. I give in return all I can—praise; for I have no money. And how ready I am to applaud any idea that seems to me sound, you will see in a moment, when you have stated your own; for I am sure that will be sound.

Listen then, Thrasymachus began. What I say is that "just" or "right" means nothing but what is to the interest of the stronger party. Well, where is your applause? You don't mean to give it me.

I will, as soon as I understand, I said. I don't see yet what you mean by right being the interest of the stronger party. For instance, Polydamas, the athlete, is stronger than we are, and it is to his interest to eat beef for the sake of his muscles; but surely you don't mean that the same diet would be good for weaker men and therefore be right for us?

You are trying to be funny, Socrates. It's a low trick to take my words in the sense you think will be most damaging.

No, no, I protested; but you must explain.

Don't you know, then, that a state may be ruled by a despot, or a democracy, or an aristocracy?

Of course.

And that the ruling element is always the strongest?

Yes.

Well then, in every case the laws are made by the ruling party in its own interest; a democracy makes democratic laws, a despot autocratic ones, and so on. By making these laws they define as "right" for their subjects whatever is for their own interest, and they call anyone who breaks them a "wrongdoer" and punish him accordingly. That is what I mean: in all states alike "right" has the same meaning, namely what is for the interest of the party established in power, and that is the strongest. So the sound conclusion is that what is "right" is the same everywhere: the interest of the stronger party.

Now I see what you mean, said I; whether it is true or not, I must try to make out. When you define right in terms of interest, you are yourself giving one of those answers you forbade to me; though, to be sure, you add "to the stronger party."

An insignificant addition, perhaps!

Its importance is not clear yet; what is clear is that we must find out whether your definition is true. I agree myself that right is in a sense a matter of interest; but when you add "to the stronger party," I don't know about that. I must consider.

Go ahead, then.

I will. Tell me this. No doubt you also think it is right to obey the men in power?

I do.

Are they infallible in every type of state, or can they sometimes make a mistake?

Of course they can make a mistake.

In framing laws, then, they may do their work well or badly?

No doubt.

Well, that is to say, when the laws they make are to their own interest; badly, when they are not?

Yes.

But the subjects are to obey any law they lay down, and they will then be doing right?

Of course.

If so, by your account, it will be right to do what is not to the interest of the stronger party, as well as what is so.

What's that you are saying?

Just what you said, I believe; but let us look again. Haven't you admitted that the rulers, when they enjoin certain acts on their subjects, sometimes mistake their own best interests, and at the same time that it is right for the subjects to obey, whatever they may enjoin?

Yes, I suppose so.

Well, that amounts to admitting that it is right to do what is not to the interest of the rulers or the stronger party. They may unwittingly enjoin what is to their own disadvantage; and you say it is right for the others to do as they are told. In that case, their duty must be the opposite of what you said, because the weaker will have been ordered to do what is against the interest of the stronger. You with your intelligence must see how that follows.

Yes, Socrates, said Polemarchus, that is undeniable.

No doubt, Cleitophon broke in, if you are to be a witness on Socrates' side.

No witness is needed, replied Polemarchus; Thrasymachus himself admits that rulers sometimes ordain acts that are to their own disadvantage, and that it is the subjects' duty to do them.

That is because Thrasymachus said it was right to do what you are told by the men in power.

Yes, but he also said that what is to the interest of the stronger party is right; and, after making both these assertions, he admitted that the stronger sometimes command the weaker subjects to act against their interests. From all which it follows that what is in the stronger's interest is no more right than what is not.

No, said Cleitophon; he meant whatever the stronger *believes* to be in his own interest. That is what the subject must do, and what Thrasymachus meant to define as right.

That was not what he said, rejoined Polemarchus.

No matter, Polemarchus, said I; if Thrasymachus

says so now, let us take him in that sense. Now, Thrasymachus, tell me, was that what you intended to say—that right means what the stronger thinks is to his interest, whether it really is so or not?

Most certainly not, he replied. Do you suppose I should speak of a man as "stronger" or "superior" at the very moment when he is making a mistake?

I did think you said as much when you admitted that rulers are not always infallible.

That is because you are a quibbler, Socrates. Would you say a man deserves to be called a physician at the moment when he makes a mistake in treating his patient and just in respect of that mistake; or a mathematician, when he does a sum wrong and just in so far as he gets a wrong result? Of course we do commonly speak of a physician or a mathematician or a scholar having made a mistake; but really none of these, I should say, is ever mistaken, in so far as he is worthy of the name we give him. So strictly speaking—and you are all for being precise—no one who practices a craft makes mistakes. A man is mistaken when his knowledge fails him; and at that moment he is no craftsman. And what is true of craftsmanship or any sort of skill is true of the ruler; though anyone might speak of a ruler making a mistake, just as he might of a physician. You must understand that I was talking in that loose way when I answered your question just now; but the precise statement is this. The ruler, in so far as he is acting as a ruler, makes no mistakes and consequently enjoins what is best for himself; and that is what the subject is to do. So, as I said at first, "right" means doing what is to the interest of the stronger.

Very well, Thrasymachus, said I. So you think I am quibbling?

I am sure you are.

You believe my questions were maliciously designed to damage your position?

I know it. But you will gain nothing by that. You cannot outwit me by cunning, and you are not the man to crush me in the open.

Bless your soul, I answered, I should not think of trying. But, to prevent any more misunderstanding, when you speak of that ruler or stronger party whose interest the weaker ought to serve, please make it clear whether you are using the words in the ordinary way or in that strict sense you have just defined.

I mean a ruler in the strictest possible sense. Now quibble away and be as malicious as you can. I want no mercy. But you are no match for me.

Do you think me mad enough to beard a lion or try to outwit a Thrasymachus?

You did try just now, he retorted, but it wasn't a success.

. . . .

Enough of this, said I. Now tell me about the physician in that strict sense you spoke of: is it his business to earn money or to treat his patients? Remember, I mean your physician who is worthy of the name.

To treat his patients.

And what of the ship's captain in the true sense? Is he a mere seaman or the commander of the crew?

The commander.

Yes, we shall not speak of him as a seaman just because he is on board a ship. That is not the point. He is called captain because of his skill and authority over the crew.

Quite true.

And each of these people has some special interest?[2]

No doubt.

And the craft in question exists for the very purpose of discovering that interest and providing for it?

Yes.

Can it equally be said of any craft that it has an interest, other than its own greatest possible perfection?

What do you mean by that?

Here is an illustration. If you ask me whether it is sufficient for the human body just to be itself, with no need of help from without, I should say, Certainly not; it has weaknesses and defects, and its condition is not all that it might be. That is precisely why the art of medicine was invented: it was designed to help the body and provide for its interests. Would not that be true?

It would.

But now take the art of medicine itself. Has that any defects or weaknesses? Does any art stand in need of some further perfection, as the eye would be imperfect without the power of vision or the ear without hearing, so that in their case an art is required that will study their interests and provide for their carrying out those functions? Has the art itself any corresponding need of some further art to remedy its defects and look after its interests; and will that further art require yet another, and so on for ever? Or will every art look after its own interests? Or, finally, is it not true that no art needs to have its weaknesses remedied or its interests studied either by another art or by itself, because no art has in itself any weakness or fault, and the only interest it is required to serve is that of its subject-matter? In itself, an art is sound and flawless, so long as it is entirely true to its own nature as an art in the strictest sense—and it is the strict sense that I want you to keep in view. Is not that true?

So it appears.

Then, said I, the art of medicine does not study its own interest, but the needs of the body, just as a groom shows his skill by caring for horses, not for the art of grooming. And so every art seeks, not its own advantage—for it has no deficiencies—but the interest of the subject on which it is exercised.

It appears so.

But surely, Thrasymachus, every art has authority and superior power over its subject.

To this he agreed, though very reluctantly.

So far as arts are concerned, then, no art ever studies or enjoins the interest of the superior or stronger party, but always that of the weaker over which it has authority.

Thrasymachus assented to this at last, though he tried to put up a fight. I then went on:

So the physician, as such, studies only the patient's interest, not his own. For as we agreed, the business of the physician, in the strict sense, is not to make money for himself, but to exercise his power over the patient's body; and the ship's captain, again, considered strictly as no mere sailor, but in command of the crew, will study and enjoin the interest of his subordinates, not his own.

He agreed reluctantly.

And so with government of any kind: no ruler, in so far as he is acting as ruler, will study or enjoin what is for his own interest. All that he says and does will be said and done with a view to what is good and proper for the subject for whom he practises his art.

. . . .

At this point, when everyone could see that Thrasymachus' definition of justice had been turned inside out, instead of making any reply, he said:

Socrates, have you a nurse?

Why do you ask such a question as that? I said. Wouldn't it be better to answer mine?

Because she lets you go about sniffling like a child whose nose wants wiping. She hasn't even taught you to know a shepherd when you see one, or his sheep either.

What makes you say that?

Why, you imagine that a herdsman studies the interests of his flocks or cattle, tending and fattening them up with some other end in view than his master's profit or his own; and so you don't see that, in politics, the genuine ruler regards his subjects exactly like sheep, and thinks of nothing else, night and day, but the good he can get out of them for himself. You are so far out in your notions of right and wrong, justice and injustice, as not to know that "right" actually means what is good for someone else, and to be "just" means serving the interest of the stronger who rules, at the cost of the subject who obeys; whereas injustice is just the reverse, asserting its authority over those innocents who are called just, so that they minister solely to their master's advantage and happiness, and not in the least degree to their own. Innocent as you are yourself, Socrates, you must see that a just man always has the worst of it. Take a private business: when a partnership is wound up, you will never find that the more honest of two partners comes off with the larger share; and in their relations to the state, when there are taxes to be paid, the honest man will pay more than the other on the same amount of property; or if there is money to be distributed, the dishonest will get it all. When either of them hold some public office, even if the just man loses in no other way, his private affairs at any rate will suffer from neglect, while his principles will not allow him to help himself from the public funds; not to mention the offence he will give to his friends and relations by refusing to sacrifice those principles to do them a good turn. Injustice has all the opposite advantages. I am speaking of the type I described just now, the man who can get the better of other people on a large scale: you must fix your eye on him, if you want to judge how much it is to one's own interest not to be just. You can see that best in the most consummate form of injustice, which rewards wrongdoing with supreme welfare and happiness and reduces its victims, if they won't retaliate in kind, to misery. That form is despotism, which uses force or fraud to plunder the goods of others, public or private, sacred or profane, and to do it in a wholesale way. If you are caught committing any one of these crimes on a small scale, you are punished and disgraced: they call it sacrilege, kidnapping, burglary, theft and brigandage. But if, besides taking their property, you turn all your countrymen into slaves, you will hear no more of those ugly names; your countrymen themselves will call you the happiest of men and bless your name, and so will everyone who hears of such a complete triumph of injustice; for when people denounce injustice, it is because they are afraid of suffering wrong, not of doing it. So true is it, Socrates, that injustice, on a grand enough scale, is superior to justice in strength and freedom and autocratic power; and "right," as I said at first, means simply what serves the interest of the stronger party; "wrong" means what is for the interest and profit of oneself.

Having deluged our ears with this torrent of words, as the man at the baths might empty a bucket over one's head, Thrasymachus meant to take himself off; but the company obliged him to stay and defend his position. I was specially urgent in my entreaties.

My good Thrasymachus, said I, do you propose to fling a doctrine like that at our heads and then go away without explaining it properly or letting us point out to you whether it is true or not? Is it so small a matter in your eyes to determine the whole course of conduct which every one of us must follow to get the best out of life?

Don't I realize it is a serious matter? he retorted.

Apparently not, said I; or else you have no consideration for us, and do not care whether we shall lead better or worse lives for being ignorant of this truth you profess to know. Do take the trouble to let us into your secret; if you treat us handsomely, you may be sure it will be a good investment; there are so many of us to show our gratitude. I will make no secret of my own conviction, which is that injustice is not more profitable than justice, even when left free to work its will unchecked. No; let your unjust man have full power to do wrong, whether by successful violence or by escaping detection; all the same he will not convince me that he will gain more than he would by being just. There may be others here who feel as I do, and set justice above injustice. It is for you to convince us that we are not well advised.

How can I? he replied. If you are not convinced by what I have just said, what more can I do for you? Do you want to be fed with my ideas out of a spoon?

God forbid! I exclaimed; not that. But I do want you to stand by your own words; or, if you shift your ground, shift it openly and stop trying to hoodwink us as you are doing now. You see, Thrasymachus, to go back to your earlier argument, in speaking of the shepherd you did not think it necessary to keep to that strict sense you laid down when you defined the genuine physician. You represent him, in his character of shepherd, as feeding up his flock, not for their own sake but for the table or the market, as if he were out to make money as a caterer or a cattle-dealer, rather than a shepherd. Surely the sole concern of the shepherd's art is to do the best for the charges put under its care; its own best interest is sufficiently provided for, so long as it does not fall short of all that shepherding should imply. On that principle it followed, I thought, that any kind of authority, in the state or in private life, must, in its character of authority, consider solely what is best for those under its care. Now what is your opinion? Do you think that the men who govern states—I mean rulers in the strict sense—have no reluctance to hold office?

I don't think so, he replied; I know it.

Well, but haven't you noticed, Thrasymachus, that in other positions of authority no one is willing to act unless he is paid wages, which he demands on the assumption that all the benefit of his action will go to his charges? Tell me: Don't we always distinguish one form of skill from another by its power to effect some particular result? Do say what you really think, so that we may get on.

Yes, that is the distinction.

And also each brings us some benefit that is peculiar to it: medicine gives health, for example; the art of navigation, safety at sea; and so on.

Yes.

And wage-earning brings us wages; that is its distinctive product. Now, speaking with that precision which you proposed, you would not say that the art of navigation is the same as the art of medicine, merely on the ground that a ship's captain regained his health on a voyage, because the sea air was good for him. No more would you identify the practice of medicine with wage-earning because a man may keep his health while earning wages, or a physician attending a case may receive a fee.

No.

And, since we agreed that the benefit obtained by each form of skill is peculiar to it, any common benefit enjoyed alike by all these practitioners must come from some further practice common to them all?

It would seem so.

Yes, we must say that if they all earn wages, they get that benefit in so far as they are engaged in wage-earning as well as in practising their several arts.

He agreed reluctantly.

This benefit, then—the receipt of wages—does not come to a man from his special art. If we are to speak strictly, the physician, as such, produces health; the builder, a house; and then each, in his further capacity of wage-earner, gets his pay. Thus every art has its own function and benefits its proper subject. But suppose the practitioner is not paid; does he then get any benefit from his art?

Clearly not.

And is he doing no good to anyone either, when he works for nothing?

No, I suppose he does some good.

Well then, Thrasymachus, it is now clear that no form of skill or authority provides for its own benefit. As we were saying some time ago, it always studies and prescribes what is good for its subject—the interest of the weaker party, not of the stronger. And that, my friend, is why I said that no one is willing to be in a position of authority and undertake to set straight other men's troubles, without demanding to be paid; because, if he is to do his work well, he will never, in his capacity of ruler, do, or command others to do, what is best for himself, but only what is best for the subject. For that reason, if he is to consent, he must have his recompense, in the shape of money or honour, or of punishment in case of refusal.

What do you mean, Socrates? asked Glaucon. I recognize two of your three kinds of reward; but I don't understand what you mean by speaking of punishment as a recompense.

Then you don't understand the recompense required by the best type of men, or their motive for accepting authority when they do consent. You surely know that a passion for honours or for money is rightly regarded as something to be ashamed of.

Yes, I do.

For that reason, I said, good men are unwilling to rule, either for money's sake or for honour. They have no wish to be called mercenary for demanding to be paid, or thieves for making a secret profit out of their office; nor yet will honours tempt them, for they are not ambitious. So they must be forced to consent under threat of penalty; that may be why a readiness to accept power under no such constraint is thought discreditable. And the heaviest penalty for declining to rule is to be ruled by someone inferior to yourself. That is the fear, I believe, that makes decent people accept power; and when they do so, they face the prospect of authority with no idea that they are coming into the enjoyment of a comfortable berth; it is forced upon them because they can find no one better than themselves, or even as good, to be entrusted with power. If there could ever be a society of perfect men, there might well be as much competition to evade office as there now is to gain it; and it would then be clearly seen that the genuine ruler's nature is to seek only the advantage of the subject, with the consequence that any man of understanding would sooner have another to do the best for him than be at the pains to do the best for that other himself. On this point, then, I entirely disagree with Thrasymachus' doctrine that right means what is to the interest of the stronger.

Chapter IV (I. 347 E–354 C)
Thrasymachus: Is Injustice More
Profitable Than Justice?

. . . .

However, I continued, we may return to that question later. Much more important is the position Thrasymachus is asserting now: that a life of injustice is to be preferred to a life of justice. Which side do you take, Glaucon? Where do you think the truth lies?

I should say that the just life is the better worth having.

You heard Thrasymachus' catalogue of all the good things in store for injustice?

I did, but I am not convinced.

Shall we try to convert him, then, supposing we can find some way to prove him wrong?

By all means.

We might answer Thrasymachus' case in a set speech of our own, drawing up a corresponding list of the advantages of justice; he would then have the right to reply, and we should make our final rejoinder; but after that we should have to count up and measure the advantages on each list, and we should need a jury to decide between us. Whereas, if we go on as before, each securing the agreement of the other side, we can combine the functions of advocate and judge. We will take whichever course you prefer.

I prefer the second, said Glaucon.

Come then, Thrasymachus, said I, let us start afresh with our questions. You say that injustice pays better than justice, when both are carried to the furthest point?

I do, he replied; and I have told you why.

And how would you describe them? I suppose you would call one of them an excellence and the other a defect?

Of course.

Justice an excellence, and injustice a defect?

Now is that likely, when I am telling you that injustice pays, and justice does not?

Then what do you say?

The opposite.

That justice is a defect?

No; rather the mark of a good-natured simpleton.

Injustice, then, implies being ill-natured?

No; I should call it good policy.

Do you think the unjust are positively superior in character and intelligence, Thrasymachus?

Yes, if they are the sort that can carry injustice to perfection and make themselves masters of whole cities and nations. Perhaps you think I was talking of pickpockets. There is profit even in that trade, if you can escape detection; but it doesn't come to much as compared with the gains I was describing.

I understand you now on that point, I replied. What astonished me was that you should class injustice with superior character and intelligence and justice with the reverse.

Well, I do, he rejoined.

That is a much more stubborn position, my friend; and it is not so easy to see how to assail it. If you would admit that injustice, however well it pays, is nevertheless, as some people think, a defect and a discreditable thing, then we could argue on generally accepted principles. But now that you have gone so far as to rank it with superior character and intelligence, obviously you will say it is an admirable thing as well as a source of strength, and has all the other qualities we have attributed to justice.

You read my thoughts like a book, he replied.

However, I went on, it is no good shirking; I must go through with the argument, so long as I can be sure you are really speaking your mind. I do believe you are not playing with us now, Thrasymachus, but stating the truth as you conceive it.

Why not refute the doctrine? he said. What does it matter to you whether I believe it or not?

It does not matter, I replied.

. . . .

Thrasymachus' assent was dragged out of him with a reluctance of which my account gives no idea. He was sweating at every pore, for the weather was hot; and I saw then what I had never seen before—Thrasymachus blushing. However, now that we had agreed that justice implies superior character and intelligence, injustice a deficiency in both respects, I went on:

Good; let us take that as settled. But we were also saying that injustice was a source of strength. Do you remember, Thrasymachus?

I do remember; only your last argument does not satisfy me, and I could say a good deal about that. But if I did, you would tell me I was haranguing you like a public meeting. So either let me speak my mind at length, or else, if you want to ask questions, ask them, and I will nod or shake my head, and say "Hm?" as we do to encourage an old woman telling us a story.

No, please, said I; don't give your assent against your real opinion.

Anything to please you, he rejoined, since you won't let me have my say. What more do you want?

Nothing, I replied. If that is what you mean to do, I will go on with my questions.

Go on, then.

Well, to continue where we left off, I will repeat my question: What is the nature and quality of justice as compared with injustice? It was suggested, I believe, that injustice is the stronger and more effective of the two; but now we have seen that justice implies superior character and intelligence, it will not be hard to show that it will also be superior in power to injustice, which implies ignorance and stupidity; that must be obvious to anyone. However, I would rather look deeper into this matter than take it as settled offhand. Would you agree that a state may be unjust and may try to enslave other states or to hold a number of others in subjection unjustly?

Of course it may, he said; above all if it is the best sort of state, which carries injustice to perfection.

I understand, said I; that was your view. But I am wondering whether a state can do without justice when it is asserting its superior power over another in that way.

Not if you are right, that justice implies intelligence; but if I am right, injustice will be needed.

I am delighted with your answer, Thrasymachus; this is much better than just nodding and shaking your head.

It is all to oblige you.

Thank you. Please add to your kindness by telling me whether any set of men—a state or an army or a band of robbers or thieves—who were acting together for some unjust purpose would be likely to succeed, if they were always trying to injure one another. Wouldn't they do better, if they did not?

Yes, they would.

Because, of course, such injuries must set them quarrelling and hating each other. Only fair treatment can make men friendly and of one mind.

Be it so, he said; I don't want to differ from you.

Thank you once more, I replied. But don't you agree that, if injustice has this effect of implanting hatred wherever it exists, it must make any set of people, whether freemen or slaves, split into factions, at feud with one another and incapable of any joint action?

Yes.

And so with any two individuals: injustice will set them at variance and make them enemies to each other as well as to everyone who is just.

It will.

And will it not keep its character and have the same effect, if it exists in a single person?

Let us suppose so.

The effect being, apparently, wherever it occurs—in a state or a family or an army or anywhere else—to make united action impossible because of factions and quarrels, and moreover to set whatever it resides in at enmity with itself as well as with any opponent and with all who are just.

Yes, certainly.

Then I suppose it will produce the same natural results in an individual. He will have a divided mind and be incapable of action, for lack of singleness of purpose; and he will be at enmity with all who are just as well as with himself?

Yes.

And "all who are just" surely includes the gods?

Let us suppose so.

The unjust man, then, will be a god-forsaken creature; the good-will of heaven will be for the just.

Enjoy your triumph, said Thrasymachus. You need not fear my contradicting you. I have no wish to give offence to the company.

· · · · · · · ·

You will make my enjoyment complete, I replied, if you will answer my further questions in the same way. We have made out so far that just men are superior in character and intelligence and more effective in action. Indeed without justice men cannot act together at all; it is not strictly true to speak of such people as ever having effected any strong action in common. Had they been thoroughly unjust, they could not have kept their hands off one another; they must have had some justice in them, enough to keep them from injuring one another at the same time with their victims. This it was that enabled them to achieve what they did achieve: their injustice only partially incapacitated them for their career of wrongdoing; if perfect, it would have disabled them for any action whatsoever. I can see that all this is true, as against your original position. But there is a further question which we postponed: Is the life of justice the better and happier life? What we have said already leaves no doubt in my mind; but we ought to consider more carefully, for this is no light matter: it is the question, what is the right way to live?

Go on, then.

I will, said I. Some things have a function;[3] a horse, for instance, is useful for certain kinds of work. Would you agree to define a thing's function in general as the work for which that thing is the only instrument or the best one?

I don't understand.

Take an example. We can see only with the eyes, hear only with the ears; and seeing and hearing might be called the functions of those organs.

Yes.

Or again, you might cut vine-shoots with a carving-knife or a chisel or many other tools, but with none so well as with a pruning-knife made for the purpose; and we may call that its function.

True.

Now, I expect, you see better what I meant by suggesting that a thing's function is the work that it alone can do, or can do better than anything else.

Yes, I will accept that definition.

Good, said I; and to take the same examples, the eye and the ear, which we said have each its particular function: have they not also a specific excellence or virtue? Is not that always the case with things that have some appointed work to do?

Yes.

Now consider: is the eye likely to do its work well, if you take away its peculiar virtue and substitute the corresponding defect?

Of course not, if you mean substituting blindness for the power of sight.

I mean whatever its virtue may be; I have not come to that yet. I am only asking, whether it is true of things with a function—eyes or ears or anything else—that there is always some specific virtue which enables them to work well; and if they are deprived of that virtue, they work badly.

I think that is true.

Then the next point is this. Has the soul a function that can be performed by nothing else? Take for example such actions as deliberating or taking charge and exercising control: is not the soul the only thing of which you can say that these are its proper and peculiar work?

That is so.

And again, living—is not that above all the function of the soul?

No doubt.

And we also speak of the soul as having a certain specific excellence or virtue?

Yes.

Then, Thrasymachus, if the soul is robbed of its peculiar virtue, it cannot possibly do its work well. It must exercise its power of controlling and taking charge well or ill according as it is itself in a good or a bad state.

That follows.

And did we not agree that the virtue of the soul is justice, and injustice its defect?

We did.

So it follows that a just soul, or in other words a just man, will live well; the unjust will not.

Apparently, according to your argument.

But living well involves well-being and happiness.

Naturally.

Then only the just man is happy; injustice will involve unhappiness.

Be it so.

But you cannot say it pays better to be unhappy.

Of course not.

Injustice then, my dear Thrasymachus, can never pay better than justice.

Well, he replied, this is a feast-day, and you may take all this as your share of the entertainment.

For which I have to thank you, Thrasymachus; you have been so gentle with me since you recovered your temper. It is my own fault if the entertainment has not been satisfactory. I have been be-having like a greedy guest, snatching a taste of every new dish that comes round before he has properly enjoyed the last. We began by looking for a defini-tion of justice: but before we had found one, I dropped that question and hurried on to ask whether or not it involved superior character and intelligence; and then, as soon as another idea cropped up, that injustice pays better, I could not refrain from pursuing that.

So now the whole conversation has left me com-pletely in the dark; for so long as I do not know what justice is, I am hardly likely to know whether or not it is a virtue, or whether it makes a man happy or unhappy.

Part II
(Books II–IV, 445 B)
Justice in the State and in
the Individual

Chapter V (II. 357 A–367 E)
The Problem Stated

. . . .

I thought that, with these words, I was quit of the discussion; but it seems this was only a prelude. Glaucon, undaunted as ever, was not content to let Thrasymachus abandon the field.

Socrates, he broke out, you have made a show of proving that justice is better than injustice in every way. Is that enough, or do you want us to be really convinced?

Certainly I do, if it rests with me.

Then you are not going the right way about it. I want to know how you classify the things we call good. Are there not some which we should wish to have, not for their consequences, but just for their own sake, such as harmless pleasures and enjoy-ments that have no further result beyond the satis-faction of the moment?

Yes, I think there are good things of that de-scription.

And also some that we value both for their own sake and for their consequences—things like knowl-edge and health and the use of our eyes?

Yes.

And a third class which would include physical training, medical treatment, earning one's bread as a doctor or otherwise—useful, but burdensome things, which we want only for the sake of the profit or other benefit they bring.

Yes, there is that third class. What then?

In which class do you place justice?

I should say, in the highest, as a thing which any-one who is to gain happiness must value both for it-self and for its results.

Well, that is not the common opinion. Most peo-ple would say it was one of those things, tiresome and disagreeable in themselves, which we cannot avoid practising for the sake of reward or a good reputation.

I know, said I; that is why Thrasymachus has been finding fault with it all this time and praising injustice. But I seem to be slow in seeing his point.

Listen to me, then, and see if you agree with mine. There was no need, I think, for Thrasymachus to yield so readily, like a snake you had charmed into submission; and nothing so far said about justice and injustice has been established to my satisfaction. I want to be told what each of them really is, and what effect each has, in itself, on the soul that harbours it, when all rewards and consequences are left out of account. So here is my plan, if you approve. I shall revive Thrasymachus' theory. First, I will state what is commonly held about the nature of justice and its origin; secondly, I shall maintain that it is always practised with reluctance, not as good in itself, but as a thing one cannot do without; and thirdly, that this reluctance is reasonable, because the life of injustice is much the better life of the two—so people say. That is not what I think myself, Socrates; only I am be-wildered by all that Thrasymachus and ever so many others have dinned into my ears; and I have never yet heard the case for justice stated as I wish to hear it. You, I believe, if anyone, can tell me what is to be said in praise of justice in and for itself; that is what I want. Accordingly, I shall set you an example by glorifying the life of injustice with all the energy that I hope you will show later in denouncing it and ex-alting justice in its stead. Will that plan suit you?

Nothing could be better, I replied. Of all subjects this is one on which a sensible man must always be glad to exchange ideas.

Good, said Glaucon. Listen then, and I will begin with my first point: the nature and origin of justice.

What people say is that to do wrong is, in itself, a desirable thing; on the other hand, it is not at all desirable to suffer wrong, and the harm to the sufferer outweighs the advantage to the doer. Consequently, when men have had a taste of both, those who have not the power to seize the advantage and escape the harm decide that they would be better off if they made a compact neither to do wrong nor to suffer it. Hence they began to make laws and covenants with one another; and whatever the law prescribed they called lawful and right. That is what right or justice is and how it came into existence; it stands halfway between the best thing of all—to do wrong with impunity—and the worst, which is to suffer wrong without the power to retaliate. So justice is accepted as a compromise, and valued, not as good in itself, but for lack of power to do wrong; no man worthy of the name, who had that power, would ever enter into such a compact with anyone; he would be mad if he did. That, Socrates, is the nature of justice according to this account, and such the circumstances in which it arose.

The next point is that men practice it against the grain, for lack of power to do wrong. How true that is, we shall best see if we imagine two men, one just, the other unjust, given full license to do whatever they like, and then follow them to observe where each will be led by his desires. We shall catch the just man taking the same road as the unjust; he will be moved by self-interest, the end which it is natural to every creature to pursue as good, until forcibly turned aside by law and custom to respect the principle of equality.

Now, the easiest way to give them that complete liberty of action would be to imagine them possessed of the talisman found by Gyges, the ancestor of the famous Lydian. The story tells how he was a shepherd in the king's service. One day there was a great storm, and the ground where his flock was feeding was rent by an earthquake. Astonished at the sight, he went down into the chasm and saw, among other wonders of which the story tells, a brazen horse, hollow, with windows in its sides. Peering in, he saw a dead body, which seemed to be of more than human size. It was naked save for a gold ring, which he took from the finger and made his way out. When the shepherds met, as they did every month, to send an account to the King of the state of his flocks, Gyges came wearing the ring. As he was sitting with the others, he happened to turn the bezel of the ring inside his hand. At once he became invisible, and his companions, to his surprise, began to speak of him as if he had left them. Then, as he was fingering the ring, he turned the bezel outwards and became visible again. With that, he set about testing the ring to see if it really had this power, and always with the same result: according as he turned the bezel inside or out he vanished and reappeared. After this discovery he contrived to be one of the messengers sent to the court. There he seduced the Queen, and with her help murdered the King and seized the throne.

Now suppose there were two such magic rings, and one were given to the just man, the other to the unjust. No one, it is commonly believed, would have such iron strength of mind as to stand fast in doing right or keep his hands off other men's goods, when he could go to the marketplace and fearlessly help himself to anything he wanted, enter houses and sleep with any woman he chose, set prisoners free and kill men at his pleasure, and in a word go about among men with the powers of a god. He would behave no better than the other; both would take the same course. Surely this would be strong proof that men do right only under compulsion; no individual thinks of it as good for him personally, since he does wrong whenever he finds he has the power. Every man believes that wrongdoing pays him personally much better, and, according to this theory, that is the truth. Granted full licence to do as he liked, people would think him a miserable fool if they found him refusing to wrong his neighbours or to touch their belongings, though in public they would keep up a pretence of praising his conduct, for fear of being wronged themselves. So much for that.

Finally, if we are really to judge between the two lives, the only way is to contrast the extremes of justice and injustice. We can best do that by imagining our two men to be perfect types, and crediting both to the full with the qualities they need for their respective ways of life. To begin with the unjust man: he must be like any consummate master of a craft, a physician or a captain, who, knowing just what his art can do, never tries to do more, and can always retrieve a false step. The unjust man, if he is to reach perfection, must be equally discreet in his criminal attempts, and he must not be found out, or we shall think him a bungler; for the highest pitch of injustice is to seem just when you are not. So we must endow our man with the full complement of injustice; we must allow him to have secured a spotless reputation for virtue while committing the blackest crimes; he must be able to retrieve any mistake, to defend himself with convincing eloquence if his misdeeds are denounced, and, when force is required, to bear down all opposition by his courage and strength and by his command of friends and money.

Now set beside this paragon the just man in his simplicity and nobleness, one who, in Aeschylus' words, "would be, not seem, the best." There must, indeed, be no such seeming; for if his character were apparent, his reputation would bring him honours and rewards, and then we should not know whether it was for their sake that he was just or for justice's sake alone. He must be stripped of everything but justice, and denied every advantage the other enjoyed. Doing no wrong, he must have the worst reputation for wrong-doing, to test whether his virtue is proof against all that comes of having a bad name; and under this lifelong imputation of wickedness, let him hold on his course of justice unwavering to the point of death. And so, when the two men have carried their justice and injustice to the last extreme, we may judge which is the happier.

My dear Glaucon, I exclaimed, how vigorously you scour these two characters clean for inspection, as if you were burnishing a couple of statues!

I am doing my best, he answered. Well, given two such characters, it is not hard, I fancy, to describe the sort of life that each of them may expect; and if the description sounds rather coarse, take it as coming from those who cry up the merits of injustice rather than from me. They will tell you that our just man will be thrown into prison, scourged and racked, will have his eyes burnt out, and, after every kind of torment, be impaled. That will teach him how much better it is to seem virtuous than to

be so. In fact those lines of Aeschylus I quoted are more fitly applied to the unjust man, who, they say, is a realist and does not live for appearances: "he would be, not seem" unjust.

reaping the harvest sown
In those deep furrows of the thoughtful heart
Whence wisdom springs.

With his reputation for virtue, he will hold offices of state, ally himself by marriage to any family he may choose, become a partner in any business, and, having no scruples about being dishonest, turn all these advantages to profit. If he is involved in a lawsuit, public or private, he will get the better of his opponents, grow rich on the proceeds, and be able to help his friends and harm his enemies. Finally, he can make sacrifices to the gods and dedicate offerings with due magnificence, and, being in a much better position than the just man to serve the gods as well as his chosen friends, he may reasonably hope to stand higher in the favour of heaven. So much better, they say, Socrates, is the life prepared for the unjust by gods and men.

Here Glaucon ended, and I was meditating a reply, when his brother Adeimantus exclaimed:

Surely, Socrates, you cannot suppose that that is all there is to be said.

Why, isn't it? said I.

The most essential part of the case has not been mentioned, he replied.

Well, I answered, there is a proverb about a brother's aid. If Glaucon has failed, it is for you to make good his shortcomings; though, so far as I am concerned, he has said quite enough to put me out of the running and leave me powerless to rescue the cause of justice.

Nonsense, said Adeimantus; there is more to be said, and you must listen to me. If we want a clear view of what I take to be Glaucon's meaning, we must study the opposite side of the case, the arguments used when justice is praised and injustice condemned. When children are told by their fathers and all their pastors and masters that it is a good thing to be just, what is commended is not justice in itself but the respectability it brings. They are to let men see how just they are, in order to gain high positions and marry well and win all the other advantages which Glaucon mentioned, since the just man owes all these to his good reputation.

In this matter of having a good name, they go farther still: they throw in the favourable opinion of heaven, and can tell us of no end of good things with which they say the gods reward piety. There is the good old Hesiod, who says the gods make the just man's oak-trees "bear acorns at the top and bees in the middle; and their sheep's fleeces are heavy with wool," and a great many other blessings of that sort. And Homer speaks in the same strain:

As when a blameless king fears the gods and up-holds right judgment; then the dark earth yields wheat and barley, and the trees are laden with fruit; the young of his flocks are strong, and the sea gives abundance of fish.

Musaeus and his son Eumolpus enlarge in still more spirited terms upon the rewards from heaven they promise to the righteous. They take them to the other world and provide them with a banquet of the Blest, where they sit for all time carousing with garlands on their heads, as if virtue could not be more nobly recompensed than by an eternity of intoxication. Others, again, carry the rewards of heaven yet a stage farther: the pious man who keeps his oaths is to have children's children and to leave a posterity after him. When they have sung the praises of justice in that strain, with more to same effect, they proceed to plunge the sinners and unrighteous men into a pool of mud in the world below, and set them to fetch water in a sieve. Even in this life, too, they give them a bad name, and make out that the unjust suffer all those penalties which Glaucon described as falling upon the good man who has a bad reputation: they can think of no others. That is how justice is recommended and injustice denounced.

Besides all this, think of the way in which justice and injustice are spoken of, not only in ordinary life, but by the poets. All with one voice reiterate that self-control and justice, admirable as they may be, are difficult and irksome, whereas vice and injustice are pleasant and very easily to be had; it is mere convention to regard them as discreditable. They tell us that dishonesty generally pays better than honesty. They will cheerfully speak of a bad man as happy and load him with honours and social esteem, provided he be rich and otherwise powerful; while they despise and disregard one who has neither power nor wealth, though all the while they acknowledge that he is the better man of the two.

Most surprising of all is what they say about the gods and virtue: that heaven itself often allots misfortunes and a hard life to the good man, and gives prosperity to the wicked. Mendicant priests and soothsayers come to the rich man's door with a story of a power they possess by the gift of heaven to atone for any offence that he or his ancestors have committed with incantations and sacrifice, agreeably accompanied by feasting. If he wishes to injure an enemy, he can, at a trifling expense, do him a hurt with equal case, whether he be an honest man or not, by means of certain invocations and spells which, as they profess, prevail upon the gods to do their bidding. In support of all these claims they call the poets to witness. Some, by way of advertising the easiness of vice, quote the words: "Unto wickedness men attain easily and in multitudes; smooth is the way and her dwelling is very near at hand. But the gods have ordained much sweat upon the path to virtue" and a long road that is rough and steep.

Others, to show that men can turn the gods from their purpose, cite Homer: "Even the gods themselves listen to entreaty. Their hearts are turned by the entreaties of men with sacrifice and humble prayers and libation and burnt offering, whensoever anyone transgresses and does amiss." They produce a whole farrago of books in which Musaeus and Orpheus, described as descendants of the Muses and the Moon, prescribe their ritual; and they persuade entire communities, as well as individuals, that, both in this life and after death, wrongdoing may be absolved and purged away by means of sacrifices and agreeable performances which they are pleased to call rites of initiation. These deliver us from punishment in the other world, where awful things are in store for all who neglect to sacrifice.

Now, my dear Socrates, when all this stuff is talked about the estimation in which virtue and vice are held by heaven and by mankind, what effect can we suppose it has upon the mind of a young man quick-witted enough to gather honey from all these flowers of popular wisdom and to draw his own conclusions as to the sort of person he should be and the way he should go in order to lead the best possible life? In all likelihood he would ask himself, in Pindar's words: "Will the way of right or the by-paths of deceit lead me to the higher fortress," where I may entrench myself for the rest of my life? For, according to what they tell me, I have nothing to gain but trouble and manifest loss from being honest, unless I also get a name for being so; whereas, if I am dishonest and provide myself with a reputation for honesty, they promise me a marvellous career. Very well, then; since "outward seeming," as wise men inform me, "overpowers the truth" and decides the question of happiness, I had better go in for appearances wholeheartedly. I must ensconce myself behind an imposing facade designed to look like virtue, and trail the fox behind me, "the cunning shifty fox"—Archilochus knew the world as well as any man. You may say it is not so easy to be wicked without ever being found out. Perhaps not; but great things are never easy. Anyhow, if we are to reach happiness, everything we have been told points to this as the road to be followed. We will form secret societies to save us from exposure; besides, there are men who teach the art of winning over popular assemblies and courts of law; so that, one way or another, by persuasion or violence, we shall get the better of our neighbours without being punished. You might object that the gods are not to be deceived and are beyond the reach of violence. But suppose that there are no gods, or that they do not concern themselves with the doings of men; why should we concern ourselves to deceive them? Or, if the gods do exist and care for mankind, all we know or have ever heard about them comes from current tradition and from the poets who recount their family history, and these same authorities also assure us that they can be won over and turned from their purpose "by sacrifice and humble prayers" and votive offerings. We must either accept both these statements or neither. If we are to accept both, we had better do wrong and use part of the proceeds to offer sacrifice. By being just we may escape the punishment of heaven, but we shall be renouncing the profits of injustice; whereas by doing wrong we shall make our profit and escape punishment into the bargain, by means of those entreaties which win over the gods when we transgress and do amiss. But then, you will say, in the other world the penalty for our misdeeds on earth will fall either upon us or upon our children's

children. We can counter that objection by reckoning on the great efficacy of mystic rites and the divinities of absolution, vouched for by the most advanced societies and by the descendants of the gods who have appeared as poets and spokesmen of heavenly inspiration.

What reason, then, remains for preferring justice to the extreme of injustice, when common belief and the best authorities promise us the fulfilment of our desires in this life and the next, if only we conceal our ill-doing under a veneer of decent behaviour? The upshot is, Socrates, that no man possessed of superior powers of mind or person or rank or wealth will set any value on justice; he is more likely to laugh when he hears it praised. So, even one who could prove my case false and were quite sure that justice is best, far from being indignant with the unjust, will be very ready to excuse them. He will know that, here and there, a man may refrain from wrong because it revolts some instinct he is graced with or because he has come to know the truth; no one else is virtuous of his own will; it is only lack of spirit or the infirmity of age or some other weakness that makes men condemn the iniquities they have not the strength to practise. This is easily seen: give such a man the power, and he will be the first to use it to the utmost.

What lies at the bottom of all this is nothing but the fact from which Glaucon, as well as I, started upon this long discourse. We put it to you, Socrates, with all respect, in this way. All you who profess to sing the praises of right conduct, from the ancient heroes whose legends have survived down to the men of the present day, have never denounced injustice or praised justice apart from the reputation, honours, and rewards they bring; but what effect either of them in itself has upon its possessor when it dwells in his soul unseen of gods or men, no poet or ordinary man has ever yet explained. No one has proved that a soul can harbour no worse evil than injustice, no greater good that justice. Had all of you said that from the first and tried to convince us from our youth up, we should not be keeping watch upon our neighbours to prevent them from doing wrong to us, but everyone would keep a far more effectual watch over himself, for fear lest by wronging others he should open his doors to the worst of all evils.

That, Socrates, is the view of justice and injustice

which Thrasymachus and, no doubt, others would state, perhaps in even stronger words. For myself, I believe it to be a gross perversion of their true worth and effect; but, as I must frankly confess, I have put the case with all the force I could muster because I want to hear the other side from you. You must not be content with proving that justice is superior to injustice; you must make clear what good or what harm each of them does to its possessor, taking it simply in itself and, as Glaucon required, leaving out of account the reputation it bears. For unless you deprive each of its true reputation and attach to it the false one, we shall say that you are praising or denouncing nothing more than the appearances in either case, and recommending us to do wrong without being found out; and that you hold with Thrasymachus that right means what is good for someone else, being the interest of the stronger, and wrong is what really pays, serving one's own interest at the expense of the weaker. You have agreed that justice belongs to that highest class of good things which are worth having not only for their consequences, but much more for their own sakes—things like sight and hearing, knowledge, and health, whose value is genuine and intrinsic, not dependent on opinion. So I want you, in commending justice, to consider only how justice, in itself, benefits a man who has it in him, and how injustice harms him, leaving rewards and reputation out of account. I might put up with others dwelling on those outward effects as a reason for praising the one and condemning the other; but from you, who have spent your life in the study of this question, I must beg leave to demand something better. You must not be content merely to prove that justice is superior to injustice, but explain how one is good, the other evil, in virtue of the intrinsic effect each has on its possessor, whether gods or men see it or not.

Chapter VI (II. 367 E–372 A)
The Rudiments of Social
Organization

. . . .

I was delighted with these speeches from Glaucon and Adeimantus, whose gifts I had always admired. How right, I exclaimed, was Glaucon's lover to begin that poem of his on your exploits at the battle of Megara by describing you two as the

> sons divine
> Of Ariston's noble line!

Like father, like sons: there must indeed be some divine quality in your nature, if you can plead the cause of injustice so eloquently and still not be convinced yourselves that it is better than justice. That you are not really convinced I am sure from all I know of your dispositions, though your words might well have left me in doubt. But the more I trust you, the harder I find it to reply. How can I come to the rescue? I have no faith in my own powers, when I remember that you were not satisfied with the proof I thought I had given to Thrasymachus that it is better to be just. And yet I cannot stand by and hear justice reviled without lifting a finger. I am afraid to commit a sin by holding aloof while I have breath and strength to say a word in its defence. So there is nothing for it but to do the best I can.

Glaucon and the others begged me to step into the breach and carry through our inquiry into the real nature of justice and injustice, and the truth about their respective advantages. So I told them what I thought. This is a very obscure question, I said, and we shall need keen sight to see our way. Now, as we are not remarkably clever, I will make a suggestion as to how we should proceed. Imagine a rather short-sighted person told to read an inscription in small letters from some way off. He would think it a godsend if someone pointed out that the same inscription was written up elsewhere on a bigger scale, so that he could first read the larger characters and then make out whether the smaller ones were the same.

No doubt, said Adeimantus; but what analogy do you see in that to our inquiry?

I will tell you. We think of justice as a quality that may exist in a whole community as well as in an individual, and the community is the bigger of the two. Possibly, then, we may find justice there in larger proportions, easier to make out. So I suggest that we should begin by inquiring what justice means in a state. Then we can go on to look for its counterpart on a smaller scale in the individual.

That seems a good plan, he agreed.

Well then, I continued, suppose we imagine a state coming into being before our eyes. We might then be able to watch the growth of justice or of injustice within it. When that is done, we may hope it will be easier to find what we are looking for.

Much easier.

Shall we try, then, to carry out this scheme? I fancy it will be no light undertaking; so you had better think twice.

No need for that, said Adeimantus. Don't waste any more time.

My notion is, said I, that a state comes into existence because no individual is self-sufficing; we all have many needs. But perhaps you can suggest some different origin for the foundation of a community?

No, I agree with you.

So, having all these needs, we call in one another's help to satisfy our various requirements; and when we have collected a number of helpers and associates to live together in one place, we call that settlement a state.

Yes.

So if one man gives another what he has to give in exchange for what he can get, it is because each finds that to do so is for his own advantage.

Certainly.

Very well, said I. Now let us build up our imaginary state from the beginning. Apparently, it will owe its existence to our needs, the first and greatest need being the provision of food to keep us alive. Next we shall want a house; and thirdly, such things as clothing.

True.

How will our state be able to supply all these demands? We shall need at least one man to be a farmer, another a builder, and a third a weaver. Will that do, or shall we add a shoemaker and one or two more to provide for our personal wants?

By all means.

The minimum state, then, will consist of four or five men.

Apparently.

Now here is a further point. Is each one of them to bring the product of his work into a common stock? Should our one farmer, for example, provide food enough for four people and spend the whole of his working time in producing corn, so as to share with the rest; or should he take no notice of them and spend only a quarter of his time on growing just enough corn for himself, and divide the other three-quarters between building his house, weaving his clothes, and making his shoes, so as to save the trouble of sharing with others and attend himself to all his own concerns?

The first plan might be the easier, replied Adeimantus.

That may very well be so, said I; for, as you spoke, it occurred to me, for one thing, that no two people are born exactly alike. There are innate differences which fit them for different occupations.

I agree.

And will a man do better working at many trades, or keeping to only one?

Keeping to one.

And there is another point: obviously work may be ruined, if you let the right time go by. The workman must wait upon the work; it will not wait upon his leisure and allow itself to be done in a spare moment. So the conclusion is that more things will be produced and the work be more easily and better done, when every man is set free from all other occupations to do, at the right time, the one thing for which he is naturally fitted.

That is certainly true.

We shall need more than four citizens, then, to supply all those necessaries we mentioned. You see, Adeimantus, if the farmer is to have a good plough and spade and other tools, he will not make them himself. No more will the builder and weaver and shoemaker make all the many implements they need. So quite a number of carpenters and smiths and other craftsmen must be enlisted. Our miniature state is beginning to grow.

It is.

Still, it will not be very large, even when we have added cowherds and shepherds to provide the farmers with oxen for the plough, and the builders as well as the farmers with draught-animals, and the weavers and shoemakers with wool and leather.

No; but it will not be so very small either.

And yet, again, it will be next to impossible to plant our city in a territory where it will need no imports. So there will have to be still another set of people, to fetch what it needs from other countries.

There will.

Moreover, if these agents take with them nothing that those other countries require in exchange, they will return as empty-handed as they went. So, besides everything wanted for consumption at home, we must produce enough goods of the right kind for the foreigners whom we depend on to supply us. That will mean increasing the number of farmers and craftsmen.

Yes.

And then, there are these agents who are to import and export all kinds of goods—merchants, as we call them. We must have them; and if they are to do business overseas, we shall need quite a number of ship-owners and others who know about that branch of trading.

We shall.

Again, in the city itself how are the various sets of producers to exchange their products? That was our object, you will remember, in forming a community and so laying the foundation of our state.

Obviously, they must buy and sell.

That will mean having a market-place, and a currency to serve as a token for purposes of exchange.

Certainly.

Now suppose a farmer, or an artisan, brings some of his produce to market at a time when no one is there who wants to exchange with him. Is he to sit there idle, when he might be at work?

No, he replied; there are people who have seen an opening here for their services. In well-ordered communities they are generally men not strong enough to be of use in any other occupation. They have to stay where they are in the market-place and take goods for money from those who want to sell, and money for goods from those who want to buy.

That, then, is the reason why our city must include a class of shopkeepers—so we call these people who sit still in the market-place to buy and sell, in contrast with merchants who travel to other countries.

Quite so.

There are also the services of yet another class, who have the physical strength for heavy work, though on intellectual grounds they are hardly worth including in our society—hired labourers, as we call them, because they sell the use of their strength for wages. They will go to make up our population.

Yes.

Well, Adeimantus, has our state now grown to its full size?

Perhaps.

Then, where in it shall we find justice or injustice? If they have come in with one of the elements we have been considering, can you say with which one?

I have no idea, Socrates; unless it be somewhere in their dealings with one another.

You may be right, I answered. Anyhow, it is a question which we shall have to face.

Chapter VII (II 372 A–374 E)
The Luxurious State

. . . .

Let us begin, then, with a picture of our citizens' manner of life, with the provision we have made for them. They will be producing corn and wine, and making clothes and shoes. When they have built their houses, they will mostly work without their coats or shoes in summer, and in winter be well shod and clothed. For their food, they will prepare flour and barley-meal for kneading and baking, and set out a grand spread of loaves and cakes on rushes or fresh leaves. Then they will lie on beds of myrtle-boughs and bryony and make merry with their children, drinking their wine after the feast with garlands on their heads and singing the praises of the gods. So they will live pleasantly together; and a prudent fear of poverty or war will keep them from begetting children beyond their means.

Here Glaucon interrupted me: You seem to expect your citizens to feast on dry bread.

True, I said; I forgot that they will have something to give it a relish, salt, no doubt, and olives, and cheese, and country stews of roots and vegetables. And for dessert we will give them figs and peas and beans; and they shall roast myrtle-berries and acorns at the fire, while they sip their wine. Leading such a healthy life in peace, they will naturally come to a good old age, and leave their children to live after them in the same manner.

That is just the sort of provender you would supply, Socrates, if you were founding a community of pigs.

Well, how are they to live, then, Glaucon?

With the ordinary comforts. Let them lie on couches and dine off tables on such dishes and sweets as we have nowadays.

Ah, I see, said I; we are to study the growth, not just of a state, but of a luxurious one. Well, there may be no harm in that; the consideration of luxury may help us to discover how justice and injustice take root in society. The community I have described seems to me the ideal one, in sound health as it were: but if you want to see one suffering from inflammation, there is nothing to hinder us. So some people, it seems, will not be satisfied to live in this simple way; they must have couches and tables and furniture of all sorts; and delicacies too, perfumes, unguents, courtesans, sweetmeats, all in plentiful variety. And besides, we must not limit ourselves now to those bare necessaries of house and clothes and shoes; we shall have to set going the arts of embroidery and painting, and collect rich materials, like gold and ivory.

Yes.

Then we must once more enlarge our community. The healthy one will not be big enough now; it must be swollen up with a whole multitude of callings not ministering to any bare necessity: hunters and fishermen, for instance; artists in sculpture, painting, and music; poets with their attendant train of professional reciters, actors, dancers, producers; and makers of all sorts of household gear, including everything for women's adornment. And we shall want more servants: children's nurses and attendants, lady's maids, barbers, cooks and confectioners. And then swineherds—there was no need for them in our original state, but we shall want them now; and a great quantity of sheep and cattle too, if people are going to live on meat.

Of course.

And with this manner of life physicians will be in much greater request.

No doubt.

The country, too, which was large enough to support the original inhabitants, will now be too small. If we are to have enough pasture and plough land, we shall have to cut off a slice of our neighbours' territory; and if they too are not content with necessaries, but give themselves up to getting unlimited wealth, they will want a slice of ours.

That is inevitable, Socrates.

So the next thing will be, Glaucon, that we shall be at war.

No doubt.

We need not say yet whether war does good or harm, but only that we have discovered its origin in desires which are the most fruitful source of evils both to individuals and to states.

Quite true.

This will mean a considerable addition to our community—a whole army, to go out to battle with any invader, in defence of all this property and of the citizens we have been describing.

Why so? Can't they defend themselves?

Not if the principle was right, which we all accepted in framing our society. You remember we agreed that no one man can practise many trades or arts satisfactorily.

True.

Well, is not the conduct of war an art, quite as important as shoemaking?

Yes.

But we would not allow our shoemaker to try to be also a farmer or weaver or builder, because we wanted our shoes well made. We gave each man one trade, for which he was naturally fitted; he would do good work, if he confined himself to that all his life, never letting the right moment slip by. Now in no form of work is efficiency so important as in war; and fighting is not so easy a business that a man can follow another trade, such as farming or shoemaking, and also be an efficient soldier. Why, even a game like draughts or dice must be studied from childhood; no one can become a fine player in his spare moments. Just taking up a shield or other weapon will not make a man capable of fighting that very day in any sort of warfare, any more than taking up a tool or implement of some kind will make a man a craftsman or an athlete, if he does not understand its use and has never been properly trained to handle it.

No; if that were so, tools would indeed be worth having.

These guardians of our state, then, inasmuch as their work is the most important of all, will need the most complete freedom from other occupations and the greatest amount of skill and practice.

I quite agree.

And also a native aptitude for their calling.

Certainly.

So it is our business to define, if we can, the natural gifts that fit men to be guardians of a commonwealth, and to select them accordingly. It will certainly be a formidable task; but we must grapple with it to the best of our power.

Yes.

Chapter VIII (II. 375 A–376 E)
The Guardian's Temperament

. . . .

Don't you think then, said I, that, for the purpose of keeping guard, a young man should have much the same temperament and qualities as a well-bred watch-dog? I mean, for instance, that both must have quick senses to detect an enemy, swiftness in pursuing him, and strength, if they have to fight when they have caught him.

Yes, they will need all those qualities.

And also courage, if they are to fight well.

Of course.

And courage, in dog or horse or any other creature, implies a spirited disposition. You must have noticed that a high spirit is unconquerable. Every soul possessed of it is fearless and indomitable in the face of any danger.

Yes, I have noticed that.

So now we know what physical qualities our Guardian must have, and also that he must be of a spirited temper.

Yes.

Then, Glaucon, how are men of that natural disposition to be kept from behaving pugnaciously to one another and to the rest of their countrymen?

It is not at all easy to see.

And yet they must be gentle to their own people and dangerous only to enemies; otherwise they will destroy themselves without waiting till others destroy them.

True.

What are we to do, then? If gentleness and a high temper are contraries, where shall we find a character to combine them? Both are necessary to make a good Guardian, but it seems they are incompatible. So we shall never have a good Guardian.

It looks like it.

Here I was perplexed, but on thinking over what we had been saying, I remarked that we deserved to be puzzled, because we had not followed up the comparison we had just drawn.

What do you mean? he asked.

We never noticed that, after all, there are natures in which these contraries are combined. They are to be found in animals, and not least in the kind we compared to our Guardian. Well-bred dogs, as you know, are by instinct perfectly gentle to people whom they know and are accustomed to, and fierce to strangers. So the combination of qualities we require for our Guardian is, after all, possible and not against nature.

Evidently.

Do you further agree that, besides this spirited temper, he must have a philosophical element in his nature?

I don't see what you mean.

This is another trait you will see in the dog. It is really remarkable how the creature gets angry at the mere sight of a stranger and welcomes anyone he knows, though he may never have been treated unkindly by the one or kindly by the other. Did that never strike you as curious?

I had not thought of it before; but that certainly is how a dog behaves.

Well, but that shows a fine instinct, which is philosophic in the true sense.

How so?

Because the only mark by which he distinguishes a friendly and an unfriendly face is that he knows the one and does not know the other; and if a creature makes that the test of what it finds congenial or otherwise, how can you deny that it has a passion for knowledge and understanding?

Of course, I cannot.

And that passion is the same thing as philosophy—the love of wisdom.

Yes.

Shall we boldly say, then, that the same is true of human beings? If a man is to be gentle towards his own people whom he knows, he must have an instinctive love of wisdom and understanding.

Agreed.

So the nature required to make a really noble Guardian of our commonwealth will be swift and strong, spirited, and philosophic.

Quite so. . . .

. . . .

Chapter X (III. 412 B–IV. 421 c)
Selection of Rulers: The Guardians'
Manner of Living

. . . .

What is the next point to be settled? Is it not the question, which of these Guardians are to be rulers and which are to obey?

No doubt.

Well, it is obvious that the elder must have authority over the young, and that the rulers must be the best.

Yes.

And as among farmers the best are those with a natural turn for farming, so, if we want the best among our Guardians, we must take those naturally fitted to watch over a commonwealth. They must have the right sort of intelligence and ability; and also they must look upon the commonwealth as their special concern—the sort of concern that is felt for something so closely bound up with oneself that its interests and fortunes, for good or ill, are held to be identical with one's own.

Exactly.

So the kind of men we must choose from among the Guardians will be those who, when we look at the whole course of their lives, are found to be full of zeal to do whatever they believe is for the good of the commonwealth and never willing to act against its interest.

Yes, they will be the men we want.

We must watch them, I think, at every age and see whether they are capable of preserving this conviction that they must do what is best for the community, never forgetting it or allowing themselves to

be either forced or bewitched into throwing it over.

How does this throwing over come about?

I will explain. When a belief passes out of the mind, a man may be willing to part with it, if it is false and he has learnt better, or unwilling, if it is true.

I see how he might be willing to let it go; but you must explain how he can be unwilling.

Where is your difficulty? Don't you agree that men are unwilling to be deprived of good, though ready enough to part with evil? Or that to be deceived about the truth is evil, to possess it good? Or don't you think that possessing truth means thinking of things as they really are?

You are right. I do agree that men are unwilling to be robbed of a true belief.

When that happens to them, then, it must be by theft, or violence, or bewitchment.

Again I do not understand.

Perhaps my metaphors are too high-flown. I call it theft when one is persuaded out of one's belief or forgets it. Argument in the one case, and time in the other, steal it away without one's knowing what is happening. You understand now?

Yes.

And by violence I mean being driven to change one's mind by pain or suffering.

That too I understand, and you are right.

And bewitchment, as I think you would agree, occurs when a man is beguiled out of his opinion by the allurements of pleasure or scared out of it under the spell of panic.

Yes, all delusions are like a sort of bewitchment.

As I said just now, then, we must find out who are the best guardians of this inward conviction that they must always do what they believe to be best for the commonwealth. We shall have to watch them from earliest childhood and set them tasks in which they would be most likely to forget or to be beguiled out of this duty. We shall then choose only those whose memory holds firm and who are proof against delusion.

Yes.

We must also subject them to ordeals of toil and pain and watch for the same qualities there. And we must observe them when exposed to the test of yet a third kind of bewitchment. As people lead colts up to alarming noises to see whether they are timid, so these young men must be brought into terrifying situations and then into scenes of pleasure, which will put them to severer proof than gold tied in the furnace. If we find one bearing himself well in all these trials and resisting every enchantment, a true guardian of himself, preserving always that perfect rhythm and harmony of being which he has acquired from his training in music and poetry, such a one will be of the greatest service to the commonwealth as well as to himself. Whenever we find one who has come unscathed through every test in childhood, youth, and manhood, we shall set him as a Ruler to watch over the commonwealth; he will be honoured in life, and after death receive the highest tribute of funeral rites and other memorials. All who do not reach this standard we must reject. And that, I think, my dear Glaucon, may be taken as an outline of the way in which we shall select Guardians to be set in authority as Rulers.

I am very much of your mind.

These, then, may properly be called Guardians in the fullest sense, who will ensure that neither foes without shall have the power, nor friends within the wish, to do harm. Those young men whom up to now we have been speaking of as Guardians, will be better described as Auxiliaries, who will enforce the decisions of the Rulers.

I agree.

. . . .

Chapter XII (IV. 427 C–434 D)
The Virtues in the State

. . . .

So now at last, son of Ariston, said I, your commonwealth is established. The next thing is to bring to bear upon it all the light you can get from any quarter, with the help of your brother and Polemarchus and all the rest, in the hope that we may see where justice is to be found in it and where injustice, how they differ, and which of the two will bring happiness to its possessor, no matter whether gods and men see that he has it or not.

Nonsense, said Glaucon; you promised to conduct the search yourself, because it would be a sin not to uphold justice by every means in your power.

That is true; I must do as you say, but you must all help.

We will.

I suspect, then, we may find what we are looking for in this way. I take it that our state, having been founded and built up on the right lines, is good in the complete sense of the word.

It must be.

Obviously, then, it is wise, brave, temperate, and just.

Obviously.

Then if we find some of these qualities in it, the remainder will be the one we have not found. It is as if we were looking somewhere for one of any four things: if we detected that one immediately, we should be satisfied; whereas if we recognized the other three first, that would be enough to indicate the thing we wanted; it could only be the remaining one. So here we have four qualities. Had we not better follow that method in looking for the one we want?

Surely.

To begin then: the first quality to come into view in our state seems to be its wisdom; and there appears to be something odd about this quality.[4]

What is there odd about it?

I think the state we have described really has wisdom; for it will be prudent in counsel, won't it?

Yes.

And prudence in counsel is clearly a form of knowledge; good counsel cannot be due to ignorance and stupidity.

Clearly.

But there are many and various kinds of knowledge in our commonwealth. There is the knowledge possessed by the carpenters or the smiths, and the knowledge how to raise crops. Are we to call the state wise and prudent on the strength of these forms of skill?

No; they would only make it good at furniture-making or working in copper or agriculture.

Well then, is there any form of knowledge, possessed by some among the citizens of our new-founded commonwealth, which will enable it to take thought, not for some particular interest, but for the best possible conduct of the state as a whole in its internal and external relations?

Yes, there is.

What is it, and where does it reside?

It is precisely that art of guardianship which resides in those Rulers whom we just now called Guardians in the full sense.

And what would you call the state on the strength of that knowledge?

Prudent and truly wise.

And do you think there will be more or fewer of these genuine Guardians in our state than there will be smiths?

Far fewer.

Fewer, in fact, than any of those other groups who are called after the kind of skill they possess?

Much fewer.

So, if a state is constituted on natural principles, the wisdom it possesses as a whole will be due to the knowledge residing in the smallest part, the one which takes the lead and governs the rest. Such knowledge is the only kind that deserves the name of wisdom, and it appears to be ordained by nature that the class privileged to possess it should be the smallest of all.

Quite true.

Here then we have more or less made out one of our four qualities and its seat in the structure of the commonwealth.

To my satisfaction, at any rate.

Next there is courage. It is not hard to discern that quality or the part of the community in which it resides so as to entitle the whole to be called brave.

Why do you say so?

Because anyone who speaks of a state as either brave or cowardly can only be thinking of that part of it which takes the field and fights in its defence; the reason being, I imagine, that the character of the state is not determined by the bravery or cowardice of the other parts.

No.

Courage, then, is another quality which a community owes to a certain part of itself. And its being brave will mean that, in this part, it possesses the power of preserving, in all circumstances, a conviction about the sort of things that it is right to be afraid of—the conviction implanted by the education which the law-giver has established. Is not that what you mean by courage?

I do not quite understand. Will you say it again?

I am saying that courage means preserving something.

Yes, but what?

The conviction, inculcated by lawfullly established education, about the sort of things which may rightly be feared. When I added "in all circumstances," I meant preserving it always and never abandoning it, whether under the influence of pain or of pleasure, of desire or of fear. If you like, I will give an illustration.

Please do.

You know how dyers who want wool to take a purple dye, first select the white wool from among all the other colours, next treat it very carefully to make it take the dye in its full brilliance, and only then dip it in the vat. Dyed in that way, wool gets a fast colour, which no washing, even with soap, will rob of its brilliance; whereas if they choose wool of any colour but white, or if they neglect to prepare it, you know what happens.

Yes, it looks washed-out and ridiculous.

That illustrates the result we were doing our best to achieve when we were choosing our fighting men and training their minds and bodies. Our only purpose was to contrive influences whereby they might take the colour of our institutions like a dye, so that, in virtue of having both the right temperament and the right education, their convictions about what ought to be feared and on all other subjects might be indelibly fixed, never to be washed out by pleasure and pain, desire and fear, solvents more terribly effective than all the soap and fuller's earth in the world. Such a power of constantly preserving, in accordance with our institutions, the right conviction about the things which ought, or ought not, to be feared, is what I call courage. That is my position, unless you have some objection to make.

None at all, he replied; if the belief were such as might be found in a slave or an animal—correct, but not produced by education—you would hardly describe it as in accordance with our institutions, and you would give it some other name than courage.

Quite true.

Then I accept your account of courage.

You will do well to accept it, at any rate as applying to the courage of the ordinary citizen; if you like we will go into it more fully some other time.

At present we are in search of justice, rather than of courage; and for that purpose we have said enough.

I quite agree.

Two qualities, I went on, still remain to be made out in our state, temperance and the object of our whole inquiry, justice. Can we discover justice without troubling ourselves further about temperance?

I do not know, and I would rather not have justice come to light first, if that means that we should not go on to consider temperance. So if you want to please me, take temperance first.

Of course I have every wish to please you.

Do go on then.

I will. At first sight, temperance seems more like some sort of concord or harmony than the other qualities did.

How so?

Temperance surely means a kind of orderliness, a control of certain pleasures and appetites. People use the expression, "master of oneself," whatever that means, and various other phrases that point the same way.

Quite true.

Is not "master of oneself" an absurd expression? A man who was master of himself would presumably be also subject to himself, and the subject would be master; for all these terms apply to the same person.

No doubt.

I think, however, the phrase means that within the man himself, in his soul, there is a better part and a worse; and that he is his own master when the part which is better by nature has the worse under its control. It is certainly a term of praise; whereas it is considered a disgrace, when, through bad breeding or bad company, the better part is overwhelmed by the worse, like a small force outnumbered by a multitude. A man in that condition is called a slave to himself and intemperate.

Probably that is what is meant.

Then now look at our newly founded state and you will find one of these two conditions realized there. You will agree that it deserves to be called master of itself, if temperance and self-mastery exist where the better part rules the worse.

Yes, I can see that is true.

It is also true that the great mass of multifarious appetites and pleasures and pains will be found to occur chiefly in children and women and slaves, and, among free men so called, in the inferior multitude; whereas the simple and moderate desires which, with the aid of reason and right belief, are guided by reflection, you will find only in a few, and those with the best inborn dispositions and the best educated.

Yes, certainly.

Do you see that this state of things will exist in your commonwealth, where the desires of the inferior multitude will be controlled by the desires and wisdom of the superior few? Hence, if any society can be called master of itself and in control of pleasures and desires, it will be ours.

Quite so.

On these grounds, then, we may describe it as temperate. Furthermore, in our state, if anywhere, the governors and the governed will share the same conviction on the question who ought to rule. Don't you think so?

I am quite sure of it.

Then, if that is their state of mind, in which of the two classes of citizens will temperance reside—in the governors or in the governed?

In both, I suppose.

So we were not wrong in divining a resemblance between temperance and some kind of harmony. Temperance is not like courage and wisdom, which made the state wise and brave by residing each in one particular part. Temperance works in a different way; it extends throughout the whole gamut of the state, producing a consonance of all its elements from the weakest to the strongest as measured by any standard you like to take—wisdom, bodily strength, numbers, or wealth. So we are entirely justified in identifying with temperance this unanimity or harmonious agreement between the naturally superior and inferior elements on the question which of the two should govern, whether in the state or in the individual.

I fully agree.

Good, said I. We have discovered in our commonwealth three out of our four qualities, to the best of our present judgment. What is the remaining one, required to make up its full complement of goodness? For clearly this will be justice.

Clearly.

Now is the moment, then, Glaucon, for us to keep the closest watch, like huntsmen standing round a covert, to make sure that justice does not slip through and vanish undetected. It must certainly be somewhere hereabouts; so keep your eyes open for a view of the quarry, and if you see it first, give me the alert.

I wish I could, he answered; but you will do better to give me a lead and not count on me for more than eyes to see what you show me.

Pray for luck, then, and follow me.

I will, if you will lead on.

The thicket looks rather impenetrable, said I; too dark for it to be easy to start up the game. However, we must push on.

Of course we must.

Here I gave the view halloo. Glaucon, I exclaimed, I believe we are on the track and the quarry is not going to escape us altogether.

That is good news.

Really, I said, we have been extremely stupid. All this time the thing has been under our very noses from the start, and we never saw it. We have been as absurd as a person who hunts for something he has all the time got in his hand. Instead of looking at the thing, we have been staring into the distance. No doubt that is why it escaped us.

What do you mean?

I believe we have been talking about the thing all this while without ever understanding that we were giving some sort of account of it.

Do come to the point. I am all ears.

Listen, then, and judge whether I am right. You remember how, when we first began to establish our commonwealth and several times since, we have laid down, as a universal principle, that everyone ought to perform the one function in the community for which his nature best suited him. Well, I believe that that principle, or some form of it, is justice.

We certainly laid that down.

Yes, and surely we have often heard people say that justice means minding one's own business and not meddling with other men's concerns; and we have often said so ourselves.

We have.

Well, my friend, it may be that this minding of one's own business, when it takes a certain form, is acutally the same thing as justice. Do you know what makes me think so?

No, tell me.

I think that this quality which makes it possible for the three we have already considered, wisdom, courage, and temperance, to take their place in the commonwealth, and so long as it remains present secures their continuance, must be the remaining one. And we said that, when three of the four were found, the one left over would be justice.

It must be so.

Well now, if we had to decide which of these qualities will contribute most to the excellence of our commonwealth, it would be hard to say whether it was the unanimity of rulers and subjects or the soldier's fidelity to the established conviction about what is, or is not, to be feared, or the watchful intelligence of the Rulers; or whether its excellence were not above all due to the observance by everyone, child or woman, slave or freeman or artisan, ruler or ruled, of this principle that each one should do his own proper work without interfering with others.

It would be hard to decide, no doubt.

It seems, then that this principle can at any rate claim to rival wisdom, temperance, and courage as conducing to the excellence of a state. And would you not say that the only possible competitor of these qualities must be justice?

Yes, undoubtedly.

Here is another thing which points to the same conclusion. The judging of law-suits is a duty that you will lay upon your Rulers, isn't it?

Of course.

And the chief aim of their decisions will be that neither party shall have what belongs to another or be deprived of what is his own.

Yes.

Because that is just?

Yes.

So here again justice admittedly means that a man should possess and concern himself with what properly belongs to him.

True.

Again, do you agree with me that no great harm would be done to the community by a general interchange of most forms of work, the carpenter and the cobbler exchanging their positions and their tools and taking on each other's jobs, or even the same man undertaking both?

Yes, there would not be much harm in that.

But I think you will also agree that another kind of interchange would be disastrous. Suppose, for instance, someone whom nature designed to be an artisan or tradesman should be emboldened by some advantage, such as wealth or command of votes or bodily strength, to try to enter the order of fighting men; or some member of that order should aspire, beyond his merits, to a seat in the council-chamber of the Guardians. Such interference and exchange of social positions and tools, or the attempt to combine all these forms of work in the same person, would be fatal to the commonwealth.

Most certainly.

Where there are three orders, then, any plurality of functions or shifting from one order to another is not merely utterly harmful to the community, but one might fairly call it the extreme of wrongdoing. And you will agree that to do the greatest of wrongs to one's own community is injustice.

Surely.

This, then, is injustice. And, conversely, let us repeat that when each order—tradesman, Auxiliary, Guardian—keeps to its own proper business in the commonwealth and does its own work, that is justice and what makes a just society.

I entirely agree.

Chapter XIII (IV. 434 D–441 C)
The Three Parts of the Soul

. . . .

We must not be too positive yet, said I. If we find that this same quality when it exists in the individual can equally be identified with justice, then we can at once give our assent; there will be no more to be said; otherwise, we shall have to look further. For the moment, we had better finish the inquiry which we began with the idea that it would be easier to make out the nature of justice in the individual if we first tried to study it in something on a larger scale. That larger thing we took to be a state, and so we set about constructing the best one

we could, being sure of finding justice in a state that was good. The discovery we made there must now be applied to the individual. If it is confirmed, all will be well; but if we find that justice in the individual is something different, we must go back to the state and test our new result. Perhaps if we brought the two cases into contact like flint and steel, we might strike out between them the spark of justice, and in its light confirm the conception in our own minds.

A good method. Let us follow it.

Now, I continued, if two things, one large, the other small, are called by the same name, they will be alike in that respect to which the common name applies. Accordingly, in so far as the quality of justice is concerned, there will be no difference between a just man and a just society.

No.

Well, but we decided that a society was just when each of the three types of human character it contained performed its own function; and again, it was temperate and brave and wise by virtue of certain other affections and states of mind of those same types.

True.

Accordingly, my friend, if we are to be justified in attributing those same virtues to the individual, we shall expect to find that the individual soul contains the same three elements and that they are affected in the same way as are the corresponding types in society.

That follows.

Here, then, we have stumbled upon another little problem: Does the soul contain these three elements or not?

Not such a very little one, I think. It may be a true saying, Socrates, that what is worth while is seldom easy.

Apparently; and let me tell you, Glaucon, it is my belief that we shall never reach the exact truth in this matter by following our present methods of discussion; the road leading to that goal is longer and more laborious. However, perhaps we can find an answer that will be up to the standard we have so far maintained in our speculations.

Is not that enough? I should be satisfied for the moment.

Well, it will more than satisfy me, I replied.

Don't be disheartened, then, but go on.

Surely, I began, we must admit that the same elements and characters that appear in the state must exist in every one of us; where else could they have come from? It would be absurd to imagine that among peoples with a reputation for a high-spirited character, like the Thracians and Scythians and northerners generally, the states have not derived that character from their individual members; or that it is otherwise with the love of knowledge, which would be ascribed chiefly to our own part of the world, or with the love of money, which one would specially connect with Phoenicia and Egypt.

Certainly.

So far, then, we have a fact which is easily recognized. But here the difficulty begins. Are we using the same part of ourselves in all these three experiences, or a different part in each? Do we gain knowledge with one part, feel anger with another, and with yet a third desire the pleasures of food, sex, and so on? Or is the whole soul at work in every impulse and in all these forms of behaviour? The difficulty is to answer that question satisfactorily.

I quite agree.

Let us approach the problem whether these elements are distinct or identical in this way. It is clear that the same thing cannot act in two opposite ways or be in two opposite states at the same time, with respect to the same part of itself, and in relation to the same object. So if we find such contradictory actions or states among the elements concerned, we shall know that more than one must have been involved.

Very well.

Consider this proposition of mine, then. Can the same thing, at the same time and with respect to the same part of itself, be at rest and in motion?

Certainly not.

We had better state this principle in still more precise terms, to guard against misunderstanding later on. Suppose a man is standing still, but moving his head and arms. We should not allow anyone to say that the same man was both at rest and in motion at the same time, but only that part of him was at rest, part in motion. Isn't that so?

Yes.

An ingenious objector might refine still further and argue that a peg-top, spinning with its peg fixed at the same spot, or indeed any body that revolves in the same place, is both at rest and in motion as a whole, but we should not agree, because the parts in respect of which such a body is moving and at rest are not the same. It contains an axis and a circumference; and in respect of the axis it is at rest inasmuch as the axis is not inclined in any direction, while in respect of the circumference it revolves; and if, while it is spinning, the axis does lean out of the perpendicular in all directions, then it is in no way at rest.

That is true.

No objection of that sort, then, will disconcert us or make us believe that the same thing can ever act or be acted upon in two opposite ways, or be two opposite things, at the same time, in respect of the same part of itself, and in relation to the same object.

I can answer for myself at any rate.

Well, anyhow, as we do not want to spend time in reviewing all such objections to make sure that they are unsound, let us proceed on this assumption, with the understanding that, if we ever come to think otherwise, all the consequences based upon it will fall to the ground.

Yes, that is a good plan.

Now, would you class such things as assent and dissent, striving after something and refusing it, attraction and repulsion, as pairs of opposite actions or states of mind—no matter which?

Yes, they are opposites.

And would you not class all appetites such as hunger and thirst, and again willing and wishing, with the affirmative members of those pairs I have just mentioned? For instance, you would say that the soul of a man who desires something is striving after it, or trying to draw to itself the thing it wishes to possess, or again, in so far as it is willing to have its want satisfied, it is giving its assent to its own longing, as if to an inward question.

Yes.

And, on the other hand, disinclination, unwillingness, and dislike, we should class on the negative side with acts of rejection or repulsion.

Of course.

That being so, shall we say that appetites form one class, the most conspicuous being those we call thirst and hunger?

Yes.

Thirst being desire for drink, hunger for food?

Yes.

Now, is thirst, just in so far as it is thirst, a desire in the soul for anything more than simply drink? Is it, for instance, thirst for hot drink or for cold, for much drink or for little, or in a word for drink of any particular kind? Is it not rather true that you will have a desire for cold drink only if you are feeling hot as well as thirsty, and for hot drink only if you are feeling cold; and if you want much drink or little, that will be because your thirst is a great thirst or a little one? But, just in itself, thirst or hunger is a desire for nothing more than its natural object, drink or food, pure and simple.

Yes, he agreed, each desire, just in itself, is simply for its own natural object. When the object is of such and such a particular kind, the desire will be correspondingly qualified.[5]

We must be careful here, or we might be troubled by the objection that no one desires mere food and drink, but always wholesome food and drink. We shall be told that what we desire is always something that is good; so if thirst is a desire, its object must be, like that of any other desire, something—drink or whatever it may be—that will be good for one.[6]

Yes, there might seem to be something in that objection.

But surely, wherever you have two correlative terms, if one is qualified, the other must always be qualified too; whereas if one is unqualified, so is the other.

I don't understand.

Well, "greater" is a relative term; and the greater is greater than the less; if it is much greater, then the less is much less; if it is greater at some moment, past or future, then the less is less at that same moment. The same principle applies to all such correlatives, like "more" and "fewer," "double" and "half"; and again to terms like "heavier" and "lighter," "quicker" and "slower," and to things like hot and cold.

Yes.

Or take the various branches of knowledge: is it not the same there? The object of knowledge pure and simple is the knowable—if that is the right word—without any qualification; whereas a particular kind of knowledge has an object of a particular kind. For example, as soon as men learnt how to build houses, their craft was distinguished from others under the name of architecture, because it had a unique character, which was itself due to the character of its object; and all other branches of craft and knowledge were distinguished in the same way.

True.

This, then, if you understand me now, is what I meant by saying that, where there are two correlatives, the one is qualified if, and only if, the other is so. I am not saying that the one must have the same quality as the other—that the science of health and disease is itself healthy and diseased, or the knowledge of good and evil is itself good and evil—but only that, as soon as you have a knowledge that is restricted to a particular kind of object, namely health and disease, the knowledge itself becomes a particular kind of knowledge. Hence we no longer call it merely knowledge, which would have for its object whatever can be known, but we add the qualification and call it medical science.

I understand now and I agree.

Now, to go back to thirst: is not that one of these relative terms? It is essentially thirst for something.

Yes, for drink.

And if the drink desired is of a certain kind, the thirst will be correspondingly qualified. But thirst which is just simply thirst is not for drink of any particular sort—much or little, good or bad—but for drink pure and simple.

Quite so.

We conclude, then, that the soul of a thirsty man, just in so far as he is thirsty, has no other wish than to drink. That is the object of its craving, and towards that it is impelled.

That is clear.

Now if there is ever something which at the same time pulls it the opposite way, that something must be an element in the soul other than the one which is thirsting and driving it like a beast to drink; in accordance with our principle that the same thing cannot behave in two opposite ways at the same time and towards the same object with the same part of itself. It is like an archer drawing the bow: it is not accurate to say that his hands are at the same time both pushing and pulling it. One hand does the pushing, the other the pulling.

Exactly.

Now, is it sometimes true that people are thirsty and yet unwilling to drink?

Yes, often.

What, then, can one say of them, if not that their soul contains something which urges them to drink and something which holds them back, and that this latter is a distinct thing and overpowers the other?

I agree.

And is it not true that the intervention of this inhibiting principle in such cases always has its origin in reflection; whereas the impulses driving and dragging the soul are engendered by external influences and abnormal conditions?

Evidently.

We shall have good reason, then, to assert that they are two distinct principles. We may call that part of the soul whereby it reflects, rational; and the other, with which it feels hunger and thirst and is distracted by sexual passion and all the other desires, we will call irrational appetite, associated with pleasure in the replenishment of certain wants.

Yes, there is good ground for that view.

Let us take it, then, that we have now distinguished two elements in the soul. What of that passionate element which makes us feel angry and indignant? Is that a third, or identical in nature with one of those two?

It might perhaps be identified with appetite.

I am more inclined to put my faith in a story I once heard about Leontius, son of Aglaion. On his way up from the Piraeus outside the north wall, he noticed the bodies of some criminals lying on the ground, with the executioner standing by them. He wanted to go and look at them, but at the same time he was disgusted and tried to turn away. He struggled for some time and covered his eyes, but at last the desire was too much for him. Opening his eyes wide, he ran up to the bodies and cried, 'There you are, curse you; feast yourselves on this lovely sight!'

Yes, I have heard that story too.

The point of it surely is that anger is sometimes in conflict with appetite, as if they were two distinct principles. Do we not often find a man whose desires would force him to go against his reason, reviling himself and indignant with this part of his nature which is trying to put constraint on him? It

is like a struggle between two factions, in which indignation takes the side of reason. But I believe you have never observed, in yourself or anyone else, indignation make common cause with appetite in behaviour which reason decides to be wrong.

No, I am sure I have not.

Again, take a man who feels he is in the wrong. The more generous his nature, the less can he be indignant at any suffering, such as hunger and cold, inflicted by the man he has injured. He recognizes such treatment as just, and, as I say, his spirit refuses to be roused against it.

That is true.

But now contrast one who thinks it is he that is being wronged. His spirit boils with resentment and sides with the right as he conceives it. Persevering all the more for the hunger and cold and other pains he suffers, it triumphs and will not give in until its gallant struggle has ended in success or death; or until the restraining voice of reason, like a shepherd calling off his dog, makes it relent.

An apt comparison, he said; and in fact it fits the relation of our Auxiliaries to the Rulers: they were to be like watch-dogs obeying the shepherds of the commonwealth.

Yes, you understand very well what I have in mind. But do you see how we have changed our view? A moment ago we were supposing this spirited element to be something of the nature of appetite; but now it appears that, when the soul is divided into factions, it is far more ready to be up in arms on the side of reason.

Quite true.

Is it, then, distinct from the rational element or only a particular form of it, so that the soul will contain no more than two elements, reason and appetite? Or is the soul like the state, which had three orders to hold it together, traders, Auxiliaries, and counsellors? Does the spirited element make a third, the natural auxiliary of reason, when not corrupted by bad upbringing?

It must be a third.

Yes, I said, provided it can be shown to be distinct from reason, as we saw it was from appetite.

That is easily proved. You can see that much in children: they are full of passionate feelings from their very birth; but some, I should say, never become rational, and most of them only late in life.

A very sound observation, said I, the truth of which may also be seen in animals. And besides, there is the witness of Homer in that line I quoted before: "He smote his breast and spoke, chiding his heart." The poet is plainly thinking of the two elements as distinct, when he makes the one which has chosen the better course after reflection rebuke the other for its unreasoning passion.

I entirely agree.

Chapter XIV (IV. 441 c–445 b)
The Virtues in the Individual

. . . .

And so, after a stormy passage, we have reached the land. We are fairly agreed that the same three elements exist alike in the state and in the individual soul.

That is so.

Does it not follow at once that state and individual will be wise or brave by virtue of the same element in each and in the same way? Both will possess in the same manner any quality that makes for excellence.

That must be true.

Then it applies to justice: we shall conclude that a man is just in the same way that a state was just. And we have surely not forgotten that justice in the state meant that each of the three orders in it was doing its own proper work. So we may henceforth bear in mind that each one of us likewise will be a just person, fulfilling his proper function, only if the several parts of our nature fulfil theirs.

Certainly.

And it will be the business of reason to rule with wisdom and forethought on behalf of the entire soul; while the spirited element ought to act as its subordinate and ally. The two will be brought into accord, as we said earlier, by that combination of mental and bodily training which will tune up one string of the instrument and relax the other, nourishing the reasoning part on the study of noble literature and allaying the other's wildness by harmony and rhythm. When both have been thus nurtured and trained to know their own true functions, they must be set in command over the appetites, which form the greater part of each man's soul and are by nature insatiably covetous. They must keep watch lest this part, by battening on the pleasures that are called bodily, should grow so great and powerful that it will no longer keep to its own work, but will try to enslave the others and usurp a dominion to which it has no right, thus turning the whole of life upside down. At the same time, those two together will be the best of guardians for the entire soul and for the body against all enemies from without: the one will take counsel, while the other will do battle, following its ruler's commands and by its own bravery giving effect to the ruler's designs.

Yes, that is all true.

And so we call an individual brave in virtue of this spirited part of his nature, when, in spite of pain or pleasure, it holds fast to the injunctions of reason about what he ought or ought not to be afraid of.

True.

And wise in virtue of that small part which rules and issues these injunctions, possessing as it does the knowledge of what is good for each of the three elements and for all of them in common.

Certainly.

And, again, temperate by reason of the unanimity and concord of all three, when there is no internal conflict between the ruling element and its two subjects, but all are agreed that reason should be ruler.

Yes, that is an exact account of temperance, whether in the state or in the individual.

Finally, a man will be just by observing the principle we have so often stated.

Necessarily.

Now is there any indistinctness in our vision of justice, that might make it seem somehow different from what we found it to be in the state?

I don't think so.

Because, if we have any lingering doubt, we might make sure by comparing it with some commonplace notions. Suppose, for instance, that a sum of money were entrusted to our state or to an individual of corresponding character and training, would anyone imagine that such a person would be specially likely to embezzle it?

No.

And would he not be incapable of sacrilege and theft, or of treachery to friend or country; never false to an oath or any other compact; the last to be guilty of adultery or of neglecting parents or the due service of the gods?

Yes.

And the reason for all this is that each part of his nature is exercising its proper function, of ruling or of being ruled.

Yes, exactly.

Are you satisfied, then, that justice is the power which produces states or individuals of whom that is true, or must we look further?

There is no need; I am quite satisfied.

And so our dream has come true—I mean the inkling we had that, by some happy chance, we had lighted upon a rudimentary form of justice from the very moment when we set about founding our commonwealth. Our principle that the born shoemaker or carpenter had better stick to his trade turns out to have been an adumbration of justice; and that is why it has helped us. But in reality justice, though evidently analogous to this principle, is not a matter of external behaviour, but of the inward self and of attending to all that is, in the fullest sense, a man's proper concern. The just man does not allow the several elements in his soul to usurp one another's functions; he is indeed one who sets his house in order, by self-mastery and discipline coming to be at peace with himself, and bringing into tune those three parts, like the terms in the proportion of a musical scale, the highest and lowest notes and the mean between them, with all the intermediate intervals. Only when he has linked these parts together in well-tempered harmony and has made himself one man instead of many, will he be ready to go about whatever he may have to do, whether it be making money and satisfying bodily wants, or business transactions, or the affairs of state. In all these fields, when he speaks of just and honourable conduct, he will mean the behaviour that helps to produce and to preserve this habit of mind; and by wisdom he will mean the knowledge which presides over such conduct. Any action which tends to break down this habit will be for him unjust; and the notions governing it he will call ignorance and folly.

This is perfectly true, Socrates.

Good, said I. I believe we should not be thought altogether mistaken, if we claimed to have discovered the just man and the just state, and wherein their justice consists.

Indeed we should not.

Shall we make that claim, then?

Yes, we will.

So be it, said I. Next, I suppose, we have to consider injustice.

Evidently.

This must surely be a sort of civil strife among the three elements, whereby they usurp and encroach upon one another's functions and some one part of the soul rises up in rebellion against the whole, claiming a supremacy to which it has no right because its nature fits it only to be the servant of the ruling principle. Such turmoil and aberration we shall, I think, identify with injustice, intemperance, cowardice, ignorance, and in a word with all wickedness.

Exactly.

And now that we know the nature of justice and injustice, we can be equally clear about what is meant by acting justly and again by unjust action and wrongdoing.

How do you mean?

Plainly, they are exactly analogous to those wholesome and unwholesome activities which respectively produce a healthy or unhealthy condition in the body; in the same way just and unjust conduct produce a just or unjust character. Justice is produced in the soul, like health in the body, by establishing the elements concerned in their natural relations of control and subordination, whereas injustice is like disease and means that this natural order is inverted.

Quite so.

It appears, then, that virtue is as it were the health and comeliness and well-being of the soul, as wickedness is disease, deformity, and weakness.

True.

And also that virtue and wickedness are brought about by one's way of life, honourable or disgraceful.

That follows.

So now it only remains to consider which is the more profitable course: to do right and live honourably and be just, whether or not anyone knows what manner of man you are, or to do wrong and be unjust, provided that you can escape the chastisement which might make you a better man.

But really, Socrates, it seems to me ridiculous to ask that question now that the nature of justice and injustice has been brought to light. People think that all the luxury and wealth and power in the world cannot make life worth living when the bodily constitution is going to rack and ruin; and are we to believe that, when the very principle whereby we live is deranged and corrupted, life will be worth living so long as a man can do as he will, and wills to do anything rather than to free himself from vice and wrongdoing and to win justice and virtue?

Yes, I replied, it is a ridiculous question.

NOTES

1. In certain lawsuits the defendant, if found guilty, was allowed to propose a penalty alternative to that demanded by the prosecution. The judges then decided which should be inflicted. The "costs" here means the fee which the sophist, unlike Socrates, expected from his pupils.
2. All the persons mentioned have some interest. The craftsman *qua* craftsman has an interest in doing his work as well as possible, which is the same thing as serving the interest of the subjects on whom his craft is exercised; and the subjects have their interest, which the craftsman is there to promote.
3. The word translated "function" is the common word for "work." Hence the need for illustrations to confine it to the narrower sense of "function," here defined for the first time.
4. Because the wisdom of the whole resides in the smallest part, as explained below.
5. The object of the following subtle argument about relative terms is to distinguish thirst as a mere blind craving for drink from a more complex desire whose object includes the pleasure or health expected to result from drinking. We thus forestall the objection that all desires have "the good" (apparent or real) for their object and include an intellectual or rational element, so that the conflict of motives might be reduced to an intellectual debate, in the same "part" of the soul, on the comparative values of two incompatible ends.
6. If this objection were admitted, it would follow that the desire would always be correspondingly qualified. It is necessary to insist that we do experience blind cravings which can be isolated from any judgement about the goodness of their object.

An Enquiry Concerning the Principles of Morals

DAVID HUME

—•—

Section I
Of the General Principles of Morals

Disputes with men, pertinaciously obstinate in their principles, are, of all others, the most irksome; except, perhaps, those with persons, entirely disingen-

From *Enquiries Concerning Human Understanding and Concerning the Principles of Morals*, edited by L. A. Selby-Bigge, 3rd edition, revised by P. H. Nidditch. Copyright © 1975 by Oxford University Press. Reprinted by permission of the publisher.

uous, who really do not believe the opinions they defend, but engage in the controversy, from affectation, from a spirit of opposition, or from a desire of showing wit and ingenuity, superior to the rest of mankind. The same blind adherence to their own arguments is to be expected in both; the same contempt of their antagonists; and the same passionate vehemence, in inforcing sophistry and falsehood. And as reasoning is not the source, whence either disputant derives his tenets; it is in vain to expect, that any logic, which speaks not to the affections, will ever engage him to embrace sounder principles.

Those who have denied the reality of moral distinctions, may be ranked among the disingenuous disputants; nor is it conceivable, that any human creature could ever seriously believe, that all characters and actions were alike entitled to the affection and regard of everyone. The difference, which nature has placed between one man and another, is so wide, and this difference is still so much farther widened, by education, example, and habit, that, where the opposite extremes come at once under our apprehension, there is no scepticism so scrupulous, and scarce any assurance so determined, as absolutely to deny all distinction between them. Let a man's insensibility be ever so great, he must often be touched with the images of Right and Wrong; and let his prejudices be ever so obstinate, he must observe, that others are susceptible of like impressions. The only way, therefore, of converting an antagonist of this kind, is to leave him to himself. For, finding that nobody keeps up the controversy with him, it is probable he will, at last, of himself, from mere weariness, come over to the side of common sense and reason.

There has been a controversy started of late, much better worth examination, concerning the general foundation of Morals; whether they be derived from Reason, or from Sentiment; whether we attain the knowledge of them by a chain of argument and induction, or by an immediate feeling and finer internal sense; whether, like all sound judgement of truth and falsehood, they should be the same to every rational intelligent being; or whether, like the perception of beauty and deformity, they be founded entirely on the particular fabric and constitution of the human species.

The ancient philosophers, though they often affirm, that virtue is nothing but conformity to reason, yet, in general, seem to consider morals as deriving their existence from taste and sentiment. On the other hand, our modern enquirers, though they also talk much of the beauty of virtue, and deformity of vice, yet have commonly endeavoured to account for these distinctions by metaphysical reasonings, and by deductions from the most abstract principles of the understanding. Such confusion reigned in these subjects, that an opposition of the greatest consequence could prevail between one system and another, and even in the parts of almost each individual system; and yet nobody, till very

lately, was ever sensible of it. The elegant Lord Shaftesbury, who first gave occasion to remark this distinction, and who, in general, adhered to the principles of the ancients, is not, himself, entirely free from the same confusion.

It must be acknowledged, that both sides of the question are susceptible of specious arguments. Moral distinctions, it may be said, are discernible by pure *reason*: else, whence the many disputes that reign in common life, as well as in philosophy, with regard to this subject: the long chain of proofs often produced on both sides; the examples cited, the authorities appealed to, the analogies employed, the fallacies detected, the inferences drawn, and the several conclusions adjusted to their proper principles. Truth is disputable; not taste: what exists in the nature of things is the standard of our judgement; what each man feels within himself is the standard of sentiment. Propositions in geometry may be proved, systems in physics may be controverted; but the harmony of verse, the tenderness of passion, the brilliancy of wit, must give immediate pleasure. No man reasons concerning another's beauty; but frequently concerning the justice or injustice of his actions. In every criminal trial the first object of the prisoner is to disprove the facts alleged, and deny the actions imputed to him: the second to prove, that, even if these actions were real, they might be justified, as innocent and lawful. It is confessedly by deductions of the understanding, that the first point is ascertained: how can we suppose that a different faculty of the mind is employed in fixing the other?

On the other hand, those who would resolve all moral determinations into *sentiment*, may endeavour to show, that it is impossible for reason ever to draw conclusions of this nature. To virtue, say they, it belongs to be *amiable*, and vice *odious*. This forms their very nature or essence. But can reason or argumentation distribute these different epithets to any subjects, and pronounce beforehand, that this must produce love, and that hatred? Or what other reason can we ever assign for these affections, but the original fabric and formation of the human mind, which is naturally adapted to receive them?

The end of all moral speculations is to teach us our duty; and, by proper representations of the deformity of vice and beauty of virtue, beget correspondent habits, and engage us to avoid the one, and embrace the other. But is this ever to be expected from inferences and conclusions of the understanding, which of themselves have no hold of the affections nor set in motion the active powers of men? They discover truths: but where the truths which they discover are indifferent, and beget no desire or aversion, they can have no influence on conduct and behaviour. What is honourable, what is fair, what is becoming, what is noble, what is generous, takes possession of the heart, and animates us to embrace and maintain it. What is intelligible, what is evident, what is probable, what is true, procures only the cool assent of the understanding; and gratifying a speculative curiosity, puts an end to our researches.

Extinguish all the warm feelings and prepossessions in favour of virtue, and all disgust or aversion to vice; render men totally indifferent towards these distinctions; and morality is no longer a practical study, nor has any tendency to regulate our lives and actions.

These arguments on each side (and many more might be produced) are so plausible, that I am apt to suspect, they may, the one as well as the other, be solid and satisfactory, and that *reason* and *sentiment* concur in almost all moral determinations and conclusions. The final sentence, it is probable, which pronounces characters and actions amiable or odious, praise-worthy or blameable; that which stamps on them the mark of honour or infamy, approbation or censure; that which renders morality an active principle and constitutes virtue our happiness, and vice our misery: it is probable, I say, that this final sentence depends on some internal sense or feeling, which nature has made universal in the whole species. For what else can have an influence of this nature? But in order to pave the way for such a sentiment, and give a proper discernment of its object, it is often necessary, we find, that much reasoning should precede, that nice distinctions be made, just conclusions drawn, distant comparisons formed, complicated relations examined, and general facts fixed and ascertained. Some species of beauty, especially the natural kinds, on their first appearance, command our affection and approbation; and where they fail of this effect, it is impossible for any reasoning to redress their influence, or adapt them bet-

ter to our taste and sentiment. But in many orders of beauty, particularly those of the finer arts, it is requisite to employ much reasoning, in order to feel the proper sentiment; and a false relish may frequently be corrected by argument and reflection. There are just grounds to conclude, that moral beauty partakes much of this latter species, and demands the assistance of our intellectual faculties, in order to give it a suitable influence on the human mind.

But though this question, concerning the general principles of morals, be curious and important, it is needless for us, at present, to employ further care in our researches concerning it. For if we can be so happy, in the course of this enquiry, as to discover the true origin of morals, it will then easily appear how far either sentiment or reason enters into all determinations of this nature.[1] In order to attain this purpose, we shall endeavour to follow a very simple method; we shall analyse that complication of mental qualities, which form what, in common life, we call Personal Merit: we shall consider every attribute of the mind, which renders a man an object either of esteem and affection, or of hatred and contempt; every habit or sentiment or faculty, which, if ascribed to any person, implies either praise or blame, and may enter into any panegyric or satire of his character and manners. The quick sensibility, which, on this head, is so universal among mankind, gives a philosopher sufficient assurance, that he can never be considerably mistaken in framing the catalogue, or incur any danger of misplacing the objects of his contemplation: he needs only enter into his own breast for a moment, and consider whether or not he should desire to have this or that quality ascribed to him, and whether such or such an imputation would proceed from a friend or an enemy. The very nature of language guides us almost infallibly in forming a judgement of this nature; and as every tongue possesses one set of words which are taken in a good sense, and another in the opposite, the least acquaintance with the idiom suffices, without any reasoning, to direct us in collecting and arranging the estimable or blameable qualities of men. The only object of reasoning is to discover the circumstances on both sides, which are common to these qualities; to observe that particular in which the estimable qualities agree on the one hand, and the blameable on the other; and thence to reach the foundation of ethics, and find those universal principles, from which all censure or approbation is ultimately derived. As this is a question of fact, not of abstract science, we can only expect success, by following the experimental method, and deducing general maxims from a comparison of particular instances. The other scientific method, where a general abstract principle is first established, and is afterwards branched out into a variety of inferences and conclusions, may be more perfect in itself, but suits less the imperfection of human nature, and is a common source of illusion and mistake in this as well as in other subjects. Men are now cured of their passion for hypotheses and systems in natural philosophy, and will hearken to no arguments but those which are derived from experience. It is full time they should attempt a like reformation in all moral disquisitions; and reject every system of ethics, however subtle or ingenious, which is not founded on fact and observation.

We shall begin our enquiry on this head by the consideration of the social virtues, Benevolence and Justice. The explication of them will probably give us an opening by which the others may be accounted for.

Section II
Of Benevolence

Part I

It may be esteemed, perhaps, a superfluous task to prove, that the benevolent or softer affections are estimable; and wherever they appear, engage the approbation and good-will of mankind. The epithets *sociable, good-natured, humane, merciful, grateful, friendly, generous, beneficent,* or their equivalents, are known in all languages, and universally express the highest merit, which *human nature* is capable of attaining. Where these amiable qualities are attended with birth and power and eminent abilities, and display themselves in the good government or useful instruction of mankind, they seem even to raise the possessors of them above the rank of *human nature,*

and make them approach in some measure to the divine. Exalted capacity, undaunted courage, prosperous success; these may only expose a hero or politician to the envy and ill-will of the public: but as soon as the praises are added of humane and beneficent; when instances are displayed of lenity, tenderness or friendship; envy itself is silent, or joins the general voice of approbation and applause.

. . . .

Part II

We may observe that, in displaying the praises of any humane, beneficent man, there is one circumstance which never fails to be amply insisted on, namely, the happiness and satisfaction, derived to society from his intercourse and good offices. To his parents, we are apt to say, he endears himself by his pious attachment and duteous care still more than by the connexions of nature. His children never feel his authority, but when employed for their advantage. With him, the ties of love are consolidated by beneficence and friendship. The ties of friendship approach, in a fond observance of each obliging office, to those of love and inclination. His domestics and dependants have in him a sure resource; and no longer dread the power of fortune, but so far as she exercises it over him. From him the hungry receive food, the naked clothing, the ignorant and slothful skill and industry. Like the sun, an inferior minister of providence he cheers, invigorates, and sustains the surrounding world.

If confined to private life, the sphere of his activity is narrower; but his influence is all benign and gentle. If exalted into a higher station, mankind and posterity reap the fruit of his labours.

As these topics of praise never fail to be employed, and with success, where we would inspire esteem for any one; may it not thence be concluded, that the utility, resulting from the social virtues, forms, at least, a *part* of their merit, and is one source of that approbation and regard so universally paid to them?

. . . .

In all determinations of morality, this circumstance of public utility is ever principally in view; and wherever disputes arise, either in philosophy or common life, concerning the bounds of duty, the question cannot, by any means, be decided with greater certainty, than by ascertaining, on any side, the true interests of mankind. If any false opinion, embraced from appearances, has been found to prevail; as soon as farther experience and sounder reasoning have given us juster notions of human affairs, we retract our first sentiment, and adjust anew the boundaries of moral good and evil.

Giving alms to common beggars is naturally praised; because it seems to carry relief to the distressed and indigent: but when we observe the encouragement thence arising to idleness and debauchery, we regard that species of charity rather as a weakness than a virtue.

Tyrannicide, or the assassination of usurpers and oppressive princes, was highly extolled in ancient times; because it both freed mankind from many of these monsters, and seemed to keep the others in awe, whom the sword or poinard could not reach. But history and experience having since convinced us, that this practice increases the jealously and cruelty of princes, a Timoleon and a Brutus, though treated with indulgence on account of prejudices of their times, are now considered as very improper models for imitation.

Liberality in princes is regarded as a mark of beneficence, but when it occurs, that the homely bread of the honest and industrious is often thereby converted into delicious cates for the idle and the prodigal, we soon retract our heedless praises. The regrets of a prince, for having lost a day, were noble and generous; but had he intended to have spent it in acts of generosity to his greedy courtiers, it was better lost than misemployed after that manner.

Luxury, or a refinement on the pleasures and conveniencies of life, had long been supposed the source of every corruption in government, and the immediate cause of faction, sedition, civil wars, and the total loss of liberty. It was, therefore, universally regarded as a vice, and was an object of declamation to all satirists, and severe moralists. Those, who prove, or attempt to prove, that such refinements rather tend to the increase of industry, civility, and arts regulate anew our *moral* as well as *political* sentiments, and represent, as laudable or innocent, what had formerly been regarded as pernicious and blameable.

Upon the whole, then, it seems undeniable, *that* nothing can bestow more merit on any human creature than the sentiment of benevolence in an eminent degree; and *that* a *part*, at least, of its merit arises from its tendency to promote the interests of our species, and bestow happiness on human society. We carry our view into the salutary consequences of such a character and disposition; and whatever has so benign an influence, and forwards so desirable an end, is beheld with complacency and pleasure. The social virtues are never regarded without their beneficial tendencies, nor viewed as barren and unfruitful. The happiness of mankind, the order of society, and harmony of families, the mutual support of friends, are always considered as the result of their gentle dominion over the breasts of men.

How considerable a *part* of their merit we ought to ascribe to their utility, will better appear from future disquisitions[2]; as well as the reason, why this circumstance has such a command over our esteem and approbation.[3]

Section III
Of Justice

Part I

That Justice is useful to society, and consequently that *part* of its merit, at least, must arise from that consideration, it would be a superfluous undertaking to prove. That public utility is the *sole* origin of justice, and that reflections on the beneficial consequences of this virtue are the *sole* foundation of its merit; this proposition, being more curious and important, will better deserve our examination and enquiry.

Let us suppose that nature has bestowed on the human race such profuse *abundance* of all *external* conveniencies, that, without any uncertainty in the event, without any care or industry on our part, every individual finds himself fully provided with whatever his most voracious appetites can want, or luxurious imagination wish or desire. His natural beauty, we shall suppose, surpasses all acquired ornaments; the perpetual clemency of the seasons renders useless all clothes or covering: the raw herbage affords him the most delicious fare; the clear fountain, the richest beverage. No laborious occupation required: no tillage: no navigation. Music, poetry, and contemplation form his sole business: conversation, mirth, and friendship his sole amusement.

It seems evident that, in such a happy state, every other social virtue would flourish, and receive tenfold increase; but the cautious, jealous virtue of justice would never once have been dreamed of. For what purpose make a partition of goods, where every one has already more than enough? Why give rise to property, where there cannot possibly be any injury? Why call this object *mine*, when upon the seizing of it by another, I need but stretch out my hand to possess myself of what is equally valuable? Justice, in that case, being totally useless, would be an idle ceremonial, and could never possibly have place in the catalogue of virtues.

We see, even in the present necessitous condition of mankind, that, wherever any benefit is bestowed by nature in an unlimited abundance, we leave it always in common among the whole human race, and make no subdivisions of right and property. Water and air, though the most necessary of all objects, are not challenged as the property of individuals; nor can any man commit injustice by the most lavish use and enjoyment of these blessings. In fertile extensive countries, with few inhabitants, land is regarded on the same footing. And no topic is so much insisted on by those, who defend the liberty of the seas, as the unexhausted use of them in navigation. Were the advantages, procured by navigation, as inexhaustible, these reasoners had never had any adversaries to refute; nor had any claims ever been advanced of a separate, exclusive dominion over the ocean.

It may happen, in some countries, at some periods, that there be established a property in water, none in land; if the latter be in greater abundance than can be used by the inhabitants, and the former be found, with difficulty, and in very small quantities.

Again; suppose, that, though the necessities of the human race continue the same as the present, yet the mind is so enlarged, and so replete with friendship and generosity, that every man has the utmost tenderness for every man, and feels no more concern for his own interest than for that of his fellows; it seems evident, that the use of justice would, in this case, be suspended by such an extensive benevolence, nor would the divisions and barriers of property and obligation have ever been thought of. Why should I bind another, by a deed or promise, to do me any good office, when I know that he is already prompted, by the strongest inclination, to seek my happiness, and would, of himself, perform the desired service; except the hurt, he thereby receives, be greater than the benefit accruing to me? in which case, he knows, that, from my innate humanity and friendship, I should be the first to oppose myself to his imprudent generosity. Why raise land-marks between my neighbour's field and mine, when my heart has made no division between our interests; but shares all his joys and sorrows with the same force and vivacity as if originally my own? Every man, upon this supposition, being a second self to another, would trust all his interests to the discretion of every man; without jealousy, without partition, without distinction. And the whole human race would form only one family; where all would lie in common, and be used freely, without regard to property; but cautiously too, with as entire regard to the necessities of each individual, as if our own interests were most intimately concerned.

In the present disposition of the human heart, it would, perhaps, be difficult to find complete instances of such enlarged affections; but still we may observe, that the case of families approaches towards it; and the stronger the mutual benevolence is among the individuals, the nearer it approaches; till all distinction of property be, in a great measure, lost and confounded among them. Between married persons, the cement of friendship is by the laws supposed so strong as to abolish all division of possessions; and has often, in reality, the force ascribed to it. And it is observable, that, during the ardour of new enthusiasms, when every principle is inflamed into extravagance, the community of goods has frequently been attempted; and nothing but experience of its inconveniencies, from the returning or disguised selfishness of men, could make the imprudent fanatics adopt anew the ideas of justice and of separate property. So true is it, that this virtue derives its existence entirely from its necessary *use* to the intercourse and social state of mankind.

To make this truth more evident, let us reverse the foregoing suppositions; and carrying everything to the opposite extreme, consider what would be the effect of these new situations. Suppose a society to fall into such want of all common necessaries, that the utmost frugality and industry cannot preserve the greater number from perishing, and the whole from extreme misery; it will readily, I believe, be admitted, that the strict laws of justice are suspended, in such a pressing emergence, and give place to the stronger motives of necessity and self-preservation. Is it any crime, after a shipwreck, to seize whatever means or instrument of safety one can lay hold of, without regard to former limitations of property? Or if a city besieged were perishing with hunger; can we imagine, that men will see any means of preservation before them, and lose their lives, from a scrupulous regard to what, in other situations, would be the rules of equity and justice? The use and tendency of that virtue is to procure happiness and security, by preserving order in society: but where the society is ready to perish from extreme necessity, no greater evil can be dreaded from violence and injustice; and every man may now provide for himself by all the means which prudence can dictate, or humanity permit. The public, even in less urgent necessities, opens granaries, without the consent of proprietors; as justly supposing, that the authority of magistracy may, consistent with equity, extend so far: but were any number of men to assemble, without the tie of laws or civil jurisdiction; would an equal partition of bread in a famine, though effected by power and even violence, be regarded as criminal or injurious?

Suppose likewise, that it should be a virtuous man's fate to fall into the society of ruffians, remote from the protection of laws and government; what conduct must he embrace in that melancholy situation? He sees such a desperate rapaciousness prevail; such a disregard to equity, such contempt of order, such stupid blindness to future consequences, as must immediately have the most tragical conclusion, and must terminate in destruction to the greater number, and in a total dissolution of society to the rest. He, meanwhile, can have no other expedient than to arm himself, to whomever the sword he seizes, or the buckler, may belong: To make provision of all means of defence and security: And his particular regard to justice being no longer of use to his own safety or that of others, he must consult the dictates of self-preservation alone, without concern for those who no longer merit his care and attention.

When any man, even in political society, renders himself by his crimes, obnoxious to the public, he is punished by the laws in his goods and person; that is, the ordinary rules of justice are, with regard to him, suspended for a moment, and it becomes equitable to inflict on him, for the *benefit* of society, what otherwise he could not suffer without wrong or injury.

The rage and violence of public war; what is it but a suspension of justice among the warring parties, who perceive, that this virtue is now no longer of any *use* or advantage to them? The laws of war, which then succeed to those of equity and justice, are rules calculated for the *advantage* and *utility* of that particular state, in which men are now placed. And were a civilized nation engaged with barbarians, who observed no rules even of war, the former must also suspend their observance of them, where they no longer serve to any purpose; and must render every action or rencounter as bloody and pernicious as possible to the first aggressors.

Thus, the rules of equity or justice depend entirely on the particular state and condition in which men are placed, and owe their origin and existence to that utility, which results to the public from their strict and regular observance. Reverse, in any considerable circumstance, the condition of men: Produce extreme abundance or extreme necessity: Implant in the human breast perfect moderation and humanity, or perfect rapaciousness and malice: By rendering justice totally *useless*, you thereby totally destroy its essence, and suspend its obligation upon mankind.

The common situation of society is a medium amidst all these extremes. We are naturally partial to ourselves, and to our friends; but are capable of learning the advantage resulting from a more equitable conduct. Few enjoyments are given us from the open and liberal hand of nature; but by art, labour, and industry, we can extract them in great abundance. Hence the ideas of property become necessary in all civil society: Hence justice derives its usefulness to the public: And hence alone arises its merit and moral obligation.

. . . .

The more we vary our views of human life, and the newer and more unusual the lights are in which we survey it, the more shall we be convinced, that the origin here assigned for the virtue of justice is real and satisfactory.

Were there a species of creatures intermingled with men, which, though rational, were possessed of such inferior strength, both of body and mind, that they were incapable of all resistance, and could never, upon the highest provocation, make us feel the effects of their resentment; the necessary consequence, I think, is that we should be bound by the laws of humanity to give gentle usage to these creatures, but should not, properly speaking, lie under any restraint of justice with regard to them, nor could they possess any right or property, exclusive of such arbitrary lords. Our intercourse with them could not be called society, which supposes a degree of equality; but absolute command on the one side, and servile obedience on the other. Whatever we covet, they must instantly resign: Our permission is the only tenure, by which they hold their possessions: Our compassion and kindness the only check, by which they curb our lawless will: And as no inconvenience ever results from the exercise of a power, so firmly established in nature, the restraints of justice and property, being totally *useless*, would never have place in so unequal a confederacy.

This is plainly the situation of men, with regard to animals; and how far these may be said to possess reason, I leave it to others to determine. The great superiority of civilized Europeans above barbarous Indians, tempted us to imagine ourselves on the same footing with regard to them, and made us throw off all restraints of justice, and even of humanity, in our treatment of them. In many nations, the female sex are reduced to like slavery, and are rendered incapable for all property, in opposition to their lordly masters. But though the males, when united, have in all countries bodily force sufficient to maintain this severe tyranny, yet such are the insinuation, address, and charms of their fair companions, that women are commonly able to break the confederacy, and share with the other sex in all the rights and privileges of society.

Were the human species so framed by nature as that each individual possessed within himself every faculty, requisite both for his own preservation and for the propagation of his kind: Were all society and intercourse cut off between man and man, by the primary intention of the supreme Creator: It seems evident, that so solitary a being would be as much incapable of justice, as of social discourse and conversation. Where mutual regards and forbearance serve to no manner of purpose, they would never direct the conduct of any reasonable man. The headlong course of the passions would be checked by no reflection on future consequences. And as each man is here supposed to love himself alone, and to depend only on himself and his own activity for safety and happiness, he would, on every occasion, to the utmost of his power, challenge the preference above every other being, to none of which he is bound by any ties, either of nature or of interest.

But suppose the conjunction of the sexes to be established in nature, a family immediately arises; and particular rules being found requisite for its subsistence, these are immediately embraced; though without comprehending the rest of mankind within their prescriptions. Suppose that several families unite together into one society, which is totally disjoined from all others, the rules, which preserve peace and order, enlarge themselves to the utmost extent of that society; but becoming then entirely useless, lose their force when carried one step farther. But again suppose, that several distinct societies maintain a kind of intercourse for mutual convenience and advantage, the boundaries of justice still grow larger, in proportion to the largeness of men's views, and the force of their mutual connexions. History, experience, reason sufficiently instruct us in this natural progress of human sentiments, and in the gradual enlargement of our regards to justice, in proportion as we become acquainted with the extensive utility of that virtue.

. . . .

Section V
Why Utility Pleases

Part I

It seems so natural a thought to ascribe to their utility the praise, which we bestow on the social virtues, that one would expect to meet with this principle everywhere in moral writers, as the chief foundation of their reasoning and enquiry. In common life, we may observe, that the circumstance of utility is always appealed to; nor is it supposed, that a greater eulogy can be given to any man, than to display his usefulness to the public, and enumerate the services, which he has performed to mankind and society. What praise, even of an inanimate form, if the regularity and elegance of its parts destroy not its fitness for any useful purpose! And how satisfactory an apology for any disproportion or seeming deformity, if we can show the necessity of that particular construction for the use intended! A ship appears more beautiful to an artist, or one moderately skilled in navigation, where its prow is wide and swelling beyond its poop, than if it were framed with a precise geometrical regularity, in contradiction to all the laws of mechanics. A building, whose doors and windows were exact squares, would hurt the eye by that very proportion; as ill adapted to the figure of a human creature, for whose service the fabric was intended. What wonder then, that a man, whose habits and conduct are hurtful to society, and dangerous or pernicious to every one who has an intercourse with him, should, on that account, be an object of disapprobation, and communicate to every spectator the strongest sentiment of disgust and hatred.

But perhaps the difficulty of accounting for these effects of usefulness, or its contrary, has kept philosophers from admitting them into their systems of ethics, and has induced them rather to employ any other principle, in explaining the origin of moral good and evil. But it is no just reason for rejecting any principle, confirmed by experience, that we cannot give a satisfactory account of its origin, nor are able to resolve it into other more general principles. And if we would employ a little thought on the present subject, we need be at no loss to account for the influence of utility, and to deduce it from principles, the most known and avowed in human nature.

From the apparent usefulness of the social virtues, it has readily been inferred by sceptics, both ancient and modern, that all moral distinctions arise from education, and were, at first, invented, and afterwards encouraged, by the art of politicians, in order to render men tractable, and subdue their natural ferocity and selfishness, which incapacitated them for society. This principle, indeed, of precept and education, must so far be owned to have a powerful influence, that it may frequently increase or diminish, beyond their natural standard, the sentiments of approbation or dislike; and may even, in particular instances, create, without any natural principle, a new sentiment of this kind; as is evident in all superstitious practices and observances: But that *all* moral affection or dislike arises from this origin, will never surely be allowed by any judicious enquirer. Had nature made no such distinction, founded on the original constitution of the mind, the words, *honourable* and *shameful, lovely* and *odious, noble* and *despicable*, had never had place in any language; nor could politicians, had they invented these terms, ever have been able to render them intelligible, or make them convey any idea to the audience. So that nothing can be more superficial than this paradox of the sceptics; and it were well, if, in the abstruser studies of logic and metaphysics, we could as easily obviate the cavils of that sect, as in the practical and more intelligible sciences of politics and morals.

The social virtues must, therefore, be allowed to have a natural beauty and amiableness, which, at first, antecedent to all precept or education, recommends them to the esteem of uninstructed mankind, and engages their affections. And as the public utility of these virtues is the chief circumstance, whence they derive their merit, it follows, that the end, which they have a tendency to promote, must be some way agreeable to us, and take hold of some natural affection. It must please, either from considerations of self-interest, or from more generous motives and regards.

It has often been asserted, that, as every man has a strong connexion with society, and perceives the impossibility of his solitary subsistence, he becomes, on that account, favourable to all those habits or principles, which promote order in society, and insure to him the quiet possession of so inestimable a blessing. As much as we value our own happiness and welfare, as much must we applaud the practice of justice and humanity, by which alone the social confederacy can be maintained, and every man reap the fruits of mutual protection and assistance.

This deduction of morals from self-love, or a regard to private interest, is an obvious thought, and has not arisen wholly from the wanton sallies and sportive assaults of the sceptics. To mention no others, Polybius, one of the gravest and most judicious, as well as most moral writers of antiquity, has assigned this selfish origin to all our sentiments of virtue. But though the solid practical sense of that author, and his aversion to all vain subtilties, render his authority on the present subject very considerable; yet is not this an affair to be decided by authority, and the voice of nature and experience seems plainly to oppose the selfish theory.

We frequently bestow praise on virtuous actions, performed in very distant ages and remote countries; where the utmost subtilty of imagination would not discover any appearance of self-interest, or find any connexion of our present happiness and security with events so widely separated from us.

A generous, a brave, a noble deed, performed by an adversary, commands our approbation; while in its consequences it may be acknowledged prejudicial to our particular interest.

Where private advantage concurs with general affection for virtue, we readily perceive and avow the mixture of these distinct sentiments, which have a very different feeling and influence on the mind. We praise, perhaps, with more alacrity, where the generous humane action contributes to our particular interest: But the topics of praise, which we insist on, are very wide of this circumstance. And we may attempt to bring over others to our sentiments, without endeavouring to convince them, that they reap any advantage from the actions which we recommend to their approbation and applause.

Frame the model of a praiseworthy character, consisting of all the most amiable moral virtues: Give instances, in which these display themselves after an eminent and extraordinary manner: You readily engage the esteem and approbation of all your audience, who never so much as enquire in what age and country the person lived, who possessed these noble qualities: A circumstance, however, of all others, the most material to self-love, or a concern for our own individual happiness.

Once on a time, a statesman, in the shock and contest of parties, prevailed so far as to procure, by his eloquence, the banishment of an able adversary; whom he secretly followed, offering him money for his support during his exile, and soothing him with topics of consolation in his misfortunes. *Alas*! cries the banished statesman, *with what regret must I leave my friends in this city, where even enemies are so generous*! Virtue, though in an enemy, here pleased him: And we also give it the just tribute of praise and approbation; nor do we retract these sentiments, when we hear, that the action passed at Athens, about two thousand years ago, and that the persons names were Eschines and Demosthenes.

What is that to me? There are few occasions, when this question is not pertinent: And had it that universal, infallible influence supposed, it would turn into ridicule every composition, and almost every conversation, which contain any praise or censure of men and manners.

It is but a weak subterfuge, when pressed by these facts and arguments, to say, that we transport ourselves, by the force of imagination, into distant ages and countries, and consider the advantage, which we should have reaped from these characters, had we been contemporaries, and had any commerce with the persons. It is not conceivable, how a *real* sentiment or passion can ever arise from a known *imaginary* interest; especially when our *real* interest is still kept in view, and is often acknowledged to be entirely distinct from the imaginary, and even sometimes opposite to it.

A man, brought to the brink of a precipice, cannot look down without trembling; and the sentiment of *imaginary* danger actuates him, in opposition to the opinion and belief of *real* safety. But the imagination is here assisted by the presence of a striking object; and yet prevails not, except to be also aided by novelty, and the unusual appearance of the object. Custom soon reconciles us to heights and precipices, and wears off these false and delusive terrors. The reverse is observable in the estimates which we form of characters and manners; and the more we habituate ourselves to an accurate scrutiny of morals, the more delicate feeling do we acquire of the most minute distinctions between vice and virtue. Such frequent occasion, indeed, have we, in common life, to pronounce all kinds of moral determinations, that no object of this kind can be new or unusual to us; nor could any *false* views or pre-possessions maintain their ground against an experience, so common and familiar. Experience being chiefly what forms the associations of ideas, it is impossible that any association could establish and support itself, in direct opposition to that principle.

Usefulness is agreeable, and engages our approbation. This is a matter of fact, confirmed by daily observation. But, *useful?* For what? For somebody's interest, surely. Whose interest then? Not our own only: For our approbation frequently extends farther. It must, therefore, be the interest of those, who are served by the character or action approved of; and these we may conclude, however remote, are not totally indifferent to us. By opening up this principle, we shall discover one great source of moral distinctions.

Part II

Self-love is a principle in human nature of such extensive energy, and the interest of each individual is, in general, so closely connected with that of the community, that those philosophers were excusable, who fancied that all our concern for the public might be resolved into a concern for our own happiness and preservation. They saw every moment, instances of approbation or blame, satisfaction or displeasure towards characters and actions; they denominated the objects of these sentiments, *virtues*, or *vices*; they observed, that the former had a tendency to increase the happiness, and the latter the misery of mankind; they asked, whether it were possible that we could have any general concern for society, or any disinterested resentment of the welfare or injury of others; they found it simpler to consider all these sentiments as modifications of self-love; and they discovered a pretence, at least, for this unity of principle, in that close union of interest, which is so observable between the public and each individual.

But notwithstanding this frequent confusion of interests, it is easy to attain what natural philosophers, after Lord Bacon, have affected to call the *experimentum crucis*, or that experiment which points out the right way in any doubt or ambiguity. We have found instances, in which private interest was

separate from public; in which it was even contrary: And yet we observed the moral sentiment to continue, notwithstanding this disjunction of interests. And whenever these distinct interests sensibly concurred, we always found a sensible increase of the sentiment, and a more warm affection to virtue, and detestation of vice, or what we properly call, *gratitude* and *revenge*. Compelled by these instances, we must renounce the theory, which accounts for every moral sentiment by the principle of self-love. We must adopt a more public affection, and allow, that the interests of society are not, even on their own account, entirely indifferent to us. Usefulness is only a tendency to a certain end; and it is a contradiction in terms, that anything pleases as means to an end, where the end itself no wise affects us. If usefulness, therefore, be a source of moral sentiment, and if this usefulness be not always considered with a reference to self; it follows, that everything, which contributes to the happiness of society, recommends itself directly to our approbation and good-will. Here is a principle, which accounts, in great part, for the origin of morality: And what need we seek for abstruse and remote systems, when there occurs one so obvious and natural?[4]

Have we any difficulty to comprehend the force of humanity and benevolence? Or to conceive, that the very aspect of happiness, joy, prosperity, gives pleasure; that of pain, suffering, sorrow, communicates uneasiness? The human countenance, says Horace, borrows smiles or tears from the human countenance. Reduce a person to solitude, and he loses all enjoyment, except either of the sensual or speculative kind; and that because the movements of his heart are not forwarded by correspondent movements in his fellow-creatures. The signs of sorrow and mourning, though arbitrary, affect us with melancholy; but the natural symptoms, tears and cries and groans, never fail to infuse compassion and uneasiness. And if the effects of misery touch us in so lively a manner; can we be supposed altogether insensible or indifferent towards its causes; when a malicious or treacherous character and behaviour are presented to us?

We enter, I shall suppose, into a convenient, warm, well-contrived apartment: We necessarily receive a pleasure from its very survey; because it presents us with the pleasing ideas of ease, satisfaction, and enjoyment. The hospitable, good-humoured, humane landlord appears. This circumstance surely must embellish the whole; nor can we easily forbear reflecting, with pleasure, on the satisfaction which results to every one from his intercourse and good-offices.

His whole family, by the freedom, ease, confidence, and calm enjoyment, diffused over their countenances, sufficiently express their happiness. I have a pleasing sympathy in the prospect of so much joy, and can never consider the source of it, without the most agreeable emotions.

He tells me, that an oppressive and powerful neighbour had attempted to dispossess him of his inheritance, and had long disturbed all his innocent and social pleasures. I feel an immediate indignation arise in me against such violence and injury.

But it is no wonder, he adds, that a private wrong should proceed from a man, who had enslaved provinces, depopulated cities, and made the field and scaffold stream with human blood. I am struck with horror at the prospect of so much misery, and am actuated by the strongest antipathy against its author.

In general, it is certain, that, wherever we go, whatever we reflect on or converse about, everything still presents us with the view of human happiness or misery, and excites in our breast a sympathetic movement of pleasure or uneasiness. In our serious occupations, in our careless amusements, this principle still exerts its active energy.

. . . .

If any man from a cold insensibility, or narrow selfishness of temper, is unaffected with the images of human happiness or misery, he must be equally indifferent to the images of vice and virtue: As, on the other hand, it is always found, that a warm concern for the interests of our species is attended with a delicate feeling of all moral distinctions; a strong resentment of injury done to men; a lively approbation of their welfare. In this particular, though great superiority is observable of one man above another; yet none are so entirely indifferent to the interest of their fellow-creatures, as to perceive no distinctions of moral good and evil, in consequence of the different tendencies of actions and principles. How, indeed, can we suppose it possible in any one, who wears a human heart, that if there be subjected

to his censure, one character or system of conduct, which is beneficial, and another which is pernicious, to his species or community, he will not so much as give a cool preference to the former, or ascribe to it the smallest merit or regard? Let us suppose such a person ever so selfish; let private interest have ingrossed ever so much his attention; yet in instances, where that is not concerned, he must unavoidably feel *some* propensity to the good of mankind, and make it an object of choice, if everything else be equal. Would any man, who is walking along, tread as willingly on another's gouty toes, whom he has no quarrel with, as on the hard flint and pavement? There is here surely a difference in the case. We surely take into consideration the happiness and misery of others, in weighing the several motives of action, and incline to the former, where no private regards draw us to seek our own promotion or advantage by the injury of our fellow-creatures. And if the principles of humanity are capable, in many instances, of influencing our actions, they must, at all times, have *some* authority over our sentiments, and give us a general approbation of what is useful to society, and blame of what is dangerous or pernicious. The degrees of these sentiments may be the subject of controversy; but the reality of their existence, one should think, must be admitted in every theory or system.

. . . .

A statesman or patriot, who serves our own country in our own time, has always a more passionate regard paid to him, than one whose beneficial influence operated on distant ages or remote nations; where the good, resulting from his generous humanity, being less connected with us, seems more obscure, and affects us with a less lively sympathy. We may own the merit to be equally great, though our sentiments are not raised to an equal height, in both cases. The judgment here corrects the inequalities of our internal emotions and perceptions; in like manner, as it preserves us from error, in the several variations of images, presented to our external senses. The same object, at a double distance, really throws on the eye a picture of but half the bulk; yet we imagine that it appears of the same size in both situations; because we know that on our approach to it, its image would expand on the eye, and that the difference consists not in the object itself, but in our position with regard to it. And, indeed, without such a correction of appearances, both in internal and external sentiment, men could never think or talk steadily on any subject; while their fluctuating situations produce a continual variation on objects, and throw them into such different and contrary lights and positions.[5]

The more we converse with mankind, and the greater social intercourse we maintain, the more shall we be familiarized to these general preferences and distinctions, without which our conversation and discourse could scarcely be rendered intelligible to each other. Every man's interest is peculiar to himself, and the aversions and desires, which result from it, cannot be supposed to affect others in a like degree. General language, therefore, being formed for general use, must be moulded on some more general views, and must affix the epithets of praise or blame, in conformity to sentiments, which arise from the general interests of the community. And if these sentiments, in most men, be not so strong as those, which have a reference to private good; yet still they must make some distinction, even in persons the most depraved and selfish; and must attach the notion of good to a beneficent conduct, and of evil to the contrary. Sympathy, we shall allow, is much fainter than our concern for ourselves, and sympathy with persons remote from us much fainter than that with persons near and contiguous; but for this very reason it is necessary for us, in our calm judgements and discourse concerning the characters of men, to neglect all these differences, and render our sentiments more public and social. Besides, that we ourselves often change our situation in this particular, we every day meet with persons who are in a situation different from us, and who could never converse with us were we to remain constantly in that position and point of view, which is peculiar to ourselves. The intercourse of sentiments, therefore, in society and conversation, makes us form some general unalterable standard, by which we may approve or disapprove of characters and manners. And though the heart takes not part entirely with those general notions, nor regulates all its love and hatred, by the universal abstract differences of vice and virtue, without regard to self, or the persons with

whom we are more intimately connected; yet have these moral differences a considerable influence, and being sufficient, at least, for discourse, serve all our purposes in company, in the pulpit, on the theatre, and in the schools.

Thus, in whatever light we take this subject, the merit, ascribed to the social virtues, appears still uniform, and arises chiefly from that regard, which the natural sentiment of benevolence engages us to pay to the interests of mankind and society. If we consider the principles of the human make, such as they appear to daily experience and observation, we must, a priori, conclude it impossible for such a creature as man to be totally indifferent to the well or ill-being of his fellow-creatures, and not readily, of himself, to pronounce, where nothing gives him any particular bias, that what promotes their happiness is good, what tends to their misery is evil, without any farther regard to consideration. Here then are the faint rudiments, at least, or outlines, of a *general* distinction between actions; and in proportion as the humanity of the person is supposed to encrease, his connexion with those who are injured or benefited, and his lively conception of their misery or happiness; his consequent censure or approbation acquires proportionable vigour. There is no necessity, that a generous action, barely mentioned in an old history or remote gazette, should communicate any strong feelings of applause and admiration. Virtue, placed at such a distance, is like a fixed star, which, though to the eye of reason it may appear as luminous as the sun in his meridian, is so infinitely removed as to affect the senses, neither with light nor heat. Bring this virtue nearer, by our acquaintance or connexion with the persons, or even by an eloquent recital of the case; our hearts are immediately caught, our sympathy enlivened, and our cool approbation converted into the warmest sentiments of friendship and regard. These seem necessary and infallible consequences of the general principles of human nature, as discovered in common life and practice.

Again; reverse these views and reasonings: Consider the matter a posteriori; and weighing the consequences, enquire if the merit of social virtue be not, in a great measure, derived from the feelings of humanity, with which it affects the spectators. It appears to be matter of fact, that the circumstance of *utility*, in all subjects, is a source of praise and approbation: That it is constantly appealed to in all moral decisions concerning the merit and demerit of actions: That it is the *sole* source of that high regard paid to justice, fidelity, honour, allegiance, and chastity: That it is inseparable from all the other social virtues, humanity, generosity, charity, affability, lenity, mercy, and moderation: And, in a word, that it is a foundation of the chief part of morals, which has a reference to mankind and our fellow-creatures.

It appears also, that, in our general approbation of characters and manners, the useful tendency of the social virtues moves us not by any regards to self-interest, but has an influence much more universal and extensive. It appears that a tendency to public good, and to the promoting of peace, harmony, and order in society, does always, by affecting the benevolent principles of our frame, engage us on the side of social virtues. And it appears, as an additional confirmation, that these principles of humanity and sympathy enter so deeply into all our sentiments, and have so powerful an influence, as may enable them to excite the strongest censure and applause. The present theory is the simple result of all these influences, each of which seems founded on uniform experience and observation.

Were it doubtful, whether there were any such principle in our nature as humanity or a concern for others, yet when we see, in numberless instances, that whatever has a tendency to promote the interests of society, is so highly approved of, we ought thence to learn the force of the benevolent principle; since it is impossible for anything to please as means to an end, where the end is totally indifferent. On the other hand, were it doubtful, whether there were, implanted in our nature, any general principle of moral blame and approbation, yet when we see, in numberless instances, the influence of humanity, we ought thence to conclude, that it is impossible, but that everything which promotes the interest of society must communicate pleasure, and what is pernicious give uneasiness. But when these different reflections and observations concur in establishing the same conclusion, must they not bestow an undisputed evidence upon it?

. . . .

Section IX
Conclusion

Part I

It may justly appear surprising that any man in so late an age, should find it requisite to prove, by elaborate reasoning, that Personal Merit consists altogether in the possession of mental qualities, *useful* or *agreeable* to the *person himself* or to *others*. It might be expected that this principle would have occurred even to the first rude, unpractised enquirers concerning morals, and been received from its own evidence, without any argument or disputation. Whatever is valuable in any kind, so naturally classes itself under the division of *useful* or *agreeable*, the *utile* or the *dulce*, that it is not easy to imagine why we should ever seek further, or consider the question as a matter of nice research or inquiry. And as every thing useful or agreeable must possess these qualities with regard either to the *person himself* or to *others*, the complete delineation or description of merit seems to be performed as naturally as a shadow is cast by the sun, or an image is reflected upon water.

. . . .

And as every quality which is useful or agreeable to ourselves or others is, in common life, allowed to be a part of personal merit; so no other will ever be received, where men judge of things by their natural, unprejudiced reason, without the delusive glosses of superstition and false religion. Celibacy, fasting, penance, mortification, self-denial, humility, silence, solitude, and the whole train of monkish virtues; for what reason are they everywhere rejected by men of sense, but because they serve to no manner of purpose; neither advance a man's fortune in the world, nor render him a more valuable member of society; neither qualify him for the entertainment of company, nor increase his power of self-enjoyment? We observe, on the contrary, that they cross all these desirable ends; stupify the understanding and harden the heart, obscure the fancy and sour the temper. We justly, therefore, transfer them to the opposite column, and place them in the catalogue of vices; nor has any superstition force sufficient among men of the world, to pervert entirely these natural sentiments. A gloomy, hair-brained enthusiast, after his death, may have a place in the calendar; but will scarcely ever be admitted, when alive, into intimacy and society, except by those who are as delirious and dismal as himself.

It seems a happiness in the present theory, that it enters not into that vulgar dispute concerning the *degrees* of benevolence or self-love, which prevail in human nature; a dispute which is never likely to have any issue, both because men, who have taken part, are not easily convinced, and because the phenomena, which can be produced on either side, are so dispersed, so uncertain, and subject to so many interpretations, that it is scarcely possible accurately to compare them, or draw from them any determinate inference or conclusion. It is sufficient for our present purpose, if it be allowed, what surely, without the greatest absurdity cannot be disputed, that there is some benevolence, however small, infused into our bosom; some spark of friendship for human kind; some particle of the dove kneaded into our frame, along with the elements of the wolf and serpent. Let these generous sentiments be supposed ever so weak; let them be insufficient to move even a hand or finger of our body, they must still direct the determinations of our mind, and where everything else is equal, produce a cool preference of what is useful and serviceable to mankind, above what is pernicious and dangerous. A *moral distinction*, therefore, immediately arises; a general sentiment of blame and approbation; a tendency, however faint, to the objects of the one, and a proportionable aversion to those of the other. Nor will those reasoners, who so earnestly maintain the predominant selfishness of human kind, be any wise scandalized at hearing of the weak sentiments of virtue implanted in our nature. On the contrary, they are found as ready to maintain the one tenet as the other; and their spirit of satire (for such it appears, rather than of corruption) naturally gives rise to both opinions; which have, indeed, a great and almost an indissoluble connexion together.

Avarice, ambition, vanity, and all passions vulgarly, though improperly, comprised under the denomination of *self-love*, are here excluded from our theory concerning the origin of morals, not because they are too weak, but because they have not a proper direction for that purpose. The notion of morals implies some sentiment common to all mankind, which recommends the same object to general approbation, and makes every man, or most men, agree in the same opinion or decision concerning it. It also implies some sentiment, so universal and comprehensive as to extend to all mankind, and render the actions and conduct, even of the persons the most remote, an object of applause or censure, according as they agree or disagree with that rule of right which is established. These two requisite circumstances belong alone to the sentiment of humanity here insisted on. The other passions produce in every breast, many strong sentiments of desire and aversion, affection and hatred; but these neither are felt so much in common, nor are so comprehensive, as to be the foundation of any general system and established theory of blame or approbation.

When a man denominates another his *enemy*, his *rival*, his *antagonist*, his *adversary*, he is understood to speak the language of self-love, and to express sentiments, peculiar to himself, and arising from his particular circumstances and situation. But when he bestows on any man the epithets of *vicious* or *odious* or *depraved*, he then speaks another language, and expresses sentiments, in which he expects all his audience are to concur with him. He must here, therefore, depart from his private and particular situation, and must choose a point of view, common to him with others; he must move some universal principle of the human frame, and touch a string to which all mankind have an accord and symphony. If he mean, therefore, to express that this man possesses qualities, whose tendency is pernicious to society, he has chosen this common point of view, and has touched the principle of humanity, in which every man, in some degree, concurs. While the human heart is compounded of the same elements as at present, it will never be wholly indifferent to public good, nor entirely unaffected with the tendency of characters and manners. And though this affection of humanity may not generally be esteemed so strong as vanity or ambition, yet, being common to all men, it can alone be the foundation of morals, or of any general system of blame or praise. One man's ambition is not another's ambition, nor will the same event or object satisfy both; but the humanity of one man is the humanity of every one, and the same object touches this passion in all human creatures.

But the sentiments, which arise from humanity, are not only the same in all human creatures, and produce the same approbation or censure; but they also comprehend all human creatures; nor is there any one whose conduct or character is not, by their means, an object to every one of censure or approbation. On the contrary, those other passions, commonly denominated selfish, both produce different sentiments in each individual, according to his particular situation; and also contemplate the greater part of mankind with the utmost indifference and unconcern. Whoever has a high regard and esteem for me flatters my vanity; whoever expresses contempt mortifies and displeases me; but as my name is known but to a small part of mankind, there are few who come within the sphere of this passion, or excite, on its account, either my affection or disgust. But if you represent a tyrannical, insolent, or barbarous behaviour, in any country or in any age of the world, I soon carry my eye to the pernicious tendency of such a conduct, and feel the sentiment of repugnance and displeasure towards it. No character can be so remote as to be, in this light, wholly indifferent to me. What is beneficial to society or to the person himself must still be preferred. And every quality or action, of every human being, must, by this means, be ranked under some class or denomination, expressive of general censure or applause.

What more, therefore, can we ask to distinguish the sentiments, dependent on humanity, from those connected with any other passion, or to satisfy us, why the former are the origin of morals, not the latter? Whatever conduct gains my approbation, by touching my humanity, procures also the applause of all mankind, by affecting the same principle in them; but what serves my avarice or ambition pleases these passions in me alone, and affects not the avarice and ambition of the rest of mankind. There is no circumstance of conduct in any man, provided it have a beneficial tendency, that is not agreeable to my humanity, however remote the person; but every man, so far removed as neither to cross nor serve my avarice and ambition, is regarded as wholly indifferent by those passions. The distinction, therefore, between these species of sentiment being so great and evident, language must soon be moulded upon it, and must invent a peculiar set of terms, in order to express those universal sentiments of censure or approbation, which arise from humanity, or from views of general usefulness and its contrary. Virtue and Vice become then known; morals are recognized; certain general ideas are framed of human conduct and behaviour; such measures are expected from men in such situations. This action is determined to be conformable to our abstract rule; that other, contrary. And by such universal principles are the particular sentiments of self-love frequently controlled and limited.

From instances of popular tumults, seditions, factions, panics, and of all passions, which are shared with a multitude, we may learn the influence of society in exciting and supporting any emotion; while the most ungovernable disorders are raised, we find, by that means, from the slightest and most frivolous occasions. Solon was no very cruel, though, perhaps, an unjust legislator, who punished neuters in civil wars; and few, I believe, would, in such cases, incur the penalty, were their affection and discourse allowed sufficient to absolve them. No selfishness, and scarce any philosophy, have there force sufficient to support a total coolness and indifference; and he must be more or less than man, who kindles not in the common blaze. What wonder then, that moral sentiments are found of such influence in life; though springing from principles, which may appear, at first sight, somewhat small and delicate? But these principles, we must remark, are social and universal; they form, in a manner, the *party* of humankind against vice or disorder, its common enemy. And as the benevolent concern for others is diffused, in a greater or less degree, over all men, and is the same in all, it occurs more frequently in discourse, is cherished by society and conversation, and the blame and approbation, consequent on it, are thereby roused from that lethargy into which they are probably lulled, in solitary and uncultivated nature. Other passions though perhaps originally stronger, yet being selfish and private, are often overpowered by its force, and yield the dominion of our breast to those social and public principles.

. . . .

Part II

Having explained the moral *approbation* attending merit or virtue, there remains nothing but briefly to consider our interested *obligation* to it, and to inquire whether every man, who has any regard to his own happiness and welfare, will not best find his account in the practice of every moral duty. If this can be clearly ascertained from the foregoing theory, we shall have the satisfaction to reflect, that we have advanced principles, which not only, it is hoped, will stand the test of reasoning and inquiry, but may contribute to the amendment of men's lives, and their improvement in morality and social virtue. And though the philosophical truth of any proposition by no means depends on its tendency to promote the interests of society; yet a man has but a bad grace, who delivers a theory, however true, which, he must confess, leads to a practice dangerous and pernicious. Why rake into those corners of nature which spread a nuisance all around? Why dig up the pestilence from the pit in which it is buried? The ingenuity of your researches may be admired, but your systems will be detested; and mankind will agree, if they cannot refute them, to sink them, at least, in eternal silence and oblivion. Truths which are *pernicious* to society, if any such there be, will yield to errors which are salutary and *advantageous*.

But what philosophical truths can be more advantageous to society, than those here delivered, which represent virtue in all her genuine and most engaging charms, and make us approach her with ease, familiarity, and affection? The dismal dress falls off, with which many divines, and some philosophers, have covered her; and nothing appears but gentleness, humanity beneficence, affability; nay, even at proper intervals, play, frolic, and gaiety. She talks not of useless austerities and rigours, suffering and self-denial. She declares that her sole purpose is to make her votaries and all mankind, during every instant of their existence, if possible, cheerful and happy; nor does she ever willingly part with any pleasure but in hopes of ample compensation in some other period of their lives. The sole trouble which she demands, is that of just calculation, and a steady preference of the greater happiness. And if any austere pretenders approach her, enemies to joy and pleasure, she either rejects them as hypocrites and deceivers; or, if she admit them in her train, they are ranked, however, among the least favoured of her votaries.

And, indeed, to drop all figurative expression, what hopes can we ever have of engaging mankind to a practice which we confess full of austerity and rigour? Or what theory of morals can ever serve any useful purpose, unless it can show, by a particular detail, that all the duties which it recommends, are also the true interest of each individual? The peculiar advantage of the foregoing system seems to be, that it furnishes proper mediums for that purpose.

That the virtues which are immediately *useful* or *agreeable* to the person possessed of them, are desirable in a view of self-interest, it would surely be superfluous to prove. Moralists, indeed, may spare themselves all the pains which they often take in recommending these duties. To what purpose collect arguments to evince that temperance is advantageous, and the excesses of pleasure hurtful. When it appears that these excesses are only denominated such, because they are hurtful; and that, if the unlimited use of strong liquors, for instance, no more impaired health or the faculties of mind and body than the use of air or water, it would not be a whit more vicious or blameable.

It seems equally superfluous to prove, that the *companionable* virtues of good manners and wit, decency and genteelness, are more desirable than the contrary qualities. Vanity alone, without any other consideration, is a sufficient motive to make us wish for the possession of these accomplishments. No man was ever willingly deficient in this particular. All our failures here proceed from bad education, want of capacity, or a perverse and unpliable disposition. Would you have your company coveted, admired, followed; rather than hated, despised, avoided? Can any one seriously deliberate in the case? As no enjoyment is sincere, without some reference to company and society; so no society can be agreeable, or even tolerable, where a man feels his presence unwelcome, and discovers all around him symptoms of disgust and aversion.

But why, in the greater society or confederacy of mankind, should not the case be the same as in particular clubs and companies? Why is it more doubtful, that the enlarged virtues of humanity, generosity, beneficence, are desirable with a view to happiness and self-interest, than the limited endowments of ingenuity and politeness? Are we apprehensive lest those social affections interfere, in a greater and more immediate degree than any other pursuits, with private utility, and cannot be gratified, without some important sacrifice of honour and advantage? If so, we are but ill-instructed in the nature of the human passions, and are more influenced by verbal distinctions than by real differences.

Whatever contradiction may vulgarly be supposed between the *selfish* and *social* sentiments or dispositions, they are really no more opposite than selfish and ambitious, selfish and revengeful, selfish and vain. It is requisite that there be an original propensity of some kind, in order to be a basis to self-love, by giving a relish to the objects of its pursuit; and none more fit for this purpose than benevolence or humanity. The goods of fortune are spent in one gratification or another; the miser who accumulates his annual income, and lends it out at interest, has really spent it in the gratification of his avarice. And it would be difficult to show why a man is more a loser by a generous action, than by any other method of expense; since the utmost which he can attain by the most elaborate selfishness, is the indulgence of some affection.

Now if life, without passion, must be altogether insipid and tiresome; let a man suppose that he has full power of modelling his own disposition, and let him deliberate what appetite or desire he would choose for the foundation of his happiness and enjoyment. Every affection, he would observe, when gratified by success, gives a satisfaction proportioned to its force and violence; but besides this advantage, common to all, the immediate feeling of benevolence and friendship, humanity and kindness, is sweet, smooth, tender, and agreeable, independent of all fortune and accidents. These virtues are besides attended with a pleasing consciousness or remembrance, and keep us in humour with ourselves as well as others; while we retain the agreeable reflection of having done our part towards mankind and society. And though all men show a jealousy of our success in the pursuits of avarice and ambition; yet are we almost sure of their good-will and good wishes, so long as we persevere in the paths of virtue,

and employ ourselves in the execution of generous plans and purposes. What other passion is there where we shall find so many advantages united; an agreeable sentiment, a pleasing consciousness, a good reputation? But of these truths, we may observe, men are, of themselves, pretty much convinced; nor are they deficient in their duty to society, because they would not wish to be generous, friendly, and humane; but because they do not feel themselves such.

Treating vice with the greatest candour, and making it all possible concessions, we must acknowledge that there is not, in any instance, the smallest pretext for giving it the preference above virtue, with a view to self-interest; except, perhaps, in the case of justice, where a man, taking things in a certain light, may often seem to be a loser by his integrity. And though it is allowed that, without a regard to property, no society could subsist; yet according to the imperfect way in which human affairs are conducted, a sensible knave, in particular incidents, may think that an act of iniquity or infidelity will make a considerable addition to his fortune, without causing any considerable breach in the social union and confederacy. That *honesty is the best policy*, may be a good general rule, but is liable to many exceptions; and he, it may perhaps be thought, conducts himself with most wisdom, who observes the general rule, and takes advantage of all the exceptions.

I must confess that, if a man think that this reasoning much requires an answer, it will be a little difficult to find any which will to him appear satisfactory and convincing. If his heart rebel not against such pernicious maxims, if he feel no reluctance to the thoughts of villainy or baseness, he has indeed lost a considerable motive to virtue; and we may expect that his practice will be answerable to his speculation. But in all ingenuous natures, the antipathy to treachery and roguery is too strong to be counterbalanced by any views of profit or pecuniary advantage. Inward peace of mind, consciousness of integrity, a satisfactory review of our own conduct; these are circumstances, very requisite to happiness, and will be cherished and cultivated by every honest man, who feels the importance of them.

Such a one has, besides, the frequent satisfaction of seeing knaves, with all their pretended cunning and abilities, betrayed by their own maxims; and while they purpose to cheat with moderation and secrecy, a tempting incident occurs, nature is frail, and they give into the snare; whence they can never extricate themselves, without a total loss of reputation, and the forfeiture of all future trust and confidence with mankind.

But were they ever so secret and successful, the honest man, if he has any tincture of philosophy, or even common observation and reflection, will discover that they themselves are, in the end, the greatest dupes, and have sacrificed the invaluable enjoyment of a character, with themselves at least, for the acquisition of worthless toys and gewgaws. How little is requisite to supply the *necessities* of nature? And in a view to *pleasure*, what comparison between the unbought satisfaction of conversation, society, study, even health and the common beauties of nature, but above all the peaceful reflection on one's own conduct; what comparison, I say, between these and the feverish, empty amusements of luxury and expense? These natural pleasures, indeed, are really without price; both because they are below all price in their attainment, and above it in their enjoyment.

Appendix I

Concerning Moral Sentiment

If the foregoing hypothesis be received, it will now be easy for us to determine the question first started,[6] concerning the general principles of morals; and though we postponed the decision of that question, lest it should then involve us in intricate speculations, which are unfit for moral discourses, we may resume it at present, and examine how far either *reason* or *sentiment* enters into all decisions of praise or censure.

One principal foundation of moral praise being supposed to lie in the usefulness of any quality or action, it is evident that *reason* must enter for a considerable share in all decisions of this kind; since nothing but that faculty can instruct us in the tendency of qualities and actions, and point out their beneficial consequences to society and to their possessor. In many cases this is an affair liable to great controversy; doubts may arise; opposite interests

may occur; and a preference must be given to one side, from very nice views, and a small overbalance of utility. This is particularly remarkable in questions with regard to justice; as is, indeed, natural to suppose, from that species of utility which attends this virtue. Were every single instance of justice, like that of benevolence, useful to society; this would be a more simple state of the case, and seldom liable to great controversy. But as single instances of justice are often pernicious in their first and immediate tendency, and as the advantage to society results only from the observance of the general rule, and from the concurrence and combination of several persons in the same equitable conduct; the case here becomes more intricate and involved. The various circumstances of society; the various consequences of any practice; the various interests which may be proposed; these, on many occasions, are doubtful, and subject to great discussion and inquiry. The object of municipal laws is to fix all the questions with regard to justice; the debates of civilians; the reflections of politicians; the precedents of history and public records, are all directed to the same purpose. And a very accurate *reason* or *judgement* is often requisite, to give the true determination, amidst such intricate doubts arising from obscure or opposite utilities.

But though reason, when fully assisted and improved, be sufficient to instruct us in the pernicious or useful tendency of qualities and actions; it is not alone sufficient to produce any moral blame or approbation. Utility is only a tendency to a certain end; and were the end totally indifferent to us, we should feel the same indifference towards the means. It is requisite a *sentiment* should here display itself, in order to give a preference to the useful above the pernicious tendencies. This sentiment can be no other than a feeling for the happiness of mankind, and a resentment of their misery; since these are the different ends which virtue and vice have a tendency to promote. Here therefore *reason* instructs us in the several tendencies of actions, and *humanity* makes a distinction in favour of those which are useful and beneficial.

This partition between the faculties of understanding and sentiment, in all moral decisions, seems clear from the preceding hypothesis. But I shall suppose that hypothesis false; it will then be requisite to look out for some other theory that may be satisfactory; and I dare venture to affirm that none such will ever be found, so long as we suppose reason to be the sole source of morals. To prove this, it will be proper to weigh the . . . following considerations.

I. It is easy for a false hypothesis to maintain some appearance of truth, while it keeps wholly in generals, makes use of undefined terms, and employs comparisons, instead of instances. This is particularly remarkable in that philosophy, which ascribes the discernment of all moral distinctions to reason alone, without the concurrence of sentiment. It is impossible that, in any particular instance, this hypothesis can so much as be rendered intelligible, whatever specious figure it may make in general declamations and discourses. Examine the crime of *ingratitude*, for instance; which has place, wherever we observe good-will, expressed and known, together with good-offices performed, on the one side, and a return of ill-will or indifference, with ill-offices or neglect on the other; anatomize all these circumstances, and examine, by your reason alone, in what consists the demerit or blame. You never will come to any issue or conclusion.

Reason judges either of *matter of fact* or of *relations*. Enquire then, *first*, where is that matter of fact which we here call *crime*; point it out; determine the time of its existence; describe its essence of nature; explain the sense or faculty to which it discovers itself. It resides in the mind of the person who is ungrateful. He must, therefore, feel it, and be conscious of it. But nothing is there, except the passion of ill-will or absolute indifference. You cannot say that these, of themselves, always, and in all circumstances, are crimes. No, they are only crimes when directed towards persons who have before expressed and displayed good-will towards us. Consequently, we may infer, that the crime of ingratitude is not any particular individual *fact*; but arises from a complication of circumstances, which, being presented to the spectator, excites the *sentiment* of blame, by the particular structure and fabric of his mind.

This representation, you say, is false. Crime, indeed, consists not in a particular *fact*, of whose reality we are assured by *reason*; but it consists in certain *moral relations*, discovered by reason, in the

same manner as we discover by reason the truths of geometry or algebra. But what are the relations, I ask, of which you here talk? In the case stated above, I see first good-will and good-offices in one person; then ill-will and ill-offices in the other. Between these, there is a relation of *contrariety*. Does the crime consist in that relation? But suppose a person bore me ill-will or did me ill-offices; and I, in return, were indifferent towards him, or did him good-offices. Here is the same relation of *contrariety*; and yet my conduct is often highly laudable. Twist and turn this matter as much as you will, you can never rest the morality on relation; but must have recourse to the decisions of sentiment.

When it is affirmed that two and three are equal to the half of ten, this relation of equality I understand perfectly. I conceive, that if ten be divided into two parts, of which one has as many units as the other; and if any of these parts be compared to two added to three, it will contain as many units as that compound number. But when you draw thence a comparison to moral relations, I own that I am altogether at a loss to understand you. A moral action, a crime, such as ingratitude, is a complicated object. Does the morality consist in the relation of its parts to each other? How? After what manner? Specify the relation: be more particular and explicit in your propositions, and you will easily see their falsehood.

No, say you, the morality consists in the relation of actions to the rule of right; and they are denominated good or ill, according as they agree or disagree with it. What then is this rule of right? In what does it consist? How is it determined? By reason, you say, which examines the moral relations of actions. So that moral relations are determined by the comparison of action to a rule. And that rule is determined by considering the moral relations of objects. Is not this fine reasoning?

All this is metaphysics, you cry. That is enough; there needs nothing more to give a strong presumption of falsehood. Yes, reply I, here are metaphysics surely; but they are all on your side, who advance an abstruse hypothesis, which can never be made intelligible, nor quadrate with any particular instance of illustration. The hypothesis which we embrace is plain. It maintains that morality is determined by sentiment. It defines virtue to be *what-*

ever mental action or quality gives to a spectator the pleasing sentiment of approbation; and vice the contrary. We then proceed to examine a plain matter of fact, to wit, what actions have this influence. We consider all the circumstances in which these actions agree, and thence endeavour to extract some general observations with regard to these sentiments. If you call this metaphysics, and find anything abstruse here, you need only conclude that your turn of mind is not suited to the moral sciences.

II. When a man, at any time, deliberates concerning his own conduct (as, whether he had better, in a particular emergence, assist a brother or a benefactor), he must consider these separate relations, with all the circumstances and situations of the persons, in order to determine the superior duty and obligation; and in order to determine the proportion of lines in any triangle, it is necessary to examine the nature of that figure, and the relations which its several parts bear to each other. But notwithstanding this appearing similarity in the two cases, there is, at bottom, an extreme difference between them. A speculative reasoner concerning triangles or circles considers the several known and given relations of the parts of these figures, and thence infers some unknown relation, which is dependent on the former. But in moral deliberations we must be acquainted beforehand with all the objects, and all their relations to each other; and from a comparison of the whole, fix our choice or approbation. No new fact to be ascertained; no new relation to be discovered. All the circumstances of the case are supposed to be laid before us, ere we can fix any sentence of blame or approbation. If any material circumstance be yet unknown or doubtful, we must first employ our inquiry or intellectual faculties to assure us of it; and must suspend for a time all moral decision or sentiment. While we are ignorant whether a man were aggressor or not, how can we determine whether the person who killed him be criminal or innocent? But after every circumstance, every relation is known, the understanding has no further room to operate, nor any object on which it could employ itself. The approbation or blame which then ensues, cannot be the work of the judgement, but of the heart; and is not a speculative proposition or affirmation, but an active feeling or sentiment. In the disquisitions of the understanding, from known circumstances and relations, we infer some new and unknown. In moral decisions, all the circumstances and relations must be previously known; and the mind, from the contemplation of the whole, feels some new impression of affection or disgust, esteem or contempt, approbation or blame.

Hence the great difference between a mistake of *fact* and one of *right*; and hence the reason why the one is commonly criminal and not the other. When Oedipus killed Laius, he was ignorant of the relation, and from circumstances, innocent and involuntary, formed erroneous opinions concerning the action which he committed. But when Nero killed Agrippina, all the relations between himself and the person, and all the circumstances of the fact, were previously known to him; but the motive of revenge, or fear, or interest, prevailed in his savage heart over the sentiments of duty and humanity. And when we express that detestation against him to which he himself, in a little time, became insensible, it is not that we see any relations, of which he was ignorant; but that, from the rectitude of our disposition, we feel sentiments against which he was hardened from flattery and a long perseverance in the most enormous crimes. In these sentiments then, not in a discovery of relations of any kind, do all moral determinations consist. Before we can pretend to form any decision of this kind, everything must be known and ascertained on the side of the object or action. Nothing remains but to feel, on our part, some sentiment of blame or approbation; whence we pronounce the action criminal or virtuous.

. . . .

V. It appears evident that the ultimate ends of human actions can never, in any case, be accounted for by *reason*, but recommend themselves entirely to the sentiments and affections of mankind, without any dependence on the intellectual faculties. Ask a man *why he uses exercise*; he will answer, *because he desires to keep his health*. If you then enquire, *why he desires health*, he will readily reply, *because sickness is painful*. If you push your enquiries farther, and desire a reason *why he hates pain*, it is impossible he can ever give any. This is an ultimate end, and is never referred to any other object.

Perhaps to your second question, *why he desires*

health, he may also reply, that *it is necessary for the exercise of his calling*. If you ask, *why he is anxious on that head*, he will answer, *because he desires to get money*. If you demand *Why? It is the instrument of pleasure*, says he. And beyond this it is an absurdity to ask for a reason. It is impossible there can be a progress *in infinitum*; and that one thing can always be a reason why another is desired. Something must be desirable on its own account, and because of its immediate accord or agreement with human sentiment and affection.

Now as virtue is an end, and is desirable on its own account, without fee or reward, merely for the immediate satisfaction which it conveys; it is requisite that there should be some sentiment which it touches, some internal taste or feeling, or whatever you please to call it, which distinguishes moral good and evil, and which embraces the one and rejects the other.

Thus the distinct boundaries and offices of *reason* and of *taste* are easily ascertained. The former conveys the knowledge of truth and falsehood: the latter gives the sentiment of beauty and deformity, vice and virtue. The one discovers objects as they really stand in nature, without addition or diminution: the other has a productive faculty, and gilding or staining all natural objects with the colours, borrowed from internal sentiment, raises in a manner a new creation. Reason being cool and disengaged, is no motive to action, and directs only the impulse received from appetite or inclination, by showing us the means of attaining happiness or avoiding misery: Taste, as it gives pleasure or pain, and thereby constitutes happiness or misery, becomes a motive to action, and is the first spring or impulse to desire and volition. From circumstances and relations, known or supposed, the former leads us to the discovery of the concealed and unknown: after all circumstances and relations are laid before us, the latter makes us feel from the whole a new sentiment of blame or approbation. The standard of the one, being founded on the nature of things, is eternal and inflexible, even by the will of the Supreme Being: the standard of the other, arising from the internal frame and constitution of animals, is ultimately derived from that Supreme Will, which bestowed on each being its peculiar nature, and arranged the several classes and orders of existence.

Appendix II

Of Self-love

There is a principle, supposed to prevail among many, which is utterly incompatible with all virtue or moral sentiment; and as it can proceed from nothing but the most depraved disposition, so in its turn it tends still further to encourage that depravity. This principle is, that all *benevolence* is mere hypocrisy, friendship a cheat, public spirit a farce, fidelity a snare to procure trust and confidence; and that while all of us, at bottom, pursue only our private interest, we wear these fair disguises, in order to put others off their guard, and expose them the more to our wiles and machinations. What heart one must be possessed of who professes such principles, and who feels no internal sentiment that belies so pernicious a theory, it is easy to imagine: and also what degree of affection and benevolence he can bear to a species whom he represents under such odious colours, and supposes so little susceptible of gratitude or any return of affection. Or if we should not ascribe these principles wholly to a corrupted heart, we must at least account for them from the most careless and precipitate examination. Superficial reasoners, indeed, observing many false pretences among mankind, and feeling, perhaps, no very strong restraint in their own disposition, might draw a general and a hasty conclusion that all is equally corrupted, and that men, different from all other animals, and indeed from all other species of existence, admit of no degrees of good or bad, but are, in every instance, the same creatures under different disguises and appearances.

There is another principle, somewhat resembling the former; which has been much insisted on by philosophers, and has been the foundation of many a system; that, whatever affection one may feel, or imagine he feels for others, no passion is, or can be disinterested; that the most generous friendship, however sincere, is a modification of self-love; and that, even unknown to ourselves, we seek only our own gratification, while we appear the most deeply engaged in schemes for the liberty and happiness of mankind. By a turn of imagination, by a refinement of reflection, by an enthusiasm of passion, we seem to take part in the interests of others, and imagine ourselves divested of all selfish considerations: but, at bottom, the most generous patriot and most niggardly miser, the bravest hero and most abject coward, have, in every action, an equal regard to their own happiness and welfare.

Whoever concludes from the seeming tendency of this opinion, that those, who make profession of it, cannot possibly feel the true sentiments of benevolence, or have any regard for genuine virtue, will often find himself, in practice, very much mistaken. Probity and honour were no strangers to Epicurus and his sect. Atticus and Horace seem to have enjoyed from nature, and cultivated by reflection, as generous and friendly dispositions as any disciple of the austerer schools. And among the modern, Hobbes and Locke, who maintained the selfish system of morals, lived irreproachable lives; though the former lay not under any restraint of religion which might supply the defects of his philosophy.

An Epicurean or a Hobbist readily allows, that there is such a thing as friendship in the world, without hypocrisy or disguise; though he may attempt, by a philosophical chymistry, to resolve the elements of this passion, if I may so speak, into those of another, and explain every affection to be self-love, twisted and moulded, by a particular turn of imagination, into a variety of appearances. But as the same turn of imagination prevails not in every man, nor gives the same direction to the original passion; this is sufficient even according to the selfish system to make the widest difference in human characters, and denominate one man virtuous and humane, another vicious and meanly interested. I esteem the man whose self-love, by whatever means, is so directed as to give him a concern for others, and render him serviceable to society: as I hate or despise him, who has no regard to any thing beyond his own gratifications and enjoyments. In vain would you suggest that these characters, though seemingly opposite, are at bottom the same, and that a very inconsiderable turn of thought forms the whole difference between them. Each character, notwithstanding these inconsiderable differences, appears to me, in practice, pretty durable and untransmutable. And I find not in this more than in other subjects, that the natural sentiments arising from the general appearances of things are easily destroyed by subtile reflections concerning the minute origin of these appearances. Does not the lively, cheerful colour of a countenance inspire me with complacency and pleasure; even though I learn from philosophy that all difference of complexion arises from the most minute differences of thickness, in the most minute parts of the skin; by means of which a superficies is qualified to reflect one of the original colours of light, and absorb the others?

But though the question concerning the universal or partial selfishness of man be not so material as is usually imagined to morality and practice, it is certainly of consequence in the speculative science of human nature, and is a proper object of curiosity and enquiry. It may not, therefore, be unsuitable, in this place, to bestow a few reflections upon it.[7]

The most obvious objection to the selfish hypothesis is, that, as it is contrary to common feeling and our most unprejudiced notions, there is required the highest stretch of philosophy to establish so extraordinary a paradox. To the most careless observer there appear to be such dispositions as benevolence and generosity; such affections as love, friendship, compassion, gratitude. These sentiments have their causes, effects, objects, and operations, marked by common language and observation, and plainly distinguished from those of the selfish passions. And as this is the obvious appearance of things, it must be admitted, till some hypothesis be discovered, which by penetrating deeper into human nature, may prove the former affections to be nothing but modifications of the latter. All attempts of this kind have hitherto proved fruitless, and seem to have proceeded entirely from that love of *simplicity* which has been the source of much false reasoning in philosophy. I shall not here enter into any detail on the present subject. Many able philosophers have shown the insufficiency of these systems. And I shall take for granted what, I believe, the smallest reflection will make evident to every impartial enquirer.

. . . .

. . . Tenderness to their offspring, in all sensible beings, is commonly able alone to counter-balance the strongest motives of self-love, and has no manner of dependance on that affection. What interest can a fond mother have in view, who loses her health by assiduous attendance on her sick child, and afterwards languishes and dies of grief, when freed, by its death, from the slavery of that attendance?

Is gratitude no affection of the human breast, or is that a word merely, without any meaning or reality? Have we no satisfaction in one man's company above another's, and no desire of the welfare of our friend, even though absence or death should prevent us from all participation in it? Or what is it commonly, that gives us any participation in it, even while alive and present, but our affection and regard to him?

These and a thousand other instances are marks of a general benevolence in human nature, where no *real* interest binds us to the object. And how an *imaginary* interest known and avowed for such, can be the origin of any passion or emotion, seems difficult to explain. No satisfactory hypothesis of this kind has yet been discovered; nor is there the smallest probability that the future industry of men will ever be attended with more favourable success.

But farther, if we consider rightly of the matter, we shall find that the hypothesis which allows of a disinterested benevolence, distinct from self-love, has really more *simplicity* in it, and is more conformable to the analogy of nature than that which pretends to resolve all friendship and humanity into this latter principle. There are bodily wants or appetites acknowledged by every one, which necessarily precede all sensual enjoyment, and carry us directly to seek possession of the object. Thus, hunger and thirst have eating and drinking for their end; and from the gratification of these primary appetites arises a pleasure, which may become the object of another species of desire or inclination that is secondary and interested. In the same manner there are mental passions by which we are impelled immediately to seek particular objects, such as fame or power, or vengeance without any regard to interest; and when these objects are attained a pleasing enjoyment ensues, as the consequence of our indulged affections. Nature must, by the internal frame and constitution of the mind, give an original propensity to fame, ere we can reap any pleasure from that acquisition, or pursue it from motives of self-love, and a desire of happiness. If I have no vanity, I take no delight in praise: if I be void of ambition, power gives me no enjoyment: if I be not angry, the punishment of an adversary is totally indifferent to me. In all these cases there is a passion which points immediately to the object, and constitutes it our good or happiness; as there are other secondary passions which afterwards arise and pursue it as a part of our happiness, when once it is constituted such by our original affections. Were there no appetite of any kind antecedent to self-love, that propensity could scarcely ever exert itself; because we should, in that case, have felt few and slender pains or pleasures, and have little misery or happiness to avoid or to pursue.

Now where is the difficulty in conceiving, that this may likewise be the case with benevolence and friendship, and that, from the original frame of our temper, we may feel a desire of another's happiness or good, which, by means of that affection, becomes our own good, and is afterwards pursued, from the combined motives of benevolence and self-enjoyment? Who sees not that vengeance, from the force alone of passion, may be so eagerly pursued, as to make us knowingly neglect every consideration of ease, interest, or safety; and, like some vindictive animals, infuse our very souls into the wounds we give an enemy; and what a malignant philosophy must it be, that will not allow to humanity and friendship the same privileges which are undisputably granted to the darker passions of enmity and resentment? Such a philosophy is more like a satyr than a true delineation or description of human nature; and may be a good foundation for paradoxical wit and raillery, but is a very bad one for any serious argument or reasoning.

NOTES

1. See Appendix I.
2. Sect. III and IV.
3. Sect. V.
4. It is needless to push our researches so far as to ask, why we have humanity or a fellow-feeling with others. It is sufficient, that this is experienced to be a principle in human nature. We must stop somewhere in our examination of causes; and there are, in every science, some general principles, beyond which we cannot hope to find any principle more general. No man is absolutely indifferent to the happiness and misery of others. The first has a natural tendency to give pleasure; the second, pain. This every one may find in himself. It is not prob-

able, that these principles can be resolved into principles more simple and universal, whatever attempts may have been made to that purpose. But if it were possible, it belongs not to the present subject; and we may here safely consider these principles as original: happy, if we can render all the consequences sufficiently plain and perspicious!

5. For a like reason, the tendencies of actions and characters, not their real accidental consequences, are alone regarded in our moral determinations or general judgements; though in our real feeling or sentiment, we cannot help paying greater regard to one whose station, joined to virtue, renders him really useful to society, than to one, who exerts the social virtues only in good intentions and benevolent affections. Separating the character from the fortune, by an easy and necessary effort of thought, we pronounce these persons alike, and give them the same general praise. The judgement corrects or endeavours to correct the appearance: But is not able entirely to prevail over sentiment.

Why is this peach-tree said to be better than that other; but because it produces more or better fruit? And would not the same praise be given it, though snails or vermin had destroyed the peaches, before they came to full maturity? In morals too, is not *the tree known by the fruit*? And cannot we easily distinguish between nature and accident, in the one case as well as in the other?

6. Sect. I.

7. Benevolence naturally divides into two kinds, the *general* and the *particular*. The first is, where we have no friendship or connexion or esteem for the person, but feel only a general sympathy with him or a compassion for his pains, and a congratulation with his pleasures. The other species of benevolence is founded on an opinion of virtue, on services done us, or on some particular connexions. Both these sentiments must be allowed real in human nature: but whether they will resolve into some nice considerations of self-love, is a question more curious than important. The former sentiment, to wit, that of general benevolence, or humanity, or sympathy, we shall have occasion frequently to treat of in the course of this enquiry; and I assume it as real, from general experience, without any other proof.

Morality and Advantage

DAVID GAUTHIER

David Gauthier (1932–   ) is a professor of philosophy at the University of Pittsburgh. His publications include *The Logic of Leviathan* and *Morals by Agreement*.

—•—

I

Hume asks, rhetorically, "what theory of morals can ever serve any useful purpose, unless it can show, by a particular detail, that all the duties which it recommends, are also the true interest of each individual?"[1]

But there are many to whom this question does not seem rhetorical. Why, they ask, do we speak the language of morality, impressing upon our fellows their duties and obligations, urging them with appeals to what is right and good, if we could speak to the same effect in the language of prudence, appealing to considerations of interest and advantage? When the poet, Ogden Nash, is moved by the muse to cry out:

O Duty,
Why hast thou not the visage of a sweetie or a cutie?[2]

we do not anticipate the reply:

O Poet,
I really am a cutie and I think you ought to know it.

The belief that duty cannot be reduced to interest, or that morality may require the agent to subordinate all considerations of advantage, is one which has withstood the assaults of contrary-minded philosophers from Plato to the present. Indeed, were it not for the conviction that only interest and advantage can motivate human actions, it would be difficult to understand philosophers contending so vigorously for the identity, or at least compatibility, of morality with prudence.

Yet if morality is not true prudence it would be wrong to suppose that those philosophers who have sought some connection between morality and advantage have been merely misguided. For it is a truism that we should all expect to be worse off if men were to substitute prudence, even of the most enlightened kind, for morality in all of their deliberations. And this truism demands not only some connection between morality and advantage, but a seemingly paradoxical connection. For if we should all expect to suffer, were men to be prudent instead of moral, then morality must contribute to advantage in a unique way, a way in which prudence—following reasons of advantage—cannot.

Thomas Hobbes is perhaps the first philosopher who tried to develop this seemingly paradoxical connection between morality and advantage. But since he could not admit that a man might ever reasonably subordinate considerations of advantage to the dictates of obligation, he was led to deny the possibility of real conflict between morality and prudence. So his argument fails to clarify the distinction between the view that claims of obligation reduce to considerations of interest and the view that claims of obligation promote advantage in a way in which considerations of interest cannot.

More recently, Kurt Baier has argued that "being moral is following rules designed to overrule self-interest whenever it is in the interest of everyone alike that everyone should set aside his interest."[3] Since prudence is following rules of (enlightened) self-interest, Baier is arguing that morality is designed to overrule prudence when it is to everyone's advantage that it do so—or, in other words, that morality contributes to advantage in a way in which prudence cannot.[4]

Baier does not actually demonstrate that morality contributes to advantage in this unique and seemingly paradoxical way. Indeed, he does not ask how it is possible that morality should do this. It is this possibility which I propose to demonstrate.

II

Let us examine the following proposition, which will be referred to as "the thesis": *Morality is a system of principles such that it is advantageous for everyone if everyone accepts and acts on it, yet acting on the system of principles requires that some persons perform disadvantageous acts.*[5]

What I wish to show is that this thesis *could be true*, that morality could possess those characteristics attributed to it by the thesis. I shall not try to show that the thesis is true—indeed, I shall argue in Section V that it presents at best an inadequate conception of morality. But it is plausible to suppose that a modified form of the thesis states a necessary, although not a sufficient, condition for a moral system.

Two phrases in the thesis require elucidation. The first is "advantageous for everyone." I use this phrase to mean that *each* person will do better if the system is accepted and acted on than if *either* no system is accepted and acted on *or* a system is accepted and acted on which is similar, save that it never requires any person to perform disadvantageous acts.

Clearly, then, the claim that it is advantageous for everyone to accept and act on the system is a very strong one; it may be so strong that no system of principles which might be generally adopted could meet it. But I shall consider in Section V one among the possible ways of weakening the claim.

The second phrase requiring elucidation is "disadvantageous acts." I use this phrase to refer to acts which, in the context of their performance, would be less advantageous to the performer than some other act open to him in the same context. The phrase does not refer to acts which merely impose on the performer some short-term disadvantage that is recouped or outweighed in the long run. Rather it refers to acts which impose a disadvantage that is never recouped. It follows that the performer may say to himself, when confronted with the requirement to perform such an act, that it would be better *for him* not to perform it.

It is essential to note that the thesis, as elucidated, does not maintain that morality is advantageous for everyone in the sense that each person will do *best* if the system of principles is accepted and acted on. Each person will do better than if no system is adopted, or than if the one particular alternative mentioned above is adopted, but not than if any alternative is adopted.

Indeed, for each person required by the system to perform some disadvantageous act, it is easy to specify a better alternative—namely, the system modified so that it does not require *him* to perform any act disadvantageous to himself. Of course, there is no reason to expect such an alternative to be better than the moral system for everyone, or in fact for anyone other than the person granted the special exemption.

A second point to note is that each person must gain more from the disadvantageous acts performed by others than he loses from the disadvantageous acts performed by himself. If this were not the case, then some person would do better if a system were adopted exactly like the moral system save that it never requires *any* person to perform disadvantageous acts. This is ruled out by the force of "advantageous for everyone."

This point may be clarified by an example. Suppose that the system contains exactly one principle. Everyone is always to tell the truth. It follows from the thesis that each person gains more from those occasions on which others tell the truth, even though it is disadvantageous to them to do so, than he loses from those occasions on which he tells the truth even though it is disadvantageous to him to do so.

Now this is not to say that each person gains by telling others the truth in order to ensure that in return they tell him the truth. Such gains would merely be the result of accepting certain short-term disadvantages (those associated with truth-telling) in order to reap long-term benefits (those associated

with being told the truth). Rather, what is required by the thesis is that those disadvantages which a person incurs in telling the truth, when he can expect neither short-term nor long-term benefits to accrue to him from truth-telling, are outweighed by those advantages he receives when others tell him the truth when they can expect no benefits to accrue to them from truth-telling.

The principle enjoins truth-telling in those cases in which whether one tells the truth or not will have no effect on whether others tell the truth. Such cases include those in which others have no way of knowing whether or not they are being told the truth. The thesis requires that the disadvantages one incurs in telling the truth in these cases are less than the advantages one receives in being told the truth by others in parallel cases; and the thesis requires that this holds for everyone.

Thus we see that although the disadvantages imposed by the system on any person are less than the advantages secured him through the imposition of disadvantages on others, yet the disadvantages are real in that incurring them is *unrelated* to receiving the advantages. The argument of long-term prudence, that I ought to incur some immediate disadvantage *so that* I shall receive compensating advantages later on, is entirely inapplicable here.

III

It will be useful to examine in some detail an example of a system which possesses those characteristics ascribed by the thesis to morality. This example, abstracted from the field of international relations, will enable us more clearly to distinguish, first, conduct based on immediate interest; second, conduct which is truly prudent; and third, conduct which promotes mutual advantage but is not prudent.

A and *B* are two nations with substantially opposed interests, who find themselves engaged in an arms race against each other. Both possess the latest in weaponry, so that each recognizes that the actual outbreak of full-scale war between them would be mutually disastrous. This recognition leads *A* and *B* to agree that each would be better off if they were mutually disarming instead of mutually arming. For mutual disarmament would preserve the balance of power between them while reducing the risk of war.

Hence A and B enter into a disarmament pact. The pact is advantageous for both if both accept and act on it, although clearly it is not advantageous for either to act on it if the other does not.

Let A be considering whether or not to adhere to the pact in some particular situation, whether or not actually to perform some act of disarmament. A will quite likely consider the act to have disadvantageous consequences. A expects to benefit, not by its own acts of disarmament, but by B's acts. Hence if A were to reason simply in terms of immediate interest, A might well decide to violate the pact.

But A's decision need be neither prudent nor reasonable. For suppose first that B is able to determine whether or not A adheres to the pact. If A violates, then B will detect the violation and will then consider what to do in the light of A's behavior. It is not to B's advantage to disarm alone; B expects to gain, not by its own acts of disarmament, but by A's acts. Hence A's violation, if known to B, leads naturally to B's counter-violation. If this continues, the effect of the pact is entirely undone, and A and B return to their mutually disadvantageous arms race. A, foreseeing this when considering whether or not to adhere to the pact in the given situation, must therefore conclude that the truly prudent course of action is to adhere.

Now suppose that B is unable to determine whether or not A adheres to the pact in the particular situation under consideration. If A judges adherence to be in itself disadvantageous, then it will decide, both on the basis of immediate interest and on the basis of prudence, to violate the pact. Since A's decision is unknown to B, it cannot affect whether or not B adheres to the pact, and so the advantage gained by A's violation is not outweighed by any consequent loss.

Therefore if A and B are prudent they will adhere to their disarmament pact whenever violation would be detectable by the other, and violate the pact whenever violation would not be detectable by the other. In other words, they will adhere openly and violate secretly. The disarmament pact between A and B thus possesses two of the characteristics ascribed by the thesis to morality. First, accepting the pact and acting on it is more advantageous for each than making no pact at all. Second, in so far as the pact stipulates that each must disarm even when disarming is undetectable by the other, it requires each to perform disadvantageous acts—acts which run counter to considerations of prudence.

One further condition must be met if the disarmament pact is to possess those characteristics ascribed by the thesis to a system of morality. It must be the case that the requirement that each party perform disadvantageous acts be essential to the advantage conferred by the pact; or, to put the matter in the way in which we expressed it earlier, both A and B must do better to adhere to this pact than to a pact which is similar save that it requires no disadvantageous acts. In terms of the example, A and B must do better to adhere to the pact than to a pact which stipulates that each must disarm only when disarming is detectable by the other.

We may plausibly suppose this condition to be met. Although A will gain by secretly retaining arms itself, it will lose by B's similar acts, and its losses may well outweigh its gains. B may equally lose more by A's secret violations than it gains by its own. So, despite the fact that prudence requires each to violate secretly, each may well do better if both adhere secretly than if both violate secretly. Supposing this to be the case, the disarmament pact is formally analogous to a moral system, as characterized by the thesis. That is, acceptance of and adherence to the pact by A and B is more advantageous for each, either than making no pact at all or than acceptance of and adherence to a pact requiring only open disarmament, and the pact requires each to perform acts of secret disarmament which are disadvantageous.

Some elementary notion, adapted for our purposes from the mathematical theory of games, may make the example even more perspicuous. Given a disarmament pact between A and B, each may pursue two pure strategies—adherence and violation. There are, then, four possible combinations of strategies, each determining a particular outcome. These outcomes can be ranked preferentially for each nation; we shall let the numerals 1 to 4 represent the ranking from first to fourth preference.

Thus we construct a simple matrix,[6] in which A's preferences are stated first:

		B	
		adheres	violates
A	adheres	2, 2	4, 1
	violates	1, 4	3, 3

The matrix does not itself show that agreement is advantageous to both, for it gives only the rankings of outcomes given the agreement. But it is plausible to assume that A and B would rank mutual violation on a par with no agreement. If we assume this, we can then indicate the value to each of making and adhering to the pact by reference to the matrix.

The matrix shows immediately that adherence to the pact is not the most advantageous possibility for either, since each prefers the outcome, if it alone violates, to the outcome of mutual adherence. It shows also that each gains less from its own violations than it loses from the other's, since each ranks mutual adherence above mutual violation.

Let us now use the matrix to show that, as we argued previously, public adherence to the pact is prudent and mutually advantageous, whereas private adherence is not prudent although mutually advantageous. Consider first the case where adherence—and so violation—are open and public.

If adherence and violation are open, then each knows the strategy chosen by the other, and can adjust its own strategy in the light of this knowledge—or, in other words, the strategies are interdependent. Suppose that each initially chooses the strategy of adherence. A notices that if it switches to violation it gains—moving from 2 to 1 in terms of preference ranking. Hence immediate interest dictates such a switch. But it notices further that if it switches, then B can also be expected to switch—moving from 4 to 3 on its preference scale. The eventual outcome would be stable, in that neither could benefit from switching from violation back to adherence. But the eventual outcome would represent not a gain for A but a loss—moving from 2 to 3 on its preference scale. Hence prudence dictates no change from the strategy of adherence. This adherence is mutually

advantageous; A and B are in precisely similar positions in terms of their pact.

Consider now the case when adherence and violation are secret and private. Neither nation knows the strategy chosen by the other, so the two strategies are independent. Suppose A is trying to decide which strategy to follow. It does not know B's choice. But it notices that if B adheres, then it pays A to violate, attaining 1 rather than 2 in terms of preference ranking. If B violates, then again it pays A to violate, attaining 3 rather than 4 on its preference scale. Hence, no matter which strategy B chooses, A will do better to violate, and so prudence dictates violation.

B of course reasons in just the same way. Hence each is moved by considerations of prudence to violate the pact, and the outcome assigns each rank 3 on its preference scale. This outcome is mutually disadvantageous to A and B, since mutual adherence would assign each rank 2 on its preference scale.

If A and B are both capable only of rational prudence, they find themselves at an impasse. The advantage of mutual adherence to the agreement when violations would be secret is not available to them, since neither can find it in his own overall interest not to violate secretly. Hence, strictly prudent nations cannot reap the maximum advantage possible from a pact of the type under examination.

Of course, what A and B will no doubt endeavor to do is eliminate the possibility of secret violations of their pact. Indeed, barring additional complications, each must find it to his advantage to make it possible for the other to detect his own violations. In other words, each must find it advantageous to ensure that their choice of strategies is interdependent, so that the pact will always be prudent for each to keep. But it may not be possible for them to ensure this, and to the extent that they cannot, prudence will prevent them from maximizing mutual advantage.

IV

We may now return to the connection of morality with advantage. Morality, if it is a system of principles of the type characterized in the thesis, requires that some persons perform acts genuinely disadvantageous to themselves, as a means to greater mutual advantage. Our example shows sufficiently that such a system is possible, and indicates more precisely its character. In particular, by an argument strictly parallel to that which we have pursued, we may show that men who are merely prudent will not perform the required disadvantageous acts. But in so violating the principles of morality, they will disadvantage themselves. Each will lose more by the violations of others than he will gain by his own violations.

Now this conclusion would be unsurprising if it were only that no man can gain if he alone is moral rather than prudent. Obviously such a man loses, for he adheres to moral principles to his own disadvantage, while others violate them also to his disadvantage. The benefit of the moral system is not one which any individual can secure for himself, since each man gains from the sacrifices of others.

What is surprising in our conclusion is that no man can ever gain if he is moral. Not only does he not gain by being moral if others are prudent, but he also does not gain by being moral if others are moral. For although he now receives the advantage of others' adherence to moral principles, he reaps the disadvantage of his own adherence. As long as his own adherence to morality is independent of what others do (and this is required to distinguish morality from prudence), he must do better to be prudent.

If all men are moral, all will do better than if all are prudent. But any one man will always do better if he is prudent than if he is moral. There is no real paradox in supposing that morality is advantageous, even though it requires the performance of disadvantageous acts.

On the supposition that morality has the characteristics ascribed to it by the thesis, is it possible to answer the question "Why should we be moral?" where "we" is taken distributively, so that the question is a compendious way of asking, for each person, "Why should I be moral?" More simply, is it possible to answer the question "Why should I be moral?"

I take it that this question, if asked seriously, demands a reason for being moral other than moral reasons themselves. It demands that moral reasons be shown to be reasons for acting by a non-circular argument. Those who would answer it, like Baier, endeavor to do so by the introduction of considerations of advantage.

Two such considerations have emerged from our discussion. The first is that if all are moral, all will do better than if all are prudent. This will serve to answer the question "Why should we be moral?" if this question is interpreted rather as "Why should we all be moral—rather than all being something else?" If we must all be the same, then each person has a reason—a prudential reason—to prefer that we all be moral.

But, so interpreted, "Why should we be moral?" is not a compendious way of asking, for each person, "Why should I be moral?" Of course, if everyone is to be whatever I am, then I should be moral. But a general answer to the question "Why should I be moral?" cannot presuppose this.

The second consideration is that any individual always does better to be prudent rather than moral, provided his choice does not determine other choices. But in so far as this answers the question "Why should I be moral?" it leads to the conclusion "I should not be moral." One feels that this is not the answer which is wanted.

We may put the matter otherwise. The individual who needs a reason for being moral which is not itself a moral reason cannot have it. There is nothing surprising about this; it would be much more surprising if such reasons could be found. For it is more than apparently paradoxical to suppose that considerations of advantage could ever of themselves justify accepting a real disadvantage.

V

I suggested in Section II that the thesis, in modified form, might provide a necessary, although not a sufficient, condition for a moral system. I want now to consider how one might characterize the man who would qualify as moral according to the thesis—I shall call him the "moral" man—and then ask what would be lacking from this characterization, in terms of some of our commonplace moral views.

The rationally prudent man is incapable of moral behavior, in even the limited sense defined by the thesis. What difference must there be between the prudent man and the "moral" man? Most simply, the "moral" man is the prudent but trustworthy man. I treat trustworthiness as the capacity which enables its possessor to adhere, and to judge that he ought to adhere, to a commitment which he has made, without regard to considerations of advantage.

The prudent but trustworthy man does not possess this capacity completely. He is capable of trustworthy behavior only in so far as he regards his *commitment* as advantageous. Thus he differs from the prudent man just in the relevant respect; he accepts arguments of the form "If it is advantageous for me to agree[7] to do x, and I do agree to do x, then I ought to do x, whether or not it then proves advantageous for me to do x."

Suppose that A and B, the parties to the disarmament pact, are prudent but trustworthy. A, considering whether or not secretly to violate the agreement, reasons that its advantage in making and keeping the agreement, provided B does so as well, is greater than its advantage in not making it. If it can assume that B reasons in the same way, then it is in a position to conclude that it ought not to violate the pact. Although violation would be advantageous, consideration of this advantage is ruled out by A's trustworthiness, given the advantage in agreeing to the pact.

The prudent but trustworthy man meets the requirements implicitly imposed by the thesis for the "moral" man. But how far does this "moral" man display two characteristics commonly associated with morality—first, a willingness to make sacrifices, and second, a concern with fairness?

Whenever a man ignores his own advantage for reasons other than those of greater advantage, he may be said to make some sacrifice. The "moral" man, in being trustworthy, is thus required to make certain sacrifices. But these are extremely limited. And—not surprisingly, given the general direction of our argument—it is quite possible that they limit the advantages which the "moral" man can secure.

Once more let us turn to our example. A and B have entered into a disarmament agreement and, being prudent but trustworthy, are faithfully carrying it out. The government of A is now informed by its scientists, however, that they have developed an effective missile defense, which will render A in-

vulnerable to attack by any of the weapons actually or potentially at B's disposal, barring unforeseen technological developments. Furthermore, this defense can be installed secretly. The government is now called upon to decide whether to violate its agreement with B, install the new defense, and, with the arms it has retained through its violation, establish its dominance over B.

A is in a type of situation quite different from that previously considered. For it is not just that A will do better by secretly violating its agreement. A reasons not only that it will do better to violate no matter what B does, but that it will do better if both violate than if both continue to adhere to the pact. A is now in a position to gain from abandoning the agreement; it no longer finds mutual adherence advantageous.

We may represent this new situation in another matrix:

		B	
		adheres	violates
	adheres	3, 2	4, 1
A			
	violates	1, 4	2, 3

We assume again that the ranking of mutual violation is the same as that of no agreement. Now had this situation obtained at the outset, no agreement would have been made, for A would have had no reason to enter into a disarmament pact. And of course had A expected this situation to come about, no agreement—or only a temporary agreement—would have been made; A would no doubt have risked the short-term dangers of the continuing arms race in the hope of securing the long-run benefit of predominance over B once its missile defense was completed. On the contrary, A expected to benefit from the agreement, but now finds that, because of its unexpected development of a missile defense, the agreement is not in fact advantageous to it.

The prudent but trustworthy man is willing to carry out his agreements, and judges that he ought to carry them out, in so far as he considers them advantageous. A is prudent but trustworthy. But is A willing to carry out its agreement to disarm, now that it no longer considers the agreement advantageous?

If *A* adheres to its agreement in this situation, it makes a sacrifice greater than any advantage it receives from the similar sacrifices of others. It makes a sacrifice greater in kind than any which can be required by a mutually advantageous agreement. It must, then, possess a capacity for trustworthy behavior greater than that ascribed to the merely prudent but trustworthy man (or nation). This capacity need not be unlimited; it need not extend to a willingness to adhere to any commitment no matter what sacrifice is involved. But it must involve a willingness to adhere to a commitment made in the expectation of advantage, should that expectation be disappointed.

I shall call the man (or nation) who is willing to adhere, and judges that he ought to adhere, to his prudentially undertaken agreements even if they prove disadvantageous to him, the trustworthy man. It is likely that there are advantages available to trustworthy men which are not available to merely prudent but trustworthy men. For there may be situations in which men can make agreements which each expects to be advantageous to him, provided he can count on the others' adhering to it whether or not their expectation of advantage is realized. But each can count on this only if all have the capacity to adhere to commitments regardless of whether the commitment actually proves advantageous. Hence, only trustworthy men who know each other to be such will be able rationally to enter into, and so to benefit from, such agreements.

Baier's view of morality departs from that stated in the thesis in that it requires trustworthy, and not merely prudent but trustworthy, men. Baier admits that "a person might do better for himself by following enlightened self-interest rather than morality."[8] This admission seems to require that morality be a system of principles which each person may expect, initially, to be advantageous to him, if adopted and adhered to by everyone, but not a system which actually is advantageous to everyone.

Our commonplace moral views do, I think support the view that the moral man must be trustworthy. Hence, we have established one modification required in the thesis, if it is to provide a more adequate set of conditions for a moral system.

But there is a much more basic respect in which the "moral" man falls short of our expectations. He is willing to temper his single-minded pursuit of advantage only by accepting the obligation to adhere to prudentially undertaken commitments. He has no real concern for the advantage of others, which would lead him to modify his pursuit of advantage when it conflicted with the similar pursuits of others. Unless he expects to gain, he is unwilling to accept restrictions on the pursuit of advantage which are intended to equalize the opportunities open to all. In other words, he has no concern with fairness.

We tend to think of the moral man as one who does not seek his own well-being by means which would deny equal well-being to his fellows. This marks him off clearly from the "moral" man, who differs from the prudent man only in that he can overcome the apparent paradox of prudence and obtain those advantages which are available only to those who can display real restraint in their pursuit of advantage.

Thus a system of principles might meet the conditions laid down in the thesis without taking any account of considerations of fairness. Such a system would contain principles for ensuring increased advantage (or expectation of advantage) to everyone, but no further principle need be present to determine the distribution of this increase.

It is possible that there are systems of principles which, if adopted and adhered to, provide advantages which strictly prudent men, however rational, cannot attain. These advantages are a function of the sacrifices which the principles impose on their adherents.

Morality may be such a system. If it is, this would explain our expectation that we should all be worse off were we to substitute prudence for morality in our deliberations. But to characterize morality as a system of principles advantageous to all is not to answer the question "Why should I be moral?" nor is it to provide for those considerations of fairness which are equally essential to our moral understanding.

NOTES

1. David Hume, *An Enquiry Concerning the Principles of Morals*, sec. ix, pt. ii.
2. Ogden Nash, "Kind of an Ode to Duty."

3. Kurt Baier, *The Moral Point of View: A Rational Basis of Ethics* (Ithaca, 1958), p. 314.

4. That this, and only this, is what he is entitled to claim may not be clear to Baier, for he supposes his account of morality to answer the question "Why should we be moral?," interpreting "we" distributively. This, as I shall argue in Sec. IV, is quite mistaken.

5. The thesis is not intended to state Baier's view of morality. I shall suggest in Sec. V that Baier's view would require substituting "everyone can expect to benefit" for "it is advantageous to everyone." The thesis is stronger and easier to discuss.

6. Those familiar with the theory of games will recognize the matrix as a variant of the Prisoner's Dilemma. In a more formal treatment, it would be appropriate to develop the relation between morality and advantage by reference to the Prisoner's Dilemma. This would require reconstructing the disarmament pact and the moral system as proper games. Here I wish only to suggest the bearing of game theory on our enterprise.

7. The word "agree" requires elucidation. It is essential not to confuse an advantage in agreeing to do x with an advantage in saying that one will do x. If it is advantageous for me to agree to do x, then there is some set of actions open to me which includes both saying that I will do x and doing x, and which is more advantageous to me than any set of actions open to me which does not include saying that I will do x. On the other hand, if it is advantageous for me to say that I will do x, then there is some set of actions open to me which includes saying that I will do x, and which is more advantageous to me than any set which does not include saying that I will do x. But this set need not include doing x.

8. Baier, *op. cit.*, p. 314.

The Law of the Jungle: Moral Alternatives and Principles of Evolution

J. L. MACKIE

WHEN PEOPLE SPEAK OF "THE law of the jungle," they usually mean unrestrained and ruthless competition, with everyone out solely for his own advantage. But the phrase was coined by Rudyard Kipling, in *The Second Jungle Book*, and he meant something very different. His law of the jungle is a law that wolves in a pack are supposed to obey. His poem says that "the strength of the Pack is the Wolf, and the strength of the Wolf is the Pack," and it states the basic principles of social co-operation. Its provisions are a judicious mixture of individualism and collectivism, prescribing graduated and qualified rights for fathers of families, mothers with cubs, and young wolves, which constitute an elementary system of welfare services. Of course, Kipling meant his poem to give moral instruction to human children, but he probably thought it was at least roughly correct as a description of the social behaviour of wolves and other wild animals. Was he right, or is the natural world the scene of unrestrained competition, of an individualistic struggle for existence?

Views not unlike those of Kipling have been presented by some recent writers on ethology, notably Robert Ardrey and Konrad Lorenz. These writers connect their accounts with a view about the process of evolution that has brought this behaviour, as well as the animals themselves, into existence. They hold that the important thing in evolution is the good of the species, or the group, rather than the good of the individual. Natural selection favours those groups and species whose members tend, no doubt through some instinctive programming, to co-operate for a common good; this would, of course, explain why wolves, for example, behave co-operatively and generously towards members of their own pack, if indeed they do.

However, this recently popular view has been keenly attacked by Richard Dawkins in his admirable and fascinating book, *The Selfish Gene*.[1] He defends an up-to-date version of the orthodox Darwinian theory of evolution, with special reference to "the biology of selfishness and altruism." One of his main theses is that there is no such thing as group selection, and that Lorenz and others who have used this as an explanation are simply wrong. This is a question of some interest to moral philosophers, particularly those who have been inclined to see human morality itself as the product of some kind of natural evolution.[2]

It is well, however, to be clear about the issue. It is not whether animals ever behave for the good of the group in the sense that this is their conscious subjective goal, that they *aim* at the well-being or survival of the whole tribe or pack: the question of motives in this conscious sense does not arise. Nor is the issue whether animals ever behave in ways which do in fact promote the well-being of the group to which they belong, or which help the species of which they are members to survive: of course they do. The controversial issue is different from both of these: it is whether the good of the group or the species would ever figure in a correct evolutionary account. That is, would any correct evolutionary account take either of the following forms?

i. The members of this species tend to do these things which assist the survival of this species because their ancestors were members of a sub-species whose members had an inheritable tendency to do these things, and as a result that sub-species survived, whereas other sub-species of the ancestral species at that time had members who tended not to do these things and as a result their sub-species did not survive.

ii. The members of this species tend to do these things which help the group of which they are members to flourish because some ancestral groups happened to have members who tended to do these things and these groups, as a result, survived better than related groups of the ancestral species whose members tended not to do these things.

In other words, the issue is this: is there natural selection by and for group survival or species survival as opposed to selection by and for individual survival (or, as we shall see, gene survival)? Is behaviour that helps the group or the species, rather than the individual animal, rewarded by the natural selection which determines the course of evolution?

However, when Dawkins denies that there is selection by and for group or species survival, it is not selection by and for individual survival that he puts in its place. Rather it is selection by and for the survival of each single gene—the genes being the unit factors of inheritance, the portions of chromosomes which replicate themselves, copy themselves as cells divide and multiply. Genes, he argues, came into existence right back at the beginning of life on earth, and all more complex organisms are to be seen as their products. We are, as he picturesquely puts it, gene-machines: our biological function is just to protect our genes, carry them around, and enable them to reproduce themselves. Hence the title of his book, *The Selfish Gene*. Of course what survives is not a token gene: each of these perishes with the cell of which it is a part. What survives is a gene-type, or rather what we might call a gene-clone, the members of a family of token genes related to one another by simple direct descent, by replication. The popularity of the notions of species selection and group selection may be due partly to confusion on this point. Since clearly it is only types united by descent, not individual organisms, that survive long enough to be of biological interest, it is easy to think that selection must be by and for species survival. But this is a mistake: genes, not species, are the types which primarily replicate themselves and are selected. Since Dawkins roughly defines the gene as "a genetic unit which is small enough to last for a number of generations and to be distributed around in the form of many copies," it is (as he admits) practically a tautology that the gene is the basic unit of natural selection and therefore, as he puts it, "the fundamental unit of self-interest," or, as we might put it less picturesquely, the primary beneficiary of natural selection. But behind this near-tautology is a synthetic truth, that this basic unit, this primary beneficiary, is a small bit of chromosome. The reason why this is so, why what is differentially effective and therefore subject to selection is a small bit of a chromosome, lies in the mechanism of sexual reproduction by way of meiosis, with crossing over between chromosomes. When male and female cells each divide before uniting at fertilization, it is not chromosomes as a whole that are randomly distributed between the parts, but sections of chromosomes. So sections of chromosomes can be separately inherited, and therefore can be differentially selected by natural selection.

The issue between gene selection, individual selection, group selection, and species selection might seem to raise some stock questions in the philosophy of science. Many thinkers have favoured reductionism of several sorts, including methodological individualism. Wholes are made up of parts, and therefore in principle whatever happens in any larger thing depends upon and is explainable in terms of what happens in and between its smaller components. But though this metaphysical individualism is correct, methodological individualism does not follow from it. It does not follow that we must always conduct our investigations and construct our explanations in terms of component parts, such as the individual members of a group or society. Scientific accounts need not be indefinitely reductive. Some wholes are obviously more accessible to us than their components. We can understand what a human being does without analysing this in terms of how each single cell in his body or his brain

behaves. Equally we can often understand what a human society does without analysing this in terms of the behaviour of each of its individual members. And the same holds quite generally: we can often understand complex wholes as units, without analysing them into their parts. So if, in the account of evolution, Dawkins's concentration upon genes were just a piece of methodological individualism or reductionism, it would be inadequately motivated. But it is not: there is a special reason for it. Dawkins's key argument is that species, populations, and groups, and individual organisms too, are as genetic units too temporary to qualify for natural selection. "They are not stable through evolutionary time. Populations are constantly blending with other populations and so losing their identity," and, what is vitally important, "are also subject to evolutionary change from within" (p. 36).

This abstract general proposition may seem obscure. But it is illustrated by a simple example which Dawkins gives (pp. 197–201).

A species of birds is parasitized by dangerous ticks. A bird can remove the ticks from most parts of its own body, but, having only a beak and no hands, it cannot get them out of the top of its own head. But one bird can remove ticks from another bird's head: there can be mutual grooming. Clearly if there were an inherited tendency for each bird to take the ticks out of any other bird's head, this would help the survival of any group in which that tendency happened to arise—for the ticks are dangerous: they can cause death. Some who believe in group selection would, therefore, expect this tendency to be favoured and to evolve and spread for this reason. But Dawkins shows that it would not. He gives appropriate names to the different "strategies," that is, the different inheritable behavioural tendencies. The strategy of grooming anyone who needs it he labels "Sucker." The strategy of accepting grooming from anyone, but never grooming anyone else, even someone who has previously groomed you, is called "Cheat." Now if in some population both these tendencies or strategies, and only these two, happen to arise, it is easy to see that the cheats will always do better than the suckers. They will be groomed when they need it, and since they will not waste their time pecking out other birds' ticks, they will have more time and energy to spare for finding food, attracting mates, building nests, and so on. Consequently the gene for the Sucker strategy will gradually die out. So the population will come to consist wholly of cheats, despite the fact that this is likely to lead to the population itself becoming extinct, if the parasites are common enough and dangerous enough, whereas a population consisting wholly of suckers would have survived. The fact that the group is open to evolutionary change from within, because of the way the internal competition between Cheat and Sucker genes works out, prevents the group from developing or even retaining a feature which would have helped the group as a whole.

This is just one illustration among many, and Dawkins's arguments on this point seem pretty conclusive. We need, as he shows, the concept of an *evolutionarily stable strategy* or *ESS* (p. 74 *et passim*). A strategy is evolutionarily stable, in relation to some alternative strategy or strategies, if it will survive indefinitely in a group in competition with those alternatives. We have just seen that where Cheat and Sucker alone are in competition, Cheat is an ESS but Sucker is not. We have also seen, from this example, that an ESS may not help a group, or the whole species, to survive and multiply. Of course we must not leap to the conclusion that an ESS never helps a group or a species: if that were so we could not explain much of the behaviour that actually occurs. Parents sacrifice themselves for their children, occasionally siblings for their siblings, and with the social insects, bees and ants and termites, their whole life is a system of communal service. But the point is that these results are not to be explained in terms of group selection. They can and must be explained as consequences of the selfishness of genes, that is, the fact that gene-clones are selected for whatever helps each gene-clone itself to survive and multiply.

But now we come to another remarkable fact. Although the gene is the hero of Dawkins's book, it is not unique either in principle or in fact. It is not the only possible subject of evolutionary natural selection, nor is it the only actual one. What is important about the gene is just that it has a certain combination of logical features. It is a replicator: in the right environment it is capable of producing multiple copies of itself: but in this process of copy-

ing some mistakes occur: and even mistaken copies—mutations—will also produce copies of themselves: and, finally, the copies produced may either survive or fail to survive. Anything that has these formal, logical, features is a possible subject of evolution by natural selection. As we have seen, individual organisms, groups, and species do not have the required formal features, though many thinkers have supposed that they do. They cannot reproduce themselves with sufficient constancy of characteristics. But Dawkins, in his last chapter, introduces another sort of replicators. These are what are often called cultural items or traits; Dawkins christens them *memes*—to make a term a bit like "genes"—because they replicate by memory and imitation (mimesis). Memes include tunes, ideas, fashions, and techniques. They require, as the environment in which they can replicate, a collection of minds, that is, brains that have the powers of imitation and memory. These brains (particularly though not exclusively human ones) are themselves the products of evolution by gene selection. But once the brains are there gene selection has done its work: given that environment, memes can themselves evolve and multiply in much the same way as genes do, in accordance with logically similar laws. But they can do so more quickly. Cultural evolution may be much faster than biological evolution. But the basic laws are the same. Memes are selfish in the same sense as genes. The explanation of the widespread flourishing of a certain meme, such as the idea of a god or the belief in hell fire, may be simply that it is an efficiently selfish meme. Something about it makes it well able to infect human minds, to take root and spread in and among them, in the same way that something about the smallpox virus makes it well able to take root and spread in human bodies. There is no need to explain the success of a meme in terms of any benefit it confers on individuals or groups; it is a replicator in its own right. Contrary to the optimistic view often taken of cultural evolution, this analogy shows that a cultural trait can evolve, not because it is advantageous to society, but simply because it is advantageous to itself. It is ironical that Kipling's phrase "the law of the jungle" has proved itself a more efficient meme than the doctrine he tried to use it to propagate.

So far I have been merely summarizing Dawkins's argument. We can now use it to answer the question from which I started. Who is right about the law of the jungle? Kipling, or those who have twisted his phrase to mean almost the opposite of what he intended? The answer is that neither party is right. The law by which nature works is not unrestrained and ruthless competition between individual organisms. But neither does it turn upon the advantages to a group, and its members, of group solidarity, mutual care and respect, and cooperation. It turns upon the self-preservation of gene-clones. This has a strong tendency to express itself in individually selfish behaviour, simply because each agent's genes are more certainly located in him than in anyone else. But it can and does express itself also in certain forms of what Broad called self-referential altruism, including special care for one's own children and perhaps one's siblings, and, as we shall see, reciprocal altruism, helping those (and only those) who help you.

But now I come to what seems to be an exception to Dawkins's main thesis, though it is generated by his own argument and illustrated by one of his own examples. We saw how, in the example of mutual grooming, if there are only suckers and cheats around, the strategy Cheat is evolutionarily stable, while the strategy Sucker is not. But Dawkins introduces a third strategy, Grudger. A grudger is rather like you and me. A grudger grooms anyone who has previously groomed him, and any stranger, but he remembers and bears a grudge against anyone who cheats him—who refuses to groom him in return for having been groomed—and the grudger refuses to groom the cheat ever again. Now when all three strategies are in play, both Cheat and Grudger are evolutionarily stable. In a population consisting largely of cheats, the cheats will do better than the others, and both suckers and grudgers will die out. But in a population that starts off with more than a certain critical proportion of grudgers, the cheats will first wipe out the suckers, but will then themselves become rare and eventually extinct: cheats can flourish only while they have suckers to take advantage of, and yet by doing so they tend to eliminate those suckers.

It is obvious, by the way, that a population con-

taining only suckers and grudgers, in any proportions, but no cheats, would simply continue as it was. Suckers and grudgers behave exactly like one another as long as there are no cheats around, so there would be no tendency for either the Sucker or the Grudger gene to do better than the other. But if there is any risk of an invasion of Cheat genes, either through mutation or through immigration, such a pattern is not evolutionarily stable, and the higher the proportion of suckers, the more rapidly the cheats would multiply.

So we have two ESSs, Cheat and Grudger. But there is a difference between these two stable strategies. If the parasites are common enough and dangerous enough, the population of cheats will itself die out, having no defence against ticks in their heads, whereas a separate population of grudgers will flourish indefinitely. Dawkins says, "If a population arrives at an ESS which drives it extinct, then it goes extinct, and that is just too bad" (p. 200). True: *but is this not group selection after all?* Of course, this will operate only if the populations are somehow isolated. But if the birds in question were distributed in geographically isolated regions, and Sucker, Cheat and Grudger tendencies appeared (after the parasites became plentiful) in randomly different proportions in these different regions, then some populations would become pure grudger populations, and others would die out, so that eventually all surviving birds would be grudgers. And they would be able to re-colonize the areas where cheat populations had perished.

Another name for grudgers is "reciprocal altruists." They act as if on the maxim "Be done by as you did." One implication of this story is that this strategy is not only evolutionarily stable within a population, it is also viable for a population as a whole. The explanation of the final situation, where all birds of this species are grudgers, lies partly in the non-viability of a population of pure cheats. So this is, as I said, a bit of group selection after all.

. . . .

What implications for human morality have such biological facts about selfishness and altruism? One is that the possibility that morality is itself a product of natural selection is not ruled out, but care would be needed in formulating a plausible speculative account of how it might have been favoured. Another is that the notion of an ESS may be a useful one for discussing questions of practical morality. Moral philosophers have already found illumination in such simple items of game theory as the Prisoners' Dilemma; perhaps these rather more complicated evolutionary "games" will prove equally instructive. Of course there is no simple transition from "is" to "ought," no direct argument from what goes on in the natural world and among non-human animals to what human beings ought to do. Dawkins himself explicitly warns against any simple transfer of conclusions. At the very end of the book he suggests that conscious foresight may enable us to develop radically new kinds of behaviour. "We are built as gene-machines and cultured as meme-machines, but we have the power to turn against our creators. We, alone on earth, can rebel against the tyranny of the selfish replicators" (p. 215). This optimistic suggestion needs fuller investigation. It must be remembered that the human race as a whole cannot act as a unit with conscious foresight. Arrow's Theorem shows that even quite small groups of rational individuals may be unable to form coherently rational preferences, let alone to act rationally. Internal competition, which in general prevents a group from being a possible subject of natural selection, is even more of an obstacle to its being a rational agent. And while we can turn against some memes, it will be only with the help and under the guidance of other memes.

This is an enormously problematic area. For the moment I turn to a smaller point. In the mutual grooming model, we saw that the Grudger strategy was, of the three strategies considered, the only one that was healthy in the long run. Now something closely resembling this strategy, reciprocal altruism, is a well-known and long-established tendency in human life. It is expressed in such formulae as that justice consists in giving everyone his due, interpreted, as Polemarchus interprets it in the first book of Plato's *Republic*, as doing good to one's friends and harm to one's enemies, or repaying good with good and evil with evil. Morality itself has been seen, for example by Edward Westermarck, as an outgrowth from the retributive emotions. But some moralists, including Socrates and Jesus, have recommended something very different from this, turning the other cheek and repaying evil with good. They have tried to substitute "Do as you would be done by" for "Be done by as you did." Now this, which in human life we characterize as a Christian spirit or perhaps as saintliness, is roughly equivalent to the strategy Dawkins has unkindly labelled "Sucker." Suckers are saints, just as grudgers are reciprocal altruists, while cheats are a hundred per cent selfish. And as Dawkins points out, the presence of suckers endangers the healthy Grudger strategy. It allows cheats to prosper, and could make them multiply to the point where they would wipe out the grudgers, and ultimately bring about the extinction of the whole population. This seems to provide fresh support for Nietzsche's view of the deplorable influence of moralities of the Christian type. But in practice there may be little danger. After two thousand years of contrary moral teaching, reciprocal altruism is still dominant in all human societies: thoroughgoing cheats and thoroughgoing saints (or suckers) are distinctly rare. The sucker slogan is an efficient meme, but the sucker behaviour pattern far less so. Saintliness is an attractive topic for preaching, but with little practical persuasive force. Whether in the long run this is to be deplored or welcomed, and whether it is alterable or not, is a larger question. To answer it we should have carefully to examine our specifically human capabilities and the structure of human societies, and also many further alternative strategies. We cannot simply apply to the human situation conclusions drawn from biological models. Nevertheless they are significant and challenging as models; it will need to be shown how and where human life diverges from them.

NOTES

1. R. Dawkins, *The Selfish Gene* (Oxford, 1976).
2. I am among these: see p. 113 of my *Ethics: Inventing Right and Wrong* (Penguin, Harmondsworth, 1977).

2. SUBJECTIVISM, RELATIVISM, AND SKEPTICISM

The Subjectivity of Values

J. L. MACKIE

—•—

1. Moral Scepticism

There are no objective values. This is a bald statement of the thesis of this chapter, but before arguing for it I shall try to clarify and restrict it in ways that may meet some objections and prevent some misunderstanding.

The statement of this thesis is liable to provoke one of the three very different reactions. Some will think it not merely false but pernicious; they will see it as a threat to morality and to everything else that is worthwhile, and they will find the presenting of such a thesis in what purports to be a book on ethics paradoxical or even outrageous. Others will regard it as a trivial truth, almost too obvious to be worth mentioning, and certainly too plain to be worth much argument. Others again will say that it is meaningless or empty, that no real issue is raised by the question whether values are or are not part of the fabric of the world. But, precisely because there can be these three different reactions, much more needs to be said.

The claim that values are not objective, are not part of the fabric of the world, is meant to include not only moral goodness, which might be most naturally equated with moral value, but also other things that could be more loosely called moral values or disvalues—rightness and wrongness, duty,

obligation, an action's being rotten and contemptible, and so on. It also includes non-moral values, notably aesthetic ones, beauty and various kinds of artistic merit. I shall not discuss these explicitly, but clearly much the same considerations apply to aesthetic and to moral values, and there would be at least some initial implausibility in a view that gave the one a different status from the other.

Since it is with moral values that I am primarily concerned, the view I am adopting may be called moral scepticism. But this name is likely to be misunderstood: "moral scepticism" might also be used as a name for either of two first order views, or perhaps for an incoherent mixture of the two. A moral sceptic might be the sort of person who says "All this talk of morality is tripe," who rejects morality and will take no notice of it. Such a person may be literally rejecting all moral judgments; he is more likely to be making moral judgments of his own, expressing a positive moral condemnation of all that conventionally passes for morality; or he may be confusing these two logically incompatible views, and saying that he rejects all morality, while he is in fact rejecting only a particular morality that is current in that society in which he has grown up. But I am not at present concerned with the merits or faults of such a position. These are first order moral views, positive or negative: the person who adopts either of them is taking a certain practical, normative, stand. By contrast, what I am discussing is a second order view, a view about the status of moral values and the nature of moral valuing, about where and how they fit into the world. These first and second order views are not merely distinct but completely independent: one could be a second order moral sceptic without being a first order one, or again the other way round. A man could hold strong moral views, and indeed ones whose content was thoroughly conventional, while believing that they were simply attitudes and policies with regard to conduct that he and other people held. Conversely, a man could reject all established morality while believing it to be an objective truth that it was evil or corrupt.

With another sort of misunderstanding moral scepticism would seem not so much pernicious as absurd. How could anyone deny that there is a difference between a kind action and a cruel one, or that a coward and a brave man behave differently in the face of danger? Of course, this is undeniable; but it is not to the point. The kinds of behaviour to which moral values and disvalues are ascribed are indeed part of the furniture of the world, and so are the natural, descriptive, differences between them; but, not perhaps, their differences in value. It is a hard fact that cruel actions differ from kind ones, and hence that we can learn, as in fact we all do, to distinguish them fairly well in practice, and to use the words "cruel" and "kind" with fairly clear descriptive meanings; but is it an equally hard fact that actions which are cruel in such a descriptive sense are to be condemned? The present issue is with regard to the objectivity specifically of value, not with regard to the objectivity of those natural, factual, differences on the basis of which differing values are assigned.

2. Subjectivism

Another name often used, as an alternative to "moral scepticism," for the view I am discussing is "subjectivism." But this too has more than one meaning. Moral subjectivism too could be a first order, normative, view, namely that everyone really ought to do whatever he thinks he should. This plainly is a (systematic) first order view; on examination it soon ceases to be plausible, but that is beside the point, for it is quite independent of the sec-

ond order thesis at present under consideration. What is more confusing is that different second order views compete for the name "subjectivism." Several of these are doctrines about the meaning of moral terms and moral statements. What is often called moral subjectivism is the doctrine that, for example, "This action is right" *means* "I approve of this action," or more generally that moral judgments are equivalent to reports of the speaker's own feelings or attitudes. But the view I am now discussing is to be distinguished in two vital respects from any such doctrine as this. First, what I have called moral scepticism is a negative doctrine, not a positive one: it says what there isn't, not what there is. It says that there do not exist entities or relations of a certain kind, objective values or requirements, which many people have believed to exist. Of course, the moral sceptic cannot leave it at that. If his position is to be at all plausible, he must give some account of how other people have fallen into what he regards as an error, and this account will have to include some positive suggestions about how values fail to be objective, about what has been mistaken for, or has led to false beliefs about, objective values. But this will be a development of his theory, not its core: its core is the negation. Secondly, what I have called moral subjectivism, is an ontological thesis, not a linguistic or conceptual one. It is not, like the other doctrine often called moral subjectivism, a view about the meanings of moral statements. Again, no doubt, if it is to be at all plausible, it will have to give some account of their meanings, and I shall say something about this in Section 7 of this chapter. . . . But this too will be a development of the theory, not its core.

It is true that those who have accepted the moral subjectivism which is the doctrine that moral judgments are equivalent to reports of the speaker's own feelings or attitudes have usually presupposed what I am calling moral scepticism. It is because they have assumed that there are no objective values that they have looked elsewhere for an analysis of what moral statements might mean, and have settled upon subjective reports. Indeed, if all our moral statements were such subjective reports, it would follow that, at least so far as we are aware, there are no objective moral values. If we were aware of them, we would say something about them. In this sense this sort of subjectivism entails moral scepticism. But the converse entailment does not hold. The denial that there are objective values does not commit one to any particular view about what moral statements mean, and certainly not to the view that they are equivalent to subjective reports. No doubt if moral values are not objective they are in some very broad sense subjective, and for this reason I would accept "moral subjectivism" as an alternative name to "moral scepticism." But subjectivism in this broad sense must be distinguished from the specific doctrine about meaning referred to above. Neither name is altogether satisfactory: we simply have to guard against the (different) misinterpretations which each may suggest.

. . . .

5. Standards of Evaluation

One way of stating the thesis that there are no objective values is to say that value statements cannot be either true or false. But this formulation, too, lends itself to misinterpretation. For there are certain kinds of value statements which undoubtedly can be true or false, even if, in the sense I intend, there are no objective values. Evaluations of many sorts are commonly made in relation to agreed and assumed standards. The classing of wool, the grading of apples, the awarding of prizes at sheepdog trials, flower shows, skating and diving championships, and even the marking of examination papers are carried out in relation to standards of quality or merit which are peculiar to each particular subject-matter or type of contest, which may be explicitly laid down but which, even if they are nowhere explicitly stated, are fairly well understood and agreed by those who are recognized as judges or experts in each particular field. Given any sufficiently determinate standards, it will be an objective issue, a matter of truth and falsehood, how well any particular specimen measures up to those standards. Comparative judgments in particular will be capable of truth and falsehood: it will be a factual question whether this sheepdog has performed better than that one.

The subjectivist about values, then, is not denying that there can be objective evaluations relative to standards, and these are as possible in the aesthetic and moral fields as in any of those just mentioned. More than this, there is an objective distinction which applies in many such fields, and yet would itself be regarded as a peculiarly moral one: the distinction between justice and injustice. In one important sense of the word it is a paradigm case of injustice if a court declares someone to be guilty of an offence of which it knows him to be innocent. More generally, a finding is unjust if it is at variance with what the relevant law and the facts together require, and particularly if it is known by the court to be so. More generally still, any award of marks, prizes, or the like is unjust if it is at variance with the agreed standards for the contest in question: if one diver's performance in fact measures up better to the accepted standards for diving than another's, it will be unjust if the latter is awarded higher marks or the prize. In this way the justice or injustice of decisions relative to standards can be a thoroughly objective matter, though there may still be a subjective element in the interpretation or application of standards. But the statement that a certain decision is thus just or unjust will not be objectively prescriptive: in so far as it can be simply true it leaves open the question whether there is any objective requirement to do what is just and to refrain from what is unjust, and equally leaves open the practical decision to act in either way.

Recognizing the objectivity of justice in relation to standards, and of evaluative judgments relative to standards, then, merely shifts the question of the objectivity of values back to the standards themselves. The subjectivist may try to make his point by insisting that there is no objective validity about the choice of standards. Yet he would clearly be wrong if he said that the choice of even the most basic standards in any field was completely arbitrary. The standards use in sheepdog trials clearly bear some relation to the work that sheepdogs are kept to do, the standards for grading apples bear some relation to what people generally want in or like about apples, and so on. On the other hand, standards are not as a rule strictly validated by such purposes. The appropriateness of standards is neither fully determinate nor totally indeterminate in relation to independently specifiable aims or desires. But however determinate it is, the objective appropriateness of standards in relation to aims or desires is no more of a threat to the denial of objective values than is the objectivity of evaluation relative to standards. In fact it is logically no different from the objectivity of goodness relative to desires. Something may be called good simply in so far as it satisfies or is such as to satisfy a certain desire; but the objectivity of such relations of satisfaction does not constitute in our sense an objective value.

6. Hypothetical and Categorical Imperatives

We may make this issue clearer by referring to Kant's distinction between hypothetical and categorical imperatives, though what he called imperatives are more naturally expressed as "ought" statements than in the imperative mood. "If you want X, do Y" (or "You ought to do Y") will be a hypothetical imperative if it is based on the supposed fact that Y is, in the circumstances, the only (or the best) available means to X, that is, on a causal relation between Y and X. The reason for doing Y lies in its causal connection with the desired end, X; the oughtness is contingent upon the desire. But "You ought to do Y" will be a categorical imperative if you ought to do Y irrespective of any such desire for any end to which Y would contribute, if the oughtness is not thus contingent upon any desire. But this distinction needs to be handled with some care. An "ought"-statement is not in this sense hypothetical merely because it incorporates a conditional clause. "If you promised to do Y, you ought to do Y" is not a hypothetical imperative merely on account of the stated if-clause; what is meant may be either a hypothetical or a categorical imperative, depending upon the implied reason for keeping the supposed promise. If this rests upon some such further unstated conditional as "If you want to be trusted another time," then it is a hypothetical imperative; if not, it is categorical. Even a desire of the agent's can figure in the antecedent of what, though conditional in grammatical form, is still in Kant's sense a categorical imperative. "If you are strongly attracted

sexually to young children you ought not to go in for school teaching" is not, in virtue of what it explicitly says, a hypothetical imperative: the avoidance of school teaching is not being offered as a means to the satisfaction of the desires in question. Of course, it could still be a hypothetical imperative, if the implied reason were a prudential one; but it could also be a categorical imperative, a moral requirement where the reason for the recommended action (strictly, avoidance) does not rest upon that action's being a means to the satisfaction of any desire that the agent is supposed to have. Not every conditional ought-statement or command, then, is a hypothetical imperative; equally, not every non-conditional one is a categorical imperative. An appropriate if-clause may be left unstated. Indeed, a simple command in the imperative mood, say a parade-ground order, which might seem most literally to qualify for the title of a categorical imperative, will hardly ever be one in the sense we need here. The implied reason for complying with such an order will almost always be some desire of the person addressed, perhaps simply the desire to keep out of the trouble. If so, such an apparently categorical order will be in our sense a hypothetical imperative. Again, an imperative remains hypothetical even if we change the "if" to "since": the fact that the desire for X is actually present does not alter the fact that the reason for doing Y is contingent upon the desire for X by way of Y's being a means to X. In Kant's own treatment, while imperatives of skill relate to desires which an agent may or may not have, imperatives of prudence relate to the desire for happiness which, Kant assumes, everyone has. So construed, imperatives of prudence are no less hypothetical than imperatives of skill, no less contingent upon desires that the agent has at the time the imperatives are addressed to him. But if we think rather of a counsel of prudence as being related to the agent's future welfare, to the satisfaction of desires that he does not yet have—not even to a present desire that his future desires should be satisfied—then a counsel of prudence is a categorical imperative, different indeed from a moral one, but analogous to it.

A categorical imperative, then, would express a reason for acting which was unconditional in the sense of not being contingent upon any present desire of the agent to whose satisfaction the recommended action would contribute as a means—or more directly: "You ought to dance," if the implied reason is just that you want to dance or like dancing, is still a hypothetical imperative. Now Kant himself held that moral judgments are categorical imperatives, or perhaps are all applications of one categorical imperative, and it can plausibly be maintained at least that many moral judgments contain a categorically imperative element. So far as ethics is concerned, my thesis that there are no objective values is specifically the denial that any such categorically imperative element is objectively valid. The objective values which I am denying would be action-directing absolutely, not contingently (in the way indicated) upon the agent's desires and inclinations.

Another way of trying to clarify this issue is to refer to moral reasoning or moral arguments. In practice, of course, such reasoning is seldom fully explicit: but let us suppose that we could make explicit the reasoning that supports some evaluative conclusion, where this conclusion has some action-guiding force that is not contingent upon desires or purposes or chosen ends. Then what I am saying is that somewhere in the input to this argument—perhaps in one or more of the premises, perhaps in some part of the form of the argument—there will be something which cannot be objectively validated—some premiss which is not capable of being simply true, or some form of argument which is not valid as a matter of general logic, whose authority or cogency is not objective, but is constituted by our choosing or deciding to think in a certain way.

7. The Claim to Objectivity

If I have succeeded in specifying precisely enough the moral values whose objectivity I am denying, my thesis may now seem to be trivially true. Of course, some will say, valuing, preferring, choosing, recommending, rejecting, condemning, and so on, are human activities, and there is no need to look for values that are prior to and logically independent of all such activities. There may be widespread

agreement in valuing, and particular value-judgments are not in general arbitrary or isolated: they typically cohere with others, or can be criticized if they do not, reasons can be given for them, and so on: but if all that the subjectivist is maintaining is that desires, ends, purposes, and the like figure somewhere in the system of reasons, and that no ends or purposes are objective as opposed to being merely inter-subjective, then this may be conceded without much fuss.

But I do not think that this should be conceded so easily. As I have said, the main tradition of European moral philosophy includes the contrary claim, that there are objective values of just the sort I have denied. I have referred already to Plato, Kant, and Sidgwick. Kant in particular holds that the categorical imperative is not only categorical and imperative but objectively so: though a rational being gives the moral law to himself, the law that he thus makes is determinate and necessary. Aristotle begins the *Nicomachean Ethics* by saying that the good is that at which all things aim, and that ethics is part of a science which he calls "politics," whose goal is not knowledge but practice; yet he does not doubt that there can be *knowledge* of what is the good for man, nor, once he has identified this as well-being or happiness, *eudaimonia*, that it can be known, rationally determined, in what happiness consists; and it is plain that he thinks that this happiness is intrinsically desirable, not good simply because it is desired. The rationalist Samuel Clarke holds that

> these eternal and necessary differences of things make it *fit and reasonable* for creatures so to act . . . even separate from the consideration of these rules being the *positive will* or *command of God*; and also antecedent to any respect or regard, expectation or apprehension, of any *particular private and personal advantage or disadvantage, reward or punishment*, either present or future. . . .

Even the sentimentalist Hutcheson defines moral goodness as "some quality apprehended in actions, which procures approbation . . . ," while saying that the moral sense by which we perceive virtue and vice has been given to us (by the Author of nature) to direct our actions. Hume indeed was on the other side, but he is still a witness to the dominance of the objectivist tradition, since he claims that when we "see that the distinction of vice and virtue is not founded merely on the relations of objects, nor is perceiv'd by reason," this "wou'd subvert all the vulgar systems of morality." And Richard Price insists that right and wrong are "real characters of actions," not "qualities of our minds," and are perceived by the understanding; he criticizes the notion of moral sense on the ground that it would make virtue an affair of taste, and moral right and wrong "nothing in the objects themselves"; he rejects Hutcheson's view because (perhaps mistakenly) he sees it as collapsing into Hume's.

But this objectivism about values is not only a feature of the philosophical tradition. It has also a firm basis in ordinary thought, and even in the meanings of moral terms. No doubt it was an extravagance for Moore to say that "good" is the name of a non-natural quality, but it would not be so far wrong to say that in moral contexts it is used as if it were the name of a supposed non-natural quality, where the description "non-natural" leaves room for the peculiar evaluative, prescriptive, intrinsically action-guiding aspects of this supposed quality. . . . Someone in a state of moral perplexity, wondering whether it would be wrong for him to engage, say, in research related to bacteriological warfare, wants to arrive at some judgment about this concrete case, his doing this work at this time in these actual circumstances; his relevant characteristics will be part of the subject of the judgment, but no relation between him and the proposed action will be part of the predicate. The question is not, for example, whether he really wants to do this work, whether it will satisfy or dissatisfy him, whether he will in the long run have a pro-attitude towards it, or even whether this is an action of a sort that he can happily and sincerely recommend in all relevantly similar cases. Nor is he even wondering just whether to recommend such action in all relevantly similar cases. He wants to know whether this course of action would be wrong in itself. Something like this is the everyday objectivist concept of which talk about non-natural qualities is a philosopher's reconstruction.

The prevalence of this tendency to objectify values—and not only moral ones—is confirmed by a pattern of thinking that we find in existentialists and those influenced by them. The denial of objective values can carry with it an extreme emotional reaction, a feeling that nothing matters at all, that life has lost its purpose. Of course this does not follow; the lack of objective values is not a good reason for abandoning subjective concern or for ceasing to want anything. But the abandonment of a belief in objective values can cause, at least temporarily, a decay of subjective concern and sense of purpose. That it does so is evidence that the people in whom this reaction occurs have been tending to objectify their concerns and purposes, have been giving them a fictitious external authority. A claim to objectivity has been so strongly associated with their subjective concerns and purposes that the collapse of the former seems to undermine the latter as well.

This view, that conceptual analysis would reveal a claim to objectivity, is sometimes dramatically confirmed by philosophers who are officially on the other side. Bertrand Russell, for example, says that "ethical propositions should be expressed in the optative mood, not in the indicative"; he defends himself effectively against the charge of inconsistency in both holding ultimate ethical valuations to be subjective and expressing emphatic opinions on ethical questions. Yet at the end he admits:

> Certainly there *seems* to be something more. Suppose, for example, that some one were to advocate the introduction of bull-fighting in this country. In opposing the proposal, I should *feel*, not only that I was expressing my desires, but that my desires in the matter are *right*, whatever that may mean. As a matter of argument, I can, I think, show that I am not guilty of any logical inconsistency in holding to the above interpretation of ethics and at the same time expressing strong ethical preferences. But in feeling I am not satisfied.

But he concludes, reasonably enough, with the remark: "I can only say that, while my own opinions as to ethics do not satisfy me, other people's satisfy me still less."

I conclude, then, that ordinary moral judgments include a claim to objectivity, an assumption that there are objective values in just the sense in which I am concerned to deny this. And I do not think it is going too far to say that this assumption has been incorporated in the basic, conventional, meanings of moral terms. Any analysis of the meanings of moral terms which omits this claim to objective, intrinsic, prescriptivity is to that extent incomplete. . . .

If second order ethics were confined, then, to linguistic and conceptual analysis, it ought to conclude that moral values at least are objective: that they are so in part of what our ordinary moral statements mean: the traditional moral concepts of the ordinary man as well as of the main line of western philosophers are concepts of objective value. But it is precisely for this reason that linguistic and conceptual analysis is not enough. The claim to objectivity, however ingrained in our language and thought, is not self-validating. It can and should be questioned. But the denial of objective values will have to be put forward not as the result of an analytic approach, but as an "error theory," a theory that although most people in making moral judgments implicitly claim, among other things, to be pointing to something objectively prescriptive, these claims are all false. It is this that makes the name "moral scepticism" appropriate.

But since this is an error theory, since it goes against assumptions ingrained in our thought and built into some of the ways in which language is used, since it conflicts with what is sometimes called common sense, it needs very solid support. It is not something we can accept lightly or casually and then quietly pass on. If we are to adopt this view, we must argue explicitly for it. Traditionally it has been supported by arguments of two main kinds, which I shall call the argument from relativity and the argument from queerness, but these can, as I shall show, be supplemented in several ways.

8. The Argument from Relativity

The argument from relativity has as its premiss the well-known variation in moral codes from one society to another and from one period to another, and also the differences in moral beliefs between different groups and classes within a complex commu-

nity. Such variation is in itself merely a truth of descriptive morality, a fact of anthropology which entails neither first order nor second order ethical views. Yet it may indirectly support second order subjectivism: radical differences between first order moral judgments make it difficult to treat those judgments as apprehensions of objective truths. But it is not the mere occurrence of disagreements that tells against the objectivity of values. Disagreement on questions in history or biology or cosmology does not show that there are no objective issues in these fields for investigators to disagree about. But such scientific disagreement results from speculative inferences or explanatory hypotheses based on inadequate evidence; and it is hardly plausible to interpret moral disagreement in the same way. Disagreement about moral codes seems to reflect people's adherence to and participation in different ways of life. The causal connection seems to be mainly that way round: it is that people approve of monogamy because they participate in a monogamous way of life rather than that they participate in a monogamous way of life because they approve of monogamy. Of course, the standards may be an idealization of the way of life from which they arise: the monogamy in which people participate may be less complete, less rigid, than that of which it leads them to approve. This is not to say that moral judgments are purely conventional. Of course there have been and are moral heretics and moral reformers, people who have turned against the established rules and practices of their own communities for moral reasons, and often for moral reasons that we would endorse. But this can usually be understood as the extension, in ways which, though new and unconventional, seemed to them to be required for consistency, of rules to which they already adhered as arising out of an existing way of life. In short, the argument from relativity has some force simply because the actual variations in the moral codes are more readily explained by the hypothesis that they reflect ways of life than by the hypothesis that they express perceptions, most of them seriously inadequate and badly distorted, of objective values.

But there is a well-known counter to this argument from relativity, namely to say that the items for which objective validity is in the first place to be claimed are not specific moral rules or codes but very general basic principles which are recognized at least implicitly to some extent in all society—such principles as provide the foundation of what Sidgwick has called different methods of ethics: the principle of universalizability, perhaps, or the rule that one ought to conform to the specific rules of any way of life in which one takes part, from which one profits, and on which one relies, or some utilitarian principle of doing what tends, or seems likely, to promote the general happiness. It is easy to show that such general principles, married with differing concrete circumstances, different existing social patterns or different preferences, will beget different specific moral rules; and there is some plausibility in the claim that the specific rules thus generated will vary from community to community or from group to group in close agreement with the actual variations in accepted codes.

The argument from relativity can be only partly countered in this way. To take this line the moral objectivist has to say that it is only in these principles that the objective moral character attaches immediately to its descriptively specified ground or subject: other moral judgments are objectively valid or true, but only derivatively and contingently—if things had been otherwise, quite different sorts of actions would have been right. And despite the prominence in recent philosophical ethics of universalization, utilitarian principles, and the like, these are very far from constituting the whole of what is actually affirmed as basic in ordinary moral thought. Much of this is concerned rather with what Hare calls "ideals" or, less kindly, "fanaticism." That is, people judge that some things are good or right, and others are bad or wrong, not because—or at any rate not only because—they exemplify some general principle for which widespread implicit acceptance could be claimed, but because something about those things arouses certain responses immediately in them, though they would arouse radically and irresolvably different responses in others. "Moral sense" or "intuition" is an initially more plausible description of what supplies many of our basic moral judgments than "reason." With regard to all these starting points of moral thinking the argument from relativity remains in full force.

9. The Argument from Queerness

Even more important, however, and certainly more generally applicable, is the argument from queerness. This has two parts, one metaphysical, the other epistemological. If there were objective values, then they would be entities or qualities or relations of a very strange sort, utterly different from anything else in the universe. Correspondingly, if we were aware of them, it would have to be by some special faculty of moral perception or intuition, utterly different from our ordinary ways of knowing everything else. These points were recognized by Moore when he spoke of non-natural qualities, and by the intuitionists in their talk about a "faculty of moral intuition." Intuitionism has long been out of favour, and it is indeed easy to point out its implausibilities. What is not so often stressed, but is more important, is that the central thesis of intuitionism is one to which any objectivist view of values is in the end committed: intuitionism merely makes unpalatably plain what other forms of objectivism wrap up. Of course the suggestion that moral judgments are made or moral problems solved by just sitting down and having an ethical intuition is a travesty of actual moral thinking. But, however complex the real process, it will require (if it is to yield authoritatively prescriptive conclusions) some input of this distinctive sort, either premises or forms of argument or both. When we ask the awkward question, how we can be aware of this authoritative prescriptivity, of the truth of these distinctively ethical premises or of the cogency of this distinctively ethical pattern of reasoning, none of our ordinary accounts of sensory perception or introspection or the framing and confirming of explanatory hypotheses or inference or logical construction or conceptual analysis, or any combination of these, will provide a satisfactory answer; "a special sort of intuition" is a lame answer, but it is the one to which the clearheaded objectivist is compelled to resort.

Indeed, the best move for the moral objectivist is not to evade this issue, but to look for companions in guilt. For example, Richard Price argues that it is not moral knowledge alone that such an empiricism as those of Locke and Hume is unable to account for, but also our knowledge and even our ideas of essence, number, identity, diversity, solidity, inertia, substance, the necessary existence and infinite extension of time and space, necessity and possibility in general, power, and causation. If the understanding, which Price defines as the faculty within us that discerns truth, is also a source of new simple ideas of so many other sorts, may it not also be a power of immediately perceiving right and wrong, which yet are real characters of actions?

This is an important counter to the argument from queerness. The only adequate reply to it would be to show how, on empiricist foundations, we can construct an account of the ideas and beliefs and knowledge that we have of all these matters. I cannot even begin to do that here, though I have undertaken some parts of the task elsewhere. I can only state my belief that satisfactory accounts of most of these can be given in empirical terms. If some supposed metaphysical necessities or essences resist such treatment, then they too should be included, along with objective values, among the targets of the argument from queerness.

. . . .

Plato's Forms give a dramatic picture of what objective values would have to be. The Form of the Good is such that knowledge of it provides the knower with both a direction and an overriding motive; something's being good both tells the person who knows this to pursue it and makes him pursue it. An objective good would be sought by anyone who was acquainted with it, not because of any contingent fact that this person, or every person, is so constituted that he desires this end, but just because the end has to-be-pursuedness somehow built into it. Similarly, if there were objective principles of right and wrong, any wrong (possible) course of action would have not-to-be-doneness somehow built into it. Or we should have something like Clarke's necessary relations of fitness between situations and actions, so that a situation would have a demand for such-and-such an action somehow built into it.

The need for an argument of this sort can be brought out by reflection on Hume's argument that "reason"—in which at this stage he includes all sorts of knowing as well as reasoning—can never be an "influencing motive of the will." Someone might object that Hume has argued unfairly from the lack of influencing power (not contingent upon desires) in ordinary objects of knowledge and ordinary reasoning, and might maintain that values differ from natural objects precisely in their power, when known, automatically to influence the will. To this Hume could, and would need to, reply that this objection involves the postulating of value-entities or value-features of quite a different order from anything else with which we are acquainted, and of a corresponding faculty with which to detect them. That is, he would have to supplement his explicit argument with what I have called the argument from queerness.

Another way of bringing out this queerness is to ask, about anything that is supposed to have some objective moral quality, how this is linked with its natural features. What is the connection between the natural fact that an action is a piece of deliberate cruelty—say, causing pain just for fun—and the moral fact that it is wrong? It cannot be an entailment, a logical or semantic necessity. Yet it is not merely that the two features occur together. The wrongness must somehow be "consequential" or "supervenient"; it is wrong because it is a piece of deliberate cruelty. But just what *in the world* is signified by this "because"? And how do we know the relation that it signifies, if this is something more than such actions being socially condemned, and condemned by us too, perhaps through our having absorbed attitudes from our social environment? It is not even sufficient to postulate a faculty which "sees" the wrongness: something must be postulated which can see at once the natural features that constitute the cruelty, and the wrongness, and the mysterious consequential link between the two. Alternatively, the intuition required might be the perception that wrongness is a higher order property belonging to certain natural properties; but what is this belonging of properties to other properties, and how can we discern it? How much simpler and more comprehensible the situation would be if we could replace the moral quality with some sort of subjective response which could be causally related to the detection of the natural features on which the supposed quality is said to be consequential.

. . . .

10. Patterns of Objectification

Considerations of these kinds suggest that it is in the end less paradoxical to reject than to retain the common-sense belief in the objectivity of moral values, provided that we can explain how this belief, if it is false, has become established and is so resistant to criticisms. This proviso is not difficult to satisfy.

On a subjectivist view, the supposedly objective values will be based in fact upon attitudes which the person has who takes himself to be recognizing and responding to those values. If we admit what Hume calls the mind's "propensity to spread itself on external objects," we can understand the supposed objectivity of moral qualities as arising from what we can call the projection or objectification of moral attitudes. This would be analogous to what is called the "pathetic fallacy," the tendency to read our feelings into their objects. If a fungus, say, fills us with disgust, we may be inclined to ascribe to the fungus itself a non-natural quality of foulness. But in moral contexts there is more than this propensity at work. Moral attitudes themselves are at least partly social in origin: socially established—and socially necessary—patterns of behaviour put pressure on individuals, and each individual tends to internalize these pressures and to join in requiring these patterns of behaviour of himself and of others. The attitudes that are objectified into moral values have indeed an external source, though not the one assigned to them by the belief in their absolute authority. Moreover, there are motives that would support objectification. We need morality to regulate interpersonal relations, to control some of the ways in which people behave towards one another, often in opposition to contrary inclinations. We therefore want our moral judgments to be authoritative for other agents as well as for ourselves: objective validity would give them the authority required. Aesthetic values are logically in the same position as moral ones; much the same metaphysical and epistemological considerations apply to them. But aesthetic values are less strongly objectified than moral ones; their subjective status, and an "error theory" with regard to such claims to objectivity as are incorporated in aesthetic judgments, will be more readily accepted, just because the motives for their objectification are less compelling.

But it would be misleading to think of the objectification of moral values as primarily the projection of feelings, as in the pathetic fallacy. More important are wants and demands. As Hobbes says, "whatsoever is the object of any man's Appetite or Desire, that is it, which he for his part calleth *Good*", and certainly both the adjective "good" and the noun "goods" are used in non-moral contexts of things because they are such as to satisfy desires. We get the notion of something's being objectively good, or having intrinsic value, by reversing the direction of dependence here, by making the desire depend upon the goodness, instead of the goodness on the desire. And this is aided by the fact that the desired thing will indeed have features that make it desired, that enable it to arouse a desire or that make it such as to satisfy some desire that is already there. It is fairly easy to confuse the way in which a thing's desirability is indeed objective with its having in our sense objective value. The fact that the word "good" serves as one of our main moral terms is a trace of this pattern of objectification.

Similarly related uses of words are covered by the distinction between hypothetical and categorical imperatives. The statement that someone "ought to" or, more strongly, "must" do such-and-such may be backed up explicitly or implicitly by reference to what he wants or to what his purposes and objects are. Again, there may be a reference to the purposes of someone else, perhaps the speaker: "You must do this"—"Why?"—"Because I want such-and-such." The moral categorical imperative which could be expressed in the same words can be seen as resulting from the suppression of the conditional clause in a hypothetical imperative without its being replaced by any such reference to the speaker's wants. The action in question is still required in something like the way in which it would be if it were appropriately related to a want, but it is no longer admitted that there is any contingent want upon which its being required depends. Again this move can be understood when we remember that at least our central and basic moral judgments represent social demands, where the source of the demand is indeterminate and diffuse. Whose demands or wants are in question, the agent's, or the speaker's, or those of an indefinite multitude of other people? All of this in a way, but there are advantages in not specifying them precisely. The speaker is expressing demands which he makes as a member of a community, which he has developed in and by participation in a joint way of life; also, what is required of this particular agent would be required of any other in a relevantly similar situation; but the agent too is expected to have internalized the relevant demands, to act as if the ends for which the action is required were his own. By suppressing any explicit reference to demands and making the imperatives categorical we facilitate conceptual moves from one such demand relation to another. The moral uses of such words as "must" and "ought" and "should", all of which are used also to express hypothetical imperatives, are traces of this pattern of objectification.

It may be objected that this explanation links normative ethics too closely with descriptive morality, with the mores or socially enforced patterns of behaviour that anthropologists record. But it can hardly be denied that moral thinking starts from the enforcement of social codes. Of course it is not confined to that. But even when moral judgments are detached from the mores of any actual society they are liable to be framed with reference to an ideal community of moral agents, such as Kant's kingdom of ends, which but for the need to give God a special place in it would have been better called a commonwealth of ends.

Another way of explaining the objectification of moral values is to say that ethics is a system of law from which the legislator has been removed. This might have derived either from the positive law of a state or from a supposed system of divine law. There can be no doubt that some features of modern European moral concepts are traceable to the theological ethics of Christianity. The stress on quasi-imperative notions, on what ought to be done or on what is wrong in a sense that is close to that of "forbidden," are surely relics of divine commands. Admittedly, the central ethical concepts for Plato and Aristotle also are in a broad sense prescriptive or intrinsically action-guiding, but in concentrating rather on "good" than on "ought" they show that their moral thought is an objectification of the desired and the satisfying rather than of the commanded. Elizabeth Anscombe has argued that modern, non-Aristotelian, concepts of *moral* obligation, *moral* duty, of what is *morally* right and

wrong, and of the *moral* sense of "ought" are survivals outside the framework of thought that made them really intelligible, namely the belief in divine law. She infers that "ought" has "become a word of mere mesmeric force," with only a "delusive appearance of content," and that we would do better to discard such terms and concepts altogether, and go back to Aristotelian ones.

There is much to be said for this view. But while we can explain some distinctive features of modern moral philosophy in this way, it would be a mistake to see the whole problem of the claim to objective prescriptivity as merely local and unnecessary, as a post-operative complication of a society from which a dominant system of theistic belief has recently been rather hastily excised. As Cudworth and Clarke and Price, for example, show, even those who still admit divine commands, or the positive law of God, may believe moral values to have an independent objective but still action-guiding authority. Responding to Plato's *Euthyphro* dilemma, they believe that God commands what he commands because it is in itself good or right, not that it is good or right merely because and in that he commands it. Otherwise God himself could not be called good. Price asks, "What can be more preposterous, than to make the Deity nothing but will; and to exalt this on the ruins of all his attributes?" The apparent objectivity of moral value is a widespread phenomenon which has more than one source: the persistence of a belief in something like divine law when the belief in the divine legislator has faded out is only one factor among others. There are several different patterns of the objectification, all of which have left characteristic traces in our actual moral concepts and moral language.

11. The General Goal of Human Life

The argument of the preceding sections is meant to apply quite generally to moral thought, but the terms in which it has been stated are largely those of the Kantian and post-Kantian tradition of English moral philosophy. To those who are more familiar with another tradition, which runs through Aristotle and Aquinas, it may seem wide of the mark. For them, the fundamental notion is that of the good for man, or the general end or goal of human life, or perhaps of a set of basic goods or primary human purposes. Moral reasoning consists partly in achieving a more adequate understanding of this basic goal (or set of goals), partly in working out the best way of pursuing and realizing it. But this approach is open to two radically different interpretations. According to one, to say that something is the good for man or the general goal of human life is just to say that this is what men in fact pursue or will find ultimately satisfying, or perhaps that it is something which, if postulated as an implicit goal, enables us to make sense of actual human strivings and to detect a coherent pattern in what would otherwise seem to be a chaotic jumble of conflicting purposes. According to the other interpretation, to say that something is the good for man or the general goal of human life is to say that this is man's proper end, that this is what he ought to be striving after, whether he in fact is or not. On the first interpretation we have a descriptive statement, on the second a normative or evaluative or prescriptive one. But this approach tends to combine the two interpretations, or to slide from one to the other, and to borrow support for what are in effect claims of the second sort from the plausibility of statements of the first sort.

I have no quarrel with this notion interpreted in the first way, I would only insert a warning that there may well be more diversity even of fundamental purposes, more variation in what different human beings will find ultimately satisfying, than the terminology of "*the* good for man" would suggest. Nor indeed, have I any quarrel with the second, prescriptive, interpretation, provided that it is recognized as subjectively prescriptive, that the speaker is here putting forward his own demands or proposals, or those of some movement that he represents, though no doubt linking these demands or proposals with what he takes to be already in the first, descriptive, sense fundamental human goals. . . . But if it is claimed that something is objectively the right or proper goal of human life, then this is tantamount to the assertion of something that is objectively categorically imperative, and comes

fairly within the scope of our previous arguments. Indeed, the running together of what I have here called the two interpretations is yet another pattern of objectification: a claim to objective prescriptivity is constructed by combining the normative element in the second interpretation with the objectivity allowed by the first, by the statement that such and such are fundamentally pursued or ultimately satisfying human goals. The argument from relativity still applies: the radical diversity of the goals that men actually pursue and find satisfying makes it implausible to construe such pursuits as resulting from an imperfect grasp of a unitary true good. So too does the argument from queerness; we can still ask what this objectively prescriptive rightness of the true goal can be, and how this is linked on the one hand with the descriptive features of this goal and on the other with the fact that it is to *some extent* an actual goal of human striving.

To meet these difficulties, the objectivist may have recourse to the purpose of God: the true purpose of human life is fixed by what God intended (or, intends) men to do and to be. Actual human strivings and satisfactions have some relation to this true end because God made men for this end and made them such as to pursue it—but only *some* relation, because of the inevitable imperfection of created beings.

I concede that if the requisite theological doctrine could be defended, a kind of objective ethical prescriptivity could be thus introduced. Since I think that theism cannot be defended, I do not regard this as any threat to my argument. . . . Those who wish to keep theism as a live option can read the arguments of the intervening chapters hypothetically, as a discussion of what we can make of morality without recourse to God, and hence of what we can say about morality if, in the end, we dispense with religious belief.

. . . .

[Editor's note: The quotation on page 757 from Samuel Clarke is from selections in D. D. Raphael ed., *British Moralists 1650–1800* (Oxford, 1969). The quotation from Bertrand Russell on page 759 is from his "Reply to Criticism" in P. A. Schlipp, ed., *The Philosophy of Bertrand Russell* (Evanston, 1944).]

Ethics and Observation

GILBERT HARMAN

Gilbert Harman (1938–   ) is the author of a number of important works on epistemology and ethics, including *Thought, Change in View*, and *The Nature of Morality*. He is a professor of philosophy at Princeton University.

———•———

The Basic Issue

Can moral principles be tested and confirmed in the way scientific principles can? Consider the principle that, if you are given a choice between five people alive and one dead or five people dead and one alive, you should always choose to have five people alive and one dead rather than the other way round. We can easily imagine examples that appear to confirm this principle. Here is one:

> You are a doctor in a hospital's emergency room when six accident victims are brought in. All six are in danger of dying but one is much worse off than the others. You can just barely save that person if you devote all of your resources to him and let the others die. Alternatively, you can save the other five if you are willing to ignore the most seriously injured person.

It would seem that in this case you, the doctor, would be right to save the five and let the other person die. So this example, taken by itself, confirms the principle under consideration. Next, consider the following case.

> You have five patients in the hospital who are dying, each in need of a separate organ. One needs a kidney, another a lung, a third a heart, and so forth. You can save all five if you take a single healthy person and remove his heart, lungs, kidneys, and so

forth, to distribute to these five patients. Just such a healthy person is in room 306. He is in the hospital for routine tests. Having seen his test results, you know that he is perfectly healthy and of the right tissue compatibility. If you do nothing, he will survive without incident; the other patients will die, however. The other five patients can be saved only if the person in Room 306 is cut up and his organs distributed. In that case, there would be one dead but five saved.

The principle in question tells us that you should cut up the patient in Room 306. But in this case, surely you must not sacrifice this innocent bystander, even to save the five other patients. Here a moral principle has been tested and disconfirmed in what may seem to be a surprising way.

This, of course, was a "thought experiment." We did not really compare a hypothesis with the world. We compared an explicit principle with our feelings about certain imagined examples. In the same way, a physicist performs thought experiments in order to compare explicit hypotheses with his "sense" of what should happen in certain situations, a "sense" that he has acquired as a result of his long working familiarity with current theory. But scientific hypotheses can also be tested in real experiments, out in the world.

Can moral principles be tested in the same way, out in the world? You can observe someone do something, but can you ever perceive the rightness or wrongness of what he does? If you round a corner and see a group of young hoodlums pour gasoline on a cat and ignite it, you do not need to *conclude* that what they are doing is wrong; you do not need to figure anything out; you can *see* that it is wrong. But is your reaction due to the actual wrongness of what you see or is it simply a reflection of your moral "sense," a "sense" that you have acquired perhaps as a result of your moral upbringing?

Observation

The issue is complicated. There are no pure observations. Observations are always "theory laden." What you perceive depends to some extent on the theory you hold, consciously or unconsciously. You see some children pour gasoline on a cat and ignite it. To really see that, you have to possess a great deal of knowledge, know about a considerable number of objects, know about people: that people pass through the life stages infant, baby, child, adolescent, adult. You must know what flesh and blood animals are, and in particular, cats. You must have some idea of life. You must know what gasoline is, what burning is, and much more. In one sense, what you "see" is a pattern of light on your retina, a shifting array of splotches, although even that is theory, and you could never adequately describe what you see in that sense. In another sense, you see what you do because of the theories you hold. Change those theories and you would see something else, given the same pattern of light.

Similarly, if you hold a moral view, whether it is held consciously or unconsciously, you will be able to perceive rightness or wrongness, goodness or badness, justice or injustice. There is no difference in this respect between moral propositions and other theoretical propositions. If there is a difference, it must be found elsewhere.

Observation depends on theory because perception involves forming a belief as a fairly direct result of observing something; you can form a belief only if you understand the relevant concepts and a concept is what it is by virtue of its role in some theory or system of beliefs. To recognize a child as a child is to employ, consciously or unconsciously, a concept that is defined by its place in a framework of the stages of human life. Similarly, burning is an empty concept apart from its theoretical connections to the concepts of heat, destruction, smoke, and fire.

Moral concepts—Right and Wrong, Good and Bad, Justice and Injustice—also have a place in your theory or system of beliefs and are the concepts they are because of their context. If we say that observation has occurred whenever an opinion is a direct result of perception, we must allow that there is moral observation, because such an opinion can be a moral opinion as easily as any other sort. In this sense, observation may be used to confirm or disconfirm moral theories. The observational opinions that, in this sense, you find yourself with can be in either agreement or conflict with your consciously explicit moral principles. When they are in conflict, you must choose between your explicit theory and observation. In ethics, as in science, you sometimes opt for theory, and say that you made an error in observation or were biased or whatever, or you sometimes opt for observation, and modify your theory.

In other words, in both science and ethics, general principles are invoked to explain particular cases and, therefore, in both science and ethics, the general principles you accept can be tested by appealing to particular judgments that certain things are right or wrong, just or unjust, and so forth; and these judgments are analogous to direct perceptual judgments about facts.

Observational Evidence

Nevertheless, observation plays a role in science that it does not seem to play in ethics. The difference is that you need to make assumptions about certain physical facts to explain the occurrence of the observations that support a scientific theory, but you do not seem to need to make assumptions about any moral facts to explain the occurrence of the so-called moral observations I have been talking about. In the moral case, it would seem that you need only make assumptions about the psychology or moral sensibility of the person making the moral observation. In the scientific case, theory is tested against the world.

The point is subtle but important. Consider a physicist making an observation to test a scientific theory. Seeing a vapor trail in a cloud chamber, he thinks, "There goes a proton." Let us suppose that this is an observation in the relevant sense, namely, an immediate judgment made in response to the situation without any conscious reasoning having taken place. Let us also suppose that his observation confirms his theory, a theory that helps give meaning to the very term "proton" as it occurs in his observational judgment. Such a confirmation rests on inferring an explanation. He can count his making the observation as confirming evidence for his theory only to the extent that it is reasonable to explain his making the observation by assuming that, not only is he in a certain psychological "set," given the theory he accepts and his beliefs about the experimental apparatus, but furthermore, there really was a proton going through the cloud chamber, causing the vapor trail, which he saw as a proton. (This is evidence for the theory to the extent that the theory can explain the proton's being there better than competing theories can.) But, if his having made that observation could have been equally well explained by his psychological set alone, without the need for any assumption about a proton, then the observation would not have been evidence for the existence of that proton and therefore would not have been evidence for the theory. His making the observation supports the theory only because, in order to explain his making the observation, it is reasonable to assume something about the world over and above the assumptions made about the observer's psychology. In particular, it is reasonable to assume that there was a proton going through the cloud chamber, causing the vapor trail.

Compare this case with one in which you make a moral judgment immediately and without conscious reasoning, say, that the children are wrong to set the cat on fire or that the doctor would be wrong to cut up one healthy patient to save five dying patients. In order to explain your making the first of these judgments, it would be reasonable to assume, perhaps, that the children really are pouring gasoline on a cat and you are seeing them do it. But, in neither case is there any obvious reason to assume anything about "moral facts," such as that it really is wrong to set the cat on fire or to cut up the patient in Room 306. Indeed, an assumption about moral facts would seem to be totally irrelevant to the explanation of your making the judgment you make. It would seem that all we need assume is that you have certain more or less well articulated moral principles that are reflected in the judgments you make, based on your moral sensibility. It seems to be completely irrelevant to our explanation whether your intuitive immediate judgment is true or false.

The observation of an event can provide observational evidence for or against a scientific theory in the sense that the truth of that observation can be relevant to a reasonable explanation of why that observation was made. A moral observation does not seem, in the same sense, to be observational evidence for or against any moral theory, since the truth or falsity of the moral observation seems to be completely irrelevant to any reasonable explanation of why that observation was made. The fact that an observation of an event was made at the time it was made is evidence not only about the observer but also about the physical facts. The fact that you made a particular moral observation when you did does not seem to be evidence about moral facts, only evidence about you and your moral sensibility. Facts about protons can affect what you observe, since a proton passing through the cloud chamber can cause a vapor trail that reflects light to your eye in a way that, given your scientific training and psychological set, leads you to judge that what you see is a proton. But there does not seem to be any way in which the actual rightness or wrongness of a given situation can have any effect on your perceptual apparatus. In this respect, ethics seems to differ from science.

In considering whether moral principles can help explain observations, it is therefore important to note an ambiguity in the word "observation." You see the children set the cat on fire and immediately think, "That's wrong." In one sense, your observation is that what the children are doing is wrong. In another sense, your observation is your thinking that thought. Moral observations might explain observations in the first sense but not in the second sense. Certain moral principles might help to explain why it was wrong of the children to set the cat on fire, but moral principles seem to be of no help in explaining your thinking that that is wrong. In the first sense of "observation," moral principles can be tested by observation—"That this act is wrong is evidence that causing unnecessary suffering is wrong." But in the second sense of "observation," moral principles cannot clearly be tested by observation, since they do not appear to help explain observations in this second sense of "observation." Moral principles do not seem to help explain your observing what you observe.

Of course, if you are already given the moral principle that it is wrong to cause unnecessary suffering, you can take your seeing the children setting the cat on fire as observational evidence that they are doing something wrong. Similarly, you can suppose that your seeing the vapor trail is observational evidence that a proton is going through the cloud chamber, if you are given the relevant physical theory. But there is an important apparent difference between the two cases. In the scientific case, your making that observation is itself evidence for the physical theory because the physical theory explains the proton, which explains the trail, which explains your observation. In the moral case, your making your observation does not seem to be evidence for the relevant moral principle because that principle does not seem to help explain your observation. The explanatory chain from principle to observation seems to be broken in morality. The moral principle may "explain" why it is wrong for the children to set the cat on fire. But the wrongness of that act does not appear to help explain the act, which you observe, itself. The explanatory chain appears to be broken in such a way that neither the moral principle nor the wrongness of the act can help explain why you observe what you observe.

A qualification may seem to be needed here. Perhaps the children perversely set the cat on fire simply "because it is wrong." Here it may seem at first that the actual wrongness of the act does help explain why they do it and therefore indirectly helps explain why you observe what you observe just as a physical theory, by explaining why the proton is producing a vapor trail, indirectly helps explain why the observer observes what he observes. But on reflection we must agree that this is probably an illusion. What explains the children's act is not clearly the actual wrongness of the act but, rather, their belief that the act is wrong. The actual rightness or wrongness of their act seems to have nothing to do with why they do it.

Observational evidence plays a part in science it does not appear to play in ethics, because scientific principles can be justified ultimately by their role in explaining observations, in the second sense of observation—by their explanatory role. Apparently, moral principles cannot be justified in the same way. It appears to be true that there can be no explana-

tory chain between moral principles and particular observings in the way that there can be such a chain between scientific principles and particular observings. Conceived as an explanatory theory, morality, unlike science, seems to be cut off from observation.

Not that every legitimate scientific hypothesis is susceptible to direct observational testing. Certain hypotheses about "black holes" in space cannot be directly tested, for example, because no signal is emitted from within a black hole. The connection with observation in such a case is indirect. And there are many similar examples. Nevertheless, seen in the large, there is the apparent difference between science and ethics we have noted. The scientific realm is accessible to observation in a way the moral realm is not.

Ethics and Mathematics

Perhaps ethics is to be compared, not with physics, but with mathematics. Perhaps such a moral principle as "You ought to keep your promises" is confirmed or disconfirmed in the way (whatever it is) in which such a mathematical principle as "$5 + 7 = 12$" is. Observation does not seem to play the role in mathematics it plays in physics. We do not and cannot perceive numbers, for example, since we cannot be in causal contact with them. We do not even understand what it would be like to be in causal contact with the number 12, say. Relations among numbers cannot have any more of an effect on our perceptual apparatus than moral facts can.

Observation, however, *is* relevant to mathematics. In explaining the observations that support a physical theory, scientists typically appeal to mathematical principles. On the other hand, one never seems to need to appeal in this way to moral principles. Since an observation is evidence for what best explains it, and since mathematics often figures in the explanations of scientific observations, there is indirect observational evidence for mathematics. There does not seem to be observational evidence, even indirectly, for basic moral principles. In explaining why certain observations have been made, we never seem to use purely moral assumptions. In this respect, then, ethics appears to differ not only from physics but also from mathematics.

Moral Explanations

NICHOLAS L. STURGEON

Nicholas L. Sturgeon (1942–   ) is a professor of philosophy at Cornell University who writes about ethics and related issues.

—●—

THERE IS ONE ARGUMENT FOR moral skepticism that I respect even though I remain unconvinced. It has sometimes been called the argument from moral diversity or relativity, but that is somewhat misleading, for the problem arises not from the diversity of moral views, but from the apparent difficulty of *settling* moral disagreements, or even of knowing what would be required to settle them, a difficulty thought to be noticeably greater than any found in settling disagreements that arise in, for example, the sciences. This provides an argument for moral skepticism because one obviously possible explanation for our difficulty in settling moral disagreements is that they are really unsettleable, that there is no way of justifying one rather than another competing view on these issues; and a possible further explanation for the unsettleability of moral disagreements, in turn, is moral nihilism, the view that on these issues there just is no fact of the matter, that the impossibility of discovering and establishing moral truths is due to there not being any.

I am, as I say, unconvinced: partly because I think this argument exaggerates the difficulty we actually find in settling moral disagreements, partly because there are alternative explanations to be considered for the difficulty we do find. Under the latter heading, for example, it certainly matters to what extent moral disagreements depend on disagreements about other questions which, however, disputed they may be, are nevertheless regarded as having ob-

jective answers: questions such as which, if any, religion is true, which account of human psychology, which theory of human society. And it also matters to what extent consideration of moral questions is in practice skewed by distorting factors such as personal interest and social ideology. These are large issues. Although it is possible to say some useful things to put them in perspective,[1] it appears impossible to settle them quickly or in any a priori way. Consideration of them is likely to have to be piecemeal and, in the short run at least, frustratingly indecisive.

These large issues are not my topic here. But I mention them, and the difficulty of settling them, to show why it is natural that moral skeptics have hoped to find some quicker way of establishing their thesis. I doubt that any exist, but some have of course been proposed. Verificationist attacks on ethics should no doubt be seen in this light, and J. L. Mackie's recent "argument from queerness" is a clear instance. (Mackie, 1977, pp. 38–42). The quicker response on which I shall concentrate, however, is neither of these, but instead an argument by Gilbert Harman designed to bring out the "basic problem" about morality, which in his view is "its apparent immunity from observational testing" and "the seeming irrelevance of observational evidence" (Harman, 1977, pp. vii, viii). Unless otherwise indicated, parenthetical page references are to Morality, Reason, and Truth: New Essays on the Foundation of Ethics). The argument is that reference to moral facts appears unnecessary for the *explanation* of our moral observations and beliefs.

Harman's view, I should say at once, is not in the end a skeptical one, and he does not view the argument I shall discuss as a decisive defense of moral skepticism or moral nihilism. Someone else might easily so regard it, however. For Harman himself

From *Morality, Reason, and Truth: New Essays on the Foundation of Ethics*, Rowman and Allanheld, 1984. Reprinted by permission of Rowman and Littlefield. Abridged and slightly revised.

regards it as creating a strong prima facie case for skepticism and nihilism, strong enough to justify calling it "the problem with ethics."[2] And he believes it shows that the only recourse for someone who wishes to avoid moral skepticism is to find defensible reductive definitions for ethical terms; so skepticism would be the obvious conclusion to draw for anyone who doubted the possibility of such definitions. I believe, however, that Harman is mistaken on both counts. I shall show that his argument for skepticism either rests on claims that most people would find quite implausible (and so cannot be what constitutes, for *them*, the problem with ethics); or else becomes just the application to ethics of a familiar *general* skeptical strategy, one which, if it works for ethics, will work equally well for unobservable theoretical entities, or for other minds, or for an external world (and so, again, can hardly be what constitutes the distinctive problem with *ethics*). I have argued elsewhere,[3] moreover, that one can in any case be a moral realist, and indeed an ethical naturalist, without believing that we are now or ever will be in possession of reductive naturalistic definitions for ethical terms.

The Problem with Ethics

Moral theories are often tested in thought experiments, against imagined examples; and, as Harman notes, trained researchers often test scientific theories in the same way. The problem, though, is that scientific theories can also be tested against the world, by observations or real experiments; and, Harman asks, "can moral principles be tested in the same way, out in the world?" (p. 765 in this book).

This would not be a very interesting or impressive challenge, of course, if it were merely a resurrection of standard verificationist worries about whether moral assertions and theories have any testable empirical implications, implications statable in some relatively austere "observational" vocabulary. One problem with that form of the challenge, as Harman points out, is that there are no "pure" observations, and in consequence no purely observational vocabulary either. But there is also a deeper problem that Harman does not mention, one that

remains even if we shelve worries about "pure" observations and, at least for the sake of argument, grant the verificationist his observational language, pretty much as it was usually conceived: that is, as lacking at the very least any obviously theoretical terminology from any recognized science, and of course as lacking any moral terminology. For then the difficulty is that moral principles fare just as well (or just as badly) against the verificationist challenge as do typical scientific principles. For it is by now a familiar point about scientific principles—principles such as Newton's law of universal gravitation or Darwin's theory of evolution—that they are entirely devoid of empirical implications when considered in isolation.[4] We do of course base observational predictions on such theories and so test them against experience, but that is because we do *not* consider them in isolation. For we can derive these predictions only by relying at the same time on a large background of additional assumptions, many of which are equally theoretical and equally incapable of being tested in isolation.

A less familiar point, because less often spelled out, is that the relation of moral principles to observation is similar in *both* these respects. Candidate moral principles—for example, that an action is wrong just in case there is something else the agent could have done that would have produced a greater balance of pleasure over pain—lack empirical implications when considered in isolation. But it is easy to derive empirical consequences from them, and thus to test them against experience, if we allow ourselves, as we do in the scientific case, to rely on a background of other assumptions of comparable status. Thus, if we conjoin the act-utilitarian principle I just cited with the further view, also untestable in isolation, that it is always wrong deliberately to kill a human being, we can deduce from these two premises together the consequence that deliberately killing a human being always produces a lesser balance of pleasure over pain than some available alternative act; and this claim is one any positivist would have conceded we know, in principle at least, how to test. If we found it to be false, moreover, then we would be forced by this empirical test to abandon at least one of the moral claims from which we derived it.

It might be thought a worrisome feature of this example, however, and a further opening for skepticism, that there could be controversy about which moral premise to abandon, and that we have not explained how our empirical test can provide an answer to *this* question. And this may be a problem. It should be a familiar problem, however, because the Duhemian commentary includes a precisely corresponding point about the scientific case: that if we are at all cautious in characterizing what we observe, then the requirement that our theories merely be *consistent* with observation is a very weak one. There are always many, perhaps indefinitely many, different mutually inconsistent ways to adjust our views to meet this constraint. Of course, in practice we are often confident of how to do it: if you are a freshman chemistry student, you do not conclude from your failure to obtain the predicted value in an experiment that it is all over for the atomic theory of gases. And the decision can be equally easy, one should note, in a moral case. Consider two examples. From the surprising moral thesis that Adolf Hitler was a morally admirable person, together with a modest piece of moral theory to the effect that no morally admirable person would, for example, instigate and oversee the degradation and death of millions of persons, one can derive the testable consequence that Hitler did not do this. But he did, so we must give up one of our premises; and the choice of which to abandon is neither difficult nor controversial.

Or, to take a less monumental example, contrived around one of Harman's own, suppose you have been thinking yourself lucky enough to live in a neighborhood in which no one would do anything wrong, at least not in public; and that the modest piece of theory you accept, this time, is that malicious cruelty, just for the hell of it, is wrong. Then, as in Harman's example, "you round a corner and see a group of young hoodlums pour gasoline on a cat and ignite it." At this point, either your confidence in the neighborhood or your principle about cruelty has got to give way. But the choice is easy, if dispiriting, so easy as hardly to require thought. As Harman says, "You do not need to *conclude* that what they are doing is wrong; you do not need to figure anything out; you can *see* that it is wrong" (p. 765 in this book). But a skeptic can still wonder

whether this practical confidence, or this "seeing," rests in either sort of case on anything more than deeply ingrained conventions of thought—respect for scientific experts, say, and for certain moral traditions—as opposed to anything answerable to the facts of the matter, any reliable strategy for getting it right about the world.

Now, Harman's challenge is interesting partly because it does not rest on these verificationist doubts about whether moral beliefs have observational implications, but even more because what it does rest on is a partial answer to the kind of general skepticism to which, as we have seen, reflection on the verificationist picture can lead. Many of our beliefs are justified, in Harman's view, by their providing or helping to provide a reasonable *explanation* of our observing what we do. It would be consistent with your failure, as a beginning student, to obtain the experimental result predicted by the gas laws, that the laws are mistaken. But a better explanation, in light of your inexperience and the general success experts have had in confirming and applying these laws, is that you made some mistake in running the experiment. So our scientific beliefs can be justified by their explanatory role; and so too, in Harman's view, can mathematical beliefs and so many commonsense beliefs about the world.

Not so, however, moral beliefs: they appear to have no such explanatory role. That is "the problem with ethics." Harman spells out his version of this contrast:

> You need to make assumptions about certain physical facts to explain the occurrence of the observations that support a scientific theory, but you do not seem to need to make assumptions about any moral facts to explain the occurrence of the so-called moral observations I have been talking about. In the moral case, it would seem that you need only make assumptions about the psychology or moral sensibility of the person making the moral observation. (p. 766 in this book).

More precisely, and applied to his own example, it might be reasonable, in order to explain your judging that the hoodlums are wrong to set the cat on fire, to assume "that the children really are pouring gasoline on a cat and you are seeing them do it." But there is no

> obvious reason to assume anything about "moral facts," such as that it is really wrong to set the cat on fire. . . . Indeed, an assumption about moral facts would seem to be totally irrelevant to the explanation of your making the judgment you make. It would seem that all we need assume is that you have certain more or less well articulated moral principles that are reflected in the judgments you make, based on your moral sensibility. (p. 767 in this book).

And Harman thinks that if we accept this conclusion, suitably generalized, then, subject to one possible qualification concerning reduction that I have discussed elsewhere,[5] we must conclude that moral theories cannot be tested against the world as scientific theories can, and that we have no reason to believe that moral facts are part of the order of nature or that there is any moral knowledge (pp. 23, 35).

My own view is that Harman is quite wrong, not in thinking that the explanatory role of our beliefs is important to their justification, but in thinking that moral beliefs play no such role.[6] I shall have to say something about the initial plausibility of Harman's thesis as applied to his own example, but part of my reason for dissenting should be apparent from the other example I just gave. We find it easy (and so does Harman [p. 108]) to conclude from the evidence not just that Hitler was not morally admirable, but that he was morally depraved. But isn't it plausible that Hitler's moral depravity—the fact of his really having been morally depraved—forms part of a reasonable explanation of why we believe he was depraved? I think so, and I shall argue concerning this and other examples that moral beliefs very commonly play the explanatory role Harman denies them. Before I can press my case, however, I need to clear up several preliminary points about just what Harman is claiming and just how his argument is intended to work.

Observation and Explanation

1. For there are several ways in which Harman's argument invites misunderstanding. One results from his focusing at the start on the question of

whether there can be moral *observations*.[7] But this question turns out to be a side issue, in no way central to his argument that moral principles cannot be tested against the world. There are a couple of reasons for this, of which the more important[8] by far is that Harman does not really require of moral facts, if belief in them is to be justified, that they figure in the explanation of moral observations. It would be enough, on the one hand, if they were needed for the explanation of moral beliefs that are not in any interesting sense observations. For example, Harman thinks belief in moral facts would be vindicated if they were needed to explain our drawing the moral conclusions we do when we reflect on hypothetical cases, but I think there is no illumination in calling these conclusions observations.[9] It would also be enough, on the other hand, if moral facts were needed for the explanation of what were clearly observations, but not moral observations. Harman thinks mathematical beliefs are justified, but he does not suggest that there are mathematical observations; it is rather that appeal to mathematical truths helps to explain why we make the physical observations we do (p. 768 in this book). Moral beliefs would surely be justified, too, if they played such a role, whether or not there are any moral observations.

So the claim is that moral facts are not needed to explain our having any of the moral beliefs we do, whether or not those beliefs are observations, and are equally unneeded to explain any of the observations we make, whether or not those observations are moral. In fact, Harman's view appears to be that moral facts aren't needed to explain anything at all: though it would perhaps be question-begging for him to begin with this strong a claim, since he grants that if there were any moral facts, then appeal to other moral facts—more general ones, for example—might be needed to explain *them* (p. 768 in this book). But he is certainly claiming, at the very least, that moral facts aren't needed to explain any nonmoral facts we have any reason to believe in.

2. Other possible misunderstandings concern what is meant in asking whether reference to moral facts is *needed* to explain moral beliefs. One warning about this question I have dealt with in my discussion of reduction elsewhere;[10] but another, about what Harman is clearly *not* asking, and about what

sort of answer I can attempt to defend to the question he is asking, I can spell out here. For Harman's question is clearly not just whether there is *an* explanation of our moral beliefs that does not mention moral facts. Almost surely there is. Equally surely, however, there is an explanation of our common-sense nonmoral beliefs that does not mention an external world: one which cites only our sensory experience, for example, together with whatever needs to be said about our psychology to explain why with that history of experience we would form just the beliefs we do. Harman means to be asking a question that will lead to skepticism about moral facts, but not to skepticism about the existence of material bodies or about well-established scientific theories of the world.

Harman illustrates the kind of question he is asking, and the kind of answer he is seeking, with an example from physics that it will be useful to keep in mind. A physicist sees a vapor trail in a cloud chamber and thinks, "There goes a proton." What explains his thinking this? Partly, of course, his psychological set, which largely depends on his beliefs about the apparatus and all the theory he has learned; but partly also, perhaps, the hypothesis that "there really was a proton going through the cloud chamber, causing the vapor trail, which he saw as a proton." We will *not* need this latter assumption, however, "if his having made that observation could have been equally well explained by his psychological set alone, without the need for any assumption about a proton" (p. 767 in this book).[11] So for reference to moral facts to be *needed* in the explanation of our beliefs and observations, is for this reference to be required for an explanation that is somehow *better* than competing explanations. Correspondingly, reference to moral facts will be unnecessary to an explanation, in Harman's view, not just because we can find some explanation that does not appeal to them, but because *no* explanation that appeals to them is any better than some competing explanation that does not.

Now, fine discriminations among competing explanations of almost anything are likely to be difficult, controversial, and provisional. Fortunately, however, my discussion of Harman's argument will not require any fine discriminations. This is because Harman's thesis, as we have seen, is *not* that moral explanations lose out by a small margin; nor is it that moral explanations, though sometimes initially promising, always turn out on further examination to be inferior to nonmoral ones. It is, rather, that reference to moral facts always looks, right from the start, to be "completely irrelevant" to the explanation of any of our observations and beliefs. And my argument will be that this is mistaken: that many moral explanations appear to be good explanations, or components in good explanations, that are not obviously undermined by anything else that we know. My suspicion, in fact, is that moral facts are needed in the sense explained, that they will turn out to belong in our best overall explanatory picture of the world, even in the long run, but I shall not attempt to establish that here. Indeed, it should be clear why I could not pretend to do so. For I have explicitly put to one side the issue (which I regard as incapable in any case of quick resolution) of whether and to what extent actual moral disagreements can be settled satisfactorily; but I assume it would count as a defect in any sort of explanation to rely on claims about which rational agreement proved unattainable. So I concede that it *could* turn out, for anything I say here, that moral explanations are all defective and should be discarded. What I shall try to show is merely that many moral explanations look reasonable enough to be in the running; and, more specifically, that nothing Harman says provides any reason for thinking they are not. This claim is surely strong enough (and controversial enough) to be worth defending.

3. It is implicit in this statement of my project, but worth noting separately, that I take Harman to be proposing an *independent* skeptical argument—independent not merely of the argument from the difficulty of settling disputed moral questions, but also of other standard arguments for moral skepticism. Otherwise his argument is not worth separate discussion. For *any* of these more familiar skeptical arguments will of course imply that moral explanations are defective, on the reasonable assumption that it would be a defect in any explanation to rely on claims as doubtful as these arguments attempt to show all moral claims to be. But if *that* is why there is a problem with moral explanations, one should surely just cite the relevant skeptical argument, rather than this derivative difficulty about moral explanations, as the basic "problem with ethics," and it is that argument we should discuss. So I take Harman's interesting suggestion to be that there is a *different* difficulty that remains even if we put other arguments for moral skepticism aside and *assume*, for the sake of argument, that there are moral facts (for example, that what the children in his example are doing is really wrong): namely, that these assumed facts *still* seem to play no explanatory role.

This understanding of Harman's thesis crucially affects my argumentative strategy in a way to which I should alert the reader in advance. For it should be clear that assessment of this thesis not merely permits, but *requires*, that we provisionally assume the existence of moral facts. I can see no way of evaluating the claim that *even if* we assumed the existence of moral facts they would still appear explanatorily irrelevant, without assuming the existence of some, to see how they would look. So I do freely assume this in each of the examples I discuss in the next section. (I have tried to choose plausible examples, moreover, moral facts most of us would be inclined to believe in if we did believe in moral facts, since those are the easiest to think about; but the precise examples don't matter, and anyone who would prefer others should feel free to substitute her own.) I grant, furthermore, that if Harman were right about the outcome of this thought experiment—that even after we assumed these facts they still looked irrelevant to the explanation of our moral beliefs and other nonmoral facts—then we might conclude with him that there were, after all, no such facts. But I claim he is wrong: that once we have provisionally assumed the existence of moral facts they *do* appear relevant, by perfectly ordinary standards, to the explanation of moral beliefs and of a good deal else besides. Does this prove that there *are* such facts? Well of course it helps support that view, but here I carefully make no claim to have shown so much. What I *show* is that any remaining reservations about the existence of moral facts must be based on those *other* skeptical arguments, of which Harman's argument is independent. In short, there may still be a "problem with ethics," but it has *nothing* special to do with moral explanations.

Moral Explanations

Now that I have explained how I understand Harman's thesis, I turn to my arguments against it. I shall first add to my example of Hitler's moral character several more in which it seems plausible to cite moral facts as part of an explanation of nonmoral facts, and in particular of people's forming the moral opinions they do. I shall then argue that Harman gives us no plausible reason to reject or ignore these explanations; I shall claim, in fact, that the same is true for his own example of the children igniting the cat. I shall conclude, finally, by attempting to diagnose the source of the disagreement between Harman and me on these issues.

My Hitler example suggests a whole range of extremely common cases that appear not to have occurred to Harman, cases in which we cite someone's moral character as part of an explanation of his or her deeds, and in which that whole story is then available as a plausible further explanation of someone's arriving at a correct assessment of that moral character. Take just one other example. Bernard DeVoto, in *The Year of Decision: 1846*, describes the efforts of American emigrants already in California to rescue another party of emigrants, the Donner Party, trapped by snows in the High Sierras, once their plight became known. At a meeting in Yerba Buena (now San Francisco), the relief efforts were put under the direction of a recent arrival, Passed Midshipman Selim Woodworth, described by a previous acquaintance as "a great busybody and ambitious of taking a command among the emigrants."[12] But Woodworth not only failed to lead rescue parties into the mountains himself, where other rescuers were counting on him (leaving children to be picked up by him, for example), but had to be "shamed, threatened and bullied" even into organizing the efforts of others willing to take the risk; he spent time arranging comforts for himself in camp, preening himself on the importance of his position; and as a predictable result of his cowardice and his exercises in vainglory, many died who might have been saved, including four known still to be alive when he turned back for the last time in mid-March.

DeVoto concludes: "Passed Midshipman

Woodworth was just no damned good" (1942, p. 442). I cite this case partly because it has so clearly the structure of an inference to a reasonable explanation. One can think of competing explanations, but the evidence points against them. It isn't, for example, that Woodworth was a basically decent person who simply proved too weak when thrust into a situation that placed heroic demands on him. He volunteered, he put no serious effort even into tasks that required no heroism, and it seems clear that concern for his own position and reputation played a much larger role in his motivation than did any concern for the people he was expected to save. If DeVoto is right about this evidence, moreover, it seems reasonable that part of the explanation of his believing that Woodworth was no damned good is just that Woodworth *was* no damned good.

DeVoto writes of course with more moral intensity (and with more of a flourish) than academic historians usually permit themselves, but it would be difficult to find a serious work of biography, for example, in which actions are not explained by appeal to moral character: sometimes by appeal to specific virtues and vices, but often enough also by appeal to a more general assessment. A different question, and perhaps a more difficult one, concerns the sort of example on which Harman concentrates, the explanation of judgments of right and wrong. Here again he appears just to have overlooked explanations in terms of moral character: a judge's thinking that it would be wrong to sentence a particular offender to the maximum prison term the law allows, for example, may be due in part to her decency and fair mindedness, which I take to be moral properties if any are. But do moral features of the action or institution being judged ever play an explanatory role? Here is an example in which they appear to. An interesting historical question is why vigorous and reasonably widespread moral opposition to slavery arose for the first time in the eighteenth and nineteenth centuries, even though slavery was a very old institution; and why this opposition arose primarily in Britain, France, and in French- and English-speaking North America, even though slavery existed throughout the New World.[13] There is a standard

answer to this question. It is that chattel slavery in British and French America, and then in the United States, was much *worse* than previous forms of slavery, and much worse than slavery in Latin America. This is, I should add, a controversial explanation. But as is often the case with historical explanations, its proponents do not claim it is the whole story, and many of its opponents grant that there may be some truth in these comparisons, and that they may after all form a small part of a larger explanation.[14] This latter concession is all I require for my example. Equally good for my purpose would be the more limited thesis which explains the growth of antislavery sentiment in the United States, between the Revolution and the Civil War, in part by saying that slavery in the United States became a more oppressive institution during that time. The appeal in these standard explanations is straightforwardly to moral facts.

What is supposed to be wrong with all these explanations? Harman says that assumptions about moral facts seem "completely irrelevant" in explaining moral observations and moral beliefs (p. 767 in this book), but on its more natural reading that claim seems pretty obviously mistaken about these examples. For it is natural to think that if a particular assumption is completely irrelevant to the explanation of a certain fact, then that fact would have obtained, and we could have explained it just as well, even if the assumption had been false.[15] But I do not believe that Hitler would have done all he did if he had not been morally depraved, nor, on the assumption that he was not depraved, can I think of any plausible explanation for his doing those things. Nor is it plausible that we would all have believed he was morally depraved even if he hadn't been. Granted, there is a tendency for writers who do not attach much weight to fascism as a social movement to want to blame its evils on a single maniacal leader, so perhaps some of them would have painted Hitler as a moral monster even if he had not been one. But this is only a tendency, and one for which many people know how to discount, so I doubt that our moral belief really is overdetermined in this way. Nor, similarly, do I believe that Woodworth's actions were overdetermined, so that he would have done just as he did even if he had been a more admirable person. I suppose one could have doubts about DeVoto's objectivity and reliability; it is obvious he dislikes Woodworth, so perhaps he would have thought him a moral loss and convinced his readers of this no matter what the man was really like. But it is more plausible that the dislike is mostly based on the same evidence that supports DeVoto's moral view of him, and that very different evidence, at any rate, would have produced a different verdict. If so, then Woodworth's moral character is part of the explanation of DeVoto's belief about his moral character.

It is more plausible of course that serious moral opposition to slavery would have emerged in Britain, France, and the United States even if slavery hadn't been worse in the modern period than before, and worse in the United States than in Latin America, and that the American antislavery movement would have grown even if slavery had not become more oppressive as the nineteenth century progressed. But that is because these moral facts are offered as at best a partial explanation of these developments in moral opinion. And if they really *are* part of the explanation, as seems plausible, then it is also plausible that whatever effect they produced was not entirely overdetermined; that, for example, the growth of the antislavery movement in the United States would at least have been somewhat slower if slavery had been and remained less bad an institution. Here again it hardly seems "completely irrelevant" to the explanation whether or not these moral facts obtained.

It is more puzzling, I grant, to consider Harman's own example in which you see the children igniting a cat and react immediately with the thought that this is wrong. Is it true, as Harman claims, that the assumption that the children are really doing something wrong is "totally irrelevant" to any reasonable explanation of your making that judgment? Would you, for example, have reacted in just the same way, with the thought that the action is wrong, even if what they were doing *hadn't* been wrong, and could we explain your reaction equally well on this assumption? Now, there is more than one way to understand this counterfactual question, and I shall return below to a reading of it that might appear favorable to Harman's view.

What I wish to point out for now is merely that there is a natural way of taking it, parallel to the way in which I have been understanding similar counterfactual questions about my own examples, on which the answer to it has to be simply: it depends. For to answer the question, I take it,[16] we must consider a situation in which what the children are doing is not wrong, but which is otherwise as much like the actual situation as possible, and then decide what your reaction would be in that situation. But since what makes their action wrong, what its wrongness *consists* in, is presumably something like its being an act of gratuitous cruelty (or, perhaps we should add, of intense cruelty, and to a helpless victim), to imagine them not doing something wrong we are going to have to imagine their action different in this respect. More cautiously and more generally, if what they are actually doing is wrong, and if moral properties are, as many writers have held, supervenient on natural ones,[17] then in order to imagine them not doing something wrong we are going to have to suppose their action different from the actual one in some of its natural features as well. So our question becomes: Even if the children had been doing something else, something just different enough not to be wrong, would you have taken them even so to be doing something wrong?

Surely there is no one answer to this question. It depends on a lot about you, including your moral views and how good you are at seeing at a glance what some children are doing. It probably depends also on a debatable moral issue; namely, just *how* different the children's action would have to be in order not to be wrong. (Is unkindness to animals, for example, also wrong?) I believe we can see how, in a case in which the answer was clearly affirmative, we might be tempted to agree with Harman that the wrongness of the action was no part of the explanation of your reaction. For suppose you are like this. You hate children. What you especially hate, moreover, is the sight of children enjoying themselves; so much so that whenever you see children having fun, you immediately assume they are up to no good. The more they seem to be enjoying themselves, furthermore, the readier you are to fasten on any pretext for thinking them engaged in real wickedness. Then it is true that even if the children had been engaged in some robust but innocent fun, you would have thought they were doing something wrong; and Harman is perhaps right[18] about you that the actual wrongness of the action you see is irrelevant to your thinking it wrong. This is because your reaction is due to a feature of the action that coincides only very accidentally with the ones that make it wrong.[19] But, of course, and fortunately, many people aren't like this (nor does Harman argue that they are). It isn't true of them, in general, that if the children had been doing something similar, although different enough not to be wrong, they would still have thought the children were doing something wrong. And it isn't true either, therefore, that the wrongness of the action is irrelevant to the explanation of why they think it wrong.

Now, one might have the sense from my discussion of all these examples, but perhaps especially from my discussion of this last one, Harman's own, that I have perversely been refusing to understand his claim about the explanatory irrelevance of moral facts in the way he intends. And perhaps I have not been understanding it as he wishes. In any case, I agree, I have certainly not been understanding the crucial counterfactual question, of whether we would have drawn the same moral conclusion even if the moral facts had been different, in the way he must intend. But I am not being perverse. I believe, as I have said, that my way of taking the question is the more natural one. And, more importantly: although there is, I grant, a reading of that question on which it will always yield the answer Harman wants—namely, that a difference in the moral facts would *not* have made a difference in our judgment—I do not believe this reading can support his argument. I must now explain why.

It will help if I contrast my general approach with his. I am approaching questions about the justification of belief in the spirit of what Quine has called "epistemology naturalized" (Quine, 1969a; see also Quine 1969b). I take this to mean that we have in general no a priori way of knowing which strategies for forming and refining our beliefs are likely to take us closer to the truth. The only way we have of proceeding is to assume the approximate truth of what seems to us the best overall theory we already have of what we are like and what the world is like, and to decide in the light of *that* what strategies of research and reasoning are likely to be reliable in producing a more nearly true overall theory. One result of applying these procedures, in turn, is likely to be the refinement or perhaps even the abandonment of parts of the tentative theory with which we began.

I take Harman's approach, too, to be an instance of this one. He says we are justified in believing in those facts that we need to assume to explain why we observe what we do. But he does not think that our knowledge of this principle about justification is a priori. Furthermore, as he knows, we cannot decide whether one explanation is better than another without relying on beliefs we already have about the world. Is it really a better explanation of the vapor trail the physicist sees in the cloud chamber to suppose that a proton caused it, as Harman suggests in his example, rather than some other charged particle? Would there, for example, have been no vapor trail in the absence of that proton? There is obviously no hope of answering such questions without assuming at least the approximate truth of some quite far-reaching microphysical theory, and our knowledge of such theories is not a priori.

But my approach differs from Harman's in one crucial way. For among the beliefs in which I have enough confidence to rely on in evaluating explanations, at least at the outset, are some moral beliefs. And I have been relying on them in the following way.[20] Harman's thesis implies that the supposed moral fact of Hitler's being morally depraved is irrelevant to the explanation of Hitler's doing what he did. (For we may suppose that if it explains his doing what he did, it also helps explain, at greater remove, Harman's belief and mine in his moral depravity.) To assess this claim, we need to conceive a situation in which Hitler was *not* morally depraved and consider the question whether in that situation he would still have done what he did. My answer is that he would not, and this answer relies on a (not very controversial) moral view: that in any world at all like the actual one, only a morally depraved person could have initiated a world war, ordered the "final solution," and done any number of other things Hitler did. That is why I believe that, if Hitler hadn't been morally depraved, he wouldn't have done those things, and hence that the fact of his moral depravity is relevant to an explanation of what he did.

Harman, however, cannot want us to rely on any such moral views in answering this counterfactual question. This comes out most clearly if we return to his example of the children igniting the cat. He claims that the wrongness of this act is irrelevant to an explanation of your thinking it wrong, that you would have *thought* it wrong even if it wasn't. My reply was that in order for the action not to be wrong it would have had to lack the feature of deliberate, intense, pointless cruelty, and that if it had differed in this way you might very well *not* have thought it wrong. I also suggested a more cautious version of this reply: that since the action is in fact wrong, and since moral properties supervene on more basic natural ones, it would have had to be different in *some* further natural respect in order not to be wrong; and that we do not know whether if it had so differed you would still have thought it wrong. Both of these replies, again, rely on moral views, the latter merely on the view that there is *something* about the natural features of the action of Harman's example that makes it wrong, the former on a more specific view as to which of these features do this.

But Harman, it is fairly clear, intends for us *not* to rely on any such moral views in evaluating his counterfactual claim. His claim is not that if the action had not been one of deliberate cruelty (or had otherwise differed in whatever way would be required to remove its wrongness), you would still have thought it wrong. It is, instead, that if the action were one of deliberate, pointless cruelty, but this *did not make it wrong*, you would still have thought it was wrong. And to return to the example of Hitler's moral character, the counterfactual claim that Harman will need in order to defend a comparable conclusion about that case is not that if Hitler had been, for example, humane and fairminded, free of nationalistic pride and racial hatred, he would still have done exactly as he did. It is, rather, that if Hitler's psychology, and anything else about his situation that could strike us as morally relevant, had been exactly as it in fact was, but this had *not constituted moral depravity*, he would still have done exactly what he did.

Now the antecedents of these two conditionals are puzzling. For one thing, both are, I believe, necessarily false. I am fairly confident, for example, that Hitler really was morally depraved;[21] and since I also accept the view that moral features supervene on more basic natural properties,[22] I take this to imply that there is no possible world in which Hitler has just the personality he in fact did, in just the situation he was in, but is not morally depraved. Any attempt to describe such a situation, moreover, will surely run up against the limits of our moral concepts—what Harman calls our "moral sensibility"—and this is no accident. For what Harman is asking us to do, in general, is to consider cases in which absolutely *everything* about the nonmoral facts that could seem morally relevant to us, in light of whatever moral theory we accept and of the concepts required for understanding that theory, is held fixed, but in which the moral judgment that our theory yields about the case is nevertheless mistaken. So it is hardly surprising that, using that theory and those concepts, we should find it difficult to conceive in any detail what such a situation would be like. It is especially not surprising when the cases in question are as paradigmatic in light of the moral outlook we in fact have as is Harman's example or, even more so, mine of Hitler's moral character. The only way we could be wrong about this latter case (assuming we have the nonmoral facts right) would be for our whole theory to be hopelessly wrong, so radically mistaken that there could be no hope of straightening it out through adjustments from within.

But I do not believe we should conclude, as we might be tempted to,[23] that we therefore know a priori that this is not so, or that we cannot understand these conditionals that are crucial to Harman's argument. Rather, now that we have seen how we have to understand them, we should grant that they are true: that if our moral theory were somehow hopelessly mistaken, but all the nonmoral facts remained exactly as they in fact are, then, since we do *accept* that moral theory, we would still draw exactly the moral conclusions we in fact do. But we should deny that any skeptical conclusion follows from this. In particular, we should deny that it follows that moral facts play no role in explaining our moral judgments.

For consider what follows from the parallel claim

about microphysics, in particular about Harman's example in which a physicist concludes from his observation of a vapor trail in a cloud chamber, and from the microphysical theory he accepts, that a free proton has passed through the chamber. The parallel claim, notice, is *not* just that if the proton had not been there the physicist would still have thought it was. This claim is implausible, for we may assume that the physicist's theory is generally correct, and it follows from that theory that if there hadn't been a proton there, then there wouldn't have been a vapor trail. But in a perfectly similar way it is implausible that if Hitler hadn't been morally depraved we would still have thought he was: for we may assume that our moral theory also is at least roughly correct, and it follows from the most central features of that theory that if Hitler hadn't been morally depraved, he wouldn't have done what he did. The *parallel* claim about the microphysical example is, instead, that if there hadn't been a proton there, but there *had* been a vapor trail, the physicist would still have concluded that a proton was present. More precisely, to maintain a perfect parallel with Harman's claims about the moral cases, the antecedent must specify that although no proton is present, absolutely *all* the non-microphysical facts that the physicist, in light of his theory, might take to be relevant to the question of whether or not a proton is present, are exactly as in the actual case. (These macrophysical facts, as we may for convenience call them, surely include everything one would normally think of as an observable fact.) Of course, we shall be unable to imagine this without imagining that the physicist's theory is pretty badly mistaken;[24] but I believe we should grant that, if the physicist's theory were somehow this badly mistaken, but all the macrophysical facts (including all the observable facts) were held fixed, then the physicist, since he does accept that theory, would still draw all the same conclusions that he actually does. That is, this conditional claim, like Harman's parallel claim about the moral cases, is true.

But no skeptical conclusions follow; nor can Harman, since he does not intend to be a skeptic about physics, think that they do. It does not follow, in the first place, that we have any reason to think the physicist's theory *is* generally mistaken. Nor does it follow, furthermore, that the hypothesis that

a proton really did pass through the cloud chamber is not part of a good explanation of the vapor trail, and hence of the physicist's thinking this has happened. This looks like a reasonable explanation, of course, only on the assumption that the physicist's theory is at least roughly true, for it is this theory that tells us, for example, what happens when charged particles pass through a supersaturated atmosphere, what other causes (if any) there might be for a similar phenomenon, and so on. But, as I say, we have not been provided with any reason for not trusting the theory to this extent.

Similarly, I conclude, we should draw no skeptical conclusions from Harman's claims about the moral cases. It is true that if our moral theory were seriously mistaken, but we still believed it, and the nonmoral facts were held fixed, we would still make just the moral judgments we do. But *this* fact by itself provides us with no reason for thinking that our moral theory is generally mistaken. Nor, again, does it imply that the fact of Hitler's really having been morally depraved forms no part of a good explanation of his doing what he did and hence, at greater remove, of our thinking him depraved. This explanation will appear reasonable, of course, only on the assumption that our accepted moral theory is at least roughly correct, for it is this theory that assures us that only a depraved person could have thought, felt, and acted as Hitler did. But, as I say, Harman's argument has provided us with no reason for not trusting our moral views to this extent, and hence with no reason for doubting that it is sometimes moral facts that explain our moral judgments.

I conclude with three comments about my argument.

1. I have tried to show that Harman's claim—that we would have held the particular moral beliefs we do even if those beliefs were untrue—admits of two readings, one of which makes it implausible, and the other of which reduces it to an application of a general skeptical strategy, a strategy which could as easily be used to produce doubt about microphysical as about moral facts. The general strategy is this. Consider any conclusion C we arrive at by relying both on some distinguishable "theory" T and on some body of evidence not being challenged, and ask whether we would have believed C

even if it had been false. The plausible answer, *if* we are allowed to rely on *T* will often be no: for if *C* had been false, then (according to *T*) the evidence would have had to be different, and in that case we wouldn't have believed *C*. (I have illustrated the plausibility of this sort of reply for all my moral examples, as well as for the microphysical one.) But the skeptic of course intends us *not* to rely on *T* in this way, and so rephrases the question: Would we have believed *C* even if it were false but all the evidence had been exactly as it in fact was? Now the answer has to be yes; and the skeptic concludes that *C* is doubtful. (It should be obvious how to extend this strategy to belief in other minds, or in an external world.) I am of course not convinced: I do not think answers to the rephrased question show anything interesting about what we know or justifiably believe. But it is enough for my purposes here that no such *general* skeptical strategy could pretend to reveal any problems peculiar to belief in *moral* facts.

2. My conclusion about Harman's argument, although it is not exactly the same, is nevertheless similar to and very much in the spirit of the Duhemian point I invoked earlier against verificationism. There the question was whether typical moral assertions have testable implications, and the answer was that they do, so long as you include additional moral assumptions of the right sort among the background theories on which you rely in evaluating these assertions. Harman's more important question is whether we should ever regard moral facts as relevant to the explanation of nonmoral facts, and in particular of our having the moral beliefs we do. But the answer, again, is that we should, so long as we are willing to hold the right sorts of *other* moral assumptions fixed in answering counterfactual questions. Neither answer shows morality to be on any shakier ground than, say, physics, for typical microphysical hypotheses, too, have testable implications, and appear relevant to explanations, only if we are willing to assume at least the approximate truth of an elaborate microphysical theory and to hold this assumption fixed in answering counterfactual questions.

3. Of course, this picture of how explanations depend on background theories, and moral explanations in particular on moral background theories, does show why someone already tempted toward

moral skepticism on other grounds (such as those I mentioned at the beginning of this essay) might find Harman's claim about moral explanations plausible. To the extent that you already have pervasive doubts about moral theories, you will also find moral facts nonexplanatory. So I grant that Harman has located a natural symptom of moral skepticism; but I am sure he has neither traced this skepticism to its roots nor provided any independent argument for it. His claim (p. 22) that we do not *in fact* cite moral facts in explanation of moral beliefs and observations cannot provide such an argument, for that claim is false. So, too, is the claim that assumptions about moral facts seem irrelevant to such explanations, for many do not. The claim that we *should* not rely on such assumptions because they *are* irrelevant, on the other hand, unless it is supported by some independent argument for moral skepticism, will just be question-begging: for the principal test of whether they are relevant, in any situation in which it appears they might be, is a counterfactual question about what would have happened if the moral fact had not obtained, and how we answer that question depends precisely upon whether we *do* rely on moral assumptions in answering it.

My own view I stated at the outset: that the only argument for moral skepticism with any independent weight is the argument from the difficulty of settling disputed moral questions. I have shown that anyone who finds Harman's claim about moral explanations plausible must already have been tempted toward skepticism by some other considerations, and I suspect that the other considerations will typically be the ones I sketched. So that is where discussion should focus. I also suggested that those considerations may provide less support for moral skepticism than is sometimes supposed, but I must reserve a thorough defense of that thesis for another occasion.[25]

NOTES

1. As, for example, in Gewirth (1960), in which there are some useful remarks about the first of them.
2. Harman's title for the entire first section of his book.

3. In the longer article of which this is an abridgement.

4. This point is generally credited to Pierre Duhem (1906, 1954). It is a prominent theme in the influential writings of W. V. O. Quine. For an especially clear application of it, see Putnam (1977).

5. See note 3.

6. Harman is careful always to say only that moral beliefs *appear* to play no such role, and since he eventually concludes that there *are* moral facts (p. 132), this caution may be more than stylistic. I shall argue that this more cautious claim, too, is mistaken (indeed, that is my central thesis). But to avoid issues about Harman's intent, I shall simply mean by "Harman's argument" the skeptical argument of his first two chapters, whether or not he means to endorse all of it. This argument surely deserves discussion in its own right in either case, especially since Harman never explains what is wrong with it.

7. He asks: "Can moral principles be tested in the same way [as scientific hypotheses can], out in the world? You can observe someone do something, but can you ever perceive the rightness or wrongness of what he does?" (p. 765 in this book).

8. The other is that Harman appears to use "observe" (and "perceive" and "see") in a surprising way. One would normally take observing (or perceiving, or seeing) something to involve *knowing* it was the case. But Harman apparently takes an observation to be *any* opinion arrived at as "a direct result of perception" (p. 5) or, at any rate (see next note), "immediately and without conscious reasoning" (p. 7). This means that observations need not even be true, much less known to be true. A consequence is that the existence of moral observations, in Harman's sense, would not be sufficient to show that there is moral knowledge, although this *would* be sufficient if "observe" were being used in a more standard sense. What I argue in the text is that the existence of moral observations (in either Harman's or the standard sense) is not *necessary* for showing that there is moral knowledge, either.

9. This sort of case does not meet Harman's characterization of an observation as an opinion that is "a direct result of perception" (p. 5), but he is surely right that moral facts would be as well vindicated if they were needed to explain our drawing conclusions about hypothetical cases as they would be if they were needed to explain observations in the narrower sense. To be sure, Harman is still confining his attention to cases in which we draw the moral conclusion from our thought experiment "immediately and without conscious reasoning" (p. 7) and it is no doubt the existence of such cases that gives purchase to talk of a "moral sense." But this feature, again, can hardly matter to the argument: would belief in moral facts be less justified if they were needed only to explain the instances in which we draw the moral conclusion *slowly*? Nor can it make any difference for that matter whether the case we are reflecting on is hypothetical: so my example in which we, quickly or slowly, draw a moral conclusion about Hitler from what we know of him, is surely relevant.

10. In the longer paper from which this is abridged. The salient point is that there are two very *different* reasons one might have for thinking that no reference to moral facts is needed in the explanation of moral beliefs. One—Harman's reason, and my target in this essay—is that no moral explanations even *seem* plausible, that reference to moral facts always strikes us as "completely irrelevant" to the explanation of moral beliefs. This claim, if true, would tend to support moral skepticism. The other, which might appeal to a "reductive" naturalist in ethics, is that any moral explanations that *do* seem plausible can be paraphrased without explanatory loss in entirely nonmoral terms. I doubt this view, too, and I argue in the longer version of this selection that no ethical naturalist need hold it. But anyone tempted by it should note that it is anyway no version of moral skepticism: for what it says is that we know *so much* about ethics that we are always able to say, in entirely nonmoral terms, exactly which natural properties the moral terms in any plausible moral explanations refer to—that's why the moral expressions are dispensable. These two reasons should not be confused with one another.

11. It is surprising that Harman does not mention the obvious intermediate possibility, which would occur to any instrumentalist: to cite the physicist's psychological set *and* the vapor trail, but say nothing about protons or other unobservables. It is *this* explanation, as I emphasize below, that is most closely parallel to an explanation of beliefs about an external world in terms of sensory experience and psychological makeup, or of moral beliefs in terms of nonmoral facts together with our "moral sensibility."

12. DeVoto (1942), p. 426; a quotation from the notebooks of Francis Parkman. The account of the entire rescue effort is on pp. 424–44.

13. What is being explained, of course is not just why people came to think slavery wrong, but why people who were not themselves slaves or in danger of being enslaved came to think it so seriously wrong as to be intolerable. There is a much larger and longer history of people who thought it wrong but tolerable, and an even longer one of people who appear not to have got past the thought that the world would be a better place without it. See Davis (1966).

14. For a version of what I am calling the standard view of slavery in the Americas, see Tannenbaum (1947). For an argument against both halves of the standard view, see Davis (1966), esp. pp. 60-61, 223-25, 262-63.

15. This counterfactual test requires qualification, but none of the plausible qualifications matters to my examples. See the longer version of this essay, and also my "Harman on Moral Explanations of Natural Facts," *The Southern Journal of Philosophy* 24 (1986), Supplementary Issue.

16. Following, informally, Stalnaker and Lewis on counterfactuals. See Stalnaker (1968) and Lewis (1973).

17. What would be generally granted is just that if there are moral properties they supervene on natural properties. But, remember, we are assuming for the sake of argument that there are.

    I think that moral properties are natural properties; and from this view it of course follows trivially that they supervene on natural properties: that, necessarily, nothing could differ in its moral properties without differing in some natural respect. But I also accept the more interesting thesis usually intended by the claim about supervenience—that there are more basic natural features such that, necessarily, once they are fixed, so are the moral properties. (In supervening on more basic natural facts of some sort, moral facts are like most natural facts. Social facts like unemployment, for example, supervene on complex histories of many individuals and their relations; and facts about the existence and properties of macroscopic physical objects—colliding billiard balls, say—clearly supervene on the microphysical constitution of the situations that include them.)

18. Not certainly right, because there is still the possibility that your reaction is to some extent overdetermined, and is to be explained partly by your sympathy for the cat and your dislike of cruelty, as well as by your hatred for children (although this last alone would have been sufficient to produce it).

We could of course rule out this possibility by making you an even less attractive character, indifferent to the suffering of animals and not offended by cruelty. But it may then be hard to imagine that such a person (whom I shall cease calling "you") could retain enough of a grip on moral thought for us to be willing to say he thought the action wrong, as opposed to saying that he merely pretended to do so. This difficulty is perhaps not unsuperable, but it is revealing. Harman says that the actual wrongness of the action is "completely irrelevant" to the explanation of the observer's reaction. Notice that what is in fact true, however, is that it is very hard to imagine someone who reacts in the way Harman describes, but whose reaction is not due, at least in part, to the actual wrongness of the action.

19. Perhaps deliberate cruelty is worse the more one enjoys it (a standard counterexample to hedonism). If so, the fact that the children are enjoying themselves makes their action worse, but presumably isn't what makes it wrong to begin with.

20. Harman of course allows us to assume the moral facts whose explanatory relevance is being assessed: that Hitler was depraved, or that what the children in his example are doing is wrong. But I have been assuming something more—something about what depravity is, and about what makes the children's action wrong. (At a minimum, in the more cautious version of my argument, I have been assuming that something about its more basic features makes it wrong, so that it could not have differed in its moral quality without differing in those other features as well.)

21. And anyway, remember, this is the sort of fact Harman allows us to assume in order to see whether, if we assume it, it will look explanatory.

22. It is about here that I have several times encountered the objection: but surely supervenient properties aren't needed to explain anything. It is a little hard, however, to see just what this objection is supposed to come to. If it includes endorsement of the conditional I here attribute to Harman, then I believe the remainder of my discussion is an adequate reply to it. If it is the claim that, because moral properties are supervenient, we can always exploit the insights in any moral explanations, however plausible, without resort to moral language, then I have already dealt with it in my discussion of reductionism (see note 10, above): the claim is probably false, but even if it is true it is no

support for Harman's view, which is not that moral explanations are plausible but reducible, but that they are totally implausible. And doubts about the causal efficacy of supervenient facts seem misplaced in any case, as attention to my earlier examples (note 17) illustrates. High unemployment causes widespread hardship, and can also bring down the rate of inflation. The masses and velocities of two colliding billiard balls causally influence the subsequent trajectories of the two balls. There is no doubt some sense in which these facts are causally efficacious in virtue of the way they supervene on—that is, are constituted out of, or causally realized by—more basic facts, but this hardly shows them inefficacious. (Nor does Harman appear to think it does: for his favored explanation of your moral belief about the burning cat, recall, appeals to psychological facts (about your moral sensibility), a biological fact (that it's a cat), and macrophysical facts (that it's on fire)—supervenient facts all, on his physicalist view and mine.) If anyone does hold to a general suspicion of causation by supervenient facts and properties, however, as Jaegwon Kim appears to (1979, pp. 47–48), it is enough to note that this suspicion cannot diagnose any special difficulty with *moral* explanations, any distinctive "problem with ethics." The "problem," arguably, will be with every discipline but fundamental physics.

23. And as I take it Philippa Foot (1978), for example, is still prepared to do, at least about paradigmatic cases.

24. If we imagine the physicist *regularly* mistaken in this way, moreover, we will have to imagine his theory not just mistaken but hopelessly so. And we can easily reproduce the other notable feature of Harman's claims about the moral cases, that what we are imagining is *necessarily* false, if we suppose that one of the physicist's (or better, chemist's) conclusion is about the microstructure of some common substance, such as water. For I agree with Saul Kripke that whatever microstructure water has is essential to it, that it has this structure in every possible world in which it exists. (Kripke, 1980, pp. 115–44.) If we are right (as we have every reason to suppose) in thinking that water is actually H_2O, therefore, the conditional, "If water were not H_2O, but all the observable, macrophysical facts were just as they actually are, chemists would still have come to *think* it was H_2O," has a necessarily false antecedent; just as, if we are right

(as we also have good reason to suppose) in thinking that Hitler was actually morally depraved, the conditional, "If Hitler were just as he was in all natural respects, but not morally depraved, we would still have *thought* he was depraved," has a necessarily false antecedent. Of course, I am not suggesting that in either case our knowledge that the antecedent is false is a priori.

These counterfactuals, because of their impossible antecedents, will have to be interpreted over worlds that are (at best) only "epistemically" possible; and, as Richard Boyd has pointed out to me, this helps to explain why anyone who accepts a causal theory of knowledge (or any theory according to which the justification of our beliefs depends on what explains our holding them) will find their truth irrelevant to the question of how much we know, either in chemistry or in morals. For although there certainly are counterfactuals that are relevant to questions about what causes what (and, hence, about what explains what), these have to be counterfactuals about real possibilities, not merely epistemic ones.

25. This essay has benefited from helpful discussion of earlier versions read at the University of Virginia, Cornell University, Franklin and Marshall College, Wayne State University, and the University of Michigan. I have been aided by a useful correspondence with Gilbert Harman; and I am grateful also for specific comments from Richard Boyd, David Brink, David Copp, Stephen Darwall, Terence Irwin, Norman Kretzmann, Ronald Nash, Peter Railton, Bruce Russell, Sydney Shoemaker, and Judith Slein.

REFERENCES

Davis, David Brion. 1966. *The Problem of Slavery in Western Culture*. Ithaca, N.Y.: Cornell University Press.

DeVoto, Bernard. 1942. *The Year of Decision: 1846*. Boston: Houghton Mifflin.

Duhem, Pierre. 1906. *The Aim and Structure of Physical Theory*, translated by Philip P. Wiener (1954). Princeton, N.J.: Princeton University Press.

Foot, Philippa. 1978. *Moral Relativism*. The Lindley Lecture, The University of Kansas, Lawrence.

Gewirth, Alan. 1960. "Positive 'Ethics' and Normative 'Science'." *The Philosophical Review* 69, 311–30.

Harman, Gilbert. 1977. *The Nature of Morality: An Introduction to Ethics*. New York: Oxford University Press.

Kim, Jaegwon. 1979. "Causality, Identity and Supervenience in the Mind-Body Problem," in Peter A. French, Theodore E. Uehling, Jr., and Howard K. Wettstein, eds., *Midwest Studies in Philosophy 4, Studies in Metaphysics*, pp. 31–49. Minneapolis: University of Minnesota Press.

Kripke, Saul. 1980. *Naming and Necessity*. Cambridge: Harvard University Press.

Lewis, David. 1973. *Counterfactuals*. Cambridge: Harvard University Press.

Mackie, J. L. 1977. *Ethics: Inventing Right and Wrong*. Harmondsworth, England: Penguin.

Putnam, Hilary. 1977. "The 'Corroboration' of Theories," in *Mathematics, Matter and Method, Philosophical Papers, Volume I*, 2d ed., pp. 250–69. Cambridge: Cambridge University Press.

Quine, W. V. O. 1969a. "Epistemology Naturalized," in *Ontological Relativity and Other Essays*, pp. 69–90. New York: Columbia University Press.

———. 1969b. "Natural Kinds," in *Ontological Relativity and Other Essays*, pp. 114–38. New York: Columbia University Press.

Stalnaker, Robert. 1968. "A Theory of Conditionals," in Nicholas Rescher, ed., *Studies in Logical Theory*. APQ Monograph No. 2. Oxford: Basil Blackwell.

Tannenbaum, Frank. 1947. *Slave and Citizen*. New York: Alfred A. Knopf.

PART VI

—•—

Puzzles and
Paradoxes

INTRODUCTION

Puzzles and paradoxes have played an important role in the history of philosophy and are both challenging and fun to think about. Of course, any philosophical problem can be considered a puzzle. But, we have in mind problems expressed in relatively few words that immediately reveal some puzzling aspect of things to which there is no obvious and clearly satisfactory solution. Most of these puzzles can be stated in the form of *paradoxes*. A paradox is an argument that *appears* to derive self-contradictory or otherwise absurd conclusions by valid reasoning from acceptable premises.

When a paradox becomes well-enough understood, whether as the result of a few moments work by an individual or the insights of successive generations of thinkers, the appearance of a valid derivation of an absurdity should disappear. In some cases, when properly understood the conclusion will cease to seem absurd. In other cases the premises will no longer seem acceptable or the reasoning will no longer seem valid. W. V. Quine calls paradoxes of the first sort *veridical*, those of the second sort *falsidical*, and those for which we can neither accept the conclusion nor spot the mistake *antinomies*. All three kinds are represented here.

Some of the puzzles are presented as paradoxes, whereas others are simply set forth as problems or puzzles. In deciding what to say about these latter problems or puzzles, students will usually find they can state their reasoning in the form of a paradox.

There is extensive literature on each of these puzzles, and we cite some of it. But, we think puzzles are most interesting if students approach them, at least at first, as occasions for unfettered thought rather than as scholarly projects. For example, in the case of Newcomb's problem we urge students to first decide what they would do in the imagined circumstances, to construct arguments justifying their choice, and, then, to try to find flaws or loopholes in their arguments—perhaps with the aid of students who support the opposite strategy. This approach is more rewarding than going to the library and looking up what the experts have said about the problem.

A. Zeno's Paradoxes

Zeno of Elea was born around 490 B.C. He was a supporter of the philosopher Parmenides, founder of the Eleatic School of Greek philosophy, who held that the particularity of individual things is an illusion. Zeno supported this view by producing arguments to show that plurality and change are really self-contradictory notions. Because most philosophers have regarded the conclusions of Zeno's arguments as absurd, they are known as paradoxes. Some fragments of Zeno's writings that contain arguments against plurality survive; the arguments against motion are known almost entirely through Aristotle's account of them in his *Physics*.

There is an excellent discussion of Zeno and his paradoxes by Gregory Vlastos in Paul Edwards's *Encyclopedia of Philosophy*. This article also contains a good bibliography. Max Black's treatment of Zeno's arguments in his *Problems of Analysis* (Ithaca, N.Y., 1954) and Adolf Grünbaum's *Modern Science and Zeno's Paradoxes* (Middletown, Conn., 1967) might be particularly useful to the student wishing to learn about these paradoxes. Here, we give versions of two of the paradoxes of motion and one of plurality. The statement of the plurality puzzle is that of Carl Ginet, professor of philosophy at Cornell University.

Achilles and the Tortoise

SUPPOSE THAT ACHILLES AND THE tortoise are having a race. Because Achilles is faster, we give the tortoise a head start of 10 yards. We suppose that the tortoise can run 1 yard in a second and that Achilles can run 10 yards in a second. It seems that Achilles will certainly catch and pass the tortoise. However, in order to pass the tortoise, Achilles must perform an endless sequence of tasks, one after the other. But it is easily seen that this is impossible.

The first task Achilles must perform is to reach the point where the tortoise starts. Call this Point 1. This takes one second. But, after Achilles does this, the tortoise is still 1 yard ahead, at what we will call Point 2.

The second task Achilles must perform is to reach Point 2, the point that the tortoise is at after Achilles completes the first task. When Achilles completes this second task, though, the tortoise is still ahead by 0.1 yard, at Point 3.

The third task Achilles must perform is to reach Point 3. After Achilles does this, though, the tortoise will still be ahead by 0.01 yard at Point 4.

We can see that after each task of this sort that Achilles performs, the tortoise will still be ahead, and there will be another task of the same sort still facing Achilles. That is, for any n (no matter how large), after Achilles has completed n tasks of this sort, he still won't have caught up with the tortoise, who will still be ahead by $\frac{1}{10}^{n-1}$ yards. But Achilles can never complete more tasks than there are numbers because we never run out of numbers. So Achilles will never catch the tortoise.

The Racecourse

It seems embarrassing enough for the advocates of motion and change that a runner so fast as Achilles can never catch a runner so slow as the tortoise. But things are worse. Achilles cannot even win a one-man race, for wherever the finish line is, he will never reach it.

—◆—

SUPPOSE ACHILLES IS TO RUN FROM the starting point S to the goal G. To do this, he must do all of the following:

1. Run to the point halfway from S to G.
2. Run from that point to the point halfway between it and G.
3. Run from that point to the point halfway between it and G.
4. Run from that point to the point halfway between it and G, etc.

The "etc." clearly goes on forever. That is, the first point is only halfway to G, the second point only three-fourths of the way to G, the third point only seven-eighths of the way to G, the fourth point only fifteen-sixteenths of the way to G, and, in general, the nth point will be only $2^n - 1/2^n$ of the way to G. Hence, Achilles will never make it to G.

The Argument Against Plurality

—◆—

A. The Main Argument:

1. If a finite spatial interval is divisible (i.e., composed of a plurality of parts), then it can be endlessly divided into ever-larger numbers of ever-smaller distinct and equal parts.

2. Therefore, any such interval is composed of infinitely many distinct and equal parts.

3. Each of these parts either (a) has some length or (b) has no length.

4. If (a), then the whole finite interval must be infinitely long.

5. If (b), then the whole finite interval must have no length.

6. Therefore, if a finite spatial interval is divisible, then either it is infinitely long or it has no length.

7. But every finite interval has a non-zero finite length.

8. Therefore, a finite spatial interval is not divisible.

B. An Argument for A.5:

1. If a finite spatial interval is composed of lengthless points, then its length must be the sum of the lengths of those points.

2. The length of any such point is zero.

3. The sum of any number of zeros (even infinitely many) is zero.

4. Therefore, if a finite spatial interval is composed of lengthless points, then its length is zero.

B. Metaphysical and Epistemological Puzzles and Paradoxes

The Paradox of Identity

Problems about the notion of identity through change have played a long and important role in philosophy. Heraclitus, a Greek philosopher of the fifth century B.C. claimed that one could not step in the same river twice because new waters were always rushing in. This supported his general view of things, which was the opposite of that of Parmenides and Zeno. They thought that Being was one thing that didn't change; he thought that Being was an incredible plurality in constant flux. Many centuries later, David Hume argued that all attributions of identity over time were based on confusion. The following argument for the absurd conclusion that nothing persists through time, although perhaps cruder than either of these great philosophers would accept, captures some of the spirit of their line of thinking about identity.

——•——

BY *IDENTITY*, WE MEAN THAT RELA-tion that obtains between each thing and it-self and that never obtains between a thing and anything else. So if *A* is identical with *B*, there is just one thing that is both *A* and *B*. For example, the man who coached the Stanford football team to Bowl victories in the mid-1970s is identical with the man who coached the San Francisco Forty-Niners to a Super Bowl victory in 1982. Thus, there is one man (Bill Walsh) who did both things. That is, there is one man who is the man who coached the Stanford football team to Bowl victories in the mid-1970s and who is the man who coached the San Francisco Forty-Niners to a Super Bowl victory in 1982.

Note that *identity* is not always used in ordinary English with this precise meaning. Sometimes, it is used to mean something like *exactly similar* or *exactly similar with respect to some important property*. Given *our* use of *identity*, for example, the term *identical twins* is self-contradictory. If *A* and *B* are twins, *A* and *B* are two individuals who are not identical in *our* official sense.

Now, given this sense of identity, there is one important principle that should be completely non-controversial:

> If *A* is identical with *B*, then *A* and *B* have exactly the same properties.

We can call this principle *The indiscernibility of the identical*. It should not be confused with Leibniz's principle of the identity of the indiscernible:

> If *A* and *B* have exactly the same properties, then *A* is identical with *B*.

This latter principle is controversial. But the first should not be. For, if *A* and *B* are identical, then there is just one thing that is both *A* and *B*, and the principle just requires that it has the properties it has, which is utterly trivial.

But, given this principle, it follows that no individual persists through time.

First, note that our principle has the consequence

788

that no individual persists through change and that the very example we used to illustrate the concept of identity makes no sense. For,

> The coach of the Stanford football team has the property of being the coach of the Stanford football team. (Obviously)
>
> The coach of the San Francisco Forty-Niners does not have the property of being the coach of the Stanford football team. (It would be a violation of NCAA rules.)

But, then it is obvious that, contrary to our example, the first cannot be identical with the second.

But, note that any individual who is alive at a certain time moment (t) has a certain exact age (n)—where n is the number of moments the individual has been alive, up to and including t. But a moment later, at t', this individual will no longer have this exact age. But, then, we see that the whole idea of persistence makes no sense, for to persist from moment to moment an individual has to change in respect to his or her exact age, but we have seen that change is ruled out.

So there is no persistence through change; no individual existing at any given time t is identical with any individual existing at any earlier or later time t'. Not only is there no individual who coached Stanford at one time and the Forty-Niners at some later time, there is not even an individual who coached Stanford to Bowl victories in different years, nor even one who coached them successive days, nor even through a single practice.

The Paradox of the Heap

This is an ancient paradox, that is most flexible. Here, we first use it to "show" that there is no such thing as a heap. Then, we use the same sort of reasoning to "show" that there is no such thing as baldness and that if it is wrong to have an abortion toward the end of a pregnancy, it is always wrong. This paradox can be used to "show" many other things. When versions of this paradox are set out as a chain of syllogisms, they have the form known in Aristotelian logic as the Sorites; the paradox is often just called by that name.

⸻⬩⸻

ONE GRAIN OF SAND IS NOT A HEAP of sand. If something is not a heap of sand, addition (or dimunition) by one grain will not make it a heap. But, then, nothing is a heap. For, by starting with one grain of sand and adding to it a grain at a time, we will never have a heap. If something arrived at by such a method is not a heap, then nothing just like it, arrived at by some other method, is a heap either. So there are no heaps of sand and the whole idea is incoherent.

Given a person who is not bald, plucking one hair never makes that person bald. For, the person is already bald before the last hair is plucked. Plucking one hair from a person who is not bald will never make that person bald. So, if we started with a man or woman with a full head of hair and plucked his or her hairs one at a time, we would never make that person bald. Thus, the whole idea of baldness is incoherent.

Everyone agrees that it is wrong to have an abortion on the last day of a normal pregnancy. But, surely, if it is wrong to have an abortion on a given day (or at a certain minute of a pregnancy or at a certain second of a pregnancy), it is equally wrong to have it the day (minute, second) before. But, then, it is equally wrong to have an abortion at each point in a pregnancy, and so, by our opening assumption, always wrong.

The Surprise Examination

W. V. Quine reports that this puzzle has been around since 1943. He discusses it in his essay "On a Supposed Antinomy," in *The Ways of Paradox* (New York, 1966). Richard Montague and David Kaplan discuss it in "A Paradox Regained," in Montague's *Formal Philosophy*, edited by R. H. Thomason, (New Haven, Conn., 1974). Both of these discussions contain bibliographies. The student who consults the literature will find it quickly gets intricate. Yet, the problem is easily grasped. Note that it is easy to generate analogous puzzles involving hangings (the version Quine discusses), air-raid drills, and other events whose unpleasantness is enhanced when they are a surprise. The version involving an examination seems most relevant to the philosophy student.

PROFESSOR *X* ANNOUNCES AT THE end of class on Friday that there will be a surprise hour-examination the following week. Student *Y* contemplates spending the weekend in study, but she hits on an argument that shows there can be no such examination. Here is her argument.

The exam cannot be on Friday. For, then, I would know Thursday after class that it was going to be on Friday, for it would not have been on Monday, Tuesday, Wednesday, or Thursday. But, then, it would not be a surprise, for I would know in advance when it was.

But, because it cannot be on Friday, it cannot be given on Thursday either. For, given that it cannot be on Friday, if it is not given Monday, Tuesday, or Wednesday, it has to be given on Thursday. So I would know after Wednesday's class that it was going to be given on Thursday, and it would not be a surprise.

But, because it cannot be given on Thursday or Friday, by similar reasoning it cannot be given on Wednesday either. And, indeed, the same reasoning works for Tuesday and Monday, too. So there will be no surprise examination, and I can relax this weekend.

Student *Y* does not study. The following Wednesday Professor *X* hands out an exam. Student *Y* is surprised, and she does quite poorly.

Goodman's New Riddle of Induction

This paradox is based on a problem introduced by Nelson Goodman in his book *Fact, Fiction and Forecast*, 2nd ed. (Indianapolis, Ind., 1965). He explains his own approach in this book, and his discussion has given rise to a voluminous literature.

———◆———

WE ORDINARILY ASSUME THAT we can confirm a general hypothesis by examination of instances and that this process of induction is useful in conducting our lives. For example, we assume that repeated observations of green emeralds and failure to observe any that are not green supports the hypothesis that all emeralds are green. Thus, it is reasonable to expect the next emerald we examine to be green if we have no other evidence to go on. But, actually, such confirmation provides no basis for forming expectations at all, and induction is quite useless.

Suppose that it is January 1, 1987, and that all emeralds examined have been green. This seems to support the hypothesis that all emeralds are green and to make it rational, other things being equal, to expect the next emerald we examine to also be green.

But, let the word *grue* apply to things just in case:

1. They are examined before January 1, 1987, and are green.
2. They have not been examined before January 1, 1987, and are blue.

All of the emeralds examined before January 1, 1987, are grue as well as green. Hence, our observations up to that time support the hypothesis that all emeralds are grue every bit as much as the hypothesis that all emeralds are green. Hence, our observations give us as much reason to expect the next emerald we examine to be grue as to expect it to be green. But, if the next emerald we examine is grue, it is also blue, and not green. So our observations give us as much reason to expect the next emerald we examine to be blue as they do to expect that it will be green. But, obviously, we could repeat the same argument to show that we have as much reason to expect the next emerald we examine to be any color other than green. E.g., we could repeat the argument by using the predicate *gred*, which applies to things examined before January 1, 1987, if they are green and to other things if they are red. So our observations give us no more reason to expect the next emerald we examine to be green than they do to expect it to be blue or red or any other color. So, contrary to what we assumed to be plausible, induction is totally useless.

C. Puzzles of Rational Choice

The Prisoner's Dilemma

This problem has been discussed in the literature on rational action for many years. The following statement is that of Carl Ginet.

——•——

TWO MEN SUSPECTED OF COMMIT-ting a crime together are arrested and placed in separate cells. They are not per-mitted to communicate with one another. Each of them is told the following:

1. You may either confess to the crime or refuse to confess.
2. If one of you confesses but the other does not, then, the one who confesses will go free and the other one will go to jail for four years.
3. If both of you confess, then, you will both go to jail for three years.
4. If neither of you confesses, then, you will both go to jail for one year.

5. The other one of you is being told these same things.

Assume that each prisoner is concerned solely with his own welfare and knows that the fewer years he spends in jail the better off he will be. Assume also that each knows that the other is like-wise concerned only with minimizing his own jail term.

In these circumstances, which alternative, to con-fess or to refuse to confess, should each prisoner choose? That is, given what each prisoner knows, which alternative would it be more rational for him to choose?

Newcomb's Problem

This problem was posed by William Newcomb, a physicist. The philosophical world first heard of it from Robert Nozick in his "Newcomb's Problem and Two Principles of Choice," which appeared in *Essays in Honor of Carl. G. Hempel*, edited by Nicholas Rescher (Dordrecht, The Netherlands: Reidel, 1970).

———◆———

APSYCHOLOGY PROFESSOR AT YOUR school has a reputation for being brilliant as well as possessed of an enormous fortune she has dedicated to her research. One day you get a request to report to her office at a certain hour. On a table are two boxes. One of them, labeled *A*, is transparent; in it you can see an enormous pile of $100 bills. The other, labeled *B*, is opaque. She tells you that there is $10,000 in transparent box *A* and that in box *B* there is either $1,000,000 or nothing. She tells you that she is going to give you a choice between:

1. Taking just what is in box *B*.
2. Taking what is in both boxes.

(Think about what you would choose given this much information.)

Then, she tells you that this is part of an experiment. During registration at the beginning of the quarter, you walked under a peculiar device that reminded you of the machines at airports that are used to prevent hijacking. You didn't think much about it at the time. But, she now informs you that this machine was something she designed and that it recorded an instant profile of your basic personality and character traits. On the basis of your profile, she made a prediction about what choice you would make, and she decided what to put in Box *B* on the basis of this prediction:

1. If she predicted you would take both, she put nothing in Box *B*.
2. If she predicted you would take only Box *B*, she put $1,000,000 in it.

(Now, think about what you would do given this much information.)

At this point you ask her how accurate her predictions have been. She says that 1,000 students have been given the choice, and she has only been wrong once. In all the other cases, students who chose both boxes got only $10,000, whereas those who chose only box *B* got $1,000,000. Then she tells you to choose. What do you do?

Kavka's Toxin Puzzle

This puzzle was introduced by Gregory S. Kavka in his paper, "The Toxin Puzzle," *Analysis* 43 (1983): 33–36. In that paper Kavka also notes relations between this puzzle and puzzles about deterrent intentions—for example, an intention, adopted in order to deter an attack, to retaliate if attacked.

———•———

A PSYCHOLOGY PROFESSOR AT YOUR school—perhaps the one also described in the discussion of Newcomb's Problem—has both a large fortune and an uncanny ability to detect intentions. In the interest of science she makes the following offer to you: "Here is this toxin. It is vile stuff. It will make you very sick for a day if you drink it—though it would not harm you in any lasting way. If tonight, at the stroke of midnight, you fully intend to drink it tomorrow at noon I will irrevocably put $1,000,000 into your bank account. To get the money it is not necessary that you actually drink the toxin; it is only necessary that you really do intend to drink it. However, you may not make any bets or promises that you will drink it, or otherwise arrange for bad effects of not drinking it. Nor may you in any way cause yourself to become irrational. To win the money what you must do, without violating such constraints, is fully to intend tonight to drink the toxin tomorrow."

Suppose you are confident that the psychologist is sincere and is a reliable detector of intentions. You think $1,000,000 is worth a day's sickness: you would gladly drink the toxin to get the money. So you are more than willing, in order to get the money, simply to intend to drink it. After all, merely intending to drink it won't even make you sick! But it occurs to you that if at midnight you expect yourself not to drink the stuff the next day you will not really intend at midnight to drink it. And then you note that even if you do intend at midnight to drink toxin the next day, and even if you thereby get rich, you will have no reason at all actually to drink the stuff come tomorrow noon: the money will already be in the bank and all that drinking would do would be to make you sick. So you would, at midnight, fully expect yourself not to drink the toxin; but then you would not really intend to drink it. Still, you very much want to intend to drink the toxin, for you very much want the money.

Can you win the money?

Quinn's Puzzle of the Self-Torturer

Suppose that you prefer option A to option B, and also prefer option B to option C. If your preferences are *transitive* it will follow that you also prefer option A to option C. We normally expect people's preferences to be transitive: if you prefer studying tonight to going to the movies, and prefer going to the movies to washing the car, then, we would normally assume, you prefer studying tonight to washing the car. But there are cases in which people seem to have intransitive preferences, and such cases can be puzzling in various ways. In his paper, "The Puzzle of the Self-Torturer," *Philosophical Studies* 59 (1990): 79–90, Warren Quinn posed a particularly striking puzzle raised by a case of intransitive preferences.

—•—

YOU HAVE AGREED TO BE PERMA-nently hooked up to a very tiny machine that administers electric shocks. (If you are wondering why you would agree to this, see below.) The machine can be set at any level from 0 to 1000: at 0 there is no shock, at 1000 the voltage is very high and the pain is terrible. Once the machine is set at a certain level it cannot be set lower, but it can be set higher. In general, at setting $n+1$ the voltage is very slightly higher than at setting n, but the difference in voltage is small enough that you cannot tell the difference between the two settings. Of course, you can easily tell the difference between setting 0 and setting 1000! (Compare: just by looking you cannot tell the difference between two very, very close shades of red; but you can certainly tell the difference between red and violet.)

You have allowed yourself to be hooked up to this machine because the experimenter has agreed to give you $10,000 simply for getting hooked up, and has also agreed to give you an additional $10,000 for each self-imposed increment in level of voltage. It is clear to you that the pain induced at level 1000 is so severe you would not choose it for any amount of money. But now that you are at level 0 you can see that you can get another $10,000 by going up to level 1, and that you will not notice the difference between level 0 and level 1. So you seem to have a very good reason to move up to level 1. And so you do. But now that you are at level 1 you can see that you can get another $10,000 by going up to level 2, and that you will not notice the difference between level 1 and level 2. So you seem to have a very good reason to move up to level 2. And so you do. But now that you are at level 2 . . .

Will a rational person end up at level 1000?

D. Paradoxes of Logic, Set Theory, and Semantics

The Paradox of the Liar

——•——

Here are two basic principles of logic:

NC—THE PRINCIPLE OF NONCONTRA-DICTION: No statement is both true and false.

EM—THE PRINCIPLE OF THE EX-CLUDED MIDDLE: Every statement is either true or false.

But now consider this statement:

(1) Statement (1) is false.

By EM (1) is either true or false. Suppose (1) is true.

Then (1) is false, for this is what (1) says. But then (1) is both true and false, contrary to NC. Thus, the supposition that (1) is true leads to a contradiction and must be denied. So we must suppose that (1) is false. But if (1) is false, then what (1) says is so, for what (1) says is that (1) is false. But then (1) is true. But then (1) is both false, and true, contrary to NC. So the supposition that (1) is false leads to a contradiction and must be denied. But now we have a contradiction. For by EM (1) is either true or false; but, by our argument, (1) is neither true nor false.

Other Versions of the Liar

There are many different versions of the liar paradox, which the student may wish to think about after coming up with some hypotheses about what to say about the first version. Here are some of them.

****

(1) Statement (2) is true.
(2) Statement (1) is false.

****

(1) Statement (1) is not true.

****

> The Statement in Box *A*
> is not true

Box *A*

****

"yields a falsehood when appended to its own quotation" yields a falsehood when appended to its own quotation.

(Quine, "The Ways of Paradox")

Russell's Paradox

This paradox, which Quine calls the most celebrated of all antinomies, was discovered by Bertrand Russell in 1901. Here is Quine's statement:

SOME CLASSES ARE MEMBERS OF themselves; some are not. For example, the class of all classes that have more than five members clearly has more than five classes as members; therefore the class is a member of itself. On the other hand, the class of all men is not a member of itself, not being a man. What of the class of all classes that are not members of themselves? Since its members are the non-self-members, it qualifies as a member of itself if and only if it is not.

Grelling's Paradox

CONSIDER THE RELATION OF DEscribing between adjectives and objects. *Red* describes an object x if and only if x is red, *Tall* describes an object if and only if X is tall, and so forth.

Among adjectives are those that describe words. For example, *7-lettered* describes the word *example* and *ambiguous* describes the word *bank*. This raises the possibility of adjectives that describe themselves, and there are many of them. For example, *14-charactered* describes itself, as do *English*, *short*, *ambiguous*, and *polysyllabic*. Let us call these words *autological*.

There are also lots of adjectives that do not apply to themselves. Among these are *long*, *German*, *monosyllabic*, and *50-lettered*. Let us call such adjectives *heterological*. That is, an adjective A is heterological if and only if A does not describe A.

Is *heterological* heterological?

Glossary of Philosophical Terms

absolutism The view that there are some types of action that are strictly prohibited by morality, no matter what the specific facts are in a particular case. Some have held, for example, that the intentional torturing or killing of an innocent person is morally impermissible no matter what bad consequences could be prevented by such an action. Absolutism is an especially strict kind of *deontological* view. It is discussed by Thomas Nagel in "War and Massacre."

accidental and **essential** A property is essential for an object if the object must have the property to exist and be the kind of thing that it is. A property is accidental if the object has the property, but doesn't have to have it to exist or be the kind of thing that it is.

Suppose Fred has short hair. That is an accidental property of his. He would still be Fred, and still be a human being, if he let his hair grow long or shaved it off completely. An essential property is one that a thing has to have to be the thing that it is, or to be the kind of thing it fundamentally is. As a human being, Fred wouldn't exist unless he had a human body, so having a human body is an essential property of his.

Statements about which properties are essential tend to be controversial. A *dualist* might disagree about our last example, arguing that Fred is fundamentally a mind that might exist without any body at all, so having a body isn't one of his essential properties. Someone who has been reading Kafka's *Metamorphoses* might argue that Fred could turn into a cockroach, so having a *human* body isn't one of his essential properties. Some philosophers argue that the metaphysical idea that underlies the accidental/essential distinction is wrong. Things belong to many kinds, that are more or less important for various classificatory purposes, but there is no kind that is more fundamental than all others apart from such purposes. Quine, a leading skeptic, gives the example of a bicyclist. If Fred is a bicyclist, is he necessarily two-legged?

analogy An analogy is a similarity between things. In an argument from analogy, one argues from known similarities to further similarities. Such arguments often occur in philosophy. In his *Dialogues Concerning Natural Religion*, David Hume considers an argument from analogy which purports to show that the universe was created by an intelligent being. The character Cleanthes claims that the world as a whole is similar to things like clocks. A clock has a variety of interrelated parts that function together in ways that serve ends. The world is also a complex of interrelated parts that function in ways that serve ends, such as providing food for human consumption. Clocks are the result of intelligent design, so, Cleanthes concludes, probably the world as a whole is also the product of intelligent design. Hume's character Philo criticizes the argument. In "The Argument from Analogy for Other Minds," Bertrand Russell uses an argument from analogy to try to justify his belief that other conscious beings exist.

Arguments from analogy are seldom airtight. It is possible for things to be very similar in some respects, but quite different in others. A loaf of bread might be about the same size and shape as a rock. But it differs considerably in weight, texture, taste, and nutritive value. A successful argument from analogy needs to defend the relevance of the known analogies to the argued for analogies.

This glossary was compiled with the assistance of Valerie Wilson. We looked to the following dictionaries of philosophy for assistance in constructing the glosses: A. R. Lacey, *A Dictionary of Philosophy* (New York: Charles Scribner's Sons, 1976); Peter A. Angeles, *Dictionary of Philosophy* (New York: Barnes and Noble, 1981); William L. Reese, *Dictionary of Philosophy and Religion* (New Jersey: Humanities Press, 1980).

analytic and **synthetic**   Analytic statements are those that are true (or false) in virtue of the way the ideas or meanings in them fit together. A standard example is "No bachelor is married." This is true simply in virtue of the meanings of the words. "No bachelor is happy," on the other hand, is synthetic. It isn't true or false just in virtue of the meanings of the words. It is true or false in virtue of the experiences of bachelors, and these can't be determined just by thinking about the meanings of the words.

The analytic/synthetic distinction is closely related to the **necessary/contingent** distinction and the **a priori/a posteriori** distinction; indeed, these three distinctions are often confused with one another. But they are not the same. The last one has to do with knowledge, the middle one with possibility, and the first one with meaning. While some philosophers think that the three distinctions amount to the same thing, others do not. Kant maintains that truths of arithmetic are a priori and necessary but not analytic. Kripke maintains that some identity statements are necessary, but not analytic or a priori.

analytical philosophy   The term "analytical philosophy" is often used for a style of doing philosophy that has been dominant throughout most of the twentieth century in Great Britain, North America, Australia, and New Zealand. This way of doing philosophy puts great emphasis on clarity, and it usually sees philosophy as a matter of clarifying important concepts in the sciences, the humanities, politics, and everyday life, rather than providing an independent source of knowledge. Analytical philosophy is often contrasted with **continental philosophy**, the sort of philosophy which has been more dominant in France, Germany, Spain, Italy, and some other European countries.

The term was first associated with the movement initiated by Bertrand Russell and G. E. Moore early in the twentieth century to reject the idealistic philosophy of F. H. Bradley, which had been influenced by the German Idealism of Hegel and others. Moore saw philosophy as the analysis of concepts. Analytical philosophy grew out of the approach and concerns of Moore and Russell, combined with the logical positivist movement and certain elements of pragmatism in America. However, the term "analytical philosophy" now refers to many philosophers who do not subscribe to the exact conceptions of philosophy held by the analysts, logical positivists, or pragmatists.

Indeed, there are really no precise conceptual or geographic boundaries separating analytical and continental philosophy. There are many analytical philosophers on the continent of Europe and many who identify themselves with continental philosophy in English-speaking countries. And there are important subgroups within each group. Within analytical philosophy, some philosophers take logic as their model, while others emphasize ordinary language. Both analytical and continental philosophers draw inspiration from the great philosophers of history, from the pre-Socratics, Plato, and Aristotle to Hume, Kant, Hegel, Marx, Mill, Frege, Husserl, James, and Dewey.

antecedent   *See* **conditionals**.

a posteriori and **a priori**   A posteriori knowledge is based on experience, on observation of how things are in the world of changing things. A priori knowledge is based on reasoning rather than observation.

Your knowledge that it is raining outside is a posteriori knowledge. It is based on your experience, your observation of what is happening outside. One couldn't figure out whether it was raining or not by just reasoning about it. Now consider the following questions: (1) Are there any married bachelors? (2) What is the sum of 38 and 27? After a bit of thought, you should conclude that there are no married bachelors, and 38 + 27 = 65. You know these things a priori. You didn't need to make any observations about what was happening. You just needed to reason.

One important question about a priori truths is whether they are all analytic, or whether there are some synthetic a priori truths. The philosopher Kant thought that (1) above was a priori and analytic, while (2) was a priori and synthetic. *See* **analytic** and **synthetic** for further discussion.

An *a priori argument* is one that uses no empirical premises. An *a priori concept* is one that is innate or could be acquired just by using one's reason.

See also **analytic** and **synthetic**; **contingent** and **necessary**; **matters of fact** and **relations of ideas**.

a priori   *See* **a posteriori** and **a priori**.

argument from analogy   *See* **analogy**.

atheism   Atheism is disbelief in a god. Strictly speaking, atheists are those who don't believe in any god or gods, but often writers will describe someone who does not believe in the god or gods in which they believe as an atheist.

basic structure   In "A Theory of Justice," John Rawls says that his theory of justice concerns a society's major social, political, and economic institutions. His examples include the existence of competitive markets, basic political liberties, and the structure of the family. Rawls calls this the *basic structure* of a society. G. A. Cohen, in "Where the Action Is," argues that there is an important ambiguity in this idea.

behaviorism   Behaviorism is used in somewhat different senses in psychology and philosophy. In psychology, behaviorism is a twentieth-century movement that maintains that the study of behavior is the best or even the only way to study mental phenomena scientifically. It is opposed to the introspective methods for the study of the mind emphasized in much psychology of the nineteenth century. This is *methodological behaviorism*. A methodological behaviorist might even believe in an immaterial mind (*see* **dualism**), but maintain nevertheless that there was no scientific way to study the immaterial mind except through its effects on observable, bodily behavior.

In philosophy, however, behaviorism opposes dualism; the term means some form of the view that the mind is nothing above and beyond behavior. *Logical behaviorists* maintain that talk about the mind can be reduced without remainder to talk about behavior. *Criteriological behaviorists* maintain that mental terms may not be completely reducible to behavioral terms, but

they can only be given meaning through ties to behavioral criteria.

Behaviorism is closely related to **functionalism**.

British Empiricism   *See* **empiricism**.

Cartesian dualism   *See* **dualism**.

cause and **effect**   We think of the world as more than just things happening; the things that happen are connected to one another, and what happens later depends on what happens earlier. We suppose that some things cause others, their effects. The notion of cause connects with other important notions, such as responsibility. We blame people for the harm they cause, not for things that just happened when they were in the vicinity. We assume that there is a cause when things go wrong—when airliners crash, or the climate changes, or the electricity goes off—and we search for an explanation that discloses the cause or causes.

Causation is intuitively a relation of dependence between events. The event which is caused, the effect, depends for its occurrence on the cause. It wouldn't have happened without it. The occurrence of the cause explains the effect. Once we see that the cause happened, we understand why the effect did.

Most philosophers agree that causal connections are **contingent** rather than **necessary**. Suppose the blowout caused the accident. Still, it was possible for the blowout to happen and the accident not to occur. After all, the world might have worked in such a way that a blowout was followed not by an accident but by the car's gradually slowing to a halt.

On one common view, however, causation implies laws of nature in the sense that causal connections are instances of such laws. So causal relations are "relatively necessary": they are contingent only insofar as the laws of nature are contingent. It may be a contingent fact that the laws of physics are what they are. But, on this view, *given* the contingent fact that the laws of nature are as they are, the accident had to happen once the blowout did.

Hume holds such a view. He claims that, at least as far as humans can comprehend things, A causing B amounts, at bottom, to the fact that events like A are always followed by events like B. Causation requires universal succession. At first this doesn't seem very plausible. After all, many blowouts don't lead to accidents. It seems more plausible if we assume that Hume is thinking of the total cause, the blowout plus all the other relevant factors that in this case led to the accident, including the design of the car and the skill of the driver. Taken this way, the universal succession analysis implies that if the blowout caused the accident, then if all of these relevant conditions were duplicated in another case, and there is a blowout, an accident would happen. If not, and if the blowout really caused the accident in the original case, there must be some relevant difference. This version of universal succession seems more plausible, but perhaps not totally convincing. Anscombe argues in "Causality and Determination" that causation does not imply this relevant difference principle.

Even if we grant the Humean relevant difference principle, there are difficulties with the idea that causation simply is universal succession. Consider what it means about the case of the blowout causing the accident. What is the real connection, according to the universal succession theory, between this particular blowout and this particular accident? It just seems to be that the blowout occurred, and then the accident occurred. That's all there really is to causation, as it pertains to these two events. All the rest that is required, on the universal succession analysis, has to do with other events—events *like* the blowout and events *like* the accident. It seems that there is more to causation than this.

Hume offers a candidate for this additional something involved in causation. He says it is really just a certain feeling we have when we have experienced many cases of events of one type being followed by events of another. When we have had this experience, our minds pass from the perception of an event of the first kind to an expectation of one of the second kind. Hume challenges us, if we are not satisfied that causation is

just universal succession together with the feeling of the mind passing from perception to expectation, to identify what else there is.

commodification   We treat some goods as subject to norms of a market: they can be bought and sold for prices that are subject to pressures of supply and demand. This is how we see, for example, cars and computers: we treat cars and computers as *commodities*. Are there moral limits to such commodification—moral limits to the appropriate scope of markets? If so, what are they and what is their justification? These are questions Debra Satz explores in her "Markets in Women's Reproductive Labor."

compatibilism and **incompatibilism**   In philosophy, the term "compatibilism" usually refers to a position in the issue of **freedom** versus **determinism**. Intuitively it seems that freedom excludes determinism, and vice versa. But this has been denied by some philosophers; they claim that acts can be *both* free *and* determined, usually adding that the traditional problem is the product of confused thinking abetted by too little attention to the meaning of words.

Hume held this position. In Section VIII of his *An Inquiry Concerning Human Understanding*, he describes his project as one of "reconciling" *liberty* with *necessity*, these being his terms for freedom and determinism. Hume said that liberty consists of acting according to the determinations of your will; that is, doing as you decide to do. A free act is not one that is *uncaused*, but one that is caused by the wants, desires, and decisions of the person who performs it. Hence an act can be both free and an instance of a universal causal principle. On this conception, an unfree act is one that one must·do *in spite of* one's own desires and decisions, rather than because of them.

Some compatibilists go further and maintain that freedom requires determinism. The idea is that for our own will to determine what we do, our decisions must cause our actions, and causation in turn requires determinism.

Given this distinction, the views of most philosophers on the issue of freedom and determinism can be located among the following possible positions.

1. **Incompatibilism**: Freedom and determinism are incompatible. This view leaves open two main theoretical options:
   a. *Libertarianism*: There are some free acts, so determinism is false.
   b. *Hard determinism*: Determinism is true, so there are no free acts.
2. **Compatibilism**: Freedom and determinism are compatible. This view is typically part of a view called *soft determinism* according to which there are free acts and determinism is also true. This view in turn comes in two varieties:
   a. There are free acts. Determinism is as a matter of fact true, but there would be free acts whether or not determinism were true.
   b. There are free acts. Determinism is true and its truth is required for freedom.
3. **Freedom is incoherent**: Freedom both requires and is incompatible with determinism, and hence makes no sense.

Some philosophers distinguish between freedom of action and free will. Free will involves more than having one's actions determined by one's decisions and desires. It involves having control over those desires and decisions themselves. Someone might have freedom, as the compatibilist understands it, without having free will. For example, a person addicted to smoking might be free in the sense that whether or not they smoke on a given occasion is determined by their own desire. But what if they don't want to have or be controlled by that desire? Do they have the power to get rid of the desire, or weaken its hold on them? This is the question of free will. The issue on whether free will is compatible or incompatible with determinism can then be raised.

conclusion   *See* **deductive argument**.

conditionals   A conditional is a kind of statement that is made out of two others. The normal form of the statements is "If *P* then *Q*." *P* is the **antecedent** and *Q* the **consequent**. "If *P*, *Q*" and "*Q*, if *P*" are stylistic variations of "If *P* then *Q*."

Conditionals can be in various tenses and in the indicative or subjunctive:

indicative: *If Susan comes to the party, then Michael brings the salad. If Susan came to the party, then Michael brought the salad. If Susan will come to the party, Michael will bring the salad.*
subjunctive: *If Susan were to come to the party, Michael would bring the salad. If Susan had come to the party, Michael would have brought the salad.*

A *counterfactual* conditional, one in which the antecedent is false, will usually be in the subjunctive if the speaker realizes that the antecedent is false.

One thing seems quite clear about conditionals: *if the antecedent is true, and the consequent false, then the conditional as a whole is false*. If Susan comes to the party, and Michael doesn't bring the salad, then all of the examples above are false. This is the basis for two clearly valid rules of inference:

Modus ponens: From *If P, then Q* and *P*, infer *Q*.
Modus tollens: From *If P, then Q* and *not-Q*, infer *not-P*.

In symbolic logic a defined symbol (often " $\rightarrow$ ") is called the conditional. The conditions under which conditional statements that involve this symbol are true are stipulated by logicians as follows:

1. Antecedent true, consequent true, conditional true;
2. Antecedent true, consequent false, conditional false;
3. Antecedent false, consequent true, conditional true;
4. Antecedent false, consequent false, conditional true.

This defined symbol, then, agrees with the ordinary language conditional on the clear case, number 2, the case that is crucial for the validity of modus ponens and modus tollens. But what about the other cases? Suppose Susan doesn't come to the party, but Michael brings that salad (antecedent false, consequent true). The symbolic logic statement,

Susan comes to the party →
                Michael brings the salad

is true in this case, because of part 3 of the definition. It isn't so clear that the ordinary language conditionals are true. Suppose that Michael says, "I brought the salad because Susan couldn't make it. If she had come, she would have brought it." Are any or all of the ordinary language conditionals listed above true in this case? or false? What of Michael's second sentence, which is also a conditional?

See **necessary** and **sufficient conditions**.

consequent   *See* **conditionals**.

consequentialism   Consequentialism is a view about what makes it right or wrong to do something. It maintains that the rightness of an action is determined by the goodness or badness of relevant consequences. **Utilitarianism** is a consequentialist theory that holds that what makes consequences better or worse is, at bottom, the welfare or happiness of sentient beings. A *deontological* ethics rejects consequentialism and holds that the rightness of action depends at least in part on things other than the goodness of relevant consequences. For example, someone who rejects consequentialism might hold that the principle under which an act is done determines whether it is right or wrong. Kant held a version of this view; *see* the Introduction to Part V.

continental philosophy   *See* **analytical philosophy**.

Continental rationalism   *See* **rationalism**.

contingent and **necessary**   Some things are facts, but would not have been facts if things had happened differently. These are contingent facts. Consider, for example, the fact that Columbus reached America in 1492. Things could have

turned out differently. If he had gotten a later start, he might not have reached America until 1493. So the fact that he arrived in 1492 is contingent. Necessary facts are those that could not have failed to be facts. The year 1492 would have occurred before the year 1493 no matter how long it took Columbus to get his act together. It is a necessary fact. Mathematical facts are a particularly clear example of necessary facts. The fact that $2 + 2 = 4$ doesn't depend on one thing happening rather than another.

Philosophers sometimes use the idea of a possible world to explain this distinction. Necessary truths are true in every possible world. Contingent truths are true in the actual world but false in some other possible worlds. Necessary falsehoods are false in the actual world and false in every other possible world, too. If one thinks of the distinction this way, one must be careful to distinguish between the truth of a sentence and the truth of what it says. It is easy to imagine a possible world in which the sentence "$2 + 2 = 4$" is false. Just imagine that the numeral "2" stood for the number three, but "4" still stands for four. But imagining the sentence to have a meaning that makes it false is not the same as imagining what it says, given its actual meaning, to be false. It is the latter that is important when we ask if it is necessary or contingent that $2 + 2 = 4$.

The distinction between the necessary and contingent is a *metaphysical* distinction. It has to do with facts or propositions and truth. It is closely related to the epistemological distinction between **a priori** and **a posteriori** and the distinction between **analytic** and **synthetic** statements. These three similar distinctions shouldn't be confused. Some philosophers claim that they are *co-extensional*. But they are not *co-intensional*, so this is a substantive philosophical claim. For example, some philosophers claim that there are mathematical facts that have nothing to do with the meanings of words, and may never be known at all, and are hence not knowable a priori, but are still necessary.

cosmogony   *See* **cosmos**.

cosmological argument   *See* **cosmos**.

cosmology   *See* **cosmos**.

cosmos   The cosmos is the universe considered as an integrated orderly system. Sometimes the cosmos is the orderly part of a larger whole, the other part being *chaos*. Any account of the origin of the universe as a whole, whether based on myth, religion, philosophy, or science is a **cosmogony**. An account of the nature and origin of the universe that is systematic is a **cosmology**. This term is used for the particular branch of physics that considers this question, and also for inquiries of a more philosophical nature. **Cosmological arguments** for the existence of God begin with very general facts about the known universe, such as causation, movement, and contingency, and then argue that God must exist, as first cause, or unmoved mover, or necessary being, to account for these facts. The first two ways of proving the existence of God listed by St. Thomas Aquinas are cosmological arguments.

deductive argument   Arguments have **premises** and a **conclusion**. The truth of the premises should provide grounds for the truth of the conclusion, so that the argument gives one who believes the premises a good reason for believing the conclusion.

  In a **valid** argument, the truth of the premises **entails** the truth of the conclusion. This means that is is impossible for the premises to be true and the conclusion false. A valid argument may have a false conclusion because validity of an argument does not imply truth of the premises. If the premises of a valid argument are true, then the argument is **sound**. Clearly the conclusion of any sound argument will be true.

  An argument that aims at *validity* is *deductive*, or *demonstrative*. *Deductive logic* provides rules of inference that exhibit valid patterns of reasoning.

  An argument can provide those who believe their premises good reason for accepting their conclusions even if it is not valid. Among arguments that are not valid, we can distinguish between strong and weak. A *strong* nondemonstrative or nondeductive argument makes the truth of the conclusion very probable. *Analogical arguments*, for example, are nondeductive but can be quite strong.

Inductive arguments involve generalizing from instances. Having noticed that a certain radio station plays rock music on a number of occasions, you may infer that it always does so, or that it is at least very likely that it will do so next time you tune in. Such inferences are not valid, but it seems that they can be quite strong and in fact the whole idea of using past experience to guide our conduct depends on them. *See* **induction, problem of**.

  Inductive logic aims at formulating rules for nondeductive reasoning analogous to those of deductive logic.

deontological ethics   *See* **consequentialism**.

determinism   Determinism is the doctrine that every event, including every intentional action of a human being, is determined by prior causes. This is usually thought to imply that there are universal, nonstatistical laws of nature covering every aspect of everything that happens. *See* **cause and effect**. Given the state of the universe at any time, these laws determine everything else that will ever happen. Some philosophers oppose determinism, because they think that the ultimate laws of nature are statistical. Others oppose it because they believe there are free actions, and that no actions can be both free and determined. *See* **freedom, compatibilism, fatalism**.

difference principle   A central idea of John Rawls's theory of justice, referred to as *the difference principle*, is that inequalities in the distribution of relevant goods are just if and only if these inequalities are needed to improve the plight of everyone, in particular of those who are the worst off. (See Rawls's second principle of justice, "A Theory of Justice," p. 606, and G. A. Cohen's formulation, "Where the Action Is," p. 620.)

distributive justice   *See* **justice**.

double effect, doctrine of   An act typically has both intended and unintended effects. For example, swatting a fly may have the intended effect of killing a fly, and the unintended effects of making a noise and waking up your brother. The latter effect may be unintended even though it is foreseen.

You knew that swatting the fly would or at least might wake your brother. That's not why you were doing it; you were doing it to get rid of the fly. Perhaps you didn't much care whether or not your brother slept. Perhaps you hated to wake him, but it was very important to you to swat the fly. In these cases, swatting the fly is the intended effect of your act, while waking your brother is merely foreseen.

According to the doctrine (or, principle) of double effect, the moral status of intended effects differs from those that are merely foreseen. This principle is sometimes appealed to as a part of a **deontological** moral theory. According to this principle, it might be wrong to swat the fly with the intention of waking up your brother, but permissible to swat the fly with the intention of killing it, knowing it would wake up your brother. A more interesting example is abortion. Some people maintain that it is wrong to act with the intention of aborting a fetus, but that nevertheless certain operations may be permissible, even though abortion of the fetus is a foreseeable result, so long as they are done for some other purpose, such as preventing the injury to a mother that continued pregnancy might involve. Some philosophers maintain the distinction makes no sense. Others believe there is a coherent distinction between intended and merely expected consequences, but doubt that it has the moral significance it is given by the doctrine of double effect.

dualism   The term "dualism" has a number of uses in philosophy, but perhaps the most common is to describe positions on the mind-body problem that hold that the mind cannot be identified with the body or part of the body, or that mental properties are not physical properties.

The form of dualism Descartes advocated is called **Cartesian dualism** or **interactive dualism**. The mind is that which is responsible for mental states of all kinds, including sensation, perception, thought, emotion, deliberation, decision, and intentional action. Some philosophers maintain that this role is played by the brain, but Descartes argued that this could not be so. His view was that the mind was a separate thing, or

substance, that causally interacted with the brain, and through it with the rest of the body and the rest of the world. Sensation and perception involve states of the world affecting states of sense organs, which in turn affect the brain, which causes the mind to be in certain states. Action involves states of mind affecting the brain, which in turn affects the body, which may interact with other things in the world.

Other forms of dualism include **epiphenomenalism**, **parallelism**, and **property dualism**. The epiphenomenalist holds that the body affects the mind, but not vice versa. The mind only appears to affect the body, because the apparent mental causes of bodily changes (like the decision to lift my arm) coincide with the true bodily causes (some change in my brain). Parallelists hold that mind and body are two substances that do not interact at all.

Property dualism maintains that the mind can be identified with the brain (or with the body as a whole), but mental properties cannot be reduced to physical ones. On this view, it is my brain which is responsible for sensation, perception, and other mental phenomena. But the fact that my brain is thinking a certain thought, for example, is an additional fact about it, one that cannot be reduced to any of its physical properties.

effect   *See* **cause** and **effect**.

empiricism   Empiricism is an epistemological position that emphasizes the importance of experience and denies or is very skeptical of claims to a priori knowledge or concepts. The empirical tradition in seventeenth-, eighteenth-, and nineteenth-century philosophy was centered in Britain, and Bacon, Locke, Berkeley, Hume, and Mill are often referred to as *British Empiricists*. *See also* **rationalism**.

entails   *See* **deductive argument**.

epiphenomenalism   *See* **dualism**.

epistemology   Epistemology is the theory of knowledge, the inquiry into its possibility, nature, and structure.

essential   *See* **accidental** and **essential**.

eudaimonia   Eudaimonia—sometimes translated "happiness" or "flourishing"—is a central concept in Aristotle's ethics. *See* "Aristotelian Ethics" in Part V.

evil, problem of   Many philosophers have thought that the existence of evil poses a problem for those who believe that there is a perfect God. A perfect God, it seems, would be able to do anything (*omnipotence*), would know everything (*omniscience*), and would have all the moral virtues, such as benevolence. If such a God created the world, why is there any evil? Does God not care if we suffer? Then God is not benevolent. Is this world the best God could make? Then God is not omnipotent. Or perhaps God wanted to do better, and had the power, but didn't quite know what to do. Then God is not omniscient. A perfect God would have made the best of all possible worlds. So, the argument goes, the existence of our imperfect world, full of sin and suffering, shows that God does not exist, or is not perfect.

The problem of evil is pressed by Philo, a main character in Hume's *Dialogues on Natural Religion*. Both Philo and his main adversary, Cleanthes, give up the idea that God is perfect. Philo concludes that while the world was probably created by an intelligent being or beings, there is no reason to attribute benevolence to that being or those beings. Cleanthes allows that God may be only finitely powerful.

Other philosophers have thought, however, that our problems with evil simply show how difficult it is for finite beings to grasp the plan of an infinitely perfect being. This is, contrary to first impressions, the best of all possible worlds. This is Leibniz's position in "God, Evil and the Best of All Possible Worlds."

extension and **intension**   Consider a **predicate** like "human being." It applies to or is true of a number of individuals, those who are human beings. The set of these individuals is the extension of the predicate. The members of this set have the property of being a human being in common.

This property (or, for some philosophers, the concept of this property) is the intension of the predicate.

Terms that have the same extension are *co-extensional*, terms that have the same intension are *co-intensional*. It seems that terms can be co-extensional without being co-intensional. Russell's example is "human being" and "featherless biped that is not a plucked chicken." These terms are not co-*int*ensional, since the property of being a human being is not the same as the property of being a featherless biped that is not a plucked chicken. But they are co-*ext*ensional. If you set aside the plucked chickens, humans are the only bipeds without feathers. (Probably their extensions are not *quite* the same; after all there are plucked turkeys, too, but Russell thought the example was close enough to being correct to make the point.)

The term "extension" is often used in an extended sense in which names and sentences have extensions as well as terms or predicates. (The terminology is due to Rudolf Carnap, while the idea it incorporates goes back to Gottlob Frege.) The extension of a name is the thing it names, the extension of a sentence is its truth value, true or false. This brings out the systematic connection between name, predicate, and sentence. The sentence "Fido is barking" will have the extension True (i.e., be true), just in case the extension of "Fido" (i.e., Fido) is a member of the extension of "is barking." That is, the extension of the parts (the name "Fido" and the predicate "is barking") determines the extension of the whole sentence. Sentences like this, their truth-value being determined by the extension of their parts, are **extensional**.

If a sentence is extensional, substitution of a name in it for another co-extensional name (or a predicate for another co-extensional predicate) won't affect the truth-value. Suppose Fido is also called "Bad-breath." Then the substitution of "Bad-breath" for "Fido" will preserve the truth-value of our sentence. If "Fido is barking" is true, so too will be "Bad-breath is barking."

Not all sentences are extensional. Consider the true sentence "Bad-breath is so called because of his smell." If we substitute the co-extensional name "Fido" for "Bad-breath" the result is "Fido is so called because of his smell." This sentence isn't true. So our original sentence, "Bad-breath is so called because of his smell," isn't extensional, but *nonextensional*.

We can generalize and say that any expression is extensional if its extension is determined by the extensions of its parts. Consider the predicate "is portrayed as a human being." Suppose this is true of Donald Duck, since he is portrayed in cartoons as having so many human characteristics. If we substitute "featherless biped" for "human being" we get the predicate "is portrayed as a featherless biped." This doesn't seem to be true of Donald, since he is always portrayed as a feathered biped.

In these examples, it seems possible to pick out the expressions that lead to the nonextensionality. In the first example it is "so called," in the second it is "portrayed as." Expressions like these that give rise to nonextensionality are often called "nonextensional contexts."

Some concepts that are very important in philosophy seem to generate nonextensional sentences. Consider "Harold believes that Cicero was a great Roman." Since "Tully" is another name for Cicero, if this sentence is extensional, it seems we should be able to substitute "Tully" for "Cicero" without changing the truth-value of the whole. But it seems that if Harold has never heard Cicero called "Tully," "Harold believes that Tully was a great Roman" would *not* be true.

The term **intensional** is used in three ways, one strict and comparatively rare, one loose and very common, and one incorrect. Strictly speaking, an expression is intensional if its intension is determined by the intensions of its parts. This is the way Carnap used the term. It is common to use it loosely, however, simply to mean "nonextensional," so that an "intensional context" means a form of words, like "so called" and "portrayed as" and "believes," that leads to nonextensional predicates and sentences. "Intensional" is often confused with "*intentional*" in the broad sense that is sometimes taken to be the mark of the mental. This is understandable, since many words that de-

scribe intentional phenomena, such as "believes," seem to be intensional, in the loose sense.

In *possible worlds semantics*, names, predicates, and sentences are said to have extensions *at* possible worlds—the set of things that the predicate applies to in the world. Sentences are also said to have extensions at worlds: their truth-values in the worlds. The intension of a predicate is a function from worlds to extensions, and the intension of a sentence is a function from worlds to truth-values.

extensional   *See* **extension**.

extrinsic   An extrinsic property is one that an object has partly in virtue of its relations to other things and their properties. A thing could lose such a property without really changing at all. For example, Omaha has the property of being the largest city in Nebraska. It could lose this property in virtue of Grand Island growing a great deal. Omaha wouldn't have to lose population to lose this property, or change in any other way. Being the largest city in Nebraska is thus an extrinsic property of Omaha. An **intrinsic** property, by contrast, is one that an object has because of the way it is in itself, independently of its relations to other things and their properties.

The distinction is often useful, because a property that we might have thought to be intrinsic turns out to be extrinsic on closer examination. It is very difficult, however, to give a really clear and precise explanation, or unchallengeable list, of intrinsic properties of ordinary, spatiotemporally extended objects.

fatalism   Fatalism is the doctrine that certain events are fated to happen, no matter what. This might mean that an event is fated to take place at a specific time, or that someone is going to do some deed, no matter what anyone does to try to prevent it. Fatalism differs from **determinism**. One way they differ is that a fatalistic view about the occurrence of a certain event does not depend on the laws of nature determining only a single course of event. There may be many possible futures that differ in many ways, but they all will include the fated event. Oedipus, for example, was (allegedly) fated to marry his mother and kill his father. This didn't mean that there was only one course of action open to him after hearing the prophecy, but that no matter which course he took, he would eventually end up doing that which he wanted most to avoid. A second way they differ is that an event may be determined by prior causes even though it was not fated to occur; for among those prior causes may be the decisions and efforts of human agents. So determinism does not entail fatalism about all events.

feminism Feminism is an intellectual, social, and political movement. The movement is very diverse, but one strand that runs through all varieties is the conviction that important intellectual, social, and political structures have been based on the assumption, sometimes implicit, sometimes quite explicit, that being fully human means being male. Reexamination of these structures from a perspective that appreciates the interests, values, styles, ideas, roles, methods, and emotions of women as well as men can lead to fruitful and in some cases radical reform. In "Knowledge, Human Interests, and Objectivity in Feminist Epistemology," Elizabeth Anderson explains and discusses feminist critiques of the idea that scientific inquiry should be "value-free."

first cause argument The first cause argument purports to prove the existence of God as the first cause. In the world we know, everything has a cause and nothing causes itself. The series of causes cannot go back to infinity, so there must be a first cause, and this is God. St. Thomas Aquinas's second way of proving the existence of God is a version of the first cause argument. Philosophers have challenged each step of the argument.

formal The formal properties of representations are distinguished from their *content* properties. "All cows are animals" and "all houses are buildings" have different contents, but the same form: *All Fs are Gs*. **Formal logic** seeks to classify inferences in terms of their formal properties. Where *P* and *Q* are sentences, any inference of the following form, known as *modus ponens*, is valid, no matter what the content is.

If P then Q
P
Therefore, Q.

Some philosophers have argued that philosophical confusion can sometimes be avoided by putting claims into the **formal mode** rather than the *material mode*. To put a claim in the formal mode is to express it, as nearly as possible, as a claim about words or other symbols, rather than about the things the words purport to stand for. "Santa Claus doesn't exist" is a claim in the material mode, which may be confused or confusing since it looks as if we are saying something about a thing, Santa Claus, who isn't really there to say anything about. Better to say " 'Santa Claus' doesn't refer to anything."

formal logic *See* **formal**.

formal mode *See* **formal**.

freedom In ordinary conversation we call people free who aren't prevented from doing what they want to do and conducting their life as they see fit. In politics and political philosophy, freedom usually means having civil or political liberty, having certain basic rights or freedoms, such as those codified in the American Bill of Rights, the Rights of Man, or the Charter of the United Nations.

In the realm of metaphysics and the philosophy of mind, the term "freedom" refers to a very basic feature of decisions or actions. When we perform an ordinary act, like drinking a cup of coffee, or going to a movie, or helping a friend, we have a feeling that our action results from our own decision and *that we could have done otherwise*. It seems that only when this is the case do we take full responsibility (blame or credit) for our actions. A person might be free in this sense, while not enjoying freedom in the sense of political liberties. A writer under house arrest, and prevented from publishing, would not enjoy basic civil liberties. But many of her actions would still be free in this metaphysical sense. She has coffee in the morning; she could have had tea. Perhaps she writes her essays even though she can't publish them. This is a free act, in that she could have gardened or stayed in bed instead; if she had chosen to do those things, no one would have forced her to write.

One fundamental question about freedom in this sense concerns its relation to **determinism**. If determinism is true, are any of our actions *really* free, or is freedom simply an illusion? This debate often turns on the exact definition of freedom. *Compatibilists* are likely to think of freedom as being able to act in accord with one's desires and decisions, even if those desires and decisions are themselves the influences of more remote causes, outside the agent. This is compatible with determinism, in that one's own desires and decisions might be the causes of one's actions, even though those desires and decisions were themselves caused by other things, and lie at the end of a chain of causes and effects that goes back to the time before the agent was born. An *incompatibilist* typically thinks of a free decision or act as one that is not caused by anything else, or is caused by the agent, independent of external causes.

The term **free will** is sometimes used to contrast with *freedom of action*. One's *will* in this sense is one's decision, choice, or dominating desire. Even if one is free to follow one's strongest desire, and hence has freedom of action in the compatibilist sense, does one have any control over those desires and choices themselves? Can one influence the strength of one's desires, or are they determined by external influences? One might be a compatibilist with respect to free action and determinism, but an incompatibilist with respect to free will and determinism.

In theological contexts, the question of free will is whether humans can have any choice if there is a god who has foreknowledge of what they will do.

free will   *See* **freedom**.

functionalism   The function of a thing is its operation within a system. It is the role the thing has, when the system is operating properly. For example, the function of a carburetor is to supply an atomized and vaporized mixture of fuel and air to the intake manifold of an internal combustion engine. One can contrast the function of a thing with its structure and the material from which it is made. The structure of a carburetor differs from that of a fuel injection system, although both have the same function and are made of the same types of materials.

Functionalism in the philosophy of mind is the view that mental states are real states definable by their functions, specifically by their causal role with respect to stimuli, other mental states, and behavior. Functionalism can be contrasted with **Cartesian dualism** and **behaviorism**. Functionalism agrees with Cartesian dualism in holding that mental states are real, but differs in that the latter maintains that the mental states are essentially states of an immaterial mind, defined by their basic nature, rather than their function. Functionalism agrees with *logical behaviorism* in seeing a definitional connection between mental states and behavior. They differ in that the logical behaviorist maintains that mental states are not real at all; the terms that seem to stand for them are just misleading ways of describing behavior. For the behaviorist, the definitions that connect stimuli, behavior, and mental states are reductive; they show how to eliminate reference to mental states in favor of reference to stimuli and behavior. For this reason, a behaviorist definition of a mental state cannot allow ineliminable reference to other mental states. The selections from Armstrong and Putnam explain and defend versions of functionalism. Nagel criticizes functionalist views in "What Is It Like to Be a Bat?"

hallucination, argument from   *See* **illusion, argument from**.

hedonism   *See* the discussion of utilitarianism in the Introduction to Part V.

ideas   There are two quite different uses of the term "idea" in philosophy. The term "idea" is used for the denizens of Plato's heaven. Sometimes *form* is used as a less misleading translation of *eidos*. Plato's ideas or forms are not parts of our minds, but objective, unchanging, immaterial entities that our minds somehow grasp and use for the classification of things in the changing world, which Plato held to be their pale imitations.

John Locke uses the term "idea" for that which the mind is immediately aware of, as distinguished from the qualities or **objects** in the external world the ideas are of. This use for the term leaves it rather vague. Idea can be the images involved in perception, or the constituents of thought. Hume calls the first **impressions**, the latter ideas, and the whole class *perceptions*. For Hume, the class of impressions includes passions (emotions) as well as sensations. So a feeling of anger would be an impression, as would the sensation of red brought about by looking at a fire truck. Later memory of the feeling of anger or the fire truck would involve the ideas of anger and red.

The conception of ideas as immediate objects of perception and thought, intervening between our minds and the ordinary objects we perceive and think about, was part of a philosophical movement, sometimes called "the way of ideas," greatly influenced by Descartes's *Meditations*. Descartes there uses a form of the **argument from illusion** to motivate the distinction between the mental phenomena we are certain of and the external reality that is represented by them.

identity   A thing is *identical* with itself and no other. If *a* is identical with *b*, then there is just one thing that is both *a* and *b*; "*a*" and "*b*" are two names for that one thing. It follows from this that the relation of identity is *transitive* (if *a* is identical with *b*, and *b* is identical with *c*, then *a* is identical with *c*), symmetrical (if *a* is identical with *b*, then *b* is identical with *a*), and confers indiscernibility (if *a* is identical with *b*, and *a* has property P, *b* has property P).

The term "identity" is not always used in this strict sense. For example, in this sense, "identical twins" are not identical—they couldn't be twins if they were, since there would be only one of them. We sometimes use identity to mean close resemblance in one respect or another. It is best, in philosophical contexts, to use identity in the way explained above and some other word, like *similar* or *resembles*, when that is what is meant.

The terms "numerical identity" and "qualitative identity" are sometimes used, but are best avoided. One needs to distinguish between the identity of qualities (red is one and the same color as rouge) and similarity with respect to a quality (the couch and the chair are both red; they are similar in respect of color), and this terminology obscures the distinction.

Some issues about identity are raised in the section on personal identity and in "The Paradox of Identity."

identity theory   David Armstrong in "The Nature of Mind" and David Lewis in "Mad Pain and Martian Pain" maintain that mental states are quite literally identical with physical states. Our concept of a mental state is of a state that occupies a certain causal role; it turns out that physical states do occupy those roles; hence, mental states are physical states. This *identity theory* is a species of **materialism**. It is also, strictly speaking, a form of **functionalism**, since it maintains that mental states are definable by their function or causal role. Many functionalists, however, think that mental states cannot be identified with physical states. They maintain that the relation is a less stringent one, **supervenience**. Functionalism in this narrower sense is often contrasted with the identity theory.

illusion, argument from   Philosophers use the term "argument from illusion" for a general type of argument and for a specific version of it. These arguments are intended to show that what we are directly aware of when we perceive ordinary things are not those ordinary things themselves. We can distinguish three such arguments: the argument from perceptual relativity, the argument from illusion, and the argument from hallucination.

The argument from perceptual relativity starts with the fact that perceptions of the same object in different circumstances involve different perceptual experiences. For example, a building seen from a great distance casts a different sized image on your retina, and creates quite a different experience, than the same building seen from a few yards away. Consider seeing a quarter held at a ninety degree angle to your line of sight, and the same quarter held at a forty-five degree angle. In the first case a round image is cast on your retina, in the second an elliptical image. The perceptual experience is different, although the object seen, the quarter, is the same. The conclusion drawn is that there is something involved in the experience besides the agent and the quarter, which are the same in both, that accounts for the difference. This is the *immediate* object of perception. Some philosophers take these objects to be ideas in the mind of the perceiver that represent the external object; *see* **representative ideas, theory of**. Others have taken them to be nonmental sense-data. Some philosophers have taken the ideas or sense-data to be materials out of which external objects are constructed, rather than representations of them.

The argument from illusion itself starts with the fact that two different objects can create the same experience. For example, a quarter held at an angle and an elliptical disk held at ninety degrees might cast exactly the same image on the retina and create the same experience. What is it that is the same? Not the objects seen, which are different. The answer again is an intervening object, which may be taken to be a subjective idea or something objective.

The argument from hallucination considers the case in which it is to one as if one were seeing an object, although there is in fact nothing at all there. This sort of case, a true hallucination, is much more unusual than those noted for the earlier two arguments. What is it that is present in our perception when there is nothing seen? It is, again, the subjective idea or the objective sense-datum.

Various forms of the argument from illusion are used in selections from Descartes, Berkeley, Hume, and Moore. It is criticized by Austin.

immaterialism   Immaterialism is the metaphysical doctrine held by Berkeley. He maintained that reality consisted entirely of minds (including God's) and ideas. Ordinary things were collections or congeries of ideas. Berkeley thought his view came closer to common sense than that of the philosophers he opposed (Descartes and Locke, for example), which implied the existence

of *material substances* in addition to minds and ideas. Berkeley explains in his *Three Dialogues Between Hylas and Philonous* that he thinks we have no evidence for material substances, that identifying ordinary things with such substances leads to skepticism, and in fact the very concept of a material substance is incoherent.

imperatives, categorical and **hypothetical**   *See* the discussion of Kantian ethics in the Introduction to Part V.

impressions   *See* **ideas**.

incompatibilism   *See* **compatibilism** and **incompatibilism**.

induction   *See* **induction, problem of** and **deductive argument**.

induction, problem of   The problem of induction, sometimes known as *Hume's problem*, has to do with justifying a very basic sort of *nondeductive* inference. We often seem to infer from observation that some sample of a population has a certain attribute to the conclusion that the next members of the population we encounter will also have that attribute. When you eat a piece of bread, for example, you are concluding from the many times in the past that bread has nourished you, that it will also do so this time. But it is conceivable that bread should have nourished in the past, but not this time. It isn't a **necessary, analytic,** or **a priori** truth that the next piece of bread you eat will be like the ones you have eaten before. How does your inference bridge the gap? It is natural to appeal to various general principles that one has discovered to hold. But, as Hume points out, the future application of principles found reliable in the past presents exactly the same problem. For example, consider the most general principle of all, that the future will be like the past. All one has really observed was that, in the past, the future was like the past. How does one know that in the future it will be? The problem of induction is stated in Hume's *An Inquiry Concerning Human Understanding*, Section IV, and discussed by Salmon, "The Problem of Induction."

inductive argument   *See* **deductive argument**.

infinity   The concept of infinity is a fascinating, tricky, and complex one. It has been used in a number of philosophical arguments, such as Zeno's arguments about motion, and in some of St. Thomas Aquinas's arguments for the existence of God. In the last two hundred years mathematicians have given us a clearer framework for thinking about infinity than earlier philosophers had, but this doesn't mean all of the puzzles and problems are easy to resolve.

Infinite means without end. Let's say that to count a collection of objects is to assign the natural numbers (1,2,3 . . .) in order to its members, so that every member is assigned a number and no number gets assigned twice. Let's say that *to finish counting a collection of objects* is to assign numbers in this way to every object in the collection. A finite collection of things is one that one could finish counting, at least theoretically, and say "it has n members" where n is some natural number. An infinite collection is one for which one could not finish counting. One can see from this that the set of natural numbers is itself infinite, for one would never finish counting it.

Assigning objects from one set to those in another, so that each object is assigned to only one object and has only one object assigned to it, is called putting the sets in a one-to-one correspondence. Sets that can be correlated in this way, are the same size—they have the same number of elements. Using this idea, modern mathematics has shown that not all infinite sets are the same size, so that one needs to distinguish among different infinite or *transcendental* numbers. The number of natural numbers is called aleph$_0$.

Somewhat surprisingly, this is also the number of even numbers, since there is a one-to-one correlation between numbers and even numbers (assign $2n$ to n). But it is not the number of points in a line for there is not a one-to-one correlation between the set of such points and the natural numbers. This is shown by a variation of Zeno's Racecourse Argument. Let the line be of length m. If we assign 1 to the point $m/2$, 2 to $m/4$, . . . n to $m/2n$, we will have paired a point from the continuum with each natural number, but no matter how long we go on, we will never assign a natural number to any of the points beyond $m/2$.

In thinking about infinity, it is important to keep certain distinctions in mind. One might have two quite different things in mind when calling a magnitude "infinite": that it goes on forever, or that the process of dividing it could go on forever. A finite distance like ten feet is not infinite in the first sense, but seems to be in the second: one could take the first half, half of what's left, and so on without end. Intuitively, one can traverse a finite, but infinitely divisible, distance in a finite amount of time, but not an infinite distance. Zeno's Racecourse Argument seems to show that one cannot even traverse a finite distance. But keeping this distinction in mind, what exactly does it show?

Aristotle distinguished between the potential and actual infinite. When we say that a distance of ten feet is infinitely divisible, we don't mean one could actually divide it into an infinite number of parts, but only that there are an infinite number of points in which one could divide it. Aristotle thought that this distinction took care of Zeno's arguments.

intension, intensional   *See* **extension**.

intentionality   An intentional act or state is one that is directed at objects and characterized by the objects at which it is directed. Intentionality in this sense is a feature not only of intentions, but of many other mental phenomena. Some philosophers take it to be the essence of mentality and consciousness. Think about how you would describe your intentions. You don't say what they look like or feel like or sound like, or what material they are made of. You say something like, "I have an intention to paint my room." You say what your intention is an intention *to do*. This essential characteristic of your intention is its **object**, the event or state of affairs it is aimed at bringing about. Similarly, if you are asked to describe your wants, you would describe *what you want*—a new car, say, or world peace. The **object** of the want or desire, the thing or state of affairs that would satisfy it, seems essential to it.

Beliefs and other **propositional attitudes** are also considered intentional. We describe our beliefs by giving the circumstances under which they are true: "Fred believes that San Francisco is the capital of California." The object of the belief is the **proposition**, *that San Francisco is the capital of California*. This proposition may be the object of the belief even if it is not true.

The term *"intentional"* should not be confused with the term "**intensional**," although they are related. Many of the concepts used to describe intentional phenomena are nonextensional, which is one meaning of intensional. For example, "Oedipus intended to marry Jocasta" is a true description of an intention of Oedipus. If we substitute "his mother" for "Jocasta," we change this truth into a falsehood. So the sentence is intensional.

interactive dualism   *See* **dualism.**

intrinsic   *See* **extrinsic.**

justice   Issues about justice are traditionally divided into issues about justice in the distribution of benefits and burdens to different individuals and groups in a society (**distributive justice**) and issues about the justice of various forms of punishment (*retributive justice*).

materialism and **physicalism**   Materialism is the doctrine that reality consists of material objects and their material, spatial, and temporal properties and relations. Narrowly construed, materialism refers to material substances and properties as conceived in eighteenth-century physics and philosophy, so that material properties are confined to the primary qualities then recognized, including figure (shape), extension (size), number, motion, and solidity. A more general term is **physicalism**, where *physical properties* are taken to be whatever properties physics postulates in the best account of the physical world. The physicalist leaves open the possibility that the fundamental properties needed by physics will not be much like the primary qualities of the materialist. A chief obstacle to materialism or physical-

ism is the mind. *Cartesian dualists* claim that the mind is an immaterial or nonphysical object; other kinds of dualists claim that at least mental properties are above and beyond the physical properties. The physicalist response has taken the form of identity theories (the mind is the brain; mental properties are physical properties), behaviorist theories (mental terms are ways of talking about behavior), and eliminative materialism (there are no minds or mental properties; the terms that seem to refer to them are just parts of a discredited theory of how people work). **Functionalism** is hard to categorize; perhaps it maintains the letter of property dualism but the spirit of physicalism.

matters of fact and **relations of ideas**   This is Hume's terminology for the **analytic/synthetic** distinction, which Hume didn't distinguish from the **a priori/a posteriori** distinction and the **necessary/contingent** distinction. Hume thought our thinking is conducted with simple ideas that are copied from impressions of external objects and complex ideas that result from combining the simple ones. The mind can put ideas together in new ways not derived from perception, so complex ideas need not correspond to external objects. These ideas also serve as the meanings of words. **Relations of ideas** are truths that simply reflect the way these ideas are related to each other and don't depend on whether the ideas actually apply to anything. Hume's examples are "that three times five is equal to the half of thirty" and "that the square of hypotenuse is equal to the square of the two sides." Such truths "are discoverable by the mere operation of thought, without dependence on what is anywhere existent in the universe." The contrary of a relation of ideas will imply a contradiction and is impossible.

In contrast, matters of fact have to do with what the world is like, and not just how ideas are related. The contrary of a matter of fact is possible and doesn't imply a contradiction. Hume's example is "that the sun will rise tomorrow." This is true, and we are quite certain of it at least most of the time. But it is true because of what happens tomorrow, not because of the way ideas are related. Its contrary, "that the sun will not rise tomorrow," is not a contradiction.

Hume maintained that only relations of ideas can be discovered a priori, and that no matter of fact can be demonstrated with only relations of ideas as premises. He argued that many principles philosophers had claimed to know a priori, such as that nothing happens without a cause, were matters of fact and could not be known that way.

Most philosophers agree that mathematical truths, like Hume's examples cited above, are necessary and knowable a priori. But many do think that they are not analytic—are not simply a matter of relations of ideas, in Hume's sense.

metaphysics Metaphysics considers very general questions about the nature of reality. It includes the study of the basic categories of things *(ontology)*. Questions such as whether there are universals, events, substances, individuals, necessary beings, possible worlds, numbers, ideal objects, abstract objects, and the like arise here. Metaphysics also includes questions about space, time, identity and change, mind and body, personal identity, causation, determinism, freedom, and the structure of action.

modus ponens *See* **conditionals.**

modus tollens *See* **conditionals.**

naive realism *See* **realism.**

naturalism Naturalism is a powerful if somewhat vague philosophical view, with both epistemological and metaphysical sides. All knowledge derives from the methods we use to study the natural world, sense-perception extended by the methods of the natural sciences. The only objects and properties that we should countenance are those that we perceive in the natural world, and those that are required to explain natural phenomena by our best theories. Thus, in the title of his *Dialogues on Natural Religion*, the word "natural" tells us that Hume will consider whether basically scientific methods of inquiry and argument can lead us to a belief in an intelligent creator.

Naturalism in ethics maintains that good and bad, right and wrong are definable in terms of natural properties, such as pleasure and pain, and that there are no special methods of knowledge for moral facts. In "Responsiblity, Reactive Attitudes, and Liberalism," Samuel Scheffler argues that the appeal of naturalism is a major source of the reluctance of many political philosophers to appeal to "a robust notion of preinstitutional desert."

natural religion The term "natural religion" occurs in Hume's *Dialogues*. It is basically opposed to *revealed religion*. Natural religion is religous belief based on the same sorts of evidence that we use in everyday life and science: observation and inference to the most plausible explanations for what is observed by principles based on experience. It is in this spirit that Cleanthes puts forward his analogical argument for the existence of an intelligent creator. In contrast, revealed religion relies on sacred texts and the authority of tradition and Church.

necessary *See* **contingent** and **necessary.**

necessary and **sufficient conditions** In the phrases "necessary condition" and "sufficient condition," the term "condition" may be used for properties, statements, propositions, events, or actions. The basic idea is always that:

A *is sufficent for* B. Having (being, doing) A is one way of having (being, doing) B; nothing more is needed. You may not need to have A to have B, for there may be other ways of having B. But A is one way.

A *is necessary for* B. Every way of having (being, doing) B involves having (being, doing) A. A may not be all you need; it may be that every way of having B involves not only having A but also something more. But you've got to have A to have B.

For example: Having a car is sufficient, but not necessary for having a vehicle. One could have a bicycle instead. But having a car is certainly enough.

Having blood is necessary for being alive, but not sufficient. A dead man can have blood; more than blood is required to be alive. But you can't do without it.

Being in England is necessary, but not sufficient, for being in London. Being in London is sufficient, but not necessary, for being in England.

Given these explanations, there is a symmetry to necessary and sufficient conditions:

if A is necessary for B, B is sufficient for A.

Indeed, if we take conditions to be statements we can say:

When: If P, then Q,
P is sufficient for Q, and Q is necessary for P.

Philosophers are often interested in finding an *analysis* of some interesting condition. This involves finding a set of conditions that are *individually necessary and jointly sufficient*. If A, B, C are individually necessary and jointly sufficient for D, then each of A, B, and C are necessary, and the conjunctive condition A & B & C is sufficient. For example, being a male, being unmarried, and being an adult are (arguably) individually necessary and jointly sufficient for being a bachelor.

It is necessary, finally, to distinguish different kinds of necessity and sufficiency. Is the relationship a matter of logic, metaphysics, the laws of nature, or something else? The necessity of blood for human life, for example, seems a matter of natural or causal necessity, not logic or metaphysics.

object   The term "object" is used in different ways by different philosophers, and one has to be careful when one encounters it. Sometimes it means any sort of things at all, whether abstract or concrete, universal or particular. On this usage numbers, people, rocks, properties, moods, propositions, and facts are all objects. Sometimes it is used for objects of thought. Sometimes it has the connotation of an ordinary material thing.

original position   *See* **veil of ignorance**.

paradox   A paradox is an argument that appears to derive absurd conclusions from acceptable premises by valid reasoning. Quine distinguishes veridical paradoxes from falsidical paradoxes and antinomies. In the case of a veridical paradox, the premises are acceptable and the reasoning valid, and we must accept the conclusion, which turns out not to be absurd under close analysis. A falsidical paradox really does have an absurd conclusion, but upon close analysis the premises turn out to be unacceptable or the reasoning invalid. An antinomy defies resolution by close analysis, for the paradox brings to the surface a real problem with part of our conceptual scheme that only revision can eliminate.

parallelism   *See* **dualism**.

particulars   *See* **universals** and **particulars**.

perceptual relativity, argument from   *See* **illusion, argument from**.

phenomenal character   *See* **qualia**.

phenomenology   Phenomenology is an approach to some philosophical issues developed by Edmund Husserl and his followers. It conceives of philosophy as the study of phenomena as revealed to consciousness, "bracketing" the assumptions of an orderly external world that are made by science and common sense. Phenomenology emphasizes the intentionality of consciousness. The term "phenomenology" is also used more loosely, to indicate a survey of experience connected with some topic conducted as a preliminary to theorizing.

physicalism   *See* **materialism**.

Platonism and **platonism**   Platonism refers to the philosophy of Plato (428–348 B.C.) and the movements specifically inspired by it. Uncapitalized, platonism has become a technical term in *ontology* for those who countenance abstract entities that are not merely abstractions from or constructions out of particulars, and specifically, in the philosophy of mathematics, for those who maintain that numbers are such objects. Although Plato was a platonist in this sense, most modern platonists do not hold many of Plato's most important doctrines in metaphysics, epistemology, and ethics.

predicate   The term "predicate" traditionally refers to the part of a sentence that characterizes the subject. In "Sally kissed Fred," "Sally" is the subject and "kissed Fred" is the predicate. Philosophers and logicians extend this notion, so that a sentence with one or more **singular terms** removed is a predicate. Predicates are 1-place, 2-place, and so forth, depending on the number of singular terms needed to make a sentence. A predicate is said to be *true of* an object or sequence of objects if a true sentence would result if terms referring to that object or those objects were inserted. From our example, we can get these predicates:

1. (1) kissed Fred.
2. (1) kissed (2)
3. Sally kissed (2)
4. (1) kissed (1).

(1) is a 1-place predicate, true of Sally and whoever else has kissed Fred. Predicate (2) is a 2-place predicate, true of the pair of Sally and Fred, and any other pair, the first of which has kissed the second. Number (3) is a 1-place predicate, true of Fred and others Sally has kissed. And (4) is a 1-place predicate, because it only takes one referring expression to complete the sentence, although it must be inserted twice. It is true of people who have kissed themselves.

The notion of a predicate does not necessarily fit very well with the categories linguists use to describe the structure of sentences. For example, the words "Sally kissed," which remain after "Fred" is removed from our sentence, giving predicate (3), are not usually considered a syntactic part of the original sentence.

premise   *See* **deductive argument**.

primary and **secondary qualities**   Locke distinguishes **ideas** from the modifications of bodies that cause ideas in us, which he calls qualities. Among qualities, he distinguishes primary qualities from secondary qualities. Primary qualities include solidity, extension (size), figure (shape),

motion, and number. Secondary qualities include colors, sounds, tastes, and smells. According to Locke, primary qualities are inseparable from objects through alteration and division, and resemble the ideas they cause. Secondary qualities are merely powers that objects have, in virtue of the primary qualities of their insensible parts, to produce ideas in us. So when we see that a poker chip has a certain shape, an idea is being produced in us that resembles the quality involved in its production, and the poker chip will continue to have some shape or other even if it is bent or melted; if it is divided its parts will have shape. When we see that the chip has a certain color, however, we are having an idea that is caused by the primary qualities of the surface of the chip, qualities which do not resemble the idea. If we divided the chip, at some point the parts would be too small to produce any color ideas at all and would be colorless.

Locke's distinction, versions of which can be found in Descartes, Galileo, and Boyle, has been a source of controversy since he first proposed it. A favorite target of critics is the idea of a quality resembling an idea, which is not easy to make much sense of. Berkeley makes this criticism and others in his *Dialogues*.

properties and **relations**   Consider these three facts:

1. Nixon was born in California.
2. Carter was born in Georgia.
3. Nixon was older than Carter.

These facts have different things in common with one another. Facts 1 and 3 are about the same people, Nixon and Carter, but involve different relations. Facts 1 and 2 are about different *individuals*, but involve the same relation.

The relation involved in 1 and 2 is *being born in*. This is a relation between people and places. Philosophers might say that 1 states that the relation *being born in* obtains between Nixon and California, 2 states that it obtains between Carter and Georgia, while 3 states that the relation *older than* obtains between Nixon and Carter.

Being born in and being older than are both binary or 2-ary relations: relations that obtain between two objects. Three important properties of 2-ary relations are *transitivity*, *symmetry*, and *reflexivity*. Suppose that *R* is a 2-ary relation. Then:

- *R* is *transitive* if it follows from the fact that *a* has *R* to *b* and *b* has *R* to *c* that *a* has *R* to *c*. For example, *being longer than* is a transitive relation: if *a* is longer than *b* and *b* is longer then *c*, then *a* is longer than *c*. However, *liking* is not transitive: from the fact that Bob likes Mary, and Mary likes Carol, it does not follow that Bob likes Carol.
- *R* is *symmetrical* if it follows from the fact that *a* has *R* to *b* that *b* has *R* to *a*. *Being a sibling of* is symmetrical; *being a brother of* is not.
- *R* is *reflexive* if it follows from that fact that *a* has *R* to *b* that *a* has *R* to *a*. If Bob is the same height as anyone at all—if he is the sort of thing that has height at all—then he is the same height as himself.

Relations that are transitive, symmetrical, and reflexive are *equivalence relations*. There are also 3-ary relations, and in principle there are *n*-ary relations for any *n*. When we say, "Nebraska City is between Omaha and Topeka," we are stating that a 3-place relation obtains between three cities. It is often useful to use variables to indicate the places of relations, so the relation here is *x is between y and z*.

It is sometimes useful to talk about the *arguments* or *parameters* of a relation. Thus one could say that the place argument (or parameter) of the relation of being born in was filled in 1 by California and in 2 by Georgia. In the example in the last paragraph, we might say that Topeka filled the *z* argument of the relation of *x is between y and z*.

When we say that a person is old, or tired, or silly, we are not saying something about a relation he stands in to someone or something else, but stating a property that he has or doesn't have by himself. Properties are 1-ary relations.

So far we have been ignoring time. Consider 4:

4. Carter lives in Georgia.

Number 4 is true now, but wasn't true when Carter was president and lived in Washington, D.C. It seems that living in is really a 3-ary relation, between people, places, and times, even though it looks like a 2-ary relation. Similarly, since people can be old, tired, or silly at one time, while being young, energetic, and serious at others, these are all really 2-ary rather than 1-ary relations. When we take time into account, we need to think of most properties as 2-ary relations between individuals and times.

property dualism   *See* **dualism**.

proposition   Consider the report, "Russell said that Hegel was confused." The phrase "that Hegel was confused" identifies a proposition, which was *what Russell said*. Others could assert the same proposition, and it could also be believed, doubted, denied, and the like. We could say, "Taylor doubted that Hegel was confused," "Moore believed that Hegel was confused," and so forth. It seems that the same proposition could be expressed in other languages, so a proposition is not just a particular sentence type. A proposition is an abstract object that has conditions of truth, and it is true or false depending on whether those conditions are met. Propositions are identified by statements and are referred to by "that-clauses," like "that Hegel was confused."

The existence and ontological status of propositions are matters of controversy. Some philosophers believe that propositions are mysterious entities that should be avoided; we should get by just talking about sentences that are true, without bringing in propositions. Among philosophers who accept the need for propositions, some think they should be defined in terms of properties, facts, possible worlds, and other more basic categories, while others think they are primitive.

propositional attitude   The propositional attitudes are those mental acts and states, such as belief, knowledge, and desire, that have truth or satisfaction conditions, so that they may be characterized by the propositions that capture those conditions. We say, for example, "Russell believed *that Hegel was confused*," characterizing

Russell's belief by a proposition that captures its truth conditions. And we say that Russell desired that *there would be no more wars*, thereby characterizing Russell's desire by a proposition that captures its satisfaction conditions.

qualia   Consider what it is like to have a headache, how it feels. It is somewhat different from what it is like to have a toothache, and vastly different from what it is like to taste a chocolate chip cookie. We try to avoid headaches because of what it is like to have them, and we try to find and eat chocolate chip cookies, because of what it is like to taste them.

What it is like to have a certain kind of experience is one aspect of that experience. Philosophers call such aspects *qualia*. Other terms that are used more or less similarly are *subjective characters*, and *phenomenal characters*.

Philosophers such as Thomas Nagel in "What Is It Like to Be a Bat?" and Frank Jackson in "What Mary Didn't Know" claim that the qualia or subjective characters of mental events and states cannot be identified with or reduced to physical aspects of those events and states. Thus even if we suppose that headaches *are* brain states, we have to admit that these brain states have nonphysical properties, their qualia. If we accept the arguments of Nagel and Jackson, we seem to have to accept some form of **dualism**. Minds may not be immaterial *things*, but at least they have immaterial *properties*, such as being in states with certain conscious aspects or qualia.

David Lewis, in "Knowing What It's Like," claims that qualia can be handled by the physicalist.

qualities   *See* **primary** and **secondary qualities**.

rationalism   Rationalism is an epistemological position that emphasizes reason as a source of knowledge itself, not merely a way of organizing and drawing further hypotheses from knowledge gotten by sense perception. **Continental rationalism** is a term sometimes applied to Descartes, Spinoza, Leibniz, and other seventeenth- and eighteenth-century philosophers. *See also* **empiricism**.

reactive attitudes   In "Freedom and Resentment," P. F. Strawson argues that we can understand moral responsibility in terms of an important class of emotions. He calls these "reactive attitudes." They are all reactions to good or ill will. The basic case is that of participant reactive attitudes—e.g., resentment and gratitude—which are reactions to the good or ill will of others toward us. Generalized, vicarious analogues of these attitudes include moral condemnation, moral indignation, and moral praise. Self-reactive attitudes include guilt and remorse. All these reactive attitudes contrast with an "objective" attitude which sees a person as subject to manipulation and positive and negative reinforcement, but not as a participant in interpersonal relationships tied to the reactive attitudes.

realism   In philosophy the term "realism" is used in a context of controversy in which the reality of objects of some category has been denied in some way, usually by claiming that the objects in question are creations or constructions of the human mind. The realist in the controversy is one who defends the status of the controversial objects. A philosopher can be a realist about one issue, while denying realism with respect to some other. The two most common contexts in which the term is used are universals and the objects of sense perception. A realist about universals holds that they are real, in the sense of not being mere names or concepts. A realist about the objects of sense perception holds that they are real, in the sense of enjoying an existence independent of the perceiving mind.

Naive realism is the view that the objects of perception not only exist, but exist just as they seem to be. This position is often taken to be refuted by the various forms of the argument from illusion. *See* **illusion, argument from**; **representative ideas, theory of**.

reason   Reason is the ability or faculty to engage in theoretical and/or practical reasoning. A number of philosophical issues are concerned with the role of reason in various spheres of human life. *Rationalists* and *empiricists* disagree about the role of reason in the formation of concepts and the development of knowledge, the latter seeing it only as an aid to experience. Kant supposed that there were fundamental principles of conduct provided by practical reason; whereas Hume argued that in the practical sphere reason "is, and ought only to be the slave of the passions." *See* **reasoning, practical** and **theoretical**.

reasoning, practical and **theoretical**   Theoretical reasoning is aimed at assessing evidence and drawing conclusions about what is true. Practical reasoning is aimed at making decisions about what to do.

reductionism   In philosophy the term "reductionism" occurs in the context of a controversy about the status of some kind of object. The reductionist maintains that talk and knowledge about such objects really amount to talk and knowledge about some class of objects that is usually thought to be quite different. Talk and knowledge about the first kind of object are *reduced* to talk and knowledge about the second kind. For example, Berkeley thought that talk and knowledge about ordinary objects were really just talk and knowledge about ideas. A philosopher can be a reductionist about some categories of objects while being a nonreductionist about others.

refers   Philosophers use a number of terms for the relationship that holds between singular terms and the objects they designate or stand for. *Refers* is used both for the relation between singular terms and what they stand for, and for the act of using a singular term to stand for something (" 'That piece of furniture' refers to the chair" versus "Jane used 'that piece of furniture' to refer to the chair"). The thing referred to is often called the *referent*. *Denotes* is most properly used for the relation between a definite description and the object that uniquely meets the descriptive part, as in " 'The author of *Waverley*' denotes Sir Walter Scott." But denotes is often simply used as a synonym of refers. The thing denoted is sometimes called the *denotation* and, less often, the *denotatum*. *Names* is used for the relation between a name and its *bearer* (or *nominatum*), as in " 'Fred' names that man." *Designate* and *stands for* are used in a very general way, as the latter

has been in this discussion. *See also* **extension** and **intension; singular term**.

relation of ideas   *See* **matters of fact** and **relations of ideas**.

relativism   The term relativism is used with reference to a body of statements or alleged truths about some sort of phenomena. The relativist maintains that these statements (1) are only true (or false) *relative* to some further factor or parameter, not explicitly mentioned in the statements themselves; (2) that this parameter is a person or group of people making the judgment, or something corresponding to a group of people such as a culture or a language; (3) hence there is no *objective* truth or falsity; that is, no truth or falsity merely concerning the objects involved in the phenomena independently of the subjects making those judgments. (In the terms explained in **properties** and **relations**, the relativist is claiming that an *n*-ary property is being treated as an (*n*-1)-ary property.

Here is an example where relativism is pretty plausible. Consider the comparative merits of the taste of food. Does the issue of whether carrots taste better or worse than cucumbers have an answer? The relativist, with regard to this issue, would say that there is an answer only *relative* to a particular taster. Carrots may taste better than cucumbers *to* Mary, while cucumbers taste better than carrots *to* Fred. The relativist would say that there is no *further* question of who is right. The question whether carrots taste better than cucumbers *simpliciter*, without further reference to a person who does the tasting, makes no sense. On the relativist view, the judgments of Fred and Mary are misconstrued if they are taken to be opinions about some nonrelative truth. Since taste is relative, there should be no room for such a dispute.

There are many types of relativism that are more controversial and so more interesting than relativism about the taste of food. *Ontological relativists* claim that existence is relative: that different languages, cultures, or conceptual schemes recognize different classes of objects and properties, and questions of existence make no sense considered outside of such *conceptual schemes*. Perhaps the most interesting example is *ethical relativism*. Ethical relativists claim that judgments of right and wrong are relative to individuals, societies, or cultures.

representative ideas, theory of The theory of representative ideas maintains that knowledge of external things is mediated by ideas in the mind of the knower that represent those things in virtue of a twofold relation they have to them. The ideas are *caused by* the external things, and *depict* those external things as having certain properties. Suppose, for example, one perceives a chair in front of one. The chair causes light to fall upon the retina in a certain pattern, which causes other events in the visual system, which ultimately cause ideas of a certain sort in the mind. This idea has certain features, which depict the object causing it to be a chair of a certain sort.

This theory allows an account of error and a treatment of the **argument from perceptual relativity** and the **argument from illusion**. The argument from perceptual relativity shows that which thing an idea represents and how it depicts that object to be do not depend just on the features of the idea, but also auxiliary beliefs. The same visual image might represent an object as elliptical or circular, depending on whether it was taken to be held at a right angle or acute angle to the line of vision. Normal errors and illusions occur when the idea caused by a thing does not accurately depict it, either because the auxiliary beliefs are wrong, or something unusual in the perceiving conditions or the perceiver's state leads to a wrong idea being produced. The more radical types of error involved in certain kinds of delusions, such as hallucinations, involve having an idea that is not caused by an external thing at all, but some disorder in the perceiver.

Fairly explicit versions of the theory of representative ideas may be found in Descartes and Locke. Berkeley, Hume, and others have criticized the theory for various reasons, including that it leads to *skepticism*, since it seems to provide no direct means of knowing the external objects, that the notion of depiction makes no sense, and that the whole picture of "double existence" is incoherent.

revealed religion *See* **natural religion**.

sceptic, skeptic "Skeptic" is an American spelling, "sceptic" the British. When a view is labeled *skeptical*, there are two things that must be ascertained, the type of skepticism and its topic. The skeptic can be advocating suspension of claims of knowledge or certainty, suspension of belief, or positive disbelief. Hume, for example, thinks that we cannot *know* through reason that the future will be like the past, but does not claim we should refrain from believing it; indeed, he thinks it is both natural to do so and impossible not to do so except for brief periods while doing philosophy. He describes this position as skeptical. Whatever type of skepticism is being advocated, a philosopher can be skeptical about some things and not others. For example, a philosopher might be skeptical about the existence of God, but not about the external world.

secondary qualities *See* **primary** and **secondary qualities**.

sense-data Some philosophers who accept that the various forms of the argument from illusion show that we do not directly perceive material objects, use the terms sense-datum and sense-data for what we do directly perceive. Unlike the terms "**idea**" or "**sensation**," the term "sense-data" does not imply that the direct objects of perception are mental, but leaves that question open. Sense-data are objects of some sort, distinguished from the act of being aware of them. Sense-data are usually supposed to have all of the properties they seem to have. Suppose, for example, you see a blue tie in a store with fluorescent lighting, it looks green and you take it to be so. A philosopher who believes in sense-data would say that you are directly aware of a sense-datum that is green; your mistake is in your inference from the fact about the sense-datum's color to the tie's color.

singular term Singular terms include proper names (John, Fred), singular definite descriptions (the author of *Waverley*, the present king of France, the square root of two), singular pronouns (I, you, she, he, it), and singular demonstrative phrases (that man, this ship). These terms all identify or purport to identify a particular object, about which something further is said.

The category "singular term" is found in philosophy and philosophical logic more than in linguistics. The category includes expressions that are syntactically quite different, like definite descriptions and names, and separates things that syntactically seem closely related, like singular and plural definite descriptions ("the governor of Maryland," "the senators from Maryland").

sophism A sophism is a bad argument presented as if it were a good one in order to deceive, mislead, or cheat someone; *sophistry* is the practice of doing this.

In Ancient Greece, the *sophists* were itinerant teachers of the fourth and fifth centuries B.C., some of whom, such as Protagoras and Gorgias, Socrates criticized vigorously. His negative view was based on the empiricism, relativism, and skepticism of their teachings; on the fact that they took a fee; and on the fact that they taught argument for the sake of persuasion and manipulation of others, rather than for the pursuit of truth.

sound *See* **deductive argument.**

subjective character *See* **qualia.**

substance The term "substance" has been used in a variety of ways in philosophy. In modern philosophy, a substance is a thing capable of independent existence. Substances are contrasted with qualities and relations, on the one hand, and complexes, on the other. These are all merely ways that substances are. Philosophers have had dramatically different opinions about what meets these conditions. Descartes thought that there were two basically different kinds of substance, material and immaterial, and there were many of each, and that no way of being material was a way of being mental and vice versa. Spinoza

thought that there was but one substance, and material and mental reality were aspects of it. (He called this thing *God*, while many of his opponents thought his view amounted to atheism.) In "Of Scepticism with Regard to the Senses," Hume treats our perceptions as substances—the ultimate, independent constituents of reality.

supervenience A set of properties *A* supervenes on another set of properties *B*, if all objects with the same *B*-properties have the same *A*-properties. Many advocates of **functionalism** maintain that although mental properties cannot be identified with physical properties (as the **identity theory** holds), they nevertheless *supervene* on them. Both the identity theorist and the supervenience theorist maintain that beings that are physically indiscernible will have the same mental properties. But the supervenience theorist allows that beings that are mentally alike, may be quite different physically. For example, a philosopher might think that agents built out of silicon-based computers, humans, and individuals from outer space with a completely different biology than ours could all have beliefs, desires, and intentions, in spite of the difference of their physical constitution and organization.

syllogism A syllogism is a valid deductive argument or argument form with two premises and a conclusion, that involves universal and existential statements involving three terms. For example:

> All *A*s are *B*s
> All *B*s are *C*s
> Therefore, all *A*s are *C*s.
>
> Some *A*s are *B*s
> No *B*s are *C*s
> Therefore some *A*s are not *C*s.

In these examples, *B* is the *middle term*; it appears in the premises to connect the terms in the conclusion, but does not itself appear in the conclusion. *A* is the *minor term* because it is the subject of the conclusion and *C* is the *major term* because it is the predicate of the conclusion. Much of the theory of syllogism was worked out by

Aristotle. The class of valid deductive arguments studied in modern logic is much larger.

synthetic   *See* **analytic** and **synthetic**.

teleological ethics   *See* **consequentialism**.

theodicy   A philosophical response on the part of a believer to the **Problem of Evil**.

transitive   *See* **properties** and **relations**.

Turing machine   A Turing machine is not a real machine one can go out and buy, but an abstract conception invented by A. M. Turing to help think about computing and computers. The machine scans a square on a tape, erases what it finds there, prints something new, moves to a new square, and goes into a new state. What it prints, where it moves, and into what state it goes are all determined by the state in which it was in the beginning and what it found on the square. Computer scientists and logicians have shown that Turing machines—given enough time and tape—can compute any function that any computer can compute. For a more complete account of Turing machines, *see* the Appendix to Hilary Putnam's "The Nature of Mental States."

types and **tokens**   How many words are in this statement?

An argument is an argument, but a good cigar is a smoke.

There are twelve word tokens, but only eight word types. There are two tokens each of the word types "an," "argument," "is," and "a" and one each of "but," "good," "cigar," and "smoke." The types are **universals**, while the tokens are **particulars**.

uniformity of nature   The principle of the uniformity of nature maintains that the same basic patterns or laws are found throughout nature; the future will be like the past, at least in terms of the basic operations of nature; and more generally the unexamined parts of nature will be like the parts that have been examined up to a certain point. This principle seems to underlie the use of past experience to form expectations about the future, but, according to Hume, it isn't itself susceptible of proof. The principle is discussed by Hume and Hempel; Goodman's new riddle of induction poses a puzzle about how this principle is to be understood.

universals and **particulars**   A particular is what we would ordinarily think of as a thing, with a particular position in space at any one time. A universal is that which particulars have in common, or may have in common. The kind, *human*, is a universal; individual people are particulars. **Types** are universals, **tokens** are particulars. Properties such as being red are universals; philosophers disagree about whether it is red things (roses, barns) that have them in common, or particular cases of the property (the redness of the rose, the redness of the barn). Not all philosophers agree that there are universals. *Nominalists* maintain that universals are just names that we apply to different objects that resemble one another; metaphysics should recognize particulars that resemble each other in various ways, but not universals above and beyond those particulars. A nominalist might claim that the type/token distinction really amounts to providing two ways of counting tokens, not two kinds of object to be counted.

use and **mention**   Ordinarily when a word appears in a statement, it is being used to talk about something else. If one wants to talk about the word itself, one has to mention it. In the statement,

The word "four" has four letters,

"four" is mentioned the first time it occurs and used the second time it occurs. When a word is mentioned, one may be talking about the **token** or the **type**.

utilitarianism   Utilitarianism is a *consequentialist* ethical theory. Utilitarianism is usually connected with the more specific doctrines of Bentham and Mill, who took the goodness of consequences to be measured by their effect on the happiness or welfare of sentient creatures.

Bentham focused on pleasure, Mill on a more abstract notion of happiness that allowed him to
maintain that "It is better to be a human being
dissatisfied than a pig satisfied; better to be
Socrates dissatisfied than a pig satisfied." For further discussion, *see* the Introduction to Part V.

valid   *See* **deductive argument**.

veil of ignorance   The term "veil of ignorance" is
sometimes used to characterize the skeptical consequences of the **theory of representative ideas**.
According to this theory, we only directly know
the contents of our own mind; these then form a
sort of veil between us and the external world.
This term is also often used in religion, to suggest a fundamental feature of the human condition: all of experience is simply a veil of ignorance
between us and what is most real, or matters
most.

The term was given a new use in ethics by
John Rawls, as an important part of his characterization of the **original position**. The original
position is a hypothetical state of affairs in which
members of a society choose the principles of justice that will govern them. This choice is to be
made behind a veil of ignorance in the sense that
the persons making this choice are not to know
their class, position, social class, intelligence,
strength, and so forth. The underlying intuition
is that by being ignorant of these specifics, these
individuals will be led to make an impartial and
fair choice.

virtue theory (virtue ethics)   This is an approach
to ethical theory that is frequently traced to
Aristotle and contrasted with approaches drawn
from, for example, Kant and Mill. A virtue theory highlights questions about the nature of those
character traits that are virtues—for example,
courage. Such questions are seen as in some way
fundamental to the theory. In "Virtue Theory
and Abortion" Rosalind Hursthouse explores the
structure of such a virtue theory and asks how it
can respond to difficult moral perplexities about
abortion.